4 TH EDITION

PHYSIOLOGY OF BEHAVIOR

Neil R. Carlson
University of Massachusetts

ALLYN AND BACON
Boston   London   Toronto   Sydney   Tokyo   Singapore

Series Editor: Diane McOscar
Series Editorial Assistant: Laura Frankenthaler
Production Administratorr: Peter Petraitis
Production Coordinator: Barbara Gracia
Editorial-Production Service: Woodstock Publishers' Services
Text Designer: Karen Mason
Cover Administrator: Linda K. Dickinson
Cover Designer: Susan Slovinsky
Manufacturing Buyer: Louise Richardson

Copyright © 1991, 1986, 1981, 1977 by Allyn and Bacon
A Division of Simon & Schuster, Inc.
160 Gould Street
Needham Heights, MA 02194-2134

LIBRARY OF CONGRESS CATALOGING-IN-PUBLICATION DATA

Carlson, Neil R.
     Physiology of behavior / Neil R. Carlson. — 4th ed.
        p.   cm.
     Includes bibliographical references.
     Includes indexes.
     ISBN 0-205-12638-3
     1. Psychophysiology.   I. Title
     [DNLM: 1. Behavior—physiology.   2. Nervous System—physiology.
     3. Psychophysiology.   WL 102 C284p]
     QP360.C35 1991
     152—dc20
     DNLM/DLC
     for Library of Congress   90–14464
                                                                CIP

Printed in the United States of America

10 9 8 7 6 5 4 3 2 1   96 95 94 93 92 91 90

This book is dedicated to

my wife, Mary,

and my children, Kerstin and Paul

CONTENTS

CHAPTER *3*   **Neural Communication: Physiology and Pharmacology   46**

CHAPTER *4*   **Structure of the Nervous System and Endocrine System   73**

CHAPTER 5   **Methods of Physiological Psychology 106**

CHAPTER *8*   **Control of Movement   242**

CHAPTER *9* **Sleep 270**

CHAPTER *10* **Reproductive Behavior: Sexual Development and Behavior 312**

CHAPTER *11*   **Reproductive Behavior: Maternal Behavior and Aggression   348**

CHAPTER *12*   **Ingestive Behavior: Drinking   377**

CHAPTER *13*   Ingestive Behavior: Eating   401

CHAPTER *18*   **Mental Disorders   577**

PREFACE

I wrote the first edition of *Physiology of Behavior* during my first sabbatical leave, at the University of Victoria on the west coast of Canada. I managed to finish the book despite the temptations posed by such delightful surroundings. I wrote the present edition—the fourth—during my third sabbatical leave, in Paris. As you can imagine, Paris and the beautiful countryside of France are full of temptations that seem designed to keep a writer away from his or her desk. Nevertheless, I managed to finish this edition, too.

I was able to stay at my desk because of the interesting work that has been done in my colleagues' laboratories. It is their creativity and hard work that gives me something to say. I am happy to report that, because there was so much for me to learn, I enjoyed writing this edition just as much as the first one. That is what makes writing new editions interesting—learning something new and then trying to find a way to convey the information to the reader.

In the preface to each of the previous editions I mentioned some of the new research methods that had recently been developed. Investigators are continuing to develop new methods—for example, new staining techniques for specific substances, new imaging methods, new recording methods, and the means for analyzing the release of neurotransmitters and neuromodulators in restricted regions of the brains of freely moving animals. Nowadays, as soon as a new method is developed in one laboratory, it is adopted by other laboratories and applied to a wide range of problems. And more and more, researchers are combining techniques that converge upon the solution to a problem. In the past, individuals tended to apply their particular research method to a problem; now they are more likely to use many methods, sometimes in collaboration with other laboratories.

In this edition, as in the previous ones, I have made some changes to the outline of the book, as a reader familar with the previous edition will discover. Some of these changes were made in response to new directions in research efforts, and some were made in response to suggestions of students and colleagues concerning pedagogy. The first part of the book is concerned with foundations: the history of the field, the structure and functions of neurons, neural communication, neuroanatomy, and research methods. The second part is concerned with inputs and outputs: the sensory systems and the motor system. The third part deals with classes of species-typical behavior: sleep, reproduction, aggression, and ingestion. Reproductive behavior is now discussed in two chapters. The first covers sexual development and behavior, and the second covers other sexually dimorphic behaviors related to reproduction: maternal behavior and aggression. Ingestive behavior is also covered in two chapters—one on drinking and one on eating. The fourth part of the book deals with learning: the anatomy of learning and the cellular basis (physiological and biochemical) of learning. Included in this section is a new chapter on reinforcement and addiction. This chapter combines some of the information in the reinforcement chapter of the previous editions with physiological and clinical research on the nature of addiction—which is obviously tied to brain mechanisms of reinforcement. The final part deals with human communication—both verbal and nonverbal—and mental disorders. Because of recent progress in research on the physiology of the anxiety disorders, I have expanded the discussion in the final chapter to include this research.

Besides updating my discussion of research, I have updated my writing. Writing is a difficult, time-consuming endeavor, and I find that I am still learning how to do it well. I have said this in the preface of every edition of this book, and it is still true. I have worked with copy editors who have ruthlessly marked up my manuscript, showing me how to do it better the next time. I keep thinking, "This time there will be nothing for the copy editor to do," but I am always proved wrong: The amount of red pencil on each page remains constant. But I do think that each time the writing is better organized, smoother, and more coherent. I agree with Graves and Hodge (1947), who say, "Good English is a matter not merely of grammar and syntax and vocabulary, but also of sense: the structure of the sentences must hold together logically. . . . [Even] phrases which can be justified both grammatically and from the point of view of sense may give [the] reader a wrong impression, or check his reading speed, tempting him to skip." Readability is not to be determined by counting syllables in words or words in sentences; it is a function of the clarity of thought and expression.

Good writing means including all steps of a logical discourse. My teaching experience has shown me that an entire lecture can be wasted if the students do not understand all of the "obvious" conclusions of a particular experiment before the next one is described. Unfortunately, puzzled students sometimes write notes feverishly, in an attempt to get the facts down so they can study them—and understand them—later. And a roomful of busy, attentive students tends to reinforce the lecturer's behavior. Many days later, though, a question from a student may reveal a lack of understanding of details long since passed, accompanied by quizzical looks from other students that confirm that they too have the same question. Painful experiences such as these have taught me to examine the logical steps between the discussion of one experiment and the next and to make sure they are explicitly stated. A textbook writer must address the students who will read the book and not simply address colleagues who are already acquainted with much of what he or she will say.

Because research on the physiology of behavior is an interdisciplinary effort, a textbook must provide the student with the background necessary for understanding a variety of approaches. I have been careful to provide enough biological background early in the book so that students

without a background in physiology can understand what is said later, while students with such a background can benefit from details that are familiar to them.

I designed this text for serious students who are willing to work. In return for their effort, I have endeavored to provide a solid foundation for further study. Those students who will not take subsequent courses in this or related fields should receive the satisfaction of a much better understanding of their own behavior. Also, they will have a greater appreciation for the forthcoming advances in medical practices related to disorders that affect a person's perception, mood, or behavior. I hope that students who carefully read this book will henceforth perceive human behavior in a new light.

ACKNOWLEDGMENTS

Although I must accept the blame for any shortcomings of the book, I want to thank colleagues who helped me by sending reprints of their work, suggesting topics that I should cover, sending photographs that have been reproduced in this book, and pointing out deficiencies in the previous edition. I thank David B. Adams, Daniel L. Alkon, Arthur P. Arnold, Gary S. Aston-Jones, Ronald J. Barfield, Allan I. Basbaum, Theodore W. Berger, Philip J. Best, Catherine Bielajew, Floyd E. Bloom, David A. Booth, M. Deric Bownds, Michael A. Bozarth, S. Marc Breedlove, William S. Cain, Lynwood G. Clemens, Suzanne H. Corkin, Donald V. Coscina, Charles A. Czeisler, Peter Dallos, Antonio R. Damasio, Julian M. Davidson, John D. Davis, Claude Desjardins, J. Anthony Deutsch, Russell L. De Valois, Marian C. Diamond, John F. Disterhoft, Peter Donovick, John E. Dowling, Réné Drucker-Colín, Robert W. Dykes, Michael S. Fanselow, Hans C. Fibiger, J. T. Fitzsimons, A. S. Fleming, Joaquin M. Fuster, Fred H. Gage, Albert M. Galaburda, Nori Geary, James Gibbs, John C. Gillin, David A. Goldfoot, Roger A. Gorski, Robert W. Goy, William T. Greenough, Charles G. Gross, Glenn I. Hatton, Kenneth M. Heilman, Jean Himms-Hagen, J. Allan Hobson, Bartley G. Hoebel, David H. Hubel, Albert J. Hudspeth, Shin-ichi T. Inouye, Barry L. Jacobs, Barbara E. Jones, Eric R. Kandel, A. Kertesz, E. B. Keverne, Doreen Kimura, Ernst Knobil, Barry R. Komisaruk, George F. Koob, H. S. Koopmans, Joseph

E. Le Doux, Sarah F. Leibowitz, William B. Levy, Robert G. Ley, John C. Liebeskind, Margaret S. Livingstone, Martha K. McClintock, Dennis J. McGinty, R. Meddis, Marek-Marsel Mesulam, Klaus A. Miczek, Richard R. Miselis, Mortimer Mishkin, Gordon J. Mogenson, John W. Money, Martin C. Moore-Ede, R. G. M. Morris, George Moushegian, Donald Novin, Michael Numan, David S. Olton, J. O'Keefe, Jaak Panksepp, M. Ian Phillips, Gian F. Poggio, Terrance E. Robinson, Robert W. Rodieck, Edmund T. Rolls, J. Peter Rosenfeld, Elliott D. Ross, Aryeh Routtenberg, Neil E. Rowland, Frederick S. Vom Saal, Yasua Sakuma, Peter B. Shizgal, Jerome M. Siegel, Gerald P. Smith, Larry R. Squire, Larry Stein, Eliot Stellar, Maurice B. Sterman, Janice R. Stevens, Edward M. Stricker, Fridolin Sulser, Bruce Svare, Larry W. Swanson, Richard F. Thompson, Michael G. Tordoff, Franco Zaccarino, Cornelius H. Vanderwolf, Gary W. VanHoesen, Elizabeth K. Warrington, Wilse B. Webb, Daniel R. Weinberger, Norman W. Weinberger, Larry Weiskrantz, Peter J. Whitehouse, Roy A. Wise, John S. Yeomans, S. M. Zeki, Stuart M. Zola-Morgan, and Irving Zucker.

Several colleagues have reviewed the manuscript of parts of this book and made suggestions for improving the final drafts. I thank Marie Banich, University of Illinois at Urbana-Champaign; Phillip J. Best, Miami University, Oxford; Charles Kutscher, Syracuse University; Donald Novin, University of California, Los Angeles; Neil E. Rowland, University of Florida; Thomas R. Scott, University of Delaware; Harold I. Siegel, Rutgers University; Bruce Svare, SUNY at Albany; Thomas Walsh, Rutgers University.

Anne Powell Anderson, Department of Psychology, Smith College, has prepared a student workbook to accompany this text. We all know how important active participation is in the learning process, and Beth's workbook provides an excellent framework for guiding the student's study behavior. Beth is an outstanding teacher, as her students will attest, and her experience has permitted her to prepare an excellent and useful guide for students. She has also prepared the Instructor's Manual, which includes an expanded test item file.

I also want to thank the people at Allyn and Bacon. Diane McOscar, my editor, provided assistance, support, and encouragement. Laura Frank-

enthaler, editorial assistant, helped gather comments and suggestions from colleagues who have read the book. Peter Petraitis, the production editor, assembled the team that designed and produced the book. Barbara Gracia, of Woodstock Publishers' Services, demonstrated her masterful skills of organization in managing the book's production. She got everything done on time, despite an extremely tight schedule. Few people realize what a difficult, demanding, and time-consuming job a production editor has with a project such as this, with hundreds of illustrations and an author who tends to procrastinate; but I do, and I thank her for all she has done. Carol Beal was my copy editor. Her attention to detail surprised me again and again; she found inconsistencies in my terminology, awkwardness in my prose, and disjunctions in my logical discourse, and she gave me a chance to fix them before anyone else saw them in print. Joanna Koperski of JAK Graphics, Ltd., Ann Larson of Precision Graphics, and Mark Lefkowitz, medical illustrator did a superb job on the art, as you can easily see.

I must also thank my family—my wife Mary, my daughter Kerstin, and my son Paul—for their support. Writing is a lonely pursuit, because one must be alone with one's thoughts for many hours of the day. We did many things together during our year in Paris, but we all would have liked to do more. I thank my family for giving me the time to read, reflect, and write without feeling that I was neglecting them too much.

I also thank Stylianos Nicolaïdis for giving me an academic home in his laboratory at the Collège de France, an institution founded by Francois I in 1535. He and his collaborators gave me the opportunity to discuss what I was working on and test my ideas on them. They also let me sit quietly at my desk and tap away at my keyboard.

I was delighted to hear from many students and colleagues who read previous editions of my book, and I hope that the dialogue will continue. Please write to me and tell me what you like and dislike about the book. My address is Department of Psychology, Tobin Hall, University of Massachusetts, Amherst Massachusetts 01003. When I write, I like to imagine that I am talking with you, the reader. If you write to me, we can make the conversation a two-way exchange.

1

Introduction

*T*he last frontier in this world—and perhaps the greatest one—lies within us. The human nervous system makes possible all that we can do, all that we can know, and all that we can experience. Its complexity is immense, and the task of studying it and understanding it dwarfs all previous explorations our species has undertaken.

Investigation of the physiology of behavior has a long history, with roots in philosophy, biology, and psychology. Philosophers have asked how we perceive and understand reality and have posed the mind-body question, which remains with us still. They have also devised the scientific method—a set of rules that permits us to ask questions about the natural world with some assurance that we will receive reliable answers. Biologists have devised experimental physiology, which provides the tools we use to investigate the workings of the body. They have also developed the framework needed to integrate findings from diverse species—the principles of natural selection, evolution, and genetics. Psychologists have devised methods of behavioral observation and analysis and have presented many of the theoretical questions that motivate much of the research being performed today.

PHILOSOPHICAL ROOTS OF PHYSIOLOGICAL PSYCHOLOGY

Philosophy ("love of wisdom") originally concerned itself with the basis of human knowledge and thought. Philosophers soon realized that in order to understand the basis of knowledge, they must understand the nature of reality, which led them to develop "natural philosophy," the predecessor of modern physical and biological science.

One of the most universal human characteristics is curiosity. We want to explain what makes things happen. In ancient times people believed that natural phenomena were caused by animating spirits. All moving objects—animals, the wind and tides, the sun, moon, and stars—were assumed to have spirits that caused them to move. For example, stones fell when they were dropped because their animating spirits wanted to be reunited with Mother Earth. As our ancestors became more sophisticated and learned more about nature, they abandoned this approach—which we call *animism*—in favor of physical explanations for inanimate moving objects. But they still used spirits to explain human behavior.

From the earliest historical times people have believed they possess souls. This belief stems from our awareness of our own existence. When we think or act, we feel as if something inside us— our mind or our soul—is thinking or deciding to act. But what is the nature of the human mind? We have physical bodies, equipped with muscles that move it and with sensory organs such as eyes and ears that perceive information about the world around us. Within our bodies the nervous system plays a central role, controlling the movements of the muscles and receiving information from the sensory organs. But what role does the mind play? Does it *control* the nervous system? Is it a *part of* the nervous system? Is it physical and tangible, like the rest of the body, or is it a spirit that will always remain hidden?

This puzzle has historically been called the *mind-body question*. Philosophers have been trying to answer it for many centuries, and more recently, scientists have taken up the task. Basically, people have followed two different approaches: dualism and monism. As we shall see, these two approaches reflect very different assumptions about the nature of reality.

Dualism

Early philosophers believed that reality was divided into two categories: the material and the spiritual. According to this belief, humans have physical bodies and nonphysical spirits, or souls. Mind and body are considered to be separate; the body is made of ordinary matter, but the mind is not. This belief is called *dualism*. But if the physical and spiritual aspects of our nature are independent, as this model suggests, then what is the purpose of having both, or in what way are they related? If the body functions independently of the soul, then what does the soul do?

The concept of soul is the cornerstone of religion; philosophers were therefore unwilling to dispense with it. Instead, they suggested that the soul controls the body. Because the eyes and ears—the primary windows to the soul—are located in the head, the probable location of the soul was presumed to be the brain. Moreover, damage to the head can lead to unconsciousness or paralysis, which suggested that the soul moved the body by controlling the operations of the brain.

In the seventeenth century the French philosopher and mathematician René Descartes attempted to explain how the soul could control the body. (See *Figure 1.1.*) Descartes believed that animals other than humans were machines. If we could understand how their parts were put together, we should be able to understand them completely. The *bodies* of humans were also machines and operated on exactly the same principles. However, unlike other animals, we had a

FIGURE 1.1

René Descartes (1596–1650), French philosopher and mathematician, at the court of Queen Christina of Sweden. Descartes's particular form of dualism (interactionism) stimulated interest in the relation between mind and body. (The Granger Collection, New York.)

God-given soul. The soul received information about the world through the body's senses, thought about what it perceived, and made decisions about actions. When it wanted to move the body, it did so by acting on the brain, which, in turn, moved the muscles.

Descartes formulated the first physiological model of behavior. He based his model on the mechanism that activated the statues in the grottoes of the Royal Gardens, just west of Paris. As a young man, he was fascinated by the hidden mechanisms that caused the statues to move and dance when visitors stepped on hidden plates. The statues were moved by hydraulic cylinders powered by water pressure. Descartes believed that the muscles of the body also worked hydraulically. When we exert a force with our limbs, our muscles appear to get larger. Descartes concluded that this enlargement occurs because fluid is pumped into the muscles through the nerves. When nerves are cut, a liquid oozes out; hence the nerves must be hollow.

What is the source of the fluid that gets pumped into the muscles? According to Descartes, it was the *cerebral ventricles*—the hollow, fluid-filled chambers of the brain. He concluded that the mechanism that directed the pressurized fluid into the appropriate nerves was the *pineal body*, a small organ situated on top of the brain stem. The pineal body acted like a little joystick: When it was tilted slightly in various directions, it opened pores that permitted fluid to enter the nerves and inflate the muscles. (See *Figure 1.2.*)

Because animals lacked souls, Descartes believed that this model completely explained their behavior. Of course, the details would have to be worked out through further study. Humans, however, possessed souls as well as bodies. The pineal gland, which controlled the movements of the pressurized fluids through the nerves to the muscles, provided the place for the soul to interact with the body. When the soul desired a particular action, it tilted the pineal gland appropriately, and the muscles needed to carry out the action became inflated.

As philosophers have subsequently noted, Descartes's theory contains a built-in contradiction. If the soul or mind is not a part of the physical

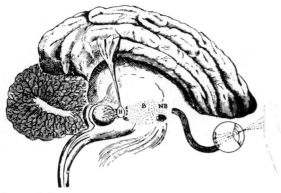

FIGURE 1.2

Descartes's theory. Descartes believed that 0018 the soul controlled the movements of the muscles through its influence on the pineal body. His explanation is modeled on the mechanism that animated statues in the Royal Gardens. More recent attempts to explain the physiology of behavior are modeled on newer devices, such as computers. (Courtesy of Historical Pictures Service, Chicago.)

world, then it cannot exert a force that moves physical objects. Thus, it cannot interact with matter. If the soul or mind possesses material properties that permit it to interact with the body, then it, like the body, is physical. Logically, we cannot have it both ways.

But the spirit of human inquiry is not easily stifled. Some philosophers after Descartes concluded that his conception of the body as a physical machine was correct as far as it went—but that it should go farther. For example, the nineteenth-century British philosopher James Mill agreed that the body was a machine but concluded that the mind was simply a part of that machine. As such, it was subject to the same physical laws as the rest of nature.

Monism

For many years philosophers tried to understand the nature of the human mind by using logic alone. Their lack of success made it clear that mere speculation is futile. If we could answer the mind-body question simply by thinking about it, philosophers would have done so long ago. Physiological psychologists take an empirical, practical, and monistic approach to the study of human nature. *Monism* is the belief that reality consists of a unified whole and, thus, that the mind is a phenomenon produced by the workings of the body. We believe that once we understand how the body works—and in particular, how the nervous system works—the mind-body problem will have been solved. What we call "mind" is a consequence of the functioning of the body and its interactions with the environment. The mind-body problem thus exists only as an abstraction. We are convinced that once we understand enough about physiology we will be able to explain how we perceive, how we think, how we remember, and how we act. We will even be able to explain the nature of our own self-awareness. Of course, only time will tell whether this belief is justified.

What can a physiological psychologist say about human self-awareness? We know that it is altered by changes in the structure or chemistry of the brain; therefore, we conclude that consciousness is a physiological function, just like behavior. We can even speculate about the usefulness of self-awareness: Consciousness and the ability to communicate seem to go hand in hand. Species like ours, with our complex social structures and enormous capacity for learning, are well served by our ability to express intentions to one another and to make requests of one another. This communication makes cooperation possible and permits us to establish customs and laws of behavior. Perhaps the ability to make plans and to communicate these plans to others is what was selected for in the evolution of consciousness. Later in this chapter, I will discuss some research that relates to the physiology of consciousness.

The question of human consciousness suggests another issue: *determinism* versus *free will*. Self-awareness seems to bring with it a feeling of control; most people believe their minds choose to make their brains do what they do. They believe that although their environment—and their physiology—affects them, they are able to act of their own free will. Because a belief in free will implies that the mind is not constrained by physiology, it is a form of dualism. This belief is unacceptable in the laboratory; physiological research is limited to those things that can be measured by physical means—matter and energy. We have no tools that permit us to study nonmaterial entities.

In our research we must act like *determinists*, looking for the physical causes of behavior.

Certainly, a belief in determinism is a belief in monism. But in addition, it is a belief that the world is an orderly place where each event is determined by the events that precede it. It is a belief that there are general principles that govern the interactions between matter and energy, and that these principles are responsible for all phenomena, both animate and inanimate. We assume that, in principle, human behavior can be explained down to the last detail by completely understanding its physiology. However, even if we someday discover all there is to know about the physiology of behavior, we will not always be able to predict a particular person's behavior on a particular occasion. In applying the physical laws governing behavior, we would have to know *everything* that is presently going on in a person's body in order to predict what he or she will do next.

From our present perspective this knowledge seems impossible to obtain, which means that for all practical purposes physiological psychology will never take all the mystery out of an individual's behavior. Even physical scientists have to confront the difference between understanding general laws and predicting the behavior of complex systems. For example, although we cannot predict where a feather will fall if we drop it from a tall building during a windstorm, no reasonable person would insist that the landing place is affected by free will on the part of the feather. A determinist would maintain that free will in humans is a myth that is bolstered by two aspects of our nature: the complexity of the human brain, which is far greater than the forces that act on a falling feather, and our own self-awareness, which makes us feel that our minds control our bodies, rather than the reverse.

I am sure that many of you do not agree with the determinist position; you may feel that you are in control of your own behavior, and you can point out—correctly—that I cannot prove otherwise. Fortunately, the issue is a philosophical and religious one that can be divorced from the scientific investigation of the physiology of behavior. If a person believes in his or her own free will, that is fine, as long as he or she *acts* like a determinist in the laboratory. We must limit the scope of our hypotheses to the methods of investigation that we have at hand. Because our techniques are physical, our explanations must also be physical. If organisms do have nonphysical minds or souls that control their behavior, the methods of physiological psychology will never detect them.

BIOLOGICAL ROOTS OF PHYSIOLOGICAL PSYCHOLOGY

Not all modern philosophers are monists, and not all believe that the human mind is based on physiological functioning. Yet scientists who study the physiology of behavior trace their intellectual ancestry to the monistic, deterministic school of philosophy. This school encouraged the development of natural scientists, who first studied living organisms in the world around them and eventually applied their techniques and principles to the study of human behavior.

Although such early natural philosophers as Aristotle speculated about the causes of behavior, René Descartes's physiological model provides a good starting place for a discussion of the biological roots of physiological psychology. His model was wrong, but it was a reasonable hypothesis, considering what was known about the body at the time. Others soon tested its predictions and found them incorrect. For example, experiments showed that the volume of a muscle does not actually increase when it contracts, as it would if it were inflated with fluid. In fact, Luigi Galvani, an eighteenth-century Italian physiologist, found that stimulation of a frog's nerve caused the muscle to which it was attached. The muscle would contract even when the muscle and the nerve attached to it were removed from the rest of the body; thus, pressurized ventricular fluid could obviously not be responsible for the contraction. (Alessandro Volta identified the stimulating event as electricity.) The value of Descartes's physiological model did not lie in whether it was right or wrong; rather, it served to focus the efforts of those who followed him on performing experiments. Thus, knowledge of the physiology of behavior began to accumulate.

Experimental Physiology

One of the most important figures in the development of experimental physiology was Johannes Müller, a nineteenth-century German physiologist. Müller was a forceful advocate of the application of experimental techniques to physiology. Previously, the activities of most natural scientists were limited to observation and classification. Although these activities are essential, Müller insisted that major advances in understanding the workings of the body would be achieved only by experimentally removing or isolating animals' organs, testing their responses to various chemicals, and otherwise altering the environment to see how the organs responded. (See *Figure 1.3.*) His most important contribution to the study of the physiology of behavior was his *doctrine of specific nerve energies.* Müller observed that although all nerves carry the same basic message—an electrical impulse—we perceive the messages of different nerves in different ways. For example, messages carried by the optic nerves produce sensations of visual images, and those carried by the auditory nerves produce sensations of sounds. How can different sensations arise from the same basic message?

The answer is that the messages occur in different channels. The portion of the brain that receives messages from the optic nerves interprets the activity as visual stimulation, even if the nerves are actually stimulated mechanically. (For example, when we rub our eyes, we see flashes of light.) Because different parts of the brain receive messages from different nerves, the brain must be functionally divided: Some parts perform some functions, and other parts perform others.

Müller's advocacy of experimentation and the logical deductions from his doctrine of specific nerve energies set the stage for performing experiments directly on the brain. Indeed, Pierre Flourens, a nineteenth-century French physiologist, did just that. Flourens removed various parts of animals' brains and observed their behavior. By seeing what the animal could no longer do, he could infer the function of the missing portion of the brain. This method is called *experimental ablation* (from the Latin *ablatus,* "carried away"). Flourens claimed to have discovered the regions of the brain that control heart rate and breathing, purposeful movements, and visual and auditory reflexes.

Soon after Flourens performed his experiments, Paul Broca, a French surgeon, applied the principle of experimental ablation to the human brain. Of course, he did not intentionally remove parts of human brains to see how they worked. Instead, he observed the behavior of people whose brains had been damaged by strokes. In 1861 he performed an autopsy on the brain of a

FIGURE 1.3
An isolated frog leg, with the nerve still attached to the muscle—a more modern version of the preparation first devised by Luigi Galvani. Johannes Müller, one of the founders of experimental physiology, advocated this type of study of various organ systems.

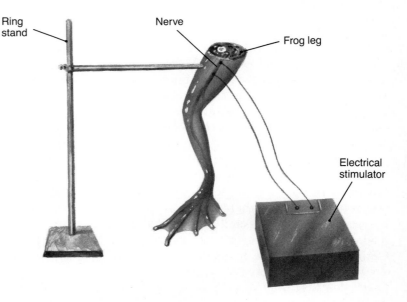

Ring stand

Nerve

Frog leg

Electrical stimulator

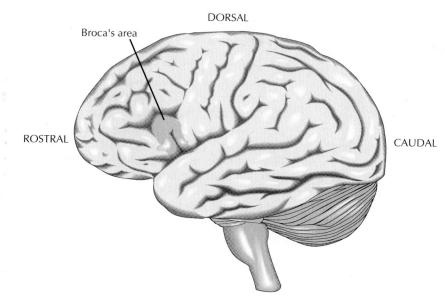

DORSAL

Broca's area

ROSTRAL

CAUDAL

FIGURE 1.4
Broca's area, a region of the brain named for French surgeon Paul Broca. Broca discovered that damage to a part of the left side of the brain disrupted a person's ability to speak.

man who had had a stroke that caused him to lose the ability to speak. Broca's observations led him to conclude that a portion of the cerebral cortex on the left side of the brain performs functions necessary for speech. (See *Figure 1.4.*) Other physicians soon obtained evidence supporting his conclusions. As you will learn, the physiological basis of speech is not localized in a particular region of the brain. Indeed, speech requires many different functions, which are organized throughout the brain. Nonetheless, the method of experimental ablation remains important to our understanding of the brains of both humans and laboratory animals.

As I mentioned earlier, Luigi Galvani used electricity to demonstrate that muscles contain the source of the energy that powers their contractions. In 1870 the German physiologists Gustav Fritsch and Eduard Hitzig used electrical stimulation as a tool for understanding the physiology of the brain. They applied weak electrical shocks to the exposed surface of a dog's cerebral cortex and observed the effects of the stimulation. They found that stimulation of different portions of a specific region of the cortex caused contraction of specific muscles on the opposite side of the body. We now refer to this region as the primary motor cortex, and we know that nerve cells there communicate directly with those that cause

muscular contractions. We also know that other regions of the brain communicate with the primary motor cortex and thus control behaviors. For example, the region that Broca found to be necessary for speech communicates with the portion of the primary motor cortex that controls the muscles of the lips, tongue, and throat, which we use to speak.

One of the most brilliant contributors to nineteenth-century science was the German physicist and physiologist Hermann von Helmholtz. Helmholtz devised a mathematical formulation of the law of conservation of energy, invented the ophthalmoscope (used to examine the retina of the eye), devised an important and influential theory of color vision and color blindness, and studied audition, music, eye movements, geometry, allergies, and the formation of ice. Although Helmholtz had studied under Müller, he opposed Müller's belief that human organs are endowed with a vital nonmaterial force that coordinates their operations. Helmholtz believed, as modern biologists do, that *all* aspects of physiology are mechanistic, subject to experimental investigation.

Helmholtz was the first scientist to attempt to measure the speed of conduction through nerves. Scientists had previously believed that such conduction was identical to the conduction that occurs in wires, traveling at approximately the speed of light. But Helmholtz found that neural conduction was much slower—only about 90 feet per second. This measurement proved that neural conduction was more than a simple electrical message, as we will see in the next chapter.

Twentieth-century developments in experimental physiology include many important inventions, such as sensitive amplifiers to detect weak electrical signals, neurochemical techniques to analyze chemical changes within and between cells, and histological techniques to see cells and their constituents. Because these developments belong to the modern era, they are discussed in detail in subsequent chapters.

Functionalism: Natural Selection and Evolution

In discussing the biological roots of physiological psychology, I have provided a brief history of the contribution of experimental physiology. Müller's insistence that biology must be an experimental science provided the starting point for an

FIGURE 1.5
Charles Darwin (1809–1882). His theory of evolution revolutionized biology and provided the basis for functionalism, a theory that strongly influenced pioneering psychologists. (North Wind Picture Archives.)

important tradition. However, other biologists continued to observe, classify, and think about what they saw, and some of them arrived at valuable conclusions. The most important of these biologists was Charles Darwin. (See *Figure 1.5.*) Darwin formulated the principle of *natural selection*, which revolutionized biology. He noted that individuals spontaneously undergo structural changes. If these changes produce favorable effects that permit the individual to reproduce more successfully, some of the individual's offspring will inherit the favorable characteristics and will themselves produce more offspring.

Darwin's theory emphasized that all of an organism's characteristics—its structure, its coloration, its behavior—have functional significance. For example, eagles have strong talons and sharp beaks because they permit the birds to catch and eat prey. Caterpillars that eat green leaves are themselves green because this color makes it difficult for birds to see them against their usual background. Mother mice construct nests because their offspring will be kept warm and out of harm's way. *Functionalism* assumes that characteristics of living organisms perform useful functions, or at least functions that were useful at one time in the history of the species. To understand the physiological basis of various behaviors, we must first understand the significance of these behaviors. We must therefore understand something about the natural history of the species being studied so that the behaviors can be seen in context.

A good example of the functional analysis of an adaptive trait was demonstrated in an experiment by Blest (1957). Certain species of moths and butterflies have spots on their wings that resemble eyes—particularly the eyes of predators such as owls. (See *Figure 1.6.*) These insects normally rely on camouflage for protection; the back of their wings, when folded, are colored like the bark of a tree. However, when a bird approaches, the insect's wings flip open, which suddenly displays the hidden eyespots. The bird then tends to fly away rather than eat the insect. Blest performed an experiment to see whether the eyespots on a moth's or butterfly's wings really disturbed birds who saw them. He placed mealworms on different backgrounds and counted how many worms

FIGURE 1.6

The owl butterfly. This butterfly displays its eyespots when approached by a bird. The bird usually will then fly away. (Cosmos/Photo Researchers Inc.)

the birds ate. Indeed, when the worms were placed on a background that contained eyespots, the birds tended to avoid them.

To understand the workings of a complex piece of machinery, one needs to know what its functions are. This principle is just as true for a living organism as it is for a mechanical device. However, an important difference exists between machines and organisms: Machines have inventors who had a purpose when they designed them, whereas organisms are the result of a long series of accidents. Thus, strictly speaking, we cannot say that any physiological mechanisms of living organisms have a *purpose*. But they have *functions*, and these we can try to determine. For example, the forelimbs shown in Figure 1.7 are adapted for different uses in different species of animals. (See *Figure 1.7*.)

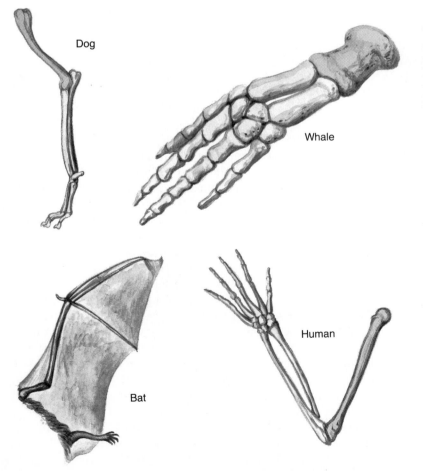

Dog

Whale

Bat

Human

FIGURE 1.7

The humerus bone, shown in color. Through the process of natural selection, this bone has been adapted to suit many different functions. (Adapted from Moore, R. *Evolution*. New York: Life Nature Library, 1964.)

The cornerstone of evolution is the principle of natural selection. Briefly, here is how the process works for sexually reproducing multicellular animals: Every organism consists of a large number of cells, each of which contains chromosomes. Chromosomes are complex molecules that contain the recipes for producing the proteins that cells need to grow and perform their functions. In essence, the chromosomes contain the blueprints for the construction (that is, the embryological development) of a particular member of a particular species. If the plans are altered, a different organism is produced.

The plans do get altered; mutations occur from time to time. Mutations are accidental changes in the chromosomes of sperms or eggs that join together and develop into new organisms. For example, cosmic radiation might strike a chromosome in a cell of a parental testis or ovary, thus producing a mutation that affects the offspring. Most mutations are deleterious: The offspring either fails to survive or survives with some sort of deficit. However, a small percentage of mutations are beneficial and confer a *selective advantage* to the organism that possesses them. That is, the animal is more likely than those without the mutation to live long enough to reproduce and hence to pass on its chromosomes (with their alteration) to its own offspring. Many different kinds of traits can confer a selective advantage. Examples include resistance to a particular disease, the ability to digest new kinds of food, more effective weapons for defense or for procurement of prey, and even a more attractive appearance to members of the opposite sex (after all, one must reproduce in order to pass on one's chromosomes).

Naturally, the traits that can be altered by mutations are physical ones; chromosomes make proteins, which affect the structure and chemistry of cells. But the *effects* of these physical alterations can be seen in an animal's behavior. Thus, the process of natural selection can indirectly act upon behavior. For example, if a particular mutation results in changes in the brain that cause a small animal to stop moving and freeze when it perceives a novel stimulus, that animal is more likely to escape undetected when a predator passes nearby. This tendency makes the animal more likely to survive and produce offspring, thus passing on its genes to future generations.

Other mutations are not immediately favorable; but because they do not put their possessors at a disadvantage, they get inherited by at least some members of the species. As a result of thousands of such mutations, the members of a particular species possess a variety of genes and are all at least somewhat different from one another. Different environments provide optimal habitats for different kinds of organisms. When the environment changes, species must adapt or run the risk of becoming extinct. If some members of the species possess assortments of genes that provide characteristics permitting them to adapt to the new environment, their genes will soon dominate, and the species will undergo changes. Thus, many mutations that do not cause immediate changes in the genetic composition of a species may at some future time provide the genetic variability that permits at least some individuals to take advantage of environmental changes.

An understanding of the principle of natural selection plays some role in the thinking of every person who undertakes research in physiological psychology. Some researchers explicitly consider the genetic mechanisms of various behaviors and the physiological processes upon which these behaviors depend. Others are concerned with comparative aspects of behavior and its physiological basis; they compare the nervous systems of animals from a variety of species in order to make hypotheses about the evolution of brain structure and the behavioral capacities that correspond to this evolutionary development. But even though many researchers are not directly involved with the problem of evolution, the principle of natural selection guides the thinking of all physiological psychologists. We ask ourselves what the selective advantage of a particular trait might be. We think about how nature might have used a physiological mechanism that already existed to perform more complex functions in more complex organisms. When we entertain hypotheses, we ask ourselves whether a particular explanation makes sense in an evolutionary perspective.

CONTRIBUTIONS OF MODERN PSYCHOLOGY

The field of physiological psychology grew out of psychology. Indeed, the first textbook of psychology, written by Wilhelm Wundt in the late nineteenth century, was titled *Principles of Physiological Psychology*. In recent years, with the explosion of information in experimental biology, scientists from other disciplines have become prominent contributors to the investigation of the physiology of behavior. The united effort of physiological psychologists, physiologists, and other neuroscientists has come about because of the realization that the ultimate function of the nervous system is *behavior*. Of course, we do things beside move—for example, we perceive, think, and remember. However, the function of perception, thinking, and remembering is that they permit us to engage in behaviors that are responsive to our environment and thus useful to our own existence.

The modern history of investigating the physiology of behavior has been written by psychologists who have combined the methods of experimental psychology with the methods of experimental physiology and have applied them to the issues that concern psychologists in general. Thus, we have studied perceptual processes, control of movement, sleep and waking, reproductive behaviors, aggressive behaviors, ingestive behaviors, learning, and communication. In recent years we have begun to study the physiology of pathological conditions, such as mental disorders.

The Goals of Research

The goal of all scientists is to explain the phenomena they study. But what do we mean by "explain"? Scientific explanation takes two forms: generalization and reduction. Most psychologists deal with *generalization.* They explain particular instances of behavior as examples of general laws, which they deduce from their experiments. For instance, most psychologists would explain a pathologically strong fear of dogs as an example of classical conditioning. Presumably, the person was frightened earlier in life by a dog. An unpleasant stimulus was paired with the sight of the animal (perhaps the person was knocked down by an exuberant dog or was attacked by a vicious one), and the subsequent sight of dogs evokes the earlier response—fear.

Most physiologists deal with *reduction.* They explain phenomena in terms of simpler phenom-

ena. For example, they may explain the movement of a muscle in terms of the changes in the membranes of muscle cells, the entry of particular chemicals, and the interactions among protein molecules within these cells. Similarly, a molecular biologist would explain these events in terms of forces that bind various molecules together and cause various parts of the molecules to be attracted to one another. In turn, the job of an atomic physicist is to describe matter and energy themselves and to account for the various forces found in nature. Practitioners of each branch of science use reduction to call on more elementary generalizations to explain the phenomena they study.

The task of the physiological psychologist is to explain behavior in physiological terms. But physiological psychologists cannot simply be reductionists. It is not enough to observe behaviors and correlate them with physiological events that occur at the same time. Identical behaviors may occur for different reasons and thus may be initiated by different physiological mechanisms. Therefore, we must understand "psychologically" why a particular behavior occurs before we can understand what physiological events made it occur.

Let me provide a specific example. Mice, like many other mammals, often build nests. Behavioral observations show that mice will build nests under two conditions: when the air temperature is low and when the animal is pregnant. A nonpregnant mouse will not build a nest if the weather is warm, whereas a pregnant mouse will build one regardless of the temperature. The same behavior occurs for different reasons. Thus, it should not be surprising that these behaviors are initiated by different physiological mechanisms, one involving changes in the levels of various hormones in the animal's blood, and another involving nerve cells that detect temperature changes. Nest building can be studied as a behavior related to the process of temperature regulation, or it can be studied in the context of parental behavior.

Sometimes, physiological mechanisms can tell us something about psychological processes. This relationship is particularly true of complex phenomena such as language, memory, and mood, which are poorly understood psychologically. For example, damage to a specific part of the brain can cause very specific impairments in a person's language abilities. The nature of these impairments suggests how these abilities are organized. For example, when the damage involves a brain region that is important in analyzing speech sounds, it also produces deficits in spelling. This finding suggests that the ability to recognize a spoken word and the ability to spell it call upon related brain mechanisms. Damage to a different region can make it impossible for people to read unfamiliar words by sounding them out but does not impair their ability to read words with which they are already familiar. This finding suggests that reading comprehension can take two routes: one that is related to speech sounds and another that is primarily visual, bypassing acoustic representation.

In practice, the research efforts of physiological psychologists involve both forms of explanation—generalization and reduction. Ideas for experiments are stimulated by the investigator's knowledge both of psychological generalizations about behavior and of physiological mechanisms. A good physiological psychologist must therefore be both a good psychologist and a good physiologist.

Understanding Self-awareness: Split Brains

I suggested earlier that our self-awareness is related to our ability to communicate verbally with each other. Several chapters will discuss research on problems related to human consciousness, including perception, memory, and verbal communication. But in this chapter I want to introduce you to some research that indicates that awareness is very much a function of the brain. Studies of humans who have undergone a particular surgical procedure demonstrate that when parts of the brain involved with verbal behavior are disconnected from parts that are involved with certain kinds of perceptions, people become unaware of these perceptions. These results suggest that the parts of the brain involved in verbal behavior play a critical role in consciousness.

The surgical procedure is one that has been used for people who have very severe epilepsy that cannot be controlled by drugs. In these people nerve cells in one side of the brain become overactive, and the overactivity is transmitted to the other side of the brain by the corpus callosum. The *corpus callosum* is a large bundle of nerve fibers that connect corresponding parts of one side of the brain with those on the other. Both sides of the brain then engage in wild activity and stimulate each other, causing a generalized epileptic seizure. These seizures can occur many times each day, preventing the patient from leading a normal life. Neurosurgeons discovered that cutting the corpus callosum (the *split-brain operation*) greatly reduced the frequency of the epileptic seizures.

Figure 1.8 shows a drawing of the split-brain operation. We see the brain sliced down the middle, from front to back, dividing it into its two symmetrical halves (the *cerebral hemispheres*). The corpus callosum is being cut by the neurosurgeon's special knife. (See *Figure 1.8.*)

Sperry (1966) and Gazzaniga and his associates (Gazzaniga, 1970; Gazzaniga and LeDoux, 1978) have studied these patients extensively. The two cerebral hemispheres receive sensory information from the opposite sides of the body and control movements of the opposite sides, too. The corpus callosum permits the two hemispheres to share information, so that each side knows what the other side is perceiving and doing. After the split-brain operation is performed, the two hemispheres are disconnected and operate independently; their sensory mechanisms, memories, and motor systems can no longer exchange information. The effects of these disconnections are not obvious to the casual observer, for the simple reason that only one hemisphere—in most people, the left—controls speech. The right hemisphere of an epileptic person with a split brain can understand speech reasonably well, but that hemisphere is poor at reading and spelling and is totally incapable of producing speech.

Because only one side of the brain can talk about what it is experiencing, most observers do not detect the independent operations of the right side of a split brain. Even the patient's left brain has to learn about the independent existence of the right brain. One of the first things that these patients say they notice after the operation is that

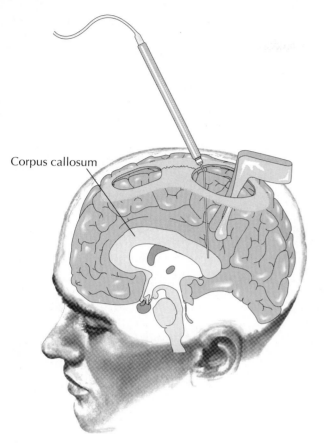

Corpus callosum

FIGURE 1.8
The split-brain operation. (Adapted from Gazzaniga, M.S. *Fundamentals of Psychology.* New York: Academic Press, 1973.)

their left hand seems to have a "mind of its own." For example, patients may find themselves putting down a book held in the left hand, even if they are reading it with great interest. This conflict occurs because the right hemisphere, which controls the left hand, cannot read and therefore finds the book boring. At other times, they surprise themselves by making obscene gestures (with the left hand) when they had not intended to. A psychologist once reported that a man with a split brain attempted to beat his wife with one hand and protect her with the other. Did he *really* want to hurt her? Yes and no, I guess.

One exception to the crossed representation of sensory information is the olfactory system. That is, when a person sniffs a flower through the left nostril, only the left brain receives a sensation of

the odor. Thus, if the right nostril of a patient with a split brain is closed, leaving the left nostril open, the patient will accurately identify odors verbally. However, if the odor enters the right nostril, the patient will say that he or she smells nothing. But, in fact, the right hemisphere *has* perceived the odor and *can* identify it. This ability can be demonstrated by asking the patient to smell an odor with the right nostril and then reach for some objects that are hidden from view by a partition. If the patient is asked to use the left hand, controlled by the hemisphere that detected the smell, he or she will select the object that corresponds to the odor—a plastic flower for a floral odor, a toy fish for a fishy odor, a model tree for the odor of pine, and so forth. But if the patient is asked to use the right hand, he or she fails this test, because the right hand is connected to the left hemisphere, which did not smell the odor. (See *Figure 1.9.*)

The effects of cutting the corpus callosum reinforce the conclusion that we become conscious of something only if information about it is able to reach the circuits that control speech, which are located in the left hemisphere. If such communication is interrupted, then some kinds of information can never reach consciousness.

The Value of Research in Physiological Psychology

Most of the research that I have described in this book involves experimentation on living animals. As you will see, many of the experiments involve surgery. In some cases parts of the animals' brains are destroyed or small metal tubes are placed there to introduce drugs or remove fluid for analysis. After an animal has participated in an experiment, it is usually killed so that its brain can be examined and analyzed.

Any time we use another species of animals for our own purposes, we should be sure that what we are doing is both humane and worthwhile. I believe that a good case can be made that research on the physiology of behavior qualifies on both counts. The first part—humane treatment—is a matter of procedure. We know how to maintain laboratory animals in good health in comfortable, sanitary conditions. We know how to administer anesthetics and analgesics so that animals do not

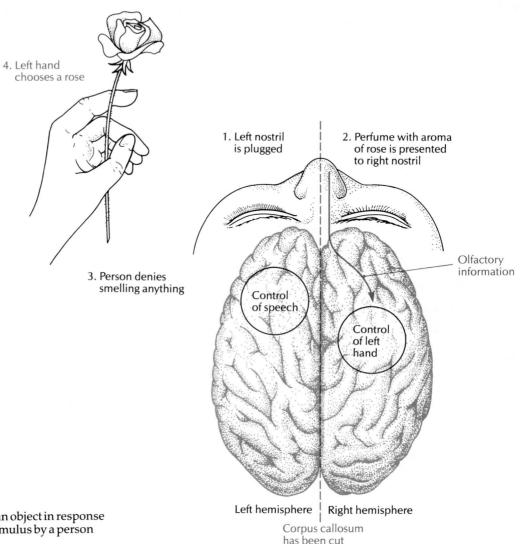

4. Left hand chooses a rose

1. Left nostril is plugged

2. Perfume with aroma of rose is presented to right nostril

3. Person denies smelling anything

Olfactory information

Control of speech

Control of left hand

Left hemisphere | Right hemisphere

Corpus callosum has been cut

FIGURE 1.9
Identification of an object in response to an olfactory stimulus by a person with a split brain.

suffer during or after surgery, and we know how to prevent infections with proper surgical procedures and the use of antibiotics. Most industrially developed societies have very strict regulations about the care of animals and also require approval of the procedures that will be used in the experiments in which they participate. There is no excuse for mistreating animals in our care. In fact, the vast majority of laboratory animals *are* treated humanely.

Whether an experiment is *worthwhile* is more difficult to say. We use animals for many pur-

poses. We eat their meat and their eggs and drink their milk; we turn their hides into leather; we extract insulin and other hormones from their organs to treat people with diseases; we train them to do useful work on farms or to entertain us. Even having a pet is a form of exploitation; it is we—not they—who decide that they will live in our homes. The fact is, we have been using other animals throughout the evolutionary history of our species (and only recently have we been worried about whether this use is humane).

If a person believes that it is wrong to use another animal in any way, regardless of the benefits to humans, there is nothing I can say to convince him or her of the value of scientific research with animals. For this person, the issue is closed from the very beginning. Moral absolutes cannot be settled logically; like religious beliefs, they can be accepted or rejected, but they cannot be proved or disproved. Therefore, I will not try to attack or defend absolute moral positions. My arguments in support of scientific research with animals are based on an evaluation of the benefits the research has to humans.

Our species is beset by many medical, mental, and behavioral problems, many of which can be solved only through biological research. I will restrict my discussion to research on the nervous system, leaving arguments about research on diseases such as cancer and infectious diseases to others. First, let us consider some of the major neurological disorders. Strokes, caused by bleeding or occlusion of a blood vessel within the brain, often leave people partly paralyzed, unable to read or write or to communicate verbally with their friends and family. Basic research on the means by which nerve cells communicate with each other has led to important discoveries about the causes of the death of brain cells. This research was not directed toward a specific practical goal; the potential benefits actually came as a surprise to the investigators.

Experiments based on these results have shown that if a blood vessel leading to the brain is occluded for a few minutes, the part of the brain that is nourished by that vessel will die. However, the brain damage can be prevented by first administering a drug that interferes with a particular kind of neural communication. (I will discuss this phenomenon in Chapter 15.) This research is important, because it may lead to medical treatments that can help reduce the brain damage caused by strokes. But it involves operating on a laboratory animal such as a rat and pinching off a blood vessel. (The animals are all anesthetized, of course.) Some of the animals will sustain brain damage, and all will be killed so that their brains can be examined. However, I think you will agree that research like this is just as legitimate as using animals for food.

Research with laboratory animals has produced important discoveries about the possible causes or potential treatments of neurological and mental disorders, including Parkinson's disease, schizophrenia, manic-depressive illness, anxiety disorders, obsessive-compulsive disorders, anorexia nervosa, obesity, and drug addictions. These problems are still with us and cause much human suffering. Unless we continue our research with laboratory animals, they will not be solved. Some people have suggested that instead of using laboratory animals in our research, we could use tissue cultures or computers. Unfortunately, tissue cultures or computers are not substitutes for living organisms. We have no way to study behavioral problems such as addictions in tissue cultures, nor can we program a computer to simulate the workings of an animal's brain. (If we could, that would mean we already had all the answers.)

The easiest way to justify research with animals is to point to actual and potential benefits to human health, as I have just done. However, I think that we can also justify this research with a less practical but perhaps equally important argument. One of the things that characterizes our species is a quest for an understanding of our world. For example, astronomers contemplate the universe and try to uncover its mysteries. Even if their discoveries never lead to practical benefits such as better drugs or faster methods of transportation, the fact that they enrich our understanding of the beginning and the fate of our universe justifies their efforts. The pursuit of knowledge is itself a worthwhile endeavor. Surely the attempt to understand the universe within us—our nervous system, which is responsible for all that we are or can be—is equally valuable.

*I*NTERIM SUMMARY

The mind-body problem has puzzled philosophers for many centuries. The naive animism of primitive cultures was soon replaced by dualism, which rejected the notion of spirits but retained a belief in a nonmaterial human soul. Modern science has adopted a monistic position—the belief that the world consists of matter and energy and that nonmaterial entities such as minds or souls are not a part of the universe. At the very least, they cannot be studied with the tools available to scientists.

A dualist, René Descartes, proposed a model of the brain based on hydraulically actuated statues. His model stimulated observations that produced important discoveries. The results of Galvani's experiments eventually led to an understanding of the nature of the message transmitted by nerves between the brain and the sensory organs and the muscles. Müller's doctrine of specific nerve energies paved the way for study of the functions of specific parts of the brain, through the methods of experimental ablation and electrical stimulation.

Darwin's theory of evolution, which was based on the concept of natural selection, provided an important contribution to modern physiological psychology. The theory asserts that we must understand the functions performed by an organ or body part or by a behavior. Through random mutations, changes in an individual's genetic material cause different proteins to be produced, which results in the alteration of some physical characteristics. If the changes confer a selective advantage on the individual, the new genes will be transmitted to more and more members of the species. Even behaviors can evolve, through the selective advantage of alterations in the structure of the nervous system.

All scientists hope to explain natural phenomena. In this context the term *explanation* has two basic meanings: generalization and reduction. Generalization refers to the classification of phenomena according to their essential features so that general laws can be formulated. For example, observing that gravitational attraction is related to the mass of two bodies and to the distance between them helps explain the movement of planets. Reduction refers to the description of phenomena in terms of more basic physical processes. For example, gravitation can be explained in terms of forces and subatomic particles.

Physiological psychologists use both generalization and reduction in explaining behavior. In large part, generalizations use the traditional methods of psychology. Reduction explains behaviors in terms of physiological events within the body—primarily within the nervous system. Thus, physiological psychology builds on the tradition of both experimental psychology and experimental physiology.

Study of the functions of the human nervous system give us hope that even the most complex mental processes may someday be understood. Cutting the corpus callosum not only splits the brain but also disconnects right-hemisphere brain functions from conscious awareness. For example, when sensory information about a particular object is presented to the right hemisphere of a person with a split brain, the person is not aware of the object but can, nevertheless, indicate by movements of the left hand that the object has been perceived. This phenomenon suggests that conscious awareness involves operations of the verbal mechanisms of the left hemisphere. Indeed, consciousness may be, in large part, a matter of our "talking to ourselves." Thus, once we understand the language functions of the brain, we may have gone a long way in understanding how the brain can be conscious of its own existence.

Research on the physiology of behavior necessarily involves the use of laboratory animals. It is incumbent on all scientists using these animals to see that they are housed comfortably and treated humanely, and laws have been enacted to ensure that they are. Such research has already produced benefits to humankind and promises to continue to do so in the future.

ORGANIZATION OF THIS BOOK

Outline

The physiology of behavior means, in large part, the role of the nervous system in the control of behavior. Thus, this book begins with the fundamentals of neurophysiology, neurochemistry, neuropharmacology, and neuroanatomy. Chapter 2 describes the cells of the nervous system and explains how neurons send messages along their axons (nerve fibers). Chapter 3 describes communication between neurons, which is almost always accomplished chemically. The release of the chemical transmitter is explained, as well as the effects it has on the cell receiving the message. Because almost all drugs that have behavioral effects produce them by influencing chemical communication between neurons, the effects of these drugs are also covered. As you will see, beside being used to treat diseases and mental disorders, drugs have become important tools in our attempts to understand the nature of brain mechanisms.

Chapter 4 outlines the anatomy of the brain and its interactions with the endocrine system. A necessary step in understanding how the brain carries out its functions is to determine which neural circuits perform which functions. Thus, in order to understand the results of research in physiological psychology, one must know at least some essentials of neuroanatomy. Chapter 5 describes the basic research methods of physiological psychology, including neuroanatomical methods, experimental ablation methods, electrical-recording methods, electrical stimulation methods, and neurochemical methods.

The second section of the book describes the physiology of perception and movement. Chapter 6 discusses vision, and Chapter 7 discusses the other sensory modalities: audition, the vestibular senses, the somatosenses, gustation, and olfaction. Chapter 8 describes the neural control of movement.

The third section of the book deals with species-typical behaviors, which are of special importance to motivation. Chapter 9 describes the physiology of sleep and waking, including sleep disorders and the control of biological rhythms. Chapter 10 describes the physiology of sexual development and mating behavior. Chapter 11 describes other behaviors involved in reproduction: aggressive behavior and the care of offspring. Chapter 12 describes the control of drinking and the internal physiological processes related to water balance; Chapter 13 describes eating and metabolism.

The fourth section of the book deals with the physiology of learning and motivation. Chapter 14 deals with the anatomy of learning, attempting to answer the question "Which parts of the brain are essential for the learning of which kinds of behavior?" Chapter 15 describes research on the physiology and biochemistry of learning—the actual nature of the structural and biochemical changes that take place in the brain as a result of experience. Chapter 16 describes research on the neural mechanisms responsible for reinforcement and drug addiction.

The final section of the book describes the anatomy and physiology of human communication and of disorders of thought and mood. Chapter 17 discusses what we have learned about the neural organization of various types of communication: listening, speaking, reading, writing, and expressing and perceiving emotions. Chapter 18 describes research on the physiology of serious mental disorders: schizophrenia, the affective disorders, and the anxiety disorders.

Some Mechanical Details

Before you begin reading the next chapter, I want to say a few things about the design of the book that may help you with your studies. I have tried to integrate the text and illustrations as closely as possible. In my experience, one of the most annoying aspects of reading some books is not knowing when to look at an illustration. When reading complicated material, I have found that sometimes I look at the figure too soon, before I have read enough to understand it; and sometimes, I look at it too late and realize that I could have made more sense of the text if I had just looked at the figure sooner. Furthermore, after looking at the illustration, I often find it difficult to return to the place where I stopped reading. Therefore, in this book you will find the figure references in boldface italics (like this: *Figure 5.6*), which means "stop reading and look at the figure." I have placed these references in the locations I think will be optimal. If you look away from the text then, you will be assured that you will not be interrupting a line of reasoning in a crucial place and will not have to reread several sentences to get going again. You will find sections like this:

"Figure 4.1 shows an alligator and a human. The alligator is certainly laid out in a linear fashion; we can draw a straight line that starts between its eyes and continues down the center of its spinal cord. (See *Figure 4.1.*)" This particular example is a trivial one and will give you no problems no matter when you look at the figure. But in other cases the material is more complex, and you will have less trouble if you know what to look for before you stop reading and examine the illustration.

You will notice that some words in the text are printed in *lightface italics* and others are printed in **boldface italics**. Lightface italics mean one of two things: Either the word is being stressed for emphasis and is not a new term, or I am pointing out a new term that I do not think you need to learn. On the other hand, a word in boldface is a new term that you should try to learn. Most of the boldfaced terms in the text are part of the vocabulary of the physiological psychologist. Often, they will be used again in a later chapter. As an aid to your studying, I have included a list of all of the boldfaced terms at the end of each chapter, along with the page number on which the term was first used. Also, the end of the text contains a glossary, which provides definitions for important terms that are used throughout the book. In addition, a comprehensive index at the end of the book provides a list of terms and topics, with page references.

The physiology of behavior is a complex subject, and this book contains many concepts and descriptions of experiments that will be new to you. At the end of each major section I have included an *interim summary*, which provides a place for you to stop and think again about what you have just read, in order to make sure that you understand the direction the discussion has gone. Taken together, these sections provide a detailed summary of the information introduced in the chapter. My students tell me that they review the interim summaries just before taking a test.

CONCLUDING REMARKS

The introduction is over. I tried to make it reasonably short so that you would not have to wait long to get to the heart of the matter. The next two chapters introduce you to the cells of the nervous system, whose structure and activities are responsible for our perceptions, memories, and actions; they make us what we are. I hope that in reading this book you will come not only to learn more about the brain but also to appreciate it for the marvelous organ it is. The brain is wonderfully complex, and perhaps the most remarkable thing about it is that we are able to use it in our attempt to understand it.

NEW TERMS

animism p. 2
cerebral hemisphere p. 12
corpus callosum p. 12
doctrine of specific nerve
    energies p. 6

dualism p. 2
experimental ablation p. 6
functionalism p. 8
generalization p. 11

monism p. 4
reduction p. 7
split-brain operation p. 12

SUGGESTED READINGS

Butterfield, H. *The Origins of Modern Science: 1300–1800*. New York: Macmillan, 1959.

Sacks, O. *The Man Who Mistook His Wife for a Hat and Other Clinical Tales*. New York: Harper & Row, 1987.

Schultz, D., and Schultz, S.E. *A History of Modern Psychology*, 4th ed. New York: Academic Press, 1987.

Springer, S.P., and Deutsch, G. *Left Brain, Right Brain*, 3rd ed. New York: W.H. Freeman and Co., 1989.

2

Structure and Functions of Cells of the Nervous System

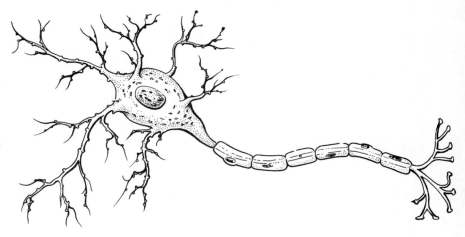

*T*he brain is the organ that moves the muscles. That may sound a bit simplistic, but ultimately, movement—or more accurately, behavior—is the primary function of the nervous system. In order to make useful movements, the brain must know what is happening outside, in the environment. Thus, the body contains cells that are specialized for detecting environmental events and others that are specialized for producing movements. Of course, complex animals such as ourselves do not react automatically to events in our environment; our brains are flexible enough so that we behave in different ways, according to present circumstances and those we experienced in the past. Besides perceiving and acting, we can remember and decide. All these abilities are made possible by the billions of cells found in the nervous system.

This chapter describes the structure and functions of the most important cells of the nervous system. Information, in the form of light, sound waves, odors, tastes, or contact with objects, is gathered from the environment by specialized cells called *sensory neurons.* Movements are accomplished by the contraction of muscles, which are controlled by *motor neurons.* (The term *motor* is used here in its original sense to refer to movement, not to a mechanical engine.) And in between sensory neurons and motor neurons come all the other 100 billion (or so) neurons that do the perceiving, learning, remembering, deciding, and controlling of complex behaviors.

In order to understand how the nervous system controls behavior, we must first understand its parts—the cells that compose it. Because this chapter deals with cells, you need not be familiar with the structure of the nervous system, which is presented in Chapter 4. However, you need to know that the nervous system consists of two basic divisions, the central nervous system and the peripheral nervous system. The *central nervous system* (CNS) consists of the parts that are encased by the bones of the skull and spinal column: the brain and the spinal cord. The *peripheral nervous system* (PNS) is found outside these bones and consists of the nerves and some of the sensory organs.

CELLS OF THE NERVOUS SYSTEM

Neurons

The neuron (nerve cell) is the information-processing and information-transmitting element of the nervous system. Before describing the particular characteristics of neurons, I will describe the structures and properties these cells have in common with other cells of the body.

Structures of Cells

Figure 2.1 illustrates a typical animal cell. (See *Figure 2.1.*) The *membrane* defines the boundary of the cell. It consists of a double layer of lipid (fatlike) molecules. Floating in the membrane are a variety of protein molecules that have special functions. Some detect substances outside the cell (such as hormones) and pass information about the presence of these substances to the interior of the cell. Others control access to the interior of the cell, permitting some substances to enter but barring others. Still others act as pumps, actively pushing certain molecules out of the cell or pulling them in. Because the membrane of the neuron is especially important in the transmission of information, its characteristics will be discussed in more detail later in this chapter.

The *nucleus* ("nut") of the cell is round or oval and is covered by the nuclear membrane. The nucleolus and the chromosomes reside here. The *nucleolus* manufactures *ribosomes,* small structures that are involved in protein synthesis. The chromosomes, which consist of long strands of *deoxyribonucleic acid* (DNA), contain the organism's genetic information. When they are active, portions of the chromosomes (*genes*) cause production of another complex molecule, *messenger ribonucleic acid* (mRNA). The mRNA leaves the nuclear membrane and attaches to ribosomes, where it causes the production of a particular protein. (See *Figure 2.2.*)

Proteins are important in cell functions. As well as providing structure, proteins serve as *enzymes,* which direct the chemical processes of a cell by controlling chemical reactions. Enzymes are special protein molecules that act as catalysts;

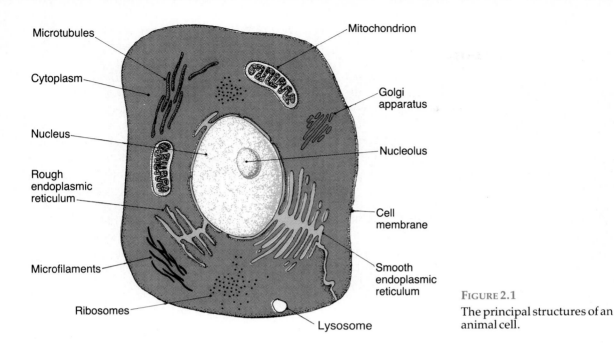

FIGURE 2.1
The principal structures of an animal cell.

that is, they cause a chemical reaction to take place without becoming a part of the final product themselves. Because cells contain the constituents needed to synthesize an enormous variety of compounds, the ones they actually do produce depend primarily on the particular enzymes that are present. Furthermore, there are enzymes that break molecules apart as well as put them together; the enzymes present in a particular region of a cell thus determine which molecules remain intact. For example,

$$A + B \underset{Y}{\overset{X}{\rightleftharpoons}} AB$$

In this reversible reaction the relative concentrations of enzymes X and Y determine whether the complex substance AB or its constituents, A and

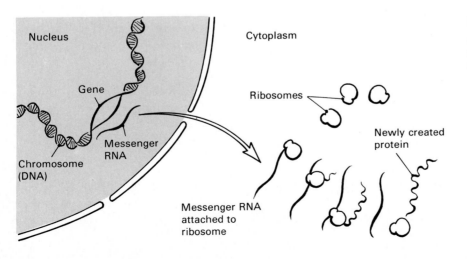

FIGURE 2.2
An overview of the process of protein synthesis, controlled by the genes.

B, will predominate. Enzyme X makes A and B join; enzyme Y splits AB apart. (Energy may also be required to make the reactions proceed.)

The bulk of the cell consists of cytoplasm. *Cytoplasm* is complex and varies considerably across types of cells, but it can be most easily characterized as a jellylike, semiliquid substance that fills the space outlined by the membrane. Cytoplasm is not static and inert; it streams and flows. It contains small specialized structures, just as the body contains specialized organs.

Mitochondria (singular: mitochondrion) are shaped like oval beads and are formed of a double membrane. The inner membrane is wrinkled, and the wrinkles make up a set of shelves *(cristae)* that fill the inside of the bead. Mitochondria perform a vital role in the economy of the cell; many of the biochemical steps involved in the extraction of energy from the breakdown of nutrients take place on the cristae. Most cell biologists believe that many eons ago mitochondria were free-living organisms, which came to "infect" larger cells. Because the mitochondria could extract energy more efficiently than the larger cells, they became useful to them and eventually became a permanent part of them. The cell provides mitochondria with nutrients, and the mitochondria provide the cell with a special molecule—*adenosine triphosphate* (ATP)—that it uses as its immediate source of energy.

Endoplasmic reticulum appears in two forms: rough and smooth. Both types consist of folded layers of membrane identical with the membrane that encloses the cell. Rough endoplasmic reticulum contains ribosomes. The protein produced by the ribosomes attached to the rough endoplasmic reticulum is destined to be transported out of the cell. For example, the hormone insulin (a protein) is manufactured there in certain cells of the pancreas. Unattached ribosomes are also distributed around the cytoplasm; the unattached variety appears to produce protein for use within the cell. The smooth endoplasmic reticulum is concerned with the transport of substances around the cytoplasm and provides channels for the segregation of various molecules involved in different cellular processes. Some complex molecules (such as those that consist of several protein molecules) are assembled there.

The *Golgi apparatus* is a special form of endoplasmic reticulum. It serves primarily as a wrapping or packaging agent. For example, secretory cells (such as those that release hormones) wrap their product in a membrane produced by the Golgi apparatus. When the cell secretes its products, the container migrates to the outer membrane of the cell, fuses with it, and bursts, spilling the product into the fluid surrounding the cell. As we will see, neurons are secretory cells; they communicate with each other by secreting chemicals by this means. The Golgi apparatus also produces *lysosomes,* small sacs that contain enzymes that break down substances no longer needed by the cell. These products are then recycled or excreted from the cell.

Arranged throughout the cell are microfilaments and microtubules. *Microfilaments* are made of the same type of long protein fibers that provide the motive force in muscles. They are found just under the membrane and give cells (especially neurons) their particular shape. They probably also control the movement of proteins that are embedded in the membrane. *Microtubules* are larger than microfilaments and consist of bundles of filaments arranged around a hollow core. They provide motive force in cells such as sperms and transport substances from place to place in other types of cells, including neurons.

Structures of Neurons

Neurons come in many shapes and varieties, according to the specialized jobs they perform. They usually have, in one form or another, the following four structures or regions: (1) cell body, or soma; (2) dendrites; (3) axon; and (4) terminal buttons.

Soma. The *soma* (cell body) contains the nucleus and much of the machinery that provides for the life processes of the cell. (See *Figure 2.3.*) Its shape varies considerably in different kinds of neurons.

Dendrites. Dendron is the Greek word for tree, and the *dendrites* of the neuron look very much like trees. (See *Figure 2.3.*) Dendrites vary in shape even more widely than do real trees; a

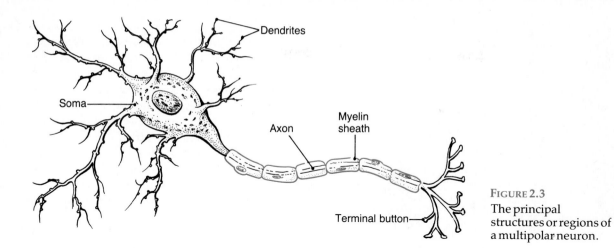

FIGURE 2.3
The principal structures or regions of a multipolar neuron.

glance at Figure 2.4 shows some of the many forms they can take. (See *Figure 2.4.*) Neurons "converse" with one another, and dendrites serve as important recipients of these messages. The messages that pass from neuron to neuron are transmitted across the **synapse,** a junction between the terminal buttons (described below) of the sending cell and a portion of the somatic or dendritic membrane of the receiving cell. The word *synapse* derives from the Greek *sunaptein,* "to join together."

Synapses on the dendrites of many neurons occur not on the branches or twigs but on little buds known as **dendritic spines.** Figure 2.5 illustrates a terminal button of the sending cell and a dendritic spine of the receiving cell. The terminal button is partly cut open so that you can see what is inside. (See *Figure 2.5.*) Synapses occur not only between a terminal button and the dendrite of another neuron but also between a terminal button and the soma of another neuron. In most cases there are no spines on the membrane of the soma; the terminal button just meets the smooth surface of the membrane. (See *Figure 2.6.*) Communication at a synapse proceeds in only one direction: from the terminal button to the membrane of the other cell.

Axon. The dendritic and somatic membranes receive messages from other cells—in some cases

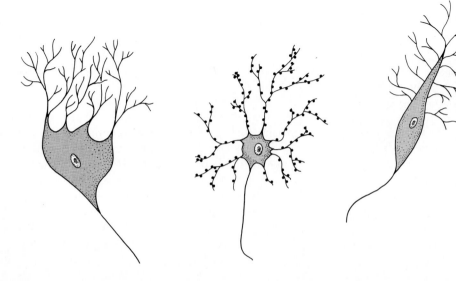

FIGURE 2.4
A sample of the variety of dendritic shapes of various types of neurons.

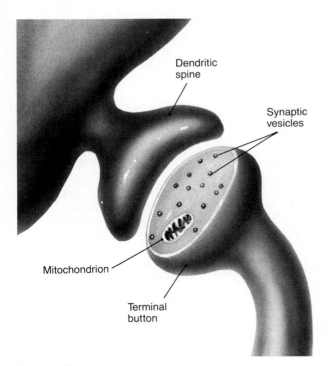

FIGURE 2.5
A synapse of a terminal button of one neuron with a dendritic spine of another.

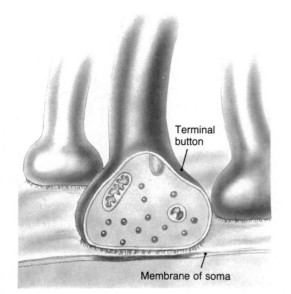

FIGURE 2.6
A synapse of a terminal button of one neuron with the somatic membrane of another.

from hundreds of other cells. These messages affect the activity of the neuron, which as a result may or may not transmit messages down its axon to other cells—those cells to which *this* neuron transmits messages. (See *Figure 2.7.*)

The *axon* is a long, slender tube. It carries information away from the cell body to the terminal buttons. The message is electrical, but as we will see, it is not carried down the axon the way a message travels down a telephone wire. Like dendrites, axons and their branches come in different shapes. In fact, the three principal types of neurons are classified according to the way in which their axons and dendrites leave the soma.

The neuron depicted in Figures 2.3 and 2.7 is the most common type found in the central nervous system; it is a *multipolar neuron.* In this type of neuron the somatic membrane gives rise to one axon but to the trunks of many dendritic trees. *Bipolar neurons* give rise to one axon and one dendritic tree, at opposite ends of the soma. (See *Figure 2.8a.*) These neurons are usually sensory; that is, they convey information from the environment to the central nervous system.

The third type of nerve cell is the *unipolar neuron.* It has only one stalk that leaves the soma and divides into two branches a short distance away. (See *Figure 2.8b.*) Unipolar neurons, like bipolar neurons, transmit information from the environment to the CNS. The arborizations farther from the CNS are dendrites; the arborizations within the CNS end in terminal buttons. The dendrites of most unipolar neurons detect sensory information applied to the skin.

Terminal Buttons. Most axons divide and branch many times. At the ends of the twigs are found little knobs called *terminal buttons,* which have a very special function: When a message is passed down the axon, the terminal buttons of the transmitting cell secrete a chemical called a *transmitter substance.* This chemical (there are many different ones in the CNS) affects the receiving cell. The effect it produces excites or inhibits the receiving cell and thus helps determine whether this cell will send a message down its axon to the cells with which it communicates. Details of this process will be described later in this chapter and in Chapter 3.

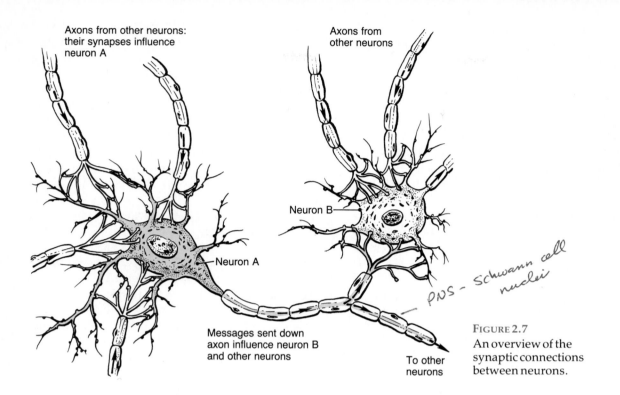

Axons from other neurons: their synapses influence neuron A

Axons from other neurons

Neuron B

Neuron A

PNS - Schwann cell nuclei

Messages sent down axon influence neuron B and other neurons

To other neurons

FIGURE 2.7
An overview of the synaptic connections between neurons.

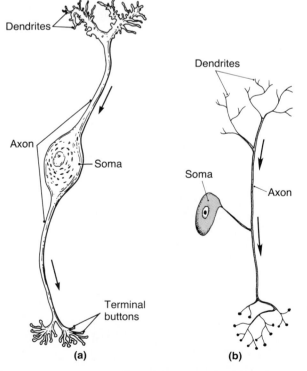

Dendrites

Axon

Soma

Dendrites

Soma

Axon

Terminal buttons

(a)

(b)

Supporting Cells

Neurons constitute only about half the volume of the CNS. The rest consists of a variety of supporting cells. Because neurons have a very high rate of metabolism but have no means of storing nutrients, they must constantly be supplied with nutrients and oxygen or they will quickly die. Unlike most other cells of the body, neurons cannot be replaced when they die; we are born with as many as we will ever have. Thus, the role played by the cells that support and protect neurons is very important to our existence.

Glia

The most important supporting cells of the central nervous system are the *neuroglia*, or "nerve glue." **Glia** (also called *glial cells*) do indeed glue the CNS together, but they do much

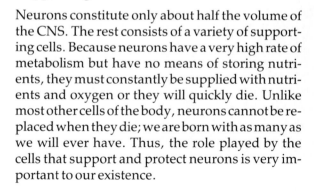

FIGURE 2.8
Neurons. (a) A bipolar neuron, primarily found in sensory systems (for example, vision and audition). (b) A unipolar neuron, found in the somatosensory system (touch, pain, and the like).

more than that. Neurons lead a very sheltered existence; they are physically and chemically buffered from the rest of the body by the glial cells. Glial cells surround neurons and hold them in place, controlling their supply of some of the chemicals they need to exchange messages with other neurons; they insulate neurons from one another so that neural messages do not get scrambled; and they even act as housekeepers, destroying and removing the carcasses of neurons that are killed by injury or that die as a result of old age.

There are several types of glial cells, each of which plays a special role in the CNS. *Astrocyte* means "star cell," and this name accurately describes the shape of these cells. Astrocytes (or *astroglia*) are rather large, as glia go, and provide physical support to neurons. Together with microglia, they also clean up debris within the brain. Finally, they chemically buffer the fluid surrounding neurons, a function that will be discussed later in this chapter.

Some of the astrocyte's processes (the arms of the star) are wrapped around blood vessels; other processes are wrapped around parts of neurons, so that the somatic and dendritic membrane of neurons is largely surrounded by astrocytes. (See *Figure 2.9.*) This arrangement suggested to the Italian histologist Camillo Golgi (1844–1926) that astrocytes supply neurons with nutrients from the capillaries and dispose of their waste products (Golgi, 1903). He thought that nutrients passed from capillaries to the cytoplasm of the astrocytes and then through the cytoplasm to the neurons, with waste products following the opposite route. As Figure 2.9 shows, this hypothesis is plausible.

However, this hypothesis has not been confirmed.

There is good evidence from the peripheral nervous system, though, that the satellite cells *do* transport substances to neurons. Lasek, Gainer, and Przybylski (1974) found that in the peripheral nervous system of the squid, neurons take up proteins that are synthesized in adjacent satellite cells. Also, some neurons lose their ability to produce the transmitter substance if the surrounding satellite cells are destroyed (Patterson and Chun, 1974).

Besides having a possible role in transporting chemicals to neurons, astrocytes serve as the matrix that holds neurons in place. They also surround and isolate synapses, apparently minimizing the dispersion of transmitter substances that are released by the terminal buttons. Thus, astrocytes provide each synapse with an isolation booth, keeping the neurons' conversations private.

Neurons occasionally die for unknown reasons or are killed by head injury, infection, or stroke. Certain kinds of astrocytes (along with the microglia) then take up the task of cleaning away the debris. These cells are able to travel around the CNS; they extend and retract their processes (*pseudopodia*, or "false feet") and glide about the way amoebas do. When they contact a piece of debris from a dead neuron, they push themselves against it, finally engulfing and digesting it. We call this process *phagocytosis* (*phagein*, "to eat"; *kutos*, "cell"). If there is a considerable amount of injured tissue to be cleaned up, astrocytes will divide and produce enough new cells to do the task.

FIGURE 2.9
Structure and location of astrocytes, whose processes surround capillaries and neurons of the central nervous system.

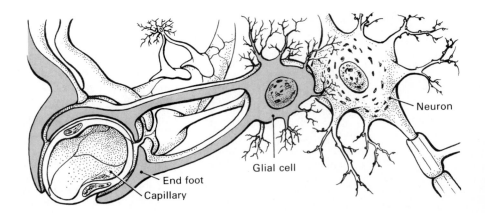

Neuron

Glial cell

End foot
Capillary

Once the dead tissue is broken down, a framework of astrocytes will be left to fill in the vacant area, and a specialized kind of astrocyte will form scar tissue, walling off the area.

Microglia are smaller than the other types of glia. They serve as phagocytes, along with the astrocytes.

Oligodendroglia are residents of the CNS, and their principal function is to provide support to axons and to produce the *myelin sheath,* which insulates most axons from one another. (Some axons are not myelinated and lack this sheath.) Myelin, 80 percent lipid and 20 percent protein, is produced by the oligodendroglia in the form of a tube surrounding the axon. This tube does not form a continuous sheath; rather, it consists of a series of segments, each approximately 1 mm long, with a small (1–2 μm) portion of uncoated axon between the segments. This bare portion of axon is called a *node of Ranvier,* after its discoverer. The myelinated axon, then, resembles a string of elongated beads. (Actually, the beads are very much elongated, their length being approximately 80 times their width.)

A given oligodendroglial cell produces several segments of myelin. During the development of the CNS, oligodendroglia form processes shaped something like canoe paddles. Each of these paddle-shaped processes then wraps many times around a segment of an axon and, while doing so, produces layers of myelin. Each paddle, then, becomes a segment of an axon's myelin sheath. (See *Figure 2.10.*)

Unmyelinated axons of the CNS are not actually naked; they are also covered by oligodendroglia. However, in this case the glial cells do not manufacture myelin; they simply wrap a process loosely around the axon and hold it in place.

Schwann Cells

In the CNS the oligodendroglia support axons and produce myelin. In the PNS the *Schwann cells* perform the same functions. Most axons in the PNS are myelinated. The myelin sheath occurs in segments, as it does in the CNS; each segment consists of a single Schwann cell, wrapped many times around the axon. In the CNS the oligodendroglia grow a number of paddle-shaped

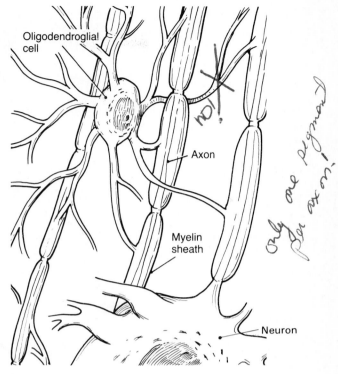

FIGURE 2.10
Oligodendroglial cell, which forms the myelin that surrounds many axons in the central nervous system. Each glial cell forms one segment of myelin for several adjacent axons.

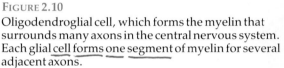

processes that wrap around a number of axons. In the PNS a Schwann cell provides myelin for only one axon, and the entire Schwann cell—not merely a part of it—surrounds the axon. (See *Figure 2.11.*)

Schwann cells also differ from their CNS counterparts, the oligodendroglia, in an important way. If damage occurs to a peripheral nerve (which consists of a bundle of many myelinated axons, all covered in a sheath of tough, elastic connective tissue), the Schwann cells aid in the digestion of the dead and dying axons. Then the Schwann cells arrange themselves in a series of cylinders that act as guides for regrowth of the axons. The distal portions of the severed axons die, but the stump of each severed axon grows sprouts, which then spread in all directions. If one of these sprouts encounters a cylinder provided by a Schwann cell, the sprout will quickly grow

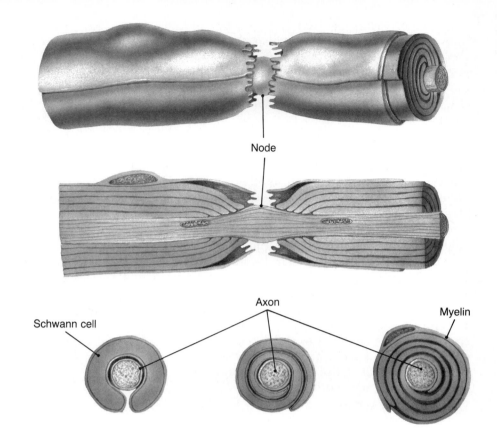

FIGURE 2.11
Schwann cells. During development, Schwann cells tightly wrap themselves many times around an individual axon in the peripheral nervous system and form one segment of the myelin sheath.

through the tube (at a rate of up to 3–4 mm a day), while the other, nonproductive sprouts wither away. If the cut ends of the nerve are still located close enough to each other, the axons will reestablish connections with the muscles and sense organs they previously served.

On the other hand, if a section of the nerve is damaged beyond repair, the axons will not be able to find their way to the original sites of innervation. In such cases neurosurgeons can sew the cut ends of the nerve together, if not too much of the nerve has been damaged. (Nerves are flexible and can be stretched a bit.) If too long a section has been lost, and if the nerve was an important one (controlling hand muscles, for example), a piece of nerve of about the same size can be taken from another part of the body. Because many nerves overlap in the area of tissue they innervate, neurosurgeons have no trouble finding a branch of a nerve that the patient can lose without ill effect. The surgeon, using a special microscope and

very delicate instruments, grafts this piece of nerve to the damaged one. Of course, the axons in the excised and transplanted piece of nerve die away, but the tubes produced by the Schwann cells guide the sprouts of the damaged nerve and help them find their way back to the hand muscles.

Unfortunately, the glial cells of the CNS are not so cooperative as the supporting cells of the PNS. If axons in the brain or spinal cord are damaged, new sprouts will form, as in the PNS. However, the budding axons encounter scar tissue produced by the astrocytes, and they cannot penetrate this barrier. Even if they could get through, the axons would not reestablish their original connections without guidance similar to that provided by the Schwann cells of the PNS. During development, axons have two modes of growth. The first mode causes them to elongate so that they reach their target, which could be as far away as the other end of the brain or spinal cord. Schwann cells provide this signal to injured axons. The second mode causes axons to stop elongating and begin sprouting terminal buttons, because they have reached their target. Liuzzi and Lasek (1987) found that even when astrocytes do not produce scar tissue, they appear to produce a chemical signal that instructs regenerating axons to begin the second mode of growth: to stop elongating and start sprouting terminal buttons. Thus, the difference in the regenerative properties of the CNS and PNS results from differences in the characteristics of the supporting cells, not from differences in the neurons.

THE BLOOD-BRAIN BARRIER

Long ago, physiologists discovered that if a dye such as trypan blue was injected into an animal's bloodstream, all tissues except the brain and spinal cord would be tinted blue. However, if the same dye is injected into the ventricles of the brain, the blue color will spread throughout the CNS (Bradbury, 1979). This experiment demonstrates that a barrier exists between the blood and the fluid that surrounds the cells of the brain—the *blood-brain barrier.*

Some substances can cross the blood-brain barrier; others cannot. Thus, it is *selectively permeable* (*per,* "through; *meare,* "to pass"). In most of the body the cells that line the capillaries do not fit together absolutely tightly. Small gaps are found between them that permit the free exchange of most substances between the blood plasma and the fluid outside the blood vessels that surrounds the cells. In the central nervous system the capillaries lack these gaps, and thus, many substances cannot leave the blood. Substances that can dissolve in lipids pass through the capillaries easily, because they simply dissolve through the membranes of the cells that line the capillaries. Other substances, such as glucose (the primary fuel of the central nervous system) must be actively transported through the capillary walls, carried by special proteins (Crone, 1965).

The messages that are conveyed from place to place in the nervous system involve movements of substances through the membranes of neurons. If the composition of the fluid that bathes neurons is changed even slightly, the transmission of these messages will be disrupted. Thus, if this fluid is not closely regulated, the brain cannot function normally. The presence of the blood-brain barrier probably makes it easier to regulate the composition of this fluid.

The blood-brain barrier is not uniform throughout the nervous system. In several places the barrier is relatively permeable, allowing substances excluded elsewhere to cross freely. For example, the *area postrema* is a part of the brain that controls vomiting. The blood-brain barrier is much weaker there, permitting this region to be more sensitive to toxic substances in the blood. A poison that enters the circulatory system from the stomach can thus stimulate this area to initiate vomiting. If the organism is lucky, the poison can be expelled from the stomach before it causes too much damage.

To a certain extent, the blood-brain barrier works both ways. That is, there is also a *brain-blood barrier.* Proteins present in the fluid bathing the cells of the brain cannot enter the blood supply and hence are not recognized by the body's immune system as belonging to that organism. Indeed, when protein is extracted from CNS myelin and is injected into an animal's blood supply, the immune system reacts by attacking tissue in the CNS as if it were foreign. The disease thus produced is called *experimental allergic encephalomyelitis,* which resembles multiple sclerosis (Swanborg, 1988).

Some investigators believe that multiple sclerosis results from virus-produced damage to the blood-brain barrier, which allows myelin protein to enter the blood supply. This invasion of a "foreign protein" mobilizes the immune system against the CNS myelin. With the insulation gone, messages being carried by the axons are no longer kept separate, and the scrambling of messages results in sensory disorders and loss of muscular control. As the disease progresses, the axons themselves are destroyed.

I NTERIM SUMMARY

All organs of the body consist of cells, which contain a quantity of clear cytoplasm, enclosed in a membrane. Embedded in the membrane are protein molecules that have special functions, such as the transport of particular substances into and out of the cell. The cytoplasm contains the nucleus, which contains the genetic information; the nucleolus (located in the nucleus), which manufactures ribosomes; the ribosomes, which serve as sites of protein synthesis; the endoplasmic reticulum, which serves as a storage reservoir and as a channel for transportation of chemicals through the cytoplasm; the Golgi apparatus, which wraps substances that the cell secretes in a membrane; microfilaments and microtubules, which compose the internal "skeleton" of the cell and provide the motive power for transporting chemicals from place to place; and the mitochondria, which serve as the location for most of the chemical reactions through which the cell extracts energy from nutrients.

Neurons receive messages directly from the environment (for example, sights, sounds, smells, and tastes) or from other neurons. They receive messages from other neurons by means of synapses, junctions between the terminal buttons of the transmitting neurons and the membrane of a dendrite or the soma of the receiving neuron. Terminal buttons are located at the ends of the axons.

Neurons are supported by the glial cells of the central nervous system and the satellite cells of the peripheral nervous system. Within the CNS, astrocytes provide the primary support and also remove debris and form scar tissue in the event of tissue damage. Microglia remove debris. Oligodendroglia form myelin, the substance that insulates axons, and also support unmyelinated axons. Within the PNS, support and myelin are provided by the Schwann cells.

In most organs molecules freely diffuse between the blood within the capillaries that serve them and the extracellular fluid that bathes their cells. The molecules pass through gaps between the cells that line the capillaries. The walls of the capillaries of the CNS lack these gaps; consequently, fewer substances can enter or leave the brain across the blood-brain barrier.

NEURAL COMMUNICATION: AN OVERVIEW

Now that you know about the basic structure of neurons, it is time to provide an overview of the ways they can interact, gathering sensory information and initiating a behavior. The example will be a very simple one, but more complex ones will be described in following chapters.

Neurons communicate through synapses. The message transmitted by a particular synapse has one of two effects: excitation or inhibition. Excitatory effects increase the likelihood that the neuron receiving them will send a message down *its* axon; inhibitory effects decrease this likelihood. Thus, the rate at which a neuron sends messages down its axons depends on the excitatory and inhibitory effects that are caused by neurons whose terminal buttons form synapses with it. For example, in Figure 2.12 neuron A can be excited by the terminal buttons of some neurons *(color)* and inhibited by the terminal buttons of others *(gray)*. The rate at which neuron A sends messages down its axon is determined by the relative activity of the excitatory and inhibitory synapses on the membrane of its soma and dendrites. A high rate of activity in the excitatory synapses will normally increase the rate at which neuron A sends messages down its axon, but this effect can be canceled by a high rate of activity in the inhibitory synapses. (See *Figure 2.12.*)

The message that is conducted down the axon, from the cell body to the terminal buttons, is electrical. Normally, there is an electrical charge across the membrane. The activity of excitatory synapses triggers an abrupt change in this charge, which is conducted down the axon to the terminal buttons. When the terminal buttons receive this message, they release a chemical that has either an excitatory or an inhibitory effect on the neurons with which they form synapses. And there the process begins again.

In order to appreciate the operation of this process, consider a simple assembly of three neurons. The first neuron is a sensory receptor that

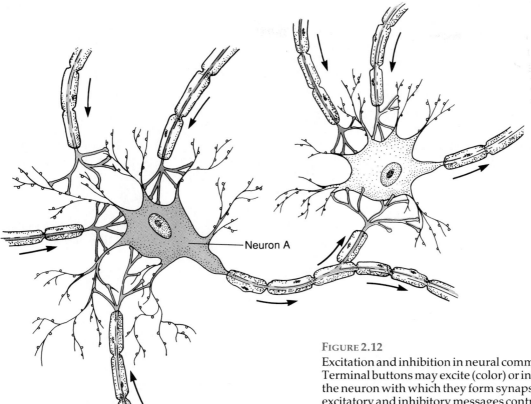

— Neuron A

FIGURE 2.12
Excitation and inhibition in neural communication. Terminal buttons may excite (color) or inhibit (gray) the neuron with which they form synapses. The excitatory and inhibitory messages control the rate of activity of the axon of neuron A.

detects painful stimuli. When its dendrites are stimulated by a pinprick, it sends messages down the axon to the terminal buttons, which are located in the spinal cord. (You will recognize this cell as a unipolar neuron; see *Figure 2.13.*) The terminal buttons of the sensory neuron release a transmitter substance that excites the somatic and dendritic membrane of the second neuron (the interneuron), causing it to send messages down its axon. In turn, its terminal buttons release a chemical that excites the third neuron (the motor neuron), which sends messages down its axon. The terminal buttons of the motor neuron synapse with the cells in a muscle. When they release their chemical, the muscle cells contract, causing a part of the body to move. This scheme represents a simplified version of what happens when a pinprick on the end of a finger causes a person to react by reflexively moving his or her arm away from the source of the pain. (See *Figure 2.13.*)

So far, all of the synaptic effects have been excitatory. Now let us complicate matters a bit to see the effect of inhibitory synapses. Suppose you are carrying a bunch of roses from your garden. As you walk, the thorns begin to prick your fingers. The pain receptors stimulate a withdrawal reflex like the one shown in Figure 2.13, which tends to make you open your hand and let go of the roses. However, because you do not want to drop your flowers, you manage to hold onto them until you have a chance to get a better, less painful grip on them. The message not to drop the roses comes through the axon of a neuron located in the brain. The terminal buttons at the end of this axon form synapses with an inhibitory neuron in the spinal cord. The terminal buttons of the inhibitory neuron release a chemical that inhibits the activity of the motor neuron. Thus, messages from the brain prevent the withdrawal reflex from operating. (See *Figure 2.14.*)

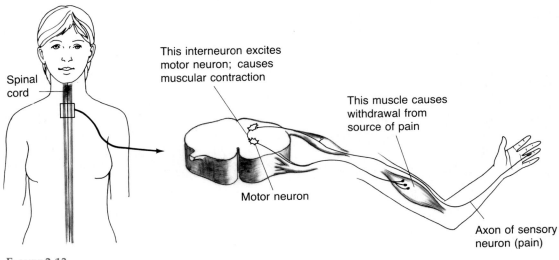

Spinal cord

This interneuron excites motor neuron; causes muscular contraction

This muscle causes withdrawal from source of pain

Motor neuron

Axon of sensory neuron (pain)

FIGURE 2.13
A withdrawal reflex, a simple example of a useful function of the nervous system.

Of course, reflexes are more complicated than this description, and the mechanisms that inhibit them are even more so. Yet this simple model, demonstrating one example of the importance of excitation and inhibition, provides an overview of the process of neural communication, which is described in more detail in this chapter and the next.

COMMUNICATION WITHIN A NEURON

The details of synaptic transmission—the communication between neurons—will be described in Chapter 3. The rest of this chapter deals with communication within a neuron—the way a message is sent from the cell body down the axon to the terminal buttons, informing them to release some transmitter substance. Although this message is electrical, the axon does not carry it the way a wire conducts electrical current. As we shall see in this section, the message is conducted by means of alterations in the membrane of the axon that cause exchanges of various chemicals between the axon and the fluid surrounding it. These exchanges produce electrical currents.

Measuring Electrical Potentials of Axons

Here we will examine the nature of the message that is conducted along the axon. To do so, we ob-

tain an axon that is large enough to work with. Fortunately, nature has provided the neuroscientist with the giant squid axon (the giant axon of a squid, not the axon of a giant squid!). This axon is about 0.5 mm in diameter, which is hundreds of times larger than the largest mammalian axon. (This large axon controls an emergency response: sudden contraction of the mantle, which squirts water through a jet and propels the squid away from a source of danger.) We place an isolated giant squid axon in a dish of seawater, in which it can exist for a day or two.

To measure the electrical charges generated by an axon, we will need to use a pair of electrodes. *Electrodes* are electrical conductors that provide a path for electricity to enter or leave a medium. One of the electrodes is a simple wire that we place in the seawater. The other one, which we use to record the message from the axon, has to be special. Because even a giant squid axon is rather small, we must use a tiny electrode that will record the membrane potential without damaging the axon. To do so, we use a microelectrode.

A *microelectrode* is simply a very small electrode, and it can be made of metal or glass. In this case we will use one made of thin glass tubing, which is heated and drawn down to an exceedingly fine point, less than a thousandth of a millimeter in diameter. Because glass will not conduct electricity, the glass microelectrode is filled

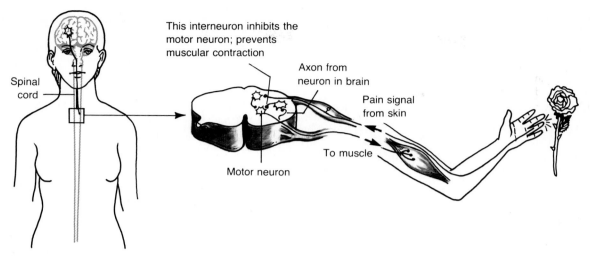

This interneuron inhibits the
motor neuron; prevents
muscular contraction

Axon from
neuron in brain

Pain signal
from skin

Spinal
cord

To muscle

Motor neuron

FIGURE 2.14
The role of inhibition. Inhibitory signals arising from the brain can prevent the
withdrawal reflex from causing the person to drop the rose.

with a liquid that conducts electricity, such as a solution of potassium chloride.

We place the wire electrode in the seawater
and insert the microelectrode into the axon. (See
Figure 2.15.) As soon as we do so, we discover that
the inside of the axon is negatively charged with
respect to the outside; the difference in charge
being 70 mV (millivolts, or thousandths of a volt).
Thus, the inside of the membrane is -70 mV. This
electrical charge is called the *membrane potential.*
The term *potential* refers to a stored-up source of

energy—in this case, electrical energy. For example, a flashlight battery that is not connected to an
electrical circuit has a *potential* charge of 1.5 V between its terminals. If we connect a light bulb to
the terminals, the potential energy is tapped and
converted into radiant energy (light). (See *Figure
2.15.*) Similarly, if we connect our electrodes—
one inside the axon and one outside it—to a very
sensitive voltmeter, we will convert the potential
energy to movement of the meter's needle. Of
course, the potential electrical energy of the

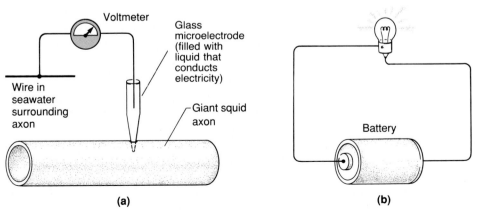

Voltmeter

Glass
microelectrode
(filled with
liquid that
conducts
electricity)

Wire in
seawater
surrounding
axon

Giant squid
axon

Battery

(a)

(b)

FIGURE 2.15
Measuring electrical charge. (a) A voltmeter detecting the charge across a membrane of
an axon. (b) A light bulb detecting the charge across the terminals of a battery.

axonal membrane is very weak compared with that of a flashlight battery.

As we shall see, the message that is conducted down the axon consists of a brief change in the membrane potential. However, this change occurs very rapidly—too rapidly for us to see if we were using a voltmeter. Thus, to study the message, we will use an *oscilloscope.* This device, like a voltmeter, measures voltages, but it also produces a record of these voltages, graphing them as a function of time. These graphs are displayed on a screen, much like the one found in a television. The vertical axis represents voltage, and the horizontal axis represents time, going from left to right.

Once we insert our microelectrode into the axon, the oscilloscope draws a straight horizontal line at −70 mV, as long as the axon is not disturbed. This electrical charge across the membrane is called, quite appropriately, the *resting potential.* Now let us disturb the resting potential and see what happens. To do so, we will use another device—an electrical stimulator that allows us to alter the membrane potential at a specific location. (See *Figure 2.16.*) The stimulator can pass current through another microelectrode that we have inserted into the axon. Because the inside of the axon is negative, a positive charge applied to the inside of the membrane produces a *depolarization.* That is, it takes away some of the electrical charge across the membrane near the electrode, reducing the membrane potential.

Let us see what happens to an axon when we artificially change the membrane potential at one point. Figure 2.17 shows a graph drawn by an oscilloscope that has been monitoring the effects of brief depolarizing stimuli. The graphs of the effects of these separate stimuli are superimposed on the same drawing so that we can compare them. We deliver a series of depolarizing stimuli, starting with a very weak one and gradually increasing their strength. Each stimulus briefly depolarizes the membrane potential a little more. Finally, after we present shock number 4, the membrane potential suddenly reverses itself, so that the inside becomes *positive* (and the outside becomes negative). The membrane potential quickly returns to normal, but first, it overshoots

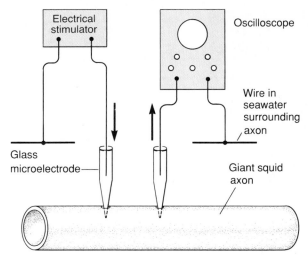

FIGURE 2.16

The means by which an axon can be stimulated while its membrane potential is being recorded.

the resting potential, becoming *hyperpolarized*— more polarized than normal—for a short time. The whole process takes about 2 msec (milliseconds). (See *Figure 2.17.*)

This phenomenon, a very rapid reversal of the membrane potential, is called the *action potential.* It constitutes the message carried by the axon from the cell body to the terminal buttons. The voltage level that triggers an action potential— which was achieved only by shock number 4—is called the *threshold of excitation.*

The Membrane Potential: Dynamic Equilibrium

To understand what causes the action potential to occur, we must first understand the reasons for the existence of the membrane potential. As we will see, this electrical charge is the result of a balance between two opposing forces: diffusion and electrostatic pressure.

The Force of Diffusion

When a spoonful of sugar is carefully poured into a container of water, it settles to the bottom. After a time the sugar dissolves, but it remains close to the bottom of the container. After a much

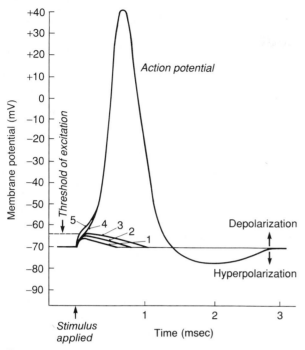

FIGURE 2.17

The results that would be seen on an oscilloscope screen if depolarizing stimuli of varying intensities were delivered to the axon shown in Figure 2.16.

The Force of Electrostatic Pressure

When some substances are dissolved in water, they split into two parts, each with an opposing electrical charge. Substances with this property are called *electrolytes;* the charged particles into which they decompose are called *ions.* Ions are of two basic types: *Cations* have a positive charge, and *anions* have a negative charge. For example, when sodium chloride (NaCl, table salt) is dissolved in water, many of the molecules split into sodium cations (Na^+) and chloride anions (Cl^-). (I find that the easiest way to keep the terms *cation* and *anion* straight is to think of the cation's plus sign as a cross, and remember the superstition of a black *cat* crossing your path.)

As you have undoubtedly learned, particles with the same kind of charge repel each other (+ repels + , and − repels −), but particles with different charges are attracted to each other (+ and − attract). Thus, anions repel anions, cations repel cations, but anions and cations attract each other. (See *Figure 2.19.*) The force exerted by this attraction or repulsion is called *electrostatic pressure.* Just as the force of diffusion moves molecules from regions of high concentration to regions of low concentration, electrostatic pressure moves ions from place to place: Cations are pushed away from regions with an excess of cat-

longer time (probably several days), the molecules of sugar distribute themselves evenly throughout the water, even if no one stirs the liquid. The process whereby molecules distribute themselves evenly throughout the medium in which they are dissolved is called *diffusion.*

When there are no forces or barriers to prevent diffusion, molecules diffuse from regions of high concentration to regions of low concentration. Molecules are constantly in motion, and their rate of movement is proportional to the temperature. Only at absolute zero [0 K (kelvin) = −273.15°C = −459.7°F] do molecules cease their random movement. At all other temperatures they move about, colliding and veering off in different directions, thus pushing each other away. The result of these collisions in the example of the sugar water is to force sugar molecules upward (and to force water molecules downward), away from the regions in which they are most concentrated. (See *Figure 2.18.*)

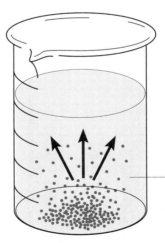

Diffusion forces sugar molecules away from region of highest concentration

FIGURE 2.18

Diffusion. The force of diffusion moves sugar molecules up until they are evenly distributed throughout the container.

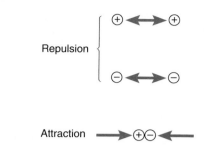

FIGURE 2.19
Electrostatic pressure. Particles with the same charge repel each other; particles with different charges attract each other.

ions, and anions are pushed away from regions with an excess of anions.

Ions in the Extracellular and Intracellular Fluid

The fluid within cells (*intracellular fluid*) and the fluid surrounding them (*extracellular fluid*) contain different ions. The forces of diffusion and electrostatic pressure contributed by these ions give rise to the membrane potential. Because the membrane potential is produced by a balance between the forces of diffusion and electrostatic pressures, to understand what produces this potential, we must know the concentration of the

various ions in the extracellular and intracellular fluids.

There are several important ions in these fluids. I will discuss four of them here: protein anions (symbolized by A^-), chloride ions (Cl^-), sodium ions (Na^+), and potassium ions (K^+). The Latin words for sodium and potassium are *natrium* and *kalium*; hence, they are abbreviated *Na* and *K*, respectively. Protein anions (A^-) are found in the intracellular fluid. Although the other three ions are found in both the intracellular and extracellular fluids, K^+ is found predominantly in the intracellular fluid, whereas Na^+ and Cl^- are found predominantly in the extracellular fluid. (See *Figure 2.20.*) The easiest way to remember which ion is found where is to recall that the fluid that surrounds our cells is similar to seawater, which is predominantly a solution of salt, NaCl. The primitive ancestors of our cells lived in the ocean; thus, the seawater was their extracellular fluid. Our extracellular fluid thus resembles seawater, produced and maintained by regulatory mechanisms that are described in Chapter 12.

Let us consider the ions in Figure 2.20, examining the forces of diffusion and electrostatic pressure exerted on each, and reasoning why each is located where it is. We can quickly dis-

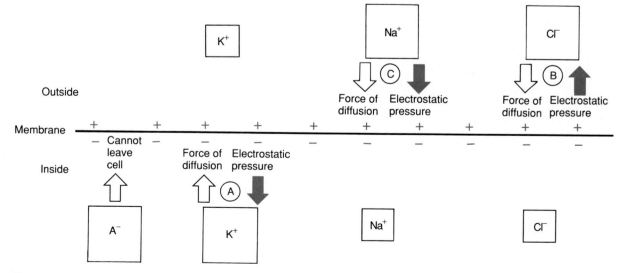

FIGURE 2.20
The relative concentration of some important ions inside and outside the neuron and the forces acting on them.

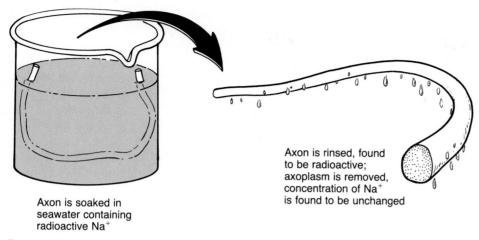

Axon is rinsed, found to be radioactive; axoplasm is removed, concentration of Na⁺ is found to be unchanged

Axon is soaked in seawater containing radioactive Na⁺

FIGURE 2.21
Experimental demonstration that the axonal membrane is permeable to Na^+.

pense with A^-, the protein anion, because this ion is too large to pass through the membrane of the axon; therefore, although its presence within the cell affects the other ions, it is located where it is because the membrane is impermeable to it.

The potassium ion K^+ is concentrated within the axon; thus, the force of diffusion tends to push it out of the cell. However, the outside of the cell is charged positively with respect to the inside, so electrostatic pressure tends to force the cation inside. Thus, the two opposing forces balance. (See *Figure 2.20* at the circled A.)

The chloride ion Cl^- is in greatest concentration outside the axon. The force of diffusion pushes it inward. However, because the inside of the axon is negatively charged, electrostatic pressure pushes the anion outward. Again, two opposing forces balance each other. (See *Figure 2.20* at the circled B.)

The sodium ion Na^+ is also in greatest concentration outside the axon, so it, like Cl^-, is pushed into the cell by the force of diffusion. But unlike chloride, the sodium ion is *positively* charged. Therefore, electrostatic pressure does *not* prevent Na^+ from entering the cell; indeed, the negative charge inside the axon *attracts* Na^+. (See *Figure 2.20* at the circled C.)

How can Na^+ remain in greatest concentration in the extracellular fluid, despite the fact that both forces (diffusion and electrostatic pressure) tend to push it inside? The simplest explanation would

be that the membrane is impermeable to Na^+, as it is to A^-, the protein anion. This possibility can be tested with the following experiment. A giant squid axon is placed in a dish of seawater containing some radioactive Na^+, is allowed to sit awhile, and is then removed and washed off. The axon is now found to be radioactive, which shows that Na^+ *can* pass through the membrane, because some of the radioactive Na^+ in the seawater found its way into the axon. (See *Figure 2.21*.)

Although the axon contains radioactive Na^+, analysis of its cytoplasm (which can be squeezed out like toothpaste from a tube) shows that the concentration of Na^+ is unchanged. This analysis indicates that although some molecules of Na^+ entered the axon, an equal number left again, keeping the concentration constant. But as we know, the forces of diffusion and electrostatic pressure tend to push Na^+ into the cell. It is easy to understand why the axon became radioactive—these forces pushed some radioactive sodium ions in. But what pushed an equal number of Na^+ ions out again, against these two forces?

The answer is this: Another force, provided by the **sodium-potassium pump,** continuously pushes Na^+ out of the axon. The sodium-potassium pump consists of complex protein molecules situated in the membrane, driven by energy provided by the mitochondria as they metabolize the cell's nutrients. These molecules exchange Na^+ for K^+, pushing three sodium ions out for every

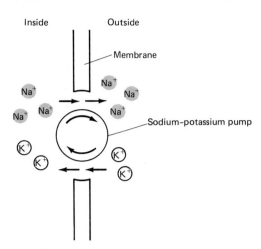

Inside   Outside

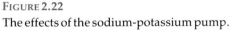

FIGURE 2.22
The effects of the sodium-potassium pump.

two potassium ions they push in. (See *Figure 2.22.*)

Because the membrane is not very permeable to Na^+, the sodium-potassium pump very effectively keeps the intracellular concentration of Na^+ low. By pumping K^+ into the cell, it also increases the intracellular concentration of K^+ somewhat. The membrane is approximately 100 times more permeable to K^+ than to Na^+, so the increase is slight; but as we will see when we study the process of neural inhibition in Chapter 3, it is very important. The sodium-potassium pump uses considerable energy: Up to 40 percent of the neuron's metabolic resources are used to operate it. Neurons, muscle cells, glia—in fact, most cells of the body—have a sodium-potassium pump in their membrane.

The Action Potential

As we saw, the forces of both diffusion and electrostatic pressure tend to push Na^+ into the cell. However, the membrane is not very permeable to this ion, and the sodium-potassium pump continuously pumps out Na^+, keeping the intracellular level of Na^+ low. But imagine what would happen if the membrane suddenly became permeable to Na^+. The forces of diffusion and electrostatic pressure would cause Na^+ to rush into the cell.

This sudden influx of positively charged ions would drastically change the membrane potential. Indeed, experiments have shown that this mechanism is precisely what causes the action potential: A brief drop in the membrane resistance to Na^+ (allowing these ions to rush into the cell) is immediately followed by a transient drop in the membrane resistance to K^+ (allowing these ions to rush out of the cell).

I said earlier that the membrane consists of a double layer of lipid molecules that contains many different kinds of protein molecules. One class of protein molecules provides a way for ions to enter or leave the cells. These molecules constitute *ion channels,* which contain gates that can open or close. When a gate is open, a particular type of ion can flow through the channel and thus can enter or leave the cell. (See *Figure 2.23.*) Neural membranes contain many thousands of ion channels. For example, the giant squid axon contains from 100 to 600 sodium channels in each square micrometer of membrane. (There are one million square micrometers in a square millimeter.) Thus, the permeability of a membrane to a particular ion at a given moment is determined by the number of ion channels that are open.

The following numbered paragraphs describe the movements of ions through the membrane during the action potential. Figure 2.24, which accompanies the description, shows only Na^+ and K^+, for the sake of simplicity. As the figure shows, the changes in the membrane potential are caused by the movements of ions immediately adjacent to the membrane. The arrows indicate the ions that

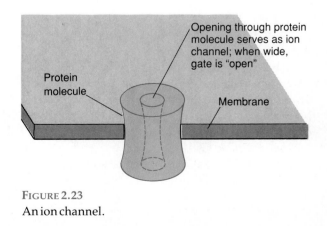

FIGURE 2.23
An ion channel.

will move between one panel and the next. The numbers on the figure correspond to the numbers of the paragraphs that follow. (See *Figure 2.24.*)

1. As soon as the threshold of excitation is reached, the sodium channels in the membrane open and Na$^+$ rushes in, propelled by the forces of diffusion and electrostatic pressure. The opening of these channels is triggered by the depolariza-tion of the membrane potential; they open at the threshold of excitation. Because these channels are opened by changes in the membrane potential, they are called *voltage-dependent ion channels.* The influx of positively charged sodium ions produces a rapid change in the membrane potential, from −70 to +50 mV.

2. At about the time the action potential

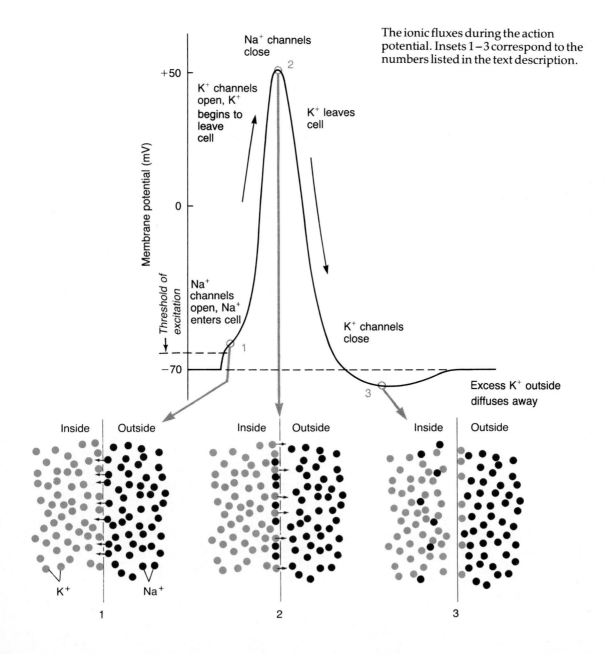

The ionic fluxes during the action potential. Insets 1−3 correspond to the numbers listed in the text description.

reaches its peak (in approximately 1 msec), the sodium channels close and the membrane once again becomes resistant to the flow of Na⁺. (Why this happens is not yet known.) By now, the voltage-dependent potassium channels in the membrane have opened, letting K⁺ ions move freely through the membrane. At the peak of the action potential the inside of the axon is now *positively* charged, so K⁺ is driven out of the cell by diffusion and by electrostatic pressure. This outflow of cations causes the membrane potential to return toward its normal value. As it does so, the potassium channels close again.

3. The membrane potential not only returns to normal but actually overshoots its resting value ($-70mV$) and only gradually returns to normal. The accumulation of K⁺ ions outside the membrane causes it to become temporarily hyperpolarized. These extra ions soon diffuse away, and the membrane potential returns to -70 mV. Eventually, the sodium-potassium pump removes the Na⁺ that leaked in and retrieves the K⁺ that leaked out.

How much ionic flow is there? When I say "Na⁺ rushes in," I do not mean that the axoplasm becomes flooded with Na⁺. Because the drop in membrane resistance to Na⁺ is so brief, and because diffusion over any appreciable distance takes some time, not too many Na⁺ molecules flow in, and not too many K⁺ molecules flow out. At the peak of the action potential a very thin layer of fluid immediately inside the axon becomes full of newly arrived Na⁺ ions; this amount is indeed enough to reverse the membrane potential. (This condition is shown at position 2 in Figure 2.24.) However, not enough time has elapsed for these ions to fill the entire axon. Before that event can take place, the Na⁺ channels close and K⁺ starts flowing out.

Experiments have shown that an action potential temporarily increases the number of Na⁺ ions inside the giant squid axon by 0.0003 percent. Although the concentration just inside the membrane is high, the total number of ions entering the cell is very small, relative to the number already there. On a short-term basis, the sodium-potassium pump is not very important. The few Na⁺ ions that manage to leak in diffuse into the

rest of the axoplasm, and the slight increase in Na⁺ concentration is hardly noticeable. However, the sodium-potassium pump is important on a long-term basis, because in many axons action potentials occur at a very high rate. Without the sodium-potassium pump the axoplasm would eventually become full of sodium ions, and the axon would no longer be able to function.

Conduction of the Action Potential

Now that we have a basic understanding of the resting membrane potential and the production of the action potential, we can consider the movement of the message down the axon, or *conduction of the action potential.* To study this phenomenon, we again make use of the giant squid axon. We attach an electrical stimulator to an electrode at one end of the axon and place recording electrodes, attached to oscilloscopes, at different distances from the stimulating electrode. Then we apply a depolarizing stimulus to the end of the axon and trigger an action potential. We record the action potential from each of the electrodes, one after the other. Thus, we see that the action potential is conducted down the axon. As it travels, it remains constant in size. (See *Figure 2.25.*)

This experiment establishes a basic law of axonal conduction: the **all-or-none law.** This law states that an action potential either occurs or it does not occur; once it has been triggered, it is transmitted down the axon to its end. It always remains the same size, without growing or diminishing. In fact, the axon will transmit an action potential in either direction, or even in both directions, if one is started in the middle of its length. However, because action potentials in living animals always start at the end attached to the soma, axons normally carry one-way traffic.

As you know, the strength of a muscular contraction can range between very weak to very forceful, and the strength of a stimulus can range from barely detectable to very intense. We know that the occurrence of action potentials in axons controls the strength of muscular contractions and represents the intensity of a physical stimulus. But if the action potential is an all-or-none event, how can it represent information that varies in a continuous fashion? The answer is simple:

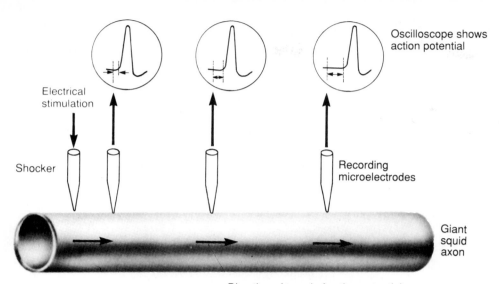

FIGURE 2.25

Conduction of the action potential. When an action potential is triggered, its size remains undiminished as it travels down the axon. The speed of conduction can be calculated from the delay between the stimulus and the action potential.

A single action potential is not the basic element of information; rather, variable information is represented by an axon's *rate of firing*. (In this context, *firing* refers to the production of action potentials.) A high rate of firing causes a strong muscular contraction, and a strong stimulus (such as a bright light) causes a high rate of firing in axons that serve the eyes. Thus, the all-or-none law is supplemented by the *rate law*. (See *Figure 2.26.*)

Action potentials are not the only kind of electrical signals that occur in neurons. As we shall see in Chapter 3, when a message is sent across a synapse, a small electrical signal is produced in the membrane of the neuron that receives the message. In order to understand this process, and to understand the way that action potentials are conducted in myelinated axons (described below), we must see how such signals other than action potentials are conducted. To do so, we produce a below-threshold depolarization (too small to produce an action potential) at one end of an axon and record its effects from electrodes placed along the axon. We find that the stimulus produces a disturbance in the membrane potential that becomes smaller as it moves away from the point of stimulation. (See *Figure 2.27.*)

The transmission of the small, below-threshold depolarization is *passive*. Neither sodium channels nor potassium channels are opening or closing. The axon is acting like an electrical cable, carrying along the current started at one end. This property of the axon follows laws discovered in the nineteenth century that describe conduction of electricity through telegraph cables laid along

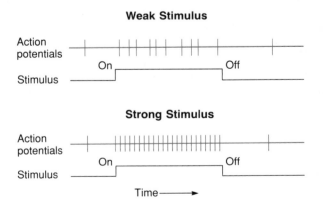

Rate of firing. The strength of a stimulus is represented by the rate of firing of an axon. The size of each action potential is always constant.

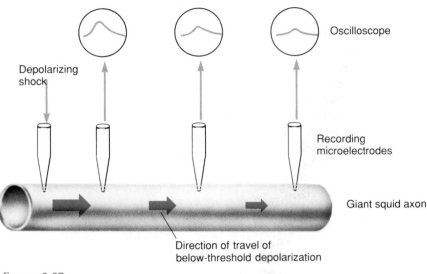

FIGURE 2.27

Decremental conduction. When a subthreshold shock is applied to the axon, the disturbance in the membrane potential is largest near the stimulating electrode and gets progressively smaller at farther distances along the axon.

the ocean floor. As a signal passes through a submarine cable, it gets smaller because of the electrical characteristics of the cable, including leakage through the insulator and resistance in the wire. Because the signal decreases in size (decrements), it is referred to as *decremental conduction.* We say that the conduction of a small depolarization by the axon follows the laws that describe the *cable properties* of the axon—the same laws that describe the electrical properties of a submarine cable. And because hyperpolarizations never trigger action potentials, these disturbances, like subthreshold depolarizations, are also transmitted by means of the passive cable properties of an axon.

Recall that all but the smallest axons in mammalian nervous systems are myelinated; segments of them are covered by a myelin sheath produced by the oligodendroglia of the CNS or the Schwann cells of the PNS. These segments are separated by portions of naked axon, the nodes of Ranvier. Conduction of an action potential in a myelinated axon is somewhat different from conduction in an unmyelinated axon.

Schwann cells (and the oligodendroglia of the CNS) wrap tightly around the axon, leaving no measurable extracellular fluid between them and the axon. The only place where a myelinated axon comes in contact with the extracellular fluid is at a node of Ranvier, where the axon is naked. In the myelinated areas there can be no inward flow of Na^+ when the sodium channels open, because there *is* no extracellular sodium. How, then, does the "action potential" travel along the area of axonal membrane covered by myelin sheath? You guessed it—cable properties. The axon passively conducts the electrical disturbance from the action potential to the next node of Ranvier. The disturbance gets smaller, but it is still large enough to trigger an action potential at the next node. The action potential gets retriggered, or repeated, at each node of Ranvier and is passed, by means of cable properties of the axon, along the myelinated area to the next node. Its conduction, hopping from node to node, is called *saltatory conduction,* from the Latin *saltare,* "to dance." (See *Figure 2.28.*)

There are two advantages to saltatory conduction. The most important one is economic. Energy must be expended by the sodium-potassium pump to get rid of the excess Na^+ that enters the axon during the action potential. The pump is given work to do all along an unmyelinated axon, because Na^+ enters everywhere. But because Na^+

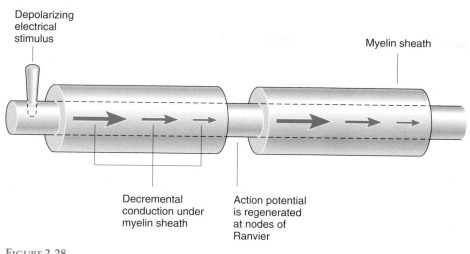

Depolarizing
electrical
stimulus

Myelin sheath

Decremental
conduction under
myelin sheath

Action potential
is regenerated
at nodes of
Ranvier

FIGURE 2.28
Saltatory conduction, showing propagation of an action potential down
a myelinated axon.

can enter a myelinated axon only at the nodes of Ranvier, much less gets in and, consequently, much less has to be pumped out again. Therefore, a myelinated axon expends much less energy to maintain its sodium balance.

The second advantage to myelin is speed. Conduction of an action potential is faster in a myelinated axon because the transmission between the nodes, which occurs by means of the axon's cable properties, is very fast. Increased speed makes it possible for an animal to react faster and (undoubtedly) to think faster. One of the ways to increase the speed of conduction is to increase size. Because it is so large, the unmyelinated squid axon, with a diameter of 500 μm, achieves a conduction velocity of approximately 35 m/sec (meters per second). However, the same speed is achieved by a myelinated cat axon with a diameter of a mere 6 μm. The fastest myelinated axon, 20 μm in diameter, can conduct action potentials at a speedy 120 m/sec, or 432 km/h (kilometers per hour). At that speed a signal can get from one end of an axon to the other without much delay.

*I*NTERIM SUMMARY

Neurons communicate by means of synapses. When a message is sent down an axon, the terminal buttons secrete a chemical that has either an excitatory or an inhibi-

tory effect on the neuron with which it communicates. Ultimately, the effects of these excitatory and inhibitory synapses cause behavior, in the form of muscular contraction.

The message conducted down an axon is called an action potential. The membranes of all cells of the body are electrically charged, but only axons can produce action potentials. The resting membrane potential occurs because various ions are located in different concentrations in the fluid inside and outside the cell. The extracellular fluid (like seawater) is rich in Na^+ and Cl^-, and the intracellular fluid is rich in K^+ and various protein anions, designated as A^-.

The cell membrane is freely permeable to water, but its permeability to various ions—in particular, Na^+ and K^+—is regulated by ion channels. When the membrane potential is at its resting value (-70 mV), the gates of the voltage-dependent sodium and potassium channels are closed. The experiment with radioactive seawater showed us that some Na^+ continuously leaks into the axon but is promptly forced out of the cell again by the sodium-potassium pump (which also forces potassium *into* the axon). When an electrical stimulator depolarizes the membrane potential of the axon so that it reaches the threshold of excitation, voltage-dependent sodium channels open and Na$^+$ rushes into the cell, driven by the force of diffusion and by electrostatic pressure. The entry of the positively charged ions further reduces the membrane potential and, indeed, causes it to reverse, so that the inside becomes positive. The opening of the sodium channels is temporary; they soon close again. The depolarization of the membrane potential caused by the influx of Na$^+$ activates voltage-dependent potassium channels, and K$^+$ leaves the axon, down its concentration gradient. The efflux of K$^+$ quickly brings the membrane potential back to its resting value.

The action potential normally begins at one end of the axon, where the axon attaches to the soma. It travels continuously down unmyelinated axons, remaining constant in size, until it reaches the terminal buttons. (When the axon divides, the action potential continues down each branch.) In myelinated axons, ions can flow through the membrane only at the nodes of Ranvier, because the axons are covered everywhere else with myelin, which isolates them from the extracellular fluid. Thus, the action potential is conducted from one node of Ranvier to the next by means of passive cable properties. When the electrical message reaches a node, voltage-dependent sodium channels open, and the action potential reaches full strength again. This mechanism saves a considerable amount of energy, because sodium-potassium pumps are not needed along the myelinated portions of the axons; and saltatory conduction is also faster.

CONCLUDING REMARKS

Now you know something about the elements of the nervous system. Like all other organs of the body, the central nervous system consists of specialized cells, each with its particular functions. The basic task of the nervous system is to detect events occurring in the environment and to respond with appropriate behaviors. The detection is accomplished by sensory neurons, and the behaviors are accomplished by muscles, which contract when told to do so by the neurons that communicate with them. Simple organisms detect only a few kinds of events and automatically respond with only a few kinds of behaviors. The nervous system of complex organisms—such as humans—contains a large number of neurons that receive messages from sensory neurons and communicate with motor neurons and with each other. Thus, the complexity of our perceptions, memories, feelings, and behaviors depends on the numbers of our neurons and the complexity of their interconnections. The next chapter considers just how neurons communicate with each other in performing their tasks.

This chapter has considered the important features of neurons, the cells that provide their support, and the action potential, the message conducted down the axon. The next chapter describes the nature of the message transmitted across synapses and the way excitatory and inhibitory influences from synapses can interact.

NEW TERMS

action potential p. 34
adenosine triphosphate p. 22
all-or-none law p. 40
anion p. 35
area postrema p. 29
astrocyte p. 26
axon p. 24
bipolar neuron p. 24

blood-brain barrier p. 29
cable properties p. 42
cation p. 35
central nervous system (CNS) p. 20
cytoplasm p. 22
dendrite p. 22
dendritic spine p. 23

deoxyribonucleic acid (DNA) p. 20
depolarization p. 34
diffusion p. 35
electrode p. 32
electrolyte p. 35
electrostatic pressure p. 35
endoplasmic reticulum p. 22

enzyme p. 20
experimental allergic
    encephalomyelitis p. 29
extracellular fluid p. 36
gene p. 20
glia p. 25
Golgi apparatus p. 22
hyperpolarization p. 34
intracellular fluid p. 36
ion p. 35
ion channel p. 38
lysosome p. 22
membrane p. 20
membrane potential p. 33
messenger ribonucleic
    acid (mRNA) p. 20

microelectrode p. 32
microfilament p. 22
microglia p. 27
microtubule p. 22
mitochondria p. 22
motor neuron p. 20
multipolar neuron p. 24
myelin sheath p. 27
node of Ranvier p. 27
nucleolus p. 20
nucleus p. 20
oligodendroglia p. 27
oscilloscope p. 34
peripheral nervous system
    (PNS) p. 20
phagocytosis p. 26

rate law p. 41
resting potential p. 34
ribosome p. 20
saltatory conduction p. 42
Schwann cell p. 27
sensory neuron p. 20
sodium-potassium
    pump p. 37
soma p. 22
synapse p. 23
terminal button p. 24
threshold of excitation p. 34
transmitter substance p. 24
unipolar neuron p. 24
voltage-dependent ion
    channel p. 39

SUGGESTED READINGS

Kandel, E.R., and Schwartz, J.H. *Principles of Neural Science,* 2nd ed. New York: Raven Press, 1985.

Kuffler, S.W., and Nicholls, J.G. *From Neuron to Brain,* 2nd edition. Sunderland, Mass.: Sinauer Associates, 1984.

Shepherd, G.M. *Neurobiology,* 2nd ed. New York: Oxford University Press, 1988.

3

Neural Communication: Physiology and Pharmacology

*C*hapter 2 discussed the resting membrane potential and described how a small decrease in this potential triggers an action potential that is conducted down the axon to the terminal buttons. This chapter discusses the nature of communication among neurons and the ways in which drugs facilitate or interfere with this communication. The interactions among neurons constitute the means by which our nervous system functions.

SYNAPTIC TRANSMISSION

As we saw in Chapter 2, neurons communicate by means of synapses, and the medium used for these one-way conversations is the chemical released by terminal buttons. These chemicals, called transmitter substances (or neurotransmitters), diffuse across the fluid-filled gap between the terminal buttons and the membranes of the neurons with which they form synapses. The transmitter substances cause a brief alteration in the membrane potential of these neurons, which produces either an excitatory or an inhibitory effect on the rate of firing of their axons.

This section begins with a discussion of the transmission of information by means of chemicals. Next, the section describes the structure of synapses and the nature of neural integration. Most of the rest of the section covers the steps involved in the process of synaptic transmission, from release of the transmitter substance to termination of the postsynaptic potential.

The Concept of Chemical Transmission

Chemicals are used to transmit information within an organism and even between them. These chemicals—transmitter substances, neuromodulators, hormones, and pheromones—control the behavior of cells, organs, or entire animals. All of these methods of transmission require the presence of cells that release the chemical and specialized protein molecules (receptors) that detect their presence.

Neurotransmitters are chemicals that are released by terminal buttons and are detected by receptors in the membrane of another neuron (or muscle fiber or gland cell) located a very short distance away. The communication at each synapse is private. *Neuromodulators* travel farther and are dispersed more widely. They, too, are released by terminal buttons but are secreted in larger amounts and diffuse much larger distances, modulating the activity of many neurons in a particular part of the brain. Some neuromodulators may even be picked up by blood vessels and distributed to other parts of the brain.

Hormones are produced in cells located in special organs, called *endocrine glands.* Endocrine glands release their hormones in much the same way that neurons release their neurotransmitters or neuromodulators. The hormones are distributed to the rest of the body through the bloodstream. Hormones affect the activity of cells by stimulating receptors located either on the surface of their membrane or deep within their nuclei. (Both types are described later in this chapter.) Some of the neurons located in the brain contain such receptors, and hormones are able to affect behavior by stimulating the receptors and changing the activity of these neurons. For example, a sex hormone, testosterone, increases the aggressiveness of most male mammals.

Pheromones are chemicals that are released into the environment through sweat, urine, or the secretions of specialized glands. The odor of these chemicals is detected by receptors in the noses of other animals. Most pheromones affect the reproductive behavior or physiology of other members of the same species. For example, pheromones can attract potential mates, arouse them sexually, inhibit their aggression, and alter the activity of their endocrine system. These interesting chemicals are discussed in more detail in Chapter 10.

This chapter will deal mostly with synaptic transmission, the private communication between a terminal button and the membrane of another cell. However, you should bear in mind that the same principles are seen in chemical communication over longer distances, and probably all of these forms of communication evolved from a common mechanism.

Structure of Synapses

As you have already learned, synapses are junctions between the terminal buttons at the ends of the axonal branches of one neuron and the membrane of another. Because a message is transmitted in only one direction, the membranes on the two sides of the synapse are named in relation to the synapse: The membrane of the terminal button (transmitting neuron) is the *presynaptic membrane,* and that of the receiving neuron is the *postsynaptic membrane.* As Figure 3.1 shows, these membranes are separated by a small gap, which varies in size from synapse to synapse but is usually around 200 Å wide. (An angström, Å, is one ten-millionth of a millimeter.) The space, called the *synaptic cleft,* contains extracellular fluid, through which the transmitter substance diffuses. (See *Figure 3.1.*)

As you may have noticed in Figure 3.1, three prominent structures are located in the cytoplasm of the terminal button: mitochondria, synaptic vesicles, and cisternae. Many of the biochemical steps in the extraction of energy from glucose take place on the cristae of the mitochondria; hence their presence near the terminal button suggests that certain processes that occur there require energy. *Synaptic vesicles* are small, rounded objects in the shape of spheres or ovoids. They appear to be packages that contain transmitter substance (the term *vesicle* means "little bladder"). They are produced in the soma and transported through the axoplasm to the terminal buttons. (See *Figure 3.1.*) In addition, the *cisternae,* which are collections of membrane similar to the Golgi apparatus, serve as recycling plants. They make synaptic vesicles out of the membrane of old vesicles that have expelled their contents into the synaptic cleft.

Evidence that the soma produces synaptic vesicles comes from a very simple experiment. If a nerve is ligated ("tied") with a bit of thread and is later examined under an electron microscope, a collection of vesicles—along with a lot of other material—will be found on the proximal (closer to soma) side of the obstruction. These vesicles are presumably produced in the Golgi apparatus, the packaging plant of the cell, and are sent down to the terminal buttons via *axoplasmic transport,* an active process by which substances are propelled along microtubules and microfilaments that run the length of the axon. These fibers also run through the terminal buttons, presumably transporting substances within them.

The postsynaptic membrane under the termi-

FIGURE 3.1
Details of a synapse.

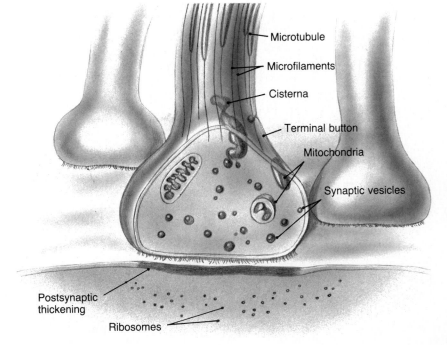

- Microtubule
- Microfilaments
- Cisterna
- Terminal button
- Mitochondria
- Synaptic vesicles
- Postsynaptic thickening
- Ribosomes

nal button is somewhat thicker than the membrane elsewhere. As we will see, it contains specialized protein molecules that detect the presence of transmitter substances in the synaptic cleft and initiate the changes in the membrane potential that excite or inhibit the rate of firing of the cell's axon. Ribosomes are found in the cytoplasm near the postsynaptic membrane. Because ribosomes are needed for protein synthesis, their presence near the postsynaptic membrane implies that protein synthesis is important for some aspect of the process of receiving messages from terminal buttons.

Neural Integration

The interaction of the effects of excitatory and inhibitory synapses on the somatic and dendritic membranes of a neuron determines the rate at which its axon fires. This interaction is called **neural integration** (*integration* means "to make whole," in the sense of combining two functions). To illustrate this process, we can perform a hypothetical experiment.

We anesthetize an animal and place a microelectrode inside the axon of a multipolar neuron in its brain (neuron C). We have chosen this hypothetical animal because the neuron receives synaptic inputs from two neurons (A and B), one inhibitory and one excitatory. We attach electrodes from two electrical stimulators to the two axons that communicate with the neuron. (See *Figure 3.2*.)

First, we stimulate axon A, one of the incoming axons, and record the membrane potential of the axon of neuron C, the postsynaptic neuron. After a brief delay the membrane potential of axon C begins to depolarize, reaches the threshold of excitation, and "fires," transmitting an action potential down its length. (See *Figure 3.3a.*) Next, we stimulate axon B. This time, we see that the effect is to *hyperpolarize* the membrane of axon C. (See *Figure 3.3b.*) Of course, hyperpolarizations never cause action potentials. Now let us see what happens when we simultaneously stimulate axons A and B. The synapses at the end of axon A cause depolarizations, and those at the end of axon B cause hyperpolarizations. These effects cancel each

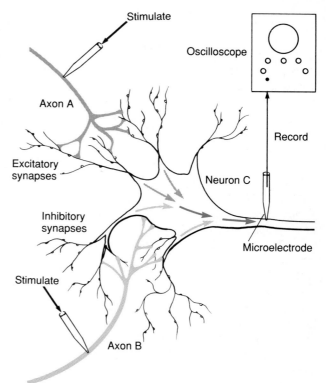

FIGURE 3.2
The means for measuring the effects of the activity of excitatory and inhibitory synapses on the rate of firing of a neuron's axon.

other; the membrane potential of axon C changes very little, and an action potential is not triggered. (See *Figure 3.3c.*)

As you just saw in Figure 3.3, when a synapse becomes active, it causes a brief change in the membrane potential of the cell with which it communicates. This change is called a postsynaptic potential because it occurs in the postsynaptic neuron. Hyperpolarizations *inhibit* the production of action potentials; hence they are called **inhibitory postsynaptic potentials** (IPSPs). Depolarizations *excite* the neuron, making action potentials more likely; hence they are called **excitatory postsynaptic potentials** (EPSPs). An individual neuron may have tens of thousands of synapses on it. Thus, the rate of firing of its axon at a particular time depends on the relative number of EPSPs and IPSPs that are produced on its membrane.

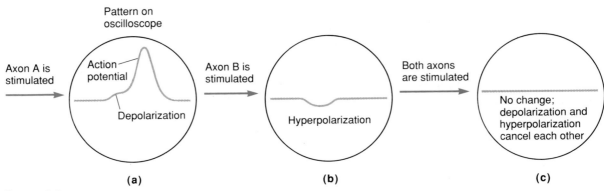

FIGURE 3.3
Excitatory and inhibitory postsynaptic potentials. (a) Action potential triggered. (b) Hyperpolarization. (c) Canceling effects.

Note that *neural* inhibition (that is, an inhibitory postsynaptic potential) does not always produce *behavioral* inhibition. For example, suppose a group of neurons inhibits a particular movement. If these neurons are inhibited, they will no longer suppress the behavior. Thus, inhibition of the inhibitory neurons makes the behavior more likely to occur. Of course, the same is true for neural excitation. Neural *excitation* of neurons that *inhibit* a behavior suppresses that behavior. For example, when we are dreaming, a particular set of inhibitory neurons in the brain becomes active and prevents us from getting up and acting out our dreams. (As we will see in Chapter 9, if these neurons are destroyed, people *will* act out their dreams.) Neurons are elements in complex circuits; without knowing the details of these circuits, one cannot predict the effects of the excitation or inhibition of one set of neurons on an organism's behavior.

Release of Transmitter Substance

When action potentials are conducted down an axon (and down all of its branches), something happens inside all of the terminal buttons: A number of synaptic vesicles filled with a transmitter substance migrate to the presynaptic membrane, adhere to it, and then break open, spilling their contents into the synaptic cleft. (See *Figure 3.4.*)

The evidence for this process comes from several different kinds of experiments. Clark, Hurlbut, and Mauro (1972) removed a muscle from a frog, along with a length of nerve that innervated it. They infused the muscle and terminal buttons with venom of the black widow spider,

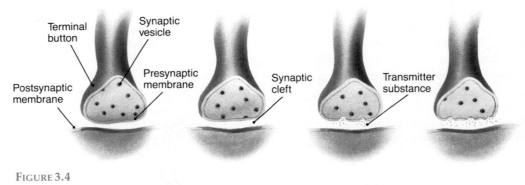

FIGURE 3.4
The release of a transmitter substance into the synaptic cleft from a terminal button.

which causes transmitter substance to be released from the terminal buttons that synapse on the muscle fibers. When they examined the terminal buttons under an electron microscope, they found that the synaptic vesicles were gone.

Heuser and colleagues (Heuser, 1977; Heuser, Reese, Dennis, Jan, Jan, and Evans, 1979) obtained even more direct evidence. Because the release of transmitter substance is a very rapid event, taking only a few milliseconds to occur, special procedures are needed to stop the action so that the details can be studied. They electrically stimulated the nerve attached to an isolated frog muscle and then dropped the muscle against a block of pure copper that had been cooled to 4 K (approximately −453°F). Contact with the supercooled metal froze the outer layer of tissue in 2 milliseconds or less. The ice held the components of the terminal buttons in place until they could be chemically stabilized and examined with an electron microscope. Figure 3.5 shows a portion of the synapse in cross section; note the vesicles that appear to be fused with the presynaptic membrane, forming the shape of an omega (Ω). (See *Figure 3.5.*)

What happens to the membrane of the synaptic vesicles after they have broken open and released the transmitter substance they contain? It appears that it is recycled. Heuser and Reese (1973) suggested that as the synaptic vesicles fuse with the presynaptic membrane and burst open, their membrane becomes incorporated into that of the terminal button, which consequently becomes larger. Therefore, if the proper size of the terminal button is to be maintained, some membrane must be removed. They obtained evidence that suggested that at the point of junction between the axon and the terminal button, little buds of membrane pinch off into the cytoplasm, in a process called *pinocytosis.* The buds of membrane migrate to the cisternae and fuse with them, adding to their membrane. Then new synaptic vesicles are produced as pieces of membrane break off the cisternae and are filled with molecules of transmitter substance. (See *Figure 3.6.*)

In their experiment Heuser and Reese used a chemical with the unlikely name *horseradish peroxidase.* As we will see, this enzyme, extracted from the horseradish plant, is useful to neurochemists and neuroanatomists. Heuser and Reese placed a frog muscle and attached nerve in a solution of horseradish peroxidase and

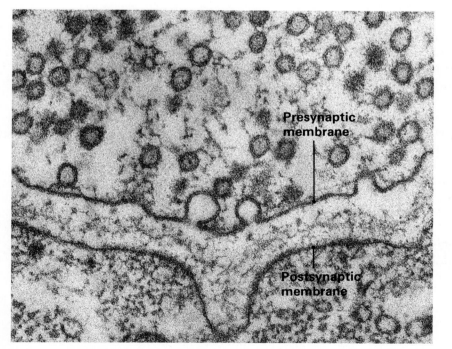

Presynaptic membrane

Postsynaptic membrane

FIGURE 3.5
A photograph from an electron microscope, showing a cross section of a synapse. The omega-shaped figures are synaptic vesicles fusing with the presynaptic membranes of terminal buttons that form synapses with frog muscle. (From Heuser, J.E., in *Society for Neuroscience Symposia, Volume II*, edited by W.M. Cowan and J.A. Ferrendelli. Bethesda, Md.: Society for Neuroscience, 1977.)

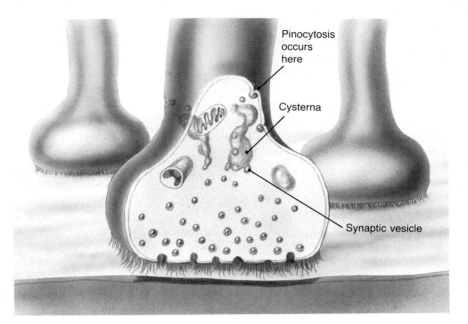

FIGURE 3.6
Recycling of the membrane of synaptic vesicles that have released neurotransmitter into the synaptic cleft.

electrically stimulated the nerve, causing the axons to fire. Shortly thereafter, they removed the muscle and nerve from the solution and treated them with chemicals that react with horseradish peroxidase, producing black spots that are visible under a microscope wherever the chemical is present in the tissue. When they chemically treated and examined the nerve tissue soon after placing it in the horseradish peroxidase solution, they found black spots inside small vesicles in the cytoplasm near the junction of the axon and terminal button. When they waited a longer time before chemically treating the tissue, they found black spots in the cisternae. When they waited even longer, they found them in the synaptic vesicles themselves. The results indicate that the horseradish peroxidase, which was taken into the cell with a bit of extracellular fluid when buds pinched off the axonal membrane during pinocytosis, was transported to the cisternae and then into the newly made synaptic vesicles.

More recent evidence confirms most of this story but contradicts part of it. Koenig and Ikeda (1989) studied the release of transmitter substance and the recycling of the membrane of synaptic vesicles in a species of fruit fly (*Drosophila melanogaster*) with an interesting genetic mutation. At 19°C everything works normally in their nervous system, but at 29°C membrane recycling ceases. Thus, the investigators were able to warm the flies, stimulate a group of axons long enough so that all synaptic vesicles in the terminal buttons had disappeared, and then cool the flies again to permit the reconstruction of the vesicles. They followed this procedure with many flies, freezing them at different times after the period of stimulation so that they could follow the recycling process.

Figure 3.7 shows photographs of the results, taken with an electron microscope. Before stimulation the terminal button was full of synaptic vesicles (sv). (In all photographs the synaptic junction is indicated by a thick arrow.) (See *Figure 3.7a*.) Stimulation at 29°C caused complete depletion of all synaptic vesicles. Two minutes after the fly was returned to 19°C, we see that pinocytosis has begun again; some buds of membrane are forming along the membrane of the terminal button (*arrowheads*). Note that the buds are not located at the active zone of the synapse; thus, they are different from the omega-shaped figures that you saw in Figure 3.5. Some of these buds (*thin arrows*) seem to be coalescing with small cisternae (*asterisks*). (See *Figure 3.7b*.) After 8 minutes of recovery the cisternae (*asterisks*) were much larger, and buds were still forming at the

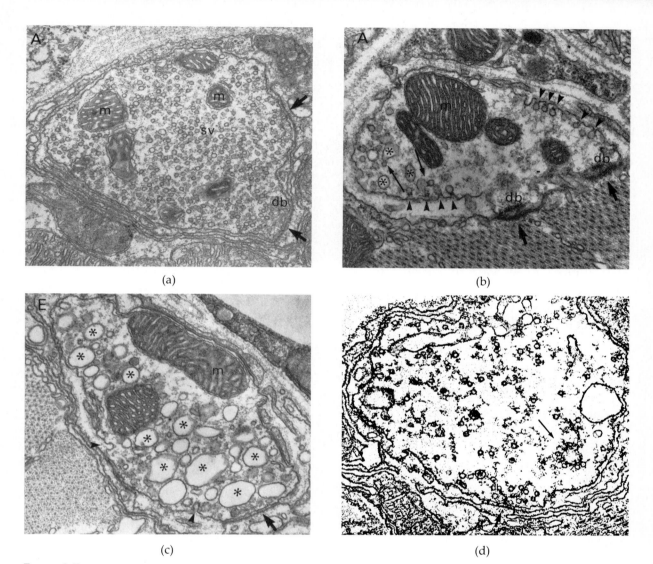

(a)

(b)

(c)

(d)

FIGURE 3.7

Photographs from an electron microscope, showing the reconstruction of synaptic vesicles after all transmitter substance has been released. (a) Appearance of a terminal button before stimulation. (b) Appearance of a terminal button after 2 minutes of recovery. (c) Appearance of a terminal button after 8 minutes of recovery. (d) Appearance of a terminal button after 12 minutes of recovery. (db = presynaptic dense body, m = mitochondria, sv = synaptic vesicles.) (From Koenig, J.H., and Ikeda, K. *The Journal of Neuroscience*, 1989, *9*, 3844–3860.)

membrane *(arrowheads)*. (See *Figure 3.7c.*) After 12 minutes most of the cisternae had disappeared, apparently replaced by newly formed synaptic vesicles. In fact, one cisterna appears to be giving birth to several vesicles *(thin arrow)*. (See *Figure 3.7d.*)

All of what we have seen in the photographs is

consistent with the recycling hypothesis of Heuser and Reese. However, one finding is not: Koenig and Ikeda did not observe an increase in the size of the terminal buttons after the synaptic vesicles had disappeared. What, then, happened to all of the membrane that coated the vesicles, and where did the buds come from? The investigators admit that there is, indeed, a mystery to be solved here. They suggest that the membranes of the synaptic vesicles may have simply dissolved as soon as they reached the presynaptic membrane, but they cannot explain where the pieces were stored or how they got put together again.

The force that moves the synaptic vesicles toward the presynaptic membrane appears to be supplied by a process similar to the one responsible for axoplasmic flow and for muscular contraction. As we will see in Chapter 8, the interaction of two proteins, actin and myosin, provides the force that contracts muscle fibers. They interact and cause a contraction when calcium ions (Ca^{2+}) enter the cell. Similarly, the entry of Ca^{2+} appears to be the event that causes synaptic vesicles to migrate to the presynaptic membrane and rupture. If the extracellular fluid is artificially depleted of Ca^{2+}, the terminal button no longer releases transmitter substance when its axon is stimulated. Studies have shown that when an action potential reaches a terminal button, voltage-dependent calcium channels open their gates and the membrane temporarily becomes permeable to Ca^{2+}. The Ca^{2+} enters the cytoplasm of the terminal button, pushed in by the force of diffusion and electrostatic pressure, just like Na^+. The entry of Ca^{2+} appears to cause microtubules to propel the synaptic vesicles to the presynaptic membrane. A calcium pump, similar in operation to the sodium-potassium pump, later removes the intracellular Ca^{2+}.

Activation of Receptors

How does the transmitter substance produce a depolarization or hyperpolarization in the postsynaptic membrane? It does so by activating special molecules attached to the postsynaptic membrane. These molecules, which are made of protein, are called **postsynaptic receptors.** When molecules of a transmitter substance diffuse across the synaptic cleft and meet a postsynaptic receptor, they attach to the receptor in the manner of keys fitting a lock. Once they attach, the postsynaptic receptors open the gates of **neurotransmitter-dependent ion channels.** Thus, the transmitter substance permits particular ions to pass through the membrane, changing the local membrane potential.

Neurotransmitters open ion channels by at least two different means. The best-known example of the first method is the nicotinic acetylcholine receptor. (Acetylcholine is a transmitter substance that will be discussed in more detail later in this chapter; I will also explain then the meaning of the term *nicotinic.*) This receptor has been studied in the organ that produces electrical current in *Torpedo,* the electric ray, where it occurs in great number. (The electric ray is a fish that generates a powerful electrical current, not a science-fiction weapon.) Acetylcholine receptors open the gates of the ion channels that permit sodium ions to enter the cell. The structure of the acetylcholine receptor is shown in Figure 3.8. Acetylcholine molecules attach to two sites located on the part of the molecule that projects into the synaptic cleft. When *both* sites are occupied by molecules of acetylcholine, the ion channel widens, permitting sodium ions to pass through. (See *Figure 3.8.*)

The second method is more complicated. Some receptors do not open ion gates directly but instead cause the production of a second messenger (the first messenger being the transmitter substance). Attached to receptors in the postsynaptic membrane at many synapses are molecules of a special protein called a **G protein.** When a molecule of the transmitter substance occupies the receptor, the G protein binds with a molecule of **GTP** (guanine triphosphate) and then moves over to activate an enzyme called **adenylate cyclase.** When adenylate cyclase becomes active, it causes ATP (adenosine triphosphate) to be converted into **cyclic AMP** (cyclic adenosine monophosphate). Cyclic AMP is the second messenger.

Cyclic AMP activates enzymes called **protein kinases;** when activated, these enzymes cause changes in the physical shape of the proteins that control the gates of the ion channels in the postsynaptic membrane. (*Kinase* translates roughly as "enzyme that causes movement.") A protein kinase makes the protein change its shape by causing it to be **phosphorylated**—to gain a phosphate ion. The change in the protein's shape opens the gate and permits ions to cross the membrane. As a consequence, a postsynaptic potential is produced. (See *Figure 3.9.*)

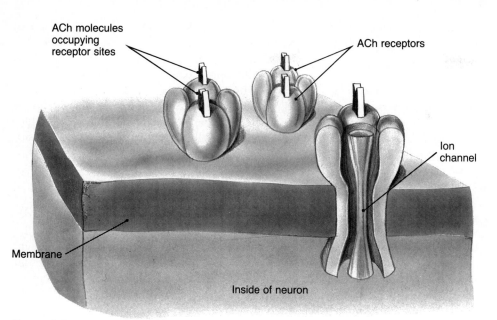

FIGURE 3.8

The acetylcholine (ACh) receptor, an example of a neurotransmitter-dependent ion channel. (Adapted from Changeux, J.-P., Devillers-Thiéry, A., and Chemouilli, P. *Science*, 1984, *225*, 1335–1345.)

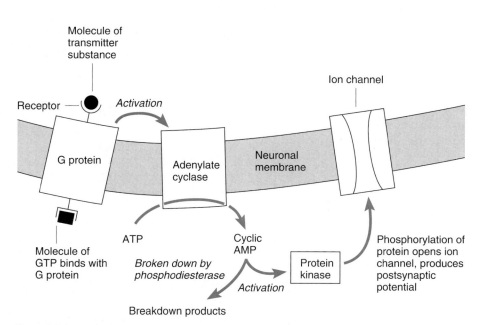

FIGURE 3.9

Indirect control of ion channels. Many neurotransmitter receptors control ion channels indirectly, by means of second-messenger cyclic AMP.

Cyclic nucleotides are destroyed soon after they are produced by an enzyme called *phosphodiesterase.* Thus, a drug that inhibits the activity of phosphodiesterase allows cyclic AMP to accumulate and keeps the ion gates open for a longer-than-usual time. In fact, many people dose themselves daily with a phosphodiesterase inhibitor, *caffeine.* This drug increases synaptic activity at some neurons, producing behavioral effects of activation and wakefulness.

I have to admit that the role of cyclic AMP in synaptic transmission is complicated and that there are many steps and names of chemicals to learn. However, it is an important process because it is the way that most receptors are coupled to ion channels. In addition, many investigators use a change in the level of cyclic AMP in a cell as an indication of whether the postsynaptic receptors have been activated.

Cyclic AMP plays a role in other processes besides the production of postsynaptic potentials. For example, it provides the means by which some hormones are able to produce changes in the physiological processes of the cells that they affect. Endocrine glands produce two classes of hormones: peptides and steroids. *Peptides* are chains of amino acids, which are linked together by special chemical links called *peptide bonds* (hence their name). For example, insulin and the hormones of the pituitary gland are peptides. *Steroids* consist of very small fat-soluble molecules that have no difficulty entering the target cells. (*Steroid* derives from *stereos,* "solid," and *oleum,* "oil." They are synthesized from cholesterol.) Examples of steroid hormones include the sex hormones secreted by the ovaries and testes and the hormones secreted by the adrenal cortex.

Peptides control physiological processes in their target cells by stimulating receptors on the surface of these cells, just as transmitter substances do. (As we shall see later in this chapter, some peptides are produced by neurons and serve as transmitter substances.) As far as we know, all receptors for peptide hormones are linked to G proteins and use cyclic AMP as a second messenger. Unlike transmitter substances, these hormones do not produce postsynaptic potentials. Instead, the cyclic AMP travels to the nucleus of the cell, where it causes changes in protein synthesis that alter the cell's physiological processes.

Because steroid hormones are soluble in lipids, they pass easily through the cell membrane. They travel to the nucleus, where they attach themselves to receptors. The receptors, stimulated by the hormone, then direct the machinery of the cell to alter its protein production. (See *Figure 3.10.*)

Postsynaptic Potentials

Because postsynaptic potentials can be either depolarizing (excitatory) or hyperpolarizing (inhibitory), the alterations in membrane permeability must be caused by the movement of particular species of ions. There are four major types of neu-

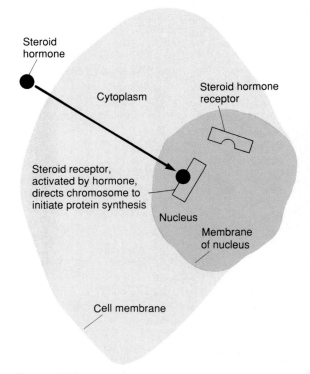

Steroid hormone

Cytoplasm

Steroid hormone receptor

Steroid receptor, activated by hormone, directs chromosome to initiate protein synthesis

Nucleus

Membrane of nucleus

Cell membrane

FIGURE 3.10

Action of steroid hormones. Steroid hormones affect their target cells by means of specialized receptors in the nucleus. Once a receptor binds with a molecule of a steroid hormone, it causes genetic mechanisms to initiate protein synthesis.

rotransmitter-dependent ion channels in the postsynaptic membrane: sodium, potassium, chloride, and calcium. The neurotransmitter-dependent sodium channel is the most important source of excitatory postsynaptic potentials. As we saw in Chapter 2, the sodium-potassium pump keeps sodium outside the cell, waiting for the forces of diffusion and electrostatic pressure to push it in. Obviously, when sodium channels are opened, the result is a depolarization—an EPSP. (See *Figure 3.11a.*)

We also saw in Chapter 2 that the sodium-potassium pump maintains a small surplus of potassium ions inside the cell. If potassium channels open, some of these cations will follow this gradient and leave the cell. Because K^+ is positively charged, its efflux will hyperpolarize the membrane, producing an IPSP. (See *Figure 3.11b.*)

At many synapses inhibitory transmitter substances open the chloride channels, instead of (or in addition to) potassium channels. The effect of opening chloride channels depends on the membrane potential of the neuron. If the membrane is at the resting potential, nothing happens, because (as we saw in Chapter 2) the forces of diffusion and electrostatic pressure balance perfectly for the chloride ion. However, if the membrane potential has already been depolarized by the activity of excitatory synapses located nearby, then the opening of chloride channels will permit Cl^- to leave the cell. The exodus of anions will bring the membrane potential back to its normal resting condition. Thus, the opening of chloride channels serves to neutralize EPSPs. (See *Figure 3.11c.*)

The fourth type of neurotransmitter-dependent ion channel is the calcium channel. Calcium ions (Ca^{2+}), being positively charged and being located in highest concentration outside the cell, act like sodium ions; that is, the opening of calcium channels depolarizes the membrane, producing EPSPs. But calcium does even more. As we saw earlier in this chapter, the entry of calcium into the terminal button triggers the migration of synaptic vesicles and the release of the transmitter substance. *Postsynaptically,* calcium binds with and activates special enzymes. These enzymes have a variety of effects, including the production of biochemical and structural changes in the postsynap-

tic neuron. As we shall see in Chapter 15, one of the ways that learning affects the connections between neurons involves changes in dendritic spines initiated by the opening of calcium channels. (See *Figure 3.11d.*)

Termination of the Postsynaptic Potential

Postsynaptic potentials are brief depolarizations or hyperpolarizations caused by the activation of

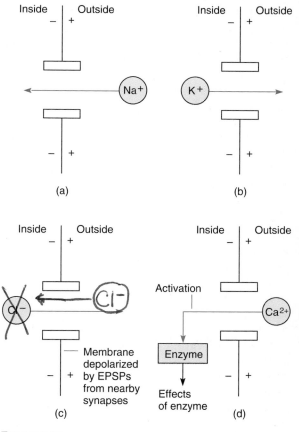

FIGURE 3.11
Ionic movements during postsynaptic potentials. (a) EPSPs produced by the influx of Na^+ through sodium channels. (b) IPSPs produced by the efflux of K^+ through sodium channels. (c) IPSPs produced by the efflux of Cl^- through chloride channels. This effect occurs only if the membrane has already been depolarized by the action of nearly excitatory synapses. (d) EPSPs produced by the influx of Ca^{2+} through calcium channels. Once inside the cell, calcium activates various enzymes and produces biochemical or structural changes.

postsynaptic receptors with molecules of a transmitter substance. They are kept brief by two mechanisms: reuptake and enzymatic deactivation.

The postsynaptic potentials produced by almost all transmitter substances are terminated by **reuptake.** This process is simply an extremely rapid removal of transmitter substance from the synaptic cleft by the terminal button. The transmitter substance does not return in the vesicles that get pinched off the membrane of the terminal button; instead, the membrane contains a pumplike mechanism that draws on the cell's energy reserves to force molecules of the transmitter substance from the synaptic cleft directly into the cytoplasm. When an action potential arrives, the terminal buttons release a small amount of transmitter substance into the synaptic cleft and then take it back, giving the postsynaptic receptors only a brief exposure to the transmitter substance.

Enzymatic deactivation is accomplished by an enzyme that destroys the transmitter molecule. As far as we know, postsynaptic potentials are terminated in this way for only one transmitter substance—*acetylcholine* (ACh). Transmission at synapses on muscle fibers and at some synapses between neurons is mediated by ACh. Postsynaptic potentials produced by ACh are short-lived because the postsynaptic membrane at these synapses contains an enzyme called **acetylcholinesterase** (AChE). AChE destroys ACh by cleaving it into its constituents, choline and acetate. Because neither of these substances is capable of activating postsynaptic receptors, the postsynaptic potential is terminated once the molecules of ACh are broken apart. AChE is an extremely energetic destroyer of ACh; one molecule of AChE will chop apart more that five thousand molecules of ACh each second.

Autoreceptors

Postsynaptic receptors detect the presence of a transmitter substance in the synaptic cleft and initiate excitatory or inhibitory postsynaptic potentials. But the postsynaptic membrane is not the only location of receptors that respond to transmitter substances. Many neurons also possess receptors that respond to the transmitter substance that *they* release, called **autoreceptors.**

Autoreceptors can be located on the membrane of any part of the cell: terminal button, axon, soma, or dendrite. In general, these receptors do not control ion channels; when stimulated by a molecule of the appropriate transmitter substance, they do not produce changes in the local membrane potential. Instead, they regulate internal processes, including the synthesis and release of the transmitter substance. In most cases the effects are inhibitory; that is, the presence of the transmitter substance in the extracellular fluid in the vicinity of the neuron causes a decrease in the rate of synthesis or release of the transmitter substance. Most investigators believe that autoreceptors are part of a regulatory system that controls the amount of transmitter substance released.

Other Types of Synapses

So far, my discussion of synaptic activity has referred only to the effects of postsynaptic excitation or inhibition. These effects occur at **axosomatic synapses** or **axodendritic synapses** (synapses between the terminal buttons of axons with somatic or dendritic membrane, respectively). Other kinds of synapses exist as well.

A junction between a terminal button and an axon of another cell (usually on or near the terminal button) is referred to as an **axoaxonic synapse.** This type of synapse does not directly contribute to neural integration, as do the axosomatic and axodendritic synapses discussed in the previous section. Instead, axoaxonic synapses alter the amount of transmitter substance released by the terminal buttons of the postsynaptic axon. They can produce presynaptic modulation: presynaptic inhibition or presynaptic facilitation.

As you know, the release of a transmitter substance by a terminal button is initiated by an action potential. Normally, a particular terminal button releases a fixed amount of transmitter substance each time an action potential arrives. However, the release of transmitter substance can be modulated by the activity of axoaxonic synapses. If the activity of the axoaxonic synapse decreases the release of the transmitter substance, the effect is

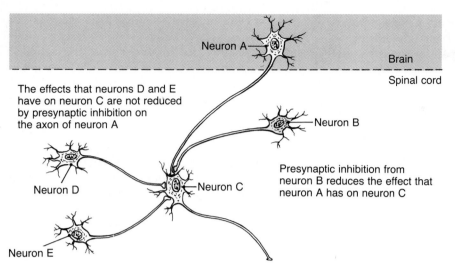

The effects that neurons D and E have on neuron C are not reduced by presynaptic inhibition on the axon of neuron A

Neuron A

Brain

Spinal cord

Neuron B

Presynaptic inhibition from neuron B reduces the effect that neuron A has on neuron C

Neuron D

Neuron C

Neuron E

FIGURE 3.12
An example of the advantage of presynaptic inhibition.

called *presynaptic inhibition.* If it increases the release, it is called *presynaptic facilitation.*

Axoaxonic synapses obviously have an effect only if the postsynaptic axon is actually firing. As an example of how these synapses might be useful, let us consider neuron B, which can exert presynaptic inhibition or facilitation on neuron A through an axoaxonic synapse. When neuron B is active, the effect of neuron A on neuron C is either reduced or augmented. But this effect is localized; the effects of neurons D and E on neuron C remain unchanged. (See *Figure 3.12.*)

Many very small neurons have extremely short processes and apparently lack axons. These neurons form ***dendrodendritic synapses,*** or synapses between dendrites. Because these neurons lack long axonal processes, they do not transmit information from place to place within the brain. Most investigators believe that they perform regulatory functions, perhaps helping to organize the activity of groups of neurons. Because these neurons are so small, they are difficult to study; thus, little is known about their function.

Some larger neurons, as well, form dendrodendritic synapses. Some of these synapses are chemical, indicated by the presence of synaptic vesicles in one of the juxtaposed dendrites and a postsynaptic thickening in the membrane of the other. Other synapses are *electrical;* the membranes meet and almost touch, forming a ***gap junction.*** The membranes on both sides of a gap junction contain channels that permit ions to diffuse from one cell to another. Thus, changes in the membrane potential of one neuron induce changes in the membrane of the other. Although most gap junctions in vertebrate synapses are dendrodendritic, axosomatic and axodendritic gap junctions also occur. Gap junctions are common in invertebrates; their function in the vertebrate nervous system is not known.

I NTERIM SUMMARY

Synapses consist of junctions between the terminal buttons of one neuron and the membrane—usually the somatic or dendritic membrane—of another. When an action potential is transmitted down an axon, the terminal buttons at the end release a transmitter substance, a chemical that produces depolarizations (EPSPs) or hyperpolarizations (IPSPs) of the postsynaptic membrane. The rate of firing of the postsynaptic cell is determined by the relative activity of the excitatory and inhibitory synapses on the membrane of its dendrites and soma.

All forms of chemical communication—including that produced by transmitter substances, neuromodulators, hormones, and pheromones—involve the release of chemicals that are detected by specialized protein receptors.

Transmitter substances are stored in synaptic vesicles, small sacs of membrane located in the cytoplasm of terminal buttons. When an action potential reaches the terminal button, the sudden depolarization causes voltage-dependent calcium channels in the membrane to open, and Ca^{2+} enters the cytoplasm. This ion catalyzes chemical reactions that propel synaptic vesicles to the inner surface of the presynaptic membrane. The vesicles fuse with the membrane and burst, spilling their contents into the synaptic cleft. The transmitter substance that is thus released diffuses through the extracellular fluid in the synaptic cleft and reaches the receptors in the postsynaptic membrane. The membrane of the synaptic vesicles is recycled through the cisternae.

When postsynaptic receptors are activated by molecules of a transmitter substance, they open neurotransmitter-dependent ion channels. They do so directly (as in the case of nicotinic acetylcholine receptors) or indirectly, through the second messenger cyclic AMP. Cyclic AMP activates protein kinases that cause proteins in the membrane to change their shape, opening the gates of ion channels. Peptide hormones also exert their effects by means of cyclic AMP, but steroid hormones stimulate receptors located within the nucleus of their target cells.

The activation of postsynaptic receptors by molecules of a transmitter substance causes the ion channels to open, resulting in a postsynaptic potential. Excitatory postsynaptic potentials occur when Na^+ enters the cell. Inhibitory postsynaptic potentials are produced by the opening of K^+ channels or Cl^- channels. The entry of Ca^{2+} produces EPSPs, but even more importantly, it activates special enzymes that cause physiological changes in the postsynaptic cell.

Postsynaptic potentials are normally brief. They are terminated by two means. In the case of acetylcholine the enzyme acetylcholinesterase, which is attached to the postsynaptic membrane, deactivates the transmitter substance, breaking it down to choline and acetate. In all other cases (as far as we know) molecules of the transmitter substance are removed from the synaptic cleft by means of a special mechanism in the membrane that pumps them back into the cytoplasm, where they can be used again. This retrieval process is called reuptake.

The presynaptic membrane, as well as the postsynaptic membrane, contains receptors that detect the presence of a transmitter substance. Presynaptic receptors, also called autoreceptors, monitor the quantity of transmitter substance that a neuron releases and apparently regulate the amount that is synthesized or released.

Axosomatic and axodendritic synapses are not the only kinds found in the nervous system. Axoaxonic synapses produce presynaptic inhibition by depolarizing the membrane of a terminal button enough so that an action potential, if it occurs, produces a smaller change in the polarization of the membrane. The result of this effect is to cause the terminal button to release a smaller quantity of its transmitter substance. Dendrodendritic synapses also occur, but their role in neural communication is not yet understood.

TRANSMITTER SUBSTANCES

Because transmitter substances have two general effects on the postsynaptic membrane—depolarization (EPSP) or hyperpolarization (IPSP)—one might expect that there would be two kinds of transmitter substances, excitatory and inhibitory. Instead, there are many different kinds. Although some do appear to be exclusively excitatory or inhibitory, others can produce either excitation or inhibition, depending on the nature of the postsynaptic receptors. The classes of transmitter substances that have been studied the most include *acetylcholine*, *monoamines*, *amino acids*, and *peptides*. This section will describe the production of transmitter substances, briefly summarize their role in behavior, and discuss their interactions with drugs.

Acetylcholine

The transmitter substance at synapses on skeletal muscles of vertebrates is acetylcholine (ACh). (These synapses are said to be *acetylcholinergic. Ergon* is the Greek word for "work.") ACh is also found in the ganglia of the autonomic nervous system and at the target organs of the parasympathetic branch of the autonomic nervous system (discussed in more detail in Chapter 4). Because ACh is found outside the central nervous system in locations that are easy to study, this transmitter substance has received much attention from neuroscientists. The fact that it has an excitatory effect on the membrane of skeletal muscle fibers and an inhibitory effect on the membrane of muscle fibers in the heart illustrates an important principle: *The effect that a transmitter substance has on the postsynaptic membrane is not determined by the chemical itself but by the nature of the postsynaptic receptors it stimulates.* ACh receptors on skeletal muscle fibers control sodium ion channels and produce depolarizations (excitations); ACh receptors on cardiac muscle fibers control potassium ion channels and produce hyperpolarizations (inhibition).

ACh is also found in the brain. It is apparently involved in learning and remembering and in controlling the stage of sleep in which dreams occur. ACh is produced by means of the following reaction:

choline acetyltransferase

acetyl CoA + choline $\longrightarrow$ acetylcholine + CoA

Choline, a substance derived from the breakdown of lipids, is taken into the neuron from the general circulation. *CoA* (coenzyme A) is a complex molecule, consisting in part of the vitamin pantothenic acid (one of the B vitamins). CoA is produced by the mitochondria, and it takes part in many reactions in the body. *Acetyl CoA* is composed of CoA with an acetate ion attached to it. (Acetate is the cation found in vinegar, also called acetic acid.) In the presence of the enzyme *choline acetyltransferase,* the acetate ion is transferred from the CoA molecule to the choline molecule, yielding a molecule of ACh and one of ordinary CoA.

A simple analogy illustrates the role of coenzymes in chemical reactions. Think of acetate as a hot dog and choline as a bun. The task of the person (enzyme) who operates the hot dog vending stand is to put a hot dog into the bun (make acetylcholine). To do so, the vendor needs a fork (coenzyme) to remove the hot dog from the boiling water. The vendor inserts the fork into the hot dog (attaches acetate to CoA) and transfers the hot dog from fork to bun.

You will recall that after being released by the terminal button, ACh is deactivated by the enzyme acetylcholinesterase (AChE), which is present in the postsynaptic membrane. The deactivation produces choline and acetate from ACh. Because the amount of choline that is picked up by the soma from the general circulation and is sent to the terminal buttons by means of axoplasmic flow is not sufficient to keep up with the loss of choline by an active synapse, choline must be recycled. After ACh is destroyed by the AChE in the postsynaptic membrane, the choline is returned to the terminal buttons by means of reuptake. There, it is converted back into ACh. This process has an efficiency of 50 percent; that is, half of the choline is retrieved and recycled.

Sometimes, too much ACh is produced—more than can be stored in the synaptic vesicles. For this reason, AChE is also present in the cytoplasm of the terminal buttons. This AChE cannot destroy the ACh that is stored in the vesicles, but it can—and does—destroy any transmitter substance produced by the cell that exceeds the storage capacity of the synaptic vesicles.

There are two different types of ACh receptors, with different molecular shapes. These receptors were identified when investigators discovered that different drugs activated or inhibited them. One class is stimulated by nicotine (a poison found in tobacco leaves), the other by muscarine (a poison found in mushrooms). Consequently, they are referred to as *nicotinic receptors* and *muscarinic receptors,* respectively. Muscle fibers contain nicotinic receptors exclusively; the central nervous system primarily contains muscarinic receptors. Nicotinic receptors are the ones I discussed earlier in this chapter; as Figure 3.8 showed, they are coupled directly to sodium channels. Muscarinic receptors are coupled by G proteins to adenylate cyclase; thus, they use cyclic

AMP as the second messenger (See Figure 3.9).

Why are there several types of receptors for a particular transmitter substance? One answer is that different receptors are coupled to different mechanisms in the postsynaptic membrane and thus have different effects on the postsynaptic cell. For example, both nicotinic and muscarinic ACh receptors detect the presence of acetylcholine, but the former is linked directly to an ion channel, whereas the latter uses cyclic AMP as a second messenger. Another answer is that some receptors contain several binding sites that detect the presence of various neuromodulators as well as the transmitter substance. For example, one type of receptor detects the presence of a neurotransmitter (GABA) and at least two neuromodulators, which alter the sensitivity of the GABA receptor. (I will discuss this receptor later in this chapter.)

The Monoamines

Epinephrine, norepinephrine, dopamine, and serotonin are four chemicals that belong to a family of compounds called **monoamines.** Because the molecular structures of these substances are similar, some drugs affect the activity of all of them, to some degree. Epinephrine, norepinephrine and dopamine, belong to a subclass of monoamines called *catecholamines.* (See *Table 3.1.*)

Norepinephrine

Because *norepinephrine* (NE), like ACh, is found in neurons in the autonomic nervous system, this neurotransmitter has received much experimental attention. I should note that *Adrenalin* and *epinephrine* are synonymous, as are *noradrenalin* and *norepinephrine.* **Epinephrine** is produced by the adrenal medulla, the central core of the adrenal glands, which are small endocrine glands located above the kidneys. It also serves as a transmitter substance in the brain, but it is of minor importance, compared with norepinephrine. *Ad renal* is Latin for "toward kidney." In Greek, one would say *epi nephron* ("upon the kidney"), hence the term *epinephrine.* The latter term has been adopted by pharmacologists, probably because the word *Adrenalin* was appropriated by a drug company as a proprietary name; therefore, to be consistent with general usage, I will refer to the transmitter substance as *norepinephrine.* The accepted adjectival form is *noradrenergic;* I suppose that *norepinephrinergic* never caught on because it is too difficult to pronounce.

Noradrenergic neurons in the brain are primarily involved in control of alertness and wakefulness; a small group of neurons located in the back part of the brain sends axons to widespread regions of the rest of the brain. Noradrenergic synapses in the central nervous system produce inhibitory postsynaptic potentials. By contrast, at the target organs of the sympathetic nervous system (discussed in Chapter 4) norepinephrine usually has an excitatory effect.

Neurons that release norepinephrine do not do so through terminal buttons on the ends of axonal branches, as most other neurons release their transmitter substances. Instead, norepinephrine is released through **axonal varicosities,** beadlike swellings of the axonal branches. These varicosities give the axonal branches of noradrenergic neurons the appearance of beaded chains. (See **Figure 3.13.**)

The synthesis of norepinephrine is somewhat more complicated than that of ACh, but each step is a simple one. The precursor molecule is modified slightly, step by step, until it achieves its final shape. Each step is controlled by a different enzyme, which adds a small part or takes one off. The precursor for both of the catecholamine transmitter substances (dopamine and norepinephrine) is **tyrosine,** an essential amino acid that we must obtain from our diet. Tyrosine receives a hydroxyl group (OH—an oxygen atom and a hydrogen atom) and becomes *L-DOPA* (L-3,4-dihydroxyphenylalanine). The enzyme that adds the

TABLE 3.1

Classification of the monoamine transmitter substances

Monoamines	
Catecholamines	*Indolamines*
Norepinephrine	Serotonin (5-HT)
Dopamine	

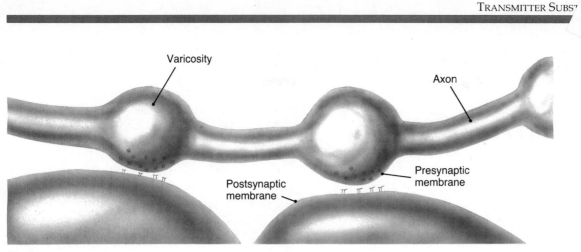

FIGURE 3.13

Axonal varicosities. Noradrenergic axons release their neurotransmitter through varicosities rather than terminal buttons.

hydroxyl group is called *tyrosine hydroxylase.* L-DOPA then loses a carboxyl group (COOH— one carbon atom, two oxygen atoms, and one hydrogen atom) through the activity of the enzyme *DOPA decarboxylase* and becomes dopamine. Finally, the enzyme *dopamine β-hydroxylase* attaches a hydroxyl group to dopamine, which becomes norepinephrine. These reactions are shown in *Figure 3.14.*

Most transmitter substances are synthesized in the cell body, packaged in synaptic vesicles, and transported down the axon to the terminal buttons. However, for norepinephrine the final step of synthesis occurs inside the vesicles themselves. The vesicles are filled with dopamine. There, the dopamine is converted to norepinephrine through the action of dopamine β-hydroxylase.

There are several types of noradrenergic receptors, identified by their differing sensitivities to various drugs. In the central nervous system β_1-noradrenergic receptors and α_1-*noradrenergic receptors* are found primarily in postsynaptic membranes; α_2-*noradrenergic receptors* serve primarily as presynaptic autoreceptors. In addition, β_2-*noradrenergic receptors* are found in the central nervous system but are apparently associated with glia and muscles in the walls of blood vessels. All four kinds of receptors are also found in various organs of the body besides the brain and are responsible for the effects of the catecholamine hormones, epinephrine and norepineph-

rine. All of these receptors are coupled to G proteins that activate adenylate cyclase.

Just as the AChE in the terminal buttons of acetylcholinergic neurons destroys ACh that is produced in excess of the amount that can be stored in the synaptic vesicles, the production of the catecholamines is regulated by an enzyme called *monoamine oxidase* (MAO). This enzyme is also found in the blood, where it deactivates amines that are present in foods such as chocolate and cheese; without such deactivation these amines could cause dangerous increases in blood pressure.

Dopamine

Like the other catecholamine transmitter substance, norepinephrine, *dopamine* (DA) appears to produce inhibitory postsynaptic potentials. Dopamine is one of the more interesting neurotransmitters because it has been implicated in several important functions, including movement, attention, and learning; thus, it is discussed in Chapters 8 and 16.

Degeneration of dopaminergic neurons that connect two parts of the brain's motor system causes *Parkinson's disease,* a movement disorder characterized by tremors, rigidity of the limbs, poor balance, and difficulty in initiating movements. The cell bodies of these neurons are located in a region of the brain called the *substantia nigra* ("black substance"). This region is normally stained black with melanin, the substance that

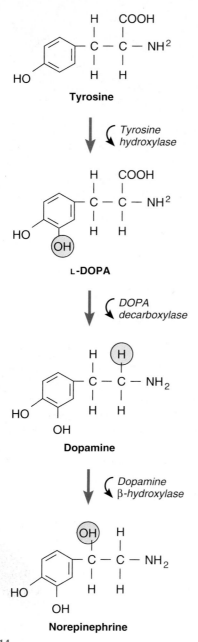

FIGURE 3.14
Biosynthesis of the catecholamines.

gives color to skin. This compound is produced by the breakdown of dopamine. (The brain damage that causes Parkinson's disease was discovered by pathologists who observed that the substantia nigra of a deceased person who had had this disorder was pale rather than black.) People with

Parkinson's disease are given L-DOPA, the precursor to dopamine. Increased levels of L-DOPA in the brain cause more dopamine to be synthesized and released by the surviving dopaminergic neurons, and the patients' symptoms are alleviated.

Dopamine has been implicated as a transmitter substance that might be involved in schizophrenia, a serious mental disorder that includes hallucinations, delusions, and disruption of normal, logical thought processes. Drugs that block the activity of dopaminergic neurons alleviate these symptoms; hence investigators have speculated that schizophrenia is produced by their overactivity. In fact, symptoms of schizophrenia are an occasional side effect of L-DOPA in patients with Parkinson's disease. Fortunately, these symptoms can usually be eliminated by reducing the dose of the drug. The physiology of schizophrenia is discussed in Chapter 18.

We have already seen the biosynthetic pathway for dopamine in Figure 3.14; this transmitter is the immediate precursor of norepinephrine. Excess dopamine in the terminal buttons is destroyed by monoamine oxidase, the same enzyme that regulates norepinephrine.

Two types of dopamine receptors have been identified: D_1 *dopamine receptors* and D_2 *dopamine receptors*. It appears that D_1 receptors are exclusively postsynaptic, whereas D_2 receptors are found both presynaptically and postsynaptically in the brain. Stimulation of D_1 receptors increases the production of cyclic AMP, whereas stimulation of D_2 receptors decreases it.

Serotonin

The third monoamine transmitter substance, *serotonin* (also called *5-HT,* or 5-hydroxytryptamine), has also received much experimental attention. Its precursor is the amino acid *tryptophan.* The enzyme *tryptophan hydroxylase* adds a hydroxyl group, producing *5-HTP* (5-hydroxytryptophan). The enzyme *5-HTP decarboxylase* removes a carboxyl group from 5-HTP, and the result is 5-HT (serotonin). (See *Figure 3.15.*)

Investigators have identified at least three different types of serotonin receptors: 5-HT_{1A}, 5-HT_{1B}, and 5-HT_2. Of these, the 5-HT_2 receptors appear to be found exclusively in postsynaptic

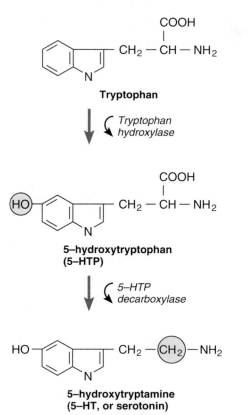

FIGURE 3.15

Biosynthesis of serotonin (5-hydroxytryptamine, or 5-HT).

membranes, whereas the others are found both presynaptically and postsynaptically.

At most synapses serotonin produces inhibitory postsynaptic potentials. In addition, its behavioral effects are also generally inhibitory. Serotonin plays a role in the regulation of mood, in the control of eating, sleep, and arousal, and in the regulation of pain. Serotonergic neurons are involved somehow in the control of dreaming. In fact, the drug LSD appears to produce hallucinations by stimulating $5\text{-}HT_2$ receptors. The drug appears to produce dreaming while the person is awake.

Amino Acid Transmitter Substances

So far, all of the transmitter substances I have described are synthesized within neurons: acetylcholine from choline, the catecholamines from the amino acid tyrosine, and serotonin from the amino acid tryptophan. Some neurons secrete simple amino acids as transmitter substances. Because amino acids are used for protein synthesis by all cells of the brain, it is difficult to prove that a particular amino acid is a transmitter substance. However, investigators suspect that at least eight amino acids may serve as transmitter substances in the mammalian central nervous system (CNS). Three of them are especially important, because they appear to be the most common transmitter substances in the CNS: glutamic acid, gamma-aminobutyric acid (GABA), and glycine.

Glutamic Acid

Because *glutamic acid* (often called *glutamate*) and gamma-amino butyric acid (GABA) are found in very simple organisms, many investigators believe that they are the first neurotransmitters to have evolved. Besides producing postsynaptic potentials by activating postsynaptic receptors, they also have direct excitatory effects (glutamic acid) and inhibitory effects (GABA) on axons; they raise or lower the threshold of excitation, thus affecting the rate at which action potentials occur. These direct effects suggest that these substances had a general modulating role even before the evolutionary development of specific receptor molecules.

Glutamic acid is found throughout the brain. In fact, it appears to be the principal excitatory transmitter substance in the brain. It is produced in abundance by the cells' metabolic processes. Oriental food often contains glutamic acid in the form of monosodium glutamate (MSG), the sodium salt of glutamic acid. Some people are especially sensitive to the effects of MSG and experience mild neurological symptoms, including temporary dizziness and numbness, after eating food that contains large amounts of the chemical.

Investigators have discovered three types of glutamate receptors, named for drugs that stimulate them, the *NMDA receptor*, the *quisqualate receptor*, and the *kainate receptor* (named for N-methyl-D-aspartate, quisqualic acid, and kainic acid, respectively). Because the NMDA receptor appears to play an important role in producing some of the synaptic changes that are responsible for learning, it will be discussed in more detail in Chapter 15.

GABA

GABA (gamma-aminobutyric acid) is produced from glutamic acid by the action of an enzyme (GAD, or glutamic acid decarboxylase) that removes a carboxyl group. GABA is an inhibitory transmitter substance, and it appears to have a widespread distribution throughout the brain and spinal cord. Two GABA receptors have been identified, $GABA_A$ and $GABA_B$.

As you know, neurons in the brain are greatly interconnected. Without the activity of inhibitory synapses these interconnections would make the brain unstable. That is, through excitatory synapses neurons would excite their neighbors, which would then excite *their* neighbors, which would then excite the originally active neurons, and so on, until most of the neurons in the brain would be firing uncontrollably. In fact, this event does sometimes occur, and we refer to it as a *seizure*. Normally, an inhibiting influence is supplied by GABA-secreting neurons, which are present in large numbers in the brain. Some investigators believe that one of the causes of epilepsy is an abnormality in the biochemistry of GABA-secreting neurons.

GABA receptors appear to be very complex; they contain sites that recognize at least two (and probably more) different transmitter substances and neuromodulators. A class of tranquilizing drugs called *benzodiazepines* appears to produce antianxiety effects by stimulating a particular site on GABA receptors. These drugs include diazepam (Valium) and chlordiazepoxide (Librium), which are used to reduce anxiety, promote sleep, reduce seizure activity, and produce muscle relaxation. When the benzodiazepine binding sites are activated, they increase the sensitivity of the receptor to GABA. Because GABA is an inhibitory transmitter substance, the effect of this increased sensitivity is to increase neural inhibition. These receptors also contain binding sites that are responsible for the effects of barbiturates and alcohol; as we shall see in Chapter 16, neuropharmacologists have discovered a drug that blocks one of these binding sites and prevents alcohol from having intoxicating effects.

Although the brain does not produce Valium or Librium, it is unlikely that the existence of benzodiazepine receptors is coincidental. Perhaps some neurons in the brain produce neuromodulators that cause a stress reaction (or reduce it) by activating or blocking the benzodiazepine receptors. In fact, two possible candidates have been found in the brain; one compound blocks the receptor and the other appears to stimulate it. More research is needed to find out whether one or both of these chemicals actually serve as neuromodulators in the brain.

Glycine

The amino acid *glycine* appears to be the inhibitory neurotransmitter in the spinal cord and lower portions of the brain. Little is known about its biosynthetic pathway; there are several possible routes, but not enough is known to decide how neurons produce glycine. The bacteria that cause tetanus (lockjaw) release a chemical that blocks the activity of glycine synapses; the removal of the inhibitory effect of these synapses causes muscles to contract continuously.

Peptides

Recent studies have discovered that the neurons of the central nervous system release a large variety of peptides. As we saw earlier in this chapter, peptides consist of two or more amino acids, linked together by peptide bonds. Like proteins, peptides are synthesized by the ribosomes according to instructions contained on the chromosomes in the nucleus.

Several different peptides are released by neurons. Some of them probably serve as transmitter substances, whereas others serve as neuromodulators. Peptides appear to play a role in controlling sensitivity to pain, regulating species-typical defensive behaviors, and regulating eating and drinking. For example, a peptide called angiotensin makes animals thirsty when they lose fluid from their blood. I will have more to say about the behavioral effects of several peptides in later chapters.

Because the synthesis of peptides is complex and must take place in the soma, these chemicals must be delivered to the terminal buttons by axoplasmic flow. Once they are released, they are deactivated by enzymes; they are not returned to the terminal buttons and recycled. All of the peptides that have been studied so far are produced from a small number of precursor molecules. These precursors are large peptides that are broken into pieces by special enzymes; a particular neuron manufactures the enzymes that it needs to break the precursor apart in the right places. The pieces of the precursor that a particular neuron uses are stored in synaptic vesicles, and the other ones are destroyed.

Recently, experimenters have discovered that many peptides are released in conjunction with a "classical" neurotransmitter (one of the ones I just described). That is, some terminal buttons contain two different types of synaptic vesicles, each filled with a different substance. We do not understand the reason for this co-release. Some investigators believe that the peptide serves to regulate the sensitivity of presynaptic or postsynaptic receptors to the neurotransmitter. One example of this interaction has been observed. The terminal buttons of the salivary nerve of the cat (which control the secretion of saliva) release both acetylcholine and a peptide called VIP. When the axons fire at a low rate, only ACh is released, and only a little saliva is secreted. At a higher rate, both ACh and VIP are secreted, and the VIP dramatically increases the sensitivity of the muscarinic receptors in the salivary gland to ACh; thus, much saliva is released. Table 3.2 lists some peptides that are known to be released along with the "classical" transmitter substances. (See *Table 3.2.*)

*I*NTERIM SUMMARY

The nervous system contains a variety of transmitter substances, each of which interacts with a specialized receptor. Those that have received the most study are acetylcholine and the monoamines: dopamine, norepinephrine, and 5-hydroxytryptamine (serotonin). The synthesis of these transmitter substances is controlled by enzymes. Several amino acids also serve as transmitter substances, the most important of which are glutamic acid (glutamate), GABA, and glycine. Glutamate serves as an excitatory transmitter substance; the others serve as inhibitory transmitter substances. Peptide transmitter substances consist of chains of

TABLE 3.2

Peptides known to be released with transmitter substances

Transmitter substance	Peptide
Acetylcholine	Vasoactive intestinal peptide (VIP)
Dopamine	Cholecystokinin (CCK)
Epinephrine	Neuropeptide Y Neurotensin
GABA	Somatostatin
Norepinephrine	Enkephalin Somatostatin Neuropeptide Y Neurotensin
Oxytocin	Enkephalin
Serotonin	Enkephalin Substance P Thyroid hormone releasing hormone (TRH)
Vasopressin	Cholecystokinin Dynorphin

Note: Several peptides (such as cholecystokinin) were first discovered in other organs; thus, their names do not reflect their function in the brain.
SOURCE: Adapted from Cooper, J.R., Bloom, F.E., and Roth, R.H., *The Biochemical Basis of Neuropharmacology*, 5th ed. New York: Oxford University Press, 1986.

amino acids. Like proteins, peptides are synthesized at the ribosomes according to sequences coded for by the chromosomes.

PHARMACOLOGY OF SYNAPSES

Investigators have discovered many drugs that act on synapses. Some of these drugs are used to study the functions of the nervous system, and some are used to treat disorders. Some are in common use, and some are found only in research laboratories. Drugs that affect synaptic transmission are classified into two general categories. Those that block or inhibit the postsynaptic effects are called *antagonists;* drugs that facilitate them are called *agonists.* (The Greek word *agon* means "contest." Thus, an *agonist* is one who takes part in the contest.)

This section will describe the basic effects of drugs on synaptic activity and give a few examples. Recall from earlier in this chapter that the sequence of synaptic activity goes like this: Transmitter substances are synthesized and stored in synaptic vesicles. When axons fire, the transmitter substances are released into the synaptic cleft, where they activate postsynaptic receptors. So that their effects are brief, they are destroyed by an enzyme or taken back into the terminal button to be recycled. The discussion of the effects of drugs in this section follows the same basic sequence.

Effects on Production of Transmitter Substances

The first step is the synthesis of the transmitter substance from its precursors. In some cases the rate of synthesis and release of a neurotransmitter is increased when a precursor is administered; in these cases the precursor itself serves as an agonist. As we saw, L-DOPA serves as a dopamine agonist. (See step 1 in *Figure 3.16.*)

The steps in the synthesis of transmitter substances are controlled by enzymes. Therefore, if a drug inactivates one of these enzymes, it will prevent the transmitter substance from being produced. For example, the drug *PCPA* (parachlorophenylalanine) blocks the enzyme tryptophan hydroxylase, which prevents synthesis of serotonin. Thus, PCPA is a serotonin antagonist. (See step 2 in *Figure 3.16.*) PCPA is sometimes used to block the activity of a tumor composed of cells that secrete serotonin.

Effects on Storage and Release of Transmitter Substances

Transmitter substances are stored in synaptic vesicles, which are transported to the presynaptic membrane, where the chemicals are released. One drug, *reserpine,* blocks the storage of the monoamines in synaptic vesicles. The transmitter substances fail to enter the synaptic vesicles and thus remain in the cytoplasm of the terminal button, where they are destroyed by MAO; hence nothing is released when the vesicles rupture against the presynaptic membrane. Reserpine is a monoamine antagonist. (See step 3 in *Figure 3.17.*)

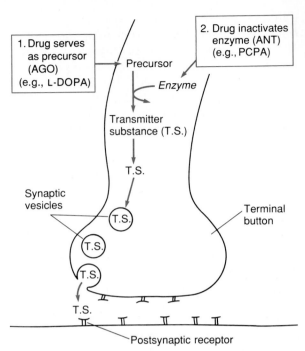

FIGURE 3.16

Effect of drugs on the production of a transmitter substance (AGO = agonist; ANT = antagonist).

This drug, which comes from the root of a shrub, was discovered over three thousand years ago in India, where it was found to be useful in treating snakebite and seemed to have a calming effect. Pieces of the root are still sold in markets in rural areas of India. In Western medicine reserpine is occasionally used to treat high blood pressure.

Some drugs act as antagonists by preventing the release of transmitter substances from the terminal button; for example, *botulinum toxin,* produced by bacteria that can grow in improperly canned food, prevents the release of ACh. Other drugs act as agonists by stimulating the release of a neurotransmitter. As we saw earlier in this chapter, the venom of the black widow spider causes acetylcholinergic terminal buttons to release ACh. (See steps 4 and 5 in *Figure 3.17.*) The effects of black widow spider venom can also be fatal, but the venom is much less toxic. In fact, most healthy adults would have to receive several bites, but infants or frail old people would be more susceptible.

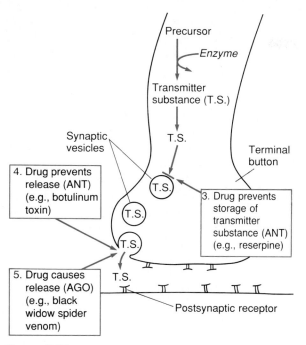

FIGURE 3.17
Effect of drugs on the storage or release of transmitter substance (AGO = agonist; ANT = antagonist).

Effects on Receptors

Once the transmitter substance is released, it must stimulate the postsynaptic receptors. Some drugs serve as agonists by binding with and activating the receptors directly, mimicking the effects of the transmitter substance. As you already know, nicotine and muscarine activate two different classes of acetylcholine receptor: nicotinic and muscarinic. Members of another category of drugs bind with the postsynaptic receptors but do *not* activate them. Because they occupy the receptors without activating them, they prevent the transmitter substance from exerting its effect and hence act as antagonists. These drugs are called *receptor blockers.* By analogy, a key that fits into a lock but does not turn it prevents it from opening, because the proper key cannot enter the lock as long as it is occupied. (See steps 6 and 7 in *Figure 3.18.*)

As you certainly know, nicotine is found in tobacco, which comes from a plant with the Latin name *Nicotiniana tabacum.* Nicotine is a very potent poison; the amount found in a single cigarette could constitute a fatal dose if it were extracted and injected into a person. Muscarine, found in the poison mushroom *Amanita muscaria,* is also fatal in low doses.

Just as two different drugs stimulate the two classes of acetylcholine receptors, two different drugs *block* them. Both were discovered in nature long ago, and both are used by modern medicine. The first, *atropine,* blocks muscarinic receptors. The drug is named after *Atropos,* the Greek fate who cut the thread of life (which a sufficient dose of atropine will certainly do). Atropine is one of several *belladonna alkaloids* extracted from a plant called the "deadly nightshade," and therein lies a tale. Many years ago, women who wanted to in-

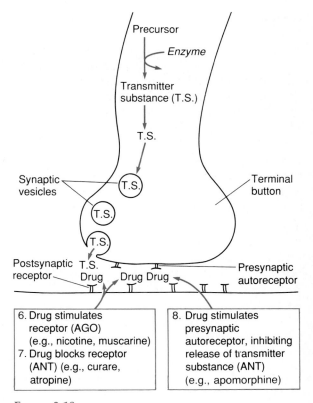

FIGURE 3.18
Effect of drugs in stimulating or blocking presynaptic or postsynaptic receptors (AGO = agonist; ANT = antagonist).

crease their attractiveness to men put drops containing belladonna alkaloids into their eyes. In fact, *belladonna* means "pretty lady." Why was the drug used this way? One of the unconscious responses that occurs when we are interested in something is dilation of our pupils. By blocking the effects of acetylcholine on the pupil, belladonna alkaloids such as atropine make the pupils dilate. This change makes a woman appear more interested in a man when she looks at him, and, of course, this apparent sign of interest makes him regard her as more attractive.

Another drug, *curare*, blocks nicotinic receptors. Because these receptors are the ones found on muscles, curare, like botulinum toxin, causes paralysis. However, its effects are much faster. The drug is extracted from several different species of plants found in South America. It was discovered long ago by people who used it to coat the tips of arrows and darts. Within minutes of being struck by one of these points, an animal collapses, ceases breathing, and dies. Nowadays, curare (and other drugs that have the same effect) are used to paralyze people who are to undergo surgery so that their muscles will relax completely and not contract when they are cut with a scalpel. An anesthetic must also be used, because a person who receives only curare will remain perfectly conscious and sensitive to pain, even though paralyzed. And, of course, a respirator must be used to supply air to the lungs.

As we saw earlier in this chapter, the presynaptic membranes of some neurons possess autoreceptors, which apparently regulate the amount of transmitter substance that is released. Because stimulation of these receptors causes less transmitter substance to be released, drugs that selectively activate them, but do not activate the postsynaptic receptors, act as antagonists. For example, low doses of *apomorphine* stimulate dopaminergic autoreceptors and thus inhibit dopamine release. (See step 8 in *Figure 3.18*.)

Effects on Reuptake or Destruction of Transmitter Substance

The next step after stimulation of the postsynaptic receptor is termination of the postsynaptic potential; molecules of the transmitter substance are de-

stroyed by an enzyme or taken back into the terminal button through the process of reuptake. Drugs can interfere with either of these processes; because they prolong the presence of the transmitter substance in the synaptic cleft (and hence in a location where they can stimulate postsynaptic receptors), both types serve as *agonists*. The postsynaptic activity of transmitter substances is terminated by active uptake mechanisms in the terminal button. Drugs that block or retard the reuptake process permit molecules of the transmitter substance to remain in the synaptic cleft for a longer time, where they produce a prolonged postsynaptic potential. Similarly, a drug that deactivates the enzyme acetylcholinesterase (AChE) permits acetylcholine to remain intact longer than usual. (See steps 9 and 10 in *Figure 3.19*.)

Both *amphetamine* and *cocaine* are potent catecholamine agonists because they retard the

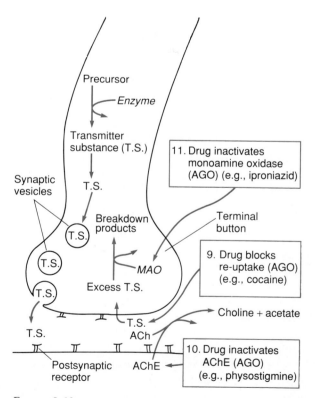

FIGURE 3.19

Effect of drugs in inhibiting reuptake or preventing the destruction of transmitter substances (AGO = agonist; ANT = antagonist).

reuptake of norepinephrine and dopamine. As we shall see in Chapter 16, the effect of these drugs on dopamine explains why they are often abused.

Drugs that deactivate or inhibit AChE are used for several purposes. Some are used as insecticides. These drugs readily kill insects but not humans and other mammals, because our blood contains enzymes that destroy them. (Insects lack the enzyme.) Other AChE inhibitors are used medically. For example, a hereditary disorder called *myasthenia gravis* is caused by gradual loss of nicotinic acetylcholine receptors on muscles. The person becomes weaker and weaker as the muscles become less responsive to the neurotransmitter. If the person is given an AChE inhibitor such as **physostigmine,** the person regains his or her strength, because the acetylcholine that is released has a more prolonged effect on the remaining receptors. Unfortunately, physostigmine eventually loses its effectiveness as more and more ACh receptors are lost.

As we saw earlier in this chapter, monoamine oxidase is present in the terminal buttons of monoaminergic synapses, where it regulates the production of the transmitter substance by destroying any extra quantities that the cell produces. Drugs that inactivate MAO allow an increased amount of transmitter substance to be released when the axon fires. An example of a MAO inhibitor is *iproniazid,* which selectively blocks the particular form of MAO that destroys serotonin; thus, it is a serotonin agonist. (See step 11 in *Figure 3.19.*)

Drugs that affect synapses find many uses; for example, they serve as poisons, antidotes to poisons, and treatments for illnesses and mental disorders. Especially important to the topic of this book, they serve as tools to help neuroscientists investigate the functions of the nervous system. You will encounter many of them in subsequent pages.

I NTERIM SUMMARY

The process of synaptic transmission entails the synthesis of the transmitter substance, its storage in synaptic vesicles, its release into the synaptic cleft, its interaction with postsynaptic receptors, and the consequent opening of ion channels in the postsynaptic membrane. The effects of the transmitter substance are then terminated by enzymatic deactivation (in the case of acetylcholine) or reuptake into the terminal button.

Each of the steps necessary for synaptic transmission can be interfered with by drugs, and a few can be stimulated. Thus, drugs can increase the pool of available precursor, block a biosynthetic enzyme, prevent the storage of transmitter substance in the synaptic vesicles, stimulate or block the release of the transmitter substance, stimulate or block postsynaptic receptors, retard reuptake, or deactivate enzymes that destroy the transmitter substance postsynaptically (acetylcholinesterase) or presynaptically (monoamine oxidase). Drugs have been used to treat neurological and psychiatric disorders, and as we will see throughout the rest of this book, they have served as important tools for investigating the functions of various classes of neurons.

C ONCLUDING REMARKS

This chapter described neural communication—the production, release, and postsynaptic effects of substances thought to serve as neurotransmitters. As you will learn in Chapter 15, neuroscientists have made considerable progress in discovering the changes in the structure of synapses that occur when learning takes place. (When you get to that chapter, your brain will be different from the way it is now, because you will have learned other things in the meantime.) We have also seen the ways that drugs can selectively affect the production and activity of these substances. Subsequent chapters describe the ways neuroscientists have used drugs to study how the brain controls behavior. For example, much of what we know about the physiology of mental disorders has come from studies using drugs that affect synaptic transmission.

So far, the focus of discussion has been on the properties of individual neurons. We know that perceiving, learning, and behaving depend on the activity of neurons, including the mechanisms described in this chapter and in Chapter 2. However, most research on the physiology of behavior deals with the functions of *circuits* of neurons, not with the details of their synaptic communi-cations. Thus, the focus of discussion must shift to the functions of neural circuits. The groundwork for this discussion will be laid in Chapter 4, which describes the anatomy of the nervous system.

NEW TERMS

acetylcholine (ACh) p. 61
acetylcholinesterase (AChE) p. 58
acetyl CoA p. 61
adenylate cyclase p. 54
agonist p. 67
amphetamine p. 70
antagonist p. 67
apomorphine p. 70
atropine p. 69
autoreceptor p. 58
axoaxonic synapse p. 58
axodendritic synapse p. 58
axonal varicosity p. 62
axoplasmic transport p. 48
axosomatic synapse p. 58
benzodiazepine p. 66
botulinum toxin p. 68
caffeine p. 56
catecholamine p. 62
choline acetyltransferase p. 61
cisterna p. 48
CoA p. 61
cocaine p. 70
curare p. 70
cyclic AMP p. 54
dendrodendritic synapse p. 59
DOPA decarboxylase p. 63
dopamine p. 63

dopamine β-hydroxylase p. 63
endocrine gland p. 47
enzymatic deactivation p. 58
epinephrine p. 62
excitatory postsynaptic
   potential (EPSP) p. 49
GABA p. 66
gap junction p. 59
glutamic acid p. 65
G protein p. 54
glycine p. 66
GTP p. 54
horseradish peroxidase p. 51
5-HT p. 64
5-HTP p. 64
5-HTP decarboxylase p. 64
inhibitory postsynaptic
   potential (IPSP) p. 49
iproniazid p. 71
L-DOPA p. 62
monoamine p. 62
monoamine oxidase
   (MAO) p. 63
muscarinic receptor p. 61
neural integration p. 49
neuromodulator p. 47
neurotransmitter-dependent
   ion channel p. 54

nicotinic receptor p. 61
norepinephrine p. 62
Parkinson's disease p. 63
PCPA p. 68
peptide p. 56
pheromone p. 47
phosphodiesterase p. 56
phosphorylation p. 54
physostigmine p. 71
pinocytosis p. 51
postsynaptic
   membrane p. 48
postsynaptic receptor p. 54
presynaptic facilitation p. 59
presynaptic inhibition p. 59
presynaptic membrane p. 48
protein kinase p. 54
receptor blocker p. 69
reserpine p. 68
reuptake p. 58
serotonin p. 64
steroid p. 56
synaptic cleft p. 48
synaptic vesicle p. 48
tryptophan p. 64
tryptophan hydroxylase p. 64
tyrosine p. 62
tyrosine hydroxylase p. 63

SUGGESTED READINGS

Cooper, J.R., Bloom, F.E., and Roth, R.H. *The Biochemical Basis of Neuropharmacology,* 4th ed. New York: Oxford University Press, 1982.

Kandel, E.R., and Schwartz, J.H. *Principles of Neural Science,* 2nd ed. New York: Raven Press, 1985.

Kuffler, S.W., and Nicholls, J.G. *From Neuron to Brain,* 2nd ed. Sunderland, Mass.: Sinauer Associates, 1984.

Shepherd, G.M. *Neurobiology,* 2nd ed. New York: Oxford University Press, 1988.

4

Structure of the Nervous System

*T*he goal of neuroscience research is to understand how the brain works. In order to understand the results of this research, you must be acquainted with the basic structure of the nervous system. The number of terms introduced in this chapter is kept to a minimum (but as you will see, the minimum is still a rather large number). With the framework you will receive from this chapter, you should have no trouble learning the material presented in subsequent chapters.

BASIC FEATURES OF THE NERVOUS SYSTEM

Before beginning a description of the nervous system, I want to discuss the terms used to describe it. The gross anatomy of the brain was described long ago, and everything that could be seen without the aid of a microscope was given a name. Early anatomists named most brain structures according to their similarity to com-

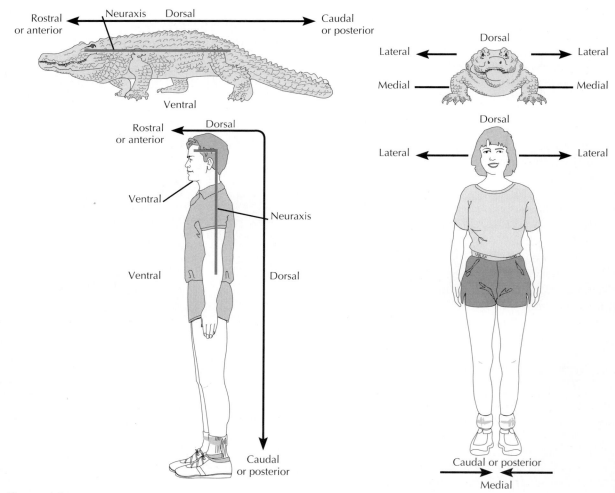

FIGURE 4.1

Side and frontal views of an alligator and a human, showing the terms used to denote anatomical directions.

monplace objects: amygdala, or "almond-shaped object"; hippocampus, or "sea horse"; genu, or "knee"; cortex, or "bark"; pons, or "bridge"; uncus, or "hook," to give a few examples. Throughout this book I will translate the names of anatomical terms as I introduce them, because the translation makes the terms more memorable. For example, knowing that *cortex* means "bark" (like the bark of a tree) will help you remember that the cortex is the outer layer of the brain.

When describing topographical features (hills, roads, rivers, etc.), we need to use terms denoting directions (for example, the road goes north and then turns to the east as it climbs the hill). Similarly, in describing structures of the nervous system and their interconnecting pathways, we must have available a set of words that define geographical relations.

Directions in the nervous system are normally described relative to the **neuraxis,** an imaginary line drawn through the spinal cord up to the front of the brain. For simplicity's sake, let us consider an animal with a straight neuraxis. Figure 4.1 shows an alligator and a human. This alligator is certainly laid out in a linear fashion; we can draw a straight line that starts between its eyes and continues down the center of its spinal cord. (See *Figure 4.1.*) The front end is **anterior,** and the tail is **posterior.** The terms *rostral* (toward the beak) and *caudal* (toward the tail) are also employed; I will more often use these latter terms. The top of the head and the back are part of the **dorsal** surface; the *ventral* (front) surface faces the ground. These directions are somewhat more complicated in the human; because we stand upright, our neuraxis bends. When we describe structures in the human brain, the terms **superior** and **inferior** are often used. The superior structure is above (dorsal to) the inferior one. The frontal views of the alligator and the human illustrate the terms **lateral** and **medial,** toward the side and toward the midline, respectively. (See *Figure 4.1.*)

Two other useful terms are *ipsilateral* and *contralateral*. **Ipsilateral** refers to structures on the same side of the body. Thus, if we say that the olfactory bulb sends axons to the *ipsilateral* hemisphere, we mean that the left olfactory bulb sends axons to the left hemisphere and the right olfactory bulb sends axons to the right hemisphere.

Contralateral refers to structures on opposite sides of the body. If we say that a particular region of the left cerebral cortex controls movements of the *contralateral* hand, we mean that the region controls movements of the right hand.

To see what is in the nervous system, we have to cut it open; to be able to convey information about what we find, we slice it in a standard way. Figure 4.2 shows a human nervous system. We can slice the nervous system in three ways:

1. Transversely, like a salami, giving us **cross sections** (also known as **frontal sections**)

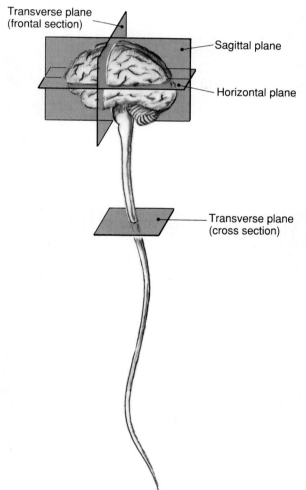

CNS

Transverse plane
(frontal section)

Sagittal plane

Horizontal plane

Transverse plane
(cross section)

FIGURE 4.2
Planes of section as they pertain to the human central nervous system.

2. Parallel to the ground, giving us *horizontal sections*
3. Perpendicular to the ground and parallel to the neuraxis, giving us *sagittal sections*

Note that because of our upright posture, cross sections of the spinal cord are actually parallel to the ground. (See *Figure 4.2.*)

An Overview

Figure 4.3 illustrates the relation of the brain and spinal cord to the head and neck of a human. Do not be concerned with unfamiliar labels on this figure; these structures will be described later. (See *Figure 4.3.*) The brain is a large mass of neurons, glia, and other supporting cells. It is the most protected organ of the body, encased in a tough, bony skull and floating in a pool of cerebrospinal fluid. The brain receives a copious supply of blood and is chemically guarded by the blood-brain barrier.

Blood Supply

The brain receives approximately 20 percent of the blood flow from the heart, and it receives it continuously. Other parts of the body, such as the

FIGURE 4.3
The relation of the brain and spinal cord to the head and neck.

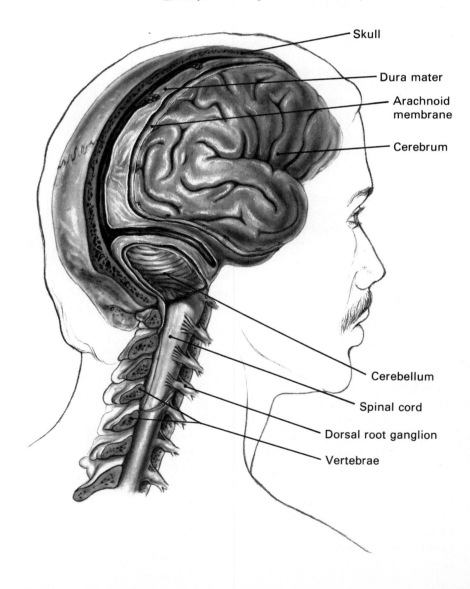

Skull

Dura mater

Arachnoid membrane

Cerebrum

Cerebellum

Spinal cord

Dorsal root ganglion

Vertebrae

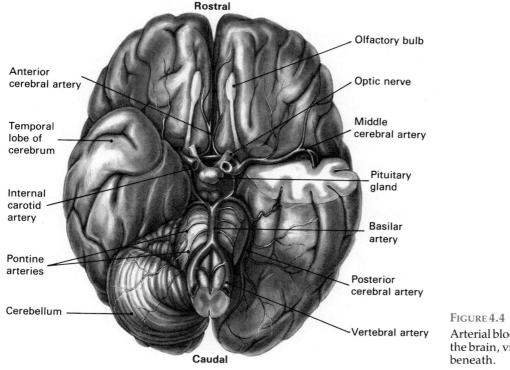

Rostral

Anterior
cerebral artery

Temporal
lobe of
cerebrum

Internal
carotid
artery

Pontine
arteries

Cerebellum

Caudal

Olfactory bulb

Optic nerve

Middle
cerebral artery

Pituitary
gland

Basilar
artery

Posterior
cerebral artery

Vertebral artery

FIGURE 4.4

Arterial blood supply to
the brain, viewed from
beneath.

skeletal muscles or digestive system, receive varying quantities of blood depending on their needs, relative to those of other regions. But the brain always receives its share. The brain cannot store its fuel (primarily glucose), nor can it temporarily extract energy without oxygen as the muscles can; therefore, a consistent blood supply is essential. A 1-second interruption of the blood flow to the brain uses up much of the dissolved oxygen; a 6-second interruption produces unconsciousness. Permanent damage occurs within a few minutes.

Circulation of blood in the body proceeds from arteries to arterioles to capillaries; the capillaries then drain into venules, which collect and become veins. The veins travel back to the heart, where the process begins again. Figure 4.4 shows a bottom view of the brain and its major arterial supply. (The spinal cord has been cut off, as have the left half of the cerebellum and the left temporal lobe.) Two major sets of arteries serve the brain: the *vertebral arteries,* which serve the caudal portion of the brain, and the *internal carotid arteries,* which serve the rostral portion. (See *Figure 4.4.*)

You can see that the blood supply is rather peculiar; major arteries join together and then separate again. Normally, there is a little mixing of blood from the rostral and caudal arterial supplies and, in the case of the rostral supply, from that of the right and left sides of the brain. But if a blood vessel becomes blocked (for example, by a blood clot), blood flow can follow alternative routes, reducing the probability of loss of blood supply and subsequent destruction of brain tissue.

Venous drainage of the brain is shown in Figure 4.5. Major veins, like major arteries, are interconnected, so that blood in some veins can flow in either direction (shown by double-ended arrows), depending on intracerebral pressures in various parts of the brain. (See *Figure 4.5.*)

Meninges

The entire nervous system—brain, spinal cord, cranial and spinal nerves, and autonomic ganglia—is covered by tough connective tissue. The protective sheaths around the brain and spi-

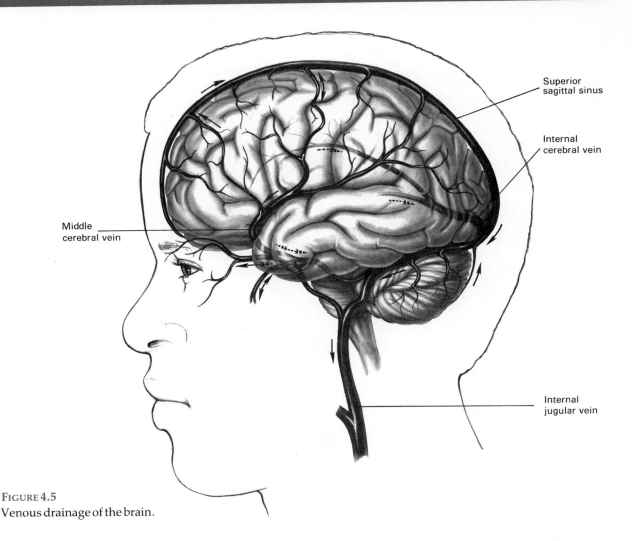

Superior
sagittal sinus

Internal
cerebral vein

Middle
cerebral vein

Internal
jugular vein

FIGURE 4.5
Venous drainage of the brain.

nal cord are referred to as the *meninges* (singular: *meninx*). The meninges consist of three layers, which are shown in Figure 4.6. The outer layer is thick, tough, and flexible but unstretchable; its name, *dura mater,* means "hard mother." The middle layer of the meninges, the *arachnoid membrane,* gets its name from the weblike appearance of the *arachnoid trabeculae* that protrude from it (from the Greek *arachnē,* meaning "spider"; *trabecula* means "track"). The arachnoid membrane is soft and spongy and lies beneath the dura mater. Closely attached to the brain and spinal cord, and following every surface convolution, is the *pia mater* ("pious mother"). The smaller surface blood vessels of the brain and spinal cord are contained within this layer. Be-

tween the pia mater and arachnoid membrane is a gap called the *subarachnoid space.* This space is filled with a liquid called *cerebrospinal fluid* (CSF). (See *Figure 4.6.*)

The peripheral nervous system (PNS) is covered with two layers of meninges. The middle layer (arachnoid membrane), with its associated pool of CSF, covers only the brain and spinal cord. Outside the central nervous system (CNS), the outer and inner layers (dura mater and pia mater) fuse and form a sheath that covers the spinal and cranial nerves and the autonomic ganglia.

In the first edition of this book I said that I did not know why the outer and inner layers of the meninges were referred to as "mothers." I received a letter from medical historians at the Department of Anatomy at UCLA that explained the name. (Sometimes, it pays to proclaim one's ignorance.) A tenth-century Persian physician, Ali ibn Abbas, used the Arabic term *al umm* to refer to the meninges. The term literally means "mother" but was used to designate any swaddling material, because Arabic lacked a specific term for the word *membrane*. The tough outer membrane was called *al umm al djafiya*, and the soft inner one was called *al umm al rigiga*. When the writings of Ali ibn Abbas were translated into Latin during the eleventh century, the translator, who was probably not familiar with the structure of the meninges, made a literal translation of *al umm*. He referred to the membranes as the "hard mother" and the "pious mother" (*pious* in the sense of "delicate"), rather than using a more appropriate Latin word.

The Ventricular System and Production of CSF

The brain is very soft and jellylike. The considerable weight of a human brain (approximately 1400 g), along with its delicate construction, necessitates that it be protected from shock. A human brain cannot even support its own weight well; it is difficult to remove and handle a fresh brain from a recently deceased human without damaging it.

Fortunately, the intact brain within a living human is well-protected. It floats in a bath of CSF contained within the subarachnoid space. Because the brain is completely immersed in liquid, its net weight is reduced to approximately 80 g;

thus, pressure on the base of the brain is considerably diminished. The CSF surrounding the brain and spinal cord also reduces the shock to the central nervous system that would be caused by sudden head movement.

The brain contains a series of hollow, interconnected chambers called *ventricles,* which are filled with CSF. (See *Figure 4.7.*) The largest chambers are the *lateral ventricles,* which are connected to the *third ventricle.* The third ventricle is located at the midline of the brain; its walls divide the surrounding part of the brain into symmetrical halves. A bridge of neural tissue called the *massa intermedia* crosses through the middle of the third ventricle and serves as a convenient reference point. The *cerebral aqueduct,* a long tube, connects the third ventricle to the *fourth ventricle.* The lateral ventricles constitute the first and second ventricles, but they are never referred to as such. (See *Figure 4.7.*)

Cerebrospinal fluid is manufactured by a special vascular structure called the *choroid plexus,* which protrudes into each of the ventricles and produces CSF from blood plasma. The CSF is produced continuously; the total volume of CSF is approximately 125 ml, and the half-life (the time it takes for half of the CSF present in the ventricular system to be replaced by fresh fluid) is about 3 hours. Therefore, several times this amount is produced by the choroid plexus each day. The continuous production of CSF means that there must be a mechanism for its removal; Figure 4.8 illustrates the production, circulation, and reabsorption of CSF.

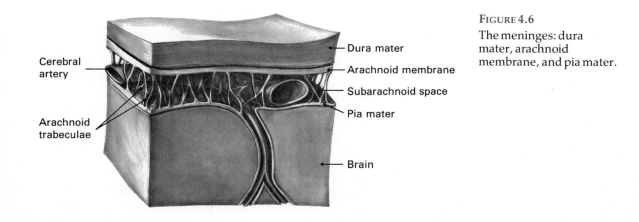

Cerebral artery · Arachnoid trabeculae · Dura mater · Arachnoid membrane · Subarachnoid space · Pia mater · Brain

FIGURE 4.6
The meninges: dura mater, arachnoid membrane, and pia mater.

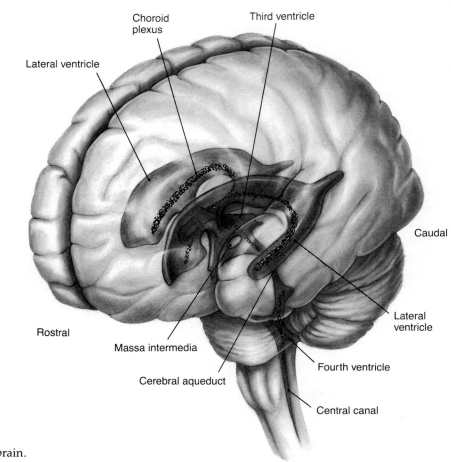

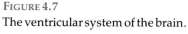

FIGURE 4.7
The ventricular system of the brain.

Figure 4.8 shows a slightly rotated midsagittal view of the central nervous system, which shows only one of the lateral ventricles. (See *Figure 4.8.*) CSF is produced by the choroid plexus of the lateral ventricles, and it flows into the third ventricle. More CSF is produced in this ventricle, which then flows through the cerebral aqueduct to the fourth ventricle, where still more CSF is produced. The CSF leaves the fourth ventricle through small openings that connect with the subarachnoid space surrounding the brain. The CSF then flows through the subarachnoid space around the central nervous system, where it is reabsorbed into the blood supply through the *arachnoid granulations.* These pouch-shaped structures protrude into the *superior sagittal sinus,* a blood vessel that drains into the veins serving the brain. (See *insert, Figure 4.8.*)

The meninges, skull, and vertebral column encase the CNS in a rigid container of fixed volume. This situation means that any growth in the mass of the brain must result in displacement of the fluid contents of the container. Hence growth of a brain tumor, depending on its location, will often deform the walls of the ventricular system, as the invading mass takes up volume previously occupied by CSF. (It is fortunate that these hollow ventricles exist; the only other fluid-filled spaces are the blood vessels, which would be constricted by a growing tumor if there were no ventricles in the brain.)

Occasionally, the flow of CSF is interrupted at some point in its route of passage. For example, the cerebral aqueduct may be blocked by a tumor. This occlusion results in greatly increased pressure within the ventricles, because the choroid

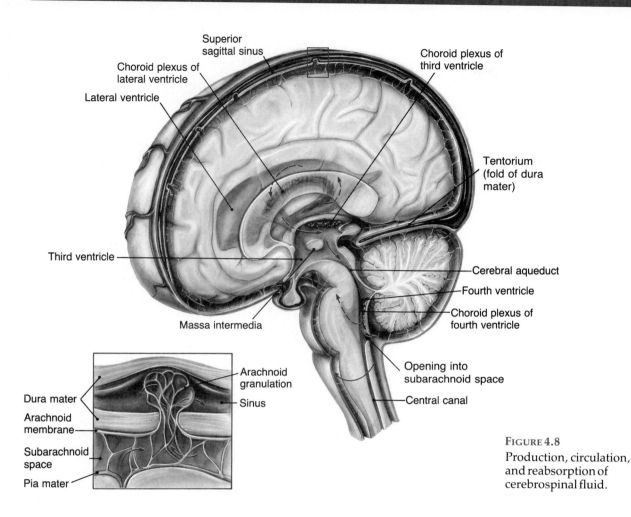

Superior
sagittal sinus

Choroid plexus of
lateral ventricle

Lateral ventricle

Choroid plexus of
third ventricle

Tentorium
(fold of dura
mater)

Third ventricle

Cerebral aqueduct

Fourth ventricle

Choroid plexus of
fourth ventricle

Massa intermedia

Opening into
subarachnoid space

Central canal

Arachnoid
granulation

Sinus

Dura mater

Arachnoid
membrane

Subarachnoid
space

Pia mater

FIGURE 4.8
Production, circulation,
and reabsorption of
cerebrospinal fluid.

plexus continues to produce CSF. The walls of the ventricles then expand and produce a condition known as **hydrocephalus** (literally, "water-head"). If the obstruction remains, and if nothing is done to reverse the increased intracerebral pressure, blood vessels will be occluded, and permanent—perhaps fatal—brain damage will occur. Fortunately, a surgeon can usually operate on the person, drilling a hole through the skull and inserting a plastic tube into one of the ventricles. The tube is then placed beneath the skin and connected to a pressure relief valve that is implanted in the abdominal cavity. When the pressure in the ventricles becomes excessive, the valve permits the CSF to escape into the abdomen, where it is eventually reabsorbed into the blood supply. Figure 4.9 shows a drawing of a brain of an infant

with a drainage tube inserted into the right lateral ventricle. (See *Figure 4.9.*)

I NTERIM SUMMARY

Anatomists have adopted a set of terms to describe the locations of parts of the body. *Anterior* is toward the head, *posterior* is toward the tail, *lateral* is toward the side, *medial* is toward the middle, *dorsal* is toward the back, and *ventral* is toward the front surface of the body. In the special case of the nervous system, *rostral* means toward the beak (or nose) and *caudal* means toward the tail. *Ipsilateral* means "same side" and *contralateral* means "other side." A cross section (or frontal section) slices the nervous

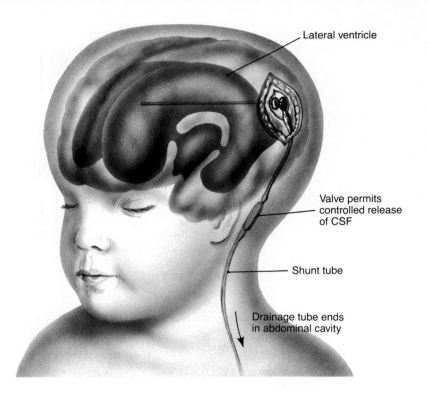

Lateral ventricle

Valve permits
controlled release
of CSF

Shunt tube

Drainage tube ends
in abdominal cavity

FIGURE 4.9
Insertion of a shunt tube to
relieve a congenital case of
hydrocephalus; the infant
was born with an abnormally
small cerebral aqueduct. The
tube will permit the
dammed-up cerebrospinal
fluid to escape.

system like a salami, a horizontal section
slices it parallel to the ground, and a sagittal
section slices it perpendicular to the ground,
parallel to the neuraxis.

The central nervous system consists of the
brain and spinal cord, and the peripheral
nervous system consists of the spinal and
cranial nerves and peripheral ganglia. The
CNS is covered with the meninges: dura mater, arachnoid membrane, and pia mater.
The space under the arachnoid membrane is
filled with cerebrospinal fluid, in which the
brain floats. The PNS is covered with only
the dura mater and pia mater. Cerebrospinal
fluid is produced in the choroid plexus of the
lateral, third, and fourth ventricles. It flows
from the two lateral ventricles into the third
ventricle, through the cerebral aqueduct
into the fourth ventricle, then into the subarachnoid space, and finally back into the
blood supply. If the flow of CSF is blocked
by a tumor or other obstruction, the result
is hydrocephalus: enlargement of the ventricles and subsequent brain damage.

THE CENTRAL NERVOUS SYSTEM

Although the brain is exceedingly complicated,
an understanding of the basic features of brain development makes it easier to learn and remember
the location of the most important structures.
With that end in mind, I introduce these features
here in the context of brain development.

The central nervous system begins its existence early in embryonic life as a hollow tube, and
it maintains this basic shape even after it is fully
developed. Early in development the central nervous system contains three interconnected chambers. These chambers become ventricles, and the
tissue that surrounds them becomes the three major parts of the brain: the *forebrain,* the *midbrain,*
and the *hindbrain.* (See *Figure 4.10a.*) Later, the
rostral chamber divides into three separate chambers, which become the two lateral ventricles and
the third ventricle. The region around the lateral
ventricles becomes the *telencephalon* ("end
brain"), and the region around the third ventricle
becomes the *diencephalon* ("interbrain"). (See
Figure 4.10b.) In its final form the chamber inside

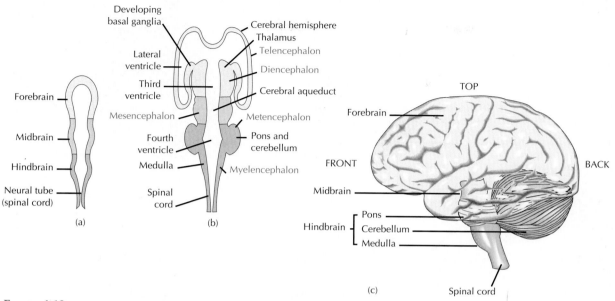

FIGURE 4.10

An outline of brain development, showing its relation to the ventricles. (a) Early development. (b) Mid development. (c) Late development, near time of birth. (Adapted from Gardner, E. *Fundamentals of Neurology*, 6th ed. Philadelphia: Saunders, 1975.)

the *mesencephalon* ("midbrain") becomes narrow, forming the cerebral aqueduct, and two structures develop in the hindbrain: the *metencephalon* ("behindbrain") and the *myelencephalon* ("marrowbrain"). (See *Figure 4.10c.*)

Figure 4.11 shows a lateral view of the developing human brain, indicating how the forebrain curls back as it develops, so that it eventually constitutes the largest component of the brain. (See *Figure 4.11.*) Finally, Table 4.1 summarizes the terms I have introduced here and mentions some of the major structures found in each part of the brain, which will be described in the remainder of the chapter. (See *Table 4.1.*)

TABLE 4.1
Anatomical subdivisions of the brain

Major Division	Ventricle	Subdivision	Principal Structures
Forebrain	Lateral	Telencephalon	Cerebral cortex Basal ganglia Limbic system
	Third	Diencephalon	Thalamus Hypothalamus
Midbrain	Cerebral aqueduct	Mesencephalon	Tectum Tegmentum
Hindbrain	Fourth	Metencephalon	Cerebellum Pons
		Myelencephalon	Medulla oblongata

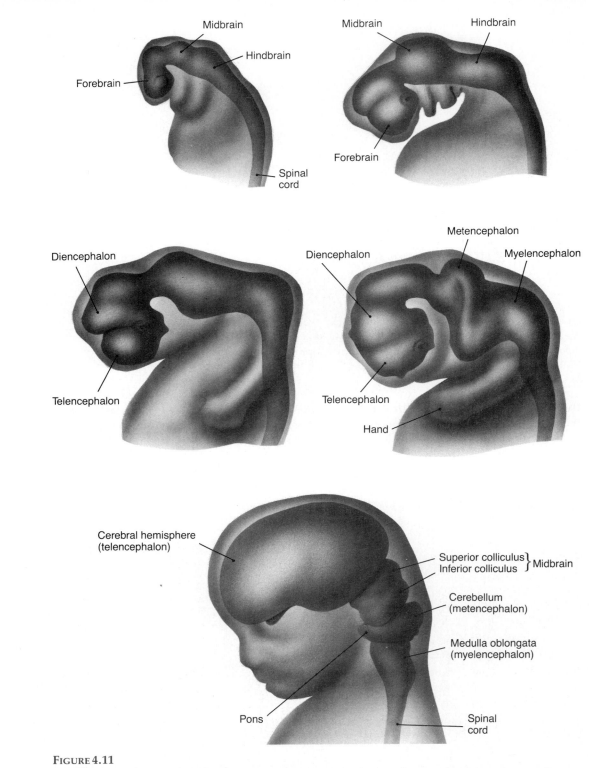

FIGURE 4.11
An outline of human brain development. (Adapted from Gardner, E. *Fundamentals of Neurology*, 6th ed. Philadelphia: Saunders, 1975.)

FRONT

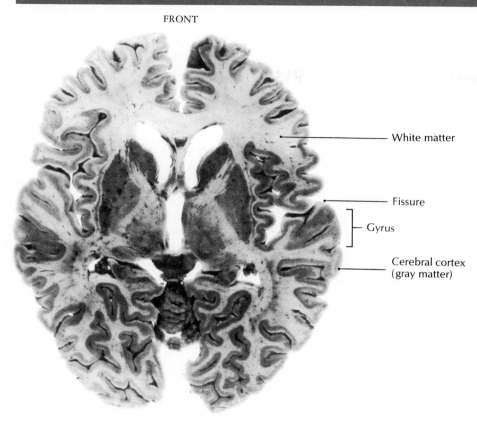

White matter

Fissure

Gyrus

Cerebral cortex
(gray matter)

FIGURE 4.12   BACK

A photograph of a slice of a human brain cut in the horizontal plane, showing fissures and gyri and the layer of cerebral cortex that follows these convolutions. (Photograph from *Structure of the Human Brain: A Photographic Atlas*, Second Edition, by Stephen J. DeArmond, Madelaine M. Fusco, and Maynard M. Dewey. Copyright © 1976 by Oxford University Press, Inc. Reprinted by permission.)

The Forebrain

As we saw, the forebrain surrounds the rostral end of the neural tube. Its two major components are the telencephalon and the diencephalon.

Telencephalon

The telencephalon includes most of the two symmetrical cerebral hemispheres that comprise the cerebrum. The cerebral hemispheres are covered by the cerebral cortex and contain the basal ganglia and the limbic system. The latter two sets of structures are primarily in the *subcortical regions* of the brain—those located deep within it, beneath the cerebral cortex.

Cerebral Cortex. *Cortex* means "bark," and the *cerebral cortex* surrounds the cerebral hemi-

spheres like the bark of a tree. In humans the cerebral cortex is greatly convoluted; these convolutions, consisting of *sulci* (small grooves), *fissures* (large grooves), and *gyri* (bulges between adjacent sulci or fissures), greatly enlarge the surface area of the cortex, compared with a smooth brain of the same size. In fact, two-thirds of the surface of the cortex is hidden in the grooves; thus, the presence of gyri and sulci triples the area of the cerebral cortex. The total surface area is approximately 2360 cm^2 (2.5 ft^2), and the thickness is approximately 3 mm. The cerebral cortex consists mostly of glia and the cell bodies, dendrites, and interconnecting axons of neurons. Because cells predominate, giving the cerebral cortex a grayish brown appearance, it is referred to as *gray matter*. (See *Figure 4.12.*) Beneath the cerebral cortex run millions of axons that connect the neurons of the cerebral cortex with those located elsewhere in the brain. The large concentration of myelin gives this tissue an opaque white appearance—hence the term *white matter*.

The surface of the cerebral hemispheres is divided into four lobes, named after the bones of the skull that overlie them. The *frontal lobe, parietal lobe, temporal lobe,* and *occipital lobe* are visible on the lateral surface and are shown in Figure 4.13. The *central sulcus* divides the frontal lobe from the parietal lobe, and the *lateral fissure* divides the temporal lobe from the overlying frontal and parietal lobes. (See *Figure 4.13.*)

Figure 4.14 shows the inner cortical surface of the right cerebral hemisphere. The cerebral cortex that covers most of the surface of the cerebral hemispheres is called the *neocortex* ("new" cortex, because it is of relatively recent evolutionary origin). Another form of cerebral cortex, the *limbic cortex,* is located around the edge of the cerebral hemispheres (*limbus* means "border"). The *cingulate gyrus,* an important region of the limbic cortex, can be seen in this figure. (See *Figure 4.14.*)

Figure 4.14 also shows the *corpus callosum,* which is the largest *commissure* (cross-hemisphere connection) in the brain. The corpus

callosum consists of axons that connect the cortex of the two cerebral hemispheres. The axons unite geographically similar regions of the two cerebral cortices. In order to slice the brain into its two symmetrical halves, one must slice through the middle of the corpus callosum. (Recall that I described the split-brain operation, in which the corpus callosum is severed, in Chapter 1.) (See *Figure 4.14.*)

The frontal lobes are specialized for the planning, execution, and control of movements. The *primary motor cortex,* immediately rostral to the central sulcus, contains neurons that participate in the control of movement. (See *Figure 4.15.*) If an experimenter places a wire on the surface of the primary motor cortex and stimulates the neurons there with a weak electrical current, the current will cause movement of a particular part of the body. Moving the wire to a different spot causes a different part of the body to move. Because the cerebral hemispheres are connected with the *opposite* sides of the body, stimulation of the right primary motor cortex moves parts of the left side of the body, and stimulation of the left cortex moves the right side.

The posterior lobes of the brain (the parietal,

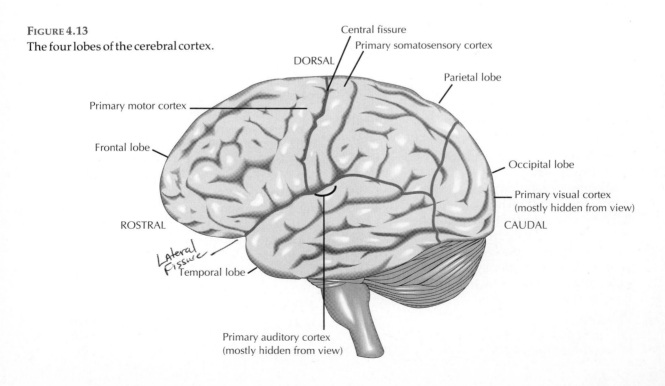

FIGURE 4.13
The four lobes of the cerebral cortex.

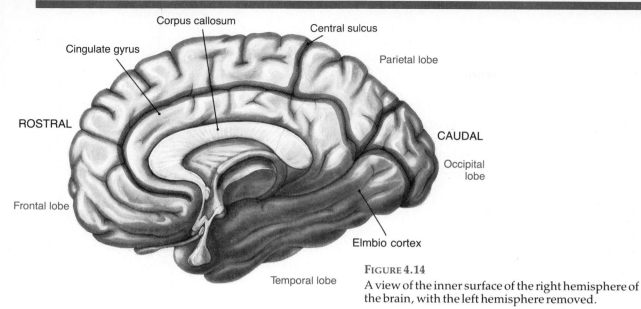

Corpus callosum

Cingulate gyrus

Central sulcus

Parietal lobe

ROSTRAL

CAUDAL

Occipital lobe

Frontal lobe

Elmbio cortex

Temporal lobe

FIGURE 4.14
A view of the inner surface of the right hemisphere of the brain, with the left hemisphere removed.

temporal, and occipital lobes) are specialized for perception. The ***primary somatosensory cortex*** lies immediately caudal to the central sulcus, right behind the primary motor cortex. This region of cerebral cortex receives information about the somatosenses ("body senses": touch, pressure, temperature, and pain). The ***primary visual cortex*** lies at the back of the occipital lobes along the calcarine fissure, mostly hidden between the two cerebral hemispheres. As its name implies, it receives visual information. The ***primary auditory cortex*** lies in the temporal lobes, mostly hidden in the lateral fissure. (See ***Figure 4.15.***)

The rest of the neocortex is referred to as ***association cortex.*** The association cortex in the frontal lobes is involved in the planning of movements; thus, neurons there control the activity of those in the primary motor cortex, which in turn

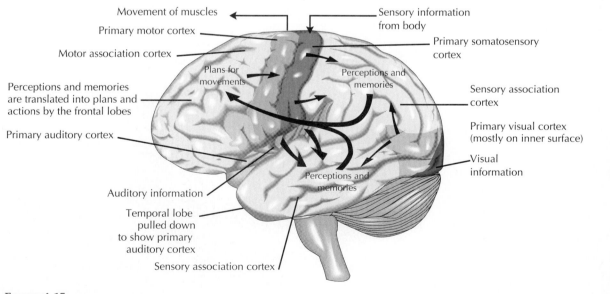

Movement of muscles

Primary motor cortex

Motor association cortex

Perceptions and memories are translated into plans and actions by the frontal lobes

Primary auditory cortex

Auditory information

Temporal lobe pulled down to show primary auditory cortex

Sensory association cortex

Plans for movements

Perceptions and memories

Perceptions and memories

Sensory information from body

Primary somatosensory cortex

Sensory association cortex

Primary visual cortex (mostly on inner surface)

Visual information

FIGURE 4.15
The relation between primary sensory and motor cortex and association cortex.

control muscular movements. The association cortex in the posterior lobes receives information from the primary sensory areas and is involved in perception and memories. The primary somatosensory cortex sends information to the somatosensory association cortex, the primary visual cortex sends information to the visual association cortex, and the primary auditory cortex sends information to the auditory association cortex. (See *Figure 4.15.*)

If people sustain damage to the somatosensory association cortex, their deficits are related to somatosensation and to the environment in general; for example, they may have difficulty perceiving the shapes of objects that they can touch but not see, they may be unable to name parts of their bodies, or they may have trouble drawing maps or following them. If people sustain damage to the visual association cortex, they will not become blind; but they may be unable to recognize objects by sight, although they can often recognize them if they feel them with their hands. If people sustain damage to the auditory association cortex, they may have difficulty perceiving speech or even producing meaningful

speech of their own. If people sustain damage to regions of the association cortex at the junction of the three posterior lobes, where the somatosensory, visual, and auditory functions overlap, they may have difficulty reading or writing.

Limbic system. The *limbic system* consists of a set of interconnected structures including several regions of the limbic cortex (already described) and a set of interconnected structures surrounding the core of the forebrain. (See *Figure 4.16.*) The two most important of these structures are the **hippocampus** ("sea horse") and the **amygdala** ("almond"), located next to the lateral ventricle in the temporal lobe. These and other parts of the limbic system are described in more detail in later chapters, where their participation in emotion, motivation, and learning are discussed.

Basal Ganglia. The *basal ganglia* are a collection of subcortical nuclei in the forebrain, which lie beneath the anterior portion of the lateral ventricles. (See *Figure 4.17.*) The basal ganglia are in-

FIGURE 4.16
A schematic, simplified drawing of the limbic system.

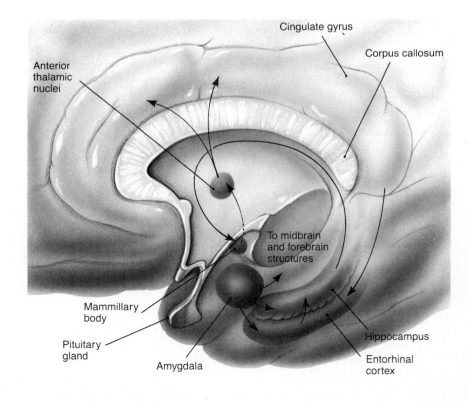

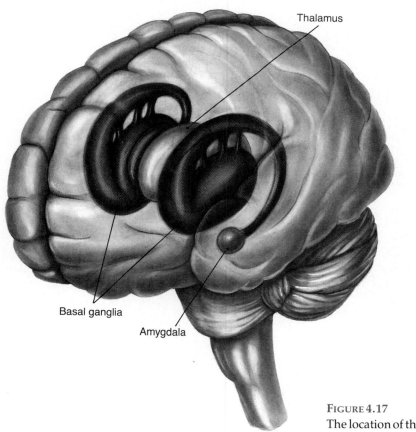

Thalamus

Basal ganglia

Amygdala

FIGURE 4.17
The location of the basal ganglia in a human brain.

volved in the control of movement. For example, Parkinson's disease is caused by degeneration of dopaminergic neurons located in the midbrain that send axons to parts of the basal ganglia. This disease consists of weakness, tremors, rigidity of the limbs, poor balance, and difficulty in initiating movements.

The amygdala, considered by some anatomists to be part of the basal ganglia, is located within the temporal lobe near its rostral tip. As we already saw, the amygdala is an important component of the limbic system. As we will see in later chapters, destruction of various parts of the amygdala inhibits the performance of defensive responses and affects reproductive behaviors.

Diencephalon

The second major division of the forebrain, the diencephalon, is situated between the telencephalon and the mesencephalon; and it surrounds the third ventricle. (See *Figure 4.18.*) Its

two most important structures are the thalamus and hypothalamus.

Thalamus.   The **thalamus** (from the Greek *thalamos*, "inner chamber") is located in the dorsal part of the diencephalon. It is a large structure with two lobes, connected by a bridge of gray matter called the *massa intermedia*, which pierces the middle of the third ventricle. (You already encountered the massa intermedia in Figure 4.7. See *Figure 4.18.*) The massa intermedia is probably not an important structure, because it is absent in the brains of some apparently normal people.

Most neural input to the cerebral cortex is received from the thalamus; indeed, much of the cortical surface can be divided into regions that receive projections from specific parts of the thalamus. *Projection fibers* are sets of axons that arise from cell bodies located in one region of the brain and synapse on neurons located within another region (that is, they project to these regions).

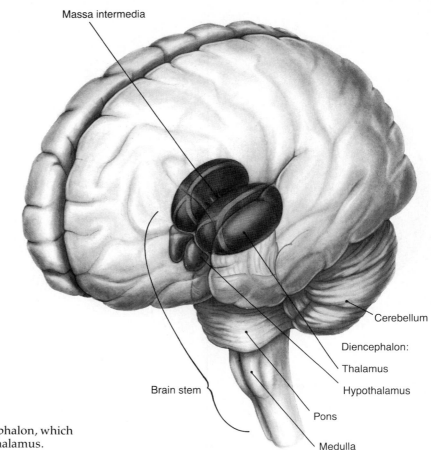

Massa intermedia

Cerebellum

Diencephalon:

Thalamus

Hypothalamus

Brain stem

Pons

Medulla

FIGURE 4.18
The location of the human diencephalon, which
includes the thalamus and hypothalamus.

The thalamus is divided into several *nuclei,*
which are groups of neurons of similar shape.
Some of these nuclei receive sensory information
from the sensory systems. The neurons in these
nuclei then relay the sensory information to specific sensory projection areas of the cerebral
cortex. For example, the *lateral geniculate nucleus*
receives information from the eye and sends
axons to the primary visual cortex, and the *medial
geniculate nucleus* receives information from the
inner ear and sends axons to the primary auditory
cortex. Other thalamic nuclei project to specific regions of the cerebral cortex, but they do not relay
primary sensory information. For example, the
ventrolateral nucleus receives information from
the cerebellum and projects to the primary motor
cortex.

Hypothalamus. The *hypothalamus* lies at the
base of the brain, under the thalamus. Although it
is a relatively small structure, it is an important
one. It controls the autonomic nervous system
and the endocrine system and organizes behaviors related to survival of the species—the so-
called four F's: fighting, feeding, fleeing, and
mating.

The hypothalamus is situated on both sides of
the inferior portion of the third ventricle. As its
name implies, it is located beneath the thalamus.
The hypothalamus is a very complex structure,
containing many nuclei and fiber tracts. Figure
4.19 indicates its location and size. Note that the
pituitary gland is attached to the base of the hypothalamus via the pituitary stalk. Just in front of the
pituitary stalk is the *optic chiasm,* the place where

half of the axons in the optic nerves (from the eyes) cross from one side of the brain to the other. (See *Figure 4.19.*) The role of the hypothalamus in the control of the four F's (and other behaviors, such as drinking and sleeping) will be considered in several chapters later in this book.

Much of the endocrine system is controlled by hormones produced by cells in the hypothalamus. A small but very crucial vascular system interconnects the hypothalamus and the *anterior pituitary gland.* Arterioles of the hypothalamus branch into capillaries that drain into small veins.

These veins travel to the anterior pituitary gland, where they branch into another set of capillaries. Therefore, substances that enter the hypothalamic capillaries of this system travel directly to the anterior pituitary gland before they are diluted in the large volume of blood in the vascular system. (See *Figure 4.20.*) The hypothalamic hormones are secreted by specialized neurons called *neurosecretory cells,* located near the base of the pituitary stalk. These hormones are carried by the blood vessels to the anterior pituitary gland and stimulate it to secrete its hormones. For example,

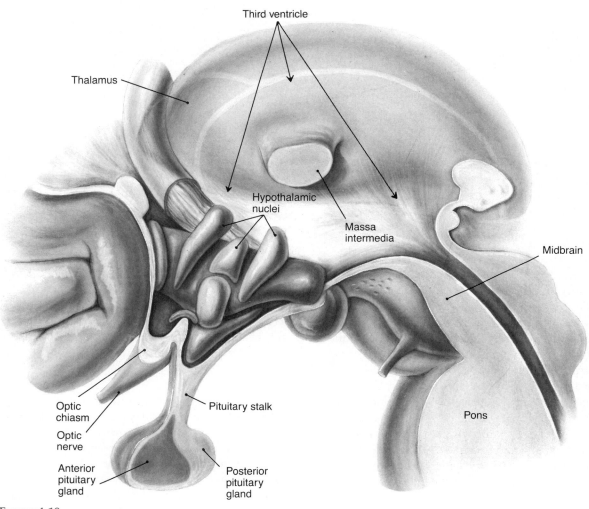

FIGURE 4.19
The regions of the hypothalamus in a human brain.

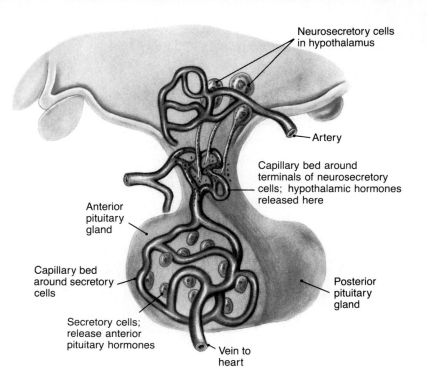

Neurosecretory cells
in hypothalamus

Artery

Capillary bed around
terminals of neurosecretory
cells; hypothalamic hormones
released here

Anterior
pituitary
gland

Capillary bed
around secretory
cells

Posterior
pituitary
gland

Secretory cells;
release anterior
pituitary hormones

Vein to
heart

FIGURE 4.20
The anterior pituitary gland, showing the portal blood supply. Hormones released by the neurosecretory cells in the hypothalamus enter capillaries and are conveyed to the anterior pituitary gland, where they control its secretion of hormones.

gonadotropin-releasing hormone causes the anterior pituitary gland to secrete the *gonadotropic hormones.*

Most of the anterior pituitary hormones control the secretions of other endocrine glands. Because of this function, the anterior pituitary gland has been called the body's "master gland." For example, the gonadotropic hormones stimulate the gonads (ovaries and testes) to release male or female sex hormones. These hormones have effects on cells throughout the body, including some in the brain. Two other anterior pituitary hormones, prolactin and somatotropic hormone (growth hormone), do not control other glands but act as the final messenger. The behavioral effects of many of the anterior pituitary hormones are discussed in later chapters.

The hypothalamus also produces the hormones of the *posterior pituitary gland* and controls their secretion. These hormones include oxytocin, which stimulates ejection of milk and uterine contractions at the time of childbirth, and vasopressin, which regulates urine output by the kidneys. They are produced by neurons in the hypothalamus whose axons travel down the pituitary stalk and terminate in the posterior pituitary gland. The hormones are carried in vesicles through the axoplasm of these neurons and collect in the terminal buttons in the posterior pituitary gland. When these axons fire, the hormone contained within their terminal buttons is liberated and enters the circulatory system.

The Mesencephalon

The mesencephalon (midbrain) surrounds the cerebral aqueduct and consists of two major parts: the tectum and the tegmentum.

Tectum

The *tectum* ("roof") is located in the dorsal portion of the mesencephalon. Its principal structures are the *superior colliculi* and *inferior colliculi,* which appear as four bumps on the surface of the *brain stem.* Figure 4.21 illustrates a dorsal view of the brain stem, with the overlying cerebrum and cerebellum removed. (The brain stem includes the diencephalon, midbrain, and hindbrain, and it is so called because it looks just like that—a stem.) (See *Figure 4.21.*) The inferior

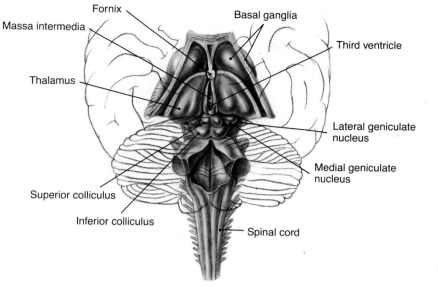

Fornix
Massa intermedia
Thalamus
Basal ganglia
Third ventricle
Lateral geniculate nucleus
Medial geniculate nucleus
Superior colliculus
Inferior colliculus
Spinal cord

FIGURE 4.21
A dorsal view of the human brain stem.

colliculi are a part of the auditory system. The superior colliculi are part of the visual system. In mammals they are primarily involved in visual reflexes and reactions to moving stimuli.

Tegmentum

The *tegmentum* ("covering") consists of the portion of the mesencephalon beneath the tectum. It includes the rostral end of the reticular formation, several nuclei controlling eye movements, the periaqueductal gray matter, the red nucleus, the substantia nigra, and the ventral tegmental area. (See *Figure 4.22.*)

The *reticular formation* is a large structure consisting of many nuclei (over ninety in all). It is also characterized by a diffuse, interconnected network of neurons with complex dendritic and axonal processes. (Indeed, *reticulum* means "little net"; early anatomists were struck by the netlike appearance of the reticular formation.) The reticular formation occupies the core of the brain stem, from the lower border of the medulla to the upper border of the midbrain. (See *Figure 4.22.*) The reticular formation receives sensory information by means of various pathways and projects axons to the cerebral cortex, thalamus, and spinal cord. It plays a role in sleep and arousal, attention, muscle tonus, movement, and various vital reflexes. Its

functions will be described in later chapters.

The *periaqueductal gray matter* is so called because it consists mostly of cell bodies of neurons ("gray matter," as contrasted with the "white matter" of axon bundles) that surround the cerebral aqueduct as it travels from the third to the fourth ventricle. The periaqueductal gray matter contains neural circuits that control sequences of movements that constitute species-typical behaviors, such as fighting and mating. As we will see in Chapter 7, opiates such as morphine decrease an organism's sensitivity to pain by stimulating receptors on neurons located in this region.

The *red nucleus* and *substantia nigra* ("black substance") are important components of the motor system. A bundle of axons that arises from the red nucleus constitutes one of the two major fiber systems that bring motor information from the brain to the spinal cord. The substantia nigra contains dopamine-secreting neurons that project to the caudate nucleus. Degeneration of these neurons causes Parkinson's disease.

The Hindbrain

The hindbrain, which surrounds the fourth ventricle, consists of two major divisions: the metencephalon and the myelencephalon.

Metencephalon

The metencephalon consists of the pons and the cerebellum.

Cerebellum.   The *cerebellum* ("little brain") resembles a miniature version of the cerebrum. It is covered by *cerebellar cortex* and has a set of *deep cerebellar nuclei* that project to its cortex and receive projections from it, just as the thalamic nuclei connect with the cerebral cortex. Figure 4.23 shows the brain stem with the cerebellum dissected away on one side to illustrate the superior, middle, and inferior *cerebellar peduncles* ("little feet"), bundles of white matter that connect the cerebellum to the pons. (See *Figure 4.23.*)

Damage to the cerebellum impairs standing, walking, or performance of coordinated movements. (A virtuoso pianist or other performing musician owes much to his or her cerebellum.) The cerebellum receives visual, auditory, vestibu-

FIGURE 4.22
A cross section through the human tegmentum.

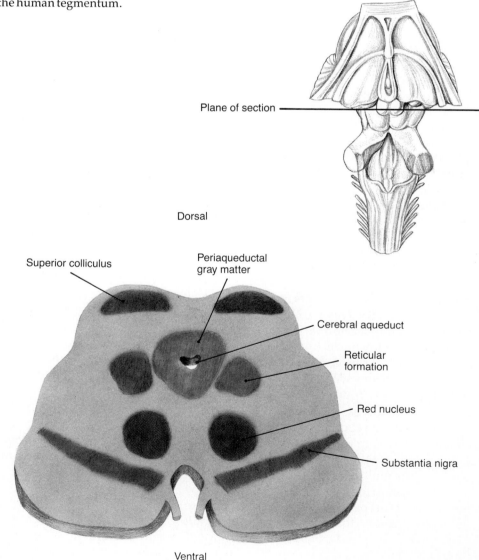

Dorsal view

Plane of section

Dorsal

Superior colliculus

Periaqueductal gray matter

Cerebral aqueduct

Reticular formation

Red nucleus

Substantia nigra

Ventral

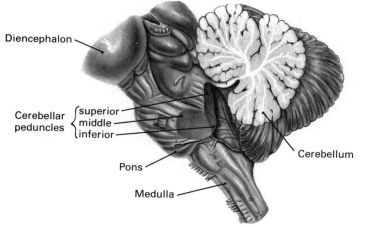

Diencephalon

Cerebellar peduncles { superior middle inferior

Pons

Medulla

Cerebellum

FIGURE 4.23
The attachment of the cerebellum to the human brain stem. Only the right cerebellar hemisphere is shown; the left has been removed to show the cerebellar peduncles.

lar, and somatosensory information, and it also receives information about individual muscular movements being directed by the brain. The cerebellum integrates this information and modifies the motor outflow, exerting a coordinating and smoothing effect on the movements. Cerebellar damage results in jerky, poorly coordinated, exaggerated movements; extensive cerebellar damage makes it impossible even to stand. As we will see in Chapter 14, recent studies have shown that the cerebellum is also involved in learning.

Pons. The *pons*, a large bulge in the brain stem, lies between the mesencephalon and medulla oblongata, immediately ventral to the cerebellum. (*Pons* means "bridge," but it does not really look like one. See *Figure 4.23.*) The pons contains, in its core, a portion of the reticular formation, including some nuclei that appear to be important in sleep and arousal.

Myelencephalon

The myelencephalon contains one major structure, the *medulla oblongata* (literally, "oblong marrow"), usually just called the *medulla.* This structure is the most caudal portion of the brain stem; its lower border is the rostral end of the spinal cord. (See *Figure 4.23.*) The medulla contains part of the reticular formation, including nuclei that control vital functions such as regulation of the cardiovascular system, respiration, and skeletal muscle tonus.

The Spinal Cord

The *spinal cord* is a long, conical structure, approximately as thick as a person's little finger. The principal function of the spinal cord is to distribute motor fibers to the effector organs of the body (glands and muscles) and to collect somatosensory information to be passed on to the brain. The spinal cord also has a certain degree of autonomy from the brain; various reflexive control circuits (some of which are described in Chapter 8) are located there.

The spinal cord is protected by the vertebral column, which is composed of twenty-four individual vertebrae of the *cervical* (neck), *thoracic* (chest), and *lumbar* (lower back) regions, and the fused vertebrae making up the *sacral* and *coccygeal* portions of the column (located in the pelvic region). The spinal cord passes through a hole in each of the vertebrae (the *spinal foramens*). Figure 4.24 illustrates the divisions and structures of the spinal cord and vertebral column. Note that the spinal cord is only about two-thirds as long as the vertebral column; the rest of the space is filled by a mass of *spinal roots* composing the *cauda equina* ("mare's tail"). (See *Figure 4.24.*)

Early in embryological development the vertebral column and spinal cord are the same length. As development progresses, the vertebral column grows faster than the spinal cord. This differential growth rate causes the spinal roots to be displaced downward; the most caudal roots travel

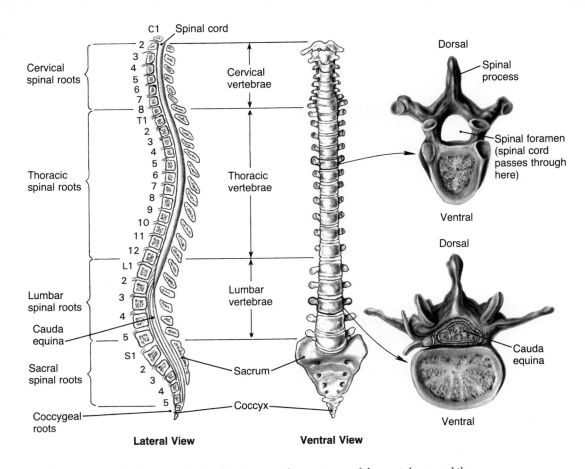

The human spinal column, with details showing the anatomy of the vertebrae and the relation between the spinal cord and spinal column.

the farthest before they emerge through openings between the vertebrae and thus compose the cauda equina. To produce the *caudal block* sometimes used in pelvic surgery or childbirth, a local anesthetic can be injected into the CSF contained within the sac of dura mater surrounding the cauda equina. The drug blocks conduction in the axons of the cauda equina.

Small bundles of fibers emerge from the spinal cord in two straight lines along its dorsolateral and ventrolateral surfaces. Groups of these bundles fuse together and become the thirty-one paired sets of *dorsal roots* and *ventral roots.* The dorsal and ventral roots join together as they pass through the intervertebral foramens and become spinal nerves. Figure 4.25 illustrates a cross section of the spinal column taken between two adja-

cent vertebrae, showing the junction of the dorsal and ventral roots in the intervertebral foramens. (See *Figure 4.25.*)

The spinal cord, like the brain, consists of white matter and gray matter. Unlike the brain's, its white matter (consisting of ascending and descending bundles of myelinated axons) is on the outside; the gray matter (mostly neural cell bodies and short, unmyelinated axons) is on the inside.

*I*NTERIM SUMMARY

The central nervous system consists of three major divisions, organized around the three chambers of the tube that develops early in embryonic life: the forebrain, the midbrain, and the hindbrain. The development of the

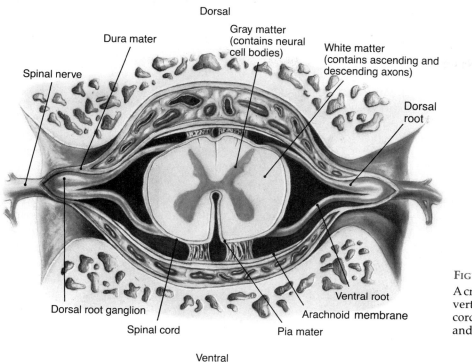

Dorsal

Dura mater

Gray matter
(contains neural
cell bodies)

White matter
(contains ascending and
descending axons)

Spinal nerve

Dorsal
root

Dorsal root ganglion

Spinal cord

Pia mater

Ventral root

Arachnoid membrane

Ventral

FIGURE 4.25

A cross section through a
vertebra, showing the spinal
cord, dorsal and ventral roots,
and spinal nerves.

CNS is illustrated in Figures 4.10 and 4.11, and Table 4.1 outlines the major divisions and subdivisions of the brain.

The forebrain, which surrounds the lateral and third ventricles, consists of the telencephalon and diencephalon. The telencephalon contains the cerebral cortex, the limbic system, and the basal ganglia. The cerebral cortex is organized into the frontal, parietal, temporal, and occipital lobes. The central sulcus divides the frontal lobe, which deals specifically with movement and the planning of movement, from the other three lobes, which deal primarily with perceiving and learning. The limbic system, which includes the limbic cortex, the hippocampus, and the amygdala, is involved in emotion, motivation, and learning. The basal ganglia participate in the control of movement. The diencephalon consists of the thalamus, which directs information to and from the cerebral cortex, and the hypothalamus, which controls the endocrine system and modulates species-typical behaviors.

The midbrain, which surrounds the cere-

bral aqueduct, consists of the tectum and tegmentum. The tectum is involved in audition and the control of visual reflexes and reactions to moving stimuli. The tegmentum contains the reticular formation, which is important in sleep, arousal, and movement; the periaqueductal gray matter, which controls various species-typical behaviors; and the red nucleus and the substantia nigra, both parts of the motor system. The hindbrain, which surrounds the fourth ventricle, contains the cerebellum, the pons, and the medulla. The cerebellum plays an important role in integrating and coordinating movements. The pons contains some nuclei that are important in sleep and arousal. The medulla oblongata, too, is involved in sleep and arousal, but it also plays a role in control of movement and in control of vital functions such as heart rate, breathing, and blood pressure.

The outer part of the spinal cord consists of white matter: axons conveying information up or down. The central gray matter contains cell bodies.

PERIPHERAL NERVOUS SYSTEM

The brain and spinal cord communicate with the rest of the body via the cranial nerves and spinal nerves. These nerves are part of the peripheral nervous system, which conveys sensory information to the central nervous system and conveys messages from the central nervous system to the body's muscles and glands.

Spinal Nerves

The *spinal nerves* begin at the junction of the dorsal and ventral roots of the spinal cord. The nerves leave the vertebral column and travel to the muscles or sensory receptors they innervate, branching repeatedly as they go. Branches of spinal nerves often follow blood vessels, especially those branches that innervate skeletal muscles. *Figure 4.26* is a dorsal view of a human, showing a few branches of the spinal nerves.

Now let us consider the pathways by which sensory information enters the spinal cord and motor information leaves it. The cell bodies of all axons that bring sensory information into the brain and spinal cord are located outside the CNS. (The sole exception is the visual system; the retina of the eye is actually a part of the brain.) These incoming axons are referred to as *afferent axons* because they "bear toward" the CNS. The cell bodies that give rise to the axons that bring somatosensory information to the spinal cord reside in the *dorsal root ganglia,* rounded swellings of the dorsal root. (Refer to *Figures 4.25 and 4.26.*) These neurons are of the unipolar type (described in Chapter 2). The axonal stalk divides close to the cell body, sending one limb into the spinal cord and the other limb out to the sensory organ. Note that all of the axons in the dorsal root convey somatosensory information.

Cell bodies that give rise to the ventral root are located within the gray matter of the spinal cord. The axons of these multipolar neurons leave the spinal cord via a ventral root, which joins a dorsal root to make a spinal nerve. The axons that leave the spinal cord through the ventral roots control muscles and glands. They are referred to as *efferent axons,* because they "bear away from" the CNS.

Cranial Nerves

Twelve pairs of *cranial nerves* leave the ventral surface of the brain. Most of these nerves serve sensory and motor functions of the head and neck region. One of them, the *tenth,* or *vagus nerve,* regulates the functions of organs in the thoracic and abdominal cavities. It is called the *vagus* ("wandering") nerve because its branches wander throughout the thoracic and abdominal cavities. (The word *vagabond* has the same root.) Figure 4.27 presents a view of the base of the brain and illustrates the cranial nerves and the structures they serve. Note that efferent (motor) fibers are drawn as solid lines and that afferent (sensory) fibers are drawn as broken lines. (See *Figure 4.27 and Table 4.2.*)

As I mentioned in the previous section, cell bodies of sensory nerve fibers that enter the brain and spinal cord (except for the visual system) are located outside the central nervous system. Somatosensory information (and the sense of taste) is received, via the cranial nerves, from unipolar neurons. Auditory, vestibular, and visual information is received via fibers of bipolar neurons (described in Chapter 2). Olfactory information is received via the *olfactory bulbs,* which receive information from the olfactory receptors in the nose. The olfactory bulbs are complex structures containing a considerable amount of neural circuitry; actually, they are part of the brain. Sensory mechanisms are described in more detail in Chapters 6 and 7.

Autonomic Nervous System

The part of the peripheral nervous system that receives sensory information from the sensory organs and that controls movements of the skeletal muscles is called the *somatic nervous system.* The other branch of the peripheral nervous system— the *autonomic nervous system* (ANS)—is concerned with regulation of smooth muscle, cardiac muscle, and glands. (*Autonomic* means "self-governing.") Smooth muscle is found in the skin (associated with hair follicles), in blood vessels, in the eyes (controlling pupil size and accommodation of the lens), and in the walls and sphincters of the gut, gallbladder, and urinary bladder. Merely

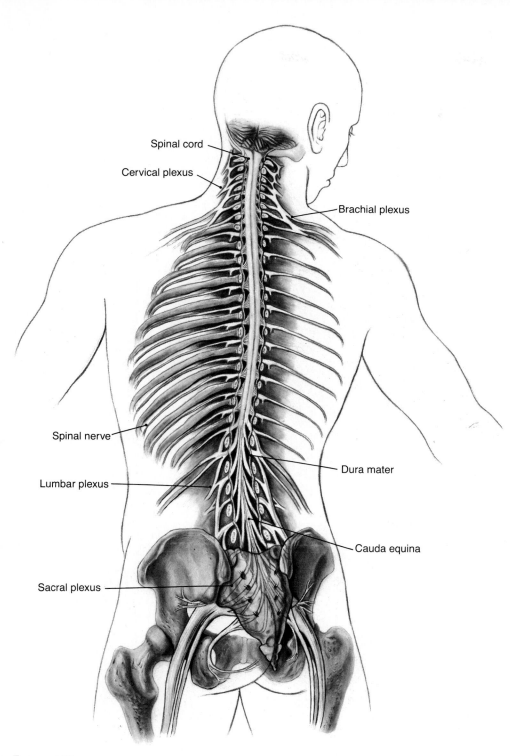

Spinal cord

Cervical plexus

Brachial plexus

Spinal nerve

Dura mater

Lumbar plexus

Cauda equina

Sacral plexus

FIGURE 4.26

A dorsal view of the human spinal cord and some of the principal spinal nerves.

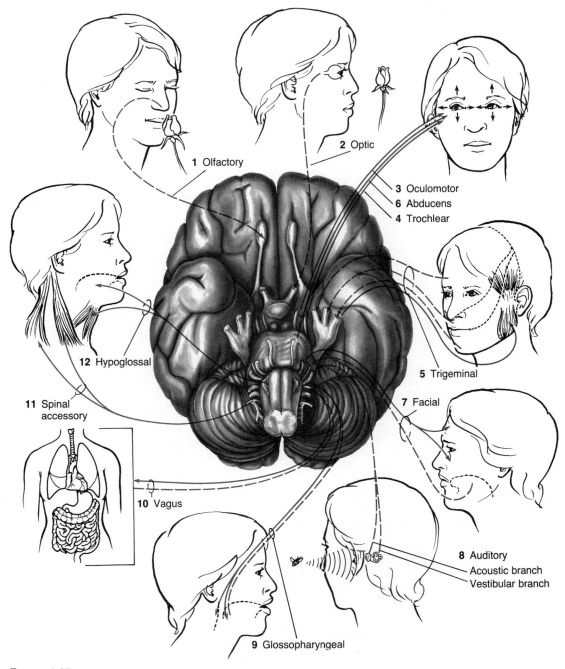

1 Olfactory
2 Optic
3 Oculomotor
6 Abducens
4 Trochlear
5 Trigeminal
7 Facial
8 Auditory
Acoustic branch
Vestibular branch
9 Glossopharyngeal
10 Vagus
11 Spinal accessory
12 Hypoglossal

FIGURE 4.27
The names, numbers, locations, and functions of the twelve cranial nerves. Solid lines denote axons that control muscles or glands; broken lines denote sensory axons.

TABLE 4.2
The cranial nerves and their functions

Number	Name	Function[a]
1	Olfactory	Olfaction (smell) **S**
2	Optic	Vision **S**
3	Occulomotor	Eye movements, control of pupil and lens, tears **MP**
4	Trochlear	Eye movements **M**
5	Trigeminal	Facial sensations, chewing **SM**
6	Abducens	Eye movements **M**
7	Facial	Facial muscles, salivary glands, taste **SMP**
8	Auditory	Acoustic branch: audition **S** Vestibular branch: balance **S**
9	Glossopharyngeal	Throat muscles, salivary glands, taste **SMP**
10	Vagus	Parasympathetic control of internal organs, sensation from internal organs, taste **SMP**
11	Spinal accessory	Head and neck muscles **M**
12	Hypoglossal	Tongue and neck muscles **M**

[a]**S**, sensory; **M**, motor; **P**, parasympathetic functions.

describing the organs innervated by the autonomic nervous system suggests the function of this system: regulation of "vegetative processes" in the body.

The ANS consists of two anatomically separate systems, the *sympathetic division* and the *parasympathetic division*. With few exceptions, organs of the body are innervated by both of these subdivisions, and each has a different effect. For example, the sympathetic division speeds the heart rate, whereas the parasympathetic division slows it.

Sympathetic Division of the ANS

The *sympathetic division* is most involved in activities associated with expenditure of energy from reserves that are stored in the body. For example, when an organism is excited, the sympathetic nervous system increases blood flow to skeletal muscles, stimulates the secretion of epinephrine (resulting in increased heart rate and a rise in blood sugar level), and causes piloerection (erection of fur in mammals who have it and production of "goose bumps" in humans).

The cell bodies of sympathetic motor neurons are located in the gray matter of the thoracic and lumbar regions of the spinal cord (hence the sympathetic nervous system is also known as the *thoracolumbar system*). The fibers of these neurons exit via the ventral roots. After joining the spinal nerves, the fibers branch off and pass into **spinal sympathetic ganglia** (not to be confused with the dorsal root ganglia). Figure 4.28 shows the relation of these ganglia to the spinal cord. Note that the various spinal sympathetic ganglia are connected to the neighboring ganglia above and below, thus forming the **sympathetic chain.** (See *Figure 4.28.*)

The axons that leave the spinal cord through the ventral root are part of the **preganglionic neurons.** With one exception, all sympathetic preganglionic axons enter the ganglia of the sympathetic chain, but not all of them synapse there. (The exception is the medulla of the adrenal gland, described below.) Some axons leave and travel to one of the other sympathetic ganglia, located among the internal organs. All sympathetic preganglionic axons form synapses with neurons located in one of the ganglia. The neurons with which they form synapses are called

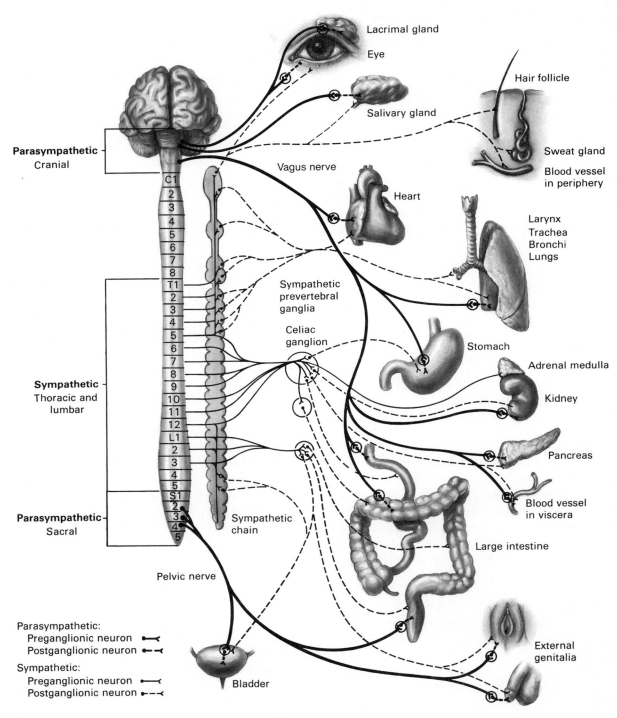

Parasympathetic
Cranial

Vagus nerve

Lacrimal gland

Eye

Salivary gland

Hair follicle

Sweat gland

Blood vessel
in periphery

Larynx
Trachea
Bronchi
Lungs

Heart

Sympathetic
prevertebral
ganglia

Celiac
ganglion

Stomach

Adrenal medulla

Kidney

Pancreas

Blood vessel
in viscera

Large intestine

Sympathetic
Thoracic and
lumbar

Sympathetic
chain

Parasympathetic
Sacral

Pelvic nerve

C1
2
3
4
5
6
7
8
T1
2
3
4
5
6
7
8
9
10
11
12
L1
2
3
4
5
S1
2
3
4
5

Parasympathetic:
    Preganglionic neuron
    Postganglionic neuron
Sympathetic:
    Preganglionic neuron
    Postganglionic neuron

Bladder

External
genitalia

Figure 4.28
The autonomic nervous system and the target organs it
serves.

postganglionic neurons. In turn, the postganglionic neurons send axons to the target organs, such as the intestines, stomach, kidneys, or sweat glands. (See *Figure 4.28.*)

The sympathetic nervous system controls the *adrenal medulla,* a set of cells located in the center of the adrenal gland. The adrenal medulla closely resembles a sympathetic ganglion. It is innervated by preganglionic axons, and its secretory cells are very similar to postganglionic sympathetic neurons. These cells secrete epinephrine and norepinephrine when they are stimulated. These hormones function chiefly as an adjunct to the direct neural effects of sympathetic activity; for example, they increase blood flow to the muscles and cause stored nutrients to be broken down into glucose within skeletal muscle cells, which increases the energy available to them.

All synapses within the sympathetic ganglia are acetylcholinergic; the terminal buttons on the target organs, belonging to the postganglionic axons, are noradrenergic. (An exception to this rule is provided by the sweat glands, which are innervated by acetylcholinergic terminal buttons.)

Parasympathetic Division of the ANS

The *parasympathetic division* of the autonomic nervous system supports activities that are involved with increases in the body's supply of stored energy. These activities include salivation, gastric and intestinal motility, secretion of digestive juices, and increased blood flow to the gastrointestinal system.

Cell bodies that give rise to preganglionic axons in the parasympathetic nervous system are located in two regions: the nuclei of some of the cranial nerves (especially the vagus nerve) and the intermediate horn of the gray matter in the sacral region of the spinal cord. Thus, the parasympathetic division of the ANS has often been referred to as the *craniosacral system.* Parasympathetic ganglia are located in the immediate vicinity of the target organs; the postganglionic fibers are therefore relatively short. The terminal buttons of both preganglionic and postganglionic neurons in the parasympathetic nervous system secrete acetylcholine.

I NTERIM SUMMARY

The spinal nerves and the cranial nerves convey sensory axons into the central nervous system and motor axons out from it. Spinal nerves are formed by the junctions of the dorsal roots, which contain incoming (afferent) axons, and the ventral roots, which contain outgoing (efferent) axons. The autonomic nervous system consists of two divisions: the sympathetic division, which controls activities that occur during excitement or exertion, such as increased heart rate; and the parasympathetic division, which controls activities that occur during relaxation, such as decreased heart rate and increased activity of the digestive system. The pathways of the autonomic nervous system contain preganglionic axons, from the brain or spinal cord to the sympathetic or parasympathetic ganglia, and postganglionic axons, from the ganglia to the target organ. The adrenal medulla, which secretes epinephrine and norepinephrine, is controlled by axons of the sympathetic nervous system.

C ONCLUDING REMARKS

Although this chapter describes only the most important features of the nervous system, I am sure that you now appreciate its complexity. This complexity should come as no surprise; after all, this system is responsible for complex functions—perceptions, memories, thoughts, and feelings.

Having studied this chapter, you should be acquainted with the pathways by which information enters and leaves the central nervous system, its major structures, and some of the functions they perform. You have also been introduced to the means by which the brain controls the endocrine system through the pituitary gland and through the nerves of the autonomic nervous system. I will have more to say about neuroanatomy in later chapters, when we deal with the physiology of particular classes of behaviors.

NEW TERMS

adrenal medulla p. 103
afferent axon p. 98
amygdala p. 88
anterior p. 75
anterior pituitary gland p. 91
arachnoid granulation p. 80
arachnoid membrane p. 78
association cortex p. 87
autonomic nervous
    system p. 98
basal ganglia p. 88
brain stem p. 92
cauda equina p. 95
caudal p. 75
caudal block p. 96
central sulcus p. 86
cerebellar cortex p. 94
cerebellar peduncle p. 94
cerebellum p. 94
cerebral aqueduct p. 79
cerebral cortex p. 85
cerebrospinal fluid p. 78
choroid plexus p. 79
cingulate gyrus p. 86
commissure p. 86
contralateral p. 75
corpus callosum p. 86
cranial nerve p. 98
cross section p. 75
deep cerebellar nuclei p. 94
diencephalon p. 82
dorsal p. 75
dorsal root p. 96
dorsal root ganglia p. 98
dura mater p. 78
efferent axon p. 98
fissure p. 85
forebrain p. 82
fourth ventricle p. 79
frontal lobe p. 86

frontal section p. 75
gyrus p. 85
hindbrain p. 82
hippocampus p. 88
horizontal section p. 76
hydrocephalus p. 81
hypothalamus p. 90
inferior p. 75
inferior colliculi p. 92
internal carotid artery p. 77
ipsilateral p. 75
lateral p. 75
lateral fissure p. 86
lateral geniculate nucleus p. 90
lateral ventricle p. 79
limbic cortex p. 86
limbic system p. 88
medial p. 75
medial geniculate nucleus p. 90
medulla oblongata p. 95
meninges (singular:
    meninx) p. 78
mesencephalon p. 83
metencephalon p. 83
midbrain p. 82
myelencephalon p. 83
neocortex p. 86
neuraxis p. 75
neurosecretory cell p. 91
nucleus p. 90
occipital lobe p. 86
olfactory bulb p. 98
optic chiasm p. 90
parasympathetic division p. 103
parietal lobe p. 86
periaqueductal
    gray matter p. 93
pia mater p. 78
pons p. 95
posterior p. 75

posterior pituitary gland p. 92
postganglionic neuron p. 103
preganglionic neuron p. 101
primary auditory cortex p. 87
primary motor cortex p. 86
primary somatosensory
    cortex p. 87
primary visual cortex p. 87
projection fiber p. 89
red nucleus p. 93
reticular formation p. 93
rostral p. 75
sagittal section p. 76
somatic nervous system p. 98
spinal cord p. 95
spinal nerve p. 98
spinal root p. 95
spinal sympathetic
    ganglia p. 101
subarachnoid space p. 78
subcortical region p. 85
substantia nigra p. 93
sulci p. 85
superior p. 75
superior colliculi p. 92
superior sagittal sinus p. 80
sympathetic chain p. 101
sympathetic division p. 101
tectum p. 92
tegmentum p. 93
telencephalon p. 82
temporal lobe p. 86
thalamus p. 89
third ventricle p. 79
vagus nerve p. 98
ventral p. 75
ventral root p. 96
ventricle p. 79
ventrolateral nucleus p. 90
vertebral artery p. 77

SUGGESTED READINGS

Barr, M.L., and Kiernan, J.A. *The Human Nervous System: An Anatomical Viewpoint*, 4th ed. Philadelphia: Harper & Row, 1983.

Brodal, A. *Neurological Anatomy in Relation to Clinical Medicine*. Oxford: Oxford University Press, 1981.

DeArmond, S.J., Fusco, M.M., and Dewey, M.M. *Structure of the Human Brain: A Photographic Atlas*. New York: Oxford University Press, 1976.

Gluhbegovic, N., and Williams, T.H. *The Human Brain: A Photographic Guide*. New York: Harper & Row, 1980.

Moyer, K.E. *Neuroanatomy*. New York: Harper & Row, 1980.

Netter, F.H. *The Ciba Collection of Medical Illustrations. Vol. 1, Nervous System*. Summit, N.J.: Ciba Pharmaceutical Products Co., 1953.

5

Methods of Physiological Psychology

Study of the physiology of behavior involves the efforts of scientists in many disciplines, including physiology, neuroanatomy, biochemistry, psychology, endocrinology, and histology. To pursue a research project in physiological psychology requires competence in many experimental techniques. Because different procedures often produce contradictory results, investigators must be familiar with the advantages and limitations of the methods they employ. Scientific investigation entails a process of asking questions of nature. The method that is used frames the question. Often we receive a puzzling answer, only to realize later that we were not asking the question we thought we were. As we will see, the best conclusions about the physiology of behavior are made by comparing the results of studies that approach the problem with different methods. The use of two or more different methods to study a particular problem is called *converging operations.* I will have more to say about this topic at the end of this chapter, after I have described the individual methods.

Physiological psychology is a biological science. Thus, most research in this area involves living organisms. Investigators must be certain that their subjects are housed in a comfortable and healthful environment and that any surgical procedures be carried out with the use of the appropriate anesthetics. In most countries governmental agencies have established rules concerning the housing and treatment of laboratory animals. In addition, professional organizations such as the American Psychological Association and the Society for Neuroscience have rules of their own.

The brain is so important that one hardly need explain the value of research designed to help us understand it. Along with the fascination of studying the organ that makes us what we are is the hope that we will discover principles of brain function that can be applied to the treatment of neurological and behavioral disorders.

NEUROANATOMICAL TECHNIQUES

Histological Procedures

The gross anatomy of the brain was described long ago, and everything that could be identified was given a name. As we saw in Chapter 4, many of these names, such as amygdala ("almond") or hippocampus ("sea horse"), described the general shape of the structures. Detailed anatomical information about the brain requires more than dissection and simple observation; it requires the use of various *histological* (tissue-preparing) techniques. As we have seen, the brain consists of billions of neurons and glial cells, the nerve cells forming distinct nuclei and fiber bundles. We cannot possibly see the details of cell structure and connections between neurons by gross examination of the brain. And even a microscope is useless without fixation and staining of the neural tissue.

Fixation

If we hope to study the tissue in the form it had at the time of the organism's death, we must destroy the autolytic enzymes (*autolytic* means "self-dissolving"), which will otherwise turn the tissue into shapeless mush. The tissue must also be preserved, to prevent its decomposition by bacteria or molds. To achieve both of these objectives, we place the neural tissue in a *fixative.* The most commonly used fixative is *formalin,* an aqueous solution of formaldehyde, a gas. Formalin halts autolysis, hardens the very soft and fragile brain, and kills any microorganisms that might destroy it.

Before the brain is fixed (that is, put into a fixative solution), it is usually perfused. *Perfusion* of tissue (literally, "a pouring through") entails removal of the blood and its replacement with another fluid. The animal's brain is perfused because better histological results are obtained when there is no blood present in the tissue. The animal whose brain is to be studied is killed with an overdose of a general anesthetic. Blood vessels are opened so that the blood can be drained from them and replaced with a dilute salt solution. The brain is removed from the skull and placed in a jar containing the fixative.

Once the brain has been fixed, the investigator must slice it into thin sections and stain various cellular structures in order to see anatomical details. Some procedures require that the tissue be stained before being sliced, but the techniques that physiological psychologists most commonly use call for sectioning first and then staining.

Therefore, I will describe the procedures in that order.

Sectioning

A *microtome* is used to slice neural tissue. This device (literally, "that which slices small") is an instrument capable of slicing tissue into very thin sections. Sections prepared for examination under a light microscope are typically 10 to 80 μm in thickness; those prepared for the electron microscope are generally cut at less than 1 μm. (A micrometer, abbreviated μm, is 1/1000 of a millimeter.) Electron microscopy will be discussed later in this chapter.

A microtome contains three parts: a knife, a platform on which to mount the tissue, and a mechanism that advances the knife (or the platform) after each slice, so that another section can be cut. Figure 5.1 shows two commonly used microtomes. The first one is a sliding microtome. The knife holder slides forward on an oiled rail and takes a section off the top of the tissue mounted on the platform. The platform automatically rises by a predetermined amount as the knife and holder are pushed back. (See *Figure 5.1a.*) To operate the rotary microtome shown on the right, you simply turn the wheel. The tissue platform moves up and down relative to the vertically mounted knife. The tissue is cut as it descends, and the platform is automatically advanced on the upstroke, moving the tissue into position for the next slice. (See *Figure 5.1b.*)

Slicing brain tissue is not quite as simple as it might at first appear. As I mentioned, raw neural tissue is very soft. Fixation in formalin will harden the brain somewhat, but it is still too soft to cut. Either of two techniques can be used to make the tissue hard enough to cut thinly: *freezing* or *embedding*.

Freezing is simplest. The tissue is chilled with a refrigeration device. Often the brain is first soaked in a sucrose (table sugar) solution, which minimizes tissue damage by preventing the formation of large ice crystals as the brain freezes.

FIGURE 5.1
Microtomes. (a) Sliding microtome.
(b) Rotary microtome.

Brain embedded in nitrocellulose

Platform rises after each slice

Knife blade slides forward

(a)

Brain mounts on face of platform

Knife blade

Turning this handle operates mechanism

Platform travels up and down, slicing brain against knife blade; after each slice, platform moves forward

(b)

The temperature of the brain must be carefully regulated; if the block of brain tissue is too cold, the tissue will shatter into little fragments. If it is too warm, a layer of tissue will be torn off rather than sliced off. Frozen sections can be cut with either sliding or rotary microtomes.

The brain can also be embedded in materials that are of sliceable consistency at room temperature, such as paraffin or nitrocellulose. Paraffin comes in various grades, according to the room temperature at which it can best be sliced. The brain is first soaked in a solvent for paraffin (such as xylene) and is then soaked in successively stronger solutions of paraffin that are kept melted in an oven. The brain is then placed in a small container of liquid paraffin, which is allowed to cool and harden. The entire block is sliced, the paraffin providing the physical support for the tissue. A rotary microtome is used to cut these sections; as the knife passes through the block, it warms it slightly, so that the sections get glued together, end to end. (See *Figure 5.2.*) It is gratifying, after having spent a lot of time preparing the tissue, to see the sections emerge in a continuous ribbon.

After the tissue is cut, the slices are usually mounted on glass microscope slides with an agent such as albumin (protein extracted from egg whites). The slides are dried and heated, which makes the albumin become insoluble and cements the tissue sections to the glass. The tissue can then be stained by putting the entire slide into various chemical solutions. The stained and mounted sections are covered with a mounting medium, and a very thin glass coverslip is placed over the sections. The mounting medium (which is thick and resinous) gradually dries out, keeping the coverslip in position.

Staining

If you looked at an unstained section of brain tissue under a microscope, you would be able to see the outlines of some large cellular masses and the more prominent fiber bundles. However, no fine details would be revealed. For this reason, the study of microscopic neuroanatomy requires special histological stains. Three basic types of stains are used for neural tissue: those that reveal cell bodies by interacting with the contents of the cytoplasm, those that selectively color myelin

FIGURE 5.2
A "ribbon" being formed as a paraffin-embedded brain is sliced on a rotary microtome.

sheaths, and those that stain the cell membrane (of the entire cell or just the axons). In addition, stains have been found that selectively color certain chemicals in the brain, including transmitter substances.

Cell-Body Stains. In the late nineteenth century Franz Nissl, a German neurologist, discovered that methylene blue, a dye derived from the distillation of coal tar, would stain the cell bodies of brain tissue. The material that takes up the dye, known as the *Nissl substance,* consists of RNA, DNA, and associated proteins located in the nucleus and scattered, in the form of granules, in the cytoplasm. Many dyes can be used to stain cell bodies, but the most frequently used is cresyl violet. Incidentally, the dyes were not developed for histological purposes but were originally manufactured for use in dyeing cloth.

The discovery of cell-body stains (also called *Nissl stains*) made it possible to identify nuclear masses in the brain. Color Plate 5.1 shows a frontal section of a cat brain stained with cresyl violet. Note that you can observe fiber bundles by their lighter appearance; they do not take up the stain. (See *Color Plate 5.1.*) The stain is not selective for *neural* cell bodies. All cells are stained, neurons and glia alike. Thus, it is up to the investigators to determine which is which—by size, shape, and location.

Myelin Stains. ***Myelin stains*** color myelin sheaths. These stains make it possible to identify fiber bundles. (What is light in Color Plate 5.1 is dark in Color Plate 5.2.) However, pathways of single fibers cannot be traced. There is simply too much intermingling of the individual fibers. (See ***Color Plate 5.2.***)

Membrane Stains. ***Membrane stains*** contain salts of various heavy metals, such as silver, uranium, or osmium, that interact with the somatic, dendritic, and axonal membranes. The ***Golgi-Cox stain*** (which uses silver) is highly selective, staining only a fraction of the neurons in a given region. Why this happens is not known, and the selectivity undoubtedly gives a biased view of the neurons that populate the region. But the selective staining makes it possible to observe the axonal and dendritic branches of individual neurons and to trace details of synaptic interconnections. Figure 5.3 shows the appearance of individual neurons of the cerebral cortex stained by a new modification of the Golgi-Cox stain. Note the individual neurons and their interconnecting processes. The large cells in the center are oligodendroglia, providing myelin sheaths for the bundles of fibers running horizontally. (See ***Figure 5.3.***)

The Histofluorescence Method. A technique discovered by Falck, Hillarp, Thieme, and Torp (1962) provided a method for precisely locating certain kinds of transmitter substances in the brain. These investigators discovered that when brain tissue was exposed to dry formaldehyde gas, noradrenergic neurons would fluoresce a bright yellow when the tissue was examined under ultraviolet light. The technique was refined and applied to the other monoamines, and investigators drew "maps" showing the distribution of the monoaminergic neurons in the central nervous system. For example, a noradrenergic map is shown in Figure 9.19. Once the location of particular types of neurons is known, it becomes possible

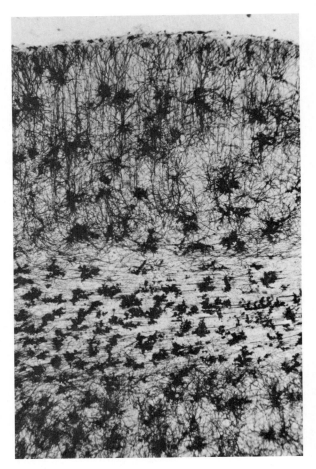

FIGURE 5.3

A section of cortex of a cat brain, stained by a modified Golgi-Cox method. (Histological material courtesy of D.N. Spinelli and J.K. Lane.)

to investigate their function. As we will see in Chapter 9, studies have shown that noradrenergic neurons play a role in alertness and vigilance.

Tracing Neural Connections

The central nervous system contains many billions of neurons, most of which are gathered together in thousands of discrete nuclei. These nuclei are interconnected by incredibly complex systems of axons. The problem of the neuroanatomist is to trace these connections and find out which nuclei are connected to which others and what route is taken by the interconnecting fibers. The problem cannot be resolved by means of histological procedures that stain all neurons, such as cell-body, membrane, or myelin stains. If we look closely at a brain that has been prepared by these means, we see only a tangled mass of neurons. Special techniques must be used to make the connections that are being investigated stand out from all of the others.

Tracing Pathways Originating in a Brain Structure

Suppose an investigator is interested in a particular nucleus in the brain and wants to know what other parts of the brain receive information from the nucleus. The technique of *amino acid autoradiography* will provide the answer. The term *autoradiography* can be translated roughly as "writing with one's own radiation." The investigator injects radioactive amino acids into a particular region of the brain and then leaves the animal alone for a day or two. During this time the cell bodies take up the radioactive amino acids and incorporate them into proteins. Some of these proteins are transported through the axons to the terminal buttons. (See *Figure 5.4.*) The animal is then killed, its brain is removed and sliced, and the sec-

tions are placed on microscope slides. The slides are taken into a darkroom, where they are coated with a photographic emulsion (the substance found on photographic film). After a wait of several weeks the slides, with their coatings of emulsion, are developed, just like photographic film. The radioactive proteins show themselves as black spots in the developed emulsion because the radioactivity exposes the emulsion, just as X-rays or light will do.

Figure 5.5 illustrates the actual appearance of the grains of exposed silver in the photographic emulsion. A solution containing radioactive amino acids (proline and leucine) was injected into a rabbit's prefrontal cortex, where it was taken up by neural cell bodies, incorporated into protein, and transported through axons to their terminal buttons. Figure 5.5a shows a Nissl-stained section through the anterior temporal lobe. Figure 5.5b shows the section viewed under *dark-field illumination,* which makes the silver grains scatter a beam of light and thus look white. You can clearly see the silver grains in the nucleus labeled Ce (the central nucleus of the amygdala). (See *Figure 5.5.*) The technique has revealed here that neurons in the prefrontal cortex of the rabbit

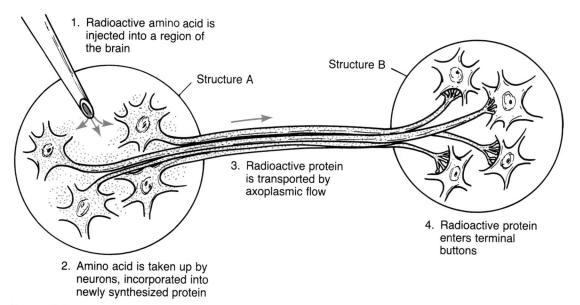

1. Radioactive amino acid is injected into a region of the brain

Structure A

Structure B

3. Radioactive protein is transported by axoplasmic flow

4. Radioactive protein enters terminal buttons

2. Amino acid is taken up by neurons, incorporated into newly synthesized protein

FIGURE 5.4

The procedure for the use of amino acid autoradiography to reveal the efferent axons of a brain region.

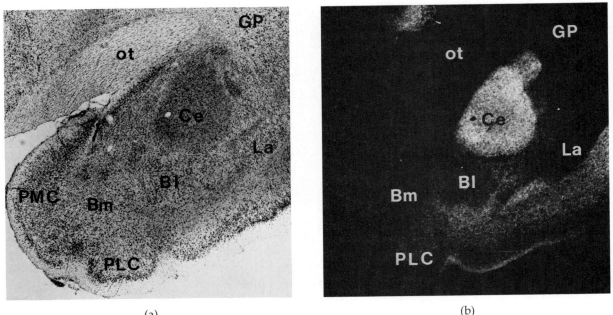

(a)   (b)

FIGURE 5.5

Amino acid autoradiography. A solution of radioactive proline and leucine was injected into the frontal cortex and was carried by axoplasmic flow to the central nucleus of the amygdala (Ce). (a) Photomicrograph taken as a standard exposure. (b) Photomicrograph taken under dark-field illumination, which shows the exposed grains of emulsion as spots of white against a dark background. GP = globus pallidus; ot = optic tract. Other abbreviations label various nuclei of the amygdala. (Reprinted with permission from Kapp, B.S., Schwaber, J.S., and Driscoll, P.A. *Neuroscience,* 1985, *15,* 327–346. Copyright © 1985, Pergamon Press, plc.)

have axons that form synapses with neurons in the central nucleus of the amygdala.

Tracing Pathways Leading to a Brain Structure

Horseradish peroxidase is a rather unlikely name for a substance that is used in neuroanatomical research. (Believe it or not, there is also a turnip peroxidase.) Horseradish peroxidase (usually called *HRP*) is an enzyme—a protein that is capable of splitting certain peroxide molecules, turning them into insoluble salts. We already saw its use (in Chapter 3) as a tracer that demonstrated the recycling of the membrane of terminal buttons during the release of transmitter substances.

Most investigators do not use pure HRP but rather a compound that contains both HRP and a substance called *wheat germ agglutinin* (WGA). When HRP (plus WGA) is injected into the brain,

it is taken up by terminal buttons and is subsequently transported by retrograde axoplasmic flow—that is, flow directed back toward the cell soma. Thus, the HRP eventually reaches the cell bodies of neurons that send axons into the region of the brain that had received the injection.

The technique works like this: Some HRP is injected into the part of the brain that is under investigation. Terminal buttons in that region take up the chemical and transport it back to the cell bodies. After a survival time of a day or two, the animal is killed, the brain is sliced, and the sections are soaked in a sequence of chemical baths that visibly mark the location of the HRP, which has been carried back to the cell bodies. Thus, the HRP technique permits identification of neurons that project axons *to* a particular region. (See *Figure 5.6.*)

Figure 5.7 illustrates the appearance of cells that have been labeled with HRP. The chemical

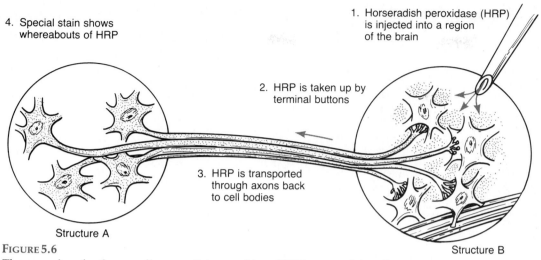

4. Special stain shows whereabouts of HRP

1. Horseradish peroxidase (HRP) is injected into a region of the brain

2. HRP is taken up by terminal buttons

3. HRP is transported through axons back to cell bodies

Structure A

Structure B

FIGURE 5.6

The procedure for the use of horseradish peroxidase (HRP) to reveal the afferent neurons that send axons to a brain region.

was injected into the medial mammillary nuclei of the hypothalamus of a rat, where it was taken up by terminal buttons. The HRP was carried back, by retrograde axoplasmic flow, to cell bodies located in the medial prefrontal cortex, shown in the photomicrograph. The results indicate that neurons in the medial mammillary nuclei receive input from neurons in to the medial prefrontal cortex. (See *Figure 5.7.*)

Together, the HRP technique and the radioactive amino acid technique permit investigators to discover the source of the inputs into a particular part of the brain and the locations to which that region sends axons. Thus, these techniques help to provide us with a "wiring diagram" of the brain.

Study of the Living Brain

Advances in X-ray techniques and computers have led to the development of several methods for studying the anatomy of the living brain. The first to be developed was called *computerized tomography* (*tomos*, "cut"; *graphein*, "to write"). This procedure, usually referred to as a *CT scan*, works as follows: The patient's head is placed in a large doughnut-shaped ring. The ring contains an X-ray tube and, directly opposite it (on the other

side of the patient's head), an X-ray detector. The X-ray beam passes through the patient's head, and the amount of radioactivity that gets through it is measured by the detector. The X-ray emitter and detector scan the head from front to back. They are then moved around the ring by a few degrees, and the transmission of radioactivity is measured again. The process is repeated until the brain has been scanned from all angles. (See *Figure 5.8.*)

The computer takes the information and plots a two-dimensional picture of a horizontal section of the brain. The patient's head is then moved up or down through the ring, and a scan is taken of another section of the brain. Figure 5.9 shows a series of these scans taken through the head of a patient who sustained a stroke that damaged portions of the right parietal and occipital lobes. (See *Figure 5.9.*)

Computerized tomography has been used extensively in the diagnosis of various pathological conditions of the brain, including tumors, blood clots, hydrocephalus, and degenerative diseases such as multiple sclerosis. The benefits to the patient are obvious; a CT scan can often tell the physician whether brain surgery is necessary. The technique is also of considerable importance to neuropsychologists, who try to infer brain func-

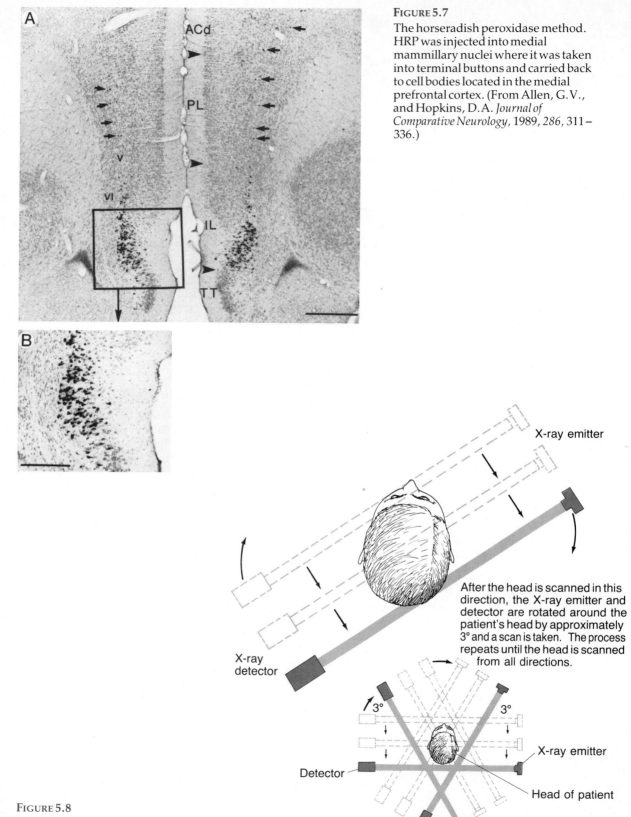

FIGURE 5.7
The horseradish peroxidase method.
HRP was injected into medial
mammillary nuclei where it was taken
into terminal buttons and carried back
to cell bodies located in the medial
prefrontal cortex. (From Allen, G.V.,
and Hopkins, D.A. *Journal of
Comparative Neurology*, 1989, *286*, 311–
336.)

ACd

PL

V

VI

IL

TT

X-ray emitter

After the head is scanned in this
direction, the X-ray emitter and
detector are rotated around the
patient's head by approximately
3° and a scan is taken. The process
repeats until the head is scanned
from all directions.

X-ray
detector

3°   3°

Detector

X-ray emitter

Head of patient

FIGURE 5.8
A computerized tomography (CT) scanner.

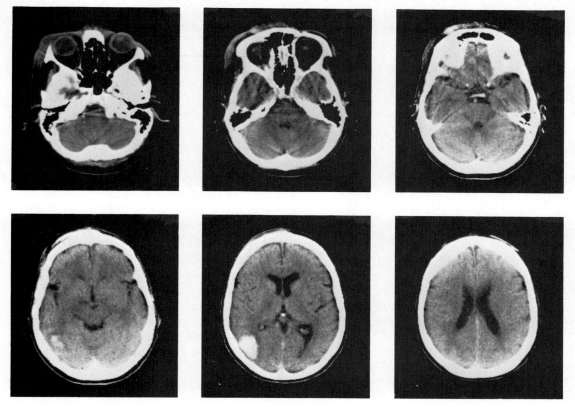

FIGURE 5.9

A series of CT scans from a patient with a lesion in the right occipital-parietal area (scan 5). The lesion appears white because it was accompanied by bleeding; blood absorbs more radiation than the surrounding brain tissue. Rostral is up, caudal is down; left and right are reversed. Scan 1 shows a section through the eyes and the base of the brain. (Courtesy of J.McA. Jones, Good Samaritan Hospital, Portland, Oregon.)

tions by studying the behavioral capacities of people who have sustained brain damage by disease or physical injury. The CT scan makes it possible for them to determine the approximate location of the lesion.

An even more detailed picture of what is inside a person's head is provided by a process called *magnetic resonance imaging* (MRI). The MRI scanner resembles a CT scanner, but it does not use X-rays. Instead, it passes an extremely strong magnetic field through the patient's head. When a person's body is placed in a strong magnetic field, the nuclei of some molecules in the body spin with a particular orientation. If a radio frequency wave is then passed through the body, these nuclei emit radio waves of their own. Different molecules emit energy at different frequencies. The MRI scanner is tuned to detect the radiation from hydrogen molecules. Because these molecules are present in different concentrations in different tis-

sues, the scanner can use the information to prepare pictures of slices of the brain. Unlike CT scans, which are limited to the horizontal plane, MRI scans can be taken in the sagittal or frontal planes, as well. (See *Figure 5.10.*)

Another technique, *positron emission tomography* (PET), permits investigators to assess the amount of metabolic activity in various parts of the brain. First, the patient receives an injection of radioactive *2-deoxyglucose* (2-DG). Because this chemical resembles glucose, it is taken into cells, especially those that are metabolically active. However, unlike glucose, 2-DG cannot be metabolized, so it accumulates within the cells. (Eventually, the chemical is broken down and leaves the cells.) The person's head is placed in a machine similar to a CT scanner. When a beam of X-rays passes through the head, the radioactive molecules of 2-DG emit a particle called a positron, which is detected by the scanner. The computer

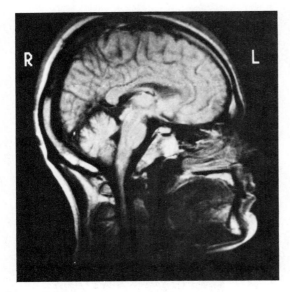

FIGURE 5.10

A midsagittal MRI scan of a human brain. (Image provided courtesy of Philips Medical Systems, Inc.)

determines which regions of the brain have taken up the radioactive substance, and it produces a picture of a slice of the brain, showing different amounts of metabolic activity. (See *Color Plate 5.3.*)

The metabolic activity of specific regions of the brain can also be estimated by a device that measures regional cerebral blood flow. If the neural activity of a particular region of the brain increases, the metabolic rate increases, too (largely as a result of increased operation of ion pumps in the membrane of the cells in that region). This increased metabolic rate dilates the arterioles in the region, which increases the local blood flow. Regional cerebral blood flow can be measured by having a person breathe air containing a measured amount of a radioactive isotope of an inert gas called *xenon* (a close relative of neon). A large array of very sensitive detectors is placed near the head, and the radioactivity of each region is measured. A computer calculates the blood flow of the region measured by each of the detectors and displays the results on a video screen. Color Plate 5.4 shows a display of the mean regional cerebral blood flow of a group of normal subjects and subjects with schizophrenia who are attempting to solve two different problems. The differences in

color indicate that the brains of the two groups of people are activated differently while they work on these tasks. (See *Color Plate 5.4.*)

The development of computers capable of calculating and presenting detailed color graphics displays has made it possible to combine images obtained by different techniques in remarkable ways. For example, Color Plate 5.5 shows a side view of the head of a seven-year-old girl who had almost continuous seizures. The source of the seizure activity in the brain was near the part of the motor cortex that controls the muscles responsible for speech and respiration, and consequently, she was unable to talk and had great difficulty breathing. The seizures could not be controlled by medication, so removal of the abnormal brain tissue was the only recourse. Because this abnormal tissue was so close to Broca's area, it was important to identify its location precisely so that a minimum of brain tissue could be removed. The image shown in the photograph was derived from a series of PET and MRI scans, presented in three dimensions, showing the area of abnormal metabolic activity. Next to it is a photograph of the same area made during the operation. As you can see, the neurosurgeon knew what to expect even before the skull was opened. (See *Color Plate 5.5.*) The operation was successful, by the way; the seizures stopped, and the girl was able to breathe without assistance.

Electron Microscopy

The light microscope is limited in its ability to resolve extremely small details. Because of the nature of light itself, magnification of more than approximately 1500 times does not add any detail. In order to see such small anatomical structures as synaptic vesicles and details of cell organelles, investigators must use an electron microscope. A beam of electrons is passed through the tissue to be examined. (The tissue must first be coated with a substance that produces detailed variations in the resistance to the passage of electrons, much like staining for light microscopy, causing various portions of the tissue to absorb light.) A shadow of tissue is then cast upon a sheet of photographic film, which is exposed by the electrons. Electron photomicrographs produced in this way can pro-

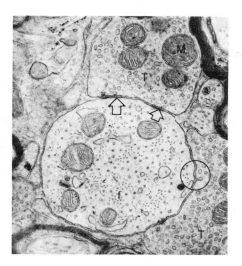

FIGURE 5.11

An electron photomicrograph of a section through an axodendritic synapse. Two synaptic regions are indicated by arrows, and a circle points out a region of pinocytosis in an adjacent terminal button, presumably representing recycling of vesicular membrane. T = terminal button; f = microfilaments; M = mitochondrion. (From Rockel, A.J., and Jones, E.G. *Journal of Comparative Neurology*, 1973, *147*, 61–92.)

vide information about structural details on the order of a few Ångström units. (See *Figure 5.11*.)

A *scanning electron microscope* provides less magnification than a standard one, which transmits the electron beam through the tissue. However, it shows objects in three dimensions. The microscope scans the tissue with a moving beam of electrons. The information received from the reflection of the beam is used to produce a remarkably detailed three-dimensional view. (See *Figure 5.12*.)

Stereotaxic Surgery

Many procedures used in neuroscience research require the investigator to place an object such as a wire or the tip of a metal cannula (tube) in a particular part of the brain. For example, the investigator might want to inject a chemical into the brain, which requires the insertion of a cannula, or to destroy a particular region of the brain, which requires the insertion of a metal electrode, through which destructive electrical current may be passed. If the investigator simply sliced the brain

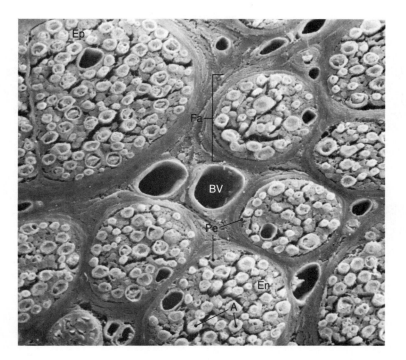

FIGURE 5.12

A scanning electron photomicrograph of the cut end of a peripheral nerve. Ep = epineurium (the connective tissue surrounding the nerve); Fa = fascicle (bundle of axons); Pe = perineurium (the connective tissue surrounding individual fascicles); En = endoneurium (the connective tissue surrounding single axons); A = axons; BV = blood vessel. (From *Tissues and Organs: A Text-Atlas of Scanning Electron Microscopy* by R.G. Kessel and R.H. Kardon. W.H. Freeman and Company. Copyright © 1979.)

open to get to the appropriate part, great damage would be done. Stereotaxic surgery permits the insertion of an object into the depths of the brain without serious damage to the overlying tissue.

Stereotaxis literally means "solid arrangement"; more specifically, it refers to the ability to locate objects in space. A stereotaxic apparatus permits the investigator to locate brain structures that are hidden from view. This device contains a holder that fixes the animal's head in a standard position and a carrier that moves an electrode or a cannula through measured distances in all three axes of space. However, in order to perform stereotaxic surgery, one must first study a stereotaxic atlas, so I will describe the atlas first.

The Stereotaxic Atlas

No two brains of animals of a given species are completely identical, but there is enough similarity among individuals to predict the location of a particular brain structure, relative to external features of the head. For instance, a particular thalamic nucleus of a rat might be so many millimeters ventral, anterior, and lateral to a point formed by the junction of several bones of the skull. Figure 5.13 shows two views of a rat skull: a drawing of the dorsal surface and, beneath it, a midsagittal view. (See *Figure 5.13.*) The junction of the coronal and sagittal *sutures* (seams between adjacent bones of the skull) is labeled *bregma.* If the animal's skull is oriented as shown in the illustration,

FIGURE 5.13
Relation of the skull sutures to a rat's brain, and the stereotaxic coordinates for an electrode placement.

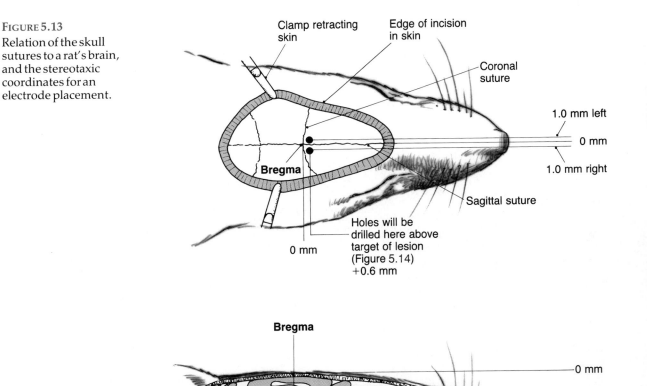

a particular region of the brain occupies a fairly constant location in space, relative to bregma. Not all atlases use bregma as the reference point, but this reference is the easiest to describe.

A *stereotaxic atlas* contains pages that correspond to frontal sections taken at various distances anterior and posterior to bregma (or another reference point). For example, the page shown in Figure 5.14 contains a drawing of a slice of the brain located 0.6 mm anterior to bregma. If we wanted to place the tip of a wire in the structure labeled F (the fornix), we would have to drill a hole through the skull 0.6 mm anterior to bregma (because the structure shows up on the 0.6-mm page) and 1.0 mm lateral to the midline. (See *Figures 5.13 and 5.14.*) The electrode would be lowered through the hole until the tip was 7.0 mm lower than the skull height at bregma. (See *Figure 5.14.*) Thus, by finding a neural structure (which we cannot see in our animal) on one of the pages of a stereotaxic atlas, we can determine the structure's location relative to bregma (which we can see). I should note that because of variations in different strains and ages of animals, the atlas gives only an

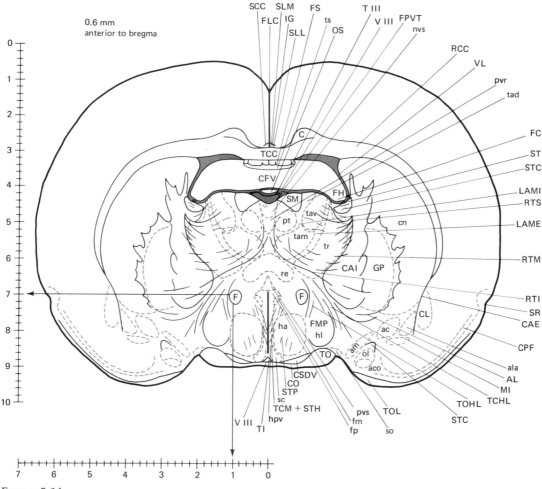

FIGURE 5.14

A page from a stereotaxic atlas of the rat brain. The scale on the side and bottom of the figure has been modified to be consistent with my description of bregma as a reference point. (From König, J.F.R., and Klippel, R.A. *The Rat Brain: A Stereotaxic Atlas of the Forebrain and Lower Parts of the Brain Stem.* Copyright 1963 by the Williams & Wilkins Co., Baltimore.)

approximate location. It is always necessary to try out a new set of coordinates, slice and stain the animal's brain, see where the lesion was made, correct the numbers, and try again.

There are human stereotaxic atlases, by the way. Sometimes, a neurosurgeon produces subcortical lesions (for example, to reduce severe tremors caused by Parkinson's disease). Usually, the surgeon uses multiple landmarks and verifies the location of the wire (or other device) inserted into the brain by taking X-rays before producing a brain lesion.

The Stereotaxic Apparatus

A *stereotaxic apparatus* operates on simple principles. The device includes a head holder, which holds the animal's skull in the proper orientation, a holder for the electrode, and a calibrated mechanism that moves the electrode holder in measured distances along the three axes: anterior-posterior, dorsal-ventral, and lateral-medial. Figure 5.15 illustrates a stereotaxic apparatus designed for small animals; various head holders can be used to outfit this device for such diverse species as rats, mice, hamsters, pigeons, and turtles. (See *Figure 5.15.*)

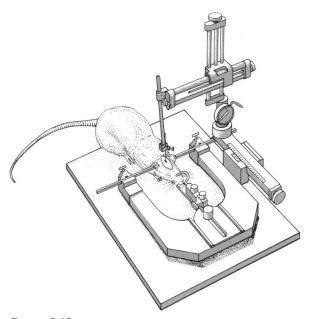

FIGURE 5.15
A stereotaxic apparatus for performing brain surgery on rats.

Once the investigator has obtained the stereotaxic coordinates, he or she anesthetizes the animal, places it in the apparatus, and cuts the scalp open. This cut exposes the skull so that the cannula or electrode can be placed with its tip on bregma. The investigator measures the location of bregma along each of the axes and moves the cannula or electrode the proper distance along the anterior-posterior and lateral-medial axes to a point just above the target. He or she then drills a hole through the skull just below the cannula or electrode and lowers the device into the brain by the proper amount. Now the tip of the cannula or electrode is in the correct position in the brain.

The next step depends upon what the investigator intends to accomplish by the surgery. In some cases the cannula or electrode is permanently implanted with acrylic plastic, a procedure that will be described later in this chapter. In other cases a chemical is infused into the brain through the cannula or an electrical current is passed through the electrode in order to stimulate or destroy brain tissue. In either of these situations the device is subsequently removed from the brain. With any of these techniques, once surgery is complete, the wound is sewed together, and the animal is taken out of the stereotaxic apparatus and allowed to recover from the anesthetic.

*I*NTERIM SUMMARY

For an examination of the details of the nervous system, the brain is perfused, and the tissue is preserved in a fixative such as formalin, is hardened by freezing or soaking in paraffin or nitrocellulose, and is then sliced by a microtome. Cell-body stains, myelin stains, or membrane stains reveal what their names imply. Tracing tracts involves the use of even more special techniques. Amino acid autoradiography reveals the place to which neurons in a particular region send their axons. Radioactive amino acids, injected into the structure in the living animal, are taken up by the neurons, incorporated into proteins, and carried down the axons to the terminal buttons. Later, the brain is sliced, and the sections are mounted on glass slides and coated with a photographic emulsion;

after a period of time the emulsion is developed. The horseradish peroxidase technique reveals the place *from which* inputs to a particular structure come. HRP is injected into the structure, where it is taken up by terminal buttons and carried back to the cell bodies. Later, a special stain shows their whereabouts.

The living human brain can be studied by several means. CT scanners use X-rays to construct images of horizontal sections through the brain. MRI scanners use a combination of a magnetic field and radio waves to construct even more detailed images in any plane. PET scanners can be used to reveal the metabolic rate of different regions of the brain after a person has received an injection of radioactive 2-DG. Regional cerebral blood flow can be measured through an array of sensitive detectors while a person breaths air containing some radioactive xenon.

Electron microscopy reveals details of the contents of cells, including their processes such as dendrites, axons, and terminal buttons. A scanning electron microscope shows the detailed three-dimensional anatomy of small structures such as nerves and sensory organs.

Stereotaxic surgery involves the use of a stereotaxic atlas, which contains drawings or photographs of slices through the brain, and a stereotaxic apparatus, a device that permits the investigator to position the tip of an electrode or cannula in a precise point in space. Usually, junctions between the bones of the skull are used as reference points to locate the desired target.

LESION PRODUCTION/ BEHAVIORAL EVALUATION

One of the most important research methods used to investigate brain functions involves destroying part of the brain and evaluating the animal's subsequent behavior. This technique is not as glamorous as many of the more recently devised techniques, but it often serves as the final test that confirms or disproves conclusions made by other methods. For example, an investigator may find that neurons in a particular part of the brain become active when the animal performs a particular behavior. This finding suggests that the structure may be at least partly responsible for that behavior. If the animal no longer performs the behavior after the structure is destroyed, we become more confident of our conclusion about the structure's responsibility for the behavior. However, if the animal still performs the behavior, we know that the structure is not necessary for its performance. It may still play a role, but not an essential one. In this situation, then, the principle of converging operations (studying a problem by two or more different methods) can be put to use.

Evaluating the Behavioral Effects of Brain Damage

A *lesion* literally refers to a wound or injury; and when a physiological psychologist destroys part of the brain, he or she usually refers to the damage as a brain lesion. The rationale for lesion studies is that the function of an area of the brain can be inferred from the behavioral capacity that is missing from the animal's repertoire after the area is destroyed. For example, if an animal can no longer see after part of the brain is destroyed, we can conclude that the destroyed area plays some role in vision.

However, we must be very careful in interpreting the effects of brain lesions. For example, how do we ascertain that the lesioned animal is blind? Does it bump into objects, or fail to run through a maze toward the light that signals the location of food, or no longer constrict its pupils to light? An animal could bump into objects because of deficits in motor coordination, it could have lost its memory for the maze problem, or it could see quite well but could have lost its visual reflexes. The experimenter must be clever enough to ask the right question, especially when studying complex processes such as hunger, attention, or memory. Even when studying simpler processes, people can be fooled. For years people thought that the albino rat was blind. (It isn't.) Think about it: How would you test to see whether a rat can see? Remember that they have vibrissae (whiskers) that can be used to detect a wall before bumping into it or the edge of a table before walking off it. They can also find their way around a room by following odor trails.

The interpretation of lesion studies is also complicated by the fact that all regions of the brain are interconnected, and no single part is wholly responsible for any one function. When a nucleus is destroyed, the lesion may also sever axons passing through the area. If a structure normally inhibits another, the observed changes in behavior might really be caused by disinhibition of that second structure. Also, we very often see a partial recovery of function some time after part of a brain is damaged. It is impossible to say whether this recovery results from a "taking over" of the function of the damaged structure by some other brain region or from repair of temporarily injured synapses. In later chapters we will see many examples of the difficulty that occurs when trying to infer the role of a brain region from the behavior of an animal lacking that region.

I should also note that histological evaluation must be made of each animal's brain lesion. Brain lesions often miss the mark, and one must verify the precise location of the brain damage after testing the animals behaviorally. The investigator may have intended to destroy structure X but may have occasionally missed, destroying nearby structure Y in some animals instead. After the behavioral observations are completed, the animals are killed, and the investigator slices and stains the animals' brains to see where the damage is. Only the data collected from the animals in which structure X was destroyed are included in the final analysis. (Sometimes, interesting results are obtained accidentally; the investigator may find that structure Y is even more important than structure X to the function being studied.)

Producing Brain Lesions

It is easy to destroy parts of the dorsal surface of the cerebral or cerebellar cortex; the animal is anesthetized, the scalp is cut, part of the skull is removed, and the cortex is brought into view. Almost always, a suction device is used to aspirate the brain tissue. To accomplish this tissue removal, the dura mater is cut away, and a glass pipette is placed on the surface of the brain. A vacuum pump attached to the pipette is used to suck away brain tissue. With practice, it is quite easy to aspirate the cortical gray matter, stopping at the underlying layer of white matter, which has a much tougher consistency.

Subcortical brain lesions are usually produced by passing electrical current through a stainless steel wire that is electrically insulated with paint or varnish except for a portion of the tip. The investigator guides the wire stereotaxically, so that its end reaches the appropriate location, and then turns on the lesion-making device. Two kinds of electrical current can be used. Direct-current (DC) devices create lesions by initiating chemical reactions whose products destroy the cells in the vicinity of the electrode tip. Radio frequency (RF) lesion-making devices produce alternating current of a very high frequency. This current does not stimulate neural tissue, nor does it cause chemical reactions. Instead, it destroys nearby cells with the heat produced by the passage of the current through the tissue, which offers electrical resistance. (See *Figure 5.16.*)

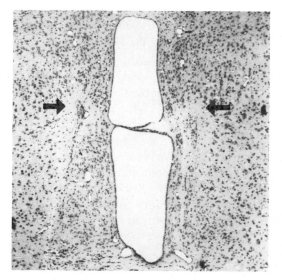

FIGURE 5.16
Radio frequency lesion. The arrows point to very small lesions produced by passing radio frequency current through the tips of stainless steel electrodes placed in the medial preoptic nucleus of a rat brain. (Frontal section, cell-body stain.) (Reprinted with permission from Pergamon Press and Turkenburg, J.L., Swaab, D.F., Endert, E., Louwerse, A.L., and van de Poll, N.E. *Brain Research Bulletin,* 1988, *21,* 215–224.)

Radio frequency lesions have a distinct advantage over DC lesions: No metal ions are left in the damaged tissue. In contrast, when DC lesions are produced, some of the electrode is left behind in the brain, because ions of metal are carried away by the electrical current. These ions can affect the surviving neurons in the vicinity of the lesion and alter the behavior of the animal (King and Frohman, 1986).

Lesions produced by means of radio frequency or direct current destroy everything in the vicinity of the electrode tip, including neuron cell bodies and the axons of neurons that pass through the region. A more selective method of producing brain lesions employs a neurotoxin ("nerve poison"), such as *kainic acid* or *ibotenic acid*. When these chemicals are injected through a cannula into a region of the brain, they destroy cell bodies in the vicinity but spare axons that are passing nearby. (See ***Figure 5.17.***) This selectivity permits the investigator to determine whether the behavioral effects of destroying a particular brain struc-

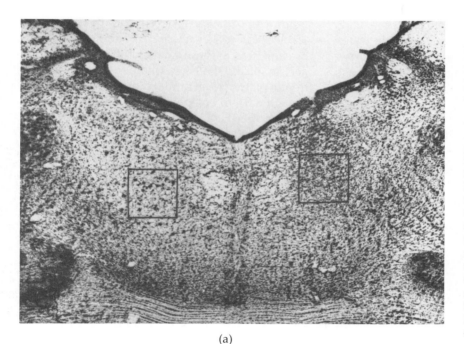

(a)

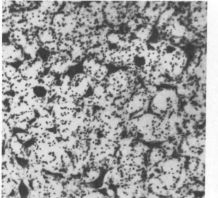

(b)

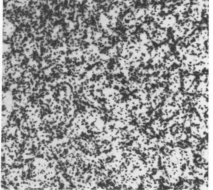

(c)

FIGURE 5.17
Neurotoxic lesion. Ibotenic acid was injected into one side of the pontine reticular formation of a cat brain. (a) Frontal section. The arrows show the path followed by the metal cannula that was used to inject the neurotoxin. The two photographs in parts b and c show the brain tissue in more detail (indicated by black squares here). (b) Normal tissue. Large neurons and small glial cells can be seen. (c) Damaged tissue. Only glial cells can be seen. (From Suzuki, S.S., Siegel, J.M., and Wu, M.-F. *Brain Research,* 1989, *484,* 78–93.)

ture occur because the cells there are killed or because the axons that pass nearby are severed. For example, RF lesions of a region of the pons abolish a particular form of sleep; thus, investigators believed that this region was involved in the production of this stage of sleep. But later studies showed that when kainic acid is used to destroy the neurons located there, the animals' sleep is *not* affected. Thus, the sleep-altering effects of RF lesions must be caused by destroying the axons that pass through the area, not the cell bodies that reside there.

Even more specific methods of lesion production are available. For example, the drug **6-hydroxydopamine** (6-HD) resembles the catecholamines norepinephrine and dopamine. You will recall that the postsynaptic effects of most neurotransmitters are terminated by re-uptake; the terminal button releases the neurotransmitter, then retrieves it. Because 6-HD resembles the catecholamines, it is taken up by the axons of neurons that secrete dopamine or norepinephrine. Once inside, the chemical poisons and kills the neurons. Thus, 6-HD can be injected directly into particular regions of the brain to kill specific populations of neurons that use one of these transmitter substances. If the investigator uses the proper concentration of 6-HD, only catecholamine-secreting neurons will be damaged.

RECORDING THE BRAIN'S ELECTRICAL ACTIVITY

Rationale

Axons produce action potentials, and terminal buttons elicit postsynaptic potentials in the membrane of the cells with which they form synapses. These electrical events can be recorded (as we have already seen), and changes in the electrical activity of a particular region can be used to determine whether that region plays a role in various behaviors. For example, recordings can be made during stimulus presentations, decision making, or motor activities. The rationale is sound; but as we will see, electrical recordings of neural activity, especially of those electrical events that might be correlated with complex behaviors, are difficult to interpret.

Recordings can be made chronically, over an

extended period of time after the animal recovers from surgery, or acutely, for a relatively short period of time during which the animal is kept anesthetized. Acute recordings, made while the animal is anesthetized, are usually restricted to studies of sensory pathways or (in conjunction with electrical stimulation of the brain) investigations of anatomical pathways in the brain (to be described in a later section of this chapter). Acute recordings seldom involve behavioral observations, since the behavioral capacity of an anesthetized animal is limited, to say the least.

Chronic electrodes can be implanted in the brain with the aid of a stereotaxic apparatus, and an electrical socket attached to the electrodes can be cemented to the animal's skull by means of an acrylic plastic that is normally used for making dental plates. Then, after recovery from surgery, the animal can be "plugged in" to the recording system. (See *Figure 5.18*.)

Electrical recordings can be taken through very small electrodes that detect the activity of one neuron (or just a few neurons) or through large electrodes that respond to the electrical activity of large populations of neurons. In either case the electrical signal detected by the electrode is quite small and must be amplified. A biological amplifier works just like the amplifiers in a stereo sys-

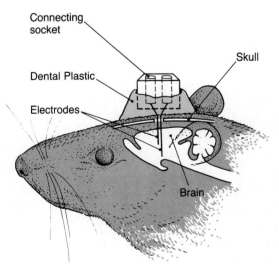

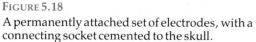

FIGURE 5.18
A permanently attached set of electrodes, with a connecting socket cemented to the skull.

tem, converting the weak signals recorded at the brain (about as weak as those produced by a phonograph cartridge) into stronger ones, large enough to be displayed on the appropriate device. Output devices vary considerably. Their basic purpose is to convert the raw data (amplified electrical signals from the brain) into a form we can perceive—usually a visual display.

Electrodes

Depending on the type of electrical signal he or she wishes to detect, the investigator constructs or purchases special electrodes. Although these electrodes come in many forms, they can be classified into two basic types: microelectrodes and macroelectrodes.

Microelectrodes

Microelectrodes have a very fine tip, small enough to record the electrical activity of individual neurons. This technique is usually called *single-unit recording* (a unit refers to an individual neuron). Microelectrodes can be constructed of fine metal wires or glass tubes. Metal electrodes are sharpened by etching them in an acid solution. Current is passed through a fine wire as it is moved in and out of the solution. The tip erodes away, leaving a very fine, sharp point. The wire (usually of tungsten or stainless steel) is then insulated with a special varnish. The very end of the tip is so sharp that it does not retain insulation and thus can record electrical signals.

As we already saw in Chapter 2, electrodes can also be constructed of fine glass tubes. Glass tubes have an interesting property. If they are heated until soft, and if the ends are pulled apart, the softened glass will stretch into a very fine filament. However, no matter how thin the filament becomes, it will still have a hole running through it. To construct glass microelectrodes, the investigator heats the middle of a length of capillary tubing (glass with an outside diameter of approximately 1 mm) and then pulls the ends sharply apart. The glass tube is drawn out finer and finer, until the tube snaps apart. The result is two microelectrodes, as shown in *Figure 5.19.* (These devices are usually produced with the aid of a special machine, called a microelectrode puller.) Glass

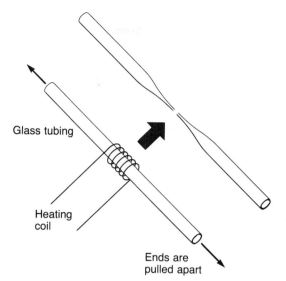

FIGURE 5.19

Micropipettes produced by heating the center portion of a length of glass capillary tubing and pulling the ends apart.

will not conduct electricity, so the microelectrode is filled with a conducting liquid, such as a solution of potassium chloride. Glass microelectrodes were used to provide the data concerning axonal conduction and synaptic transmission described in Chapters 2 and 3.

Macroelectrodes

Macroelectrodes, which record the activity of a very large number of neurons, are not nearly so difficult to make or to use. They can be constructed from a variety of materials: Stainless steel or platinum wires, insulated except for the tip, can be inserted into the brain or placed on top of it. Small balls of metal can be placed on the surface of the brain. Wires can be attached to screws that are driven into holes in the skull. Flat disks of silver or gold can be attached to the scalp with an electrically conductive paste. (The last type of electrode is used for recordings of the electroencephalographic activity from the human head, discussed in a subsequent section of this chapter.)

Macroelectrodes do not detect the activity of individual neurons; rather, the records obtained with these devices represent the postsynaptic potentials of many thousands—or millions—of cells in the area of the electrode. Recordings taken from the scalp, especially, represent the electrical activity of an enormous number of neurons.

Output Devices

After being amplified, electrical signals from the nervous system must be displayed so that we can see them and measure them. Obviously, we cannot directly observe the electrical activity from an amplifier; just as a sound system is useless without speakers or headphones, so a biological amplifier is useless without an output device.

Oscilloscope

In Chapter 2, I described the basic principle of an *oscilloscope*, which plots electrical potentials as a function of time. Figure 5.20 shows the display unit of an oscilloscope, the cathode ray tube. This device contains an electron gun, which emits a focused stream of electrons toward the face of the tube. A special surface on the inside of the glass converts some of the energy of the electrons into a visible spot of light. Electrons are negatively charged and are thus attracted to positively charged objects and repelled by negatively charged ones. The plates arranged above and be-

low the electron beam, and on each side, can be electrically charged, thus deflecting the beam and directing it to various places on the face of the tube. The dot can thus be moved independently by the horizontal and vertical deflection plates. (See *Figure 5.20*.)

The deflection plates that move the beam horizontally are usually attached to a timing circuit that sweeps the beam from left to right at a constant speed. Simultaneously, the output of the biological amplifier moves the beam up and down. We thus obtain a graph of electrical activity as a function of time.

To illustrate the use of an oscilloscope for the recording of single-unit activity, consider the procedure shown in Figure 5.21. A light is flashed in front of the cat, and at the same time, the dot on the oscilloscope is started across the screen, moving from left to right. Thus, the vertical axis represents the electrical signal from a neuron and the horizontal axis represents time. Suppose we record from a cell in the visual cortex that responds to a light flash by giving a burst of action potentials. If we move the beam slowly, we will see the record of this event on the face of the oscilloscope as vertical lines superimposed on a horizontal one. If we move the beam rapidly, we will see the shapes of the individual action potentials. (See *Figure 5.21*.)

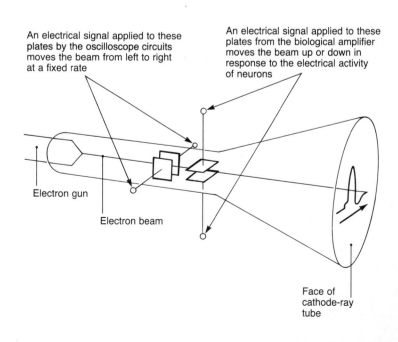

FIGURE 5.20
A simplified drawing of the cathode ray tube from an oscilloscope.

An electrical signal applied to these plates by the oscilloscope circuits moves the beam from left to right at a fixed rate

An electrical signal applied to these plates from the biological amplifier moves the beam up or down in response to the electrical activity of neurons

Electron gun

Electron beam

Face of cathode-ray tube

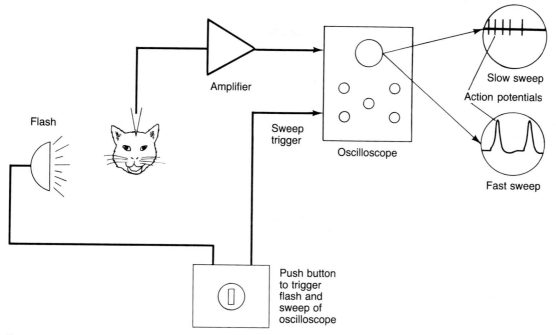

FIGURE 5.21
The means by which the responses of single units to a flash of light can be recorded.

You might wonder how the illustrated display can be seen; after all, the display consists of a moving dot, and I have shown a continuous line. The explanation is that most oscilloscope screens exhibit *persistence;* as the dot moves, it leaves a trace of its pathway behind, which slowly fades away.

When recording single-unit activity, the investigator usually also attachs the output of the amplifier to a loudspeaker. When an investigator lowers a microelectrode through the brain, he or she must stop before the optimal recording point, to allow the brain tissue, which has been pushed down by the progress of the electrode, to spring back up. If the electrode goes down too far, the cell will probably be injured or killed by the electrode when the tissue moves up. Therefore, the investigator must detect the firing of a cell as soon as possible, so that he or she can stop moving the electrode before damage is done. Our ears are much more efficient than our eyes in extracting the faint signal of a firing neuron from the random background noise. We can hear the ticking, snapping sound of single-unit activity from the loudspeaker long before we can see the action potentials on the face of the oscilloscope. Our auditory system does an excellent job of extracting signal from noise.

Oscilloscopes are also ideal for the display of evoked potentials. *Evoked potentials* are electrical changes in the brain that are *evoked* by a stimulus, such as a sound or a flash of light. They are recordings made through macroelectrodes and should not be confused with *action* potentials, which occur in single axons. When a stimulus is presented to an organism, a series of electrical events is initiated at the receptor organ. This activity is conducted into the brain, where it propagates through sensory pathways. If a macroelectrode is placed in or near one of these pathways, it will detect the electrical activity evoked by the stimulus. For example, we might place a scalp electrode on the back of a person's head and present a flash of light, while simultaneously triggering the sweep of an oscilloscope. Figure 5.22 shows such an experiment, along with the evoked potential from the visual cortex, recorded through the skull and scalp. (See *Figure 5.22.*)

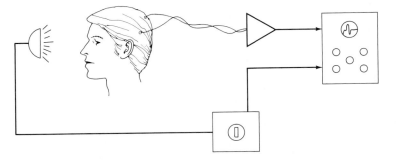

FIGURE 5.22

The means by which electrical potentials in the brain, evoked by a flash of light, can be recorded from the human scalp.

Ink-Writing Oscillograph

Oscilloscopes are most useful in the display of phasic activity, such as an evoked potential, that occurs during a relatively brief period of time. If neural activity is continuously recorded and displayed on an oscilloscope screen, it will be seen as a series of successive sweeps of the beam, presenting a rather confusing picture. A much better device for such a purpose is the ink-writing oscillograph (often called a *polygraph*).

The time base of the polygraph is provided by a mechanism that moves a very long strip of paper past a series of pens. Essentially, the pens are the pointers of large voltmeters, moving up and down in response to the electrical signal sent to them by the biological amplifiers. Figure 5.23 illustrates a record of electrical activity recorded from macroelectrodes attached to various loca-

tions on a person's scalp. (See *Figure 5.23.*) Such records are called *electroencephalograms* (EEGs), or "writings of electricity from the head." They can be used to diagnose epilepsy or brain tumors, or to study the stages of sleep and wakefulness, which are associated with characteristic patterns of electrical activity. I should note that many modern polygraphs do not use ink; they print electrostatically or with heated pens on specially treated paper, or they are collected by a computer and displayed on a video screen. Nevertheless, their principle of operation is the same.

Figure 5.24 shows the EEG recorded from the hippocampus of a rat during sleep and during the performance of various behaviors while awake. You will see that the pattern of activity changes drastically during different behaviors. (See *Figure 5.24.*)

FIGURE 5.23

A record from an ink-writing oscillograph.

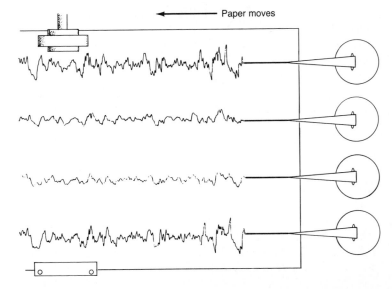

Paper moves

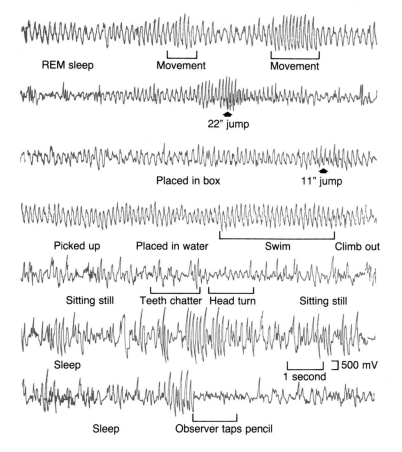

FIGURE 5.24

EEG activity from the rat hippocampus, recorded during various behaviors. (From Whishaw, I.Q., and Vanderwolf, C.H. *Behavioral Biology,* 1973, *8,* 461–484.)

Computers

Electrophysiological data are often stored in computers, which can also be used to display the data. A computer can convert the analog signal (one that can continuously vary, like the EEG) received from the biological amplifier into a series of numbers (digital values). Figure 5.25 illustrates how an evoked potential can be represented by a series of digital values. Each point represents the voltage of the analog signal at successive millisecond intervals. The values were obtained from a rat's brain through screws attached to the skull, were stored in a computer, and were then displayed on the screen of an oscilloscope. (See *Figure 5.25.*)

A computer can do more than display the data; it can perform many kinds of analyses as well. For example, it can compute the delay between the presentation of a stimulus and the occurrence of an evoked potential, or it can count the number of action potentials that a stimulus produces in a single unit.

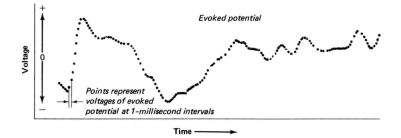

FIGURE 5.25

An evoked potential as represented by a display of points digitized by and stored in a computer.

STIMULATION OF THE BRAIN

Neural activity can be elicited by electrical or chemical stimulation of the brain. In Chapter 2 I described the way action potentials could be produced by delivering electrical pulses to an axon. Various neural structures can also be stimulated through electrodes or metal cannulas inserted into the brain.

Electrical and Chemical Stimulation

Electrical stimulation simply involves passing an electrical current through a wire inserted into the brain, as you saw in Figure 5.18. Chemical stimulation is usually accomplished by injecting a small amount of an excitatory amino acid such as kainic acid or glutamic acid into the brain. As you learned in Chapter 3, the principal excitatory transmitter substance in the brain is glutamic acid, and both of these substances stimulate glutamate receptors, thus activating the neurons on which these receptors are located.

Injections of chemicals into the brain can be done chronically, so that the animal's behavior can be observed several times. A metal cannula (a guide cannula) is placed in an animal's brain and its top is cemented to the skull. At a later date a smaller cannula of measured length is placed inside the guide cannula, and a chemical is injected into the brain while the animal moves about freely. (See *Figure 5.26.*)

The principal disadvantage of chemical stimulation is that it is more complicated than electrical stimulation; it requires cannulas, tubes, special pumps or syringes, and sterile solutions of excitatory amino acids. However, chemical stimulation has a distinct advantage over electrical stimulation: It activates cell bodies but not axons. Because only cell bodies (and their dendrites, of course) contain glutamate receptors, we can be assured that an injection of an excitatory amino acid into a particular region of the brain excites the cells there but not the axons that happen to pass through the region. Thus, the effects of chemical stimulation are more localized than the effects of electrical stimulation.

You may have noticed that I just said that kainic acid, which I described earlier as a neurotoxin, can be used to stimulate neurons. These two uses are not really contradictory. In fact, kainic acid kills neurons by stimulating them to death, through a phenomenon called *excitotoxicity.* Thus, large doses of a concentrated solution kill neurons, whereas small doses of a dilute solution simply stimulate them.

Identification of Neural Connections

Electrical stimulation can be used to find whether neurons in two parts of the brain are connected; thus, it can be used to answer neuroanatomical questions. If stimulation delivered through an electrode in structure A changes the electrical activity of neurons in structure B, then the structures must be connected. Both excitatory and inhibitory connections can be detected; the former will increase the rate of neural firing and the latter will decrease it.

Electrical Stimulation During Neurosurgery

One of the more interesting uses of electrical stimulation of the brain was developed by the late Wilder Penfield (see Penfield and Jasper, 1954) to treat focal-seizure disorders. These problems are produced by localized regions of neural tissue that periodically irritate the surrounding areas, triggering epileptic seizures (wild, sustained firing of cerebral neurons, resulting in some behavioral disruption). If severe cases of focal epilepsy do not respond to medication, surgical excision of the focus may be necessary. The focus is identified by means of EEG recordings before surgery and is confirmed by EEG recordings during surgery, after the brain is exposed. (As we saw in an earlier section, it can also be identified by special imaging techniques.)

Patients undergoing open-head surgery first have their heads shaved. Then a local anesthetic is administered to the scalp along the line that will be followed by the incision. A general anesthetic is not used, because the method requires that the patient be awake and conscious during surgery. The surgeon cuts the scalp and saws through the skull under the cut so that a piece of skull can then be removed. Next, the surgeon cuts and folds back the dura mater, exposing the brain itself.

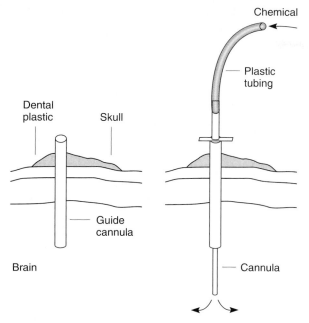

FIGURE 5.26

An intracranial cannula. A guide cannula is permanently attached to the skull, and at a later time a thinner cannula can be inserted through the guide cannula into the brain. Chemicals can be infused into the brain through this device.

When removing an epileptic focus, the surgeon wants to cut away all the abnormal tissue, while sparing neural tissue that performs important functions, such as the comprehension and production of speech. For this reason, Penfield first stimulated parts of the brain to determine which regions he could safely remove, before removing the seizure focus. Penfield touched the tip of a metal electrode to various parts of the brain and observed the effects of stimulation on the patient's behavior. For example, stimulation of the primary motor cortex produced movement, and stimulation of the primary auditory cortex elicited reports of the presence of buzzing noises. Stimulation of portions of the temporal lobe and frontal lobe stopped the patient's ongoing speech and disrupted the ability to understand what the surgeon and his associates were saying.

After the surgeon removes the region of the brain that contains the seizure focus, the dura mater is sewn back together and the piece of skull is replaced.

Besides giving patients relief from their epileptic attacks, the procedure provided Penfield with interesting data. As he stimulated various parts of the brain, he noted the effect and placed a sterile piece of paper, on which a number was written, on the point stimulated. When various points had been stimulated, Penfield photographed the exposed brain with its numbered locations before removing the slips of paper and proceeding with the surgery. After the operation, he could then compare the recorded notes with the photograph of the patient's brain, showing the location of the points of stimulation. (See *Figure 5.27*.)

The Use of Brain Stimulation in Behavioral Studies

Stimulation of the brain of an unanesthetized, freely moving animal often produces behavioral changes. For example, hypothalamic stimulation can elicit behaviors such as feeding, drinking,

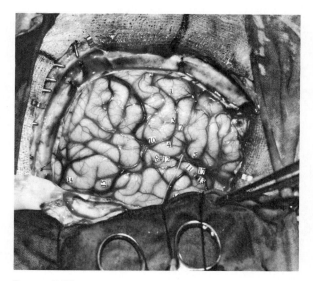

FIGURE 5.27

The appearance of the cortical surface of a conscious patient whose brain has been stimulated. The points of stimulation are indicated by the numbered tags placed there by the surgeon. (From Case M.M., in Wilder Penfield, *The Mystery of the Mind: A Critical Study of Consciousness and the Human Brain*, with Discussions by William Feindel, Charles Hendel, and Charles Symonds. Copyright © 1975 by Princeton University Press. Figure 4, p. 24 reprinted with permission of Princeton University Press.)

grooming, attack, or escape, which suggests that the hypothalamus is involved in their control. Stimulation of the caudate nucleus often halts on-going behavior, which suggests that this structure is involved in motor inhibition. Brain stimulation can serve as a signal for a learned task or can even serve as a rewarding or punishing event, as we will see in Chapter 16.

There are problems in interpreting the significance of the effects of brain stimulation, especially when it is produced with electricity. An electrical stimulus (usually a series of pulses) can never duplicate the natural neural processes that go on in the brain. The normal interplay of spatial and temporal patterns of excitation and inhibition is destroyed by the artificial stimulation of an area. Electrical brain stimulation is probably as natural as attaching ropes to the arms of the members of an orchestra and then shaking all the ropes simultaneously to see what they can play. In fact, local stimulation is sometimes used to produce a "temporary lesion," by which the region is put out of commission by the meaningless artificial stimulation. The surprising finding is that stimulation so often *does* produce orderly changes in behavior.

CHEMICAL TECHNIQUES

A growing number of investigations into the physiological bases of behavior use various chemical techniques. The importance of these techniques will be made obvious to you as you read the rest of this book. In this section I will only mention some of the basic procedures.

Microiontophoresis

The principal method for identifying receptors that respond to particular transmitter substances involves electrical recording along with a chemical technique called *microiontophoresis*.

When postsynaptic receptors are exposed to the appropriate transmitter substance, they change the permeability of the membrane to various ions, resulting in excitatory or inhibitory postsynaptic potentials. These potentials increase or decrease the cell's firing rate. To determine which transmitter substances a particular neuron responds to, an investigator uses a ***multi-***

barreled micropipette. This device consists of two or more glass microelectrodes (also called *micropipettes*), bundled together so that their tips are close to one another.

Figure 5.28 illustrates a seven-barreled micropipette glued to a recording microelectrode. Each of the seven micropipettes can be filled with transmitter substances, neuromodulators, hormones, or drugs. The pH (acid-base balance) of the solutions in the micropipettes is adjusted so that the chemicals ionize. Then when an electrical current is passed through one of the micropipettes, some molecules of the substance will be discharged. The injection of extremely small quantities of a chemical in this way is called ***microiontophoresis*** (*iontophoresis* means "ion carrying," from *pherein*, "to bear or carry"). (See ***Figure 5.28.***)

The recording microelectrode detects the neural activity of the cell that is being exposed to

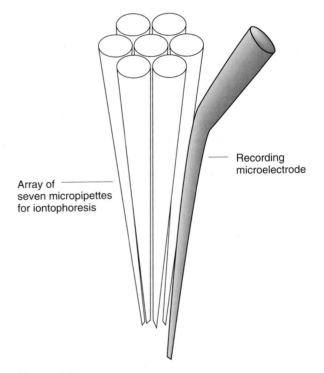

Array of seven micropipettes for iontophoresis

Recording microelectrode

FIGURE 5.28

Microiontophoresis. Molecules of different chemicals are carried out of the seven micropipettes by an electrical current. The recording microelectrode records the activity of the neuron and determines whether it responds to the chemical.

one of the chemicals placed in the micropipettes—for example, a particular hormone. If the neuron changes its firing rate when some of the hormone is ejected from the micropipette, we can conclude that the neuron contains receptors for the hormone.

Chemical Analysis of Local Brain Regions

Sometimes, an investigator wants to know how much of a particular compound is present in a particular region of the brain. For example, the investigator might suspect that a particular drug increases the release of a particular transmitter substance in that region. One way to determine whether the drug has that effect is to administer the drug to an animal and soon afterward kill it, remove the brain, cut out a small piece of brain containing the region of interest, and analyze this piece chemically. In fact, many studies have followed this procedure.

Several methods now enable investigators to perform an ongoing analysis of the substances present in the extracellular fluid that surrounds the cells of the brain. In recent years many laboratories have adopted one of them, called **microdialysis.** *Dialysis* is a process in which substances are separated by means of an artificial membrane that is permeable to some molecules but not others. A microdialysis probe consists of a small metal tube that introduces a solution into a section of dialysis tubing—a piece of artificial membrane shaped in the form of a cylinder. Another small metal tube leads the solution away after it has circulated through the pouch. A drawing of such a probe is shown in *Figure 5.29.*

The tip of the probe is placed in the animal's brain in the location of interest. A small amount of a solution similar to cerebrospinal fluid is pumped through one of the small metal tubes into the dialysis tubing. The fluid circulates through the dialysis tubing and passes through the second metal tube, where it is collected in a miniature vial attached to a holder mounted on the animal's head. As the fluid passes through the dialysis tubing, it collects molecules from the extracellular fluid of the brain, which are pushed across the membrane by the force of diffusion. Every few minutes, the

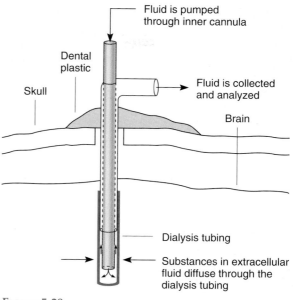

FIGURE 5.29

Microdialysis. Artificial cerebrospinal fluid is slowly infused into the microdialysis tube, where it picks up molecules that diffuse in from the extracellular fluid. The fluid is then collected in a small vial attached to the animal's head.

vial is removed so that its contents can be analyzed, and a clean vial is put in its place.

The solution that has passed through the dialysis tubing is analyzed by an extremely sensitive analytical method called *high-precision liquid chromatography* (HPLC). The method is so sensitive that it can detect transmitter substances (and their breakdown products) that have been released by the terminal buttons and have escaped from the synaptic cleft into the rest of the extracellular fluid. (Remember that most of the transmitter substance that is released is taken back into the terminal buttons.) As we shall see in Chapter 16, experiments using microdialysis have shown that many addictive drugs, including cocaine, alcohol, and nicotine, cause the release of dopamine in a particular region of the brain.

Immunological Techniques

The body's immune system has the ability to produce antibodies in response to antigens. *Antigens* are proteins (or peptides), such as those found on the surface of viruses. *Antibodies,* which are also proteins, are produced by white blood cells to destroy invading microorganisms. Antibodies are located on the surface of white blood cells, in the way neurotransmitter receptors are located on the surface of neurons. When the antigens present on the surface of a virus come into contact with the antibodies that recognize them, the antibodies trigger an attack on the virus by the white blood cells.

Special techniques developed by cell biologists permit them to produce antibodies to a wide variety of molecules. For example, they can produce antibodies to peptide hormones or to enzymes used in the synthesis of particular transmitter substances, such as choline acetyltransferase, the enzyme that produces acetylcholine. These antibody molecules can be attached to molecules of special dyes that emit light when they are exposed to ultraviolet light. To determine where the substance is located in the brain, the investigator places fresh slices of brain tissue in a solution that contains the antibody/dye molecules. The antibodies attach themselves to their antigen—the peptide or the enzyme. When the investigator examines the slices with a microscope under ultraviolet light, he or she can see which parts of the brain—even which individual neurons—contain the antigen. (See *Color Plate 5.6.*)

The technique I just described is an ***immunohistochemical procedure.*** (*Immuno-* refers to the antigen-antibody interaction of the immune system, and *histo-* refers to tissue.) As investigators develop ways to produce antibodies to more and more substances, including peptide neurotransmitters, neuromodulators, and hormones, immunohistochemical techniques are becoming increasingly important in neuroscience research.

Behavioral Effects of Drugs

Chapter 3 described various chemicals that mimic a particular transmitter substance, that inhibit or facilitate its production, or that prevent its destruction or re-uptake. Investigators often use these substances to determine the behavioral consequences of stimulating or inhibiting the effects of a particular neurotransmitter. For example, parachlorophenylalanine (PCPA) prevents the synthesis of serotonin and produces insomnia (at least temporarily), which suggests the involvement of this transmitter substance in sleep. As we saw earlier in this chapter, drugs can be injected directly into localized regions of the brain, which will affect only certain populations of neurons.

Radioactive Tracers

Radioactive tracers are radioactive chemicals that become incorporated into chemical processes within cells. They provide the investigator with a labeled substance whose location can be followed by various means. We saw one of the most important uses of radioactive tracers in amino acid autoradiography, which uses anterograde axoplasmic flow to trace the pathways followed by axons of neurons that reside in some particular region of the brain. I will describe some basic techniques here, with particular procedures to follow in later chapters.

Determining the Rate of Chemical Reactions

Radioactive chemicals can be used to determine the rate of incorporation of a given substance in various chemical reactions. For example, if we want to determine the relative rates of protein synthesis in various neural structures, we could inject an animal with a measured amount of radioactive amino acids, the building blocks of proteins. After waiting for a few days, we would kill the animal, dissect the brain, and extract the protein. The amount of radioactivity in the protein extracted from a particular portion of brain tissue would tell us how much of that protein had been constructed since the radioactive amino acid had been administered. "Old" protein would not be radioactive; only "new" protein would be radioactive. The amount of radioactivity in a given amount of protein would tell us how much of that protein was "new."

Special Autoradiographic Techniques

Many hormones and neuromodulators have behavioral effects. Presumably, these chemicals produce their behavioral effects by affecting the activity of groups of neurons in the brain. A special autoradiographic technique can be used to locate these neurons. Suppose we were interested in finding out which neurons are stimulated by estradiol, a female sex hormone. We could inject an animal with radioactive estradiol, wait awhile, then kill the animal, remove and slice the brain, place the sections on microscope slides, and prepare autoradiographs by coating the sections with a photographic emulsion. (The technique of autoradiography is described in the section on amino acid autoradiography.) If some neurons selectively take up the estradiol, they will have become radioactive, and these neurons will be covered by black spots in the developed photographic emulsion.

As we saw earlier in this chapter, the PET scanner uses radioactive 2-deoxyglucose (2-DG), in conjunction with a beam of radiation. Rat brains are too small to examine in a PET scanner, but a simpler technique, which incorporates 2-DG and autoradiography, can be used to assess the metabolism of various regions of even such a small brain. The experimenter injects radioactive 2-DG into the animal and permits the radioactive compound to be taken into cells. Because 2-DG resembles glucose, the most active cells take up the largest amounts. The experimenter then kills the animal, removes the brain, slices it, and prepares it for autoradiography. Those regions of the brain that were most active contain the most radioactivity; they show this radioactivity in the form of dark spots in the developed emulsion. Figure 5.30 shows an autoradiograph of a slice of a rat brain; the dark spots at the bottom (indicated by the arrow) are nuclei with an especially high metabolic rate. Chapter 9 describes these nuclei and their function. (See *Figure 5.30.*)

Receptor-Binding Studies

Radioactive tracers can be used to measure the relative number of receptors for a particular transmitter substance, neuromodulator, or hormone in a particular part of the brain. First, the investigator obtains a brain and removes the part of the brain in which he or she is interested. The tissue is then homogenized—broken up into very small

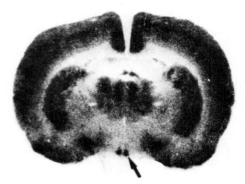

FIGURE 5.30

A 2-DG autoradiograph, showing especially high regions of activity in the pair of nuclei in the hypothalamus, at the base of the brain. (From Schwartz, W.J., and Gainer, H. *Science*, 1977, *197*, 1089–1091.)

pieces—and suspended in a thick, viscous liquid. Next, the liquid is placed in a centrifuge, where the various components of the tissue are separated according to their specific gravity. One layer of the liquid contains cell membranes, with their attached receptors. The contents of this layer are extracted and placed in a test tube for analysis.

A radioactive *ligand* is added to the test tube. A *ligand* (from *ligare,* "to bind") is a chemical that is capable of binding to a receptor. For example, acetylcholine is the natural ligand for nicotinic acetylcholine receptors, and nicotine is an artificial ligand. The radioactive ligand is allowed to bind with any receptors that are present in the test tube, and then the membrane fragments are washed so that the unattached molecules of the radioactive ligand are removed from the solution. Finally, the radioactivity of the membrane fragments is measured; the higher the radioactivity, the more receptors there must be.

Radioactive ligands can also be used to study the distribution of particular receptors in the brain. The radioactive ligand is administered to the animal, and after a short while, the brain is prepared for autoradiography. The regions that contain the receptor in question will show themselves on the autoradiogram. Figure 5.31 shows an autoradiogram of a horizontal section of a rat brain made after the animal was administered a radioactive ligand for opiate receptors. (See *Figure 5.31.*)

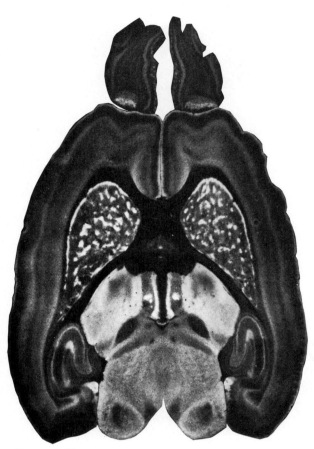

FIGURE 5.31
An autoradiogram of a rat brain (horizontal section, rostral is at top) that has been encubated in a solution containing a radioactive ligand for opiate receptors. The receptors are indicated by white areas. (From Herkenham, M.A., and Pert, C.B. *Journal of Neuroscience*, 1982, *2*, 1129–1149. Reprinted by permission of the *Journal of Neuroscience*.)

INTERIM SUMMARY

Brain lesions can be produced electrically, by passing direct current or radio frequency current through a metal electrode that is insulated except for the tip. Radio frequency lesions are better, because no metal ions are left in the brain. Brain lesions can also be produced chemically, by injecting an excitatory amino acid such as kainic acid or ibotenic acid, which stimulates neurons so much that they die. These lesions spare axons that happen to be passing through the region. Some neurotoxins will destroy only particular

kinds of neurons; for example, 6-HD kills catecholaminergic neurons. After brain lesions are made, both their location and extent must be verified through histological examination.

Electrical recordings can be made through macroelectrodes, which record the postsynaptic activity of a large number of neurons in a particular region, or through microelectrodes, which record postsynaptic potentials or action potentials of individual neurons. Oscilloscopes, ink-writing oscillographs, or computers are used to display the data. Of course, computers can analyze the data as well as display them.

The brain can be stimulated electrically, through a metal electrode, or chemically, by infusing a dilute solution of an excitatory amino acid that activates glutamate receptors. Connections between neurons in two regions of the brain can be identified by stimulating one region electrically and recording the activity in the other region. Even human brains can be stimulated during neurosurgery.

Microiontophoresis permits an investigator to infuse extremely small quantities of neurotransmitters, neuromodulators, hormones, or drugs in the vicinity of a neuron and record its response to the chemical. The secretions of cells in a particular region of the brain can be analyzed by dissecting that region postmortem or by placing a microdialysis probe in the brain and analyzing the substances that the fluid picks up from the brain. Immunological techniques permit the investigator to stain peptides and proteins, including enzymes involved in the synthesis or breakdown of compounds by neurons in the brain.

Radioactive tracers can be used to measure the rate of various chemical processes, such as the synthesis of particular proteins. Autoradiography can be used, along with the administration of radioactive 2-DG, to measure the regional metabolic rate in the brains of laboratory animals. The numbers and locations of particular receptors can be assessed by using a radioactive ligand for that type of receptor.

CONCLUDING REMARKS

In this chapter I referred to the strategy of converging operations. The results of any single research method are not definitive; each method has its limitations and ambiguities. Yet when several methods all yield the same conclusion—when their results *converge*—we can be much more confident that the conclusion is correct.

Let me give an example. Investigators have determined that the sexual behavior of female rats is stimulated by estradiol. Suppose we wanted to know about the location of the estradiol-sensitive neurons in the brain. I have already described the use of autoradiography to determine which neurons selectively take up this hormone. These neurons are located in several parts of the brain, but particularly in the ventromedial nucleus of the hypothalamus. Consider what other methods, described in this chapter, could be used to confirm these results. We might use stereotaxic surgery to destroy the ventromedial nucleus, predicting that the lesion would abolish the behavioral effects of estradiol on female sexual behavior. (We might want to destroy the nucleus with a neurotoxin such as kainic acid to be sure that the effects are not caused by destroying axons that pass through the region.) We might record the activity of these neurons while we infused estradiol into the region with a micropipette, expecting that their activity would change. We might administer a small amount of estradiol directly into the ventromedial nucleus with a small cannula, predicting that the hormone would stimulate sexual behavior. If these experiments produced consistent results, we might decide to investigate the connections of the neurons in the ventromedial hypothalamus with neurons elsewhere in the brain. To investigate, we would use amino acid autoradiography to see where their axons terminated and would then make lesions in *those* regions to see whether they affected sexual behavior. And so on.

As we will see in Chapter 10, these studies *have* been performed, and the results were as predicted. The rest of this book describes the efforts that have been made to understand the physiology of behavior. The quest involves many different methods, all devoted to a common goal. This chapter has introduced you to the most important methods used in neuroscience research, so you should have no trouble understanding the experiments described in later chapters of the book. I hope that you have also learned enough so that you will be able to understand the rationale behind most experimental procedures you might read about in scientific journals or other books.

NEW TERMS

amino acid
    autoradiography p. 111
bregma p. 118
computerized tomography
    (CT) p. 113
converging operations p. 107
2-deoxyglucose (2-DG) p. 115
electroencephalogram p. 128
evoked potential p. 127
fixative p. 107
formalin p. 107
Golgi-Cox stain p. 110

horseradish peroxidase p. 112
6-hydroxydopamine p. 124
immunohistochemical
    procedure p. 134
ligand p. 135
macroelectrode p. 125
magnetic resonance
    imaging (MRI) p. 115
membrane stain p. 110
microdialysis p. 133
microelectrode p. 125
microiontophoresis p. 132

microtome p. 108
multibarreled micro-pipette p. 132
myelin stain p. 110
Nissl substance p. 109
oscilloscope p. 126
perfusion p. 107
positron emission tomography
    (PET) p. 115
scanning electron microscope p. 117
single-unit recording p. 125
stereotaxic apparatus p. 120
stereotaxic atlas p. 119

SUGGESTED READINGS

Laboratory Manuals

Skinner, J.E. *Neuroscience: A Laboratory Manual.* Philadelphia: Saunders, 1971.

Webster, W.G. *Principles of Research Methodology in Physiological Psychology.* New York: Harper & Row, 1975.

Wellman, P. *Laboratory Exercises in Physiological Psychology.* Boston: Allyn and Bacon, 1986.

Stereotaxic Atlases

Koenig, J.F.R., and Klippel, R.A. *The Rat Brain: A Stereotaxic Atlas of the Forebrain and Lower Parts of the Brain Stem.* Baltimore: Williams & Wilkins, 1963.

Paxinos, G., and Watson, C. *The Rat Brain in Stereotaxic Coordinates.* Sydney: Academic Press, 1982

Slotnick, B.M., and Leonard, C.M. *A Stereotaxic Atlas of the Albino Mouse Forebrain.* Rockville, Md.: Public Health Service, 1975. (U.S. Government Printing Office Stock Number 017–024–00491–0.)

Snider, R.S., and Niemer, W.T. *A Stereotaxic Atlas of the Cat Brain.* Chicago: University of Chicago Press, 1961.

6

Vision

*A*s we saw in Chapter 4, the brain performs two major functions: It controls the movements of the muscles, producing useful behaviors, and it regulates the body's internal environment. In order to perform both these tasks, the brain must be informed about what is happening both in the external environment and within the body. Such information is received by the sensory systems. This chapter and the next are devoted to a discussion of the ways in which sensory organs detect changes in the environment and the ways in which the brain interprets neural signals from these organs.

People often say that we have five senses: sight, hearing, smell, taste, and touch. Actually, we have more than five, but even experts disagree about how the lines between the various categories should be drawn. Certainly, we should add the vestibular senses; as well as providing us with auditory information, the inner ear supplies information about head orientation and movement. The sense of touch (or, more accurately, *somatosensation*) detects changes in pressure, warmth, cold, vibration, limb position, and events that damage tissue (that is, produce pain). Everyone agrees that we can detect these stimuli; the issue is whether or not they are detected by separate senses.

This chapter considers vision, the sensory modality that receives the most attention from psychologists, anatomists, and physiologists. One reason for this attention derives from the fascinating complexity of the sensory organs of vision and the relatively large proportion of the brain that is devoted to the analysis of visual information. Another reason, I am sure, is that vision is so important to us as individuals. A natural fascination with such a rich source of information about the world leads to curiosity about how this sensory modality works. Chapter 7 deals with the other sensory modalities: audition, the somatosenses, the vestibular senses, gustation, and olfaction.

TRANSDUCTION AND SENSORY CODING

Before studying the particulars of vision, you should understand some general properties of sensory systems. This section considers the means by which neurons detect environmental changes and the ways in which these changes are encoded in the nervous system.

We receive information about the environment from sensory receptors, specialized neurons that detect a variety of physical events. Stimuli impinge on the receptors and, through various processes, alter their membrane potentials. This process is known as *sensory transduction* because sensory events are *transduced* ("transferred") into changes in the cells' membrane potential. These electrical changes are called *receptor potentials.* Most receptors lack axons; a portion of their somatic membrane forms synapses with the dendrites of other neurons. Receptor potentials affect the release of transmitter substances and hence modify the pattern of firing in neurons with which these cells form synapses. Ultimately, the information reaches the brain. (See *Figure 6.1, top.*) The exception to this scheme is provided by the receptors for the somatosenses (including the muscle and joint senses), which are sensitive to pressure, stretch, temperature, vibration, and stimuli that damage tissue. These receptors consist of unipolar neurons with specialized dendrites whose membrane potentials are depolarized by the stimuli they detect. The depolarizations increase the rate of firing of the cells' axons. The axons convey sensory information to the central nervous system. (See *Figure 6.1, bottom.*)

Each sensory modality (or submodality) possesses different types of receptors, which detect the presence of particular chemicals or different forms of energy; examples of the types of stimuli that are detected are presented in *Table 6.1.*

The transduction of sensory information into receptor potentials, and then into changes in neural firing, entails a form of code. The concept of *sensory coding* deserves some discussion. A code consists of a set of rules whereby information may be transformed from one set of symbols into another. For example, a verbal message can be encoded in the pattern of electrical charges in the memory of a digital computer. In the nervous system sensory information is coded by two basic means: spatial coding and temporal coding. *Spatial coding* is used by all sensory modalities,

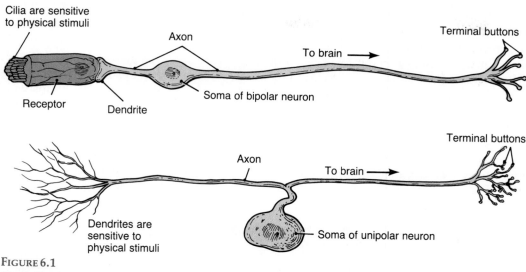

FIGURE 6.1

Bipolar (*top*) and unipolar (*bottom*) sensory neurons. Bipolar sensory neurons receive sensory information from receptors that lack axons; the dendrites of unipolar sensory neurons are themselves sensitive to physical stimuli.

TABLE 6.1

The types of transduction accomplished by the sense organs

Sense Organ	Nature of the Stimulus Transduced
Eye	Light (radiant energy)
Ear (cochlea)	Rapid, periodic changes in air pressure (mechanical energy)
Vestibular system	Tilt of head; rotation of head (mechanical energy)
Tongue (taste)	Recognition of molecular shape
Nose (odor)	Recognition of molecular shape (?)
Skin, internal organs	Touch: movement of skin (mechanical energy) Warmth and coolness: thermal energy Vibration: movement of skin (mechanical energy) Pain: damage to body tissue (chemical reaction)
Muscle	Stretch, changes in muscle length (mechanical energy)

with the possible exception of olfaction. The principle is quite simple: Different stimuli alter the activity of different neurons. For example, different receptors detect pressure applied to different parts of the body; thus, different sets of axons entering the spinal cord become active when a particular part of the skin is touched. The anatomical specificity is maintained up to the somatosensory cortex; neurons there receive information from receptors located in different parts of the skin. Similarly, photoreceptors in different parts of the retina are stimulated by light reflected from different parts of the scene and send information to neurons in different parts of the brain.

But we can perceive more than the presence of a stimulus and its location. As we saw in Chapter 2, intensity of stimulation is encoded by the rate of neural firing; the more intense the stimulus is, the faster the axon fires. This method of specifying information is called **temporal coding.** Possibly, the nervous system uses more complex temporal codes than simple rate; for example, it might use temporal *patterns* such as those used in Morse code. However, no experimental evidence indicates that such coding schemes exist.

A problem we encounter when we consider sensory coding is the identification of the ultimate destination of the information. Where does the message go? We must be careful not to seek a decoder that looks at the neural representation of sensory information and interprets the pattern. If we do so, we commit the error of looking for a *homunculus*, a ''little person'' who resides in our heads, looking at and interpreting the activity of cortical neurons, the way a person might look at a display panel of some piece of complex machinery. The problem with the homunculus approach is that we must go on to explain how the homunculus works, which reintroduces the origi-

nal problem. The best strategy is to keep in mind that the function of perception is the control of behavior. Some stimuli cause immediate responses; others cause neural changes (that is, produce memories) that may affect the organism's behavior at a later date. Whether immediate or delayed (or both), the pattern of neural activity produced by a particular stimulus causes a change in the patterns of activity of the motor systems controlling behavior. Finding out how all that works provides enough of a challenge without inserting a

FIGURE 6.2
The electromagnetic spectrum.

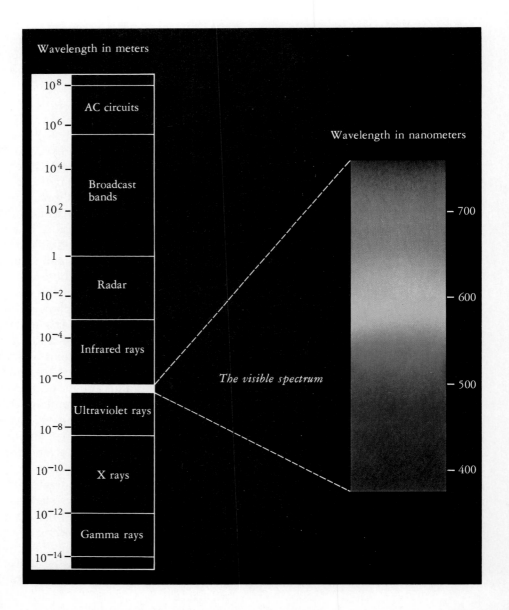

homunculus between perception and action.

With this introduction to the general characteristics of sensory processing accomplished, we will now turn to a specific channel—vision.

THE STIMULUS

As we all know, our eyes detect the presence of light. For humans, light is a narrow band of the electromagnetic spectrum. Electromagnetic radiation with a wavelength of between 380 and 760 nm (a nanometer, nm, is one billionth of a meter) is visible to us. (See *Figure 6.2.*) Other animals can detect different ranges of electromagnetic radiation. For example, a rattlesnake can detect its prey by means of infrared radiation; thus, it can locate warm-blooded animals in the dark. The range of wavelengths we call *light* is not qualitatively different from the rest of the electromagnetic spectrum; it is simply the part of the continuum that we humans can see.

Physicists have discovered that light has two properties. It acts as a continuous wave, with a particular frequency (and wavelength); and it also acts as if it were composed of small packages of energy, called *photons.* When physicists study optics, they find it best to think of light as a wave of radiant energy. When physicists study the interaction between light and molecules (that is, the study of the chemical basis of vision), they find it best to think of light as a stream of photons. Physicists have learned to live with this paradox, so I suppose the rest of us should, too.

First, let us consider light as a continuous wave of radiant energy. Light travels at a constant speed of approximately 300,000 km (186,000 miles) per second. Thus, if the frequency of oscillation of the wave varies, the distance between the peaks of the waves will similarly vary, but in inverse fashion. Slower oscillations lead to longer wavelengths, and faster ones to shorter wavelengths. Wavelength determines one of the perceptual dimensions of light: its *hue.* The visible spectrum displays the range of hues that our eyes can detect.

Light can also vary in intensity. If the intensity of the electromagnetic signal is increased, the stimulus appears to increase in *brightness,* the second of the perceptual dimensions of light. The third dimension, *saturation,* refers to the relative

purity of the light that is being perceived. If all the radiation is of one wavelength, the perceived color is pure, or fully saturated. Conversely, if the radiation contains all wavelengths, it produces no sensation of hue—it appears white. Colors with intermediate amounts of saturation consist of different mixtures. Figure 6.3 shows some color samples, all with the same hue but with different levels of brightness and saturation. (See *Figure 6.3.*)

When investigators study the transduction of visual stimuli, they refer to photons, or discrete particles of energy, that are absorbed by the photopigment in the rods and cones in the retina. (I will discuss these receptor cells shortly.) A more intense stimulus emits a greater number of photons than a less intense one in a given period of time, which means that the photopigment will absorb more photons. On the other hand, when investigators study color perception, they refer to the absorption of light of various wavelengths. Both approaches are correct, but obviously, they each reveal only part of the actual nature of light.

THE RECEPTIVE ORGAN

The Eyes

The eyes are suspended in the *orbits,* bony pockets in the front of the skull. They are moved by six extraocular muscles attached to the tough, fibrous outer coat of the eye, called the *sclera*. (See *Figure 6.4.*) Normally, we cannot look behind our eyeballs and see these muscles, because their attachments to the eyes are hidden by the *conjunctiva.* These mucous membranes line the eyelid and fold back to attach to the eye (thus preventing a contact lens that has slipped off the cornea from "falling behind the eye"). Figure 6.5 illustrates the external and internal anatomy of the eye. (See *Figure 6.5.*)

The outer layer of most of the eye, the sclera, is opaque and does not permit entry of light. However, the *cornea,* the outer layer at the front of the eye, is transparent and admits light. The amount of light that enters is regulated by the size of the *pupil,* which is formed by the opening in the iris. The *iris* consists of a ring of muscles situated behind the cornea. It contains two bands of muscles, the dilator (whose contraction enlarges the pupil)

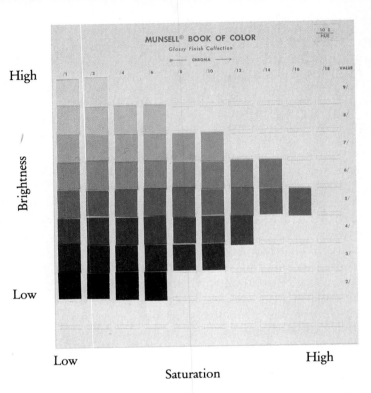

FIGURE 6.3

Examples of colors with the same dominant wavelength (hue), but different saturations and brightnesses. (Courtesy of Munsell Color Corporation.)

and the sphincter (whose contraction reduces it). The sphincter is innervated by acetylcholinergic fibers of the parasympathetic nervous system; acetylcholinergic blockers (for example, belladonna alkaloids such as atropine) thus dilate the pupil by relaxing the sphincter of the iris. As we saw in Chapter 3, belladonna received its name from this effect.

The *lens* is situated immediately behind the iris. It consists of a series of transparent, onionlike layers. Its shape can be altered by contraction of the *ciliary muscles.* Because of the tension of elastic fibers that suspend it, the lens is normally relatively flat. In its flat state the lens focuses the image of distant objects on the *retina,* the light-sensitive tissue layer that lines the inner portion of the eye. When the ciliary muscles contract, tension is taken off these fibers, and the lens springs back to its normally rounded shape. Therefore, movements of the ciliary muscles determine whether the lens focuses images of near or distant objects on the retina, a process called *accommodation.*

Accommodation is usually integrated with *convergence* ("turning together") of the eyes.

When we look at a near object, the eyes turn inward, so that the two images of the object fall on corresponding portions of the retinas. Convergence and accommodation normally occur together, so that the object on which the eyes are focused is also the object on which the eyes converge. If you hold a pencil in front of you and focus on a distant object, you will see two blurry pencils. If you then focus on the pencil, you will get two blurry views of the background. Control of eye movement is a very complicated process; as we study the process, we realize that it takes a sophisticated computer to accomplish what our brain does in moving the eyes.

After passing through the lens, light traverses the main part of the eye, which contains the vitreous humor. *Vitreous humor* ("glassy liquid") is a clear, gelatinous substance that gives the eye its bulk. After passing through the vitreous humor, light falls on the retina. In the retina are located the receptor cells, the *rods* and *cones* (named for their shapes), collectively known as *photoreceptors.* The human retina contains approximately 120 million rods and 6 million cones. Although they

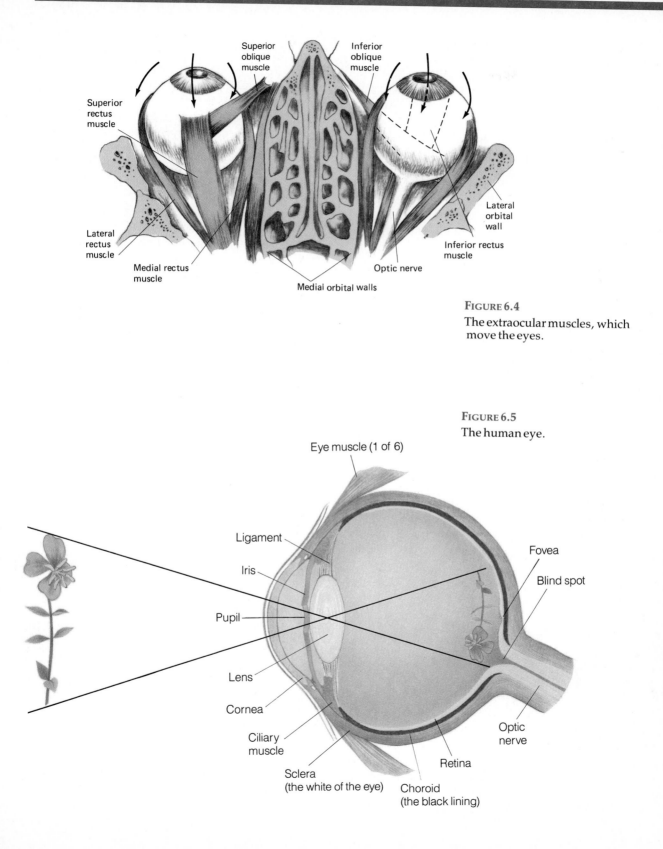

FIGURE 6.4
The extraocular muscles, which move the eyes.

FIGURE 6.5
The human eye.

are greatly outnumbered, cones provide us with most of the information about our environment. In particular, they are responsible for our daytime vision. They provide us with information about small features in the environment and thus are the source of vision of the highest sharpness, or *acuity* (from *acus*, meaning "needle"). The *fovea*, or central region of the retina, which mediates our most acute vision, contains only cones. Cones are also responsible for color vision—our ability to discriminate light of different wavelengths. Although rods do not detect different colors and provide vision of poor acuity, they are more sensitive to light. In a very dimly lighted environment we use our rod vision; therefore, in dim light we are color-blind and lack foveal vision. You have probably noticed, while out on a dark night, that looking directly at a dim, distant light (that is, placing the image of the light on the fovea) causes it to disappear.

Another feature of the retina is the *optic disk*, where the axons conveying visual information gather together and leave the eye through the optic nerve. The optic disk produces a *blind spot*, because no receptors are located there. We do not normally perceive our blind spots, but their presence can be demonstrated. If you have not found yours, you may want to try the exercise described in *Figure 6.6.*

Close examination of the retina shows that it consists of several layers of neuron cell bodies, their axons and dendrites, and the photoreceptors. Figure 6.16 illustrates a cross section through the primate retina. The drawing includes many different types of cells, which will be described in more detail later. Major types of cells are indicated by different colors, and within each type different subtypes are indicated by differences in shading. The first thing to note is that the retina is divided into three main layers: the photoreceptive layer, the bipolar cell layer, and the ganglion cell layer. Note that the photoreceptors are at the *back* of the retina; light must pass through the overlying layers to get to them. Fortunately, these layers are transparent. (Refer to *Figure 6.16.*)

The photoreceptors form synapses with *bipolar cells* (shades of red and pink). In turn, these neurons form synapses with the *ganglion cells* (shades of green), whose axons travel through the optic nerves to the brain. In addition, the *outer plexiform layer* of the retina contains *horizontal cells* (shades of blue), and the *inner plexiform layer* contains *amacrine cells* (shades of brown), both of which transmit information in a direction parallel to the surface of the retina and thus combine messages from adjacent photoreceptors. The functions of these connections will be described later in this chapter. (Refer to *Figure 6.16.*)

Photoreceptors

Figure 6.7 shows a drawing of a rod and a cone. Note that each photoreceptor consists of an outer segment connected by a cilium to the inner segment, which contains the nucleus. (See *Figure*

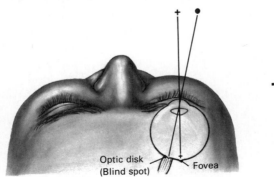

FIGURE 6.6
A test for the blind spot. With your left eye closed, look at the + with your right eye and move the page nearer and farther from you. When the page is about 20 cm from your face, the black circle disappears, because its image falls on the blind spot of your right eye.

6.7.) The outer segment contains several hundred **lamellae,** thin plates of membrane. (*Lamella* is the diminutive form of *lamina,* "thin layer.") Although the outer segments of both types of receptors are layered, there is a basic difference. Rods contain free-floating disks, whereas the lamellae of the cones consist of one continuous, folded membrane.

The first step in the process of transduction of light involves a special chemical called a **photopigment.** Photopigments consist of two parts, an **opsin** (a protein) and **retinal** (a lipid). There are several forms of opsin; for example, the photopigment of human rods, **rhodopsin,** consists of *rod opsin* plus retinal. (*Rhod-* actually refers to the Greek *rhodon,* "rose," and not to *rod.* Before it is bleached by the action of light, rhodopsin has a pinkish hue.) Molecules of photopigments are embedded in the membrane of the lamellae; a single human rod contains approximately 10 million rhodopsin molecules.

Retinal is synthesized from *retinol* (vitamin A), which explains why carrots, rich in retinol, are said to be good for your eyesight. Retinal is a molecule with a long chain that is capable of bending at a specific point. The straight-chained form of retinal is called *all-trans retinal;* the form with a bend is called *11-cis retinal.* The bent form, 11-*cis* retinal, is the only form of retinal capable of attaching to rod opsin to form rhodopsin. However, the 11-*cis* form of retinal is unstable; it can exist only in the dark. When a molecule of rhodopsin is exposed to light (that is, when it absorbs a photon), the bend in the retinal chain straightens out, and the retinal assumes the all-*trans* form. Because rod opsin cannot remain attached to all-*trans* retinal, the rhodopsin breaks into its two constituents. When it does so, it changes from its rosy color to a pale yellow; hence we say that the light *bleaches* the photopigment. (See *Figure 6.8.*)

The splitting of the photopigment causes a sudden decrease in the sodium permeability of the outer membrane of the photoreceptor, which hyperpolarizes the membrane. This change in the membrane potential constitutes the receptor potential. The system is exquisitely sensitive; the absorption of a single photon by a single molecule of photopigment can produce a detectable receptor potential.

Investigators have found that the bleaching of one rhodopsin molecule causes 50,000 molecules of cyclic GMP to disappear (Woodruff and Bownds, 1979). You will recall from Chapter 3 that cyclic nucleotides such as cyclic AMP and cyclic GMP serve as second messengers in many neurons, mediating the postsynaptic effects of transmitter substances. In the dark, molecules of cyclic GMP hold ion channels open in the membrane of the photoreceptor that permit sodium, magnesium, and calcium ions to enter (Yau and Baylor,

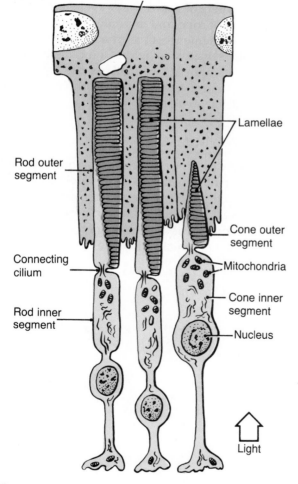

Fragment detached from rod outer segment during normal loss and regeneration of lamellae

Lamellae

Rod outer segment

Connecting cilium

Rod inner segment

Cone outer segment

Mitochondria

Cone inner segment

Nucleus

Light

FIGURE 6.7

Photoreceptors. (Redrawn from Young, R.W., Visual cells. Copyright 1970 by Scientific American, Inc. All rights reserved.)

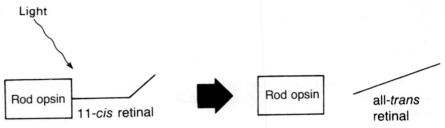

FIGURE 6.8

Bleaching of a photopigment. When light strikes rhodopsin, the 11-*cis* retinal straightens, becoming all-*trans* retinal, and detaches from the rod opsin. This event liberates energy, which initiates the steps that produce a receptor potential.

1989). Because of the constant inflow of cations, the membrane potential is normally around −40 mV rather than the more typical −70 mV. When a photon bleaches a photopigment molecule, a set of chemical reactions causes the activation of hundreds of molecules of phosphodiesterase, which, in turn, destroy thousands of molecules of cyclic GMP. With the number of molecules of cyclic GMP diminished, many of the ion channels close. The sodium conductivity of the membrane consequently falls, and it becomes hyperpolarized. Eventually, the phosphodiesterase itself disappears (or is deactivated), new cyclic GMP is synthesized, and the membrane potential returns to normal. (See *Figure 6.9.*)

In humans and most old-world primates, photoreceptors contain four different opsins (rod opsin and three kinds of cone opsins), which bind with retinal to produce four different photopigments. Each of these compounds most readily absorbs light of a particular wavelength. A particular type of cone contains only one of the three cone photopigments; thus, the three cones are maximally sensitive to light of long, medium, or short wavelength. As we shall see, the visual system uses information from these three types of cones to achieve color vision.

*I*NTERIM SUMMARY

Freely moving animals such as ourselves require information about the environment in order to survive. Energy or molecules of particular chemicals cause receptor potentials in the neurons in our sensory organs. The receptor potentials alter the rate of firing of

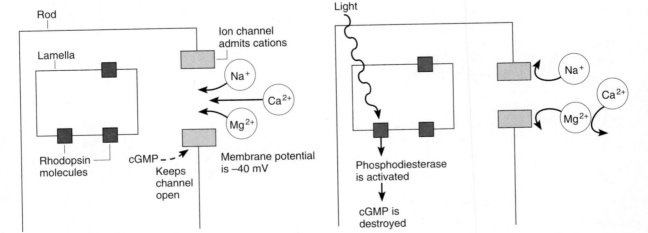

FIGURE 6.9

Transduction. A hypothetical explanation for the production of receptor potentials in photoreceptors.

axons that communicate sensory information to the brain. The nervous system employs two basic schemes of sensory coding: spatial coding and temporal coding.

The photoreceptors in the eyes are the rods and cones. The extraocular muscles move the eyes so that images of the environment fall on corresponding parts of each retina. Accommodation is accomplished by the ciliary muscles, which change the shape of the lens. Photoreceptors communicate synaptically with bipolar cells, which communicate synaptically with ganglion cells. In addition, horizontal cells (located in the outer plexiform layer) and amacrine cells (located in the inner plexiform layer) combine messages from adjacent photoreceptors.

When light strikes a molecule of photopigment in a photoreceptor, the 11-*cis* retinal molecule straightens out, becoming all-*trans* retinal, which detaches from the opsin molecule. This detachment initiates a series of chemical reactions that result in the destruction of cyclic GMP, closing ion channels that are normally in the open state. The decreased influx of cations produces the receptor potential—hyperpolarization of the photoreceptor membrane.

CONNECTIONS BETWEEN EYE AND BRAIN

The best word to describe the first level of analysis of the retinal image would be *mosaic*. Literally, a *mosaic* is a picture consisting of a large number of discrete elements—for example, bits of glass or ceramic. The cornea and lens of the eye cast an image of the environment on the retinal photoreceptors, each of which responds to the intensity of the light that falls on it. The connection of photoreceptors to ganglion cells (whose axons transmit visual information over the optic nerves) does not occur on a one-to-one basis. At the periphery of the retina many individual receptors converge on a single ganglion cell. Foveal vision is more direct, with approximately equal numbers of ganglion cells and cones. These receptor-to-axon relationships accord very well with the fact that our foveal (central) vision is most acute, but our peripheral

vision is much less precise. In a sense, the pieces constituting the mosaic get larger as one goes from fovea to periphery, and the image transmitted to the brain becomes correspondingly cruder. (See *Figure 6.10*.)

The retina also contains neural circuitry that encodes the visual information in a more complex way. However, before we examine the nature of this level of coding, we should become acquainted with the anatomy of the ascending visual system.

The axons of the retinal ganglion cells ascend to the brain through the optic nerves and eventually reach the *dorsal lateral geniculate nucleus* of the thalamus. The terminal buttons of these axons form synapses with cells in this nucleus, which in

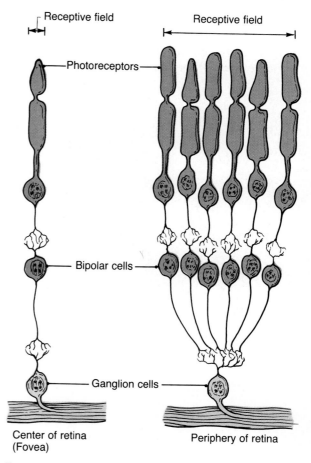

FIGURE 6.10

Central versus peripheral acuity. Ganglion cells in the fovea receive input from a smaller number of photoreceptors than those in the periphery and hence provide more acute visual information.

turn send their axons via the *optic radiations* to the primary visual cortex—the region surrounding the *calcarine fissure* (*calcarine* means "spur-shaped") in the medial and posterior occipital lobe. The primary visual cortex is often called the *striate cortex* because it contains a dark-staining layer *(striation)* of cells. (See *Figure 6.11.*)

Figure 6.12 shows a diagrammatical view of the human brain as observed from below. The optic nerves join together at the base of the brain to form the *optic chiasm* (*khiasma* means "cross"). There, axons from ganglion cells serving the inner halves of the retina (the nasal sides) cross through the chiasm and ascend to the dorsal lateral geniculate nucleus of the opposite side of the brain. (See *Figure 6.12.*) The lens inverts the image of the world projected on the retina (and similarly reverses left and right). Therefore, because the axons from the nasal halves of the retinas cross to the other side of the brain, each hemisphere receives information from the contralateral half (opposite side) of the visual scene. That is, if a person looks straight ahead, the right hemisphere receives information from the left half of the visual field, and the left hemisphere receives information from the right. (See *Figure 6.12.*)

Each dorsal lateral geniculate nucleus then projects to the ipsilateral (same-side) visual cortex; as a matter of fact, the lateral geniculate nuclei provide the only subcortical input to the primary visual cortex of primates. Because there is a considerable amount of overlap in the visual fields of the two eyes, many cortical regions receive information about the same point in the visual field from both eyes.

Figure 6.13 shows the actual appearance of the base of the brain, with neural tissue dissected away so that the optic radiations can be seen. Note the heavy projection to the upper lip of the calcarine fissure. (See *Figure 6.13.*)

Ignoring for a moment the complexities of coding that take place in the retina, we find that the visual system maintains the spatial code seen on the retinal mosaic all the way up to the visual cortex. There is a *retinotopic representation* on the cortex (*topos* means "place" in Greek). That is, stimulation of a particular region of the retina excites neurons in a particular region of the primary visual cortex, and adjacent retinal regions excite adjacent cortical areas. If a small portion of the striate cortex is damaged, the result will be a small blind spot *(scotoma)* in the visual field; the location of the blind spot depends on the location of the lesion. In addition, if a two-dimensional array of electrodes is placed over the human visual cortex, the person will report "seeing" geometrical shapes that correspond to the pattern of electrodes that are stimulated (Dobelle, Mladejovsky, and Girvin, 1974). This study was carried out on blind people to see whether it would be possible to provide visual prostheses. (A *prosthesis*, literally an "addition," is an artificial device made to take the place of a missing or damaged part of the body.) Unfortunately, long-term electrical stimulation causes tissue damage, thus ruling out the use of such synthetic replacement parts in the immediate future, so some other way will have to be found to stimulate cortical neurons.

The retinal surface is not represented on the vi-

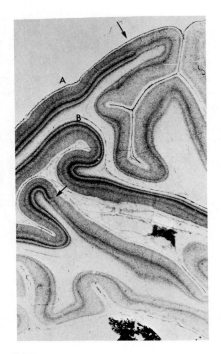

FIGURE 6.11

A photomicrograph of a cross section through the striate cortex of a rhesus macaque monkey. The ends of the striate cortex are shown by arrows. (From Hubel, D.H., and Wiesel, T.N. *Proceedings of the Royal Society of London, B.*, 1977, *198*, 1–59.)

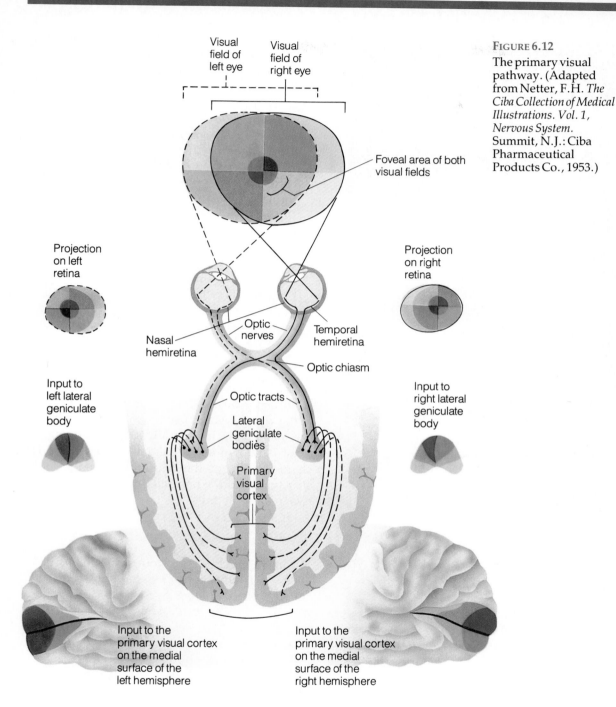

Visual field of left eye

Visual field of right eye

Foveal area of both visual fields

FIGURE 6.12
The primary visual pathway. (Adapted from Netter, F.H. *The Ciba Collection of Medical Illustrations. Vol. 1, Nervous System.* Summit, N.J.: Ciba Pharmaceutical Products Co., 1953.)

Projection on left retina

Projection on right retina

Nasal hemiretina

Optic nerves

Temporal hemiretina

Optic chiasm

Input to left lateral geniculate body

Optic tracts

Lateral geniculate bodies

Primary visual cortex

Input to right lateral geniculate body

Input to the primary visual cortex on the medial surface of the left hemisphere

Input to the primary visual cortex on the medial surface of the right hemisphere

sual cortex in a linear fashion, though; the picture is much distorted. It is as if a picture were printed on a sheet of rubber that was then stretched in various directions. The center of the sheet is stretched the most; foveal vision, with its great acuity, takes up approximately 25 percent of the

visual cortex. (The area of the visual field that is detected by the fovea is approximately the size of a large grape held at arm's length.)

Besides the primary retino-geniculo-striate pathway, there are five other pathways taken by fibers from the retina:

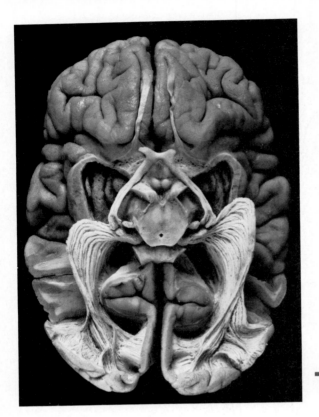

FIGURE 6.13
The base of the brain, with tissue dissected away so that the projections (optic radiations) between the dorsal lateral geniculate nucleus and the primary visual cortex are visible. (From Gluhbegovic, N., and Williams, T.H. *The Human Brain: A Photographic Atlas.* Hagerstown, Md.: Harper & Row, 1980.)

1. *Suprachiasmatic nucleus.* This region of the hypothalamus controls behaviors and physiological processes that vary across the day/night cycle. Input from the retina synchronizes its activity. (This structure will be discussed in Chapter 9.)
2. *Accessory optic nuclei.* These nuclei, located in the brain stem, play a role in coordinating eye movements that compensate for head movements, thus keeping the eyes "on track" (Ito, 1977). This system also involves the floccular region of the cerebellum, discussed in Chapter 8.

3. *Pretectum.* This pathway terminates near the superior colliculus and plays a role in the control of pupillary size (Sprague, Berlucchi, and Rizzolatti, 1973).
4. *Superior colliculus.* The superior colliculus plays a role in attention to visual stimuli and control of eye movements. This structure sends fibers to various areas of the visual association cortex but not to the primary visual cortex. The superior colliculus also receives information from most areas of the visual cortex.
5. *Ventral lateral geniculate nucleus.* The dorsal lateral geniculate nucleus is the principal relay station between the retina and the striate cortex. The ventral lateral geniculate nucleus also receives direct visual input but relays it only to subcortical structures: the pretectum, superior colliculus, pontine nuclei, and suprachiasmatic nucleus. Its function is not known.

ANALYSIS OF VISUAL FORM

This section describes the anatomy and functions of the visual system, from retinal ganglion cell to the visual association cortex. I will summarize what is known about the nature and response characteristics of the neurons located in each structure, and the nature of the connections between the structures.

Two Visual Systems

Recent research (Livingstone and Hubel, 1987, 1988; Zeki and Shipp, 1988) has shown that the primate visual system consists of two parallel, largely independent systems: the *magnocellular system* and the *parvocellular system*. (As I will explain later, the two systems get their names from different layers of the dorsal lateral geniculate nucleus.) The magnocellular system appears to have evolved earlier. It is found in all mammals, and it deals with the analysis of form, movement, and depth. The parvocellular system is seen only in primates. It is involved with color perception and with the detection of fine details. Specific damage to the parvocellular system in monkeys, produced by a chemical (an acrylamide monomer) that destroys retinal ganglion cells that contribute to the parvocellular system, causes loss of color vision and the ability to detect fine details (Merigan and Eskin, 1986; Merigan, 1989).

Mammals other than primates have little or no color vision and cannot see fine details. However, they have excellent depth perception, can detect small differences in brightness, and are sensitive to movement. The visual systems of primates possess these characteristics too, but they can also detect differences in color and fine details that cannot be discriminated by other mammals. These additional abilities are very useful for animals that exploit a wide range of habitats and foodstuffs; for example, an animal with color vision can easily discriminate ripe fruit from unripe fruit and from the green leaves of the tree. Livingstone and Hubel (1987) have demonstrated the independence of these two systems in humans by showing that people cannot use color cues alone to perceive movement or depth. That is, we can easily perceive the shape of a red figure on a green background; but when a red figure *moves* against a green background of the same brightness, we fail to perceive its motion. Instead of seeming to move, it seems to disappear and reappear from place to place. Similarly, the perception of depth disappears when a figure shows differences in color but not brightness. For example, the drawing in Figure 6.14, rendered in black and white, looks like a pile of three-dimensional objects. When rendered in red lines against a green background, it loses all of its apparent depth and simply looks like a jumble of lines. (See *Figure 6.14.*)

Why does the perception of movement or depth disappear? It does so because the parvocellular system, which detects colors, evolved after the magnocellular system was already in place. The visual system already knew how to perceive depth and movement, so there was no reason to duplicate that function in the new system. (Nature tends to be efficient.) When two colors, such as red and green, are chosen to be identical in their apparent brightness, they look exactly the same to the color-blind magnocellular system. Since they look the same, they cannot be seen to move or to give rise to the perception of depth. The parvocellular system does see the difference, but it cannot contribute to the perception of movement or depth.

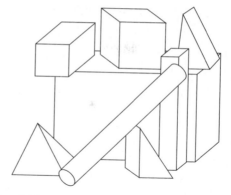

Figure 6.14

Lack of depth perception by the parvocellular system. When this figure is presented as green lines against a red background with the same brightness, the appearance of three-dimensionality disappears; the drawing looks like a jumble of lines. (Reprinted with permission from Livingstone, M., and Hubel, D. *Science,* 1988, *240,* 740–749. Copyright 1988 by the American Association for the Advancement of Science.)

Why, you might ask, do I not *show* you a picture of red lines against a green background and let you see the phenomenon for yourself? Unfortunately, that would not work. It is very difficult to find colors of red and green ink that appear absolutely identical in brightness; and if they are not identical, the magnocellular system will detect the difference. Each person perceives the brightness of different colors in a slightly different way, so that even if the inks were matched for one person, they would be different for another. To demonstrate the independence of color vision and perception of motion and depth, Livingstone and Hubel had to fine-tune the displays for each of their subjects.

Receptive Fields and Feature Detection

The portion of the visual field to which a single neuron responds is called its *receptive field.* Obviously, the receptive field of a photoreceptor is determined by its location on the retinal mosaic. The receptive fields of neurons in subsequent levels of the visual pathways are determined by the details of their anatomical connections with the photoreceptors and with each other. As we have seen, a retinotopic representation is maintained up to the level of the visual cortex. Thus, the receptive fields of neurons in adjacent parts of the visual cortex are themselves adjacent; in other words, neighboring neurons respond to stimuli in adjacent parts of the visual field. In general, cells that respond to foveal stimulation have small receptive fields, whereas those that respond to stimulation of the peripheral retina have larger ones. But an even more important characteristic of neurons in the visual system is that they respond most vigorously when the eye is presented with a particular pattern of light and dark, such as a line segment of a given orientation and length. The neurons respond best to particular visual *features*; hence they are referred to as *feature detectors.*

The identification of a cell's receptive field and the type of stimulus to which it responds best is accomplished by a procedure called *mapping.* The animal is anesthetized and placed in front of a projection screen or a display terminal attached to a computer. A contact lens is usually placed on its eye to compensate for the paralysis of the ciliary muscle (which controls the lens) and thus to focus images properly on the retina. Recordings of action potentials are taken from single neurons while a visual stimulus moves around on the screen. The receptive field is defined as the area of the visual field in which the stimulus elicits a response from the cell. The "best" stimulus is determined by the shape of the visual stimulus that produces the largest response. In this case *response* means a change in the rate of firing; the change can be either an increase or a decrease, because information can be coded by a decreased rate of firing as well as by an increased rate. Obviously, because the experimenter can never try out all possible visual stimuli, all that he or she can say is that the stimulus that produces the largest response is the best of the ones that were tried.

Retinal Ganglion Cells

The first neurons in the visual system that have axons capable of producing action potentials are the retinal ganglion cells.

Description of Receptive Fields

Kuffler (1952, 1953), recording from ganglion cells in the retina of the cat, discovered that their receptive field consists of a roughly circular center, surrounded by a ring. In his experiments cells responded in opposite manner to light in the two regions of each receptive field, a characteristic that is now called *opponent coding.* A spot of light presented to the central field (*center*) produced a burst of unit activity. However, when the spot was moved to the surrounding field (*surround*), the cell ceased firing, but it began firing vigorously for a while when the spot of light was turned off. The cell thus responded in a center-on, surround-off manner. For convenience, these cells are referred to as *on-center cells.* Kuffler also identified cells that give the opposite response; inhibition when the center was illuminated, and excitation when the surrounding field was illuminated. (As you might expect, they are referred to as *off-center cells.*) Simultaneous presentation of a stimulus to both center and surround of either type of cell produced little or no response. Therefore, these ganglion cells compare the brightness of the center spot with its surround, giving the greatest response when the contrast is maximal. (See *Figure 6.15.*)

Enroth-Cugell and Robson (1966), studying the retina of the cat, found that not all retinal ganglion cells show this cancellation effect. Those that did show a null position (that is, center + surround stimulation counterbalancing each other) they called *X cells;* those that did not they called *Y cells.* The X cells and Y cells differ in several ways. The axons of X cells conduct relatively slowly and display a sustained response (*tonic response*) to a continuous stimulus in their receptive field, which tends to be small. These cells do not respond well to rapidly moving stimuli. Many of them respond differentially to stimuli of different hues. In contrast, the axons of Y cells conduct relatively rapidly, and the cells show a brisk response to the onset of the stimulus but quickly cease responding to a continuous stimulus (*phasic response*). The Y cells' receptive fields are larger than those of X cells, and they respond best to rapidly moving stimuli. In addition, they are not sensitive to different hues.

Subsequent research revealed that primate retinas also contain two distinct categories of ganglion cells (Leventhal, Rodieck, and Dreher, 1981). In fact, these two types of ganglion cells form the starting points of the parvocellular and

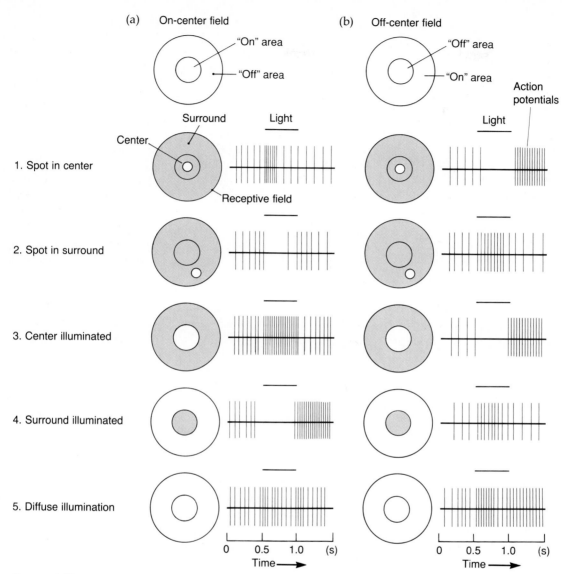

FIGURE 6.15

Responses of retinal ganglion cells with center-on (*a*) and center-off (*b*) receptive fields to various stimuli. (Adapted from Kandel, E.R., and Schwartz, J.H. *Principles of Neural Science.* New York: Elsevier Science Publishing Co., 1982; after Kuffler, S.W. *Cold Spring Harbor Symposium for Quantitative Biology,* 1952, *17,* 281–292.)

magnocellular systems. The **A cells** are Y-like; they have large receptive fields, produce phasic responses to visual stimuli, are especially sensitive to motion, and are insensitive to differences in hue. Their dendritic fields are large, and their shape has earned them the name *parasol ganglion cell.* (See *Figure 6.16.*) Type A cells constitute approximately 10 percent of the population of gan-

glion cells in the retina (Perry, Oehler, and Cowey, 1984). They send their axons to the dorsal lateral geniculate nucleus, with collaterals projecting to the superior colliculus.

The second category of ganglion cells in the primate retina, **B cells,** are X-like. They have small receptive fields, produce tonic, sustained responses to visual stimuli, and are generally not

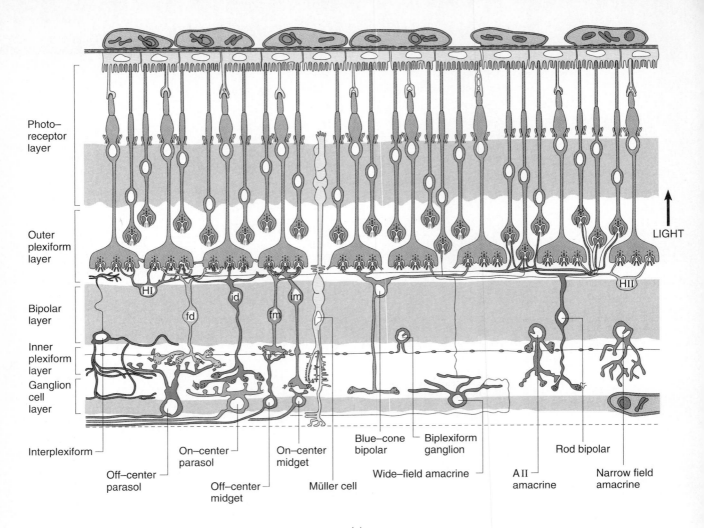

Photo–
receptor
layer

Outer
plexiform
layer

Bipolar
layer

Inner
plexiform
layer

Ganglion
cell
layer

LIGHT

HI

fd

id

fm

im

HII

Interplexiform

Off–center
parasol

On–center
parasol

Off–center
midget

On–center
midget

Müller cell

Blue–cone
bipolar

Wide–field amacrine

Biplexiform
ganglion

A II
amacrine

Rod bipolar

Narrow field
amacrine

(a)

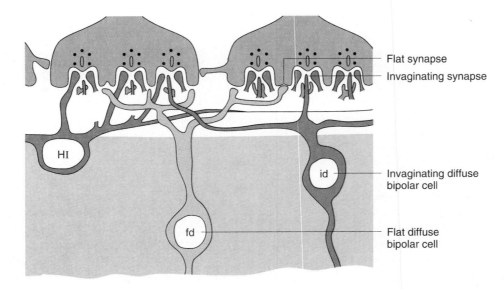

Flat synapse

Invaginating synapse

Invaginating diffuse
bipolar cell

Flat diffuse
bipolar cell

HI

id

fd

(b)

sensitive to motion. Many of them are sensitive to different hues. Because their dendritic fields are small, they are referred to as *midget ganglion cells.* (See *Figure 6.16.*) Perry, Oehler, and Cowey (1984) estimate that type B cells constitute approximately 80 percent of the population of retinal ganglion cells. Their axons go exclusively to the dorsal lateral geniculate nucleus.

The remaining 10 percent of the retinal ganglion cells consist of at least eight different types (Rodieck, 1988). One of them, the *biplexiform ganglion cell,* makes synaptic connections with rods as well as with bipolar cells and ganglion cells (Mariani, 1982). (See *Figure 6.16.*)

The response characteristics of A and B cells suggest that B cells (midget ganglion cells) supply information for color perception and perception of fine detail, whereas A cells (parasol ganglion cells) supply information about moving stimuli. At present, not enough is known about the characteristics of the other types of ganglion cells to speculate about their functions.

Retinal Circuitry of Center/ Surround Receptive Fields

Investigators have made considerable progress in relating the circuitry of retinal neurons to their functional characteristics. So many investigators have contributed to this story that I will simply refer you to Dowling (1987) and Rodieck (1988) for specific references. The primate retina contains at least seven different types of bipolar cells, six of which are described here. Four major types of bipolar cells form synaptic connections with cones: *invaginating diffuse, flat diffuse, invaginating midget,* and *flat midget.* **Invaginating bipolar cells** send a dendrite into a cup-shaped indentation in the photoreceptor, whereas **flat bipolar cells** present dendrites to the base of the photoreceptor adjacent to the indentation. (See *inset, Figure 6.16.*) **Diffuse bipolar cells** have wide dendritic fields that form synapses with six or seven cones, whereas **midget bipolar cells** have

small dendritic fields that are restricted to one cone. In addition, *blue-cone bipolar cells* form synapses with cones that detect short wavelengths of light. Rods make connections only with **rod bipolar cells,** by means of invaginating-type synapses. (See *Figure 6.16.*)

The primate retina contains two different types of horizontal cells, HI and HII. *HI cells* form synapses with rods and with all three types of cones; thus, they appear to be concerned only with monochromatic vision. In contrast, *HII cells* form synapses only with cones, and their pattern of connection suggests that a given HII cell receives information from only one type of cone; thus, they appear to be concerned with color vision. All horizontal cells form invaginating-type synapses. (See *inset, Figure 6.16.*)

Amacrine cells connect with the axons of bipolar cells and the dendrites of ganglion cells. There are approximately twenty different types of them. Three are shown in Figure 6.16: *wide-field, narrow-field,* and *AII.* AII amacrine cells provide communication between rod bipolar cells and on-center ganglion cells (to be described shortly). The function of the other types of amacrine cells is not yet known. (See *Figure 6.16.*)

As we already saw, ganglion cells have different response characteristics. Kuffler (1952, 1953) discovered the distinction between on-center and off-center cells. *On-center* ganglion cells form synaptic connections with *invaginating-type* bipolar cells in the *inner* half of the inner plexiform layer. *Off-center* ganglion cells form synaptic connections with *flat-type* bipolar cells in the *outer* half of the inner plexiform layer (Rodieck, 1988). *Parasol* (type A) and *midget* (type B) ganglion cells receive information from *diffuse* and *midget* bipolar cells, respectively. (See *Figure 6.16.*)

The retina also contains a type of cell that is not part of the classical circuitry, the *interplexiform cell.* The connections of this type of cell vary in different species, and at the present little can be said about its connections in old world primates. Their function may be to remove inhibitory interactions in the retina under low-light conditions. When plenty of light is available, these inhibitory interactions help produce a sharper image; but when the light is dim, they are counterproductive (Dowling, 1979).

◀ FIGURE 6.16
The cells of the primate retina. (Adapted with permission from Rodieck, R.W. The primate retina. In *Comparative Primate Biology. Volume 4: Neurosciences,* edited by H.D. Steklis and J. Erwin. New York: A.R. Liss, 1988.)

In recent years much has been learned about the neurotransmitters utilized by neurons in the retina (see Daw, Brunker, and Parkinson, 1989, for a review). The transmission of the message from photoreceptors through bipolar cells to ganglion cells appears to be accomplished with excitatory amino acids. In particular, the photoreceptors liberate glutamate. Inhibition (as we have seen, light can have inhibitory as well as excitatory effects on the firing rate of ganglion cells) is accomplished by the means of glycine. In addition, dopamine and many peptides have been discovered in the retina, but their specific functions are not yet known.

Lateral Geniculate Nucleus

The dorsal lateral geniculate nucleus receives inputs from the retinal ganglion cells. This thalamic nucleus receives its name from its resemblance to a bent knee (*genu* means "knee"). The nucleus on each side of the brain contains six layers of neurons. Each layer receives input from only one eye: layers 2, 3, and 5 from the ipsilateral eye, and layers 1, 4, and 6 from the contralateral eye. The topographical arrangement of receptive fields of the retinal ganglion cells is maintained by the neurons in the lateral geniculate nucleus; each of the six layers contains a complete map of the retina. The neurons in layers 1 and 2 contain larger cell bodies than those in the remaining four layers. For this reason, the inner two layers are called the *magnocellular layers* and the outer four layers are called the *parvocellular layers* (*parvo-* refers to the small size of the cells). (See *Figure 6.17*.)

As I explained earlier in this section, the distinction between the magnocellular and parvocellular system is an important one. The magnocellular layers are found in all mammals, whereas the parvocellular layers are found only in primates. Neurons in the magnocellular layers receive input from type A ganglion cells, whereas those in the parvocellular layers receive input from type B ganglion cells. You will recall that type B ganglion cells receive color-coded information and are connected to smaller numbers of photoreceptors. These facts explain why the neurons in the parvocellular layers are involved with the detection of fine details and with color vision.

Indeed, recordings of the response character-

FIGURE 6.17

A photomicrograph of a section through the right lateral geniculate nucleus of a rhesus monkey (cresyl violet stain). Layers 1, 4, and 6 receive input from the contralateral (left) eye, and layers 2, 3, and 5 receive input from the ipsilateral (right) eye. The receptive fields of all six layers are in almost perfect registration; cells located along the line of the unlabeled arrow have receptive fields centered on the same point. (From Hubel, D.H., Wiesel, T.N., and Le Vay, S. *Philosophical Transactions of the Royal Society of London, B.*, 1977, *278*, 131–163.)

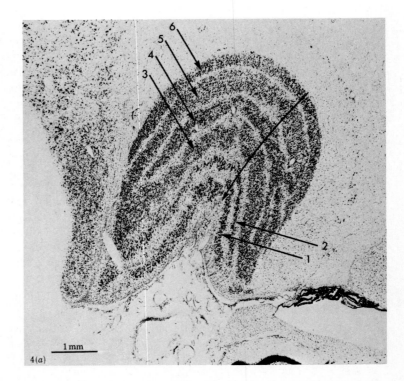

TABLE 6.2

Properties of the magnocellular and parvocellular divisions of the visual system

Property	Magnocellular Division	Parvocellular Division
Color	No	Yes
Sensitivity to contrast	High	Low
Spatial resolution	Low	High
Temporal resolution	Fast (transient response)	Slow (sustained response)

SOURCE: Adapted from Livingstone, M.S., and Hubel, D.H. *Journal of Neuroscience,* 1987, *7,* 3416–3468.

istics of neurons in the dorsal lateral geniculate nucleus have shown that the parvocellular and magnocellular layers receive very different types of information (Livingstone and Hubel, 1987). Many neurons in the parvocellular layers respond to different hues. For example, they might be excited by a red light shone on the center of their re-

ceptive field and inhibited by a green light. They also show high spatial resolution and low temporal resolution; that is, are able to distinguish between small visual features, but their response is slow and prolonged. In contrast, cells in the magnocellular layers are color-blind, are not able to detect fine details, and respond in a transient (Y-like) manner to a visual stimulus. And although they appear to be responsible for vision of lower acuity, they are able to detect smaller contrasts between light and dark. (See *Table 6.2.*)

Primary Visual Cortex

Anatomy and Inputs

The primary visual cortex consists of six principal layers (and several sublayers), arranged in bands parallel to the surface. These layers contain the nuclei of cell bodies and dendritic trees that show up as bands of light or dark in sections of tissue that have been dyed with a cell-body stain. (See *Figure 6.18.*)

In primates, axons from the dorsal lateral geniculate nucleus terminate on cortical neurons in

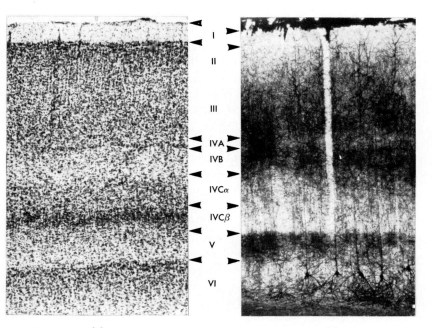

(a)   (b)

FIGURE 6.18

A photomicrograph of a small section of striate cortex. (a) Individual neurons, stained with a membrane stain. (b) The six principal layers and the sublayers, stained with a cell-body stain. (From Lund, J.S. *Journal of Comparative Neurology,* 1987, *257,* 60–92.)

layer 4C. Neurons in the parvocellular layers send their axons to the deeper part of this layer (to layer 4Cβ), which in turn send their axons to layer 4B. The axons of neurons in the magnocellular layers terminate just above them, in layer 4Cα. From there, the information is relayed to the lower part of layer 3 and then to layers 2 and 3 (Hubel and Wiesel, 1972; Lund and Boothe, 1975).

An unusual characteristic of the primate striate cortex was discovered by Wong-Riley (1978). She found that a stain for a mitochondrial enzyme called *cytochrome oxidase* showed a patchy distribution. Subsequent research with the stain (Horton and Hubel, 1980; Humphrey and Hendrickson, 1980) revealed the presence of a polka-dot pattern of dark columns extending through layers 2 and 3 and (more faintly) layers 5 and 6. The columns, which the authors called **blobs,** are oval in cross section, approximately 150×200 μm in diameter and spaced at 0.5-mm intervals. They receive a weak input from the dorsal lateral geniculate nucleus (apparently from neurons located between the parvocellular and magnocellular layers), and a strong input from layer 4Cβ (Fitzpatrick, Itoh, and Diamond, 1983; Livingstone and Hubel, 1987).

Figure 6.19 shows a photograph of a slice through the visual cortex of a macaque monkey that has been flattened out and stained for cytochrome oxidase. You can clearly see the blobs within the striate cortex. Because the curvature of the cortex prevents it from being perfectly flattened, some of the tissue is missing in the center of the slice. (See *Figure 6.19.*)

Feature Detection

The pioneering studies of David Hubel and Torsten Wiesel at Harvard University during the 1960s began a revolution in the study of the physiology of visual perception (see Hubel and Wiesel, 1977, 1979). Hubel and Wiesel discovered that neurons in the visual cortex did not simply respond to spots of light; they selectively responded to specific *features* of the visual world.

As would be expected, neurons in layer 4C of the striate cortex have response properties like those of the dorsal lateral geniculate nucleus that provides input to this layer: circular receptive fields organized in a center/surround fashion.

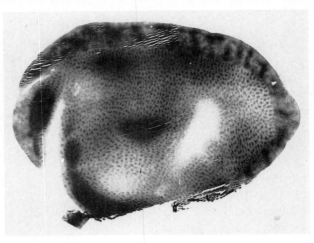

FIGURE 6.19

A photomicrograph of a slice through the primary visual cortex of a macaque monkey, parallel to the surface. The blobs have been stained with cytochrome oxidase. (From Hubel, D.H., and Livingstone, M.S. *Journal of Neuroscience,* 1989, *7,* 3378–3415.)

However, neurons in the other layers have more interesting properties. Most show the greatest response when a line with a particular *orientation* is placed in their receptive field. That is, some neurons respond best to a vertical line, some to a horizontal line, and some to a line oriented somewhere in between. The selectivity of different neurons varies, but in general, their response falls off when the line tilts by more than 10 degrees. (For comparison's sake, the angle between the hands of a clock at one o'clock is 30 degrees.)

Some orientation-sensitive neurons have receptive fields organized in an opponent fashion. Hubel and Wiesel referred to them as **simple cells.** For example, a line of a particular orientation (say, a dark 45-degree line against a white background) might excite the cell if placed in the center of the receptive field but inhibit it if moved away from the center. (See *Figure 6.20a.*) Another type of neuron, which they referred to as **complex cells,** had larger receptive fields. These neurons, like simple cells, responded best to a line of a particular orientation but did not show an inhibitory surround; that is, they continued to respond while the line was moved within the receptive field. In fact, many complex cells responded best to movement of the line perpendicular to its angle of orientation. In addition, they responded equally well to white lines against black backgrounds and black

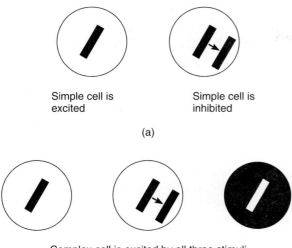

Simple cell is excited

Simple cell is inhibited

(a)

Complex cell is excited by all three stimuli

(b)

FIGURE 6.20
Response characteristics of neurons in the primary visual cortex. (a) Simple cell. (b) Complex cell.

lines against white backgrounds. (See *Figure 6.20b.*)

Hubel and Wiesel also reported the presence of **hypercomplex cells.** These cells, like complex cells, responded best to lines of a particular orientation located anywhere within their receptive field. They are located in the same layers of cortex. However, unlike the response of complex cells, their response diminished or even disappeared altogether if the line was so long that it extended outside the receptive field. (See *Figure 6.21.*)

The terms *simple, complex,* and *hypercomplex* suggest a hierarchy of feature detection—that simple cells provide the input to complex cells and that complex cells provide the input to hypercomplex cells. However, we now know that this hypothesis is incorrect. The distinctions between these three types of neurons are important, but they are not what Hubel and Wiesel originally thought them to be.

Modular Organization

Most investigators believe that the brain is organized in modules, which probably range in size from a hundred thousand to a few million neurons. Each module receives information from other modules, performs some calculations, and then passes the results to other modules. In recent years investigators have been learning the characteristics of the modules that are found in the visual cortex (De Valois and De Valois, 1988; Livingstone and Hubel, 1988). The primary visual cortex consists of approximately 2500 modules, each approximately 0.5×0.7 mm and containing approximately 150,000 neurons. The neurons in each module are devoted to the analysis of a particular portion of the visual field. (In a sense, these blocks are the "tiles" that constitute the mosaic of the primary visual cortex.) The modules actually consist of two segments, each centered around a cytochrome oxidase-rich blob. The neurons in layer 4Cα and 4Cβ, which receive information directly from the dorsal lateral geniculate nucleus, are strictly *monocular;* that is, they respond to visual stimulation presented to the right or left eye,

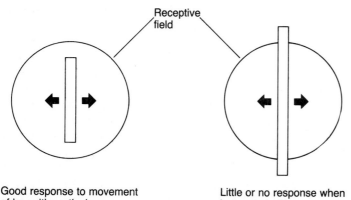

Receptive field

Good response to movement of bar with particular orientation

Little or no response when bar extends beyond receptive field

FIGURE 6.21
Complex and hypercomplex cells. The characteristics of these cells differ in terms of the effects of stimuli outside their receptive fields.

but not to both. One of the halves of each module receives input from the left eye and the other receives it from the right eye. Eighty percent of the neurons in the other layers of the cortex are *binocular*, responding to stimulation presented to either eye; obviously, then, the two halves of the module must exchange information. (See *Figure 6.22.*)

Although the neurons in a given module have receptive fields centered around approximately the same location, they differ in several ways (Livingstone and Hubel, 1982). First, the neurons in the blobs are generally not sensitive to orientation; that is, they will respond to lines presented at any angle of orientation. However, most of these neurons are sensitive to another dimension: color. (The specific way these neurons encode color will be described in a later section of this chapter.) Outside the blob neurons show orientation sensitivity and, in the case of complex cells, sensitivity to movement.

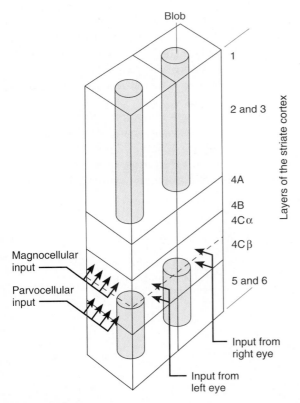

FIGURE 6.22
One of the modules of the primary visual cortex.

Each module of the striate cortex, then, contains neurons devoted to the detection of colors, movements, and lines or edges of particular orientations within a specific portion of the visual field. Within a module the response characteristics of the neurons are arranged systematically. That is, if a neuron in a particular location responds best to a line oriented at an angle of 45°, then a neuron located a short distance away will respond best to a line with an orientation of 50°, and so on. Each 25 μm of lateral movement within the striate cortex encounters neurons that respond to lines rotated by 10°. As we travel across both halves of a module, we will encounter two 180° rotations in the orientations of lines that best stimulate the neurons.

A study by Hubel, Wiesel, and Stryker (1978) demonstrated the pattern of preference for lines of a particular orientation throughout the primary visual cortex. The investigators injected a monkey with radioactive 2-deoxyglucose (2-DG) and then presented a pattern of vertical stripes, moving back and forth from left to right. The injected chemical resembles normal glucose and hence is taken up in greatest quantities by neurons that have the highest metabolic rate. However, unlike glucose, 2-DG cannot be metabolized and, in addition, cannot leave the cell once it enters. Thus, the procedure labels metabolically active cells with radioactivity. The monkey was killed, its brain was sliced, and the sections were examined by means of autoradiography.

Because the retina was stimulated with a pattern of vertical lines in this experiment, those cortical neurons that respond best to lines of this orientation should have fired at the highest rate and hence should have been the most active metabolically. Therefore, they should also be the most radioactive. Those cells that respond best to lines of other orientations should contain relatively small amounts of radioactivity.

Figure 6.23 shows a slice through the striate cortex taken perpendicular to the surface. Note that columns of neurons, approximately 0.5 mm apart, were labeled with radioactive 2-DG, indicating that they responded best to vertically oriented lines. In contrast, neurons in layer 4C were uniformly dark, because they responded to any stimulus that passed through the center of their

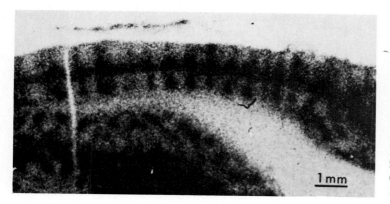

FIGURE 6.23
An autoradiograph of a cross section through the striate cortex of a rhesus monkey that had been given an injection of [³H]-2-deoxyglucose and had been exposed to a moving pattern of vertical stripes. (From Hubel, D.H., Wiesel, T.N., and Stryker, M.P. *Journal of Comparative Neurology*, 1978, *177*, 361–380.)

receptive field. (See *Figure 6.23.*)

Each module of the striate cortex is rectangular. As we just saw, orientation sensitivity systematically varies along one dimension. What about the other? The short answer is *spatial frequency*. But in order to explain what that term means, I will need to explain some concepts that may not be familiar to you.

Spatial Frequency

It turns out that although many neurons in the striate cortex do respond when the eye is presented with stimuli such as lines and bars, the best stimulus for these neurons is a *sine-wave grating* (De Valois, Albrecht, and Thorell, 1978). Figure 6.24 compares a sine-wave grating with a more familiar square-wave grating. A square-wave grating consists of a simple set of rectangular bars that vary in brightness; the brightness along the length of a line perpendicular to them would vary in a stepwise (square-wave) fashion. (See *Figure 6.24a.*) A sine-wave grating looks like a series of fuzzy, unfocused parallel bars. Along any line perpendicular to the long axis of the grating, the brightness varies according to a sine-wave function. (See *Figure 6.24b.*)

A sine-wave grating is designated by its *spatial frequency.* We are accustomed to frequencies (for example, of sound waves or radio waves) being expressed in terms of distance (such as cycles per meter). Because the image of a stimulus on the retina varies in size according to how close it is to the eye, *visual angle* is generally used instead of the physical distance between adjacent cycles. Thus, the spatial frequency of a visual stimulus is

(a)

(b)

FIGURE 6.24
Parallel gratings. (a) Square-wave grating. (b) Sine-wave grating. (From De Valois, R.L., and De Valois, K.K. *Spatial Vision*. New York: Oxford University Press, 1988.)

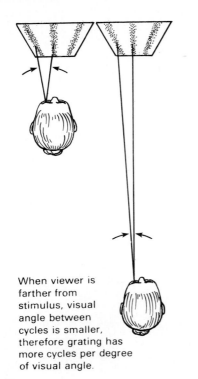

When viewer is
farther from
stimulus, visual
angle between
cycles is smaller,
therefore grating has
more cycles per degree
of visual angle.

FIGURE 6.25
The concepts of visual angle and spatial frequency.
Angles are drawn between the sine waves, with the
apex at the viewer's eye. The *visual angle* between
adjacent sine waves is smaller when the observer is
farther from the stimulus.

measured in cycles per degree of visual angle. (See
Figure 6.25.)

Most neurons in the striate cortex respond best
when a sine-wave grating of a particular spatial
frequency is placed in the appropriate part of the
visual field. For orientation-sensitive neurons the
grating must be aligned at the appropriate angle of
orientation. In most cases a neuron's receptive
field is large enough to include between 1.5 and
3.5 cycles of the grating (De Valois, Thorell, and
Albrecht, 1985).

You will recall that Hubel, Wiesel, and Stryker
(1978) used 2-DG autoradiography to demonstrate the regular pattern of orientation columns
in the visual cortex. In a similar study, Tootell,
Silverman, and De Valois (1981) injected cats with
radioactive 2-DG and presented each with a
sine-wave-grating pattern of a particular spatial
frequency, ranging from 0.25 to 2.0 cycles per degree. Control animals saw patterns containing all

of these frequencies. The investigators presented
the patterns in all orientations and moved them in
all directions, so that no subset of orientation-sensitive neurons would be selectively stimulated.
They then killed the animals, treated slices of the
visual cortex with a photographic emulsion, and
later developed these exposures. Figure 6.26
shows examples of their results. In the experimental animals they found evidence of radioactivity in discrete bands approximately 1.0 mm apart
(top). In contrast, they observed uniform labeling
in the cortex of the control cats, who saw all
freqencies *(bottom)*. (See *Figure 6.26.*) Thus, neurons in the striate cortex of the cat appear to be arranged according to sensitivity to particular spatial frequencies.

The layout of the modules is somewhat more
complex in the primate striate cortex than in the
cat striate cortex. If a series of low–spatial–
frequency gratings (at all orientations) is shown to
a monkey treated with radioactive 2-DG, the pattern of radioactivity indicates that the neurons in
the blobs were activated. In contrast, if a monkey
is shown a series of gratings at a higher spatial frequency, then a doughnutlike pattern of radioactivity is seen, with a blob forming the hole of each
doughnut (Tootell, Silverman, Switkes, and De
Valois, 1982). These findings, and those of a subsequent study in which the response characteristics of single cortical neurons were recorded, indicate that the neurons within blobs respond to the
lowest spatial frequencies and that higher frequencies stimulate cells farther away from the
blob (De Valois and De Valois, 1988).

Although Livingstone and Hubel originally
believed that neurons within blobs were insensitive to orientation and that neurons outside blobs
were insensitive to changes in hue, more recent
studies indicate otherwise (Thorell, De Valois,
and Albrecht, 1984; Silverman, Grosof, De Valois,
and Elfar, 1989). When blob neurons are tested
with low-frequency sine-wave gratings (as opposed to lines or square-wave gratings), they
show orientation sensitivity; and when nonblob
neurons are tested with high-frequency sine-
wave gratings, they show sensitivity to differences in hue. However, the relative differences in
the sensitivity of these two populations to hue
mean that, for all practical purposes, blob cells
serve color vision and nonblob cells do not.

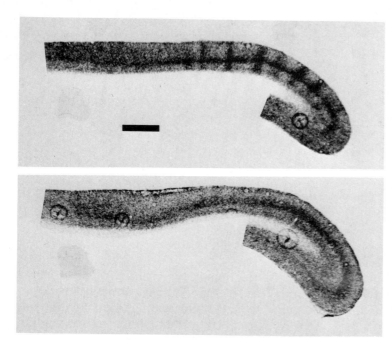

FIGURE 6.26
2-DG autoradiographs of cat visual cortex. *Top:* Experimental cat presented with a sine-wave grating of 2.0 cycles per degree. *Bottom:* Control cat presented with a sine-wave grating containing many different spatial frequencies. (Reprinted with permission from Tootell, R.B., Silverman, M.S., and De Valois, R.L. *Science,* 1981, *214,* 813–815. Copyright 1981 by the American Association for the Advancement of Science.)

Analysis of Form: The Role of Fourier Analysis

You have just patiently (I hope) read a section describing the response characteristics of neurons in the striate cortex to a type of stimulus you have probably never seen before: a sine-wave grating. Now it is time to try to explain *why* the visual system seems to be wired in such a way as to detect such esoteric features. A nineteenth-century French physicist, Jean Fourier, discovered that any repetitive waveform, no matter how complex, could be shown to be the sum of a series of *sine waves* of different frequencies and amplitudes. *Sine waves* are smooth, repeating curves that are produced by plotting the vertical location of a point on a continuously rotating circle as a function of time. They can vary in *frequency* (the speed at which the circle is rotated) and *amplitude* (the size of the circle). The location of a point along a single cycle of a sine wave is specified by its *phase.* The peak is at 0°, the middle of the cycle is at 90°, the trough is at 180°, and the middle of the cycle occurs again at 270°. The end of the cycle, 360°, is the same as the beginning of the next one. (See *Figure 6.27.*)

The dissection of a waveform into its elementary components is called a *Fourier analysis.* For example, Fourier analysis reveals that the complex wave shown in color in Figure 6.28 is actually the sum of the three simple sine waves shown below. Note that the starting points of the three sine waves are different; that is, they vary in their phase. (See *Figure 6.28.*) Later, mathematicians discovered that even nonrepetitive waveforms could be produced by adding a series of sine waves.

A Fourier analysis can be made of a visual stimulus. For example, consider the photograph shown in Figure 6.29. If we take a thin horizontal slice through it, we get a line that varies in brightness, much like one of the lines that constitute a television picture. If we measure the brightness of all points on this line, we can draw a graph of changes in brightness along the length of it. (See *Figure 6.29.*) If slices are taken horizontally and vertically, a two-dimensional analysis can be made that will represent the information in the scene. The result of the analysis is a series of numbers that can be used to reconstruct the original image.

The visual system appears to perform a sort of Fourier analysis. However, instead of an analysis of whole slices of the scene, as Figure 6.29 shows, the analysis in the striate cortex is restricted to a very small part of the visual field—the portion detected by a single module. Each module contains

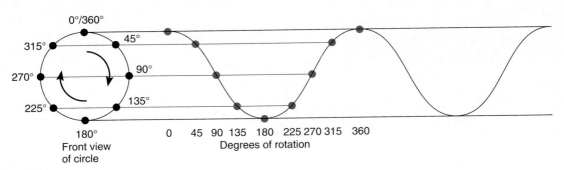

FIGURE 6.27

The origin of a sine wave. The location of a given point on a sine wave (its phase) is given in degrees, corresponding to the rotation of a point on a circle that defines the sine wave.

cells that look at their receptive field and detect the presence of a few cycles of variations in brightness at particular spatial frequencies at particular orientations. The information from these modules is then sent to the visual association cortex for further analysis. (I will have more to say about that analysis later.)

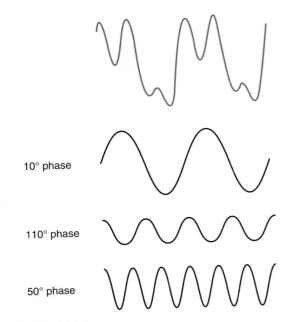

FIGURE 6.28

Fourier analysis. The complex waveform (color) is composed of the three sine waves (black), starting at different phase angles. (From De Valois, R.L., and De Valois, K.K. *Spatial Vision*. New York: Oxford University Press, 1988.)

The neurons in the visual cortex that Hubel and Wiesel classified as *simple* and *complex* both respond to sine-wave gratings, but in different ways. You will recall that a simple cell responds to a line segment of a particular orientation located in the center of the cell's receptive field. For example, a particular simple cell might give an excitatory response to a black bar with an orientation of 45 degrees against a white background. If so, it will give an inhibitory response to a white bar against a black background. In contrast, a complex cell responds to a line segment of a particular orientation located anywhere in the receptive field, and it responds equally well to black bars against white backgrounds and white bars against black backgrounds. (See *Figure 6.30a*.) A similar distinction holds for sine-wave gratings. The response of a simple cell changes when the bars of a sine-wave grating are moved to different positions within the receptive field (when the *phase* of the grating is varied); complex cells give an unchanging response. Thus, simple cells are *phase-sensitive*, whereas complex cells are *phase-insensitive*. (See *Figure 6.30b*.)

Albrecht (1978) mapped the shapes of receptive fields of simple cells by observing their response while moving a very thin flickering line of the appropriate orientation through their receptive fields. He found that many of them had multiple inhibitory and excitatory regions surrounding the center. The profile of the excitatory and inhibitory regions of such neurons looked like a modulated sine wave—precisely what would be

FIGURE 6.29

A graph of the variation in brightness of a slice of a photograph. The information could be stored in a computer, and the pure sine-wave frequencies in the waveform could be calculated by Fourier analysis.

Simple cell is
excited

Complex cell
is excited

Bright bar in center
of receptive field

Simple cell is
excited

Complex cell
is excited

Bright bar in center
of receptive field

Simple cell is
inhibited

Complex cell
is excited

Bright bar outside
center of receptive field

(a)

Simple cell is
inhibited
(phase dependence)
Complex cell
is excited
(phase independence)

Dark bar in center
of receptive field

(b)

FIGURE 6.30

Relation of simple and complex cells to spatial frequency analysis. (a) Responses to a vertical bar of light. (b) Responses to a vertical sine-wave grating. Note that simple cells are excited only when light falls on the center of the receptive field. Complex cells are excited even when light falls in the surrounding portion of their receptive field. In terms of sine-wave gratings they are *phase-insensitive*.

167

needed to detect a few cycles of a sine-wave grating. (See *Figure 6.31.*)

Why does the striate cortex contain both simple (phase-sensitive) and complex (phase-insensitive) neurons? A likely explanation is that phase-sensitive cells are needed to specify the precise locations of edges of objects and of specific details within them. Low-frequency-sensitive, phase-sensitive (simple) cells encode the location of objects in the environment, while high-frequency-sensitive, phase-insensitive (complex) cells encode the texture of objects and backgrounds, which tend to consist of repetitive patterns. With regard to texture the particular location of the bumps and grooves is not important; for example, we do not need to know the details of grains of sand on the beach or wrinkles in the bark of a tree. Thus, complex cells can efficiently signal the presence of texture of a particular degree of roughness without having to keep track of all the details. Of course, if we need to study the details of a textured object, we can do so by scanning it piece by piece with our foveal vision.

Another question: What is the role of neurons that Hubel and Wiesel referred to as hypercomplex? More recent research indicates that these cells do not consist of a separate category but represent the end of a continuum. The response of many neurons, both simple and complex, is inhibited when a stimulus is presented outside its primary receptive field. Some neurons are inhibited by a considerable amount; others are inhibited very little. The importance of this inhibition to visual perception is not yet known.

Yet another question may have occurred to you: If both simple and complex cells are actually sensitive to portions of sine-wave gratings, why do they respond to lines? The answer is given by a Fourier analysis of a line. Actually, I will describe the analysis of a square-wave grating, because that is simpler, but the same principle applies to a single line. As Figure 6.32 shows, the brightness of a series of light and dark rectangular bars varies in a stepwise fashion when it is measured perpendicular to their long axis—hence the term *square-wave* grating. If the frequency of a square wave is *f*, then its Fourier analysis shows that it consists of a sine wave of frequency *f* plus diminishing amounts of sine waves with frequencies 3*f*, 5*f*, 7*f*, and so on. Figure 6.32 shows the results of adding 3*f*, 5*f*, and 7*f* to a sine wave with the basic frequency. The resulting waveform begins to look more and more like a square wave. (See *Figure 6.32.*)

As you can see from Figure 6.32 the Fourier analysis of a square-wave grating contains

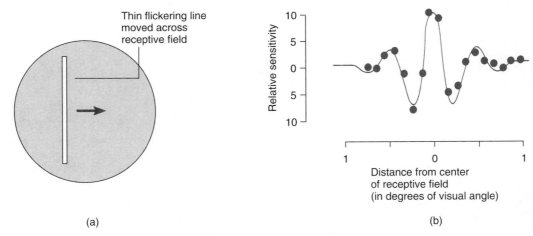

(a)   (b)

FIGURE 6.31

The experiment by Albrecht, 1978. (a) The stimulus presented to the animal. (b) The response of a simple cell in the primary visual cortex. (Adapted from De Valois, R.L., and De Valois, K.K. *Spatial Vision.* New York: Oxford University Press, 1988.)

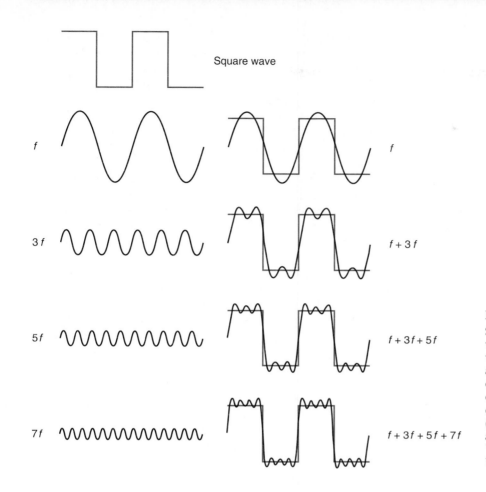

FIGURE 6.32
Synthesis of a square-wave grating. A square-wave grating can be approximated by adding odd-numbered multiples of the basic frequency, in decreasing amplitude. (From De Valois, R.L., and De Valois, K.K. *Spatial Vision.* New York: Oxford University Press, 1988.)

frequencies much higher than the basic one. Similarly, a line or an abrupt edge contains high frequencies. Thus, when investigators use lines or thick bars as stimuli, they will excite neurons sensitive to a wide range of spatial frequencies. Although a line or a bar seems like a very simple stimulus, it turns out to be a complex one, given the type of analysis performed by the striate cortex.

Although spatial frequency may still seem to you to be a rather abstract concept, many experiments have confirmed that the concept plays a central role in visual perception. (De Valois and De Valois, 1988, summarize many of them.) Here, I will describe just one example. Look at the two pictures in *Figure 6.33.* You can see that the photograph on the right looks much more like the face of Abraham Lincoln than the one on the left. And yet both photographs contain the same information.

The creators of the photographs, Harmon and Julesz (1973), used a computer to construct the figure on the left, which consists of a series of squares, each representing the average brightness of a portion of a picture of Lincoln. The one on the right is simply a transformation of the first one, in which high frequencies have been removed. As you saw in Figure 6.32, sharp edges contain high spatial frequencies. In the case of the left-hand picture these frequencies have nothing to do with the information contained in the original picture; thus, they can be seen as visual "noise." The filtration process (accomplished by a computer performing a Fourier analysis) removes this noise—and makes the image much clearer to the human visual system. Presumably, the high frequencies produced by the edges of the squares in the left-hand figure stimulate neurons in the striate cortex that are tuned to high spatial fre-

FIGURE 6.33

Spatial filtering. Both pictures contain the same amount of low-frequency information, but extraneous high-frequency information has been filtered from the picture on the right. If you look at the pictures from across the room, they look identical. (From Harmon, L.D., and Julesz, B. *Science*, 1973, *180*, 1191–1197. Copyright 1973 by the American Association for the Advancement of Science.)

quencies. When the visual association cortex receives this noisy information, it has difficulty perceiving the underlying form.

If you want to watch the effect of filtering the extraneous high-frequency noise, try the following demonstration. Put the book down and look at the figures from across the room. The distance "erases" the high frequencies, because they exceed the resolving power of the eye, and the two pictures look identical. Now walk toward the book, focusing on the left-hand figure. As you get closer, the higher frequencies reappear and the face on the left gets harder and harder to recognize. (See *Figure 6.33.*)

Stereoscopic Depth Perception: Disparity Detectors

As we have seen, neurons in the primate striate cortex encode information about orientation, spatial frequency, and color. We saw that many of these neurons are binocular, responding to visual stimulation of either eye. Many binocular cells, especially those found in layer 4B (which receives information from the magnocellular system), have response patterns that appear to contribute to the perception of depth (Poggio and Poggio, 1984). Some of them will respond only when both eyes are simultaneously stimulated and will not respond to stimulation of one eye alone (Poggio and Fischer, 1977; Clarke and Whitteridge, 1978). Others have identical receptive fields with respect to both eyes, but in most cases the cells respond most vigorously when each eye sees a stimulus in a slightly *different* location. That

is, the neurons respond to **retinal disparity,** a stimulus that produces images on slightly different parts of the retina of each eye.

We perceive depth by many means, most of which involve cues that can be detected monocularly, by one eye alone. For example, perspective, relative retinal size, loss of detail through the effects of atmospheric haze, and relative apparent movement of retinal images as we move our heads all contribute to depth perception and do not require binocular vision. However, binocular vision provides a vivid perception of depth through the process of **stereopsis.** If you have used a stereoscope (such as a View Master) or seen a three-dimensional movie, you know what I mean.

Stereopsis (literally, "solid appearance") requires binocular retinal disparity of some elements of a visual stimulus. When you fix your gaze on an object in the middle distance, the convergence of your eyes causes that point, and other points an equal distance away from you, to fall on identical portions of each retina. These points fall on the *fixation plane.* (Actually, because the equidistant points fall on a portion of a sphere, the term *plane* is a misnomer.) This phenomenon is easy to demonstrate. Hold your hands in front of you, one at arm's length and the other at half that distance from your face. Extend a finger from each hand and focus on the farther one. You will see two images of the nearer one. Now slowly move the nearer finger away from you until it lies alongside the other. As you do so, you will see the two images of the moving finger merge. The cues for stereopsis are provided by stimuli located just off the fixation plane, which stimulate slightly different parts of the retina of each eye. As we saw, some neurons respond selectively to just this occurrence.

Investigators have found that the visual cortex contains two classes of neurons that are sensitive to retinal disparity. The first class responds with an increase or decrease in firing rate to a limited range of retinal disparity ($\pm 0.2°$ for the excitatory cells and $\pm 0.4°$ for the inhibitory cells). The response of these neurons is shown in the left portion of Figure 6.34. (See *Figure 6.34, left.*) The second class of neurons selectively responds to stimuli nearer than or farther away than the fixation plane. (See *Figure 6.34, right.*)

The biological significance of these cells receives support from the finding that there are two classes of people who have difficulty in judging the distance of objects by means of binocular cues: Some of them misjudge objects in front of the fixation plane (closer to them); others have difficulty with objects that are behind it (Richards, 1977). It

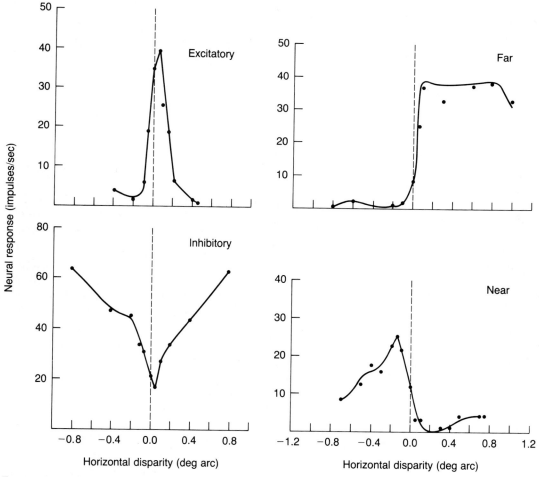

FIGURE 6.34

Responses of neurons in the visual cortex to horizontal disparity in stimuli presented to both eyes. *Left:* Maximal excitatory (*top*) or inhibitory (*bottom*) response to a particular amount of disparity. *Right:* Specific response to far (*top*) or near (*bottom*) stimulus. (Reproduced, with permission, from Poggio, G.F., and Poggio, T. *Annual Review of Neuroscience*, Volume 7, © 1984 by Annual Reviews Inc.)

seems likely that people with this affliction lack either "near-detecting" or "far-detecting" neurons. Another category of people can easily judge which of two objects is farther from them when both objects are almost the same distance but, surprisingly, have trouble judging which is closer when one object is much closer to them than the other (Jones, 1977). Presumably, these people are able to respond to small disparities by means of the finely tuned disparity detectors whose response was shown in the left half of Figure 6.34.

Visual Association Cortex

Perception of objects and of the totality of the visual scene do not take place in the striate cortex. Each cortical module responds to only part of the information present in the visual field, and for perceptions of objects to take place, information from these individual modules must be combined. That combination takes place in the visual association cortex.

Prestriate Cortex

Neurons in the striate cortex send axons to other regions of the cortex, primarily to the first level of the visual association cortex, the *prestriate cortex. Prestriate* is a misleading term, because it actually comes after striate cortex, rather than before it, in the analysis of visual information. (For this reason some investigators use the term *circumstriate* cortex, because it surrounds the striate cortex.) Zeki and his colleagues (see Zeki and Shipp, 1988) have studied the prestriate cortex in some detail.

The striate cortex is sometimes referred to as *area V1*, because it is the sole projection area of the dorsal lateral geniculate nucleus. Neurons in V1 send axons to three regions of the prestriate cortex, which have been designated as *areas V2, V3*, and *V5*. In addition, another region of the prestriate cortex, *area V3A*, receives projections from neurons in V3 but not directly from V1. (See *Figure 6.35.*)

Each of these five areas, V2, V3, V3A, V4, and V5, contains one or more independent representations of the visual field. The interesting thing about these areas is that because of the details of their connections with neurons in V1 (striate cortex), their neurons respond to different visual features (Zeki, 1978b; Zeki and Shipp, 1988).

As we saw earlier in this chapter, type A (parasol) and type B (midget) ganglion cells receive different types of information from the photoreceptors, and they project to different layers of the dorsal lateral geniculate nucleus: type A to the magnocellular layers and type B to the parvocellular layers. In turn, neurons in the magnocellular layers project to different layers of the striate cortex (V1). The distinction between the magnocellular and parvocellular systems continues into the prestriate cortex. As Wong-Riley (1978) discovered, a stain for cytochrome oxidase reveals the presence of discrete columns (*blobs*) in the striate cortex. The same stain reveals the presence of alternating thick and thin stripes in area V2 (Livingstone and Hubel, 1982; Tootel, Silverman, De Valois, and Jacobs, 1983). Different regions of V2 receive input from different parts of V1: The thick stripes receive input from layer 4B of the striate cortex (magnocellular system), the thin stripes receive input from the blobs (parvocellular system), and the regions between the stripes receive input from the "interblob" regions of cortical layers 2 and 3 (parvocellular system). (See *Figure 6.36.*)

The response characteristics of neurons in specific regions of area V2 are very different (Hubel and Livingstone, 1987). As would be suggested by the nature of their connections with area V1, neurons in the thick stripes of area V2 show orientation selectivity. In addition, many of them show strong responses to variations in retinal disparity and thus undoubtedly participate in stereopsis. Neurons in the thin stripes resemble those in the V1 blobs; they show no orientation selectivity, and most respond to color. Neurons in the regions between the stripes are orientation-selective but do not respond to particular directions of movements. The response characteristics of neurons in area V2 to sine-wave gratings of different frequencies are not yet known. (See *Figure 6.36.*)

Area V3 appears to be a part of the magnocellular system and probably deals with the analysis of form. It receives input from layer 4B of the striate cortex and from the thick stripes of V2, and its neurons are sensitive to orientation but not to color (Zeki, 1978a, 1978b). The functional difference between areas V3 and V3A is not yet understood. (See *Figure 6.36.*)

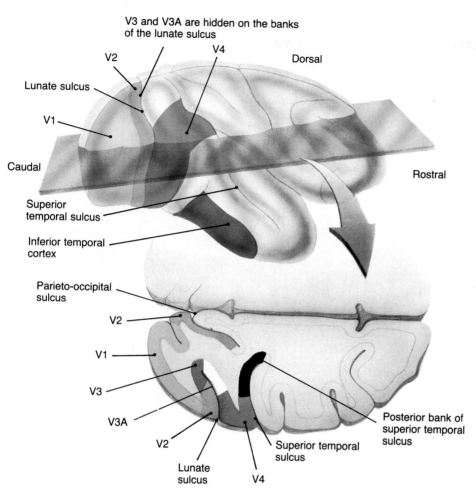

FIGURE 6.35

Areas of visual association cortex of the rhesus monkey brain. (Adapted from Zeki, S.M. *Journal of Physiology*, 1978, *277*, 227–244.)

According to Zeki (1980), area V4 seems to be specialized for color. It receives input from the thin stripes of area V2, and most of its cells are color-sensitive. However, it also receives input from the interstripe regions of area V2, and some neurons show orientation sensitivity (Zeki, 1988). The relation between color and form analysis in this region of visual cortex is not yet known. (See *Figure 6.36*.)

Area V5, located on the posterior bank of the superior temporal sulcus, is specialized for the analysis of movement. More is known about this region of prestriate cortex than any other. Area V5 receives input only from the magnocellular system—directly from movement-sensitive complex cells in layer 4B of the striate cortex, from the thick stripes of area V2, and from area V3 (Maunsell and Van Essen, 1983). It also receives input from the superior colliculus—directly and from projections relayed through the pulvinar, a nucleus of the thalamus. (See *Figure 6.36*.) Lesions of area V5 in monkeys disrupt perception of motion (Siegel and Andersen, 1986). In addition, damage to the prestriate cortex of the posterior temporal lobe has been reported to produce "motion blindness" in humans (Hess, Baker, and Zihl, 1989).

Zeki and Shipp (1988) injected horseradish peroxidase into area V5 and found that retrograde transport of the enzyme produced a patchy pat-

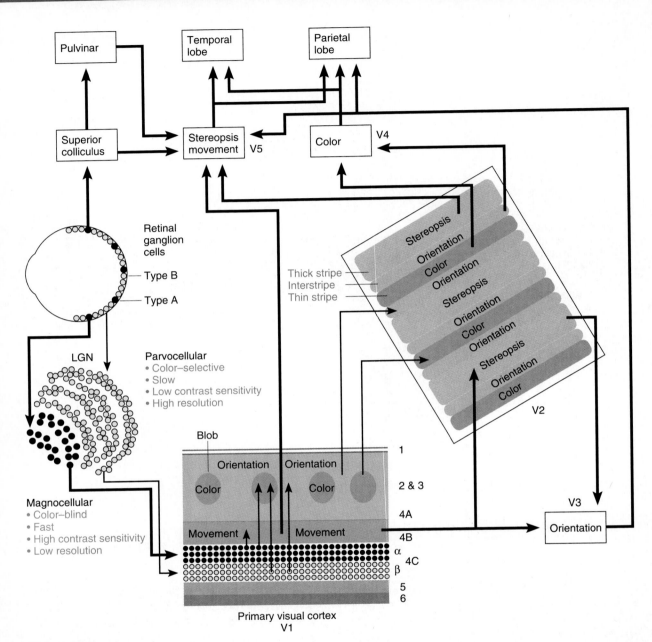

FIGURE 6.36
A summary of the parvocellular and magnocellular visual systems. (Adapted from Livingstone, M., and Hubel, D. *Science*, 1988, *240*, 740–749.)

tern in area V1, similar to the pattern produced by a stain for cytochrome oxidase. However, the patches did *not* correspond to the blobs, so it appears that the organization of cortical modules is even more complex than was originally believed. Figure 6.37 shows a photograph of a slice through V1 from a treated monkey taken parallel to the sur-

face, stained for the presence of horseradish peroxidase. (See *Figure 6.37.*)

The input from the superior colliculus turns out to be important; Rodman, Gross, and Albright (1989) found that destruction of the striate cortex does not eliminate the movement sensitivity of V5 neurons but that subsequent destruction of the

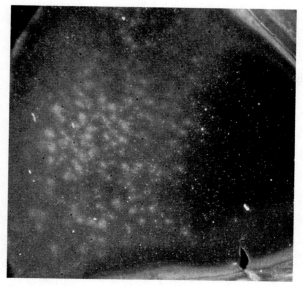

FIGURE 6.37

A slice through V1 (primary visual cortex), stained for horseradish peroxidase (golden color), showing the location of neurons whose axons project to area V5. Reprinted with permission from Zeki, S. and Shipp, S. *Nature*, Vol. 335, pp. 311–317. Copyright © 1988 Macmillan Magazines Ltd.

terclockwise fashion. The neurons in adjacent portions of each rectangle have motion sensitivities oriented in opposite directions. (See *Figure 6.38.*)

As we have seen, neurons in the modules of area V1 respond to different features of small parts of the visual field: to color, to spatial frequency, to orientation, to binocular disparity, and to movement (and, possibly, to other features that have not yet been discovered). Each module then sends different kinds of information to different regions of the visual association cortex, each containing at least one map of the visual field. Zeki (1984) suggests that this system permits interactions among similar kinds of features. As we shall see later in this chapter, the placement of color-sensitive neurons together in one cortical area (area V4) permits interactions that provide the basis for phenomena such as color constancy. In addition, the placement of movement-sensitive neurons in another cortical area (area V5) may provide the circuitry that enables the visual system to extract information about form from movement—for example, the ability to perceive elements moving in a particular direction as belonging to the same object.

superior colliculus does. What, then, is accomplished by the input from the striate cortex? One possibility is suggested by Segraves, Goldberg, Deng, Bruce, Ungerleider, and Mishkin (1987), who found that although monkeys could detect movement after lesions of the striate cortex, they showed difficulty estimating its *rate*.

Albright, Desimone, and Gross (1984) mapped the characteristics of movement-sensitive neurons in area V5. They found that all V5 neurons responded better to moving stimuli than to stationary ones, and that most of them gave the same response regardless of the color or shape of the test stimulus. Most neurons showed directional sensitivity; that is, they responded only to movements in a particular direction. They also found that, like the striate cortex, area V5 is divided into modules. Figure 6.38 shows the hypothetical organization of these modules. Each module consists of a pair of rectangles, arranged side by side. Moving along the long axis, one encounters neurons with directional sensitivities that vary systematically, in a clockwise or coun-

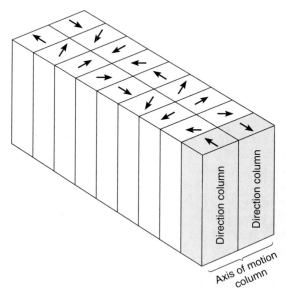

FIGURE 6.38

A hypothetical model of a cortical module in area V5 of prestriate cortex. (From Albright, T.D., Desimone, R., and Gross, C.G. *Journal of Neurophysiology*, 1984, *51*, 16–31.)

Inferior Temporal Cortex

In primates the prestriate cortex represents an intermediate level of visual analysis. The highest level of analysis, analysis of visual patterns and identification of particular objects, appears to take place in a region of the brain called the *inferior temporal cortex,* located on the ventral half of the temporal lobe. (Refer to *Figure 6.35.*) This area of association cortex receives inputs from the prestriate cortex and from various thalamic nuclei, especially the pulvinar. Presumably, it is here that analyses of form, movement, depth, and color are brought together and perceptions of three-dimensional objects and backgrounds are achieved. In many ways it is the most interesting region of all, because neural circuits here "learn" to detect stimuli with particular shapes, regardless of their size or location. For that reason I will discuss it only briefly here and postpone a more complete discussion until Chapter 14, which deals with the anatomy of learning and memory.

An example of the role of the inferior temporal cortex in perception is illustrated in an experiment by Iwai and Mishkin (1969). These investigators trained rhesus monkeys to discriminate between a plus sign and a square. (Correct responses were reinforced with a small piece of food.) Then they removed the inferior temporal cortex bilaterally and found that the monkeys required several hundred trials to relearn the task. Iwai, Osawa, and Umitsu (1979) found that slight differences in the stimuli disrupted the performance of monkeys with lesions of the inferior temporal cortex. Although the animals could be retrained to discriminate between the original stimuli, they failed to discriminate between the same patterns when they were superimposed on a different background. (See *Figure 6.39.*)

Many studies have investigated the functions of the primate inferior temporal cortex. In general, they respond best to three-dimensional objects (or photographs of them) rather than to simple stimuli, such as spots, lines, or sine-wave gratings. For example, some respond best to a photograph of a hand, some to a profile of a monkey's face, and some to the front of a monkey's face. Destruction of visual association cortex in the temporal lobes of humans results in deficits in visual perception; these deficits will be discussed in the last section of this chapter.

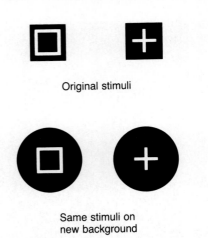

Original stimuli

Same stimuli on
new background

FIGURE 6.39
Visual stimuli. After bilateral removal of the inferior temporal cortex, monkeys who had learned to discriminate between the top pair of stimuli failed to discriminate between the bottom pair.

Parietal Cortex

As we just saw, the prestriate cortex sends information to the association cortex of the inferior temporal gyrus, the location in which object perception appears to take place. In addition, areas V3, V4, and V5 send information to the parietal lobe. The parietal lobe is involved in spatial perception, and it is through these connections that it receives its visual input. Damage to the parietal lobes disrupts performance on a variety of tasks that require perceiving and remembering the locations of objects (Ungerleider and Mishkin, 1982).

A particularly interesting phenomenon called *Balint's syndrome* occurs in humans who have sustained bilateral damage to the parieto-occipital region (Balint, 1909; Damasio, 1985). Such damage usually occurs when a person undergoes a period of very low blood pressure, which produces anoxia in regions of the brain between the areas irrigated by major arteries, where the blood supply is not especially rich. The parieto-occipital region, situated between the areas supplied by the middle and posterior cerebral arteries, is one of these areas. Balint's syndrome consists of three major symptoms: optic ataxia, ocular apraxia, and simultanagnosia. All three symptoms are related to spatial perception.

Optic ataxia is a deficit in reaching for objects under visual guidance (*ataxia* comes from the

Greek word for "disorderly"). A person with Balint's syndrome might be able to perceive and recognize a particular object, but when he or she tries to reach for it, the movement is often misdirected. ***Ocular apraxia*** (literally "without visual action") is a deficit of visual scanning. If a person with Balint's syndrome looks around a room filled with objects, he or she will see an occasional item and will be able to perceive it normally. However, the patient will not be able to maintain fixation; his or her eyes will begin to wander and another object will come into view for a time. The person is unable to make a systematic scan of the contents of the room and will not be able to perceive the location of the objects he or she sees. If an object moves, or if a light flashes, the person may report seeing something but will not be able to make an eye movement that directs the gaze toward the target.

Simultanagnosia is the most interesting of the three symptoms. As I just mentioned, if the gaze of a person with Balint's syndrome happens to fall on an object, he or she will perceive it. But *only one object* will be perceived at a time. For example, if an examiner holds either a comb or a pen in front of a patient's eyes, the patient will recognize the object. But if the examiner holds a pen and a comb together (for example, so that they form the legs of an X), the patient will see either the comb or the pen, not both. The existence of simultanagnosia means that perception of separate objects takes place at least somewhat independently, even when the outlines of the objects overlap in the visual field.

*I*NTERIM SUMMARY

Visual information from the retina reaches the primary visual cortex surrounding the calcarine fissure by means of the dorsal lateral geniculate nuclei. Several other regions of the brain, including the suprachiasmatic nucleus of the hypothalamus, the accessory optic nuclei of the brain stem, the pretectum, the superior colliculus, and the ventral lateral geniculate nucleus, also receive visual information. These latter regions help regulate activity during the day/night cycle, coordinate eye and head movements, control attention to visual stimuli, and regulate the size of the pupils.

Research by Livingstone and Hubel suggests that the primate visual system contains two major components, named after layers of the dorsal lateral geniculate nucleus: the magnocellular system (more primitive; color-blind; sensitive to movement, depth, and small differences in brightness) and the parvocellular system (more recent, color-sensitive, and able to discriminate finer details).

Most ganglion cells respond in an opposing center/surround fashion, with excitation to light in one region and inhibition to light in the other. Type A cells (parasol) are large and contribute to the magnocellular system. Type B cells (midget) contribute to the parvocellular system. On-center ganglion cells receive input from invaginating-type bipolar cells in the inner half of the inner plexiform layer; off-center ganglion cells receive input from flat-type bipolar cells in the outer half of the inner plexiform layer.

The dorsal lateral geniculate nucleus consists of six layers of neurons, each containing a map of half of the retina of one eye; three layers are devoted to each eye. The inner two layers are magnocellular, and the outer four are parvocellular. The neurons send axons to the primary visual cortex.

Projections from the parvocellular and magnocellular layers terminate in different layers of the striate cortex. The striate cortex is organized into modules, each surrounding a pair of blobs, which are revealed by a stain for cytochrome oxidase. Each half of a module receives information from one eye; but because information is shared, most of the neurons respond to input to both eyes. The neurons in the blobs are sensitive to color and to low spatial frequencies, whereas those between the blobs are sensitive to high spatial frequencies and (relatively) insensitive to color. In addition, different cells respond to sine-wave gratings of different orientations. The visual system appears to perform an analysis similar to a Fourier analysis as it codes visual information in a scene.

Hubel and Wiesel discovered two types of neurons in the striate cortex: simple and complex. Subsequent research has revealed that simple cells are sensitive to phase and will show different responses if a grating is moved, whereas complex cells are insensitive to phase. It appears that phase-sensitive cells specify locations of edges of objects and features, whereas phase-insensitive cells encode texture.

The visual cortex also contains neurons that serve as disparity detectors, which respond maximally when a visual stimulus falls on not-quite-corresponding portions of the two retinas. Some of these neurons detect objects closer to the observer than the fixation plane, others detect objects farther away, and others detect very small disparities in either direction.

The prestriate cortex receives information from the primary visual cortex and from the superior colliculus. It is divided into distinct regions in which reside neurons with special functions. Area V2 shows thick and thin stripes when stained for cytochrome oxidase. The thick stripes receive input from the magnocellular system and show sensitivity to orientation and retinal disparity. The thin stripes receive information from the blobs in area V1 and show color sensitivity. The interstripe regions receive magnocellular information and are sensitive to orientation. Area V3 receives magnocellular information. Area V4 neurons receive input from both the thin stripes and the interstripe regions of area V2 and respond to color. Neurons in area V5 receive input from the magnocellular system of area V1, from the thick stripes of area V2, from area V3, and from the superior colliculus. This area plays an important role in the perception of movement. Its modular organization is beginning to be understood.

The prestriate cortex sends information on to two regions of association cortex: the inferior temporal gyrus and the parietal lobe. Both lesion studies and electrical-recording studies indicate that object perception takes place in the inferior temporal lobe, whereas the perception of the spatial location of objects takes place in the parietal lobe. Balint's syndrome, which is caused by bilateral damage to the parieto-occipital region, includes the symptoms of optic ataxia, ocular apraxia, and simultanagnosia.

COLOR VISION

Various theories of color vision have been proposed for many years—long before it was possible to disprove or validate them by physiological means. In 1802 Thomas Young, a British physicist and physician, proposed that the eye detected different colors because it contained three types of receptors, each sensitive to a single hue. His theory was referred to as the *trichromatic* (three-color) *theory*. It was suggested by the fact that, for a human observer, any color can be reproduced by mixing various quantities of three colors judiciously selected from different points along the spectrum.

I must emphasize that *color mixing* is different from *pigment mixing*. If we combine yellow and blue pigments (as when we mix paints), the resulting mixture is green. Color mixing refers to the addition of two or more light sources. If we shine a beam of red light and a beam of bluish green light together on a white screen, we will see yellow light. If we mix yellow and blue light, we get white light. When white appears on a color television screen, it actually consists of tiny dots of red, blue, and green light. (See *Figures 6.40 and 6.41.*)

Another fact of color perception suggested to a German physiologist, Ewald Hering (1905/1965), that hue might be represented in the visual system as *opponent colors*. Humans have long regarded yellow, blue, red, and green as primary colors. (Black and white are primary, too, but we perceive them as colorless.) All other colors can be described as mixtures of these primary colors. The trichromatic system cannot explain why *yellow* is included in this group. In addition, some colors appear to blend, whereas others do not. For example, one can speak of a bluish green or a yellowish green, and orange appears to have both red and yellow qualities. Purple resembles both red and blue. However, we cannot conceive of a greenish red or a bluish yellow; these colors seem to be op-

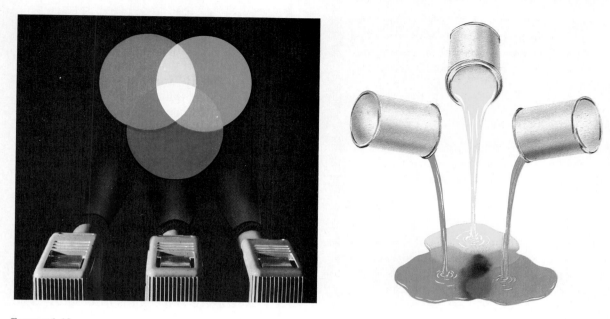

FIGURE 6.40

Additive color mixing and paint mixing. When blue, red, and green light of the proper intensity are all shone together, the result is white light. When red, blue, and yellow paints are mixed together, the result is a dark gray. (Photo courtesy of GATF.)

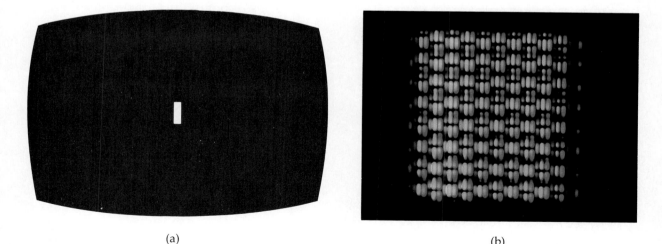

(a)   (b)

FIGURE 6.41

Color coding. The television screen demonstrates—in reverse—the principle of color coding by the three types of cones in the retina. (a) A small white rectangle shown in the middle of the screen. (b) An enlargement of the same white rectangle. Note that the screen displays only red, blue, and green spots of light. At a distance these colors blend and produce white light.

posite each other. Again, these facts are not explained by the trichromatic theory. As we shall see, the visual system uses both trichromatic and oppent-color systems to encode information related to color.

Color Coding in the Retina

Just as the circuitry of the retina gives rise to the center/surround response characteristics of the ganglion cells, it also gives rise to opponent-color coding.

Photoreceptors

Physiological investigations of retinal photoreceptors in higher primates have found that Young was right: Three different types of photoreceptors (three different types of cones) are responsible for color vision. Investigators have studied the absorption characteristics of individual photoreceptors, determining the amount of light of different wavelengths that is absorbed by the photopigments. These characteristics are controlled by the particular opsin a photoreceptor contains; different opsins absorb particular wavelengths more readily. Figure 6.42 shows the absorption characteristics of the four types of photoreceptors in the human retina: rods and the three types of cones. (See *Figure 6.42.*)

The peak sensitivities of the three types of cones are approximately 420 nm (blue-violet), 530

nm (green), and 560 nm (yellow-green). The peak sensitivity of the short-wavelength cone is actually 440 nm in the intact eye, because the lens absorbs some short-wavelength light. For convenience, the short-, medium-, and long-wavelength cones are traditionally called "blue," "green," and "red" cones. The retina contains approximately equal numbers of "red" and "green" cones but a much smaller number of "blue" cones (approximately 8 percent of the total). (See *Figure 6.43.*)

Genetic defects in color vision appear to result from anomalies in one or more of the three types of cones (Boynton, 1979; Nathans, Piantanida, Eddy, Shows, and Hogness, 1986). The first two kinds of defective color vision described here involve genes on the X chromosome; thus, because males have only one X chromosome, they are much more likely to have this disorder. People with *protanopia* ("first-color defect") confuse red and green. They see the world in shades of yellow and blue; both red and green look yellowish to them. Their visual acuity is normal, which suggests that their retinas do not lack "red" or "green" cones. This fact, and their sensitivity to lights of different wavelengths, suggests that their "red" cones are filled with "green" cone opsin. People with *deuteranopia* ("second-color defect") also confuse red and green. Their "green" cones appear to be filled with "red" cone opsin.

FIGURE 6.42
Relative absorbance of light of various wavelengths by rods and the three types of cones in the human retina. (From Dartnall, H.J.A., Bowmaker, J.K., and Mollon, J.D. Human visual pigments: Microspectrophotometric results from the eyes of seven persons. *Proceedings of the Royal Society of London, B.*, 1983, 220, 115–130.)

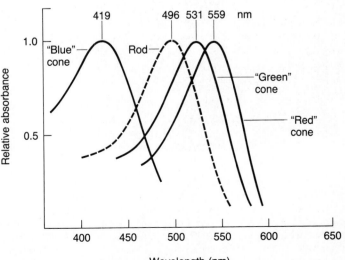

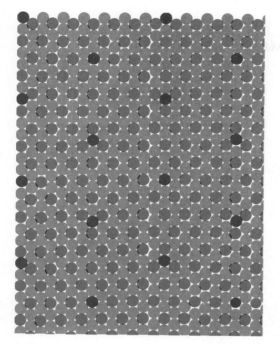

FIGURE 6.43

A possible arrangement of "blue," "red," and "green" cones in the human retina, based on the model proposed by Walraven (1974).

Tritanopia ("third-color defect") is rare, affecting fewer than 1 in 10,000 people. This disorder involves a faulty gene that is not located on an X chromosome; thus, it is equally prevalent in males and females. People with tritanopia have difficulty with hues of short wavelengths and see the world in greens and reds. To them, a clear blue sky is a bright green, and yellow looks pink. Their retinas appear to lack "blue" cones. Because the retina contains so few of these cones, their absence does not noticeably affect visual acuity.

Retinal Ganglion Cells

At the level of the retinal ganglion cell, the three-color code gets translated into an opponent-color system. Daw (1968) and Gouras (1968) found that these neurons respond specifically to pairs of primary colors, with red opposing green and blue opposing yellow. Most receptive fields of color-sensitive ganglion cells are arranged in a center/surround fashion. For example, a cell might be excited by red and inhibited by green in the center, while showing the opposite response in the sur-

rounding ring. Other ganglion cells that receive input from cones do not respond differentially to different wavelengths but simply encode relative brightness in the center and surround.

The response characteristics of retinal ganglion cells to light of different wavelengths are obviously determined by the retinal circuitry. Figure 6.44 shows a schematic representation of the relation between the three types of cones and the two major types of color-coding ganglion cells. A third type of ganglion cells responds to light of any wavelength; these cells provide high-acuity monochromatic (black and white) information. No attempt is made to show the actual circuitry; the arrows refer merely to the effects of the photic stimulation. (See *Figure 6.44*.)

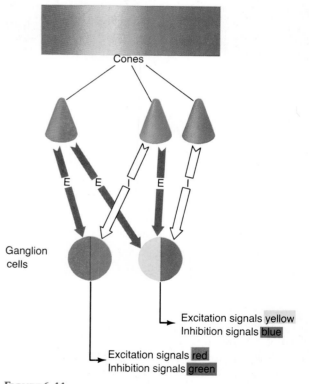

FIGURE 6.44

Color coding in the retina. The trichromatic coding of the cones ("red," "green," and "blue") is transformed into the opponent-process coding of the retinal ganglion cells (red/green and yellow/blue). The arrows labeled E and I represent neural circuitry within the retina that translates excitation of a cone into excitation or inhibition of a ganglion cell.

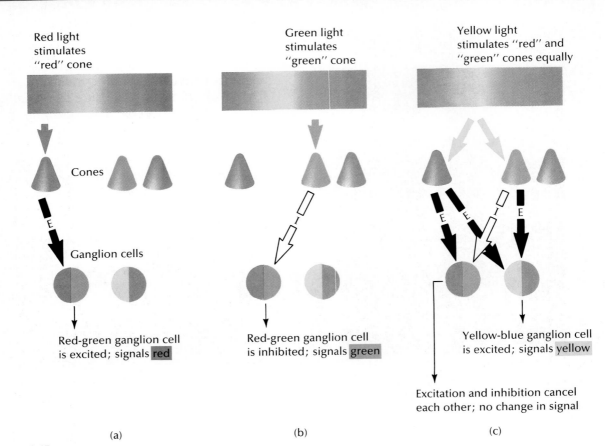

Red light
stimulates
"red" cone

Green light
stimulates
"green" cone

Yellow light
stimulates "red" and
"green" cones equally

Cones

Ganglion cells

Red-green ganglion cell
is excited; signals red

Red-green ganglion cell
is inhibited; signals green

Yellow-blue ganglion cell
is excited; signals yellow

Excitation and inhibition cancel
each other; no change in signal

(a)   (b)   (c)

FIGURE 6.45

Color coding in the retina. (a) Red light stimulating a "red" cone, which causes
excitation of a red/green ganglion cell. (b) Green light stimulating a "green" cone, which
causes inhibition of a red/green ganglion cell. (c) Yellow light stimulating "red" and
"green" cones equally but not affecting "blue" cones. The stimulation of "red' and
"green" cones causes excitation of a yellow/blue ganglion cell. The arrows labeled E and
I represent neural circuitry within the retina that translates excitation of a cone into
excitation or inhibition of a ganglion cell. For clarity, only some of the circuits are
shown.

Figure 6.45 helps explain how particular hues
are detected by the red, green, and blue cones and
translated into excitation or inhibition of the red-
green and yellow-blue ganglion cells. Detection
and coding of pure red, green, or blue light is the
easiest to understand. For example, red light
excites red cones, which causes the excitation of
red-green ganglion cells. (See *Figure 6.45a.*) Now
consider the effect of yellow light. Because the
wavelength that produces the sensation of yellow
is intermediate between red and green, it will
stimulate both red and green cones about equally.
Yellow-blue ganglion cells are excited by both red
and green cones, so their rate of firing increases.

However, red-green ganglion cells are excited by
red and inhibited by green, so their firing rate does
not change. The brain detects an increased firing
rate from the axons of yellow-blue ganglion cells,
which it interprets as yellow. (See *Figure 6.45b.*)

The opponent-color system employed by the
ganglion cells explains why we can imagine a yellowish red (orange) but not a yellowish blue. The
brain perceives yellowish red when the activity of
both yellow-blue and red-green ganglion cells increase. But for the brain to perceive a yellowish
blue, the activity of yellow-blue ganglion cells
would have to increase and decrease at the same
time, which they obviously cannot do.

Color Coding in the Lateral Geniculate Nucleus

Parvocellular neurons in the primate dorsal lateral geniculate nucleus encode color in the same way that retinal ganglion cells do, in opponent fashion, with complementary colors. De Valois, Abramov, and Jacobs (1966), recording action potentials from neurons in the lateral geniculate nucleus, found two major types of opponent cells: red-green detectors and blue-yellow detectors. Each type of detector responded in excitatory or inhibitory fashion to one of the pair of colors in the center and in the opposite manner to that color in the surround. Figure 6.46 shows the rate of firing of these types of cells as a function of the wavelength of a spot of light presented to the center of their receptive fields. (See *Figure 6.46.*)

Color Coding in the Cortex

As we saw earlier, neurons within the blobs in the primary visual cortex respond to colors. Like the ganglion cells in the retina and the parvocellular

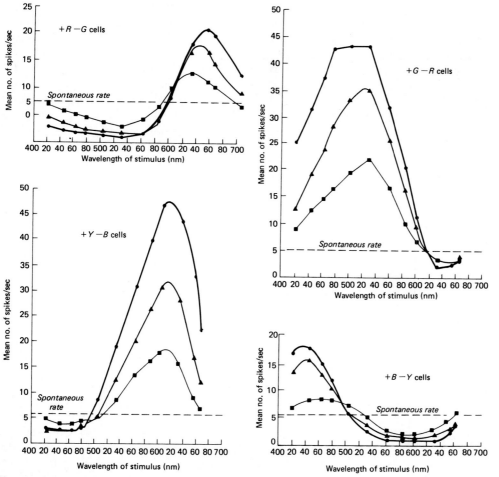

FIGURE 6.46

Responses recorded from single neurons in the lateral geniculate nucleus to light of various wavelengths. These neurons appear to encode color in an opponent-process fashion. *Spontaneous rate* refers to the baseline rate of neural firing in the absence of stimulation. R = red; G = green; Y = yellow; B = blue; + = excitation; j = inhibition. (From De Valois, R.L., Abramov, I., and Jacobs, G.H. *Journal of the Optical Society of America*, 1966, 56, 966–977.)

neurons in the dorsal lateral geniculate nucleus, they respond in opponent fashion. We saw that neurons in the blobs send axons through area V2 to area V4. Zeki (1980) found that neurons in area V4 respond selectively to colors, often in opponent fashion, but their response characteristics are much more complex. Unlike the neurons we have encountered so far, these neurons respond to a *variety* of wavelengths, not just those that correspond to red, green, yellow, and blue. Some neurons respond very selectively, their response rate dropping by a factor of 2 when the stimulus is as little as 10 nm away from their peak sensitivity.

Lesions of a restricted region of the human prestriate cortex can cause complete loss of color vision without disrupting visual acuity; the patients describe their vision as resembling a black-and-white film (Damasio, Yamada, Damasio, Corbett, and McKee, 1980). It seems likely that these lesions destroy the analog of V4, but not enough is known about the anatomy of the human visual system to be certain.

Most neurons in the visual system respond best to brightness *contrast* rather than absolute levels of brightness. Thus, the perceived brightness of a particular stimulus depends on the relative amounts of light received from it and from other parts of the scene. The perceived color of a stimulus is similarly influenced by the surrounding scene (Land, 1974). For example, the appearance of the colors of objects remains much the same whether we observe them under artificial light, under an overcast sky, or at noon on a cloudless day. This fact means that our visual system does not simply respond according to the wavelength of the light reflected by objects in each part of the visual field; instead, it compensates for the source of the light. This compensation appears to be made by simultaneously comparing the color composition of each point in the visual field with the mean of all the other points. If the average level of long-wavelength light is high (as it would be if an object were illuminated by the light of a setting sun), then some long-wavelength light is "subtracted out" of the perception of each point in the scene.

Using a procedure devised by Land (1977), Zeki (1980) dramatically demonstrated the role of area V4 in this phenomenon. After locating a neuron in V4 that responded to red light, he placed a special display panel in front of the monkey. The display contained rectangular patches of paper of different colors. (The display is referred to as a *Mondrian,* because it resembles the style of paintings made by this artist.) He adjusted the position of the display so that a patch of red paper fell in the neuron's receptive field. The neuron responded. Then he illuminated the display panel with red light. Under these conditions the red patch loses its vivid red appearance to a human observer. Even though its receptive field was flooded with red light, the neuron did *not* respond. Similarly, the neuron failed to respond when he illuminated the display panel with green or blue light. Only when he shone all three lights on the panel (simulating white light) did the neuron respond. This is an important finding, because only when all three lights are used will the red patch appear as a vivid red to an observer. The response of the neuron in V4 thus correlates with the perception of the color red, not simply with the presence of light of a particular wavelength. (See *Figure 6.47.*)

As Zeki (1984) notes, neurons in the retina, in the dorsal lateral geniculate nucleus, and in the striate cortex act like *wavelength detectors;* they respond according to the wavelength of light that falls on their receptive field and are not affected by light falling on the receptive fields of their neighbors. In contrast, neurons in area V4 act like *color detectors,* showing a response that is adjusted by the light falling on the rest of the visual field. His discovery appears to mark the transition between color sensation and color perception.

*I*NTERIM SUMMARY

Color vision occurs as a result of information provided by three types of cones, each of which is sensitive to light of a certain wavelength: long, medium, or short. Color-sensitive ganglion cells respond in an opposing center/surround fashion to the pairs of primary colors: red and green, and blue and yellow.

The absorption characteristics of the cones are determined by the particular opsin that their photopigment contains. Most forms of defective color vision appear to be caused by alterations in cone opsins. The "red" cones

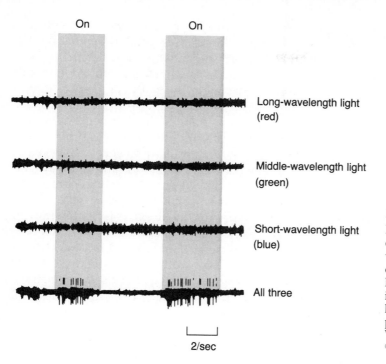

On   On

Long-wavelength light
(red)

Middle-wavelength light
(green)

Short-wavelength light
(blue)

All three

2/sec

FIGURE 6.47
Response of a single neuron in area V4
of the rhesus monkey visual cortex
whose receptive field included a red-
colored patch on a multihued
Mondrian when the entire display was
illuminated with red, green, or blue
light or with all three. (Reprinted by
permission from Zeki, S.M., *Nature*,
Vol. 284, pp. 412–418. Copyright
© 1980 Macmillan Journals Limited.)

of people with protanopia are filled with "green" cone opsin, and the "green" cones of people with deuteranopia are filled with "red" cone opsin. The retinas of people with tritanopia appear to lack "blue" cones.

The color-sensitive cells of the dorsal lateral geniculate nucleus respond to red/green or yellow/blue in an opposing center/surround fashion. These neurons send information about color to the blobs in the primary visual cortex, which send information to area V4 of the prestriate cortex. Neurons in V4 respond selectively to a wide range of wavelengths and are not particularly responsive to spatial features of visual stimuli, such as orientation. The Mondrian experiment tells us that the responses of neurons in V4 closely correspond to some of the more complex phenomena of color perception. Neurons there encode *color*, not *wavelength*.

EFFECTS OF BRAIN DAMAGE ON HUMAN VISUAL PERCEPTION

Damage to portions of the visual system of the human brain have given investigators some insights into the anatomy and physiology of visual per-

ception. In general, the results have been consistent with what has been learned from experiments with other primates.

Blindsight

Damage to the eyes, optic nerves, optic tracts, lateral geniculate nucleus, optic radiations, or primary visual cortex results in loss of vision in particular portions of the visual field or in complete blindness if the damage is total. However, an interesting phenomenon is seen in people with damage to the optic radiations or primary visual cortex that spares the projections from the lateral geniculate nucleus to the superior colliculus.

It has long been recognized that damage to the optic radiations or primary visual cortex on one side of the brain causes blindness in the contralateral visual field. That is, if the right side of the brain is damaged, the patient will be blind to everything located to the left when he or she looks straight ahead. However, Weiskrantz and his colleagues (Weiskrantz, Warrington, Sanders, and Marshall, 1974; Weiskrantz, 1987) found that if an object is placed in the patient's blind field and the patient is asked to reach for it, he or she will be able to do so rather accurately. In fact, if the investigator presents objects of different sizes, the patient will open his or her hand wider when reaching for large objects than for small ones. The patients are surprised to find their hands repeatedly coming in contact with an object in what appears to them as darkness; they say that they see nothing there. The patient is also sensitive to movement and, to a certain extent, the orientation of objects in the blind field.

This phenomenon, which Weiskrantz called **blindsight,** probably depends on the connections between the superior colliculus and the prestriate cortex. As we saw earlier, Rodman, Gross, and Albright (1989) found that neurons in area V5 did not lose their ability to detect movement after destruction of the striate cortex, but they did lose this ability after the superior colliculus was subsequently destroyed. Whether area V5 or another area is responsible for some aspects of the residual vision in blindsight is not yet known.

Besides telling us something about the functions of the various parts of the visual system, the phenomenon of blindsight also shows that visual information can control behavior without producing a conscious sensation. Although the superior colliculi send visual information to parts of the brain that guide hand movements, they do not appear to send them to parts of the brain responsible for conscious awareness. Perhaps that phenomenon is a more recent evolutionary development. I will have more to say about this topic in Chapters 14 and 16, which discuss memory and human communication.

Visual Agnosias

As I mentioned earlier in this chapter, damage to different parts of the circumstriate cortex can cause achromatopsia (complete loss of color perception) or loss of sensitivity to movement. In addition, damage to the visual association cortex can cause a category of deficits known as **visual agnosia.** Agnosia ("failure to know") refers to an inability to identify or perceive a stimulus by means of a particular sensory modality, even though its details can be detected by means of that modality and the person retains relatively normal intellectual capacity. *Apperceptive* agnosias are failures in high-level perception, whereas *associative* agnosias are disconnections between these perceptions and verbal systems. The distinction will be described in more detail shortly.

People with visual agnosia cannot identify or perceive common objects by sight, even though they have relatively normal visual acuity (Warrington and James, 1988). In some cases they can read small print but fail to recognize a common object, such as a wristwatch. However, if they are permitted to hold the object (say, the wristwatch), they can immediately recognize it by touch and say what it is. Thus, they have not lost their memory for the object or forgotten how to say its name. You will note that in the first sentence of this paragraph I said inability to "identify or perceive." Normally, we think of these words as being almost synonymous; it seems that if we can perceive something, we can also identify it. However, we will see that associative visual agnosia involves reasonably normal perception but impaired ability to identify what is perceived.

Apperceptive Visual Agnosia

Apperceptive visual agnosia is a perceptual problem caused by brain damage. Although the person may have normal visual acuity, he or she cannot successfully recognize objects visually by their shape. For example, a patient studied by Benson and Greenberg (1969) was initially believed to be blind but was subsequently observed to navigate his wheelchair around the halls of the hospital. Testing revealed that his visual fields were full (there were no scotomas) and that he could pick up threads placed on a sheet of white paper. He could discriminate among stimuli that differed in size, brightness, or hue but could not distinguish those that differed only in shape.

A common symptom of visual agnosia is **prosopagnosia,** an inability to recognize faces (*prosopon* means "face"). Prosopagnosia is a subtle deficit that can occur even when a person has no apparent difficulty recognizing common objects visually. Some investigators have speculated that facial recognition is mediated by special circuits in the brain that are devoted to the specific analysis of facial features. However, several observations suggest that the distinction between prosopagnosia and agnosia for common objects is quantitative, not qualitative; that is, visual agnosia for common objects is simply a more severe deficit, caused by more extensive damage to the relevant parts of the visual association cortex. Alexander and Albert (1983) note that although prosopagnosia can be seen without visual-object agnosia, all patients with visual-object agnosia also have prosopagnosia.

Damasio, Damasio, and Van Hoesen (1982) describe three patients with prosopagnosia who could recognize familiar objects but had difficulty discriminating between particular objects of the same class. For example, none of them could recognize their own car, although they could tell a car from other types of motorized vehicles. One of them could find her own car in a parking lot only by reading all the license plates until she found her own. Another patient, a farmer, could no longer recognize his cows (Bornstein, Stroka, and Munitz, 1969). Although it is conceivable that the evolutionary process could have selected for neural mechanisms specialized for the recognition of faces of members of our own species, it is unlikely that it could have done so for the shapes of cars and cows. We can probably conclude that prosopagnosia is simply a relatively mild form of visual-object agnosia; faces are particularly complex stimuli.

From studies of their own patients and from a review of the literature, Damasio, Damasio, and Van Hoesen (1982) conclude that apperceptive visual agnosias are most commonly caused by bilateral damage to the medial portion of the occipital and posterior temporal cortex, which includes regions of prestriate cortex. The syndrome is relatively rare, because bilateral damage to the same relatively small portion of the brain is uncommon. If the lesion is too large, it will invade the optic radiations that lie immediately beneath the cortex and thus produce blindness. From experiments with monkeys we might predict that bilateral lesions of the inferior temporal cortex (on the lateral surface of the brain) would also produce deficits in visual perception.

Associative Visual Agnosia

A person with apperceptive agnosia who cannot recognize common objects also cannot draw them or copy other people's drawings; thus, we properly speak of a deficit in perception. How-ever, people with an ***associative visual agnosia*** appear to be able to perceive normally but cannot name what they have seen. For example, a patient studied by Ratcliff and Newcombe (1982) could copy a drawing of an anchor (much better than I could have done). Thus, he could perceive the shape of the anchor. However, he could not recognize what he had just drawn. When asked on another occasion to draw (not copy) a picture of an anchor, he could not do so. Although he could *copy* a real image of an anchor, he apparently could not form his own mental image of one. (See ***Figure 6.48.***) When asked (on yet another occasion) to define *anchor*, he said "a brake for ships," so we can conclude that he knew what the word meant.

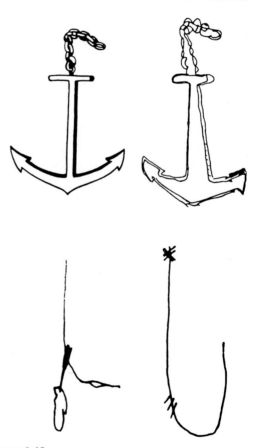

FIGURE 6.48

Associative visual agnosia. The patient successfully copied an anchor (*top*) but failed on two attempts to comply with a request to "draw an anchor" (*bottom*). (From Ratcliff, G., and Newcombe, F., in *Normality and Pathology in Cognitive Functions*, edited by A.W. Ellis. London: Academic Press, 1982.)

Associative visual agnosia appears to involve difficulty in transferring visual information to verbal mechanisms. That is, the person perceives the object well enough to draw it, but his or her verbal mechanisms do not receive the necessary information to produce the appropriate word. (If this concept seems puzzling or difficult to believe, do not despair. I will describe similar phenomena in more detail in Chapter 16.) David Margolin and I studied a man who had sustained brain damage from an inflammatory disease that affected his cerebral blood vessels. (The damage was diffuse, so we could not make any conclusions about the anatomy of his disorder.) He suffered from an apparent visual agnosia, failing to identify most pictures of objects. However, he sometimes made unintentional gestures when he was studying a picture that gave him enough of a clue that he could identify it. For example, on one occasion while he was puzzling over a picture of a cow, he started making movements with both hands that were unmistakably ones he would make if he were milking a cow. He looked at his hands and said, ''Oh, a cow!'' (He was a farmer, by the way.)

We might speculate that his perceptual mechanisms, in the visual association cortex, were relatively normal but that connections between these mechanisms and the speech mechanisms of the left hemisphere were disrupted. However, the connections between the perceptual mechanisms and the motor mechanisms of the frontal lobe were spared, permitting him to make appropriate movements when looking at some pictures. (See *Figure 6.49.*) In fact, a particularly observant and conscientious speech therapist helped the patient learn how to read by these means. She taught him the manual alphabet used by deaf people, in which letters are represented by particular hand and finger movements. (This system is commonly called *finger spelling.*) He could then look at individual letters of words he could not read, make the appropriate movements, observe the sequence of letters that he spelled, and decode the word.

The anatomical basis of associative visual agnosia has not been clearly established. Many investigators believe that the syndrome is caused by damage to white matter underlying the occipital and temporal lobes. The disruption of these axons disconnects regions of the brain that mediate vi-

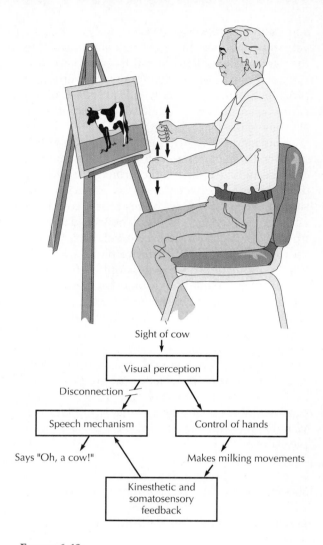

FIGURE 6.49
Associative visual agnosia. A patient was able to identify a picture of a cow by observing himself make milking movements.

sual perception from those that are needed for verbalization.

INTERIM SUMMARY

Damage to the visual system up to the striate cortex produces blindness in all or part of the visual field. However, damage limited to the striate cortex or to the optic radiations leading to them produces a syndrome called blindsight. People with blindsight deny seeing anything in the blind part of their visual field but can nevertheless point to objects located there and discriminate their size and orientation. They are also sensitive to movement. However, although their behavior can be affected by objects in their blind field, they have no conscious awareness of the presence of these objects.

Studies with humans who have sustained damage to the visual association cortex have discovered two basic forms of visual agnosia. Apperceptive visual agnosia involves difficulty in perceiving the shapes of objects, even though the fine details can often be detected. Achromatopsia, lack of color vision, often accompanies this disorder and probably results from damage to the human equivalent of V4. Prosopagnosia, failure to recognize faces, has traditionally been regarded as a separate disorder, but it probably represents a mild form of apperceptive visual agnosia. The second basic form of visual agnosia, associative visual agnosia, is characterized by relatively good object perception but the inability to name what has been perceived. This disorder is probably caused by damage to axons that connect the visual association cortex with regions of the brain that are important for verbalization.

CONCLUDING REMARKS

Vision has long fascinated people, and research on this topic has occupied the efforts of many investigators and undoubtedly will continue to do so for many years. As you have seen in this chapter, biochemists are studying the process of sensory transduction, neuroanatomists are studying the details of neural connections in the retina, thalamus, midbrain, and neocortex, and other neuroscientists are studying the response characteristics of neurons in these structures. The functions of various regions of the visual association cortex are beginning to be mapped out, and neurologists and neuropyschologists are beginning to be able to characterize the nature of visual deficits in people with brain damage and to relate these deficits to research with laboratory animals. In the next chapter we will have a look at the anatomy and functions of the other senses.

NEW TERMS

accommodation p. 144
A cell p. 155
amacrine cell p. 146
apperceptive visual agnosia p. 186
associative visual agnosia p. 187
Balint's syndrome p. 176
B cell p. 155
bipolar cell p. 146
blindsight p. 186
blob p. 160
brightness p. 143
calcarine fissure p. 150
ciliary muscle p. 144
complex cell p. 160
cone p. 144
conjunctiva p. 143

convergence p. 144
cornea p. 143
deuteranopia p. 180
diffuse bipolar cell p. 157
dorsal lateral geniculate nucleus p. 149
feature detector p. 154
flat bipolar cell p. 157
fovea p. 146
ganglion cell p. 146
homunculus p. 142
horizontal cell p. 146
hue p. 143
hypercomplex cell p. 161
inferior temporal cortex p. 176
inner plexiform layer p. 146
invaginating bipolar cell p. 157
iris p. 143

lamella p. 147
lens p. 144
magnocellular layer p. 158
midget bipolar cell p. 157
midget ganglion cell p. 157
ocular apraxia p. 177
off-center cell p. 154
on-center cell p. 154
opponent coding p. 154
opsin p. 147
optic ataxia p. 176
optic chiasm p. 150
optic disk p. 146
optic radiations p. 150
orbit p. 143
outer plexiform layer p. 146
parasol ganglion cell p. 155
parvocellular layer p. 158

phase p. 165
photon p. 143
photopigment p. 147
photoreceptor p. 144
prestriate cortex p. 172
prosopagnosia p. 186
protanopia p. 180
pupil p. 143
receptive field p. 153
receptor potential p. 140
retina p. 144
retinal p. 147

retinal disparity p. 170
retinotopic representation p. 150
rhodopsin p. 147
rod p. 144
rod bipolar cell p. 157
saturation p. 143
sclera p. 143
sensory coding p. 140
sensory transduction p. 140
simple cell p. 160
simultanagnosia p. 176

sine wave p. 165
sine-wave grating p. 163
spatial coding p. 140
spatial frequency p. 163
stereopsis p. 170
striate cortex p. 150
temporal coding p. 141
tritanopia p. 181
visual agnosia p. 186
visual angle p. 163
vitreous humor p. 144

SUGGESTED READINGS

Boynton, R.M. *Human Color Vision.* New York: Holt, Rinehart and Winston, 1979.

De Valois, R.L., and De Valois, K.K. *Spatial Vision.* New York: Oxford University Press, 1988.

Dowling, J.E. *The Retina: An Approachable Part of the Brain.* Cambridge, Mass.: Harvard University Press, 1987.

Gregory, R.L. *Eye and Brain.* New York: McGraw-Hill, 1978.

Katsuki, Y., Norgren, R., and Sato, M. *Brain Mechanisms of Sensation.* New York: John Wiley & Sons, 1981.

Lund, J.S. Anatomical organization of macaque monkey striate visual cortex. *Annual Review of Neuroscience,* 1988, *11,* 253–288.

Maunsell, J.H.R., and Newsome, W.T. Visual processing in monkey extrastriate cortex. *Annual Review of Neuroscience,* 1987, *10,* 363–402.

Movshon, J.A., and Van Sluyters, R.C. Visual neural development. *Annual Review of Neuroscience,* 1984, *7,* 477–522.

Poggio, G.F., and Poggio, T. The analysis of stereopsis. *Annual Review of Neuroscience,* 1984, *7,* 379–412.

Rodieck, R.W. The primate retina. In *Comparative Primate Biology. Volume 4: Neurosciences,* edited by H.D. Steklis and J. Erwin. New York: A.R. Liss, 1988.

Yau, K.-W., and Baylor, D.A. Cyclic GMP-activated conductance of retinal photoreceptor cells. *Annual Review of Neuroscience,* 1989, *12,* 289–328.

7

Audition, Vestibular Senses, Somatosenses, Gustation, and Olfaction

*O*ne chapter was devoted to vision, but the rest of the sensory modalities must share a chapter. This unequal allocation of space reflects the relative importance of vision to our species and the relative amount of research that has been devoted to it. This chapter considers audition, the vestibular senses, the somatosenses (including kinesthesia), pain perception, gustation, and olfaction.

AUDITION

For most people, audition is the second most important sense. The value of verbal communication makes it even more important than vision in some respects; for example, a blind person can join others in conversation far more easily than a deaf person can. Acoustic stimuli also provide information about things that are hidden from view, and our ears work just as well in the dark.

The Stimulus

We hear sounds, which are produced by objects that vibrate and set the molecules of the air into motion. When an object vibrates, its movements cause the air surrounding it alternately to condense and rarefy (pull apart), producing waves that travel away from the object at approximately 700 miles per hour. If the vibration ranges between approximately 30 and 20,000 times per second, these waves will stimulate receptive cells in our ears and will be perceived as sounds. We can also stimulate these receptors by placing a vibrating object against the bones of the head, bypassing air conduction altogether.

In Chapter 6 we saw that light has three perceptual dimensions—hue, brightness, and saturation—which correspond to three physical dimensions. Similarly, sounds vary in their pitch, loudness, and timbre. The perceived *pitch* of an auditory stimulus is determined by the frequency of vibration, which is measured in *hertz* (Hz), or cycles per second. (The term honors Heinrich Hertz, a nineteenth-century German physicist.) *Loudness* is a function of intensity—the degree to which the condensations and rarefactions of air differ from each other. More vigorous vibrations of an object produce more intense sound waves and, hence, louder ones. *Timbre* provides information about the nature of the particular sound—for example, the sound of an oboe or a train whistle. Most natural acoustic stimuli are complex, consisting of several different frequencies of vibration. The particular mixture determines the sound's timbre. (See *Figure 7.1.*)

The eye is a *synthetic* organ (literally, "a putting together"). When two different wavelengths of light are mixed, we perceive a single color. For example, when we see a mixture of red and bluish green light, we perceive pure yellow light and cannot detect either of the two constituents. In

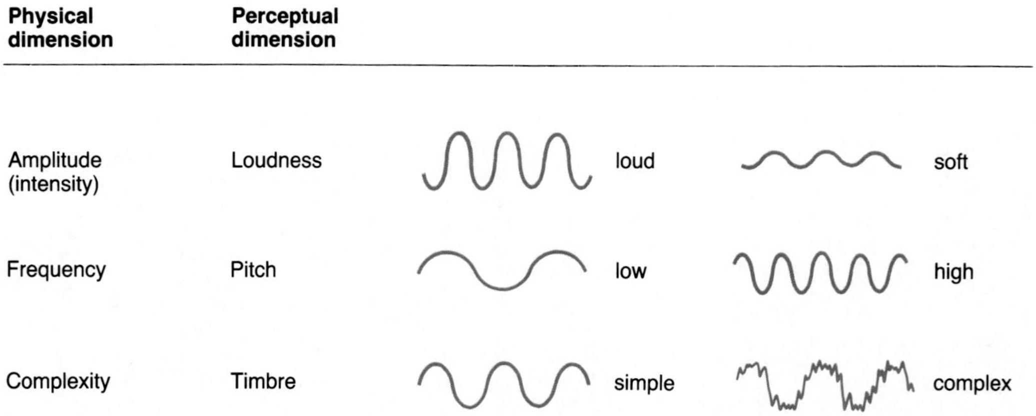

Physical dimension	Perceptual dimension				
Amplitude (intensity)	Loudness		loud		soft
Frequency	Pitch		low		high
Complexity	Timbre		simple		complex

FIGURE 7.1
The physical and perceptual dimensions of sound waves.

contrast, the ear is an *analytical* organ (from *analuein*, "to undo"). When two different frequencies of sound waves are mixed, we do not perceive an intermediate tone; instead, we hear both original tones. As we will see, the ability of our auditory system to detect the individual component frequencies of a complex tone gives us the capacity to identify the nature of particular sounds, such as those of different musical instruments.

Anatomy of the Ear

Figure 7.2 shows a section through the ear and auditory canal and illustrates the apparatus of the middle and inner ear. (See *Figure 7.2.*) Sound is funneled via the *pinna* (external ear) through the *external auditory canal* to the **tympanic membrane** (eardrum), which vibrates with the sound. We are

not very good at moving our ears, but by orienting our heads, we can modify the sound that finally reaches the receptors. A muscle in the tympanic membrane (the *tensor tympani*) can alter the membrane's tension and thus control the amount of sound that is permitted to pass through to the middle ear.

The *middle ear* consists of a hollow region behind the tympanic membrane, approximately 2 ml in volume. It contains the bones of the middle ear, called the **ossicles,** which are set into vibration by the tympanic membrane. The **malleus** (hammer) connects with the tympanic membrane and transmits vibrations via the **incus** (anvil) and **stapes** (stirrup) to the **cochlea,** the structure that contains the receptors. The baseplate of the stapes presses against the membrane behind the **oval window,** the opening in the bony process surrounding the cochlea. (See *Figures 7.2 and 7.3.*)

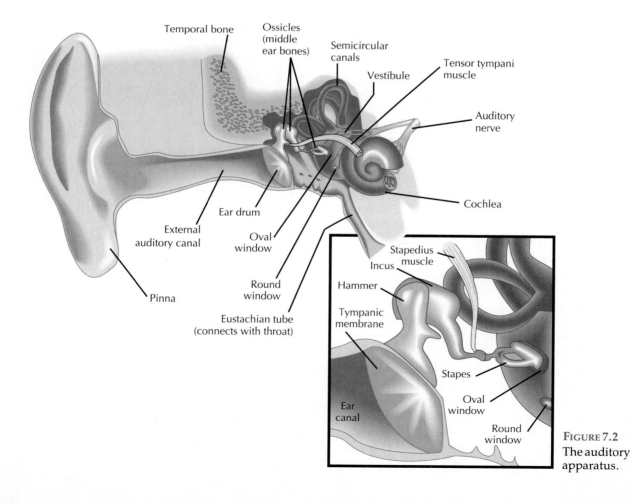

FIGURE 7.2
The auditory apparatus.

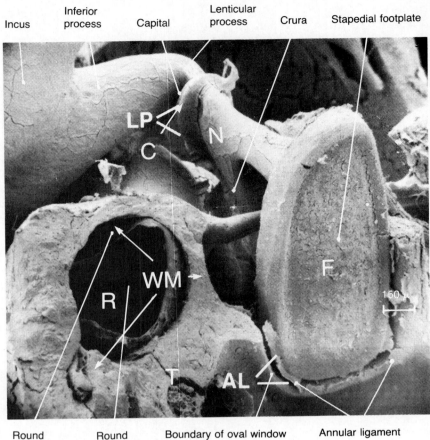

Incus   Inferior process   Capital   Lenticular process   Crura   Stapedial footplate

Round window membrane   Round window   Boundary of oval window   Annular ligament

FIGURE 7.3

A scanning electron micrograph of the stapes and the round window. (From *Tissues and Organs: A Text-Atlas of Scanning Electron Microscopy.* By Richard G. Kessel and Randy H. Kardon. Copyright © 1979 by W.H. Freeman and Company. Reprinted with permission.)

The *stapedial muscle,* when contracted, directs the baseplate of the stapes away from its normal point of attachment to the oval window, hence dampening the vibration passed on to the receptive cells. This response occurs when loud noises are presented to the ear, and it may serve to protect the inner ear from damage.

The cochlea is part of the *inner ear.* It is filled with fluid; therefore, sounds transmitted through the air must be transferred into a liquid medium. This process is normally very inefficient—99.9 percent of the energy of airborne sound would be reflected away if the air impinged directly against the oval window of the cochlea. (If you have ever swum underwater, you have probably noted how quiet it is there; most of the sound arising in the air is reflected off the surface of the water.) The chain of ossicles serves as an extremely efficient means of energy transmission. The bones provide a me-

chanical advantage, with the baseplate of the stapes making smaller but more forceful excursions against the oval window than the tympanic membrane makes against the malleus.

The name *cochlea* comes from the Greek word *kokhlos,* or "land snail." It is indeed snail-shaped, consisting of two and three-quarters turns of a gradually tapering cylinder. The cochlea is divided longitudinally into three sections, as shown in *Figure 7.4.* The receptive organ, known as the **organ of Corti,** consists of the *basilar membrane,* the *hair cells,* and the *tectorial membrane.* The auditory receptor cells are called **hair cells,** and they are anchored, via rodlike **Deiters's cells,** to the **basilar membrane.** The cilia of the hair cells pass through the *reticular membrane,* and the ends of some of them attach to the fairly rigid **tectorial membrane,** which projects overhead like a shelf. (See *Figure 7.4.*) Sound waves cause the basilar membrane to

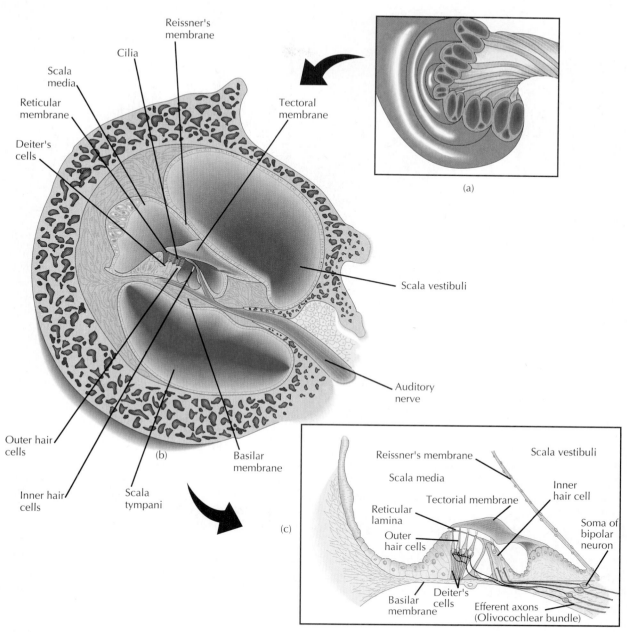

FIGURE 7.4
A cross section through the cochlea, showing the organ of Corti.

move relative to the tectorial membrane, which bends the cilia of the hair cells. This bending produces receptor potentials.

If the cochlea were a closed system, no vibration would be transmitted through the oval window, because liquids are essentially incompressible. However, there is a membrane-covered opening, the *round window,* which allows the fluid contents of the cochlea to move back and forth. The baseplate of the stapes presses against the membrane behind the oval window, thus increasing the hydrostatic pressure within the

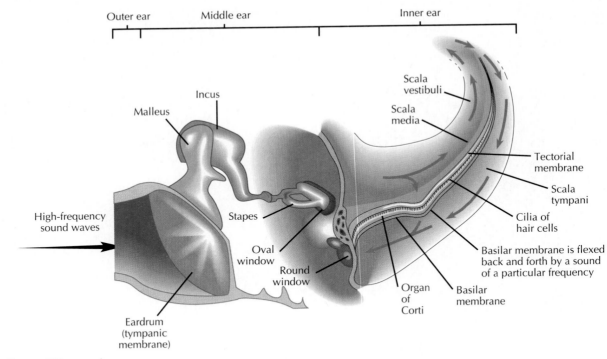

FIGURE 7.5
Stimulation of the organ of Corti. Sound waves transmitted through the oval window
deform a portion of the basilar membrane.

vestibule, a chamber to which the cochlea is attached. The *scala vestibuli* (literally, the stairway of the vestibule) connects with the vestibule and conducts the pressure around the turns of the cochlea. (See *Figure 7.5.*)

In recent years much progress has been made in studies of the way that the organ of Corti converts mechanical energy into neural activity. Georg von Békésy, in a lifetime of brilliant studies on the cochleas of various animals, from human cadavers to elephants, found that the vibratory energy exerted on the oval window results in deformations in the shape of the basilar membrane called *traveling waves* (von Békésy, 1960). If you have ever taken hold of the end of a rope or garden hose and shaken it up and down, you have produced traveling waves. Because of the physical properties of different parts of the basilar membrane and its interaction with the surrounding fluids, sounds of different frequencies produce the greatest amount of deformation in different regions of the basilar membrane: high-

frequencies at the end nearest the oval window, and low-frequencies at the opposite end.

Figure 7.5 shows this process in a cochlea that has been partially straightened out. The baseplate of the stapes vibrates against the membrane behind the oval window and introduces sound waves of high or low frequency into the scala vestibuli. The vibrations cause part of the basilar membrane to flex back and forth, transmitting the pressure waves into the *scala tympani,* which lies beneath. Pressure changes in the scala tympani are transmitted to the membrane of the round window, which moves in and out in a manner opposite to the movements of the oval window. (See *Figure 7.5.*)

Auditory Hair Cells and the Transduction of Auditory Information

Two types of auditory receptors, *inner* and *outer* auditory hair cells, lie on the inside and outside of the cochlear coils, respectively. Hair cells contain

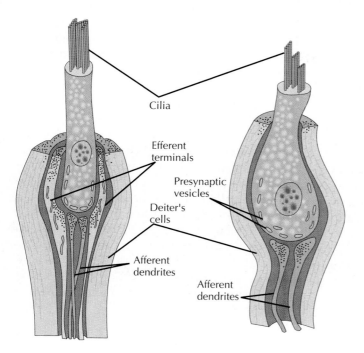

Cilia

Efferent
terminals

Presynaptic
vesicles

Deiter's
cells

Afferent
dendrites

Afferent
dendrites

FIGURE 7.6
The auditory hair cells.

cilia ("eyelashes"), fine hairlike appendages, which are arranged in rows, according to height. The human cochlea contains 3400 inner hair cells and 12,000 outer hair cells. Figure 7.6 illustrates these cells and their supporting Deiters's cells. (See *Figure 7.6.*) The hair cells form synapses with dendrites of neurons that give rise to the auditory nerve axons. Figure 7.7 shows the actual appearance of the inner and outer hair cells and the reticular membrane in a photograph taken by means of a scanning electron microscope, which shows excellent three-dimensional detail. Note the three rows of outer hair cells on the right and the single row of inner hair cells on the left. (See *Figure 7.7.*)

Sound waves cause both the basilar membrane and the tectorial membrane to flex up and down. Because the fulcra (turning points) of these two membranes are located in different

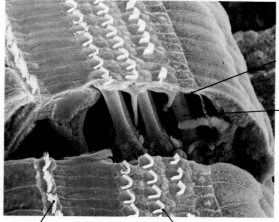

Cilia of inner hair cells   Cilia of outer hair cells

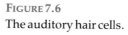

Reticular membrane

Hair cell

FIGURE 7.7
A scanning electron photomicrograph of a portion of the organ of Corti, showing the cilia of the inner and outer hair cells. (Photomicrograph courtesy of I. Hunter-Duvar, The Hospital for Sick Children, Toronto, Ontario.)

places, and because the tips of the outer hair cells are attached to the tectorial membrane, the vibrations bend the cilia in one direction or the other. (See *Figure 7.8.*) The cilia of the inner hair cells do not touch the overlying tectorial membrane, but the relative movement of the two membranes causes the fluid within the cochlea to flow past them and makes them bend back and forth, too.

Cilia contain actin filaments, which make them stiff and rigid (Flock, 1977). Adjacent cilia are linked to each other at their tip. Thus, movement of the bundle of cilia in the direction of the tallest of them stretches the linking fibers, whereas movement in the opposite direction relaxes them. (See *Figure 7.9.*)

The bending of the bundle of cilia causes receptor potentials. The resting potential of an auditory hair cell is approximately -60 mV. When the

bundle of cilia is moved toward the tallest one, the flow of K^+ into the cell increases, the membrane depolarizes, and the release of neurotransmitter increases. When the bundle is moved in the opposite direction, the influx of K^+ decreases, the membrane hyperpolarizes, and the release of neurotransmitter decreases. (See *Figure 7.9.*) Hudspeth (1982, 1985) showed that the tips of the cilia contain ion channels. Each cilium appears to contain three to seven channels, for a total of approximately one hundred per bundle. When the bundle is straight, approximately 20 percent of the ion channels are open. When the bundle moves toward the tallest one, the increased tension on the connecting fibers pulls more ion channels open and causes depolarization. When the bundle moves in the opposite direction, the relaxation of the fibers allows the opened ion channels to close. (See *Figure 7.10.*)

The Auditory Pathway

Connections with the Cochlear Nerve

The organ of Corti sends auditory information to the brain by means of the *cochlear nerve,* a branch of the auditory nerve (eighth cranial nerve). The neurons that give rise to the afferent axons that travel through this nerve are of the bipolar type. Their cell bodies reside in the *cochlear nerve ganglion.* (This ganglion is also called the *spiral ganglion,* because it consists of clumps of cell bodies arranged in a spiral caused by the curling of the cochlea.) These neurons have axonal processes, capable of sustaining action potentials, that protrude from both ends of the soma. The end of one process acts like a dendrite, responding with excitatory postsynaptic potentials when the transmitter substance is released by the auditory hair cells. The excitatory postsynaptic potentials trigger action potentials in the auditory nerve axons, which forms synapses with neurons in the medulla. (See *Figure 7.4c.*)

Each cochlear nerve contains approximately 50,000 afferent axons. The dendrites of approximately 95 percent of these axons form synapses with the inner hair cells. Most afferent fibers make contact with only one inner hair cell, but each inner hair cell forms synapses with approximately 20 fibers (Spoendlin, 1973; Keithley and

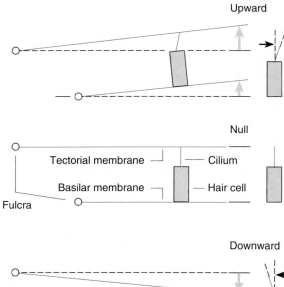

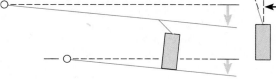

FIGURE 7.8

A schematic explanation of the fact that vibrations of the basilar membrane cause bending of the cilia of the hair cells. (Adapted from Gulick, W.L., Gescheider, G.A., and Frisina, R.D. *Hearing: Physiological Acoustics, Neural Coding, and Psychoacoustics.* New York: Oxford University Press, 1989.)

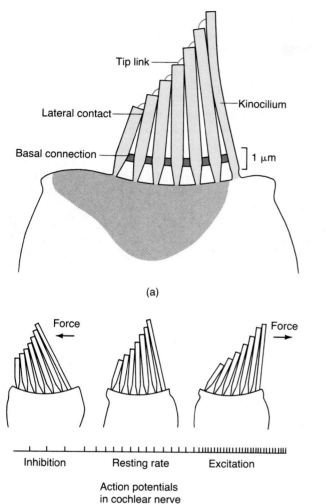

(a)

(b)

FIGURE 7.9

Cilia of auditory hair cells. (a) Their appearance. (b) Transduction. Movement of the bundle stretches or relaxes tension on the links between the tips of adjacent cilia and changes the rate of firing of the afferent axon. (Adapted from Howard, J., Roberts, W.M., and Hudspeth, A.J. *Annual Review of Biophysics and Biophysical Chemistry*, 1988, *17*, 99–124.)

have been unable to obtain single-unit recordings from them. The fibers branch considerably, each one serving approximately 10 outer hair cells. Thus, although the inner hair cells represent only 22 percent of the total number of receptive cells, their connections with auditory nerves suggest that they are of primary importance in the transmission of auditory information to the central nervous system.

Physiological and behavioral studies confirm the inferences made from the synaptic connections of the two types of hair cells: The inner hair cells are necessary for normal hearing. In fact, Deol and Gluecksohn-Waelsch (1979) found that a mutant strain of mice whose cochleas contain *only* outer hair cells apparently cannot hear at all. Some investigators currently believe that the outer hair cells are involved in altering the mechanical characteristics of the basilar membrane, thus directly influencing the effects of sound vibrations on the inner hair cells. I will discuss this possibility in the section on the anatomical coding of pitch.

The cochlear nerve contains efferent axons as well as afferent ones. The source of the efferent axons is the superior olivary complex, a group of nuclei in the medulla; thus, the efferent fibers con-

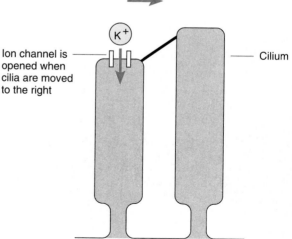

FIGURE 7.10

Transduction. Tension on the links between adjacent cilia opens ion channels, resulting in entry of potassium ions, which depolarizes the membrane potential.

Schreiber, 1987). The axons that receive information from the inner hair cells are thick and myelinated. The other 5 percent of the sensory fibers in the cochlear nerve form synapses with the much more numerous outer hair cells. These fibers are thin and unmyelinated, and so far, investigators

stitute the *olivocochlear bundle.* The fibers form synapses directly on outer hair cells and on the dendrites that serve the inner hair cells. (Refer to *Figures 7.4c and 7.6.*) The transmitter substance at the afferent synapses appears to be an excitatory amino acid such as glutamate or aspartate. The efferent terminal buttons secrete acetylcholine, which appears to have an inhibitory effect on the hair cells.

The Central Auditory System

The anatomy of the auditory system is more complicated than that of the visual system. Rather than give a detailed verbal description of the pathways, I will refer you to *Figure 7.11.* Note that axons enter the *cochlear nuclei* of the medulla and

synapse there. Most of the neurons in the cochlear nuclei send axons to the *superior olivary complex,* also located in the medulla. Neurons there project axons through a large bundle of axons called the *lateral lemniscus* to the inferior colliculus, located in the dorsal midbrain. Neurons there project to the medial geniculate nucleus, which sends axons to the auditory cortex of the temporal lobe. Many synapses along the way complicate the story. Each hemisphere receives information from both ears but primarily from the contralateral one. And auditory information is relayed to the cerebellum and reticular formation as well.

If we unrolled the basilar membrane into a flat strip and followed afferent axons serving successive points along its length, we would reach suc-

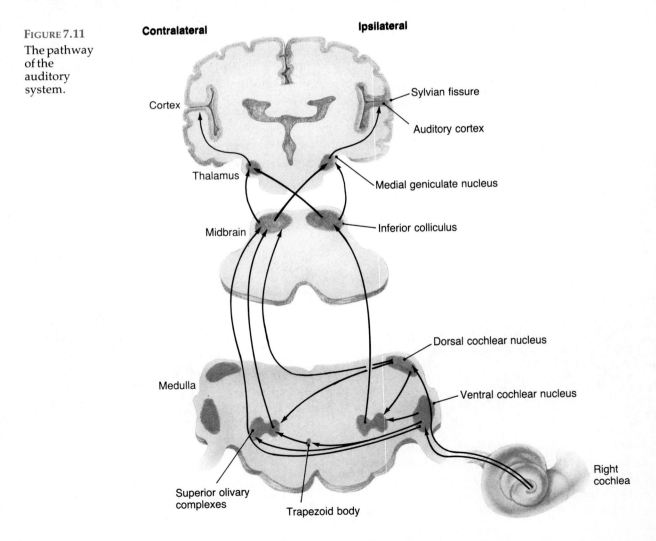

FIGURE 7.11 The pathway of the auditory system.

Contralateral

Ipsilateral

Cortex

Sylvian fissure

Auditory cortex

Thalamus

Medial geniculate nucleus

Midbrain

Inferior colliculus

Medulla

Dorsal cochlear nucleus

Ventral cochlear nucleus

Right cochlea

Superior olivary complexes

Trapezoid body

cessive points in the nuclei of the auditory system and ultimately successive points along the surface of the primary auditory cortex. The *basal* end of the basilar membrane (the end toward the oval window) is represented most medially in the auditory cortex, and the *apical* end is represented most laterally there. Because, as we will see, different parts of the basilar membrane respond best to different frequencies of sound, this relationship between cortex and basilar membrane is referred to as **tonotopic representation** (*tonos* means "tone" and *topos* means "place").

Neurons in the primary auditory cortex send axons to the auditory association cortex. In Chapter 4, we saw that the primary auditory cortex lies hidden on the inside of the lateral fissure, and that the auditory association cortex lies on the superior part of the temporal lobe.

Detection of Pitch

As we have seen, the perceptual dimension of pitch corresponds to the physical dimension of frequency. The cochlea detects frequency by two means: High and medium frequencies are coded anatomically (spatially), and low frequencies are coded temporally, by the rate of axonal firing.

Anatomical Coding of Pitch

The work of von Békésy has shown us that because of the mechanical construction of the cochlea and basilar membrane, acoustic stimuli of different frequencies cause different parts of the basilar membrane to flex back and forth. Figure 7.12 illustrates the amount of deformation along the length of the basilar membrane produced by stimulation with tones of various frequencies. Note that higher frequencies produce more displacement at the basal end of the membrane (the end closest to the stapes). (See *Figure 7.12.*)

Evidence for spatial coding of pitch comes from several sources. High doses of the antibiotic drugs kanamycin and neomycin produce degeneration of the auditory hair cells. Damage to auditory hair cells begins at the basal end of the cochlea and progresses toward the apical end; this pattern can be verified by killing experimental animals after dosing them with the antibiotic for varying amounts of time. Longer exposures to the drug

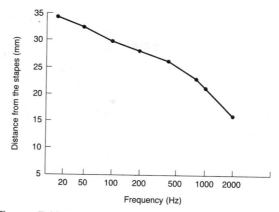

FIGURE 7.12

Anatomical coding of pitch. Stimuli of different frequencies maximally deform different regions of the basilar membrane. (From von Békésy, G. *Journal of the Acoustical Society of America*, 1949, *21*, 233–245.)

are associated with increased progress of hair cell damage down the basilar membrane. Stebbins, Miller, Johnsson, and Hawkins (1969) found that the progressive death of hair cells induced by an antibiotic closely parallels a progressive hearing loss: The highest frequencies are the first to go, and the lowest are the last.

The work of von Békésy indicated that although the basilar membrane codes for frequency along its length, the coding was not very specific. His studies, and those of investigators who followed him, indicated that a given frequency causes a large region of the basilar membrane to be deformed. This finding contrasted with the observation that people can detect changes in frequency of only 2 or 3 Hz. For several years investigators believed that sharpening had to occur within the neural components of the auditory system. They proposed various schemes whereby a broad distribution of stimulation could result in a sharpened response, perhaps by means of a process called *lateral inhibition*. This phenomenon is found in the nervous system of several different species, including (probably) the mammalian retina. It consists of mutual inhibition of sensory neurons with their neighbors, such that the neurons receiving the strongest signal inhibit those near them receiving weaker ones. The result of this process exaggerates the difference between strong and weak signals.

However, even early studies posed some problems for the "sharpening" hypothesis. For example, Katsuki (1961) made recordings from single axons in the cochlear nerve and single neurons in various parts of the auditory system and found no evidence of sharpening. Figure 7.13 shows some V-shaped *auditory tuning curves.* The data were collected as follows: The investigator located an axon with a microelectrode and presented tones of various frequencies and intensities. For each cell he plotted points that corresponded to the least intense tone that gave a response at a given frequency. The V shapes indicate that at higher intensities (the top of the V-shaped curves) a given axon responds to a wider range of frequencies. At low intensities (the bottom of the V-shaped curves) a given axon responds to a very limited range of frequencies. (See *Figure 7.13.*) The tuning curves received from the cochlear nerve were at least as precise as those found in the medial geniculate nucleus. Where, then, did the sharpening take place? Certainly, it did not take place after the cochlea.

Neural sharpening does not appear to take place within the cochlea, either. As we saw, the inner hair cells provide the auditory information that is transmitted through the auditory nerve, and the axons that form synapses with them do not branch; each one serves only one inner hair cell. Thus, there is no opportunity for lateral inhibition to take place; each inner hair cell sends information over its own private lines.

The answer appears to be that the sharpening is accomplished mechanically, on the basilar membrane itself. Because of technical limitations, von Békésy had to observe the cochleas of animals that were no longer living or, at best, cochleas that had been damaged by the procedure necessary to make the measurements. More recently, investigators have used much more sensitive—and less damaging—procedures to observe movements of the basilar membrane in response to different frequencies of sound. It appears that the point of maximum vibration of the basilar membrane to a particular frequency is very precisely localized.

The source of this localization is still not completely understood. For one thing, the cilia of the hair cells differ in length and stiffness from one basilar membrane to another, which would affect their response frequency. For another, it appears that outer hair cells participate in active processes that shape the mechanical characteristics of the basilar membrane. Outer hair cells are not only sensory transducers but also contractile elements, like muscle fibers. When they are exposed to an electrical current, or when acetylcholine is placed on them, they contract by up to 20 percent of their length. Because the tips of their cilia are embedded in the tectorial membrane, contraction would affect the response properties of the inner hair

FIGURE 7.13

Tuning curves of single units in various portions of the auditory system. dB = decibel; kHz = kilohertz (1000 Hz). (From Katsuki, Y., in *Sensory Communication,* edited by W.A. Rosenblith. Copyright 1961 by MIT Press.)

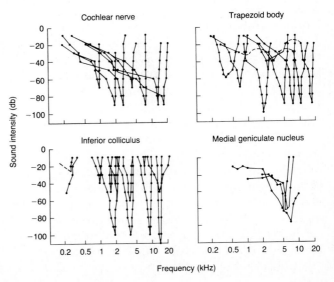

cells. Kemp (1978) discovered that when brief sounds are presented to a normal cochlea, it produces a sound itself, which can be detected with a microphone. Presumably, this sound is produced by contraction of the outer hair cells. Most investigators believe that the signals that cause contraction of the outer hair cells come partly from the olivocochlear bundle and partly from local circuits of neurons within the organ of Corti. But as we have seen, any neural sharpening that occurs there must involve only the outer hair cells.

Temporal Coding of Pitch

We have seen that frequency is nicely encoded in a spatial manner on the basilar membrane. However, the lowest frequencies do not appear to be accounted for in this manner. Kiang (1965) was unable to find any cells that responded best to frequencies of less than 200 Hz. How, then, can animals distinguish low frequencies? It appears that lower frequencies are encoded by neural firing that is synchronized to the movements of the apical end of the basilar membrane. The neurons fire in time with the sonic vibrations.

Miller and Taylor (1948) provided good evidence that pitch can be encoded by synchronized firing of the auditory hair cells. These investigators presented *white noise* (sound containing all frequencies, similar to the hissing sound you hear between FM radio stations) to human observers. When the investigators rapidly switched the white noise on and off, the observers reported that they heard a tone corresponding to the frequency of pulsation. The white noise, containing all frequencies, stimulated the entire length of the basilar membrane, so the frequency that was detected could not be coded for by place. The only frequency-specific information the auditory system could have had was the firing rate of cochlear nerve axons.

Detection of Loudness

The auditory system is incredibly sensitive to sound vibrations. Wilska (1935) used an ingenious procedure to estimate the smallest vibration to produce a perceptible sound. He glued a small wooden rod to a volunteer's tympanic membrane (temporarily, of course) and made the rod vibrate

longitudinally by means of an electromagnetic coil that could be energized with alternating current. He could vary the frequency and intensity of the current, which consequently changed the perceived pitch and loudness of the stimulus. Wilska observed the rod under a microscope and measured the distance it moved in vibration. This movement was related to the amount of electrical current used, so that he could calculate the extremely minute vibrations of the eardrum that were too small to detect under the microscope. The astonishing result was that in order for the subject to detect a sound, the eardrum needed to be vibrated a distance of less than the diameter of a hydrogen atom. Thus, in very quiet environments a young and healthy ear is limited in its ability to detect sounds in the air by the masking noise of blood rushing through the cranial blood vessels, rather than by the sensitivity of the auditory system itself. More recent studies using modern instruments have essentially confirmed Wilska's measurements. The softest sounds that can be detected appear to move the tip of the hair cells by between 1 and 100 picometers (trillionths of a meter). The softest sound we can detect is (I hesitate to say it) on the order of one 100-trillionth of the loudest sound that will not damage the inner ear (Uttal, 1973).

The axons of the cochlear nerve appear to encode loudness by rate. More intense vibrations produce a more intense shearing force on the cilia of the auditory hair cells, presumably causing them to release more transmitter substance, resulting in a higher rate of firing by the cochlear nerve axons. This explanation seems simple for the axons that encode pitch anatomically; in this case pitch is encoded by which neurons fire, and loudness is encoded by their rate of firing. However, the neurons that encode lower frequencies do so by their rate of firing. If they fire more frequently, they signal a higher pitch. Therefore, most investigators believe that the loudness of low-frequency sounds is encoded by the *number* of axons that are active at a given time.

Detection of Timbre

Although laboratory investigations of the auditory system often employ pure sine waves as stimuli, these waves are seldom encountered outside the laboratory. Instead, we hear sounds with a rich mixture of frequencies—sounds of complex timbre. For example, consider the sound of a clarinet playing a particular note. If we hear it, we can easily say that it is a clarinet and not a flute or a violin. The reason we can do so is that these three instruments produce sounds of different timbre, which our auditory system can distinguish.

Figure 7.14 shows the waveform from a clarinet playing a steady note (*top*). The shape of the waveform repeats itself regularly at the *fundamental frequency,* which corresponds to the perceived pitch of the note. A Fourier analysis of the waveform shows that it actually consists of a series of sine waves that includes the fundamental frequency and many *overtones,* multiples of the fundamental frequency. Different instruments produce overtones with different intensities. (See *Figure 7.14.*) Electronic synthesizers simulate the sounds of real instruments by producing a series of overtones of the proper intensities, mixing them, and passing them through a loudspeaker.

When the basilar membrane is stimulated by the sound of a clarinet, different portions respond to each of the overtones. This response produces a unique anatomically coded pattern of activity in the cochlear nerve, which is subsequently identified by the auditory system of the brain. Just how this analysis is done is not known and probably will not be known for many years. When you consider that we can listen to an orchestra playing and identify several instruments that are playing simultaneously, you can appreciate the complexity of the analysis performed by the auditory system.

Feature Detection in the Auditory System

So far, I have discussed coding of only pitch, loudness, and timbre (the last of which is actually a complex frequency analysis). The auditory system also responds to other qualities of acoustic stimuli. For example, our ears are very good at determining whether the source of a sound is to the right or left of us. (To discriminate front from back, we merely turn our heads, transforming the discrimination into a left-right decision.) Two separate physiological mechanisms detect the location of sound sources: We use phase differences for

low frequencies (less than approximately 3000 Hz) and intensity differences for higher frequencies. Stevens and Newman (1936) found that localization is worst at approximately 3000 Hz, presumably because both mechanisms are rather inefficient at that frequency.

Localization by Means of Arrival Time and Phase Differences

If we are blindfolded, we can still determine the location of a stimulus that emits a click with

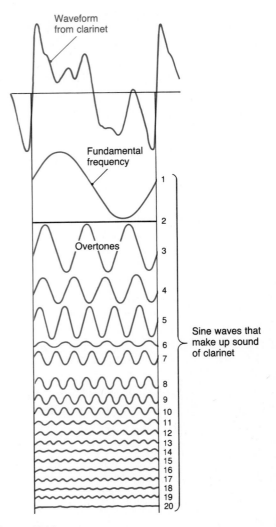

FIGURE 7.14
The shape of a sound wave from a clarinet (*top*) and the individual frequencies into which it can be analyzed. (Reprinted from *Stereo Review,* copyright © 1977 by Diamandis Communications Inc.)

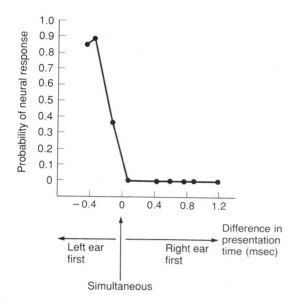

FIGURE 7.15

Neural responses to binaural pairs of clicks presented at slightly different times to the two ears. (From Moushegian, G., Rupert, A.L., and Langford, T.L. *Journal of Neurophysiology*, 1967, *30*, 1239–1261.)

rather good accuracy. We do so because neurons respond selectively to different *arrival times* of the sound waves at the left and right ears. If the source of the click is to the right or left of the midline, the sound pressure wave will reach one ear sooner and initiate action potentials there first. Only if the stimulus is straight ahead will the ears be stimulated simultaneously. Many neurons in the auditory system are *binaural*, responding to sounds presented to either ear. (Their counterparts in the visual system are the *binocular* neurons.) Some of

these neurons, especially those in the superior olivary complex of the medulla, respond according to the difference in arrival times of sound waves produced by clicks presented to both ears. Their response rates reflect differences as small as a fraction of a millisecond. For example, Figure 7.15 shows the graph of a cell that responded most vigorously when the first of a pair of binaural clicks is presented first to the left ear. (See *Figure 7.15.*)

We detect the source of continuous low-pitched sounds by means of phase differences. *Phase differences* refer to the simultaneous arrival, at each ear, of different portions (phases) of the oscillating sound wave. For example, if we assume that sound travels at 700 mi/h through the air (the actual value depends on temperature, barometric pressure, and humidity), adjacent cycles of a 1000-Hz tone are 12.3 in. apart. Thus, if the source of the sound is located to one side of the head, one eardrum is pulled out while the other is pushed in. (See *Figure 7.16.*) If some auditory neurons respond only during a particular phase of a sound wave, a tone presented by a sound source closer to one ear than the other would produce firing patterns of axons from the two ears that are slightly out of synchrony.

Indeed, some auditory neurons do fire only during a particular phase of a sound wave (that is, during a particular portion of the cycle). Figure 7.17 illustrates this phenomenon, called *phase locking.* The sine wave at the top of the diagram represents the vibration of the basilar membrane produced by a pure tone. Line B shows the response of a cell that responds to every wave. Lines

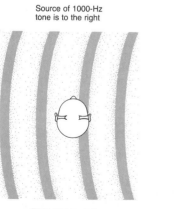

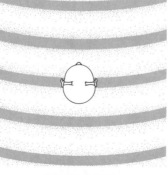

FIGURE 7.16

Phase differences. *Left:* When a 1000-Hz tone is located to one side of the head, the eardrums vibrate out of phase. *Right:* When a 1000-Hz tone is located to the front or back of the head, the eardrums vibrate in phase.

C and D show responses of cells that do not respond to every wave; however, when they fire, they do so only during the same portion of the cycle. (See *Figure 7.17.*)

Rose, Brugge, Anderson, and Hind (1967) found evidence of phase locking in axons of the cochlear nerve. The graphs shown in Figure 7.18 are called *frequency histograms*. Note the regular peaks. (See *Figure 7.18.*) The horizontal axes represent the time between two successive action potentials. To construct such plots, we find an active axon and turn on the stimulus. We start a clock as soon as an action potential is recorded and stop it when we detect another one. We then note the time, reset the clock, and see how long it takes for another action potential to occur. (Of course, being poor mortals, we engage the services of a computer to do the timing and recording for us.) After we have recorded and timed for a while, we will have a series of numbers—interspike in-

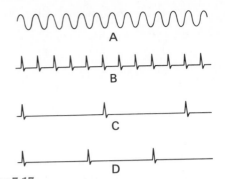

FIGURE 7.17

Phase locking. A represents the stimulus; B, C, and D represent the responses of different neurons.

tervals. We see that the numbers are clustered: For a cell stimulated with a 1000-Hz tone, the interspike intervals tend to be 1, 2, 3, 4 (etc.) msec. We find very few at 1.5, 2.5, 3.5 (etc.) msec. The number of times each interval was seen is

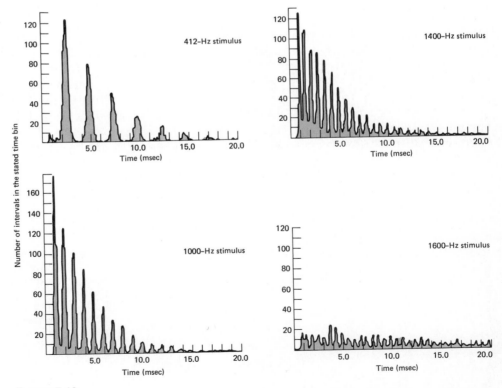

FIGURE 7.18

Evidence that individual auditory nerve axons show phase locking to pure tones. (From Rose, J.E., Brugge, J.F., Anderson, D.J., and Hind, J.E. *Journal of Neurophysiology,* 1967, 30, 769–793.)

plotted in Figure 7.18. Note, especially, the graph for the 1000-Hz tone, with its regular clusters at even 1-msec intervals. (See *Figure 7.18.*) The cells clearly "lock on" to a portion of the wave of vibration, even if they do not always fire at the same rate.

The auditory system uses the differences in firing times of phase-locked neurons to localize the source of a continuous sound, just as it localizes the source of a single click. Moushegian and Rupert (1974) recorded the activity of single neurons in the superior olivary complex while presenting a pair of 650-Hz tones, one to each ear. The rate of firing of some neurons varied with the phase difference between the two tones. Thus, these neurons provide information that can be used to detect the location of sources of low-frequency tones.

A possible mechanism to explain the ability of the nervous system to detect very short delays in the arrival times of two signals was first proposed by Jeffress (1948). He suggested that neurons received information from two sets of axons coming from the two ears. Each neuron served as a *coincidence detector*; it responded only if it simultaneously received signals from synapses be-

longing to both sets of axons. If a signal reached the two ears simultaneously, neurons in the middle of the array would fire. If, however, the signal reached one ear before the other, then neurons farther away from the "early" ear would be stimulated. (See *Figure 7.19.*)

In fact, that is exactly how the mechanism works. Carr and Konishi (1989) obtained anatomical evidence in support of Jeffress's hypothesis from the brain of the barn owl, a nocturnal bird that can very accurately detect the source of a sound (such as that made by an unfortunate mouse). Figure 7.20 shows a drawing of the distribution of the branches of two axons, one from each ear, projecting to the nucleus laminaris, the barn owl analog of the mammalian medial superior olive. As you can see, axons from the ipsilateral and contralateral ears penetrate the nucleus from opposite directions; therefore, dorsally located neurons within the nucleus are stimulated by sounds that first reach the contralateral ear. (See *Figure 7.20.*) Carr and Konishi recorded from single units within the nucleus and found that the response characteristics of the neurons located there were perfectly consistent with these anatomical facts.

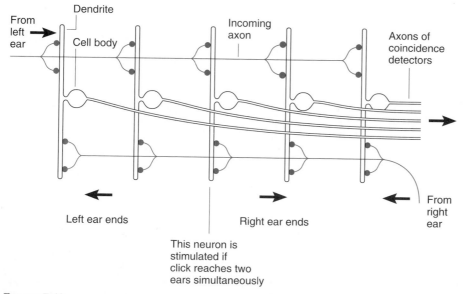

FIGURE 7.19
A model of a coincidence detector that can determine differences in arrival times at each ear of an auditory stimulus.

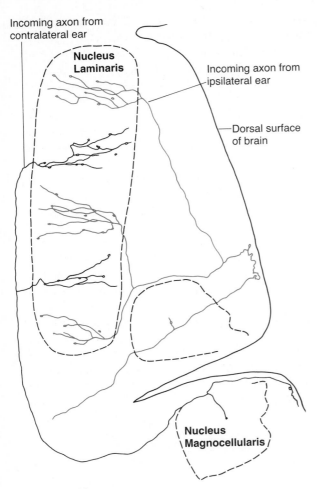

FIGURE 7.20
Evidence for a coincidence detector in the brain of a barn owl. Compare the branches of the axons with those of Figure 7.19. The drawing was prepared from microscopic examination of sections of stained tissue. (Adapted from Carr, C.E., and Konishi, M. *Proceedings of the National Academy of Sciences, USA*, 1989, *85*, 8311–8315.)

Localization by Means of Intensity Differences

The auditory system cannot readily detect binaural phase differences of high-frequency stimuli; the differences in phases of such rapid sine waves are just too short to be measured by the neurons. However, high-frequency stimuli that occur to the right or left of the midline stimulate the ears unequally. The head absorbs high frequencies, producing a "sonic shadow," so that the ear oppo-

site the source of the sound receives less intense stimulation. Some neurons in the auditory system respond differentially to binaural stimuli of different intensity in each ear, which means that they provide information that can be used to detect the source of tones of high frequency.

The neurons that detect binaural differences in loudness are located in the superior olivary complex. But whereas neurons that detect binaural differences in phase or arrival time are located in the *medial* superior olivary complex, these neurons are located in the *lateral* superior olivary complex. Information from both sets of neurons is sent to other levels of the auditory system.

Detection of Other Features

The auditory system also detects other features, but the mechanisms are not nearly so well defined. Various studies (Whitfield and Evans, 1965; Saitoh, Maruyama, and Kudoh, 1981) have found cells that respond only to the onset or cessation of a sound (or to both), to changes in pitch or intensity (sometimes only to changes in one direction), or to complex stimuli that contain a variety of frequencies. More recently, McKenna, Weinberger, and Diamond (1989) found that when they presented a series of different tones, some neurons in the primary auditory cortex responded to a particular frequency only in a particular context; for example, they would respond if the tone were the last in a series but not if it were the first. Thus, neurons in the auditory cortex encode rather complex features. Because data are scanty so far, we have no real conception of the coding mechanism that the brain uses for these changes or even of precisely what features are coded.

Behavioral Functions of the Auditory System

Destruction of the primary visual cortex leads to blindness. In contrast, destruction of the auditory cortex—even in humans—does not impair simple intensity or frequency discriminations.

Neff (1977) reviewed a large number of studies that he and his colleagues performed with cats and monkeys to investigate the role of various levels of the auditory system in auditory discrimination, localization, and lateralization (the ability to discriminate to which ear a monaural stimulus is presented). To measure the animals' ability to discriminate between different acoustic stimuli, they placed them in a *shuttle box,* an apparatus with two chambers separated by a doorway. When the experimenters presented one stimulus (S$^+$), the animals had several seconds to cross to the other side; otherwise, they would receive a shock to their feet through the floor that would continue until they escaped to the other chamber. When the experimenters presented the other stimulus (S$^-$), the animals were required to do nothing; this stimulus was not followed by a foot shock. If the animals were able to discriminate between S$^+$ and S$^-$, they soon learned to enter the opposite chamber during the former and stay put during the latter.

In other studies Neff and his colleagues evaluated the animals' ability to localize the sources of sounds by placing them in a wire cage, briefly presenting a sound through one of two loudspeakers in front of them, and then letting them leave the cage. If they approached the speaker that had just made a sound, they would find some food. (See *Figure 7.21.*) In yet another set of studies, intended to test the animals' ability to determine which ear receives an acoustic stimulus, they fitted the animals with earphones and placed them in a shuttle box. Stimuli presented to one ear served as S$^+$, and those presented to the other ear served as S$^-$.

Their results were as follows: Bilateral removal of all areas of the auditory cortex (both primary auditory cortex and auditory association cortex) did not prevent the animals from learning to detect tones of different frequencies or intensities. However, they could not discriminate between different "tunes" or temporal patterns of acoustic stimuli, they could not detect changes in the duration of tones, they could not localize the source of sounds, they could not detect changes in complex sounds, and they could not determine which ear was stimulated. *Unilateral* removal of the auditory cortex abolished only the ability to localize sounds and to determine which ear was stimulated.

Bilateral destruction of the brachium of the inferior colliculus (which abolishes all auditory input to the medial geniculate nuclei but leaves the brain stem structures intact) does not affect the animals' ability to detect sounds (even very soft ones), but it impairs the ability to detect *differences* in the intensity of sounds and abolishes frequency discrimination. Thus, these two functions must require the thalamus (but not the cortex). Neff and his colleagues also destroyed the lateral lemniscus, which abolishes auditory input to the inferior colliculi. These animals appeared to be deaf. They could learn to respond to very loud tones, but these tones might be detected by nonauditory means; perhaps the animals *felt* vibrations taking place in their ears.

As we saw in the previous chapter, lesions of the visual association cortex in humans can produce visual agnosias. Similarly, lesions of the auditory association cortex can produce auditory agnosias, the inability to comprehend the mean-

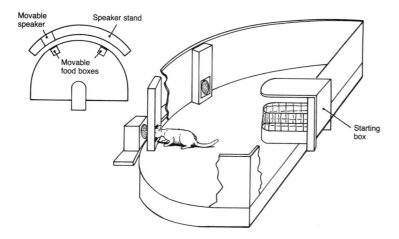

FIGURE 7.21
The experimental apparatus used by Neff and his colleagues to investigate localization of sound sources. (From Neff, W.D. *Annals of Otology, Rhinology and Laryngology,* 1977, *86,* 500–506.)

ing of sounds. If the lesion occurs in the left hemisphere, the person will sustain a particular form of language disorder. If it occurs in the right hemisphere, the person will be unable to recognize the nature or location of nonspeech sounds. Because of the importance of audition to language, these topics are discussed in much more detail in Chapter 17.

INTERIM SUMMARY

The receptive organ for audition is the organ of Corti, located on the basilar membrane. When sound strikes the tympanic membrane, it sets the ossicles into motion, and the baseplate of the stapes pushes against the membrane behind the oval window. Pressure changes thus applied to the fluid within the cochlea cause a portion of the basilar membrane to flex, which causes the basilar membrane to move laterally with respect to the tectorial membrane that overhangs it. This movement pulls directly on the cilia of the outer hair cells and causes movements in the fluid within the cochlea that causes the cilia of the outer hair cells to wave back and forth. These mechanical forces open ion channels in the tips of the hair cells and thus produce receptor potentials.

The hair cells form synapses with the dendrites of the bipolar neurons whose axons give rise to the cochlear branch of the eighth cranial nerve. The central auditory system involves several brain stem nuclei, including the cochlear nuclei, superior olivary complexes, and inferior colliculi. The medial geniculate nucleus relays auditory information to the primary auditory cortex on the medial surface of the temporal lobe.

Pitch is encoded by two means. High-frequency sounds cause the base of the basilar membrane (near the oval window) to flex; lower-frequency sounds cause the apex (opposite end) to flex. Because high and low frequencies thus stimulate different groups of auditory hair cells, frequency is encoded anatomically. The lowest frequencies cause the apex of the basilar membrane to flex back and forth in time with the acoustic vibra-

tions. Possibly, the outer hair cells act as motive elements as well as sensory transducers, contracting in response to activity of the efferent axons and modifying the mechanical properties of the basilar membrane.

The auditory system is analytical in its operation. That is, it can discriminate between sounds with different timbres by detecting the individual overtones that constitute the sounds and producing unique patterns of neural firing in the auditory system.

Left-right localization is performed by analyzing binaural differences in arrival time, in phase relations, and in intensity. The location of sources of brief sounds (such as clicks) and sounds of frequencies below approximately 3000 Hz is detected by neurons in the lateral superior olivary complex, which respond most vigorously when one ear receives the click first, or when the phase of a sine wave received by one ear leads that received by the other. The location of sources of high-frequency sounds is detected by neurons in the medial superior olivary complex, which respond most vigorously when one organ of Corti is stimulated more intensely than the other. Removal of both the primary auditory cortex and the auditory association cortex does not affect the ability to detect differences in frequency or intensity; thus, this analysis must be performed by subcortical components of the auditory system. However, the cortical removal does impair localization of the source of sounds and discrimination between different "tunes," changes in the duration of sounds, and changes in complex sounds.

VESTIBULAR SYSTEM

The Stimuli

The vestibular system has two components: the vestibular sacs and the semicircular canals. They represent the second and third components of the *bony labyrinths*. (We just studied the first component, the cochlea.) The *vestibular sacs* respond to the force of gravity and inform the brain about the head's orientation. The *semicircular canals* respond to angular acceleration—changes in the rotation of the head—but not to steady rotation.

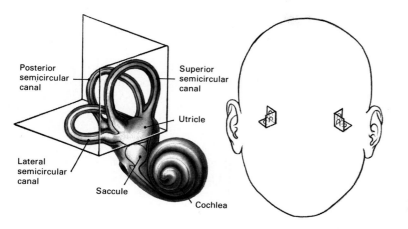

FIGURE 7.22
The bony labyrinths of the inner ear.

They also respond (but rather weakly) to changes in position or to linear acceleration.

The functions of the vestibular system include balance, maintenance of the head in an upright position, and adjustment of eye movement to compensate for head movements. Vestibular stimulation does not produce any readily definable sensation; certain low-frequency stimulation of the vestibular sacs can produce nausea, and stimulation of the semicircular canals can produce dizziness and rhythmic eye movements (*nystagmus*). However, we receive no primary sensation from these organs, as we do from the organs of audition and vision, for example.

Anatomy of the Vestibular Apparatus

Figure 7.22 shows the bony labyrinths, which include the cochlea, the semicircular canals, and the two vestibular sacs: the *utricle* ("little pouch")

and the *saccule* ("little sack"). (See *Figure 7.22.*) The semicircular canals approximate the three major planes of the head: sagittal, transverse, and horizontal. Receptors in each canal respond maximally to angular acceleration in one plane. Figure 7.23 shows cross sections through one semicircular canal. The semicircular canal consists of a membranous canal floating within a bony one; the membranous canal contains endolymph and floats within perilymph. An enlargement called the *ampulla* contains the organ in which the sensory receptors reside. The sensory receptors are hair cells similar to those found in the cochlea. Their cilia are embedded in a gelatinous mass called the *cupula,* which blocks part of the ampulla. (See *Figure 7.23.*)

In order to explain the effects of angular acceleration on the semicircular canals, I will first describe an "experiment." If we place a glass of water on the exact center of a turntable and then start

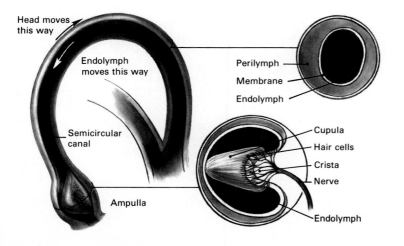

FIGURE 7.23
Cross sections through one semicircular canal.

the turntable spinning, the water in the glass will, at first, remain stationary (the glass will move with respect to the water it contains). Eventually, however, the water will begin rotating with the container. If we then stop the turntable, the water will continue spinning for a while, because of its inertia.

The semicircular canals operate on the same principle. The endolymph within these canals, like the water in the glass, resists movement when the head begins to rotate. This inertial resistance pushes the endolymph against the cupula, causing it to bend, until the fluid begins to move at the same speed as the head. If the head rotation is then stopped, the endolymph, still circulating through the canal, pushes the cupula the other way. Angular acceleration is thus translated into bending of the crista, which exerts a shearing force on the cilia of the hair cells. (Of course, unlike the glass of water in my example, we do not normally spin around in circles; the semicircular canals measure very slight and very brief rotations of the head.)

The vestibular sacs (the utricle and saccule) work very differently. These organs are roughly circular, and each contains a patch of receptive tissue. The receptive tissue is located on the ''floor'' of the utricle and on the ''wall'' of the saccule when the head is in an upright position. The receptive tissue, like that of the semicircular canals and cochlea, contains hair cells. The cilia of these receptors are embedded in an overlying gelatinous mass, which contains something rather unusual: *otoconia,* which are small crystals of calcium carbonate. (See *Figure 7.24.*) The weight of the crystals causes the gelatinous mass to shift in position as the orientation of the head changes. Thus, movement produces a shearing force on the cilia of the receptive hair cells.

Anatomy of the Receptor Cells

The hair cells of the semicircular canal and vestibular sacs have similar structures, and both resemble those found in the cochlea. Two types of cells appear in both organs. The type 1 hair cell is embedded in a dendritic process (called a *calyx*) similar in shape to an eggcup. Transmission appears

FIGURE 7.24
The receptive tissue of the utricle and saccule.

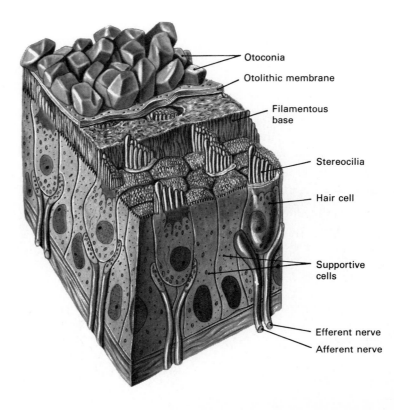

Otoconia

Otolithic membrane

Filamentous base

Stereocilia

Hair cell

Supportive cells

Efferent nerve

Afferent nerve

Type 1

Stereocilia

Kinocilium

Calyx of
afferent
dendrite

Efferent
axon

Afferent
dendrite

Type 2

Stereocilia

Kinocilium

Afferent
dendrite

Efferent axon

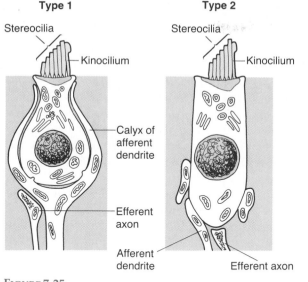

FIGURE 7.25
The two types of vestibular hair cells.

to be chemically mediated across slight indentations, indicated by the small arrows in the drawing. (See *Figure 7.25.*) Efferent terminal buttons (apparently acetylcholinergic) synapse on the outside of the calyx but not on the type 1 hair cell itself. Type 2 hair cells are not surrounded by a calyx; they synapse with both afferent dendrites and efferent terminal buttons. Hair cells of both types may synapse with branches of the same dendrite. (See *Figure 7.25.*) Each hair cell contains one long *kinocilium* and several *stereocilia*, which de-

crease in size away from the kinocilium. (Early in fetal development the hair cells of the auditory system possess kinocilia, too, but they eventually disappear.)

Hudspeth and Jacobs (1979) used microscopic techniques to determine the function of the kinocilium. Figure 7.26 shows the appearance of a normal hair cell of a bullfrog saccule (*left*) and one in which they pulled the kinocilium away from the stereocilia (*right*). (See *Figure 7.26.*) They found that removing the kinocilium or bending it away had no effect on the receptor potentials. Their results suggest that the kinocilium does not play a direct role in transduction but probably serves as a mechanical link between the stereocilia and the rest of the receptive organ.

The hair cells of the crista in a semicircular canal are all oriented in one direction, and they are thus sensitive to movement of the cupula in one direction. When head rotation causes the cupula to bend toward the utricle, the hair cells are stimulated, which produces an increased firing rate of the associated afferent neurons in the *vestibular nerve*. Bending of the cupula in the opposite direction produces a slight decrease in firing rate. Thus, the semicircular canals of the right and left ear together provide information about the magnitude and direction of angular rotation of the head. (See *Figure 7.27.*)

The hair cells of the utricle and saccule are oriented in various directions; thus, different groups of hair cells signal different angles of head tilt. (See *Figure 7.28.*)

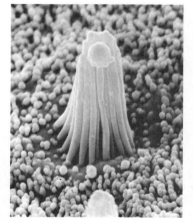

FIGURE 7.26
Left: Oblique view of a normal bundle of vestibular hair cells, with an intact kinocilium. *Right:* Top view of a bundle of hair cells from which the kinocilium has been detached. (From Hudspeth, A.J., and Jacobs, R. *Proceedings of the National Academy of Sciences, USA,* 1979, *76,* 1506–1509.)

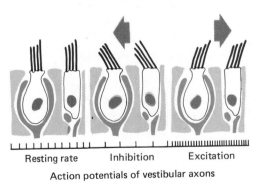

Resting rate   Inhibition   Excitation

Action potentials of vestibular axons

Figure 7.27
Coding of direction of movement. The rate of firing of axons of the vestibular nerve is increased or decreased, depending on the direction of displacement of the cilia of the vestibular hair cells. (Adapted from Ades, H.W., and Engström, H., in *The Role of the Vestibular Organs in the Exploration of Space*, edited by A. Graybill. U.S. Naval School of Medicine: NASA SP-77, 1965.)

Transduction of Vestibular Information

As we saw in previous sections, the hair cells of the vestibular apparatus apparently produce a receptor potential in response to a shearing force across the cilia, and they pass this information on to the afferent neurons by means of chemical transmission. The transduction mechanism appears to be identical to the one that occurs in the auditory hair cells.

The Vestibular Pathway

Connections with the Vestibular Nerve

The vestibular and cochlear nerves constitute the two branches of the eighth cranial nerve (auditory nerve). The bipolar cell bodies that give rise to the afferent axons of the vestibular nerve are located in the *vestibular ganglion,* which appears as a nodule on the vestibular nerve. Efferent axons arise from cell bodies in the cerebellum and medulla and inhibit the activity of the vestibular hair cells. The firing rate of these axons changes during tactile stimulation, somatic movement, and eye movements (Goldberg and Fernandez, 1975), but their function is not known.

The Central Vestibular System

Figure 7.29 illustrates the afferent and efferent axons of the vestibular system. (See *Figure 7.29.*) Most of the afferent axons of the vestibular nerve synapse within the four vestibular nuclei, but some axons travel to the cerebellum. Neurons of the vestibular nuclei send their axons to the cerebellum, spinal cord, medulla, and pons. (See *Figure 7.29.*) There also appear to be vestibular projections to the temporal cortex, but the precise pathways have not been determined. Most investigators believe that the cortical projections are responsible for feelings of dizziness; the activity of projections to the lower brain stem can produce the nausea and vomiting that accompany motion sickness. Projections to brain stem nuclei controlling neck muscles are clearly involved in maintaining an upright position of the head.

Perhaps the most interesting connections are those to the cranial nerve nuclei (third, fourth, and sixth) that control the eye muscles. As we walk or (especially) run, the head is jarred quite a bit. The vestibular system exerts direct control on eye movement, to compensate for the sudden head movements. This process, called the *vestibulo-ocular reflex,* maintains a fairly steady retinal image. Test this reflex yourself: Look at a distant object and hit yourself (gently) on the side of the head. Note that your image of the world jumps a bit, but not too much. People who have suffered vestibular damage, and who lack the vestibulo-ocular reflex, have difficulty seeing anything

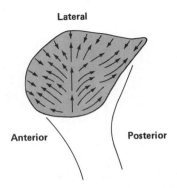

Lateral

Anterior   Posterior

Figure 7.28
Arrangement of hair cells. Hair cells in different regions of the utricle are sensitive to shearing forces in different directions. (Adapted from Flock, A. *Journal of Cell Biology*, 1964, 22, 413–431.)

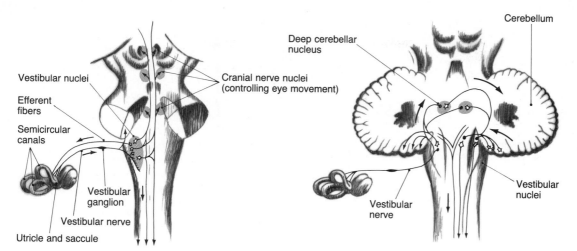

FIGURE 7.29

The pathways followed by neurons in the vestibular system. (Adapted with permission from McGraw-Hill Book Co. from *The Human Nervous System,* 2nd ed. by Noback and Demarest. Copyright 1975, by McGraw-Hill, Inc.)

while walking or running. Everything becomes a blur of movement.

*I*NTERIM SUMMARY

The semicircular canals are filled with fluid. When the head begins rotating or comes to rest after rotation, inertia causes the fluid to push the cupula to one side or the other. This movement exerts a shearing force on the crista, the organ containing the vestibular hair cells. The vestibular sacs contain a patch of receptive tissue that contains hair cells whose cilia are embedded in a gelatinous mass. The weight of the otoconia in the gelatinous mass shifts when the head tilts, causing a shearing force on some of the cilia of the hair cells.

Each hair cell contains one long kinocilium and several stereocilia. Transduction appears to involve only the stereocilia, because removal of the kinocilium has no apparent effect on receptor potentials of vestibular hair cells.

The vestibular hair cells form synapses with dendrites of bipolar neurons whose axons travel through the vestibular nerve. The receptors also receive efferent terminal buttons from neurons located in the cerebel-

lum and medulla, but the function of these connections is not known. Vestibular information is received by the vestibular nuclei in the medulla, which relay it on to the cerebellum, spinal cord, medulla, pons, and temporal cortex. These pathways are responsible for control of posture, head movements, eye movements, and the puzzling phenomenon of motion sickness.

SOMATOSENSES

The somatosenses provide information about what is happening on the surface of our body and inside it. The *cutaneous senses* (skin senses) include several submodalities commonly referred to as *touch*. *Kinesthesia* provides information about body position and movement and arises from receptors in joints, tendons, and muscles. The muscle receptors are discussed in this section and in Chapter 8. The *organic senses* arise from receptors in and around the internal organs, providing us with unpleasant sensations, such as stomachaches or gallbladder attacks, or pleasurable ones, such as those provided by a warm drink on a cold winter day. Because the cutaneous senses are the most studied of the somatosenses, both perceptually and physiologically, I will devote most of my discussion to them.

The Stimuli

The cutaneous senses respond to several different types of stimuli: pressure, vibration, heating, cooling, and events that cause tissue damage (and hence, pain). Feelings of pressure are caused by mechanical deformation of the skin. Vibration is produced in the laboratory or clinic by tuning forks or mechanical devices, but it more commonly occurs when we move our fingers across a rough surface. Thus, we use vibration sensitivity to judge an object's roughness. Obviously, sensations of warmth and coolness are produced by objects that change skin temperature from normal. Sensations of pain can be caused by many different types of stimuli, but it appears that most cause at least some tissue damage.

Kinesthesia is provided by stretch receptors in skeletal muscles that report changes in muscle length to the central nervous system and by stretch receptors in tendons that measure the force being exerted by the muscles. Receptors within joints between adjacent bones respond to the magnitude and direction of limb movement. The muscle length detectors (sensory endings on the *intrafusal muscle fibers*) do not give rise to conscious sensations; their information is used to control movement. These receptors will be discussed separately in Chapter 8.

Organic sensitivity is provided by receptors in the linings of muscles, outer layers of the gastrointestinal system and other internal organs, and linings of the abdominal and thoracic cavities. Many of these tissues are sensitive only to stretch and do not report sensations when cut, burned, or crushed. In addition, the stomach and esophagus are responsive to heat and cold and to some chemicals.

Anatomy of the Skin and Its Receptive Organs

The skin is a complex and vital organ of the body—one that we tend to take for granted. We cannot survive without it; extensive skin burns are fatal. Our cells, which must be bathed by a warm fluid, are protected from the hostile environment by the skin's outer layers. The skin participates in thermoregulation by producing sweat, thus cooling the body, or by restricting its circulation of blood, thus conserving heat. Its appearance varies widely across the body, from mucous membrane to hairy skin to the smooth, hairless skin of the palms and the soles of the feet.

Skin consists of subcutaneous tissue, dermis, and epidermis and contains various receptors scattered throughout these layers. Figures 7.30 and 7.31 show cross sections through hairy and *glabrous* skin (hairless skin, such as we have on our fingertips and palms). Hairy skin contains unencapsulated (free) nerve endings and Ruffini corpuscles (described below). Free nerve endings are found just below the surface of the skin, in a basketwork around the base of hair follicles and around the emergence of hair shafts from the skin. (See *Figure 7.30.*)

Glabrous skin contains a more complex mixture of free nerve endings and axons that terminate within specialized end organs. The increased complexity probably reflects the fact that we use the palms of our hands and the inside surfaces of our fingers to explore the environment actively: We use them to hold and touch objects. In contrast, the rest of our body most often contacts the environment passively; that is, other things come in contact with it. Over the years investigators have described a large number of cutaneous receptors, but subsequent research has shown many of them to be artifacts of the staining process used to reveal the microscopic structure of the skin. (*Artifact* means "made by art"—hence artificially introduced, not normally existing in the tissue.) Other specialized end organs have been shown to be variants of a single form, changing shape as a function of age. Iggo and Andres (1982) describe five major types of organized endings.

Pacinian corpuscles are the largest sensory end organs in the body. Their size, approximately 0.5 mm × 1.0 mm, makes them visible to the naked eye. They are found in the dermis of glabrous skin and in the external genitalia, mammary glands, and various internal organs. These receptors consist of up to seventy onionlike layers wrapped around the dendritic endings of a single myelinated fiber. (See *Figure 7.31.*) They are especially sensitive to touch, with each axon giving a burst of responses when the corpuscle is moved relative to it. The inside of the corpuscle is filled with a viscous substance that offers some resis-

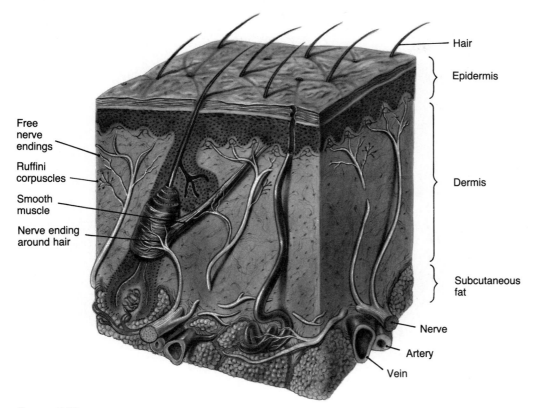

Hair

Epidermis

Dermis

Subcutaneous fat

Nerve

Artery

Vein

Free nerve endings

Ruffini corpuscles

Smooth muscle

Nerve ending around hair

FIGURE 7.30
A cross section through hairy skin, showing the cutaneous receptors located there.

tance to the movement of the nerve ending inside. This construction gives the Pacinian corpuscle its special response characteristics: Pacinian corpuscles respond to vibration.

Ruffini corpuscles, found primarily in hairy skin, look rather like Pacinian corpuscles, but they are smaller and are covered by only three or four layers. They respond to low-frequency vibration, or "flutter." (See *Figure 7.30.*)

Meissner's corpuscles are found in *papillae* ("nipples"), small elevations of the dermis that project up into the epidermis. These end organs are innervated by between two and six axons. They respond to mechanical stimuli. (See *Figure 7.31.*)

Merkel's disks are found at the base of the epidermis, in the same general locations as Meissner's corpuscles, adjacent to sweat ducts. The disks are single, flattened dendritic endings that lie adjacent to specialized epithelial cells called

Merkel's cells. Merkel's disks are found in hairy skin as well as glabrous skin. They respond to mechanical stimuli. (See *Figure 7.31.*)

Krause end bulbs are found in *mucocutaneous zones*—the junctions between mucous membrane and dry skin, such as the edge of the lips, eyelids, glans penis, and clitoris. They consist of loops of unmyelinated axons similar in appearance to balls of yarn. Each end bulb contains the endings of two to six axons. They probably respond to mechanical stimuli.

Anatomy of Kinesthetic Receptive Organs

A schematic view of a skeletal muscle is shown in *Figure 7.32.* Four kinds of information are received by afferent axons of the muscle and tendon:

1. The sensory endings on the intrafusal muscle fibers signal muscle length.

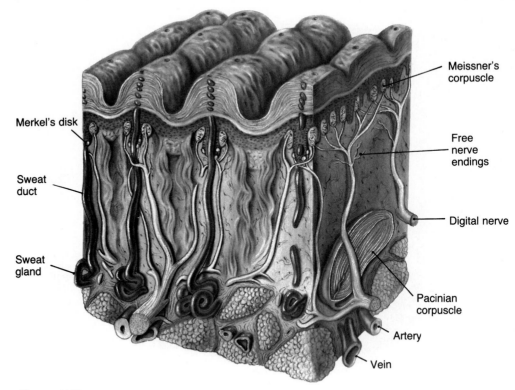

Merkel's disk

Sweat duct

Sweat gland

Meissner's corpuscle

Free nerve endings

Digital nerve

Pacinian corpuscle

Artery

Vein

FIGURE 7.31

A cross section through glabrous (hairless) skin, showing the cutaneous receptors located there.

2. The sensory endings within the *Golgi tendon organ* at the muscle-tendon junction respond to tension exerted by the muscle on the tendon.

3. The membranous covering of the muscle (*fascia*) contains Pacinian corpuscles. These receptors apparently signal deep pressure exerted upon muscles, which can be felt even if the overlying cutaneous receptors are anesthetized or denervated.

4. Throughout the muscle and its overlying fascia are distributed free nerve endings, which generally follow the blood supply. These receptors presumably signal pain that accompanies prolonged exertion or muscle cramps.

The tissue that lines the joints contains free nerve endings and encapsulated receptors, such as Pacinian corpuscles. The encapsulated endings presumably mediate sensitivity to joint movement and position; stimulation of the free nerve endings produces pain (such as that which accompanies arthritis). Pacinian corpuscles and free nerve endings are also found in the outer layers of various internal organs and give rise to organic sensations.

Transduction of Cutaneous Stimulation

Originally, investigators believed that different submodalities of the somatosenses were mediated by different types of receptors (Von Frey, 1906). This belief was challenged by other investigators, who asserted that the different categories of receptors were *not* specialized functionally, and that different submodalities were represented by the pattern of axonal firing (Sinclair, 1967). As we will see, the most recent evidence suggests that receptors *are* specialized functionally, and that the anatomical projections of different classes of re-

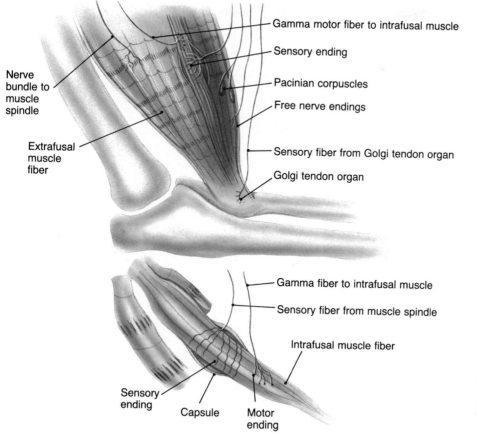

Gamma motor fiber to intrafusal muscle

Sensory ending

Pacinian corpuscles

Free nerve endings

Sensory fiber from Golgi tendon organ

Golgi tendon organ

Nerve bundle to muscle spindle

Extrafusal muscle fiber

Gamma fiber to intrafusal muscle

Sensory fiber from muscle spindle

Intrafusal muscle fiber

Sensory ending

Capsule

Motor ending

FIGURE 7.32
A skeletal muscle and its sense receptors.

Mechanical Stimulation

Sensitivity to pressure and vibration are caused by movement of the skin. The skin is sensitive only to deformation, or bending, and not to pressure exerted evenly across its surface. For example, if you dipped your finger into a pool of mercury, pressure would be exerted on all portions of your skin below the surface of the liquid. Nevertheless, you would feel only a ring of sensation, at the air-mercury junction. This is the only part of the skin that is bent, and it is here that skin receptors are stimulated. (Because mercury is poisonous if it enters a break in the skin, please do not try this demonstration—just imagine it.)

Mechanical stimuli appear to be transduced by a variety of receptors, both encapsulated and unencapsulated. The best-studied one is the

ceptors are segregated up to the level of the somatosensory cortex.

Pacinian corpuscle, which is primarily a detector of vibration. This organ responds to bending, relative to the axon that enters it. If the onionlike layers are dissected away, this receptor still responds to bending of the naked axon; thus, the transducer is the terminal itself (Loewenstein and Rathkamp, 1958). The receptor potential is proportional to the degree of bending. If the threshold of excitation is exceeded, an action potential is produced at the first node of Ranvier. Loewenstein and Mendelson (1965) have shown that the layers of the corpuscle alter the mechanical characteristics of the organ, so that the axon responds briefly when the intact organ is bent and again when it is released. Thus, it is sensitive to vibration but not to steady pressure.

The bending of the tip of the nerve ending in a Pacinian corpuscle appears to produce a receptor potential by opening ion channels in the membrane. These channels appear to be anchored to protein filaments beneath the membrane and have long carbohydrate chains attached to them. When a mechanical stimulus changes the shape of the nerve ending, tension is exerted on the carbohydrate chains, which pulls the channel open. (See *Figure 7.33.*) Most investigators believe that the encapsulated endings serve only to modify the physical stimulus transduced by the axons that enter them.

Adaptation. Investigators have known for a long time that a moderate, constant stimulus applied to the skin fails to produce any sensation after it has been present for a while. We not only ignore the pressure of a wristwatch but also cannot feel it at all if we keep our arm still (assuming that the band is not painfully tight). Physiological studies have shown that the reason for the lack of sensation is the absence of receptor firing; the receptors adapt to a constant stimulus.

This adaptation is not a result of any "fatigue" of physical or chemical processes within the receptor. Adaptation can be explained as a function of the mechanical construction of the receptors and their relationship to skin and (in some cases) end organs. As we saw earlier, the axons of Pacinian corpuscles respond once when the receptor is bent and again when it is released, because of the way the nerve ending "floats" within

the viscous interior of the corpuscle. Therefore, these receptors adapt almost immediately to a constant stimulus. Most other axons adapt more slowly. Nafe and Wagoner (1941) recorded the sensations reported by human subjects as a stimulus weight gradually moved downward, deforming the skin. Pressure was reported until the weight finally stopped moving. When the weight was increased, pressure was reported until downward movement stopped again. Pressure sensations were also briefly recorded when the weight was removed, while the surface of the skin regained its normal shape.

Responsiveness to Moving Stimuli. A moderate, constant, nondamaging stimulus is rarely of any importance to an organism, so this adaptation mechanism is useful. Our cutaneous senses are used much more often to analyze shapes and textures of stimulus objects moving with respect to the surface of the skin. Sometimes, the object itself moves, but more often, we do the moving ourselves. If I placed an object in your palm and asked you to keep your hand still, you would have a great deal of difficulty recognizing the object by touch alone. If I said you could now move your hand, you would manipulate the object, letting its surface slide across your palm and the pads of your fingers. You would be able to describe its three-dimensional shape, hardness, texture, slipperiness, and so on. (Obviously, your motor system must cooperate, and you need kinesthetic sensation from your muscles and joints, besides the cutaneous information.) If you squeeze the object and feel a lot of well-localized pressure in return, it is hard. If you feel a less intense, more diffuse pressure in return, it is soft. If it produces vibrations as it moves over the ridges on your fingers, it is rough. If very little effort is needed to move the object while pressing it against your skin, it is slippery. If it does not produce vibrations as it moves across your skin, but moves in a jerky fashion, and if it takes effort to remove your fingers from its surface, it is sticky.

Temperature

Feelings of warmth and coolness are relative, not absolute (except at the extremes). There is a temperature level that, for a particular region of

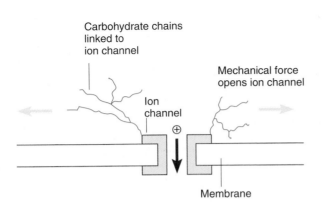

FIGURE 7.33

A hypothetical explanation of transduction of somatosensory information. Mechanical force on carbohydrate chains linked to ion channels open the channels, permitting the entry of anions, which depolarizes the membrane potential.

skin, will produce a sensation of temperature neutrality—neither warmth nor coolness. This neutral point is not an absolute value but depends on the prior history of thermal stimulation of that area. If the temperature of a region of skin is raised by a few degrees, the initial feeling of warmth is replaced by one of neutrality. If the skin temperature is lowered to its initial value, it now feels cool. Thus, increases in temperature lower the sensitivity of warmth receptors and raise the sensitivity of cold receptors. The converse holds for decreases in skin temperature. This adaptation to ambient temperature can be easily demonstrated by placing one hand in a bucket of warm water and the other in a bucket of cool water until some adaptation has taken place. If you then simultaneously immerse both hands in water at room temperature, it will feel warm to one hand and cool to the other.

Thermal receptors are difficult to study, because changes in temperature alter the metabolic activity, and also the rate of axonal firing, of a variety of cells. For example, a receptor that responds to pressure might produce varying amounts of activity in response to the same mechanical stimulus, depending upon the temperature. Nevertheless, most investigators agree that changes in temperature are detected by free nerve endings, and that warmth and coolness are detected by different populations of receptors (Sinclair, 1981). The transduction of temperature changes into the rate of axonal firing has not yet been explained.

An ingenious experiment by Bazett, McGlone, Williams, and Lufkin (1932) showed long ago that receptors for warmth and cold lie at different depths in the skin. The investigators lifted the prepuce (foreskin) of uncircumcised males with dull fishhooks. They applied thermal stimuli on one side of the folded skin and recorded the rate at which the temperature changes were transmitted through the skin by placing small temperature sensors on the opposite side. They then correlated these observations with verbal reports of warmth and coolness. The investigators concluded that cold receptors were close to the skin and that warmth receptors were located deeper in the tissue. (This experiment shows the extremities to which scientists will go to obtain information—pun intended.)

Pain

The story of pain is quite different from that of temperature and pressure; the analysis of this sensation is extremely difficult. It is obvious that our awareness of pain and our emotional reaction to it are controlled by mechanisms within the brain. For example, we can have a tooth removed painlessly while under hypnosis, which has no effect on the stimulation of pain receptors. Stimuli that produce pain also tend to trigger species-typical escape and withdrawal responses. Subjectively, these stimuli *hurt*, and we try hard to avoid them. However, sometimes we are better off ignoring pain and getting on with other tasks. In fact, our brains possess mechanisms that can reduce pain, largely through the activity of special opiatelike peptides. These mechanisms are described in more detail in a later section of this chapter.

Most investigators identify pain reception with the networks of free nerve endings in the skin. Pain appears to be produced by a variety of procedures. Intense mechanical stimulation activates a class of high-threshold receptors that produce a sensation of pain. However, most painful stimuli cause tissue damage, which suggests that pain is also caused by the release of a chemical by injured cells (Besson, Guilbaud, Abdelmoumene, and Chaouch, 1982). When cells are damaged, they very rapidly synthesize a **prostaglandin,** a category of hormones first discovered in the prostate gland. This chemical sensitizes free nerve endings to another chemical, histamine, which is also released by damaged cells. (The analgesic effect of aspirin occurs by virtue of the fact that it interferes with the synthesis of prostaglandins.)

The Somatosensory Pathways

Somatosensory axons enter the central nervous system via spinal nerves and cranial nerves, principally the trigeminal nerve (fifth cranial nerve). The cell bodies of the unipolar neurons are located in the dorsal root ganglia and cranial nerve ganglia. Two anatomically distinct systems begin at this point: the lemniscal system, which conveys precisely localized information from mechanical receptors, and the spinothalamic system, which

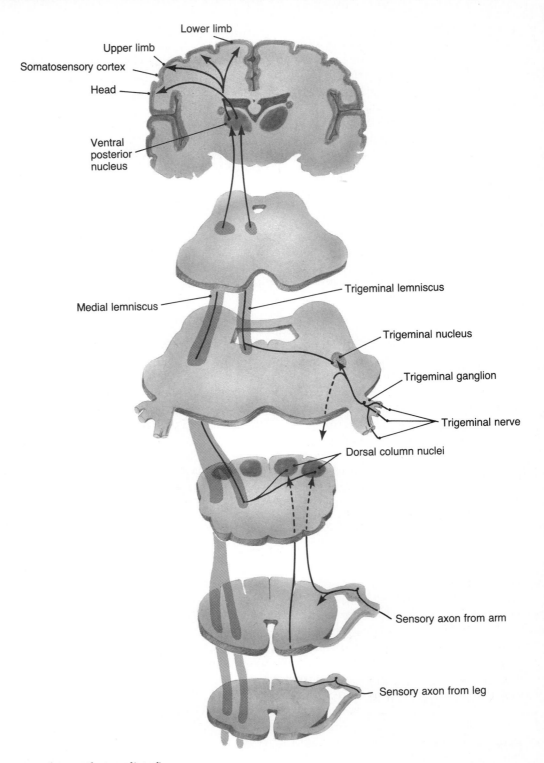

FIGURE 7.34

The lemniscal system: pathways that mediate fine touch, fine pressure, and kinesthetic feedback from the muscle and joint receptors.

carries less precisely localized information from pain and temperature receptors.

Lemniscal System

Figure 7.34 shows the *lemniscal system.* The first-order neuron has a very long axon. In the case of spinal afferent neurons, the axon ascends through the *dorsal columns* to the *dorsal column nuclei* of the medulla. (See *Figure 7.34.*) These axons are the longest nerve axons of the body; a touch receptor in the big toe is on one end of a single axon that stretches all the way to the medulla. Fibers of the second-order neurons decussate (cross to the opposite side of the brain) and travel through the *medial lemniscus* to the ventral posterior nuclei of the thalamus. (Do not confuse the medial lemniscus, which conveys somatosensory information, with the lateral lemniscus, which conveys auditory information.) The neurons synapse there, and third-order neurons project to the somatosensory cortex, located on the postcentral gyrus of the parietal lobe. (See *Figure 7.34.*)

Most touch receptors rostral to the ears send information via the trigeminal, facial, and vagus nerves. Let us consider the major pathway, from the trigeminal nerve. This pathway is almost a replica of the dorsal column pathway. Most second-order neurons decussate and travel via the *trigeminal lemniscus* (parallel to the medial lemniscus) to the ventral posterior nuclei. The third-order axons project to the somatosensory cortex. (See *Figure 7.34.*)

Spinothalamic and Reticulothalamic Pathways

Figure 7.35 illustrates the *spinothalamic system* and its offshoot, the *reticulothalamic system,* which carry information about temperature and pain. (See *Figure 7.35.*) The afferent axons synapse as soon as they enter the central nervous system, either in the dorsal horn of the spinal cord or in the nucleus of the trigeminal nerve.

Second-order neurons decussate immediately; some ascend via the spinothalamic (or trigeminothalamic) tracts directly to the ventral posterior and parafascicular nuclei of the thalamus. Others follow a diffuse, polysynaptic pathway through the reticular formation. Note

that axons of the spinothalamic tract also give off branches to the reticular formation as they pass by. (See *Figure 7.35.*) The somatosensory cortex does not appear to receive direct, third-order input from pain receptors, as it does from the other somatosensory receptors.

Kinesthetic and Organic Inputs

The cell bodies of kinesthetic receptors, like those of cutaneous receptors, reside within the dorsal root ganglia or cranial nerve ganglia. Kinesthetic axons are carried in the same nerves that convey motor fibers to the skeletal muscles. Organic sensitivity is conveyed over axons that travel with efferent axons of the autonomic nervous system and thus pass (without synapsing) through the autonomic ganglia on their way to the central nervous system. In general, organic pain is conveyed along with efferent sympathetic fibers, whereas nonpainful stimuli arising from the internal organs are transmitted via nerves that contain parasympathetic efferent axons.

Somatosensory Cortex

Figure 7.36 shows a lateral view of a monkey brain, with a drawing vaguely resembling two monkeys. These drawings roughly indicate which parts of the body project to which areas of primary and secondary somatosensory cortex (part of the somatosensory association cortex) of the parietal lobe. The mapping of the body on the surface of the cortex is called *somatotopic representation.* (You are already familiar with the retinotopic representation of the visual system and the tonotopic representation of the auditory system.) Note that a relatively large amount of cortical tissue is given to representation of fingers and lips, corresponding to the greater tactile sensitivity of these regions. (See *Figure 7.36.*) More recent evidence suggests that somatotopic representation on the cerebral cortex is even more complex.

You will recall from Chapter 6 that the primary visual cortex contains columns of modules, each of which responds to particular features, such as orientation, ocular dominance, or spatial frequency, within a restricted part of the visual field. The somatosensory cortex also has a modular organization, which was first described by Mountcastle (1957) before it was found in the vi-

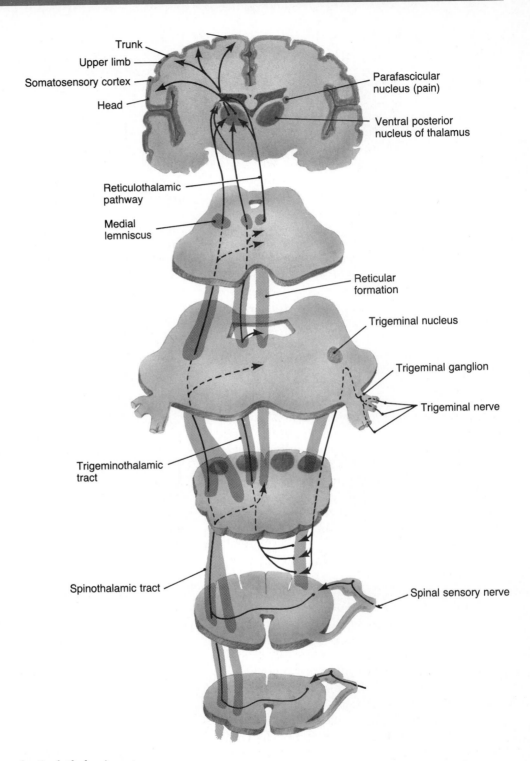

FIGURE 7.35

The spinothalamic and reticulothalamic systems:
pathways that mediate temperature sensitivity and
pain.

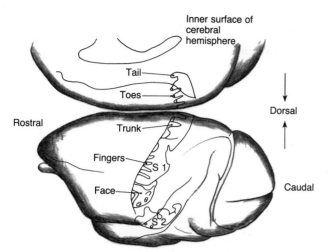

FIGURE 7.36

Sensory animunculi on the monkey brain, indicating the regions of the body that send cutaneous information to particular areas of the somatosensory cortex. (Adapted from Woolsey, C.N., in *Biological and Biochemical Bases of Behavior*, edited by H.F. Harlow and C.N. Woolsey. Madison: University of Wisconsin Press, 1958.)

sual and auditory cortex. Within a module (originally referred to as a *column*) neurons respond to a particular type of stimulus (for example, temperature or pressure) applied to a particular part of the body.

Dykes (1983) has reviewed research that indicates that the primary and secondary somatosensory cortical areas are divided into at least five (and perhaps as many as ten) different maps of the body surface. Within each map cells respond to a particular submodality of somatosensory receptors. So far, separate areas have been identified that respond to slowly adapting cutaneous receptors, rapidly adapting cutaneous receptors, receptors that detect changes in muscle length, receptors located in the joints, and Pacinian corpuscles. Figure 7.37 shows an example of the precise boundary between cortical neurons that respond to muscle receptors and those that respond to cutaneous receptors (Dykes, Rasmusson, and Hoeltzell, 1980). The photograph shows a Nissl-stained slice perpendicular to the surface of the primary somatosensory cortex. (The two white spots are lesions that the investigators made to enable them

to localize the cells from which they recorded.) The diagram shows the path of the microelectrode as it passed through successive columns. The crosshatched bar indicates no response, the dark-colored bar indicates responses from deep structures (elicited by massaging a muscle or moving a joint), and the light-colored bar indicates responses from cutaneous stimulation (elicited by touching and stroking the skin). (See *Figure 7.37*.)

As you learned in Chapter 6, Zeki and his colleagues have shown that the circumstriate cortex consists of several subareas, each of which contains an independent representation of the visual field. They found that one area responds specifically to color, another to movement, and two others to orientation. The somatosensory cortex appears to follow a similar scheme: Each cortical map of the body contains neurons that respond to a specific submodality of stimulation. Undoubtedly, further investigations will provide more accurate functional maps of the cortical subareas of both of these sensory systems.

Perception of Pain

Pain is a curious phenomenon. It is more than a mere sensation; it can be defined only by some sort of withdrawal reaction or, in humans, by verbal report. Pain can be modified by opiates, by hypnosis, by the administration of pharmacologically inert sugar pills, by emotions, and even by other forms of stimulation, such as acupuncture. Recent research efforts have made remarkable progress in discovering the physiological bases of these phenomena.

The importance of emotional and other "psychological" factors in the perception of pain (documented by Sternbach, 1968) suggests that there must be neural mechanisms that modify either the transmission of pain or the translation of central pain messages into unpleasant feelings. As we will see, there is excellent evidence for both types of interactions.

We might reasonably ask *why* we experience pain. In most cases pain serves a constructive role. For example, people who have congenital insensitivity to pain suffer an abnormally large number of injuries, such as cuts and burns. One woman eventually died because she did not make the

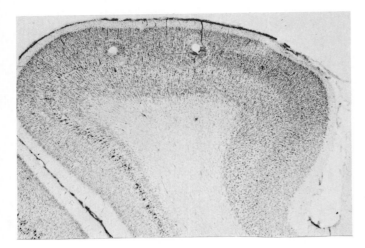

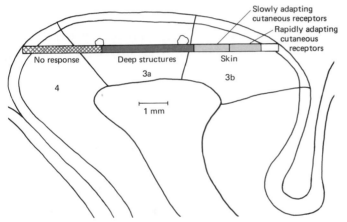

FIGURE 7.37
Response characteristics of neurons in the somatosensory cortex. Different regions contain neurons that receive information from different classes of receptors. The white spots in the photomicrograph are lesions the experimenters made to permit them to reconstruct the path of the microelectrode. The regions marked 3a, 3b, and 4 are histologically distinct areas of somatosensory cortex. (From Dykes, R.W., Rasmusson, D.D., and Hoeltzell, P.B. *Journal of Neurophysiology*, 1980, 43, 1527–1545.)

shifts in posture that we normally do when our joints start to ache. As a consequence, she suffered damage to the spine that ultimately resulted in death. Other people have died from ruptured appendixes and ensuing abdominal infections that they did not feel (Sternbach, 1968). I am sure that a person who is passing a kidney stone would not find much comfort in the fact that pain does more good than ill; but pain is, nevertheless, very important to our existence.

Some environmental events diminish the perception of pain. For example, Beecher (1959) noted that wounded American soldiers back from the battle at Anzio, Italy, during World War II reported that they felt no pain from their wounds—they did not even want medication. It would appear that their perception of pain was diminished by the relief they felt from surviving such an ordeal. There are other instances in which people still report the perception of pain but are not bothered by it. Some tranquilizers have this effect.

Physiological evidence provides a clear distinction between the perception and tolerance of pain. Mark, Ervin, and Yakovlev (1962) made stereotaxically placed lesions in the thalamus in an attempt to relieve the pain of patients suffering from the advanced stages of cancer. Damage to the sensory relay nuclei (the ventral posteromedial and ventral posterolateral thalamic nuclei) produced a loss of cutaneous senses: touch, temperature, and superficial cutaneous pain. Lesions in the parafascicular nucleus and in the intralaminar nucleus were more successful; they abolished deep pain but not cutaneous sensitivity. Finally, destruction of the dorsomedial and anterior thalamic nuclei left both cutaneous sensitivity and the perception of pain intact. However, patients with these lesions were not bothered by the pain—the emotional component was diminished. It is noteworthy that these nuclei are intimately involved with the limbic system and that the dorsomedial nuclei project to the prefrontal cortex, the most anterior region of the frontal association cortex. Removal of this region (**prefrontal lobotomy**) also reduces the emotional aspects of pain perception.

Clearly, pain perception and pain tolerance are separate phenomena. It appears that the intralaminar and parafascicular nuclei are necessary for the perception of pain, and that the dorsomedial and anterior thalamic nuclei, limbic system, and prefrontal cortex mediate its emotional component.

The study by Mark and his colleagues confirms the long-standing supposition that there are two types of pain: a rapidly felt "sharp" pain and a more gradual, but more unpleasant, "dull" pain. If you have ever stubbed your toe, you know what I mean. The first flash of pain subsides fairly quickly, to be replaced by another that is longer-lived and more poorly localized. Because lesions of the ventral posteromedial and ventral posterolateral thalamic nuclei abolished pain felt from pinpricks, but not deep-seated pain, we might infer that the "bright pain" component but not the "dull pain" component is mediated by these nuclei.

The Endogenous Opiates

For many years investigators have known that perception of pain can be modified by environmental stimuli. Recent work, beginning in the 1970s, has revealed the existence of neural circuits whose activity can produce **analgesia,** a decreased sensitivity to pain (from *an,* "not," and *algos,* "pain"). A variety of environmental stimuli can activate these analgesia-producing circuits. An important component of these mechanisms is a class of neuromodulators called the **endogenous opiates** or, more simply, **opioids.** (*Endogenous* means "produced from within.")

Discovery of Opiate Receptors. As you know, opiates such as morphine produce analgesia. Several years ago, it became clear that they did so by means of direct effects on the brain. In particular, microinjections of morphine into the periaqueductal gray matter of the midbrain produce analgesia, whereas injections into many other regions are ineffective (Tsou and Jang, 1964; Herz, Albus,

Metys, Schubert, and Teschemacher, 1970). Pert, Snowman, and Snyder (1974) discovered that neurons in the brain contain specialized receptors that respond to opiates. They homogenized the brains of rats and extracted portions of cell membranes. They incubated the membranes with radioactive naloxone and dihydromorphine, rinsed them, and found that the membranes became radioactive. (*Naloxone* is a drug that reverses the effects of opiates, and dihydromorphine is a synthetic opiate.) The finding that these two drugs both bind with molecules in fragments of postsynaptic neural membrane is strong evidence for the existence of specific opiate receptors. Naloxone blocks the effects of opiates by binding with, but not activating, the receptors.

Classes of Opiatelike Peptides. Of course, nature did not put opiate receptors in the brain for the amusement of neuroscientists. If there are receptors in the brain, then the brain must produce its own chemicals to occupy these receptors. And, in fact, it does. Terenius and Wahlström (1975) reported the existence of a substance in human cerebrospinal fluid that had a specific affinity for opiate receptors that had been extracted from rat brain. They called this chemical *morphinelike factor.*

Hughes, Smith, Kosterlitz, Fothergill, Morgan, and Morris (1975) found that the brain produces two morphinelike factors, which they identified as very small peptide chains, each containing five amino acids. They gave them the name **enkephalin** (from the Greek *kephale,* "head"). They synthesized these substances and found that the artificial compounds acted as potent opiates. The two enkephalins (labeled *Leu*-enkephalin and *Met*-enkephalin) were found to bind with opiate receptors even more effectively than morphine.

We now know that Leu- and Met-enkephalin, which contain the amino acid leucine or methionine, respectively, are only two members of a family of endogenous opiate peptides (opioids), all of which are synthesized from one of three large peptides that serve as precursors. Cells that produce one of the endogenous opiates synthesize them and also synthesize specialized enzymes that cut the precursor apart at specific locations. The active fragments are stored in vesicles, and the unneeded ones are destroyed. The first, *Pro-*

opiomelanocortin, gives rise to several hormones found in the pituitary gland, only one of which serves an opiatelike function (β-*endorphin*). The second precursor, *Pro-enkephalin,* gives rise only to enkephalins, of which there are several types. The third precursor, *Pro-dynorphin,* gives rise to several different kinds of **dynorphins,** another class of opiates that are active in the brain.

Besides producing several different opiates, the brain contains several different types of opiate receptors (Akil, Watson, Young, Lewis, Khachaturian, and Walker, 1984; Cooper, Bloom, and Roth, 1987). Like the nicotinic and muscarinic acetylcholine receptors, these receptors have been defined by the categories of chemicals that bind to them. The μ (mu) receptor is found in the neural pathways mediating pain. (Naloxone blocks these receptors.) The δ (delta) receptor is found in the limbic system and may play a role in regulation of mood. The κ (kappa) receptor is found in the cerebral cortex and may be involved with the sedative effects of the opiates. The σ (sigma) receptor is found in the hippocampus, and the ε (epsilon) receptor is found in the base of the brain, in and around the hypothalamus.

The Anatomy of Opiate-Induced Analgesia

Electrical stimulation of particular locations within the brain can cause analgesia, which can even be profound enough to serve as an anesthetic for surgery in rats (Reynolds, 1969). The most effective locations appear to be within the periaqueductal gray matter and in the rostroventral medulla. For example, Mayer and Liebeskind (1974) reported that electrical stimulation of the periaqueductal gray matter produced analgesia in rats equivalent to that produced by at least 10 milligrams of morphine per kilogram of body weight, which is a large dose. The rats did not react to pain of any kind; the authors pinched their tails and paws, applied electrical shocks to their feet, and applied heat to their tails.

Analgesic brain stimulation apparently triggers the neural mechanisms that reduce pain. These mechanisms are normally stimulated through more natural means, which will be discussed later in this section. We now know that the periaqueductal gray matter and the rostroventral medulla are two components of a pain-at-tenuating circuit. Activity of this circuit inhibits the firing of neurons in the dorsal horn of the spinal cord gray matter, whose axons give rise to the spinothalamic tract. Thus, this activity directly diminishes the signal that gives rise to sensations of pain.

Basbaum and Fields (1978) summarized their work and that of others and proposed a neural circuit that mediates opiate-induced analgesia. A more recent review (Basbaum and Fields, 1984) elaborated (and complicated) their original model. Basically, they propose the following: Endogenous opiates (released by environmental stimuli or administered as a drug) stimulate opiate receptors on neurons in the periaqueductal gray matter. As we have already seen, electrical stimulation of this region or microinjection of opiates into it produces analgesia. In addition, microinjection of naloxone into the periaqueductal gray matter blocks the analgesic effect of the systemic injection of opiates (Yeung and Rudy, 1980), and administration of morphine increases the neural activity in this region (Criswell and Rogers, 1978; Urca and Nahin, 1978). The relevant receptor type appears to be the μ receptor (Smith, Perrotti, Crisp, Cabral, Long, and Scalzitti, 1988). Because the effect of opiates appears to be inhibitory (Nicoll, Alger, and Nicoll, 1980), Basbaum and Fields propose that the neurons that contain opiate receptors are themselves inhibitory interneurons. Thus, the administration of opiates activates the neurons on which these interneurons synapse. (See *Figure 7.38.*)

Neurons in the periaqueductal gray matter send axons to the rostroventral medulla, especially to the **nucleus raphe magnus.** The terminal buttons of these neurons appear to release an excitatory peptide transmitter substance called *neurotensin* (Beitz, 1982b). Fang, Moreau, and Fields (1987) found that microinjections of neurotensin into the nucleus raphe magnus cause analgesia, which strongly suggests that this portion of the pathway is, indeed, mediated by neurons that secrete this peptide. (See *Figure 7.38.*)

The neurons in the nucleus raphe magnus send axons through the **dorsolateral columns** to the dorsal horn of the spinal cord gray matter. If these tracts are destroyed, injections of morphine

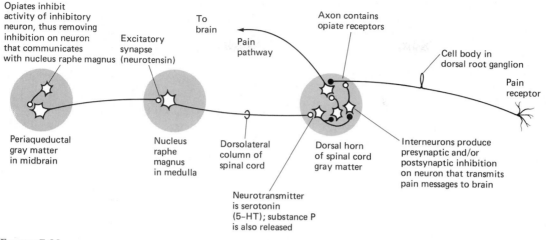

FIGURE 7.38

The neural circuit that mediates opiate-induced analgesia, as hypothesized by Basbaum and Fields (1978).

no longer produce analgesia. The raphe neurons secrete serotonin; thus, administration of PCPA (which prevents the biosynthesis of serotonin) also abolishes morphine-produced analgesia.

The neural circuitry within the dorsal gray matter of the spinal cord is not well understood. Basbaum and Fields (1984) review evidence that suggests that the inhibitory effects of the descending serotonergic neurons may be mediated by means of either presynaptic or postsynaptic inhibition, probably involving one or two interneurons that use various neurotransmitters. To further complicate matters, the raphe neurons that project to the spinal cord appear to release a peptide (substance P) along with serotonin, and the incoming pain-receptive axons in this area contain opiate receptors. Thus, endogenous opiates may mediate presynaptic inhibition there. (See *Figure 7.38.*)

Presumably, an important input to this system is mediated chemically by endogenous opiates that are released by neurosecretory cells. These chemicals are carried through the blood supply to the periaqueductal gray matter, where they stimulate opiate receptors. The periaqueductal gray matter receives inputs from the frontal cortex, amygdala, and hypothalamus (Beitz, 1982a; Mantyh, 1983). These inputs permit learning and emotional reactions to affect an animal's responsiveness to pain. In addition, pain-responsive re-

gions of the brain stem and spinal cord also send axons to the periaqueductal gray matter, which may account for the fact that painful stimulation can itself diminish further sensitivity to pain (Gebhardt, 1982).

Analgesia that is produced by electrical stimulation of the brain is partly, but not completely, mediated by endogenous opiates. Akil, Mayer, and Liebeskind (1976) found that naloxone reduces the analgesic effect of stimulation of the periaqueductal gray matter but does not completely eliminate it. This finding suggested that there are at least two brain mechanisms for analgesia: one that involves the release of endogenous opiates and one that does not. Indeed, Nichols, Thorn, and Berntson (1989) found that an injection of naloxone (which blocks μ receptors) would block analgesia produced by stimulation of the *ventral* but not the *dorsal* periaqueductal gray matter, so these two systems are both anatomically and biochemically distinct.

Biological Significance of Analgesia

It appears that a considerable amount of neural circuitry is devoted to reducing the intensity of pain. What functions do these circuits perform? When an animal encounters a noxious stimulus, it usually stops what it is doing and engages in withdrawal or escape behaviors. Obviously, these responses are quite appropriate. However, they are sometimes counterproductive. For example, if an animal sustains a wound that causes chronic pain, a tendency to engage in withdrawal responses will interfere with its performance of everyday activities, such as obtaining food. Thus, chronic, unavoidable pain would best be diminished.

Another useful function of analgesia is the suppression of pain during important behaviors such as fighting or mating. For example, males fighting for access to females during mating season will fail to pass on their genes if pain elicits withdrawal responses that interfere with fighting. As we will see, these conditions *do* diminish pain.

First, let us consider the effects of unavoidable pain. Several experiments have shown that analgesia can be produced by the application of painful stimuli or even by the presence of nonpainful stimuli that have been paired with painful ones. For example, Maier, Drugan, and Grau (1982) administered inescapable shocks to rats' tails or administered shocks that the animals could learn to escape by making a response. Although both groups of animals received the same amount of shock, only those that received *inescapable* shocks showed analgesia. That is, when their pain sensitivity was tested, it was found to be lower than that of control subjects. The analgesia was abolished by administration of naloxone, which indicates that it was mediated by the release of endogenous opiates. The results make good sense, biologically. If pain is escapable, it serves to motivate the animal to make appropriate responses. If it occurs whatever the animal does, then a reduction in pain sensitivity is in the animal's best interest.

Fanselow (1979) found that a well-known behavioral phenomenon is related to pain-induced analgesia. Normally, animals prefer signaled foot shock to nonsignaled foot shock. That is, a shock that is preceded by the sound of a buzzer is preferred to a sudden foot shock that comes out of the blue. The preference for signaled foot shock is eliminated by naloxone injections; then the rats no longer care whether the shocks come with a warning. Presumably, the warning stimulus causes endogenous opiates to be secreted, which makes signaled shock less painful than nonsignaled shock.

Pain can be reduced by stimulating regions other than those that hurt. For example, people often rub or scratch the area around a wound, in an apparent attempt to diminish the severity of the pain. And as you know, acupuncturists insert needles into various parts of the body in order to reduce pain. The needle is usually then rotated, thus stimulating axons and nerve endings in the vicinity. Often, the region that is stimulated is far removed from the region that becomes less sensitive to pain.

Several experimental studies have shown that acupuncture does, indeed, produce analgesia (Mann, Bowsher, Mumford, Lipton, and Miles, 1973; Gaw, Chang, and Shaw, 1975). Mayer, Price, Rafii, and Barber (1976) reported that the analgesic effects of acupuncture could be blocked by naloxone. However, when pain was reduced by hypnotic suggestion, naloxone had no effect. Thus, acupuncture, but not hypnosis, appears to cause analgesia through the release of endogenous opiates.

There is evidence that engaging in behaviors that are important to survival also reduces sensitivity to pain. For example, Komisaruk and Larsson (1971) found that gentle probing of a rat's vagina with a glass rod produced analgesia. Such probing also increases the activity of neurons in the periaqueductal gray matter and decreases the responsiveness of neurons in the ventrobasal thalamus to painful stimulation (Komisaruk and Steinman, 1987). The phenomenon also occurs in humans; Whipple and Komisaruk (1988) found that self-administered vaginal stimulation reduces sensitivity to painful stimuli but not to neutral tactile stimuli. Presumably, copulation triggers analgesic mechanisms. The adaptive significance of this phenomenon is clear: Painful stimuli encountered during the course of copulation are less likely to cause the behavior to be interrupted; thus, the changes of pregnancy are increased.

Pain can also be reduced, at least in some people, by administering a *placebo,* or pharmacologically inert substance. (The term *placebo* comes from *placere,* which means "to please." The physician pleases an anxious patient by giving him or her an innocuous substance.) The pain reduction seems to be mediated by endogenous opiates, because it is blocked by naloxone (Levine, Gordon, and Fields, 1979). Somehow, when some patients take a medication that they think will reduce pain, it does so *pharmacologically*, by triggering the release of endogenous opiates. This pharmacological effect is eliminated by the opiate receptor-blocker naloxone. Thus, for some people a placebo is not pharmacologically "inert." The placebo effect is probably mediated through the connections of the frontal cortex with the periaqueductal gray matter.

INTERIM SUMMARY

Cutaneous sensory information is provided by specialized receptors in the skin. Pacinian corpuscles provide information about vibration. Ruffini corpuscles, similar to Pacinian corpuscles but considerably smaller, respond to low-frequency vibration, usually referred to as "flutter." Meissner's corpuscles, found in papillae and innervated by several axons, respond to mechanical stimuli. Merkel's disks, also found in papillae, consist of single, flattened dendritic endings next to specialized epithelial cells. They respond to mechanical stimulation. Krause end bulbs, found in the junction between mucous membrane and dry skin (mucocutaneous zones), consist of loops of unmyelinated axons. They probably respond to mechanical stimuli. Painful stimuli are detected primarily by free nerve endings.

Sensory endings in the Golgi tendon organs detect muscular tension, and sensory endings in the intrafusal muscle fibers detect changes in muscle length. Free nerve endings and Pacinian corpuscles are found in the fascia covering the muscles and in the tissue lining the joints, and the body of the muscles contains free nerve endings.

Our somatosensory system is most sensitive to changes in mechanical stimuli. Unless the skin is moving, we do not detect nonpainful stimuli, because the receptors adapt to constant mechanical pressure. Temperature receptors also adapt; moderate changes in skin temperature are soon perceived as "neutral," and deviations above or below this temperature are perceived as warmth or coolness.

Precise, well-localized somatosensory information is conveyed by the lemniscal system, which includes the pathway through the dorsal columns and their nuclei and the medial lemniscus, connecting the dorsal column nuclei with the ventral posterior nuclei of the thalamus. A similar pathway connects the sensory axons of the trigeminal nerve with the trigeminal nuclei and connects these nuclei with the thalamus. Information about pain and temperature ascends the spinal cord through the spinothalamic system, which sends offshoots through the reticulothalamic system. Organic sensibility reaches the central nervous system by means of axons that travel through nerves of the autonomic nervous systems.

The neurons in the primary somatosensory cortex are topographically arranged, according to the part of the body from which they receive sensory information (somatotopic representation). Columns within the somatosensory cortex respond to a particular type of stimulus from a particular region of the body. Recent studies have shown that different types of somatosensory receptors send their information to separate areas of the somatosensory cortex.

Pain perception is not a simple function of stimulation of pain receptors; it is a complex phenomenon that can be modified by experience and the immediate environment. Lesion studies have shown that pain perception involves the parafascicular and intralaminar nuclei of the thalamus, and that a person's emotional response to pain involves the limbic system and the prefrontal cortex, which receives projections from the dorsomedial thalamus.

Just as we have mechanisms to perceive pain, we have mechanisms to reduce it—to produce analgesia. Under the appropriate circumstances neurons in the periaqueductal gray matter are stimulated through synaptic connections with the frontal cortex, amygdala, and hypothalamus. In addition, some neurosecretory cells in the brain release enkephalins, a class of endogenous opiates. These neuromodulators activate receptors on neurons in the periaqueductal gray matter and provide additional stimulation of neurons in this region. Connections from the periaqueductal gray matter to the nucleus raphe magnus of the medulla activate serotonergic neurons located there. These neurons send axons through the dorsolateral columns to the dorsal horn of the spinal cord gray matter, where they cause either presynaptic or postsynaptic inhibition of neurons whose axons transmit pain information to the brain.

Analgesia occurs when it is important for an animal to continue a behavior that would tend to be inhibited by pain—for example, mating or fighting. In addition, inescapable pain activates brain mechanisms that produce analgesia, but escapable pain does not. This distinction makes sense: If the pain is escapable, its sensation should not be blunted but should serve to motivate the animal's efforts to escape. Because the endogenous opiates are found in several regions of the brain that are apparently not involved in pain perception, these neuromodulators undoubtedly serve functions besides analgesia. The fact that many people have chosen to self-administer opiates extracted from the opium poppy attests to its potency as a reinforcer of behavior.

GUSTATION

The stimuli we have encountered so far produce receptor potentials by imparting physical energy: thermal, photic, or kinetic. However, the stimuli received by the last two senses to be studied, gustation and olfaction, interact with their receptors chemically.

The Stimuli

Gustation is clearly related to eating; this sense modality helps us determine the nature of things we put in our mouth. For a substance to be tasted, molecules of it must dissolve in the saliva and stimulate the taste receptors on the tongue. Tastes of different substances vary, but much less than we generally realize. There are only four qualities of taste: *bitterness, sourness, sweetness,* and *saltiness.* Flavor, as opposed to taste, is a composite of olfaction and gustation. Much of the flavor of a steak depends on its odor; to an *anosmic* person (one who lacks the sense of smell) or to a person whose nostrils are stopped up, an onion tastes like an apple, and a steak tastes like salty cardboard.

Most vertebrates possess gustatory systems that respond to all four taste qualities. (An exception is the cat, which does not detect sweetness.) Clearly, sweetness receptors are food detectors. Most sweet-tasting foods, such as fruits and some vegetables, are safe to eat. Saltiness receptors detect the presence of sodium chloride. In some environments inadequate amounts of this mineral are obtained from the usual source of food, so sodium chloride detectors help the animal detect its presence. Injuries that cause bleeding rapidly deplete an organism of its supply of sodium, so the ability to find it quickly can be critical.

Most species of animals will readily ingest substances that taste sweet or somewhat salty. However, they will tend to avoid substances that taste sour or bitter. Because of bacterial activity, many foods become acidic when they spoil. The acidity tastes sour and causes an avoidance reaction. (Of course, we have learned to make highly preferred mixtures of sweet and sour, such as lemonade.) Bitterness is almost universally avoided and cannot easily be improved by adding some sweetness. Many plants produce poisonous alkaloids, which protect them from being eaten by animals. Alkaloids taste bitter; thus, the bitterness receptor undoubtedly serves to warn animals away from these chemicals.

Anatomy of the Taste Buds and Gustatory Cells

The tongue, palate, pharynx, and larynx contain approximately 10,000 taste buds. Most of these receptive organs are arranged around *papillae,* small protuberances of the tongue. *Fungiform papillae,* located on the anterior two-thirds of the tongue, contain up to eight taste buds, along with receptors for pressure, touch, and temperature. *Foliate papillae* consist of up to eight parallel folds along each edge of the back of the tongue. Approximately 1300 taste buds are located in these folds.

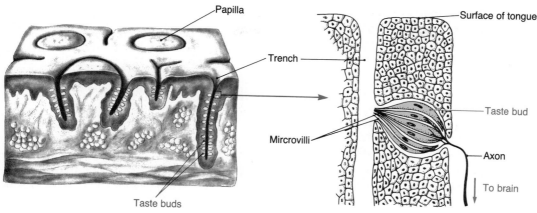

FIGURE 7.39

Left: Papillae on the surface of the tongue. *Right:* A taste bud.

Circumvallate papillae, arranged in an inverted V on the posterior third of the tongue, contain approximately 250 taste buds. They are shaped like little plateaus surrounded by moatlike trenches. Taste buds consist of groups of 20–50 receptor cells, arranged somewhat like the segments of an orange. Cilia are located at the end of each cell and project through the opening of the taste bud (the pore) into the saliva that coats the tongue. Figure 7.39 shows the appearance of a circumvallate papilla; a cross section through the surrounding trench contains a taste bud. (See *Figure 7.39.*)

Taste buds that respond to the different taste qualities have different distributions on the tongue. The tip of the tongue is most sensitive to sweetness and saltiness, the sides are most sensitive to sourness, and the back of the tongue, throat, and soft palate are most sensitive to bitterness. (See *Figure 7.40.*) This distribution explains why saccharin, an artificial sweetener that tastes both sweet and bitter to some people, produces a sensation of sweetness on the front of the tongue when it is first tasted and then a sensation of bitterness in the back of the mouth when it is swallowed.

Taste receptors form synapses with dendrites of sensory neurons that convey gustatory information to the brain. The receptors have a life span of only ten days. They quickly wear out, being directly exposed to a rather hostile environment. As they degenerate, they are replaced by newly developed cells; the afferent dendrite is passed on to

the new cell (Beidler, 1970). The presence of vesicles within the cytoplasm of the receptor cell around the synaptic region suggests that transmission at this synapse is chemical.

Transduction of Gustatory Information

It seems most likely that transduction of taste is similar to the chemical transmission that takes place at synapses: The tasted molecule binds with

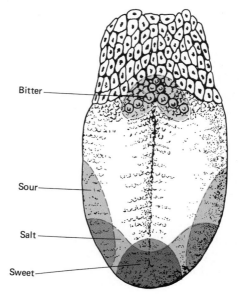

FIGURE 7.40

Different regions of the tongue are especially sensitive to different tastes.

the receptor and produces changes in membrane permeability that cause receptor potentials. Different substances bind with different types of receptors, producing different taste sensations.

To taste salty, a substance must ionize. Although the best stimulus for saltiness receptors is sodium chloride (NaCl), a variety of salts containing metallic cations (such as Na^+, K^+, and Li^+) with a halogen or other small anion (such as Cl^-, Br^-, SO_4^{2-}, or NO_3^-) taste salty. Sourness receptors probably respond to the hydrogen ions present in acidic solutions. However, because the sourness of a particular acid is not simply a function of the concentration of hydrogen ions, the anions must have an effect, as well. Bitter and sweet substances are more difficult to characterize. The typical stimulus for bitterness is a plant alkaloid such as quinine; for sweetness it is a sugar such as glucose or fructose. The fact that some molecules elicit both sensations suggests that bitterness and sweetness receptors may be similar. For example, the Seville orange rind contains a glycoside (complex sugar) that tastes extremely bitter; the addition of a hydrogen ion to the molecule makes it taste intensely sweet (Horowitz and Gentili, 1974). Some amino acids taste sweet. Indeed, the commercial sweetener aspartame consists simply of two amino acids, aspartate and phenylalanine.

The receptor molecules for at least some taste qualities appear to control potassium channels. These channels are normally open but become closed when sour or bitter stimuli are present (Kinnamon and Roper, 1988). Cyclic AMP appears to serve as a second messenger in the transduction process; Striem, Pace, Zehavi, Naim, and Lancet (1989) found that sweet stimuli increase cyclic AMP synthesis, and Avenet, Hoffman, and Lindemann (1988) found that cyclic AMP closes the K^+ channels.

Kinnamon, Dionne, and Beam (1988) suggest that sourness is detected by sites on potassium channels in the membrane of taste cells. Presumably, hydrogen ions bind with these sites and close the channels, thus depolarizing the membrane. Detection of saltiness is accomplished by sodium channels; the influx of Na^+ directly affects the membrane potential (Avenet and Lindemann, 1989; Roper, 1989).

The Gustatory Pathway

Gustatory information is transmitted through three cranial nerves. Information from the anterior part of the tongue travels through the *chorda tympani,* a branch of the seventh cranial nerve (facial nerve). Taste receptors in the posterior part of the tongue send information through the lingual (tongue) branch of the ninth cranial nerve (glossopharyngeal nerve); the tenth cranial nerve (vagus nerve) carries information from receptors of the palate and epiglottis. The chorda tympani gets its name because it passes through the middle ear just beneath the tympanic membrane. Because of its convenient location, it is accessible to a recording or stimulating electrode. Investigators have even recorded from this nerve during the course of human ear operations.

The first relay station for taste is the *nucleus of the solitary tract,* located in the medulla. (As we will see in Chapter 9, this region may also play a role in sleep.) In primates the taste-sensitive neurons of this nucleus send their axons to the ventral posteromedial thalamic nucleus, a nucleus that also receives somatosensory information received from the trigeminal nerve (Beckstead, Morse, and Norgren, 1980). Thalamic taste-sensitive neurons send their axons to the primary gustatory cortex, which is located in the frontal insular and opercular cortex (Pritchard, Hamilton, Morse, and Norgren, 1986). Unlike most other sense modalities, taste is ipsilaterally represented in the brain. (See *Figure 7.41.*)

Gustatory information also reaches the amygdala and the hypothalamus and adjacent basal forebrain (Nauta, 1964; Russchen, Amaral, and Price, 1986). Many investigators believe that the hypothalamic pathway plays a role in mediating the reinforcing effects of sweet and salty tastes. In fact, some neurons in the hypothalamus respond to sweet stimuli only when the animal is hungry (Rolls, Murzi, Yaxley, Thorpe, and Simpson, 1986). I will discuss this phenomenon in more detail in Chapter 13.

Neural Coding of Taste

Almost all fibers in the chorda tympani respond to more than one taste quality, and many respond to

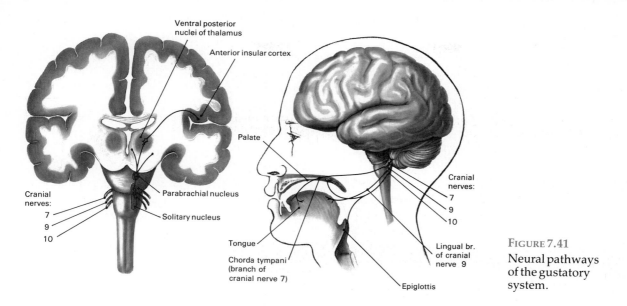

FIGURE 7.41
Neural pathways
of the gustatory
system.

changes in temperature, as well. However, most show a preference for one of the four qualities (sweet, salty, sour, or bitter). Figure 7.42 shows the average responses of fibers in the rat chorda tympani and glossopharyngeal nerve to sucrose (S), NaCl (N), HCl (H), quinine (Q), and water (W), as recorded by Nowlis and Frank (1977). These investigators stimulated three different kinds of taste buds (circumvallate, foliate, and fungiform) and found the same general types of responses from each of them. (See *Figure 7.42.*)

Similar kinds of response patterns are found in the nucleus of the solitary tract (Doetsch and Erickson, 1970). These neurons respond to even more qualities of taste. Funakoshi and Ninomiya (1977) reported data from cortical taste neurons in dogs and rats. Of sixty neurons from which they recorded, more than one-third responded to only

one of the five taste stimuli that were used; another third responded to only two of them. Ten of the neurons tested were excited by one stimulus and inhibited by another. In the monkey, Pritchard, Hamilton, and Norgren (1989) found a similar sharpening at each relay station of the gustatory system. The sharpest (and most prevalent) coding was that of neurons in the orbitofrontal cortex to the taste of glucose.

Yamamoto, Yuyama, and Kawamura (1981) attempted to determine whether the taste qualities were represented in different parts of the cortex. In general, they were. Dilute hydrochloric acid and quinine tended to stimulate neurons in adjacent regions at one end of the cortical taste area; sucrose stimulated neurons located at the opposite end. Neurons that were sensitive to sodium chloride were spread throughout the area.

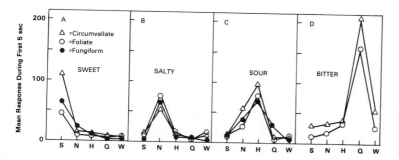

FIGURE 7.42
Mean number of responses recorded from axons in the chorda tympani and glossopharyngeal nerve during the first 5 seconds after the application of sweet, salty, sour, and bitter stimuli. The response characteristics of the axons are categorized as sweet, salty, sour, or bitter. (From Nowlis, G.H., and Frank, M., in *Olfaction and Taste 6*, edited by J. LeMagnen and P. MacLeod. Washington, D.C.: Information Retrieval, 1977.)

*I*NTERIM SUMMARY

Taste receptors detect only four sensory qualities: bitterness, sourness, sweetness, and saltiness. Bitter foods often contain plant alkaloids, many of which are poisonous. Sour foods have usually undergone bacterial fermentation, which can produce toxins. On the other hand, sweet foods (such as fruits) are usually nutritious and safe to eat, and salty foods contain an essential cation, sodium. The fact that people in affluent cultures today tend to ingest excessive amounts of sweet and salty foods suggests that stimulation of these neurons is naturally reinforcing. The means of transduction of gustatory information is not known. Presumably, the mechanism utilizes receptors similar to those that detect hormones and transmitter substances.

Gustatory information from the anterior part of the tongue travels through the chorda tympani, a branch of the facial nerve that passes beneath the eardrum on its way to the brain. The posterior part of the tongue sends gustatory information through the glossopharyngeal nerve, and the palate and epiglottis send gustatory information through the vagus nerve. Gustatory information is received by the nucleus of the solitary tract (located in the medulla) and is relayed to the thalamic taste area, to the primary gustatory cortex of the opercular and insular cortex, and then to the orbitofrontal cortex, amygdala, hypothalamus, and basal forebrain.

OLFACTION

Olfaction, the second chemical sense, helps us identify food and avoid food that has spoiled and is unfit to eat. It helps the members of many species identify receptive mates. For humans, olfaction is the most enigmatic of all sensory modalities. Odors have a peculiar ability to evoke memories, often vague ones that seem to have occurred in the distant past. Although people can discriminate among many thousands of different odors, we lack a good vocabulary to describe them. It is relatively easy to describe sights we have seen or sounds we have heard, but the description of an odor is difficult. At best, we can say it smells like something else. Thus, the olfactory system appears to be specialized for *identifying things*, not for analyzing particular qualities. As we will see, the search for odor primaries, like those of taste, vision, and audition, has not yet progressed very far.

The Stimulus

The stimulus for odor consists of volatile substances having a molecular weight in the range of approximately 15 to 300. Almost all odorous compounds are organic. However, many substances that meet these criteria have no odor at all, and we do not yet know why.

Anatomy of the Olfactory Apparatus

Our olfactory receptors reside within two patches of mucous membrane (*olfactory epithelium*), each having an area of about 1 square inch. The olfactory epithelium is located at the top of the nasal cavity, as shown in *Figure 7.43.* Less than 10 percent of the air that enters the nostrils reaches the olfactory epithelium; a sniff is needed to sweep air upward into the nasal cavity so that it reaches the olfactory receptors.

The inset in Figure 7.43 illustrates a group of olfactory receptor cells, along with their supporting cells. (See *inset, Figure 7.43.*) Olfactory receptor cells are bipolar neurons whose cell bodies lie within the olfactory mucosa that lines the *cribriform plate*, a bone at the base of the rostral part of the brain. There is a constant turnover of olfactory receptor cells, as there is of gustatory receptor cells; their life cycle is approximately 60 days. The cells send a process toward the surface of the mucosa, which divides into several cilia that penetrate the layer of mucus. Odorous molecules must dissolve in the mucus and stimulate receptor molecules on the olfactory cilia. The axons of olfactory receptor cells enter the skull through small holes in the cribriform ("perforated") plate. The olfactory mucosa also contains free nerve endings of trigeminal nerve axons; these nerve endings presumably mediate sensations of pain that can be produced by sniffing some irritating chemicals, such as ammonia.

The *olfactory bulbs* lie at the base of the brain

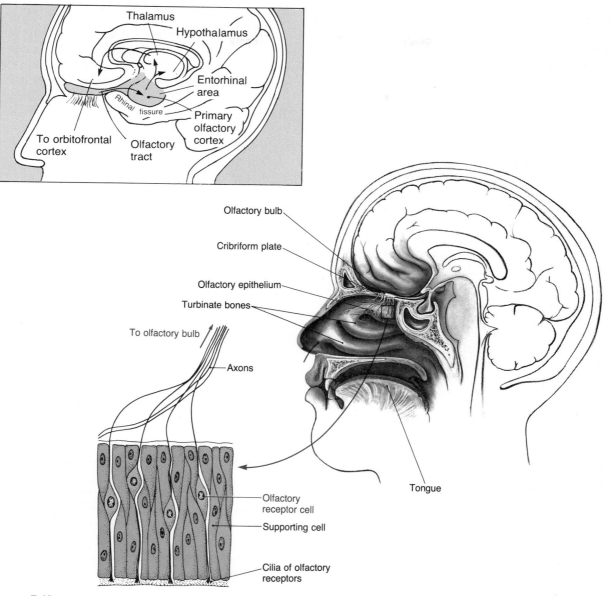

FIGURE 7.43
The olfactory system.

on the ends of the stalklike olfactory tracts. The axons of the olfactory receptors terminate in the olfactory bulbs, where they synapse with dendrites of *mitral cells* (named for their resemblance to a bishop's miter). These synapses take place in the complex axonal and dendritic arborizations called *olfactory glomeruli* (from *glomus*, "ball"). There are approximately ten thousand glomeruli, each of which receives input from a bundle of approximately one thousand axons. The axons of the mitral cells travel to the rest of the brain through the olfactory tracts. Some of these axons synapse in the brain; whereas others cross the brain, enter the other olfactory nerve, and synapse in the contralateral olfactory bulb.

Olfactory tract axons project directly to the primary olfactory cortex, which is on the pyriform cortex, a part of the limbic lobe. (See *Figure 7.43*.) The pyriform cortex projects to the hypothalamus and to the dorsomedial thalamus, which projects to the orbitofrontal cortex (Cain, 1988). As you may recall, the orbitofrontal cortex also receives gustatory information; thus, it may be involved in the combining of taste and olfaction into flavor. The hypothalamus also receives a considerable amount of olfactory information, which is probably important for the acceptance or rejection of food and for the olfactory control of reproductive processes seen in many species of mammals.

Most mammals (but probably not adult humans) have another organ that responds to olfactory stimuli: the *vomeronasal organ*. Because it plays an important role in animals' responses to odors that affect reproductive physiology and behavior, its structure and function are described in Chapter 10.

Efferent fibers from several locations in the brain enter the olfactory bulbs. The synapses of these fibers appear to be inhibitory, but their role in the processing of olfactory information is a mystery. However, the brain controls the effects of olfactory stimuli in a more obvious way: We can sniff the air, maximizing the exposure of our olfactory epithelium to the odor molecules, or we can pinch our nostrils and breathe through the mouth, thus producing minimal olfactory stimulation.

Transduction of Olfactory Information

The means by which odor molecules produce receptor potentials is unknown. Investigators assume that olfactory cilia contain receptor molecules (like those found on taste receptors and synaptic membranes) that are stimulated by odor molecules. The resting potential of olfactory neurons is approximately -45 mV, which is relatively weak. Stimulation with odorous molecules opens one or more ion channels, causing the neurons to depolarize slowly and increasing the firing rate of their axons (Lancet, 1986). The ion channels appear to be controlled by cyclic AMP. In fact, Jones and Reed (1989) have identified a protein, which they call G_{olf}, that connects olfactory receptor molecules to an enzyme that stimulates adenylate cyclase, thus producing cyclic AMP.

Coding of Odor Quality

Although investigators have made many attempts to identify odor primaries corresponding to the sweet, sour, bitter, and salty qualities of taste, we still cannot say with any assurance how odor quality is encoded. This lack of knowledge about coding at the peripheral level certainly hampers research on the central coding of olfactory information.

The search for primary olfactory qualities is stimulated primarily because it is easier to conceive of coding the overwhelming number of discriminable odors by a few primary dimensions than by a myriad of different types of receptors. After all, new substances with new odors are synthesized every year, and it would be unreasonable to expect that we have already evolved specific receptors for all of the odors yet to be experienced. However, it is possible that there really *is* a very large number of specific receptor molecules and that odor primaries do not exist. If we consider the immune system, this possibility does not seem so farfetched. The immune system uses receptor molecules to identify various antigens. Hood (1982) has estimated that more than 10 million different antigens could potentially be recognized, each by a different receptor. Perhaps the recognition of different odors is similarly individualized.

Researchers have not yet abandoned the possibility that odors may be sorted according to some classification scheme that uses a more limited number of receptor types. First, some people have very specific anosmias; they cannot detect certain odors (Lancet, 1986). At least one specific anosmia has been shown to be genetically produced (Wysocki and Beauchamp, 1984). This phenomenon suggests that there are various receptor types and that these people lack one or more kinds of specific receptors. Second, we humans seem to be able to reach some agreements about the similarities of odors. Classifications such as fruity, pinelike, and musky make sense to most of us, and we are willing to say that there is more similarity between the odors of pine oil and cedar oil than between the odors of skunk and limes. However, no coherent, testable theory exists that organizes olfactory qualities and explains differences among them.

Cain (1988) notes that although most odors are

produced by mixtures of many different chemicals, we identify them as belonging to particular objects. For example, the smell of coffee, fried bacon, and cigarette smoke each are made of up to several hundred different types of molecules. Although each of these odors is a mixture, we recognize them as being unique—we do not detect the individual components. This fact suggests that olfaction, like vision, is synthetic. (You will recall that we perceive a mixture of red light and bluish green light as pure yellow light; we do not perceive either of the components.) However, if the smell of coffee, fried bacon, and cigarette smoke are mixed together, we still recognize all three odors; thus, the olfactory system also has the characteristics of an analytic sensory modality, like audition. Obviously, these apparently contradictory facts will have to be resolved somehow.

Recordings of Neural Responses to Olfactory Stimuli

Unfortunately, recordings taken from single olfactory receptors have not helped to identify "odor primaries." Mathews (1972) recorded from nineteen olfactory receptors of the tortoise, stimulating them with twenty-seven different odors. Two of the receptors responded to only one odor, one responded to two odors, and sixteen responded to three or more odors. He found similar response characteristics in neurons in the olfactory bulb. Gesteland (1978) found that no two olfactory receptors responded alike. He reported that although two similar odors might produce similar responses in different cells, a brief search would invariably find another cell that made a sharp distinction between the odors, and the original cells would respond differently to another pair of odors.

Recordings in more central levels of the olfactory system show that neural responses tend to be more finely tuned to particular odors. For example, Tanabe, Iino, Ooshima, and Takagi (1974) and Tanabe, Iino, and Takagi (1975) found that neurons in the olfactory area of the orbitofrontal cortex of monkeys were more selective. Of the forty cells from which they recorded, half responded to only one odor, and decreasing numbers responded to two, three, or four different odors. None responded to more than five odors. The results suggest that cortical neurons respond selectively to particular patterns of activity in neurons in more peripheral parts of the olfactory system. The nature of the coding system is unknown.

Stewart, Kauer, and Shepherd (1979) used the 2-deoxyglucose (2-DG) autoradiographic technique (described in Chapter 5) to investigate the responses of neurons in the olfactory bulb. Their results suggest that specific odors may produce responses of neurons in particular regions. They injected rats with radioactive 2-DG and exposed them to a particular odor. Then they killed the rats, removed and sliced their olfactory bulbs, and used a photographic emulsion to find the radioactivity. The results indicated that different odors increased the metabolic activity (and, presumably, the synaptic activity) of different specific regions of the olfactory bulbs. The distribution of radioactivity in the olfactory bulbs of twenty-seven rats is shown in Figure 7.44. Six were exposed to the odor of camphor (colored areas), and twenty-one were exposed to amyl acetate (unfilled outlines). (See *Figure 7.44.*)

The results suggest that odor quality may be represented spatially by neurons in the olfactory system. Only further research will reveal whether this procedure can be used to identify categories of olfactory qualities.

I NTERIM SUMMARY

The olfactory receptors consist of bipolar neurons located in the olfactory epithelium that lines the roof of the nasal sinuses, on the bone that underlies the frontal lobes. The receptors send processes toward the surface of the mucosa, which divide into cilia. The membranes of these cilia appear to contain receptors that detect aromatic molecules dissolved in the air that sweeps past the olfactory mucosa. The axons of the olfactory receptors pass through the perforations of the cribriform plate and form synapses with the dendrites of the mitral cells of the olfactory bulbs. These neurons send axons through the olfactory tracts to the brain, principally to the amygdala, ventral frontal

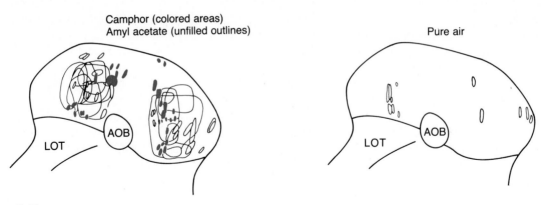

Camphor (colored areas)
Amyl acetate (unfilled outlines)

Pure air

FIGURE 7.44

Composite drawings prepared from 2-DG autoradiographs of rat olfactory bulbs after the animals were exposed to camphor (*left*, colored areas), amyl acetate (*left*, unfilled outlines), or pure air (*right*, unfilled outlines). LOT = lateral olfactory tract; AOB = accessory olfactory bulb. (From Stewart, W.B., Kauer, J.S., and Shepherd, G.M. *Journal of Comparative Neurology*, 1979, *185*, 715–734.)

neocortex, and the limbic cortex. Some axons travel to the thalamic taste area and may be responsible for at least some of the convergence of olfactory and gustatory information into the perception of flavor.

We do not know the nature of olfactory receptor molecules or how aromatic molecules produce membrane potentials. Attempts to analyze odor primaries similar to the four primary tastes have met with failure. Somehow, the olfactory system has the properties of both a synthetic and an analytic sensory modality. Studies using 2-DG autoradiography have suggested that different odors excite neurons in particular regions of the olfactory bulbs, but we do not yet know whether these results imply the existence of a spatial code or what its rules are.

CONCLUDING REMARKS

This chapter and Chapter 6 have summarized our knowledge of the physiology of sensation and perception. Obviously, far more is known than what I have been able to summarize here, but you now are familiar with the basic anatomy and physiology of the sensory modalities and the types of research issues that investigators are currently studying. The rest of the book deals with organisms' behaviors. Chapter 8 introduces the motor system, and the chapters that follow discuss particular classes of behavior. Some of the mechanisms and neural connections that you learned about here will be discussed again, as we see how various stimuli control organisms' behaviors.

NEW TERMS

SUGGESTED READINGS

Audition

Edelman, G.M., Gall, W.E., and Cowan, W.M. *Auditory Functions.* New York: John Wiley & Sons, 1988.

Gulick, W.L., Gescheider, G.A., and Frisina, R.D. *Hearing: Physiological Acoustics, Neural Coding, and Psychoacoustics.* New York: Oxford University Press, 1989.

Howard, J., Roberts, W.M., and Hudspeth, A.J. Mechanoelectrical transduction by hair cells. *Annual Review of Biophysics and Biophysical Chemistry,* 1988, *17*, 99–124.

Møller, A.R. *Auditory Physiology.* New York: Academic Press, 1983.

Roberts, W.M., Howard, J., and Hudspeth, A.J. Hair cells: Transduction, tuning, and transmission in the inner ear. *Annual Review of Cell Biology,* 1988, *4*, 63–92.

Somatosenses

Akil, H., Watson, S.J., Young, E., Lewis, M.E., Khachaturian, H., and Walker, J.M. Endogenous opioids: Biology and function. *Annual Review of Neuroscience,* 1984, *7*, 223–256.

Basbaum, A.I., and Fields, H.L. Endogenous pain control systems: Brainstem spinal pathways and endorphin circuitry. *Annual Review of Neuroscience,* 1984, *7*, 309–338.

Darian-Smith, I. Touch in primates. *Annual Review of Psychology,* 1982, *33*, 155–194.

Dubner, R., and Bennett, G.J. Spinal and trigeminal mechanisms of nociception. *Annual Review of Neuroscience,* 1983, *6*, 381–418.

Iggo, A., and Andres, K.H. Morphology of cutaneous receptors. *Annual Review of Neuroscience,* 1982, *5*, 1–32.

Olfaction and Gustation

Bruch, R.C., Kalinoski, D.L., and Kare, M.R. Biochemistry of vertebrate olfaction and taste. *Annual Review of Nutrition,* 1988, *8*, 21–42.

Roper, S.D. The cell biology of vertebrate taste receptors. *Annual Review of Neuroscience,* 1989, *12*, 329–354.

Lancet, D. Vertebrate olfactory reception. *Annual Review of Neuroscience,* 1986, *9*, 329–355.

Travers, J.B., Travers, S.P., and Norgren, R. Gustatory neural processing in the hindbrain. *Annual Review of Neuroscience,* 1987, *10*, 595–632.

8

Control of Movement

*S*o far, I have described the nature of neural communication, the basic structure of the nervous system, and the physiology of perception. Now it is time to consider the ultimate function of the nervous system: control of behavior. The brain is the organ that moves the muscles. It does many other things, but all of them are secondary to making our bodies move. This chapter describes the principles of muscular contraction, some reflex circuitry within the spinal cord, and the means by which the brain initiates behaviors. The rest of the book describes the physiology of particular categories of behaviors and the ways in which our behaviors can be modified by experience.

MUSCLES

Mammals have three types of muscles: skeletal muscle, smooth muscle, and cardiac muscle.

Skeletal Muscle

Skeletal muscles are the ones that move us (our skeletons) around and thus are responsible for our behavior. Most of them are attached to bones at each end and move the bones when they contract. (Exceptions include eye muscles and some abdominal muscles, which are attached to bone at one end only.) Muscles are fastened to bones via *tendons,* strong bands of connective tissue. Several different classes of movement can be accomplished by the skeletal muscles, but I will refer principally to two of them: flexion and extension. Contraction of a flexor muscle produces *flexion,* the drawing in of a limb. *Extension,* which is the opposite movement, is produced by contraction of extensor muscles. These are the so-called *antigravity muscles*—the ones we use to stand up. When a four-legged animal lifts a paw, the movement is one of flexion. Putting it back down is one of extension. Sometimes, people say they "flex" their muscles. This is an incorrect use of the term. Muscles *contract;* limbs *flex.* Bodybuilders show off their arm muscles by simultaneously contracting the flexor and extensor muscles of that limb.

Anatomy

The detailed structure of a skeletal muscle is shown in *Figure 8.1.* As you can see, it consists of two types of muscle fibers. The *extrafusal muscle fibers* are served by axons of the *alpha motor neurons.* Contraction of these fibers provides the muscle's motive force. The *intrafusal muscle fibers* are specialized sensory organs that are served by two axons, one sensory and one motor. (These organs are also called *muscle spindles* because of their shape. In fact, the Latin word *fusus* means "spindle"; hence *intrafusal* muscle fibers are found within the spindles, and *extrafusal* muscle fibers are found outside them.)

The central region (*capsule*) of the intrafusal muscle fiber contains sensory endings that are sensitive to stretch applied to the muscle fiber. Actually, there are two types of intrafusal muscle fibers, but for simplicity's sake only one kind is shown here. The efferent axon of the *gamma motor neuron* causes the intrafusal muscle fiber to contract; however, this contraction contributes an insubstantial amount of force. As we will see, the function of this contraction is to modify the sensitivity of the fiber's afferent ending to stretch.

A single myelinated axon of an alpha motor neuron serves several extrafusal muscle fibers. In primates the number of muscle fibers served by a single axon varies considerably, depending on the precision with which the muscle can be controlled. In muscles that move the fingers or eyes the ratio can be less than one to ten; in muscles that move the leg it can be one to several hundred. An alpha motor neuron, its axon, and associated extrafusal muscle fibers constitute a *motor unit.*

A single muscle fiber consists of a bundle of *myofibrils,* each of which consists of overlapping strands of *actin* and *myosin.* The small protrusions on the myosin filaments (*myosin cross bridges*) are the motile elements that interact with the actin filaments and produce muscular contractions. (See *Figure 8.1.*) The regions in which the actin and myosin filaments overlap produce dark stripes, or *striations;* hence skeletal muscle is often referred to as *striated muscle.*

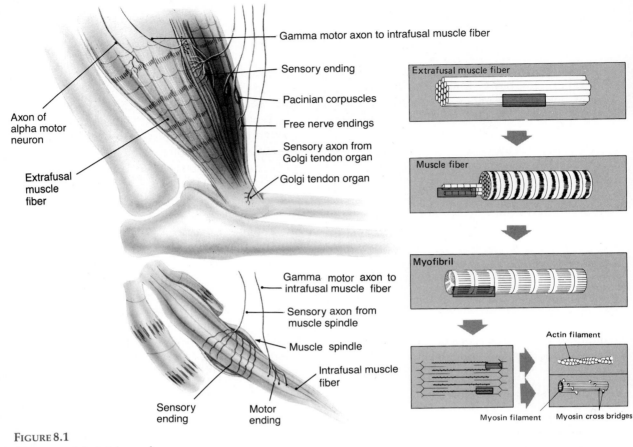

Figure 8.1
Anatomy of skeletal muscle.

The Physical Basis of Muscular Contraction

The synapse between the terminal button of an efferent neuron and the membrane of a muscle fiber is called a *neuromuscular junction.* The terminal buttons of the neurons synapse on *motor endplates,* located in grooves along the surface of the muscle fibers. When an axon fires, acetylcholine is liberated by the terminal buttons and produces a depolarization of the postsynaptic membrane (*endplate potential*). The endplate potential is much larger than an excitatory postsynaptic potential in synapses between neurons; an endplate potential *always* causes the muscle fiber to fire, propagating the potential along its length. This action potential induces a contraction, or *twitch,* of the muscle fiber.

The depolarization of a muscle fiber opens the gates of voltage-dependent calcium channels, permitting calcium ions to enter the cytoplasm.

This event triggers the contraction. Calcium acts as a cofactor that permits the myofibrils to extract energy from the ATP that is present in the cytoplasm. The myosin cross bridges alternately attach to the actin strands, bend in one direction, detach themselves, bend back, reattach to the actin at a point farther down the strand, and so on. Thus, the cross bridges "row" along the actin filaments. Figure 8.2 illustrates this rowing sequence and shows how this sequence results in shortening the muscle fiber. (See *Figure 8.2.*)

A single impulse of a motor neuron produces a single twitch of a muscle fiber. The physical effects of the twitch last considerably longer than will the action potential, because of the elasticity of the muscle and the time required to rid the cell of calcium. (Like sodium, calcium is actively extruded by a pump situated in the membrane.) Figure 8.3 shows how the physical effects of a series of action

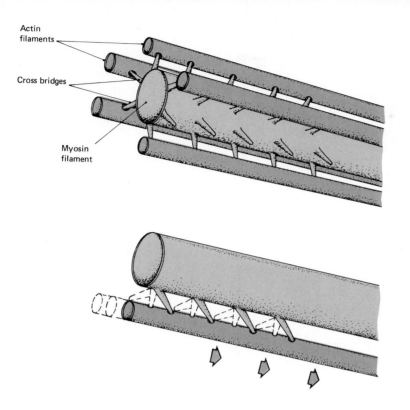

Actin filaments

Cross bridges

Myosin filament

FIGURE 8.2
The mechanism by which muscles contract. (a) Location of the myosin cross bridges. (b) The myosin cross bridges performing "rowing" movements, which cause the actin and myosin filaments to move relative to each other. (Adapted from Anthony, C.P., and Kolthoff, N.J. *Textbook of Anatomy and Physiology,* 8th ed. St. Louis: C.V. Mosby, 1971.)

potentials can overlap, causing a sustained contraction by the muscle fiber. A single motor unit in a leg muscle of a cat can raise a 100-gram weight, which attests to the remarkable strength of the contractile mechanism. (See *Figure 8.3.*)

As you know from your own experience, muscular contraction is not an all-or-nothing phenomenon, as are the twitches of the constituent muscle fibers. Obviously, strength of muscular contraction is determined by the average rate of firing of the various motor units. If, at a given moment, many units are firing, the contraction will be forceful. If few are firing, the contraction will be weak.

Sensory Feedback from Muscles

As we saw, the intrafusal muscle fibers contain sensory endings that are sensitive to stretch. The intrafusal muscle fibers are arranged in parallel with the extrafusal muscle fibers. Therefore, they are stretched when the muscle lengthens and are relaxed when it shortens. Thus, even though these afferent neurons are *stretch receptors,* they serve as *muscle length detectors.* This distinction is important. Stretch receptors are also located within the tendons, in the **Golgi tendon organ.**

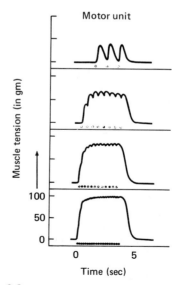

FIGURE 8.3
Action potentials and contractions. A rapid succession of action potentials can cause a muscle fiber to produce a sustained contraction. Each dot represents an individual action potential. [Adapted from Devanandan, M.S., Eccles, R.M., and Westerman, R.A. *Journal of Physiology (London),* 1965, *178,* 359–367.]

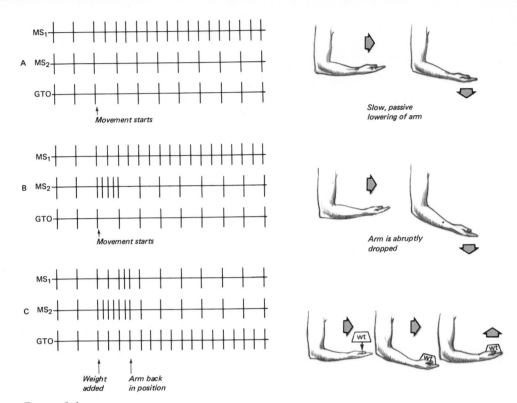

FIGURE 8.4

Effects of arm movements on the firing of muscle and tendon afferent axons. (a) Slow passive extension of the arm. (b) Rapid extension of the arm. (c) Addition of a weight to an arm held in a horizontal position. MS$_1$ and MS$_2$ are two types of muscle spindles; GTO is an afferent fiber from the Golgi tendon organ.

These receptors detect the total amount of stretch exerted by the muscle, through its tendons, on the bones to which the muscle is attached. The stretch receptors of the Golgi tendon organ encode the degree of stretch by the rate of firing. They respond not to a muscle's length but to how hard it is pulling. In contrast, the receptors on intrafusal muscle fibers detect muscle length, not tension.

Figure 8.4 shows the response of afferent axons of the muscle spindles and Golgi tendon organ to various types of movements. Figure 8.4a shows the effects of passive lengthening of muscles, the kind of movement that would be seen if your forearm, held in a completely relaxed fashion, were slowly lowered by someone who was supporting it. The rate of firing of one type of muscle spindle afferent neuron (MS$_1$) increases, while the activity of the afferent of the Golgi tendon organ (GTO) remains unchanged. (See *Figure 8.4a.*) Figure 8.4b shows the results when the arm is dropped quickly; note that this time the second type of muscle spindle afferent neuron (MS$_2$) fires a rapid burst of impulses. This fiber, then, signals rapid changes in muscle length. (See *Figure 8.4b.*) Figure 8.4c shows what would happen if a weight were suddenly dropped into your hand while your forearm was held parallel to the ground. Neurons MS$_1$ and MS$_2$ (especially MS$_2$, which responds to rapid changes in muscle length) briefly fire, because your arm lowers briefly and then comes back to the original position. The Golgi tendon organ, monitoring the strength of contraction, fires in proportion to the stress on the muscle, so it increases its rate of firing as soon as the weight is added. (See *Figure 8.4c.*)

Smooth Muscle

Our bodies contain two types of *smooth muscle,* both of which are controlled by the autonomic nervous system. *Multiunit smooth muscles* are found in large arteries, around hair follicles (where they produce *piloerection,* or fluffing of fur), and in the eye (controlling lens adjustment and pupillary dilation). This type of smooth muscle is normally inactive, but it will contract in response to neural stimulation or to certain hormones. In contrast, *single-unit smooth muscles* normally contract in a rhythmical fashion. Some of these cells spontaneously produce *pacemaker potentials,* which we can regard as self-initiated excitatory postsynaptic potentials. These slow potentials elicit action potentials, which are propagated by adjacent smooth muscle fibers, causing a wave of muscular contraction. The efferent nerve supply (and various hormones) can modulate the rhythmical rate, increasing or decreasing it. Single-unit smooth muscles are found chiefly in the gastrointestinal system, uterus, and small blood vessels.

Cardiac Muscle

As its name implies, *cardiac muscle* is found in the heart. This type of muscle looks somewhat like striated muscle but acts like single-unit smooth muscle. The heart beats regularly, even if it is denervated. Neural activity and certain hormones (especially the catecholamines) serve to modulate the heart rate. A group of cells in the *pacemaker* of the heart are rhythmically active and initiate the contractions of cardiac muscle that constitute the heartbeat.

*I*NTERIM SUMMARY

Our bodies possess skeletal muscle, smooth muscle, and cardiac muscle. Skeletal muscles contain extrafusal muscle fibers, which provide the force of contraction. The alpha motor neurons form synapses with the extrafusal muscle fibers and control their contraction. Skeletal muscles also contain intrafusal muscle fibers, which detect changes in muscle length. The length of the intrafusal muscle fiber, and hence its sensitivity to increases in muscle length, is controlled by the gamma motor neuron. Besides the intrafusal muscle fibers, the muscles contain stretch receptors in the Golgi tendon organs, located at the ends of the muscles.

The force of muscular contraction is provided by long protein molecules called actin and myosin, arranged in overlapping parallel arrays. When an action potential, initiated by the synapse at the motor endplate, causes Ca^{2+} to enter the muscle fiber, the myofibrils extract energy from ATP and cause a twitch of the muscle fiber, producing a ratchetlike "rowing" movement of the myosin cross bridges.

Smooth muscle is controlled by the autonomic nervous system through direct neural connections and indirectly through the endocrine system. Multiunit smooth muscles contract only in response to neural or hormonal stimulation. In contrast, single-unit smooth muscles normally contract rhythmically, but their rate is controlled by the autonomic nervous system. Cardiac muscle also contracts spontaneously, and its rate of contraction, too, is influenced by the autonomic nervous system.

REFLEX CONTROL OF MOVEMENT

Although behaviors are controlled by the brain, the spinal cord possesses a certain degree of autonomy. Particular kinds of somatosensory stimuli can elicit rapid responses through neural connections located within the spinal cord. These reflexes constitute the simplest level of motor integration.

The Monosynaptic Stretch Reflex

The activity of the simplest functional neural pathway in the body is easy to demonstrate. Sit on a surface high enough to allow your legs to dangle freely and have someone lightly tap your patellar tendon, just below the kneecap. This stimulus briefly stretches your quadriceps muscle, on the top of your thigh. The stretch causes the muscle to contract, which makes your leg kick forward. (I am sure few of you will bother with this demonstration, because you are already familiar with it; most physical examinations include a test of this reflex.) The time interval between the tendon tap and the start of the leg extension is about 50 milliseconds. That interval is too short for the involvement of the brain; it would take considerably longer for sensory information to be relayed to the brain and for motor information to be relayed back. For example, suppose a person is asked to move his or her leg as quickly as possible after being *touched* on the knee. This response would not be reflexive but would involve sensory and motor mechanisms of the brain. In this case the interval between the stimulus and the start of the response would be several times greater than the time required for the patellar reflex.

Obviously, the patellar reflex as such has no utility; no selective advantage is bestowed upon animals that kick a limb when a tendon is tapped. However, if a more natural stimulus is applied, the utility of this mechanism becomes apparent. Figure 8.5 shows the effects of placing a weight in a person's hand. This time I have included a piece of the spinal cord, with its roots, to show the neural circuit that composes the **monosynaptic stretch reflex.** First, follow the circuit: Starting at the muscle spindle, afferent impulses are conducted to

ferent impulses are conducted to terminal buttons in the gray matter of the spinal cord. These terminal buttons synapse on an alpha motor neuron that innervates the extrafusal muscle fibers of the same muscle. Only one synapse is encountered along the route from receptor to effector—hence the term *monosynaptic*. (See **Figure 8.5.**)

Now consider a useful function this reflex performs. If the weight the person is holding is increased, the forearm begins to move down. This movement lengthens the muscle and increases the firing rate of the muscle spindle afferent neurons, whose terminal buttons then stimulate the alpha motor neurons, increasing their rate of firing. Consequently, the strength of the muscular contraction increases, and the arm pulls the weight up. (See **Figure 8.5.**)

Another important role played by the monosynaptic stretch reflex is control of posture. In order to stand, we must keep our center of gravity above our feet, or we will fall. As we stand, we tend to oscillate back and forth, and from side to side. Our vestibular sacs and our visual system play an important role in the maintenance of pos-

FIGURE 8.5
The monosynaptic stretch reflex. (a) Neural circuit. (b) A useful function.

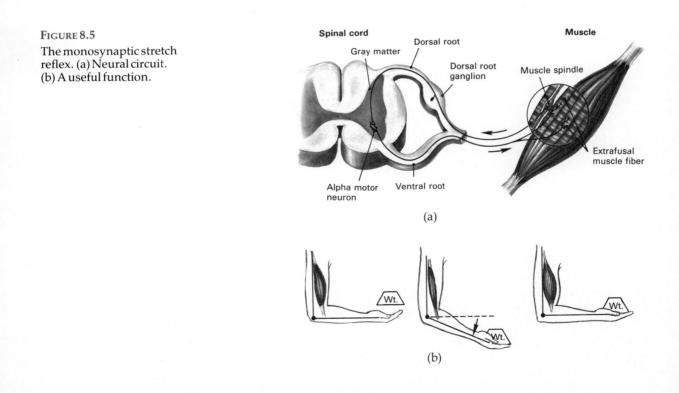

(a)

(b)

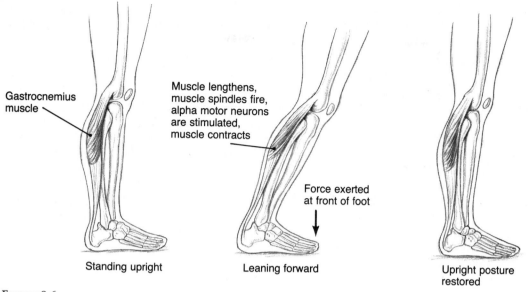

FIGURE 8.6
The role of the monosynaptic stretch reflex in postural control.

ture. However, these systems are aided by the activity of the monosynaptic stretch reflex. For example, consider what happens when a person begins to lean forward. The large calf muscle (gastrocnemius) is stretched, and this stretching elicits compensatory muscular contraction that pushes the toes down, thus restoring upright posture. (See *Figure 8.6.*)

The Gamma Motor System

The muscle spindles are very sensitive to changes in muscle length; they will increase their rate of firing when the muscle is lengthened by a very small amount. The interesting thing is that this detection mechanism is adjustable. Remember that the ends of the intrafusal muscle fibers can be contracted by activity of the associated efferent axons of the gamma motor neurons; their rate of firing determines the degree of contraction. When the muscle spindles are relaxed, they are relatively insensitive to stretch. However, when the gamma motor neurons are active, they become shorter and hence become much more sensitive to changes in muscle length. This property of adjustable sensitivity simplifies the role of the brain in controlling movement. The more control that can

occur in the spinal cord, the fewer messages must be sent to and from the brain.

We already saw that the afferent axons of the muscle spindle help maintain limb position even when the load carried by the limb is altered. Efferent control of the muscle spindles permits these muscle length detectors to assist in changes in limb position, as well. Consider a single muscle spindle. When its efferent axon is completely silent, the spindle is completely relaxed and extended. As the firing rate of the efferent axon increases, the spindle gets shorter and shorter. If, simultaneously, the rest of the entire muscle also gets shorter, there will be no stretch on the central region that contains the sensory endings, and the afferent axon will not respond. However, if the muscle spindle contracts faster than does the muscle as a whole, there will be a considerable amount of afferent activity.

The motor system makes use of this phenomenon in the following way: When commands from the brain are issued to move a limb, both the alpha motor neurons and the gamma motor neurons are activated. The alpha motor neurons start the muscle contracting. If there is little resistance, both the extrafusal and the intrafusal muscle fibers will contract at approximately the same rate, and little

FIGURE 8.7

Evidence that the muscle begins moving before action potentials occur in the sensory endings of the muscle spindle. This evidence proves that the alpha motor neurons directly initiate the movement. [From Vallbo, Å.B. *Journal of Physiology (London)*, 1971, *218*, 405–431.]

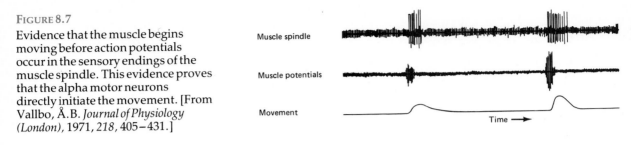

activity will be seen from the afferent axons of the muscle spindle. However, if the limb meets with resistance, the intrafusal muscle fibers will shorten more than the extrafusal muscle fibers, and hence sensory axons will begin to fire and cause the monosynaptic stretch reflex to strengthen the contraction. Thus, the brain makes use of the gamma motor system in moving the limbs. By establishing a rate of firing in the *gamma motor system*, the brain controls the length of the muscle spindles and, indirectly, the length of the entire muscle.

Physiologists formerly thought that only the gamma motor neurons were activated to initiate movements, and that the alpha motor neurons were stimulated solely by the afferent axons of the muscle spindles. However, Vallbo (1971) put small electrodes into his own peripheral nerves and found that when he contracted the muscle that was innervated by the nerve, the contraction always preceded the activity of the afferent axon of the muscle spindle. Thus, the alpha motor neurons must have been activated directly by the brain, because the movement started before the afferent impulses were observed. (See *Figure 8.7.*)

Polysynaptic Reflexes

The monosynaptic stretch reflex is the only spinal reflex that we know of that involves only one synapse. All others are *polysynaptic*. Examples include relatively simple ones, like limb withdrawal in response to pain, and relatively complex ones, like the ejaculation of semen. Spinal reflexes do not exist in isolation; they are normally controlled by the brain. For example, Chapter 2 described how inhibition from the brain can prevent a person from dropping a bunch of roses with thorns, even though the painful stimuli received by the fingers serve to cause reflexive extension of the fingers. This section will describe some general principles by which polysynaptic spinal reflexes operate.

Before I begin the discussion, I should mention that the simple circuit diagrams used here (including the one you just looked at in Figure 8.5) are much too simple. Reflex circuits are typically shown as a single chain of neurons, but in reality most reflexes involve thousands of neurons. Each axon usually synapses on many neurons, and each neuron receives synapses from many different axons.

As we previously saw, the afferent axons from the Golgi tendon organ serve as detectors of muscle stretch. There are two populations of afferent axons from the Golgi tendon organ, with different sensitivities to stretch. The more sensitive afferent axons tell the brain how hard the muscle is pulling. The less sensitive ones have an additional function. Their terminal buttons synapse on spinal cord *interneurons,* neurons that reside entirely within the gray matter of the spinal cord and serve to interconnect other spinal neurons. These interneurons synapse on the alpha motor neurons serving the same muscle. The terminal buttons liberate glycine and hence produce inhibitory postsynaptic potentials on the motor neurons. (See *Figure 8.8.*) The function of this reflex pathway is to decrease the strength of muscular contraction when there is danger of damage to the tendons or bones to which the muscles are attached. Weight lifters can lift heavier weights if their Golgi tendon organs are deactivated with injections of a local anesthetic, but they run the risk of pulling the tendon away from the bone or even breaking the bone.

The discovery of the inhibitory Golgi tendon organ reflex provided the first real evidence of neural inhibition, long before the synaptic mechanisms were understood. A *decerebrate* cat,

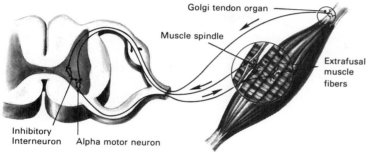

FIGURE 8.8
Polysynaptic inhibitory reflex. Input from the Golgi tendon organ can cause inhibitory postsynaptic potentials to occur on the alpha motor neuron.

whose brain stem has been cut through, exhibits a phenomenon known as ***decerebrate rigidity.*** The animal's back is arched, and its legs are extended stiffly from its body. This rigidity results from excitation originating in the caudal reticular formation, which greatly facilitates all stretch reflexes, especially of extensor muscles, by increasing the activity of the gamma motor system. Rostral to the brain stem transection is an inhibitory region of the reticular formation, which normally counterbalances the excitatory one. The transection removes the inhibitory influence, leaving only the excitatory one. If you attempt to flex the outstretched leg of a decerebrate cat, you will meet with increasing resistance, which suddenly melts away, allowing the limb to flex. It almost feels as though you were closing the blade of a pocketknife—hence the term ***clasp-knife reflex.*** The sudden release is, of course, mediated by activation of the Golgi tendon organ reflex.

Even the monosynaptic stretch reflex serves as the basis of polysynaptic reflexes. Muscles are arranged in opposing pairs. The ***agonist*** moves the limb in the direction being studied, and because muscles cannot push back, the ***antagonist*** muscle must move the limb back in the opposite direction. Consider this finding: When a stretch reflex is elicited in the agonist, it contracts quickly, thus causing the antagonist to lengthen. It would appear, then, that the antagonist is presented with a stimulus that should elicit *its* stretch reflex. And yet the antagonist relaxes instead. Let us see why.

Afferent axons of the muscle spindles, besides sending terminal buttons to the alpha motor neuron and to the brain, also synapse on inhibitory interneurons. The terminal buttons of these interneurons synapse on the alpha motor neurons that innervate the antagonistic muscle. (See ***Figure 8.9.***) Thus, a stretch reflex excites the agonist and *inhibits the antagonist,* so that the limb can move in the direction controlled by the stimulated muscle.

FIGURE 8.9
Secondary reflexes. Firing of the muscle spindle causes excitation on the alpha motor neuron of the agonist and inhibition on the antagonist.

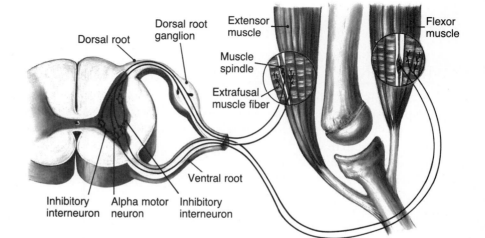

*I*NTERIM SUMMARY

Reflexes are simple circuits of sensory neurons, interneurons (usually), and efferent neurons that control simple responses to particular stimuli. In the monosynaptic stretch reflex the terminal buttons of axons that receive sensory information from the intrafusal muscle fibers synapse with alpha motor neurons that innervate the same muscle. Thus, a sudden lengthening of the muscle causes the muscle to contract. By setting the length of the intrafusal muscle fibers, and hence their sensitivity to increases in muscle length, the motor system of the brain can control limb position. Changes in a weight being held that cause the limb to move will be quickly compensated for by means of the monosynaptic stretch reflex.

Polysynaptic reflexes contain at least one interneuron between the sensory neuron and the motor neuron. For example, when a strong muscular contraction threatens to damage muscles or limbs, the increased rate of firing of the afferent axons of Golgi tendon organs stimulates inhibitory interneurons, which inhibit the alpha motor neurons of those muscles. And when the afferent axons of intrafusal muscle fibers fire, they excite inhibitory interneurons that slow the rate of firing of the alpha motor neurons that serve the antagonistic muscles, which causes the antagonist to relax, permitting the agonist to contract.

CONTROL OF MOVEMENT
BY THE BRAIN

Movements can be initiated by several means. For example, rapid stretch of a muscle triggers the monosynaptic stretch reflex, a stumble triggers righting reflexes, and the rapid approach of an object toward the face causes a startle response, a complex reflex consisting of movements of several muscle groups. Other stimuli initiate sequences of movements that we have previously learned. For example, the presence of food causes eating, and the sight of a loved one evokes a hug and a kiss. Because there is no single cause of behavior, we cannot find a single starting point in our search for the neural mechanisms that control movement.

The brain and spinal cord include several different motor systems, each of which can simultaneously control particular kinds of movements. For example, a person can walk and talk with a friend simultaneously. While doing so, he or she can make gestures with the hands to emphasize a point, scratch an itch, brush away a fly, wipe sweat off his or her forehead, and so on. Walking, postural adjustments, talking, movement of the arms, and movements of the fingers all involve different specialized motor systems.

Organization of Motor Cortex

The primary motor cortex lies on the precentral gyrus, just rostral to the central sulcus. Stimulation studies (including those in awake humans) have shown that the activity of particular parts of the primary motor cortex causes movements of particular parts of the body. Figure 8.10 shows a *motor homunculus* based on the observations of Penfield and Rasmussen (1950). Note that a disproportionate amount of cortical area is devoted to movements of the fingers and muscles used for speech. (See *Figure 8.10.*)

The principal cortical input to the primary motor cortex is the frontal association cortex, located rostral to it. Lesion studies (some of which I will describe later in this chapter) indicate that the planning of most complex behaviors takes place here. These plans are executed by the primary motor cortex, which directly controls particular movements. In turn, the frontal association cortex receives axons from association areas of the occipital, temporal, and parietal cortex. As we saw, the occipital and temporal lobes contain the visual association cortex, and the temporal lobe also contains the auditory association cortex. And as we will see later, the association cortex of the parietal lobes is responsible for a person's perception of space. Thus, the frontal association cortex receives information about the environment (including memories previously acquired by means of vision, audition, and somatosensation) from the posterior lobes and uses this in-

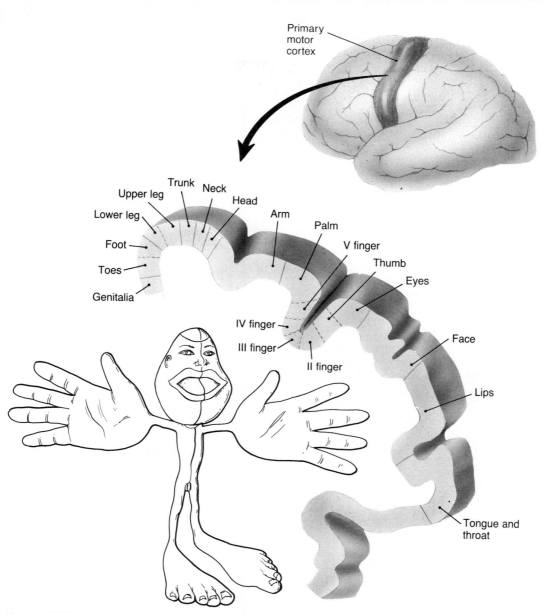

FIGURE 8.10

A motor homunculus. Stimulation of various regions of the primary motor cortex causes movement in muscles of various parts of the body.

formation to plan movements. Because the parietal lobes contain spatial information, the pathway from them to the frontal lobes is especially important in controlling both locomotion and arm and hand movements. After all, meaningful locomotion requires us to know where we are, and mean-ingful movements of our arms and hands require us to know where objects are located in space. (See *Figure 8.11.*)

The primary motor cortex also receives projections from the adjacent primary soma-tosensory cortex, located just across the central

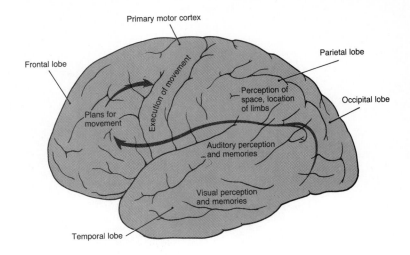

FIGURE 8.11
Cortical control of movement. The posterior association cortex is involved with perceptions and memories; the frontal association cortex is involved with plans for movement.

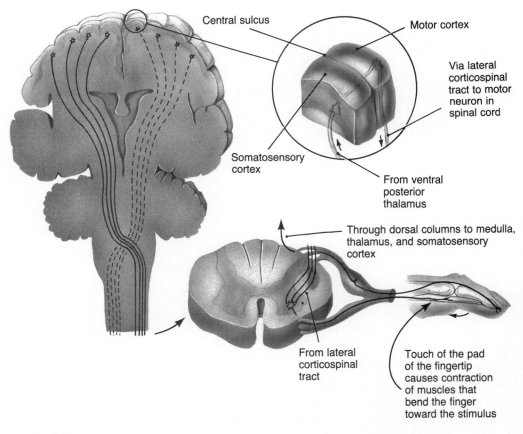

FIGURE 8.12
Connections between the primary somatosensory cortex and the primary motor cortex. These connections are important for control of the fingers in grasping and manipulating objects.

sulcus. The connections between these two areas are quite specific: Neurons in the primary somatosensory cortex that respond to stimuli applied to a particular part of the body send axons to neurons in the primary motor cortex that move muscles in the same part of the body. For example, Asanuma and Rosén (1972) and Rosén and Asanuma (1972) found that somatosensory neurons that respond to a touch on the back of the thumb send axons to motor neurons that cause thumb extension, and somatosensory neurons that respond to a touch on the ball of the thumb send axons to motor neurons that cause thumb flexion. (See *Figure 8.12.*) This organization appears to provide rapid feedback to the motor system during manipulation of objects.

Evidence that supports this suggestion was obtained by Evarts (1974), who recorded the activity of single neurons in the precentral gyrus of monkeys. He trained his subjects to move a lever back and forth by means of wrist flexions and extensions. When the monkeys made the movements in the correct amount of time, they received a squirt of grape juice, a drink they appeared to enjoy. Figure 8.13 shows the experimental preparation as well as the relationship between lever movement and the firing of a cortical neuron. Note that the firing of this neuron is nicely related to the movement, with the rate increasing during flexion. (See *Figure 8.13.*) Evarts trained monkeys to produce a hand movement in response to a flash of a light or to a tactile stimulus delivered through the handle. He found that neurons in the motor cortex began firing 100 msec after a visual stimulus but responded as soon as 25 msec after a tactile stimulus. These results confirm the conclusion that hand and finger movements are controlled by somatosensory feedback received by neurons in the postcentral gyrus.

Cortical Control of Movement

Neurons in the primary motor cortex control movements by four different pathways. They directly control the corticospinal and corticobulbar pathways and indirectly control two sets of pathways that originate in the brain stem, which will be described later in this section.

The *corticospinal pathway* consists of axons of cortical neurons that terminate in the gray matter of the spinal cord. The largest concentration of cell bodies of these neurons is located in the pri-

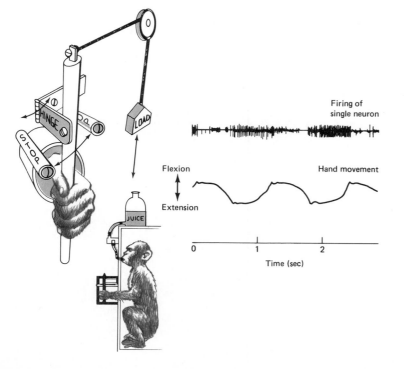

FIGURE 8.13

The relation between firing of single neurons in the motor cortex and hand movements. The single-unit records are redrawn from the original data and are therefore only approximate representations. (Redrawn from Evarts, E.V. *Journal of Neurophysiology*, 1968, 31, 14–27.)

mary motor cortex, but the parietal and temporal lobes also send fibers through the corticospinal pathway. The axons leave the cortex and travel through subcortical white matter to the ventral midbrain, where they enter the cerebral peduncles. They leave the peduncles in the medulla and join the *pyramidal tracts,* so-called because of their shape. At the level of the caudal medulla, most of the fibers decussate (cross over) and descend through the contralateral spinal cord,

forming the *lateral corticospinal tract.* The rest of the fibers descend through the ipsilateral spinal cord, forming the *ventral corticospinal tract.* (See black portion of *Figure 8.14.*)

The axons in the lateral corticospinal tract originate in the arm and hand region of the primary motor cortex. They control the motor neurons in the ventral horn of the spinal cord gray matter. These motor neurons control the muscles of the distal limbs, including those that move the arms,

FIGURE 8.14
The corticospinal pathways (black) and corticobulbar pathway (color).

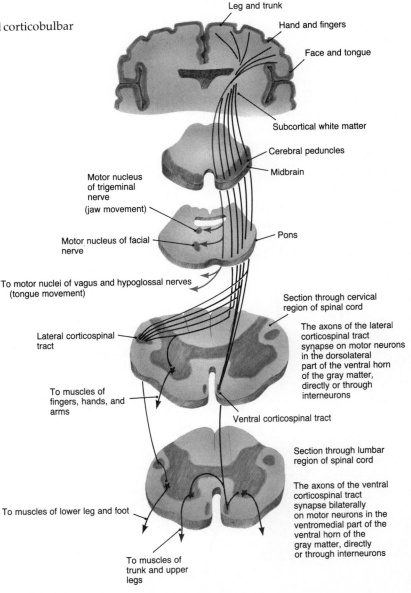

Leg and trunk

Hand and fingers

Face and tongue

Subcortical white matter

Cerebral peduncles

Midbrain

Motor nucleus of trigeminal nerve (jaw movement)

Pons

Motor nucleus of facial nerve

To motor nuclei of vagus and hypoglossal nerves (tongue movement)

Section through cervical region of spinal cord

The axons of the lateral corticospinal tract synapse on motor neurons in the dorsolateral part of the ventral horn of the gray matter, directly or through interneurons

Lateral corticospinal tract

To muscles of fingers, hands, and arms

Ventral corticospinal tract

Section through lumbar region of spinal cord

The axons of the ventral corticospinal tract synapse bilaterally on motor neurons in the ventromedial part of the ventral horn of the gray matter, directly or through interneurons

To muscles of lower leg and foot

To muscles of trunk and upper legs

hands, and fingers. (See *Figure 8.14.*)

The axons in the ventral corticospinal tract originate in the trunk region of the primary motor cortex. They descend to the appropriate region of the spinal cord and divide, sending terminal buttons into both sides of the gray matter. They control motor neurons that move the muscles of the trunk. (See *Figure 8.14.*)

Lawrence and Kuypers (1968a) cut both pyramidal tracts in monkeys in order to assess their motor functions. Within six to ten hours after recovery from the anesthesia, the animals were able to sit upright, but their arms hung loosely from their shoulders. Within a day they could stand, hold the cage bars with their hands, and even climb a little. By six weeks the monkeys could walk and climb rapidly. Thus, posture and locomotion were not disturbed. However, the animals' manual dexterity was poor. They could reach for objects and grasp them, but they used their fingers together as if they were wearing mittens; they could not manipulate their fingers independently to pick up small pieces of food. And once they had grasped food with their hand, they had difficulty releasing their grip. They usually had to use their mouth to pry their hand open. In contrast, they had no difficulty releasing their grip when they were climbing the bars of their cage.

The results confirm what we would predict from the anatomical connections: The corticospinal pathway controls hand and finger movements and is indispensable for moving the fingers independently when reaching and manipulating. Postural adjustments of the trunk and use of the limbs for reaching and locomotion are unaffected; therefore, these types of movements are controlled by other systems. Because the monkeys had difficulty releasing their grasp when they picked up objects but did not have trouble doing so when climbing the walls of the cage, we may conclude that the same behavior (opening the hand) is controlled by different brain mechanisms in different contexts.

The *corticobulbar pathway* projects to the medulla (sometimes called the *bulb*). This pathway is similar to the corticospinal pathway, except that it terminates in the motor nuclei of the fifth, seventh, tenth, and twelfth cranial nerves (the trigeminal, facial, vagus, and hypoglossal nerves). (In this context, *bulb* refers to the medulla.) These nerves control movements of the face and tongue. (See color lines in *Figure 8.14.*)

Two sets of pathways originate in the brain stem and terminate in the spinal cord gray matter: the ventromedial pathways and the rubrospinal tract. Through indirect connections the primary motor cortex can affect the activity of both sets of pathways. The first set, the *ventromedial pathways,* includes the *vestibulospinal tracts,* the *tectospinal tracts,* and the *reticulospinal tracts.* Neurons of all three of these tracts control motor neurons in the ventromedial part of the spinal cord gray matter. Thus, they primarily control movements of the trunk and proximal limb muscles. The cell bodies of neurons of the vestibulospinal tracts are located in the vestibular nuclei. As you might expect, this system plays a role in the control of posture. The cell bodies of neurons in the tectospinal tracts are located in the superior colliculus and are involved in coordinating head and trunk movements with eye movements. The cell bodies of neurons of the reticulospinal tracts are located in many nuclei in the brain stem and midbrain reticular formation. These neurons control several automatic functions, such as muscle tonus, respiration, coughing, and sneezing; but they are also involved in behaviors under direct neocortical control, such as walking. (See black lines in *Figure 8.15.*)

You will recall that Lawrence and Kuypers (1968a) found no deficits in postural movements after they had destroyed both the right and left pyramidal tracts. Presumably, the animals maintained their control of posture through the ventromedial pathways. The second study confirmed this speculation. Lawrence and Kuypers (1968b) cut the ventromedial fibers of some of the animals that had previously received bilateral pyramidal tract lesions. These animals showed severe impairments in posture. After a long recovery period they could eventually stand with great difficulty but could not take more than a few steps without falling. When they reached for food, their upper arms hung at their sides. Thus, we can conclude that the ventromedial pathways control the muscles of the trunk and proximal limbs, with supplementary control of the trunk muscles coming from the ventral corticospinal tract.

The second major pathway from the brain stem to the spinal cord gray matter is the *rubrospinal tract,* which originates in the red nucleus (*nucleus ruber*) of the midbrain. The red nucleus receives its most important inputs from the motor cortex and cerebellum. Axons of the rubrospinal tracts terminate on motor neurons in the spinal cord that control movements of forelimb and hindlimb muscles. (They do not control the muscles that move the fingers.) (See *Figure 8.15.*)

Lawrence and Kuypers (1968b) destroyed the rubrospinal tract *unilaterally* in some of the animals that had previously received bilateral lesions of the pyramidal tract. The rubrospinal tract lesion severely affected the animals' use of the ipsilateral arm. The arm tended to hang straight from the shoulder, with hand and fingers extended. If they could reach food only with the affected arm, they made a raking movement with the arm as a whole, bending their elbow and wrist as the food approached their mouth. The arm movement was

FIGURE 8.15
The ventromedial pathways (black) and the rubrospinal tract (color).

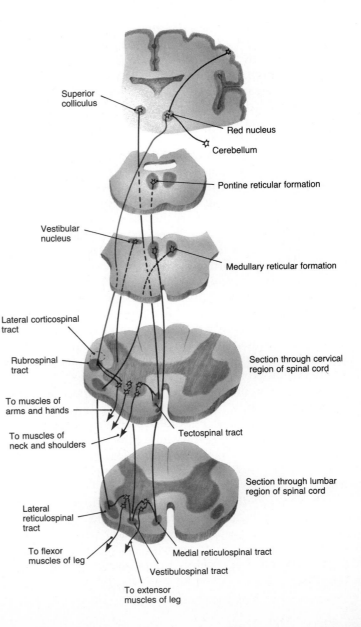

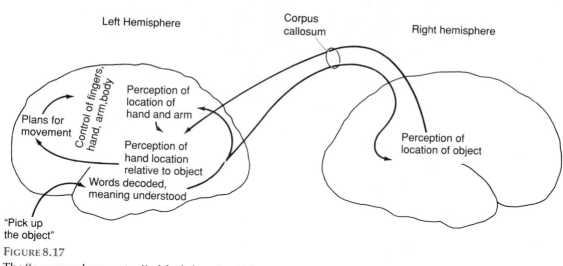

Left Hemisphere

Corpus callosum

Right hemisphere

Plans for movement

Control of fingers, hand, arm, body

Perception of location of hand and arm

Perception of hand location relative to object

Words decoded, meaning understood

"Pick up the object"

Perception of location of object

FIGURE 8.17
The "command apparatus" of the left parietal lobe.

arm cannot. (See lesion A in *Figure 8.16.*)

A similar form of limb apraxia is caused by damage to the anterior left hemisphere, sometimes called *sympathetic apraxia.* The damage causes a primary motor impairment of the right arm and hand: full or partial paralysis. As with anterior callosal lesions, the damage also causes apraxia of the left arm. The term *sympathetic* was originally adopted because the clumsiness of the left hand appeared to be a "sympathetic" response to the paralysis of the right one. (See lesion B in *Figure 8.16.*)

The third form of limb apraxia is *left parietal apraxia,* caused by lesions of the posterior left hemisphere. These lesions involve both limbs. The posterior parietal lobe contains areas of association cortex that receive information from the surrounding sensory association cortex of the occipital, temporal, and anterior parietal lobes. (See lesion C in *Figure 8.16.*)

From the effects of parietal lobe lesions in humans and monkeys, Mountcastle, Lynch, Georgopoulos, Sakata, and Acuna (1975) suggest that this region contains a sensory representation of the surrounding environment and keeps track of the location of objects in the environment and the location of the organism's body parts in relation to them. Because the right parietal lobe is especially important for perception of three-dimensional space, information about location of objects

external to the person is probably supplied from this region. According to Mountcastle and his colleagues, the left parietal region serves as a "command apparatus for the operation of the limbs, hands, and eyes within immediate extrapersonal space." For example, when a person hears a command to reach for a particular object, the meaning of the request is decoded by the left auditory association cortex and is passed on to the left parietal association cortex. Using information received from the right parietal association cortex about the spatial location of the object, neural circuits in the left parietal association cortex assess the relative location of the person's hand and the object and send information about the starting and ending coordinates to the left premotor cortex. There, the sequence of muscular contractions necessary to perform the movement is organized, and this sequence is executed through the primary motor cortex and its connections with the spinal cord and subcortical motor systems. (See *Figure 8.17.*)

Constructional Apraxia
Constructional apraxia is caused by lesions of the right hemisphere, particularly the right parietal lobe. People with this disorder do not have difficulty making most types of skilled movements with their arms and hands. They have no trouble using objects properly, imitating their use, or pretending to use them. However, they have trouble

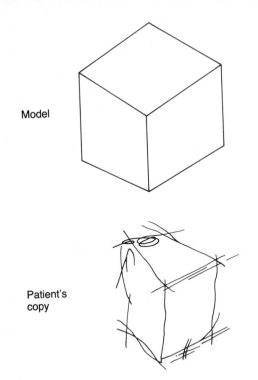

FIGURE 8.18
Attempt to copy a cube by a patient with constructional apraxia caused by a lesion of the right parietal lobe. (From *Fundamentals of Human Neuropsychology*, by B. Kolb and I.Q. Whishaw. W.H. Freeman and Company. Copyright © 1980.)

drawing pictures or assembling objects from elements such as toy building blocks.

The primary deficit in constructional apraxia appears to involve the ability to perceive and imagine geometrical relations. Because of this deficit, a person cannot draw a picture, say, of a cube, because he or she cannot imagine what the lines and angles of a cube look like, not because of difficulty controlling the movements of his or her arm and hand. (See *Figure 8.18.*) Besides being unable to draw accurately, a person with constructional apraxia invariably has trouble with other tasks involving spatial perception, such as following a map.

The Basal Ganglia

The basal ganglia constitute an important component of the motor system. We know they are important because their destruction by disease or injury causes severe motor deficits. The motor nuclei of the basal ganglia include the caudate nucleus, putamen, and globus pallidus. The basal ganglia receive inputs from the neocortex and cerebellum. They also communicate with various nuclei located in and beneath the thalamus, the red nucleus, the substantia nigra, and parts of the brain stem reticular formation. Through these connections they influence the activity of the corticospinal, rubrospinal, and ventromedial systems. (See *Figure 8.19.*)

We already saw in Chapter 3 that degeneration of the nigrostriatal bundle, the dopaminergic pathway from the substantia nigra of the midbrain to the caudate nucleus and putamen (the *neostriatum*), causes Parkinson's disease. The primary disorder is slowness of movement and difficulty in stopping one behavior and starting

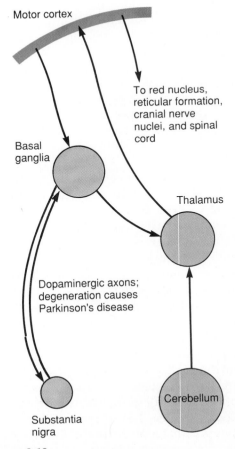

FIGURE 8.19
Some important interconnections of the basal ganglia.

another. These deficits are seen in all muscle groups—those controlling fingers, hands, arms, and trunk. For example, once a person with Parkinson's disease is seated, he or she finds it difficult to arise. Once the person begins walking, he or she has difficulty stopping. Thus, a person with Parkinson's disease cannot easily pace back and forth across a room. Reaching for an object can be accurate, but the movement usually begins only after a considerable delay. Writing is slow and labored, and as it progresses, the letters get smaller and smaller. Postural movements are impaired. If someone bumps into a normal person who is standing, he or she will quickly move to restore balance—for example, by taking a step in the direction of the impending fall or by reaching out with the arms to grasp onto a piece of furniture. However, a person with Parkinson's disease fails to do so and simply falls. A person with this disorder is even unlikely to put out his or her arms to break the fall.

Parkinson's disease also produces a resting tremor—vibratory movements of the arms and hands that diminish somewhat when the individual makes purposeful movements. The tremor is accompanied by rigidity; the joints appear stiff. However, the tremor and rigidity are not the cause of the slow movements. Although the slowness appears to be caused by degeneration of the nigrostriatal bundle, the rigidity and tremor probably occur because of damage to neurons in other pathways. Indeed, experimental studies with laboratory animals have found that damage to the substantia nigra produces hypoactivity but not tremors. The tremors probably originate in a feedback circuit consisting of a loop of neurons from the ventral thalamus to the motor cortex and back again. Neurons in the ventral thalamus fire in synchrony with the vibratory movements of the tremor, and stereotaxic lesions of this area can eliminate or reduce the tremor and rigidity (Dray, 1980). However, the lesions do not affect the slowness of movement.

Recent research has suggested that Parkinson's disease may be caused by toxins that are present in the environment, caused by faulty metabolism, or produced by unrecognized infectious disorders. Several years ago, a few young people developed symptoms of Parkinson's disease after taking illicit drugs that had been pre-pared in "underground" laboratories. Unfortunately, the drugs were contaminated with small amounts of a chemical called MPTP, which had the effect of destroying dopaminergic neurons of the substantia nigra (Langston, Ballard, Tetrud, and Irwin, 1983). Further investigation showed that the damage occurs when enzymes present in dopaminergic neurons convert MPTP into an extremely toxic compound called MPP^+. Studies with laboratory animals revealed that injections of a drug that inhibits MAO (the enzyme that breaks down the monoamines, including dopamine) protects against the damage caused by MPTP (Langston, Irwin, Langston, and Forno, 1984). Presumably, MAO is responsible for converting MPTP into MPP^+. In fact, a recent clinical trial with deprenyl, a MAO inhibitor, was so encouraging that many patients with Parkinson's disease are now receiving the drug. If the drug retards the rate of degeneration of dopaminergic neurons, it will be the most important discovery since L-DOPA for the treatment of this disorder.

Another basal ganglia disease, *Huntington's chorea,* is caused by degeneration of the caudate nucleus and putamen, especially of GABAergic and acetylcholinergic neurons. (See *Color Plates 8.1* and *8.2*.) Whereas Parkinson's disease causes a poverty of movements, Huntington's chorea causes uncontrollable ones, especially jerky limb movements. (*Chorea* derives from the Greek *khoros,* meaning "dance.") The movements of Huntington's chorea look like fragments of purposeful movements but occur involuntarily. The disease is progressive and eventually causes death.

A complete description of these two syndromes is much more complicated than my brief outline, but we can easily see that the basal ganglia can either inhibit or facilitate movements.

Mainly on the basis of clinical observations of patients with motor disorders, Kornhuber (1974) suggests that the basal ganglia may play a special role in the control of slow, smooth movements. DeLong (1974) obtained some electrophysiological evidence that supports Kornhuber's hypothesis. He found that a majority of the neurons in the putamen fire before and during slow movements but not before and during rapid ones.

Damage to the caudate nucleus or putamen generally causes symptoms of *release;* the patients exhibit rigidity (excessive muscular contraction) or uncontrollable movements of the limbs or facial muscles. Damage to the globus pallidus or ventral thalamus generally causes symptoms of *deficiency*, such as *akinesia* (lack of movement) or mutism (failure to talk). Thus, the caudate nucleus and putamen appear to be inhibitory in function, and the globus pallidus and ventral thalamus appear to be excitatory. In Parkinson's disease the slowness of movement probably occurs because degeneration of the nigrostriatal bundle disrupts an inhibitory input to the caudate nucleus (you will recall that dopamine is an inhibitory transmitter substance). Loss of inhibition increases the inhibitory function of the caudate nucleus, and movements become slower.

The Cerebellum

The cerebellum is an important part of the motor system. When it is damaged, people's movements become jerky, erratic, and uncoordinated. The cerebellum consists of two hemispheres that contain several deep nuclei situated beneath the wrinkled and folded cerebellar cortex. Thus, the cerebellum resembles the cerebrum in miniature. (See *Figure 8.20.*) The *flocculonodular lobe*, located at the caudal end of the cerebellum, receives input from the vestibular system and projects axons to the vestibular nucleus. You will not be surprised to learn that this system is involved in postural reflexes. (See black lines, *Figure 8.21.*) The *vermis* ("worm"), located on the midline, receives cutaneous and kinesthetic information from the spinal cord and sends its outputs to the *fastigial nucleus* (one of the set of deep cerebellar nuclei). Neurons in the fastigial nucleus send axons to the vestibular nucleus and to motor nuclei in the reticular formation. Thus, they influence behavior through the vestibulospinal and reticulospinal tracts, two of the three ventromedial pathways. (See gray lines, *Figure 8.21.*)

The rest of the cerebellar cortex receives inputs (relayed through nuclei in the pons) from the cerebral cortex, including the primary motor cortex and all regions of association cortex. The interme-

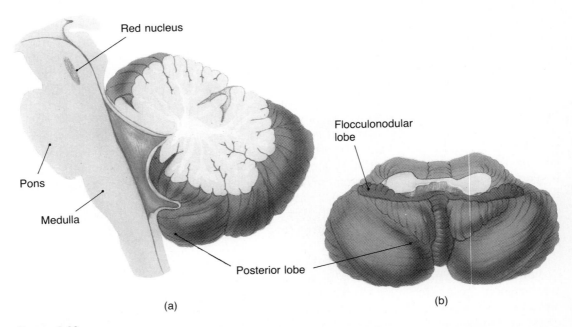

(a)

(b)

FIGURE 8.20
The cerebellar cortex. (a) Lateral view, showing right hemisphere. (b) Ventral view.

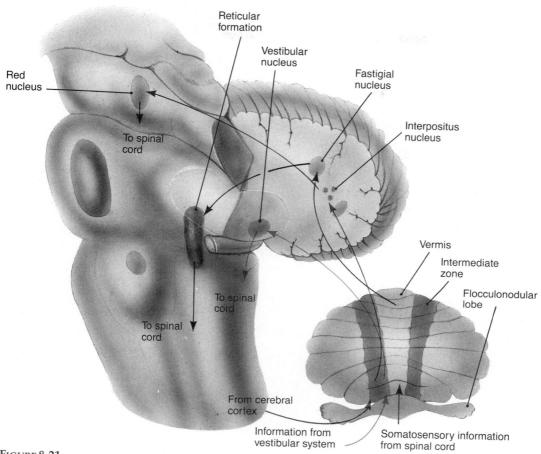

Red
nucleus

Reticular
formation

Vestibular
nucleus

Fastigial
nucleus

Interpositus
nucleus

To spinal
cord

To spinal
cord

To spinal
cord

Vermis

Intermediate
zone

Flocculonodular
lobe

From cerebral
cortex

Information from
vestibular system

Somatosensory information
from spinal cord

FIGURE 8.21
The flocculonodular lobe, vermis, and intermediate zone of the cerebellum.
These systems are involved in control of the vestibulospinal system (black
lines), reticulospinal system (gray lines), and rubrospinal system (color lines).

diate zone of the cerebellar cortex projects to the
interpositus nucleus, which in turn projects to the
red nucleus. Thus, the intermediate zone influences the activity of the rubrospinal system. (See
color lines, ***Figure 8.21.***)

The lateral zone of the cerebellum sends axons
to the ***dentate nucleus.*** From there, some axons
travel to the red nucleus; thus, the lateral zone,
like the intermediate zone, influences the
rubrospinal system. The dentate nucleus also
sends axons to the ventrolateral thalamus, which
provides the primary source of subcortical projections to the primary motor cortex. Through this
projection the lateral zone helps control rapid,

skilled movements. Movements are initiated by
neurons in the frontal association cortex, which
control neurons in the primary motor cortex. Both
regions send information about the intended
movement to the lateral zone of the cerebellum,
via the ***pontine nucleus.*** The cerebellum smooths
and integrates the movements through its connections with the primary motor cortex, via the
dentate nucleus and ventrolateral thalamus. (See
Figure 8.22.)

In humans, lesions of different regions of the
cerebellum produce different symptoms. Damage to the flocculonodular lobe or vermis causes
disturbances in posture and balance. Damage to

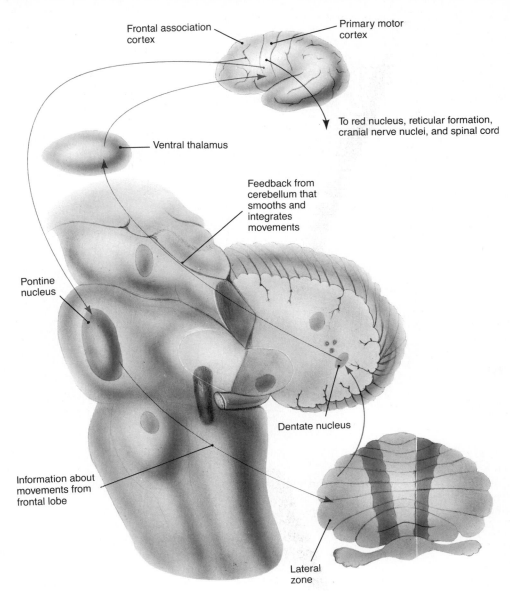

Frontal association cortex

Primary motor cortex

To red nucleus, reticular formation, cranial nerve nuclei, and spinal cord

Ventral thalamus

Feedback from cerebellum that smooths and integrates movements

Pontine nucleus

Dentate nucleus

Information about movements from frontal lobe

Lateral zone

Figure 8.22
The lateral zone of the cerebellum. It receives information about impending movements from the frontal lobe, and it helps smooth and integrate the movement through its connections to the primary motor cortex through the dentate nucleus and ventral thalamus.

the intermediate zone produces deficits in movements controlled by the rubrospinal system. The principal symptom is limb rigidity. Damage to the lateral zone causes weakness and *decomposition of movement*. For example, if a person attempts to bring the hand to the mouth, he or she will make separate movements of the joints of the shoulder, elbow, and wrist instead of performing simultaneous smooth movements.

Lesions of the lateral zone of the cerebellar cortex also appear to impair the timing of rapid *ballistic* movements. Ballistic (literally, "throwing") movements occur too fast to be modified by feedback. The sequence of muscular movements must then be programmed in advance, and the individual muscles must be activated at the proper times. You might like to try this common neurological test. Have a friend place his or her finger in front of your face, about three quarters of an arm's length away. While your friend slowly moves his or her finger around to serve as a moving target, alternately touch your nose and your friend's finger as rapidly as you can. If your cerebellum is normal, you can successfully hit your nose and your friend's finger without too much trouble. People with lateral cerebellar damage have great difficulty; they tend to miss the examiner's hand and poke themselves in the eye. (I have often wondered why neurologists do not adopt a less dangerous test.)

When we make rapid, aimed movements, we cannot rely on feedback to stop the movement when we reach the target. By the time we perceive that our finger has reached the proper place, it is too late to stop the movement, and we will overshoot the target if we try to stop it then. Instead of relying on feedback, the movement appears to be timed. We estimate the distance between our hand and the target, and our cerebellum calculates the amount of time that the muscles will have to be turned on. After the proper amount of time the cerebellum briefly turns on antagonistic muscles to stop the movement. In fact, Kornhuber (1974) suggests that one of the primary functions of the cerebellum is timing the duration of rapid movements. Obviously, learning must play a role in controlling such movements.

The cerebellum also appears to integrate successive *sequences* of movements that must be performed one after the other. For example, Holmes (1939) reported that one of his patients said, "The movements of my left arm are done subconsciously, but I have to think out each movement of the right [affected] arm. I come to a dead stop in turning and have to think before I start again." Thach (1978) obtained experimental evidence that corroborates this role. He found that many neurons in the dentate nuclei (which receive inputs from the lateral zone of the cerebellar cortex) showed response patterns that predicted the *next* movement in a sequence rather than the one that was currently taking place. Presumably, the cerebellum was planning these movements.

The Reticular Formation

The reticular formation consists of a large number of nuclei located in the core of the medulla, pons, and midbrain. The reticular formation controls the activity of the gamma motor system and hence regulates muscle tonus. In addition, the pons and medulla contain several nuclei with specific motor functions. For example, different locations in the medulla control automatic or semiautomatic responses such as respiration, sneezing, coughing, and vomiting. As we saw, the ventromedial pathways originate in the superior colliculi, vestibular nuclei, and reticular formation. Thus, the reticular formation plays a role in the control of posture.

The reticular formation also plays a role in locomotion. Stimulation of the ***mesencephalic locomotor region,*** located ventral to the inferior colliculus, causes a cat to make pacing movements (Shik and Orlovsky, 1976). The mesencephalic locomotor region does not send fibers directly to the spinal cord but apparently controls the activity of reticulospinal tract neurons.

Other motor functions of the reticular formation are also being discovered. Siegel and McGinty (1977) recorded from thirty-five single neurons in the reticular formation of unanesthetized, freely moving cats. Thirty-two of these neurons responded during *specific* movements of the head, tongue, facial muscles, ears, forepaw, or shoulder. The specific nature of the relations suggests that the neurons play some role in controlling the movements. For example, one neuron responded when the tongue moved out and to the left. The function of these neurons and the range of movements they control are not yet known.

I NTERIM SUMMARY

The motor systems of the brain are complex. (Having read this section, you do not need me to tell you that.) A good way to review the systems is through an example. While following my description, you might want to look at Table 8.1 and Figures 8.14 and 8.15 again. Suppose you see, out of the corner of your eye, that something is moving. You quickly turn your head and eyes toward the source of the movement and discover that a vase of flowers on a table someone has just bumped is ready to fall. You quickly reach forward, grab it, and restore it to a stable upright position. (For simplicity's sake I will assume that you are right-handed.)

The rapid movement of your head and eyes is controlled by mechanisms that involve the superior colliculi and nearby nuclei. The head movement and corresponding movement of the trunk are mediated by the tectospinal tract. You perceive the tipping vase because of the activity of neurons in your visual association cortex. Your visual association cortex also contributes information about depth to your right parietal lobe, whose association cortex determines the exact spatial location of the vase. Your left parietal lobe uses the spatial information, together with its own record of the location of your hand, to compute the path your hand must travel to intercept the vase. The information is relayed to your left frontal lobe, where the motor association cortex starts the movement. Because the movement will have to be a ballistic one, the cerebellum controls its timing, based on information it receives from the association cortex of the frontal and parietal lobes. Your hand stops just as it touches the vase, and connections between the somatosensory cortex and the primary motor cortex initiate a reflex that closes your hand around the vase.

The movement of your hand is controlled through a cooperation between the corticospinal, rubrospinal, and ventromedial pathways. Even before your hand moves, the ventral corticospinal tract and the ventromedial pathways (vestibulospinal and reticulospinal system, largely under the influence of the basal ganglia) begin adjusting your posture so that you will not fall forward when you suddenly reach in front of you.

Depending on how far forward you will have to reach, the reticulospinal tract may even cause one leg to step forward in order to take your weight. The rubrospinal tract controls the muscles of your upper arm, and the lateral corticospinal tract controls your finger and hand movements. Perhaps you say, triumphantly, "I got it!" The corticobulbar pathway, under the control of speech mechanisms in the left hemisphere, causes the muscles of your vocal apparatus to say these words.

A person with apraxia will have difficulty making controlled movements of the limb in response to a verbal request. Most cases of apraxia are produced by lesions of the left parietal lobe, which sends information about the requested movement to the left frontal association cortex. This region directly controls movement of the right limb by activating neurons in the left primary motor cortex and indirectly controls movement of the left limb by sending information to the right frontal association cortex. Damage to the left frontal association cortex or its connections with the right hemisphere also produce apraxia.

CONCLUDING REMARKS

We have now studied the basic physiology and pharmacology of cells of the nervous system, neuroanatomy, research methods, the physiology of sensation and perception, and the control of movements. In the remainder of the book we will consider particular classes of behaviors: sleep cycles, reproductive behavior, aggressive behavior, ingestive behavior, the acquisition of learned behaviors, addictive behaviors, communicative behaviors, and the abnormal behaviors that constitute mental disorders.

NEW TERMS

actin p. 243
agonist p. 251
akinesia p. 264
alpha motor neuron p. 243
antagonist p. 251
apraxia p. 259
callosal apraxia p. 260
cardiac muscle p. 247
chorea p. 263
clasp-knife reflex p. 251
constructional
    apraxia p. 261
corticobulbar
    pathway p. 257
corticospinal
    pathway p. 255
decerebrate p. 250
decerebrate rigidity p. 251
dentate nucleus p. 265
endplate potential p. 244
extension p. 243

extrafusal muscle fiber p. 243
fastigial nucleus p. 264
flexion p. 243
flocculonodular lobe p. 264
gamma motor neuron p. 243
Golgi tendon organ p. 246
Huntington's chorea p. 263
interneuron p. 250
interpositus nucleus p. 265
intrafusal muscle fiber p. 243
lateral corticospinal tract p. 256
left parietal apraxia p. 261
mesencephalic locomotor
    region p. 267
monosynaptic stretch
    reflex p. 248
motor endplate p. 244
motor unit p. 243
multiunit smooth
    muscle p. 246

myofibril p. 243
myosin p. 243
neuromuscular
    junction p. 244
pacemaker potential p. 247
pontine nucleus p. 265
pyramidal tract p. 256
reticulospinal tract p. 257
rubrospinal tract p. 258
single-unit smooth
    muscle p. 247
skeletal muscle p. 243
smooth muscle p. 246
striated muscle p. 243
sympathetic apraxia p. 261
tectospinal tract p. 257
ventral corticospinal
    tract p. 256
ventromedial pathway p. 257
vermis p. 264
vestibulospinal tract p. 257

SUGGESTED READINGS

Kandel, E.R., and Schwartz, J.H. *Principles of Neural Science,* 2nd ed. New York: Raven Press, 1985.

Kolb, B., and Whishaw, I.Q. *Fundamentals of Human Neuropsychology,* 3rd ed. New York: W.H. Freeman, 1989.

Schneider, J.S., and Lidsky, T.I. *Basal Ganglia and Behavior: Sensory Aspects and Motor Functioning.* Bern: Hans Huber, 1987.

Shepherd, G.M. *Neurobiology,* 2nd ed. New York: Oxford University Press, 1988.

9

Sleep

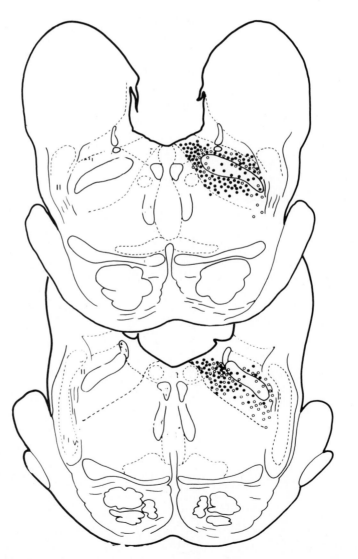

Why do we sleep? Why do we spend at least one-third of our lives doing something that provides most of us with only a few fleeting memories? I will attempt to answer this question in several ways. In the first part of this chapter I will describe what is known about the phenomenon of sleep: How much do we sleep? What do we do while asleep? What happens if we do not get enough sleep? What factors affect the duration and quality of sleep? How effective are sleeping medications? Does sleep perform a restorative function? What do we know about sleepwalking and other sleep-related disorders? In the second part of the chapter I will discuss the mechanism that controls daily rhythms of sleep and activity. In the third I will describe the search for the chemicals and the neural circuits that control sleep and wakefulness.

A PHYSIOLOGICAL AND BEHAVIORAL DESCRIPTION

Sleep is a behavior. That statement may seem peculiar, because we usually think of behaviors as activities that involve movements, such as walking or talking. Movements do occur during sleep, but except for the rapid eye movements that accompany a particular stage, sleep is not distinguished by movement. What characterizes sleep is that the insistent urge of sleepiness forces us to seek out a quiet, comfortable place, lie down, and remain there for several hours. Because we remember very little about what happens while we sleep, we tend to think of sleep more as a state of consciousness than as a behavior. The change in consciousness is undeniable, but it should not prevent us from noticing the behavioral changes.

Stages of Sleep

The best research on human sleep is conducted in a sleep laboratory. A sleep laboratory, which is usually located at a university or medical center, consists of one or several small bedrooms adjacent to an observation room, where the experimenter spends the night (trying to stay awake). The experimenter prepares the sleeper for electro-

physiological measurements by pasting electrodes to the scalp to monitor the electroencephalogram (EEG) and to the chin to monitor muscle activity, recorded as the *electromyogram* (EMG). Electrodes pasted around the eyes monitor eye movements, recorded as the *electro-oculogram* (EOG). In addition, other electrodes and transducing devices can be used to monitor autonomic measures such as heart rate, respiration, and skin conductance. Wires from the electrodes are bundled together in a "ponytail," which is then plugged into a junction box at the head of the bed. (See *Figure 9.1.*)

During wakefulness the EEG of a normal person shows two basic patterns of activity: *alpha activity* and *beta activity*. **Alpha activity** consists of regular, medium-frequency waves of 8–12 Hz. The brain produces this activity when a person is resting quietly, not particularly aroused or excited and not engaged in strenuous mental activity (such as problem solving). Although alpha waves sometimes occur when a person's eyes are open, they are much more prevalent when the eyes are closed. The other type of waking EEG pattern, **beta activity,** consists of irregular, mostly low-amplitude waves of 13–30 Hz. This activity occurs when a person is alert and attentive to events in

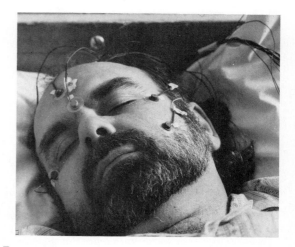

FIGURE 9.1
A subject prepared for a night's sleep in a sleep laboratory. (Woodfin Camp Associates.)

the environment or is thinking actively. (See *Figure 9.2.*)

What is the significance of these two types of waveforms? As we saw in Chapter 5, the EEG is a recording of the summed postsynaptic activity of cerebral neurons (mostly, neurons in the cerebral cortex). Therefore, a low-frequency, high-voltage EEG (alpha activity, as opposed to beta activity) reflects neural *synchrony.* These waves are pro-

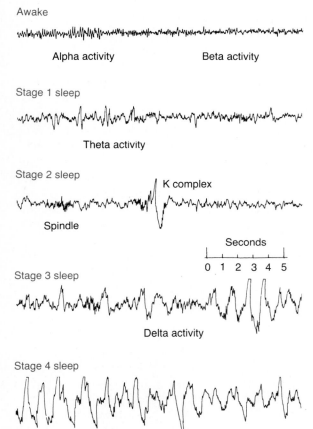

FIGURE 9.2

An EEG recording of the stages of sleep. (From Horne, J.A. *Why We Sleep: The Functions of Sleep in Humans and Other Mammals.* Oxford, England: Oxford University Press, 1988. Copyright 1988 Oxford University Press. By permission of the Oxford University Press.)

duced by a regular, synchronized pattern of activity in a large number of neurons. The activity of individual neurons is analogous to a large number of people chanting the same words together (speaking *synchronously*). Similarly, beta activity is referred to as *desynchrony;* it is like a large number of people broken into many small groups, each carrying on an individual conversation.

The analogy helps explain why desynchrony is generally assumed to represent activation, whereas synchrony reflects a resting or depressed state. A group of people who are all chanting the same message will process very little information; only one message is being produced. On the other hand, a desynchronized group will process and transmit many different messages. The alert, waking state of the brain is more like the desynchronized group of people, with much information processing going on. During synchrony the neurons of the resting brain (especially the cortex) quietly murmur the same message in unison.

Let us follow the progress of a volunteer—a male college student—in a sleep laboratory. The experimenter attaches the electrodes, turns the lights off, and closes the door. Our subject becomes drowsy and soon enters stage 1 sleep, marked by the presence of some *theta activity* (3.5–7.5 Hz). This stage is actually a transition between sleep and wakefulness; if we watch our volunteer's eyelids, we will see that from time to time they slowly open and close, and his eyes roll upward and downward. (See *Figure 9.2.*) About 10 minutes later he enters stage 2 sleep. The EEG during this stage is generally irregular but contains periods of theta activity, *sleep spindles*, and *K complexes*. *Sleep spindles* are short bursts of waves of 12–14 Hz, which occur between two and five times a minute during stages 1–4 of sleep. Some investigators believe that they represent the activity of a mechanism that decreases the brain's sensitivity to sensory input and thus keeps the person asleep (Silverstein and Levy, 1976; Bowersox, Kaitin, and Dement, 1985). The sleep of older people contains fewer sleep spindles and is generally accompanied by more awakenings during the night. *K complexes* are sudden, sharp waveforms, which, unlike sleep spindles, are usually found only during stage 2 sleep. They spontaneously occur at the rate of approximately one per minute but can often be triggered by noises. Some investigators believe that they, too, represent mechnisms involved in keeping the person asleep (Halasz, Pal, and Rajna, 1985). (See *Figure 9.2.*)

The subject is sleeping soundly now; but if awakened, he might report that he has not been asleep. This phenomenon is often reported by nurses who awaken loudly snoring patients early in the night (probably to give them a sleeping pill) and find that the patients insist they were lying there awake all the time. About 15 minutes later the subject enters stage 3 sleep, signaled by the occurrence of high-amplitude *delta activity* (less than 3.5 Hz). The distinction between stage 3 and stage 4 is not clear-cut; stage 3 contains 20–50 percent delta activity, and stage 4 contains more than 50 percent. (See *Figure 9.2.*)

About 90 minutes after the beginning of sleep (and about 45 minutes after the onset of stage 4 sleep), we notice an abrupt change in a number of physiological measures recorded from our subject. The EEG suddenly becomes mostly desynchronized, with a sprinkling of theta waves, very similar to the record obtained during stage 1 sleep. (See *Figure 9.2.*) We also note that his eyes are rapidly darting back and forth beneath his closed eyelids. We can see this activity in the EOG, recorded from electrodes pasted to the skin around his eyes, or we can observe the eye movements directly. The cornea produces a bulge in the closed eyelids that can be seen to move about. We also see that the EMG becomes silent; there is a profound loss of muscle tonus. If we try to elicit a stretch reflex by tapping our subject on a tendon with a rubber hammer, we find that he is completely unresponsive. However, we do occasionally see brief twitching movements of the hands and feet, and our subject probably has an erection.

This peculiar stage of sleep is quite distinct from the quiet sleep we saw earlier. It is usually referred to as *REM sleep* (for the *r*apid *e*ye *m*ovements that characterize it). It has also been called *paradoxical sleep,* because of the presence of an aroused, "waking" EEG during sleep. The term *paradoxical* merely reflects people's surprise at observing an unexpected phenomenon, but the years since its first discovery (reported by Aserinsky and Kleitman in 1955) have blunted the surprise value.

At this point, I should introduce some terminology. Stages 1–4 are usually referred to as *non-REM sleep.* Stages 3 and 4 are referred to as *slow-wave sleep,* because of the presence of delta activity. As we will see, research has focused on the role of REM sleep and of slow-wave sleep; most investigators believe that the other stages of non-REM sleep, stages 1 and 2, are less important than the others. By some criteria stage 4 is the deepest stage of sleep; only loud noises will cause a person to awaken, and when awakened, the person acts groggy and confused. During REM sleep a person may not react to noises, but he or she is easily aroused by meaningful stimuli, such as the sound of his or her name. Also, when awakened from REM sleep, a person appears alert and attentive.

If we arouse our volunteer during REM sleep and ask him what was going on, he will almost certainly report that he had been dreaming. The dreams of REM sleep tend to be narrative in form; there is a storylike progression of events. If we wake him during slow-wave sleep and ask, "Were you dreaming?" he will most likely say, "No." However, if we question him more carefully, he might report the presence of a thought, an image, or some emotion. I will return to this issue later.

During the rest of the night our subject's sleep alternates between periods of REM and slow-wave sleep. Each cycle is approximately 90 minutes long, containing a 20- to 30-minute bout of REM sleep. Thus, an 8-hour sleep will contain four or five periods of REM sleep. Figure 9.3 shows a graph of a typical night's sleep. Note that most slow-wave sleep (stages 3 and 4) occurs during the first half of night. Subsequent bouts of non-REM sleep contain more and more stage 2 sleep, and bouts of REM sleep (indicated by the colored horizontal bars) become more prolonged. (See *Figure 9.3.*)

The regular 90-minute cycles of REM sleep suggest that a brain mechanism alternately causes REM and slow-wave sleep. Normally, a period of slow-wave sleep must precede REM sleep. In addition, there seems to be a refractory period after each occurrence or REM sleep, during which time REM sleep cannot take place again. In fact, the cyclical nature of REM sleep appears to be controlled by a "clock" in the brain that also controls an activity cycle that continues through waking. The first

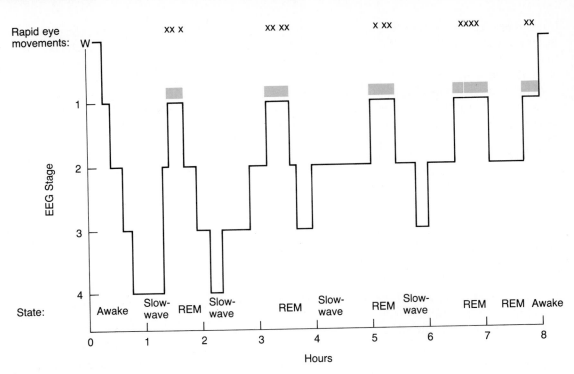

FIGURE 9.3

A typical pattern of the stages of sleep during a single night. (From Hartmann, E. *The Biology of Dreaming*, 1967. Courtesy of Charles C. Thomas, Publisher, Springfield, Illinois.)

suggestion that a 90-minute activity cycle occurs throughout the day came from the observation that infants who are fed on demand show regular feeding patterns (Kleitman, 1961). Later studies found 90-minute cycles of rest and activity, including such activities as eating, drinking, smoking, heart rate, oxygen consumption, stomach motility, urine production, and performance on various tasks that make demands upon a person's ability to pay attention. Kleitman termed this phenomenon the *basic rest-activity cycle (BRAC).* (See Kleitman, 1982, for a review.) As we will see later in this chapter, an internal "clock" in the medulla causes regular changes in activity and alertness during the day and controls periods of slow-wave and REM sleep at night.

During REM sleep we become paralyzed; most of our spinal and cranial motor neurons are strongly inhibited. (Obviously, the ones that control respiration and eye movements are spared.) At the same time, the brain is very active. Cerebral blood flow and oxygen consumption are acceler-

ated. In addition, a male's penis will become at least partially erect, and a female's vaginal secretions will increase. However, Fisher, Gross, and Zuch (1965) found that in males genital changes do not signify that the person is experiencing a dream with sexual content. (Of course, people can have dreams with frank sexual content. In males some of them culminate in ejaculation—the so-called nocturnal emissions, or "wet dreams." Females, too, sometimes experience orgasm during sleep.)

The fact that penile erections occur during REM sleep, independent of sexual arousal, has been used clinically to assess the causes of impotence (Karacan, Salis, and Williams, 1978). A subject sleeps in the laboratory with a device attached to his penis that measures its circumference. If penile enlargement occurs during REM sleep, then his failure to obtain an erection during attempts at intercourse is not caused by physiological problems such as nerve damage or a circulatory disorder. Often, once a man finds out that he is physiologically capable of achieving an erection, the knowledge is therapeutic in itself. (A neurologist told me that there is a less expensive way to gather the same data. The patient obtains a strip of postage stamps, moistens them, and applies them around his penis before going to bed. In the morning he checks to see whether the perforations are broken.)

The important differences between REM and slow-wave sleep are listed in *Table 9.1.*

Mental Activity During Sleep

Although sleep is a period during which we do not respond very much to the environment, it is incorrect to refer to sleep as a state of unconsciousness. During sleep our consciousness is certainly different from consciousness during waking, but we *are* conscious. In the morning we usually forget what we experienced while asleep, and in retrospect we recall a period of "unconsciousness." However, when experimenters wake sleeping subjects, the reports that the subjects give make it clear that they were conscious.

Some people insist that they never dream. They are wrong; everyone dreams. What does happen, however, is that most dreams are subsequently forgotten. Unless a person awakens during or immediately after a dream, the dream will not be remembered. Many people who thought they had not had a dream for years have been startled by the vivid narrations they were able to supply when roused during REM sleep in the laboratory. Even the most vivid experiences can be completely erased from consciousness. I am sure that many of you have had the experience of waking during a particularly vivid dream. You decide to tell your friends about it, and you start to review what you will say. As you do so, the memory just slips away. You can't remember the slightest detail of the dream, which was so vivid and real just a few seconds ago. You may feel that if you could remember just one thing about it, everything would come back. Understanding this phenomenon would probably help us understand the more general issue of learning and forgetting.

Although narrative, storylike dreaming occurs during REM sleep, mental activity also accompanies slow-wave sleep. Some of the most terrifying nightmares occur during slow-wave sleep, especially in stage 4 sleep (Fisher, Byrne, Edwards, and Kahn, 1970). If people are awakened from slow-wave sleep, they are unlikely to report a storylike dream. Instead, they are likely to report a situation, such as being crushed or suffocated, or simply a feeling of fear or dread. This common sensation is reflected in the terms that some languages use for describing what we call a *nightmare.* For example, in French the word is *cauchemar,* or "pressing devil." Figure 9.4 shows a victim of a nightmare (undoubtedly in the throes of stage 4 slow-wave sleep) being squashed by an *incubus* (from the Latin *incubare,* "to lie upon"). (See *Figure 9.4.*)

I NTERIM SUMMARY

Sleep is generally regarded as a state, but it is, nevertheless, a behavior. As we will see later in this chapter, we do not sleep because our brains "run down"; instead, active brain mechanisms cause us to engage in the behavior of sleep. The stages of non-REM sleep, stages 1 through 4, are defined by EEG activity. Slow-wave sleep (stages 3 and 4) are the two deepest stages. Alertness consists of desynchronized beta activity (13–30 Hz); relaxation and drowsiness consist of alpha activity (8–12 Hz). Stage 1 sleep consists of alternating periods of alpha activity, irregular fast activity, and theta activity (3.5–7.5 Hz); the EEG of stage 2 sleep lacks alpha activity

TABLE 9.1
Principal characteristics of REM and slow-wave sleep

REM Sleep	Slow-Wave Sleep
EEG desynchrony	EEG synchrony
Lack of muscle tonus	Moderate muscle tonus
Rapid eye movements	Slow or absent eye movements
Penile erection or vaginal secretion	Lack of genital activity
PGO waves	Lack of PGO waves
Narrative-type dreams	Static dreams

FIGURE 9.4

The Nightmare, 1781, by Henry Fuseli, Swiss, 1741–1825. (Gift of Mr. and Mrs. Bert L. Smokler and Mr. and Mrs. Lawrence A. Fleischman, Acc. No. 55.5. Courtesy of The Detroit Institute of Arts.)

but contains sleep spindles (short periods of 12–14 Hz activity) and occasional K complexes; stage 3 sleep consists of 20–50 percent delta activity (less than 3.5 Hz); and stage 4 sleep consists of more than 50 percent delta activity. About 90 minutes after the beginning of sleep, people enter REM sleep. Cycles of REM and slow-wave sleep alternate with a period of approximately 90 minutes.

WHY DO WE SLEEP?

We all know how insistent the urge to sleep can be and how uncomfortable we feel when we have to resist it and stay awake. With the exception of the effects of severe pain and the need to breathe, sleepiness is probably the most insistent drive. People can commit suicide by refusing to eat or drink, but even the most stoical person cannot indefinitely defy the urge to sleep. Sleep will come, sooner or later, no matter how hard a person tries to stay awake. However, despite the insistent nature of sleepiness, researchers have not yet found a simple answer to the question posed in the title of this section.

Investigators have suggested many hypotheses about the functions of sleep, but most of them are variations on two themes:

1. Sleep is an adaptive response—a behavior that serves a useful purpose. For example, sleep prevents an animal from wasting energy during a time of day when food is not available. This hypothesis suggests that the function of sleep is important but not physiologically necessary.

2. Sleep is a period of restoration, during which certain anabolic physiological processes occur. The wear and tear caused by activity during waking is repaired during sleep. This hypothesis conceives of sleep as a physiologically necessary function, just as vital as eating and drinking.

In this section I will consider these two general hypotheses. Although the evidence is not yet conclusive, sleep probably accomplishes *both* functions.

Sleep as an Adaptive Response

Some investigators believe that the best way to understand sleep is to see it as a useful behavior that we have inherited from our ancestors. For example, Webb (1975, 1982) suggests that sleep might not have special restorative properties but might simply be a behavior that keeps an animal out of harm's way when there is nothing important to do. We can imagine that our primitive ancestors benefited from irresistible periods of sleep that kept them from stumbling around in the dark, when predators were harder to see, when food was difficult to find, and when injuries were more likely to occur.

Many animals obtain food during only part of the day-night cycle. These animals profit from a period of inactivity, during which less energy is expended. In fact, animals who have safe hiding places (for example, rabbits) sleep a lot, unless they are very small and need to eat much of the time (for example, shrews). Large predators such as lions can safely sleep wherever and whenever they choose, and indeed, they sleep many hours of the day. In contrast, large animals who are preyed upon and have no place to hide (for example, cattle) sleep very little. Presumably, they must remain awake to be alert for predators. Allison and Chichetti (1976) found that *body weight* and *danger of being attacked* accounted for 58 percent of the variability in length of sleep among species. Meddis (1983) found some additional factors, including *relative size of the cerebral hemispheres* and *relative brain maturity at birth*. Species with larger brains (relative to their body size) slept more, and species whose infants are born with immature brains (like our own) spent more time in REM sleep.

The fact that sleeping time is related to features of an animal's adaptive specialization is certainly consistent with the hypothesis that sleep is a useful behavior. If sleep simply served a restorative function, then a species' sleeping time should be related to factors that cause wear and tear, such as activity level or expenditure of energy, not to danger of being attached. But as we shall see later, the relation of sleeping time to variables such as the relative size of the cerebral hemispheres *is* consistent with the restorative hypothesis.

Some investigators have used comparative data, obtained from a variety of species, to argue *against* the adaptive hypothesis. They note that sleep is a universal phenomenon among vertebrates. As far as we know, all mammals and birds sleep (Durie, 1981). Reptiles also sleep, and fish and amphibians enter periods of quiescence that can probably be called sleep. However, only warm-blooded vertebrates (mammals and birds) exhibit unequivocal REM sleep, with EEG signs of desynchrony along with rapid eye movements. (Obviously, birds such as flamingos, which sleep while perched on one leg, do not lose tone in the muscles they use to remain standing.) Thus, REM sleep appears to be of recent phylogenetic origin. This special form of sleep will be discussed separately, in a later section.

Sleep is found in some species of mammals that would seem to be better off without it. For example, the Indus dolphin (*Platanista indi*) lives in the muddy waters of the Indus estuary in Pakistan (Pilleri, 1979). Over the years it has become blind, presumably because vision is not useful in the animal's environment. (It has an excellent sonar system, which it uses to navigate and find prey.) However, despite the dangers caused by sleeping, sleep has not disappeared. The Indus dolphin never stops swimming; doing so would result in injury, because of the dangerous currents and the vast quantities of debris carried by the river during the monsoon season. Pilleri captured two dolphins and studied their habits. He found that they slept a total of 7 hours a day, in naps of 4–60 seconds each. If sleep were simply an adaptive response, why was it not eliminated (as vision was) through the process of natural selection?

Some other species of marine mammals have developed an extraordinary pattern of sleep: The cerebral hemispheres take turns sleeping, presumably because that strategy always permits at least one hemisphere to be alert. The bottlenose dolphin (*Tursiops truncatus*) and the porpoise (*Phocoena phocoena*) both sleep this way (Mukhametov, 1984). Figure 9.5 shows the EEG records from the two hemispheres; note that slow-wave sleep occurs independently in the left and right hemispheres. (See *Figure 9.5*.)

Undoubtedly, sleep *does* serve as a useful behavior. The fact that sleeping time varies with environmental factors suggests that sleep is not simply a response to physiological need. But its presence in all species of mammals and birds suggests that at least a certain amount of sleep is physiologically necessary.

Sleep as a Restorative Process

Most investigators believe that sleep accomplishes some sort of restoration from the effects of wear and tear that occur during wakefulness. However, until recently, evidence for this hypothesis was very thin, indeed. In fact, sleep does not seem to be necessary for keeping the body in

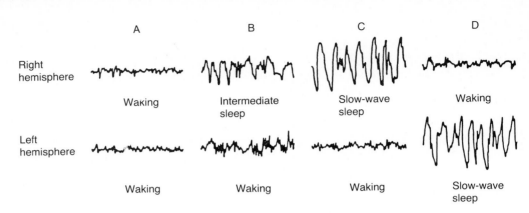

Right hemisphere

Waking

Intermediate sleep

Slow-wave sleep

Waking

Left hemisphere

Waking

Waking

Waking

Slow-wave sleep

FIGURE 9.5

Sleep in a dolphin. The two hemispheres sleep independently, presumably so that the animal remains behaviorally alert. (Adapted from Mukhametov, L.M., in *Sleep Mechanisms*, edited by A.A. Borbély and J.L. Valatx. Munich: Springer-Verlag, 1984.)

good condition (at least, in our own species). However, it *does* appear to be needed to keep the brain functioning normally. (For convenience, I will talk about the "body" and the "brain" in the following section, even though we all know that the brain is a part of the body.)

Effects of Sleep Deprivation

When we are forced to miss a night's sleep, we become very sleepy. The fact that sleepiness is so motivating suggests that sleep is a necessity of life. If so, it should be possible to deprive people or laboratory animals of sleep and see what capacities are disrupted. We should then be able to infer the role that sleep plays. However, the results of sleep deprivation studies have not revealed as much as investigators had originally hoped.

Studies with Humans.   There is a distinct difference between sleepiness and tiredness. We might want to rest after playing tennis or after having a vigorous swim, but that feeling is quite different from the sleepiness we feel at the end of a day—a sleepiness that occurs even if we have been relatively inactive. What we should do, therefore, to study the role of sleep (as opposed to the restorative function of rest) is to have our subjects rest without sleeping. Unfortunately, that is not possible. When Kleitman first began studying sleep in the early 1920s, he hoped to have subjects undress and lie quietly in bed. They would remain awake so that he could observe the effects of

"pure" sleep deprivation. It did not work. People cannot stay awake without engaging in physical activity, no matter how hard they try. So Kleitman had to accept that because his subjects could stay awake only by being active, they were rest-deprived as well as sleep-deprived.

Sleep deprivation studies found that subjects do not show a steady progression of sleepiness throughout the deprivation period. They are sleepiest at night, but they recover considerably during the day. After two or three sleepless days subjects generally do not report significant increases in sleepiness, although the cycle of sleepiness continues, with the peak occurring at night.

Deprivation studies have not obtained persuasive evidence that sleep is needed to keep the body functioning normally. Horne (1978) reviewed over fifty experiments in which humans had been deprived of sleep. He reported that most of them found no evidence of a physiological stress response. If people are subjected to treatments that begin to cause illness or damage to various organ systems, changes can be seen in such physiological measures as blood levels of cortisol and epinephrine, blood sedimentation rate, and packed blood cell volume. Generally, these changes did not occur; when evidence of stress was obtained, it was associated with stressful situations independent of sleep deprivation. In addition, sleep deprivation does not interfere with people's ability to perform physical exercise.

For example, Takeuchi, Davis, Plyley, Good, and Shephard (1985) found that three days of sleep deprivation did not affect people's general athletic ability, measured by grip strength, leg strength, running speed, and jumping.

Although sleep deprivation does not seem to damage the body, and sleep does not seem to be necessary for athletic exercise, it is possible that sleep is required for normal brain functioning. Most studies have shown that sleep-deprived subjects are able to perform normally on most intellectual tasks, as long as the tasks are short. They have difficulty with prolonged, boring tasks, but if they are properly motivated, their performance on short tasks seems to be as good as that of rested subjects. Thus, the major effect of sleep deprivation appears to be intense feelings of sleepiness but no serious deterioration in mental capacities. Any problems that do occur seem to be caused by motivational changes induced by sleepiness, not by the inability to function normally.

The problem with these conclusions is that it is difficult to distinguish between motivational changes caused by sleepiness and impairments in brain functions. Several studies suggest that even if motivation is taken into account, people perform more poorly on tasks that require a high level of cortical functioning after two days of sleep deprivation. For example, Horne and Pettitt (1985) had subjects perform a vigilance task that required them to listen to a series of tones and indicate when they heard one that was slightly different from the others. A technique derived from signal detection theory (Green and Swets, 1966) permits the measurement of a subject's ability to detect the stimulus, independent of any effects that motivation may have on the subject's willingness to report hearing a stimulus that may or may not have been present.

Horne and Pettitt first trained their subjects on the detection task, to reduce the likelihood that any practice they gained during the period of deprivation would compensate for possible deterioration. To be sure that the pretraining was successful, they also used a control group of subjects who were not sleep-deprived. One group of sleep-deprived subjects received only the payment promised for their participation; another received cash bonuses for good performance. These incentives

increased during the deprivation session; the stakes were doubled on the second day and redoubled on the third day. By the last day the subjects had the opportunity to obtain several hundred pounds sterling for good performance. The subjects (young graduate students) appeared to be well motivated and eager to win the money. However, the experimenters were obliged to pay them very little; their performance became very bad. Figure 9.6 shows the results; you can see that the high-incentive group performed better during the first two days, but by the third day they were doing just as poorly as the low-incentive group. (See *Figure 9.6*.)

Sleep deprivation produces other signs of impaired cerebral functioning. For example, most studies have found that after a few days of sleep deprivation people begin to report perceptual distortions or even hallucinations. For example, Morris, Williams, and Lubin (1960) reported that sleep-deprived subjects made statements such as "The floor seems wavy," "That black mark looked like it was changing into different rock formations," or "I thought steam was rising from the

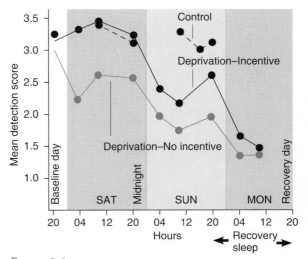

FIGURE 9.6

Alertness (ability to detect a signal) in sleep-deprived and non-sleep-deprived subjects. A high-incentive condition facilitated performance, but only temporarily. (Adapted from Horne, J. A. *Why We Sleep: The Functions of Sleep in Humans and Other Mammals.* Oxford, England: Oxford University Press, 1988. Copyright 1988 Oxford University Press. By permission of the Oxford University Press.)

floor, so I tested my eyes to check whether it was real.'' The effects on a subject without a history of mental illness are never particularly severe—the subjects will realize that the perceptual distortions and hallucinations are not real—but they do suggest that sleep deprivation adversely affects cerebral functioning.

What happens to sleep-deprived subjects after they are permitted to sleep again? Most of them sleep longer the next night or two, but they never regain all of the sleep they lost. In one remarkable case a seventeen-year-old boy stayed awake for 264 hours so that he could obtain a place in the *Guinness Book of World Records* (Gulevich, Dement, and Johnson, 1966). After his ordeal the boy slept for a little less than 15 hours and awoke feeling fine. He slept slightly more than 10 hours the second night and just under 9 hours the third. Almost 67 hours were never made up. However, percentage of recovery was not equal for all stages of sleep. Only 7 percent of stages 1 and 2 were made up, but 68 percent of stage 4 slow-wave sleep and 53 percent of REM sleep were made up.

Other studies (for example, Kales et al., 1970) have found similar results; after total sleep deprivation, subjects show an increased amount of REM sleep and (especially) deep slow-wave sleep. Thus, perhaps, these two stages of sleep are the two most important.

As I mentioned earlier, REM sleep will be discussed later. But what do we know about slow-wave sleep? As you have learned, it is characterized by delta waves—slow, high-amplitude oscillations of the EEG. Buchsbaum, Mendelson, Duncan, Coppola, Kelsoe, and Gillin (1982) used a special EEG machine that permits a computer to draw a map showing the location of particular forms of electrical activity in the brain. As Figure 9.7 indicates, the intense delta activity that occurs during stage 3 and stage 4 sleep takes place primarily in the frontal lobes. (See *Figure 9.7*.)

What happens during slow-wave sleep that makes it important? Both cerebral metabolic rate and cerebral blood flow decline during slow-wave sleep, falling to about 75 percent of the waking level during stage 4 sleep (Sakai, Meyer, Karacan, Derman, and Yamamoto, 1979). In particular, the regions marked by the highest amounts of delta waves decline the most. As we know from behavioral observation, people are unreactive to all but intense stimuli during slow-wave sleep and, if awakened, act groggy and confused. In fact, Liv-

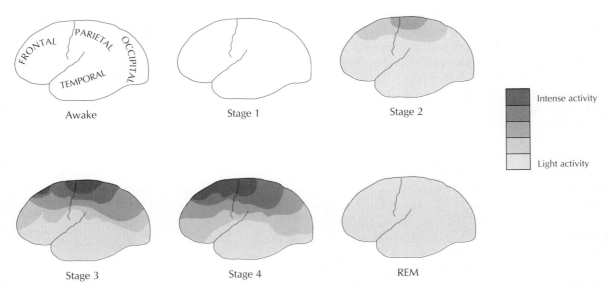

FIGURE 9.7
Relative amounts of slow-wave activity in the brain during various stages of sleep. (From Buchsbaum, M.S., Mendelson, W.B., Duncan, W.C., Coppola, R., Kelsoe, J., and Gillin, J.C. *Sleep*, 1982, *5*, 248–255.)

ingstone and Hubel (1981) found that during slow-wave sleep neurons in the visual cortex stopped responding to visual stimuli. As they noted, the results could be interpreted in two ways: Either "the muffling of sensory input during sleep serves to insulate the animal from its environment, to permit uninterrupted sleep, or . . . sensory systems also need to rest, and the decreased responsiveness we see reflects whatever recuperative processes the brain undergoes during sleep" (p. 561).

Studies with Laboratory Animals. Until recently, sleep deprivation studies with animals have provided us with little insight into the role of sleep. Because animals cannot be "persuaded" to stay awake, it is especially difficult to separate the effects of sleep deprivation from those caused by the method used to keep the animals awake. We can ask a human volunteer to try to stay awake and can expect some cooperation. He or she will say, "I'm getting sleepy—help me to stay awake." However, animals are interested only in getting to sleep and must constantly be stimulated—and hence, stressed. A study by Rechtschaffen, Gilliland, Bergmann, and Winter (1983) attempted to control for the effects of forced exercise that are necessary to keep an animal from sleeping. They constructed a circular platform on which two rats lived, each restrained in a plastic cage. When the platform was rotated by an electrical motor, the rats were forced to walk to avoid falling into a pool of water. (See *Figure 9.8.*)

Rechtschaffen and his colleagues employed a *yoked-control* procedure to deprive one rat of sleep but force both members of the pair to exercise an equal amount of time. They used a computer to record both rats' EEGs and EMGs so that they could detect both slow-wave and REM sleep. One rat served as the experimental (sleep-deprived) animal, and the other served as the yoked control. As soon as the EEG record indicated that the experimental animal was falling asleep, the computer turned on the motor that rotated the disk, forcing both animals to exercise. Because the platform rotated whenever the experimental animal started to sleep, the procedure reduced the experimental animal's total sleep time by 87 percent. However, the sleep time of the yoked-con-

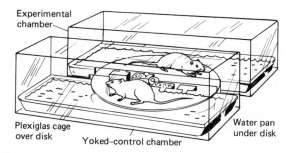

FIGURE 9.8

The apparatus used to deprive rats of sleep. Whenever one of the pair of rats in the experimental chambers fell asleep, the turntable was rotated until the animal was awake for 6 seconds. (Redrawn from Rechtschaffen, A., Gilliland, M.A., Bergmann, B.M., and Winter, J.B. *Science,* 1983, *221,* 182–184.)

trol rat was reduced by only 31 percent. Eight pairs of rats were placed in the apparatus for a period of 5 to 33 days.

The effects of sleep deprivation were severe. The experimental animals looked sick and apparently stopped grooming their fur. They became weak and uncoordinated and often fell off the disk. Three animals died and four others were killed because death appeared imminent. On autopsy, several of the experimental animals were found to have had enlarged adrenal glands, stomach ulcers, fluid in the lungs and trachea, or internal hemorrhage. Because no signs of infection were detected, these findings suggest that the pathological conditions were induced by stress.

This experiment suggests that forced exercise that occurs just after an animal falls asleep produces severe stress that eventually is fatal. Thus, we must seriously consider the possibility that sleep performs a vital physiological function. However, it could be that the stressful event is forced exercise that occurs immediately after the onset of sleep, not the loss of sleep that this exercise causes. Being forced to begin walking just after falling asleep is undoubtedly more stressful than being forced to walk while awake or after having been asleep for some time. The experiment provides important evidence, but further investigation is needed to determine the nature of the physiological role that sleep plays.

Clearly, the effects of sleep deprivation are less drastic in humans than in rats. Several hypotheses could account for this difference. Perhaps human sleep deprivation studies have just not continued long enough to cause serious harm. Perhaps the physiology of humans and rats is different, and sleep is simply less important for humans than for rats. However, sleep has an ancient evolutionary history, and the similarities in the sleep of various species of mammals are much greater than the differences. Perhaps (as Horne, 1988, suggests) the procedures used to keep humans and rats awake cause different amounts of stress. A human in a sleep deprivation study knows that he or she is being watched carefully by the experimenters and that no serious harm will occur. The subject also knows that even though the experience is somewhat of an ordeal, it will soon be over, and he or she will be able to sleep again. In contrast, the rat knows only that its environment has suddenly become very hostile. Every time it sleeps, it is forced to walk or fall into the water. It probably feels miserable from the lack of sleep and has no way of knowing whether the ordeal will ever end. In a similar situation, perhaps a person would suffer ill effects, also. (In fact, sleep deprivation was an important component of the brainwashing techniques used to persuade captured American servicemen to change their political beliefs during the Korean War.)

Effects of Exercise on Sleep

Sleep deprivation studies with humans suggest that the brain may need slow-wave sleep in order to recover from the day's activities but that the rest of the body does not. Another way to determine whether sleep is needed for restoration of physiological functioning is to look at the effects of daytime activity on nighttime sleep. If the function of sleep is to repair the effects of activity during waking hours, then we should expect that sleep and exercise are related. That is, we should sleep more after a day of vigorous exercise than after a day spent quietly at an office desk.

In fact, the relation between sleep and exercise is not very compelling. First, let me give you an example of a study with positive results. Shapiro, Bortz, Mitchell, Bartel, and Jooste (1981) carefully examined the sleep of trained athletes who competed in a 92-km (approximately 57-mi) marathon. Obviously, participation in the race re-

quired a drastic increase in energy expenditure. During the next two nights the participants slept more than they did before the race: increases of 18 and 27 percent, respectively, for the two nights. However, when slow-wave sleep is considered separately, the increase is much more impressive: 40 and 45 percent. The participants actually spent *less* time in REM sleep during the two nights after the race. These results suggest that slow-wave sleep, in particular, is important for recuperation after vigorous activity.

However, several studies have shown that *decreased* activity does not substantially reduce the amount of time a person sleeps. For example, Ryback and Lewis (1971) found no changes in slow-wave or REM sleep of healthy subjects who spent six weeks resting in bed. If sleep repairs wear and tear, we would expect these people to sleep less. Adey, Bors, and Porter (1968) studied the sleep of *completely* immobile quadriplegics and paraplegics and found only a small decrease in slow-wave sleep as compared with normal people.

Horne (1981, 1988) notes that although some studies (such as that by Shapiro and his colleagues) have found that exercise increases slow-wave sleep, others have not. Two variables seem to determine whether positive results are obtained: the temperature and humidity in which the exercise occurs, and the fitness of the subjects. If the temperature and the humidity are high and if the subjects are athletically fit, positive results are likely. Horne suggested that the important variable might be whether the exercise succeeded in heating the body. Exercise in a hot, humid environment would be more likely to do so, and an athletically fit subject would be more likely to be able to exercise long enough for his or her body to heat.

To test this hypothesis, Horne and Staff (1983) had subjects exercise on a treadmill. They ran on the treadmill either slowly for a long time or quickly for a short time. (The total amount of energy expenditure in the two conditions was equivalent.) The short, vigorous exercise raised body temperature by 2°C, and the long, slow exercise raised it by only 0.8°C. A third group simply sat in a warm bath, which raised their body temperature by 2°C. All subjects quickly cooled down again after ending their exercise or leaving the warm bath.

All subjects spent the night in the laboratory, where their sleep was recorded. The results supported the hypothesis that heating was the variable that links exercise to sleep: The slow-wave sleep of the vigorous exercisers rose by 25 percent, and that of the subjects warmed by the bath rose 20 percent. The slow-wave sleep of the subjects who exercised slowly was unchanged.

In a follow-up study Horne and Moore (1985) had subjects exercise vigorously, as they did in the previous experiment. Some subjects were cooled by electric fans, and their skin was periodically sprayed with water. Their body temperature rose only 1°C. That night, the slow-wave sleep of the "hot exercised" subjects rose by 25 percent, whereas that of the "cool exercised" subjects was unchanged. Horne (1988) now believes that the increased body temperature itself is not the significant factor but that an increase in brain temperature is. Perhaps, he says, an increase in brain temperature raises its metabolic rate and hence its demand for more slow-wave sleep. A preliminary study suggests that this hypothesis may have some merit. Horne and Harley (1988) warmed subjects heads and faces with a hair dryer, which raised their brain temperature by an estimated 1°C. Four of the six subjects showed an increase in slow-wave sleep the next night. Clearly, further research is needed.

Effects of Mental Activity on Sleep

If slow-wave sleep permits the brain to rest and recover from its daily activity, then we might expect that increased cerebral activity would cause an increase in slow-wave sleep. Indeed, as we just saw, that is precisely the way that Horne interprets the effects of increased body temperature. First of all, tasks that demand alertness and mental activity do increase glucose metabolism in the brain, as measured by a PET scanner (Roland, 1984). The most significant increases are seen in the frontal lobes, where delta activity is most intense during slow-wave sleep.

In an ingenious study Horne and Minard (1985) found a way to increase mental activity without affecting physical activity and without causing stress. The investigators told subjects to show up for an experiment in which they were supposed to take some tests designed to test read-ing skills. In fact, when the subjects turned up, they were told that the plans had been changed. They were invited for a day out, at the expense of the experimenters. (Not surprisingly, the subjects willingly accepted.) They spent the day visiting an art exhibition, a shopping center, a museum, an amusement park, a zoo, and an interesting mansion. After a scenic drive through the countryside they watched a movie in a local theater. They were driven from place to place and certainly did not become overheated by exercise. After the movie they returned to the sleep laboratory. They said they were tired, and they readily fell asleep. Their sleep duration was normal, and they awoke feeling refreshed. However, their slow-wave sleep—particularly, stage 4 sleep—was increased.

Does Physical Restoration Occur During Sleep?

The evidence that I have reviewed so far suggests that slow-wave sleep is not necessary for restoration of the body but that it may be necessary for restoration of the brain. I have discussed the effects of sleep deprivation and the effects of physical and mental activity on sleep. One other approach remains: to see whether physiological changes occur during sleep that suggest that restoration and repair takes place at that time.

Investigators who believe that the body repairs itself during sleep point to evidence for restorative processes during sleep. The most important finding is the fact that the secretion of growth hormone occurs only during sleep. (Growth hormone is, of course, important for stimulating children's growth, but it also has functions in adults.) The sleep-dependent secretion of growth hormone is significant, because this hormone increases the ability of amino acids, the constituents of proteins, to enter cells. Undoubtedly, protein synthesis is an important aspect of restoration of body tissue, because proteins are relatively fragile and must constantly be renewed and replaced.

Growth hormone (GH) is secreted shortly after the first occurrence of delta activity in slow-wave sleep (Takahashi, 1979). This fact would seem to support the hypothesis that physical wear and tear are repaired during sleep. However, children younger than four years of age, and many older people, do not secrete GH only during sleep (Carlson, Gillin, Gorden, and Snyder, 1972; Finklestein, Roffwarg, Boyar, Kream, and Hellman, 1972). Furthermore, the correlation between sleep and GH secretion breaks down for many pathological conditions, including various pituitary disorders, dwarfism, narcolepsy (a sleep disorder that will be discussed later in this chapter), schizophrenia, and depression (Takahashi, 1979). Finally, the secretion of GH in some mammals does not appear to be tied to slow-wave sleep (Quabbe, 1977).

In any event, as Horne (1988) points out, GH facilitates protein synthesis only if amino acids are freely available, and that is the case only for about 5 hours after a meal. After that time the amino acids have become incorporated into protein, have been oxidized, or have been converted into fats and stored in the body's adipose tissue. Most people eat several hours before going to bed, so during most of the night the pool of available amino acids is low.

The story is different for other animals. For example, Nicolaïdis, Danguir, and Mather (1979) provided rats with a little niche in their cages in which they could curl up and sleep. Under these conditions rats seldom nibbled (as they normally do in a laboratory cage where food is freely available), and their periods of sleep became tightly coupled to their meals; small meals were followed by short sleeps, and large meals by long sleeps. Thus, sleep does provide animals such as rats with the opportunity for restoration.

A study by Clugston and Garlick (1982) actually measured protein turnover in the human body, using a method that involved the intravenous infusion of a radioactive amino acid, leucine. The subjects ate twelve small meals, from 8 A.M. to 7 P.M.; night was a period of fasting, as it is for most of us. The investigators found that the breakdown of protein was approximately the same during the day and during the night. However, the rate of protein synthesis was higher than that of breakdown during the day but lower during the night. Thus, it appears that people build up their supply of protein while they are awake, not while they are asleep.

Perhaps for some species, such as the rat, sleep provides the sole opportunity for tissue restoration. When rats are awake, they are actively doing something: foraging for food, seeking sexual partners, grooming, eating, drinking, or otherwise keeping occupied. The only time that they really rest is when they are asleep. However, we humans are able to rest during the day. We are capable of sitting quietly (as I am doing now, and as you will be doing when you read this chapter). In fact, our metabolic rate is only about 9 percent lower during sleep than it is during quiet wakefulness (Reich, Geyer, and Karnovsky, 1972). Thus, we probably do not sleep for physical rest as much as for the opportunity it gives our brain to rest.

The Functions of REM Sleep

Clearly, REM sleep is a time of intense physiological activity. The eyes dart about rapidly, the heart rate shows sudden accelerations and decelerations, breathing becomes irregular, and the brain becomes more active. It would be unreasonable to expect that REM sleep has the same functions as slow-wave sleep. An early report on the effects of REM sleep deprivation (Dement, 1960) observed that as the deprivation progressed, subjects had to be awakened from REM sleep more frequently; the "pressure" to enter REM sleep built up. Furthermore, after several days of REM sleep deprivation subjects would show a *rebound phenomenon* when permitted to sleep normally; they spent a much greater-than-normal percentage of the recovery night in REM sleep. This rebound suggests that there is a need for a certain amount of REM sleep—that REM sleep is controlled by a regulatory mechanism. If selective deprivation causes a deficiency in REM sleep, the deficiency is made up later, when uninterrupted sleep is permitted.

How have investigators explained the occurrence of REM sleep? The similarities between REM sleep and waking have led some investigators to suggest that REM sleep permits an animal to become more sensitive to its environment and avoid being surprised by predators (Snyder, 1966). (You will recall that during REM sleep humans are more sensitive to meaningful stimuli, such as the sound of their name.) Others have suggested that REM sleep has a special role in learning. Some investigators suggest that memories of events of the previous day—especially those dealing with emotionally related information—are consolidated and integrated with existing memories (Greenberg and Pearlman, 1974); others have suggested that this time is utilized to accomplish the opposite function—to flush useless information from memory, to prevent the storage of useless clutter (Newman and Evans, 1965; Crick and Mitchison, 1983). Another investigator (Jouvet, 1980) suggests that REM sleep helps integrate learned and instinctive behaviors—it provides a time to modify species-typical behaviors according to the experience gained in the past day. The fact that the sleep of infants consists mainly of REM sleep has suggested to others that this stage is associated with brain development (Roffwarg, Muzio, and Dement, 1966). The association could go either way; brain development could cause REM sleep (perhaps to tidy up after spurts of neural growth), or REM sleep could be setting the stage for brain growth to occur.

As you can see, many hypotheses have been advanced to explain the rather puzzling phenomenon of REM sleep. In the previous paragraph I mentioned four categories: vigilance, learning (either consolidation or flushing), species-typical reprogramming, and brain development. It is probably safe to say that when there are so many hypothetical explanations for a phenomenon, we do not know very much about its causes. So far, none of the hypotheses have been either unambiguously supported or proved wrong. REM sleep deprivation, given after a session of training, does impair learning—especially of complicated tasks—but the effect is not very large (McGrath and Cohen, 1978; Smith, 1985). Similarly, a training session does increase REM sleep—especially early in the sleep period. Thus, the learning hypothesis receives a certain amount of support. The vigilance and reprogramming hypotheses have not been developed enough to make specific predictions that can be tested experimentally. The developmental hypothesis is supported by the fact that infant animals born with well-developed brains (such as guinea pigs) spend proportionally less time in REM sleep than infant animals born with less-developed brains (such as rats, cats, or humans).

Now for some experimental evidence. Because REM sleep occurs only after a period of slow-wave sleep, it is possible to deprive a subject (human or laboratory animal) of REM sleep by awakening it only at the beginning of each period of REM sleep. Control subjects are awakened the same number of times, at random intervals, and thus engage in both REM and slow-wave sleep.

In general, REM sleep deprivation has little or no effect on a person's ability to learn or to remember what was previously learned. But a few studies suggest that learning related to emotionally significant material may be affected. Greenberg, Pillard, and Pearlman (1972) had subjects view a film that generally produces anxiety in the observers (a particularly gruesome circumcision rite performed with stone knives by members of a remote South Sea Island tribe). Normally, people who see the film twice show less anxiety during the second viewing. The investigators found that subjects who were permitted to engage in REM sleep between the first and second viewings of the film showed less anxiety the second time than subjects who were deprived of REM sleep. In addition, Breger, Hunter, and Lane (1971) found that the dream content of subjects viewing the film was affected by the anxiety-producing material. Taken together, the studies suggest that REM sleep (and perhaps the dreaming that occurs then) somehow assists people to come to grips with newly learned information that has emotional consequences. As we all know, things generally seem less disturbing after a good night's sleep.

The calming effect of REM sleep appears to be contradicted by a puzzling phenomenon. The symptoms of people with severe, psychotic depression are *reduced* when they are deprived of REM sleep. In addition, treatments that reduce the symptoms of depression, such as antidepressant drugs and electroconvulsive therapy, also suppress REM sleep (Vogel, Vogel, McAbee, and Thurmond, 1980; Vogel, Buffenstein, Minter, and Hennessey, 1990). (These results will be discussed in more detail in Chapter 18.) If REM sleep helps people assimilate emotionally relevant information, why should REM sleep deprivation relieve the symptoms of people who are suffering from a serious emotional disorder?

Although experiments with human subjects have not provided strong evidence that REM sleep plays an important role in memory, studies with laboratory animals have shown that REM sleep deprivation retards memory formation and that learning a new task causes an increase in REM sleep. For example, Bloch, Hennevin, and Leconte (1977) gave rats daily training trials in a complex maze. They found that the experience enhanced subsequent REM sleep. Moreover, daily performance was related to subsequent REM sleep. The lower curve in Figure 9.9 shows REM sleep as a percentage of total sleep. The upper curve illustrates the animals' performance in the maze. The largest increase in running speed (possibly representing the largest increase in learning) was accompanied by the largest amount of REM sleep. Also note that once the task was well learned (after day 6), REM sleep declined back to baseline levels. (See *Figure 9.9.*)

Although REM sleep may facilitate learning in some way, animals deprived of REM sleep are able to learn. This fact leaves open the possibility that REM sleep is only indirectly related to learning—that the functions it performs make it easier for an animal to learn but are not directly involved in the memory process. One possibility is that during REM sleep the information that has been learned during the day becomes more solidly integrated with already-learned information, which would make the new memories more easily accessible later. An experiment by Hennevin, Hars, and Bloch (1989) supports this hypothesis. They note that previous studies showed that stimu-lation of the midbrain reticular formation facili-tates learning of a maze task when it is delivered immediately after the animal runs through the maze. The stimulation causes an increase in the activity of the neocortex, which presumably is re-sponsible for the effect. They found that stimu-lation given later, during a subsequent period of REM sleep, had the same effect, whereas stimu-lation during slow-wave sleep or during wakeful-ness long after the training trial had no effect. Pre-sumably, the cortical activation during REM sleep facilitated whatever memory-related functions were taking place then.

A particularly interesting case of brain damage suggests that whatever the functions of REM sleep may be, they do not appear to be necessary for survival. Lavie, Pratt, Scharf, Peled, and Brown (1984) reported that a 33-year-old man whose head was injured by shrapnel at age 20 en-gaged in almost no REM sleep. In the sleep labora-tory the man slept an average of $4\frac{1}{2}$ hours. On 3 of 8 nights he engaged in no REM sleep; the average on the other 5 nights was approximately 6 min-utes. The pieces of metal damaged the pons, left temporal lobe, and left thalamus. As we shall see later in this chapter, the pons seems to be the part of the brain that controls REM sleep. The almost complete lack of REM sleep did not appear to cause serious side effects. After receiving his in-jury, the man completed high school, attended law school, and began practicing law.

FIGURE 9.9
Percentage of sleep time spent in REM sleep (*lower curve*) as a function of maze-learning performance (*upper curve*). (From Bloch, V., Hennevin, E., and Leconte, P., in *Neurobiology of Sleep and Memory*, edited by R.R. Drucker-Colin and J.L. McGaugh. New York: Academic Press, 1978.)

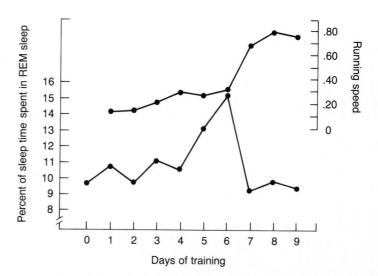

*I*NTERIM SUMMARY

Thurs 3.21

The two principal explanations for sleep are that sleep serves as an adaptive response or that it provides a period of restoration. The fact that a species' degree of safety and rate of metabolism are related to the amount of sleep it engages in supports the adaptive hypothesis, but the fact that all vertebrates sleep, including some that would seem to be better off without it, does not.

The effects of several days of sleep deprivation are not devastating to humans; the primary finding is intense sleepiness, difficulty performing tasks that require prolonged concentration, and perceptual distortions and (sometimes) mild hallucinations. The occurrence of perceptual changes, and the fact that even very attractive incentives cannot prevent the decrements in performance, suggests that sleep deprivation does impair cerebral functioning. Deep slow-wave sleep appears to be the most important stage, and perhaps its function is to permit the brain (but not necessarily the rest of the body) to recuperate. Animals who are sleep-deprived eventually die, but we cannot be sure that the stress is caused by lack of sleep or by the procedure needed to keep them awake.

Exercise can increase the amount of slow-wave sleep a person receives, but the effect appears to occur only if the brain temperature rises; it can be abolished by cooling the person during exercise or induced by warming the head. Perhaps, then, the fundamental cause is an increase in brain metabolism. Growth hormone normally is secreted only during slow-wave sleep, but the significance of this fact is uncertain, since the blood level of amino acids during sleep is normally low in in humans. In smaller animals such as rats, a meal is normally followed by a bout of sleep.

The function of REM sleep is even less certain than that of slow-wave sleep. It may promote vigilance, learning, species-typical reprogramming, or brain development. So far, the evidence is inconclusive, although several studies have shown a modest relation between REM sleep and learning.

DISORDERS OF SLEEP

Insomnia

Insomnia is a problem that affects at least 20 percent of the population at some time (Raybin and Detre, 1969), but unfortunately, little is known about its causes. At the onset I must emphasize that there is no single definition of insomnia that can apply to all people. The amount of sleep that individuals require is quite variable. A short sleeper may feel fine with 5 hours; a long sleeper may still feel unrefreshed after 10 hours of sleep. Insomnia must be defined in relation to a person's particular sleep needs. Some short sleepers have sought medical assistance because they thought that they were supposed to get more sleep, even though they felt fine. These people should be reassured that whatever amount of sleep seems to be enough *is* enough. Meddis, Pearson, and Langford (1973) reported the case of a seventy-year-old woman who slept approximately 1 hour each day (documented by sessions in a sleep laboratory). She felt fine and was of the opinion that most people "wasted much time" in bed.

Ironically, the most important cause of insomnia seems to be sleeping medication. Insomnia is not a disease that can be corrected with a medicine, in the way that diabetes can be treated with insulin. Insomnia is a symptom. If it is caused by pain or discomfort, the physical ailment that leads to the sleeplessness should be treated. If it is secondary to personal problems or psychological disorders, these problems should be dealt with directly. Patients who receive a sleeping medication develop a tolerance to the drug and suffer rebound symptoms if it is withdrawn (Weitzman, 1981). That is, the drug loses its effectiveness, so the patient requests larger doses from the physician. If the patient attempts to sleep without the accustomed medication or even takes a smaller dose one night, he or she is likely to experience a withdrawal effect: a severe disturbance of sleep. The patient becomes convinced that the insomnia is even worse than before and turns to more medication for relief. This common syndrome is called *drug dependency insomnia.* Kales, Scharf, Kales, and Soldatos (1979) found that withdrawal of some sleeping medications produced a rebound insomnia after the drugs were used for as few as three nights.

Most patients who receive a prescription for a sleeping medication are given one on the basis of their own description of their symptoms. That is, they tell their physician that they sleep very little at night, and the drug is prescribed on the basis of this testimony. Very few patients are observed during a night's sleep in a sleep laboratory; thus, insomnia is one of the few medical problems that physicians treat without having direct clinical evidence for its existence. But studies on the sleep of people who complain of insomnia show that most of them grossly underestimate the amount of time they actually sleep. Many patients with chronic insomnia report in the morning that they slept very little, or not at all, even though the EEG record shows that they slept for 6 or 7 hours (Weitzman, 1981). The U.S. Institute of Medicine (1979) found that most insomniacs, even without sleeping medication, fall asleep in less than 30 minutes and sleep for at least 6 hours. *With* sleeping medication they obtained less than a 15-minute reduction in falling asleep, and their sleep length was increased by only about 30 minutes. Given the unfortunate side effects, sleeping medication does not seem to be worthwhile.

Some people suffer from an interesting, but unfortunate, form of "pseudoinsomnia": They dream that they are awake. They do not dream that they are running around in some Alice-in-Wonderland fantasy but that they are lying in bed, trying unsuccessfully to fall asleep. In the morning their memories are of a night of insomnia, and they feel as unrefreshed as if they had really been awake.

Another form of insomnia—a true one, not a pseudoinsomnia—is caused by the inability to sleep and breathe at the same time. Patients with this disorder, called *sleep apnea,* fall asleep and then cease to breathe. (Nearly all people have occasional episodes of sleep apnea—especially people who snore—but not to the extent that it interferes with sleep.) During a period of sleep apnea the level of carbon dioxide in the blood stimulates chemoreceptors, and the person wakes up, gasping for air. The oxygen level of the blood returns to normal, the person falls asleep, and the whole cy-

cle begins again. Fortunately, many cases of sleep apnea are caused by an obstruction of the airway that can be corrected surgically.

Occasionally, infants are found dead in their cribs without any apparent signs of illness, victims of the *sudden infant death syndrome* (*SIDS*). Many investigators believe that one of the principal causes for SIDS is sleep apnea; in these cases, however, the infants are *not* awakened by a high level of carbon dioxide in the blood. For example, Kahn et al., (1988) studied the records of infants who had spent a night in a sleep laboratory and who subsequently died of SIDS. They found that compared with the records of normal infants, the records of SIDS victims showed longer periods of apnea during stage 4 sleep and less likelihood of sighing before a period of apnea. (Short periods of apnea are common in infants, children, and adults.) Unfortunately, although the differences were statistically significant, they were not large enough to be useful for clinical prediction. Gould, Lee, and Morelock (1988) believe that vulnerability to SIDS occurs when mechanisms controlling sleep mature before those that reflexively control breathing. Sudden infant deaths begin to occur around the time that an infant's naps begin to coalesce into a long period of sleep of 8 hours or more. If at this time the brain mechanisms that control respiration are not yet mature enough, the challenge of having to sustain breathing during such a long period of sleep may not be met.

Evidence suggests that a susceptibility to SIDS is inherited; parents and siblings of some infants who have died of SIDS do not respond normally to increases in carbon dioxide (Kelly, Walker, Cahen, and Shannon, 1980; Schiffman, Westlake, Santiago, and Edelman, 1980). Often infants who die of SIDS show signs of a low-grade illness, which may increase the tissue need for oxygen while simultaneously depressing respiratory mechanisms. Many infants' lives have been saved by monitoring devices that sound an alarm when a susceptible infant stops breathing during sleep, thus waking the parents in time for them to revive the child.

Problems Associated with REM Sleep

Narcolepsy is a neurological disorder characterized by sleep (or some of its components) at inappropriate times. The symptoms can be described in terms of what we know about the phenomena of sleep. The primary symptom of narcolepsy is the *sleep attack* (*narke* means "numbness," and *lepsis* means "seizure"). The narcoleptic sleep attack is an overwhelming urge to sleep that can happen at any time but occurs most often under monotonous, boring conditions. Sleep (which appears to be entirely normal) usually lasts for 2 to 5 minutes. The person usually wakes up feeling refreshed.

Another symptom of narcolepsy—in fact, the most striking one—is *cataplexy* (from *kata*, "down," and *plexis*, "stroke"). During a cataplectic attack a person will suddenly wilt and fall like a sack of flour. The person will lie there, conscious, for a few seconds to several minutes. What apparently happens is that one of the phenomena of REM sleep—muscular paralysis—occurs at an inappropriate time. You will recall that the EMG indicates a loss of muscle tonus during REM sleep. As we will see later, this loss of tonus is caused by massive inhibition of motor neurons. When muscular paralysis occurs during waking, the victim of a cataplectic attack falls as suddenly as if a switch had been thrown.

Cataplexy is quite different from a narcoleptic sleep attack; it is usually precipitated by strong emotion or by sudden physical effort, especially if the patient is caught unawares. Laughter, anger, or trying to catch a suddenly thrown object can trigger a cataplectic attack. Common situations that bring on cataplexy are attempting to discipline one's children or making love (a particularly awkward time to become paralyzed). Completely spontaneous attacks are rare.

REM sleep paralysis sometimes intrudes into waking, but at a time that does not present any physical danger—just before or just after normal sleep, when a person is already lying down. This symptom of narcolepsy is referred to as *sleep paralysis,* an inability to move just before the onset of sleep or upon waking in the morning. A person can be snapped out of sleep paralysis by being touched or by hearing someone call his or her name. Sometimes, the mental components of REM sleep intrude into sleep paralysis; that is, the person dreams while lying awake, paralyzed. These episodes—called *hypnagogic hallucinations* if they occur before falling asleep, and

hypnapompic hallucinations if they occur just after waking in the morning—are often alarming or even terrifying. (These terms come from the Greek words *hupnos,* "sleep," plus *agogos,* "leading," or *pompos,* "sending.")

Almost certainly, narcolepsy is produced by a brain abnormality that causes the neural mechanisms responsible for various aspects of REM sleep to become active at inappropriate times. Indeed, Rechtschaffen, Wolpert, Dement, Mitchell, and Fisher (1963) found that narcoleptic patients generally skip the slow-wave sleep that normally begins a night's sleep; instead, they go directly into REM sleep from waking. This finding suggests a deficiency in control over the brain mechanisms that produce REM sleep. Narcolepsy appears to be a genetic disorder. Kessler, Guilleminault, and Dement (1974) found that relatives of narcoleptic patients are sixty times more likely to have this disorder themselves, as compared with people from the general population; and almost all narcoleptics have a particular antigen, called HLA-DR2, in their blood (Juji, Satake, Honda, and Doi, 1984). Researchers have even successfully bred dogs that are afflicted with narcolepsy (Foutz, Mitler, Cavalli-Sforza, and Dement, 1979). The dogs show evidence of biochemical abnormalities in regions of the brain that control REM sleep (Fruhstorfer et al., 1989; Miller et al., 1990). (These regions will be discussed later in this chapter.)

The symptoms of narcolepsy can be successfully treated with drugs, which suggests that the disorder may result from abnormalities in neurotransmitter synthesis, release, or reuptake or receptor sensitivity. Sleep attacks are diminished by stimulants such as amphetamine, a catecholamine agonist, and the REM sleep phenomena (cataplexy, sleep paralysis, and hypnagogic and hypnapompic hallucinations) can be alleviated by imipramine, which facilitates both serotonergic and catecholaminergic activity. Most often, the drugs are given together.

A few years ago, Schenck, Bundlie, Ettinger, and Mahowald (1986) reported the existence of an interesting disorder. The formal name is *REM sleep behavioral disorder*, but a better name is **REM without atonia.** As you now know, REM sleep is accompanied by paralysis. Despite the fact that the motor cortex and subcortical motor systems are extremely active (McCarley and Hobson, 1979), people are unable to move at this time. The fact that they are dreaming suggests the possibility that but for the paralysis, they would act out their dreams. Indeed, they would. The behavior of people who exhibit REM without atonia corresponds with the contents of their dreams. Consider the following case:

I was a halfback playing football, and after the quarterback received the ball from the center he lateraled it sideways to me and I'm supposed to go around end and cut back over tackle and—this is very vivid—as I cut back over tackle there is this big 280-pound tackle waiting, so I, according to football rules, was to give him my shoulder and bounce him out of the way . . . when I came to I was standing in front of our dresser and I had [gotten up out of bed and run and] knocked lamps, mirrors and everything off the dresser, hit my head against the wall and my knee against the dresser. (Schenck, Bundlie, Ettinger, and Mahowald, 1986.)

As we shall see later in this chapter, the neural circuitry that controls the paralysis that accompanies REM sleep has been discovered in studies with laboratory animals. In humans REM without atonia seems to be produced by damage to the brain stem—perhaps to the same regions (Culebras and Moore, 1989).

Problems Associated with Slow-Wave Sleep

Some maladaptive behaviors occur during slow-wave sleep, especially during its deepest phase, stage 4. These behaviors include bedwetting *(nocturnal enuresis)*, sleepwalking *(somnambulism)*, and night terrors *(pavor nocturnus)*. All three events occur most frequently in children. Bedwetting can often be cured by training methods, such as having a bell ring when the first few drops of urine are detected in the bed sheet by a special electronic circuit (a few drops usually precede the ensuing flood). Night terrors consist of anguished screams, trembling, a rapid pulse, and usually no memory for what caused the terror. Night terrors and somnambulism usu-

ally cure themselves as the child gets older. Neither of these phenomena is related to REM sleep; a sleepwalking person is *not* acting out a dream. Most authorities firmly advise that the best treatment for these two disorders is no treatment at all. There is no evidence that they are associated (at least in childhood) with mental disorders or personality variables.

INTERIM SUMMARY

Although many people believe that they do not obtain as much sleep as they would like, insomnia is not a disease. Insomnia can be caused by depression, pain, illness, or even excited anticipation of a pleasurable event. Far too many people receive sleeping medications, which often lead to a condition called drug dependency insomnia. Sometimes, insomnia is caused by sleep apnea, which can often be corrected surgically. When sleep apnea occurs in infants, it can lead to sudden infant death; hence the respiration rate of susceptible infants should be monitored electronically until they are old enough to be past danger.

Narcolepsy is characterized by four symptoms. *Sleep attacks* consist of overwhelming urges to sleep for a few minutes. *Cataplexy* is sudden paralysis, during which the person remains conscious. *Sleep paralysis* is similar to cataplexy, but it occurs just before sleep or upon waking. *Hypnagogic* or *hypnapompic hallucinations* are dreams that occur during periods of sleep paralysis, just before or after a night's sleep. Sleep attacks are treated with stimulants such as amphetamine, and the other symptoms are treated with drugs such as imipramine. Studies with narcoleptic dogs suggest that the disorder may involve biochemical abnormalities in the brain. Another disorder associated with REM sleep, REM without atonia, occurs because of damage to brain stem mechanisms that produce paralysis during REM sleep.

During slow-wave sleep, especially during stage 4, some people are afflicted by bedwetting (nocturnal enuresis), sleepwalking (somnambulism), or night terrors (pavor nocturnus). These problems are most common in children, who usually outgrow them. Only if they occur in adults do they suggest the existence of a physical or psychological disorder.

BIOLOGICAL CLOCKS

Much of our behavior follows regular rhythms. For example, we saw that the stages of sleep are organized around a 90-minute cycle of REM and slow-wave sleep. The same rhythm continues during the day as the basic rest-activity cycle (BRAC). And, of course, our daily pattern of sleep and waking follows a 24-hour cycle. In recent years investigators have learned much about the neural mechanisms responsible for these rhythms.

Circadian Rhythms and Zeitgebers

Daily rhythms in behavior and physiological processes are found throughout the plant and animal world. These cycles are generally called *circadian rhythms.* (*Circa* means "about," and *dies* means "day"; therefore, a circadian rhythm is one that varies on a 24-hour cycle.) Some circadian rhythms, such as the rate of plant growth, are a di-

rect consequence of variations in the level of illumination and have no relevance to the study of sleep. However, other rhythms are controlled by mechanisms within the organism. For example, Figure 9.10 shows the activity of a rat during various conditions of illumination. Each horizontal line represents 24 hours. Vertical tick marks represent the animal's activity in a running wheel. The upper portion of the figure shows the activity of the rat during a normal day-night cycle, with alternating 12-hour periods of light and dark. Notice that the animal is active during the night, which is normal for a rat. (See *Figure 9.10.*)

Next, the day was moved forward by 6 hours; the animal's activity cycle quickly followed the change. (See *Figure 9.10.*) Finally, dim lights were left on continuously. The cyclical pattern in the rat's activity remained. Because there were no cycles in the rat's environment, the source of rhythmicity must be located within the animal; that is, the animal must contain an internal, biological clock. You can see that the rat's clock was not set precisely to 24 hours; when the illumination was held constant, the clock ran a bit slow. The animal began its bout of activity about 1 hour later each day. (See *Figure 9.10.*)

The phenomenon illustrated in Figure 9.10 is typical of the circadian rhythms shown by many

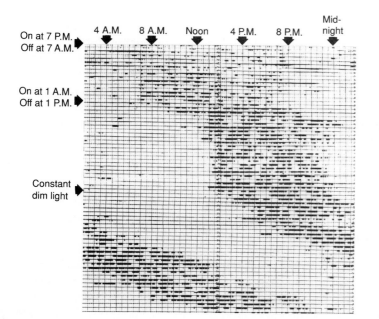

On at 7 P.M. Off at 7 A.M.

On at 1 A.M. Off at 1 P.M.

Constant dim light

4 A.M.   8 A.M.   Noon   4 P.M.   8 P.M.   Midnight

FIGURE 9.10

Wheel-running activity of a rat. Note that the animal's activity occurs at "night" (that is, during the 12 hours the light is off) and that the active period is reset when the light period is changed. When the animal is maintained in constant dim illumination, it displays a free-running activity cycle of approximately 25 hours. (From Groblewski, T.A., Nuñez, A., and Gold, R.M. Paper presented at the meeting of the Eastern Psychological Association, April 1980.)

species. A free-running clock, with a cycle a little longer than 24 hours, controls some biological functions—in this case, motor activity. Regular daily variation in the level of illumination (that is, sunlight and darkness) normally keeps the clock adjusted to 24 hours. In the parlance of scientists who study circadian rhythms, light serves as a *zeitgeber* (German for "time giver"); it synchronizes the endogenous rhythm. Studies with many species of animals have shown that if they are maintained in constant darkness, a brief flash of light will reset their internal clock, advancing or retarding it, depending upon when the light flash occurs (Aschoff, 1979). In the absence of light cycles other environmental stimuli (such as fluctuations in temperature) can serve as zeitgebers, synchronizing the animal's rhythms.

Like other animals, humans exhibit circadian rhythms. Our normal period of inactivity begins several hours after the start of the dark portion of the day-night cycle and persists for a variable amount of time into the light portion. Without the benefits of modern civilization we would probably go to sleep earlier and get up earlier than we do; we use artificial lights to delay our bedtime and window shades to extend our time for sleep. Under constant illumination our biological clocks will run free, gaining or losing time like a not-too-accurate watch. Different people have different cycle lengths, but most people in that situation will begin to live a "day" that is approximately 25 hours long.

Discovery of the Suprachiasmatic Nucleus

It has been suspected for some time that the biological clocks of mammals are neural mechanisms and that light is the primary zeitgeber. If rats are blinded, their activity cycles become free running (Browman, 1937; Richter, 1965). The observation that medial hypothalamic lesions abolished a rat's activity cycles (Richter, 1965, 1967) suggested that the clock may be located there.

Researchers working independently in two laboratories (Moore and Eichler, 1972; Stephan and Zucker, 1972) later discovered that the primary biological clock of the rat is located in the *suprachiasmatic nucleus* (SCN) of the hypothalamus; they found that lesions disrupted circadian rhythms of wheel running, drinking, and hor-

monal secretion. The SCN also provides the primary control over the timing of sleep cycles. Rats are nocturnal animals; they sleep during the day and forage and feed at night. Lesions of the SCN abolish this pattern; sleep occurs in bouts randomly dispersed throughout both day and night (Ibuka and Kawamura, 1975; Stephan and Nuñez, 1977). However, rats with SCN lesions still obtain the same amount of sleep that normal animals do. The lesions disrupt the circadian pattern but do not affect the total amount of sleep.

Figure 9.11 shows the suprachiasmatic nuclei in a transverse section through the hypothalamus of a mouse; they appear as two clusters of dark-staining neurons at the base of the brain, just above the optic chiasm. (See *Figure 9.11.*) The suprachiasmatic nuclei of the rat consist of approximately ten thousand small neurons, tightly packed into a volume of between 0.1 and 0.3 mm^3 (Meijer and Rietveld, 1989). The dendrites of these neurons form synapses with each other—a phenomenon that is found only in this part of the hypothalamus and that undoubtedly relates to the special function of these nuclei. A group of neurons is found clustered around the capillaries that serve the SCN. These neurons contain a large amount of rough endoplasmic reticulum, which suggests that they may be neurosecretory cells (Card, Riley, and Moore, 1980; Moore, Card, and Riley, 1980). Thus, some of the control that the SCN exerts over other parts of the brain may be accomplished by the secretion of neuromodulators.

Because light is the primary zeitgeber for most mammals' activity cycles, one would expect that the SCN receives fibers from the visual system. Indeed, autoradiographic techniques have revealed a direct projection of fibers from the retina to the SCN (Hendrickson, Wagoner, and Cowan, 1972). If you look carefully at Figure 9.11, you can see small dark spots within the optic chiasm, just ventral and medial to the base of the SCN; these are cell bodies of oligodendroglia that serve axons that enter the SCN and provide information from the retina. (See *Figure 9.11.*)

As we saw earlier, pulses of light reset an animal's circadian rhythms. So do pulses of electrical stimulation delivered directly to the SCN; presumably, these pulses simulate the effects of light (Rusak and Groos, 1982). The input to the SCN from the retina appears to be mediated by means

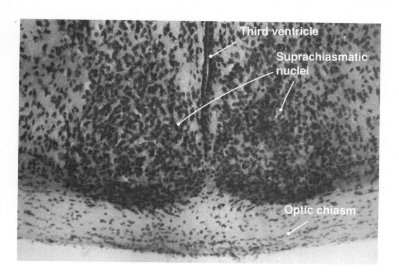

Third ventricle

Suprachiasmatic nuclei

Optic chiasm

FIGURE 9.11

A transverse section through a mouse brain, showing the location and appearance of the suprachiasmatic nuclei. Cresyl violet stain.

of an excitatory amino acid (Cahill and Menaker, 1989). In fact, an injection of glutamic acid directly into the SCN causes a shift in the timing of circadian rhythms, just as pulses of light or electrical stimulation do (Meijer, van der Zee, and Dietz, 1988).

The SCN also receives visual input indirectly, from the *intergeniculate leaflet* and the *ventral lateral geniculate nucleus* (Card and Moore, 1982, 1984). (You will recall from Chapter 6 that the *dorsal* lateral geniculate nucleus sends visual information to the striate cortex.) The input from the thalamus is mediated by a transmitter substance called *neuropeptide Y*. The geniculohypothalamic pathways appear to play a role in the effects of light on the SCN; electrical stimulation of the intergeniculate leaflet or microinfusion of neuropeptide Y directly into the SCN shifts the timing of circadian rhythms (Meijer, Rusak, and Harrington, 1984). If the geniculohypothalamic pathways are cut, an animal's circadian rhythms are still reset by changes in the light-dark cycle, but the changes occur more slowly (Rusak and Boulos, 1981). Thus, the direct pathway from the retina to the SCN and the indirect pathway through the thalamus both mediate the effects of light as a zeitgeber. Undoubtedly, there are some differences in their functions, but they have not yet been discovered.

Besides receiving fibers from the visual system, the SCN also receives input from the various regions of the diencephalon and brain stem (Meijer and Rietveld, 1989). Input from the raphe nuclei appears to be particularly important. When these nuclei are destroyed and the animals are placed in continuous light or dark, they continue to show circadian rhythms, but the rhythms are disrupted or diminished in amplitude (Block and Zucker, 1976; Levine, Rosenwasser, Yanovski, and Adler, 1986). The role that this input plays is still unknown.

How does the SCN control drinking, eating, sleep cycles, and hormone secretion? Neurons of the SCN project caudally to the midbrain and to other hypothalamic nuclei, dorsally to other diencephalic regions, and rostrally to other hypothalamic nuclei and to the septum (Swanson and Cowan, 1975; Sofroniew and Weindl, 1978). Knife cuts that interrupt the caudal efferent axons of the SCN abolish hormonal rhythms, including those that control estrous cycles in female rats (Moore and Eichler, 1972), but they do not affect cycles of feeding, drinking, and activity (Nuñez and Casati, 1979). These cycles are disrupted only by large semicircular knife cuts around most of the SCN (Meijer and Rietveld, 1989).

As I mentioned earlier, the anatomy of the SCN suggests that some of its control over the rest of the brain may be mediated by the secretion of neuromodulators. Lehman et al. (1987) obtained evidence that supports this suggestion. They destroyed the SCN and then transplanted a new set of nuclei, obtained from donor animals. The grafts succeeded in reestablishing circadian rhythms, even though very few efferent connections were observed. Ralph, Foster, Davis, and Menaker (1990) found that such transplants could establish circadian rhythms within 6 or 7 days. Thus, either the SCN needs very few connections with the rest of the brain to exert its control, or that control is mediated through the secretion of neuro-modulators.

Although experimental studies have obviously not been done, it appears likely that the primary biological clock that controls human sleep and waking cycles is also located in the SCN. Humans certainly have circadian rhythms, and these rhythms are affected by exposure to light—even ordinary room light (Czeisler, Kronauer, Allan, Duffy, Jewett, Brown, and Ronda, 1989). Anatomical studies clearly show that humans have suprachiasmatic nuclei (Lydic, Schoene, Czeisler, and Moore-Ede, 1980). In addition, brain tumors that damage the region of the SCN have been reported to produce disorders in sleep-waking cycles (Fulton and Bailey, 1929). Of course, these tumors damage a wide area of the hypothalamus, and we cannot be sure that the SCN damage is critical.

Evidence That Circadian Rhythms Originate in the SCN

Obviously, the SCN is the crucial element in the generation of endogenous circadian rhythms.

And yet the evidence presented so far does not prove that the cycles *originate* there; it is conceivable that they could originate elsewhere, be passed on to the SCN, and from there be distributed to the rest of the brain. But as it turns out, the SCN *is* the source of the rhythms.

A study by Schwartz and Gainer (1977) nicely demonstrated day-night fluctuations in the activity of the SCN. These investigators injected rats with radioactive 2-deoxyglucose (2-DG). As you will recall, this chemical is structurally similar to ordinary glucose; thus, it is taken up by cells that are metabolically active. However, it cannot be utilized, nor can it leave the cell. Therefore, metabolically active cells will accumulate radioactivity. (This technique was also used in a study on the visual mechanisms of the cerebral cortex, reported in Chapter 6.)

The investigators injected some rats with radioactive 2-DG during the day and injected others at night. The animals were then killed, and autoradiographs of cross sections through the brain were prepared. Figure 9.12 shows photographs of two of these cross sections. Note the evidence of radioactivity (and hence a high metabolic rate) in the SCN of the brain that was injected during the day (*left*). (See *Figure 9.12.*)

Schwartz and his colleagues (Schwartz, Reppert, Eagan, and Moore-Ede, 1983) found a similar pattern of activity in the SCN of squirrel monkeys, which are diurnal animals (active during the day). These results suggest that it is not dif-

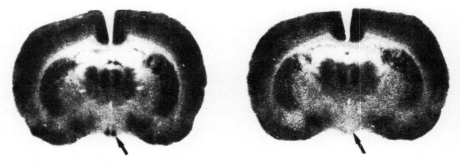

FIGURE 9.12
Autoradiographs of transverse sections through the brains of rats that had been injected with carbon 14-labeled 2-deoxyglucose during the day (*left*) and the night (*right*). The dark region at the base of the brain (*arrows*) indicates increased metabolic activity of the suprachiasmatic nuclei. (From Schwartz, W.J., and Gainer, H. *Science*, 1977, *197*, 1089–1091.)

ferences in the SCN that determine whether an animal is nocturnal or diurnal but differences elsewhere in the brain. The SCN keeps track of day and night, but it is up to mechanisms located elsewhere to determine when the animal is to be awake or asleep.

Recordings of electrical activity support the conclusions made from other approaches. Inouye and Kawamura (1979) recorded the activity of neurons in the hypothalamus and in other parts of the brain, such as the caudate nucleus. Neurons in both regions showed a regular fluctuation in firing rate across day-night cycles. Presumably, these fluctuations were controlled by the SCN. However, when knife cuts completely separated the hypothalamus from the rest of the brain, the firing rate of neurons in the caudate nucleus became constant, while those of hypothalamic neurons remained cyclical. (See *Figure 9.13*.)

The Nature of the Clock

All clocks must have a time base. Mechanical clocks use flywheels or pendulums; electronic clocks use quartz crystals. The SCN, too, must contain a physiological mechanism that parses time into units. So far, we do not know what this mechanism is. One hypothesis suggests that a time base may be provided by the synthesis of proteins (Jacklet, 1978). Perhaps cells begin to synthesize protein, and as the level of this product rises, negative feedback shuts down the synthetic process. The protein is then degraded or dispersed over time, and the low level of protein permits the cycle to begin again. The presence of the protein could affect some property of neurons in the region (for example, their membrane permeability) and alter their rate of firing.

Evidence concerning this hypothesis is mixed. Inouye, Takahashi, Wollnik, and Turek (1988) injected *anisomycin*, a drug that temporarily inhibits protein synthesis, into the SCN. The injection reset the timing of free-running circadian rhythms. However, Scammell, Schwartz, and Smith (1989) used an autoradiographic technique to measure the rate of protein synthesis in the rat SCN across the day-night cycle and failed to observe any circadian rhythms.

The "ticking" of the biological clock within the SCN could involve interactions of circuits of neu-

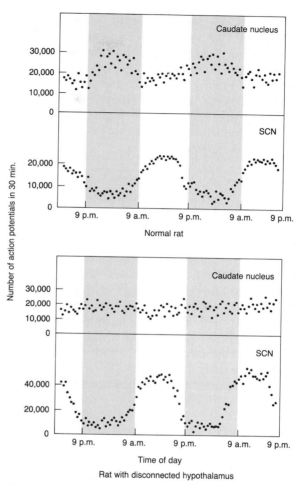

FIGURE 9.13

Activity of single units in the caudate nucleus and suprachiasmatic nucleus in an intact rat (*top*) and in a rat whose hypothalamus had been surgically disconnected (*bottom*). (Previously unpublished graph courtesy of S.T. Inouye.)

rons, or it could be intrinsic to individual neurons themselves. Evidence suggests the latter—that each neuron contains a clock. Moore and Bernstein (1989) studied the prenatal and postnatal development of the SCN in the rat. Previous reports (Reppert and Schwartz, 1984) had shown that circadian rhythms in glucose metabolism are found in these nuclei prenatally, as early as the nineteenth day after conception. However, Moore and Bernstein found that at this time the SCN contains fewer than one synapse per neuron, which seems to indicate that the neurons are "ticking" independently. In addition, Schwartz,

Gross, and Morton (1987) found that continuous infusion of TTX (tetrodotoxin), a drug that prevents action potentials by blocking voltage-dependent ion channels, abolishes circadian rhythms. However, the drug does not appear to stop the "ticking" of the individual cells; when the infusions are stopped, the animals' circadian rhythms continued as if the clock had been running the whole time.

Evidence for Other Biological Clocks

The SCN is not the only biological clock in the mammalian nervous system. For example, the basic rest-activity cycle (which controls the occurrence of REM sleep) is considerably shorter than 24 hours; in humans, it has a 90-minute period. In addition, Fuller, Lydic, Sulzman, Albers, Tepper, and Moore-Ede (1981) found that destruction of the SCN in squirrel monkeys abolished circadian rhythms in sleep-activity patterns but did not affect daily rhythms in body temperature. Thus, the biological clock that controls body temperature must be located outside the SCN. However, even these clocks are controlled to some extent by the SCN. Satinoff and Prosser (1988) found that although SCN lesions did not abolish daily rhythms in body temperature, the length of the cycle changed.

Animals who are fed on a regular daily schedule will soon become active just before the feeding time. This anticipation obviously depends upon some internal clock, because it occurs in the absence of environmental cues. Boulos, Rosenwasser, and Terman (1980) found that rats showed this anticipation even after their SCN was destroyed; therefore, another clock must be able to perform this function. (See *Figure 9.14.*)

Although the SCN has an intrinsic rhythm of approximately 24 hours, it plays a role in much longer rhythms. Male hamsters show annual rhythms of testosterone secretion, which appear to be based upon the amount of light that occurs each day. Their breeding season begins as the day length increases and ends when it decreases. Lesions of the SCN abolish these annual breeding cycles; the animals' testes then secrete testosterone all year (Rusak and Morin, 1976). Possibly, the lesions disrupt these annual cycles because they

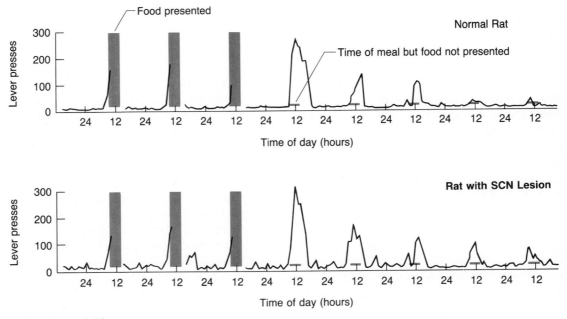

FIGURE 9.14
Anticipation of a meal. After being fed at the same time each day, both a normal rat (*top*) and a rat with bilateral SCN lesions (*bottom*) increase their lever-pressing activity at the customary time for feeding. (From Boulos, Z., Rosenwasser, A.M., and Terman, M. *Behavioral Brain Research*, 1980, *1*, 39–65.)

destroy the 24-hour clock against which the daily light period is measured to determine the season. That is, if the light period is considerably shorter than 12 hours, the season is winter; if it is considerably longer than 12 hours, the season is summer.

Much progress has been made in the investigation of the neural mechanisms of biological rhythms during the past few years. The unanswered questions concern the nature of the physiological processes that provide the underlying rhythm, the location of biological clocks other than the SCN, and the means by which these clocks influence cyclic behaviors such as sleep and waking.

*I*NTERIM SUMMARY

Our daily lives are characterized by cycles in physical activity, sleep, body temperature, secretion of hormones, and many other physiological changes. Circadian rhythms, those with a period of approximately one day, are controlled by biological clocks in the brain. The principal biological clock appears to be located in the suprachiasmatic nuclei of the hypothalamus; lesions of these nuclei disrupt most circadian rhythms, and the activity of neurons located there correlates with the day-night cycle. Light serves as a zeitgeber for most circadian rhythms. That is, the biological clocks tend to run a bit slow, with a period of approximately 25 hours. The sight of sunlight in the morning is conveyed from the retina to the SCN, resetting the clock to the start of a new cycle. We do not know how biological clocks keep time, although some investigators suggest that the rate of protein synthesis times the individual "ticks."

PHYSIOLOGICAL MECHANISMS OF SLEEP AND WAKING

So far, I have discussed the nature of sleep, its functions, problems associated with it, and the control of biological rhythms. Now it is time to see what researchers have discovered about the physiological mechanisms that are responsible for the behavior of sleep.

Factors That Trigger Sleep

As we have seen, sleep is *regulated;* that is, if an organism is deprived of slow-wave sleep or REM sleep, the organism will make up at least part of the missed sleep when permitted to do so. In addition, the amount of slow-wave sleep that a person obtains during a daytime nap is deducted from the amount of slow-wave sleep he or she obtains the next night (Karacan, Williams, Finley, and Hursch, 1970). These facts suggest that some physiological mechanism monitors the amount of sleep that an organism receives. What might this mechanism be?

The most obvious explanation would be that the body produces either *sleep-promoting substances* during wakefulness or *wakefulness-promoting* substances during sleep. For example, a sleep-promoting substance might accumulate in the blood during wakefulness and be destroyed during sleep. The longer someone is awake, the longer he or she has to sleep in order to deactivate this substance. Obviously, because slow-wave sleep and REM sleep are mostly independent of each other, there would have to be two substances, one for each stage of sleep. Alternatively, sleep could be regulated by a *wakefulness-promoting* substance. This substance would be used up during wakefulness and be manufactured only during sleep. A *decline* in the blood level of this substance would cause sleepiness.

Evidence suggests that these hypotheses are false. De Andres, Gutierrez-Rivas, Nava, and Reinoso-Suarez (1976) attached a second head to a dog and found that the two brains slept independently. If sleep and wakefulness were controlled by factors present in the blood, one would expect that the sleep cycles of the two brains would be synchronized. (Of course, the second head was neurally isolated from the rest of the body and had no control of the animal's behavior.) Reports of human Siamese twins with a common cerebral blood supply have been mixed; Lenard and Schulte (1972) reported that such twins have independent sleep cycles, whereas Lahmeyer (1988) found that the similarity in the cycles of another set of Siamese twins was higher than would be expected by chance. But perhaps the strongest evidence against a hypothetical blood-borne sleep-promoting (or wakefulness-promoting) substance comes from the sleep of dolphins and porpoises. As we saw earlier, the cerebral hemispheres of these animals sleep at different times (Mukhametov, 1984). If their sleep were controlled by *blood-borne* chemicals, the hemispheres should sleep at the same time.

These observations suggest that if sleep is controlled by chemicals, these chemicals are produced within the brain and remain there. As we saw, evidence seems to support the hypothesis that slow-wave sleep serves as a period of rest and recuperation for the cerebral hemispheres. Perhaps chemicals produced by the brain serve as neuromodulators, activating neural circuits responsible for sleep (or deactivating circuits necessary for wakefulness).

The most obvious approach would be to transfer cerebrospinal fluid from a sleepy animal to one that is not and see whether the recipient animal became sleepy. Because the barrier between the brain and the cerebrospinal fluid is weaker than the blood-brain barrier, such experiments might reveal the existence of chemicals produced by the brain. Although experiments performed early in this century seemed to have been successful (Piéron, 1913), subsequent research indicated that the injection of any substance into an animal's cerebral ventricles changes their patterns of sleep; and when control groups are used, positive results are not seen.

In a fifty-two page article that cites over four hundred papers, Borbély and Tobler (1989) report that the search for endogenous sleep-promoting substances has not yet yielded unambiguous results. Some very potent sleep-promoting substances have been found, such as the *muramyl peptides* discovered by Krueger, Pappenheimer, and Karnovski (1982a), who extracted 30 micrograms from 4.5 tons of human urine. This substance, which appears to be produced by bacteria present in the intestine, was subsequently analyzed and synthesized (Krueger, Pappenheimer, and Karnovsky, 1982b). The muramyl peptides appear to exert their sleep-promoting effect by causing glial cells present in the brain to release *interleukin-1* (IL-1), a peptide that plays a role in the immune response (Krueger, et al., 1987). One of the effects of IL-1 is hyperthermia (increased

body temperature), which is one of the means by which the body fights an infection. As we saw earlier, even short-term increases in brain temperature cause increases in slow-wave sleep. Thus, although some studies have shown that acetaminophen (an aspirinlike drug) reduces the effect of muramyl peptides on body temperature without eliminating their sleep-promoting effect, it still seems likely that they produced an increase in *brain* temperature (Shoham and Krueger, 1988).

As we saw earlier, Nicolaïdis, Danguir, and Mather (1979) found that in rats periods of sleep were closely related to the size of the meal that they had just eaten. Subsequently, Danguir and Nicolaïdis (1980) found that both slow-wave and REM sleep were related to food intake, but in different ways. A meal rich in proteins caused an increase in REM sleep, whereas a meal rich in carbohydrates caused an increase in slow-wave sleep. Fats had no effect on sleep. Further studies suggested that the results may have been mediated by hormones that are secreted when these substances are ingested. For example, the administration of insulin, which is secreted in response to a meal rich in carbohydrates, selectively increased slow-wave sleep, and the administration of insulin antiserum reduced it (Danguir and Nicolaïdis, 1984). On the other hand, the administration of *somatostatin*, somatostatin, a hormone that is secreted in response to a meal rich in proteins, selectively increased REM sleep, and, yes, the administration of somatostatin antiserum reduced it (Danguir, 1986, 1988). These hormones were all administered in small quantities by infusion into the cerebrospinal fluid, so their effects were produced by their actions on receptors in the brain. Whether these hormones affect sleep directly or whether they do so by altering other aspects of metabolism controlled by the brain is not yet known.

Whatever their mechanisms may be, the effects of insulin and somatostatin should probably be regarded as *modulating* sleep rather than controlling it. First, evidence indicates that blood-borne chemicals do not seem to be responsible for the primary control of sleep. Second, the effects of starvation are very different in humans and rats. If rats are starved, their slow-wave sleep decreases, as would be predicted by the results of the experiments by Danguir and his colleagues (Jacobs and McGinty, 1971). However, if humans are starved, their slow-wave sleep *increases* (MacFadyen, Oswald, and Lewis, 1973). Clearly, we need to know more about the relation between nutrition and sleep.

We should not conclude that because an endogenous sleep-promoting (or wakefulness-promoting) substance has not yet been unambiguously identified in the brain means that there is none to be found there; after all, there are undoubtedly many thousands of chemicals present in the fluid that bathes the cells of the brain. The fact that sleep is regulated means that *something* has to keep track of the sleep debt, and it is difficult (at least for me) to imagine what that something would be if it were not a chemical. Perhaps it is a chemical that accumulates *inside* individual neurons in the brain; if so, it will probably take some time before investigators succeed in identifying it.

Neural Control of Arousal

As we have seen, sleep is not a unitary condition but consists of several different stages with very different characteristics. Wakefulness, too, is nonuniform; sometimes, we are alert and attentive, and sometimes, we fail to notice much about what is happening around us. Of course, sleepiness has an effect on wakefulness; if we are fighting to stay awake, the struggle might impair our ability to concentrate on other things. But everyday observations suggest that even when we are not sleepy, our alertness can vary. For example, when we observe something very interesting (or frightening, or simply surprising), we feel ourselves become more activated and aware of our surroundings.

The Reticular Formation

Experimental evidence suggests that the brain stem contains circuits of neurons that can increase an animal's level of alertness and activation— what is commonly referred to as *arousal*. In 1949 Moruzzi and Magoun found that electrical stimulation of the brain stem reticular formation produced arousal. The reticular formation, which occupies the central core of the brain stem, receives collateral axons from ascending sensory pathways. Presumably, sensory input, the event that normally produces arousal, activates the reticular formation by means of these collateral axons. The activated reticular formation then arouses the cerebral cortex by means of direct axonal connections and by connections relayed through various nuclei of the thalamus.

Lindsley, Schreiner, Knowles, and Magoun (1950) obtained evidence that the arousing effect of sensory stimulation is indeed mediated through the reticular formation. They made lesions that disrupted the direct sensory pathways that run through the pons and midbrain. They found that tactile stimulation would still arouse these animals. Because the lesions destroyed the direct sensory pathways (which go to the thalamus, and from there to the somatosensory cortex), the arousal was obviously mediated by the indirect projections through the reticular formation. Although the animals presumably could not "feel" the stimulation, they nevertheless were aroused by it. In contrast, when the investigators made lesions that destroyed the reticular formation, sensory stimulation produced only a very brief period of arousal. (See *Figure 9.15.*)

Recording studies soon provided evidence that supported the stimulation and lesion studies. Multiple-unit activity (the action potentials of a large population of neurons located near the tip of the recording electrode) showed a relation between arousal and the firing rate of neurons in the reticular formation. For example, Machne, Calma, and Magoun (1955) found that neurons in the reticular formation increased their firing rate when cats were aroused by stimulating a peripheral nerve, and Bambridge and Gijsbers (1977) found a correlation between behavioral arousal and multiple-unit activity of the reticular formation in unrestrained cats.

The reticular formation is an extensive and complex brain structure, and once its role in arousal was well accepted, investigators attempted to find out the specific location of the arousal mechanisms. They began to study single-unit activity in freely moving cats, which allows for maximum specificity. Unfortunately, careful study of the activity patterns of individual neurons failed to support the hypothesis that the re-

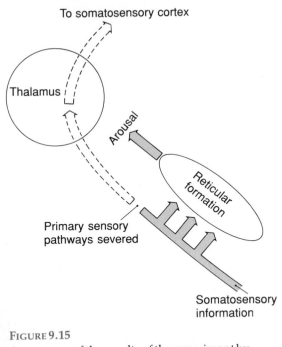

To somatosensory cortex

Thalamus

Arousal

Reticular formation

Primary sensory pathways severed

Somatosensory information

FIGURE 9.15
A summary of the results of the experiment by Lindsley and colleagues (1950).

ticular formation performs a general arousal function. Investigators found, instead, that the activity of individual neurons was closely related to specific movements of the eyes, ears, face, head, body, and limbs (Siegel, 1979, 1983). Their response rate was not related to general levels of arousal or to sleep-waking cycles.

Siegel (1979, 1983) suggests two reasons for the discrepancy. First, relations between movements and single-unit activity obviously cannot be observed in anesthetized or physically restrained cats. Many studies have used such cats and consequently have failed to observe the animals' behavior. Second, multiple-unit recording averages the activity of many neurons. If different groups of neurons are active during different types of movements, then the population *as a whole* may respond nonspecifically, which may lead the investigator to conclude erroneously that *all* of them are responding nonspecifically. Siegel explains the increased activity of neurons in the reticular formation in terms of their relation to movement. For example, suppose that an investigator finds that multiple-unit activity increases

when a cat anticipates receiving a painful foot shock or receiving some food. Because both events can be thought of as "arousing," the investigator may conclude that the units mediate nonspecific arousal. However, the results could actually have been produced by two different groups of neurons: one group that fires during ear flattening (a response that cats commonly make when they are fearful) and another group that fires during the postural adjustments the cat makes in anticipation of obtaining food.

The Noradrenergic System of the Locus Coeruleus

Although the reticular formation as a whole appears to be primarily involved in the control of movement, a small nucleus found there appears to have a profound effect on arousal. Investigators have long known that catecholamine agonists such as amphetamine produce arousal and sleeplessness. These effects appear to be mediated by the noradrenergic system of the *locus coeruleus,* located in the dorsal pons. Neurons of the locus coeruleus send axons that branch widely, terminating in the neocortex, hippocampus, thalamus, cerebellar cortex, pons, and medulla; thus, they potentially affect widespread and important regions of the brain. (See *Figure 9.16.*) Jones, Bobillier, and Jouvet (1969) made a lesion that interrupted the ascending axons from the neurons of the rostral locus coeruleus. They found that the animals' REM sleep and slow-wave sleep increased dramatically. Thus, there is evidence that the ascending noradrenergic system is involved in arousal (or at least in the suppression of sleep).

More recent studies have clarified the role that the locus coeruleus appears to play in arousal. Aston-Jones and Bloom (1981a) recorded from noradrenergic neurons of the locus coeruleus across the sleep-waking cycle in unrestrained rats. As Figure 9.17 shows, these neurons exhibited an excellent relation to behavioral arousal. Note the decline in firing rate before and during sleep and the abrupt increase when the animal wakes. The rate of firing of neurons in the locus coeruleus falls almost to zero during REM sleep and increases dramatically when the animal wakes. As we shall see later in this chapter, these facts suggest that

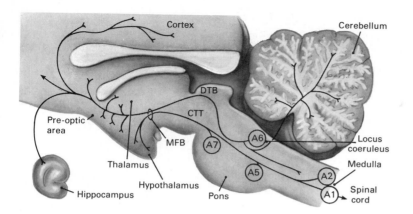

FIGURE 9.16

The principal noradrenergic pathways. CTT = central tegmental tract; DTB = dorsal tegmental bundle; MFB = medial forebrain bundle.

these neurons play a role in controlling REM sleep. (See *Figure 9.17.*)

Aston-Jones and Bloom (1981a, 1981b) found that when they aroused the animals by sudden environmental stimuli during sleep or quiet wakefulness, the noradrenergic neurons suddenly increased their activity. In addition, they increased their rate of firing approximately 3 seconds before waking (as defined by changes in the EMG record). Thus, these neurons may well be involved in arousal. However, the firing rate of these neurons was very low while the animals were grooming or drinking sweetened water—activities that are accompanied by a high level of arousal. The authors suggested that the activity of noradrenergic neurons showed a better correlation with *vigilance* than with arousal. That is, at times when the animals were sensitive to external

stimuli, the neurons were found to be firing at a high rate.

Aston-Jones and his colleagues suggest that the specific physiological function of noradrenergic neurons is to increase the animal's sensitivity to environmental stimuli (Aston-Jones, 1985). Several studies support this conclusion. Electrical stimulation of the locus coeruleus or application of norepinephrine by means of microiontophoresis makes neurons that receive noradrenergic projections become more responsive to external stimuli (Foote, Bloom, and Aston-Jones, 1983; Waterhouse et al., 1988). As we saw earlier, noradrenergic neurons send axons throughout the brain and thus are in a position to influence a vast number of neurons.

Aston-Jones, Ennis, Pieribone, Nickell, and Shipley (1986) injected horseradish peroxidase in

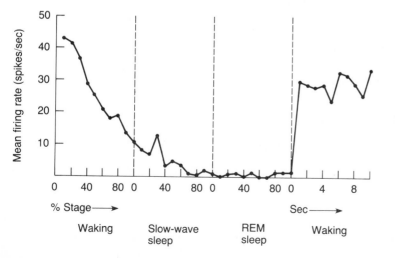

FIGURE 9.17

Activity of noradrenergic neurons in the locus coeruleus of freely moving cats during various stages of sleep and waking. (From Aston-Jones, G., and Bloom, F.E. *The Journal of Neuroscience*, 1981, *1*, 876–886. Copyright 1981, The Society for Neuroscience.)

the locus coeruleus in order to determine the sources of its afferent inputs. To their surprise, they found only two significant inputs: a nucleus in the ventrolateral medulla and another in the dorsomedial medulla. Ennis and Aston-Jones (1986, 1988) recorded single-unit activity in the locus coeruleus while electrically stimulating the two regions of the medulla that project to it. They found that one input produced excitation while the other produced inhibition. Obviously, the next step will be to investigate the sources of input to *these* regions. The excitatory input appears to be able to increase an animal's vigilance, and the inhibitory one to decrease it. In addition, as you will see in the last section of this chapter, the event that triggers the onset of REM sleep appears to be the cessation of activity in the locus coeruleus and the raphe nuclei. Perhaps, then, knowing more about the region of the medulla that provides inhibitory input to the locus coeruleus will tell us something about the control of REM sleep.

Neural Control of Slow-Wave Sleep

Although researchers have made considerable progress in identifying the neural circuits responsible for REM sleep (discussed in the final section of this chapter), relatively little is known about the neural control of slow-wave sleep. This state of af-

fairs is somewhat ironic, given the fact that slow-wave sleep appears to be the most important stage of sleep. Two parts of the brain have been implicated in slow-wave sleep: the nucleus of the solitary tract and the basal forebrain region.

The Nucleus of the Solitary Tract

The *nucleus of the solitary tract* is a structure located in the medulla that receives taste information and visceral sensation. (You already learned about this structure in Chapter 7.) Surprisingly, it may also play a role in sleep. Berlucchi, Maffei, Moruzzi, and Strata (1964) cooled the medulla by placing a metal plate on the floor of the fourth ventricle, through which a cold liquid could be circulated. The cooling, which produces a temporary lesion, resulted in behavioral and EEG arousal, even if the cat was previously asleep. This study suggests that the activity of some region of the medulla is necessary for sleep.

Magnes, Moruzzi, and Pompeiano (1961) stimulated the region of the nucleus of the solitary tract with low-frequency electrical current. The stimulation had a synchronizing effect on the cat's EEG, which is usually synonymous with sleepiness. Figure 9.18 shows the effects of such stimulation on the EEG. The tick marks on the lower line represent the stimulation; note that the cortical synchrony continues even after the stimulation is turned off. (See *Figure 9.18.*)

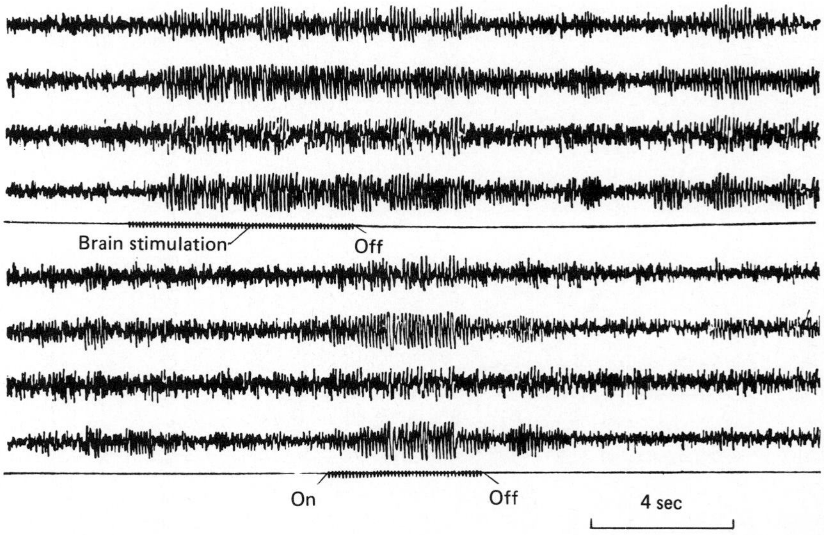

FIGURE 9.18
The effects of electrical stimulation in the region of the nucleus of the solitary tract. (From Magnes, J., Moruzzi, G., and Pompeiano, O. *Archives Italiennes de Biologie*, 1961, 99, 33–67.)

The nucleus of the solitary tract receives sensory information from the tongue and from various internal organs. Bonvallet and Sigg (1958) found that stimulation of the vagus nerve (which sends fibers to this region) produces EEG synchrony. Pompeiano and Swett (1962) stimulated cutaneous nerves in unanesthetized, freely moving cats and found that repetitive, low-frequency stimulation produced EEG synchrony when the cat was in a relatively quiet state. They subsequently found that neurons in the medulla fired in response to this nerve stimulation (Pompeiano and Swett, 1963). Kukorelli and Juhasz (1977) found that electrical stimulation of the intestines, which send information to the nucleus of the solitary tract, increased sleep. This increase occurred even in cats who were deprived of food and would normally be alert and active.

It seems likely that the calming effects of gentle rocking (which usually soothes a baby) are mediated by neurons in the nucleus of the solitary tract. Perhaps we can also thus account for the fact that a large meal makes us sleepy, because the nucleus of the solitary tract receives sensory inputs from the digestive tract.

Few studies have recorded the activity of single neurons in the nucleus of the solitary tract. One that did found that more than half of them increased their firing rate during (but not prior to) slow-wave sleep (Eguchi and Satoh, 1980). These results suggest that although the nucleus of the solitary tract may play some role in slow-wave sleep, it is probably not the place that *produces* sleep; if it were, we would expect that the neurons located there would increase their rate of firing just before sleep occurred, not after it had already commenced.

The Basal Forebrain Region

The *basal forebrain region*—an area of the forebrain that includes the preoptic area, located just rostral to the hypothalamus—also appears to play a role in sleep. Nauta (1946) found that destruction of this area produced total insomnia in rats. The animals subsequently fell into a coma and died; the average survival time was only three days. McGinty and Sterman (1968) found that cats reacted somewhat differently; the animals did not become sleepless until several days after the le-

sion was made. Two of the cats, whose sleep was totally suppressed, died within ten days. Infusions of kainic acid, which destroys cell bodies without damaging axons passing through the region, also suppresses sleep (Szymusiak and McGinty, 1986b).

The effects of the lesion experiments are corroborated by the effects of electrical stimulation of the basal forebrain region. Sterman and Clemente (1962a, 1962b) found that electrical stimulation of this region produced cortical synchrony and drowsiness in unanesthetized, freely moving cats. The average latency period between stimulation and EEG synchrony was 30 seconds; often the effect was immediate. Behavioral sleep frequently followed.

Szymusiak and McGinty (1986a) recorded the activity of single neurons in the basal forebrain of cats. The found that some neurons were more active during non-REM sleep than waking, some were more active during waking than non-REM sleep, and some showed no change in rate. In all cases the rate of activity was similar during waking and REM sleep. In a follow-up study Szymusiak and McGinty (1989) found that all of the neurons that became active during sleep had slowly conducting axons and sent projections both to other forebrain structures and to the brain stem. The exact location of these projections was not determined.

One part of the basal forebrain, the preoptic area, contains neurons that are involved in temperature regulation. Some of these neurons are directly sensitive to changes in brain temperature, and some receive information from thermosensors located in the skin. Warming of the preoptic area produces drowsiness and EEG synchrony (Roberts and Robinson, 1969; Benedek, Obal, Lelkes, and Obal, 1982). Thus, a more "natural" stimulation mimics the effects of electrical stimulation. The excessive sleepiness that accompanies a fever may be produced by this mechanism. Perhaps the connections between the preoptic area and thermosensors in the skin account for the drowsiness and lassitude we feel on a hot day. In fact, Pavlov (1923) noted that when thermal stimulation of the skin was used as a stimulus in studies of classical conditioning, the dogs he was training often fell asleep.

Neural Control of REM Sleep

As we saw earlier in this chapter, REM sleep consists of desynchronized EEG activity, muscular paralysis, rapid eye movements, and (in humans, at least) increased genital activity. In laboratory animals REM sleep also includes *PGO waves*. **PGO waves** (for *p*ons, *g*eniculate, and *o*ccipital) are the first manifestation of REM sleep. They consist of brief, phasic bursts of electrical activity that originate in the pons and are propagated to the lateral geniculate nuclei and then to the primary visual (occipital) cortex. They undoubtedly occur also in humans, but obviously, curiosity is not a good enough reason to place electrodes within a human brain. Figure 9.19 shows the typical onset of REM sleep, recorded in a cat. The first sign of an impending bout of REM sleep is the presence of PGO waves—in this case, recorded from electrodes implanted in the lateral geniculate nucleus. Next, the EEG becomes desynchronized, and then muscular activity ceases and rapid eye movements commence. (See *Figure 9.19.*)

As we shall see, REM sleep is controlled by mechanisms located within the brain stem—primarily within the pons. The executive mechanism (that is, the one whose activity turns on the various components of REM sleep) is acetylcholinergic. It is normally inhibited by the serotonergic neurons of the raphe nuclei and the noradrenergic neurons of the locus coeruleus.

Acetylcholine

Drugs that excite acetylcholinergic synapses facilitate REM sleep. Stoyva and Metcalf (1968) found that people who have been exposed to organophosphate insecticides, which inhibit acetylcholinesterase (AChE) and therefore increase the postsynaptic effects of acetylcholine, spend an increased time in REM sleep. In a controlled experiment Sitaram, Wyatt, Dawson, and Gillin (1976) administered intravenous injections of an AChE inhibitor (physostigmine) to human subjects during sleep. If the subjects were in slow-wave sleep, the injections induced REM sleep. Sitaram, Moore, and Gillin (1978) compared the effects of an AChE inhibitor (arecoline), a muscarinic blocker (scopolamine) and a placebo on REM sleep. Relative to the placebo, the acetylcholinergic agonist (arecoline) shortened the interval between periods of REM sleep, and the cholinergic antagonist (scopolamine) lengthened it.

Jasper and Tessier (1969) analyzed the levels of acetylcholine that had been released by terminal buttons in the cat cerebral cortex. The levels were highest during waking and REM sleep and were lowest during slow-wave sleep. This finding suggests that the activity of acetylcholinergic neurons is related to the desynchrony seen in these two states.

The brain contains several acetylcholinergic pathways. A group of cells within the medial septal nucleus and the diagonal band project to the hippocampus. Another group, located in and around the nucleus basalis, projects to the amygdala and neocortex (Mesulam, Mufson, Wainer, and Levey, 1983). In the brain stem, acetylcholinergic neurons are found in the dorsolateral pons, primarily in the *pedunculopontine tegmental nucleus* (PPT) and *laterodorsal tegmental nucleus* (LDT) (Jones and Beaudet, 1987). These neurons project to the thalamus, hippocampus, hypothalamus, and cingulate cortex. Acetylcholinergic neurons are also found in the cranial motor nerve nuclei and in the medullary reticular formation; the latter project into the spinal cord.

The effects of acetylcholine on REM sleep take place in the pons. If a small amount of an acetylcholinergic agonist is infused into the pons, the animal will exhibit PGO waves alone, muscular paralysis alone, or all the signs of REM sleep, depending on the location of the infusion (Katayama, DeWitt, Becker, and Hayes, 1986; Callaway, Lydic, Baghdoyan, and Hobson, 1987). The neurons that give rise to these waves are cholinergic and are found in the immediate vicinity of the superior cerebellar peduncle, in the laterodorsal pons. Figure 9.20 contains a series of

FIGURE 9.19

Onset of REM sleep in a cat. The arrows indicate the onset of PGO waves, EEG desynchrony, loss of muscular activity, and rapid eye movements. LG = lateral geniculate nucleus; EOG = electro-oculogram (eye movements). (Adapted from Steriade, M., Paré, D., Bouhassira, D., Deschênes, M., and Oakson, G. *Journal of Neuroscience*, 1989, *9*, 2215–2229.) Reprinted by permission of the *Journal of Neuroscience*.

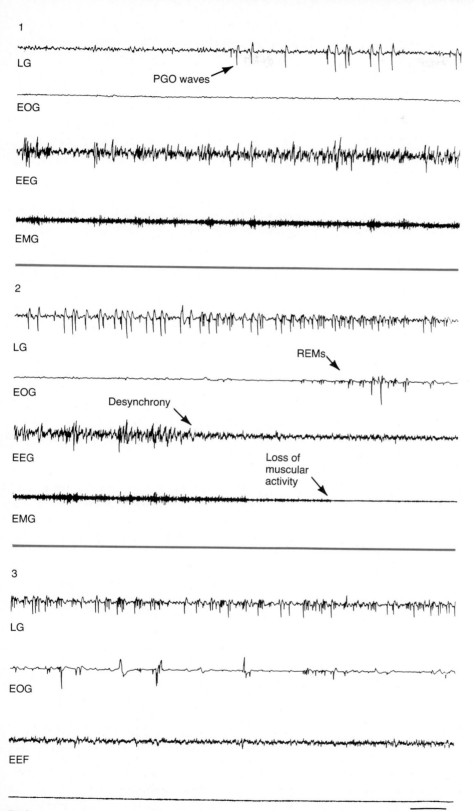

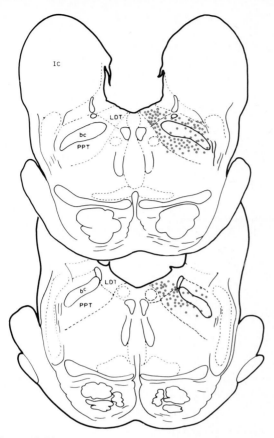

FIGURE 9.20
Acetylcholinergic neurons in the brain stem of the cat (colored circles) as revealed by a stain for choline acetyltransferase. (Adapted from Jones, B.E., and Baudet, A. *Journal of Comparative Neurology*, 1987, *261*, 15–32.)

drawings through the brain stem of a cat, prepared by Jones and Beaudet (1987). The location of acetylcholinergic cell bodies, detected by a stain for choline acetyltransferase (the enzyme that is responsible for the production of acetylcholine) is shown by colored circles. As you can see by comparing the labels on the left side with the filled circles on the right, most of these neurons are found in the LDT and the PPT. (See *Figure 9.20*.)

Figure 9.21 shows the intracellularly recorded activity of a single unit in the pons during the transition from slow-wave sleep to REM sleep (McCarley, 1989). The upper tracings show the EMG, the EEG, PGO waves (recorded in the lateral ge-

niculate nucleus), and the EOG. The fifth tracing shows the membrane potential of the neuron in the pons, and the bottom tracing shows the action potentials of this neuron sampled at four different times, as indicated by the colored brackets. As you can see, the membrane potential of the neuron became more and more depolarized during the transition from slow-wave to REM sleep, which caused its rate of activity to increase. (See *Figure 9.21*.)

Destruction of the region of the pons that contains acetylcholinergic neurons drastically reduces REM sleep. Webster and Jones (1988) made lesions by infusing kainic acid into this region. They found that the amount of REM sleep that remained was directly related to the number of cholinergic neurons that were spared. Figure 9.22 shows a photomicrograph through the pons of a normal cat (a) and a cat with a kainic acid lesion (b). Acetylcholinergic neurons show up as black granules. As you can see, few of them remain in the cat with the lesion. (See *Figure 9.22*.)

If the acetylcholinergic neurons in the dorsolateral pons are responsible for the onset of REM sleep, how do they control each of its components, PGO waves, rapid eye movements, cortical desynchrony, and muscular paralysis? The control of PGO waves appears to be direct; Sakai and Jouvet (1980) found that pontine neurons that showed bursts of activity just before each PGO wave had direct connections with the lateral geniculate nucleus. Webster and Jones (1988) suggest that the control of rapid eye movements may be achieved by projections from the dorsolateral pons to the superior colliculus and the medullary reticular formation, and the control of cortical desynchrony by projections to several thalamic nuclei, including those that have widespread projections to the cerebral cortex.

The muscular paralysis that accompanies REM sleep is a particularly interesting phenomenon. As we saw earlier, some patients with lesions in the brain stem fail to become paralyzed during REM sleep and thus act out their dreams. (As you will recall, the phenomenon is called *REM without atonia*.) The same thing happens—that is, assuming that cats dream—when a lesion is placed just caudal to the region of the dorsolateral pons that contains the acetylcholinergic neurons.

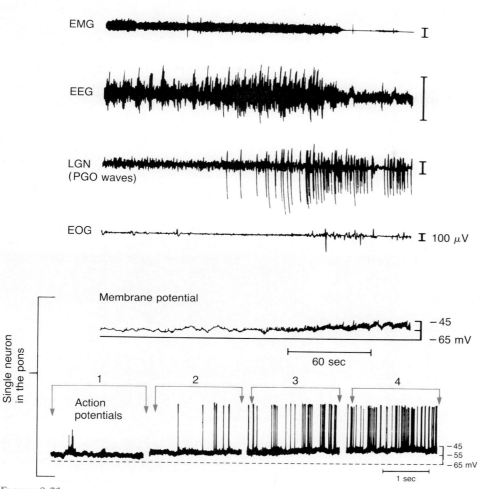

FIGURE 9.21

Activity of a single neuron in the pons during the onset of REM sleep. The upper four tracings show approximately 4 min of EMG activity, cortical EEG activity, PGO waves, and EOG activity. The tracing labeled "Membrane potential" shows the gradual depolarization of the single unit in the pons; and the bottom tracing, labeled "Action potentials," shows the gradually increasing rate of firing of the unit. The times at which these expanded samples of single-unit activity were taken are indicated by the color brackets. (Adapted from McCarley, R.W., in *Principles and Practices of Sleep Disorders in Medicine*, edited by M.H. Kryger, T. Roth, and W.C. Dement. New York: Saunders, 1989.)

To a naive observer, the cat, which is standing, looks awake since it may attack unknown enemies, play with an absent mouse, or display flight behavior. There are orienting movements of the head or eyes toward imaginary stimuli, although the animal does not respond to visual or auditory stimuli. These extraordinary episodes . . . are a good argument that "dreaming" occurs during [REM sleep] in the cat. (Jouvet, 1972, pp. 236–237)

Jouvet's lesions interrupted the caudally projecting axons of the acetylcholinergic neurons of

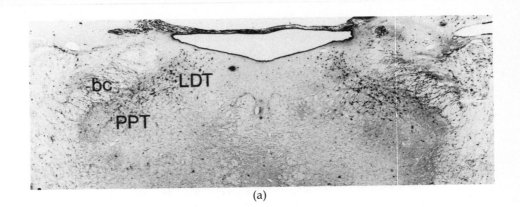

(a)

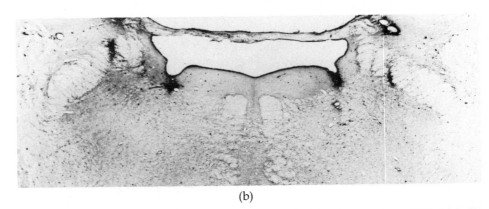

(b)

FIGURE 9.22
Destruction of acetylcholine-secreting neurons in the pons. (a) A section through the pons of an intact brain. (b) A section through the pons after infusions of kainic acid. Acetylcholine-secreting neurons show up as black spots in (a). LDT = lateral tegmental nucleus; PPT = pedunculopontine tegmental nucleus; bc = brachium conjunctivum. (From Jones, B.E., and Webster, H.H. *Brain Research*, 1988, *451*, 13–32.)

the dorsolateral pons—in particular, a set of neurons located just outside the locus coeruleus. These neurons travel to the *magnocellular nucleus* in the medial medulla (Sakai, 1980). Kanamori, Sakai, and Jouvet (1980) recorded from single neurons in the magnocellular nucleus in unrestrained cats and found that they became active during REM sleep, showing intense increases during PGO waves and bursts of rapid eye movements, and Sakai (1980) found that electrical stimulation there caused paralysis. Chemically produced lesions of this nucleus produce REM without atonia (Schenkel and Siegel, 1989). The axons of the medullary neurons project to the spi-

nal cord. Morales, Boxer, and Chase (1987) made intracellular recordings of motor neurons in the spinal cord and discovered a unique class of large-amplitude inhibitory postsynaptic potentials that were present only during REM sleep.

Serotonin and Norepinephrine

As you will recall from the earlier discussion of narcolepsy, serotonergic and noradrenergic agonists have inhibitory effects on REM sleep. In addition, the rate of activity in the serotonergic neurons of the raphe nuclei and the noradrenergic neurons of the locus coeruleus are at their very lowest levels during sleep. The pattern of firing of

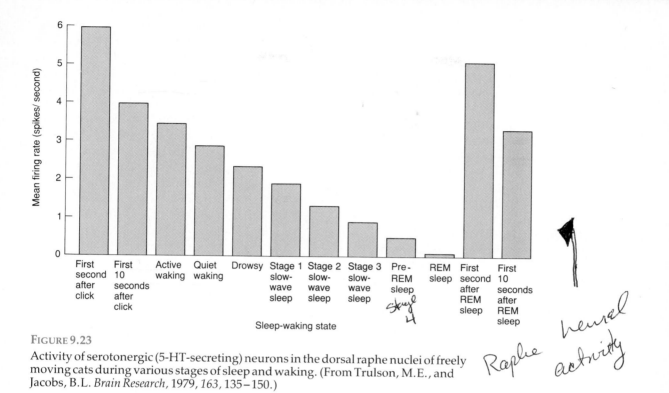

FIGURE 9.23

Activity of serotonergic (5-HT-secreting) neurons in the dorsal raphe nuclei of freely moving cats during various stages of sleep and waking. (From Trulson, M.E., and Jacobs, B.L. *Brain Research*, 1979, *163*, 135–150.)

noradrenergic neurons of the locus coeruleus was already presented in Figure 9.17. Figure 9.23 shows the activity of serotonergic neurons, recorded by Trulson and Jacobs (1979). As you can see, these neurons were most active during waking. Their firing rate declined during slow-wave sleep and became virtually zero during REM sleep. However, once the period of REM sleep ended, the neurons temporarily became very active again. (See *Figure 9.23*.)

Figure 9.24 shows the very close linkage between the activity of a single unit in the dorsal raphe nucleus and the occurrence of PGO waves, the first manifestation of REM sleep (Lydic, McCarley, and Hobson, 1983). Note that the PGO waves occur only when the serotonergic neuron is silent. (See *Figure 9.24*.)

The evidence I have just cited strongly suggests that inhibitory effects of the locus coeruleus and the dorsal raphe nuclei normally prevent

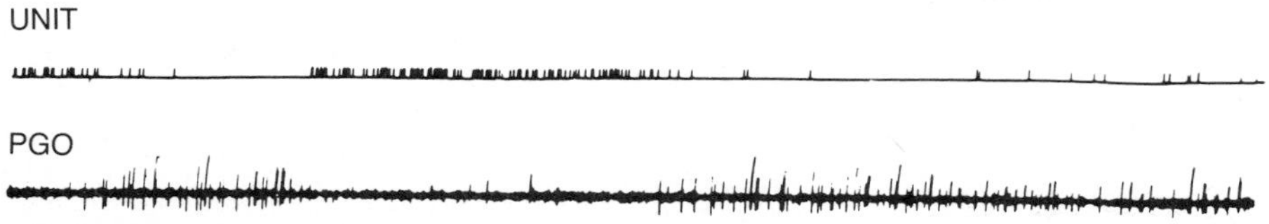

UNIT

PGO

FIGURE 9.24

Activity of a single unit in the dorsal raphe nucleus. Note that the activity is *inversely* related to the occurrence of PGO waves, the first sign of REM sleep. (Adapted from Lydic, R., McCarley, R.W., and Hobson, J.A. *Brain Research*, 1983, *274*, 365–370.)

REM sleep from occurring, and that the event that triggers a bout of REM sleep is a decrease of activity in these nuclei. In fact, infusion of a noradrenergic antagonist directly into the rostrolateral pons causes an increase in REM sleep (Denlinger, Patarca, and Hobson, 1988), and stimulation of the dorsal raphe nucleus inhibits it (Jacobs, Asher, and Dement, 1973). Acetylcholinergic neurons in the dorsolateral pons receive both serotonergic and noradrenergic inputs (Sakai, 1985).

So far, we have seen that REM sleep occurs when acetylcholinergic neurons in the dorsolateral pons become active. That event occurs when serotonergic and noradrenergic neurons in the raphe nuclei and the locus coeruleus become silent. But what makes these neurons become silent? And is there an excitatory input to the dorsolateral pons as well as the inhibitory ones, which *increases* at the beginning of REM sleep? Where is the pacemaker that controls the cycles of REM and slow-wave sleep, and how is this connected to the neurons in the dorsolateral pons? Research efforts will probably answer these questions in the next few years.

*I*NTERIM SUMMARY

The fact that the amount of sleep is regulated suggests that sleep-promoting substances (produced during wakefulness) or wakefulness-promoting substances (produced during sleep) may exist. The sleeping pattern of the dolphin brain and studies with artificial or natural Siamese twins suggest that such substances do not accumulate in the blood. They may accumulate in the brain, but so far, attempts to find them have not been successful. Nutrition appears to modulate sleep; in particular, amino acids promote REM sleep and carbohydrates promote slow-wave sleep, perhaps through the intermediaries of somatostatin and insulin.

Contrary to earlier beliefs, the reticular formation is involved in movement, not in generalized arousal. However, the noradrenergic neurons of the locus coeruleus do seem to be involved in controlling vigilance. This nucleus has only two inputs, one inhibitory and one excitatory, so we can anticipate that research will discover the mechanisms that control its activity.

Slow-wave sleep is promoted by the nucleus of the solitary tract and the basal forebrain, but so far, no one has been able to discover a more comprehensive set of neural circuits that explain just what role these structures play. REM sleep occurs when the activity of acetylcholinergic neurons in the dorsolateral pons increases; some of these neurons control PGO waves, some initiate cortical arousal, and others produce rapid eye movements. Atonia (muscular paralysis that prevents our acting out our dreams) is produced by a group of acetylcholinergic neurons located near the locus coeruleus that activates neurons in the magnocellular nucleus of the medulla, which in turn produce inhibition of motor neurons in the spinal cord.

The noradrenergic neurons of the locus coeruleus and the serotonergic neurons of the raphe nuclei have inhibitory effects on the acetylcholinergic neurons of the pons that are responsible for REM sleep. Bouts of REM sleep begin only after the activity of the noradrenergic and serotonergic neurons ceases; whether this is the only event that triggers REM sleep or whether direct excitation of acetylcholinergic neurons also occurs is not yet known.

*C*ONCLUDING REMARKS

Sleep is one of our most intriguing behaviors. In fact, slow-wave sleep and REM sleep probably should be regarded as two different behaviors, performing two different sets of functions. Slow-wave sleep may help the brain recuperate from the work it has done, and REM sleep may be involved in intergrating experiences of the previous day with older information. Malfunctions of REM sleep mechanisms can produce several different disorders; people can become paralyzed while awake or can fail to become paralyzed during sleep and act out their dreams.

So far, the search for chemicals that produce sleep has identified some possible candidates, but a specific role has has not been established for any of them. The suprachiasmatic nucleus controls our circadian rhythms of sleep and waking—and other behaviors as well. In addition, a clock in the caudal brain stem controls our cycles of REM and slow-wave sleep and seems to be responsible for fluctuations in wakefulness during the day. The past few years have provided us with much information about the physiology of sleep and waking, but the basic process still remains a mystery.

NEW TERMS

alpha activity p. 271
basal forebrain region p. 303
basic rest-activity cycle
    (BRAC) p. 274
beta activity p. 271
cataplexy p. 289
circadian rhythm p. 291
delta activity p. 273
desynchrony p. 272
drug dependency
    insomnia p. 287
electromyogram p. 271
electro-oculogram p. 271
hypnagogic
    hallucination p. 289

hypnapompic
    hallucination p. 289
interleukin-1 p. 298
K complex p. 272
laterodorsal tegmental
    nucleus (LDT) p. 304
locus coeruleus p. 300
magnocellular nucleus p. 308
narcolepsy p. 288
neuropeptide Y p. 293
non-REM sleep p. 273
nucleus of the solitary tract p. 302
pedunculopontine tegmental
    nucleus (PPT) p. 304

PGO wave p. 304
rebound phenomenon p. 284
REM sleep p. 273
REM without atonia p. 289
sleep apnea p. 288
sleep attack p. 289
sleep paralysis p. 289
sleep spindle p. 272
slow-wave sleep p. 273
suprachiasmatic
    nucleus p. 292
synchrony p. 272
theta activity p. 272
zeitgeber p. 292

SUGGESTED READINGS

Cohen, D.B. *Sleep and Dreaming: Origins, Nature and Functions.* Oxford: Pergamon Press, 1979.

Horne, J. *Why We Sleep: The Functions of Sleep in Humans and Other Mammals.* Oxford: Oxford University Press, 1988.

Kryger, M.H., Roth, T., and Dement, W.C. *Principles and Practices of Sleep Disorders in Medicine.* New York: W.B. Saunders Co., 1989.

Moore-Ede, M.C., Sulzman, F.M., and Fuller, C.A. *The Clocks that Time Us.* Cambridge, Mass.: Harvard University Press, 1982.

10

Reproductive Behavior: Sexual Development and Behavior

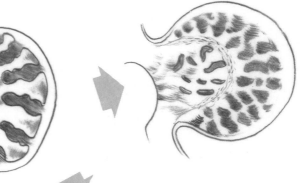

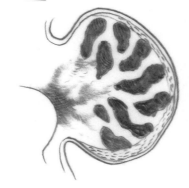

*R*eproductive behaviors constitute the most important category of social behaviors, because without them most species would not survive. Reproductive behaviors—including courting, mating, parental behavior, and most forms of aggressive behaviors—are the most striking categories of *sexually dimorphic behaviors*, that is, behaviors that differ in males and females (*di* + *morphous*, "two forms"). As you will see, hormones play a very special role in the control of these behaviors—more so than in any others. Although hormones affect many physiological processes, their effects on behaviors are generally indirect; that is, the hormones affect some physiological characteristics of the body, and these changes affect behavior. In contrast, the hormones that affect sexually dimorphic behaviors do so directly, by stimulating neurons in the central nervous system that control these behaviors. Thus, sexual dimorphism in behavior is largely accomplished by the existence of different levels of sex hormones in males and females.

This chapter begins by discussing sexual development, sexual behavior, and the effects of hormones on both development and behavior. Next, the chapter discusses evidence concerning the neural control of sexual behavior and the ways in which hormones interact with the nervous system to affect behavior.

SEXUAL DEVELOPMENT

A person's chromosomal sex is determined at the time of fertilization. However, this event is merely the first in a series of steps that culminate in the development of a male or female. This section considers the major features of sexual development.

Production of Gametes and Fertilization

All cells of the body (other than sperms or ova) contain twenty-three pairs of chromosomes, including a pair of sex chromosomes. The genetic information that programs the development of a human is contained in the DNA that constitutes these chromosomes. (We pride ourselves on our ability to miniaturize computer circuits on silicon chips; but that accomplishment looks primitive when we consider the blueprint for a human being, which is too small to be seen by the naked eye.) The nature of the sex chromosomes determines an individual's sex. There are two types of these chromosomes: X and Y chromosomes. The cells of females contain two of one type, making them XX cells. The cells of males contain one of each, making them XY cells. Thus, it is the possession of a Y chromosome that distinguishes the cells of a male from those of a female.

We can observe the twenty-three pairs of human chromosomes by scraping epithelial cells from the mucous membrane of the inside of the cheek. Among these cells will be some that are in the process of division. During cell division, which is called *mitosis,* the chromosomes duplicate themselves, thus giving each of the two daughter cells the entire complement of genetic material. (When cells divide, the products of the division are called *daughter cells,* regardless of the sex of the donor.) Figure 10.1 shows this process. For simplicity's sake, the cells shown in the figure contain only two pairs of chromosomes, rather than twenty-three. (See *Figure 10.1.*) Once cellular division has begun, the culture is treated with colchicine, a drug that dissolves the spindle fibers that pull the chromosomes apart and thus halts the process in the phase shown in part C. (See *Figure 10.1.*)

The dividing cells now contain a double set of twenty-three pairs of chromosomes in the nucleus, straightened out and easy to see. The cells are then squashed, so as to flatten the chromosomes, and the genetic material is stained. Then many cells are searched until one is found in which all the chromosomes can readily be seen. A photograph is taken, and pictures of the individual chromosomes are cut out and rearranged according to size. Thus, the numbers assigned to the chromosomes represent their relative sizes. Figure 10.2 illustrates a set of human chromosomes prepared in this way, before and after rearrangement. Remember that we can see twice as many chromosomes as the cell normally contains, because the process of cell division was arrested just before the members of a duplicated chromosome,

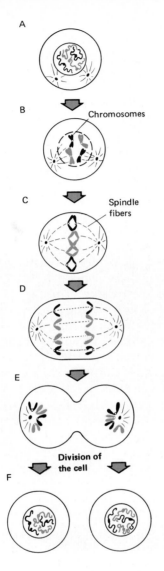

FIGURE 10.1

Mitosis, the process by which a somatic cell replicates itself. (From Orians, G.H. *The Study of Life*. Boston: Allyn and Bacon, 1973.)

joined near the center, would normally separate and travel to each of the daughter cells. We know that the cell shown in this figure came from a male, because we can see a Y chromosome (the smallest chromosome of all). (See *Figure 10.2.*)

The production of **gametes** (ova and sperms; *gamein* means "to marry") entails a different form of cell division, called **meiosis.** This process produces cells that contain only one member of each

of the twenty-three pairs of chromosomes. The development of a human begins when a single sperm and ovum join, sharing their twenty-three single chromosomes to reconstitute the twenty-three pairs. Somehow, each chromosome finds its partner and joins it.

Fertilization is the union of a single sperm with a single ovum, thus combining their genetic material. Because women have XX cells, all of their ova contain a single X chromosome (along with twenty-two other single chromosomes, of course). Because men have XY cells, half of their sperms are X bearing and half are Y bearing. Thus, the gender of the offspring is determined by the sperm that fertilizes the ovum. If it is X bearing, the offspring will be female. If it is Y bearing, it will be male. (See *Figure 10.3.*)

Development of the Gonads

Men and women differ in many ways: Their bodies are different, parts of their brains are different, and their reproductive behaviors are different. Are all these differences encoded on the tiny Y chromosome, the sole piece of genetic material that distinguishes males from females? The answer is no. The cells of both males and females contain the genetic information needed to develop the bodies of either sex. It is the hormonal exposure, both before and after birth, that is responsible for our sexual dimorphism.

The first sex organs to differentiate are the **gonads** (from the Greek *gonos,* meaning "procreation"), which become ovaries or testes. At first, male and female embryos are identical. Their gonads, which begin developing during the fifth and sixth week after the mother's last menstrual cycle, are undifferentiated. In this state they. are referred to as **primordial gonads** (*primordial* means "first begun"). But during the seventh and eighth weeks the gonads differentiate; either the cells of the cortex (the outer layers) develop into ovaries, or the cells of the medulla (the inner layers) develop into testes. (See *Figure 10.4.*)

The differentiation of the primordial gonads is controlled by the presence or absence of a protein called the **H-Y antigen** (Haseltine and Ohno, 1981). This protein was discovered by researchers investigating the factors that control the compati-

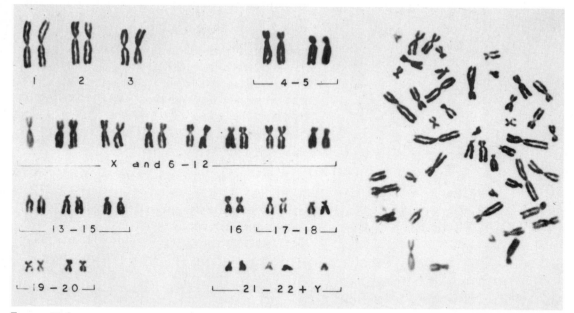

FIGURE 10.2

A karyotype of a cell whose division was arrested in metaphase (phase C of Figure 10.1). (From Money, J., and Ehrhardt, A. *Man & Woman, Boy & Girl.* Copyright 1972 by The Johns Hopkins University Press, Baltimore, Maryland. By permission.)

bility of different tissues with respect to transplantation. They discovered that female mice would reject grafts of skin from males because an antigen (a type of protein) was present on the surface of male cells. Further studies found that the important function of the H-Y antigen is an organizational effect on cells of the primordial gonads. When it stimulates receptors on the surface of these cells, it causes the gonads to develop as testes. If the protein is not present, or if an experimenter administers an antibody to the H-Y antigen, the primordial gonads develop into ovaries. As you may have expected, production of the H-Y antigen is controlled by a gene on the Y chromosome.

Development of the Internal Sex Organs

The production of H-Y antigen, and the ensuing development of testes, is the sole effect of the Y chromosome that is known to directly affect sexual development. Once the gonads have developed, a series of events is set into action that deter-

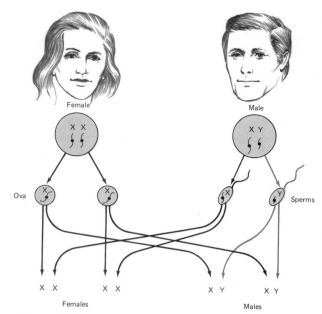

FIGURE 10.3

Determination of gender. The gender of the offspring depends on whether the sperm cell that fertilizes the ovum carries an X or a Y chromosome.

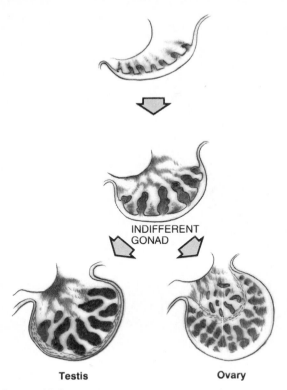

INDIFFERENT GONAD

Testis   **Ovary**

FIGURE 10.4

Development of the gonads (testes and ovaries).
(Adapted from Burns, R.K., in *Analysis of Development*,
edited by B.H. Willier, P.A. Weiss, and V. Hamberger.
Philadelphia: Saunders, 1955.)

mines the individual's gender. These events are directed by hormones secreted by the gonads and, later, by other endocrine glands as well. These hormones affect sexual development (and, as we shall see later, sexual behavior as well) in two ways. During prenatal development they have *organizational effects,* which influence the development of a person's sex organs and brain. The second role of sex hormones is their *activational effect.* For example, hormones activate the production of sperms, make erection and ejaculation possible, and induce ovulation. Because the bodies of adult males and females have been organized differently, sex hormones will have different activational effects in the two sexes.

As we just saw, prior to the seventh week the embryonic gonads are unisexual but *bipotential,* capable of assuming either form. In contrast, the

other internal sex organs are *bisexual;* that is, all embryos contain the precursors for both female and male sex organs. However, during the third month of gestation only one of these precursors develops; the other withers away. The precursor of the internal female sex organs, which develops into the *fimbriae* and *Fallopian tubes,* the *uterus,* and the *inner two-thirds of the vagina,* is called the *Müllerian system.* (See *Figure 10.5.*) The precursor of the internal male sex organs, which develops into the *epididymis, vas deferens, seminal vesicles,* and *prostate,* is called the *Wolffian system.* (See *Figure 10.5.*)

The gender of the internal sex organs of a fetus is determined by the presence or absence of testes. That is, if testes are present, the Wolffian system develops. If they are not, the Müllerian system develops. The Müllerian (female) system needs no hormonal stimulus from the gonads to develop; it just normally does so. In contrast, the cells of the Wolffian (male) system do not develop unless they are stimulated by a hormone. Thus, testes secrete two classes of hormones. A peptide hormone called *Müllerian-inhibiting substance* does exactly what its name says: It prevents the Müllerian system from developing. It therefore has a *defeminizing effect. Androgens* (primarily testosterone and dihydrotestosterone) stimulate the development of the Wolffian system. (This class of hormone is also aptly named: *andros* means "man," and *gennan* means "to produce.") Androgens have a *masculinizing effect.*

As you will recall from Chapter 3, hormones exert their effects on target cells by stimulating the appropriate hormone receptor. Thus, the precursor of the male internal sex organs, the Wolffian system, contain androgen receptors that are coupled to cellular mechanisms that promote growth and division. In contrast, the cells of the Müllerian system contain receptors for Müllerian-inhibiting substance that somehow *prevent* growth and division.

Experiments with laboratory animals have shown that ovaries are not necessary for the development of the Müllerian system. This finding has led to the dictum "Nature's impulse is to create a female." A genetic anomaly demonstrates the validity of this statement in humans. People with *Turner's syndrome* have only one sex chro-

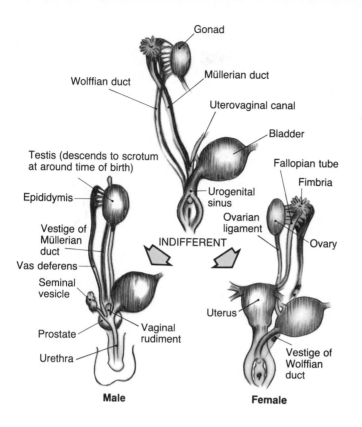

FIGURE 10.5

Development of the internal sex organs. (Adapted from Corning, H.K. *Lehrbuch der Entwicklungsgeschichte des Menschen.* Munich: J.F. Bergman, 1921.)

mosome: an X chromosome. (Thus, instead of having XX cells, they have X0 cells.) Apparently, the ovum that gives rise to such an individual is fertilized by a sperm that lost its sex chromosome during meiosis. Because a Y chromosome is not present, H-Y antigen is not produced, and testes do not develop. In addition, because only one X chromosome is present, ovaries are not produced, either. (For some reason, two X chromosomes are needed to produce ovaries.) Even though they have no gonads at all, people with Turner's syndrome develop into females, with normal female internal sex organs. Of course, they cannot bear children, because without ovaries they cannot produce ova.

Development of the External Genitalia

The external genitalia are the visible sex organs, including the penis and scrotum in males and the labia, clitoris, and outer part of the vagina in females. Whereas male and female internal sex organs develop from two different sets of precursors, the external genitalia, like the gonads, develop from a single set of bipotential primordia, capable of assuming either male or female form. Figure 10.6 illustrates the development of male and female external genitalia from the bipotential genital primordia. Note that the *primordial phallus* gives rise to the glans penis or to the clitoris; the *genital swelling* gives rise to the scrotum or to the labia majora; and the *genital tubercle* gives rise to the shaft of the penis or to the labia minora and outer third of the vagina. (See *Figure 10.6.*)

Without hormonal stimulation the external genitalia will become female, regardless of the organism's chromosomal sex; female sex hormones are not needed. However, the presence of androgens is necessary for masculine development. Thus, the presence or absence of testes determines whether a person's external genitalia are male or female. As you might predict, therefore, people with Turner's syndrome have female external genitalia even though they lack ovaries.

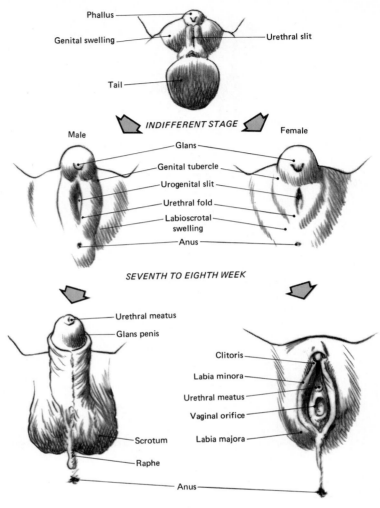

FIGURE 10.6
Development of the external genitalia. (Adapted from Spaulding, M.H., in *Contributions to Embryology*, Vol. 13. Washington, D.C.: Carnegie Institute of Washington, 1921.)

Figure 10.7 summarizes the factors that control the development of the gonads, internal sex organs, and genitalia. (See *Figure 10.7.*)

Sexual Maturation

The *primary* sex characteristics include the gonads, internal sex organs, and external genitalia. These organs are present at birth. The *secondary* sex characteristics, such as enlarged breasts and widened hips or a beard and deep voice, do not appear until puberty. Without seeing genitals, we must guess the sex of a prepubescent child from his or her haircut and clothing; the bodies of young boys and girls are rather similar. However,

at puberty the gonads are stimulated to produce their hormones, and these hormones cause the person to mature sexually. The onset of puberty occurs when cells in the hypothalamus secrete *gonadotropin-releasing hormones* (GnRH), which stimulate the production and release of two *gonadotropic hormones* by the anterior pituitary gland. The gonadotropic ("gonad-turning") hormones stimulate the gonads to produce *their* hormones, which are ultimately responsible for sexual maturation. (See *Figure 10.8.*)

The two gonadotropic hormones are *follicle-stimulating hormone* (FSH) and *luteinizing hormone* (LH), named for the effects they produce in the female (production of a *follicle* and its subse-

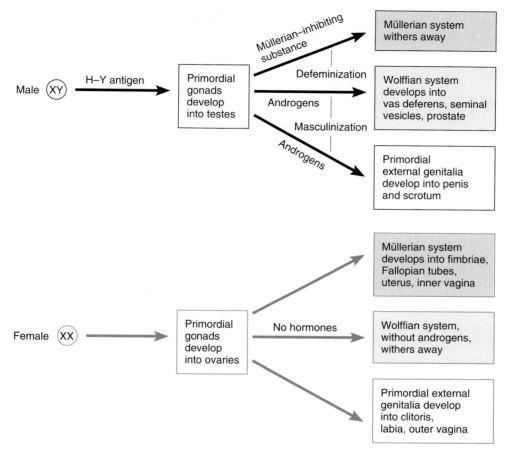

FIGURE 10.7

Hormonal control of masculinization and defeminization of the internal sex organs and external genitalia.

quent *luteinization,* to be described in the next section of this chapter). However, the same hormones are produced in the male, where they stimulate the testes to produce sperms and to secrete testosterone. If male and female pituitary glands are exchanged in rats, the ovaries and testes respond perfectly to the hormones secreted by the new glands (Harris and Jacobsohn, 1951–1952).

In response to the gonadotropic hormones (usually called *gonadotropins*), the gonads secrete sex steroid hormones. The ovaries produce **estradiol,** one of a class of hormones known as **estrogens.** The testes chiefly produce **testosterone** (an androgen). Both types of glands also produce a small amount of the hormones of the other sex. The gonadal hormones have effects on many

parts of the body. Both estradiol and testosterone initiate closure of the *epiphyses* (growing portions of the bones) and thus halt skeletal growth. Estradiol also causes breast development, growth of the lining of the uterus, changes in the deposition of body fat, and maturation of the female genitalia. Testosterone stimulates growth of facial, axillary (underarm), and pubic hair; lowers the voice; alters the hairline on the head (often causing baldness later in life); stimulates muscular development; and causes genital growth. This description leaves out two of the female secondary characteristics: axillary and pubic hair. These characteristics are produced not by estrogens but rather by **androstenedione,** an androgen secreted by the cortex of the adrenal glands. Even a male who is castrated (whose testes are removed) be-

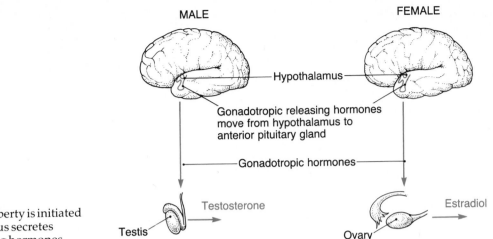

FIGURE 10.8
Sexual maturation. Puberty is initiated when the hypothalamus secretes gonadotropin-releasing hormones.

TABLE 10.1
Classification of sex hormones

Class	Principal Hormone in Humans (Where Produced)	Examples of Effects
Androgens	Testosterone (testes)	Maturation of male genitalia; production of sperms, growth of facial, pubic, and axillary hair; muscular development; enlargement of larynx, inhibition of bone growth
	Androstenedione (adrenal glands)	In females, growth of pubic and axillary hair; less important than testosterone in males
Estrogens	Estradiol (ovaries)	Maturation of female genitalia; growth of breasts; alterations in fat deposits; growth of uterine lining; inhibition of bone growth
Gestagens	Progesterone (ovaries)	Maintenance of uterine lining
Hypothalamic hormones	Gonadotropin-releasing hormone	Stimulates release of gonadotropins
Gonadotropins	Follicle-stimulating hormone (anterior pituitary)	Development of ovarian follicle
	Luteinizing hormone	Ovulation; development of corpus luteum
Other hormones	Prolactin	Milk production; male refractory period (?)
	Oxytocin	Milk ejection

fore puberty will grow axillary and pubic hair, stimulated by his own androstenedione. (See *Table 10.1.*)

The bipotentiality of many of the secondary sex characteristics remains throughout life. If a man is treated with an estrogen (for example, to control an androgen-dependent tumor), he will grow breasts, and his facial hair will become finer and softer. However, his voice will remain low, because the enlargement of the larynx is permanent. Conversely, a woman who receives high levels of an androgen (usually from a tumor that secretes androstenedione) will grow a beard, and her voice will become lower.

*I*NTERIM SUMMARY

Gender is determined by the sex chromosomes: XX produces a female, and XY produces a male. Males are produced by the action of a gene on the Y chromosome that contains the code for the production of a protein, the H-Y antigen, that causes the primordial gonads to become testes. The testes secrete two kinds of hormones that cause a male to develop. Androgens stimulate the development of the Wolffian system (masculinization), and Müllerian-inhibiting substance suppresses the development of the Müllerian system (defeminization). The external genitalia develop from common precursors. In the absence of gonadal hormones the precursors develop the female form; in the presence of androgens they develop the male form (masculinization). By default, the body is female ("Nature's impulse . . ."); only by the actions of testicular hormones does it become male. Masculinization and defeminization are referred to as *organizational* effects of hormones; *activational* effects occur after development is complete. A person with Turner's syndrome (X0) fails to develop gonads but nevertheless develops female internal sex organs and external genitalia.

Sexual maturity occurs when the hypothalamus begins secreting gonadotropin-releasing hormone, which stimulates the secretion of follicle-stimulating hormone and luteinizing hormone by the anterior pituitary gland. These hormones stimulate the gonads to secrete their hormones, which cause the genitals to mature and cause the body to develop the secondary sex characteristics (activational effects).

HORMONAL CONTROL OF SEX-RELATED BEHAVIOR

We have seen that hormones are responsible for *sexual dimorphism* (male-female differences) in the structure of the body and its organs. Hormones have organizational and activational effects on the internal sex organs, genitals, and secondary sex characteristics. Naturally, all of these effects influence a person's behavior. Simply having the physique and genitals of a man or a woman exerts a powerful effect. But hormones do more than give us masculine or feminine bodies; they also affect behavior by interacting directly with the nervous system. Androgens present during prenatal development affect the development of the nervous system. In addition, sex hormones have activational effects on the adult nervous system, influencing physiological processes and behavior. This section considers some of these effects.

Hormonal Control of Female Reproductive Cycles

Menstrual and Estrous Cycles

The reproductive cycle of female primates is called a *menstrual cycle* (from *mensis*, meaning "month"). Females of other species of mammals also have reproductive cycles, called *estrous cycles. Estrus* means "gadfly"; when a female rat is in estrus, her hormonal condition goads her to act differently than she does at other times. (For that matter, it goads male rats to act differently, too.) The primary feature that distinguishes menstrual cycles from estrous cycles is the monthly growth and loss of the lining of the uterus. The other features are approximately the same.

Menstrual cycles and estrous cycles consist of a sequence of events that are controlled by hormonal secretions of the pituitary gland and ovaries. These glands interact, the secretions of one affecting those of the other. A cycle begins with the secretion of gonadotropins by the anterior pituitary gland. These hormones (especially FSH) stimulate the growth of *ovarian follicles,* small spheres of epithelial cells surrounding each ovum. Women normally produce one ovarian follicle each month; if two are produced and fertilized, dizygotic (fraternal) twins will develop. As ovarian follicles mature, they secrete estradiol, which causes the growth of the lining of the uterus in preparation for implantation of the ovum, should it be fertilized by a sperm. Feedback from the increasing level of estradiol eventually triggers the release of a surge of LH by the anterior pituitary gland. (See *Figure 10.9.*)

The LH surge causes *ovulation:* The ovarian follicle ruptures, releasing the ovum. Under the continued influence of LH the ruptured ovarian follicle becomes a *corpus luteum* ("yellow body"), which produces estradiol and *progesterone.* (See *Figure 10.9.*) The latter hormone promotes pregnancy *(gestation).* It maintains the lining of the uterus, and it inhibits the ovaries from producing another follicle. Meanwhile, the ovum, which is released directly into the fluid contained in the abdominal cavity, enters one of the Fallopian tubes and begins its progress toward the uterus. The ovum is directed into the Fallopian tube by the "rowing" action of the ciliated cells of the fimbria, which form a fringe around the opening. This

process works remarkably well; women who have lost an ovary on one side and a Fallopian tube on the other have nevertheless become pregnant. Obviously, their ova had to find their way across the abdominal cavity and into the Fallopian tube on the other side. If an ovum meets sperm cells during its travel down the Fallopian tube and becomes fertilized, it begins to divide, and several days later it attaches itself to the uterine wall.

If the ovum is not fertilized, or if it is fertilized too late for it to develop sufficiently by the time it gets to the uterus, the corpus luteum will stop producing estradiol and progesterone, and the lining of the walls of the uterus will slough off. Menstruation will commence. (See *Figure 10.10.*)

Control of Gonadotropin Secretion by the Ovaries

As we have just seen, ovulation occurs when the blood level of estradiol, secreted by an ovarian follicle, reaches a critical level. In primates this effect of estradiol takes place in the anterior pituitary gland. The anterior pituitary gland is controlled by the hypothalamus, which secretes releasing hormones into the portal blood supply. Gonadotropin-releasing hormone (GnRH), which controls the secretion of gonadotropins, is produced by neurons located in the *arcuate nucleus* of the hypothalamus, which forms a small arch around the base of the pituitary stalk. These

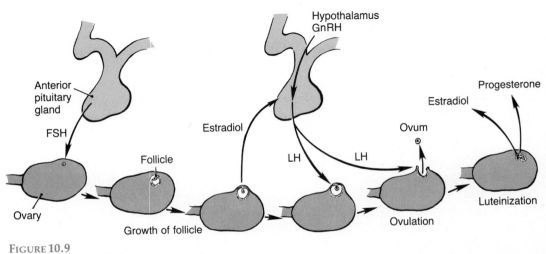

FIGURE 10.9
Neuroendocrine control of the menstrual cycle.

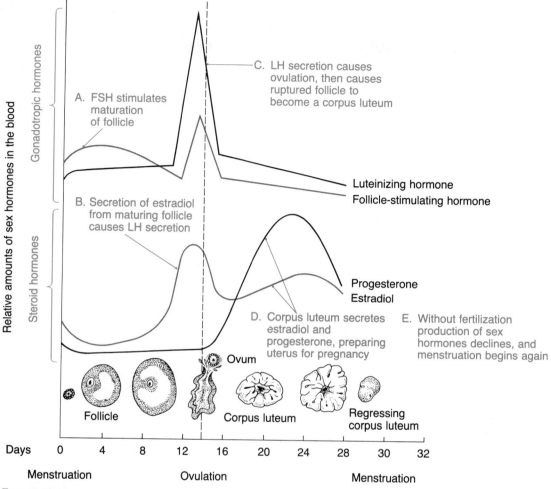

Gonadotropic hormones

Steroid hormones

Relative amounts of sex hormones in the blood

A. FSH stimulates maturation of follicle

C. LH secretion causes ovulation, then causes ruptured follicle to become a corpus luteum

B. Secretion of estradiol from maturing follicle causes LH secretion

Luteinizing hormone
Follicle-stimulating hormone

Progesterone
Estradiol

D. Corpus luteum secretes estradiol and progesterone, preparing uterus for pregnancy

E. Without fertilization production of sex hormones declines, and menstruation begins again

Ovum

Follicle   Corpus luteum   Regressing corpus luteum

Days   0   4   8   12   16   20   24   28   30   32

Menstruation   Ovulation   Menstruation

FIGURE 10.10

The hormonal and physical elements of the menstrual cycle.

neurons are controlled by an internal clock that stimulates them to secrete a pulse of GnRH every hour, causing the anterior pituitary gland to release similar pulses of gonadotropins (Pohl and Knobil, 1982). (See *Figure 10.11*.) For some reason the timing of the clock is important; if pulses of GnRH occur too fast or too slow, normal 28-day menstrual cycles will not occur (Knobil, 1987). The clock is present in primates at birth but soon stops, only to be started again at the time of puberty (Plant, 1986).

During the early part of the menstrual cycle the gonadotropins secreted by the anterior pituitary gland stimulate the development of an ovarian

follicle. The cells of the ripening ovarian follicle secrete estradiol; when the blood level of this hormone reaches a critical level of 200 pg/ml for two days, it stimulates a surge of gonadotropins, which causes ovulation. (A picogram, abbreviated pg, is one trillionth of a gram.) The estradiol acts directly on the pituitary gland, stimulating it to produce the preovulatory LH surge.

The arcuate nucleus continues to secrete pulses of GnRH even after ovulation has occurred. However, the progesterone secreted by the corpus luteum inhibits the effects of the gonadotropins on the ovaries and prevents another ovarian follicle from developing. If fertilization

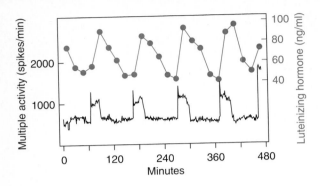

FIGURE 10.11
Cyclic changes in multiple-unit activity in the arcuate nucleus (color), and plasma levels of luteinizing hormone (black). An internal clock appears to control the secretion of gonadotropin-releasing hormone (GnRH). (Adapted from Wilson, R.C., Kesner, J.S., Kaufman, J.-M., Uemura, T., Akema, T., and Knobil, E. *Neuroendocrinology*, 1984, *39*, 256–260. With permission of S. Karger AG, Basel.)

does not occur, the corpus luteum dies in approximately 14 days, and the level of progesterone falls. As we saw, this fall causes the lining of the uterus to slough off. It also removes the inhibiting effect of progesterone on the ovaries, which permits the development of a new ovarian follicle. Thus, the length of a menstrual cycle is controlled by the ovaries; it takes 14 days for a new ovarian follicle to develop and produce a critical amount of estradiol, and a corpus luteum lives and produces progesterone for 14 days more.

Hormonal Control of Sexual Behavior of Laboratory Animals

The interactions between sex hormones and development of the human brain are difficult to study. We must turn to two sources of information: experiments with animals and various developmental disorders in humans, which serve as nature's own "experiments." Let us first consider the evidence gathered from research with laboratory animals.

Male Sexual Behavior

For fertilization to occur, a male mammal must emit sperm-containing semen into the female's vagina. Some male mammals are ready and willing to do so any season of the year, depending only on the receptivity of the female. Others, such as deer, are seasonal breeders, becoming sexually active only at certain times of the year. In fact, during the off-season their testes regress and produce almost no testosterone.

Male sexual behavior is quite varied, although the essential features of *intromission* (entry of the penis into the female's vagina), *pelvic thrusting* (rhythmic movement of the hindquarters, causing genital friction), and *ejaculation* (discharge of semen) are characteristic of all male mammals. Humans, of course, have invented all kinds of copulatory and noncopulatory sexual behavior. For example, the pelvic movements leading to ejaculation may be performed by the woman, and sex play can lead to orgasm without intromission.

The sexual behavior of rats has been studied more than that of any other laboratory animal. When a male rat encounters a receptive female, he will spend some time nuzzling her and sniffing and licking her genitals, mount her, and engage in pelvic thrusting. He will mount her several times, achieving intromission on most of the mountings. After eight to fifteen intromissions approximately 1 minute apart (each lasting only about one-quarter of a second), the male will ejaculate. At the time of ejaculation he shows a deep pelvic thrust and arches backward. The copulatory behavior of a mouse is similar and even more dramatic. During the final intromission the male takes all four feet off the floor, climbing completely on top of the female. When he ejaculates, he quivers and falls sideways to the ground. (Sometimes, the female falls with him.)

The male rat (along with many other male mammals) is most responsive to females who are in estrus ("in heat"). Males will ignore a female whose ovaries have been removed, but an injection of estradiol will restore her sex appeal (and also change her behavior toward the male). The stimuli that arouse a male rat's sexual interest include her odor and her behavior. In some species visible changes, such as the swollen sex skin in the genital region of a female monkey, also affect sex appeal.

After ejaculating, the male refrains from sexual activity for a period of time (minutes, in the rat). Most mammals will return to copulate again and again, showing a longer pause, called a *refractory period,* after each ejaculation. (The term comes from the Latin *refringere,* "to break off.") An interesting phenomenon occurs in some mammals. If a male, after finally becoming "exhausted" by repeated copulation with the same female, is presented with a new female, he begins to respond quickly—often as fast as he did in his initial contact with the first female. Successive introductions of new females can keep up his performance for prolonged periods of time. The fact that some males show a renewal of interest in sexual behavior with a new female and a good memory for females already copulated with are undoubtedly useful for species in which a single male inseminates all the members of his harem. Other mammalian species with approximately equal numbers of reproductively active males and females are less likely to act this way.

This phenomenon I have just described, also seen in roosters, is usually called the *Coolidge effect.* The following story is reputed to be true, but I cannot vouch for that fact. (If it is not true, it ought to be.) The late former U.S. president Calvin Coolidge and his wife were touring a farm, when Mrs. Coolidge asked the farmer whether the continuous and vigorous sexual activity among the flock of hens was the work of just one rooster. The reply was yes. "You might point that out to Mr. Coolidge," she said. The president then asked the farmer whether a different hen was involved each time. The answer, again, was yes. "You might point that out to Mrs. Coolidge," he said.

Sexual behavior of male rodents depends on testosterone, a fact that has long been recognized (Bermant and Davidson, 1974). If a male rat is castrated (that is, if his testes are removed), his sexual activity eventually ceases. However, the behavior can be reinstated by injections of testosterone. I will describe the neural basis of this activational effect later in this chapter.

The refractory period that occurs after an ejaculation may be produced, at least in part, by *prolactin,* a hormone normally associated with females. (Prolactin stimulates milk production.) First, prolactin is released by male rats after ejaculation. Oaknin, Rodriguez del Castillo, Guerra, Battaner, and Mas (1989) decapitated male rats after they had participated in various as-

pects of copulatory behavior and analyzed the level of several hormones in their blood. Immediately after ejaculation their blood level of prolactin rose sharply, to almost four times the baseline level. Second, prolactin has an inhibitory effect on male sexual behavior. For example, Kalra, Simpkins, Luttge, and Kalra (1983) found that the transplantation of a prolactin-secreting tumor into male rats suppressed their sexual behavior. In addition, most men with an abnormally high level of prolactin in their blood show sexual dysfunctions (Perryman and Thorner, 1981). Possibly, then, prolactin is secreted during ejaculation and inhibits further sexual activity during the refractory period.

Female Sexual Behavior

The mammalian female is generally described as being the passive participant in copulation. It is true that in many species the female's role during mounting and intromission is merely to assume a posture that exposes her genitals to the male. This behavior is called the *lordosis* response (from the Greek *lordos,* meaning "bent backward"). The female will also move her tail away (if she has one) and stand rigidly enough to support the weight of the male.

The behavior of a female laboratory animal in initiating copulation is often very active, however. Certainly, if copulation with a nonestrous rodent is attempted, she will either actively flee or rebuff the male. But when she is in a receptive state, she will often approach the male, nuzzle him, sniff his genitals, and show behaviors characteristic of her species. For example, a female rat will exhibit quick, short, hopping movements and rapid ear wiggling, which male rats find irresistible (McClintock and Adler, 1978).

Sexual behavior of female rodents depends on the gonadal hormones present during estrus: estradiol and progesterone. In rats estradiol increases about 40 hours before the female becomes receptive; and just before receptivity occurs, the corpus luteum begins secreting large quantities of progesterone (Feder, 1981). Although sexual receptivity can be produced in ovariectomized rodents by administering large doses of estradiol alone, the most effective treatment duplicates the normal sequence of hormones: a small amount of estradiol, followed by progesterone. Progesterone alone is ineffective; thus, the estradiol "primes" its effectiveness. Priming with estradiol takes about 16–24 hours, after which an injection of progesterone produces receptive behaviors within an hour (Lisk, 1978). The neural mechanisms that are responsible for these effects will be described later in this chapter.

Organizational Effects of Androgens on Behavior: Masculinization and Defeminization

The dictum "Nature's impulse is to create a female" applies to sexual behavior as well as to sex organs. That is, if a rodent brain is *not* exposed to androgens during a critical period of development, the animal will engage in female sexual behavior as an adult (if it is given estradiol and progesterone then). Fortunately for experimenters, this critical time comes shortly after birth for rats and for several other species of rodents, who are born in a rather immature condition. Thus, if a male rat is castrated immediately after birth, permitted to grow to adulthood, and then given injections of estradiol and progesterone, it will respond to the presence of another male by arching its back and presenting its hindquarters. It will act as if it were a female (Blaustein and Olster, 1989).

In contrast, if a rodent brain is exposed to androgens during development, two phenomena occur: behavioral defeminization and behavioral masculinization. *Behavioral defeminization* refers to the organizational effect of androgens that prevents the animal from displaying female sexual behavior in adulthood. As we shall see later, this effect is accomplished by suppressing the development of neural circuits controlling female sexual behavior. For example, if a female rodent is ovariectomized and given an injection of testosterone immediately after birth, she will *not* respond to a male rat when, as an adult, she is given injections of estradiol and progesterone. *Behavioral masculinization* refers to the organizational effect of androgens that enables animals to engage in male sexual behavior in adulthood. This effect is accomplished by stimulating the development of neural circuits controlling male sexual behavior. For example, if the female rodent in my previous example is given testosterone in adulthood, rather than estradiol and progester-

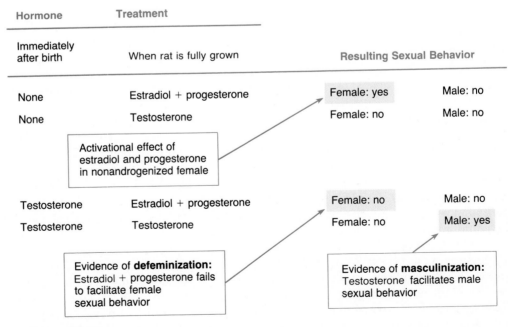

Figure 10.12
Organizational effects of testosterone. Around the time of birth, testosterone masculinizes and defeminizes rodents' sexual behavior.

one, she will mount and attempt to copulate with a receptive female. (See Feder, 1984, for references to specific studies.) (See *Figure 10.12.*)

The two organizational effects of androgens on the brain—behavioral masculinization and behavioral defeminization—are of course stimulated by testosterone, but they are also, in part, accomplished by intracellular *estradiol*. Testosterone can be converted into estradiol by a process called **aromatization.** (In chemistry an *aromatic compound* is one that contains a particular six-carbon ring.) Aromatization is accomplished by an enzyme called, appropriately, an *aromatase.* Many cells of the brain contain aromatase, and when molecules of testosterone enter them, they are converted into estradiol. The molecules of estradiol travel to the nucleus, bind with estrogen receptors, and trigger physiological changes that affect development. It appears that defeminization is largely accomplished by the stimulation of estrogen receptors, whereas masculinization is accomplished by the stimulation of both androgen and estrogen receptors. Masculinization involves both aromatization and the direct effect of testosterone on androgen receptors (McEwen, 1983; Parsons, Rainbow, and McEwen, 1984). (See *Figure 10.13.*)

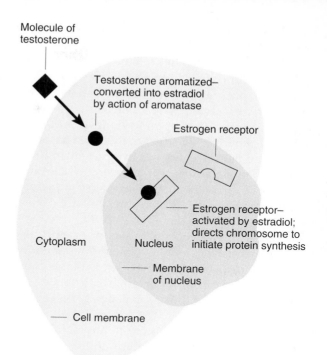

FIGURE 10.13

Aromatization. In some cells the effects of testosterone are carried out by an estrogen. Testosterone is aromatized into estradiol, which activates estrogen receptors in the nucleus.

Effects of Pheromones

Hormones transmit messages from one part of the body (the secreting gland) to another (the target tissue). Another class of chemicals, called *pheromones,* carries messages from one animal to another. These chemicals, like hormones, affect reproductive behavior. Karlson and Luscher (1959) coined the term, from *pherein,* "to carry," and *horman,* "to excite." Pheromones are released by one animal and directly affect the physiology or behavior of another. Most pheromones are detected by means of olfaction, but some are ingested or absorbed through the skin.

Pheromones can affect reproductive physiology or behavior. First, let us consider the effects on reproductive physiology. When groups of female mice are housed together, their estrous cycles slow down and eventually stop. This phenomenon is known as the *Lee-Boot effect* (van der Lee and Boot, 1955). If groups of females are exposed to the odor of a male (or of his urine), they begin cycling again, and their cycles tend to be synchronized. This phenomenon is known as the *Whitten effect* (Whitten, 1959). The *Vandenbergh effect* (Vandenbergh, Whitsett, and Lombardi, 1975) is the acceleration of the onset of puberty in a female rodent, caused by the odor of a male. Both the Whitten effect and the Vandenbergh effect are caused by a pheromone present only in the urine of intact adult males; the urine of a juvenile or castrated male has no effect. Thus, the production of the pheromone requires the presence of testosterone.

The *Bruce effect* (Bruce, 1960a, 1960b) is a particularly interesting phenomenon: When a recently impregnated female mouse encounters a normal male mouse other than the one with which she mated, the pregnancy is very likely to fail. This effect, too, is caused by a substance secreted in the urine of intact males—but not of males that have been castrated. Thus, a male mouse is able to kill the genetic material of another male and subsequently impregnate the female himself.

These four effects of pheromones on reproductive cycles appear to be mediated by the *vomeronasal organ,* which consists of a small group of sensory receptors arranged around a pouch connected by a duct to the nasal passage. The vomeronasal organ, which is present in all orders of mammals except for cetaceans (whales and dolphins), projects to the *accessory olfactory bulb,* immediately behind the olfactory bulb (Wysocki, 1979). (See *Figure 10.14.*) The vomeronasal organ probably does not detect airborne molecules, as the olfactory epithelium does, but instead is sensitive to nonvolatile compounds found in urine or other substances. In fact, stimulation of the nasopalatine nerve causes fluid to be pumped into the vomeronasal organ, which exposes the receptors to any substances that may be present (Meredith and O'Connell, 1979).

Removal of the accessory olfactory bulb disrupts the Lee-Boot effect (Reynolds and Keverne, 1979), the Whitten effect (Johns, Feder, Komisaruk, and Mayer, 1978), the Vandenbergh effect (Kaneko, Debski, Wilson, and Whitten, 1980), and the Bruce effect (Bellringer, Pratt, and Keverne, 1980); thus, this organ is essential for these phenomena. The accessory olfactory bulb sends axons to the *medial nucleus of the amygdala,* which in turn projects to the preoptic area and anterior hypothalamus, to the ventromedial nucleus of the hypothalamus, and to the bed nucleus of the stria terminalis (Halpern, 1987).

Keverne (1982) has suggested that the effects of pheromones on reproductive cycles are mediated by changes in the level of dopamine release in the hypothalamus, which in turn affects the secretion of prolactin by the anterior pituitary gland. As you will recall from Chapter 4, the hypothalamus controls the secretions of the anterior pituitary gland by secreting its own hormones. Unlike most other anterior pituitary hormones, prolactin is under *inhibitory* control; that is, unless the hypothalamus secretes an inhibitory hormone, prolactin is released spontaneously. In this case the inhibitory hormone is dopamine, which serves as a transmitter substance elsewhere in the brain. In general, pheromones present in female urine decrease hypothalamic dopamine release and thus increase prolactin secretion. Pheromones present in male urine do the opposite: They increase dopamine and decrease prolactin. For example, Reynolds and Keverne (1979) found that an injection of bromocriptine, which stimulates dopamine receptors, blocks the Lee-Boot effect (slowing of estrous cycles). In contrast, Lomas and Keverne (1982) found that bromocriptine *produces* the Vandenbergh effect (acceleration of puberty).

Li, Kaba, Saito, and Seto (1989) obtained elec-

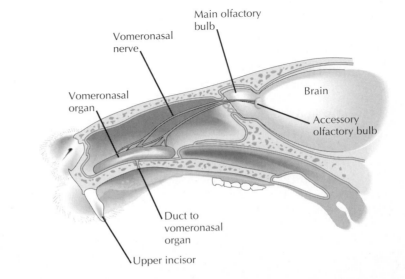

trophysiological evidence for a link between the accessory olfactory bulb and activity of neurosecretory cells in the arcuate nucleus of the hypothalamus, which control the anterior pituitary gland. The investigators found that electrical stimulation of the accessory olfactory bulb produced excitation in single neurons in the arcuate nucleus. This excitation could be blocked by injections of a local anesthetic in the medial amygdala; thus, the medial amygdala is part of the pathway from the accessory olfactory bulb to the arcuate nucleus. The anatomical details of this pathway are not yet known.

The Bruce effect involves learning; the female obviously learns to recognize the odor of the male with which she mates, because his odor will not cause her to abort if she encounters it later. This learning appears to involve the activity of a set of noradrenergic axons that enter the olfactory bulb and form synapses with both the main and accessory olfactory bulb. Keverne and de la Riva (1982) found that after these axons had been destroyed with infusions of 6-hydroxydopamine (6-HD), a female mouse would not learn to recognize the odor of the male that mated with her; *his* odor would cause her to abort.

It is possible that the stimuli associated with copulation trigger the noradrenergic mechanism and "imprint" the odor of the male on the female, ensuring that she will not abort if she later encounters his odor. Rosser and Keverne (1985) found that vaginal stimulation increases the activity in the noradrenergic axons that serve the olfactory bulbs. As other studies have shown (Gray, Freeman, and Skinner, 1986; Leon, 1987), the release of norepinephrine in the olfactory bulbs is necessary for olfactory learning. (This phenomenon will be described in more detail in Chapter 15.)

Besides having effects on reproductive cycles, some pheromones directly affect behavior. For example, pheromones present in the vaginal secretions of female hamsters stimulate sexual behavior in males. Males are attracted to the secretions of females, and they sniff and lick the female's genitals before copulating. In fact, there seem to be two categories of pheromones, one detected by the vomeronasal organ and another detected by the olfactory epithelium. Mating behav-

ior of male hamsters is disrupted only if both the primary and accessory olfactory systems are interrupted (Powers and Winans, 1975; Winans and Powers, 1977). Deafferentation of the primary olfactory system is accomplished by rinsing the olfactory epithelium with zinc sulfate; deafferentation of the accessory olfactory system is accomplished by cutting the vomeronasal nerve.

As we saw, both the primary and accessory olfactory systems send fibers to the medial nucleus of the amygdala. Lehman and Winans (1982) used autoradiography to identify the precise projection regions of these systems: They injected radioactive amino acids into the primary and accessory olfactory bulbs and examined sections of the amygdala. Next, they made lesions of the amygdala of male hamsters that destroyed both sets of projections and found that the animals no longer engaged in sexual behavior. Thus, the amygdala is part of the system that mediates the effects of pheromones on the sexual behavior of male hamsters.

The effectiveness of sex attractants depends on androgens; Gregory, Engle, and Pfaff (1975) found that castration decreased males' interest in the odor of females. Significantly, cells in the medial nucleus of the amygdala—especially that of the male—contain androgen receptors (Roselli, Handa, and Resko, 1989). Thus, if the results of all these studies are taken together, a coherent picture emerges: Androgens activate neural circuits in the medial nucleus of the amygdala, so that they respond to the odor of vaginal secretions, detected by means of the olfactory bulbs and vomeronasal organs. This excitation is then passed on to neural circuits involved in sexual arousal. (Their location is discussed later in this chapter.)

Two types of sex attractant pheromones are present in the vaginal secretions of female hamsters: dimethyl disulfide, which is detected by the main olfactory system (Singer, Agosta, O'Connell, Pfaffman, Bowen, and Field, 1976), and a substance with a high molecular weight that has not yet been analyzed (Singer, Clancy, Macrides, and Agosta, 1984). The odor of dimethyl disulfide serves to attract the male to the female. Then, as the male sniffs and licks her genitals, the high-molecular-weight pheromone stimulates the vomeronasal organ and produces mounting. Treating the olfactory mucosa with zinc sulfate eliminates the effectiveness of dimethyl disulfide but not the high-molecular-weight pheromone; cutting the vomeronasal nerve does the opposite (Clancy, Macrides, Singer, and Agosta, 1984; O'Connell and Meredith, 1984).

It appears that at least some pheromone-related phenomena occur in humans. McClintock (1971) studied the menstrual cycles of women attending an all-female college. She found that women who spent a large amount of time together tended to have synchronized cycles—their menstrual periods began within a day or two of each other. In addition, women who regularly spent some time in the presence of men tended to have shorter cycles than those who rarely spent time with (smelled?) men.

Russell, Switz, and Thompson (1977) obtained direct evidence that olfactory stimuli can synchronize women's menstrual cycles. The investigators collected daily samples of a woman's underarm sweat. They dissolved the samples in alcohol and swabbed them on the upper lips of a group of women three times each week, in the order in which they were originally taken. The cycles of the women who received the extract (but not those of control subjects whose lips were swabbed with pure alcohol) began to synchronize with the cycle of the odor donor.

Because studies have shown that the accessory olfactory system appears to mediate the effects of pheromones on reproductive cycles of rodents, the question arises as to whether the effects of olfactory stimuli on human reproductive cycles are also mediated by this system. The answer appears to be no. Most investigators agree that vomeronasal organs can be found in human fetuses, but functioning vomeronasal organs are not found in adults (Johnson, Josephson, and Hawke, 1985; Nakashima, Kimmelman, and Snow, 1985). Thus, the pheromonal control of human reproductive cycles would seem to be mediated by the main olfactory system.

What about human sexual attractants? So far, there is no evidence that they exist. (Imagine how delighted perfume makers would be if some were found.) Keverne and Michael (1971) obtained evidence suggesting that olfactory stimuli affect sexual attraction in laboratory primates, which suggested that a similar phenomenon might occur in humans. They reported that a mixture of short-chain fatty acids was secreted by a female monkey's vagina around the time of ovulation. When they swabbed these compounds on the genital regions of ovariectomized females, males became more sexually interested in them. These results suggested that the chemicals served as sexual-attractant pheromones, which would encourage sexual intercourse during the time the female is most likely to become pregnant.

However, Goldfoot, Krevetz, Goy, and Freeman (1976) tested the hypothesized sexual attractant and found that it had no effect on the females' attractiveness to males. In addition, they found that the fatty acids were actually secreted in greatest quantity during the luteal (postovulatory) phase of the menstrual cycle, when copulatory activity is at a low point. In subsequent studies Goldfoot and his colleagues (reported by Goldfoot, 1981) presented male monkeys with blocks of wood that had been swabbed with various substances. They found that sexually *inexperienced* males did not pay special attention to blocks of wood that contained the vaginal secretions from a female monkey at midcycle. However, sexually *experienced* males did sniff them more than blocks of wood containing other odors. These results suggest that the experienced males had learned to recognize the odor of a preovulatory female, not that the secretions produced then act as an automatic sexual attractant. The role of olfactory stimuli as discriminative cues is different from—and much more complex than—pheromonal control of male sexual interest by chemicals secreted by the female.

Some investigators have studied the possibility that odors produced by vaginal secretions may affect a woman's sexual attractiveness. Doty, Ford, Preti, and Huggins (1975) found that both males and females rated these odors as unpleasant, although secretions obtained around the time of ovulation were rated as less unpleasant. Thus, a woman's menstrual cycle appears to affect the odor of her vaginal secretions, but there is no direct evidence that these changes increase her sexual attractiveness.

Although there is currently no evidence that pheromones play a role in sexual attraction in higher primates, the familiar odor of a sex partner may have a positive effect on sexual arousal. We are not generally conscious of the fact, but we can identify other people on the basis of olfactory cues. For example, a study by Russell (1976) found that people were able to distinguish by odor between T-shirts that they had worn and those previously worn by other people. They could also tell whether the unknown owner of a T-shirt was male or female. Thus, it is likely that men and women can *learn* to be attracted by their partners' characteristic odors. However, this is a different phenomenon from the responses produced by pheromones, which apparently need not be learned.

Human Sexual Behavior

Human sexual behavior, like that of other mammals, is influenced by the activational effects of gonadal hormones. However, as we will see, the effects are different. Men and women are much more similar in their responses to sex hormones than are other male and female mammals.

Organizational Effects of Prenatal Androgens

A myth that should be dispelled immediately is that men and women would exchange their behavioral roles if their hormonal balances were reversed (subject, of course, to anatomical differences). Nothing of the sort would happen. Castrating a heterosexual man and giving him female sex hormones would not make him become homosexual. His body would change and he would lose the ability to have sexual intercourse, but he would not become interested in assuming the female role in sexual activity. Similarly, removing a heterosexual woman's ovaries and giving her testosterone would not make her lose her sexual interest in men or want to engage in sexual activity with other women. She would not even lose her sex drive (although men might be turned off by her beard and husky voice). In fact, she may become even *more* interested in sex than she was before.

As we shall see later in this chapter, prenatal androgenization does affect development of the human brain; there are parts of the brain that differ in men and women. Thus, androgens may have defeminizing and masculinizing effects on

human sexual behavior, just as they do in other mammals. However, the data we have so far are not conclusive. Even if prenatal androgenization does influence human sexual behavior, the effect is certainly different from that which occurs in laboratory animals. The most important reason for this difference is that, unlike rodents, human males and females do not exhibit rigidly different sexual behaviors. That statement might sound foolish to you. "Of course," you say to yourself, "men and women have different sex behavior." But think about what men and women do, in contrast to other mammals. Male rats mount, intromit, and perform pelvic thrusts. Female rats arch their backs, move their tails, and stand still. Their copulatory behaviors are very stereotyped and very different. All males basically copulate the same way, and so do all females.

The behavior of humans during sexual intercourse shares an important element with other species, namely, the movement of the penis in the vagina. However, this movement can be accomplished by the man, the woman, or both of them. There is no single pattern of movements that all humans are obliged to follow in order to copulate; human sexual activity comes in a variety of forms. Except for the obvious effects of anatomical differences, we cannot characterize particular sets of movements as "male" or "female."

What *does* distinguish between heterosexual men and women is *the gender of their preferred sex partner.* Heterosexual men prefer women, and heterosexual women prefer men. A person's sexual orientation is not defined by the particular behaviors he or she performs but by the gender of the partner with whom he or she performs them. Therefore, if the brain of a human fetus is altered by exposure to testosterone, we would not expect this alteration to affect particular *behaviors*. Rather, we might expect it to affect whether the person is sexually attracted to men or to women. This possibility will be explored in the next section and later in this chapter, when I discuss sexual preferences.

Prenatal Androgenization of Human Females. Evidence suggests that prenatal androgenization can affect human social behavior and sexual orientation, as well as anatomy. In a disorder known as the ***adrenogenital syndrome,*** the adrenal glands secrete abnormal amounts of androgens. (Note that the word is *adreno*genital, because of the involvement of the adrenal glands, not *andro*genital.) The secretion of androgens begins prenatally; thus, the syndrome causes prenatal androgenization. Boys born with adrenogenital syndrome develop normally; the extra androgen does not seem to have significant effects. However, a girl with adrenogenital syndrome will be born with an enlarged clitoris, and her labia may be partly fused together. (Remember that the scrotum and labia majora develop from the same primordia.) If the masculinization of the genitals is pronounced, surgery will be performed to correct them. In any event, once the syndrome is identified, the person will be given a synthetic hormone that suppresses the abnormal secretion of androgens.

Money, Schwartz, and Lewis (1984) studied thirty young women with a history of adrenogenital syndrome. They had all been born with enlarged clitorises and partly fused labia, which led to the diagnosis. (A few mild cases were not diagnosed for several years.) Once the diagnosis was made, they were medically treated and, if necessary, genital surgery was performed. Money and his colleagues asked the young women to describe their sexual orientation. Eleven of the women (37 percent of the total) described themselves as bisexual or homosexual, twelve (40 percent) said they were exclusively heterosexual, and seven (23 percent) refused to talk about their sex lives. If the noncommittal women are excluded from the sample, the percentage of homo- or bisexuality rises to 48 percent.

The Kinsey report on sexuality in women (Kinsey, Pomeroy, Martin, and Gebhard, 1953) reported that approximately 10 percent of American women had had some sexual contact with another woman by the age of twenty; in the sample of androgenized women, the percentage was approximately four times as high. The results therefore suggest that the exposure of a female fetus to abnormally high levels of androgens does affect sexual orientation. A plausible explanation is that the effect takes place in the brain, but we must remember that the androgens also affect the genitals; possibly, this fact played a role in shaping the development of the girls' sexual orientation. If the

differences seen in sexual orientation *were* caused by effects of the prenatal androgens on brain development, then we could reasonably conclude that they occur in males, too. That is, they would support the hypothesis that male sexual orientation is at least partly determined by masculinization (and defeminization) of the human brain.

Because controlled experiments cannot be performed on humans, some investigators have turned to our close relatives to see whether prenatal androgenization has enduring behavioral effects. Goy, Bercovitch, and McBrair (1988) administered injections of testosterone to pregnant monkeys. The testosterone entered the blood supply of the fetuses and masculinized them. Female infants that had been androgenized early during fetal development were born with masculinized genitals; the genitals of those that had been androgenized later were normal. *Both* groups showed differences in their sociosexual interactions with peers, displaying a higher proportion of malelike behavior than normal females did. For example, even as young adults, the group with normal genitals continued to mount their peers significantly more than normal females did. The results suggest that genital changes cannot account for all the behavioral effects of prenatal androgenization in primates. Whether *human* primates share these characteristics is, of course, another question.

Failure of Androgenization in Human Males. Nature has performed the equivalent of the prenatal castration experiment in humans (Money and Ehrhardt, 1972). Some people are insensitive to androgens; they have **androgen insensitivity syndrome,** one of the more aptly named disorders. The cause of androgen insensitivity syndrome is a genetic mutation that prevents the formation of functioning androgen receptors. The primordial gonads of a genetic male with androgen insensitivity syndrome become testes and secrete Müllerian-inhibiting substance and androgens. However, only the Müllerian-inhibiting substance has an effect on development. Because the cells cannot respond to the androgens, the person develops female external genitalia. The Müllerian-inhibiting substance prevents the female internal sex organs from developing, though; the uterus fails to develop and the vagina is shallow.

If an individual with this syndrome is raised as a girl, all is well. Normally, the testes are removed because they often become cancerous; but if they are not, the body will become feminized at the time of puberty by the small amounts of estradiol produced by the testes. (If the testes are removed, the person will be given estradiol.) At adulthood the individual will function sexually as a woman, although surgical lengthening of the vagina may be necessary. Women with this syndrome report average sex drives, including normal frequency of orgasm in intercourse. Most marry and lead normal sex lives. Of course, lacking a uterus and ovaries, they cannot have children.

In the previous subsection of this chapter I described a study on adrenogenital syndrome by Money, Schwartz, and Lewis (1984). They also examined a group of fifteen young women with androgen insensitivity syndrome. Only two of these women (7 percent) reported having had sexual contact with another women, and in both cases they had also had sexual contact with men. Thus, people in whom androgenization cannot take place are very unlikely to develop sexual interest in women, even though their sex chromosomes are XY and they are born with testes.

The powerful effect of the lack of androgen receptors is shown in Figure 10.15. This photograph certainly illustrates why it would be a tragedy to raise such an individual as a boy, even though the person has XY sex chromosomes. The woman in this figure lacks pubic hair and axillary hair, because in women these traits are normally stimulated by androstenedione, and without androgen receptors this hormone has no effect. (See *Figure 10.15*.)

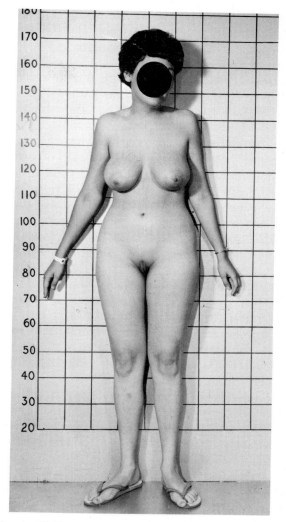

FIGURE 10.15

An XY female displaying androgen insensitivity syndrome. The absence of pubic hair can be explained by the person's insensitivity to androstenedione. (From Money, J., and Ehrhardt, A.A. *Man & Woman, Boy & Girl.* Copyright 1973 by The Johns Hopkins University Press, Baltimore, Maryland. By permission.)

Activational Effects of Sex Hormones on Women's Sexual Behavior

As we saw, the sexual behavior of female mammals other than higher primates is controlled by gonadal hormones. However, this is not the case for women. Although estradiol and progesterone may influence sexual activity, they do not *control* it. Most women do not exhibit large changes in receptivity during their menstrual cycle, as laboratory rodents do. As we saw, a female rat will copulate only during estrus, when her estradiol and progesterone levels are high. However, women can become sexually aroused at any time of their menstrual cycle. This is not to say that gonadal hormones have *no* effects in women. In general, women are more likely to engage in autosexual activity (masturbation, sexual fantasies, and arousal from books and films) or to initiate sexual activity with their partners at the time of ovulation. This peak does not occur in women who are taking birth control pills, presumably because the pills prevent ovulation and the accompanying hormonal fluctuations (Adams, Gold, and Burt, 1978; Morris, Udry, Khan-Dawood, and Dawood, 1987).

The relatively minor effects of female gonadal hormones are exemplified by the results of ovariectomy on women's sexual activity. Ovariectomy, sometimes carried out when a hysterectomy is performed, does not abolish a woman's interest in sexual activity, nor does menopause, nature's own "ovariectomy." Loss of estradiol may produce vaginal dryness, which can make intercourse painful, but this effect on sexual behavior is obviously an indirect one. (It can be alleviated by the use of a lubricating jelly or eliminated by the administration of estradiol pills.)

Another difference between women and animals with estrous cycles is indicated by their contrasting reactions to androgens. Testosterone usually produces a small increase in malelike mounting behavior in female rats, even if they were not androgenized early in life. However, androgens do not stimulate *male* sexual behavior in women. On the contrary, in heterosexual women these hormones appear to increase heterosexual desire.

Evidence for an activational effect of androgens on women's sexual behavior comes from a study by Persky, Lief, Strauss, Miller, and O'Brien (1978). These investigators studied the sexual activity and blood levels of gonadal hormones in married couples over a period of three menstrual cycles. They rated the husbands' and wives' responsivity (willingness to engage in sexual activity) and initiation (instigation of sexual activity). The husband's testosterone level was correlated with mutual interest in sexual activity, whether initiated by the husband or the wife. Frequency of intercourse over the entire cycle was related to the wife's peak testosterone level during ovulation. In addition, the wives reported more sexual gratification when their testosterone levels were high, and women with high baseline levels of testosterone tended to report greater satisfaction with sexual activity.

Although experiments with humans are not possible, research on the effects of hormones on female sexual behavior has been performed with rhesus macaques, a common species of laboratory monkey. In general, results have confirmed a role for androgens in the sexual behavior of this species. Everitt, Herbert, and Hamer (1972) found that removal of the adrenal glands decreased the sexual interest of female rhesus macaques who had previously been ovariectomized. The effect was seen most strikingly in the animals' soliciting behavior—what researchers have called *proceptivity*. Removal of the adrenal glands had a much smaller effect on *receptivity*—the animal's willingness to engage in sexual activity with a male who initiates the behavior. Administration of testosterone reinstituted these behaviors to normal levels.

Activational Effects of Sex Hormones in Men

Although women and female rodents are very different in their behavioral responsiveness to sex hormones, men and male rodents (and other mammals, for that matter) resemble each other in their behavioral responsiveness to testosterone. With normal levels they can be potent and fertile; without testosterone sperm production ceases, and sooner or later, so does sexual activity. Some investigators have said that the sexual activity of humans is "emancipated" from the effects of hormones. In one sense this is true. Men who have been castrated for medical reasons do report a continuing interest in sexual activity with their wives. Even if sexual activity no longer takes the form of intercourse, other types of sexual contact can occur.

Davidson, Camargo, and Smith (1979) performed a double-blind study that demonstrates the activational effects of testosterone on men's sexual activity. Their subjects were married men with the *hypogonadal syndrome,* whose testes failed to produce adequate amounts of testosterone. The investigators administered injections of testosterone (high or low doses) or a placebo and asked the subjects to keep a written log of their sexual activities. They found that the testosterone (particularly the high dose) significantly increased the frequency of these activities.

The decline in copulatory ability after

castration varies considerably among individuals, even of the same species. Most rats cease to copulate within a few weeks, but some retain this ability for up to five months (Davidson, 1966). Because the average life span of a rat is a little over two years, this performance compares favorably with that of castrated humans, taking the different life spans into account. As reported by Money and Ehrhardt (1972), some men lose potency immediately, whereas others show a slow, gradual decline over several years. Perhaps at least some of the variability is a function of prior experience; practice may not only "make perfect" but may also forestall a decline in function. Although there is no direct evidence with respect to this possibility in humans, Rosenblatt and Aronson (1958a, 1958b) found that high levels of sexual activity before castration substantially prolonged subsequent potency in cats.

Testosterone not only affects sexual activity but also is affected by it—or even by thinking about it. A scientist stationed on a remote island (Anonymous, 1970) removed his beard with an electrical shaver each day and weighed the clippings. Just before he left for visits to the mainland (and to female company), his beard began growing faster. Because rate of beard growth is related to androgen levels, the effect indicates that his anticipation of sexual activity stimulated testosterone production. Confirming these results, Hellhammer, Hubert, and Schurmeyer (1985) found that watching an erotic film increased men's testosterone level.

Sexual Orientation

What controls a person's sexual orientation, the gender of the preferred sex partner? Some people are exclusively homosexual, being attracted only to partners of the same sex; some are bisexual, being attracted to members of both sexes; and some are heterosexual, being attracted only to partners of the other sex. Many humans (especially males) who are essentially heterosexual engage in homosexual episodes sometime during their lives. In some societies homosexual behavior is the norm during adolescence, followed by marriage and a normal heterosexual relationship (Money and Ehrhardt, 1972). Although many animals occasionally engage in sexual activity with a member of the same sex, *exclusive* homosexuality appears to occur only in humans (Ehrhardt and Meyer-Bahlburg, 1981).

Some investigators believe that homosexuality is a result of childhood experiences, especially interactions between the child and parents. A large-scale study of several hundred male and female homosexuals reported by Bell, Weinberg, and Hammersmith (1981) attempted to assess the effects of these factors. The researchers found no evidence that homosexuals had been raised by domineering mothers or submissive fathers, as some clinicians had suggested. The best predictor of adult homosexuality was a self-report of homosexual feelings, which usually preceded homosexual activity by three years. The investigators concluded that their data did not support social explanations for homosexuality but were consistent with the possibility that homosexuality is at least partly biologically determined.

Suspecting that male homosexuality might be caused by differences in levels of gonadal hormones, investigators have measured them in homosexuals and heterosexuals. Some early studies reported differences, but most investigators now believe that the results were biased by the stress experienced by homosexual people who felt harassed by society. This stress lowered the subjects' androgen levels. It appears that well-adjusted male homosexuals have normal levels of gonadal hormones (Tourney, 1980).

Given what we now know about the effects of gonadal hormones, we would not predict that their activational effects are responsible for a person's homosexuality. After all, androgens appear to be important for the sexual desire and activity of both men and women. Therefore, the activational effects of sex hormones are probably the same in homosexuals and heterosexuals. However, we saw earlier that the organizational effects of androgens bias the later sexual proclivities of many species of animals. Therefore, if homosexuality does have a physiological cause, it is more likely to be a more subtle difference in brain structure caused by the presence or absence of prenatal androgenization.

As we saw, men and women do not differ from one another so much in their sexual *behavior* as in the gender of their sex partners. The same comparison is true for heterosexual and homosexual people; the gender of their partner, not the kind of sexual activity they engage in, distinguishes them. Therefore, if prenatal androgenization influences human brain development, the effects are likely to be seen in a person's choice of sex partner, not in the form of his or her sexual behavior. You will recall that exposure of a developing rodent brain to androgens causes masculinization or defeminization, depending on the time during which the exposure occurs. By analogy, we might predict that androgenization would defeminize a human female's choice of partner, making her less likely to choose a male, and also masculinize her choice, making her more likely to choose a female. As we saw earlier, this often happens when a human female fetus is exposed to high levels of androgens. Perhaps, then, the brains of male homosexuals are neither masculinized nor defeminized, those of female homosexuals are masculinized and defeminized, and those of bisexuals are masculinized but not defeminized. Of course, these are *speculations* that so far cannot be supported by human data; they are not *conclusions*. They should be regarded as suggestions to guide future research.

A study by Gladue, Green, and Hellman (1984) obtained evidence that suggests that the pituitary glands of homosexual males may be less defeminized than those of heterosexual males. As you learned, when the concentration of estradiol reaches a critical level, it stimulates the anterior pituitary gland to release some LH. Gladue and his colleagues injected adult male homosexuals, male heterosexuals, and female heterosexuals with an estrogen. The blood levels of LH in the women showed a dramatic rise; those of the heterosexual men did not. The change in blood levels of LH in the homosexual men was intermediate; they showed a statistically significant increase, but one smaller than that of the women. Certainly, we cannot conclude that the men's homosexuality was caused by differences in the response of their pituitary glands to estrogens. However, the results suggest that the homosexual men's pituitary glands (and hence their brains) may have received less exposure to androgens during some critical stage of prenatal development. This decreased exposure may have increased the likelihood of their

developing a preference for male sex partners later.

These results are interesting but puzzling. In monkeys, at least, the male pituitary gland is able to function like that of a female. Norman and Spies (1986) castrated male rhesus monkeys and transplanted a set of ovaries into their bodies. The ovaries began to show a normal twenty-eight-day ovulatory cycle, which obviously means that the male pituitary gland was able to respond to a rise in estradiol level with a surge of LH. These results suggest that the anterior pituitary gland is not affected by prenatal androgens. These results will have to be reconciled with those of Gladue and his colleagues.

A study performed with laboratory animals suggests that prenatal stress can alter adult sexual behavior. Ward (1972) subjected pregnant rats to periods of stress by confining them and exposing them to a bright light. This treatment increased the amount of stress-related steroid hormones secreted by the mothers' adrenal cortex. A later study (Ward and Weisz, 1980) confirmed that this treatment suppresses androgen production in male fetuses. The male rats born to the stressed mothers had smaller external genitalia as adults. Compared with normal control subjects, the animals were less likely to display male sexual behavior and were more likely to display female sexual behavior when they were given injections of estradiol and progesterone. Other studies have shown that besides having behavioral effects, prenatal stress reduces the size of a part of the forebrain that is normally larger in males than in females (Anderson, Fleming, Rhees, and Kinghorn, 1986.) Although we cannot assume that prenatal stress in humans has similar effects on the brain and behavior, the results of these studies are consistent with the hypothesis that male homosexuality may be related to events that interfere with androgenization.

Several studies have shown that prenatal events can increase the incidence of *male* sexual behavior in *female* rats. For example, Clemens (1971) found that the probability of malelike mounting behavior was highest in female rats that shared their mother's uterus with several brothers; fewer brothers resulted in less male sexual behavior. Presumably, the females were partially androgenized by their brothers' testosterone. Because humans rarely have company in the uterus, this factor apparently is not of much importance in human female homosexuality.

For some people homosexuality is immoral; others regard it as a mental disorder. However, both of these characterizations have been denounced by professional mental health organizations. It is clear that homosexuals can be as happy and as well adjusted as heterosexuals (Bell and Weinberg, 1978). If the hypotheses I have outlined here are correct, then homosexuals are no more responsible for their sexual orientation than heterosexuals are. The question "Why does someone become homosexual?" will probably be answered when we find out why someone becomes *heterosexual*.

*I*NTERIM SUMMARY

The female reproductive cycle (menstrual cycle or estrous cycle) begins with the maturation of one or more ovarian follicles, which occurs in response to the secretion of FSH by the anterior pituitary gland. As the ovarian follicle matures, it secretes estradiol, which causes the lining of the uterus to develop. When estradiol reaches a critical level, it causes the pituitary gland to secrete a surge of LH, triggering ovulation. The empty ovarian follicle becomes a corpus luteum, under the continued influence of LH, and secretes estradiol and progesterone. If pregnancy does not occur, the corpus luteum dies and stops producing hormones, and menstruation begins.

In most mammals female sexual behavior is the norm, just as the female body and female sex organs are the norm. That is, unless prenatal androgens masculinize and defeminize the animal's brain, its sexual behavior will be feminine. Behavioral masculinization refers to the androgen-stimulated development of neural circuits that respond to testosterone in adulthood, producing male sexual behavior. Behavioral defeminization refers to the inhibitory effects of androgens on the development of neural circuits that respond to estradiol and progesterone in adulthood, producing female sexual behavior.

The sexual behavior of males of all mammalian species appears to depend on the presence of androgens. Prolactin has an inhibitory effect and may be involved in the refractory period that follows ejaculation. Female mammals other than primates depend primarily on estradiol and progesterone and will copulate only during the period of estrus, when the levels of these hormones are high. In particular, estradiol has a priming effect on the subsequent appearance of progesterone.

Pheromones can affect sexual physiology and behavior. Odorants present in the urine of female mice affect their estrous cycles, lengthening and eventually stopping them (Lee-Boot effect). Odorants present in the urine of male mice abolish these effects and cause the females' cycles to become synchronized. They can also accelerate the onset of puberty in females (Vandenbergh effect). In addition, the odor of the urine from a male other than the one that impregnated the female mouse will cause her to abort (Bruce effect). The Bruce effect involves learning the odor of the male that impregnates the female, and the activity of a noradrenergic input to the olfactory bulb is involved in this learning. In general, pheromonal effects produced by odors of male urine involve an increase in dopamine and a decrease in prolactin, whereas those produced by odors of female urine involve the opposite changes.

In the hamster the attractiveness of an estrous female to the male derives in part from chemicals present in her vaginal secretions, detected by the olfactory epithelium and vomeronasal organ. Connections between the olfactory system and the amygdala appear to be important in stimulating male sexual behavior. Although some studies have shown that odors can play a role in the sexual attractiveness of female monkeys, it does not appear that the effect is caused by pheromones, which involve automatic responses to particular chemicals.

The behavioral effects of prenatal androgenization in humans, if any, are not well understood. Studies of prenatally androgenized girls suggest that organizational effects may well influence the development of sexual orientation. Testosterone has an activational effect on the sexual behavior of men, just as it does on the behavior of other male mammals. Women do not require estradiol or progesterone in order to experience sexual interest and engage in sexual behavior, although these hormones may affect the quality and intensity of their sex drive. Instead, the most important activational effect on women's sex drives seems to be provided by androgens.

Sexual orientation (that is, heterosexuality or homosexuality) may be influenced by prenatal androgenization, but conclusive evidence is lacking. One study found that the LH response of homosexual men was intermediate to that of heterosexual males and females, which suggests a lesser degree of prenatal androgenization. In addition, events that cause stress to a pregnant rat can interfere with defeminization of the sexual behavior of her male offspring.

NEURAL CONTROL OF SEXUAL BEHAVIOR

Spinal Mechanisms

Some sexual responses are controlled by neural circuits contained within the spinal cord. For example, genital stimulation can elicit sexual movements and postures in female cats and rats even after their spinal cord is transected below the brain (Beach, 1967; Hart, 1969). In males dogs with spinal cord transections genital stimulation can produce erection and ejaculation (Hart, 1967). Thus, the brain is not required for these reflexes.

In humans, too, erection and ejaculation are controlled by spinal reflexes. Men with spinal damage have become fathers when their wives have been artificially inseminated with semen obtained by mechanical stimulation (Hart, 1978). Because the spinal damage prevents sensory information from reaching the brain, they do not experience an orgasm as a result; and thus, they are unaware of the erection and ejaculation unless they see it happening. However, they do occasionally experience a "phantom erection" along with an orgasm, despite penile quiescence (Money, 1960; Comarr, 1970). Nothing happens to their genitals or internal sex organs, but the spontaneous activity of various brain mechanisms gives rise to feelings of arousal and orgasm.

Evidence obtained by Chung, McVary, and McKenna (1988) suggests that, at least in the rat, the ejaculatory reflex does not depend on androgens. They found that an ejaculatory response could be triggered by gentle, rhythmic stimulation of the end of the urethra with a small catheter that had been placed inside it. Castration had no effect on the magnitude of the response, although it did reduce the size of penile erections. The investigators also found that a similar response could be produced in female rats (intact or ovariectomized), shown by rhythmic contractions of the vagina. The results suggest that male and female "orgasmic" responses are controlled by similar mechanisms. (The word *orgasmic* is in quotation marks, because we have no way of determining how rats feel.)

Although there may be more similarities in the sexual reflexes of males and females than had previously been suspected, Breedlove and Arnold (1980, 1983), discovered striking sex differences in the size of a nucleus in the ventral horn of the lumbar region of the spinal cord of rats. This structure, called the **spinal nucleus of the bulbocavernosus** (SNB), contains motor neurons whose axons innervate the bulbocavernosus muscle, which is attached to the base of the penis and is involved in sexual activity. Although the muscle is not present in female rats, it is present in both sexes in humans. (It is usually called the *sphincter vaginae* in women.)

Breedlove, Jacobson, Gorski, and Arnold (1982) found that if female rats were injected with testosterone on the second day after birth, the spinal nucleus of the bulbocavernosus would develop. Conversely, if male rats were treated prenatally by injecting the pregnant females with drugs that inhibit the effects of androgens and were then castrated postnatally, the SNB would

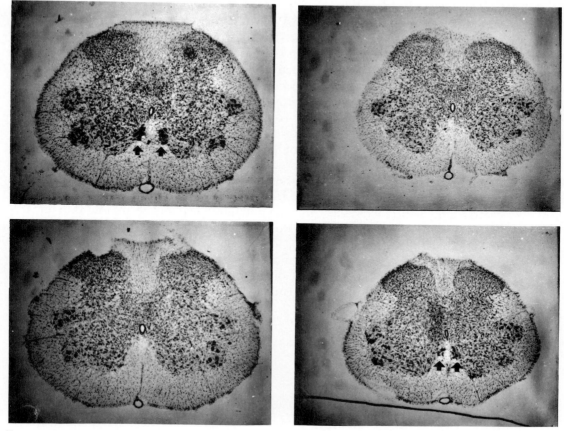

FIGURE 10.16

Photomicrographs of sections of the rat spinal cord through the region of the spinal nucleus of the bulbocavernosus. *Top left:* Normal male. *Top right:* Normal female. *Bottom left:* Castrated male treated with an antiandrogen prenatally. *Bottom right:* Androgenized female. (From Breedlove, S.M., and Arnold, A. *Journal of Neuroscience,* 1983, *3,* 417–423; 424–432. Copyright © 1983, Society for Neuroscience.)

not develop. Figure 10.16 shows photographs of sections of the rat spinal cord. The nuclei (*arrows*) are present in normal males (a) and androgenized females (b) but not in normal females (c) or nonandrogenized males (d). (See *Figure 10.16.*)

Arnold and his colleagues found that the effect of androgens is to prevent cell death (Arnold and Jordan, 1988). During most of prenatal development the SNB has similar numbers of neurons in males and females. Then a day or two before birth, the number of neurons in the female SNB begins to decline. By ten days of age the number has fallen to about one-third that in males. The androgens appear somehow to facilitate synaptic contacts of other neurons with the ones in the

SNB, which keeps the neurons alive (Matsumoto, Micevych, and Arnold, 1988).

Brain Mechanisms

Males

The *medial preoptic area* (MPA), located just rostral to the hypothalamus, is the forebrain region most critical for male sexual behavior. (As we will see in Chapter 11, it is also critical for other sexually dimorphic behavior such as territorial aggression.) Electrical stimulation of this region elicits male copulatory behavior (Malsbury, 1971). The act of copulation increases the metabolic activity of the MPA, as measured by the level of *Na,K-ATPase,* the enzyme that operates the sodium-potassium pump (Oaknin, Rodriguez del Castillo, Guerra, Battaner, and Mas, 1989).

Destruction of the MPA permanently abolishes male sexual behavior (Heimer and Larsson, 1966/1967). Lesions made with a neurotoxin that kills cell bodies without damaging axons passing through the region are just as effective; thus, the MPA itself is the critical structure (Hansen, Köhler, and Ross, 1982). The effects of MPA lesions are permanent, and they occur in rats, hamsters, mice, guinea pigs, gerbils, dogs, cats, goats, rhesus monkeys, lizards, and fish (Sachs and Meisel, 1988). (See *Figure 10.17.*)

Lordosis behavior in female rats is not abolished by preoptic area lesions; in fact, it is facilitated. However, the occasional mounting behavior seen in normal females disappears after lesions of the preoptic region (Singer, 1968). Thus, the MPA is part of a mechanism controlling male sexual behavior in *both* sexes.

Androgens exert both organizational and activational effects on neurons in the medial preoptic area. First, let us consider the activational effects. If a male rat is castrated in adulthood, its sexual behavior will cease. However, the behavior can be reinstated by implanting a small amount of testosterone directly into the medial preoptic area (Davidson, 1980). This region has been shown to contain a high concentration of nuclear androgen receptors in the male rat brain—more than five times as many as are found in females (Roselli, Handa, and Resko, 1989).

What about the organizational effects of androgens on brain development? Gorski, Gordon, Shryne, and Southam (1978) discovered a nucleus within the MPA of the rat that is three to

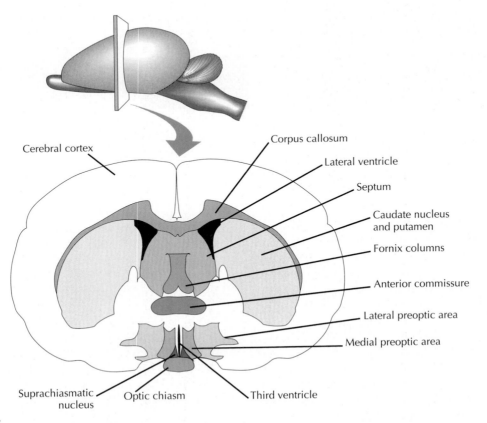

Cerebral cortex

Corpus callosum

Lateral ventricle

Septum

Caudate nucleus and putamen

Fornix columns

Anterior commissure

Lateral preoptic area

Medial preoptic area

Suprachiasmatic nucleus

Optic chiasm

Third ventricle

FIGURE 10.17

A cross section through the rat brain showing the location of the medial preoptic area. (Adapted from Paxinos, G., and Watson, C. *The Brain in Stereotaxic Coordinates.* Sydney: Academic Press, 1982. Redrawn with permission.)

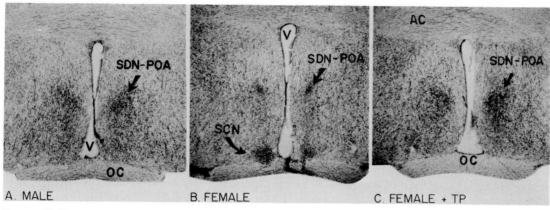

Photomicrographs of sections through the preoptic area of the rat brain. (a) Normal male. (b) Normal female. (c) Androgenized female. SDN-POA = sexually dimorphic nucleus of the preoptic area; OC = optic chiasm; V = third ventricle; SCN = suprachiasmatic nucleus; AC = anterior commissure. (From Gorski, R.A., in *Neuroendocrine Perspectives*, Vol. 2, edited by E.E. Müller and R.M. MacLeod. Amsterdam: Elsevier-North Holland, 1983.)

seven times larger in males than in females. This area is called (appropriately enough) the *sexually dimorphic nucleus* (SDN) of the preoptic area. (See *Figure 10.18.*)

Gorski and his colleagues found that the sex-related size difference in the sexually dimorphic nucleus was the result of an organizational effect of androgens; the nucleus was 50 percent smaller in rats that had been castrated immediately after birth. Jacobson, Csernus, Shryne, and Gorski (1981) found that the effect of castration on the size of the nucleus could be reversed by giving the rats injections of testosterone. More recent studies (Bloch and Gorski, 1988) have found that the sexually dimorphic nuclei can be subdivided into smaller parts. The size of some of these parts decreases when a male is castrated, which indicates that sex hormones can have *activational* effects on brain structure as well as *organizational* ones.

In the section on sexual orientation I mentioned that Anderson, Fleming, Rhees, and Kinghorn (1986) found that the size of the SDN in male rats was reduced by prenatal stress. They also found that volume of the SDN in an individual male rat (both stressed and unstressed) was directly related to the animal's level of sexual activity. In addition, lesions of the SDN decrease masculine sexual behavior in normal male rats or in females who were androgenized shortly after

birth (Turkenburg et al., 1988; De Jonge et al., 1989). Thus, SDN appears to be play an important role in male sexual behavior.

Why, exactly, do lesions of the medial preoptic area disrupt male sexual behavior? The evidence suggests that genital reflexes themselves are not affected. Stefanick and Davidson (1987) found that MPA lesions did not affect the response of a rat's penis to mechanical stimulation. Nor does sexual interest disappear; rats with MPA lesions will continue to pursue an estrous female and sniff her genital region (Heimer and Larsson, 1966/1967; Giantonio, Lund, and Gerall, 1970). Vacas, Lowenstein, and Cardinali (1982) found that male monkeys with MPA lesions continued to masturbate and to press a lever that caused a female monkey to be delivered to their cage. They also seemed sexually excited by the presence of the female, but they did *not* copulate with her. These results are interesting but puzzling. The medial preoptic area appears to be involved somehow in directing sexual behavior toward a female, but precisely how it does so is still a mystery.

Neurons in the medial preoptic area send axons to the lateral tegmental field of the midbrain (just dorsal and medial to the substantia nigra), and destruction of these axons or the lateral tegmental field disrupt male sexual behavior (Scouten, Burrell, Palmer, and Caganske, 1980;

Brackett and Edwards, 1984). These results suggests that the medial preoptic area exerts its effect by controlling motor mechanisms in the midbrain; however, little is known about these mechanisms.

The medial preoptic area of the human brain is sexually dimorphic, too (Swaab and Fliers, 1985; Allen, Hines, Shryne, and Gorski, 1989). Swaab and Hofman (1988) measured the size of this nucleus in the brains of deceased fetuses, children, and adults. They found that although the SDN could be distinguished in the brain of a fetus at midpregnancy, no sex differences were shown until about four years of age, at which time the SDN of females showed a decline in size. In addition, the SDN of both males and females decreased in size later in life. Incidentally, they studied the brains of nine homosexual men (who had died from AIDS) and found no evidence that their sexually dimorphic nuclei were any smaller than those of other men.

The medial preoptic area contains peptide receptors and neurons that secrete peptides. In a review Dornan and Malsbury (1989) listed twenty peptides that are found there. It is reasonable to suppose that some of them play a role in male sexual behavior. In fact, evidence suggests that several of them do, including prolactin, which, as we saw earlier, may play a role in the refractory period that follows ejaculation. Because the data on most of these peptides are still preliminary, I will refer you to the review by Dornan and Malsbury rather than discuss them here.

Other parts of the brain play a role in sexual behavior, too. The temporal lobes of the brain appear to play a role in the modulation of sexual arousal and in its direction toward an appropriate goal object, especially in higher mammals. (This role undoubtedly occurs in females as well as males.) We have already seen (in Chapter 6) that the temporal cortex plays a role in the visual recognition of objects. Monkeys with temporal lobe damage can "see" objects; they can orient in space quite normally and can pick up small objects. However, they cannot visually discriminate nuts and bolts from raisins and other small pieces of food. They must put everything into their mouth first, rejecting inedible objects and chewing and swallowing the edible ones. Temporal lobe damage also appears to impair an animal's ability to choose an appropriate sex object; male cats with these brain lesions have been reported to attempt copulation with everything in sight—the experimenter, a teddy bear, furniture—everything that is remotely mountable (Schreiner and Kling, 1956; Green, Clemente, and DeGroot, 1957).

In humans temporal lobe dysfunctions are often correlated with decreased sex drives. For example, focal epilepsy (brain seizures that originate from localized, irritative lesions) of the temporal lobes is sometimes associated with lack of interest in sexual activity (Blumer, 1975; Blumer and Walker, 1975). Usually, if the seizures are successfully treated by medication or by surgical removal of the affected tissue, the person attains normal sexual interest.

Kolarsky, Freund, Machek, and Polak (1967) examined the cases of men with sexual disorders and found a strong correlation between the disorders and actual or presumptive temporal lobe damage, especially if the damage occurred early in life. It is interesting to note that unusual sexual activities, such as fetishes, pedophilias (sexual interest in children), and transvestism are much more common in men than in women (Masters, Johnson, and Kolodny, 1982). We do not know whether the cause for this discrepancy is biological or cultural (or both).

Females

The one part of the brain that is most critical for performance of female sexual behavior is the *ventromedial nucleus of the hypothalamus* (VMH). Female rats with bilateral lesions of the ventromedial nuclei will not display lordosis behavior, even if they are treated with estradiol and progesterone. In fact, when trapped in a corner by a male rat, they will attack him (Pfaff and Sakuma, 1979). The critical region appears to be the anterior third of the VMH (Richmond and Clemens, 1988). (See *Figure 10.19.*) Conversely, electrical stimulation of the ventromedial nucleus facilitates female sexual behavior (Pfaff and Sakuma, 1979).

As we saw earlier, sexual behavior of female rats is activated by a priming dose of estradiol, followed by progesterone. Both of these hormones exert their behavioral effects on neurons located in the VMH. Rubin and Barfield (1980) implanted

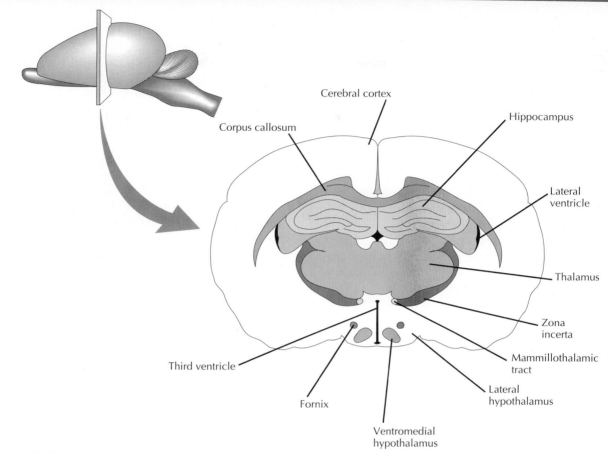

FIGURE 10.19

A cross section through the rat brain showing the location of the ventromedial nucleus of the hypothalamus.

minute quantities of estradiol bilaterally into the ventromedial nuclei of ovariectomized female rats. Next, they administered an injection of progesterone. The rats exhibited proceptive and receptive sexual behaviors when males were present: darting, hopping, ear wiggling, and lordosis. These results indicate that the priming effects of estradiol on female sexual behavior occur in the VMH. Pleim and Barfield (1988) administered priming doses of estradiol through injection or implantation beneath the animals' skin. Two days later, they placed a small amount of progesterone directly into the VMH. The animals showed increased proceptive and receptive sexual behavior. Thus, the effects of progesterone, too, take place in the VMH.

Autoradiographic studies have found that estrogen receptors are located in the medial preoptic area, ventromedial hypothalamus, amygdala, lateral septum, and periaqueductal gray matter in all mammals that have been examined so far (Pfaff and Schwartz-Giblin, 1988). The brains of both males and females contain these receptors; however, Rainbow, Parsons, and McEwen (1982) found that compared with female rat brains, male rat brains contained 58 percent fewer estrogen receptors in the medial preoptic area and 61 percent fewer progesterone receptors in the ventromedial nucleus of the hypothalamus. Presumably, these differences are among the defeminizing effects that androgens have on the developing brain.

The priming effect of estradiol is fairly straightforward: Estradiol increases the production of progesterone receptors. Blaustein and Feder (1979) administered estradiol to ovariectomized guinea pigs and found a 150 percent increase in the number of progesterone receptors in the hypothalamus. Presumably, the estradiol activates genetic mechanisms in the nucleus that are responsible for the production of progesterone receptors. In a subsequent study Blaustein and Feder (1980) administered a priming dose of estradiol and then followed it 40 hours later with an injection of progesterone. They killed animals at varying times after the progesterone injection and examined the number of progesterone receptors in the nucleus of cells of the basal forebrain. They observed a rapid increase and then a more gradual decline. (See *Figure 10.20.*)

Figure 10.21 shows two slices through the arcuate nucleus of ovariectomized guinea pigs, stained for progesterone receptors. One of the animals had previously received a priming dose of estradiol; the other had not. You probably will not need to read the figure caption to see which is which. (See *Figure 10.21.*)

The neurons of the ventromedial nucleus send axons to the *periaqueductal gray matter* (PAG) of the midbrain, surrounding the cerebral aqueduct (Krieger, Conrad, and Pfaff, 1979). This region, too, has been implicated in female sexual behavior; Sakuma and Pfaff (1979a, 1979b) found that

electrical stimulation of the PAG facilitates lordosis in female rats and that lesions there disrupt it. In addition, Sakuma and Pfaff (1980a, 1980b) found that estradiol treatment or electrical stimulation of the ventromedial nuclei increased the firing rate of neurons in the PAG.

Sakuma and Akaishi (1987) identified neurons in the VMH of ovariectomized female rats that sent axons to the PAG by electrically stimulating the PAG and recording short-latency responses in the anterior VMH. They found that the excitability of these neurons was increased by estradiol. Thus, the neurons in the VMH that send axons to the PAG are estradiol-sensitive.

The communication between the ventromedial nucleus of the hypothalamus and the periaqueductal gray matter is apparently not simply by means of neurotransmission. Harlan, Shivers, Kow, and Pfaff (1982) found evidence that axoplasmic transport from the neurons in the VMH plays a role in mediating the effects of estradiol on lordosis. The investigators infused colchicine into the ventromedial nuclei of ovariectomized rats 24 hours before giving them an injection of estradiol. As we saw at the beginning of this chapter, colchicine blocks cell division by dissolving the spindle fibers that pull the chromosomes apart. In addition, colchicine disrupts the microtubules that are necessary for fast axoplasmic flow. These fibers run the length of the axon and transport substances toward the terminal buttons. Harlan and colleagues found that the colchicine delayed the stimulating effects of estradiol on lordosis by two days. Presumably, the effects of the colchicine wore off in this amount of time. (See *Figure 10.22.*)

The substance transported through the axons of the VMH neurons toward the PAG appears to be a protein. Meisel and Pfaff (1986) implanted anisomycin, a drug that interferes with protein synthesis, into the VMH and found that estradiol no longer stimulated lordosis behavior. In a subsequent study Mobbs, Harlan, Burrous, and Pfaff (1988) found that estradiol stimulates neurons in the VMH to produce a particular protein (not yet analyzed) and transport it to the PAG. The function of this protein is not yet known, but presumably, it affects the activity of neurons in the PAG.

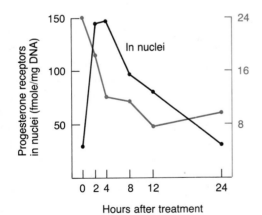

FIGURE 10.20

Quantity of progesterone receptors in the nuclei of female guinea pigs after receiving an injection of progesterone 40 hours subsequent to a priming dose of estradiol. fmol = femtomole, or one quadrillionth (10^{-15}) of a mole, a basic unit of molecular weight. (Adapted from Blaustein, J.D., and Feder, H.H. *Endocrinology*, 1980, *106*, 1061–1069. Copyright © 1980, The Encocrine Society.)

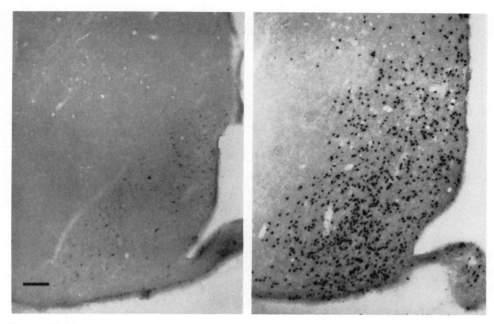

FIGURE 10.21

Photomicrographs of sections through the arcuate nucleus of ovariectomized guinea pigs, stained for progesterone receptors. (a) No priming. (b) After receiving a priming dose of estradiol. (From Blaustein, J.D., King, J.C., Toft, D.O. and Turcotte. *Brain Research*, 1988, *474* 1–15.)

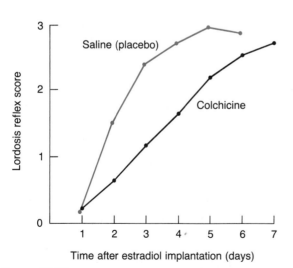

FIGURE 10.22

Amount of lordosis behavior after receiving implants of estradiol in rats treated with colchicine or a placebo. (From Harlan, R.E., Shivers, B.D., Kow, L.-M., and Pfaff, D.W. *Brain Research*, 1982, *238*, 153–157.)

The neurons of the periaqueductal gray matter send axons to the reticular formation of the medulla (Krieger and Pfaff, 1980). Cells there send axons to the spinal cord. It seems likely that this pathway is the final link between the hormone-sensitive neurons in the ventromedial nucleus of the hypothalamus and the muscles that are responsible for female sexual behavior.

INTERIM SUMMARY

Some sexual reflexes, such as erection, ejaculation, and lordosis, are organized by neural circuits in the spinal cord. The "orgasmic" reflex appears to be similar in males and females and does not depend on the stimulating effect of androgens.

Two nuclei in the nervous system develop only if a rodent is exposed to androgens early in life: the spinal nucleus of the bulbocavernosus, located in the spinal cord, and the sexually dimorphic nucleus, located in the medial preoptic area of the forebrain.

The sex difference in the size of the spinal nucleus is caused by the disappearance of neurons in the female spinal cord around the time of birth. The sexually dimorphic nucleus of the MPA is found in humans, as well.

The medial preoptic area is the forebrain region most critical for male sexual behavior. Stimulation of this area produces copulatory behavior; lesioning permanently abolishes it. Neurons in the MPA contain testosterone receptors. Copulatory activity causes an increase in the metabolic activity of this region. Implantation of testosterone directly into the MPA reinstates copulatory behavior that was previously abolished by castration in adulthood. The size of the sexually dimorphic nucleus (part of the MPA) is reduced by prenatal stress and correlates with an animal's level of sexual behavior. Several peptides are found in the MPA, and some of them, such as prolactin, may play a role in male sexual behavior.

The temporal lobe, which plays a role in visual recognition, also plays a role in recognition of appropriate sex objects. Laboratory animals with temporal lobectomies and humans with temporal lobe abnormalities are more likely than normal individuals to exhibit abnormal sexual behavior.

The most important forebrain region for female sexual behavior is the ventromedial nucleus of the hypothalamus. Its destruction abolishes copulatory behavior, and its stimulation facilitates the behavior. Both estradiol and progesterone exert their facilitating effects on female sexual behavior in this region; implantation of these hormones in the ventromedial nucleus of ovariectomized animals reinstates both receptive and proceptive sexual behavior. Autoradiographic studies confirm the existence of progesterone and estrogen receptors there. Estradiol injections facilitate the activating effects of progesterone on female sexual behavior. These priming effects are caused by the ability of estradiol to increase production of progesterone receptors in the hypothalamus.

The estradiol-sensitive neurons of the ventromedial nucleus send axons to the periaqueductal gray matter of the midbrain; presumably, neurons in the midbrain, through their connections with the medullary reticular formation, control the particular responses that constitute female sexual behavior. The stimulating effects that neurons of the ventromedial nucleus of the hypothalamus have on the periaqueductal gray matter may involve a special protein that is produced in the cell bodies and transported through their axons.

CONCLUDING REMARKS

Fortunately for the survival of our species, sexual behavior continues to interest most of us. (I suspect it will continue to do so in future generations.) As we have seen in this chapter, the hormonal and neural interactions that influence and control sexual development and behavior are indeed complex, but research efforts have made great progress in unfolding a fascinating story. The next chapter discusses other behaviors that are strongly influenced by sex hormones and thus are expressed differently in males and females: parental behavior and aggressive behavior.

NEW TERMS

accessory olfactory bulb p. 328
activational effect p. 316
adrenogenital syndrome p. 331
androgen p. 316
androgen insensitivity
    syndrome p. 332
androstenedione p. 319
arcuate nucleus p. 322
aromatization p. 327
Bruce effect p. 327
Coolidge effect p. 325
corpus luteum p. 322
defeminizing effect p. 316
estradiol p. 319
estrogen p. 319
estrous cycle p. 321
follicle-stimulating hormone
    (FSH) p. 318
gamete p. 314
gonad p. 314

gonadotropic hormone p. 318
gonadotropin-releasing
    hormone p. 318
H-Y antigen p. 314
Lee-Boot effect p. 327
lordosis p. 325
luteinizing hormone
    (LH) p. 318
masculinizing effect p. 316
medial nucleus of the
    amygdala p. 328
medial preoptic area
    (MPA) p. 339
meiosis p. 314
menstrual cycle p. 321
mitosis p. 313
Müllerian-inhibiting
    substance p. 316
Müllerian system p. 316
organizational effect p. 316

ovarian follicle p. 322
periaqueductal gray
    matter (PAG) p. 344
pheromone p. 327
primordial gonad p. 314
progesterone p. 322
prolactin p. 325
refractory period p. 325
sexually dimorphic behavior p. 313
sexually dimorphic nucleus p. 341
spinal nucleus of the
    bulbocavernosus (SNB) p. 338
testosterone p. 319
Turner's syndrome p. 316
Vandenbergh effect p. 327
ventromedial nucleus of the
    hypothalamus (VMH) p. 342
vomeronasal organ p. 328
Whitten effect p. 327
Wolffian system p. 316

SUGGESTED READINGS

Halpern, M. The organization and function of the vomeronasal system. *Annual Review of Neuroscience*, 1987, *10*, 325–362.

Kelley, D.B. Sexually dimorphic behaviors. *Annual Review of Neuroscience*, 1988, *11*, 225–252.

Knobil, E., and Neill, J. *The Physiology of Reproduction.* New York: Raven Press, 1988.

Martini, L., and Ganong, W.F. *Frontiers in Neuroendocrinology, Vol. 10.* New York: Raven Press, 1988.

Money, J., and Ehrhardt, A.A. *Man & Woman, Boy & Girl.* Baltimore: Johns Hopkins University Press, 1972.

Pfaff, D.W. *The Physiological Mechanisms of Motivation.* New York: Springer-Verlag, 1982.

Rosen, R.C., and Beck, J.G. *Patterns of Sexual Arousal.* New York: Guilford Press, 1988.

11

Reproductive Behavior: Maternal Behavior and Aggression

*S*exually dimorphic behaviors occur because of different roles played by males and females; thus, these behaviors are, in one way or another, related to reproduction. Mating, the most important sexually dimorphic behavior, was discussed in Chapter 10. This chapter describes research on the physiology of two other categories of sexually dimorphic behavior: maternal behavior and aggression. Obviously, the care of offspring is a reproductive behavior; in all species of mammals and birds infants must be protected and (in most cases) fed by the parents. Most forms of aggressive behavior, too, are related to reproduction. Males compete with each other for access to females or for territory to which they can attract them. Females compete with each other for sites on which they can build nests, and they fiercely defend their offspring against other animals.

MATERNAL BEHAVIOR

In most mammalian species reproductive behavior takes place after the offspring are born, as well as at the time they are conceived. This section examines the role of hormones in the initiation and maintenance of maternal behavior and the role of the neural circuits that are responsible for their expression. Most of the research has involved rodents; less is known about the neural and endocrine bases of maternal behavior in primates.

In focusing on maternal behavior, I do not deny the existence of paternal behavior, but male parental behavior is most prominent in higher primates such as humans—and we know little about the neurological basis of human parental behavior. Male rodents do not show parental behavior except under special circumstances. There are, of course, other classes of animals (for example, many species of fish) in which the male takes care of the young, and in many species of birds the task of caring for the offspring is shared equally. However, neural mechanisms of parental behavior have not received much study in these species.

Maternal Behavior in Rodents

The final test of the fitness of an animal's genes is the number of offspring that survive to a repro-

ductive age. Just as the process of natural selection favors reproductively competent animals, it also favors those that care adequately for their young (if their young in fact require any care). Rat and mouse pups certainly do require care; they cannot survive without a mother who attends to their needs.

At birth rats and mice resemble fetuses. The infants are blind (their eyes are still shut), and they can only helplessly wriggle. They are poikilothermous ("cold-blooded"); their brain is not yet developed enough to regulate body temperature. They even lack the ability to release their own urine and feces spontaneously and must be helped to do so by their mother. As we will see shortly, this phenomenon actually serves a useful function.

Why are most rodent neonates born in such an immature state? We might speculate as follows: In the case of rodents natural selection has undoubtedly favored organisms that produce a large number of young. The result is large litters, spaced closely together. For example, a mouse can carry a litter of twelve (or even more) pups. A pregnant mouse looks like she swallowed a golf ball; one cannot imagine the animal carrying any more weight than she does. Therefore, if mice gave birth to young that were larger and more mature, they would have to carry a smaller number of them. Also, the sooner the uterus is cleared out, the sooner the mouse can become pregnant again.

During gestation female rats and mice build nests. The form this structure takes depends on the material available for its construction. In the laboratory the animals are usually given strips of paper or lengths of rope or twine. A good *brood nest*, as it is called, is shown in Figure 11.1. This nest is made of hemp rope, a piece of which is shown below the nest. The mouse laboriously shredded the rope and then wove an enclosed nest, with a small hole for access to the interior. (See *Figure 11.1.*)

At the time of *parturition* (delivery of offspring) the female begins to groom and lick the area around the vagina. As a pup begins to emerge, she assists the uterine contractions by pulling the pup out with her teeth. She then eats the placenta and umbilical cord and cleans off the fetal

FIGURE 11.1

A mouse's brood nest. Beside it is a length of the kind of rope the mouse used to construct it.

membranes—a quite delicate operation. (A newborn pup looks like it is sealed in very thin plastic wrap.) After all the pups are born and cleaned up, the mother will probably nurse them. Milk is usually present very near the time of birth.

Periodically, the mother licks the pups' anogenital region, stimulating reflexive urination and defecation. Friedman and Bruno (1976) have shown the utility of this mechanism. They noted that a lactating female rat produces approximately 48 gm of milk (containing approximately 35 ml of water) on the tenth day of lactation. They injected some of the pups with tritiated (radioactive) water and later found radioactivity in the mother and in the litter mates. Friedman and Bruno calculated that a lactating rat normally consumes 21 ml of water in the urine of her young, thus recycling approximately two-thirds of the water she gives to the pups in the form of milk. The water, traded back and forth between mother and young, serves as a vehicle for the nutrients—fats, protein, and

sugar—contained in milk. Because the milk production of a lactating rat each day is approximately 14 percent of her body weight (for a human weighing 120 lb, that would be around 2 gal), the recycling is extremely useful, especially when the availability of water is a problem.

Besides cleaning, nursing, and purging her offspring, a female rodent will retrieve pups if they leave or are removed from the nest. The mother will even construct another nest in a new location and move her litter there, should the conditions at the old site become unfavorable (for example, when an inconsiderate experimenter puts a heat lamp over it). The way a female rodent picks up her pup is quite consistent: She gingerly grasps the animal by the back, managing not to injure it with her very sharp teeth. (I can personally attest to the ease with which these teeth can penetrate skin.) She then carries the pup with a characteristic prancing walk, her head held high. (See *Figure 11.2*.) The pup is brought back to the nest and is left there. The female then leaves the nest again to search for another pup. She continues to retrieve

FIGURE 11.2

A female mouse carrying one of her pups.

pups until she finds no more; she does not count her pups and stop retrieving when they are all back. A mouse or rat will usually accept all the pups she is offered, if they are young enough. I once observed two lactating female mice with nests in corners of the same cage, diagonally opposite each other. I disturbed their nests, which triggered a long bout of retrieving, during which each mother stole youngsters from the other's nest. The mothers kept up their exchange for a long time, passing each other in the middle of the cage.

Maternal behavior begins to wane as the pups become more active and begin to look more like adults. At around sixteen to eighteen days of age they are able to get about easily by themselves, and they begin to obtain their own food. The mother ceases to retrieve them when they leave the nest and will eventually run away from them if they attempt to nurse.

Stimuli That Elicit and Maintain Maternal Behavior

As we have seen in Chapter 10, most sexually dimorphic behaviors are controlled by the organizational and activational effects of sex hormones. Maternal behavior is somewhat different in this respect. First, there is no evidence that organizational effects of hormones play a role; as we shall see, under the proper conditions even males will take care of infants. (Obviously, they cannot provide them with milk.) Second, although maternal behavior is affected by hormones, it is not *controlled* by them.

Most virgin female rats will begin to retrieve and care for young pups after having infants placed with them for several days—a process called sensitization or *concaveation* (Wiesner and Sheard, 1933). And once the rats are sensitized, they will thereafter take care of pups as soon as they encounter them; sensitization lasts for a lifetime.

Olfaction plays an important role in sensitization. A virgin female rat does not normally approach a rat pup; in fact, when it encounters one, it retreats from the pup as if it were repelled by the pup's odor. Fleming and Rosenblatt (1974) con-

firmed that the avoidance is, indeed, based on smell. They rinsed the olfactory mucosa of virgin female rats with zinc sulfate, which eliminates olfactory sensitivity. The treatment abolished the animals' natural aversion to the pups, and soon they started taking care of them. Thus, sensitization involves overcoming a natural aversion to the odor of pups.

Fleming, Vaccarino, Tambosso, and Chee (1979) found that cutting the vomeronasal nerve, which disrupts the accessory olfactory system, also facilitates the responsiveness of virgin females to pups. Thus, both the primary and the accessory olfactory systems play a role in olfactory control of maternal behavior. You will recall that both the primary and accessory olfactory systems project to the medial amygdala. Fleming, Vaccarino, and Luebke (1980) found that lesions of the medial amygdala also facilitated responsiveness, as did lesions of the *stria terminalis,* a fiber bundle that connects the medial amygdala with various forebrain regions, including the medial preoptic area (MPA). (As we will see, the MPA is essential for maternal behavior.) Note that lesions of the amygdala or stria terminalis do not abolish the sense of smell; they only abolish the animals' aversion to the smell of pups.

Sensitization involves more than learning to tolerate the odor of pups; it also involves learning to be *attracted* to their odor. An experiment by Dickinson and Keverne (1988) suggests that this learning involves activity of noradrenergic axons that innervate the olfactory bulbs. As you will recall from Chapter 10, the activity of these axons plays a role in the Bruce effect; the release of norepinephrine in the olfactory bulbs appears to "imprint" the odor of the male that impregnates a female mouse so that the odor will not later cause the female to abort. Perhaps the activity of these axons, increased by the vaginal stimulation that occurs during delivery, "imprints" the odor of pups on the female and prevents her from avoiding them. Dickinson and Keverne operated on virgin female mice and destroyed these axons with 6-hydroxydopamine (6-HD). The mice did not take care of mouse pups that were presented to them; in fact, they killed them. However, if the lesions were made in a mother mouse after she had given birth, they had no effect; presumably, the odor had already been "imprinted," and she had no need of further learning.

The most important sense modality in the *initiation* of maternal behavior appears to be olfaction. However, other sense modalities are involved in its control. For example, mouse, rat, and hamster pups emit at least two different kinds of ultrasonic calls (Noirot, 1972). These sounds cannot be heard by humans; they have to be translated into lower frequencies by a special device (a "bat detector") in order to be perceived by the experimenter. Of course, the mother can hear these calls. When a pup gets cold (as it would if it were removed from the nest), it emits a characteristic call that brings the mother out of her nest. The sound is so effective that female mice have been observed to chew the cover off a loudspeaker that is transmitting a recording of this call. Once out of the nest, the female uses olfactory cues as well as auditory ones to find the pups; she can find a buried, anesthetized baby mouse that is unable to make any noise. The second call is made in response to rough handling. When a mother hears this sound, she stops what she is doing. Typically, it is she who is administering the rough handling, and the distress call makes her stop. The mechanism undoubtedly plays an important role in training mother mice to handle pups properly.

Stern (1989a, 1989b) reviews experimental findings that indicate that somatosensation also plays an important role in the maintenance and control of maternal behavior. She notes that most maternal behaviors include the use of the mouth: nuzzling, licking, and carrying pups; building and repairing nests; attacking and biting intruders. Many of these behaviors are initiated by somatosensory information received by the region around the mouth as the mother sniffs the pups and nuzzles them with her mouth. For example, when the region around the mouth (the *perioral region*) is desensitized by cutting nerves or injecting a local anesthetic, female rats are less likely to lick their pups, retrieve them, build or repair a nest, or attack an intruder. Tactile feedback from the pups against the mother's ventral surface is important, too. When the regions around pups' mouths are anesthetized so that they cannot root against their mother, she will not show the crouching posture that is necessary for nursing. She will, however, retrieve them and lick them.

Stern suggests that both distal and proximal cues interact to produce the entire complement of maternal behavior. Distal cues (the sight, sound, and odor of pups) attract the mother to them and arouse contact-seeking behaviors. These behaviors lead to perioral contact, which triggers nuzzling, licking, and hovering. The proximity of the mother leads the pups to root against her ventral surface, which stimulates a crouching posture that presents her nipples to them. (See *Figure 11.3.*)

Hormonal Control of Maternal Behavior

As we have just seen, hormones are not essential for the activation of maternal behavior; mere ex-

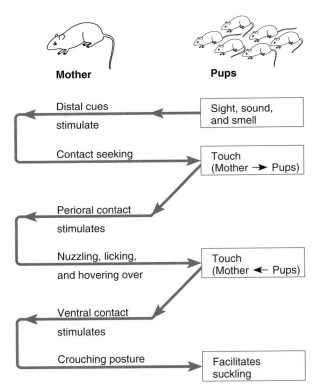

FIGURE 11.3

A proposed model of sensory regulation of the maternal behavior of a female rat. (Redrawn from Stern, J.M., in *Ethoexperimental Approaches to the Study of Behavior*, edited by D.C. Blanchard, S. Parmigiani, and P.F. Brain. The Hague: Nijhoff Publishing Co., 1989.)

posure to pups will accomplish that. (Of course, hormones are necessary for milk production.) However, many aspects of maternal behavior are facilitated by hormones. Nest-building behavior is facilitated by progesterone, the principal hormone of pregnancy. Lisk, Pretlow, and Friedman (1969) found that nonpregnant female mice built brood nests after a pellet of progesterone was implanted under the skin. The pellet slowly dissolved, maintaining a continuously high level of progesterone. The enhanced nest building was suppressed by the administration of estradiol. After parturition mothers continue to maintain their nests, and they construct new nests if necessary, even though their blood level of progesterone is very low then. Voci and Carlson (1973) found that hypothalamic implants of prolactin as well as progesterone facilitated nest building in mice. Presumably, nest building can be facilitated by either hormone: progesterone during pregnancy and prolactin after parturition. (Prolactin, produced by the anterior pituitary gland, is responsible for milk production.)

Although pregnant female rats will not immediately care for foster pups that are given to them during pregnancy, they will do so as soon as their pups are born. Mayer and Rosenblatt (1984) found that maternal behavior of female rats was not

activated until shortly before birth. If the animals were tested between 3.5 and 6.5 hours prepartum, only 25 percent of them responded. However, if they were tested less than 3.5 hours prepartum, virtually all of them did.

As we saw earlier, the vaginal stimulation that occurs during parturition may be one of the events that triggers a female rodent's responsiveness to her offspring. Another event could be a change in hormonal level. Figure 11.4 shows the levels of the three hormones that have been implicated in maternal behavior: estradiol, progesterone, and prolactin. Note that just before parturition the level of estradiol begins rising, then the level of progesterone falls dramatically, followed by a sharp increase in prolactin. (See *Figure 11.4.*) If ovariectomized virgin female rats are given estradiol, progesterone, and prolactin in a pattern that duplicates this sequence, the time it takes to sensitize their maternal behavior is drastically reduced (Moltz, Lubin, Leon, and Numan, 1970; Bridges, 1984; Stern and McDonald, 1989). In fact, prolactin itself is not necessary, because the administration of progesterone and estradiol by themselves will stimulate prolactin secretion (Amenomori, Chen, and Meites, 1970).

Fleming, Cheung, Myhal, and Kessler (1989) found that the administration of progesterone

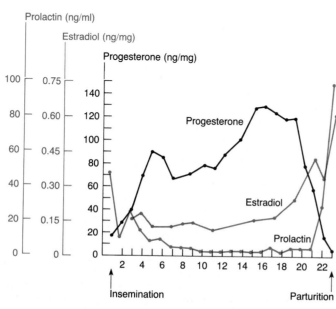

FIGURE 11.4

Blood levels of progesterone, estradiol, and prolactin in pregnant rats. (From Rosenblatt, J.S., Siegel, H.I., and Mayer, A.D. *Advances in the Study of Behavior*, 1979, *10*, 225–311.)

and estradiol had effects similar to those produced by concaveation. First, the hormone-treated rats became less timid in a strange environment that contained novel odors. Second, the animals spent more time near a jar containing some bedding material removed from a nest containing a lactating female and her pups. These effects may indeed be the ones that occur during sensitization: The animal is no longer repelled by (frightened by?) the strange odor of pups and, indeed, comes to prefer the smell.

It is interesting that the sequence of hormones that facilitates the development of maternal behavior (progesterone followed by estradiol) is the same as the one that produces estrous behavior. (However, its time course is much longer; hormonal facilitation of maternal behavior takes at least fourteen days.) Although investigators agree that the removal of progesterone and the administration of estradiol are important, they have not reached a consensus about whether prolactin is necessary. Bridges, DiBiase, Loundes, and Doherty (1985) found that a sequence of progesterone and estradiol stimulated maternal behavior only when the pituitary gland was present; when it was not (and hence when prolactin could not be secreted), the hormones had no effect. However, a subsequent study from the same laboratory (Bridges and Ronsheim, 1990) found that under certain conditions, the administration of progesterone and estradiol can stimulate maternal behavior even when the secretion of prolactin is prevented by a drug. Thus, although prolactin can facilitate maternal behavior, its presence is not essential.

Another hormone that has been implicated in the facilitation of maternal behavior is oxytocin. This hormone has several effects, including release of milk and contraction of the uterus. Thus, it is secreted just before and during birth and throughout the lactation period. Besides serving as a hormone, oxytocin is released as a neurotransmitter in the brain (Buijs and Van Heerikhuize, 1982). Infusion of oxytocin directly into the cerebral ventricles facilitates the maternal behavior of virgin female rats (Pedersen, Ascher, Monroe, and Prange, 1982), whereas infusion of an oxytocin antiserum disrupts it (Pedersen, Caldwell, Johnson, Fort, and Prange, 1985).

Neural Control of Maternal Behavior

The most critical brain region responsible for maternal behavior appears to be the medial preoptic area. Numan (1974) found that lesions of the MPA or knife cuts that isolated this region from the medial forebrain bundle disrupted both nest building and pup care. The mothers simply ignored their offspring. However, female sexual behavior was unaffected by these lesions. You will recall that male sexual behavior, but not female sexual behavior, is also disrupted by lesions of the MPA.

As you learned earlier, in the discussion of the neural basis of male sexual behavior, the MPA sends axons to the midbrain. Numan and his colleagues found that the pathway critical for maternal behavior runs from the MPA to the lateral preoptic area and from there to the *ventral tegmental area* of the midbrain. (As we will see in later chapters, this brain region, which contains dopaminergic neurons, plays a role in several species-typical behaviors, such as drinking and aggressive behavior, and in reinforcement.) Numan and Smith (1984) found that knife cuts that interrupted the connections between the medial and lateral preoptic areas disrupted maternal behavior, and so did knife cuts posterior to the lateral preoptic area or lesions of the ventral tegmental area.

As we saw earlier, Stern (1989a, 1989b) points out that more attention should be paid to the role of tactile stimuli on maternal behavior, especially around the mother's mouth. She notes that the involvement of the ventral tegmental area in maternal behavior may be related to its role in other behaviors involving the mouth, including food hoarding, drinking, and aggressive behavior that involves biting.

The medial preoptic area appears to be the place where estradiol affects maternal behavior. The MPA contains estrogen receptors (Pfaff and Keiner, 1973), and Giordano and Rosenblatt (1986) found that the concentration of estrogen receptors in the MPA increases during pregnancy. Direct implants of estradiol in the MPA facilitate maternal behavior (Numan, Rosenblatt, and Komisaruk, 1977), whereas injection of an anti-estrogen chemical in the MPA blocks it (Adieh, Mayer, and Rosenblatt, 1986).

As we just saw, olfactory deafferentation, lesions of the medial amygdala, or lesions of the stria terminalis (which connects the medial amygdala with the medial preoptic area) all facilitate maternal behavior in virgin female rats by eliminating the inhibitory effects caused by the odor of pups. Perhaps the stimulating effect of estradiol on the medial preoptic area works in a similar fashion, removing the inhibitory influence of the amygdala. (See *Figure 11.5*.)

We also saw that oxytocin has a facilitatory effect on maternal behavior. The main source of oxytocin-secreting neurons is the supraoptic and paraventricular nuclei. Salm, Modney, and Hatton (1988) found that the exposure of virgin female rats to pups caused profound changes in the microstructure of the supraoptic nuclei. Insel and Harbaugh (1989) destroyed the paraventricular nucleus during late pregnancy and found that the animals' subsequent maternal behavior was disrupted. However, when they made lesions after the pups had been born and the female had had experience taking care of them, the lesions had no effect.

Other parts of the brain are involved in the control of maternal behavior. For example, lesions of various parts of the limbic system will disrupt the sequence, but not the elements, of maternal behavior. Slotnick (1967) found that lesions of the cingulate cortex in rats scrambled the normal sequence of pup retrieval. The mother would pick up a pup, enter the nest, walk out again still carrying the pup, drop it, try to nurse one pup outside the nest, remove pups from the nest, and, in general, act confused. The individual behavioral acts that make up pup care (for example, picking up the pup and licking its anogenital region) were still present, which suggests that the lesions did not affect "motivation," but the behaviors appeared to occur at random. Carlson and Thomas (1968) observed an even more severe deficit after lesions of the septum in mice. Besides exhibiting a disordered sequence of pup retrieval, the mice failed to build nests. The deficit in nest building was not restricted to behavior that was stimulated hormonally. Normal mice, both males and females, will build nests to conserve body heat if the ambient temperature falls. I have found that when mice with septal lesions are placed in a refrigerator, they fail to build nests. (I should note that the refrigerated mice seemed to thrive in the cold, even without a nest to keep them warm.)

The septum and medial preoptic area are interconnected; these connections probably explain the lack of nest building and disorganized pup retrieval seen in rodents with septal lesions. An-

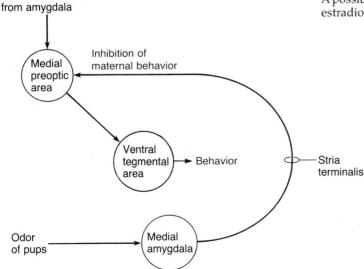

FIGURE 11.5
A possible explanation of the facilitating effects of estradiol on maternal behavior.

Estradiol injection removes inhibition from amygdala

Medial preoptic area

Inhibition of maternal behavior

Ventral tegmental area — Behavior

Stria terminalis

Odor of pups

Medial amygdala

other possible reason for the disrupting effects of septal lesions is the role of this structure in controlling the neural activity of another part of the limbic system, the hippocampus. As we will see in Chapter 14, the hippocampus plays a role in spatial perception; animals with hippocampal lesions or lesions that disconnect the septum and hippocampus have difficulty finding their way around their environment. This effect may explain why rats and mice with septal lesions do not build nests and have trouble retrieving: They do not recognize a "home" site in their cage. Perhaps the hippocampal-septal system communicates with the medial preoptic area, controlling the species-typical maternal behaviors according to the animal's location in its environment.

Human Maternal Behavior

Certainly, the behavior of human parents (both maternal and paternal) is not controlled by innate factors, as it is in some other species. Learning seems to be much more important than hormonal activation. (After all, adoptive mothers—and fathers, too—are perfectly capable of taking care of their infants.) Thus, I have little to say about the physiology of human maternal behavior. However, some investigators have suggested that even humans possess an innate tendency to care for their offspring, which is triggered by a specific experience soon after birth. In some mammalian species mothers will accept and care for their infants only if they are able to see and smell their offspring during the first day of life. For example, Klopfer, Adams, and Klopfer (1964) reported that if a lamb is removed from its mother immediately after birth and is brought back a day later, the mother will reject it. However, if she is in contact with her lamb for just a few minutes after birth, she will accept it and care for it when it is given back to her the next day. This phenomenon is called *bonding.*

Klaus, Jerauld, Krieger, McAlpine, Steffa, and Kennell (1972) reported that bonding also occurs in humans when an infant is placed naked against its mother's skin soon after it is born. The experimenters tested mothers who were having their first child. Women in the control group experienced what was then the usual hospital procedure, seeing their babies for a short time at birth and feeding them (by bottle) five times a day. Mothers in the extended-contact group received their babies for an hour soon after birth and for 5 hours each afternoon on the next three days. Thus, these mothers were in contact with their babies for 16 hours more than the mothers in the control group. A month later, the mothers were interviewed during their infant's one-month checkup. The mothers in the extended-contact group acted more concerned about their babies, holding and fondling them slightly more than the mothers in the control group. Small differences in the behavior of the two groups of mothers were still present as long as two years later. As a result of studies like this one, many hospitals have changed their procedures to ensure that a mother becomes "bonded" to her infant; the baby is placed against its mother's abdomen so that skin-to-skin contact occurs.

Although the study by Klaus and colleagues is interesting, the conditions were not controlled well enough to prove that a maternal bond develops this early. The mothers in the experimental group were aware that they were being treated differently, because they had their babies with them longer than other mothers who shared the rooms. In addition, nurses may have inadvertently communicated to them that it was important to spend more time with their infants. Either of these variables may have accounted for the fact that they were observed to interact with their babies slightly more a few months later. In fact, recent research conducted under more carefully controlled conditions has failed to confirm the results of the earlier studies. For example, Svejda, Campos, and Emde (1980) first made sure that the mothers in their study who received extended contact with their babies did not perceive themselves as "special." These investigators found that extended contact had no effect on interactions between mothers and their infants. Grossmann, Thane, and Grossmann (1981) did succeed in finding an effect of bonding in a carefully controlled study, but the effect was small and disappeared by the tenth day after the baby had been born. Therefore, although a mother's first contact with her child can undoubtedly be a pleasurable and memorable experience, there is no conclusive evidence that this event instigates a physiological reaction that increases her attentiveness to her child.

INTERIM SUMMARY

Many species must care for their offspring. Among rodents, this duty falls to the mother, who must build a nest, deliver her own pups, clean them, keep them warm, nurse them, and retrieve them if they are moved out of the nest. They must even induce their pups' urination and defecation, and their ingestion of the urine recycles water, which is often a scarce commodity.

Exposure to young pups (concaveation) stimulates maternal behavior within a few days. Apparently, the odor of pups elicits handling and licking, whereas the sound of their distress calls elicits nest building. Unsensitized virgin female rats appear to be repelled by the odor of pups, but deafferentation of the olfactory system with zinc sulfate abolishes this aversion and causes the animals to begin caring for pups more quickly. The inhibitory effect of the odor of pups may be mediated by the accessory olfactory system; cutting the vomeronasal nerve facilitates maternal behavior. Both components of the olfactory system project to the medial amygdala. Lesions of the medial amygdala or the stria terminalis also facilitate maternal responsiveness. Therefore, the inhibitory effects of olfaction on maternal behavior may be mediated by the pathway from the olfactory system to the medial amygdala to the medial preoptic area, via the stria terminalis. Excitatory effects of olfaction are seen, too; females learn to recognize the odor of their pups, and this learning involves the activity of noradrenergic input to the olfactory bulbs. Tactile stimulation of the mother's perioral region elicits nuzzling, licking, and hovering over pups; subsequent contact of the pups with the mother's ventral surface elicits crouching, which facilitates nursing.

Nest building appears to be facilitated by progesterone during pregnancy and by prolactin during the lactation period. Estradiol, prolactin, and oxytocin have been implicated in the facilitation of maternal behavior.

The medial preoptic area is the most important forebrain structure for maternal behavior, and the ventral tegmental area of the midbrain is the most important brain stem structure. The involvement of the ventral tegmental area in behaviors involving the mouth may be important in this regard. Neurons in the medial preoptic area send axons to the lateral preoptic area, which then sends axons caudally to the ventral tegmental area; if these connections are interrupted bilaterally, rats cease providing maternal care of offspring. Destruction of the paraventricular nucleus, one of the sources of oxytocin, disrupts the onset of maternal behavior but does not affect maternal behavior of rats that have had experience caring for their young. Even the exposure to pups alters the microscopic structure of the supraoptic nucleus, another source of oxytocin.

Lesions of the cingulate cortex or septum disrupt the sequence of maternal behavior without affecting the animal's willingness to emit appropriate component behavioral acts. The effects of septal lesions may occur because the medial septum plays an important role in controlling the activity of the hippocampus, which is necessary for spatial perception.

The one aspect of human maternal behavior that appeared to be innately determined was a phenomenon called bonding, which occurs in other female mammals, such as sheep. However, more recent studies suggest that women need not experience direct skin contact with their babies soon after birth in order to form close attachments with them.

AGGRESSIVE BEHAVIOR

Almost all species of animals engage in aggressive behaviors, which involve threatening gestures or actual attack directed toward another animal. Aggressive behaviors are species-typical;

that is, the patterns of movements (for example, posturing, biting, striking, and hissing) are organized by neural circuits whose development is largely programmed by an animal's genes. Most aggressive behaviors are sexually dimorphic and are related to reproduction. For example, aggressive behaviors that gain access to mates, defend territory needed to provide a site for building a nest, or defend offspring against intruders can all be regarded as reproductive behaviors. Because the reproductive roles of males and females differ, their aggressive behaviors differ also.

Although aggressive behaviors can be regarded as sexually dimorphic, the behaviors themselves are identical in males and females. What differs is the situations in which these behaviors occur and, in some cases, the hormones that arouse or inhibit these behaviors. Thus, we would not expect to see sex differences in the neural circuits responsible for the execution of aggressive behaviors, but we *would* expect to find differences in the brain mechanisms that, in response to hormonal conditions and environmental stimuli, excite or inhibit these circuits.

Nature and Functions of Aggressive Behaviors

Aggressive behavior can take different forms and can be provoked by different situations. First, I will describe the behaviors and their neural organization. Later, I will discuss the situations that provoke these behaviors and the role that hormones play in regulating their occurrence.

In cats and rodents (the species most often studied in the laboratory), aggressive behavior takes three basic forms: *offense, defense,* and *predation* (Adams, 1986). **Offensive behaviors** consist of physical assaults of one animal on another. When threatened or attacked, an animal often exhibits **defensive behaviors.** Defensive behaviors can consist of actual attacks, or they may simply involve **threat behaviors,** which consist of postures or gestures that warn the adversary to leave or become the target of an attack. (Alternatively, the threatened animal might show **submissive behaviors,** which indicate that it will not challenge the other animal.) In the natural environment

most animals display far more threats than actual attacks. Threat behaviors are useful in reinforcing social hierarchies in organized groups of animals or in warning intruders away from an animal's territory. They have the advantage of not involving actual fighting, which can harm one or both of the combatants. **Predation** is the attack of a member of one species on that of another, usually because the latter serves as food for the former.

In rodents and cats offensive behaviors consist of displays of sideways postures and biting and kicking attacks. Defensive behaviors consist of upright posturing with boxing movements in rodents, and of hissing, arching the back, and striking with the claws of the forelimbs in cats. While engaged in either offensive or defensive behaviors, the animals appear to be extremely aroused and excited, and the activity of their autonomic nervous system is high. In contrast, predatory behaviors are much more "cold-blooded"; they consist of an efficient bite to the neck and are not accompanied by a high level of autonomic activation.

Neural Control of Aggressive Behavior

As we shall see in this section, the three major types of aggressive behavior—offense, defense, and predation—are controlled by different brain mechanisms, which implies that the behaviors are at least somewhat independent. The neural control of aggressive behavior is hierarchical. That is, the particular muscular movements an animal makes in attacking or defending itself are programmed by neural circuits in the midbrain. These circuits are controlled by neurons located in the forebrain. Whether an animal attacks depends on many factors, including the nature of the eliciting stimuli in the environment and the animal's previous experience. The activity of the midbrain circuits appears to be controlled by the hypothalamus and the limbic system (especially the amygdala), which also influence many other species-typical behaviors. And, of course, the activity of the limbic system is controlled by perceptual systems that detect the status of the environment, including the presence of other animals.

Attack Elicited by Electrical Brain Stimulation

Electrical stimulation of localized regions of the brain can elicit the three major patterns of aggressive behavior: offense, defense, and predation. The offensive attack elicited by brain stimulation is dramatic. Cats who display this behavior adopt a "Halloween-cat" posture, with arched back, erect fur on the back and neck, dilated pupils, and bared teeth. If another cat is nearby, it will be attacked. However, rather than have one cat attack another, experimenters generally use rats to serve as subjects of the aggression. When the current is passed through the electrode, the cat will viciously attack a nearby rat with its claws, sometimes screaming as it does so. If the stimulation continues, the cat will often begin biting the rat. We cannot know how the cat feels, but it acts as if it were extremely angry.

In cats the defensive behavior evoked by electrical brain stimulation can consist of threat gestures, including flattening of the ears, arching of the back, and hissing and growling, or it can consist of actual attack, which usually involves striking with the claws of the forelimbs.

The behaviors seen during predation are quite different from those seen during offensive or defensive attack. Predation is not accompanied by a strong display of rage. A cat stalks a rat and suddenly pounces on it, directing powerful bites to the head and neck region. The cat does not growl or scream, and it stops attacking once the rat ceases to move. This type of attack appears more cold-blooded and ruthless than affective attack. (It is more likely to kill the rat, too.) It may seem surprising that a cat should need any special treatment to induce it to attack a rat, but most laboratory cats do *not* spontaneously attack rats.

Although predation obtains food, the brain mechanisms that organize predatory behavior are not identical to those that organize eating; these two sets of mechanisms can be excited independently. Roberts and Kiess (1964) implanted stimulating electrodes in the brains of cats in a location that produced predatory attack. (These cats were not natural rat killers.) The experimenters taught the cats to run through a maze in order to obtain a rat to attack. However, the animals would do so only while the brain stimulation was turned on; when it was off, they would not seek out the rat. When the brain stimulation was turned on, a hungry cat would even leave a dish of food to run through the maze and attack the rat, which it would *not* subsequently eat. Therefore, predatory attack is not synonymous with feeding. It provides a means for carnivores to obtain food, but the neural mechanisms for attack and eating are different.

As we all know, a cat will often stalk and kill rodents and birds even when it is not hungry; it seems to enjoy this activity independent of its food-getting utility. In contrast, animals who are fighting do not act as if they were "happy." Panksepp (1971a) observed a significant difference in rats' preference for receiving electrical brain stimulation that elicits predatory attack or affective attack. If he turned on the stimulation that produced affective attack but permitted the rats to press a lever to turn it off, they quickly learned to do so. Thus, brain stimulation that elicits affective attack appears to be aversive. In contrast, rats quickly learned to press a lever that turned *on* stimulation that elicited predatory attack. Thus, brain stimulation that elicits predatory attack appears to be reinforcing.

Midbrain

Two parts of the midbrain, the periaqueductal gray matter and the ventral tegmental area, are involved in the organization of aggressive behaviors. Offensive behavior appears to be controlled by neurons in the ventral tegmental area, and defensive behavior and predation appear to be controlled by neurons in the periaqueductal gray matter. One study suggests that neurons controlling defensive behavior are located dorsal to those that control predatory behavior.

First, let us consider offensive behavior. The best evidence that the ventral tegmental area of the midbrain is involved in these behaviors comes from a study by Adams (1986), who made lesions in the ventral tegmental area of rats and tested the animals' offensive, defensive, and predatory behavior. The experimenter used only rats who had previously exhibited spontaneous offensive and predatory behavior. Offensive behavior was tested by introducing an adult male rat into the subjects' home cage and observing whether they showed the typical sideways posture and a bite-and-kick attack. Defense was tested by placing the subjects with another male into a cage with an electrified grid floor and seeing whether the animal assumed an upright posture and "boxed" with the other rat. Predation was tested by placing a mouse in the animal's cage. The lesions disrupted only offensive attack; predation and defensive behavior were unaffected.

Defensive behavior involves neurons in the periaqueductal gray matter (PAG). Lesions of the PAG disrupt defensive shock-induced boxing in male rats (Edwards and Adams, 1974), but they do not disrupt offensive attack (Mos et al., 1983). In addition, electrical stimulation of the PAG produces defensive behavior in cats: ear flattening, hissing, growling, and striking with the claws (Shaikh and Siegel, 1989). Defensive threat and defensive attack appear to be controlled by neurons in two different regions of the PAG. Carrive, Dampney, and Bandler (1987) placed homocysteic acid, a chemical that activates excitatory amino acid receptors, into the anterior part of the PAG and observed threat behavior (posturing and vocalization) but no striking movements with the limbs. (The injection of homocysteic acid produces effects very similar to those of electrical stimulation, except that only neurons with excitatory amino acid receptors are activated.) In contrast, Carrive, Bandler, and Dampney (1989) found that injections of homocysteic acid in the *posterior* PAG elicited the limb movements and changes in the autonomic nervous system that occur when a cat goes from a defensive display to an attack. (The animals had been decerebrated, so the entire behavioral sequence could not be observed.)

Depaulis, Bandler, and Vergnes (1989) observed similar results in rats. They injected a small amount of kainic acid into the PAG, using guide tubes that had already been cemented into position on the animals' head. (Large amounts of kainic acid destroy neurons, but the small quantities that Depaulis and his colleagues used simply stimulated excitatory amino acid receptors.) The rats showed an immediate alerting response, their rate of respiration increased, and a few

showed some signs of agitation. The animals were then placed in a test cage and another rat was introduced. If the intruder approached the subject from the side contralateral to the injection of the excitatory amino acid, the subject showed a defensive posture. Normally, a defensive posture is shown only if the approaching animal is attacking; in this experiment the approaches by the intruder were nonaggressive. (See *Figure 11.6.*)

The fact that only contralateral approaches produced defensive reactions suggests that the injection of the excitatory amino acid did not simply make the animals become more fearful. If that had been the case, then they would have reacted to an approach from either direction. Instead, it appears that the injection sensitized a circuit of neurons that produce a specific response (defensive behavior) to a specific stimulus (the approach of another rat). In fact, Depaulis and his colleagues went on to test the reaction of the rats to being touched with the bristles of a small paintbrush. The animals reacted only when the side of the body contralateral to the injection was touched, and touches to the head were most likely to provoke a response, followed by the foreleg and the flank. Touches to the hind leg produced no reaction. (See *Figure 11.7.*) This difference in

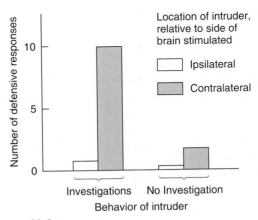

FIGURE 11.6
Effects of chemical stimulation of the periaqueductal gray matter on defensive attack when an intruder approaches ipsilateral or contralateral to the site of the stimulation. (Adapted from Depaulis, A., Bandler, R., and Vergnes, M. *Brain Research*, 1989, *486*, 121–132.)

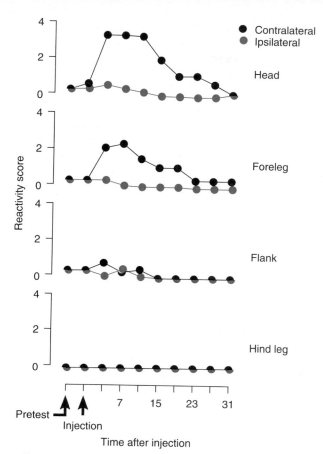

FIGURE 11.7
Reactivity to tactile stimulation delivered to various parts of a rat's body ipsilateral or contralateral to the site of chemical stimulation of the periaqueductal gray matter. (Adapted from Depaulis, A., Bandler, R., and Vergnes, M. *Brain Research*, 1989, *486*, 121–132.)

excitability may reflect the fact that when one rat attacks another, it is more likely to direct its attack to the front part of the body.

Defensive behaviors appear to be modulated by endogenous opioid peptides. Shaikh, Shaikh, and Siegel (1988) implanted thin stainless steel cannulas into the PAG of cats. The cannulas were coated with an insulating material, except for the tips. They could be used either for electrical stimulation or as guides for injecting a chemical directly into the brain. The experimenters found that defensive behaviors, elicited by electrical stimulation of the PAG, could be inhibited by the injection of a synthetic opioid into the same site. In

contrast, Shaikh and Siegel (1989) found that an injection of naloxone, a drug that blocks opiate receptors, *facilitated* defensive behavior. What is the functional significance of the inhibitory effect of opiates on defensive behavior? As we saw earlier, opioid peptides are secreted when an animal is engaged in important species-typical behaviors such as mating. In mating the secretion of opiates may help ensure that the animal will not engage in defensive behaviors that would interfere with procreation.

Predatory behavior, like defensive behavior, appears to be controlled by neurons in the periaqueductal gray matter. Shaikh and Siegel (1989) found that electrical stimulation of the *ventral* PAG produced predatory behavior in cats, whereas stimulation of the *dorsal* PAG produced defensive behavior. Lesions of the PAG abolish the killing bite of a predator, but they do not prevent the animal from stalking and lunging toward the prey (Waldbillig, 1979).

Hypothalamus

Aggressive behaviors can be elicited by stimulation of the hypothalamus as well as the midbrain. In general, stimulation of the medial hypothalamus produces offensive behavior, stimulation of the dorsal hypothalamus produces defensive behavior, and stimulation of the lateral hypothalamus produces predation (Flynn, Vanegas, Foote, and Edwards, 1970; Clemente and Chase, 1973).

Hypothalamic stimulation appears to produce attack by increasing the activity of axons that project caudally to the midbrain. Lesions that disconnect the hypothalamus from the midbrain abolish aggressive behavior elicited by hypothalamic stimulation (Ellison and Flynn, 1968). However, hypothalamic lesions do not abolish offense, defense, or predation, although the likelihood or the vigor of the behavior may change (Ellison and Flynn, 1968; Adams, 1971, 1979). Thus, although the hypothalamus may play a role in determining when aggressive behaviors occur, it does not directly control the behaviors.

MacDonnell and Flynn (1966) demonstrated the facilitative effect of hypothalamic stimulation on a reflex that appears to be a component of predatory attack. They observed that a cat normally turns its head away when a stick is touched to the side of its cheek. However, when they simultaneously stimulated the cat's hypothalamus through an electrode that normally elicited a predatory attack, the animal instead turned toward the stick so that the object met its lips. When this contact occurred, the cat's mouth opened. (See *Figure 11.8*.) At low levels of stimulation a rather small region of the cat's face produced this set of responses when touched; but as the intensity increased, the sequence could be elicited by touching the cat farther and farther from the front of its mouth.

Bandler and Flynn (1972) observed a similar in-

teraction in a reflex component of defensive attack. They found that when a cat's hypothalamus was electrically stimulated, it showed a reflexive striking movement when a specific region of its front leg was touched. When they increased the intensity of the hypothalamic stimulation, the reflex could be elicited by touching more widespread areas of the cat's leg. The reflex could be triggered by touching either leg, but a more vigorous reaction was produced by touching the leg contralateral to the hypothalamic stimulation. Thus, the effects resemble those seen by Depaulis, Bandler, and Vergnes (1989) when they stimulated the PAG.

Most extensive region from which head-orienting response could be elicited during brain stimulation

Region from which jaw-opening response could be elicited during brain stimulation

FIGURE 11.8

Stimulus control of a component of attack behavior. Tactile stimuli applied to the cat's face cause head turning or mouth opening during electrical stimulation of the hypothalamus. (From MacDonnell, M.F., and Flynn, J.P. *Science*, 1966, *152*, 1406–1408. Copyright 1966 by the American Association for the Advancement of Science.)

Amygdala

The amygdaloid complex is located in the rostromedial temporal lobe. It contains several nuclei, divided into two principal groups: the *corticomedial nuclei* (phylogenetically older) and the *basolateral nuclei* (evolved more recently). Neurons in the corticomedial nuclei send axons through the stria terminalis to the hypothalamus and other forebrain structures; neurons in the basolateral nuclei send axons through the more diffuse *ventral amygdalofugal pathway* (*amygdalofugal* means "amygdala fleeing"). The ventral amygdalofugal pathway reaches the hypothalamus, preoptic region, and septal nuclei, and it also sends fibers to the midbrain tegmentum and periaqueductal gray matter. The amygdala receives inputs from the olfactory system, temporal neocortex, thalamus, midbrain, and hypothalamus. Electrical recordings have shown that the amygdala is responsive to a variety of sensory stimuli. The anatomy of the amygdala thus provides a basis for its role in modulating hypothalamic-midbrain mechanisms in aggressive and defensive behavior. (See *Figure 11.9*.)

The corticomedial amygdala appears to play a role in the control of predatory attack. Its influence is inhibitory. Vergnes (1975, 1976) found that lesions of the corticomedial amygdala, or of the stria terminalis, which connects this region with the basal forebrain and hypothalamus, dramatically increased predatory behavior in rats. Defensive attack was not altered. Thus, the lesions appear to have removed the inhibitory control.

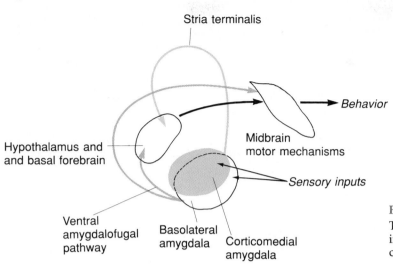

Stria terminalis

Behavior

Hypothalamus and
and basal forebrain

Midbrain
motor mechanisms

Sensory inputs

Ventral
amygdalofugal
pathway

Basolateral
amygdala

Corticomedial
amygdala

FIGURE 11.9
The amygdaloid complex and some of its
important afferent and efferent
connections.

A study by Bolhuis, Fitzgerald, Dijk, and
Koolhaas (1984) obtained evidence that the corticomedial amygdala plays a special role in defensive attack. When an animal suffers a defeat from
an opponent, the next time it confronts that animal or another dominant male, it is less likely to
fight and more likely to act submissively. The investigators arranged fights between males and bilaterally destroyed the corticomedial amygdala of
the animal that was defeated. They found that the
next time the animal met the opponent, it fought
just as much as it did previously; it did *not* show
submissive behavior. In a follow-up study Luiten,
Koolhaas, de Boer, and Koopmans (1985) found
that rats with corticomedial amygdala lesions
showed no fear response when the dominant rat
was present.

The principal role of the basolateral amygdala
in aggressive behavior appears to be an excitatory
influence on defensive attack. Stimulation of the
basolateral amygdala with electricity or with an
excitatory amino acid produces affective attack,
and lesions of the lateral nucleus (a part of the
basolateral nuclei) decrease the defensive attack
elicited by foot shock but do not affect predatory
attack (Hilton and Zbrozyna, 1963; Vergnes, 1976;
Al-Maskati and Zbrozyna, 1989). Hilton and
Zbrozyna found that electrical stimulation of the
amygdala produced defensive attack even after
the stria terminalis had been cut. Thus, the excita-

tory influence of the basolateral amygdala must be
conveyed by the ventral amygdalofugal pathway.
The influence could be mediated by connections
with the hypothalamus, the periaqueductal gray
matter, or both.

As we saw in Chapter 10, the amygdala contains estrogen and androgen receptors and receives input from the primary and accessory olfactory systems. Lesions of the amygdala reduce a
male hamster's attraction to the odor of the urine
of receptive females and remove the inhibitory effects of the odor of rat pups on the behavior of virgin female rats. As we will see in Chapter 14, the
amygdala plays a role in learning about harmful
stimuli. In particular, it is involved in learning to
make defensive responses, both behavioral and
autonomic, in the presence of a stimulus that was
previously associated with aversive stimuli. The
effects of lesions or electrical stimulation of the
amygdala on aggressive behaviors are certainly
consistent with this general function. Future
studies will have to focus on specific nuclei, which
have specific inputs and outputs and, undoubtedly, have specific roles.

*I*NTERIM SUMMARY

Aggressive behaviors are species-typical
and serve useful functions most of the time.
Its primary forms are offense, defense, and

predation. In addition, animals may exhibit threat or submissive behaviors, which may avoid an actual fight.

Electrical stimulation of the brain can produce all three types of aggressive behavior, which supports observations that they are species-typical in nature. The ventral tegmental area of the midbrain appears to be involved in the control of offensive behavior; lesions there abolish this behavior without affecting defense or predation. The periaqueductal gray matter appears to be involved in defensive behavior and predation. Stimulation of the anterior PAG with an excitatory amino acid elicits defensive threat behavior, whereas stimulation of the posterior PAG elicits defensive attack. The stimulation clearly does not simply make the animal more fearful; unilateral stimulation elicits threat only to an animal that approaches from the contralateral side. Defensive behaviors are inhibited by an opioid injected into the PAG. Stimulation of the ventral PAG produced predation, whereas lesions abolish the killing bite without affecting stalking and lunging behavior.

The hypothalamus helps control the occurrence of aggressive behaviors. In general, offense, defense, and predation are produced by stimulation of the medial, dorsal, and lateral regions of the hypothalamus.

The amygdala is also involved in aggressive behavior through its projections to the basal forebrain (including the hypothalamus) and midbrain. The corticomedial amygdala inhibits predatory attack through the connections of the stria terminalis with the basal forebrain, and it also appears to be involved in recognizing an animal that has previously defeated it. The basolateral amygdala appears to facilitate affective attack through the connections of the ventral amygdalofugal pathway with the hypothalamus and midbrain. Estrogen and androgen receptors in the amygdala undoubtedly mediate the influences of these classes of hormones on species-typical behaviors, including aggressive behavior.

Hormonal Control of Aggressive Behavior

With the exception of self-defense and predatory aggression, most instances of aggressive behavior are in some way related to reproduction. For example, males of some species establish territories that attract females during the breeding season. To do so, they must defend them against the intrusion of other males. Even in species in which breeding does not depend on the establishment of a territory, males may compete for access to females, which also involves aggressive behavior. Females, too, often compete with other females for space in which to build nests or dens in which to rear their offspring, and they will defend their offspring against the intrusion of other animals. As you learned in Chapter 10, most reproductive behaviors are controlled by the organizational and activational effects of hormones; thus, we should not be surprised that most forms of aggressive behavior, like mating, are affected by hormones.

Intermale Aggression

Adult males of many species fight for territory or access to females. In laboratory rodents androgen secretion occurs prenatally, decreases, and then increases again at the time of puberty. Intermale aggressiveness also begins around the time of puberty, which suggests that the behavior is controlled by neural circuits that are stimulated by androgens. Indeed, many years ago Beeman (1947) found that castration reduced aggressiveness and that injections of testosterone reinstated it.

We saw in Chapter 10 that early androgenization has an *organizational effect*. The secretion of androgens early in development modifies the developing brain, making neural circuits that control male sexual behavior become more responsive to testosterone. Similarly, early androgenization has an organizational effect that stimulates the development of testosterone-sensitive neural circuits that facilitate intermale aggression. Conner and Levine (1969) compared intermale aggression in rats that had been castrated immediately after birth with that of rats that were not castrated until after puberty. Injections of testosterone produced aggressive behavior only in the rats that had been castrated later in life; the injections were ineffective in those that had been castrated neonatally. Thus, the testosterone had an *activational effect* only in those animals in which an organizational effect had occurred. Edwards (1968) found that androgen-sensitive neural circuits could be masculinized in females. He noted that injections of testosterone during adulthood increased the aggressiveness of female mice that had received an injection of testosterone immediately after birth. However, females that had received placebo injections immediately after birth did *not* respond to injections of testosterone as adults. (See *Figure 11.10.*)

More recent evidence has shown that prolonged administration of testosterone will eventually induce intermale aggression even in rodents that were castrated immediately after birth. Data reviewed by vom Saal (1983) show that exposure to androgens early in life decreases the amount of exposure that is necessary to activate aggressive behavior later in life. Thus, early androgenization *sensitizes* the neural circuits— the earlier the androgenization, the more effective the sensitization. The organizational effect of androgens on intermale aggressiveness is important, but it is not an all-or-none phenomenon.

As we saw in Chapter 10, when a pregnant female is subjected to stress, her male offspring show less male sexual behavior, presumably because the stress interferes with the prenatal secretion of androgens. Kinsley and Svare (1986) found that prenatal stress also reduces intermale aggression. They subjected pregnant female mice to stress by restraining them several times in a plastic tube that was placed under bright lights. The male offspring were tested as adults for intermale aggression by placing them in a cage with an unfamiliar male. The prenatally stressed animals were much less likely than the control animals to attack the intruder. Thus, a treatment that interferes with prenatal masculinization of sexual behavior also interferes with the masculinization of aggressive behavior.

An interesting experiment by Albert, Petrovic, and Walsh (1989a) showed how the effects of testosterone interact with an animal's experience. They castrated adult male rats and then implanted empty capsules or capsules containing testosterone. All the animals were housed in pairs containing one testosterone-treated rat and one untreated rat. Half of these pairs were given competitive experience—they were deprived of food for two days and then were given access to a drinking tube that contained a tasty liquid diet. The tube was arranged so that only one rat at a time could drink from it. Testosterone had a clear effect on the animal's competitive behavior; the rats

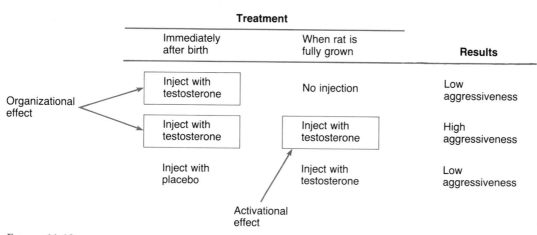

FIGURE 11.10

Organizational and activational effects of testosterone on social aggression demonstrated by Conner and Levine (1969).

with the testosterone implants fought with their cagemates and dominated the access to the tube. (See *Figure 11.11.*)

Next, the experimenters separated the pairs of animals and tested them all for intermale aggression by introducing a strange rat into the cage. The strange rat was smaller than the animal being tested, and it had been given an injection of a benzodiazepine tranquilizer so that it would not provoke a defensive reaction by attacking the test animal. Only one group of rats attacked the intruder: the testosterone-treated animals that had had experience competing with another rat. (See *Figure 11.12.*) This experiment indicates that testosterone increases an animal's competitive behavior but does not, in the absence of previous experience with aggressive behavior, increase the probability of noncompetitive attack.

Another type of experience increases the probability of intermale aggression: cohabitation with a female. Albert, Dyson, Walsh, and Petrovic (1988) castrated adult male rats and then implanted empty capsules or capsules containing testosterone. Next, they housed them individually with a normal male or female partner. Each week for four weeks they removed the partner and tested the experimental animal's aggressive behavior by introducing a strange male, who was

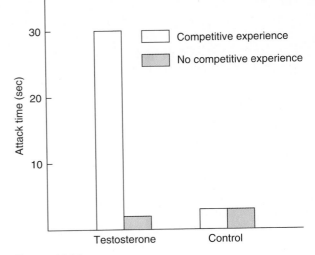

FIGURE 11.12

Effects of testosterone on aggressive behavior of rats with and without competitive experience. (Adapted from Albert, D.J., Petrovic, D.M., and Walsh, M.L. *Physiology and Behavior*, 1989, 45, 723–727.)

100 g lighter and had been given an injection of a benzodiazepine tranquilizer (as we saw in the experiment I just described). Figure 11.13 presents the data. You can see that all males housed with a female were more aggressive than those housed with a male, but testosterone enhanced this effect. (See *Figure 11.13.*)

We also saw in Chapter 10 that androgens stimulate male sexual behavior by interacting with androgen receptors in neurons located in the medial preoptic area. This region also appears to be important in mediating the effects of androgens on intermale aggression. Bean and Conner (1978) found that implanting testosterone in the medial preoptic area reinstated intermale aggression in castrated male rats. Presumably, the testosterone directly activated the behavior by stimulating the androgen-sensitive neurons located there.

The medial preoptic area (MPA) appears to be involved in several behaviors related to reproduction: male sexual behavior, maternal behavior, and intermale aggression. As we saw earlier, both male sexual behavior and maternal behavior appear to involve projections from the MPA to the region of the ventral tegmental area of the

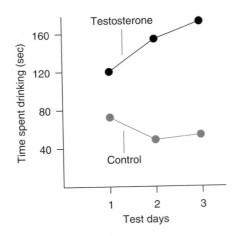

FIGURE 11.11

Effects of testosterone on time spent drinking a liquid diet in competition with another rat. (Adapted from Albert, D.J., Petrovic, D.M., and Walsh, M.L. *Physiology and Behavior*, 1989, 45, 723–727.)

midbrain. We also saw that the lesions of the ventral tegmental area abolish offensive behavior (but not defensive behavior or predation). I suspect that the connections between the MPA and the ventral tegmental area are important for the effects of androgens on intermale aggression, although there is not yet, to my knowledge, any experimental evidence to support this hypothesis.

Androgens do not appear to have direct effects on defensive behavior. Adams (1983) found that male and female rats respond similarly to opponents that attack them. In addition, Korn and Moyer (1968) reported that males and females do not differ in their response to handling by an ex-

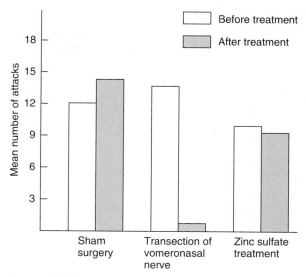

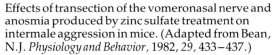

FIGURE 11.14

Effects of transection of the vomeronasal nerve and anosmia produced by zinc sulfate treatment on intermale aggression in mice. (Adapted from Bean, N.J. *Physiology and Behavior*, 1982, *29*, 433–437.)

perimenter. This finding makes perfect sense. It is reasonable that offensive behavior (usually seen in competition for territory or for access to females) should be related to androgens, just as sexual activity is. However, an animal is most likely to survive if it is prepared to defend itself at any time.

Males readily attack other males but usually do not attack females. Their ability to discriminate the sex of the intruder appears to be based on odor. Bean (1982) found that intermale aggression was abolished in mice by cutting the vomeronasal nerve. Rinsing the olfactory epithelium with zinc sulfate (which deafferents the primary olfactory system) had no effect. (See *Figure 11.14.*) Thus, intermale aggression of mice (and probably of other species of rodents) depends on a pheromonal stimulus. Undoubtedly, the medial amygdala plays a role in modulating this effect, as it does in all other phenomena controlled by pheromones. Further research is needed to support this assumption.

Pheromones also appear to be responsible for the inhibition of a male's attack on a female. If the urine of female mice is painted on a male mouse, it will not be attacked if it is introduced into another

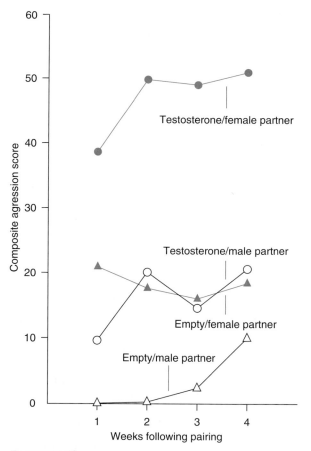

FIGURE 11.13

Effects of testosterone on the aggressive behavior of male rats housed with a male or a female partner. (Adapted from Albert, D.J., Dyson, E.M., Walsh, M.L., and Petrovic, D.M. *Physiology and Behavior*, 1988, *44*, 735–740.)

male's cage (Dixon and Mackintosh, 1971; Dixon, 1973). Evans, Mackintosh, Kennedy, and Robertson (1978) attempted to extract and analyze the compound responsible for the inhibitory effect. They were not able to identify the substance, but they did establish that it was not very volatile.

Interfemale Aggression

Many researchers have concluded that in most species females are less aggressive than males. Indeed, when two adult female rodents meet in a neutral territory, they are unlikely to fight, whereas adult males are very likely to do so. Interfemale aggression, like intermale aggression, appears to be dependent on testosterone. Van de Poll, Taminiau, Endert, and Louwerse (1988) ovariectomized female rats and then gave them daily injections of testosterone, estradiol, or a placebo for fourteen days. The animals were then placed in a test cage and an unfamiliar female was introduced. As Figure 11.15 shows, testosterone increased aggressiveness, whereas estradiol had no effect. (See *Figure 11.15.*)

As we saw in the previous section, females will become as aggressive as males if they are given testosterone immediately after birth. Apparently, a certain amount of prenatal androgenization occurs naturally. Most rodent fetuses share their mother's uterus with brothers and sisters, arranged in a row like peas in a pod. A female mouse may have zero, one, or two brothers adjacent to her. Researchers refer to these females as 0M, 1M, or 2M, respectively. (See *Figure 11.16.*) Being next to a male fetus has an effect on a female's blood levels of androgens prenatally. Vom Saal and Bronson (1980b) found that females located between two males had significantly higher levels of testosterone in their blood than females located between two females (or between a female and the end of the uterus).

When they are tested as adults, 2M females are more likely to exhibit interfemale aggressiveness. Vom Saal (1983) suggests that this phenomenon may have ecological significance. When the environment becomes crowded, the more aggressive 2M females are more likely to defend their territory against other females and successfully reproduce. Vom Saal and Bronson (1980a) found that the small amount of androgenization the 2M rats receive as fetuses has no deleterious effect on their fertility or maternal behavior.

As we saw in the previous section, when a male rat is housed with a female, its level of intermale aggression increases. A similar phenomenon occurs in female rats. Albert, Dyson, Petrovic, and Walsh (1988) housed female rats with castrated rats that had been given subcutaneous implants of testosterone. (The animals were castrated so that the females would not become pregnant.) After twelve days of cohabitation the females were tested each week for the next ten weeks for interfemale aggression by removing the male and introducing an unfamiliar female. The experimenters found that the experience increased the females' tendency to attack another female. In a follow-up study Albert, Petrovic, and Walsh (1989b) found that this effect was abolished by ovariectomy. (See *Figure 11.17.*) Thus, estradiol, progesterone, or ovarian testosterone is necessary for this effect to occur. Further studies will be needed to identify the relevant hormone(s).

Normal female rodents are just as likely as males to attack juveniles that are introduced into their cage. This behavior appears to be under the control of androgens. Gray, Whitsett, and Ziesenis (1978) found that ovariectomy abolished attacks by female mice on juveniles. Injections of

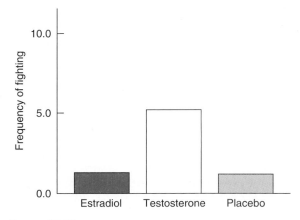

FIGURE 11.15
Effects of estradiol and testosterone on interfemale aggression in rats. (Adapted from van de Poll, N.E., Taminiau, M.S., Endert, E., and Louwerse, A.L. *International Journal of Neuroscience*, 1988, *41*, 271–286.)

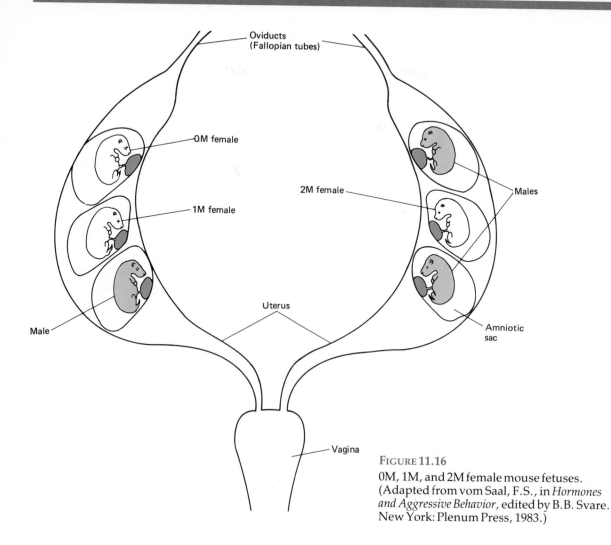

FIGURE 11.16

0M, 1M, and 2M female mouse fetuses. (Adapted from vom Saal, F.S., in *Hormones and Aggressive Behavior*, edited by B.B. Svare. New York: Plenum Press, 1983.)

estradiol or progesterone did not reinstate the behavior, but injections of testosterone did. Therefore, the small amount of testosterone produced by the ovaries appears to stimulate the attack by female mice on juveniles.

The females of some species of mammals are more aggressive than males. For example, female hamsters are aggressive at all times except during estrus. Their aggressiveness is apparently not hormone-dependent. Indeed, the only effect that hormones have on this behavior is inhibitory. Floody and Pfaff (1977) found that after being ovariectomized, female hamsters were continuously aggressive. Because the operation eliminated their period of estrus, it also eliminated their period of nonaggressiveness. When the experimenters administered estradiol and progesterone (the hormones that produce estrus), the animals became both sexually receptive and nonaggressive. Injections of estradiol, progesterone, or testosterone alone had no effect. The investigators suggested that the inhibitory effects of estradiol and progesterone on aggressive behavior are indirect—the hormones stimulate sexual behavior, which competes with aggressiveness.

Females of some primate species (for example, rhesus monkeys and baboons) are more likely to engage in fights around the time of ovulation (Carpenter, 1942; Saayman, 1971). This phenomenon is probably caused by their increased sexual interest and consequent proximity to males. As Carpenter noted, "She actively approaches males

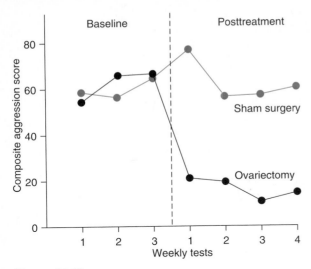

FIGURE 11.17

Effects of ovariectomy on interfemale aggression of rats that had been housed with sterile but sexually active males. (Adapted from Albert, D.J., Petrovic, D.M., and Walsh, M.L. *Physiology and Behavior*, 1989, *45*, 225–228.)

and must overcome their usual resistance to close association, hence she becomes an object of attacks by them'' (p. 136). Another period of fighting occurs just before menstruation (Sassenrath, Powell, and Hendrickx, 1973; Mallow, 1979). During this time females tend to attack other females. The story in chimpanzees is different; around the time of ovulation sexually receptive females are *less* likely to be attacked by dominant animals (Crawford, 1940).

Researchers have studied the possibility that irritability and aggressiveness may increase in women just before the time of menstruation, as it does in some other primate species. Floody (1983) reviewed the literature on the so-called *premenstrual syndrome* (PMS). Almost all studies that observed actual aggressiveness, primarily of women in institutions, found decreases around the time of ovulation and increases just before menstruation. Clearly, the changes in irritability are not universal; some women experience little or no mood shift before menstruation. And even if changes in mood occur, most women do not actually become aggressive. Whereas women with a history of criminal behavior (such as those in

prison) may indeed exhibit premenstrual aggressiveness, emotionally stable women may fail to show even a small increase in aggressiveness (Persky, 1974). Depending on their history and temperament, different people respond differently to similar physiological changes.

Maternal Aggression

Most parents who actively raise their offspring will vigorously defend them against intruders. In laboratory rodents the responsible parent is the female, so the most commonly studied form of parental defense is maternal aggression. Female mice very effectively defend their young, driving away intruding adults of either sex. Counterattacks by the intruder are rare (Svare, Betteridge, Katz, and Samuels, 1981). Whereas strange males who encounter each other engage in mutual investigation for a minute or two before fighting begins, the attack of a lactating female on an intruder is immediate (Svare, 1983).

Maternal aggressiveness actually begins during pregnancy. It, like maternal nest building, appears to be stimulated by progesterone. The onset of aggressiveness in pregnant mice occurs when progesterone levels begin to rise significantly (Mann, Konen, and Svare, 1984); cervical stimulation, which stimulates a temporary increase in progesterone secretion, also provokes a period of aggressiveness (Noirot, Goyens, and Buhot, 1975). Toward the end of pregnancy the level of progesterone falls, but aggressiveness continues. The reason for the continued aggressiveness is not clear. A surge in testosterone, which occurs just before parturition, may be responsible (Barkley, Geschwind, and Bradford, 1979).

Immediately after birth, for a period of approximately 48 hours, female mice become completely docile; they do not attack intruders (Ghiraldi and Svare, 1989). As Svare (1989) notes, it is at this time that female mice typically mate again; thus, the fact that they do not attack a male is biologically significant. This phenomenon is probably caused by the high level of estradiol that is present at that time. Ghiraldi and Svare found that ovariectomy just before parturition shortened the period of docility by 24 hours, and administration of estradiol restored it.

The tendency for a lactating female mouse to

attack a stranger is not a direct effect of ovarian or pituitary hormones; it is induced by stimuli provided by her offspring. If the newborn mice are removed, the mother fails to become aggressive. Two activating stimuli appear to be important: suckling and odors. First, let us consider the tactile stimulation produced by suckling. Normally, maternal aggressiveness begins after the mother has suckled her young for 48 hours. If the mother's nipples are surgically removed, she does not become aggressive, even if pups are present (Svare and Gandelman, 1976; Gandelman and Simon, 1980). These two studies also showed that although virgin female mice will begin exhibiting maternal behavior when they are housed with pups, they fail to show maternal aggression unless they are given daily injections of estrogen and progesterone, which causes their nipples to develop.

Suckling triggers the secretion of several hormones, including oxytocin, prolactin, and estradiol. However, these hormones are not responsible for the stimulating effect of suckling on maternal aggressiveness; removal of the ovaries, adrenal glands, or pituitary gland does not disrupt maternal aggressiveness (Svare, Mann, Broida, and Michael, 1982).

Maternal aggressiveness also requires olfactory stimulation. If pups are removed for 5 hours, aggressiveness decreases; but it is reinstated by reexposure to the pups for 5–10 minutes. Suckling is not necessary for this phenomenon; aggressiveness returns even if the pups are placed behind a wire screen (Svare and Gandelman, 1973).

Bean and Wysocki (1989) confirmed the importance of olfactory stimuli. They removed the vomeronasal organ from virgin female mice and then placed them with males. The animals became pregnant, delivered their offspring, and nursed and cared for them normally. However, they showed no maternal aggression toward unfamiliar male intruders. There are at least two reasons why removal of the vomeronasal organ disrupted maternal aggression. First, the operation could have eliminated the animal's sensitivity to olfactory stimuli from the pups that stimulate the behavior. Alternatively, the operation could have eliminated their sensitivity to the olfactory stimuli provided by the intruding males,

which provokes the attack. Bean and Wysocki did not test the aggressiveness of the females during pregnancy. It would be interesting to do so in order to see whether attacks that are not dependent on the odor of pups would still occur.

Prenatal exposure to androgens appears to have an organizational effect on maternal aggression. As we saw in the previous section, female mice who were located between two males in the uterus (2M females) are more likely to attack other females and are more responsive to the activating effects of androgens in adulthood. Vom Saal and Bronson (1980a) also found that 2M females are more maternally aggressive than 0M females. Kinsley, Konen, Miele, Ghiraldi, and Svare (1986) found that they were also more likely to exhibit aggressiveness during pregnancy.

Lactating female mice do not attack infants, but they vigorously attack juveniles or adults. The presence of hair appears to be an important distinguishing feature. Svare and Gandelman (1973) found that a lactating female will not attack a fourteen-day-old juvenile whose hair has been shaved off, but it will attack one with hair. Females are also more likely to attack unfamiliar intruders than familiar ones. Svare and Gandelman housed male mice for several days behind a wire mesh partition in the cage of a lactating female. When these mice were introduced into the female's cage, they were not attacked, whereas unfamiliar males were. The most important stimulus by which familiar males are recognized appears to be olfactory; Lynds (1976) found that when familiar intruders were coated with the urine of strangers, lactating females vigorously attacked them.

Infanticide

Although the evolutionary process has selected parents who nurture and defend their young, adults—both male and female—sometimes kill infants, including their own. Although this behavior may appear to be aberrant and maladaptive, under some circumstances it has survival value for the species.

Hrdy (1977), in a report of infanticide among langurs (a primate species), suggested that the killing of infants by a male who was not the father "is a reproductive strategy whereby the usurping male increases his own reproductive success at the expense of the former leader (presumably the father of the infant killed)" (p. 48). Because lactation suppresses a female's fertility, she is unlikely to become pregnant by the new male. However, when the male kills her offspring, she soon becomes fertile and thus capable of becoming pregnant by him. (The male tends *not* to kill his own offspring.)

You will recall a related phenomenon that I mentioned in Chapter 10: the Bruce effect (Bruce, 1960a, 1960b). When a newly pregnant mouse encounters the odor of a strange male, she tends to abort spontaneously. Thus, the male unintentionally kills her yet-unborn offspring, making it possible for him to impregnate her and propagate his own genes.

Vom Saal (1985) discovered that the tendency of male mice to kill infants is regulated by copulation. He found that after male mice successfully copulated and ejaculated, the likelihood of infanticide increased within a few days, but then decreased nineteen days later, around the time that the pups would be born. In fact, the males not only did not kill pups, they actually cared for them, just as their mothers do. This docility and solicitude lasted until about fifty days after the time of copulation, which is about the time that the pups would be weaned. Thus, the act of ejaculation initiates a series of events that increases the likelihood that a would-be father mouse kills the infants of other males but not his own.

The timing of these behavioral changes is remarkable. What internal mechanism keeps track of the nineteen-day gestation period of the female? Perrigo, Bryant, and vom Saal (1990) found that however this mechanism works, it does so by counting days, not hours. They permitted male mice to copulate and then divided them into two groups, which they put in rooms with light/dark cycles of different lengths: 22 or 27 hours. They found that the reduction in the likelihood of infanticide occurred after approximately eighteen "days," whether the days were short or long. It will be interesting to discover the mechanism that permits the mouse brain to count to eighteen.

Androgens have an effect on infanticide by male rodents. Gandelman and vom Saal (1975)

found that castration decreased the occurrence of infanticide by male mice and increased the occurrence of "maternal" behavior. These effects were reversed by replacement therapy with testosterone.

The organizational effect of androgens early in development appears to be paradoxical: Increased exposure of male rodents to androgens before or immediately after birth *inhibits* infanticide in adulthood. Vom Saal (1983) compared the behavior of adult 2M male mice (those that were located between two brothers prenatally) with 0M male mice. The 2M mice, which received a larger dose of prenatal androgens, were more likely to care for pups than kill them, whereas the 0M mice were more likely to kill them than care for them. Perrigo, Bryant, and vom Saal (1989) offer a possible explanation for this effect. They suggest that two effects of prenatal androgenization—an increase in intermale aggression and a decrease in infanticide—are related. The increased intermale aggression raises the likelihood that the animal will succeed in dominating other males and defending a territory that includes several females, which he, of course, will impregnate. Thus, because most of the litters he encounters are his own, the best strategy is not to kill pups.

Female rodents sometimes kill their own pups. Obviously, infanticide by males and females must occur for different reasons. Indeed, female infanticide appears to achieve at least two advantages: It decreases crowding, and it helps attain an optimal litter size. The first hypothetical advantage was supported by Calhoun (1962), who reported that severe crowding greatly increased the incidence of female infanticide in rats. Presumably, this behavior helped prevent the crowding from increasing still further. Gandelman and Simon (1978) obtained data that supported the second hypothetical advantage. They adjusted the size of litters of newborn mice to either twelve or sixteen pups by adding foster pups or removing them. In both groups the mean number of surviving offspring was nine. The mothers with sixteen pups tended to kill more than those with twelve pups. The smallest pups were most likely to be killed. Because these pups were probably the least fit, the behavior tends to select for an optimally sized litter that consists of the healthiest pups. (Mice have ten nipples, which suggests that the optimal size is ten or less.)

Effects of Androgens on Human Aggressive Behavior

Boys are generally more aggressive than girls. This is as true of three-to-six-year-old children as it is of seven-to-ten-year-old children (D'Andrade, 1966). Clearly, Western society tolerates assertiveness and aggressive behavior from boys more than girls. However, if socialization were the *sole* cause of the sex difference in aggressive behavior, we would expect that the difference between older boys and girls, who have been exposed to socializing stimuli longer, would be larger than that between younger boys and girls. Because this is not the case, D'Andrade's finding suggests that biological differences such as those produced by prenatal androgenization may be at least partly responsible for the increased aggressive behavior in males.

I have already reviewed some of the evidence concerning intermale aggression in laboratory animals, and we saw that androgens have strong organizational and activational effects. Prenatal androgenization increases aggressive behavior in all species that have been studied, including primates. Therefore, if androgens did not affect aggressive behavior in humans, our species would be exceptional. Boys' testosterone levels begin to increase during the early teens, at which time aggressive behavior and intermale fighting also increase (Mazur, 1983). Of course, boys' social status changes during puberty, and their testosterone affects their muscles as well as their brains; so we cannot be sure that the effect is hormonally produced, or if it is, that it is mediated neurally.

Males of many species can be gentled by castration. This observation has led authorities to castrate convicted male sex offenders. Investigators have reported that both heterosexual and homosexual aggressive attacks disappear, along with the offender's sex drive (Hawke, 1951; Sturup, 1961; Laschet, 1973). However, the studies typically lack appropriate control groups and do not always measure aggressive behavior di-

rectly. Hawke (1951) reported the following:

> Many of these individuals so treated were . . . very brutal in attacks on small children. They were very unstable and would create a disturbance at every opportunity. After castration, they became stabilized, and those who cannot be paroled are good useful citizens in the institution. In our experimental work, we have administered Testosterone, the male hormone [to some castrates] . . . . In a number of cases, after we had treated them for a period of two or three weeks, the floor supervisor would call me up and ask if I would not be willing to stop administering Testosterone to certain individuals who had reverted to all of their anti-social tendencies, were attacking small children, starting fights, breaking windows and destroying furniture. We would stop the administration of Testosterone in these individuals, and within a few days they would be restabilized and cause no further ward disturbances. We have felt that this proves the male hormone is the exciting factor in these cases. (p. 222)

Because the studies with castrated males were not performed with the appropriate double-blind controls, we cannot conclude that testosterone was the responsible agent for the increase in aggressive behavior. Certainly, the conclusion that it was is a reasonable one, but it must be determined scientifically. However, ethical standards that have been adopted by the panels that review human biomedical research will probably prevent studies that could provide a definitive answer. First, we must decide whether castration is justified in cases of brutal aggression. Second, even if a violent man is castrated and his violence ceases, can we ethically subject other people to possible harm by administering replacement doses of testosterone?

Some cases of aggressiveness—especially sexual assault—have been treated with drugs that have antiandrogenic effects (Gagne, 1981; Bradford, 1983). The rationale is based on animal research (reviewed in this chapter and in Chapter 10) that indicates that androgens promote male sexual behavior and intermale aggression. Clearly, treatment with drugs is preferable to castration, because it is not irreversible.

Another way to approach the problem is to examine the testosterone levels of people who exhibit varying levels of aggressive behavior. However, even though this approach poses fewer ethical problems, it presents methodological ones. First, let me review the evidence. Kreuz and Rose (1972) measured the testosterone levels of twenty-one male prisoners with a history of violent crime and found that the androgen levels were not related to their level of violence in prison. However, the hormone *was* related to their history of aggressive behavior during adolescence. Another study (Ehrenkranz, Bliss, and Sheard, 1974) compared three groups of prisoners: (1) socially dominant but unaggressive men, who had been convicted of nonviolent crimes; (2) chronically aggressive men, who had been convicted of violent crimes; and (3) nonaggressive, nondominant men. The testosterone levels of groups 1 and 2 were both high compared with that of the third group. Thus, this study suggests that testosterone may promote nonaggressive dominance (leadership without bullying) as well as aggressive behavior. On the other hand, perhaps testosterone simply promotes dominance in men. Those who are able to achieve dominance nonviolently do so, but those who are not intelligent or socially adept enough resort to cruder means.

The methodological problem with all correlational studies like the ones I just cited is that a man's environment can affect his testosterone level. For example, Mazur and Lamb (1980) found that men who decisively lost a tennis match had significantly lower blood levels of testosterone an hour later, and men who won had significantly higher levels. Similar effects were found in college wrestlers who won or lost competitive matches (Elias, 1981). Thus, we cannot be sure that high testosterone levels *caused* some prisoners to become dominant or violent; perhaps their success increased their testosterone levels relative to those of the prisoners they dominated.

An interesting set of experiments with another species of primates may have some relevance to human aggression. As you undoubtedly know,

alcohol intake is often associated with aggression in humans. Alcohol increases intermale aggression in dominant male squirrel monkeys, but only during the mating season, when their blood level of testosterone is two to three times higher than during the nonmating season (Winslow and Miczek, 1985, 1988). Alcohol does *not* increase the aggressive behavior of subordinate monkeys. These studies suggest that the effects of alcohol interact with both social status and with testosterone. This suggestion was confirmed by Winslow, Ellingoe, and Miczek (1988), who tested monkeys during the nonmating season. They found that alcohol increased the aggressive behavior of dominant monkeys only if they were also given injections of testosterone. However, these treatments were ineffective in subordinate monkeys, who had presumably learned not to be aggressive. The next step will be to find the neural mechanisms that are responsible for these interactions.

*I*NTERIM SUMMARY

Because many aggressive behaviors are related to reproduction, they are influenced by hormones, especially sex steroid hormones. Androgens primarily affect offensive attack; they are not necessary for defensive behaviors, which are shown by females as well as males. In males androgens have organizational and activational effects on offensive attack, just as they have on male sexual behavior. Prolonged exposure to androgens during adulthood eventually produces offensive aggression even in nonandrogenized animals, so organizational effects are not absolutely necessary. Prenatal stress reduces the incidence of intermale aggression.

The activational effects of androgens interact with those of experience; they increase competitiveness but do not increase intermale aggression unless an animal has had experience competing with (and defeating) another male. Cohabitation with a female also increases intermale aggression, even if increases in testosterone are prevented by castration and replacement therapy. The effects of androgens on intermale aggression appear to be mediated by the medial preoptic area. The inhibition of an attack by a male on a female mouse is mediated by her odor, perhaps through the connections of the accessory olfactory system with the medial nucleus of the amygdala. Recognition of the odor of a male is necessary for stimulating an attack; cutting of the vomeronasal nerve abolishes intermale aggression.

Female aggressiveness is more common than was previously believed. For example, female hamsters are normally aggressive but become less so when high levels of progesterone and estradiol promote estrus. In contrast, female primates are most likely to fight around the time of ovulation, perhaps because their increased sexual interest brings them closer to males. Although some women report irritability just before menstruation, the phenomenon is not universal.

Although interfemale aggression is far less prevalent than intermale aggression, the two behaviors seem similar; both behaviors are stimulated by testosterone, and an androgenized 2M female is more likely to be aggressive than her 0M sisters. Cohabitation with a male also increases interfemale aggressiveness, even when the female does not become pregnant. The attack by female rodents on juveniles is apparently controlled by androgens secreted by their ovaries.

Maternal aggression is a very swift and effective behavior. It begins during pregnancy, apparently triggered by the secretion of progesterone. After parturition maternal aggression is stimulated by the tactile feedback from suckling, and it can be stimulated in a virgin female whose nipples have been stimulated to grow by hormonal treatment. The odor of pups is also necessary. Maternal aggressiveness is abolished by removal of the vomeronasal organ, but it is not clear whether this operation removes the stimulating effect of the pups on aggressiveness or prevents the odor of an unfamiliar male from triggering an attack. Prenatal androgens have an organizational effect on maternal aggression; 2M females are more likely than 0M females to display maternal aggression. Although lactating females will not attack pups that belong to other females, they will attack juveniles (male or female) with hair.

Infanticide by male mice is regulated by copulation; after ejaculating, the males become more likely to kill infants, but around the time that their pups would be born, this tendency is suppressed. In males, infanticide is promoted by androgens; its occurrence is decreased by castration. However, prenatal androgens appear to suppress this behavior in females; 2M females are *less* likely to show this behavior than their 0M sisters; thus the nature of the development of this form of aggressive behavior is not well understood. Female infanticide appears to promote optimal litter size and tends to weed out less healthy offspring.

Androgens apparently promote aggressive behavior in humans, but this topic is more difficult to study in our species than in laboratory animals. Differences in testosterone levels have been observed in criminals with a history of violence, but we cannot be sure whether higher androgen levels promote violence or whether successful aggression increases androgen levels. Studies with monkeys suggest that testosterone and alcohol have synergistic effects, particularly in dominant animals. Perhaps these effects are related to the fact that some men with a history of violent behavior become more aggressive when they drink.

CONCLUDING REMARKS

Parental behavior and aggressive behavior are important categories of species-typical behavior. For the survival of most species of mammals, maternal behavior is just as important as mating. Aggression also promotes reproduction; it serves to disperse members of a species, to provide mating opportunities for the most vigorous males, to provide nesting space for the most vigorous females, and to reduce litters to their optimal size. Our understanding of the different types of aggression, the conditions under which they occur, and their neural and hormonal basis complements our knowledge of the physiology of other species-typical behaviors. Perhaps someday we will be able to use this knowledge to reduce the incidence of human violence, but at present the application of data obtained from animals to humans seems premature.

The next two chapters discuss other behaviors important to our survival: drinking and eating. However, the only beverage discussed in Chapter 12 is water. This book discusses alcohol drinking, too, but not until Chapter 16, which considers the physiology of addictive behaviors.

NEW TERMS

basolateral nuclei p. 362
bonding p. 356
concaveation p. 351
corticomedial nuclei p. 362
defensive behavior p. 358

offensive behavior p. 358
predation p. 358
stria terminalis p. 351
submissive behavior p. 358

threat behavior p. 358
ventral amygdalofugal
  pathway p. 362
ventral tegmental area p. 354

SUGGESTED READINGS

Knobil, E., and Neill, J. *The Physiology of Reproduction*. New York: Raven Press, 1988.

Krasnegor, N.A., and Bridges, R.S. *Mammalian Parenting: Biological and Behavioral Determinants*. New York: Oxford University Press, 1989.

Levine, S., and Brush, F.R. *Psychoendocrinology*. New York: Academic Press, 1989.

Parmigiani, S., Mainardi, D., and Brain, P. *House Mouse Aggression: A Model for Understanding the Evolution of Social Behavior*. London: Gordon and Breach, 1989.

Simmel, E.C., Hahn, M.E., and Walters, J.K. *Aggressive Behavior: Genetic and Neural Approaches*. Hillsdale, N.J.: Lawrence Erlbaum Associates, 1983.

Svare, B.B. *Hormones and Aggressive Behavior*. New York: Plenum Press, 1983.

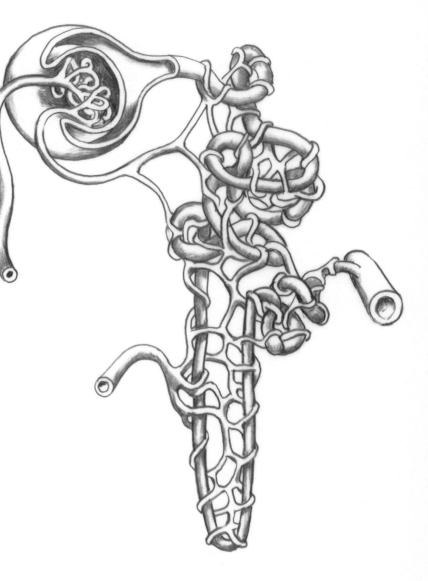

Ingestive Behavior: Drinking

As the French physiologist Claude Bernard (1813–1878) said, "The constancy of the internal milieu is a necessary condition for a free life." This famous quote succinctly says what organisms must do to be able to exist in environments hostile to the living cells that compose them (that is, to live a "free life"): They must regulate the nature of the internal fluid that bathes their cells.

The physiological characteristics of the cells that constitute our bodies evolved long ago, when these cells floated freely in the ocean. In essence, what the evolutionary process has accomplished is the ability to make our own seawater to surround our cells, to add to this seawater the oxygen and nutrients that our cells need, and to remove from it waste products that would otherwise poison them. To perform these functions, we have digestive, respiratory, circulatory, and excretory systems. We also have the behaviors necessary for finding and ingesting food and water.

Regulation of the fluid that bathes our cells is part of a process called *homeostasis* ("similar standing"). This chapter discusses the means by which we mammals achieve homeostatic control of the vital characteristics of our extracellular fluid through our *ingestive behavior:* intake of food, water, and minerals such as sodium. First, we will examine the general nature of regulatory mechanisms; then we will consider our drinking and eating behavior.

THE NATURE OF PHYSIOLOGICAL REGULATORY MECHANISMS

A physiological regulatory mechanism is one that maintains the constancy of some internal characteristic of the organism in the face of external variability—for example, maintenance of a constant body temperature despite changes in the ambient temperature. A regulatory mechanism contains four essential features: the *system variable* (the characteristic to be regulated), a *set point* (the optimal value of the system variable), a *detector* that monitors the value of the system variable, and a *correctional mechanism* that restores the system variable to the set point.

An example of a regulatory system is a room whose temperature is regulated by a thermostatically controlled heater. The system variable is the air temperature of the room, and the detector for this variable is a thermostat. This device can be adjusted so that contacts of a switch will be closed when the temperature falls below a preset value (the set point). Closure of the contacts turns on the correctional mechanism—the coils of the heater. (See *Figure 12.1.*)

If the room cools below the set point of the thermostat, the thermostat turns the heater on, which warms the room. The rise in room temperature causes the thermostat to turn the heater off. Because the activity of the correctional mechanism (heat production) feeds back to the thermostat and causes it to turn the heater off, this process is called *negative feedback.* Negative feedback is an essential characteristic of all regulatory systems.

This chapter and Chapter 13 consider regulatory systems that involve ingestive behaviors: drinking and eating. These behaviors are correctional mechanisms that replenish the body's depleted stores of water or nutrients. Because of the delay between ingestion and replenishment of the depleted stores, ingestive behaviors are controlled by *satiety mechanisms* as well as by detectors that monitor the system variables. Satiety mechanisms are required because of the physiology of our digestive system. For example, suppose you exercise in a hot, dry environment and lose body water. The loss of water causes internal detectors to initiate the correctional mechanism— drinking. You quickly drink a glass or two of water and then stop. What stops your ingestive behavior? The water is still in your digestive system, not yet in the fluid surrounding your cells, where it is needed. Therefore, although drinking was initiated by detectors that measure your body's need for water, *it was stopped by other means.* There must be a satiety mechanism that says, in effect, "Stop—this water, when absorbed by the digestive system into the blood, will eventually replenish the body's need." Satiety mechanisms monitor the activity of the correctional mechanism (in this case, drinking), not the system variables themselves. When a sufficient amount of drink-

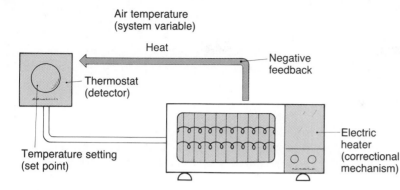

FIGURE 12.1
An example of a regulatory system.

ing occurs, the satiety mechanisms stop further drinking *in anticipation* of the replenishment that will occur later. (See *Figure 12.2.*)

SOME FACTS ABOUT FLUID BALANCE

Before you can understand the physiological control of drinking, you must know something about the fluid compartments of the body and their relations with each other. And to understand these facts, you must also know something about the functions of the kidney.

The Fluid Compartments of the Body

The body contains four major fluid compartments: one compartment of intracellular fluid and three compartments of extracellular fluid. Approximately two-thirds of the body's water is contained in the *intracellular fluid*—the fluid portion of the cytoplasm of cells. The rest is *extracellular*

fluid, which includes the *intravascular fluid* (the blood plasma), the cerebrospinal fluid, and the *interstitial fluid. Interstitial* means "standing between"; indeed, the interstitial fluid stands between our cells—it is the "seawater" that bathes them. For the purposes of this chapter I will ignore the cerebrospinal fluid and concentrate on the other three compartments. (See *Figure 12.3.*)

The fluid compartments are coupled to each other and are separated by semipermeable barriers, which permit the passage of some substances but not others. The walls of the capillaries separate the intravascular fluid (blood plasma) from the interstitial fluid, and the cell membranes separate the interstitial fluid from the intracellular fluid. Therefore, if one compartment loses water and its osmotic pressure consequently increases, water is drawn from the other compartments by osmosis.

Two of the fluid compartments of the body must be kept within precise limits—the intracel-

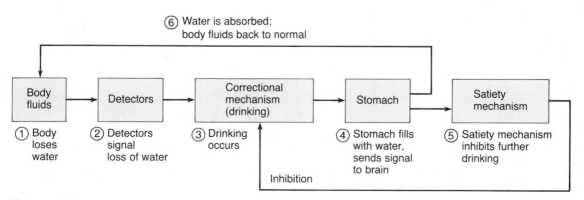

FIGURE 12.2
An outline of the system that controls drinking.

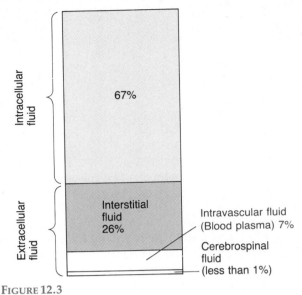

FIGURE 12.3
The relative size of the body's fluid compartments.

lular fluid and the intravascular fluid. The intracellular fluid is controlled by the concentration of solutes in the interstitial fluid. (*Solutes* are the solid substances dissolved in a solution.) Normally, the interstitial fluid is *isotonic* (from *isos*, "same," and *tonos*, "tension") with the intracellular fluid. That is, the concentration of solutes in the cells and in the interstitial fluid that bathes them is balanced, so that water does not tend to move into or out of the cells. If the interstitial fluid loses water (becomes more concentrated, or *hypertonic*), water will then move out of the cells, through osmosis. On the other hand, if the interstitial fluid gains water (becomes more dilute, or *hypotonic*), water will move into the cells. Either condition endangers cells; a loss of water deprives them of the ability to perform many chemical reactions, and a gain of water can cause their membrane to rupture. Thus, the concentration of the interstitial fluid must be closely regulated.

The volume of the blood plasma must be closely regulated because of the mechanics of the operation of the heart. If the blood volume falls too low, the heart can no longer pump the blood effectively; if the volume is not restored, heart failure will result. This condition is called *hypovolemia*, literally "low volume of the blood" (-*emia* comes

from the Greek *haima*, "blood"). The vascular system of the body can make some adjustments for loss of blood volume by contracting the muscles in smaller veins and arteries, thereby presenting a smaller space for the blood to fill, but this correctional mechanism has definite limits.

The volume of the interstitial fluid need not be regulated closely. The most important reason is that when the volumes of the intracellular and intravascular fluid compartments are kept within normal limits, the volume of the extracellular fluid will automatically stay within its normal limits. Only in certain pathological conditions—such as capillary damage, heart failure, or a very low level of protein in the blood—will the volume of the interstitial fluid become abnormally high. (There is no way for it to become abnormally low without the other fluid compartments becoming abnormal.) However, although the *volume* of the interstitial fluid is normally not a matter of concern, its *tonicity* (solute concentration) must be closely regulated, because this variable is what determines whether water flows into cells or out of them.

As we shall see, the intracellular fluid and the blood volume are monitored by two different sets of receptors. A single set of receptors would not work, because it is possible for one of these fluid compartments to be changed without affecting the other. For example, a loss of blood (obviously) reduces the volume of the intravascular fluid, but it has no effect on the volume of the intracellular fluid. On the other hand, a salty meal will increase the solute concentration of the interstitial fluid and draw water out of the cells. These cells will remain dehydrated even after the kidney has gotten rid of the excess sodium (and a quantity of water to flush it away) and restored the blood volume back to normal. Thus, the body needs a set of receptors measuring blood volume and another measuring cell volume.

Just as there are two sets of receptors, there are two sets of correctional mechanisms. One set involves the ingestion and excretion of water, and the other involves the ingestion and excretion of sodium. Obviously, the excretions of water and sodium are accomplished by the kidney, and the ingestion of these substances is accomplished by the behavior of eating salt (or foods containing salt) and drinking water.

Most of the time, we drink more water than our body needs, and the excess is excreted by the kidneys. Similarly, we ingest more sodium than we need, and the kidneys get rid of the surplus. Thus, if we want to understand the means of regulating our water and sodium balance, we must understand what the kidneys do and how they are controlled.

The Kidneys

A human kidney consists of approximately a million functional units called **nephrons.** Each nephron extracts fluid from the blood and carries it, through collecting ducts, to the **ureter.** The ureter, in turn, connects the kidney to the urinary bladder, where urine is stored until it can be released at a convenient time. (This behavior, which physiol-ogists politely refer to as *micturition,* from the Latin word for "urinate," has absolutely nothing to do with regulation. Once the urine is in the bladder, it is out of the body as far as the three fluid compartments are concerned.) (See *Figure 12.4.*)

The kidneys control the amount of water and sodium that the body excretes, which controls both the volume and the concentration (tonicity) of the extracellular fluid. If we drink a large amount of water and must get rid of the excess, our kidneys pass a large quantity of urine to the bladder. Similarly, if we eat salty food and must get rid of the excess sodium, our kidneys extract the sodium from our blood and pass it on to the bladder. However, if the organism has lost water through evaporation, the kidneys conserve water, producing a small quantity of urine. In addition, if the body becomes deficient in sodium, the

FIGURE 12.4

Anatomy of the kidney and an individual nephron. (From Orians, G.H. *The Study of Life.* Boston: Allyn and Bacon, 1973.)

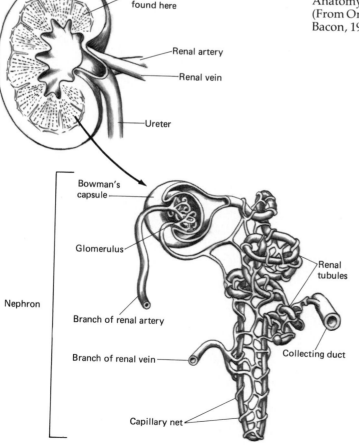

Nephrons are found here

Renal artery

Renal vein

Ureter

Bowman's capsule

Glomerulus

Nephron

Branch of renal artery

Branch of renal vein

Renal tubules

Collecting duct

Capillary net

kidneys will begin to excrete a very small amount in the urine.

The amounts of sodium and water that the kidneys excrete are controlled by two hormones: aldosterone and antidiuretic hormone. Sodium excretion is controlled by *aldosterone,* a steroid hormone secreted by the adrenal cortex. High levels of aldosterone cause the kidneys to retain sodium in the body—to pass very little sodium on to the bladder. Thus, if the body contains too much sodium, the level of aldosterone secretion falls and sodium is excreted in the urine. If too little salt is present, a high aldosterone level causes it to be conserved. (See *Figure 12.5.*)

The excretion of water by the kidneys is controlled by a hormone called *vasopressin.* The name of this hormone is unfortunate, because it does not describe its primary function, which is to instruct the kidneys how much water to retain. High levels of vasopressin will cause the kidneys to retain as much water as possible, only excreting as much as is needed to rid the body of the waste products of metabolism. The term *vasopressin* refers to its ability under certain circumstances to cause blood vessels to contract (*vas* means "vessel" in Latin). A better term is *antidiuretic hormone.* (*Diuresis* comes from the Greek *dia,* "through," and *ouron,* "urine"; thus, *anti*diuretic hormone reduces the production of urine.) Nevertheless, vasopressin is the name that most physiologists use.

Vasopressin is a peptide hormone secreted by the posterior pituitary gland. It is produced in the cell bodies of neurons located in two nuclei of the hypothalamus: the *supraoptic nucleus* and the *paraventricular nucleus.* The hormone is stored in vesicles and travels through axons to the posterior pituitary gland, where it collects in the terminal buttons. When the neurons in the supraoptic and paraventricular nuclei become active, their terminal buttons release vasopressin, which enters the blood supply. Thus, the production, storage, and release of vasopressin is exactly like that of any peptide transmitter substance, except that it affects receptors in another part of the body, not in a membrane across a synaptic cleft.

If we drink more water than our body needs, the posterior pituitary gland stops secreting vasopressin, and the kidneys excrete the excess water. If we become dehydrated, the posterior pituitary gland increases vasopressin secretion, and the kidneys excrete a minimum amount of water. (See *Figure 12.5.*)

So far, I have been talking only about system variables and correctional mechanisms. What about detectors? It turns out that some of the same detectors that control the secretion of aldosterone and vasopressin (and thus control the excretion of

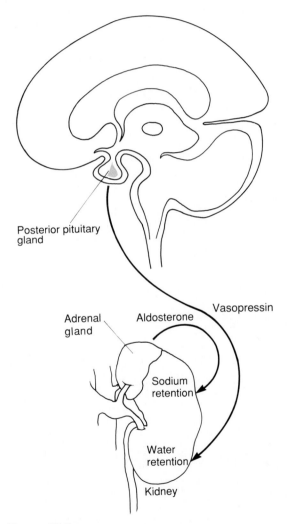

FIGURE 12.5
Hormonal control of the kidney. Aldosterone, secreted by the cortex of the adrenal gland, causes sodium retention by the kidney. Vasopressin, secreted by the posterior pituitary gland, causes water retention.

sodium and water by the kidneys) also control the intake of water and salt. Thus, I will discuss them in the next section.

*I*NTERIM SUMMARY

A regulatory system contains four features: a system variable (the variable that is regulated), a set point (the optimal value of the system variable), a detector to measure the system variable, and a correctional mechanism to change it. Physiological regulatory systems, such as control of body fluids and nutrients, require a satiety mechanism to anticipate the effects of the correctional mechanism, because the changes brought about by eating and drinking occur only after a considerable period of time.

The body contains three major fluid compartments: the intracellular fluid, the interstitial fluid, and the intravascular fluid. Sodium and water can easily pass between the intravascular fluid and the interstitial fluid, but sodium cannot penetrate the cell membrane. The solute concentration of the interstitial fluid must be closely regulated. If it becomes hypertonic, cells lose water; if it becomes hypotonic, they gain water. The volume of the intravascular fluid (blood plasma) must also be kept within bounds.

The kidneys regulate the excretion of water and sodium; in the process of excreting water, waste products are carried away by the urine. Aldosterone, a steroid hormone released by the adrenal cortex, causes sodium retention. Vasopressin, a peptide hormone produced by the supraoptic and paraventricular nuclei and released by the posterior pituitary gland, causes water retention.

DRINKING AND SALT APPETITE

As we just saw, in order for our bodies to function properly, the volume of two fluid compartments—intracellular and intravascular—must be regulated. Most of the time, we ingest more water and sodium than we need, and the kidneys excrete the excess. However, if the levels of water or sodium fall too low, correctional mechanisms—drinking of water or ingestion of sodium—are activated. Everyone is familiar with the sensation of thirst, which occurs when we need to ingest water. However, a salt appetite is much more rare, because it is difficult for people *not* to get enough sodium in their diet, even if they do not put extra salt on their food. Nevertheless, the mechanisms to increase sodium intake exist, even though they are seldom called upon in members of our species.

Because loss of water from either the intracellular or intravascular fluid compartments stimulates drinking, researchers have adopted the terms *osmometric thirst* and *volumetric thirst* to describe them. The term *volumetric* is clear—it refers to the metering (measuring) of the volume of the blood plasma. The term *osmometric* requires more explanation, which I will provide in the next section. The term *thirst* means different things in different circumstances. Its original definition referred to a sensation that people say they have when they are dehydrated. Here I use it in a descriptive sense. Because we do not know how experimental animals feel, *thirst* simply means a tendency to seek water and to ingest it.

Osmometric Thirst

Osmometric thirst occurs when the tonicity (solute concentration) of the interstitial fluid increases. This event draws water out of the cells, and they shrink in volume. The term *osmometric* refers to the fact that the detectors are actually responding to (metering) differences in concentration of the intracellular fluid and the interstitial fluid that surrounds them.

The existence of neurons that respond to changes in the solute concentration of the interstitial fluid was first hypothesized by Verney (1947), who called them ***osmoreceptors.*** Verney found that an infusion of hypertonic sodium chloride into a dog's carotid artery would stimulate the secretion of vasopressin and thus cause the kidneys to decrease their excretion of water. Figure 12.6 shows how the injection caused an almost immediate decrease in the production of urine. (See *Figure 12.6.*)

Verney hypothesized that osmoreceptors were neurons whose firing rate was affected by

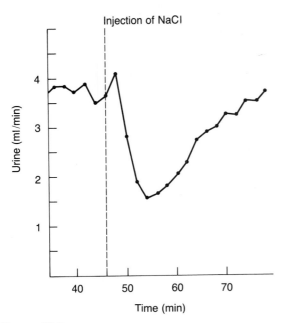

FIGURE 12.6

Effects of an injection of hypertonic saline solution into a dog's carotid artery. The solution removed water from cells in the brain and caused the posterior pituitary gland to secrete vasopressin. The hormone caused water to be retained by the kidneys, reducing the flow of urine. (From Verney, E.G. *Proceedings of the Royal Society of London, B.*, 1947, *135*, 25–106.)

their level of hydration. That is, if the interstitial fluid surrounding them became more concentrated, they would lose water through osmosis. The shrinkage would cause them to alter their firing rate, which would send signals to the neurons that control the rate of vasopressin secretion. (See *Figure 12.7.*) As we shall see, more recent studies have confirmed that osmoreceptors do exist and that they can initiate drinking as well as vasopressin secretion.

Before I discuss the evidence concerning the existence and location of osmoreceptors, I want to say more about the conditions that cause osmotic thirst. Our bodies lose water continuously, primarily through evaporation. Each breath exposes the moist inner surfaces of the respiratory system to the air; thus, each breath causes the loss of a small amount of water. In addition, our skin is not completely waterproof; some water finds its way through the layers of the skin and evaporates from

the surface. The moisture lost through evaporation is, of course, pure distilled water. (Sweating loses water, too; but because it loses salt along with the water, it produces a sodium need as well.) When we lose water through evaporation, we lose it from all fluid compartments, intracellular, interstitial, and intravascular. Thus, normal dehydration produces both *osmometric* and *volumetric* thirst.

Figure 12.8 illustrates how the loss of water through evaporation depletes both the intracellular and intravascular fluid compartments. For the sake of simplicity, only a few cells are shown, and the volume of the interstitial fluid is greatly exaggerated. Water is lost directly from the interstitial fluid, which becomes slightly more concentrated than either the intracellular or the intravascular fluid. Thus, water is drawn from both the cells and the blood plasma. When enough water is lost from the cells, the secretion of vasopressin will be stimulated, and urine production will diminish. Eventually, the loss of water from the cells and the blood plasma will be great enough that both osmometric and volumetric thirst will be produced. (See *Figure 12.8.*)

If evaporation were the only way that the distribution of water in the three fluid compartments could be disturbed, then we would not need two kinds of detectors to stimulate thirst. However, it is possible to incur a loss of intracellular fluid without losing intravascular fluid. (And as we shall see in the next section, the opposite condition is possible, too.)

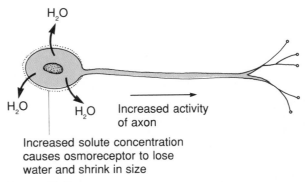

FIGURE 12.7

A hypothetical explanation of the workings of an osmoreceptor.

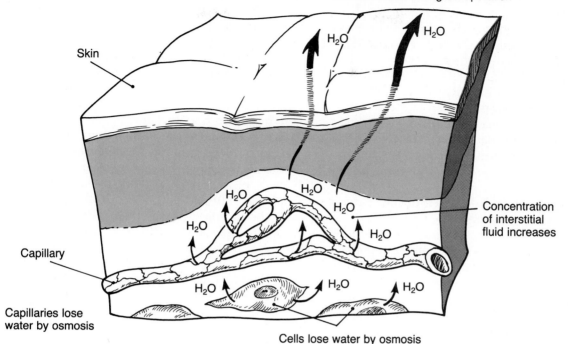

Loss of water through evaporation

Skin

H_2O

H_2O

Concentration
of interstitial
fluid increases

H_2O H_2O

H_2O

H_2O

H_2O

H_2O

Capillary

H_2O H_2O H_2O

Capillaries lose
water by osmosis

Cells lose water by osmosis

FIGURE 12.8
The loss of water through evaporation.

The most common way to incur a separate intracellular fluid loss is to eat a salty meal. The salt is absorbed from the digestive system into the blood plasma; hence the blood plasma becomes hypertonic. This condition draws water from the interstitial fluid, which makes this compartment become hypertonic, too, and thus causes water to leave the cells. As the blood plasma increases in volume, the kidneys begin excreting large amounts of both sodium and water. Eventually, the excess sodium is excreted, along with the water that was taken from the interstitial and intracellular fluid. The net result is a loss of water from the cells. *At no time did the volume of the blood plasma fall;* in fact, it was temporarily higher than normal, which is what triggered the excretion of sodium and water by the kidneys. (The mechanism responsible for the increased excretion will be discussed in the section on volumetric thirst.)

As we saw earlier, Verney hypothesized that the loss of water by the cells of the body is the stimulus that produces osmometric thirst. Fitzsimons

(1972) obtained evidence that supports Verney's hypothesis by demonstrating that the stimulus for osmometric thirst is not simply a change in the solute concentration of the interstitial fluid but the *effect* that these changes have on the water content of the cells. Fitzsimons removed the kidneys of a group of rats to prevent the kidneys from eliminating water or any of the substances he administered to the animals. Next, he injected the animals with hypertonic solutions of substances that can enter cells (such as glucose and urea) or substances that cannot (such as sodium chloride, sodium sulfate, and sucrose—table sugar). All of the substances that he injected would increase the solute concentration of the interstitial fluid. However, only the substances that *cannot* enter cells would draw water from them. For example, an increased concentration of urea in the interstitial fluid has no effect on cells because the urea freely diffuses into them, and a concentration gradient is not set up.

In fact, the only animals that drank excessively

were those that received substances that could not enter the cells and hence drew water from them; thus, cell dehydration is the stimulus for osmometric thirst. Fitzsimons found that an injection of urea (but not glucose or other substances that can enter cells) produced a small amount of drinking. The reason for this effect is that urea passes slowly through the blood-brain barrier. Therefore, an injection of urea produces a slight, and temporary, dehydration of the brain. The fact that *brain* dehydration produces drinking suggested that the osmoreceptors that produce thirst are located there.

Fitzsimons was not the first to obtain evidence that osmoreceptors were located in the brain. Andersson (1953) found that injections of hypertonic saline solution into the rostrolateral hypothalamus produced drinking but not vasopressin release, whereas injections into caudal hypothalamic regions stimulated vasopressin secretion but not thirst. Thus, different sets of receptors appear to mediate drinking and vasopressin release in response to hypertonicity.

An extensive mapping study by Peck and Blass (1975) suggested that the osmoreceptors that stimulate thirst in rats are located in the preoptic area and the anterior hypothalamus. They found that injections of hypertonic sucrose there produced drinking. (See *Figure 12.9.*) In addition, Blass and Epstein (1971) found that when a rat was made thirsty by giving it a subcutaneous injection of hypertonic saline, drinking could be inhibited by injecting water into the preoptic area. Presumably, the water turned off the signal for thirst at the detectors. (This manipulation was similar to what would happen if we heated the

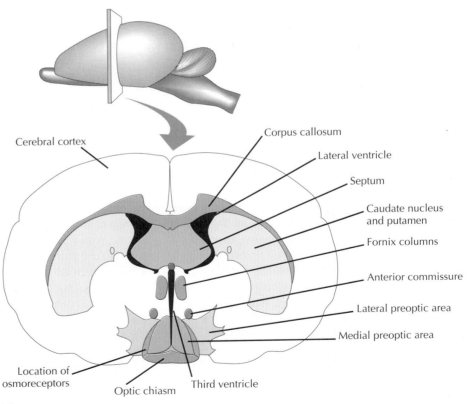

Cerebral cortex

Corpus callosum

Lateral ventricle

Septum

Caudate nucleus and putamen

Fornix columns

Anterior commissure

Lateral preoptic area

Medial preoptic area

Location of osmoreceptors

Optic chiasm

Third ventricle

FIGURE 12.9
The lateral preoptic area and the lateral hypothalamus. Injection of hypertonic sucrose in this region produces drinking, presumably by stimulating osmoreceptors located there. (Adapted from Paxinos, G., and Watson, C. *The Rat Brain in Stereotaxic Coordinates.* Sydney: Academic Press, 1982. Redrawn with permission.)

thermostat in a cold room; we would "fool" the thermostat and cause it to turn off the furnace.)

Many electrophysiological studies have found evidence of neurons whose firing rate is altered by infusions of hypertonic solutions. Arnauld, Dufy, and Vincent (1975) and Blank and Wayner (1975) found that water deprivation or systemic injections of hypertonic saline produce responses of neurons in the preoptic area. Subsequently, Silva and Boulant (1984) confirmed that the preoptic area contained osmoreceptors and not simply neurons that receive input from osmoreceptors located elsewhere. The investigators prepared a slice of live brain tissue from the preoptic area and recorded the activity of single neurons in the slice. When the solution that bathed the tissue was made hypertonic by the addition of solutes, the firing rate of the neurons changed.

There is still considerable uncertainty about the location of the osmoreceptors that stimulate vasopressin secretion. Most investigators believe that these osmoreceptors are not the ones that stimulate drinking. Some evidence suggests that the region immediately rostral to the antero-ventral tip of the third ventricle contains these receptors, and other evidence suggests that they are located in the *circumventricular organs* or perhaps even in the supraoptic nucleus, which contains most of the neurons that synthesize vasopressin (Baylis and Thompson, 1988). (I will describe the circumventricular organs and the region around the anteroventral third ventricle in the section that discusses brain mechanisms.)

Osmoreceptors *outside* the brain may also control vasopressin release. For example, when a thirsty animal drinks, vasopressin secretion is inhibited even before substantial amounts of water leave the digestive system (Nicolaïdis, 1969). Thus, these receptors perform an anticipatory role, similar to that of satiety, which was discussed earlier in this chapter. Where could these receptors be? One possibility is that they are on the tongue, which would be in a position to detect the presence of water in the mouth. Another possibility is that they are in the throat and are activated by the passage of water or by the action of the throat muscles responsible for swallowing. Alternatively, they could be located in the walls of the stomach or in the small intestine, which receives water from the stomach soon after it is swallowed. Finally, they could be in the liver.

Before I settle this mystery, I should describe two important parts of the body to you: the small intestine and the liver. The first part of the small intestine, which receives food and water from the stomach, is called the **duodenum.** The original Greek name for this part of the gut was *dodekadaktulon,* or "twelve fingers long." In fact, the duodenum is twelve finger *widths* long. The walls of the duodenum contain receptors, some of which may communicate with the brain through the nerves that serve the intestine. The liver is the first organ to receive substances from the digestive system. It receives them through the *hepatic portal system,* a special vascular system. Water and nutrients enter the blood supply through capillaries located in the small intestine. These capillaries collect into larger and larger veins and finally into the **hepatic portal vein,** which travels to the liver and branches into capillaries again. (See *Figure 12.10.*)

And now, the answer to the mystery. It appears that the immediate inhibitory effect of drinking on vasopressin secretion is caused by the act of drinking itself. The receptors that produce this effect do not appear to be on the tongue; in a study with human subjects Geelen et al. (1984) found that gargling water did not affect vasopressin secretion. However, the act of drinking a *hypertonic* saline solution did, at least for a few minutes. These results suggest that receptors in the throat (or perhaps the neurons in the brain that control the act of swallowing) detect the fact that water has been swallowed and inhibit the neurons of the supraoptic and paraventricular nuclei that are responsible for vasopressin secretion. The fact that drinking a hypertonic saline solution temporarily inhibited the secretion of vasopressin suggests that the anticipatory mechanism has only short-term effects; presumably, long-term inhibition must be produced by the presence of water in the digestive system.

The source of this long-term inhibition may be the liver. Haeberich (1968) found that the infusion of water or a hypertonic solution of sodium chloride into the hepatic portal vein, which leads to the liver, produced increases or decreases in urine production. Later, Chwalbinski-Moneta (1979)

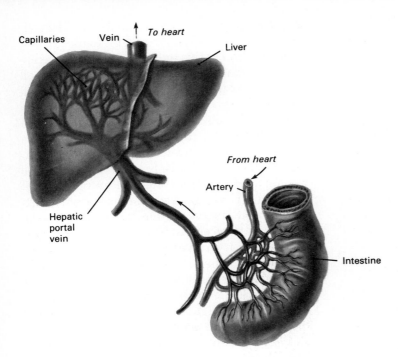

Capillaries

Vein

To heart

Liver

From heart

Artery

Hepatic
portal
vein

Intestine

FIGURE 12.10
The hepatic portal blood supply. The liver receives water, minerals, and nutrients from the digestive system through this system.

replicated these results, making direct measurements of vasopressin in the blood. Single-unit recording studies by Niijima (1969) had already shown that the liver contains osmoreceptive neurons; presumably these neurons, which are connected to the brain through the vagus nerve, inform the brain about the solute concentration of the blood plasma being received from the digestive system. The connection between the vagus nerve and the neurosecretory cells of the hypothalamus appears to follow a pathway similar to that followed by the gustatory system (Rogers and Novin, 1983).

Volumetric Thirst

Volumetric thirst occurs when the volume of the blood plasma—the intravascular volume—decreases. As we saw earlier, when we lose water through evaporation, we lose it from all three fluid compartments, intracellular, interstitial, and intravascular. Thus, evaporation produces both volumetric thirst and osmometric thirst. If evaporation were the only way that our body lost fluids, we would not need to have drinking mechanisms controlled by detectors that monitor blood vol-

ume. However, it is possible to incur a loss in intravascular volume without affecting the interstitial compartment. Loss of blood, vomiting, and diarrhea all cause hypovolemia without depleting the intracellular fluid.

Loss of blood is the most obvious cause of pure volumetric thirst. From the earliest recorded history, reports of battles note that the wounded survivors called out for water. (More prosaically, vomiting or diarrhea rids the body of isotonic fluid and hence lowers the volume of the intravascular fluid.) Thus, volumetric thirst provides a second line of defense against a loss of water should damage occur to the osmometric system, and it provides the means for the loss of isotonic fluid to instigate drinking. In addition, because hypovolemia involves a loss of sodium as well as water (that is, the sodium that was contained in the isotonic fluid that was lost), volumetric thirst leads to a salt appetite.

The easiest way to produce hypovolemia in experimental animals such as rats would be to remove some of their blood. A less drastic procedure is to inject a *colloid* into the animal's abdominal cavity or under the loose skin of the back (Fitzsimons, 1961). Colloids are gluelike substances (from the Greek *kolla*, "glue") made of large molecules that cannot cross cell membranes. Thus, they stay in the abdominal cavity or in the space under the skin. Because the solution of molecules is hypertonic, it draws extracellular fluid out of tissue. The fluid that leaves the blood plasma is isotonic; as water molecules move down the concentration gradient produced by the colloid, they draw sodium chloride with them. Initially, the water comes from the interstitial fluid; but as the volume of this fluid space decreases, the pressure of the blood causes fluid from the blood plasma to begin to fill the vacant space. Fluid does *not* leave the cells, because the solute concentration of the interstitial fluid remains stable. Within an hour the posterior pituitary gland begins to release vasopressin, and urine volume drops. At about the same time the animal begins to drink, and it continues to do so until most of the volume of fluid stolen from the extracellular fluid has been replaced.

Let us look at a specific experiment that produced volumetric thirst. Fitzsimons (1961) injected a colloid called *polyethylene glycol* into the abdominal cavity of rats and later drained the fluid that accumulated, ridding the body of the colloid along with the water and sodium chloride it had drawn from the extracellular fluid. The loss of water caused a considerable thirst; the animals drank water copiously. One or two days later, he presented the rats with both water and a hypertonic 1.8 percent saline solution, which rats normally refuse to drink. This time, the rats avidly consumed the saline solution. Why did they do so? The procedure had removed both water and salt, so they needed both substances to restore their fluid compartments to normal. Thus, the loss of salt induced a strong *salt appetite.*

What detectors are responsible for initiating volumetric thirst and a salt appetite? In fact, there are at least two sets of receptors that accomplish this dual function: one in the kidneys, and one in the heart and large blood vessels.

The Role of Angiotensin

The kidneys contain cells that are able to detect decreases in flow of blood to the kidneys. The primary cause of a reduced flow of blood is a loss of blood volume; thus, these cells detect the pres-

ence of hypovolemia. When the flow of blood to the kidneys decreases, these cells secrete an enzyme called *renin.* Renin enters the blood, where it catalyzes the conversion of a protein called *angiotensinogen* into a hormone called *angiotensin.* (In fact, there are two forms of angiotensin. Angiotensinogen becomes angiotensin I, which is quickly converted by an enzyme to angiotensin II. The active form is angiotensin II, which I shall abbreviate as *AII.*)

Angiotensin II has several physiological effects: It stimulates the adrenal cortex to secrete aldosterone, it stimulates the posterior pituitary gland to secrete vasopressin, and it increases blood pressure by causing the muscles in the small arteries to contract. (Recall that the presence of aldosterone inhibits the kidneys from excreting sodium, and the presence of vasopressin inhibits them from excreting water.) In addition, it has two behavioral effects: It initiates both drinking and a salt appetite. Therefore, a reduction in the flow of blood to the kidneys causes water and sodium to be retained by the body, helps compensate for their loss by reducing the size of the blood vessels, and encourages the animal to find and ingest both water and salt. (See *Figure 12.11.*)

Angiotensin and Food-Related Drinking

Although research on the physiology of drinking has generally focused on drinking caused by need (that is, by hypovolemia or by cellular dehydration), most drinking occurs *in anticipation* of actual need, during meals (de Castro, 1988; Kraly, 1990). For two reasons, eating produces a need for water. First, eating causes water to be diverted from the rest of the body into the stomach and small intestine, where it is needed for the digestive process (Lepkovsky et al., 1957). Second, once food is absorbed (especially salty food or food rich in amino acids), it increases the solute concentration of the blood plasma and thus induces an osmometric thirst. In fact, animals do not wait until they need the water; they drink it with their meal. Fitzsimons and Le Magnen (1969) found that when rats were switched from a high-carbohydrate diet to a high-protein diet, they increased their water intake. At first, they drank most of the water *after* the meal, when the osmotic demands were being felt. However, within a few

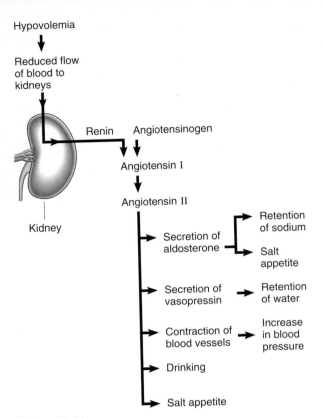

FIGURE 12.11
Detection of hypovolemia by the kidney and the renin-angiotensin system.

days the animals began drinking more water with the meals. They apparently learned the association of the new diet with subsequent thirst and drank in anticipation of that thirst.

According to research by Kraly and his colleagues, food-related drinking appears to involve angiotensin. The movement of water into the digestive system during and after a meal causes hypovolemia (Nose, Morita, Yawata, and Norimoto, 1986). As we just saw, hypovolemia stimulates the kidneys to secrete renin, which results in increased blood levels of angiotensin II. Kraly and Corneilson (1990) found that when they prevented the synthesis of angiotensin II with captopril (a drug that blocks the enzyme responsible for converting angiotensin I to angiotensin II), rats drank less water with their meals.

Food-related drinking also involves histamine, a compound that serves as a transmitter substance in the brain and as a hormone-like messenger in the rest of the body. When an animal eats, cells in the stomach release histamine. If, prior to eating a meal, a rat is given drugs that block histamine receptors, the animal will drink much less water with that meal (Kraly and Specht, 1984). In addition, an injection of histamine will itself cause drinking (Kraly, 1983). Kraly and Corneilson (1990) suggest that thirst provoked by histamine may involve angiotensin. They note that the secretion of renin is controlled by histamine receptors on cells in the kidney (Radke et al., 1986), and they found that blocking the synthesis of angiotensin II with captopril abolished the stimulating effect of histamine on drinking. Perhaps, then, the entry of food into the stomach causes the release of histamine, which stimulates the secretion of renin by the kidneys. The renin catalyzes the synthesis of angiotensin, which activates drinking mechanisms in the brain.

Atrial Baroreceptors

The second set of receptors for volumetric thirst lies within the heart. Physiologists had long known that the atria of the heart (the parts that receive blood from the veins) contain sensory neurons that detect stretch. The atria are passively filled with blood being returned from the body by the veins. The more blood that is present, the fuller the atria become just before each contraction of the heart. Thus, when the volume of the blood plasma falls, the stretch receptors within the atria will detect the change. These receptors occupy the best possible location to detect the presence of hypovolemia.

Fitzsimons and Moore-Gillon (1980) showed that information from these receptors can stimulate thirst. They operated on dogs and placed a small balloon in the inferior vena cava, the vein that brings blood from most of the body (excluding the head and arms) to the heart. When the balloon was inflated, it reduced the flow of blood to the heart and thus lowered the amount of blood that entered the right atrium. Within 30 minutes the dogs began to drink. The effect occurred even when the investigators administered *saralasin*, a drug that blocks angiotensin receptors; thus, it was not produced by secretion of renin by the kidneys. In another experiment Moore-Gillon and Fitzsimons (1982) implanted a small balloon in the junction between one of the large veins from the lungs and the left atrium of the heart. (They removed the part of the lung served by the vein so that inflating the balloon had no effect on the flow of blood into the heart.) Inflation of the balloon directly stimulated stretch receptors in the left atrium—and reduced the amount of water that the animals drank.

Salt Appetite

You will recall from Chapter 7 that the tongue contains four types of taste receptors, which provide the sensations of sweetness, bitterness, sourness, and saltiness. As we have seen, the reason our tongue has receptors that specifically detect the presence of sodium chloride is that this mineral plays a vital role in maintaining our fluid balance. A fall in the body's level of sodium makes it impossible to maintain the intravascular fluid at its proper level.

I already mentioned that angiotensin induces a salt appetite. Actually, the joint effect of two hormones, angiotensin and aldosterone, are normally responsible for the induction of sodium-seeking behavior. Sakai, Nicolaïdis, and Epstein (1986) induced a sodium need by giving rats an injection of a drug (furosemide) that causes the kidneys to excrete sodium and feeding them a diet that contains very little sodium. After such a treatment rats will drink a 3 percent sodium chloride solution, which they normally avoid. (A 3 percent NaCl solution is more than three times as salty as seawater.) The investigators found that when they administered drugs that block both AII receptors and aldosterone receptors, the animals drank none of the NaCl solution; injections of either drug alone diminished, but did not eliminate, the response. (See *Figure 12.12*.) Although the two hormones appear to act independently, their effects can combine. Epstein and Sakai (1987) found that low doses of angiotensin or aldosterone, given separately, would not induce a salt appetite in rats; but when the two hormones given together, the animals ingested large amounts of salt.

I NTERIM SUMMARY

Osmometric thirst occurs when the interstitial fluid becomes hypertonic, drawing water out of cells. This event, which can be caused by evaporation of water from the body or by ingestion of a salty meal, is detected by specialized neurons in the preoptic area and anterior hypothalamus. These neurons increase vasopressin secretion and stimulate drinking. The act of drinking itself temporarily inhibits the secretion of vasopressin. Osmoreceptors in the liver may also play a role in this inhibition.

Volumetric thirst occurs when a fall in blood flow to the kidneys stimulates the secretion of renin, which converts plasma angiotensinogen to angiotensin I, which becomes AII. AII stimulates the secretion of aldosterone (which conserves salt, needed to keep up the plasma volume), increases blood pressure, and causes drinking and a sodium appetite.

Much drinking occurs with meals, in anticipation of the need for water produced by

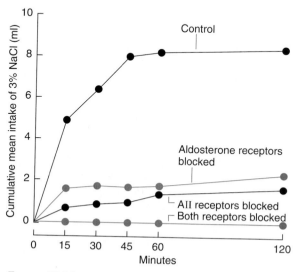

FIGURE 12.12
Effects of blocking aldosterone receptors, angiotensin (AII) receptors, or both, on salt intake of rats. (Adapted from Sakai, R.R., Nicolaïdis, S., and Epstein, A.N. *American Journal of Physiology,* 1986, *251,* R762–R768.)

the digestive process and the addition of solutes to the body's fluid compartments. The hypovolemia that accompanies a meal induces drinking through the release of AII, which may be triggered by the release of histamine by cells in the stomach.

Volumetric drinking can be stimulated independently of AII, by a set of baroreceptors receptors in the atria of the heart that sends messages to the brain. Salt appetite is also stimulated by angiotensin; AII and aldosterone together produce much more salt intake than either one alone.

NEURAL MECHANISMS OF THIRST AND SALT APPETITE

As we saw, the osmoreceptors responsible for thirst appear to be located in the preoptic area and the anterior hypothalamus. The regions that play an important role in volumetric drinking and salt appetite also appear to be located in the forebrain. However, the picture of the neural circuitry that has been obtained so far is still fuzzy; at best, we can say that some structures have been implicated in the physiological and behavioral control of fluid balance, but the exact roles these structures play is still uncertain.

Control of Osmometric Thirst

Lesions of the preoptic area, which destroy the osmoreceptors located there, interfere with osmometric drinking but do not completely abolish it (Peck and Novin, 1971; Coburn and Stricker, 1978). It is possible that additional osmoreceptors are located elsewhere in the brain, and that these receptors can stimulate drinking.

The next structure involved in osmometric drinking is the *zona incerta.* This region is an oblong extension of the midbrain reticular formation; its posterior end is in the midbrain, between the substantia nigra and the ventral tegmental area, and its anterior end is in the diencephalon, just lateral and dorsal to the paraventricular nuclei of the hypothalamus. (Refer to *Figure 10.19.*)

Huang and Mogenson (1972) found that electrical stimulation of the rostral zona incerta elicited drinking in rats. Walsh and Grossman (1978)

found that lesions of the zona incerta caused a profound deficit in osmometric drinking; injections of hypertonic sodium chloride did not induce drinking. In addition, rats with these lesions did not drink when they were given an injection of angiotensin, either, but they *did* drink if they were given an injection of polyethylene glycol. Thus, damage to the zona incerta also disrupts the hormonal stimulus for volumetric thirst but not the neural one.

Mok and Mogenson (1986) recorded from single neurons in the zona incerta. They found that injections of hypertonic saline, hypertonic sucrose, or distilled water into the preoptic area changed the firing rate of these neurons. They also found that a unilateral injection of a local anesthetic into the zona incerta would prevent an injection of hypertonic saline from producing drinking when the saline was injected into the *ipsilateral* preoptic area but not when it was injected into the *contralateral* preoptic area. These results imply that the osmoreceptors in the preoptic area stimulate drinking by activating neurons in the ipsilateral zona incerta.

The zona incerta sends axons to many brain structures involved in movement, including the basal ganglia, the brain stem reticular formation, the red nucleus, the periaqueductal gray matter, and the ventral horn of the spinal cord (Ricardo, 1981). Thus, it appears to be in an excellent position to influence drinking behavior.

Control of Volumetric Thirst

As we saw earlier in this chapter, two mechanisms detect hypovolemia and produce thirst: the renin-secreting cells of the kidneys, and the stretch receptors in the atria of the heart. Of these two mechanisms, the renin-angiotensin system has received much more attention.

The Renin-Angiotensin System

Although angiotensin has been studied for many years, only recently have scientists developed radioimmunoassay techniques sensitive enough to measure the level of AII in small samples of an animal's blood. Van Eekelen and Phillips (1988), in an experiment with rats, continuously infused AII into a vein, periodically sampled blood from an artery, and analyzed the amount of AII that was present. They found that the animals, who were free to move around, did not drink until the blood level of AII reached a level of approximately 450 pg/ml. (A *picogram,* abbreviated *pg,* is a trillionth of a gram, or 10^{-12}. The prefix *pico-* comes from the Italian word *piccolo,* ''small.'') A blood level of AII of 450 pg/ml occurs normally when a rat has been deprived of water for approximately 48 hours. Thus, it is possible that the ability of the renin-angiotensin system to produce drinking is important only in emergencies.

Angiotensin is a peptide composed of eight amino acids, and as far as we know, all peptides that directly affect behavior do so by interacting with specific receptors in neural membranes. Therefore, researchers hypothesized that the brain contains neurons that initiate thirst when they detect the presence of angiotensin. Because angiotensin does not cross the blood-brain barrier (Volicer and Loew, 1975), a likely site of action would be one of the regions of the brain where this barrier is low. Angiotensin could leave the capillaries in one of these regions, enter the interstitial fluid, and stimulate angiotensin receptors. Indeed, Mendelsohn, Quirion, Saavedra, Aguilera, and Catt (1984) found that neurons in several organs located in the boundary between the ventricles and the brain contain angiotensin receptors.

The *circumventricular organs,* as these organs are called, are isolated from the rest of the brain by glial cells and have a rich supply of capillaries. These capillaries have fenestrations, like capillaries elsewhere in the body, but unlike those in the rest of the brain. (See *Figure 12.13.*) Thus, peptide hormones such as angiotensin can enter the interstitial fluid of the circumventricular organs but are kept from entering the rest of the brain by their glial cell barriers. (See *Figure 12.14.*)

Although all of the circumventricular organs contain AII receptors, one of them, the *subfornical organ (SFO),* appears to be the site of action of angiotensin in the blood. This structure gets its name from its location, just below the commissure of the ventral fornix. (See *Figure 12.14.*)

Evidence clearly indicates that the subfornical organ is the site of action of angiotensin. Simpson, Epstein, and Camardo (1978) found that very low doses of angiotensin injected directly into the SFO caused drinking and that destruction of the SFO or injection of saralasin, which blocks AII receptors, abolished the drinking response to injections of angiotensin into the blood. Phillips and Felix (1976) found that microiontophoretic injections of angiotensin into the SFO increased the firing rate of single neurons located there. Kadekaro, et

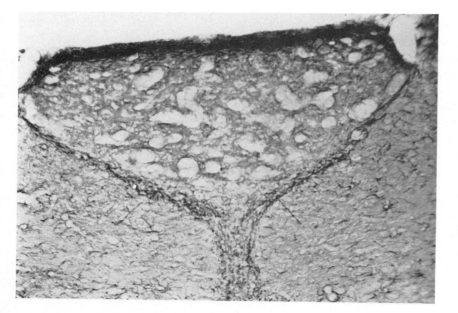

FIGURE 12.13

A photomicrograph of a circumventricular organ (the area postrema), showing the rich supply of blood vessels (which appear as holes in the tissue) and the thin line of glial cells (arrows) that isolate the organ from the rest of the brain. (Reprinted with permission from Phillips, M.I., in *Circumventricular Organs and Body Fluids, Vol. III,* edited by P. Gross. Boca Raton, Fla.: CRC Press, 1987. Copyright CRC Press, Inc. Boca Raton, Fla.)

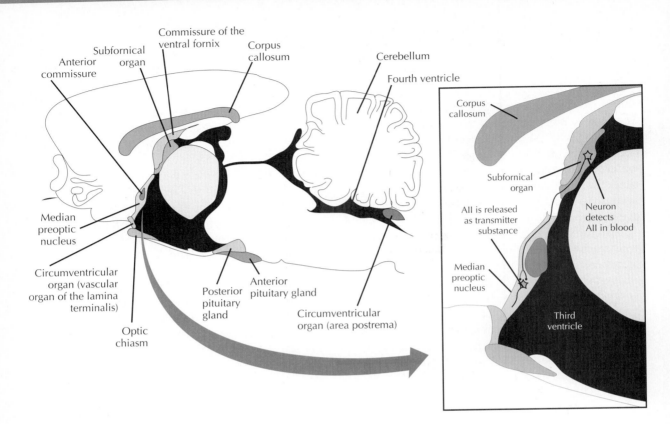

FIGURE 12.14
A sagittal section of the rat brain, showing the location of the circumventricular organs. Inset: A hypothetical circuit connecting the subfornical organ with the median preoptic nucleus.

al. (1989) found that an intravenous injection of AII caused the metabolic activity of the SFO to increase, even when the axons connecting the SFO with the rest of the brain had been cut. (They used the technique of 2-DG autoradiography, described in Chapter 5, to assess metabolic activity.) Thus, AII directly activates the neurons of the SFO.

The subfornical organ, being primarily an organ that detects the presence of a hormone in the blood, has few neural inputs but sends axons to several parts of the brain. As Miselis, Weiss, and Shapiro (1987) note, the outputs of the SFO fall into three categories: endocrine, autonomic, and behavioral. As we saw earlier, angiotensin has four major effects: It stimulates aldosterone secretion, it stimulates vasopressin secretion, it increases blood pressure, and it causes drinking.

The first of these effects, aldosterone secretion, occurs directly in the adrenal cortex. The other three involve the brain. The *endocrine outputs* of the SFO include axons that project to the neurons in the supraoptic and paraventricular nuclei that are responsible for production and secretion of the posterior pituitary hormones, vasopressin and oxytocin. (The reason for the connection with the vasopressin neurons is obvious, but the function of the connection with the oxytocin neurons is still not understood.) The *autonomic outputs* include axons that project to the cells of the paraventricular nucleus and other parts of the hypothalamus, which in turn send axons to brain stem nuclei that control the sympathetic and parasympathetic nervous system. This system is responsible for the effects of angiotensin on blood pressure. The most important *behavioral outputs,* which control drinking, are probably those to a region of the basal forebrain just in front of the ventral portion of the anterior third ventricle.

Let us consider the behavioral outputs of the SFO—the efferent connections that are responsible for its effects on drinking. Lind, Thunhorst, and Johnson (1984) reported some interesting results. They found that lesions of the ventral stalk of the SFO, which destroys its efferent connections, abolished the drinking response that is produced by injecting AII into a vein. However, these lesions had only a small effect on the drinking response that is produced by injecting AII into the third ventricle. These results indicate that angiotensin receptors located elsewhere in the brain are capable of stimulating drinking.

In fact, it appears that these receptors are located in the ***median preoptic nucleus*** (not to be confused with the *medial* preoptic nucleus), which is shaped like half a doughnut, wrapped around the front of the anterior commissure, a fiber bundle that connects the amygdala and anterior temporal lobe. (See inset, *Figure 12.14.*) The median preoptic nucleus is on the *brain* side of the blood-brain barrier; thus, its AII receptors are never exposed to angiotensin present in the blood. Only when angiotensin is injected directly into the third ventricle can it reach them.

If angiotensin cannot get from the blood to the median preoptic nucleus, what is the point of having AII receptors there? Lind and Johnson (1982) proposed the following answer: When neurons in the SFO are stimulated by the presence of angiotensin in the blood, a message is sent down their axons to the neurons in the median preoptic nucleus. The terminal buttons of these axons release angiotensin *as a transmitter substance.* Thus, the AII receptors in the median preoptic nucleus are not there to detect the presence of a hormone; instead, they are postsynaptic receptors for a peptide transmitter substance that just happens to be a hormone, too.

There is considerable evidence to support Lind and Johnson's hypothesis. For example, after the median preoptic nucleus has been destroyed, injections of AII into the blood or the third ventricle have no effect on drinking (Johnson and Cunningham, 1987). In addition, Nelson

and Johnson (1985) prepared a vertical slice of the rat brain, parallel to the midline, and placed the slice in a liquid medium that kept the cells alive for a while. They electrically stimulated neurons in the SFO and found that single neurons in the median preoptic nucleus responded to this stimulation. The responses of the neurons in the median preoptic nucleus were abolished by the application of saralasin, which blocks AII receptors. (See inset, *Figure 12.14.*)

The Atrial Stretch Receptor System

You will recall that the secretion of renin (and its conversion to angiotensin) is only one of the two ways that hypovolemia produces thirst. The other way is through activation of stretch receptors located in the atria of the heart. Little is known about the neural pathways that connect these receptors to brain mechanisms that control the behavior of drinking. One study suggests that part of this pathway may lie in the basal forebrain. Thornton, de Beaurepaire, and Nicolaïdis (1984) recorded the activity of single neurons in the medial anterior hypothalamus, just in front of the anteroventral third ventricle, in rats. They found that the neurons were sensitive to changes in blood pressure that occurred spontaneously or were induced by temporary removal of small amounts of blood from a vein. Possibly, these neurons receive information from stretch receptors located in the atria of the heart, and they may be part of a neural circuit responsible for volumetric thirst. More research will be needed to make a definitive conclusion.

Control of Salt Appetite

As we saw earlier, a sodium deficiency stimulates a salt appetite in two ways, through the action of aldosterone and of angiotensin on the brain. A sodium deficiency produces hypovolemia, and thus, the detectors that stimulate salt appetite are the same ones that stimulate volumetric thirst. The available evidence suggests that angiotensin produces a salt appetite the same way it produces thirst—by stimulating AII receptors in the subfornical organ. In fact, some of the studies I cited in the section on the brain mechanisms of angiotensin on thirst also looked at salt appetite and found similar effects. I did not mention these results at the time because the discussion was complicated enough as it was.

As we saw earlier, the zona incerta plays a critical role in osmometric drinking and drinking stimulated by angiotensin. It also appears to play a role in the development of salt appetite. Grossman and Grossman (1978) found that when a hypertonic sodium chloride solution is presented to sodium-depleted rats with lesions of the zona incerta, the animals will consume much less salt than a normal animal will. Conversely, electrical stimulation of parts of the zona incerta will induce salt intake (Gentil, Mogenson, and Stevenson, 1971).

The medial amygdala appears to play a critical role in salt appetite evoked by aldosterone. The medial nucleus contains aldosterone receptors (Coirini, Magarinos, DeNicola, Rainbow, and McEwen, 1985). Schulkin, Marini, and Epstein (1989) found that lesions of the medial amygdala specifically abolished the effects of aldosterone on salt intake. However, when the investigators induced a sodium deficiency (with a sodium-deficient diet combined with an injection of furosemide, which causes the kidneys to excrete sodium), the rats ingested a normal amount of a sodium chloride solution. Presumably, the salt appetite was stimulated by the angiotensin system. (See *Figure 12.15*.)

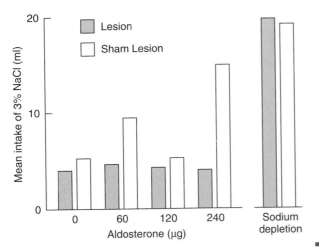

FIGURE 12.15
Effects of lesions of the medial amygdala on salt intake of rats produced by aldosterone or sodium depletion. (Adapted from Schulkin, J., Marini, J., and Epstein, A.N. *Behavioral Neuroscience*, 1989, *103*, 178–185.)

*I*NTERIM SUMMARY

Osmometric thirst is stimulated by osmoreceptors in the anterior basal forebrain. These neurons send axons to the zona incerta. Electrical stimulation of the zona incerta causes drinking. Lesions of this region depress osmometric drinking and drinking provoked by angiotensin but not by polyethylene glycol; thus, the only thirst that the zona incerta is *not* involved in is thirst provoked by the atrial stretch receptors. The zona incerta sends axons to many parts of the brain involved in motor control.

Volumetric thirst stimulated by AII involves the subfornical organ. Neurons there possess angiotensin receptors; when they are stimulated, the terminal buttons of their axons release AII (as a transmitter substance) in the median preoptic nucleus. Neurons there send axons to brain mechanisms involved in the behavior of drinking. AII also produces changes in blood pressure and secretion of the posterior pituitary hormones through the connections of the subfornical organ with the brain stem and the supraoptic and paraventricular nuclei.

The atrial stretch receptor system may stimulate thirst through connections with the neurons in the medial hypothalamus, just in front of the anteroventral third ventricle. The subfornical organ appears to be involved in salt appetite induced by AII, and the medial amygdala appears to be involved in salt appetite induced by aldosterone. The zona incerta appears to be the next relay for sodium appetite; lesions there decrease salt intake, whereas stimulation increases it.

MECHANISMS OF SATIETY

As I explained in the first part of this chapter, an anticipatory mechanism, which we call satiety, is needed to stop drinking even before the system variables (cellular dehydration or hypovolemia) have been restored. In this section I will consider satiety produced by drinking and satiety caused by ingestion of sodium chloride.

Drinking

Normally, when a thirsty animal is given the opportunity to drink, it will rapidly drink enough water to restore its loss and then stop. In most cases satiety occurs before substantial amounts of water are absorbed from the digestive system. For example, a dog consumes the water it needs within 2–3 minutes (Adolph, 1939). However, replenishment of the water previously lost from the blood plasma does not begin for 10–12 minutes and is not completed until 40–45 minutes (Ramsay, Rolls, and Wood, 1977). As we saw earlier, receptors in the throat (and undoubtedly somewhere else in the digestive system) are responsible for the inhibition of vasopressin secretion produced by drinking. Perhaps these same receptors are responsible for satiety.

Receptors in the mouth and throat *do* influence the amount of water an organism drinks, but their effects are secondary to those of receptors in the stomach, small intestine, and liver. Receptors in each of these locations send a signal to the brain that water has been received and is therefore making progress along the way to absorption. Miller, Sampliner, and Woodrow (1957) allowed thirsty rats to drink 14 ml of water or administered it directly into the stomach through a tube that had previously been placed there. At various times after the preload the rats were permitted to drink. As Figure 12.16 shows, rats who received the 14-ml preload by mouth drank less than those that received it directly into the stomach. In other words, water placed directly into the stomach is less satiating than water that gets there after being tasted and swallowed. Thus, receptors in the mouth and throat play a role in satiety. (See *Figure 12.16*.)

It is clear, however, that satiety produced by receptors in the mouth and throat does not last long. Many studies, dating from Bernard (1856), have shown that when water that an animal drinks is not allowed to reach the stomach, an animal may pause for a while the first time it drinks but will soon resume drinking and will continue to do so until it is exhausted. These experiments

used a surgical procedure called an ***esophageal fistula.*** (A *fistula* is an abnormal or artificial opening between one hollow organ and the outside of the body.) An esophageal fistula causes water that is swallowed to fall to the ground. (After the animal's behavior has been tested, the experimenter puts water directly into its stomach.)

Hall (1973) and Hall and Blass (1977) obtained evidence that receptors in the stomach are less important for satiety than those of the duodenum or liver. They prepared a noose out of fine fishing line, passed it around the ***pylorus,*** the junction of the small intestine with the stomach, and threaded the line through a plastic tube. They brought the end of the tube through the rat's skin and fastened it to the top of the rat's head. The experimenters could tighten and loosen the noose

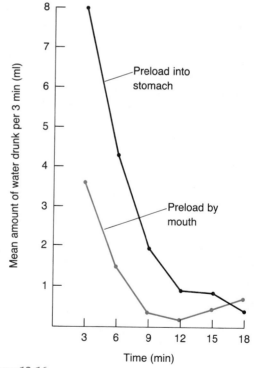

FIGURE 12.16

Effects of receiving 14 ml of water by mouth or through a tube inserted into the stomach on subsequent drinking of thirsty rats. (From Miller, N.E., Sampliner, R.I., and Woodrow, P. *Journal of Comparative and Physiological Psychology*, 1957, *50*, 1–5. Copyright 1957 by the American Psycological Association. Reprinted with permission of the author.)

without disturbing the rats. (See *Figure 12.17.*) When the experimenters tightened the noose, the pylorus closed, and contents of the stomach could not enter the intestine. When water could not leave the stomach, thirsty rats drank *more* water than when the noose was open. These results suggest that signals from the small intestine or liver are important in satiety; the noose prevented water from reaching them, thus preventing these signals from being sent.

At present, I know of no evidence that indicates that receptors in the duodenum are involved in satiety, although they well may be. However, there is good evidence that the liver plays such a role. Kozlowski and Drzewiecki (1973) obtained evidence supporting this hypothesis. They infused water into the hepatic portal vein, which conveys blood from the intestine to the liver. The infusions inhibited osmometric drinking initiated by injections of hypertonic saline. (As we saw earlier, these infusions also inhibit vasopressin secretion.) In addition, Smith and Jerome (1983) found that when they cut the branch of the vagus nerve that connects the liver to the brain, thirsty rats drank more water than normal. Presumably, the increase occurred because the operation interrupted the communication of inhibitory signals from the liver to the brain.

Salt Appetite

Satiety associated with salt intake has received less attention than satiety associated with drinking, but some general conclusions can be made. First, although an animal identifies the presence of sodium in the diet by tasting it, receptors in the mouth do not appear to play a role in satiety; a sodium-deficient rat will continue to drink a concentrated salt solution if a gastric fistula allows it to escape from the stomach (Mook, 1969). In addition, stomach or duodenal receptors do not appear to be important; an injection of a salt solution directly into the stomach of a sodium-deficient rat does not have an immediate effect on salt appetite, although it will inhibit sodium intake after a delay of several hours (Wolf, Schulkin, and Simson, 1984).

Tordoff, Schulkin, and Friedman (1987) induced a sodium need in rats with a combination of a low-sodium diet and a drug (furosemide) that causes the kidneys to excrete sodium. They placed catheters into the animals' hepatic portal vein and jugular vein. Thus, they were able to make injections into the veins while the animals were moving around freely. They found that an injection of a hypertonic sodium chloride solution into the hepatic portal vein, which directly enters the liver, would reduce the amount of salt solution that an animal would drink, whereas an injection into the jugular vein did not. (By the time the salt they injected into the jugular vein got around to the liver, it had been diluted and dispersed through a large volume of blood.) Thus, the experiment provides excellent evidence that the liver detects the presence of sodium in the blood it receives from the digestive system and sends a satiety signal to the brain.

Another satiety signal for salt appetite comes from a hormone secreted in what might seem to be an unlikely place: the atria of the heart. As we saw earlier, the atria of the heart provide a perfect location to detect a fall in blood volume. Similarly, they provide a perfect location to detect a *rise* in blood volume.

De Bold and his colleagues discovered that a hormone, ***atrial natriuretic peptide*** (ANP), is secreted by the atria of the heart (De Bold, Borenstein, Veres, and Sonnenberg, 1981; De Bold, 1985). The term *natriuretic* (not the easiest word to pronounce) comes from the fact that the hormone promotes the excretion of sodium (in Latin, *natrium*) by the kidneys. ANP appears to be an emergency backup system that helps prevent disastrously high volumes of blood plasma. The hormone is secreted when the atria are stretched more than usual by the presence of too much fluid in the blood plasma. Because plasma volume is largely controlled by the sodium concentration, eliminating sodium is obviously a useful response. But ANP does more than produce sodium excretion; it also increases the excretion of water, inhibits the secretion of renin, vasopressin, and aldosterone, and inhibits sodium appetite. (See Tarjan, Denton, and Weisinger, 1988, for a review.) ANP receptors are found in the adrenal medulla, the pituitary gland, and the brain; pre-

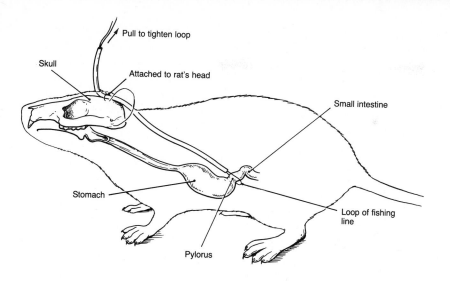

FIGURE 12.17
The procedure used by Hall and Blass (1977) to prevent water from leaving the stomach.

sumably, these sites are responsible for the effects of the hormone on the endocrine system and on behavior (Quirion, 1989).

INTERIM SUMMARY

Although receptors in the mouth and throat play a role in anticipatory satiety produced by drinking, the most important detectors appear to be in the duodenum or liver; when the pylorus is held shut, an animal drinks more than when it is open. Water infused into the hepatic portal vein will inhibit osmometric drinking, and water-deprived rats will drink more water if the hepatic branch of the vagus nerve is cut. Thus, osmoreceptors in the liver appear to play a role in satiety for drinking.

Although receptors on the tongue detect the presence of salt for a sodium-depleted animal, their stimulation does not produce satiety; that occurs only when the salt solution is permitted to accumulate in the stomach. Here, too, osmoreceptors in the liver play a role; an infusion of hypertonic sodium chloride into the hepatic portal vein reduces the intake of a sodium chloride solution by a sodium-depleted rat.

The atria of the heart secrete a peptide hormone, atrial natriuretic peptide, that is secreted in response to severe hypervolemia. It stimulates sodium excretion by the kidneys and inhibits the secretion of renin, vasopressin, and aldosterone, and inhibits sodium appetite.

CONCLUDING REMARKS

The regulation of water and mineral balance in the body is vital; if our cells lose or gain too much water, or if the volume of our blood increases or decreases too much, we cannot survive. As you have learned, the evolutionary process has selected the mechanisms needed to regulate these variables: detectors that monitor all the important system variables and correctional mechanisms that restore them to their set points.

Because of the vital importance of water and mineral balance, some of the control mechanisms are redundant. For example, both the angiotensin system and the baroreceptors in the heart initiate drinking in response to a fall in blood volume. In addition, single detection mechanisms can control several correctional mechanisms, all of which cooperate to achieve the same effect. For example, angiotensin contracts blood vessels, stimulates the secretion of aldosterone (which instructs the kidneys to conserve sodium and stimulates brain mechanisms that cause a sodium appetite), and through its effects on the brain, increases blood pressure and provokes drinking. The regulatory systems of the body do what they need to, and they do it well.

The next chapter describes research on the mechansisms that control what—and how much—we eat.

NEW TERMS

aldosterone p. 382
angiotensin p. 389
angiotensinogen p. 389
atrial natriuretic
    peptide p. 398
colloid p. 388
correctional
    mechanism p. 378
detector p. 378
duodenum p. 387
esophageal fistula p. 397
extracellular fluid p. 379
hepatic portal vein p. 387
homeostasis p. 378
hypertonic p. 380

hypotonic p. 380
hypovolemia p. 380
ingestive behavior p. 378
interstitial fluid p. 379
intracellular fluid p. 379
intravascular fluid p. 379
isotonic p. 380
median preoptic
    nucleus p. 395
negative feedback p. 378
nephron p. 381
osmometric thirst p. 383
osmoreceptor p. 383
paraventricular
    nucleus p. 382

polyethylene glycol p. 389
pylorus p. 397
renin p. 389
salt appetite p. 389
saralasin p. 390
satiety mechanism p. 378
set point p. 378
subfornical organ
    (SFO) p. 393
supraoptic nucleus p. 382
system variable p. 378
ureter p. 381
vasopressin p. 382
volumetric thirst p. 388
zona incerta p. 392

SUGGESTED READINGS

De Caro, G., Epstein, A.N., and Massi, M. *The Physiology of Thirst and Sodium Appetite.* New York: Plenum Publishing Co., 1986.

Gross, P. *Circumventricular Organs and Body Fluids. Vol. III.* Boca Raton, Fla.: CRC Press, 1987.

Rolls, B.J., and Rolls, E.T. *Thirst.* Cambridge, England: Cambridge University Press, 1982.

Stricker, E.M. *Handbook of Behavioral Neurobiology. Vol. 10. Neurobiology of Food and Fluid Intake.* New York: Plenum Press, 1990.

13

Ingestive Behavior: Eating

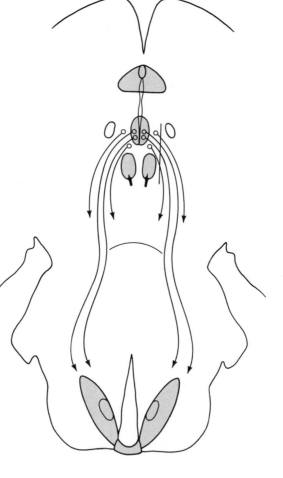

Clearly, eating is one of the most important things we do—and it can also be one of the most pleasurable. Much of what an animal learns to do is motivated by the constant struggle to obtain food; thus, the need to ingest undoubtedly shaped the evolutionary development of our own species. After having read Chapter 12, in which you saw that the signals that cause thirst are well understood, you may be surprised to learn that we still are not sure just what the system variables for hunger are. Control of ingestive behavior is even more complicated than the control of drinking and sodium intake. We can achieve water balance by the intake of two ingredients: water and sodium chloride. When we eat, we must obtain adequate amounts of carbohydrates, fats, amino acids, vitamins, and minerals other than sodium. Thus, our food-ingestive behaviors are more complex, and so are the physiological mechanisms that control them.

This chapter describes research on the control of eating: metabolism, regulation of body weight, the environmental and physiological factors that begin and stop a meal, and the neural mechanisms that monitor the nutritional state of our bodies and control our ingestive behavior. It also describes the most serious eating disorders, obesity and anorexia nervosa. Despite all the effort that has gone into understanding the physiology of ingestive behavior, these disorders are still difficult to treat. Our best hope of finding effective treatments is achieving a better understanding of the physiology of metabolism and ingestive behavior.

SOME FACTS ABOUT METABOLISM

As you saw in Chapter 12, you must know something about the fluid compartments of the body and the functions of the kidney in order to understand the physiology of drinking. Thus, you will not be surprised that this chapter begins with a discussion of metabolism. Your first inclination may be to skip over this section; but if you do so, you will find that you will not understand experiments that are described later. For example, the system variables that cause an animal to seek food

and eat it are obviously related to the animal's metabolism. This section will discuss only as much about this subject as you will need to understand these experiments.

Absorption, Fasting, and the Two Nutrient Reservoirs

When we eat, we incorporate into our own bodies molecules that were once part of other living organisms, plant and animal. We ingest these molecules for two reasons: to construct and maintain our own organs, and to obtain energy for muscular movements and for keeping our bodies warm. In other words, we need both building blocks and fuel. Although food used for building blocks is essential, I will discuss only the food used for fuel, because most of the molecules we eat get "burned" to provide energy for movement and heating.

Energy for movement and heat is extracted from nutrients by a set of chemical reactions that take place in the mitochondria of each of our cells. In order to understand the research described in this chapter, all you have to know about these reactions is that they accept a limited number of fuels (which I will discuss later) and produce water and carbon dioxide as waste products. In the process they provide cells with energy. In order to stay alive, cells must be supplied with one or more of these fuels and with oxygen to metabolize them. If a cell is deprived of nutrients or oxygen, it soon dies.

Obviously, the fuels come from the digestive tract, and their presence there is a result of eating. But the digestive tract is sometimes empty; in fact, most of us wake up in the morning in that condition. So there has to be a reservoir that stores nutrients to keep the cells of the body nourished when the gut is empty. Indeed, there are two reservoirs—one short-term and the other long-term. The short-term reservoir stores carbohydrates, and the long-term reservoir stores fats.

The short-term reservoir is located in the cells of the liver and the muscles, and it is filled with a complex, insoluble carbohydrate called *glycogen.* Let us consider the cells in the liver first. These cells convert glucose (a simple, soluble carbohydrate) into glycogen and store the glycogen. They are stimulated to do so by the presence of *insulin,* a peptide hormone produced by the pancreas. Thus, when glucose and insulin are present in the blood, some of the glucose is used as a fuel, and some of it is stored as glycogen. Later, when all of the food has been absorbed from the digestive tract, the level of glucose in the blood begins to fall.

The fall in glucose is detected by cells in the brain, which cause an increase in the activity of sympathetic axons that innervate the pancreas. This increase in activity inhibits the secretion of insulin and causes another set of cells of the pancreas to begin secreting a different peptide hormone, *glucagon.* The effect of glucagon is opposite that of insulin; it converts glycogen into glucose. (Unfortunately, the terms *glucose, glycogen,* and *glucagon* are similar enough that it is easy to confuse them. Even worse, you will soon encounter another one, *glycerol.*) (See *Figure 13.1.*) Thus, the liver soaks up excess glucose and stores it as glycogen when plenty of glucose is available, and it releases glucose from its reservoir when the digestive tract becomes empty and the level of glucose in the blood begins to fall.

The carbohydrate reservoir in the liver is primarily reserved for the central nervous system (CNS). When you wake in the morning, your brain is being fed by your liver, which is in the process of converting glycogen to glucose and releasing it into the blood. The glucose reaches the CNS, where it is absorbed and metabolized by the neurons and the glia. This process can continue for a few hours, until all of the carbohydrate reservoir in the liver is used up. (The average liver holds approximately 300 calories of carbohydrate.) Usually, we eat some food before this reservoir gets depleted, which permits us to refill it. But if we do not eat, the CNS has to start living on the products of the long-term reservoir.

But before I discuss the long-term reservoir, I should say something about the second short-term carbohydrate reservoir—the one located in the muscles. Our muscles provide us with the ability to act, and sometimes, we must act very vigorously. For example, if we begin to run, our metabolic rate increases so much that the liver cannot keep up with the demands of the muscles.

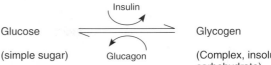

FIGURE 13.1
Effects of insulin and glucagon on glucose and glycogen.

Even a full digestive system will not help, because vigorous exercise shunts so much blood to the muscles that the process of digestion virtually comes to a halt. Thus, the muscles have their own private short-term carbohydrate reservoir. The reservoir is rather small, and it serves mainly as a fuel for quick bursts of muscular effort.

The long-term reservoir is filled with fats, or, more precisely, with **triglycerides.** Triglycerides are complex molecules that contain *glycerol* (a soluble carbohydrate, also called *glycerine*) combined with three *fatty acids* (stearic acid, oleic acid, and palmitic acid). Adipose tissue (fat tissue) is found beneath the skin and in various locations in the abdominal cavity. It consists of cells capable of absorbing nutrients from the blood, converting them to triglycerides, and storing them. They can expand in size enormously; in fact, the primary physical difference between an obese person and a person of normal weight is the size of their fat cells, which is determined by the amount of triglycerides that these cells contain.

The long-term fat reservoir is obviously what keeps us alive during a prolonged fast. Once our short-term carbohydrate reservoir is depleted, fat cells start converting triglycerides into fuels that the cells can use and releasing these fuels into the bloodstream. But the fat reservoir is used on a short-term basis, as well. As I said earlier, when we wake in the morning with an empty digestive tract, our brain (in fact, all of the central nervous system) is living on glucose released by the liver. But what about the other cells of the body? They are living on fatty acids, leaving the glucose for the brain. As you will recall from Chapter 4, the sympathetic nervous system is primarily involved in the breakdown and utilization of stored nutrients. During the fasting phase there is an increase in the activity of the sympathetic axons that innervate adipose tissue, the pancreas, and the adrenal me-

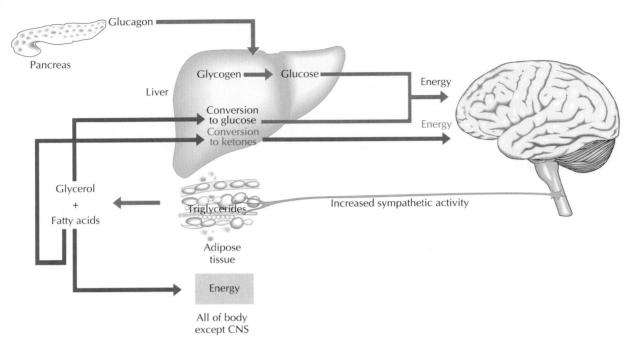

FIGURE 13.2
The fasting phase of metabolism. The pathway shown in color is active only after prolonged fasting.

dulla. All three effects (direct neural stimulation, secretion of glucagon, and secretion of catecholamines) cause triglycerides in the long-term fat reservoir to be broken down into glycerol and fatty acids. The fatty acids can be directly metabolized by cells in all of the body *except the brain,* which needs glucose. That leaves glycerol. The liver takes up glycerol and converts it to glucose. That glucose, obviously, is available to the brain.

If you have followed the discussion so far, you may be asking *why* the cells of the rest of the body treat the brain so kindly, letting it consume almost all the glucose that the liver releases from its carbohydrate reservoir and constructs from glycerol. That is a good question. The answer, fortunately, is simple: Insulin has several other functions besides causing glucose to be converted to glycogen. One of these functions is the control of the entry of glucose into cells. Glucose easily dissolves in water, but it will not dissolve in fats. Cell membranes are made of lipids (fatlike substances); thus, glucose cannot directly pass through them. In order for glucose to be taken into a cell, it must be transported there by an active mechanism in the membrane, similar in principle to the sodium-potassium pump and to the mechanisms responsible for the reuptake of transmitter substances. This glucose transport mechanism is controlled by insulin receptors in the membrane; only when insulin is present can glucose be pumped into the cell. But the cells of the nervous system are an exception to this rule; *they do not need insulin to absorb glucose.*

Figure 13.2 reviews what I have said so far about the metabolism that takes place while the digestive tract is empty, which physiologists refer to as the ***fasting phase*** of metabolism. A fall in the blood glucose level causes the pancreas to stop secreting insulin and to start secreting glucagon. The absence of insulin means that most of the cells of the body can no longer use glucose; thus, all the glucose present in the blood is reserved for the central nervous system. The presence of glucagon instructs the liver to start drawing on the short-term carbohydrate reservoir—to start converting its glycogen into glucose. The presence of glucagon, along with increased activity of the sympathetic nervous system, instructs fat cells to start drawing on the long-term fat reservoir—to start breaking down triglycerides into fatty acids and glycerol. Most of the body lives on the fatty acids, and the glycerol is converted into glucose by the liver, which gets used by the brain. (See the black lines in *Figure 13.2.*)

One more detail should be added to the picture I have presented. If fasting continues long enough so that the liver's short-term carbohydrate reservoir is depleted, the liver starts producing another fuel for the central nervous system from the long-term fat reservoir. As you already know, the cells of the central nervous system cannot use fatty acids. They can, however, use another substance, called *ketones.* During prolonged fasting the liver converts some of the fatty acids present in the blood into ketones, which supplement the brain's diet. (See the color lines in *Figure 13.2.*)

The phase of metabolism that occurs when food is present in the digestive tract is called the *absorptive phase.* Now that you understand the fasting phase, this one is simple. Suppose that we eat a balanced meal of proteins, carbohydrates, and fats. The proteins are broken down into amino acids and the carbohydrates are broken down into glucose. The fats basically remain as fats. Let us consider each of these three nutrients.

1. As we start absorbing the nutrients, the level of glucose in the blood rises. This rise is detected by cells in the brain, which causes the activity of the sympathetic nervous system to decrease and the activity of the parasympathetic nervous system to increase. This change tells the pancreas to stop secreting glucagon and to begin secreting insulin. The insulin permits all the cells of the body to use glucose as a fuel. Extra glucose is converted into glycogen, which fills the short-term carbohydrate reservoir. If some glucose is left over, fat cells absorb it and convert it to triglycerides.

2. A small proportion of the amino acids received from the digestive tract are used as building blocks to construct proteins and polypeptides; the rest are converted to fats and stored in adipose tissue.

3. Fats are not used at this time; they are simply stored in adipose tissue. (See *Figure 13.3.*)

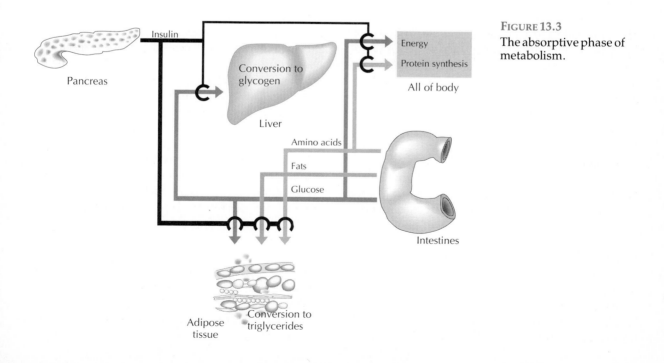

FIGURE 13.3
The absorptive phase of metabolism.

Insulin

Conversion to glycogen

Pancreas

Liver

Energy

Protein synthesis

All of body

Amino acids

Fats

Glucose

Intestines

Adipose tissue

Conversion to triglycerides

Is Body Weight Regulated?

No one questions the fact that body fluids are regulated, but some people have suggested that body weight might not be. The reason for this suggestion is easy to see: Many people are obese, and some of those who are not say that they have to make a real effort to remain thin. If body weight is truly regulated, then we might expect that people should get hungry only when they need to eat and should stop eating when they have eaten enough. But obviously, we sometimes eat when we are not really hungry, and we continue to eat even when we have had enough.

There are several reasons to explain the apparent failure of the body to regulate weight. First, as we shall see, some of the eating habits imposed on us by our society interfere with regulatory mechanisms that evolved in different types of environments. Second, regulation is not as bad as it may seem. The fact that many people show visible fat in their abdomens or in their hips and thighs does not mean that their body weights are not regulated; it may only mean that the amount of fat that is normal for them is higher than what we find esthetically pleasing nowadays. Consider the purpose of fat—to provide a reservoir that can be drawn upon in time of need. In the past (and in the present, in some parts of the world), the supply of food was (is) unreliable. When certain plants were in season, when the fish were running in the river, or when migratory animals were passing through the region, there was plenty to eat. At other times people ate very little and made up the difference by living off their fat. If they had not stored some fat during the good seasons, they would have died during times when food was harder to find.

As we will see in the section on eating disorders near the end of this chapter, heredity plays an important role in determining a person's body size and shape. Primarily because of genetic differences, some people are just naturally fatter than others. In other words, people's "set points" can vary. The reasons for these differences and their implications for control of body weight will be discussed later.

The best evidence that body weight is regulated comes from studies that indicate that changes in diet cause compensatory changes in behavior or in metabolism. For example, if people or laboratory animals eat more than usual, they gain weight, but not as much as would be predicted from their new diet. Similarly, if people or laboratory animals eat less than usual, the amount of weight they lose is less than one would predict. Thus, overeating causes energy to be squandered, and undereating causes it to be conserved. For example, Bray (1969) had a group of volunteers eat a diet that caused them to lose 3 percent of their body weight. Their rate of oxygen consumption, which indicates their rate of metabolism, went down 17 percent. Changes in metabolic rate are primarily caused by changes in the rate at which we produce heat and lose it to the environment. The more heat we lose, the more we burn calories that would otherwise be stored in the form of fat.

The experiments that best demonstrate the nature of regulation are those done with laboratory animals, because their environments and their behavior can be controlled precisely, and their physiological processes can be closely observed. First, it is clear that caloric intake is controlled. For example, if animals are given a diet with fewer calories, they soon eat more of it; whereas if they are given a richer diet, they begin to eat less. In addition, if the animal's energy balance is altered, its food intake will follow suit. For example, if a rat is put into a cold environment, where it must expend more energy to keep warm, its food intake will increase and its body weight will remain stable. If it is put into a warmer environment, it will compensate by eating less.

What, exactly, is the system variable that permits the body weight of most organisms to remain relatively stable? It seems highly unlikely that body *weight* itself is regulated—this variable would have to be measured by detectors in the soles of our feet or (for those of us who are more sedentary) in the skin of our buttocks. What is more likely is that some variable related to body fat is regulated. The basic difference between obese and nonobese people is the amount of fat stored in their adipose tissue. Perhaps fat tissue provides a signal to the brain that indicates how much of it there is. If so, the signal is almost certainly some sort of chemical, because cutting the nerves that serve the fat tissue in an animal's body do not affect its body weight.

There is good evidence that the amount of body fat is regulated. Liebelt, Bordelon, and Liebelt (1973) described several studies they performed to investigate the regulation of adipose tissue. When a piece of adipose tissue is transplanted from one mouse into another, the transplanted tissue normally withers away, even when the two mice are genetically identical, so there is no question of tissue rejection. However, when the experimenters first removed some of the adipose tissue belonging to the recipient animals, the transplants were accepted. In other words, when the total amount of fat tissue in the recipient mouse was surgically reduced, an implant grew—presumably in response to chemical signals encouraging growth of such tissue. Furthermore, when mice were given a brain lesion that causes overeating and subsequent obesity (I will discuss this phenomenon later), their bodies accepted a graft of adipose tissue while they were gaining weight, as though the lesion had raised the adipose tissue set point.

Another piece of evidence suggests that body fat is regulated. If animals are force-fed through a tube placed in their stomach so that they become fat, they will subsequently reduce their food intake until their weight returns to normal levels (Hoebel and Teitelbaum, 1966; Steffens, 1975). A possible explanation for this finding is that the excessive amount of body fat produces a signal that causes the animal to reduce its intake of food until its weight returns to normal.

As you might expect, several investigators have tried to identify a chemical signal that is produced by adipose tissue. For example, Cook et al. (1987) found that fat tissue produces a protein that they named *adipsin,* and Knoll (1982) isolated an appetite-suppressing glycoprotein from human blood that he named *satietin.* In a more recent attempt Harris, Bruch, and Martin (1989) removed fat tissue from rats that they had overfed by 200 percent for 6–12 days. They were able to extract a substance, probably a protein, that inhibits growth of fat cells. Further studies will have to be performed to determine whether one or more of these substances actually do tell the brain how much fat the body possesses.

*I*NTERIM SUMMARY

Metabolism consists of two phases. During the absorptive phase we receive glucose, amino acids, and fats from the intestines. The blood level of insulin is high, which permits all cells to metabolize glucose. In addition, the liver and the muscles convert glucose to glycogen, which replenishes the short-term reservoir. Excess carbohydrates and amino acids are converted to fats, and fats are placed into the long-term reservoir in the adipose tissue.

During the fasting phase the activity of the parasympathetic nervous system falls and the activity of the sympathetic nervous system increases. In response, the level of insulin falls, and the level of glucagon and the adrenal catecholamines rises. These events cause liver glycogen to be converted to glucose and triglycerides to be broken down into glycerol and fatty acids. In the absence of insulin only the central nervous system can use the glucose available in the blood; the rest of the body lives on fatty acids. Glycerol is converted to glucose by the liver; and if fasting continues long enough to deplete the short-term carbohydrate reservoir, some fatty acids are converted to ketones for use by the brain.

Body weight (or, more likely, quantity of adipose tissue) is regulated, although the amount of fat people's bodies contain can vary widely. Both people and laboratory animals will eat less of a rich diet and more of a diet low in calories, and they will change their food intake if their metabolic requirements change. Transplantation studies suggest that fat tissue may produce signals that can be monitored by the brain. Three different chemicals have been extracted from blood and from fat tissue; one or more of them may convey this signal.

WHAT STARTS A MEAL?

The heading to this section is a very simple question, but the answer is complex. The short answer, I suppose, is that we still are not sure, but that will not stop me from writing more. In fact, many factors start a meal, including the presence of appetizing food, the company of people who are eating, or the words "It's time to eat!" More fundamentally, there must be some sort of signal that tells the brain that the supply of nutrients has gotten low, and that it is time to begin looking for, and ingesting, some food. This section considers all of these factors.

Before I begin, I will point out that the physiological signals that cause a meal to begin need not be the ones that cause it to end. As I said in the discussion of regulatory systems at the beginning of this chapter, there is a considerable delay between the act of eating (the correctional mechanism) and a change in the system variable. We may start eating because the supply of nutrients has fallen below a certain level, but we certainly do not stop eating because the level of those nutrients has been restored to normal. In fact, we stop eating long before that happens, because digestion takes several hours. Thus, the signals for hunger and satiety are sure to be different.

Social and Environmental Factors

Most people, if they were asked why they eat, would say that they do so because they get hungry. By that, they probably mean that something happens inside their body that provides a sensation that makes them want to eat. In other words, we tend to think of eating as something provoked by physiological factors. But often, we eat because of habit or because of some stimuli present in our environment. These stimuli include a clock indicating that it is time to eat, the sight of a plate of food, the smell of food cooking in the kitchen, or the presence of other people. Many studies have shown that eating can be classically conditioned in both humans and laboratory animals. For example, Weingarten (1983) presented hungry rats with a buzzer and a light (CS$^+$) followed by food six times a day for eleven days. Another stimulus, a tone (CS$^-$), was turned on intermittently between meals. During test days following the training, he periodically turned on the CS$^+$ and the CS$^-$ and observed the animals' eating behavior. The rats began eating within 5 seconds after the

CS$^+$ was presented, even when they were satiated, but did not react to the CS$^-$. Birch, McPhee, Sullivan, and Johnson (1989) observed a similar phenomenon in nursery school children. Thus, it seems reasonable to suppose that stimuli naturally associated with eating can provoke a meal.

One of the most important appetite stimulators is the taste of food. As we saw in Chapter 7, sweetness detectors on our tongue are probably there because they helped our ancestors identify food that was safe to eat. Even when we are not particularly hungry, we tend to find a sweet taste pleasant, and eating something sweet tends to increase our appetite. For example, Brala and Hagen (1983) had college students drink a milk shake, which was sweetened with either aspartame (a low-calorie artificial sweetener) or with sugar. Half of the subjects first rinsed their mouths with gymnemic acid, a chemical that blocks the perception of sweetness; to them, the milk shake did not taste sweet. Ninety minutes later, the subjects were offered a platter containing a variety of snack food. The subjects who had experienced a sweet taste from the milk shake reported feeling hungrier and, in fact, ate more than those who did not. Thus, a sweet taste can increase subsequent food intake.

The same phenomenon occurs in laboratory animals. For example, Tordoff (1988) found that rats who were given some saccharin to drink during the first two hours of the dark cycle ate 10–15 percent more food than those who were simply given water to drink. (Rats, being nocturnal creatures, eat most of their food after the lights go off.) The fact that a sweet taste stimulates appetite suggests that drinking diet soda may make it more difficult for a person trying to lose weight to keep on his or her diet; although the soda certainly does not contribute calories, it may make the person hungrier. In fact, rats fed a tasty diet get fatter if saccharin is put in their drinking water (Powley and Berthoud, 1985).

Another variable that affects appetite is the meal schedule. When a rat is free to eat whenever it wants, the size of the meal is primarily determined by external factors, such as the taste and texture of the food. However, the *time* of the next meal is related to the size of the one just eaten; that is, if a rat eats a large meal, it waits longer until the next one (Le Magnen and Tallon, 1963, 1966). Unlike many other animals, we humans tend to take our meals at fixed times: soon after waking, at midday, and in the evening. This custom makes it difficult for us to adjust the timing of our meals, as other animals can do. What we do instead is adjust the *size* of our meals. If we have eaten recently or if the previous meal was large, we tend to eat a smaller meal (Jiang and Hunt, 1983; de Castro, McCormick, Pedersen, and Kreitzman, 1986). The difference between our pattern and that of animals such as rats seems to be caused by our habit of eating at fixed times. If people live in isolation, away from cues that indicate the time of day, their meal patterns resemble those of rats: The bigger the meal, the longer they wait until the next one (Bernstein, 1981).

The presence of other people is yet another factor that strongly affects our eating behavior. De Castro and de Castro (1989) asked people to keep diaries that listed all the food they ate during a seven-day period and the number of other people who were present while they were eating. The investigators found that the amount of food eaten was directly related to the number of other people who were present—the more people present, the more the subjects ate. In addition, the correlation that is normally seen between the time since the previous meal and the size of the present meal was observed only when the subjects ate alone; when other people were present, the correlation was abolished.

Dietary Selection: Responding to the Consequences

Animals need to obtain a variety of different nutrients: carbohydrates, fats, essential amino acids, minerals, and various chemicals that the body cannot make, which we call vitamins. Some animals can get along well eating only one type of food. For example, the physiology of a koala is perfectly suited to a diet of eucalyptus leaves, and that of a giant panda to bamboo shoots. Predators can count on their prey to get a balanced diet and, by eating them, obtain all the nutrients, vitamins, and minerals they need. But animals that eat only one type of food will be limited by the distribution

of their food; you will not find koalas where there are not eucalyptus trees, nor giant pandas where there are not bamboo forests. Similarly, predators are utterly dependent on their prey.

It is probably not a coincidence that two of the most successful species on earth, humans and rats, are omnivores. (Please excuse the comparison.) Omnivores ("all-devouring creatures") are liberated from dependency on a particular type of food. However, as always, with freedom comes responsibility. The metabolism of omnivores is such that no single food will provide all essential nutrients. Thus, it is advantageous to eat many different kinds of foods. As we shall see, we tend to do that, naturally. But in some situations, when the foods available at a particular time and place lack an essential nutrient, such as a vitamin or mineral, the animal must make special efforts to find a food that supplies what is needed. In addition, omnivores are exposed to foods that may contain toxic substances. All plants produce chemicals designed by the evolutionary process to poison animals (primarily insects) that might eat them. Most of these poisons are harmless to mammals, but some are not. In addition, food that has been infected with various types of bacteria or molds can become toxic. Thus, omnivores must learn to avoid foods that might cause harm.

Let us consider the tendency to obtain a varied diet. Most of us find a meal that consists of moderate quantities of several different foods to be more interesting than a huge platter of only one food. If we eat a single food, we soon become tired of it, a phenomenon that has been labeled *sensory-specific satiety.* Le Magnen (1956) demonstrated this phenomenon elegantly. He fed rats a diet to which he could add a flavoring. He let the rats eat one flavor for 30 minutes. By that time they had pretty much stopped eating. He replaced the dish with a second flavor, and the rats began eating again. He presented a total of four different flavors (of the same basic food, remember) and found that the rats would eat a meal that was two to three times larger than a 2-hour meal consisting of a single course. Rolls, Rowe, Rolls, Kingston, Megson, and Gunary (1981) observed the same phenomenon in humans; they found that people would eat a larger meal when they were offered four types of sandwich fillings or four different flavors of yogurt. Obviously, the phenomenon of sensory-specific satiety encourages the consumption of a varied diet.

Of course, it is not enough simply to get a varied diet. Foods differ in their ability to provide needed calories and specific nutrients. Omnivores are able to learn about the consequences of eating different kinds of food. For example, Sclafani and Nissenbaum (1988) showed that rats can learn which flavors provide them with calories. The investigators gave rats flavored water to drink. On some days the water was cherry-flavored; on other days it was grape-flavored. The rats drank the flavored water from a special drinking tube that permitted the experimenters to detect each lick that the animals took. As the animals drank the flavored water, an automatic pump delivered either water or a nutritive starch solution into their stomachs, through tubes that had been previously placed there. For each rat a particular flavor was paired with the injection of the starch solution. After four days of training the rats were permitted to chose between the two flavors. They overwhelmingly chose the flavor that had been paired with the starch infusions; thus, rats are able to learn which flavor is associated with the delivery of a nutritive substance to their stomach.

As we saw in Chapter 7, most mammals come provided with specialized receptors that detect substances that are possibly poisonous. Our tongue contains receptors that detect alkaloids and acids (the bitterness and sourness detectors), many of which are poisonous. Thus, we tend to reject bitter or sour tastes. (As we shall see, this tendency is controlled by mechanisms in the brain stem; thus, it is undoubtedly a very primitive reaction.) But taste tells us about the nature of food only when it is in the mouth, so taste provides us with a limited range of information. Much more information is provided by the olfactory system. Although there are many odors that almost everyone finds disgusting, such as the smell of rotten meat (you'll be able to think of some others), studies with infants suggest that there are no odors that are innately repulsive (Engen, 1974, 1982). Thus, they appear to be learned. Some, undoubtedly, are learned socially. We see that our parents find an odor disgusting, and we learn to do so, too.

But others are learned by direct experience of the consequences of ingestion.

If an animal encounters a particular food, eats it, becomes sick, and survives, the animal will avoid eating that food afterward. That is, the animal will have formed a *conditioned flavor aversion.* The aversion can be formed simply on the basis of taste; but more often, olfaction is also involved, because flavor is a composite of taste and olfaction. The phenomenon was first experimentally demonstrated by Garcia and Koelling (1966). The investigators let rats taste some saccharin and then injected them with lithium chloride, which produces nausea. (Rats cannot vomit, but their behavior indicates that lithium chloride makes them feel ill.) Afterward, the rats refused to drink saccharin. Other studies have shown that conditioned aversions can readily be formed to the complex flavors of particular foods, which are the composites of odors and tastes.

If a rat encounters a new and potentially interesting food, it only takes a small nibble of the food. If the food contained something toxic, and if it survives its subsequent illness, it will never eat that food again. But if it does *not* get ill, it will take a larger meal the next time; it acts as if it has learned that the food is safe. Humans, too, can form conditioned flavor aversions. These aversions can sometimes occur by chance. A friend of mine often took trips on airplanes with her parents when she was a child. Unfortunately, she usually got airsick. Just before takeoff, her mother would give her some spearmint-flavored chewing gum to help relieve the pressure on her eardrums that would occur when the plane ascended. Yes, she developed a conditioned flavor aversion to spearmint gum. In fact, the odor of the gum still makes her feel nauseated. A more serious problem is encountered by patients undergoing chemotherapy for cancer. The drugs they are given often cause nausea, and the patients can form an aversion to the foods they eat during the course of therapy (Bernstein, 1978).

Rozin and Kalat (1971) describe an interesting phenomenon: Conditioned flavor aversions can motivate an animal to find a nutrient that it needs. As we saw in Chapter 12, if a rat is fed a food that is deficient in sodium, it will develop a sodium appetite and will seek foods that contain sodium, which it is able to taste. This tendency need not be learned; it is innate. However, rats (and humans) cannot innately recognize the flavor of vital ingredients of the diet, such as vitamins or minerals other than sodium. If a rat is fed a food that is deficient in a particular vitamin, such as thiamine, it will become ill. Its illness will cause the formation of a conditioned aversion to that food. If it is offered another, it will eat it; and if it gets well after eating that food (because it contains the ingredient lacking in its diet), it will learn to prefer that food over the old one.

Thus, we omnivores are endowed with some innate tendencies and with the ability to learn from our experience with particular foods. These tendencies and abilities permit us to obtain the nutrients we need from an enormous variety of foodstuffs, while avoiding foods that could be dangerous to us. Later in this chapter, I will discuss the physiology of sensory-specific satiety and conditioned flavor aversions.

Depletion of Nutrients

Even though environmental factors play a role in starting and controlling a meal—especially in our own species—physiological factors also play an important role. For example, we saw in the previous section that many species of animals (including our own, if clocks and dinner bells are not present) eat soon after a small meal but wait longer after a large one. This fact suggests that hunger is inversely related to the amount of nutrients left over from the previous meal.

Most investigators believe that the physiological signal that initiates a meal is a fall in level of available nutrients in the blood. As you learned earlier in this chapter, during the absorptive phase of metabolism we live on food that is being absorbed from the digestive tract. After that, we start drawing on our two nutrient reservoirs: The brain lives on glucose provided by the carbohydrate reservoir, and the rest of the body lives on fatty acids provided by the fat reservoir. Although the needs of the cells of the body are being met, the level of nutrients in the blood falls slightly. And later, when the carbohydrate reservoir of the liver is depleted and all the body must live on the fat reservoir, the level decreases slightly again. Surely,

then, these decreases in the nutrient content of the blood provide the physiological stimulus for hunger.

The Glucostatic Hypothesis

But what nutrient is measured, and *how* is it measured? For several reasons the most obvious candidate is glucose. To begin with, glucose is the primary fuel during the absorptive phase of metabolism; thus, when it is plentiful, the animal does not need to eat. In addition, a drop in the level of blood glucose is the event that inhibits the secretion of insulin and stimulates sympathetic activity, thus triggering the fasting phase of metabolism. If a fall in glucose is responsible for the fasting phase of metabolism, perhaps it is responsible for hunger, too. Finally, because the brain controls eating, it seems reasonable that hunger might be triggered by a decrease in the brain's primary fuel.

The hypothesis that the signal for hunger is a fall in blood glucose is called the **glucostatic hypothesis** (Mayer, 1955). A *glucostat* is assumed to be a neuron that measures blood glucose the way a thermostat measures temperature. The glucostatic hypothesis suggests that the firing rate of glucostats is related to the level of glucose in the interstitial fluid. A fall in the level of glucose produces a signal in these neurons that stimulates food seeking and eating.

Louis-Sylvestre and Le Magnen (1980) devised a procedure that permitted them to continuously analyze the level of glucose in a rat's blood. They withdrew 15 μl of blood each minute from a catheter implanted in a rat's jugular vein and replaced it with an equal amount of blood from a donor rat; thus, the subject's blood volume was not reduced. They found that the blood glucose level fell by 6–8 percent approximately 6 or 7 minutes before each meal. Several minutes after the start of the meal, the blood glucose level rose, and another meal was not taken until the blood glucose level fell again. (See *Figure 13.4.*)

If food is not available when an animal would normally eat, its blood glucose falls, and it eats more when it can finally obtain some food. The amount of food eaten is closely related to the fall in the blood glucose level. Larue-Achagiotis and Le Magnen (1985) took the food away from rats for 3

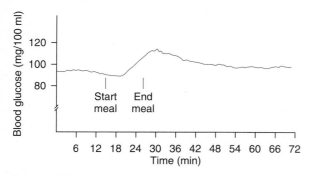

FIGURE 13.4

Blood glucose level before, during, and after a spontaneous meal of a rat. (Adapted from Le Magnen, J. *Hunger.* Cambridge, England: Cambridge University Press, 1985.)

hours at various times of the night and day. During the day, when rats normally eat very little anyway, the blood glucose level fell only slightly; and the rats ate very little when the food was given back to them. However, when the food was taken away during the night, the decrease in blood glucose level was much greater, and the rats ate much more. A similar phenomenon is seen in humans. Bellisle, Lucas, Amrani, and Le Magnen (1984) found that when people skip breakfast, their blood glucose level is lower at lunch time, and they eat a larger lunch.

Evidence suggests that the fall in blood glucose just before a spontaneous meal is not just *related* to the onset of a meal, it is the *cause* of it. Campfield, Brandon, and Smith (1985) continuously monitored the blood glucose level of rats. If they injected a very small amount of glucose into their veins when they detected a decline in the blood glucose level, the predicted meal was postponed. It was as if the injection removed the hunger signal.

As you know, insulin is necessary for the utilization of glucose; if it is not present, the mechanism that transports glucose into cells cannot function. Thus, hunger is related to the level of insulin in the blood as well as to the level of glucose. Continuous infusion of insulin makes animals overeat and become obese, because the hormone causes most of the glucose to be stored in fat tissue and prevents it from being released again; hence the animals must eat more fre-

quently in order to keep up their blood glucose level. Figure 13.5 shows the effects of a continuous infusion of insulin on food intake and body weight in rats. Note that after the infusion is stopped, the animals eat very little food until they lose most of the weight they gained. This recovery provides further evidence that body fat is regulated. (See *Figure 13.5*.)

In the previous section I discussed the fact that the sight, smell, and taste of food can stimulate appetite. One of the reasons for this phenomenon is the so-called *cephalic phase* ("head" phase) of food intake (Powley, 1977). When we eat, or even when we encounter stimuli normally associated with eating, many changes occur in our body. These changes (which include the phenomena that Pavlov was studying when he discovered classical conditioning) prepare our digestive system and related organs for the ingestion of a meal. The changes include salivation, secretion of gastric acid, and secretion of insulin. One of these responses—the secretion of insulin—has an important effect on appetite. The secretion of insulin, triggered by the stimuli associated with eating, switches the body from the fasting phase to the absorptive phase of metabolism. Fat tissue stops releasing fatty acids, and all cells start using the glucose present in the blood. Of course, this

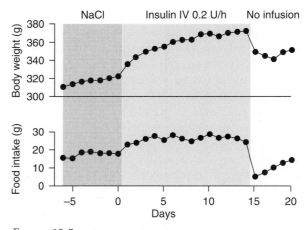

FIGURE 13.5

Effects on continuous intravenous infusion of insulin on the body weight and food intake of rats. (Adapted from Larue-Achagiotis, C., and Le Magnen, J. *Appetite,* 1985, *6*, 319–329.)

soon causes a further fall in the blood glucose level, which causes an increase in hunger.

I think you can see why a snack has an appetizing effect. The taste—especially if it is sweet—initiates the cephalic phase. The increased secretion of insulin causes a fall in the blood sugar level, and the person (or the animal) becomes hungrier.

Beyond the Glucostatic Hypothesis

More recent evidence suggests that although a fall in the level of glucose may be the most important physiological signal for hunger, it is not the only one. After all, our cells can use other nutrients besides glucose. If animals eat a meal low in carbohydrates but high in proteins and fats, they still manage to eat a relatively constant amount of calories, even though their blood glucose level is reduced slightly. If their eating were solely controlled by the level of glucose in their blood, they would be expected to overeat and get fat.

An experiment by Friedman, Tordoff, and Ramirez (1986) suggests that fatty acid metabolism, as well as glucose metabolism, plays a role in hunger. They used two drugs that interfere with glucose or fatty acid metabolism. One of them you are already familiar with, 2-deoxyglucose (2-DG), because I have described several experiments that used radioactive 2-DG in conjunction with PET scanners or autoradiography to study the metabolic rate of different parts of the brain. When (nonradioactive) 2-DG is given in large doses, it interferes with glucose metabolism by competing with glucose for access to the mechanism that transports glucose through the cell membrane and for access to the enzymes that metabolize glucose. Another chemical, *methyl palmoxirate* (MP), interferes with the metabolism of fatty acids by interfering with their transport into mitochondria, where they are normally metabolized.

Friedman and his colleagues found that a moderate dose of 2-DG or a moderate dose of MP had little effect on food intake when they were given alone. However, when the chemicals were given together, food intake increased significantly. (See *Figure 13.6.*) Presumably, when the

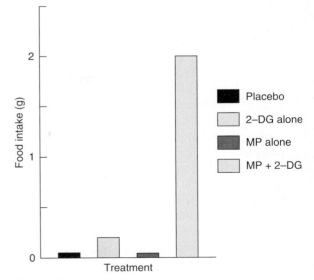

FIGURE 13.6

Effects of methyl palmoxirate (MP) and 2-deoxyglucose (2-DG) on food intake of rats. Intake is significantly stimulated only when both fatty acid and carbohydrate metabolism are impaired. (Adapted from Friedman, M.I., Tordoff, M.G., and Ramirez, I. *Brain Research Bulletin*, 1986, *17*, 855–859.)

metabolism of only one fuel was reduced, the animal simply relied more heavily on the other type of fuel. The investigators also found that if rats were fed a diet high in fats but low in carbohydrates, treatment with MP alone caused food intake to increase. With no carbohydrates for the animals to fall back on, a treatment that interferes with fatty acid metabolism is enough to stimulate eating.

Nicolaïdis (1974, 1987) has proposed the *ischymetric hypothesis* of hunger (from the Greek word *ischis*, "power"). He suggests that a set of neurons—somewhere—serve as witnesses that testify to the rest of the nervous system about the level of nutrients available in the blood. Presumably, these neurons are like all other neurons and can burn the same fuels as they can. However, the firing rate of their axons is very sensitive to their metabolic rate. If the level of fuels falls, their metabolic rate falls too; and the change in the firing rate of their axons tells other neurons that it is time to start thinking about the next meal.

Detectors

As you have just seen, evidence suggests that both glucose and fatty acids provide important physiological signals for hunger. Possibly amino acids do, too, but less is known about the importance of amino acids in the body's metabolism. One of the problems in studying amino acids is that they are essential for protein synthesis. Thus, a diet low in amino acids interferes with many biological processes. Similarly, a diet that is very high in amino acids produces toxic waste products. Thus, experimental manipulations in the amino acid content of diets cause effects unrelated to energy metabolism. For that reason experimenters have concentrated on carbohydrates and lipids.

For years investigators have assumed that the detectors for hunger are neurons located in the brain and have looked for them there. Indeed, they have succeeded in finding them in the brain but have had difficulty confirming their importance in the control of feeding. For example, Blass and Kraly (1974) destroyed the lateral hypothalamus, which contains most of the brain's glucose receptors. After recovering from the short-term effects of the surgery, the rats' eating behavior continued to be controlled by nutritional factors. For example, they also ate more when they were given a low-calorie diet and ate less when they were given a high-calorie diet. They ate more or less when their metabolic rate was raised or lowered by changing the room temperature. Thus, although the lateral hypothalamus does contain glucose receptors, they are not necessary for the regulation of food intake. Obviously, there must be some detectors located elsewhere. Eating is vital; thus, it would not be surprising if the evolutionary process favored the development of more than one set of detectors capable of stimulating this behavior.

The brain is not the only organ that contains glucose receptors; evidence suggests that glucose receptors in the liver play a role in the control of food intake. Russek (1971) noted that although intravenous (IV) injections of glucose had little effect on food intake, *intraperitoneal (IP)* injections (that is, into the abdominal cavity) suppressed eating. This observation certainly does not favor the hypothesis that all the glucose receptors that control food intake are located in the brain. An IV injection of glucose raises the blood sugar level, but an IP injection has little effect. Conversely, most of the glucose injected into the abdominal cavity is taken up by the liver and stored as glycogen. The finding that the glucose injected intraperitoneally probably got no farther than the liver but nevertheless inhibited eating suggested to Russek that the liver might contain receptors that were sensitive to glucose. Perhaps these receptors send signals to the brain that activate mechanisms that control eating.

To test this hypothesis, Russek attached two chronic cannulas in a dog, one in the hepatic portal vein (the system that carries blood from the intestines to the liver) and another in the jugular vein, located in the neck. Injection in the jugular vein introduces a substance into the general circulation. By the time the substance reaches the liver, it is already diluted by the blood. In contrast, injection in the hepatic portal vein introduces a substance directly into the liver. An injection of glucose into the hepatic portal vein produced long-lasting satiety, whereas a similar injection into the jugular vein had no effect on food intake. Since then, many other studies (for example, Novin, Robinson, Culbreth, and Tordoff, 1983) have confirmed these results.

Of course, I am getting ahead of myself by describing experiments dealing with satiety; that is the topic of the next section. But the original studies with the liver looked at the effects of turning off hunger, not producing it. A study by Novin, VanderWeele, and Rezek (1973) suggested that receptors in the liver can stimulate hunger as well as produce satiety; when these cells are deprived of nutrients, they cause eating. The investigators infused 2-DG into the hepatic portal vein. (Because the animals had been eating a high-carbohydrate, low-fat diet, the 2-DG effectively starved the cells of the liver.) They found that the intraportal infusions of 2-DG caused immediate eating. The effect appeared to be mediated by the neural connections between the liver and the brain, because it was largely eliminated by cutting the vagus nerve.

Electrophysiological studies have found glucose-sensitive receptors in the liver that send information through afferent fibers in the vagus nerve (Niijima, 1969, 1982). These receptors appear to provide "hunger" signals; they fire at a high rate when the level of glucose in the hepatic portal blood is low and fire at a low rate when the glucose level is high.

If an important hunger signal is received by the brain from the liver via the vagus nerve, then cutting this nerve should abolish these signals and decrease eating. However, several experiments have shown that hepatic denervation does not prevent hunger. For example, Tordoff, Hopfenbeck, and Novin (1982) found that cutting the hepatic branch of the vagus nerve had little effect on eating. Therefore, we must conclude that even if the liver does play a role in hunger, it is not the *sole* source of hunger signals.

There is good evidence for interactions between hepatic and hypothalamic glucose receptors. Shimizu, Oomura, Novin, Grijalva, and Cooper (1983) used multibarreled glass micropipettes for recording and for microiontophoretic injection of glucose to identify glucose receptors in the brain. When they located a neuron that responded to glucose (with a decrease in response rate), they injected glucose into the hepatic portal vein. Most of the hypothalamic glucose receptors also decreased their firing rate when glucose was presented to the liver. This convergence of information suggests that in the absence of either brain or liver glucose receptors, hunger can be evoked by activity of the other system.

*I*NTERIM SUMMARY

Many stimuli, environmental and physiological, can initiate a meal. Stimuli associated with eating—such as clocks pointing to lunchtime or dinnertime, the smell or sight of food, or (especially) the taste of food—increase appetite. The fact that a sweet taste is an especially potent appetizer suggests that drinking artificially sweetened beverages may be counterproductive in the long run. The size of a meal taken by a rat (or a person living in isolation) determines the interval until the next one. In contrast, most people eat at relatively fixed times but vary their intake according to how much (or when) they ate the previous meal. The presence of other people tends to increase our

meal and removes the controlling effect of the previous meal.

Omnivores are naturally attracted to sweet tastes and avoid sour or bitter ones. In addition, they can learn to avoid (form an aversion to) the flavors of foods that make them ill. If they eat a diet that lacks an essential ingredient, their illness produces an aversion to their present diet and motivates them to seek another. If that diet cures them, they learn to prefer it.

The primary physiological signal for hunger appears to be a fall in the level of nutrients in the blood. A few minutes before each meal, the blood level of glucose falls, and the meal can be postponed by infusing a small amount of glucose into the blood. The cephalic phase of a meal, stimulated by the presence of food, includes the secretion of insulin. This hormone stimulates appetite by causing the blood glucose level to fall.

Although glucose is probably the most important signal, it is not the only one. Studies with inhibitors of the metabolism of glucose fatty acids indicate that both of these nutrients are involved. Nutrient-sensitive detectors are located in both the brain and the liver; both probably play a role in detecting a fall in the blood level of nutrients.

WHAT STOPS A MEAL?

The search for the signals that stop a meal follows the pathway traveled by ingested food: the eyes, nose, and mouth; the stomach; the duodenum; and the liver. Each of these locations provides a signal to the brain that indicates that food has been ingested and is progressing on the way toward absorption. To discover the nature of the detectors in these locations and their effects on behavior, experimenters "trick" the organism by taking food out of the digestive system, placing food there, or surgically disconnecting receptors along the digestive tract from the brain.

Head Factors

The term *head factors* refers to several sets of receptors located in the head: the eyes, the nose, the tongue, and the throat. Information about the appearance, odor, taste, texture, and temperature of food has some automatic effects on food intake, but most of the effects involve learning. Satiety can be produced by head factors alone, but this effect is weak and short-lived. (I refer to satiety for an entire meal, not sensory-specific satiety, which was discussed earlier.) In Chapter 12 we saw that a thirsty animal with an esophageal or gastric fistula (which prevents swallowed water from reaching the stomach) will drink until it is exhausted; thus, little or no satiety for water is produced by head factors. In contrast, when an animal with an esophageal fistula sham-eats the first time, it does not eat indefinitely. (*Sham feeding* is the term used to describe the fact that the food is swallowed but leaves the digestive system before it can be digested.) Instead, the animal swallows a meal-sized amount of food and then stops eating (Janowitz and Grossman, 1949). However, it soon returns to eat again, which indicates that the satiety produced by head factors is short-lived and normally must be superseded by satiety factors caused by the presence of food in the digestive system.

Undoubtedly, the most important role of head factors in satiety is the fact that taste and odor of food can serve as stimuli that permit animals to learn about the caloric contents of different foods. Thus, animals can learn to adjust their intake according to the caloric value of what they are eating. Mather, Nicolaïdis, and Booth (1978) found that rats learned to eat less of a food with a particular flavor when the eating of that food was accompanied by intravenous infusions of glucose, which supplied extra calories.

Gastric Factors

Although most people associate feelings of hunger with "hunger pangs" in the stomach and feelings of satiety with an impression of gastric fullness, the stomach is not necessary for feelings of hunger. Humans whose stomachs have been removed because of cancer or the presence of large ulcers still periodically get hungry (Ingelfinger, 1944). Of necessity, these people eat frequent, small meals; in fact, a large meal causes nausea and discomfort, apparently because the

duodenum quickly fills up. However, although the stomach may not be especially important in producing hunger, it does appear to play an important role in satiety.

Investigators have known for a long time that a hungry animal will eat less if nutrients are injected directly into its stomach just before it is given access to food (Berkun, Kessen, and Miller, 1952). What is the nature of this signal? One possibility is that stretch detectors in the walls of the stomach simply respond to the pressure of food. However, Young and Deutsch (1980) found that when a hungry rat ate all the food it wanted, the pressure within the stomach remained remarkably constant; it did *not* show an increase at the end of the meal that would be expected if pressure were providing a satiety signal.

In fact, the stomach appears to contain receptors that can detect the presence of nutrients. Davis and Campbell (1973) allowed rats to eat their fill, and shortly thereafter, they removed food from the rats' stomachs through an implanted tube. When the rats were permitted to eat again, they ate almost exactly the same amount of food that had been taken out. This finding suggests that animals are able to monitor the amount of food in their stomachs.

Deutsch and Gonzalez (1980) confirmed and extended these findings. They operated on rats and attached an inflatable cuff around the pylorus—something that looked like a miniature blood pressure cuff. The cuff could be inflated by remote control, which would cause it to compress the pylorus, preventing the stomach from emptying. (As we saw in Chapter 12, Hall and Blass used a similar device, in which a noose of fishing line could be tightened to prevent water from leaving the stomach.) With their device Deutsch and Gonzalez could confine food to the stomach, eliminating the possible influence of receptors in the intestine or liver. After observations were made, the cuff could be deflated so that the stomach would empty normally.

Each day, the investigators inflated the pyloric cuff and gave the rats a 30-minute opportunity to drink a commercial high-calorie liquid diet. Because the rats had not eaten for 15 hours, they readily consumed the liquid diet. After the meal the investigators removed 5 ml of the stomach's contents through an implanted tube. On some days they replaced the contents with a saline solution, and on others they let the rats eat without intervention. The rats adjusted their food intake perfectly, compensating for the calories that were removed but ignoring the added nonnutritive saline solution. The results indicate that animals can monitor the total amount of nutrients received by the stomach. They do not do so simply by measuring the volume of the food there, because they are not fooled by the infusion of a saline solution. And the detection takes place in the stomach, not the intestine, because the pyloric cuff keeps all the food in the stomach.

So far, I have been giving the impression that chemical receptors in the stomach send a signal to the brain that automatically controls food intake. However, that is not the case. Even when a rat (or a human) eats normally, without having an experimenter take food out of its stomach, a change in the caloric content of a diet is not detected immediately. That is, if a new food is introduced that is higher or lower in calories than the animal's accustomed food, the animal will not immediately change its intake to compensate for the change in concentration; the compensation takes a few days (Janowitz and Hollander, 1955; Booth, 1981).

Deutsch (1983) found that signals from the stomach could control food intake *only when the animal was familiar with the food it was eating*. If the rat ate familiar food, it would eat the amount required to replace any food removed by the experimenter. However, if a novel flavor was added to the food, the animal did *not* compensate for the food that was removed. After several days experience with the new flavor, the animals began compensating again. Thus, it appears that rats use feedback from the metabolic consequences of a particular food to calibrate the signal the brain receives from the stomach. The flavor of the food identifies it, and that tells the brain how to handle the signal coming from the stomach. Oral and olfactory signals are necessary for an animal to be able to use gastric signals.

How are the signals transmitted from the stomach to the brain? The most likely route would be the gastric branch of the vagus nerve. Indeed, the vagus nerve does convey emergency signals from stretch receptors in the walls of the stomach.

Gonzalez and Deutsch (1981) equipped rats with pyloric cuffs and found that the animals would stop eating when they injected a large amount of saline into their stomach. Almost certainly, this inhibitory effect is not satiety but simply discomfort; the rats' stomachs were simply too full to accept any food. When the animals' vagus nerves were severed, though, an injection of saline into the stomach would *not* inhibit eating.

Although the emergency signal from the stomach's stretch receptors is conveyed neurally, the signal from the stomach's nutrient receptors to the brain appears to be conveyed hormonally. Gonzalez and Deutsch found that even after the rats' vagus nerves were severed, the animals would increase their food intake to compensate for food that the experimenters had removed from their stomachs. Thus, information about nutrients in the stomach is not conveyed to the brain through the vagus nerve.

Possibly, afferent fibers through the sympathetic nerves that connect the stomach to the spinal cord may convey nutritional information to the brain, but an experiment by Koopmans (1981) suggests that the route is hormonal, not neural. He transplanted a large section of the gastrointestinal system from one rat to another: stomach, duodenum, and jejunum (the middle part of the small intestine), with the pancreas attached. (The rats were genetically identical members of an inbred strain, so there was no problem with tissue rejection.) He did *not* remove any organs from the recipient rat. He attached the end of the transplanted jejunum to the side of the recipient's own jejunum and prepared an opening into the extra stomach so that he could insert food into it. (See *Figure 13.7.*)

Koopmans found that when he infused various foods into the extra stomach, the animal ate less than it normally would; saline injections did not have this effect. Rats whose extra stomachs received 8 ml of a commercial liquid diet ate only half as much as those whose extra stomachs received 8 ml of saline. The effect occurred even when a pyloric noose prevented food from leaving the stomach, which rules out the effects of intestinal receptors or the absorption of nutrients into the blood. Because the transplanted gastrointestinal system had no neural connec-

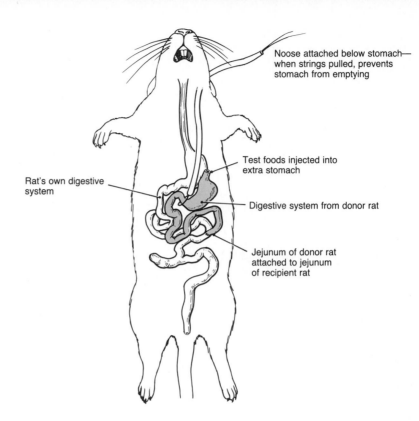

Noose attached below stomach—
when strings pulled, prevents
stomach from emptying

Test foods injected into
extra stomach

Digestive system from donor rat

Jejunum of donor rat
attached to jejunum
of recipient rat

Rat's own digestive
system

FIGURE 13.7
Implantation of an extra stomach
and small intestine in a rat,
performed by Koopmans (1981).

tion with the recipient animal, the effect must have been chemically (probably hormonally) mediated.

Intestinal Factors

After food reaches the stomach, it is mixed with hydrochloric acid and pepsin, an enzyme that breaks proteins into their constituent amino acids. As digestion proceeds, food is gradually introduced into the duodenum. There, the food is mixed with bile and pancreatic enzymes, which continue the digestive process. The duodenum controls the rate of stomach emptying by secreting a peptide hormone called *cholecystokinin* (CCK). This hormone receives its name from the fact that it causes the gallbladder (cholecyst) to contract, injecting bile into the duodenum. (Bile breaks down fats into small particles so that they can be absorbed from the intestines.) CCK is secreted in response to the presence of fats, which are detected by receptors in the walls of the

duodenum. In addition to stimulating contraction of the gallbladder, CCK causes the pylorus to contract and inhibits gastric contractions, thus keeping the stomach from giving it more food.

Obviously, the blood level of CCK must be related to the amount of nutrients (particularly fats) that the duodenum receives from the stomach. Thus, this hormone could potentially provide a satiety signal to the brain, telling it that the duodenum was receiving food from the stomach. In fact, many studies have indeed found that injections of CCK suppress eating (Gibbs, Young, and Smith, 1973a; Smith, Gibbs, and Kulkosky, 1982). Because CCK cannot cross the blood-brain barrier, its site of action must be either outside the central nervous system or in one of the circumventricular organs (like that of angiotensin).

In fact, CCK seems to act peripherally. Smith, Gibbs, and Kulkosky (1982) reported that the inhibitory effect of CCK on food intake was abolished by cutting the gastric branch of the vagus nerve, which disconnects the stomach from the brain. Evidence suggests that the pylorus, a region rich in CCK receptors, may be an important site of action. Moran, Shnayder, Hostetler, and McHugh (1989) removed rats' pyloruses, attaching the stomach directly to the cut end of the duodenum. After the surgery the suppressive effect of CCK on the animals' eating was significantly decreased. However, by 2–3 months after the surgery the junction between the stomach and the duodenum had grown new CCK receptors, and the hormone again suppressed food intake. (See *Figure 13.8*.)

The suppressive effect of CCK on eating is well established. However, several investigators have questioned whether the suppression is caused by *aversion* or by *satiety*. That is, CCK might simply make the animals feel nauseated, so they stop eating. Deutsch and Hardy (1977) found that when an injection of CCK was paired with a particular flavor, rats formed a conditioned aversion to that flavor. In addition, Moore and Deutsch (1985) found that an injection of an *antiemetic* drug (one that suppresses nausea and vomiting) diminished the inhibitory effect of CCK on eating. Antiemetics also reduce a conditioned taste aversion established by an injection of lithium chloride, which supports the suggestion that the effect of CCK is not true satiety (Coil, Hankins, Jenden,

and Garcia, 1978). Finally, McCann, Verbalis, and Stricker (1989) found that several chemicals known to produce nausea, including lithium chloride, copper sulfate, and apomorphine, cause a release of oxytocin by the posterior pituitary gland; thus, they consider oxytocin release an indicator of malaise. They found that injections of CCK, too, cause a release of oxytocin.

It is possible, of course, that the doses of CCK that produce aversion are higher than those that are necessary to suppress eating. If that is true, then the fact that high doses produce an aversion is irrelevant. After all, high doses of ordinary substances such as sugar or salt can make an animal sick. However, an experiment by Reidelberger, Kalogeris, and Solomon (1989) suggests that this explanation is not correct. The authors infused CCK into dogs' veins while simultaneously monitoring the level of the hormone in the animals' blood. (CCK is destroyed very rapidly; thus, even if an experimenter knows how much CCK has been injected, he or she does not know how much is present in the blood.) The investigators found that a dose of CCK that was large enough to suppress eating raised the blood CCK level by approximately 60 pmol (picomoles). In contrast, a normal meal raises the blood level of CCK by only 2 pmol. Thus, the amount of CCK that is released by the duodenum during a normal meal does *not* appear to be enough to suppress eating.

You might be asking yourself why I have been devoting so much space (and so much of your time) to CCK if the available evidence suggests that it is not a factor in satiety. There are three reasons. First, the CCK story points out that it is sometimes difficult to determine whether a naturally occurring substance plays a particular role in behavior. Satiety is especially difficult to study, because eating can be inhibited by many treatments, including those that produce pain or nausea. Second, an enormous amount of research effort has been devoted to the subject. Possibly, you will hear about the "satiating effects" of CCK later on, and a summary and critique of the research here may be helpful. Finally, CCK is also found in the brain.

Several studies have shown that the brain contains CCK, that it is synthesized there, and that some neurons contain CCK receptors (Rehfeld,

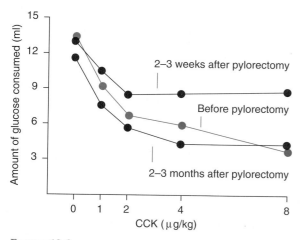

FIGURE 13.8

Effects of cholecystokinin (CCK) on the amount of glucose consumed by dogs before and after removal of the pyloric region. (Based on data from Moran, Shnayder, Hostetler, and McHugh, 1989.)

1978; Goltermann, Rehfeld, and Røigaard-Petersen, 1980; Zarbin, Innis, Wamsley, Snyder, and Kuhar, 1983). By now you have probably become accustomed to the fact that chemicals that serve as hormones are also used as neurotransmitters or neuromodulators by the brain. We do not yet know what CCK does in the brain. Some experiments have shown that infusion of CCK into the cerebral ventricles suppresses feeding, whereas others have not (Griesbacher, Leighton, Hill, and Hughes, 1989). Thus, the "CCK story" is unfinished. The CCK found in the brain obviously does something, and once we find out what it does, we will know more about brain functions.

Liver Factors

Satiety produced by head factors and gastric factors is anticipatory; that is, these factors predict that the food in the digestive system will, when absorbed, eventually restore the system variables that cause hunger. Food in the mouth or stomach does not restore the body's store of nutrients. Not until nutrients are absorbed from the intestines are the internal system variables that cause hunger returned to normal. The last stage of satiety appears to occur in the liver, which is the first organ to learn that food is finally being received from the intestines.

We have already seen (in the section that discussed the detectors that give rise to hunger) several studies that have shown that the infusion of nutrients into the hepatic portal vein produce satiety. Tordoff and Friedman (1988) demonstrated that this effect seems to be localized in the liver. They infused small amounts of two nutrients, glucose and fructose, into the hepatic portal vein. The amounts they used were similar to those that are produced when a meal is being digested. Both nutrients reduced the amount of food that the rats ate. Almost certainly, the signal was detected by the liver. First, neither the glucose nor the fructose increased the animals' blood level of glucose, free fatty acids, glycerol, or ketones; thus, the infusions did not provide a signal that could be detected directly by nutrient receptors in the brain. Second, fructose cannot cross the blood-brain barrier and is metabolized very poorly by cells in

the rest of the body (Park, Johnson, Wright, and Bastel, 1957; Van den Berghe, 1978). However, fructose can be readily metabolized by the liver. Therefore, the results strongly suggest that when the liver receives nutrients from the intestines, it sends a signal to the brain that produces satiety. (More accurately, the signal *continues* the satiety that was already started by head factors and gastric factors.)

As we saw in the previous section, we cannot necessarily conclude that a treatment produces *satiety* just because it inhibits eating. Fortunately, the effects of infusions of nutrients into the hepatic portal vein do not appear to be aversive. Tordoff and Friedman (1986) infused either a saline solution or a solution of glucose into the hepatic portal blood supply of rats while the animals were eating. The two solutions were randomly paired with two nonnutritive flavors added to their food: chicken or chocolate. As expected, the glucose suppressed eating. In addition, when the rats were permitted to choose between the two flavors of food, they preferred the one associated with the glucose infusion. Thus, not only is the infusion not aversive, it is actually reinforcing. As we saw earlier, Sclafani and Nissenbaum (1988) found that an infusion of starch into the stomach produced a preference for a flavor associated with the infusion; thus, the brain interprets the signals from the stomach and the liver not simply as satiety signals but as signals that a beneficial event has occurred.

INTERIM SUMMARY

Because of the long delay between swallowing food and digesting it, the regulation of food intake requires a satiety mechanism; without it, we would overeat and damage our stomachs. The feedback produced by tasting, smelling, and swallowing food provides the first satiety signal, but unless this signal is followed by feedback from the stomach indicating that food has arrived there, the animal will eat again. The stomach contains nutrient detectors that tell the brain how much food has been received. If some food is removed from the stomach, the animal eats enough to replace it, even if the experimenter tries to fool the animal by injecting an equal volume of a saline solution. However, the signal from the stomach must be calibrated; the animal must have eaten the food before in order to learn what its nutritional value is. Although an emergency signal from stretch receptors in the walls of the stomach are carried to the brain by the vagus nerve, the information about the nutrient content seems to be conveyed by means of a hormone.

Several investigators have suggested that cholecystokinin, released by the duodenum when it receives fat-rich food from the stomach, provides a satiety signal. The inhibitory effect of CCK on eating appears to be mediated by receptors in the pylorus. However, studies have shown that CCK has an aversive effect, and that the quantities that must be administered in order to suppress feeding far exceed the levels that occur naturally after eating a meal. CCK and CCK receptors are present in the brain; what they do is not yet known.

The final satiety signal comes from the liver, which detects that nutrients are being received from the intestines. The signal from the liver can even be used to reinforce the consumption of a particular flavor.

NEURAL MECHANISMS

Brain Stem

Ingestive behaviors are phylogenetically ancient; obviously, all our ancestors ate and drank or died. Thus, we should expect that the basic ingestive behaviors of chewing and swallowing are programmed by phylogenetically ancient brain circuits. Indeed, studies have shown that these behaviors can be performed by decerebrate rats, whose brains were transected between the diencephalon and the midbrain (Norgren and Grill, 1982). Of course, they cannot approach and eat food; the experimenters must place food, in liquid form, into their mouth. Decerebrate animals can distinguish between different tastes; they drink and swallow sweet or slightly salty liquids and spit out bitter ones. They even respond to hunger and satiety cues. They drink more sucrose after

having been deprived of food for 24 hours, and they drink less of it if some sucrose is injected directly into their stomachs.

As you learned in Chapter 7, gustatory information reaches the brain through three cranial nerves (the seventh, ninth, and tenth). The first synapse is in the nucleus of the solitary tract, which is situated in the dorsal medulla. This nucleus also receives information from the internal organs, including the stomach and the liver; thus, it is in a position to monitor hunger and satiety signals. The caudal brain stem also appears to contain nutrient-sensitive receptors. Ritter, Slusser, and Stone (1981) injected cold cream into the cerebral aqueduct, which blocked communication between the third and fourth ventricles. Next, they injected a drug called 5-TG (which, like 2-DG, inhibits glucose metabolism) into either the third ventricle or the fourth ventricle. Injections into the fourth ventricle stimulated eating, but injections into the third ventricle (located in the middle of the hypothalamus) had no effect. Thus, it appears that even the brain stem contains the circuitry necessary for integrating hunger and satiety signals and controlling the acceptance or rejection of food.

Scott and his colleagues have performed a series of experiments that indicate that in rats the coding of gustatory information in the brain stem is changed by the physiological condition of the animal and by its prior experience with particular foods. For example, Jacobs, Mark, and Scott (1988) examined the pattern of the response of neurons in the nucleus of the solitary tract to various types of gustatory stimuli. They found that when they induced a sodium deficiency, the response pattern to sodium chloride changed so that it resembled the pattern seen when they presented sucrose. Thus, to a rat with a sodium appetite, "salty" tastes "sweet" (or, as the authors suggest, it simply tastes "good"). In addition, Chang and Scott (1984) found that after animals had developed a conditioned aversion to saccharin by pairing it with injections of lithium chloride, the response pattern for saccharin changed. Normally, the pattern resembled that of sucrose; after the aversion was established, it resembled that of quinine. What was coded as "good" now came to be coded as "bad."

Although coding of "good" and "bad" tastes occurs in the brain stem, conditioned flavor aversions are abolished by lesions of the basolateral amygdala (Kemble and Nagel, 1973; Nachman and Ashe, 1974). Thus, one might expect that the learning takes place in the amygdala, and the changes in the response patterns recorded in the nucleus of the solitary tract simply reflect these changes. However, Mark and Scott (1988) found that pairing saccharin with an injection of lithium chloride changed the response patterns of these neurons in decerebrate rats, even though the animals did not show a conditioned flavor aversion. Thus, we can conclude that although the changes take place in the brain stem, the amygdala is necessary for *expressing* an aversion. The learning takes place in one part of the brain, but another part is required for the learning to affect behavior.

Hypothalamus

Discoveries made in the 1940s and 1950s focused the attention of researchers interested in ingestive behavior on two regions of the hypothalamus: the lateral area and the ventromedial nucleus. For many years investigators believed that these two regions controlled hunger and satiety, respectively; one was the accelerator, and the other was the brake. The basic findings were these: After the lateral hypothalamus was destroyed, animals stopped eating or drinking (Anand and Brobeck, 1951; Teitelbaum and Stellar, 1954). Electrical stimulation of the same region would produce eating, drinking, or both behaviors. Conversely, lesions of the ventromedial nucleus of the hypothalamus produced overeating that led to gross obesity, whereas electrical stimulation suppressed eating (Hetherington and Ranson, 1942). The story was too simple, of course. Although the lateral hypothalamus appears to play a role in the control of food intake, we are not certain that the ventromedial nucleus plays a role in satiety.

Ventromedial Hypothalamus/ Paraventricular Nucleus

One of the most striking effects of a localized brain lesion is the overeating and obesity that is produced by a lesion of the ventromedial hypo-

thalamus (VMH). The most plausible explanation for a lesion causing an increase in eating is that it damages satiety mechanisms in the brain, and this explanation was accepted for many years. However, the *VMH syndrome* (the set of behaviors that accompany these lesions) turns out to be much more complex than a loss of inhibitory control of eating. Animals with VMH lesions are "finicky"; they will not overeat if some quinine is added to their diet (Ferguson and Keesey, 1975). If given a choice of different diets, animals with VMH lesions will primarily overeat carbohydrates (Sclafani and Aravich, 1983). In addition to affecting behavior, VMH lesions disrupt the control of the autonomic nervous system. In particular, they cause an increase in parasympathetic activity of the vagus nerve, which stimulates the secretion of insulin and inhibits the secretion of glucagon and adrenal catecholamines (Weingarten, Chang, and McDonald, 1985). Thus, the liver and adipose tissue of an animal with a VMH lesion are unable to release their nutrients during the fasting phase of metabolism; consequently, the animal *has* to eat to keep up the supply of nutrients in its blood.

The VMH syndrome is complex anatomically as well as behaviorally. Sclafani (1971) made knife cuts parallel to the midline, just lateral to the ventromedial nucleus, and found that the animals overate, just as they do with lesions of the VMH. More detailed studies found that these knife cuts interrupted efferent axons from the paraventricular nucleus (PVN) as well as those from the VMH itself (Gold, Jones, Sawchenko, and Kapatos, 1977). The axons from the PVN pass through the edge of the VMH; thus, VMH lesions disrupt the connections of the PVN.

Kirchgessner and Sclafani (1988) found that the destination of the axons from the VMH and the PVN seems to be the nucleus of the solitary tract and the dorsal motor nucleus of the vagus. (See *Figure 13.9.*) As you know, the nucleus of the solitary tract receives nutrient-related information from the tongue, liver, and stomach; thus, changes in its activity could affect an animal's intake of food. The dorsal motor nucleus of the vagus nerve controls the activity of the parasympathetic axons that stimulate insulin secretion; thus, the increased insulin secretion produced by

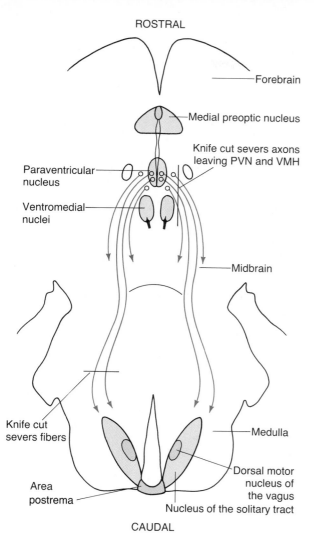

ROSTRAL

Forebrain

Medial preoptic nucleus

Knife cut severs axons leaving PVN and VMH

Paraventricular nucleus

Ventromedial nuclei

Midbrain

Knife cut severs fibers

Medulla

Dorsal motor nucleus of the vagus

Area postrema

Nucleus of the solitary tract

CAUDAL

FIGURE 13.9

An outline of the connections between the paraventricular nucleus, ventromedial nucleus, and the medulla that may be involved in the effects of ventromedial lesions on food intake. (Adapted from Kirchgessner, A.L., and Sclafani, A. *Physiology and Behavior*, 1988, 42, 517–528.)

VMH lesions may be caused by disruption of this pathway.

Most of the research interest in the VMH syndrome in recent years has focused on the role of the paraventricular nucleus. (See *Figure 13.10.*) You learned earlier in this chapter that the PVN is involved in control of the posterior pituitary gland. This nucleus also appears to play an impor-

tant role in carbohydrate intake. Rats, being nocturnal animals, generally sleep and fast during the day; then, when night comes, they take their first big meal. This meal tends to be high in carbohydrates, which are the most easily digested and metabolized nutrients; later meals are higher in fats and protein (Leibowitz, Weiss, and Shor-Posner, 1988). This carbohydrate appetite appears to be under the control of neurons in the paraventricular nucleus.

Two neurotransmitters play an important role in the medial hypothalamus in appetite for carbohydrates. Norepinephrine (NE) stimulates carbohydrate intake, and serotonin (5-HT) inhibits it. Stanley, Schwartz, Hernandez, Hoebel, and Leibowitz (1989) placed a microdialysis probe in the paraventricular nucleus of rats and recorded the level of extracellular NE across the sleep-waking cycle. (Microdialysis was described in Chapter 5.) The investigators found that the level of NE showed a sharp rise just after the onset of the dark phase of the light cycle, at about the time when the animals ate their first meal. (See *Figure 13.11.*)

Leibowitz, Weiss, Yee, and Tretter (1985) found that microinfusion of NE into the PVN stimulates eating, especially of carbohydrates. (See *Figure 13.12.*) In fact, if clonidine (a drug that stimulates noradrenergic α_2 receptors) is continuously infused into the PVN, the animal will overeat and get fat; and if AMPT (a drug that blocks the synthesis of NE) is infused, the animal will undereat and lose weight (Yee, MacLow, Chan, and Leibowitz, 1987). It is not clear whether the effects of NE stimulate eating directly or whether they do so indirectly, by increasing the secretion of insulin by the pancreas. Sawchenko, Gold, and Leibowitz (1981) found that after they cut the branch of the vagus nerve that serves the pancreas, animals showed a smaller intake of food when they put NE in the PVN, which suggests that at least part of the effect may be caused by hormonal changes.

So far, little is known about the control of NE secretion in the PVN. As we saw in Chapter 9 ("Sleep"), the locus coeruleus, the primary source of the noradrenergic axons to the PVN, is itself controlled by two regions of the medulla. Perhaps the activity of the noradrenergic neurons is regulated by signals from nutrient receptors in the

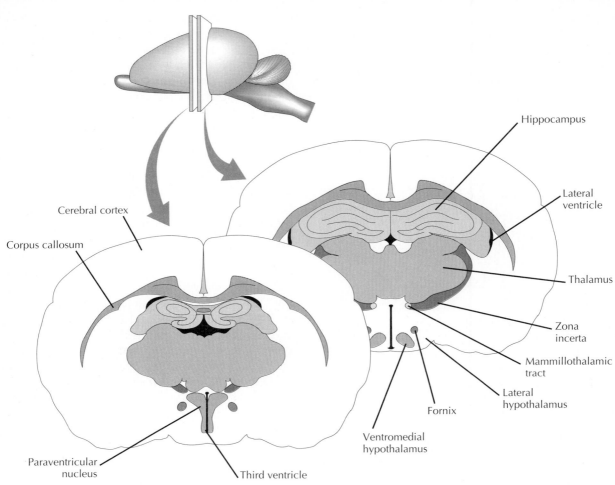

Figure 13.10
Cross sections through the rat brain, showing the location of the paraventricular nucleus, zona incerta, and the ventromedial nuclei of the hypothalamus. (Adapted from Paxinos, G., and Watson, C. *The Brain in Stereotaxic Coordinates.* Sydney: Academic Press, 1982. Redrawn with permission.)

brain stem and liver, by taste signals from the tongue, and by information from the supra-chiasmatic nucleus that the active period of the light-dark cycle has begun.

The release of another transmitter substance, 5-HT, has an effect opposite that of NE: It *inhibits* the eating of carbohydrates. Experiments using the microdialysis procedure suggest that 5-HT is released throughout the hypothalamus when a rat eats its first meal during the active portion of the light-dark cycle (Schwartz, McClane, Hernandez, and Hoebel, 1989; Stanley, Schwartz, Hernandez, Leibowitz, and Hoebel, 1989).

Leibowitz, Weiss, Walsh, and Viswanath (1989) found that infusion of 5-HT into the PVN reduces the amount of carbohydrates that rats eat but has little effect on the intake of fats and proteins. In addition, this suppressive effect occurs only during the animals' first meal, just after the onset of the dark cycle. In contrast, drugs that destroy serotonergic neurons, inhibit the synthesis of 5-HT, or block 5-HT receptors increase food intake, especially carbohydrates (Breisch, Zemlan, and Hoebel, 1976; Saller and Stricker, 1976; Stallone and Nicolaïdis, 1989). A 5-HT agonist, *fenfluramine,* is commonly used to suppress appe-

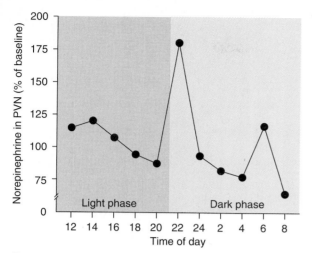

FIGURE 13.11

Extracellular norepinephrine levels in the paraventricular nucleus during the light and dark phases of the day-night cycle, as measured by microdialysis. (Adapted from Stanley, B.G., Schwartz, D.H., Hernandez, L., Hoebel, B.G., and Leibowitz, S.F. *Life Sciences*, 1989, *45*, 275–282.)

tite in obese people who are trying to lose weight. This drug appears to exert its effects by facilitating the effects of 5-HT in the hypothalamus.

Lateral Hypothalamus

For approximately two decades after the discovery that lesions of the lateral hypothalamus abolished eating behavior, most investigators subscribed to the hypothesis that this region was a "feeding center." (Refer to *Figure 13.10.*) During the 1970s researchers finally began to pay attention to the fact that rats with these lesions have other types of behavioral impairments. In fact, they hardly move at all and pay little attention to stimuli around them. Stricker and Zigmond (1976) reviewed the existing evidence and concluded that the behavioral effects of lateral hypothalamic lesions, including the suppression of eating, was produced by damage to dopaminergic axons of the nigrostriatal bundle that passes through this region, which is known to play a role in the control of movement. However, subsequent research showed that neurotoxic lesions made with ibotenic acid, which kills cells while sparing axons passing through the region, produces a long-lasting decrease in food intake and

body weight (Winn, Tarbuck, and Dunnett, 1984; Dunnett, Lane, and Winn, 1985). The lesions did not affect dopamine levels in the forebrain. Thus, the neurons of the lateral hypothalamus, as well as the axons passing through this region, appear to play a role in the control of ingestive behavior.

Another piece of evidence indicating that the lateral hypothalamus plays a role in ingestive behavior is the fact that a neurotransmitter (or neuromodulator) called *neuropeptide Y* is an extremely potent stimulator of food intake (Levine and Morley, 1984). An infusion of this substance into the hypothalamus causes frantic, ravenous eating. Early studies suggested that the site of action of this compound was the paraventricular nucleus (which suggests that this discussion should have been included in the previous section), but recent experiments indicate a more lateral site of action. Stanley, Magdalin, and Leibowitz (1989) used very fine metal cannulas to infuse extremely small quantities (10 μl) of neuropeptide Y into various regions of the hypothalamus. They found that the most effective site was in the mid-lateral hypothalamus. Sahu, Kalra, and Kalra (1988) found that hypothalamic levels of neuropeptide Y are increased by food deprivation and lowered by eating. Beyond that fact, little is known about the

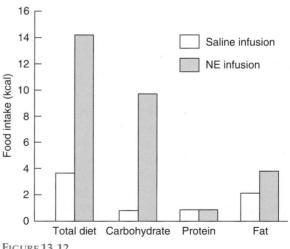

FIGURE 13.12

Effects of infusion of norepinephrine into the paraventricular nucleus on intake of carbohydrate, protein, and fat. (Adapted from Leibowitz, S.F., Weiss, G.F., Yee, F., and Tretter, J.B. *Brain Research Bulletin*, 1985, *14*, 561–567.)

physiological conditions that cause the release of neuropeptide Y or of the neural circuitry responsible for carrying out its effects.

You may recall from Chapter 9 that neuropeptide Y is also the neurotransmitter the thalamus uses to communicate visual information to the suprachiasmatic nucleus. Because eating is one of the behaviors affected by circadian rhythms (which are controlled by the suprachiasmatic nucleus), the use of neuropeptide Y by these two systems may not simply be a coincidence. We can hope that further studies will find connections between neuropeptide Y–sensitive neurons and those that control the behavior of eating.

As I mentioned in the section describing the glucostatic hypothesis, many neurons in the hypothalamus act as glucoreceptors; that is, they change their firing rate when glucose is infused in their vicinity. Most of these glucose-sensitive neurons are located in the lateral hypothalamus (Oomura, 1976). Himmi, Boyer, and Orsini (1988) found that many neurons in the lateral hypothalamus change their firing rate in response to spontaneous fluctuations in the level of glucose in the blood supply to the brain or to fluctuations produced by glucose infusions. These neurons may be involved in the control of eating, in the control of hormones that regulate metabolism, or both.

Rolls and his colleagues (see Rolls, 1986) have studied the response characteristics of single neurons in the lateral hypothalamus and substantia innominata (a nearby region in the basal forebrain). Burton, Rolls, and Mora (1976) found that some neurons located there respond to either the sight or the taste of food, but do so *only if the animal is hungry.* These neurons may be involved in the motivational aspects of eating. In support of this suggestion Rolls, Murzi, Yaxley, Thorpe, and Simpson (1986) found that the firing rate of these neurons was related to sensory-specific satiety. For example, one neuron showed a high rate of firing when the monkey was shown a peanut, a banana, an orange, or a syringe that was used to squirt a glucose solution into its mouth. The animal was then given repeated drinks of the glucose solution. At first, it drank the solution enthusiastically, but after a while, acceptance turned to rejection. At the same time, the neuron responded

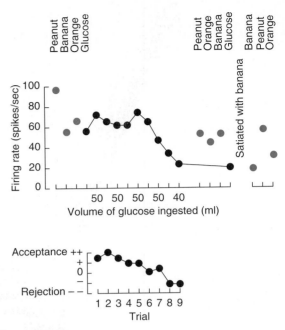

FIGURE 13.13

Sensory-specific satiety. The graph plots the firing rate of a single neuron in a monkey's lateral hypothalamus when the animal is shown various foods. The smaller graph at the right indicates ratings of the monkey's acceptance or rejection of the glucose solution, presented nine times. (Adapted from Rolls, E.T., Murzi, E., Yaxley, S., Thorpe, S.J., and Simpson, S.J. *Brain Research,* 1986, *368,* 79–86.)

less and less when the monkey was shown the syringe. However, the neuron still responded to the sight of a peanut, an orange, or a banana. The monkey was then allowed to eat all the banana it wanted. The neuron stopped responding to the sight of the banana, but it still responded to the sight of the peanut. It pretty much stopped responding to the sight of an orange, too, but perhaps after drinking 440 ml of a glucose solution and eating all the banana one wants, an orange provides less of a flavor contrast than a peanut does. (See *Figure 13.13.*)

*I*NTERIM SUMMARY

The brain stem contains neural circuits that are able to control acceptance or rejection of sweet or bitter foods and can even be modulated by satiation or physiological hunger signals, such as a decrease in glucose metabolism. Neurons in the nucleus of the solitary tract appear to encode "good" and "bad" tastes; they change their response from "saltiness" to "good" when the animal is sodium-deficient, and they change their response from "sweet" to "bad" when saccharin is paired with an injection of lithium chloride. These changes can take place in a decerebrate rat, even though the basolateral amygdala is necessary for the expression of a conditioned flavor aversion.

Lesions of the ventromedial hypothalamus produce overeating and obesity, and electrical stimulation of this area inhibits eating. However, this region is not a simple "satiety center." The lesions make an animal finicky and increase the secretion of insulin (thus forcing the animal to eat more). Some (perhaps most) of the VMH syndrome is caused by damage to fibers from the PVN to the nucleus of the solitary tract and the dorsal motor nucleus of the vagus.

The first meal of the active portion of the dark-light cycle tends to be high in carbohydrates. It is preceded by a large increase in norepinephrine in the PVN. In addition, when NE is infused into the PVN, the animal eats—especially carbohydrates. The response may be a result of changes in the activity of the autonomic nervous system, direct stimulation of circuits that control eating, or both.

Another transmitter substance, 5-HT, has an inhibitory effect on eating in the PVN. This hormone is secreted during mealtime, which suggests that it may play a role in satiety. The most common appetite suppressant, fenfluramine, is a 5-HT agonist.

Lesions of the lateral hypothalamus abolish eating (along with many other behaviors), and stimulation elicits it. Although many of the behavioral effects involve dopamine-secreting axons that pass through this region, experiments with neurotoxic lesions indicate that the lateral hypothalamus, by itself, plays an excitatory role in eating. When infused into the mid–lateral hypothalamus, neuropeptide Y stimulates vigorous eating. The lateral hypothalamus contains glucose receptors and neurons whose firing rate increases when food-related stimuli are presented and the animal is hungry. Studies with sensory-specific satiety show that the activity of these neurons is closely tied to food-related motivation.

EATING DISORDERS

Unfortunately, some people are susceptible to eating disorders. Some people grow obese, even though our society regards this condition as unattractive and in spite of the fact that obese people tend to have more health problems—and to die sooner—than people of normal weight. Other people (especially young women) can become obsessed with losing weight, eating little and increasing their activity level until their body weight becomes extremely low—often fatally so. Has what we have learned about the physiology of appetite helped us understand these conditions?

Obesity

There are undoubtedly many causes of obesity, including learning and innate or acquired differences in metabolism. The behavior of eating, like most other behaviors, is subject to modification through learning. Unfortunately, many aspects of modern, industrialized societies tend to weaken physiological controls over eating. For example, as children we learn to eat what is put on our plates; indeed, many children are praised for eating all that they have been given and punished for failing to do so. As Birch, McPhee, Shoba, Steinberg, and Krehbiel (1987) showed, the effect of this kind of training can be to make children less sensitive to the nutrient content of their diet. As we get older, our metabolic requirements decrease; and if we continue to eat as we did when we were younger, we tend to accumulate fat. The inhibitory signals associated with food consumption are certainly not absolute; they can be overridden by habit or by the simple pleasure of ingesting good-tasting food. In fact, the typical arrangement of meals into courses followed by a dessert inhibits the development of sensory-specific satiety and encourages increased food intake. An earlier section in this chapter, "Social and Environmental Factors," discussed some other environmental variables that can encourage overeating.

Obesity is extremely difficult to treat; the enormous financial success of diet books, fat farms, and weight reduction programs attests to the trouble people have losing weight. Kramer, Jeffery, Forster, and Snell (1989) reported that four to five years after participating in a fifteen-week behavioral weight loss program, fewer than 3 percent of the participants managed to maintain the weight loss they had achieved during the program. Even drastic means such as gastric and intestinal surgery (designed to limit the amount of food that the stomach can hold or to prevent food from being fully digested before it is eliminated) are not the answer. These procedures have risks of their own, often produce unpleasant side effects, and have a failure rate of at least 40 percent (Kral, 1989).

Many psychological variables have been suggested as causes of obesity, including field dependence, lack of impulse control, poor ability to delay gratification, and maladaptive eating styles (primarily eating too fast). However, in a review of the literature Rodin, Schank, and Striegel-Moore (1989) found that none of these suggestions have received empirical support. Rodin and her colleagues also found that unhappiness and depression seem to be the *effects* of obesity, not its causes, and that dieting behavior seems to make the problem worse. (As we shall see later in this section, repeated bouts of weight loss and gain make subsequent weight loss more difficult to achieve.)

One reason that many people have so much difficulty losing weight is that metabolic factors appear to play an important role in obesity. For example, Rodin and her colleagues described the case of a 312-pound woman who joined a weight loss program and managed to lose 120 pounds in a year. Despite the fact that she ate less than 1200 calories a day, she did not lose any more weight, even 18 months later. In fact, many obese people do not eat excessive amounts of food. Rodin and her colleagues found that most studies comparing the amounts of food eaten by obese people and people of normal weight failed to show a significant difference.

Almost all excess body weight is carried in the form of fat. Normally, we carry a certain amount of fat in our long-term nutrient reservoir, making deposits and withdrawals each day during the absorptive and fasting phases of metabolism but keeping the total amount stable. Obesity occurs when deposits exceed withdrawals. We expend energy in two basic ways: through exercise (muscular activity) and through the production of heat. Actually, *most* of our energy expenditure is in the form of heat production; if food intake were kept constant, an obese person would have to increase his or her activity level tremendously in order to lower his or her body weight (Segal and Pi-Sunyer, 1989). Of course, exercise brings with it many benefits, such as cardiovascular fitness and a sense of well-being, so it is a worthwhile endeavor for people of all body weights.

Just as cars differ in their fuel efficiency, so do people. Rose and Williams (1961) studied pairs of people who were matched for weight, height, age, and activity. Some of these matched pairs differed by a factor of two in the number of calories they ate each day. People with an efficient metabolism have calories left over to deposit in the long-term nutrient reservoir; thus, they have difficulty keeping this reservoir from growing. In contrast, people with an inefficient metabolism can eat large meals without getting fat.

Nonobese people respond to overeating very differently from obese people. For example, Sims and Horton (1968) enlisted the participation of some prison inmates in an experiment to determine the effects of overeating on body weight. The subjects, men of normal weight, were fed varied and tasty meals several times a day and were asked to eat all they could. Some participants ate up to 8000 calories a day, an enormous quantity for relatively sedentary people. Their weight gain was rather modest, and at the end of the experiment, when the subjects were permitted to select their own diet, they quickly returned to their normal weights.

Differences in metabolism appear to have a hereditary basis. Stunkard et al. (1986) found that the body weight of a sample of people who had been adopted as infants was highly correlated with their *biological* parents but not with their *adoptive* parents. A similar study comparing adopted people with their full and half siblings (with whom they had not been raised) also obtained evidence for genetic factors in obesity (Sørensen, Price, Stunkard, and Schulsinger, 1989). In a review of the literature Bouchard (1989) concluded that heredity probably played a role in people's resting metabolic rate, in the amount of heat produced by the body after a meal, in the energy expended during exercise, and (perhaps) in the proportion of carbohydrates, proteins, and fats they chose in their diets.

Why are there genetic differences in metabolic efficiency? James and Trayhurn (1981) suggest that under some environmental conditions metabolic efficiency is advantageous. That is, in places where food is only intermittently available in sufficient quantities, being able to stay alive on small amounts of food and to store up extra nutrients in the form of fat when food becomes available for a while is a highly adaptive trait. Therefore, people's metabolic rates may reflect the nature of the environment experienced by their ancestors. For example, physically active lactating women in Gambia manage to maintain their weight on only 1500 calories per day (Whitehead et al., 1978). This efficiency allows people to survive in environments in which food is scarce. However, in a society that produces an abundance of food, an inefficient metabolism is a definite advantage.

Another factor—this one nonhereditary—can influence people's metabolism. Many obese people diet and then relapse, thus undergoing large changes in body weight. Some investigators have suggested that starvation causes the body's metabolism to become more efficient. For example, Brownell, Greenwood, Stellar, and Shrager (1986) fed rats a diet that made them become obese and then restricted their food intake until their body weights returned to normal. Then they made the rats fat again and reduced their food intake again. The first time, the rats became fat within 46 days and returned to normal within 21 days. The second time, they became fat in only 14 days but required 46 days to lose the excess weight. Clearly, the experience of gaining and los-

ing large amounts of body weight altered the animals' metabolic efficiency.

Steen, Oppliger, and Brownell (1988) obtained evidence that the same phenomenon (which we can call the "yo-yo" effect) takes place in humans. They measured the resting metabolic rate in two groups of high school wrestlers: those who fasted just before a meet and binged afterwards, and those who did not. (The motive for fasting just before a match is to qualify for a lower-weight group, where the competition is presumably less challenging.) The investigators found that wrestlers who fasted and binged had a resting metabolic rate 14 percent lower than those who did not. Possibly, these people will have difficulty maintaining a normal body weight as they get older.

In normal animals overeating causes a rise in metabolic rate, which partly compensates for the increased intake of calories. Rothwell and Stock (1979) fed rats a very palatable diet consisting of supermarket "junk" foods such as potato chips and cookies, which caused them to increase their daily caloric intake greatly. Despite an average caloric increase of 80 percent, weight gain was only 27 percent higher than that of control animals. For this effect to occur, the animals would have had to increase their energy expenditure by approximately 100 percent. Indeed, their resting oxygen consumption was consistently higher than that of control animals. However, the increase was probably not caused by an increase in physical activity, because the animals were housed in pairs in small cages, and they would have had to walk 6 km per day to expend this much energy.

This phenomenon occurs in humans, as well. Welle, Nair, and Campbell (1989) had human subjects overeat by 1600 calories per day for ten days. At the end of that time their metabolic rate had increased by 22 percent. Even a single meal—or stimuli associated with eating—can cause a rise in metabolic rate. LeBlanc and Cabanac (1989) placed human subjects in an chamber so that they could continuously monitor their oxygen consumption and, thereby, calculate their metabolic rate. They found that eating a sugar pie or tasting it, chewing it, and spitting it out again caused an increase in metabolic rate. Even when the subjects simply went through the motions of eating—

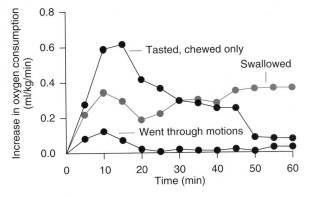

FIGURE 13.14

Effects of eating a sugar pie, tasting and chewing it only, or simply going through the motions on the metabolic rate of human subjects, as measured by oxygen consumption. (Adapted from LeBlanc, J., and Cabanac, M. *Physiology and Behavior*, 1989, 46, 479–482.)

moving their hands to their mouths and making chewing and swallowing motions—their metabolic rates increased slightly. (See *Figure 13.14*.)

What are the physiological differences between people with efficient and inefficient metabolisms? So far, no one knows for sure. Research with laboratory animals has focused on specialized adipose cells that convert calories of food directly into heat. These cells are especially important for hibernating animals, who must warm up before they can wake in the spring. Heat production by this tissue is called ***nonshivering thermogenesis*** (*thermo,* "heat"; *genesis,* "creation"). These specialized fat cells are rich in mitochondria, which serve as sites of fuel breakdown and heat production (Nichols, 1979). The mitochondria give the fat a brown appearance, which gives this tissue the name ***brown adipose tissue.*** (The fat tissue that comprises the body's long-term nutrient reservoir is called *white* adipose tissue.)

The metabolism of these cells is controlled by β-noradrenergic receptors on their membranes (Bukowiecki, Folléa, Vallières, and Leblanc, 1978); thus β-noradrenergic agonists such as norepinephrine or isoproterenol activate nonshivering thermogenesis (heat production), and β-noradrenergic antagonists such as propranolol inhibit it. Rothwell and Stock (1979)

found that injections of propranolol reduced the resting oxygen consumption of the rats eating the rich supermarket diet but not that of the normally fed rats. In addition, injection of norepinephrine, which activates brown adipose tissue, caused more of a temperature rise in the skin of these rats.

In rats, feeding-induced thermogenesis appears to be mediated primarily by the activity of the brown adipose tissue. For example, Glick, Teague, and Bray (1981) found that a single meal increased the metabolism of brown adipose tissue by up to 200 percent. Studies have shown that the brown adipose tissue of an obese strain of rats does not respond to a meal (Triandafillou and Himms-Hagen, 1983); thus, at least one form of genetic obesity is accompanied by deficient meal-induced thermogenesis.

The excitatory effect of a meal on the metabolic activity of brown adipose is controlled by the medial hypothalamus. After the medial hypothalamus has been surgically destroyed, a meal no longer produces a rise in the temperature of the brown adipose tissue (Hogan, Himms-Hagen, and Coscina, 1985). The PVN appears to be the most critical region. Freeman and Wellman (1987) found that electrical stimulation of the PVN increased the temperature of brown adipose tissue, and Amir (1990) confirmed these findings using an infusion of glutamate, which stimulates neurons but not axons passing through the area.

What about human obesity? Although humans do possess some brown adipose tissue, investigators disagree about its role in meal-induced thermogenesis and obesity (Himms-Hagen, 1980; Blaza, 1983). Clearly, metabolic differences are an important cause of human obesity, but the sources of these differences are not yet known.

Anorexia Nervosa/Bulimia Nervosa

Most people, if they have an eating problem, tend to overeat. However, some people, especially young adolescent women, have the opposite problem: They eat too little, even to the point of starvation. This disorder is called ***anorexia nervosa.*** The literal meaning of the word *anorexia* suggests a loss of appetite, but people with this disorder are usually interested in—even preoccupied with—food. They may enjoy preparing meals for others to consume, collect recipes, and even hoard food that they do not eat. Broberg and Bernstein (1989) presented anorexic and lean (but nonanorexic) young women with a warm, appetizing cinnamon roll. They cut the roll and said that they could eat it if they wanted. For the next 10 minutes the experimenters withdrew blood samples and analyzed the insulin content. They found that both groups of subjects showed an increase in insulin level; surprisingly, the increase was even higher in the anorexic subjects. Thus, we cannot conclude that anorexics are simply unresponsive to food. (See *Figure 13.15.*) Incidentally, as you might expect, the normal subjects ate the roll, but the anorexics did not, saying that they were not hungry.

Although anorexics may not be oblivious to the effects of food, they express an intense fear of becoming obese, which continues even if they become dangerously thin. Many exercise by cycling, running, or almost constant walking and pacing. Sometimes, their control of food intake fails, and they gorge themselves with food, a phenomenon known as **bulimia** (from *bous*, "ox," and *limos*,

"hunger"). These binges are usually followed by self-induced vomiting or use of laxatives, along with feelings of depression and guilt (Mawson, 1974; Halmi, 1978). Sometimes, bulimia occurs by itself, without anorexia, in which case it is referred to as *bulimia nervosa.*

The fact that anorexia nervosa is seen primarily in young women has prompted both biological and social explanations. Most psychologists favor the latter, concluding that the emphasis our society places on slimness—especially in women—is responsible for this disorder. However, the success of psychotherapy is not especially encouraging; Patton (1989) reported that four years after being treated, only half of the patients can be considered fully recovered. Twenty-five percent are improved, and the remaining 25 percent still have severe problems. About one patient in thirty dies of the disorder. Many anorexics suffer from osteoporosis, and bone fractures are common. When the weight loss becomes severe enough, they cease menstruating. Two disturbing reports (Artmann, Grau, Adelman, Schleiffer, 1985; Lankenau, Swigar, Bhimani, Luchins, and Quinlon, 1985) indicate that CT scans revealed enlarged ventricles and widened sulci, which indicates loss of brain tissue. The widened sulci, but not the enlarged ventricles, apparently return to normal after recovery.

As you might suspect, many investigators have suggested that anorexia and bulimia may be caused by biochemical or structural abnormalities in the brain mechanisms that control metabolism or eating. In a review of the literature Fava, Copeland, Schweiger, and Herzog (1989) reported that studies have found evidence for changes in NE, 5-HT, and opioids in people with anorexia nervosa, and changes in NE and 5-HT in people with bulimia nervosa. Many studies have reported changes in endocrine levels of anorexic patients, but these changes are probably effects of the disorder, not causes. In most cases, when a patient recovers, the endocrine system returns to normal. The authors also report that the anorexic drug fenfluramine is often successful in treating bulimia nervosa, but no reliable treatment has been found for anorexia nervosa.

Anorexia nervosa is a serious condition; understanding its causes is more than an academic

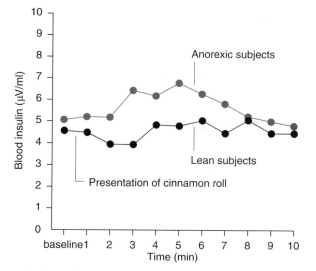

FIGURE 13.15
Effects of the sight and smell of a warm cinnamon roll on insulin secretion in anorexic women and thin, nonanorexic women. (Adapted from Broberg, D.J., and Bernstein, I.L. *Physiology and Behavior*, 1989, *45*, 871–874.)

matter. We can hope that research on the biological and social control of feeding and metabolism will help us understand this puzzling and dangerous disorder.

INTERIM SUMMARY

Two sets of eating disorders, obesity and anorexia/bulimia nervosa, present serious health problems. Although environmental effects, such as learning to eat everything on the plate and arranging food in appetizing courses, may contribute to overeating, the most important cause appears to be an efficient metabolism, which permits fat to accumulate easily. Metabolic rates are controlled by hereditary and environmental factors. Ironically, dieting—especially repeated bouts of weight changes—may promote an increase in metabolic efficiency and make further weight loss more difficult to achieve. The "yo-yo" effect has been demonstrated both in rats and humans.

When we overeat, our metabolic rate goes up, which helps burn off some of the additional calories. In rats the most important furnace for these calories is the brown adipose tissue, whose activity is regulated by the VMH, through its control of the sympathetic axons. However, the physiological causes of the differences in people's metabolism are not yet known.

Anorexia nervosa is a serious—even life-threatening—disorder. Although anorexic patients avoid eating, they often remain preoccupied with food, and their insulin level rises when they are presented with an appetizing stimulus. Researchers are beginning to study possible abnormalities in the regulation of transmitter substances and neuropeptides that seem to play a role in normal control of feeding to see whether medical treatments can be discovered.

CONCLUDING REMARKS

As I said in the introduction to this chapter, less is known about the system variables involved in the control of eating than in the control of drinking. This difference is not due to a lack of effort on the part of researchers; in fact, more people are studying the physiology of hunger than the physiology of thirst. The problem is that regulating our nutrient reservoirs is more complicated than regulating the concentration of the interstitial fluid and the volume of the blood plasma. We must have adequate supplies of carbohydrates, proteins, and fats to fulfill our present needs, and we must also have enough of these substances stored away to tide us over for several days should food not be available. There are many different factors that produce hunger and many that produce satiety. Thus, because changes in one factor can compensate for changes in another, it is impossible to study just a single factor in isolation.

A complete understanding of the physiology of hunger will not be acheived easily, but I do believe that it will be achieved. And with it will come an understanding of the causes of eating disorders such as obesity and anorexia nervosa.

In the next chapter we shift our focus from the study of regulatory mechanisms to the study of the brain mechanisms that make it possible for us to profit from experience—to learn and remember.

NEW TERMS

absorptive phase
   (of metabolism) p. 405
anorexia nervosa p. 430
brown adipose tissue p. 430
bulimia p. 431
cephalic phase p. 412
cholecystokinin (CCK) p. 418
conditioned flavor aversion p. 410

fasting phase
   (of metabolism) p. 404
fatty acid p. 403
glucagon p. 403
glucostatic hypothesis p. 411
glycerol p. 403
glycogen p. 402
insulin p. 402

intraperitoneal (IP) p. 414
ketone p. 405
neuropeptide Y p. 425
nonshivering
   thermogenesis p. 430
sensory-specific satiety p. 410
sham feeding p. 416
triglyceride p. 403

SUGGESTED READINGS

Keesey, R.E., and Powley, T.L. The regulation of body weight. *Annual Review of Psychology,* 1986, *37,* 109–134.

Le Magnen, J. *Hunger.* Cambridge, England: Cambridge University Press, 1985.

Ritter, R.C., Ritter, S., and Barnes, C.D. *Feeding Behavior: Neural and Humoral Controls.* New York: Academic Press, 1986.

Stricker, E. *Handbook of Behavioral Neurobiology. Vol. 10.: Neurobiology of Food and Water Intake.* New York: Plenum Press, 1990.

Walsh, B.T. *Eating Disorders.* Washington, D.C., American Psychiatric Press, 1988.

Winick, M. *Control of Appetite.* New York: John Wiley & Sons, 1988.

14

Anatomy of Memory

*E*xperiences change us; encounters with our environment alter our behavior, presumably by modifying our nervous system. Until recently, the search for the neural basis of memory has seemed disappointingly slow. The brain is complex, and so is learning. Although the individual changes that occur within the cells of the brain may be relatively simple, the brain consists of many billions of neurons. Therefore, isolating and identifying the particular changes that are responsible for a particular memory is exceedingly difficult. Similarly, although the elements of a particular learning task may be simple, its implications for an organism may be complex. The behavior that the investigator observes and measures may be only one of many that change as a result of an experience. However, despite the difficulties, the long years of work finally seem to be paying off. New approaches and new methods have evolved from old ones, and real progress has been made in understanding the anatomy and physiology of learning and remembering.

This chapter discusses research on the anatomy of learning; it describes investigations that have attempted to determine which parts of the brain are involved in learning. Chapter 15 discusses what we have learned about the structural and biochemical changes that occur in the nervous system when learning takes place.

THE NATURE OF MEMORY

We use the word *memory* as if it described a tangible object—a note we make to ourselves and put away for future reference. However, when we say we *store* memories and later *retrieve* them, we are speaking metaphorically. Although it is convenient to describe memories as if they were notes placed in filing cabinets, this is certainly not the way experiences are reflected within the brain. Experiences are not "stored"; they change the way we perceive, perform, think, and plan. They do so by physically changing the structure of the nervous system, altering neural circuits that participate in perceiving, performing, thinking, and planning.

As I said in Chapter 2, the primary function of the brain is to move the muscles—to produce useful behaviors. The primary function of the ability to learn is to develop behaviors that are adapted to an ever-changing environment. The ability to learn permits us to find food when we are hungry, warmth when we are cold, companions when we are lonely. It also permits us to avoid objects or situations that might harm us. However, the fact that the ultimate function of learning is a useful change in behavior does not mean that learning takes place only in the parts of the brain that control movement. Learning can take at least three basic forms: perceptual learning, stimulus-response learning, and motor learning. More complex forms of learning also exist; for example, we have the ability to remember the *relations* between large numbers of objects and events, including the many different stimuli (and our responses to them) that constitute particular episodes in our lives. As we will see, this category of learning has been given many names, and investigators still disagree about its exact characteristics. For convenience, I will refer to it as relational learning. Let us look at each of these types of learning.

Perceptual learning is the ability to learn to recognize stimuli that have been seen before and to distinguish them from similar ones. The primary function of this type of learning is the identification and categorization of objects (including other members of our own species) and situations. Unless we have learned to recognize something, we cannot learn how we should behave with respect to it—we will not profit from our experiences with it, and profiting from experience is what learning is all about.

Each of our sensory systems is capable of perceptual learning. We can learn to recognize objects by their visual appearance, the sounds they make, how they feel, or how they smell. We can recognize people by the shape of their faces, the movements they make when they walk, or the sound of their voices. When we hear people talk, we can recognize the words they are saying and, perhaps, their emotional state. As we shall see, perceptual learning appears to be accomplished by changes in the sensory association cortex. That is, learning to recognize complex visual stimuli involves changes in the visual association cortex, learning to recognize complex auditory stimuli involves changes in the auditory association cortex, and so on. (Very simple stimuli, such as changes in brightness, do not require the neocortex; learning that involves these stimuli can be accomplished by subcortical components of the sensory systems.)

Stimulus-response learning is the ability to learn to perform a particular behavior when a particular stimulus is present. The behavior could be an automatic response such as a defensive reflex, or it could be a complicated sequence of movements that was learned previously. Stimulus-response learning includes two major categories of learning that have been studied by psychologists: *classical conditioning* and *instrumental conditioning*.

Classical conditioning is a form of learning in which an unimportant stimulus acquires the properties of an important one. It involves an *association between two stimuli.* A stimulus that previously had little effect on behavior becomes able to evoke a reflexive, species-typical behavior. For example, we flinch when we see a balloon being overinflated near our face. The flinch is a species-typical defensive reaction that serves to protect our eyes. Normally, this reaction occurs when we hear a loud noise, when something rapidly approaches our face, or when our eyes or the skin around them is touched; we do not have to learn to make this response. We respond this way when we see an overinflated balloon because of our prior experience with bursting balloons. Sometime in the past, probably when we were children, an overinflated balloon burst near our face, and the blast of air elicited a defensive flinch. Through classical conditioning the stimulus that preceded the blast of air—the sight of an overinflated balloon—became an elicitor of flinching.

The names that have been assigned to the stimuli and responses that constitute classical

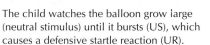

The child watches the balloon grow large (neutral stimulus) until it bursts (US), which causes a defensive startle reaction (UR).

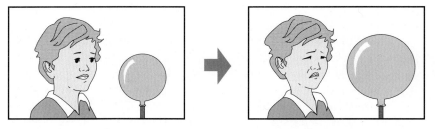

After the child's first experience with a bursting balloon, the mere sight of an inflating balloon (CS) elicits a defensive reaction (CR).

Figure 14.1
The process of classical conditioning.

conditioning are shown in Figure 14.1. I will use these terms repeatedly in this chapter and in Chapter 15, so it is worth your while learning them now. The blast of air, the original eliciting stimulus, is called the **unconditional stimulus** (US): It unconditionally elicits the species-typical response. The response of flinching is called the **unconditional response** (UR). After a person has had a few experiences with bursting balloons, the sight of the inflated balloon—the **conditional stimulus** (CS)—comes to elicit flinching, which is now called the **conditional response** (CR): The response is conditional on the pairing of the conditional and unconditional stimuli. (See **Figure 14.1.**)

Classical conditioning occurs when a neutral stimulus is followed by one that automatically elicits a response. It enables organisms to learn to make species-typical responses under new conditions. Thus, classical conditioning serves to prepare an organism for a forthcoming event. For example, a warning signal can permit the organism to defend itself against harm; stimuli associated with a potential mate can cause it to emit a response that serves as a sexual display; and stimuli associated with food can cause secretion of saliva, digestive juices, and insulin. (We saw examples of classically conditioned responses of the digestive system in Chapter 13.)

A particularly important effect of classical conditioning is the establishment of **conditioned emotional responses.** After having had pleasant or unpleasant experiences with particular objects, with particular people, or in particular locations, we experience emotional reactions when we again encounter these objects, people, or places. For example, if we encounter someone we had an unpleasant argument with, the sight of that person (or the sound of his or her voice) is likely to produce some of the same reactions of the autonomic nervous system that occurred during the argument. We feel the effects of these responses, and we recognize the presence of an unpleasant emotion.

How does classical conditioning work? Figure 14.2 shows a simplified neural circuit that could account for this type of learning. I will use an example that I will discuss in more detail later in this chapter, a defensive eyeblink response of a rabbit.

A small puff of air directed toward the eye can trigger this reflex; thus, a puff of air serves as a US. There are many potential CSs. The diagram shows two possible ones, a 1000-Hz tone and a 5000-Hz tone. For the sake of simplicity, we will pretend that the auditory system contains two neurons, each one responding with action potentials when one of these two tones is detected. We will also pretend that the somatosensory system contains only one neuron, which responds when the eye receives a puff of air. Finally, we will pretend that the motor system contains three neurons that control three responses: blinking, ear wiggling, and nose twitching. In a real nervous system the somatosensory and auditory systems could detect a very large number of different stimuli, and the motor system could control a very large number of different responses. However, the principles are much easier to understand in a simple diagram. (See **Figure 14.2.**)

Now let us see how the circuit works. If we present a 1000-Hz tone, we find that the animal makes no reaction, because the synapses connecting the tone-sensitive neuron with the neurons of the motor system are weak. However, if we present a puff of air to the eye, the eye blinks. This occurs because the process of evolution has provided a strong synapse between the somatosensory neuron and the motor neuron that causes a blink (synapse P, for "puff"). The synapse is strong because it is useful to close one's eyelid when one's eye is threatened. To establish classical conditioning, we first present the 1000-Hz tone and then almost immediately follow it with a puff of air. After we repeat these pairs of stimuli several times, we find that we can dispense with the air puff; the 1000-Hz tone produces the blink all by itself.

Over forty years ago, Hebb proposed a rule that might explain how neurons are changed by experience in a way that would cause changes in behavior (Hebb, 1949). The **Hebb rule** says, "When an axon of cell A is near enough to excite cell B or repeatedly or persistently takes part in firing it, some growth process or metabolic change takes place in one or both cells such that A's efficiency, as one of the cells firing B, is increased" (p. 62). How would the Hebb rule apply to our circuit? If the 1000-Hz tone is presented first, then weak

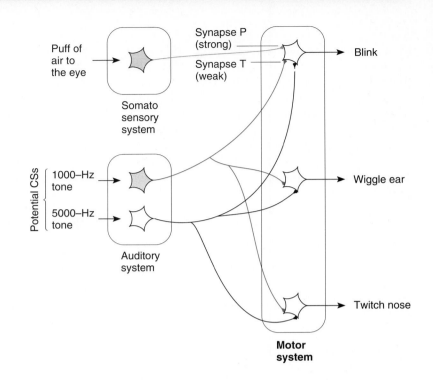

FIGURE 14.2
A simple neural model of classical
conditioning. When the 1000-Hz
tone is presented just before the puff
of air to the eye, synapse T is
strengthened.

synapse T (for "tone") becomes active. If the puff
is presented immediately afterward, then strong
synapse P becomes active and makes the motor
neuron fire. The act of firing then strengthens all
synapses with the motor neuron *that have just been
active*. Of course, this means synapse T. After several pairings of the stimuli, and several incre-
ments of strengthening, synapse T becomes
strong enough to cause the motor neuron to fire by
itself. Learning has occurred. (See *Figure 14.2.*)

When Hebb formulated his rule, he was unable to determine whether it was true or false.
Now, finally, enough progress has been made in
laboratory techniques that the strength of individual synapses can be determined, and investigators are studying the physiological bases of learning. In fact, Chapter 15 is devoted to such studies.

The second major class of stimulus-response
learning is *instrumental conditioning* (also called
operant conditioning). Whereas classical conditioning involves automatic, species-typical responses, instrumental conditioning involves behaviors that have been learned. And whereas
classical conditioning involves an association between two stimuli, instrumental conditioning in-

volves an *association between a response and a stimulus.* Instrumental conditioning is a more flexible
and adaptive form of learning. It permits an organism to adjust its behavior according to the consequences of that behavior. That is, when a behavior is followed by favorable consequences, the
behavior tends to occur more frequently; when it
is followed by unfavorable consequences, it tends
to occur less frequently. Collectively, "favorable
consequences" are referred to as *reinforcing stimuli*, and "unfavorable consequences" are referred
to as *punishing stimuli.* For example, a response
that enables a hungry organism to find food will
be reinforced, and a response that causes pain will
be punished.

Because most physiological investigations of
instrumental conditioning have been devoted to
reinforcement rather than punishment, I will restrict my discussion to this phenomenon. Briefly
stated, reinforcement causes changes in an animal's nervous system that increase the likelihood
that a particular stimulus will elicit a particular response. For example, when a hungry rat is first
put in an operant chamber, it is not very likely to
press the lever mounted on a wall. However, if it

does press the lever, and if it receives a piece of food immediately afterward, the likelihood of making another response increases. Put another way, reinforcement causes the sight of the lever to serve as the stimulus that elicits the lever-pressing response. It is not accurate to say simply that a particular *movement* becomes more frequent. If no lever is present, a rat that has learned to press one will not wave its paw around in the air. The *sight of a lever* is needed to produce the response. Thus, the process of reinforcement establishes a connection between neural circuits involved in perception (the sight of the lever) and those involved in movement (the act of lever pressing).

How might instrumental conditioning work? Figure 14.3 provides a possible model. Our rat's visual system contains two neurons. One fires when the rat sees a lever, and the other fires when it sees a water bottle. (Again, we will keep things simple. Besides providing the brain with only a few neurons, we will ignore the role of hunger, which would certainly have an important effect

on learning and performance.) The motor system contains three neurons. The first produces the movements needed to press the lever, the second makes the rat's ears wiggle, and the third makes it stand on its hind legs. Another neuron is part of a reinforcement system. This neuron is activated when good things happen. For example, if the rat is hungry and it receives some food, that is a good thing. (I will say a little more about the reinforcement system later in this chapter and will discuss it in much more detail in Chapter 16, which deals with reinforcement and addictive behaviors.) (See *Figure 14.3.*)

I am sure you see the similarity between Figure 14.3 and Figure 14.2. Initially, synapse L (for "lever") is too weak to cause the motor neuron to fire. Thus, the sight of the lever does not make the rat press it. However, eventually the rat happens to wander over and press the lever. (Psychologists have developed special procedures to get rats to perform unlikely behaviors such as lever pressing, but there is no reason to concern ourselves

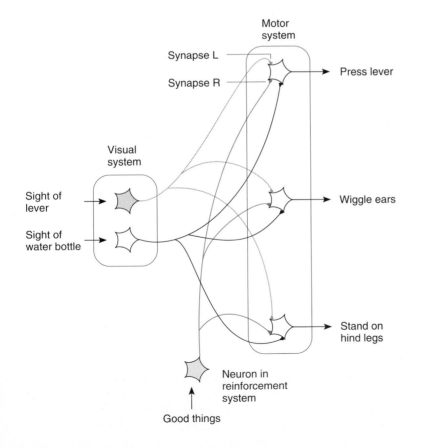

FIGURE 14.3
A simple neural model of instrumental conditioning. When the animal sees the lever, presses it, and something good happens, the activity of the reinforcement system strengthens synapse L.

with this issue here.) The lever press causes a piece of food to be delivered to the rat, who quickly eats it. This "good thing" is detected by the reinforcement system, which makes synapses with all the motor neurons. When synapse R (for "reinforcement") is active, it causes the strengthening of all synapses that have just fired *if the postsynaptic neuron has also just fired*. In this case it is synapse L on the neuron that produces the lever press that gets strengthened. Once synapse L is sufficiently strengthened, the sight of the lever elicits the lever press. (See *Figure 14.3.*)

The third major category of learning, *motor learning,* is actually a special form of stimulus-response learning; for that reason I will not discuss it separately in this chapter. For simplicity's sake, we can think of perceptual learning as the establishment of changes within the sensory systems of the brain, stimulus-response learning as the establishment of connections between sensory systems and motor systems, and motor learning as the establishment of changes within motor systems. But, in fact, motor learning cannot occur without sensory guidance from the environment. For example, most skilled movements involve interactions with objects: bicycles, pinball machines, knitting needles, and so on. Even skilled movements we make by ourselves, such as solitary dance steps, involve feedback from the joints, muscles, vestibular apparatus, eyes, and contact between the feet and the floor. Motor learning differs from other forms of learning primarily in the degree to which new forms of behavior are learned; the more novel the behavior, the more that neural circuits in the motor systems of the brain must be modified. (See *Figure 14.4.*)

The three forms of learning I have described so far consist primarily of changes in one sensory system, between one sensory system and the motor system, or in the motor system. But obviously, learning is usually more complex than that. We are able to learn the *relations* among individual stimuli. For example, a somewhat more complex form of perceptual learning involves connections between different areas of the association cortex. When we hear the sound of a cat meowing in the dark, we can imagine what a cat looks like and what it would feel like if we stroked its fur. Obviously, the neural circuits in the auditory associa-

tion cortex that recognize the meow are somehow connected to corresponding circuits in the visual association cortex and the somatosensory association cortex. These interconnections, too, are accomplished as a result of learning.

Perception of spatial location also involves learning about the relations among many stimuli. For example, consider what we must learn in order to become familiar with the contents of a room. Of course, we must learn to recognize each of the objects. In addition, we must learn the relative locations of the objects with respect to each other. Thus, when we are located in a particular place in the room, our perceptions of these objects and their locations relative to us tell us exactly where we are.

Other types of learning, such as our ability to remember a sequence of events, requires that we keep track of not only individual stimuli but also the order in which they occur. As we will see later in this chapter, a special system that involves the hippocampus and related structures appears to perform coordinating functions that are necessary for many types of learning that go beyond single regions of the cerebral cortex.

INTERIM SUMMARY

Learning produces changes in the way we perceive, act, think, and feel. It does so by producing changes in the nervous system in the circuits responsible for perception, in those responsible for the control of movement, and in connections between the two.

Perceptual learning consists primarily of changes in perceptual systems that make it possible for us to recognize stimuli so that we can respond to them appropriately. Stimulus-response learning consists of connections between perceptual and motor systems. The most important forms are classical and instrumental conditioning. Classical conditioning occurs when a neutral stimulus is followed by an unconditional stimulus (US) that naturally elicits an unconditional response (UR). After this pairing, the neutral stimulus becomes a conditional stimulus (CS); it now elicits the conditional response (CR) by itself. If these responses

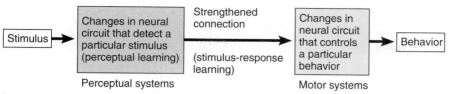

FIGURE 14.4

An overview of perceptual, stimulus-response, and motor learning.

include significant activity of the autonomic nervous system, we call them conditioned emotional responses.

Instrumental conditioning occurs when a response is followed by a reinforcing stimulus, such as a drink of water for a thirsty animal. The reinforcing stimulus increases the likelihood that the other stimuli present when the response was made will evoke the response. Both forms of stimulus-response learning may occur as a result of strengthened synaptic connections, as described by the Hebb rule.

Motor learning, although it may primarily involve changes within neural circuits that control movement, is guided by sensory stimuli; thus, it is actually a form of stimulus-response learning. Relational learning is the most complex form of learning. It includes the ability to recognize objects through more than one sensory modality, to recognize the relative location of objects in the environment, and to remember the sequence in which events occurred during particular episodes.

PERCEPTUAL LEARNING

This section describes research on perceptual learning. Because visual learning has received more attention than any other form of perceptual learning, I will concentrate on this sensory modality.

Visual Learning

In mammals with large and complex brains objects are recognized visually by circuits of neurons in the visual association cortex. As we saw in Chapter 6, the primary visual cortex receives information from the lateral geniculate nucleus of the thalamus. Within the primary visual cortex individual modules of neurons analyze information from restricted regions of the visual scene that pertain to movement, orientation, color, binocular disparity, and spatial frequency. Information about each of these attributes is collected in subregions of the prestriate cortex, which surrounds the primary visual cortex (striate cortex). For example, area V3 is devoted to the analysis of orientation, area V4 to the analysis of color, and area V5 to the analysis of movement.

After analyzing particular attributes of the visual scene, the subregions of the prestriate cortex send the results of their analysis to the inferior temporal cortex, where the information is combined, producing neural activity that corresponds to the perception of particular three-dimensional objects. (See *Figure 14.5*.)

Lesion Studies

Long ago, Klüver and Bucy (1939) discovered that monkeys with bilateral lesions of the temporal lobes (including subcortical structures as well as the neocortex) had difficulty perceiving visual stimuli. They referred to the phenomenon as "psychic blindness." The animals could move around in their environment and could see well enough to pick up small objects. However, they had great difficulty *recognizing* what they saw. They would pick up items from a tray containing small edible and inedible objects, bring them to their mouth, and then eat the pieces of food and drop the pieces of hardware. They also showed no signs of fear to visual stimuli that normal monkeys avoid, such as snakes.

Mishkin (1966) showed that if visual information were prevented from reaching the inferior

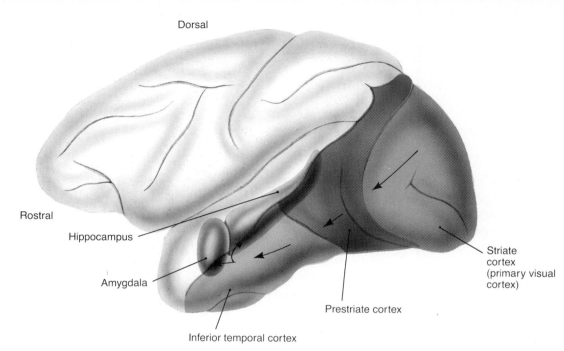

Dorsal

Rostral

Hippocampus

Amygdala

Inferior temporal cortex

Prestriate cortex

Striate cortex (primary visual cortex)

FIGURE 14.5
The major divisions of the visual cortex of the rhesus monkey. The arrows indicate the primary direction of the flow of information.

temporal cortex, monkeys lost the ability to distinguish between different visual patterns. First, he removed the striate cortex on one side of the brain and tested the animals' ability to discriminate between visual patterns. They performed well. Next, he removed the contralateral inferior temporal cortex; again, no deficit. Finally, he cut the corpus callosum, which isolated the remaining inferior temporal cortex from the remaining primary visual cortex. This time, the animals could no longer perform the visual discrimination task. Therefore, we can conclude that the inferior temporal cortex is necessary for visual pattern discrimination and that it must receive information from the primary visual cortex. (See *Figure 14.6.*)

Subsequent studies have shown that the two major regions of the inferior temporal cortex perform different functions. The region bordering the prestriate cortex is necessary for perception of simple shapes; its removal impairs monkeys' ability to discriminate among different two-dimensional patterns (Blake, Jarvis, and Mishkin, 1977). In contrast, removal of the region closer to the

rostral end of the temporal lobe area impairs monkeys' ability to discriminate among different *three-dimensional* objects. Mishkin and his colleagues (reported by Mishkin, 1982) trained monkeys on a *delayed nonmatching-to-sample task*. They showed monkeys a small three-dimensional object (the *sample*) from a large collection of "junk objects" assembled for that purpose. The monkeys moved the object aside to uncover and eat a peanut placed in a small well underneath. After a 10-second delay the experimenters showed the monkeys two objects: the one they had just seen and a new one. If the monkeys moved the *new* object, they found another peanut; but none was to be found under the old one. A different stimulus was used on each trial. This task is easy for monkeys to perform; they learn it within a few days. (See *Figure 14.7.*)

After the preliminary training Mishkin and his colleagues removed the inferior temporal cortex bilaterally. After surgery the animals required 1500 trials to relearn the task; and even then, they did not quite attain the criterion of 90 percent correct. After administering these retraining trials,

Left hemisphere   Right hemisphere

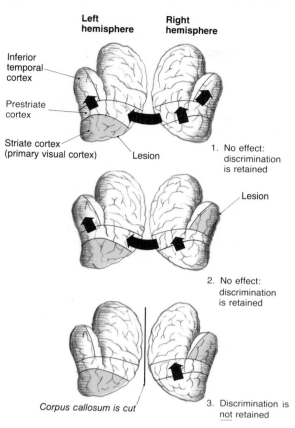

Inferior temporal cortex

Prestriate cortex

Striate cortex (primary visual cortex)   Lesion

Lesion

Corpus callosum is cut

1. No effect: discrimination is retained

2. No effect: discrimination is retained

3. Discrimination is not retained

FIGURE 14.6

The procedure used by Mishkin (1966). Not all of the control groups used in the experiment are shown here. (Adapted from Mishkin, M., in *Frontiers in Physiological Psychology*, edited by R.W. Russell. New York: Academic Press, 1966.)

the experimenters tested the monkeys with delays longer than 10 seconds. The monkeys with lesions of the inferior temporal cortex performed poorly when the delay was lengthened. Thus, the inferior temporal cortex plays an important role in a monkey's ability to remember a particular three-dimensional object.

Recording Studies

The conclusions from the lesion studies are supported by an electrophysiological study by Fuster and Jervey (1981), who obtained evidence that neurons in the inferior temporal cortex retain information about a just-perceived stimulus. They turned on a colored light (yellow, green, red, or blue) behind a translucent disk (the sample stimulus), turned it off, and, after a delay interval, turned on yellow, green, red, and blue lights behind four other disks (the matching stimuli). (See *Figure 14.8.*) If the monkey pressed the disk whose color matched the one it had just seen, it received a piece of food.

While the monkeys were performing this task, the experimenters recorded the activity of single neurons in the inferior temporal cortex. Some neurons responded selectively to color, maintaining a high response rate during the delay interval. For example, Figure 14.9 shows data from a neuron that responded to red light, but not to green light, during a 16-second delay interval. The horizontal lines above each graph represent

Movable shutter

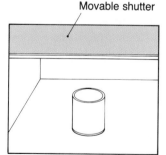

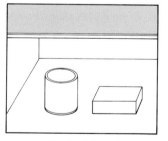

Sample interval
Shutter is opened, monkey obtains food from well underneath by moving object aside

Delay interval
Shutter is closed

Choice interval
Shutter is opened, food is hidden under novel object

FIGURE 14.7

The delayed nonmatching-to-sample procedure used by Mishkin and his colleagues (reported by Mishkin, 1982).

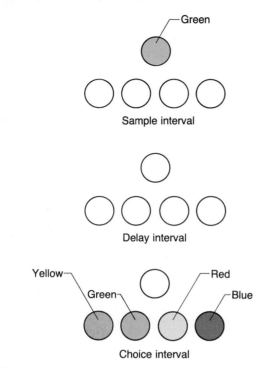

FIGURE 14.8

The delayed matching-to-sample procedure used by Fuster and Jervey (1981).

individual trials; vertical tick marks represent action potentials. The graphs beneath the horizontal lines are sums of the individual trials, showing the total responses during successive intervals. As you can see, when the sample stimulus consisted of a red light, the neuron became active and remained active even after the sample stimulus went off. (See *Figure 14.9.*) Under normal conditions a stimulus causes a neuron to respond briefly. Thus, the sustained response during the delay interval suggests that the neuron is participating in remembering a just-perceived stimulus.

More recently, Fuster (1990) modified the delayed matching-to-sample task slightly, placing a small gray symbol in the middle of the sample disk. The shape of the symbol indicated whether or not the matching response would be based on the color of the disk. That is, the gray symbol told the monkeys whether they should pay attention to the color. Fuster found neurons in the inferior temporal cortex that responded to various aspects of the task. For example, some neurons re-

sponded only when one of the gray symbols was present. The most interesting neurons were those that responded to a particular color even during the delay interval but did so only when the gray symbol indicated that the color was relevant and therefore should be remembered. These results provide even more support for the suggestion that visual memories are maintained in the inferior temporal cortex.

Some neurons in the inferior temporal cortex show remarkable specificity in their response characteristics, which suggests that they are part of circuits that detect the presence of specific stimuli. For example, Desimone, Albright, Gross, and Bruce (1984) found neurons in this region that responded to such stimuli as hands and faces. Figure 14.10 shows the response of a neuron that responded best to a profile view of another monkey's face. Other neurons responded best to full face views. (See *Figure 14.10.*)

Rolls and his colleagues (reported in Rolls, 1989) have studied the responses of neurons in the inferior temporal cortex of monkeys to the sight of monkey's faces. Neurons that specifically respond to the sight of faces are not scattered throughout the visual association cortex; instead, they are localized in a particular region, which suggests that face recognition may be a specialty of that region.

Neurons that respond to the sight of faces tend to have excitatory responses with a latency of 80–160 msec after the presentation of the stimulus, and the responses of some of them remain constant even if the picture is blurred or changed in color, size, or distance (Rolls and Baylis, 1986). (See *Figure 14.11.*) Baylis, Rolls, and Leonard (1985) found that most of these neurons are sensitive to differences between faces, which suggests that the circuits of which they are a part are responsible for a monkey's ability to recognize particular individuals.

Rolls, Baylis, Hasselmo, and Nalwa (1989) found that as monkeys became familiar with particular faces, the response characteristics of some face-sensitive neurons in the inferior temporal cortex changed. They presented monkeys with pictures of human and monkey faces on the screen of a video monitor. They found that many cells showed changes in their response character-

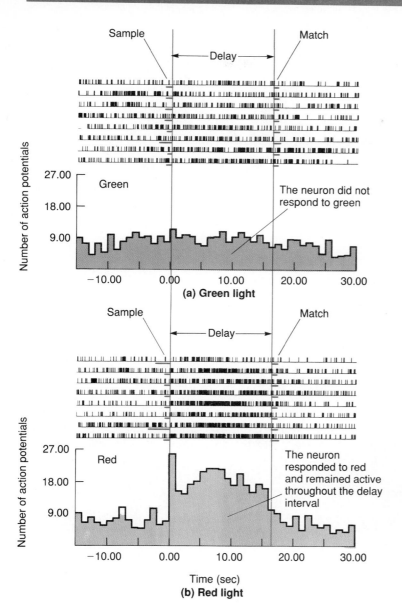

Sample · Match

←— Delay —→

Number of action potentials

27.00

18.00

9.00

Green

The neuron did not respond to green

−10.00   0.00   10.00   20.00   30.00

(a) Green light

Sample · Match

←— Delay —→

Number of action potentials

27.00

18.00

9.00

Red

The neuron responded to red and remained active throughout the delay interval

−10.00   0.00   10.00   20.00   30.00

Time (sec)

(b) Red light

FIGURE 14.9

Responses of a single unit during the presentation of the sample stimulus, the delay interval, and the presentation of matching stimuli in the experiment outlined in Figure 14.8. (From Fuster, J.M., in *Conditioning: Representation of Involved Neural Functions*, edited by C.D. Woody. New York: Plenum Press, 1982.)

istic when new faces were shown to the monkey. For example, in one experiment they showed the same set of five faces, one at a time, for several trials. Most neurons showed rather stable responses. Then the experimenters introduced a new face into the series. After one or two presentations the response pattern to the familiar faces changed. This finding suggests that learning caused a "rewiring" of the neural circuits.

Modeling the Brain's Ability to Learn: Neural Networks

The results of the electrical-recording study by Rolls and his colleagues strongly suggest that the inferior temporal cortex is an important site of visual perceptual learning, and that perception is not simply a result of analysis by prewired circuits. That is, experience changes the wiring, and these wiring changes represent what is learned.

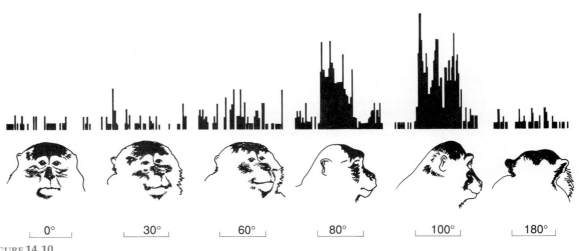

0°   30°   60°   80°   100°   180°

FIGURE 14.10

Responses of a single neuron in the inferior temporal cortex to photographs of a monkey's face, oriented at different angles to the viewer. Each stimulus was presented for 2.5 seconds, as indicated by the color bars. The height of the vertical black bars indicates the number of the times the neuron fired during each interval of time. (From Desimone, R., Albright, T.D., Gross, C.G., and Bruce, D. *Journal of Neuroscience*, 1984, *4*, 2051–2062. Reprinted by permission of the *Journal of Neuroscience*.)

(a)

(b)

FIGURE 14.11

Examples of photographs of faces that produced similar responses in face-sensitive neurons in the inferior temporal cortex. (a) Faces of different sizes. (b) Faces of reduced and reversed contrast. (From Rolls, E.T., and Baylis, G.C. *Experimental Brain Research*, 1986, *65*, 38–48.)

But why should the presentation of a new face alter the way neurons respond to faces that the monkey is already familiar with?

A possible answer comes from a recent approach to modeling the function of neural circuits, called *neural networks.* Investigators have discovered that when they construct a network of simple elements, interconnected in certain ways, the network does some surprising things. (The authors of neural networks use computers to model them; they do not construct actual networks with electrical components.) The elements are given properties like those of neurons. They are connected to each other through junctions similar to synapses. Like synapses, these junctions can have either excitatory or inhibitory effects. When an element receives a critical amount of excitation, it sends a message to the elements with which it communicates, and so on. Some of the elements of a network have input lines that can receive signals from the "outside," which could represent a sensory organ or the information received from another network. Other elements have output lines, which communicate with other networks or control muscles, producing behavior. Thus, particular patterns of input can represent particular stimuli, and particular patterns of output can represent responses. (See *Figure 14.12.*)

Neural networks can be taught to recognize particular stimuli. For example, an author of a neural network can specify that the connections between elements are strengthened by an unconditional stimulus or by a reinforcement system. Or they can use other techniques to teach a network to recognize a particular stimulus. In this case the networks receive only one input pattern (there is no "reinforcing stimulus"), but inhibitory elements within the circuit refine the response the network makes to a particular input. Networks such as these are "shown" a particular stimulus by being presented with a particular pattern of activity on the input lines, and their output is monitored. The first time a particular stimulus is presented, the output elements respond weakly and nonspecifically; but after it is presented several times, a strong and reliable output pattern emerges. The network can be shown more and more stimuli, producing unique output patterns for each of them.

The characteristics of neural networks are similar to many of those exhibited by real nervous systems, which is what makes them exciting to scientists interested in the neural basis of learning. For example, neural networks show generalization, discrimination, and graceful degradation. *Generalization* refers to the ability to recognize similarities between stimuli. For example, suppose that a network has learned to recognize a few very different stimuli. If we then show it a stimulus that resembles one it knows, its output pattern will closely resemble the pattern it produces when it is shown the stimulus it already knows. *Discrimination* refers to the ability to recognize differences between stimuli. If we show a network several similar stimuli, it will learn to distinguish among them, producing very different output patterns to each of them. Finally, *graceful degradation* refers to the fact that random damage to elements of a neural network or to their connections ("synapses") does not bring the network to a crashing halt. Instead, the performance of the network deteriorates, at a level proportional to the amount of damage. These three phenomena, gen-

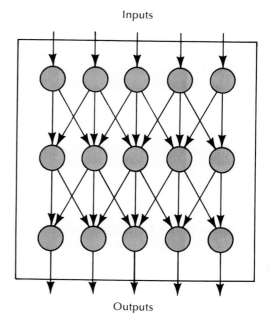

Inputs

Outputs

FIGURE 14.12

A very simple neural network, used as a model of brain function. The connections (arrows) can be excitatory or inhibitory, depending on the particular model.

eralization, discrimination, and graceful degradation, also characterize the way that our brains work.

Obviously, because the brain is made of networks of neurons, learning occurs in neural networks. The question is whether the neural networks that scientists construct work the same way that the brain does, and the only way to find that out is to learn the detailed anatomy of real neural circuits and the physiological characteristics of individual neurons and synaptic connections. As more is learned about these subjects, more realistic models of neural networks can be constructed. The reason that neural networks have captured the imagination of neuroscientists is that even though investigators have been working with them for only a few years, and thus the state of the art is still relatively primitive, the resemblance of these model networks to the workings of the nervous system is uncanny. In just a few years investigators have constructed many models, including those that recognize patterns, learn names of objects, control the finger movements used by a typist, read words, and learn the past tenses of English verbs (Rumelhart, McClelland, and the PDP Research Group, 1986). Of course, with only a few years of experience with this new approach we cannot be sure that it will live up to its promise. In my decision to describe the approach to you, I am obviously betting that it will; I expect to be writing about neural networks for some years to come.

Investigators studying the properties of neural networks emphasize that they are dealing with the *microstructure* of the brain—with the functions performed by individual modules. The brain contains a large number of networks—probably many thousands of them—each devoted to performing individual functions. The networks probably exist in a sort of hierarchy, with some controlling the functions of others and regulating the exchanges of information between them. Thus, understanding the operations of individual neural networks will never reveal all we need to know about the functions of the brain. We will also need to know the organization of the brain—the relations between the individual networks of which it is constructed. We will need to know the *macrostructure* of the brain as well as its microstruc-

ture. In fact, most of this chapter is devoted to macrostructure.

So what about the face-sensitive neurons in the inferior temporal cortex? Rolls (1989) suggests that the findings that he and his colleagues have obtained are exactly what would be predicted if they were recording from neurons that were elements in a neural network devoted to learning to recognize particular faces. Somehow, other neural networks in the prestriate cortex do a rough sorting, sending information about stimuli that resemble faces to the face-sensitive region of the inferior temporal cortex. Because of the type of input they receive, and because of the details of their circuitry, the neural networks in this region learn to discriminate among different faces and continue to recognize them (that is, demonstrate generalization) even when the face is near or far, clear or blurry. The output of this region is sent to other parts of the brain, where learning about the significance of these faces takes place. For example, some faces might belong to aggressive monkeys that should be avoided, some might belong to friendly sex partners, and so on.

Other Types of Perceptual Learning

Although visual learning has received more attention than other forms of perceptual learning, it is clear that perceptual learning of stimuli presented to the other sense modalities involves changes in neural networks located in other areas of sensory association cortex. I will discuss two examples, one of auditory learning and one of tactual learning.

An experiment by Diamond and Weinberger (1989) showed that an auditory learning task affects the responses of single neurons in the auditory association cortex. They presented cats with a series of tones of different frequencies and recorded the rate of neural firing to each frequency. Then they trained the animals in a classical conditioning task in which the CS was a tone of 14 kHz. They found that the training changed the pattern of the neurons' response to tones of various frequencies. Figure 14.13 shows one such cell. The pretraining response is shown in black, and the posttraining response is shown in color. As you

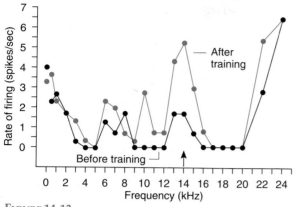

FIGURE 14.13

Rate of firing of a single neuron in the auditory association cortex to tones of various frequencies before and after classical conditioning. The CS was a tone of 14 kHz (arrow). (Adapted from Diamond, D.M., and Weinberger, N.M. *Behavioral Neuroscience*, 1989, *103*, 471–494.)

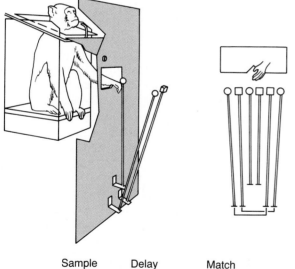

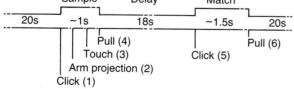

FIGURE 14.14

The experimental procedure used by Koch and Fuster (1989). (From Koch, K.W., and Fuster, J.M. *Experimental Brain Research*, 1989, *76*, 292–306.)

can see, the training more than doubled the responsiveness of this neuron to a 14-kHz tone. (See *Figure 14.13.*)

Koch and Fuster (1989) performed an interesting experiment in which they recorded the electrical activity of single neurons in the somatosensory association cortex of the parietal lobe. They taught monkeys a tactile delayed matching-to-sample task. The animals were placed in front of a panel that had a cutout through which they could reach and feel (but not see) solid objects mounted on the ends of movable rods. A click indicated that a trial started. They then reached out and felt the sample (a sphere or a cube), pulled it toward them, and let it go. The sample then retracted out of reach. After an 18-second delay interval, another click indicated that the choice was to be made. The monkeys reached through the hole, felt for the stimulus that matched the sample, and pulled it. If the response was correct, they received a drink of fruit juice through a tube positioned near their mouths. (See *Figure 14.14.*)

Koch and Fuster recorded the activity of single neurons in the somatosensory association cortex during the performance of the task. Like Rolls and his colleagues, they found that the activity of the neurons was similar to what would be expected if this part of the brain contained a neural network responsible for perceptual learning. They found that some of the neurons responded selectively to one stimulus or the other; some of them even continued their activity during the delay interval. Because the discriminative stimuli were not present at that time, the continued activity appears to reflect a memory of the just-perceived stimulus.

*I*NTERIM SUMMARY

Perceptual learning occurs as a result of changes in synaptic connections within the sensory association cortex. Damage to a monkey's inferior temporal cortex—the highest level of visual association cortex—disrupts the animal's ability to perceive three-dimensional objects, as tested by a delayed nonmatching-to-sample test. Electrical-recording studies have shown that some neurons in the inferior temporal cortex encode the information presented during the sample period of a delayed matching-to-sample task and continue to fire during the delay interval. Other recording studies have shown that some neurons respond preferentially to particular complex stimuli, including faces. When new stimuli are presented, the response patterns of some neurons in the inferior temporal cortex change, which indicates that "rewiring" may be taking place.

Recently, investigators have begun to construct models of neural networks, in which interconnected elements that have some of the known properties of neurons are presented with "stimuli" encoded by particular patterns of inputs to the network. Although these networks are very simple, they have been found to be capable of simulating many characteristics of the brain, including perceptual and stimulus-response learning.

Although most attention has been paid to visual learning, studies with auditory and somatosensory learning have yielded similar results. One study found that presenting a particular tone as a CS increased the sensitivity of some neurons in the auditory association cortex to this tone. Another study found that a tactile delayed matching-to-sample task produced sustained activity in some neurons that persisted throughout the delay interval, presumably representing the memory for that stimulus.

STIMULUS-RESPONSE LEARNING

Most learning occurs as a result of the establishment of new connections between perceptual systems and motor mechanisms; thus, most learning comes under the heading of stimulus-response learning. Even "pure" perceptual learning often involves making responses, although the responses may not be apparent to observers. For example, when we see something new, we might not make a response that other people can see, but we may *think* about it, and thinking is a form of behavior. Because much of our thinking involves the use of words (talking to ourselves "in our head"), I

will postpone further discussion of this topic until Chapter 17, which considers the nature of human communication.

Although instrumental conditioning is probably the most important form of stimulus-response learning in the daily lives of most species of mammals, more progress has been made in the understanding of the neurobiology of classical conditioning and relational learning. Thus, my discussion will necessarily reflect the attention that these forms of learning have received. This section will discuss two forms of classical conditioning, and the next one will discuss the role of the hippocampal system in relational learning.

Conditioned Emotional Responses

One part of the brain—the amygdala—appears to play a special role in physiological and behavioral reactions to objects and situations that have special biological significance, such as those that warn of pain or other unpleasant consequences or signify the presence of food, water, salt, potential mates or rivals, or infants in need of care. As we have already seen in previous chapters, the amygdala is involved in the effects of pheromones on reproductive physiology and behavior (including maternal behavior), in the control of aggression, in salt appetite, and in the learning and expression of conditioned flavor aversions. This section will describe research on the role of the amygdala in classical conditioning involving aversive stimuli.

In the first section of this chapter I described a special category of classical conditioning, the conditioned emotional response. A conditioned emotional response consists of a set of physiological and behavioral responses that are produced by a CS that has been paired with an aversive stimulus, such as one that produces pain. Aversive stimuli elicit many responses, both specific and nonspecific. For example, a painful stimulus applied to an animal's paw will elicit a specific defensive reflex: The animal will move its leg in a way that withdraws its paw from the source of the pain. But other, nonspecific responses will also occur. Some of these responses are controlled by the autonomic nervous system. For example, the animal's pupils will dilate, its heart rate will increase, its blood pressure will increase, its adrenal glands will secrete stress-related hormones, and so on. Other nonspecific responses involve the control of skeletal muscles. Depending on the animal's species and the nature of the aversive stimulus, it may run away or it may stop moving and "freeze" in place.

If an animal learns to make a specific response that avoids contact with the aversive stimulus (or at least minimizes its painful effect), most of the nonspecific responses will eventually disappear. That is, if the animal learns a successful coping response, the emotional responses will no longer occur. For example, if an animal learns to retract its paw every time a warning stimulus occurs and learns how to avoid receiving a painful stimulus, it will no longer show pupillary dilation, changes in heart rate, or any of the other responses it showed at the beginning of the training. The situation is under control and no longer provokes an emotional reaction. In contrast, if an aversive stimulus follows a CS no matter what the animal does, the animal will continue to display a conditioned emotional response. You can imagine your own emotional response to the buzzing sound of a flying wasp if on several occasions you were stung after hearing this sound.

Emotional responses can be conditioned to a variety of stimuli, simple or complex. For example, the perception of a simple stimulus such as the buzz of a wasp can probably be accomplished by subcortical structures and does not require the presence of the auditory cortex. However, the perception of a complex visual stimulus such as the sight of a menacing stranger armed with a loaded revolver would certainly require the participation of the inferior temporal cortex. Thus, different perceptual systems are connected to the neural circuits that control the emotional responses. To simplify the task of identifying the circuits responsible for the acquisition of conditioned emotional responses, most investigators have used simple stimuli that can be analyzed subcortically. Presumably, what they learn is relevant to situations including more complex stimuli. The results of their studies should help us understand the nature of human emotional reactions and perhaps provide hints about ways that harmful effects of stress can be reduced.

The role of the amygdala in conditioned emotional responses was suspected for a long time. For example, Roldan, Alvarez-Pelaez, and Fernandez deMolina (1974) found that electrical stimulation of the amygdala elicited defensive reactions, including "initial attention, retraction and lowering of the head, flattening of ears, crouching, dilation of pupils, piloerection [erection of hairs in the animal's fur], and growling or hissing" (p. 780).

Anatomical evidence suggests that the amygdala serves as a focal point between sensory systems and effector systems that are responsible for hormonal, autonomic, and behavioral components of conditioned emotional responses. Because stimulus-response learning occurs as a result of changes in the strength of connections between sensory and motor systems, the amygdala would seem to be a good place to begin to look for neural circuits involved in learning a conditioned emotional response.

LeDoux and his colleagues have extensively studied classically conditioned emotional responses in rats by using an auditory stimulus as a CS and a brief electrical shock to the feet as a US. In their studies they presented an 800-Hz tone for 10 seconds and then delivered a brief (0.5 second) shock to the floor on which the animals were standing. (See *Figure 14.15.*) By itself, the shock produces an *unconditional* emotional response: The animal jumps into the air, its heart rate and blood pressure increase, and its adrenal glands secrete catecholamines and corticosterone. The experimenters presented several pairings of CS and US, which establishes classical conditioning.

The investigators tested conditioned emotional responses the next day by presenting the CS

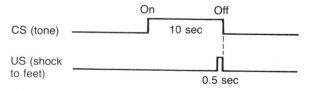

FIGURE 14.15
The procedure used to produce conditioned emotional responses.

(the 800-Hz) tone several times and measuring the animals' blood pressure and heart rate and observing its behavior. In normal animals the CS produces an increase in heart rate and blood pressure and behavioral arrest—a species-typical defensive response called *freezing*. That is, the animals act as if they were expecting to receive a shock.

Although the amygdala receives auditory information from both the thalamus and the auditory cortex, for simple auditory stimuli the thalamic input appears to be the important one. Lesions of the primary auditory cortex do not disrupt the learning of a conditioned emotional response, but thalamic lesions do (LeDoux, Sakaguchi, and Reis, 1984). The critical part of the thalamus appears to be the *medial division of the medial geniculate nucleus* (MGM). (See *Figure 14.16.*) As you will recall from Chapters 4 and 7, the medial geniculate nucleus of the thalamus receives auditory information from the inferior colliculus and passes it on to the primary auditory cortex. However, unlike the rest of the medial geniculate nucleus, the MGM projects only to other subcortical structures, including the amygdala (LeDoux, Ruggiero, and Reis, 1985). LeDoux, Iwata, Pearl, and Reis (1986) found that axon-sparing neurotoxic lesions of the MGM disrupted the acquisition of both autonomic and behavioral conditioned emotional responses (blood pressure changes and freezing, respectively). The lesions had no effect on defensive learning cued by a visual stimulus, so the effect appears to be specific to the auditory system.

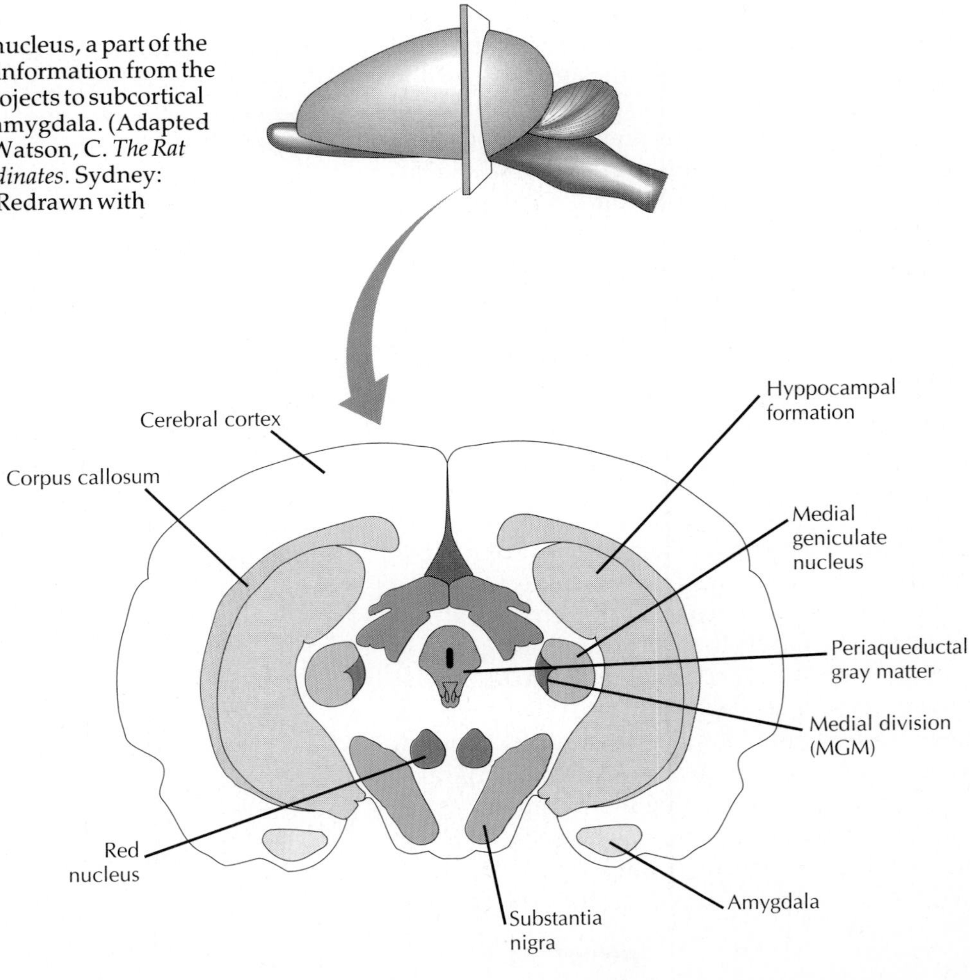

FIGURE 14.16

The medial geniculate nucleus, a part of the thalamus that receives information from the auditory system and projects to subcortical regions, including the amygdala. (Adapted from Paxinos, G., and Watson, C. *The Rat Brain in Stereotaxic Coordinates.* Sydney: Academic Press, 1982. Redrawn with permission.)

Iwata, LeDoux, Meeley, Arneric, and Reis (1986) found that disrupting the connection between the MGM and the amygdala prevents the learning of a conditioned emotional response to an auditory stimulus. The critical part of the amygdala appears to be the *central nucleus*. Iwata, Chida, and LeDoux (1987) found that stimulation of the central nucleus with an excitatory amino acid caused increases in heart rate and blood pressure. In fact, long-term stimulation of the central amygdala produces gastric ulcers (Henke, 1982), and its destruction helps prevent the development of ulcers in a stressful situation (Ray, Henke, and Sullivan, 1987).

The central nucleus of the amygdala sends axons to many regions of the brain, including the basal forebrain, lateral hypothalamus, periaqueductal gray matter, and medulla. LeDoux, Iwata, Cicchetti, and Reis (1988) made neurotoxic lesions of two of these projection regions, the lateral hypothalamus and the caudal periaqueductal gray matter, and examined their effects on the autonomic and behavioral components of a conditioned emotional response. They found that lesions of the lateral hypothalamus interfered with the change in blood pressure, whereas lesions of the periaqueductal gray matter interfered with the freezing response. Thus, different mechanisms, both under the control of the central nucleus of the amygdala, are responsible for the autonomic and behavioral components of conditioned emotional responses.

Recent anatomical studies have shown that the central nucleus of the amygdala projects to other parts of the brain involved in reactions to aversive stimuli: adrenergic cells in the ventrolateral medulla, which are involved in control of the sympathetic nervous system; the dorsal motor nucleus of the vagus nerve, which is involved in control of the parasympathetic nervous system; and the parvocellular division of the paraventricular nucleus of the hypothalamus, which is involved in the secretion of stress-related hormones (Cassell and Gray, 1989; Danielsen, Magnuson, and Gray, 1989; Gray, Carney, and Magnuson, 1989). It seems likely that these connections, too, are involved in the expression of conditioned emotional responses.

Although most of the experiments investiga-ting the role of the central nucleus of the amygdala in conditioned emotional responses have used auditory stimuli, results from studies using stimuli of other sensory modalities are consistent with the ones I have reviewed. For example, lesions of the central nucleus disrupt conditioned responses evoked by visual or olfactory stimuli that have been paired with a foot shock (Hitchcock and Davis, 1986; Sananes and Campbell, 1989).

Having traced a neural circuit necessary for learning a conditioned emotional response to an auditory CS (MGM to central nucleus of the amygdala to various effector mechanisms), we can ask where the structural changes responsible for this learning are located. If you recall the discussion of the neural basis of classical conditioning earlier in this chapter, you will remember that a likely mechanism involves the interaction between synapses conveying information about the CS and the US. Thus, we would predict that learning takes place in a location that receives both auditory (tone) and somatosensory (foot shock) information.

LeDoux, Ruggiero, Forest, Stornetta, and Reis (1987) performed an anatomical study to find where information concerning these two senses might overlap. Using anterograde-tracing techniques, they found that neurons in both the inferior colliculus and the dorsal spinal cord sent axons to the medial division of the medial geniculate nucleus (MGM). (These two regions provide auditory and somatosensory information, respectively.) Thus, perhaps the synaptic changes responsible for emotional responses classically conditioned to an auditory stimulus take place in the MGM.

These anatomical findings are consistent with the results of a single-unit-recording study by Weinberger and his colleagues (reported by Weinberger, 1982) showing that neurons in the MGM increased their responsiveness to the auditory CS after this stimulus was paired with an aversive US. Figure 14.17 shows the responses of a single neuron in this nucleus during ten trials of a control procedure and ten trials of conditioning (two trials per graph). During the control procedure the tone (CS) and the shock (US) were presented at random intervals and were not paired. During conditioning the tone was followed by the

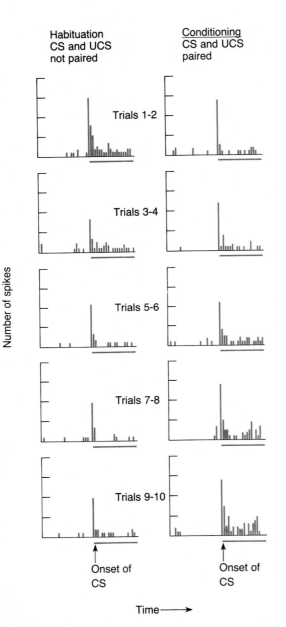

Habituation
CS and UCS
not paired

Conditioning
CS and UCS
paired

Trials 1-2

Trials 3-4

Trials 5-6

Trials 7-8

Trials 9-10

Number of spikes

Onset of
CS

Onset of
CS

Time ⟶

FIGURE 14.17
Responses of a single neuron in the magnocellular
medial geniculate nucleus during aversive classical
conditioning. (From Weinberger, N.M., in
Conditioning: Representation of Involved Neural Functions,
edited by C.D. Woody. New York: Plenum Press,
1982.)

shock. The data show that during the control procedure the neuron initially responded to the tone
(indicated by the color horizontal line), but this response soon habituated. However, once conditioning trials began, the neuron quickly began
responding during the tone. (See *Figure 14.17.*)

More recently, Supple and Kapp (1989) recorded the activity of neurons in the MGM while
they trained the animals with a *differential classical
conditioning procedure.* One tone (the CS$^+$) was always followed by a shock; the other (the CS$^-$) was
not. Eventually, the animals made conditional responses to the CS$^+$ but not to the CS$^-$. Before
training took place, neurons in the MGM responded identically to the two stimuli, but after
learning had taken place, the investigators found
two categories of neurons: one that responded
when the CS$^+$ was presented, and one that responded when the CS$^-$ was presented. Thus, it
appears that the learning procedure caused the
development of circuits of neurons in the MGM
that signaled the presence of the two conditional
stimuli.

Applegate, Frysinger, Kapp, and Gallagher
(1982) found that the responsiveness of neurons
in the central nucleus also changes during classical conditioning. (See *Figure 14.18.*) Because the
amygdala receives input from neurons in the thalamus, we cannot be sure whether these results
indicate that learning modifies synaptic connections in the amygdala, too, or whether they simply reflect the changes that take place in the thalamus. Possibly, changes could be occurring in both
locations.

In the past few years the amygdala has received much attention from neuroscientists interested in learning and memory. Because of its position as a focal point in the neural mechanisms
involved in learned responses to aversive stimuli,
it will undoubtedly continue to receive this attention. (See *Figure 14.19.*)

Conditioned Nictitating
Membrane Response

In recent years several laboratories have been investigating the neural circuitry responsible for a
classically conditioned defensive response in the
rabbit: the nictitating membrane response. The

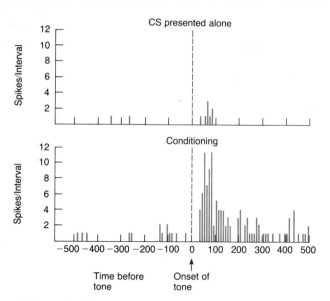

FIGURE 14.18

Multiple-unit activity in the central nucleus of the amygdala during habituation of the orienting response and during conditioning and extinction of the bradycardia response. (Adapted from Kapp, B.S., Gallagher, M., Applegate, C.D., and Frysinger, R.C., in *Conditioning: Representation of Involved Neural Functions*, edited by C.D. Woody. New York: Plenum Press, 1982.)

advantage of this response is that the neural circuitry is simple; in fact, more is known about it than any other learned response in mammals. The work is important because it raises the possibility that studies in the near future will be able to identify the biochemical and structural changes in neurons that are responsible for memory (the top-

ic of Chapter 15). When the pathways necessary for a particular form of learning are understood, investigators know where to look for changes. The synaptic changes that are responsible for the classically conditioned nictitating membrane response are not yet known, but what has been discovered so far tends to support the Hebb rule.

The experiments cited in this section use a procedure developed by Gormezano (1972). The *nictitating membrane* (from *nictare*, "to wink") is a tough inner eyelid possessed by many mammals, birds, and fish. Each eye has one nictitating membrane, which moves laterally across the eye, from the nasal side to the temporal side. When a stimulus threatens the animal's eye, the nictitating membrane sweeps across the eye, covering it. In order to record movement of the membrane, the experimenter attaches a loop of nylon thread to its edge and then places the animal in a restraining cage. A lever mounted on a small movement transducer is attached to the loop of thread. When the membrane moves, it causes the lever to move, which activates the transducer. (See *Figure 14.20.*) Most investigators send an electrical signal from the transducer to a computer and use it to monitor the response.

Unconditional responses of the nictitating membrane are elicited by presenting a somatosensory stimulus to the eye, such as a puff of air. The conditional stimulus is usually a tone. In most cases the experimenter turns on the tone (CS) and then 250 msec later turns on the unconditional stimulus (US). The CS and the US are then terminated simultaneously. At first, the animal makes only unconditional responses, but then it begins

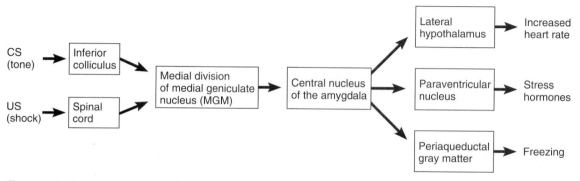

FIGURE 14.19

A summary of some of the circuitry involved in an auditory conditioned emotional response.

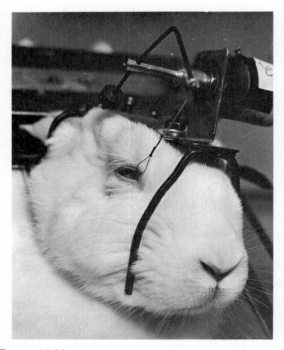

FIGURE 14.20

A rabbit prepared for measurement of the nictitating membrane response.

The circuit responsible for the unconditional response is simple. Somatosensory information concerning the unconditional stimulus (such as a puff of air) is transmitted through the fifth cranial nerve (trigeminal nerve) to a particular region of the *sensory trigeminal nucleus* (Berthier and Moore, 1983). Second-order neurons in this nucleus send axons to the *accessory abducens nucleus,* which contains the motor neurons that cause contraction of the retractor bulbi. (See the dotted black line in *Figure 14.22.*)

For classical conditioning to take place, there must be a convergence of information concerning the CS and the US in the same location. That convergence takes place in the cerebellum. Two laboratories independently discovered that lesions in either of two places within the cerebellum—a particular region of the cerebellar cortex or the ***interpositus nucleus***—abolished conditional nictitating membrane responses but not unconditional ones. That is, although the rabbits would continue to make unconditional nictitating

to move its nictitating membrane in anticipation of the puff of air. These anticipatory responses are conditional responses, and they gradually occur earlier and earlier in the interval between the CS and the US. Obviously, if they occur before the US does, they are being triggered by the CS. (See *Figure 14.21.*)

Movement of the rabbit's nictitating membrane is controlled by a special muscle, which runs parallel to the optic nerve. Contraction of this muscle, called the ***retractor bulbi*** (*bulbus,* "onion," refers to the eye), pulls the eye back into its socket, and the natural elasticity of the nictitating membrane causes it to wipe across the eye. The sixth cranial nerve (abducens nerve) innervates the retractor bulbi, and the neurons that send axons to this muscle lie in the ***accessory abducens nucleus,*** just adjacent to the abducens nucleus in the caudal pons (Powell, Berthier, and Moore, 1979). Therefore, the pathways by which conditional or unconditional nictitating membrane responses are produced must terminate in this region.

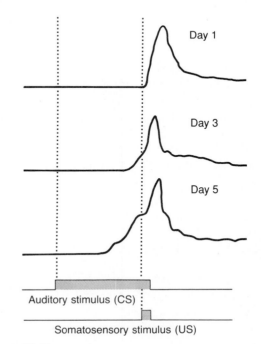

FIGURE 14.21

Acquisition of a classically conditioned nictitating membrane response. (Graphs courtesy of J.W. Moore.)

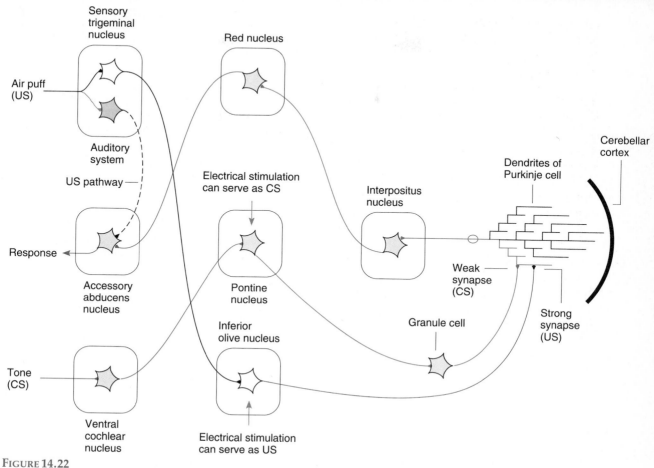

FIGURE 14.22

The proposed neural pathway responsible for a classically conditioned nictitating membrane response. The pathway for the unconditional response is shown as a dotted black line; the pathway for the conditional response is shown as a color line.

membrane responses when a puff of air was directed to their eye, they no longer made conditional (learned) responses to a tone that had been paired with the puff of air (McCormick and Thompson, 1984; Yeo, Hardiman, and Glickstein, 1984). In addition, recordings of the activity of single neurons in the interpositus nucleus and in the cerebellar cortex showed response patterns that were closely correlated with the shape of the conditional nictitating membrane response. (See *Figure 14.23.*) Finally, electrical stimulation of the interpositus nucleus produced nictitating membrane responses.

Figure 14.22 shows the circuit that is hypothesized to be responsible for the conditional (learned) response, as proposed by Thompson (1989). *Granule cells* in the cerebellar cortex receive information about the CS (tone) from a pathway that includes the *cochlear nucleus* and the *pontine nucleus*. This information is then transmitted to the dendrites of the *Purkinje cells*, which provide the output of the cerebellar cortex. Information about the US (air puff) is transmitted from the sensory trigeminal nucleus to the *inferior olive*, and from there to another region on the dendrites of the Purkinje cells. Presumably, the joint activity of the two sets of synapses with the dendrites of the Purkinje cells strengthens the one transmitting auditory information (the CS). The axons of the Purkinje cells transmit information to the interpositus nucleus. From there, information is transmitted to the *red nucleus* of the pons, then to the accessory abducens nucleus, and finally to the retractor bulbi muscle. (Refer to *Figure 14.22.*)

The circuitry I have just described has been discovered through the efforts of many investigators. For example, the importance of the inferior olive was originally discovered by McCormick and Thompson (1982); that of the red nucleus by Rosenfield and Moore (1983); and that of the pontine nucleus by Steinmetz et al. (1987). The experiments that have been performed to uncover the details of the learning-related circuitry within the cerebellum are particularly interesting. To confirm the location of the neural circuit that introduces the CS to the cerebellum, Steinmetz, Rosen, Chapman, Lavond, and Thompson (1986) attempted to classically condition the nictitating membrane response, using electrical stimulation of the pontine nuclei as a CS and air puff as a US. The training succeeded; the animals learned the task as if a real auditory stimulus had been presented.

A similar study confirmed the location of the neural circuit that introduces the US. Mauk, Steinmetz, and Thompson (1986) found that electrical stimulation of different locations in the inferior olive produced various movements, such as head turning, eyelid closure, or leg movements. This finding indicates that the synapses of the olivary neurons on the dendrites of the Purkinje cells are "strong." When the experimenters paired this stimulation with auditory stimuli (presenting the auditory CS first, of course), the behavioral response, whatever it was, became conditioned to the CS. These results confirm those of an experiment by McCormick, Steinmetz, and Thompson (1985), who made lesions of the part of the inferior olive that receives somatosensory information from the face and transmits it to the cerebellum. The animals acted as if the US no longer existed. If they had previously been trained, the conditional response gradually disappeared, as if extinction were taking place. If the animals had not previously been trained, they were unable to acquire a classically conditioned response.

As you might have predicted, experimenters have even tried to establish a classically conditioned response entirely through artificial stimu-

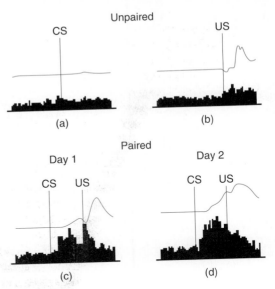

FIGURE 14.23

Responses of groups of neurons in the interpositus nucleus of the rabbit cerebellum during classical conditioning. The curves at the top of each figure indicate the nictitating membrane response. Note that the neurons respond only when a conditional (learned) response is made. (a) CS presented alone. (b) US presented alone. (c) First day of training, CS and US paired. (c) Second day of training. (From McCormick, D.A., and Thompson, R.F. *Journal of Neuroscience,* 1984, 4 2811–2822.)

lation. Steinmetz, Lavond, and Thompson (1989) paired stimulation of the pontine nucleus (CS) with stimulation of the inferior olive (US). They found that whatever unconditional response was produced by the olivary stimulation became classically conditioned to the pontine stimulation. And the pairing worked only when the CS was presented first; if the US was presented first, or if the delay between CS and US was too long, conditioning did not occur. Natural stimuli work this way, too. (Refer to *Figure 14.22.*)

The goals of many neuroscientists are not only to find the neural circuits responsible for learning but also to discover the structural and biochemical changes that take place within the neurons in these circuits. The recent research on the neuroanatomy of simple classical conditioning is especially important, because it appears to have identified structures involved in a particular form of stimulus-response learning. With the hundreds of millions of neurons in even the smallest mammalian brain, discovering the structural basis of learning is even more difficult than finding the proverbial needle in a haystack. However, the research described in this section has helped divide the haystack into much smaller and more manageable pieces. Perhaps in the next few years investigators will begin to discover what kinds of changes occur in neurons in these parts of the brain during classical conditioning.

INTERIM SUMMARY

Conditioned emotional responses are a special category of classical conditioning in which the conditional response involves defensive behavior and activity of the autonomic nervous system. The central nucleus of the amygdala plays a critical role in this type of learning, because it receives sensory information from several sensory modalities and controls behavioral, autonomic, and hormonal responses related to fear-producing stimuli. Neuroanatomical-tracing studies, lesion studies, electrical-recording studies, and electrical-stimulation studies indicate that conditioned emotional responses using a simple auditory stimulus involve the medial division of the medial geniculate nucleus (MGM). Somatosensory (US) and auditory (CS) information converge there, and apparently, learning-related changes take place there, too. The information is passed to the central nucleus of the amygdala, where it is directed toward neural circuits responsible for various components of the conditioned emotional response.

In the past few years much progress has been made in tracing the neural circuits that are responsible for a rabbit's learning of a classically conditioned nictitating membrane response. A puff of air directed to the eye causes the unconditional response by means of the following circuit: The trigeminal nerve conveys the somatosensory information to the sensory trigeminal nucleus. Neurons there send axons to the accessory abducens nucleus, which contains the motor neurons that control the retractor bulbi, the muscle that retracts the eye and permits the nictitating membrane to sweep across the eye.

The conditional response involves the participation of neurons in the cerebellum. Information about the unconditional stimulus (air puff) reaches the dendrites of Purkinje cells in the cerebellar cortex through the inferior olive of the medulla. Information about the conditional stimulus (tone) is passed through the cochlear nucleus and the pontine nucleus to granule cells in the cerebellar cortex. These cells pass the information on to the dendrites of the Purkinje cells. If the auditory input (weak synapses) to the Purkinje cells is immediately followed by the somatosensory input (strong synapses), the former get strengthened, resulting in classical conditioning. Information about a conditional response is transmitted from the Purkinje cells to the interpositus nucleus, to the red nucleus of the pons, and finally to the accessory abducens nucleus. Knowing the circuitry responsible for a learned response will help investigators discover the nature of the synaptic changes that are responsible for learning.

RELATIONAL LEARNING

So far, I have been discussing relatively simple forms of learning, which can be understood as changes in neural networks that detect the presence of particular stimuli, or as strengthened connections between neurons that convey sensory information and those that produce responses. But most forms of learning are more complex; most memories of real objects and events are related to other memories. Seeing a photograph of an old friend may remind you of the sound of the person's name and of the movements you have to make to pronounce it. You may also be reminded of things you have done with your friend: places you have visited, conversations you have had, experiences you have shared. Each of these memories can contain a series of events, complete with sights and sounds, which you will be able to recall in the proper sequence. Obviously, the neural circuits in the inferotemporal cortex that recognize your friend's face are connected to circuits in many other parts of the brain, and these circuits are connected to many others.

One of the most dramatic and intriguing phenomena caused by brain damage is *anterograde amnesia*, which, at first glance, appears to be the inability to learn new information. However, when we examine the phenomenon more carefully, we find that the basic abilities of perceptual learning, sensory-response learning, and motor learning are intact, but that complex relational learning, of the type I just described, is gone. This section discusses the nature of anterograde amnesia in humans, its anatomical basis, and related research in laboratory animals.

Human Anterograde Amnesia

The term **anterograde amnesia** refers to difficulty in learning new information. A person with pure anterograde amnesia can remember events that occurred in the past, during the time before the brain damage occurred, but cannot retain information he or she encountered *after* the damage. In contrast, **retrograde amnesia** refers to inability to remember events that happened *before* the brain damage occurred. (See *Figure 14.24.*) As we shall see, pure anterograde amnesia is rare; usually, there is also a retrograde amnesia for events that occurred for a period of time before the brain damage occurred.

In 1889 Sergei Korsakoff, a Russian physician, first described a severe memory impairment caused by brain damage, and the disorder was given his name. The most profound symptom of

Korsakoff's syndrome is a severe anterograde amnesia: The patients appear to be unable to form new memories, although they can still remember old ones. They can converse normally and can remember events that happened long before their brain damage occurred, but they cannot remember events that occur afterward.

Korsakoff's syndrome is usually a result of chronic alcoholism. The disorder actually results from a thiamine (vitamin B_1) deficiency caused by the alcoholism (Adams, 1969; Haas, 1988). Because alcoholics receive a substantial number of calories from the alcohol they ingest, they usually eat a poor diet, so their vitamin intake is consequently low. Furthermore, alcohol appears to interfere with intestinal absorption of thiamine and the ensuing deficiency produces brain damage. I will discuss the location of the brain damage that causes Korsakoff's syndrome later in this chapter.

Anterograde amnesia can also be caused by damage to the temporal lobes. Scoville and Milner (1957) reported that bilateral removal of the medial temporal lobe produced a memory impairment in humans that was apparently identical to that seen in Korsakoff's syndrome. Thirty operations had been performed on psychotic patients in an attempt to alleviate their mental disorder, but it was not until this operation was performed on patient H.M. that the anterograde amnesia was discovered. The psychotic patients' behaviors were already so disturbed that amnesia was not detected. However, patient H.M. was reasonably intelligent and was not psychotic; therefore, his postoperative deficit was discovered immediately. He received the surgery in an attempt to treat his very severe epilepsy, which could not be controlled even by high doses of anticonvulsant medication.

The surgery successfully treated H.M.'s seizure disorder, but it became apparent that he suffered a serious memory impairment. Subsequently, Scoville and Milner (1957) examined eight of the psychotic patients who were able to cooperate with them. Careful testing revealed that some of these patients also had anterograde amnesia; the deficit appeared to occur only when the hippocampus was removed. Thus, they concluded that the hippocampus was the critical structure destroyed by the surgery. Later in this

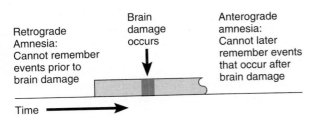

Retrograde Amnesia: Cannot remember events prior to brain damage

Brain damage occurs

Anterograde amnesia: Cannot later remember events that occur after brain damage

Time

FIGURE 14.24
A schematic definition of retrograde amnesia and anterograde amnesia.

chapter, I will say more about the anatomical basis of anterograde amnesia caused by temporal lobe damage.

Basic Description

In order for you to understand more fully the nature of anterograde amnesia, I will discuss the case of patient H.M. in more detail (Milner, Corkin, and Teuber, 1968; Milner, 1970; Corkin, Sullivan, Twitchell, and Grove, 1981). Patient H.M. has been extensively studied because his amnesia is relatively pure. His intellectual ability and his immediate verbal memory appear to be normal. He can repeat seven numbers forward and five numbers backward; and he can carry on conversations, rephrase sentences, and perform mental arithmetic. He has a retrograde amnesia for events that occurred during several years preceding the operation, but he can recall older memories very well. He showed no personality change after the operation, and he appears to be generally polite and well-mannered.

However, since the operation, H.M. has been unable to learn anything new. He cannot identify by name people he met since the operation (performed in 1953, when he was twenty-seven years old), nor can he find his way back home if he leaves his house. (His family moved to a new house after his operation, and he has been unable to learn how to get around in the new neighborhood.) He is aware of his disorder and often says something like this:

> Every day is alone in itself, whatever enjoyment I've had, and whatever sorrow I've had . . . . Right now, I'm wondering. Have I done or said anything amiss? You see, at this moment everything looks clear to me, but what happened just before? That's what worries me. It's like waking from a dream; I just don't remember. (Milner, 1970, p. 37)

H.M. is capable of remembering a small amount of verbal information as long as he is not distracted; constant rehearsal can keep information in his immediate memory for a long time. However, rehearsal does not appear to have any long-term effects; if he is distracted for a moment, he will completely forget whatever he had been rehearsing. He works very well at repetitive tasks.

Indeed, because he so quickly forgets what previously happened, he does not become bored easily. He can endlessly reread the same magazine or laugh at the same jokes, finding them fresh and new each time. His time is typically spent solving crossword puzzles and watching television.

From these findings Milner and her colleagues made the following conclusions:

1. *The hippocampus is not the location of long-term memories; nor is it necessary for the retrieval of long-term memories.* If it were, H.M. would not have been able to remember events from early in his life, he would not know how to talk, he would not know how to dress himself, and so on.

2. *The hippocampus is not the location of immediate (short-term) memories.* If it were, H.M. would not be able to carry on a conversation, because he would not remember what the other person said long enough to think of a reply.

3. *The hippocampus is involved in converting immediate (short-term) memories into long-term memories.* This conclusion is based on a particular hypothesis of memory function: that our immediate memory of an event is retained by neural activity, and that long-term memories consist of relatively permanent biochemical or structural changes in neurons. The conclusion seems a reasonable explanation for the fact that when presented with new information, H.M. seems to understand it and remember it as long as he thinks about it, but that a permanent record of the information is just never made.

As we will see, these three conclusions are too simple. Subsequent research on patients with anterograde amnesia indicates that the facts are more complicated—and more interesting—than they first appeared to be. But in order to appreciate the significance of the findings of more recent research, we must understand these three conclusions and remember the facts that led to them.

Spared Learning Abilities

H.M.'s memory deficit is striking and dramatic. However, when he and other patients with anterograde amnesia are more carefully studied, it becomes apparent that the amnesia does not represent a total failure in learning ability. When the patients are appropriately trained and tested, we find that they are capable of perceptual learning, sensory-response learning, and motor learning.

First, let us consider perceptual learning. Figure 14.25 shows two sample items from a test of the ability to recognize broken drawings; note how the drawings are successively more complete. (See *Figure 14.25.*) Subjects are first shown the least complete version (version I) of each of twenty different drawings. If they do not recognize a figure (and most people do not recognize version I), they are shown more complete versions until they identify it. One hour later, the subjects are tested again for retention, starting with version I. H.M. was given this test and, when retested an hour later, showed considerable improvement (Milner, 1970). When he was retested four months later, he *still* showed this improve-

FIGURE 14.26
The mirror-drawing task.

ment. His performance was not as good as that of normal control subjects, but he showed unmistakable evidence of long-term retention.

Milner (1965) presented H.M. with a mirror-drawing task. This procedure requires the subject to trace the outline of a figure (in this case, a star) with a pencil while looking at the figure in a mirror. (See *Figure 14.26.*) The task may seem simple, but it is actually rather difficult and requires some practice to perform well. With practice H.M. became proficient at mirror drawing; his errors were reduced considerably during the first session, and his improvement was retained on subsequent days of testing. Thus, long-term memories were certainly established.

Investigators have succeeded in teaching amnesic subjects a wide variety of tasks. For example, Weiskrantz and Warrington (1979) found that amnesic subjects could acquire a classically conditioned eyeblink response. Sidman, Stoddard, and Mohr (1968) successfully trained patient H.M. on a visual discrimination task in which pennies were given for correct responses. Johnson, Kim, and Risse (1985) played unfamiliar melodies from Korean songs to amnesic patients and found that when they were tested later, they preferred these

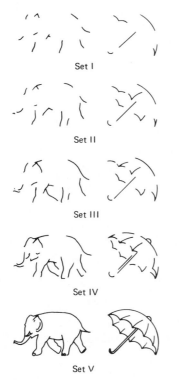

FIGURE 14.25
Examples of broken drawings. (Reprinted with permission of author and publisher from Gollin, E.S. Developmental studies of visual recognition of incomplete objects. *Perceptual and Motor Skills*, 1960, *11*, 289–298.)

melodies to ones they had not heard before. The experimenters also presented photographs of two men along with stories of their lives: One man was dishonest, mean, and vicious, and the other was nice enough to invite home to dinner. Twenty days later, the amnesic patients said they liked the picture of the "nice" man better than the "nasty" one.

If amnesic patients can learn tasks like these, you might ask, why do we call them *amnesic?* The answer is this: Although the patients can learn to perform these tasks, they do not remember anything about having learned them. They do not remember the experimenters, the room in which the training took place, the apparatus that was used, or any events that occurred during the training. Thus, although the amnesic patients in the study by Johnson, Kim, and Risse liked some melodies better, they did not recognize that they had heard them before; nor did they remember having seen the pictures of the two young men. Similarly, in the experiment by Sidman, Stoddard, and Mohr, although H.M. learned to make the correct response (press a panel with a picture of a circle on it), he was unable to recall having done so. In fact, once H.M. had learned the task, the experimenters interrupted him, had him count his pennies (to distract him for a little while), and then asked him to say what he was supposed to do. He

had absolutely no idea. But when they turned on the stimuli again, he immediately made the correct response.

Analysis of Anterograde Amnesia

The distinction between what people with anterograde amnesia can and cannot learn is obviously important, because it reflects the basic organization of the learning process. Clearly, there are at least two different types of memories. Investigators have proposed many different hypotheses to account for the pattern of deficits seen in anterograde amnesia. Some of the terms they have employed are shown in *Table 14.1.*

Many hypothetical explanations about the nature of anterograde amnesia focus on the distinction between verbal and nonverbal behavior. For example, Squire and his colleagues (Squire, Shimamura, and Amaral, 1989) suggest that patients with anterograde amnesia are unable to form ***declarative memories,*** which they define as memories "explicitly available to conscious recollection as facts, events, or specific stimuli" (p. 218). The term *declarative* obviously comes from *declare,* which means "to proclaim; to announce." The term reflects the fact that patients with anterograde amnesia cannot talk about experiences that they have had since the time of their brain

---

TABLE 14.1

Terms that have been used to describe two types of memory (not all are synonymous)

Names		Authors
Knowing how	Knowing that	Ryle (1949)
Procedural memory	Declarative memory	Winograd (1975)
Taxon	Locale	O'Keefe and Nadel (1978)
Reference memory	Working memory	Olton, Becker, and Handelmann (1979)
Automatic recollection	Conscious recollection	Baddeley (1982)
Semantic memory	Cognitive mediation	Warrington and Weiskrantz (1982)
Habit	Memory	Mishkin, Malamut, and Bachevalier (1984)
Dispositional memory	Representational memory	Thomas (1984)
Implicit memory	Explicit memory	Graf and Schacter (1985)
Nondeclarative memory	Declarative memory	Benzing and Squire (1989)

Source: Adapted from Squire, L.R. *Memory and Brain*. New York: Oxford University Press, 1987.

damage. In their definition, Squire and his colleagues do not use the word *verbal*, but the term *consciousness* implies verbal awareness; if we are aware of something, then we are able to talk about it.

Clearly, verbal learning is disrupted in anterograde amnesia. Gabrieli, Cohen, and Corkin (1988) found that patient H.M. does not seem to have learned any words that have been introduced into the English language since his surgery. For example, he defined *biodegradable* as "two grades," *flower child* as "a young person who grows flowers," and *soul food* as "forgiveness." As the authors noted, for H.M. modern-day English is partly a foreign language.

But if the learning deficit of people with anterograde amnesia were simply a verbal deficit, then we would predict that similar damage to the brains of members of other species would not affect their ability to learn. After all, they cannot talk. But as we shall see later in this chapter, nonverbal animals can have anterograde amnesia, too. Therefore, we must look beyond a verbal-nonverbal distinction to understand what functions have been disrupted. As the title for this section ("Relational Learning") suggests, the deficit might be a loss of the ability to learn complex relations. For example, consider the fact that patient H.M. can successfully learn several different kinds of perceptual or stimulus-response tasks. He can learn to recognize a particular stimulus or to make a particular response whenever a particular stimulus appears. However, if we ask him later whether he remembers the room where the testing took place, he will say no. He has no memory for the many other stimuli that were also present at the time: the experimenter, the room, the apparatus, the words that were spoken, and so on.

What is the difference between learning to perform a particular response when a particular stimulus is present and being able to remember that an experience occurred? In the first case learning would seem to consist of strengthened connections between neurons that perceive a stimulus and neurons that control a behavior. This basic capacity is not damaged in people with anterograde amnesia. But to be able to talk about an event later, a person must have learned much more. The person must have learned the *relation* between the stimuli that were present at the time and the sequence of events that occurred during the episode. When the person is asked about the episode later, he or she is able to picture the scene and describe it. Anterograde amnesia appears to be a loss of the ability to learn about complex relations between many stimuli, including the order of their occurrence in time.

Anatomy of Anterograde Amnesia

The phenomenon of anterograde amnesia—and its implications for the nature of relational learning—has led investigators to study the phenomenon in laboratory animals. But before I review behavioral research with laboratory animals (which has provided some very interesting results), we should examine the brain damage that produces anterograde amnesia. One fact is clear: Damage to the hippocampus, or to regions that supply its inputs and receive its outputs, causes anterograde amnesia. As you will recall, Scoville and Milner (1957) studied patients who had received temporal lobectomies and concluded that anterograde amnesia occurred only when the hippocampus was bilaterally damaged. After many years of controversy researchers have finally concluded that they were right.

Anatomy of the Hippocampal Formation. I will spare you the controversy and present the most conclusive evidence that is available from anatomical studies with both humans and laboratory animals. But first I will present some relevant anatomy. The *hippocampal formation* is a specialized region of the limbic cortex located in the temporal lobe. Because the hippocampal formation is folded in one dimension and then curved in another, it has a complex, three-dimensional shape. Thus, it is difficult to show what it looks like with a diagram on a two-dimensional sheet of paper. I must confess that I looked at diagrams of the hippocampus for many years without ever really being able to picture its structure in three dimensions. Finally, I read an article on the anatomy of the hippocampal formation that presented a set of drawings that showed its embryonic development, and the picture became clearer. I have based my illustrations on that article (Swanson, Köhler, and Björklund, 1987). The next few para-

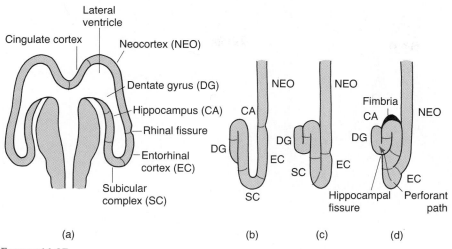

FIGURE 14.27

Development of the hippocampal formation. (a) Horizontal section of the developing brain. (b) Ammon's horn folding back on itself. (c) Dentate gyrus folding forward. (d) Formation of the perforant path and the fimbria. (Adapted from Swanson, L.W., Köhler, C., and Björklund, A., in *Handbook of Chemical Neuroanatomy. Vol. 5.: Integrated Systems of the CNS, Part I.* Amsterdam: Elsevier Science Publishers, 1987.)

graphs give many details about neuroanatomy; in fact, this is probably the most concentrated dose you will receive in this book outside of Chapter 4. Let me assure you that learning this information is worthwhile; you will use some of what you learn immediately afterward in this chapter, and the rest will come up again in Chapter 15.

Figure 14.27 shows the development of the hippocampal formation, which includes the *entorhinal cortex,* the three subdivisions of the *subicular complex,* the hippocampus itself, and the *dentate gyrus.* The drawings illustrate a rat brain, but the development of a human brain is very similar. The hippocampus is also called "Ammon's horn," or, in Latin, *cornu ammonis.* That fact may seem like a piece of trivia, but it explains why its two major divisions are called *CA1* and *CA3.* (CA2 and CA4 exist, too, but we will not need to talk about them.) Figure 14.27a shows a horizontal section of the developing brain that you may remember from Chapter 4. In the temporal lobe the *rhinal fissure* marks the border between the neocortex and the hippocampal formation, which is composed of limbic cortex. Going medially from the rhinal fissure, we encounter the entorhinal cortex, the subicular complex, the hip-

pocampus (Ammon's horn), and the dentate gyrus. (See *Figure 14.27a.*)

Figures 14.27b, 14.27c, and 14.27d show the further development of the hippocampal formation. First, Ammon's horn folds back on itself; then the dentate gyrus folds forward. Axons of neurons in the entorhinal cortex grow toward the dentate gyrus, forming the *perforant path* (which *perforates* the hippocampal fissure). The *fimbria* forms on the rostral fold of Ammon's horn. This structure consists of a bundle of axons that becomes the *fornix* after it detaches itself from the hippocampal formation. It connects the hippocampal formation with the basal forebrain, diencephalon, and brain stem. (See *Figures 14.27b–14.27d.*)

Figure 14.28 shows a photomicrograph of a horizontal section through the hippocampal formation of a rat brain and an accompanying drawing that shows its intrinsic connections. The major neocortical inputs and outputs of the hippocampal formation are channeled through the entorhinal cortex. Neurons in the entorhinal cortex relay incoming information through the perforant path to the *granule cells* of the dentate gyrus. These neurons then send axons to field CA3,

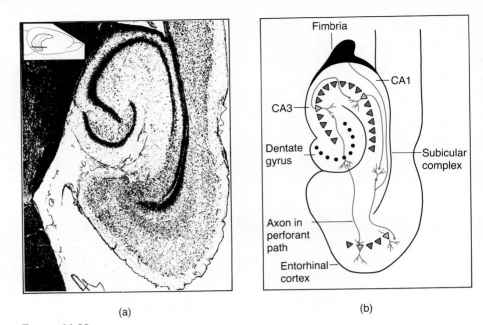

(a)   (b)

FIGURE 14.28

Connections of the components of the hippocampal formation. (Photograph from Swanson, L.W., Köhler, C., and Björklund, A., in *Handbook of Chemical Neuroanatomy. Vol. 5.: Integrated Systems of the CNS, Part I.* Amsterdam: Elsevier Science Publishers, 1987.)

where they form synapses with the *pyramidal cells.* These cells send axons to the adjacent field CA1, where they synapse with other pyramidal cells. CA1 pyramidal cells send axons to the subicular complex, which, in turn, sends axons back to the entorhinal cortex, where the circuit started. (See *Figure 14.28.*)

Figure 14.29 shows the connections of the hippocampal system with the neocortex. (This figure illustrates a monkey brain, because the neocortex of this animal is much more developed and differentiated than that of a rat.) As you can see, all association areas of the brain send information to, and receive information from, the hippocampal formation. In primates much of the communication between the hippocampal formation and the neocortex passes through a band of cortex surrounding the entorhinal cortex. (See *Figure 14.29.*)

I mentioned that the hippocampus also communicates with subcortical regions of the brain through the fimbria/fornix. Outgoing axons in this bundle mainly belong to neurons in the subicular complex; incoming ones synapse with neurons throughout the hippocampal complex. The subcortical outputs go to the lateral septum, the mammillary bodies, and the anterior thalamus. The subcortical inputs include serotonergic axons from the raphe nuclei, noradrenergic axons from the locus coeruleus, and acetylcholinergic axons from the medial septum. Each of these three neurotransmitters has a profound effect on the activity of the hippocampal formation. The hippocampal formation also receives information from the amygdala; several nuclei of the amygdala send axons directly to the entorhinal cortex.

FIGURE 14.29 ▶

Inputs and outputs of the hippocampal formation in the monkey brain. The regions at the top of the figure communicate with the entorhinal cortex through a region of cortex that surrounds it; those at the bottom communicate with the entorhinal cortex directly. (Adapted from Squire, L.R., Shimamura, A.P., and Amaral, D.G., in *Neural Models of Plasticity: Experimental and Theoretical Approaches,* edited by J.H. Byrne and W.O. Berry. San Diego: Academic Press, 1989.)

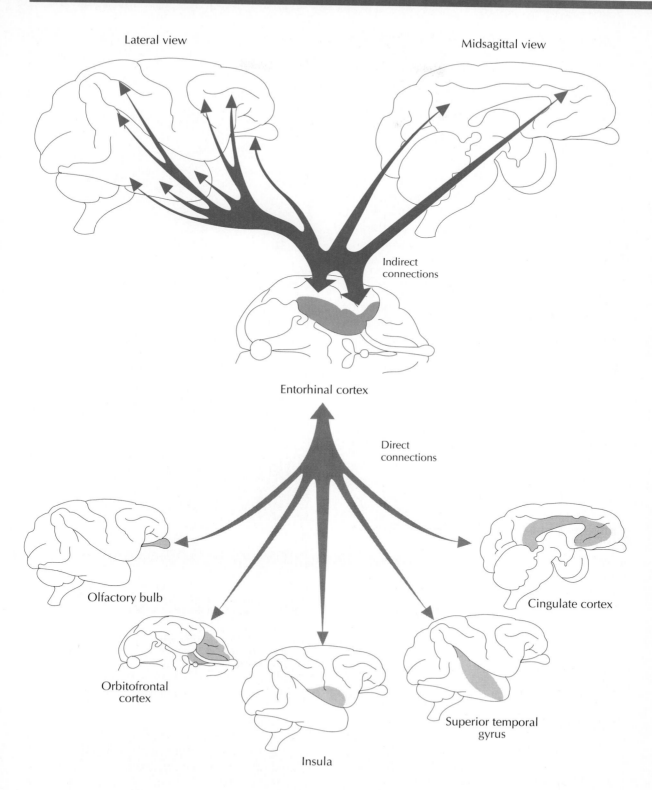

Lateral view

Midsagittal view

Indirect
connections

Entorhinal cortex

Direct
connections

Olfactory bulb

Cingulate cortex

Orbitofrontal
cortex

Superior temporal
gyrus

Insula

Evidence for the Role of the Hippocampus. The clearest evidence that damage to the hippocampal formation produces anterograde amnesia comes from a case studied by Zola-Morgan, Squire, and Amaral (1986). Patient R.B., a 52-year-old man with a history of heart trouble, sustained a cardiac arrest. Although his heart was successfully restarted, the period of anoxia caused by the temporary halt in blood flow caused brain damage. The primary symptom of this brain damage was a permanent anterograde amnesia, which Zola-Morgan and his colleagues carefully documented. Five years after the onset of the amnesia, R.B. died of heart failure. His family gave permission for histological examination of his brain.

The investigators discovered that field CA1 of the hippocampal formation was gone; its neurons had completely degenerated. (In Chapter 15 I will come back to the fact that this part of the brain is particularly susceptible to damage from anoxia.) Figure 14.30 shows two photomicrographs, one of a section through a normal hippocampus and one of a section through that of patient R.B. Although the sections were taken at slightly different angles, you will have no difficulty seeing the difference in the appearance of field CA1 in the two brains. (See *Figure 14.30.*)

This single case indicates that hippocampal damage can cause anterograde amnesia. However, it does not rule out the possibility that other structures are also involved. One possible structure is the amygdala. In studies with monkeys Mishkin (1978, 1982) found evidence that damage to either the hippocampus or the amygdala alone had only a small effect on a test of memory but that combined damage to the hippocampus *and* the amygdala produced a severe deficit. Thus, he hypothesized that human anterograde amnesia is caused by damage to both of these structures. (In fact, H.M.'s surgery destroyed his amygdala as well as his hippocampus.)

The case of patient R.B. does not support this conclusion; Zola-Morgan and his colleagues looked at the amygdala carefully and found no evidence of damage. Perhaps, then, the hippocampus and amygdala have different functions in monkeys and humans. Neuroscientists would not be happy if this were the case; we would all like

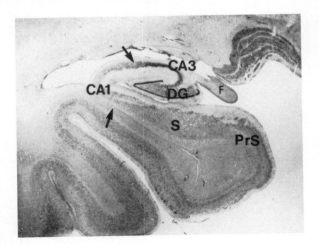

(a)

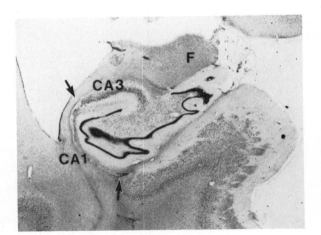

(b)

FIGURE 14.30

Damage to field CA1 caused by anoxia. (a) Section through a normal hippocampus. (b) Section through the hippocampus of patient R.B. The pyramidal cells of field CA1 (between the two arrowheads) have degenerated. DG = dentate gyrus, PrS = presubiculum, S = subiculum, F = fornix. (From Squire, L.R., in *Molecules to Models: Advances in Neurosciences* edited by K.L. Kelner and D.E. Koshland. Washington, D.C.: American Association for the Advancement of Science, 1989.)

to think that studying the brain functions of monkeys will tell us something useful about the human brain. Fortunately, Zola-Morgan, Squire, and Amaral (1989a) obtained evidence showing that even in monkeys, the amygdala need not be damaged to produce severe anterograde amnesia. They pointed out that when amygdala lesions are produced in a monkey's brain, the surgeon invariably damages the cortex surrounding the entorhinal cortex. As we saw in the review of the anatomy of the hippocampal formation, most connections between the neocortex and the hippocampal formation pass through this region of the cortex. Thus, these connections are disrupted in the course of surgically destroying the amygdala. The amygdala lesions, besides destroying the amygdala, cause further damage to the hippocampal complex.

Zola-Morgan and his colleagues tested several groups of monkeys on a memory task. They found that stereotaxic lesions of the amygdala, which did not damage the adjacent cortex, had no effect on tests of anterograde amnesia and did not worsen an animal's performance when they were combined with hippocampal lesions. And in a follow-up study Zola-Morgan, Squire, Amaral, and Suzuki (1989) found that lesions of the cortex surrounding the entorhinal cortex would, by themselves, cause a severe memory impairment. Deprived of its cortical inputs and outputs, the hippocampal formation was unable to function normally. Thus, although the amygdala certainly plays a role in memory (as we saw earlier in this chapter), its destruction does not appear to contribute to anterograde amnesia.

We can conclude that bilateral lesions of the medial temporal lobes cause anterograde amnesia because they damage the hippocampal formation, but what about Korsakoff's syndrome? You will recall that I promised earlier to discuss the anatomy of this disorder. The two parts of the brain most often damaged in cases of Korsakoff's syndrome are the *mammillary bodies* and the *mediodorsal nucleus* of the thalamus. Most of the efferent axons of the fornix columns, which originate in the subicular complex, terminate in the mammillary bodies. Thus, it would be theoretically tidy to conclude that mammillary body lesions cause Korsakoff's syndrome, and that they do so because they interrupt an important output of the hippocampal system, which we know to be involved in anterograde amnesia.

Unfortunately, facts do not always follow theories the way we would like them to. Victor, Ad-ams, and Collins (1971) studied the autopsies of patients with Korsakoff's syndrome and concluded that amnesia was more reliably associated with damage to the mediodorsal nucleus of the thalamus than with damage to the mammillary bodies. This conclusion seemed to be bolstered by a report by Squire and Moore (1979) that a man with damage to the mediodorsal nucleus caused by a freak injury developed anterograde amnesia. However, a more careful study of this patient with advanced MRI (magnetic resonance imaging) techniques (Squire, Amaral, Zola-Morgan, Kritchevsky, and Press, 1989) showed that his brain damage was more extensive than previously suspected; among other things, it included the mammillary bodies. In a thorough review of the literature Markowitsch (1988) concluded that because all cases of Korsakoff's syndrome are accompanied by damage to many structures in the brain, the available evidence does not permit us to conclude that a single structure (outside the hippocampal formation) is uniquely responsible for producing anterograde amnesia. We will probably have to turn to studies with animals, where precisely localized brain damage can be produced.

In fact, experimenters have examined the effects of lesions of either the mediodorsal thalamic nucleus or the columns of the fornix (or the mammillary bodies, to which they project) in monkeys. These lesions do produce memory deficits, but they are not as severe as those seen in humans with Korsakoff's syndrome (Zola-Morgan and Squire, 1985a; Murray, Davidson, Gaffan, Olton, and Suomi, 1989; Zola-Morgan, Squire, and Amaral, 1989b). Thus, the anatomy of Korsakoff's syndrome is still uncertain; more research is needed to settle the issue definitively.

Studies of the Hippocampal Formation in Laboratory Animals

The discovery that hippocampal lesions produced anterograde amnesia in humans stimulated interest in the exact role that this structure plays in the learning process. To pursue this interest, many investigators turned to studies with laboratory animals.

Spatial Perception and Learning

After the discovery that lesions of the hippocampus caused anterograde amnesia, experimenters began making lesions of the hippocampus in animals and testing their learning ability. They quickly found that the animals remained capable of learning most tasks. At the time they were surprised, and some even thought that the hippocampus had different functions in humans than it had in other animals. We now realize that most of the learning tasks that the animals were given tested simple sensory-response learning, which even humans with anterograde amnesia can do well. But from the beginning consistent deficits were seen in tasks that required the animals to learn to navigate through space. In particular, hippocampal lesions impaired animals' ability to learn complex mazes.

Remembering Places Visited. Olton and Samuelson (1976) devised a task that requires rats to remember where they have just been and discovered that hippocampal lesions impaired performance even more than they do on a standard maze task. The investigators placed the rats on a circular platform located at the junction of eight arms, which radiated away from the center like the spokes of a wheel. (See *Figure 14.31.*) The entire maze was elevated high enough above the ground that the rats would not jump to the floor. Before placing the rats on the platform in the center, the experimenters put a piece of food at the end of each of the arms. The rats (who were hungry, of course) were permitted to explore the maze and eat the food. The animals soon learned to retrieve the food efficiently, entering each arm once. After twenty trials most animals did not enter an arm from which they had already obtained food during that session. A later study (Olton, Collison, and Werz, 1977) showed that rats could perform well even when they were prevented from following a fixed sequence of visits to the arms; thus, they had to remember where they had been, not simply follow the same pattern of responses each time. Control procedures in several studies ruled out the possibility that rats simply smelled their own odor in arms they had previously visited.

The radial-arm maze is symmetrical, and few

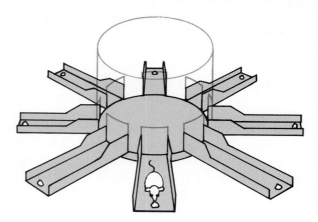

FIGURE 14.31
An eight-arm radial maze.

cues are present to distinguish one part of the apparatus from another. It is clear that if a rat can see objects in the environment around the maze, it uses these objects for navigation. For example, O'Keefe and Conway (1980) attached objects to the inside of a black curtain that surrounded a maze and found that the animals kept track of their location with respect to these objects. When the experimenters moved the stimuli as a group, maintaining their relative positions, the animals reoriented their responses accordingly. That is, if they had already visited an arm that pointed toward a particular object, they would avoid whatever arm pointed toward that object after the experimenters had rotated the visual stimuli outside the maze. However, when the experimenters interchanged the stimuli so that they were arranged in a new order, the animals' performance was disrupted. (Imagine how disoriented you might be if you entered a familiar room and found that the windows, doors, and furniture were in new positions.)

The radial-arm-maze task uses a behavioral capacity that is well developed in rats. Rats are scavengers and often find food in different locations each day. Thus, they must be able to find their way around the environment efficiently, not getting lost and not revisiting too soon a place where they previously found food. Of course, they must also learn which places in the environment are likely to contain food and visit them occasionally. Although these two abilities might appear to require the same brain functions, they do not. Let us consider the ability to avoid revisiting a place where food was just found. Olton and his colleagues (reviewed by Olton, 1983) found that lesions of the hippocampus, fimbria/fornix, or entorhinal cortex severely disrupted the ability of rats to visit the arms of a radial maze efficiently. In fact, their postoperative performance reached chance levels; they acted as if they had no memory of which arms they had previously entered. They eventually obtained all the food, but only after entering many of the arms repeatedly.

Thus, hippocampal lesions disrupt animals' ability to remember the places they have just visited. However, this deficit does not impair the second type of learning—learning to visit locations that sometimes contain food and to avoid visiting locations that never do. Olton and Papas (1979) demonstrated this distinction in a single experiment. They trained rats in a seventeen-arm radial maze. Before each session eight of the arms were baited with food; the other nine arms were *never* baited. Although rats with lesions of the fimbria/fornix visited the baited arms randomly, failing to avoid visiting the ones in which they had just eaten, they learned to stay away from the nine arms that never contained food. They apparently could not remember where they had just been, but they could learn which locations regularly contained food.

On the basis of such results, Olton (1983) has suggested that lesions of the hippocampus or its connections impair working memory but leave reference memory relatively intact. *Working memory* consists of information about things that have just happened, which are useful in the immediate future but which change from day to day. Thus, it is "erasable" memory that is replaced on a regular basis. *Reference memory* is more permanent memory, produced by consistent conditions. For example, my remembering where I parked my car in the parking lot *today* is working memory. Tomorrow I will park in a new place and remember that. However, my remembering that when I come to work I park in lot number 40 is reference memory, which is unchanging. As you can see, there is some similarity between this distinction and the one Squire has made between *declarative* and *nondeclarative* memory. Of course, a

rat cannot "declare" that it knows how to perform a particular task.

Whether or not the deficit caused by lesions of the hippocampal formation is one of working memory, the hippocampal formation does certainly play a special role in spatial perception. Morris, Garrud, Rawlins, and O'Keefe (1982) trained rats to perform a task that required them to find a particular location in space solely by means of visual cues external to the apparatus. The "maze" consisted of a circular pool, 1.3 meters in diameter, filled with a mixture of water and milk. The milk hid the location of a small platform, situated just beneath the surface of the liquid. The experimenters put the rats into the milky water and let them swim until they encountered the hidden platform and climbed onto it. They released the rats from a new position on each trial. After a few trials normal rats learned to swim directly to the hidden platform from wherever they were released. However, rats with hippocampal lesions swam in what appeared to be an aimless fashion until they encountered the platform. Figure 14.32 shows the performance of three rats: a normal rat, one with a neocortical lesion (to control for the fact that removal of the hippocampus entails damage to the overlying neocortex), and one with a hippocampal lesion. The results speak for themselves. (See *Figure 14.32*.)

The experiment by Morris and his colleagues provides evidence that the hippocampus is involved in long-term (reference) memory for spatial locations as well as in a temporary, immediate (working) memory for places just visited. This evidence contrasts with Olton and Papas's finding that rats with hippocampal lesions learned to avoid visits to the nine arms of a seventeen-arm maze that were never baited with food. Perhaps the rats in this study learned to avoid the nine empty arms by means of subtle differences in the construction of the individual arms, not by means of their spatial location.

Recording Studies: Neurons That Respond to Particular Places. One of the most intriguing discoveries about the hippocampal formation was made by O'Keefe and Dostrovsky (1971), who recorded the activity of individual neurons in the hippocampus as an animal moved around the en-

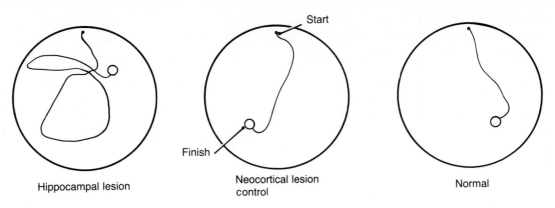

Start

Finish

Hippocampal lesion

Neocortical lesion
control

Normal

FIGURE 14.32

Effects of hippocampal lesions and neocortical control lesions on performance in the
circular "milk maze." The small circle marks the location of the submerged platform.
(Reprinted by permission from Morris, R.G.M., Garrud, P., Rawlins, J.N.P., and O'Keefe,
J. *Nature*, 1982, *297*, 681–683. Copyright © 1982, Macmillan Journals Limited.)

vironment. The experimenters found that some
neurons fired at a high rate only when the rat was
in a particular location. Different neurons had
different *spatial receptive fields;* that is, they responded in different locations. For obvious reasons these neurons were named ***place cells.***
When, for example, a rat is exploring a radial-arm
maze, place cells in its hippocampus respond to
places defined in relation to objects in the environment outside the maze (for example, lighting fix-
tures, cabinets, and racks of cages). If a particular
place cell is active when the rat is at the end of the
arm that points north, it will continue to fire in the
end of the northern arm, even after the maze is
rotated so that a different arm points north.

Muller and Kubie (1987) examined the spatial
receptive fields of hippocampal place cells in different environments. They found that if environments differed only in size, the receptive fields
would be found in the same relative locations.
However, if the environments differed in shape,
the locations of the receptive fields would change
in unpredictable ways. If they placed a barrier in
the middle of a neuron's receptive field, the shape
of the field would change; but if the barrier was
outside the field, no change would occur.

Hippocampal place cells are obviously guided
by visual stimuli, because their receptive fields
change when objects outside an environment are
moved. They also receive internally generated

stimuli. Hill and Best (1981) deafened and blindfolded rats and found that the spatial receptive fields of most of their place cells remained
constant—even when they rotated the maze. At
first, the experimenters were surprised and puzzled by the results, but then it occurred to them
that the animals may have been keeping track of
where they were by feedback from proprioceptive
cues. The rats may have been keeping track of
their starting point, left and right turns, and so on,
which kept resetting their "mental map." To test
this hypothesis, Hill and Best wrapped their
deafened and blindfolded rats in a towel, spun
them around, and then placed them in the maze.
(If you have ever played blindman's buff or pin-
the-tail-on-the-donkey, you will understand
how disorienting this treatment is.) The experimenter's hypothesis was correct; after the rats
had been spun, the receptive fields of their place
cells were disrupted.

McNaughton, Leonard, and Chen (1989) illustrated this phenomenon by using a slightly different procedure. They let rats become familiar with
an eight-arm radial maze and then found single
neurons in the hippocampus that had spatial receptive fields. Next, they introduced the rats into
the maze in complete darkness, using different
starting points on each trial. Because the animals
could no longer see the cues outside the maze,
they could not tell which way the arms of the maze

| Previous day | Phase 1: Lights out before rat placed in maze | Phase 2: Lights on | Phase 3: Lights out again |

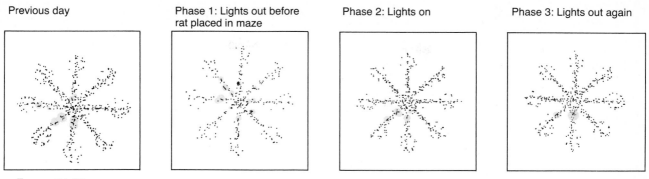

FIGURE 14.33

Spatial receptive fields of a neuron in the hippocampus in a radial-arm maze. Black dots represent places visited. Color circles represent the firing of the neuron; the size of the circle is proportional to the rate of firing. (From McNaughton, B.L., Leonard, B., and Chen, L. *Psychobiology*, 1989, 17, 236–246.)

were oriented with respect to the room. Indeed, the receptive fields of the place cells were disrupted. Then the experimenters turned on the lights briefly, showing the rats the environmental cues that surrounded the maze. The receptive fields now reoriented themselves, and they continued to respond appropriately even when the lights were turned off again.

Figure 14.33 illustrates the results, recorded from a single place cell. Each record indicates the places visited by the rats (black dots) and the activity of the neuron (colored circles). The size of a given circle is proportional to the rate at which the neuron fired. As you can see, this neuron normally fired when the rat was in the center part of the arms pointing south and southwest. (For convenience, I am assuming that up is north.) When the rat was tested in the dark, this neuron fired near the entrance of each of the arms. After the light was turned on, the normal pattern reestablished itself, and it continued even when the light was turned off again. (See *Figure 14.33*.)

McNaughton and his colleagues obtained evidence that the parietal cortex provides the information that the hippocampal formation needs to remain oriented in an environment even after the animal is not able to see the cues that normally guide it. They recorded from single neurons in the parietal cortex and found that their responses encoded various types of spatial information provided by movements that the rat made. For exam-

ple, some responded when the rat turned left or right, some when it moved toward the center or toward the outside of the maze, and so on. Presumably, the hippocampus makes use of this information to keep track of its location in the maze when the external cues are not visible.

The hippocampus appears to receive spatial information through the entorhinal cortex, not through the fornix. Miller and Best (1980) found that lesions of the entorhinal cortex severely disrupted the spatial receptive fields of hippocampal place cells, but that lesions of the fornix had a much smaller effect. In addition, Rose (1983) found that single granule cells in the dentate gyrus (which receive input from the entorhinal cortex) also had spatial receptive fields. But even though the fornix may not bring spatial information into the hippocampal formation, it does affect the functioning of this structure; as we have seen, lesions of the fornix disrupt performance of a radial-maze task.

The fact that neurons in the hippocampal formation have spatial receptive fields does not mean that each neuron encodes a particular location. Instead, this information is undoubtedly represented by particular *patterns* of activity in neural networks within the hippocampal formation. In fact, investigators have been attempting to construct models that will help us understand how the hippocampus accomplishes this task. I will say more about this subject a little later.

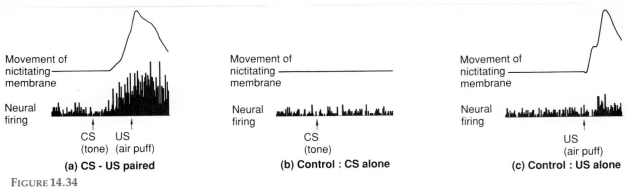

FIGURE 14.34

Pattern of firing of single neurons in the rabbit hippocampus along with a record of the movement of the nictitating membrane. (a) Conditional responses of a trained rabbit. Note that the response and neural firing begin before the unconditional stimulus. (b) Lack of response from a rabbit presented with the tone alone. (c) Unconditional response of a rabbit presented with the puff of air alone. Note that the activity of the hippocampal neurons does not increase with the unconditional response. (From Berger, T.W., Rinaldi, P.C., Weisz, D.J., and Thompson, R.F. *Journal of Neurophysiology*, 1983, *50*, 1197–1219.)

Nonspatial Functions of the Hippocampal Formation

So far, all of the experiments I have described with laboratory animals have been related to spatial perception and learning. As we saw in the discussion of human anterograde amnesia, although people with hippocampal damage also have difficulty finding their way around, anterograde amnesia in both humans and laboratory animals includes many deficits not related to space. For example, monkeys with lesions of the hippocampal formation and humans with anterograde amnesia perform similarly on a variety of memory tasks (Zola-Morgan and Squire, 1985b; Squire, Zola-Morgan, and Chen, 1988). In particular, the hippocampal lesions disrupted the monkeys' ability to remember a three-dimensional stimulus they had just seen for more than a few seconds.

Several studies by Berger and his colleagues (reviewed by Berger, Berry, and Thompson, 1986) have shown that neurons in the hippocampus respond not only to an animal's location in the environment. They also respond when the animal makes a learned response, but not an unlearned one. Berger and his colleagues recorded from single neurons in the hippocampus while they trained the animals to make classically conditioned nictitating membrane responses. They dis-

covered that the pattern of unit activity recorded from these neurons was closely correlated with the movement of the membrane during a conditional response but *not* during an unconditional response elicited by the puff of air alone.

Figure 14.34 shows the pattern of firing (series of vertical bars) of a single hippocampal neuron, along with a graph of the movement of the nictitating membrane, recorded by the transducer. The record in Figure 14.34a is from a rabbit that had learned to make a conditional response to the tone; the fact that the membrane began to move before the puff of air was presented indicates that the response was a learned one, not one elicited by the air. Note the good correspondence between the firing pattern of the neuron and the movement of the nictitating membrane. The response of the neuron precedes the movement by approximately 40 msec. (See *Figure 14.34a.*) The other two records are from a rabbit that was presented with a tone (CS) or a puff of air (US), but not both. Note that under these conditions the hippocampal neuron does not alter its rate of firing. (See *Figures 14.34b and 14.34c.*)

Although the hippocampus is *informed* about the execution of a conditional response, it does not appear to play a direct role in learning that response. Solomon and Moore (1975) found that rabbits with bilateral hippocampal lesions learned a conditional nictitating membrane response as rapidly as nonlesioned animals. However, Weisz, Solomon, and Thompson (1980) found that when a delay is imposed between the CS and the US (the tone and the air puff), hippocampal lesions prevented the learning of a conditional response. Perhaps the hippocampal formation helps the animal remember the conditional stimulus during the delay interval. In addition, Berger and Orr (1983) found that hippocampal lesions disrupted the reversal of a differential classical conditioning task. The rabbits were presented tones of two different frequencies, only one of which (CS$^+$) was followed by the puff of air (US). The CS$^-$ was presented by itself, alone. Berger and Orr found that the hippocampal lesions had no effect on learning the discrimination; but when they reversed the significance of the two stimuli, changing the old CS$^+$ to a CS$^-$ and vice versa, the lesioned animals took over three times as long to change their response pattern. These results suggest that the hippocampus plays a role in *unlearning* to make a response to one stimulus and learning to make it to another instead.

The Role of the Hippocampus in Relational Learning

As we saw earlier, people with anterograde amnesia can learn to recognize new stimuli, can learn new responses, and can learn to make a particular response when a particular stimulus is presented. What they cannot do is to talk about what they have learned. Anterograde amnesia appears to be a loss of the ability to learn about complex relations between many stimuli, including the order of their occurrence in time. How does research with laboratory animals help us understand this process?

Many investigators have come to the conclusion that the deficit in spatial learning produced by hippocampal lesions is caused by a failure to learn complex relations. For example, according to Wiener, Paul, and Eichenbaum (1989), "An emerging consensus . . . has indicated that the hippocampus is critical to learning and memory over a large range of information modalities that share a common demand for representing relationships among multiple independent percepts, but not for acquiring independent stimulus-rein-

forcement associations" (p. 2761). Sutherland and Rudy (1989) present a "configurational association theory," which suggests that the hippocampal system "combines the representations of elementary stimulus events to construct unique representations and allows for the formation of associations between these configural representations and other elementary representations" (p. 129).

I think it is likely that the original function of the hippocampus was to help the animal learn to navigate in the environment. Let us consider how this might be accomplished. For example, suppose you are standing in an environment similar to the circular "milk maze" I described earlier: a large field covered with grass, surrounded by distinctive objects, such as trees and buildings. You are familiar with the environment, having walked across it and played games on it many times. If someone blindfolds you and then picks you up and drops you somewhere on the field, you will recognize your location as soon as you remove the blindfold. Your location is defined by the *configuration* of objects you see—the *relation* they have with respect to each other. You will get a different view of these objects from each position on the field. Of course, if there are distinctive objects present on the field itself (trees, garbage cans, drinking fountains), the task will be even easier, because you can judge your position relative to nearby objects as well as distant ones.

Many experiments have shown that hippocampal lesions disrupt the performance of tasks that require the animal to remember relations among stimuli, rather than individual stimuli. For example, Rudy and Sutherland (1989) trained rats on a *conditional discrimination task.* A conditional discrimination is one in which a response to a particular stimulus is reinforced under one condition but not under another. Thus, a response depends on the *relation* between stimuli. They trained rats to press a lever when a light was present *or* when a tone was present, but not when both were present at the same time. This task cannot be learned simply by establishing connections between the visual system and the motor system, and between the auditory system and the motor system. Instead, some circuits must detect the occurrence of particular patterns of activity in both the visual system and the motor system and *inhibit* a response.

As you have undoubtedly guessed, Rudy and Sutherland found that rats with hippocampal lesions were unable to learn this task. That is, they readily learned to respond when either the light or the tone was present, but they failed to learn *not to respond* when they were present at the same time.

In the experiment by Rudy and Sutherland the contextual stimulus was the joint presence of a light and a tone. Another contextual stimulus is *time*. Several experiments have shown that the hippocampal formation is involved in an animal's ability to distinguish between situations that differ only in terms of time. For example, Aggleton, Hunt, and Rawlins (1986) constructed a Y-shaped maze with fifty different interchangeable arms that could be attached to the stem. Training consisted of fifty trials. The animal was placed in the stem of the maze and was permitted to enter one of the arms, where it received a piece of food. The rat was then removed from the maze, and the experimenters prepared for the next trial by removing the nonreinforced arm and attaching a new one from the set of fifty. Thus, the maze contained a familiar arm in which the rat had just received food, and an unfamiliar one. The position of the arms was varied randomly from trial to trial, so that the animals could not simply learn to enter the left or the right arm. Hence the task was to enter the arm they had not entered before. (See *Figure 14.35.*)

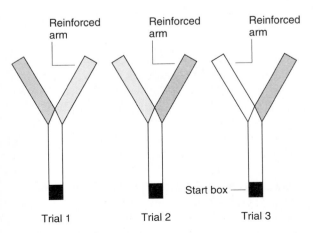

FIGURE 14.35
The procedure of the experiment by Aggleton, Hunt, and Rawlins (1986).

Rats with hippocampal lesions had no difficulty learning this problem; they could easily distinguish between an arm they had previously visited and one that they had never visited before.

The task by Aggleton and his colleagues does not require the animals to learn relations; it only requires them to distinguish old from new. Raffaele and Olton (1988) trained rats in a task that differed in one important way: The same two arms were used on all trials. This meant that the animals had to remember which arm they had found food in *on the previous trial*. They had already entered each of the arms on many occasions, so their choice had to be based on a contextual stimulus: time. Damage to the hippocampal complex prevented animals from learning the task.

How can we put all the information about the hippocampal complex together? As you will recall, the hippocampal complex receives information from all regions of the sensory association cortex and from the motor association cortex of the frontal lobe. It also receives information from the amygdala concerning odors and dangerous stimuli and, as we saw a few paragraphs earlier, from neural circuits involved in classical conditioning. Thus, the hippocampal complex knows what is going on in the environment, where the animal is located, and what responses it has just made. It probably also knows about the animal's emotional state: whether the animal is hungry, sexually aroused, frightened, and so on. Thus, when something happens, the hippocampal system has all the information necessary to put that event into the proper context.

Let us work through two learning tasks for which the hippocampal system is needed. First, let us consider Rudy and Sutherland's conditional discrimination experiment. The animals learn to press the lever when either the light or the tone is present; the hippocampus is not needed for this task. But then the experimenters introduce some trials in which the light and the tone are present simultaneously. The hippocampal formation detects the presence of the light and the tone and, through its connections that go back to the neocortex, informs the rest of the brain that a new situation has just occurred. Because the animal never receives food when it responds in this situation, the information received from the hippocampal formation begins to modify connections in the neocortex. Eventually, the animal learns not to respond to the compound stimulus of light plus tone.

For the second example we will return to anterograde amnesia in humans. Consider a normal person learning to press a panel with a picture of a circle on it, as patient H.M. did. While the person is seated in front of the apparatus, his or her hippocampal formation receives information about the context in which the learning is taking place: the room, the other people present, the person's mood, and so on. These pieces of information are collected together and are somehow "attached" to the patterns of activity in many different parts of the brain. Later, when the person is asked about the task, the question reactivates the pattern of activity in the hippocampus, which causes the retrieval of the memory of the episode, pieces of which are stored all over the brain. Patient H.M., lacking a functioning hippocampal system, has nothing that can put together the individual pieces of information, so he is unable to remember the episode.

You will recognize, of course, that this hypothetical explanation is vague about many parts of the process. For example, how does asking someone a question reactivate the pattern of activity in the hippocampus? And how, exactly, are pieces of information collected together and attached to sets of neural circuits? Obviously, we need to think about these questions, design clever experiments to obtain useful information, think about the questions in light of the new information, design more clever experiments. . . .

Rolls (1989) presents a hypothetical model of the role of the hippocampal formation in learning and memory that may prove to be useful. He suggests that the hippocampal system is a neural network that functions as an *autoassociator*. Each part of the hippocampal system—dentate gyrus, field CA3, field CA1, and the three parts of the subicular complex—successively analyzes information and passes the results of its analysis on to the next part. An autoassociative network quickly and efficiently learns to recognize particular patterns of inputs and produces a unique output for each pattern. Then if a similar pattern is presented later—or if parts of the pattern are presented— the network produces the appropriate output. Presumably, the activity of hippocampal "place"

neurons represents the activation of circuits that recognize the pattern of stimuli received when an animal is in a particular location. The computations performed by the hippocampal complex guide the formation of complex memories by establishing connections within and between different regions of association cortex. They also make it possible to retrieve this information later, by reactivating the circuits formed by these connections.

I left one more puzzle for the end of this discussion: that of retrograde amnesia. I already told you that people with anterograde amnesia inevitably have some retrograde amnesia. For example, Squire, Haist, and Shimamura (1989) found that the period of retrograde amnesia in patients with anterograde amnesia (including some known to have hippocampal damage) lasted approximately fifteen years. That is, the patients are unable to remember events for several years before the time of their brain damage but can remember events from the remote past. This finding means that the hippocampal system is involved in the retrieval of relatively young declarative memories but is not needed for the retrieval of old ones. What happens over the course of several years that makes declarative memories accessible without the use of the hippocampal complex? Is it simply a matter of practice—does the act of remembering something again and again, over the period of years, somehow reinforce that memory so that it can be more easily retrieved later? When we can answer this question, we will really know something about the memory process.

INTERIM SUMMARY

Brain damage can produce anterograde amnesia, which consists of the inability to remember events that happen after the damage occurs, even though immediate memory (such as that needed to carry on a conversation) is largely intact. The patients also have a retrograde amnesia of several years' duration but can remember information from the distant past. Ordinary stimulus-response learning does not appear to be impaired; people can learn to recognize new stimuli, they are capable of instrumental and classical conditioning, and they can acquire conditioned emotional responses. However, they are not capable of *declarative learning*—of describing events that happen to them. They are also unable to learn the meanings of words they did not know before the brain damage took place.

Although other structures may be involved, researchers are now confident that the primary cause of anterograde amnesia is damage to the hippocampal formation or to its inputs and outputs. The entorhinal cortex receives information from all regions of the association cortex, through its connections with a ring of cortex that surrounds it. Neurons in the entorhinal cortex send axons through the perforant path to the dentate gyrus. From there information is transmitted to field CA3 and then field CA1 of the hippocampus, then to the subicular complex, and finally back to the entorhinal cortex. Subcortical inputs and outputs to the hippocampal formation pass through the fimbria/fornix system.

Studies with laboratory animals indicate that damage to the hippocampal formation disrupts the ability to learn spatial relations and to distinguish events that have just occurred from those that have occurred at another time. The basic deficit appears to be an inability to distinguish among different contexts, which includes positions in space and in time. Although the animals can learn simple discrimination tasks, they cannot learn conditional discrimination tasks, in which a stimulus has different meanings in different contexts.

The hippocampal formation contains neurons that respond when the animal is in a particular location, which implies that the hippocampus contains neural networks that keep track of the relations among stimuli in the environment that define the animal's location. Much of this information is received from the parietal cortex. The hippocampal formation is also informed about learned responses that the animal is about to make; electrical activity there is closely correlated with the movement of the conditioned nictitating membrane response. Per-

haps this information helps the animal determine the context in which it is performing the behavior; hippocampal lesions disrupt reversal of a differential classical conditioning task but not its original acquisition.

The original role of the hippocampal formation may well have been to provide animals with the ability to orient in space, keeping track of the multiple stimuli that define spatial location; but it is clear that its role has expanded to learning relations among nonspatial stimuli and situations, as well. Presumably, people with anterograde amnesia can no longer learn about episodes in their lives because their inability to distinguish one context from another prevents the elements that make up an episode from being tied together.

CONCLUDING REMARKS

Learning involves changes in neurons, and the location of the changes depends on the nature of what is being learned. Learning to perceive visual stimuli involves neurons in the visual association cortex, especially the inferior temporal cortex. Learning to respond to biologically relevant stimuli that control species-typical defensive behaviors or conditioned food aversions involves neurons in various nuclei of the amygdala. Learning a classically conditioned nictitating membrane response involves a circuit of neurons in the cerebellum and brain stem. The progess that has been made in recent years in finding these circuits of neurons will provide investigators with the opportunity to determine just what kinds of changes neurons undergo when the organism learns something.

The hippocampus plays an important role in spatial perception and memory and may also serve as a temporary repository for memories. In the next chapter I describe some recent research devoted to discovering the changes in neural connections that may be responsible for storing memories of recent events—including those that take place in the hippocampus.

NEW TERMS

accessory abducens
    nucleus p. 456
anterograde amnesia p. 460
CA1 p. 465
CA3 p. 465
classical conditioning p. 436
conditional response
    (CR) p. 437
conditional stimulus
    (CS) p. 437
conditioned emotional
    response p. 437
declarative memory p. 463

dentate gyrus p. 465
entorhinal cortex p. 465
fimbria p. 465
Hebb rule p. 437
hippocampal formation p. 464
instrumental conditioning p. 438
interpositus nucleus p. 456
Korsakoff's syndrome p. 460
medial division of the medial
    geniculate nucleus (MGM) p. 452
neural network p. 447
nictitating membrane p. 455
perforant path p. 465

place cell p. 472
punishing stimulus p. 438
reference memory p. 471
reinforcing stimulus p. 438
retractor bulbi p. 456
retrograde amnesia p. 460
subicular complex p. 465
unconditional response
    (UR) p. 437
unconditional stimulus
    (US) p. 437
working memory p. 471

SUGGESTED READINGS

Byrne, J.H., and Berry, W.O. *Neural Models of Plasticity: Experimental and Theoretical Approaches.* San Diego, Cal.: Academic Press, 1989.

Changeux, J.-P., and Konishi, M. *The Neural and Molecular Bases of Learning.* Chichester, England: John Wiley & Sons, 1987.

Isaacson, R.L., and Pribram, K.H. *The Hippocampus. Vol. 4.* New York: Plenum Press, 1986.

Imbert, M. *Models of Visual Perception: From Natural to Artificial.* Oxford: Oxford University Press, 1989.

Olton, D.S., and Kesner, R.P. *Neurobiology of Comparative Cognition.* Hillsdale, N.J.: Lawrence Erlbaum Associates, 1989.

Rumelhart, D.E., McClellan, J.L., and the PDP Research Group. *Parallel Distributed Processing: Explorations in the Microstructure of Cognition.* Cambridge, Mass.: MIT Press, 1986.

Squire, L.R. *Memory and Brain.* New York: Oxford University Press, 1987.

15

Physiology and Biochemistry of Memory

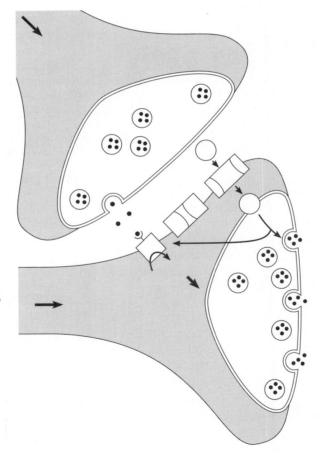

*C*hapter 14 discussed the anatomy of memory. We saw that there are three types of learning: perceptual learning, sensory-response learning, and motor learning. We saw that perceptual learning involves changes in networks of neurons located in the sensory association cortex, and that both sensory-response learning and motor learning involve the strengthening of connections between particular sensory and motor systems. In addition, relational learning, a special form of sensory-response learning, makes it possible to learn configurations of stimuli and to tie particular experiences to the context in which they occur. This type of learning involves the establishment of interconnections between sensory and motor systems in many parts of the brain, guided by the hippocampal formation.

Chapter 14 described the strengthening of synapses as the basis of learning but left open the question of just how this strengthening occurs. This chapter discusses research on the nature of the physiological changes responsible for learning.

THE CONSOLIDATION PROCESS

In the discussion of anterograde amnesia in the section on relational learning in Chapter 14, I described the distinction between immediate and long-term memory without describing them more specifically. Now it is time to examine their characteristics more carefully.

Two Stages of Memory

Many psychologists believe that learning consists of at least two stages: short-term memory and long-term memory. They conceive of short-term memory as a means of storing a limited amount of information temporarily and long-term memory as a means of storing an unlimited amount (or at least an enormously large amount) of information permanently. For example, if someone dictated seven numbers to you, you could probably repeat them back; if someone dictated fifteen numbers, you would not be able to do so. However, you could certainly *memorize* fifteen numbers if you

studied and rehearsed them long enough. Thus, a simple model of the memory process says that sensory information enters short-term memory, rehearsal keeps it there, and eventually, the information makes its way into long-term memory, where it is permanently stored. The conversion of short-term memories into long-term memories has been called *consolidation,* because the memories are "made solid," so to speak. (See *Figure 15.1.*)

If such a model is correct, it implies that we need to seek two different types of storage. Perhaps, as many investigators have suggested, short-term memory consists of neural activity, and long-term memory consists of synaptic changes. In fact, the original explanation for anterograde amnesia caused by brain damage was that both short-term memory and long-term memory were intact, but that the consolidation process that links them was faulty. But as we saw in Chapter 14, people with anterograde amnesia have no difficulty with nondeclarative stimulus-response learning. Clearly, their long-term memory *can* acquire new information.

The problem with the simple consolidation hypothesis of memory is that it ignores the fact that there are at least two types of short-term memory. One type, which some psychologists have called *working memory,* is an active process. It is actually a kind of private behavior, involving repetition of new information, recollection of old information, manipulation of images, and otherwise thinking about the information that has just been perceived. For example, if you try to memorize a telephone number, you will actively repeat

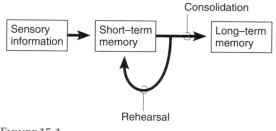

FIGURE 15.1

A simple model of the learning process.

the number to yourself. In doing so, you are undoubtedly using the same brain mechanisms that are involved in talking to other people, although you may not actually move your lips. (I will discuss these mechanisms in Chapter 17.) You may also call upon information that is already in long-term memory. If you notice that the number contains the month and day you were born, you will use that fact to remember the number more easily.

The other type of short-term memory is passive. We do not think about it; it operates automatically and produces short-term changes that may or may not result in long-term ones. Presumably, this type of short-term memory leads to nondeclarative long-term memory. Passive short-term memory is involved in simple stimulus-response learning, such as the acquisition of a pattern discrimination.

Both types of short-term memory, active and passive, undoubtedly involve neural activity. Thus, if something disrupts neural activity in the brain, it should "erase" short-term memory without necessarily affecting long-term memory, which involves structural changes. In fact, short-term memories can be disrupted in several ways. For example, if a person receives a head injury that causes a loss of consciousness, he or she is likely to have a short period of retrograde amnesia for the events that occurred just prior to the injury. Often, a football player that receives a head injury forgets the play that led to his injury, and a person who receives a concussion in an automobile accident cannot remember how the accident occurred. Obviously, head injuries are not useful tools of laboratory research, but many investigators have made use of a treatment, originally devised as a therapy for mental illness, which causes retrograde amnesia.

Experimental Retrograde Amnesia

During the 1930s Ugo Cerletti, an Italian psychiatrist, developed a technique called *electroconvulsive therapy (ECT).* The procedure entails passing a brief electrical current through electrodes attached to a person's head. The effect of the current is to induce a seizure similar to that which occurs naturally in people with epilepsy. The original purpose of the procedure was to alleviate the symptoms of schizophrenia, but clin-

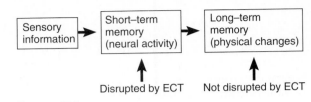

FIGURE 15.2
A simple explanation of the effects of electroconvulsive therapy on learning.

icians soon found that ECT had little effect on the hallucinations and delusions they hoped to reduce. However, they did discover that ECT improved the mood of people with severe depression. Because depression can be a fatal condition (a significant number of depressed people commit suicide), ECT is still used today to treat some patients. But that is another story, which I will discuss in Chapter 18.

The relevance of seizures produced by ECT to the topic of this chapter is that patients who receive it inevitably forget events that occurred shortly before the seizure. That is, they show a retrograde amnesia. Perhaps the seizure disrupts ongoing short-term memories, preventing their consolidation into long-term memory. Many studies with patients undergoing ECT have documented the amnestic (amnesia-producing) effect of the seizure. (See *Figure 15.2.*)

As you might expect, experimental seizures have been employed by many investigators to study the consolidation process in animals. (When used experimentally, the technique is more appropriately called electroconvulsive *shock*, ECS, rather than electroconvulsive *therapy*.) The procedure most commonly used to test for consolidation employs a *passive-avoidance task.* For example, Chorover and Schiller (1965) used an apparatus consisting of a chamber with a grid floor, in the middle of which was a small wooden platform. (See *Figure 15.3.*) The experimenters placed rats on the platform and gave them a brief foot shock as soon as they left it and stepped onto the floor. They removed the animals from the chamber and put them back into their home cage. The next day they placed the rats on the platform again. This time the animals stayed put; they showed that they remembered receiving the painful shock after stepping down the previous day.

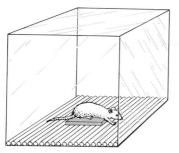

FIGURE 15.3

The step-down apparatus for testing retention of a passive-avoidance response.

(The animals avoid the possibility of receiving another shock by remaining *passive,* which explains the name given to this type of task.)

Because the rats learned the task after a single trial, the experimenters knew precisely when the punishing stimulus (the foot shock) occurred. Chorover and Schiller trained several groups of rats in this way, following the foot shock with an artificially induced seizure. Several days before the experimental session, they pierced the rats' ears and fitted them with a set of earrings made from metal dress snaps. They attached wires to these earrings before placing the rats on the platform. After the rats stepped off the platform and received a foot shock, the experimenters passed a brief pulse of electricity through the wires. The current passed through the rats' brains and induced a seizure. Different groups of rats received seizures at different time intervals after the foot shock. Figure 15.4 shows the data. Animals that received ECS within a few seconds after the punishing foot shock stepped off the platform quickly the next day; they did not appear to remember the experience. However, as the interval between the foot shock and the seizure increased, more and more subjects remained on the platform when tested the next day. The results suggest that in rats an electrically induced seizure disrupts the consolidation of short-term memories if it occurs within a few seconds of an experience. (See *Figure 15.4.*)

Most studies using ECS with laboratory animals have found that the period of retrograde amnesia is very short—on the order of a few seconds. In fact, some studies indicate that if an animal is already familiar with the chamber in which it is

trained (so that it need not learn about the environment), the ECS must be given less than a second after the animal steps down, or it will remember the experience the next day (McGaugh and Herz, 1972). These findings contrast with the retrograde amnesia seen in humans who receive ECT, which is generally much longer.

In fact, two different types of short-term memory are probably involved. The passive-avoidance task is clearly a test of nondeclarative memory, whereas humans are typically given declarative memory tests, such as lists of words to memorize. Thus, the comparison is not simply between two species; it is also between two types of learning. An early observation reported by therapists who were administering ECT to humans suggests that even in humans, nondeclarative memories are more resistant to the amnesic effects of the seizures. The therapists reported that even though the patients remembered nothing about the procedure that had taken place in the room where the ECS was given (that is, they had a "declarative amnesia"), they acted fearful when they entered the room for their next treatment and sometimes reported that they felt as if something bad had happened there. Thus, the ECS did not prevent

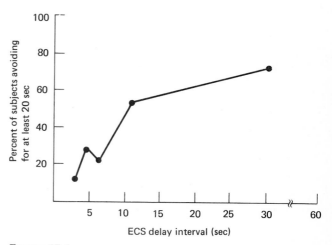

FIGURE 15.4

Effects of ECS delay interval on passive-avoidance performance. (From Chorover, S.L., and Schiller, P.H. *Journal of Comparative and Physiological Psychology,* 1965, *59,* 73–78. Copyright 1965 by the American Psychological Association. Reprinted by permission of the author.)

the formation of a conditioned emotional response. It appears that the seizures disrupted the neural activity responsible for the short-term declarative memories but had much less effect on the nondeclarative ones.

The simplest explanation for the amnestic effects of a seizure is that short-term memories consist of neural activity in circuits that encode the stimuli that were just perceived and that the seizure—a bout of wild, uncontrolled neural firing—disrupts this activity. In nondeclarative memories such as the passive-avoidance task, the most important sensory information relates to the act of stepping down and feeling something painful with the feet. The particular pattern of neural firing encodes the details of the experience. If a seizure disrupts this pattern before consolidation has taken place, the memory is irretrievably lost.

Unfortunately, we cannot be certain that the simplest explanation of the effects of a seizure is correct. We now know that seizures are especially disruptive of hippocampal functioning and that they even produce permanent damage. This fact makes it difficult to interpret the results of electroconvulsive shock on learning. Nowadays, scientists interested in the physiology of learning rarely use electroconvulsive shock, because it has not taught us as much about the learning process as we had hoped.

The Nature of Short-Term Memory

Almost certainly, the same types of structural changes are responsible for both declarative and nondeclarative long-term memories—that is, strengthening of synaptic connections. However, the process is different. As we saw, the short-term memory (working memory) that gives rise to declarative long-term memories is a private behavior, which obviously must involve the activity of neural circuits located throughout the brain. Thus, the declarative long-term memories take longer to become established and involve more complex changes in the brain.

Nondeclarative learning that occurs gradually, over the course of several trials (such as most forms of classical or instrumental conditioning), probably occurs as a result of small changes in the nervous system that are produced each time the stimuli are presented (or each time the response is reinforced). Short-term memory for this type of learning may not last more than a few seconds.

The short-term phase of declarative learning takes longer than that of nondeclarative learning because it involves private behaviors. Some experiments I discussed in Chapter 14 provide evidence that remembering a stimulus that was just perceived involves neural activity. For example, you will recall that Fuster and Jervey (1981) found that neurons in the inferior temporal cortex of monkeys were excited by the sample stimulus in a visual delayed matching-to-sample task and continued to fire for the duration of the delay interval, even after the stimulus was turned off. We can speculate that a particular sample stimulus activated a particular set of neural circuits, and their continued activity constituted the short-term memory. Once the matching stimuli were presented and the animal made its choice, the activity was no longer needed.

Because the animals in Fuster and Jervey's experiment saw the same set of stimuli again and again, the short-term memory consisted of the activation of neural circuits that had already been established. Most stimuli we perceive are probably hybrids, consisting of familiar and unfamiliar components. Thus, the short-term neural representations of them are also hybrids. In fact, Miller (1956) discovered that people can remember, on the average, about seven independent pieces of information in their short-term (working) memory: seven numbers, seven letters, seven words, or seven tones with a particular pitch. But if we can remember and think about only seven pieces of information at a time, how can we manage to write novels, design buildings, or even carry on a simple conversation? The answer comes in a particular form of encoding of information that Miller called *chunking*.

Chunking refers to the fact that a large component of short-term memory consists of activated long-term memory. That is, if a stimulus is identical to (or strongly resembles) one that we are already familiar with, the details of the stimulus do not have to be explicitly placed in short-term memory; all that needs to be done is to activate some circuits that are already there. For example, suppose that I briefly showed you a photograph of your own house and asked you to draw it from memory; you would easily be able to do so. Obviously, the mental image you would base your drawing on would come from long-term memory that was activated by the sight of the photograph. Suppose, instead, that I showed you a photograph of a house *similar* to your own but having some different details. Now you would base your drawing on your long-term memory of your house, with a few changes coming from the differences you had noted and stored in short-term memory. This is why I referred to short-term working memory in the previous paragraph as a *hybrid*.

As we have seen, declarative and nondeclarative short-term memories differ considerably in their complexity and in their duration. In declarative short-term memory the sensory activity may give rise to complex private behaviors that affect what is ultimately learned. In nondeclarative short-term memory the neural activity may barely outlast the activity in the sensory system. But in any case, we can be certain of one thing: Long-term memory is always initiated by neural activity. Thus, if short-term memory consists of temporary neural activity and long-term memory consists of physical changes in synaptic connections, the question we need to ask is how neural activity can produce structural changes. The rest of this chapter is devoted to this issue.

*I*NTERIM SUMMARY

Many psychologists believe that learning takes place in two stages: Immediate short-term memories eventually become consolidated into long-term memories. However, the short-term memory that leads to declarative long-term memories is probably different from that which leads to nondeclarative memories. Declarative short-term memory (often called "working memory") is actually a form of private behavior, in which we rehearse information and otherwise think about it. Clearly, this form of memory can last for a considerable amount of time, which helps explain the disruptive effects of electroconvulsive therapy on human memory. Although we have no way of knowing what other animals "think" about, they presumably have a similar form of short-term memory. In contrast, nondeclarative short-term

memory, involving simple stimulus-response learning, is much shorter and is less vulnerable to the effects of electroconvulsive shock.

Short-term memory of both kinds undoubtedly consists of neural activity. In most cases short-term memory is a hybrid of new and old information ("chunking"), and thus it includes activation of neural circuits that encode information that has already become part of long-term memory.

THE PHYSIOLOGY OF LONG-TERM MEMORY

A logical way to discover the physical changes that occur in the nervous system when learning takes place would be to teach animals something and then examine their nervous system carefully, comparing them with those of animals that had not received the training. Unfortunately, there are many practical problems with this approach. For one thing, the brain is exceedingly complex, and no two brains are exactly alike. Thus, unless we know exactly where to look, we are unlikely to find any significant differences between two groups of brains. Even if we do discover some differences, we cannot be sure that they were a direct result of learning. For example, if the learning task exposes the animals to stress or causes them to increase their activity, their brains could change as a result of factors not specific to the learning itself.

In this section we will examine three approaches to the study of the physiology of long-term memory: making the learning experience very important for the animal; using an organism with a simple nervous system; and artificially stimulating a part of the nervous system, duplicating (one hopes) the effects of the neural activity that initiates long-term memory.

Effects of Experience on the Structure of the Nervous System

More than twenty-five years ago, Rosenzweig and his colleagues began a research program designed to circumvent this problem by teaching animals *many* things and comparing their brains with those of animals that learned very little (see Rosenzweig, 1984, for a review). That way they might be able to see the kinds of changes that learning produces, even though they would not be able to determine which changes were caused by which experiences. The experimenters divided litters of rats and placed the animals into two kinds of environments: enriched and impoverished. The enriched environment contained such things as running wheels, ladders, slides, and "toys" that the animals could explore and manipulate. The experimenters changed these objects every day to maximize the animals' experiences and thus ensure that they would learn as much as possible. The impoverished environments were plain cages in a dimly illuminated, quiet room.

Rosenzweig and his colleagues found many differences in the brains of animals raised in the two environments. The brains of rats raised in the enriched environment had a thicker cortex, a better capillary supply, more glial cells, more protein content, and more acetylcholinesterase (and, by inference, more acetylcholine-secreting terminal buttons). As we will see later in this chapter, acetylcholine appears to play a role in learning; thus, this last finding may be especially noteworthy. Subsequent studies have found changes on a microanatomical level as well. Turner and Greenough (1985) observed an increase in the size of synapses and approximately 25 percent more synapses per neuron, and Greenough and Volkmar (1973) observed that neurons had larger and more complex dendritic trees. Changes occur even in the adult brain; Sirevaag, Black, Shafron, and Greenough (1988) found that when rats were placed in an enriched environment between the ages of thirty and sixty days (young adulthood), the capillaries in their visual cortex grew more branches and their surface area increased, presumably to accommodate the growth of neural processes stimulated by the experience.

These studies provided evidence that learning produces changes in the nervous system that we can detect by present methods. Of course, it is possible that the particular changes that have been observed do not themselves represent memories but are simply a result of better health or some other nonspecific effect of living in a more stimulating environment. In fact, the "enriched" laboratory environment is undoubtedly more normal than the impoverished one, compared with the environment in which wild rats live. Thus, it might be more fair to say that an impoverished environment leads to a thinner cortex, poorer capillary supply, and so on. However, there is no reason *not* to believe that at least some of the differences between the two groups of animals are a direct result of learning. The next step is to train animals to perform particular tasks and look for changes in those parts of the brain that receive the relevant stimuli and that control the relevant responses.

Findings of several experiments suggest that learning itself can increase the complexity of neural connections. For example, Spinelli and Jensen (1979) and Spinelli, Jensen, and DiPrisco (1980) trained kittens on an avoidance task in which a visual stimulus warned the animals that unless they lifted their paw, they would receive a mild shock to their forearm in a few seconds. The investigators found extensive changes in the response properties of neurons in the visual cortex, somatosensory cortex, and motor cortex. For example, a warning stimulus presented to one eye told the animals that the avoidance response should be made, and a "safety" stimulus presented to the other eye told them that nothing was going to happen. The experimenters found that a large number of neurons in the side of the somatosensory cortex opposite to the trained foreleg responded to the warning stimulus. They also found anatomical changes in the somatosensory cortex, including increased dendritic branching, as shown in Figure 15.5. The photomicrograph on the left is from "untrained" somatosensory cortex; the one on the right is from "trained" cortex. (See *Figure 15.5.*)

Spinelli and his colleagues studied kittens because they found that similar training failed to produce detectable changes in the brains of adult cats. Presumably, the changes in the brain produced by one small experience were simply lost among all the other changes that had taken place. Training the animals while their brains were still developing appears to have magnified the effects of the experience.

Greenough, Juraska, and Volkmar (1979) succeeded in finding specific learning-induced changes in the brains of adult animals. They gave rats extensive training in a series of mazes, which

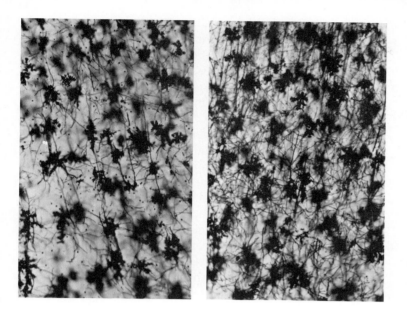

FIGURE 15.5
Dendrites of neurons from "untrained" somatosensory cortex (*left*) and "trained" somatosensory cortex (*right*). Golgi-Cox stain. (From Spinelli, D.N., Jensen, F.E., and DiPrisco, G.V. *Experimental Neurology*, 1980, *62*, 1–11.)

contrasted with the relative lack of visual stimulation received by the control animals. The investigators found larger dendritic fields in the animals' visual cortex. Of course, the changes could have been caused by factors not specific to learning, such as increased exercise or changes in hormone levels. However, Chang and Greenough (1982) showed that the changes were caused by visual stimulation received during training. They divided the rats' cerebral hemispheres by cutting the corpus callosum and placed an opaque contact lens on one eye. This treatment permitted visual information from the maze training to reach only one hemisphere. Changes in dendritic fields were seen only on the side of the brain that received the increased visual stimulation.

As you learned in Chapter 14, considerable progress has been made in finding the precise neurons involved in the classical conditioning of the nictitating membrane response. Perhaps some day investigators will be able to detect changes in these neurons and relate them directly to the circuitry responsible for the learning task.

The studies reviewed in this subsection have shown us that single learning tasks do not produce changes in the brain that we can detect with our current technology unless very young animals are used. If adult animals are trained on an extended series of tasks, changes can be detected,

but these changes cannot be said to be a result of any particular experience. We have seen that experience can certainly affect the nervous system, producing changes in the number of synapses and the complexity of dendritic branching; but clearly, another approach is needed to be able to relate particular changes to the establishment of particular memories.

Learning in a Simple Nervous System

One way to avoid the difficulties in trying to find learning-induced changes in the nervous system is to study animals with simple nervous systems. For several years researchers have been studying *Aplysia californica* (the sea hare), a shell-less marine mollusk. They have discovered much about the physiological basis of habituation, sensitization, and, recently, about classical conditioning, as well.

Habituation and Sensitization of the Retraction Response

Behavioral studies of *Aplysia* have focused on the external organs of the mantle cavity: the gill, mantle shelf, and siphon. The gill exchanges gases with seawater, thus obtaining oxygen and releasing carbon dioxide. The mantle shelf is a

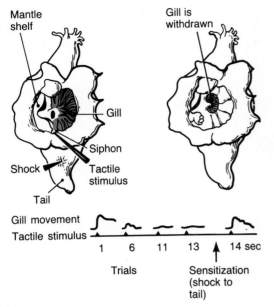

FIGURE 15.6

Habituation and sensitization of the gill withdrawal response. (From Kandel, E.R., and Schwartz, J.H. *Science*, 1982, *218*, 433–443. Copyright 1982 by the American Association for the Advancement of Science.)

protective sheet that forms a funnellike siphon at its posterior end. Normally, movements of the mantle cause water to be pumped into and out of the mantle cavity. (See *Figure 15.6*.)

When the siphon or mantle shelf is touched, all three external organs retract into the mantle cavity. This defensive response presumably serves to protect these appendages from harm. When a weak stimulus is applied repeatedly to one location (say, the siphon), the response eventually disappears; that is, it *habituates*. This habituation is specific to a particular afferent pathway; if the experimenter now stimulates another location (say, the mantle shelf), the siphon, mantle shelf, and gill will all retract. In contrast to habituation, *sensitization* is a more general phenomenon. The presentation of a noxious stimulus, such as an electrical shock applied to the tail, will increase the amplitude of withdrawal responses elicited by gentle touch of any part of the mantle cavity area. Figure 15.6 shows habituation of the gill withdrawal response after one, six, eleven, and thirteen gentle tactile stimuli applied to the siphon,

followed by sensitization of this response produced by an electrical shock to the tail (Kandel and Schwartz, 1982). (See *Figure 15.6*.)

Kandel and his colleagues (for specific references, see Kandel and Schwartz, 1982) have identified most of the neurons that participate in the withdrawal reflex. They have located five motor neurons that innervate the gill, seven that innervate the siphon, and one that innervates both. Two groups of twenty-four sensory neurons, one group serving the mantle shelf and one group serving the skin of the siphon, activate these motor neurons. In addition, several interneurons produce excitation or inhibition. Habituation is caused by a decrease in the release of transmitter substance by the sensory neurons, and sensitization is caused by an increase in its release.

Sensitization is produced by serotonin-secreting facilitatory interneurons that form axoaxonic synapses with sensory neurons. These interneurons are activated by noxious stimuli, such as a shock delivered to the tail. Their activity produces presynaptic facilitation; that is, they cause the terminal buttons with which they form synapses to release more of their transmitter substance when they fire. This means that the next time the sensory neuron in the siphon skin is stimulated, it produces a gill withdrawal. (See *Figure 15.7*.)

Kandel and his colleagues found that the increase in the release of transmitter substance is caused by an increase in the amount of calcium that enters the terminal button. You will recall from Chapter 3 that the release of a transmitter substance is triggered by the entry of calcium ions into the terminal buttons, which activates protein molecules that propel the synaptic vesicles to the presynaptic membrane. In the excitatory axoaxonic synapses of *Aplysia* the presence of a molecule of 5-HT at a receptor activates the adenylate cyclase with which the receptor is coupled. This activation causes the production of cyclic AMP, which activates a protein kinase that *closes* nearby potassium channels. This closure sets the stage for an increased release of transmitter substance.

Let us see why. You will recall from Chapter 3 that the rapid repolarization of an action potential is caused by the movement of the potassium ion

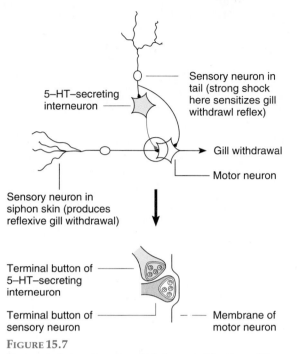

5–HT–secreting interneuron

Sensory neuron in tail (strong shock here sensitizes gill withdrawl reflex)

Gill withdrawal

Motor neuron

Sensory neuron in siphon skin (produces reflexive gill withdrawal)

Terminal button of 5–HT–secreting interneuron

Terminal button of sensory neuron

Membrane of motor neuron

FIGURE 15.7

The neural circuit responsible for sensitization of the gill withdrawal response. (Adapted from Kandel, E.R., and Schwartz, J.H. *Science*, 1982, *218*, 433–443.)

(K⁺) out of the cell. (See *Figure 15.8*.) Obviously, K^+ can leave the cell only if the potassium channels are open. But we just saw that the presence of 5-HT causes potassium channels to close; thus, K^+ leaves the cell much more slowly than normally, and the duration of the action potential is prolonged. And during the time that the cell is depolarized, voltage-dependent ion channels are open, permitting calcium ions (Ca^{2+}) to enter the cell. The increased concentration of Ca^{2+} in the terminal button causes an increased release of transmitter substance. (See *Figure 15.9*.)

Classical Conditioning of the Withdrawal Response

It turns out that the mechanism discovered by Kandel and his colleagues applies to classical conditioning as well as to sensitization. Let us examine the behavior. Withdrawal of the siphon and gill can be classically conditioned by presenting a light touch to the siphon or mantle (CS) and then presenting a strong electrical shock to the tail (US). In fact, the response can be differentially conditioned. Carew, Hawkins, and Kandel (1983) applied gentle tactile stimuli to two different

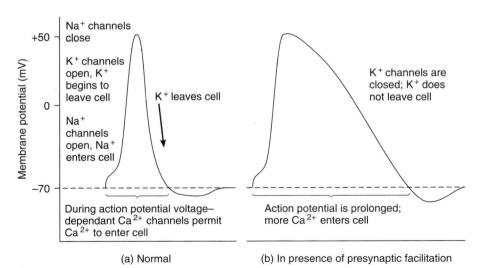

FIGURE 15.8

Role of K^+ efflux during the action potential. (a) A normal action potential. (b) A long-duration action potential, caused by a reduced rate of K^+ efflux.

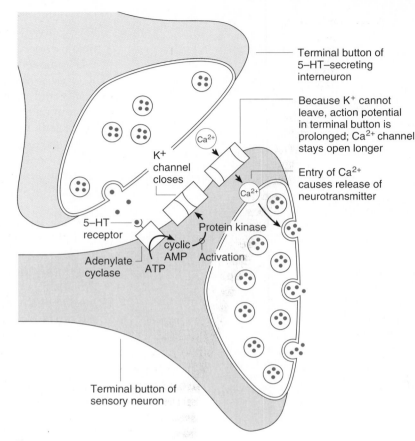

Terminal button of
5–HT–secreting
interneuron

Because K$^+$ cannot
leave, action potential
in terminal button is
prolonged; Ca^{2+} channel
stays open longer

Entry of Ca^{2+}
causes release of
neurotransmitter

Ca^{2+}

Ca^{2+}

K$^+$
channel
closes

5–HT
receptor

Protein kinase

Adenylate
cyclase

ATP

cyclic
AMP

Activation

Terminal button of
sensory neuron

FIGURE 15.9

The mechanism believed to be responsible for sensitization of the gill
withdrawal response. Release of 5-HT by the interneuron causes K$^+$
channels in the terminal button of the sensory neuron to close, thus
prolonging the action potential, the influx of Ca^{2+}, and the release of the
neurotransmitter.

places, the siphon and mantle, but followed only
one of these stimuli (CS$^+$) with a noxious shock;
the other stimulus (CS$^-$) was never followed by
shock. (See *Figure 15.10.*) After fifteen training
trials the CS$^+$ produced a strong withdrawal reaction, but the CS$^-$ did not.

Classical conditioning can be accomplished in
an isolated central nervous system. Hawkins,
Abrams, Carew, and Kandel (1983) separated the
Aplysia central nervous system from the rest of the
animal, leaving it attached to the tail. They
inserted stimulating electrodes into two sensory
neurons serving the skin of the siphon and inserted a recording electrode into a motor neuron
that innervates the siphon. (You can see the advantage of using an animal with such a simple ner-

vous system.) They used the stimulating electrodes to present conditional stimuli, and they
recorded the activity of the siphon motor neuron
(the response). Stimulation of one neuron in the
intact nervous system (CS$^+$) was paired with the
unconditional stimulus, a shock to the tail. Stimulation of the other neuron (CS$^-$) was not. The
procedure worked: Within five trials the CS$^+$
produced conditional responses (increased
excitatory postsynaptic potentials), but the CS$^-$
did not.

Hawkins and his colleagues then followed the
same training procedure and measured the efflux
of potassium from the terminal button caused by
stimulating each of the sensory neurons. They
found that stimulating the "paired" neuron (CS$^+$)

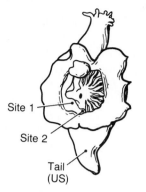

FIGURE 15.10

Differential classical conditioning of the siphon withdrawal reflex. CS^+ and CS^- are tactile stimuli applied to different portions of the siphon and mantle.

produced a smaller outward flow of potassium than stimulating the "unpaired" neuron (CS^-), which indicates that the potassium channels were closed. As you can see, these effects are similar to those produced by sensitization. The investigators suggested that when a sensory neuron and a serotonergic facilitatory interneuron are activated at the same time, the synapses between the CS^+ neuron and the motor neuron are strengthened. (See *Figure 15.11*.)

But what is the mechanism by which the facilitatory interneuron strengthens the synapses that belong to the CS^+ neuron but not the CS^- neuron? Byrne and Gingrich (1989) suggest the following model. First, an action potential in the CS^+ neuron opens voltage-dependent calcium channels, and some Ca^{2+} enters the cell. The intracellular Ca^{2+} then causes the release of the transmitter substance but also "primes" the adenylate cyclase, making it more sensitive to the action of the 5-HT receptor. When the US is presented, the facilitatory interneuron releases 5-HT. The primed adenylate cyclase produces more cyclic AMP than it does in the unprimed state, which results in the closure of more potassium channels, the entry of more calcium, and the release of more transmitter substance. Presumably, the priming effect of the calcium on the adenylate cyclase lasts only for a short time; if the US occurs too late, the 5-HT will arrive at the receptor too late to cause a large influx of calcium. (See *Figure 15.12*.)

Most investigators agree that long-term classical conditioning probably involves structural changes in synapses as well as changes in the adenylate cyclase molecule. For example, Montarolo et al. (1986) found that long-term sensitization occurs only when protein synthesis is permitted to take place. They produced sensitization by di-

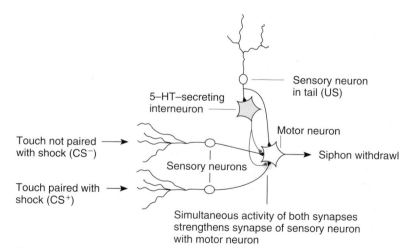

FIGURE 15.11

A hypothetical circuit responsible for differential classical conditioning of the siphon withdrawal response. (Adapted from Byrne, J.H., and Gingrich, K.J., in *Neural Models of Plasticity: Experimental and Theoretical Approaches*, edited by J.H. Byrne and W.O. Berry. San Diego: Academic Press, 1989.)

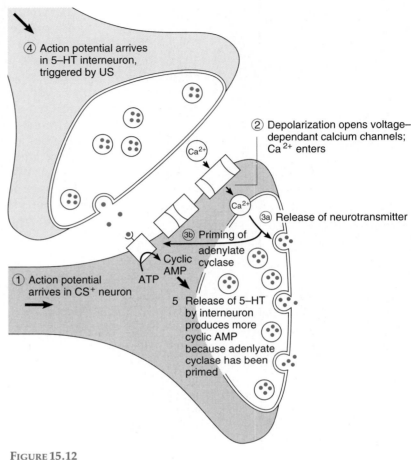

④ Action potential arrives
in 5–HT interneuron,
triggered by US

② Depolarization opens voltage–
dependant calcium channels;
Ca²⁺ enters

Ca²⁺

Ca²⁺

③a Release of neurotransmitter

③b Priming of
adenylate
cyclase

Cyclic
AMP

① Action potential
arrives in CS⁺ neuron

ATP

5 Release of 5–HT
by interneuron
produces more
cyclic AMP
because adenlyate
cyclase has been
primed

FIGURE 15.12
The mechanism believed to be responsible for differential classical
conditioning of the siphon withdrawal response. (Adapted from Byrne,
J.H., and Gingrich, K.J., in *Neural Models of Plasticity: Experimental and
Theoretical Approaches,* edited by J.H. Byrne and W.O. Berry. San Diego:
Academic Press, 1989.)

rectly applying 5-HT to the synapses of sensory
neurons. If they also applied drugs that interfere
with protein synthesis, long-term sensitization
did not occur. However, if they applied the drugs
an hour later, the drugs had no effect on sensitization. Thus, protein synthesis is needed to initiate
the change, but it is no longer required once the
change has taken place. It seems likely that the
proteins that are synthesized play a role in producing structural changes in the synapses. In fact,
Bailey and Chen (1989) found that long-term sensitization produced an increase in the length of active zones and the number of synaptic vesicles at
the synapses of sensory neurons. It remains to be

seen whether these changes would be prevented
by the inhibition of protein synthesis. (See *Figure
15.13.*)

*I*NTERIM SUMMARY

Experiences can affect the structure of the
nervous system, especially if they occur in
young animals. Rats raised in an enriched
environment, full of objects and hap-
penings, have larger brains than those
raised in an impoverished environment,
with a thicker cortex, more dendritic spines,
a higher level of acetylcholinesterase, and

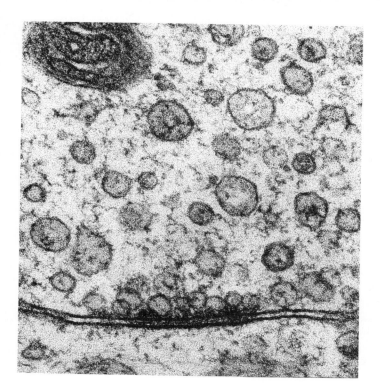

FIGURE 15.13

The active zone at a synapse in *Aplysia*. Synaptic vesicles are clustered above the presynaptic membrane. (From Bailey, C.H., Kandel, E.R., and Chen, M. *Journal of Neurophysiology*, 1981, *46*, 356–368.)

more synapses. Visual information obtained during a series of maze problems causes increased complexity only in the part of the visual cortex that receives the information. Kittens trained in a simple avoidance task have more dendritic branching in the region of the somatosensory cortex devoted to analysis of the unconditional stimulus and more neurons devoted to analysis of the visual discriminative stimuli.

Some researchers have investigated the cellular mechanisms of learning in organisms with simple nervous systems in the hope that what they discover will help others understand such mechanisms in more complex organisms. Both the sensitization of the habituated retraction response in *Aplysia* and its classical conditioning appear to be caused by serotonergic facilitatory interneurons that form synapses with the terminal buttons of sensory neurons. Sensitization occurs when an electric shock to the tail activates the serotonergic neurons. The release of 5-HT causes the production of cy-

clic AMP in the terminal buttons of the sensory neuron, which closes potassium channels and thus prolongs action potentials triggered by tactile stimulation. Longer action potentials result in the entry of more calcium and, therefore, the release of more transmitter substance.

Classical conditioning occurs when a CS is followed by a US. Action potentials in the sensory neuron (CS) cause the entry of calcium, which "primes" the molecules of adenylate cyclase. If a US immediately follows, the terminal buttons of facilitatory interneurons release 5-HT, which activates the molecules of adenylate cyclase. Because these molecules have already been "primed," they cause the production of more cyclic AMP than usual, which closes more potassium channels than usual. This results in the entry of more calcium and the release of more transmitter substance, which triggers a CR.

Studies with drugs that inhibit protein synthesis indicate that long-term sensitization (and, presumably, long-term classical conditioning) occurs only when protein synthesis can take place. Long-term sensitization produces larger synapses and a greater number of synaptic vesicles, which may be the results of this protein synthesis. Further research is needed to determine whether the events that take place in the cells of *Aplysia* will help us understand the cellular changes that learning produces in the mammalian nervous system.

Long-Term Potentiation

Recently, many investigators have begun studying the effects of electrical stimulation on structural changes in synaptic connections, based on the conviction that all long-term memories must be initiated by neural activity. This approach has proved to be extremely useful; it has taught us much about the plasticity of the nervous system and, as a bonus, has yielded interesting facts about the physiology of the hippocampal system.

The Phenomenon

Electrical stimulation of circuits within the hippocampal formation can lead to long-term physiological changes that may very well be among those responsible for learning. Lømo (1966) discovered that intense electrical stimulation of the perforant path caused a long-term increase in the magnitude of excitatory postsynaptic potentials in the dentate gyrus; this increase has come to be called *long-term potentiation.* (The word *potentiate* means "to strengthen, to make more potent.")

Figure 15.14 shows a typical procedure for producing long-term potentiation. A stimulating electrode is placed in the perforant path, and a recording electrode is placed in the dentate gyrus, near the granule cells. (See *Figure 15.14.*) First, a single pulse of electrical stimulation is delivered to the perforant path, and the resulting population EPSP is recorded in the dentate gyrus. The *population EPSP* is an extracellular measurement of the excitatory postsynaptic potentials (EPSP) produced by the synapses of the perforant path axons with the dentate granule cells. The size of the first population EPSP indicates the strength of the synaptic connections before long-term poten-

tiation has taken place. Long-term potentiation is induced by stimulating the axons in the perforant path with a burst of approximately one hundred pulses of electrical stimulation, delivered within a few seconds. Evidence that long-term potentiation has occurred is obtained by periodically delivering single pulses to the perforant path and recording the response in the dentate gyrus. (See *Figure 15.15.*)

Long-term potentiation can be produced in fields CA3 and CA1 as well as in the dentate gyrus and the neocortex (Perkins and Teyler, 1988; Brown, Ganong, Kairiss, Keenan, and Kelso, 1989). It can last for several months (Bliss and Lømo, 1973). Even more importantly, long-term potentiation can involve the interaction between different synapses on a particular neuron. That is, when weak and strong synapses to a single neuron are stimulated at approximately the same time, the weak synapse becomes strengthened. As we saw in Chapter 14, this is exactly what Hebb (1949) suggested was the basis of long-term learning.

One of the first experiments to demonstrate this phenomenon was performed by Levy and

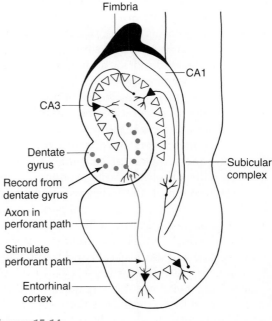

FIGURE 15.14

Some of the intrinsic circuitry of the hippocampal formation.

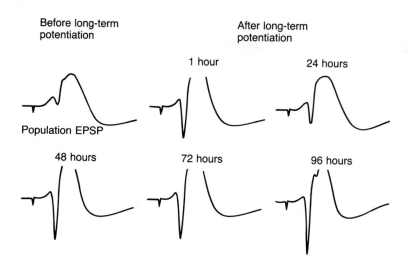

Before long-term potentiation

After long-term potentiation

1 hour

24 hours

Population EPSP

48 hours

72 hours

96 hours

FIGURE 15.15

Population EPSPs recorded from the dentate gyrus before and after electrical stimulation that led to long-term potentiation. Note that the tops of some of the waves are missing. (From Berger, T.W. *Science*, 1984, *224*, 627–630. Copyright 1984 by the American Association for the Advancement of Science.)

Steward (1983). The investigators stimulated rats' entorhinal cortex bilaterally and recorded excitatory postsynaptic potentials in the dentate gyrus on one side. The dentate gyrus receives afferent axons from the entorhinal cortex on both sides of the brain, but the contralateral projections are sparse and weak. In fact, stimulation of the entorhinal cortex does not excite the contralateral dentate gyrus enough to produce long-term potentiation there. Levy and Steward stimulated the entorhinal cortex on both sides of the brain and found that if the ipsilateral stimulation occurred simultaneously with the contralateral stimulation, or if it followed it by 20 msec or less, facilitation occurred. That is, the pairing increased the synaptic strength of the weak contralateral projections. Levy and Steward called the phenomenon *associative long-term potentiation,* because it was produced by the association (in time) between the activity of the two synapses. As you can see, these contingencies resemble what is presumed to occur during classical conditioning. (See *Figure 15.16.*)

Long-term potentiation can be produced in isolated slices of the hippocampal formation as well as in the brains of living animals, which makes it possible to stimulate and record from individual neurons and to analyze biochemical changes. The brain is removed from the skull, the

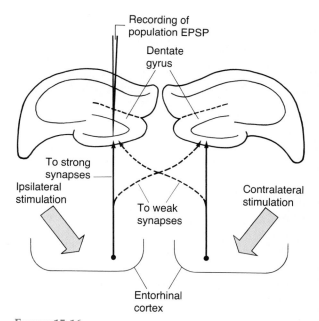

Recording of population EPSP

Dentate gyrus

To strong synapses

Ipsilateral stimulation

To weak synapses

Contralateral stimulation

Entorhinal cortex

FIGURE 15.16

The procedure of Levy and Steward that demonstrated associative long-term potentiation. *Condition 1.* Repeated contralateral stimulation (weak synapses): no change in population EPSP. *Condition 2.* Repeated contralateral stimulation (weak synapses) followed by ipsilateral stimulation (strong synapses): increased population EPSP in response to contralateral stimulation when presented alone. (Adapted from Levy, W.B., and Steward, O. *Neuroscience*, 1983, *8*, 791–797.)

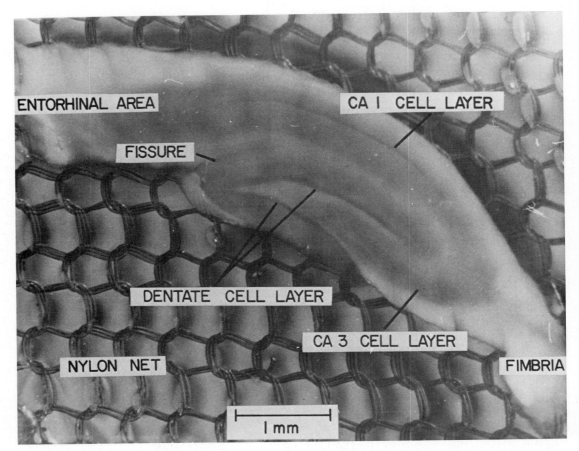

FIGURE 15.17
A photograph of a hippocampal slice in a tissue chamber. (From Teyler, T.J. *Brain Research Bulletin*, 1980, *5*, 391–403.)

hippocampal complex is dissected, and slices are placed in a temperature-controlled chamber filled with liquid that resembles interstitial fluid. Figure 15.17 shows a 400-μm slice of hippocampal formation being maintained in a tissue chamber. Under optimal conditions a slice remains alive for up to 40 hours. (See *Figure 15.17.*)

Many experiments have demonstrated that associative long-term potentiation can take place in hippocampal slices. For example, Chattarji, Stanton, and Sejnowski (1989) stimulated two sets of axons: the mossy fiber axons that connect the dentate gyrus with field CA3 and the collateral axons arising from other pyramidal cells in CA3. The mossy fiber axons *(strong input)* received bursts of stimulation, whereas the collateral axons

(weak input) received single pulses of stimulation. The investigators recorded the effects of stimulation from the layer that contains the cell bodies of the CA3 neurons. (See *Figure 15.18.*) They found that when the weak input and the strong input were stimulated together, the response of the CA3 pyramidal cells to the weak input increased.

Even *differential* associative long-term potentiation has been demonstrated in hippocampal slices. Kelso and Brown (1986) stimulated two different weak inputs (W1 and W2) and one strong input (S) to pyramidal cells in the CA1 field. In some cases they paired W1 with S; in others they paired W2 with S. They found that only the paired weak stimulus was strengthened. (See *Figure 15.19.*) These results indicate that the pairing did

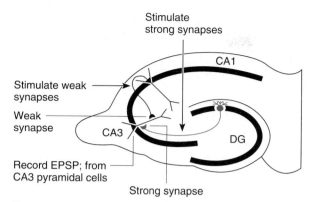

FIGURE 15.18

The procedure of the experiment by Chattarji, Stanton, and Sejnowski (1989). (Adapted from Chattarji, S., Stanton, P.K., and Sejnowski, T.J. *Brain Research*, 1989, *95*, 145–150.)

not simply make the CA1 pyramidal cells become more sensitive to *all* its inputs. Thus, the strengthening occurs in specific synapses.

Physiology and Biochemistry of Long-Term Potentiation

Long-term potentiation could be caused by several different means. It could be produced presynaptically, through increased release of transmitter substance; or it could be produced postsynaptically, through an increased number of receptors, increased ability of the receptors to activate changes in the permeability of the postsynaptic membrane, or increased communication between the region of the postsynaptic membrane and the rest of the neuron. It could also be produced by an increased number of synapses, which would involve both presynaptic and postsynaptic changes. Although it remains possible that long-term potentiation involves the production of new synapses, the evidence we have today suggests that the relevant changes are postsynaptic—that they occur in dendritic spines on pyramidal cells in the hippocampus or on granule cells of the dentate gyrus.

Long-term potentiation occurs when a sufficient amount of calcium enters a neuron. Lynch, Larson, Kelso, Barrionuevo, and Schottler (1984) demonstrated the importance of this calcium influx by injecting EGTA directly into hippocampal

pyramidal cells. This chemical binds with calcium and makes it insoluble, destroying its biological activity. The EGTA blocked the establishment of long-term potentiation in the injected cells; their excitability was not increased by high-frequency stimulation of axons that formed synapses with them. However, neighboring cells, which were not injected with EGTA, showed long-term potentiation.

Lynch and his colleagues (Lynch, Muller, Seubert, and Larson, 1988) suggest a possible mechanism for long-term potentiation. They propose that the entry of calcium into the dendritic spine causes structural changes in the dendritic spine. A high-molecular-weight protein called *spectrin* is found inside dendritic spines, where it appears to serve as a framework that supports the structure of the spine. This protein is broken down by a calcium-dependent proteolytic ("protein dissolving") enzyme called *calpain,* which is also found in dendritic spines (Perlmutter, et al., 1988). The proteolytic activity of calpain is blocked by a chemical called *leupeptin.* Researchers Staubli, Larson, Thibault, Baudry, and Lynch (1988) found that when they infused leupeptin into rats' lateral ventricles, electrical stimulation

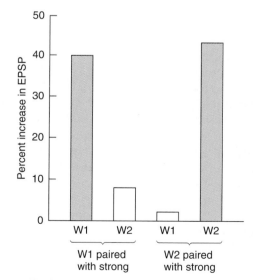

FIGURE 15.19

Differential associative long-term potentiation. (Data from Kelso, S.R., and Brown, T.H. *Science*, 1986, *232*, 85–87.)

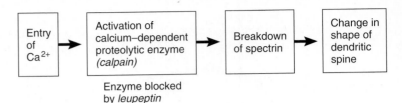

FIGURE 15.20

A summary of the hypothesized role of calpain and spectrin in long-term potentiation.

of the hippocampus no longer produced long-term potentiation. Thus, long-term potentiation appears to require the breakdown of spectrin. (See *Figure 15.20.*)

Lynch and his colleagues hypothesize that the breakdown of spectrin causes changes in the shape of dendritic spines that reduce the electrical resistance between the spine and the dendrite; thus, a postsynaptic potential produced in the dendritic spine will have a larger effect on the rest of the cell. In fact, several investigators have found that long-term potentiation changes the shape of dendritic spines. In particular, more concave spines are found, the average surface area of dendritic spines increases, and the stems that connect the spines with the dendrites become shorter and wider (Desmond and Levy, 1988). The latter two changes would increase the effectiveness of the synapse. (See *Figure 15.21.*)

Evidence suggests that protein synthesis, as well as the breakdown of protein, may play a role in long-term potentiation. Krug, Lössner, and Ott (1984) and Stanton and Sarvey (1984) found that drugs that block protein synthesis also block long-term potentiation. Fazeli, Errington, Dolphin, and Bliss (1988) inserted cannula into the dentate gyrus that permitted them to analyze the contents of the interstitial fluid. When the investigators induced long-term potentiation through electrical stimulation, they observed an increase in protein release by the tissue approximately 1 hour later. The administration of a drug that prevents long-term potentiation blocked the release of protein; thus, the stimulation itself was not responsible for its release. (The drug, AP5, will be discussed later.) The nature and function of this protein is not known.

Clearly, long-term potentiation requires some

sort of additive effect. That is, a series of pulses delivered at a high rate all in one burst will produce long-term potentiation, but the same number of pulses given at a slow rate will not. The most likely explanation for this difference is that each pulse produces an aftereffect that dissipates with time. If the next pulse comes before the aftereffect fades away, its own effect will be amplified. Thus, each pulse "primes" the following one.

Although earlier studies investigating the nature of long-term potentiation used bursts of approximately one hundred pulses, later studies discovered that if the interval between pulses is chosen carefully, much less stimulation is required. Staubli and Lynch (1987) found that stimulation that duplicated the natural pattern of firing that occurs in hippocampal pyramidal cells

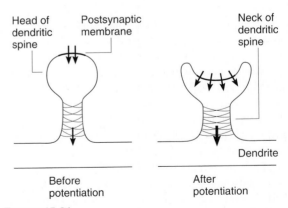

FIGURE 15.21

Changes in the shape of dendritic spines that may be produced by long-term potentiation. (Adapted from Desmond, N.L., and Levy, W.B., in *Long-term Potentiation: From Biophysics to Behavior*, edited by P.W. Landfield and S. Deadwyler. New York: A.R. Liss, 1988.)

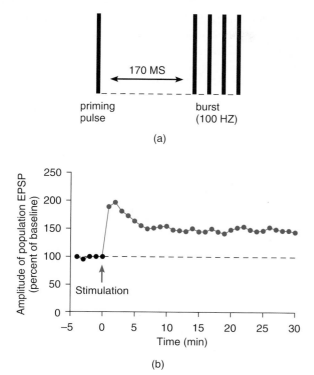

(a)

(b)

FIGURE 15.22

Long-term potentiation produced by four pulses of stimulation presented 170 msec after a priming pulse. (a) Pattern of the electrical stimulation. (b) Population EPSP. (Adapted from Diamond, D.M., Dunwiddie, T.V., and Rose, G.M. *Journal of Neuroscience*, 1988, *8*, 4079–4088.)

was much more effective than simple repetitive bursts. (I will describe this pattern of firing, called a *theta rhythm*, later in this chapter.) In fact, Diamond, Dunwiddie, and Rose (1988) were able to produce long-term potentiation with as few as five pulses of electrical stimulation: a priming pulse followed 170 msec later by a burst of four pulses. (See *Figure 15.22*.)

Experiments have made it clear that the priming effect consists of a depolarization of the postsynaptic membrane. If depolarization is prevented by hyperpolarizing the pyramidal cell with an intracellular electrode, synaptic strengthening does not occur (Malinow and Miller, 1986). In fact, all that has to happen for long-term potentiation to take place is for terminal buttons to be activated while the dendrite of the postsynaptic neurons is depolarized. Kelso, Ganong, and

Brown (1986) found that if they simultaneously stimulated axons that formed synapses with CA1 neurons and artificially depolarized the neurons with an intracellular electrode, the synapses became stronger. However, if the stimulation of the synapses and the depolarization of the neuron occurred at different times, no effect was seen; thus, the two events had to occur together.

Experiments such as the ones I just described indicate that long-term potentiation requires two events: activation of synapses and depolarization of the postsynaptic neuron. The explanation for this phenomenon, at least in some parts of the hippocampal formation, lies in the characteristics of a very special receptor. One of the most important excitatory neurotransmitters in the brain is glutamic acid (usually referred to as *glutamate*). As you have already learned, many neurotransmitters are detected by more than one type of receptors. For example, there are two major types of acetylcholine receptors—nicotinic and muscarinic, named for the agonists that best stimulate them. Similarly, there are several different types of glutamate receptors, also named for their agonists. One of them, the NMDA receptor (short for *N*-methyl-D-aspartate), plays a critical role in long-term potentiation.

The ***NMDA receptor*** has some unusual properties (see Cotman, Monaghan, and Ganong, 1988, for a review). It is found in the hippocampal formation, especially in field CA1. The NMDA receptor controls a calcium ion channel. However, this channel is normally blocked by magnesium ions (Mg^{2+}), which prevents calcium ions from entering the cell, even when the receptor is stimulated by glutamate. But if the postsynaptic membrane is depolarized (say, by the activity of other, non-NMDA receptors), the Mg^{2+} is ejected from the ion channel, and the channel is free to admit Ca^{2+} ions. Thus, calcium ions enter the cells through the channels controlled by NMDA receptors only when glutamate is present *and* when the postsynaptic membrane is already depolarized. As we just saw, the entry of calcium into the dendritic spines is the event that initiates the physical changes responsible for long-term potentiation. (See *Figure 15.23*.)

The strongest evidence implicating NMDA receptors in long-term potentiation comes from re-

Priming
Molecule of glutamate stimulates NMDA receptor, opens calcium channel, but magnesium ion blocks channel

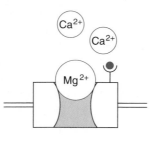

(a)

EPSP arrives from non–NMDA receptors; depolarization evicts magnesium ion, but glutamate molecule is gone; calcium channel is closed

(b)

Potentiation
Molecule of glutamate stimulates NMDA receptor, opens calcium channel

Because membrane is still depolarized, magnesium ion is still gone; calcium enters, activates calpain, initiates changes in dendritic spine

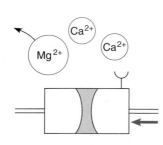

(c)

The mechanism through which NMDA receptors are believed to be responsible for long-term potentiation. (a) Priming with glutamate. (b) Eviction of Mg^{2+} ions by an EPSP from ion channels controlled by non-NMDA glutamate receptors. (c) Potentiation.

search with drugs that block NMDA receptors, such as AP5 (2-amino-5-phosphonopentanoate). AP5 prevents the establishment of long-term potentiation in field CA1 and the dentate gyrus. However, it has no effect on long-term potentiation that has already been established (Brown, Ganong, Kairiss, Keenan, and Kelso, 1989).

I think that considering what you already know about associative long-term potentiation,

you can anticipate the role that NMDA receptors play in this phenomenon. If weak synapses are active by themselves, nothing happens, because the membrane of the dendritic spine does not depolarize sufficiently for the calcium channels controlled by the NMDA receptors to open. (Remember that in order for these channels to open, the postsynaptic membrane must depolarize and displace the Mg^{2+} ions that normally block them.) However, if strong synapses on the same dendrite are active at the same time, then the postsynaptic membrane will become depolarized enough for calcium to enter the ion channels controlled by the NMDA receptors. Thus, the special properties of NMDA receptors account not only for the existence of long-term potentiation but also for its associative nature.

NMDA receptors are present in highest concentrations in field CA1 of the hippocampus, but they are also found in the dentate gyrus, the neocortex, parts of the basal ganglia, and the lateral septum. Very few NMDA receptors are found in the region of field CA3 that receives input from the dentate gyrus (Monaghan and Cotman, 1985).

The high concentration of NMDA receptors in field CA1 probably explains the fact that an episode of anoxia can damage this region. (Chapter 14 discussed the case of patient R.B., who had anterograde amnesia caused by degeneration of CA1.) Disturbances of various kinds, including seizures, anoxia, or hypoglycemia, cause the release of glutamate at abnormally high levels. Within a few minutes the presence of glutamate begins to destroy neurons (see Rothman and Olney, 1987, for a review). However, if an animal is first treated with a drug that blocks NMDA receptors, a period of anoxia is much less likely to produce brain damage.

You will recall that interpretation of the effects of electroconvulsive shock on learning is complicated by the fact that seizures can produce hippocampal damage. Labruyere et al., (1986) found that this damage can be prevented by the application of drugs that block NMDA receptors, which suggests that the damage is caused by the overstimulation of these receptors. In fact, Rogers, Barnes, Mitchell, and Tilson (1989) found that 45 minutes of sustained electrical stimulation of the perforant path caused severe degeneration of pyramidal neurons in the hippocampal formation, especially in field CA1. Pretreatment with an NMDA antagonist greatly reduced this destruction.

Another form of brain damage may also involve NMDA receptors. Huntington's chorea, a fatal inherited disease discussed in Chapter 8, is caused by degeneration of neurons in the basal ganglia. The pattern of degeneration resembles that produced by the administration of NMDA receptor agonists (Beal et al., 1986). Therefore, the disease may involve the abnormal release of glutamate and subsequent overstimulation of NMDA receptors.

The fact that NMDA receptors are found in very low concentrations in the region of field CA3 that receives input from the dentate gyrus suggests that they cannot be responsible for long-term potentiation there. In fact, although AP5, the blocker of the NMDA receptor, prevents the establishment of long-term potentiation in field CA1 and in the dentate gyrus, it has no effect in field CA3 (Harris and Cotman, 1986; Errington, Lynch, and Bliss, 1987). Another mechanism must be responsible for the development of long-term potentiation in this region.

A study by Buzsáki and Gage (1988) indicates that the subcortical inputs to the hippocampal system that enter through the fornix are essential for the establishment of long-term potentiation. The most important inputs include acetylcholinergic axons from neurons in the medial septum, noradrenergic axons from neurons in the locus coeruleus, and serotonergic axons from the raphe nuclei. Buzsáki and Gage cut the fornix of rats and several months later implanted electrodes in the perforant path and dentate gyrus. They found that stimulation of the perforant path led to long-term potentiation in control animals but not in those with fornix transections.

Which of the inputs to the hippocampal formation are important? Although all of the inputs may be important, the strongest case can be made for the involvement of norepinephrine. The administration of propranolol, a drug that blocks noradrenergic β receptors, prevents the development of long-term potential in field CA3. In addition, the infusion of norepinephrine or drugs that stimulate β receptors facilitates long-term potentiation in both field CA3 and the dentate gyrus. The effect of norepinephrine appears to be mediated by an increased influx of Ca^{2+} into the cells (see Johnston, Hopkins, and Gray, 1989, for a review). Therefore, noradrenergic β receptors, as well as NMDA receptors, appear to play a role in long-term potentiation in parts of the hippocampal formation.

Acetylcholine, too, may influence long-term potentiation. Robinson and Racine (1982) found that stimulation of the medial septum (which contains the cell bodies of acetylcholine-secreting axons that terminate in the hippocampal formation) facilitated the formation of long-term potentiation in the dentate gyrus. Acetylcholine appears to be the transmitter substance that controls the presence of hippocampal theta activity. As we shall see in the next subsection, theta activity modulates the formation of long-term potentiation in the intact nervous system, which suggests that the role of acetylcholine may be important.

Relation to Learning

I have spent several pages discussing the physiology of long-term potentiation in the hippocampal formation because this phenomenon appears to play a role in learning. Thus, understanding long-term potentiation will probably help us understand how learning takes place. Several experiments have found that the phenomenon of long-term potentiation is more than a laboratory curiosity; it is directly related to learning in the intact animal.

As we saw in Chapter 14, pyramidal cells in the hippocampal formation respond when the animal is present in particular locations. The sensory information reaches the dentate gyrus from the entorhinal cortex by means of the perforant path. If learning about complex environments produces changes in the hippocampal formation similar to those caused by electrical stimulation, then learning should alter the excitability of granule cells in the dentate gyrus. In fact, they do. Sharp, McNaughton, and Barnes (1983) measured the population EPSP in the dentate gyrus in response to a single shock delivered to the perforant path. Next, they placed the rats in an enriched environment filled with boxes, ramps, and other objects.

They found that this experience increased the extracellular population spike by 48 percent. Thus, an animal's experience can affect synaptic strength in the hippocampal formation.

Although the hippocampus is not necessary for the classical conditioning of a nictitating membrane response, you will recall from Chapter 14 that cells there respond in a pattern that conforms to the shape of the conditional response. Thus, it is not surprising that classical conditioning, too, affects synaptic strength in the hippocampal formation. Weisz, Clark, Yank, Thompson, and Solomon (1982) found that the amplitude of the population EPSP in the dentate gyrus doubled during the course of classical conditioning of the nictitating membrane response. (See *Figure 15.24.*) In addition, LoTurco, Coulter, and Alkon (1988) found similar effects in field CA1.

If the kinds of neural changes seen in long-term potentiation are really those that take place during learning, then treatments that interfere with long-term potentiation should also interfere with the ability to learn tasks that involve the hippocampal formation. As we saw in Chapter 14, the hippocampal formation is involved in learning spatially guided tasks. Morris, Anderson, Lynch, and Baudry (1986) found that performance of a spatially guided task (the Morris "milk maze") was disrupted by chronic infusion of AP5 (the blocker of the NMDA receptor) into the lateral

ventricles. Figure 15.25 shows the effects of AP5 and a control injection of saline on two rats' performances in the maze. For this test the pedestal was removed after eight days of training, and the rats were placed in the maze and permitted to swim for 60 minutes. The control animals concentrated their search in the quadrant of the pool that previously contained the platform, whereas the rats that had been infused with AP5 appeared to search the maze in a random fashion. (See *Figure 15.25.*)

Several studies have shown that long-term potentiation can *impair* learning. For example, McNaughton, Barnes, Rao, Baldwin, and Rasmussen (1986) found that high-frequency stimulation of the perforant path disrupted the learning of a spatially guided task. The authors suggest that the reason for the deficit was that the artificial stimulation produced changes in a large number of synapses in the hippocampal formation, leaving very few synapses available for encoding the new information. These results emphasize the fact that information is stored in the form of a *pattern* of synaptic changes. Almost certainly, these changes involve only a small proportion of the synapses in the hippocampal formation.

I mentioned earlier that long-term potentiation can most easily be established when the pattern of stimulation matches a rhythm normally found in the hippocampal formation. Green and

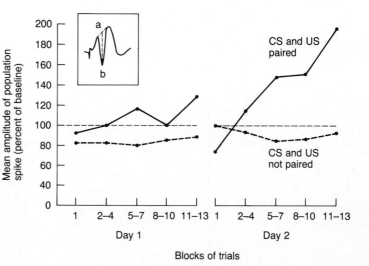

FIGURE 15.24
Amplitude of the extracellular population spike in the dentate gyrus of a rabbit during classical conditioning of the nictitating membrane response. The inset indicates the method of measuring the extracellular population spike. (From Weisz, D.J., Clark, G.A., Yank, B., Thompson, R.F., and Solomon, P.R., in *Conditioning: Representation of Involved Neural Functions,* edited by C.D. Woody. New York: Plenum Press, 1982.)

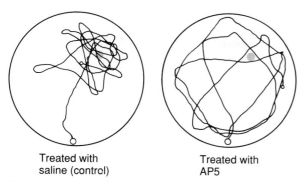

Treated with
saline (control)

Treated with
AP5

FIGURE 15.25

Performance of rats treated with saline or AP5 (a drug that blocks NMDA receptors) on the Morris "milk maze." (Adapted from Morris, R.G.M., Anderson, E., Lynch, G., and Baudry, M. *Nature*, 1986, *319*, 774–776).

Arduini (1954) discovered that the hippocampus produces a regular rhythmical pattern of electrical activity called ***theta activity***—medium-amplitude, medium-frequency (5–8 Hz) waves. The rhythm is controlled by acetylcholinergic neurons in the medial septum that send axons to the hippocampal formation via the fornix (Petsche, Stumpf, and Gogolák, 1962). Thus, drugs that block acetylcholine receptors abolish these rhythms.

Vanderwolf and his colleagues (Vanderwolf, 1969; Vanderwolf, Kramis, Gillespie, and Bland, 1975) observed that hippocampal theta activity is closely related to the type of behavior the animal is performing. In rats, *theta behaviors* are associated with exploration or investigation; they include such behaviors as walking, running, rearing up on the hind legs, sniffing, and manipulating objects with the forepaws. They also occur during REM sleep (when the animal is dreaming?). *Nontheta behaviors* are not involved with exploration; they include alert immobility ("freezing"), drinking, and various self-directed behaviors.

Many investigators believe that the presence of theta is correlated with the acquisition of sensory information by the hippocampal formation. When a rat investigates odors in the environment, its rate of sniffing is synchronized with the waves of its hippocampal theta rhythm (Wiener, Paul, and Eichenbaum, 1989). Also, when pulses of electrical stimulation are delivered to the perforant pathway in synchrony with the peaks of the theta waves, long-term potentiation can be established more easily (Pavlides, Greenstein, Grudman, and Winson, 1988).

Buzsáki (1989) suggests that during theta rhythms information is sampled by the dentate gyrus and CA3 field. Then after the bout of exploration is over, the cessation of the theta rhythms permits the information to be transferred to the CA1 field and, ultimately, to the rest of the brain.

In recent years the phenomenon of long-term potentiation has received a considerable amount of attention from scientists interested in the cellular basis of learning, and their interest appears to be justified. The fact that long-term potentiation can be produced in the cerebral cortex as well as in the hippocampal formation suggests that the mechanisms that underlie this phenomenon may be widespread in the brain. The discovery of the functions of the NMDA receptor provides solid evidence for a mechanism that produces the type of synapse that Hebb predicted over forty years ago. However, other mechanisms must also exist; for example, we know very little about how norepinephrine and acetylcholine affect synaptic changes, and learning can probably take place in parts of the brain that neither contain NMDA receptors nor receive inputs from the noradrenergic or acetylcholinergic systems. But the progress that has been made so far is encouraging.

*I*NTERIM SUMMARY

The study of long-term potentiation in the hippocampal formation has suggested a mechanism that might be responsible for at least some forms of long-term memory. As we saw in Chapter 14, a circuit of neurons passes through the hippocampal formation, from the entorhinal cortex to the dentate gyrus to field CA3 to field CA1 to the subiculum and back to the entorhinal cortex. High-frequency stimulation of the axons in this circuit strengthens synapses; it leads to an increase in the size of the EPSPs in the dendritic spines of the postsynaptic neurons. Associative long-term potentiation can also occur, in which weak synapses are strengthened by the action of strong ones. In fact, the only requirement for long-term potentiation is that the postsynaptic membrane be depolarized at the same time the synapses are active.

Long-term potentiation, like long-term sensitization and classical conditioning in *Aplysia,* is initiated by the entry of calcium into the postsynaptic neuron. The calcium appears to activate a proteolytic enzyme (calpain) that causes changes in the structure of the dendritic spine by breaking apart a protein called spectrin. These changes decrease the electrical resistance between the spine and the rest of the dendrite, thus increasing the effect of EPSPs on the dendritic membrane potential.

In field CA1 and in the dentate gyrus, NMDA receptors play a special role in long-term potentiation. These receptors, sensitive to glutamate, control calcium channels but can open them only if the membrane is already depolarized. Thus, the combination of membrane depolarization (from a priming pulse or from the activity of a strong synapse nearby) and activation of an NMDA receptor causes the entry of calcium ions, producing long-term potentiation. The special sensitivity of field CA1 to the damaging effects of anoxia, hypoglycemia, and seizures is a result of the high concentration of NMDA receptors there.

Norepinephrine and acetylcholine also appear to play a role in long-term potentiation. The stimulation of β receptors facilitates long-term potentiation in field CA3, and drugs that block these receptors prevent its formation. Stimulation of the medial septum, which causes the release of acetylcholine in the hippocampal formation, facilitates the formation of long-term potentiation in the hippocampal formation.

Long-term potentiation appears to be related to learning. When rats are exposed to novel, complex environments, or when rabbits are trained with a classical conditioning procedure, the extracellular population spike in the dentate gyrus increases, just as it does when the entorhinal cortex is subjected to high-frequency stimulation. Hippocampal theta activity, controlled by ace-

tylcholinergic neurons in the medial septum, appears to be a time during which the hippocampus receives and stores sensory input. In addition, the establishment of long-term potentiation is modulated by the presence of theta waves.

EFFECTS OF NEUROTRANSMITTERS AND NEUROMODULATORS

Researchers have suggested that several neurotransmitters and neuromodulators play a role in learning: the catecholamines, acetylcholine, the endogenous opioids, and various other neuropeptides, such as ACTH, vasopressin, substance P, cholecystokinin, somatostatin, and neuropeptide Y (McGaugh, 1989). Although learning is certainly complex, it seems unlikely that *all* of these substance are involved in learning in an important way. Dopaminergic neurons appears to be an important part of the process of reinforcement. Because Chapter 16 describes their role of dopamine in reinforcement and addiction, I will not discuss dopamine in this chapter. We saw earlier in this chapter that the release of glutamate is involved in long-term potentiation. Acetylcholine, too, seems to play an important role; drugs that affect acetylcholinergic synapses also affect learning. Peptide neuromodulators may also affect learning. The evidence for the role of the endogenous opiates is the strongest and least controversial and seems to be related to the effects of norepinephrine.

Acetylcholine

J.A. Deutsch has suggested that acetylcholinergic neurons may play an important role in learning. He and his colleagues performed several studies during the 1960s and 1970s (reviewed by Deutsch, 1983) that support this suggestion. In particular, they found that drugs that affect transmission at ACh-secreting synapses impair or facilitate learning, depending on when these drugs are administered.

Interest in acetylcholinergic neurons has been rekindled in recent years by the discovery that the loss of ACh-secreting terminal buttons may be related to human dementia. The term *dementia* derives from the Latin word for "madness." However, in current usage it refers to deterioration of intellectual abilities resulting from an organic brain disorder. The most common form of dementia is *Alzheimer's disease,* which occurs in approximately 5 percent of the population above the age of 65. It is characterized by progressive loss of memory and other mental functions. At first, the person may have difficulty remembering appointments and sometimes fails to think of words or people's names. As time passes, he or she shows increasing confusion and increasing difficulty with tasks such as balancing a checkbook. The memory deficit most critically involves recent events, and it thus resembles the anterograde amnesia of Korsakoff's syndrome. If the person ventures outside alone, he or she is likely to get lost. Eventually, the person becomes bedridden and completely helpless and finally succumbs (Van Hoesen and Damasio, 1987).

Alzheimer's disease produces severe degeneration of the hippocampus and neocortex, especially the association cortex of the frontal and temporal lobes. Color Plate 15.1 shows a normal brain; Color Plate 15.2 shows the brain of a patient with Alzheimer's disease. You can see how much wider the sulci are, especially in the frontal and temporal lobes, indicating substantial loss of cortical tissue. (See **Color Plates 15.1** and **15.2**).

Several studies have shown that the level of acetylcholine is very much reduced in the brains of patients with Alzheimer's disease. The cell bodies of ACh-secreting neurons reside in subcortical areas, not in the neocortex or hippocampus itself. The cell bodies of neurons that project to the neocortex are located in the *nucleus basalis,* located in the basal forebrain near the preoptic area, and those that project to the hippocampus are located in the medial septum. Both of these nuclei appear to degenerate in the brains of patients with Alzheimer's disease (Nakano and Hirano, 1982; Whitehouse et al., 1982).

Despite the undeniable fact that Alzheimer's disease causes the degeneration of acetylcholinergic neurons, studies indicate that the damage to acetylcholinergic neurons is not unique; the disease also causes damage to neurons that secrete norepinephrine, serotonin, glutamate, and several peptides (Van Hoesen and Damasio,

1987). The loss of these neurons could also be responsible for the memory loss seen in Alzheimer's disease. For example, Hyman, Van Hoesen, Damasio, and Barnes (1984) found that the glutamate-secreting neurons that give rise to the perforant path (from the entorhinal cortex to the dentate gyrus) degenerate in Alzheimer's disease. In fact, Hyman, Van Hoesen, and Damasio (1987) found an 83 percent reduction in the level of glutamate in the portion of the dentate gyrus that receives this input. Obviously, this damage would produce memory deficits even without damage to acetylcholinergic neurons. As you have already learned, if the hippocampal formation is deprived of its input, the result is a severe anterograde amnesia.

The precursor of dopamine, L-DOPA, has been successfully used to treat the symptoms of Parkinson's disease, which is caused by degeneration of dopaminergic neurons. Thus, because Alzheimer's disease includes degeneration of ACh-secreting neurons, it occurred to investigators to try to improve patients' cognitive performance with choline, the precursor of acetylcholine, or with *its* precursor, lecithin. These treatments have not been very successful in either healthy elderly people or patients with Alzheimer's disease (Bartus, Dean, Beer, and Lippa, 1982). However, because a few studies reported some promising results with infusion of a cholinergic agonist directly into the cerebral ventricles, a collaborative double-blind study was established at several medical centers to see whether this procedure would help people with Alzheimer's disease (Harbaugh et al., 1989). Unfortunately, it did not. As the authors concluded, "the degree of improvement was not sufficient to justify further treatment of Alzheimer's disease patients by intracerebroventricular infusion of benthanechol chloride" (p. 481). Given what we know about the damage of noncholinergic neurons in the brains of Alzheimer's patients, these results are disappointing but hardly surprising.

Despite the fact that acetylcholinergic neurons do not provide the key to Alzheimer's disease, the experiments that were prompted by the discovery of basal forebrain degeneration have provided interesting information. Several studies have shown that memory impairments can be produced in humans and laboratory animals by administering drugs that block muscarinic ACh receptors. For example, Drachman and Leavitt (1974) found that scopolamine, administered to normal young human subjects, selectively impaired recent memory without affecting recall of old memories. Sitaram, Weingartner, and Gillin (1978) found that arecoline (a drug that stimulates muscarinic receptors) facilitated the learning of a list of words, whereas scopolamine retarded it. Thus, the level of ACh activity does indeed affect people's learning ability.

We have already seen that the acetylcholinergic input to the hippocampal formation is important in learning. The control of acetylcholinergic neurons in the medial septum of hippocampal theta rhythms may determine whether the hippocampus "remembers" events that are currently happening.

Although the exact role that acetylcholine plays in the neocortex is not yet known, evidence suggests that it is involved in learning there, too. For example, Fibiger, Murray, and Phillips (1983) destroyed the nucleus basalis in rats and trained them in a sixteen-arm radial maze. The lesions decreased neocortical choline acetyltransferase activity by 50 percent but did not affect the hippocampal levels of this enzyme; thus, the lesions damaged the acetylcholinergic input to the neocortex but not to the hippocampus. At the beginning of each session nine of the arms were baited with food; the other seven never were. The rats learned to avoid entering arms in which they had just obtained food (thus showing good working memory). However, their reference memory was poor; they did not learn to avoid entering arms that were never baited. The rats' performance could be improved to near-normal levels by injections of physostigmine, an ACh agonist. These intriguing results suggest that ACh may play complementary roles in the hippocampus and neocortex: In the hippocampus it may be involved in memory for recent events, whereas in the neocortex it may be involved in the formation of long-term memory.

In Chapter 14 I described an experiment by Diamond and Weinberger (1989) that showed that when a tone of a particular frequency was used as a conditional stimulus in a classical conditioning task, single neurons in the auditory association cortex became more responsive to that frequency. Metherate and Weinberger (1989) found that an infusion of acetylcholine paired with the presentation of a particular frequency had a similar effect. Whether the phenomenon they observed is directly related to the effects of ACh on learning remains to be seen.

Several studies have shown that transplantation of cells from the basal forebrain into the hippocampus or neocortex can partially reverse the effects of damage to cholinergic input to these regions (see Buzsáki and Gage, 1988, for a review). For example, Welner, Dunnett, Salamone, MacLean, and Iversen (1988) produced lesions of the nucleus basalis that resulted in poor performance on a spatial alternation test of memory. They implanted some acetylcholinergic cells from the basal forebrain of embryonic rats into three sites in the neocortex on each side of the brain. Because the cells came from brains that were still in the process of developing, they grew in the host brain and began secreting acetylcholine. The transplantation of cholinergic cells (but not noncholinergic cells) reduced the impairment caused by the nucleus basalis lesions.

Similar studies have shown that transplantation of embryonic cells from the medial septum to the hippocampus can restore theta activity that is lost by cutting the fornix (Buzsáki, Gage, and Czopf, 1987). The transplants can also restore spatial receptive fields (Shapiro et al., 1989). They can even reduce memory deficits caused by fornix lesions. Nilsson, Shapiro, Gage, Olton, and Björklund (1987) found that a transplant of septal tissue into the hippocampus improved the performance of rats with fornix lesions on the Morris "milk maze" task. Figure 15.26 shows the performance of a normal rat, a rat with a fornix lesion, and a rat with a fornix lesion and a transplant during a 2-minute test in which the platform was removed. (See *Figure 15.26.*)

Opioids and Norepinephrine

As you have already learned, opiates have important effects on behavior. In general, they decrease sensitivity to pain and inhibit species-typical defensive responses that interfere with the perfor-

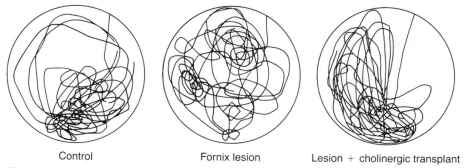

Control   Fornix lesion   Lesion + cholinergic transplant

FIGURE 15.26

The effects of fornix lesions and transplants of fetal brain tissue on performance of the Morris "milk maze." (From Nilsson, O.G., Shapiro, M.L., Gage, F.H., Olton, D.S., and Björklund, A. *Experimental Brain Research*, 1987, *67*, 195–215.)

mance of other behaviors, such as fighting or mating. Because opiates appear to affect different behaviors in different ways, and because they can have punishing effects on behavior as well as the more usual reinforcing effects (Jacquet, 1973), it has proved difficult to determine just what effect these substances have on learning. Before investigators can be certain that opiates directly influence the formation of memories, they must control for unconditional effects of these substances on the performance of various classes of behaviors and for possible reinforcing or punishing effects.

The clearest effects of opiates on learning have shown that it disrupts learning of behaviors motivated by aversive stimuli, such as conditioned emotional responses or conditioned avoidance tasks. For example, Gallagher, Kapp, McNall, and Pascoe (1981) found that injection of an opiate agonist into the central nucleus of the amygdala impaired the acquisition of a conditioned emotional response, whereas naloxone, an opiate receptor blocker, facilitated it. (You will remember from Chapter 14 that the central nucleus of the amygdala is an important component of neural circuits responsible for the learning of conditioned emotional responses.) Opiate antagonists have no effect on an animal's sensitivity to pain and, when injected into the amygdala, neither do opiate agonists (Goldstein, Pryor, Otis, and Larsen, 1976; Rodgers, 1978). Thus, these drugs did not affect learning simply by changing the effectiveness of the shock (US).

We might ask *why* opioids have an inhibitory effect on learning that is motivated by aversive stimuli. The answer may lie in the fact that the endogenous opioids are released while an animal is engaging in behaviors with important survival value, such as mating or fighting in defense of one's territory or one's offspring. Because the opioids suppress the acquisition of defensive responses, their release during survival activity makes it more likely that an animal will continue the mating sequence or the fighting and not be frightened away.

In the amygdala, at least, the opioids may produce their behavioral effects by blocking the release of norepinephrine. If the noradrenergic input to the amygdala is destroyed, naloxone no longer has a facilitatory effect on learning (Gallagher, Rapp, and Fanelli, 1985). McGaugh, Introini-Collison, and Nagahara (1988) found that the memory-enhancing effects of naloxone on an avoidance task were abolished by injections of drugs that block noradrenergic β receptors.

As we saw in Chapter 10, the activity of noradrenergic terminals in the olfactory bulb, triggered by vaginal stimulation, is necessary for a female mouse to remember the odor of the male with which she mates. This learning ensures that his odor, if she encounters it during her subsequent pregnancy, will not cause her to abort (the Bruce effect). Several studies have shown the importance of norepinephrine to olfactory learning early in the life of a rat.

Rat pups learn to recognize the odor of their mother, which is necessary for them to orient toward her and attach to her nipples. This learning can be simulated by stroking a pup with a soft brush while presenting an olfactory stimulus. Later, the animals show a preference for the odor to which they were exposed. Early olfactory learning causes changes in the olfactory bulb, as shown by 2-DG autoradiography, electrophysiological, and anatomical studies (Sullivan and Leon, 1987; Woo, Coopersmith, and Leon, 1987; Wilson and Leon, 1988). The effects of the learning can be found in adulthood; thus, it is clearly long-term learning.

Nakamura, Kimura, and Sakaguchi (1987) showed that tactile stimulation increases the activity of noradrenergic neurons in the locus coeruleus, which innervate the olfactory bulbs. Sullivan, Wilson, and Leon (1989) found that the stimulation of noradrenergic receptors not only is essential for early olfactory learning but also can duplicate the effects of the tactile stimulus (US). The investigators assessed the effects of propranolol, a drug that blocks noradrenergic β receptors, and isoproterenol, a drug that stimulates them. They found that propranolol blocked both learning and the physiological changes in the olfactory bulb that normally occur after the olfactory stimulus has been paired with the tactile stimulation. Conversely, pairing an odor with an injection of isoproterenol (with no tactile stimulus) was sufficient to produce both olfactory learning and the physiological changes in the olfactory bulbs.

Although we do not yet understand the mechanism by which norepinephrine facilitates learning, we have a few hints. As we saw in Chapter 9, norepinephrine is involved in vigilance and attentiveness to stimuli, and the effect of direct application of norepinephrine to a neuron is to increase its responsiveness to its inputs. Clearly, this effect could increase the likelihood that a neuron receiving information will be altered physiologically and therefore participate in learning. And as we saw earlier in this chapter, norepinephrine facilitates long-term potentiation in the dentate gyrus and CA3 field of the hippocampal formation. Thus, it appears to contribute to learning in several different systems.

Collier, Quirk, and Routtenberg (1987) have obtained evidence for a particularly interesting property of endogenous opiates: the editing of memory. They trained rats in a spatial delayed matching-to-sample task in an eight-arm radial maze. On the first trial one arm was baited with food (the sample arm), and the rats were placed on the center platform and permitted to find the food. Twenty minutes later, the same arm was baited again, and the rats were placed on the center platform again. A correct response would be to enter the arm that contained food on the first trial. Each day a different arm was baited on the two trials. Within fifteen to twenty-five days the rats learned the task; on the second trial they approached the correct arm.

Once the rats had learned the task, the experimenters implanted a stimulating electrode in the granule cell layer of the dentate gyrus. After the animals recovered from the surgery, the experimenters tested the effects of 10 seconds of low-intensity electrical stimulation through the electrodes immediately after the first trial. The stimulation appeared to "erase" the animals' memory of the location of the baited arm; they entered an average of four and one-half arms before finding the food, which is about what would be expected by chance. Granule cells of the dentate gyrus and their axons, the mossy fibers, appear to contain dynorphin, an endogenous opioid (Gall, Brecha, Karten, and Chang, 1981). To test their hypothesis that the effects of the stimulation were mediated by the release of opiates, Collier and his colleagues pretreated some animals with naloxone, which blocks opiate receptors. Indeed, the naloxone prevented the amnestic effect of the electrical stimulation; these animals performed almost perfectly.

As we have seen in this chapter and the previous chapter, the hippocampal system seems to play an important role in detecting contextual relations among stimuli, including the time and place during which events occur. This role involves the hippocampus in remembering what happened on the last trial of a task that involves the same set of stimuli—what Olton (1983) calls "working memory." For this mechanism to work, there must be some means to erase old information when new information is presented. The findings of Collier and his colleagues suggest that the erasure may be produced by the release of opioids. Of course, this suggestion is speculative; further studies will have to be performed to confirm or refute it.

INTERIM SUMMARY

Acetylcholinergic neurons appear to participate in the learning process; acetylcholine agonists and antagonists can facilitate or hinder learning. An early symptom of Alzheimer's disease, which eventually produces degeneration of the hippocampus and cerebral cortex, is loss of memory. Although some of the memory loss may be related to the loss of ACh-secreting neurons, many other neurons degenerate, too, including the glutamate-secreting neurons of the perforant path.

Damage to the nucleus basalis, which contains the ACh-secreting neurons that innervate the cerebral cortex, disrupt reference memory but not working memory in a radial-arm-maze task. The implantation of brain tissue, removed from the basal forebrain of fetal rats, into the neocortex or hippocampus can improve the learning ability of rats with basal forebrain or fornix lesions, respectively, which implies that the secretion of acetylcholine in these structures is important in learning.

Learning is also affected by the endogenous opiates. An opiate agonist injected into the central nucleus of the amygdala impairs the acquisition of a classically conditioned decrease in heart rate, whereas an opiate antagonist injected there facilitates it. Many studies have shown that opiates can either facilitate or retard the rate of learning; but because opiates have reinforcing effects of their own, we cannot yet be sure what conclusions to draw from these experiments. Another study found that electrical stimulation of the dentate gyrus erased working memory in a radial-arm-maze task. However, when the rats were pretreated with the opiate receptor blocker naloxone, the stimulation did not have an amnestic effect. The results suggest that opiates may perform some role in determining when information temporarily stored in the hippocampus gets erased.

CONCLUDING REMARKS

Investigators have employed many different approaches to study the physiology of learning. Finally, after many years of study, some of these approaches are beginning to pay off. We now have evidence that experience can produce physiological changes in the brain, and the details of some kinds of changes (for example, those that accompany long-term potentiation in mammals and learning in *Aplysia*) are being uncovered. Almost certainly, many neurotransmitters and neuromodulators are involved in learning. So far, investigators have obtained good evidence that dopamine, glutamate, acetylcholine, and the endogenous opiates are important, and epinephrine and norepinephrine are probably important as well. The physiology of learning is such an important (and interesting) topic that many laboratories are currently investigating different phenomena, making it difficult for physiologists to keep informed about major new research. As you can see from the dates of the articles I cited in this chapter, many of the experiments I described to you I just learned about myself. My hope is that this chapter has covered enough of the field to give you an appreciation for the problems encountered in such research and for the fruits of the investigators' efforts.

The next chapter discusses a topic related to learning: physiological mechanisms of reinforcement. These mechanisms are responsible for sensory-response learning and, as we shall see, for the ability of some substances to cause addictions.

NEW TERMS

Alzheimer's disease p. 505
associative long-term
    potentiation p. 495
calpain p. 497
consolidation p. 481
dementia p. 504

electroconvulsive therapy
    (ECT) p. 482
leupeptin p. 497
long-term potentiation p. 494
NMDA receptor p. 499

nucleus basalis p. 505
passive-avoidance task p. 482
population EPSP p. 494
spectrin p. 497
theta activity p. 503

SUGGESTED READINGS

Byrne, J.H., and Berry, W.O. *Neural Models of Plasticity: Experimental and Theoretical Approaches.* San Diego, Calif.: Academic Press, 1989.

Changeux, J.-P., and Konishi, M. *The Neural and Molecular Bases of Learning.* Chichester, England: John Wiley & Sons, 1987.

Cotman, C.W., Monaghan, D.T., and Ganong, A.H. Excitatory amino acid neurotransmission: NMDA receptors and Hebb-type synaptic plasticity. *Annual Review of Neuroscience,* 1988, *11*, 61–80.

Landfield, P.W., and Deadwyler, S. *Long-term Potentiation: From Biophysics to Behavior.* New York: A.R. Liss, 1988.

Matthies, H. Neurobiological aspects of learning and memory. *Annual Review of Psychology,* 1989, *40*, 1989.

McGaugh, J.L. Involvement of hormonal and neuromodulatory systems in the regulation of memory storage. *Annual Review of Neuroscience,* 1989, *12*, 255–288.

Squire, L.R. *Memory and Brain.* New York: Oxford University Press, 1987.

16

Reinforcement and Addiction

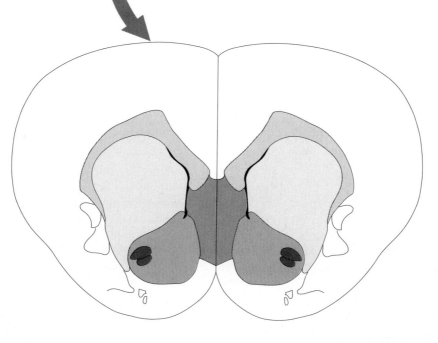

The process of reinforcement enables us to profit from experience by shaping our behaviors according to their consequences. Reinforcing stimuli, and stimuli that are associated with them, motivate us. As we saw in Chapter 14, instrumental conditioning involves the establishment of connections between perceptual mechanisms and motor mechanisms, under the control of a reinforcement system. This chapter discusses the nature of that system.

Although the ideal function of the reinforcement system is to determine when responses have favorable outcomes, our species has discovered substances that stimulate this system artificially. Thus, taking these substances produces a reinforcing effect, often to our detriment. The topic of the second part of this chapter is addiction to substances that stimulate the reinforcement system.

REINFORCEMENT

The discovery of reinforcing brain stimulation, one of the most fascinating discoveries in the history of neuroscience, was made by accident. This discovery captured the imagination of many writers, who warned of a future in which a totalitarian state would put electrodes in the brains of its subjects so that rewards could be given for correct behaviors—or even for correct thoughts. People no longer worry about this prospect of mass neurosurgery, but it is still fascinating to contemplate the fact that the reinforcing effects of things that give us pleasure seem to act on specific circuits in the brain.

Discovery of Reinforcing Brain Stimulation

In 1954 James Olds was trying to determine whether electrical stimulation of the reticular formation might increase arousal and thus facilitate learning. He was assisted in this project by Peter Milner, who was a graduate student at the time. Olds had heard a talk by Neal Miller that described the aversive effects of electrical stimulation of the brain. Therefore, he decided to make sure that

stimulation of the reticular formation was not aversive—if it were, the effects of this stimulation on the speed of learning would be difficult to assess. Fortunately for the investigators, one of the electrodes missed its target; the tip wound up some millimeters away, probably in the hypothalamus. (Unfortunately, the brain of the animal was lost, so histological verification could not be obtained.) If all of the electrodes had reached their intended target, Olds and Milner would not have discovered what they did.

Here is Olds's description of what happened when he tested this animal to see if the brain stimulation was aversive:

> I applied a brief train of 60-cycle sine-wave electrical current whenever the animal entered one corner of the enclosure. The animal did not stay away from the corner, but rather came back quickly after a brief sortie which followed the first stimulation and came back even more quickly after a briefer sortie which followed the second stimulation. By the time the third electrical stimulus had been applied the animal seemed indubitably to be "coming back for more." (Olds, 1973, p. 81)

Olds and Milner were intrigued and excited by this result. They implanted electrodes in the brains of a group of rats and allowed the animals to administer their own stimulation by pressing a lever-operated switch in an operant chamber. (See *Figure 16.1.*) The animals readily pressed the lever; in their initial study Olds and Milner (1954) reported response rates of over seven hundred per hour. (The self-administration of electrical brain stimulation is usually referred to as *self-stimulation.*) In subsequent studies rates of many thousands of responses per hour have been obtained. Clearly, electrical stimulation of the brain can be a very potent reinforcer.

The anatomy of reinforcement will be discussed in a later section of this chapter. Here I will note only that electrical stimulation of many parts of the brain can reinforce behavior. In general, stimulation of parts of the limbic system and motor system are effective, but the best and most reli-

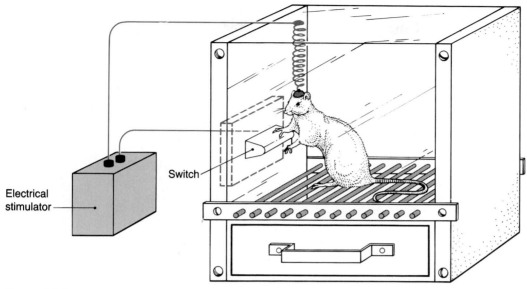

FIGURE 16.1
An operant chamber with a lever, used in studies of the effects of reinforcing brain stimulation.

able location is the *medial forebrain bundle* (MFB), a bundle of axons that travel in a rostral-caudal axis from the midbrain to the rostral basal forebrain. The MFB passes through the lateral hypothalamus, and it is in this region that most investigators place the tips of their electrodes. The MFB contains long ascending and descending axons that interconnect forebrain and midbrain structures, and short axons that connect adjacent regions. It also contains ascending dopaminergic, noradrenergic, and serotonergic axons on their way from the brain stem to their diencephalic and telencephalic projection areas. As we will see later in this chapter, recent studies suggest that a particular subset of these fibers is responsible for the reinforcing effects of stimulation of the MFB.

How Brain Stimulation Reinforces Behavior

Almost all investigators believe that the electrical stimulation of the medial forebrain bundle is reinforcing because it activates the same system that is activated by natural reinforcers, such as food, water, or sexual contact. The reinforcement system must perform two functions: detect the presence of a reinforcing stimulus, and strengthen the con-

nections between the neurons that detect the discriminative stimulus (such as the sight of a lever) and the neurons that produce the instrumental response (a lever press). (See *Figure 16.2.*)

Detection of a reinforcing event is not a simple matter; a stimulus that serves as a reinforcer on one occasion may fail to do so on another. For example, the presence of food will reinforce the behavior of a hungry organism but not one that has just eaten. Thus, the reinforcement system does not simply detect particular stimuli; it must also monitor the state of the organism to determine whether a given stimulus should serve as a reinforcer.

There is a less complicated possibility. Many psychologists prefer to define reinforcers as stimuli that provide an opportunity to perform a behavior rather than as pleasurable stimuli (Premack, 1965). In this view *eating*—not the presence of food—is the reinforcing event. Eating occurs only when the organism is hungry; therefore, the presence of food will not reinforce the behavior of a satiated organism, because the organism does not eat. In fact, it is a general principle that *reinforcing stimuli are elicitors of behavior* (Donahoe, Crowley, Millard, and Stickney, 1982). If this characterization is correct, then the rein-

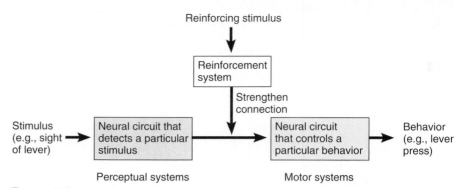

FIGURE 16.2
An overview of the functions of the reinforcement system.

forcement system does not have to detect environmental stimuli and compare them with the animal's motivational condition; instead, it only has to monitor the animal's behavior. The reinforcement system is activated by feedback from making an appetitive response such as eating, drinking, or mating; and this system strengthens the link between the discriminative stimulus and the instrumental response. (See *Figure 16.3.*)

If this model of the reinforcement system is correct, then we might expect that reinforcing brain stimulation would be related to the elicitation of responses. In fact, it is; reinforcing brain stimulation almost always elicits appetitive responses. For example, if the tip of an electrode is placed in a rat's MFB and the experimenter turns on the stimulator, the animal will engage in species-typical behaviors such as eating, drinking, fighting, copulation, gnawing on wooden blocks, carrying of objects, or shredding of nesting material. Which of these behaviors the animal performs depends on the location of the electrode and the objects that are present in its environment. If no objects are present, the rat will engage in sniffing and frantic exploratory behavior. If the rat is given the opportunity to turn on the stimulator itself by pressing a lever, it will eagerly do so. Thus, activation of neural circuits that produce appetitive behaviors is reinforcing.

Electrical stimulation of some parts of the brain causes aversive effects, not reinforcing ones. If an animal presses a lever that delivers aversive electrical stimulation, it will avoid pressing it again—in other words, the lever pressing is punished. It

will also learn to make a response that turns off such stimulation or prevents it from happening. In general, aversive brain stimulation, like reinforcing brain stimulation, elicits species-typical behaviors; but these behaviors tend to be negative ones, such as defense, attack, or attempts to escape. Thus, activation of neural circuits that produce escape or avoidance behaviors is punishing.

Anatomy of Reinforcement

An animal's behavior can be reinforced by electrical stimulation of many parts of the brain, including the olfactory bulb, prefrontal cortex, nucleus accumbens, caudate nucleus, putamen, various thalamic nuclei, reticular formation, amygdala, ventral tegmental area, substantia nigra, locus coeruleus, and, of course, the MFB (Olds and Fobes, 1981). The finding that stimulation of so many structures is reinforcing suggests that more than one system is involved in reinforcement.

In the past several years investigators have made considerable progress in identifying the neural systems that mediate reinforcement. We now know that dopaminergic neurons play a critical role and that the axons that are activated by stimulation of the MFB descend to brain stem structures, including a nucleus that contains dopaminergic neurons. In addition, the endogenous opiates have been shown to play a role in reinforcement, perhaps by modulating the effectiveness or activity of dopamine-secreting neurons. It is likely that other systems of neurons, which do

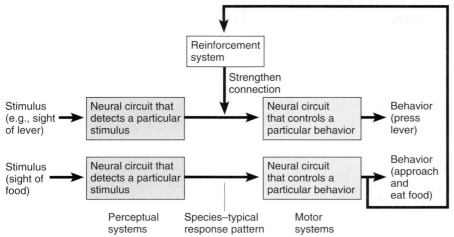

Feedback from appetitive response

Reinforcement system

Strengthen connection

Stimulus (e.g., sight of lever) → Neural circuit that detects a particular stimulus → Neural circuit that controls a particular behavior → Behavior (press lever)

Stimulus (sight of food) → Neural circuit that detects a particular stimulus → Neural circuit that controls a particular behavior → Behavior (approach and eat food)

Perceptual systems   Species–typical response pattern   Motor systems

FIGURE 16.3

A schematic explanation of reinforcement. Reinforcement may be detected by feedback from the behavior elicited by the reinforcing stimulus.

not contain dopaminergic axons, mediate reinforcing effects, too, but I shall restrict my discussion to the dopaminergic system, because this is the one that has also been implicated in drug addiction.

Anatomy of Dopaminergic Pathways

As we saw in Chapter 5, the development of the histofluorescence techniques permitted investigators to trace the pathways of mono-aminergic neurons. They soon discovered that the distribution of reinforcing electrode sites nicely coincided with the distribution of catechol-aminergic neurons—those that secrete norepinephrine and dopamine. That is, brain stimulation through electrodes whose tips were placed in fiber bundles that contained catecholaminergic axons or in structures that received catecholaminergic projections generally had reinforcing effects. Furthermore, the administration of amphetamine, a potent catecholamine agonist, greatly increased the rate at which animals would respond for reinforcing brain stimulation (Stein, 1964). These findings suggested that catecholaminergic neurons participate in the process of reinforcement. Although some investigators believed that noradrenergic neurons were directly involved in reinforcement, experiments

performed over the course of several years have indicated that they do not play an important role.

There are several systems of neurons whose terminal buttons secrete dopamine. The major pathways begin in the substantia nigra and the ventral tegmental area (Lindvall, 1979; Fallon, 1988). The *nigrostriatal system* starts in the *pars compacta* of the substantia nigra and projects to the *neostriatum*—the caudate nucleus and putamen. As we saw in Chapters 4 and 8, this system is important in the control of movement; its degeneration results in Parkinson's disease. The ***tegmentostriatal system*** begins in the ventral tegmental area and projects to the ***nucleus accumbens,*** a region of the *paleostriatum*, located in the basal forebrain rostral to the preoptic area and immediately adjacent to the septum. (See ***Figure 16.4.***) As we will see, this system appears to play the most important role in reinforcement. The *mesolimbic/mesocortical system* begins in both the substantia nigra and the ventral tegmental area and projects to several forebrain regions of the cortex and limbic system, including the olfactory tubercle, septum, amygdala, lateral and medial prefrontal cortex, and entorhinal cortex. (See ***Figure 16.5.***) Note that the major catecholaminergic pathways pass through the MFB on their way forward. Thus, stimulation of the MFB

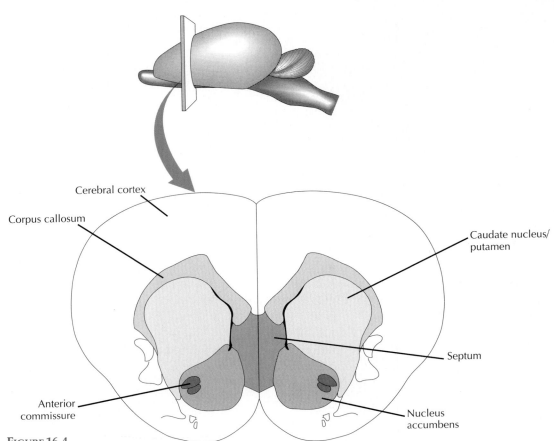

FIGURE 16.4

A section through a rat brain, showing the location of the nucleus accumbens. (Adapted from Paxinos, G., and Watson, C. *The Rat Brain in Stereotaxic Coordinates.* Sydney: Academic Press, 1982.)

could potentially activate axons of all of these systems.

There are five other dopaminergic pathways: one in the retina; one in the olfactory bulb; one that projects from the zona incerta to the medial preoptic area, hypothalamus, and septum; one that projects from the periaqueductal gray matter to the medial thalamus and hypothalamus; and one that projects from the hypothalamus to the pituitary stalk. So far, none of these pathways have been implicated in reinforcement.

Effects of Systemic Administration of Dopamine Antagonists

Studies with drugs that block dopamine receptors clearly indicate that dopamine is involved in reinforcement—provided not only by electrical stimulation of the brain but also by natural rein-

forcing stimuli. The discovery of the antipsychotic drugs, which exert their therapeutic effects by blocking dopamine receptors, gave researchers a tool to investigate the role of dopaminergic activity in reinforcement. (The role of these synapses in schizophrenia will be discussed in Chapter 18.)

Many studies have shown that drugs that block dopamine receptors also block the process of reinforcement. For example, Rolls, Rolls, Kelly, Shaw, Wood, and Dale (1974) trained rats to press a lever for several different types of reinforcement, including brain stimulation, food, and water, and then administered a drug that blocks dopamine receptors (spiroperidol). They found that the drug suppressed the animals' instrumental responding. However, we cannot determine from studies such as this one whether the animals stopped responding because the food, water, or

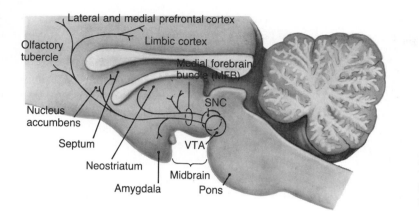

FIGURE 16.5
The principal dopaminergic pathways. SN = substantia nigra; VTA = ventral tegmental area.

electrical stimulation was no longer reinforcing, or whether they stopped because the drug interfered with motor systems that controlled their behavior. The drug could have simply made it difficult for the animal to move.

Other studies have shown that the drugs do block reinforcement and do not simply produce motor side effects. They interfere with movement if they are given in high enough doses, but this effect is not responsible for the suppression of instrumental responses. A study by Fouriezos and Wise (1976) supported the hypothesis that dopaminergic synapses are involved in reinforcement. They trained rats to press a lever for electrical brain stimulation and then gave them injections of pimozide (a drug that blocks dopamine receptors). If an animal's behavior is reinforced, and if the reinforcement is then terminated (for example, by disconnecting the food-dispensing

mechanism), the animal will respond for a while and then gradually cease to respond. In other words, the behavior *extinguishes,* but not immediately. (*Extinction* refers to the decline of nonreinforced responses.) When the rats were placed in the operant chamber, they began pressing at a normal rate but soon slowed down; their behavior resembled that of rats placed on an extinction schedule. (See *Figure 16.6.*)

Several studies have used conditioning tasks in which motor performance is not an issue. If an animal receives food (or another reinforcer) in a particular location, it will return to that location later. In other words, reinforcement in a particular place produces a ***conditioned place preference.*** Spyraki, Fibiger, and Phillips (1982a) trained two groups of hungry rats in a conditioned place preference task. On alternate days, the rats were placed in each of two chambers. They received

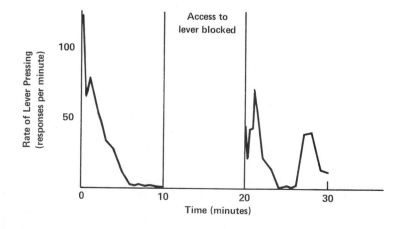

FIGURE 16.6
Lever-pressing responses made by a rat that had received an injection of pimozide, a blocker of dopamine receptors. Note that the rate of responding is high early in the session. (From Fouriezos, G., and Wise, R.A. *Brain Research,* 1976, *103,* 377–380.)

food in one chamber but not the other. After eight days of training, the animals were permitted to chose between the two chambers. Rats in the control group, which received an injection of saline just before each day's training, chose the chamber where they had received food. Rats in the experimental group, which received an injection of haloperidol, showed no preference. Thus, a dopamine receptor does prevent the establishment of a conditioned place preference.

Spyraki and her colleagues noted that when food was present in the chamber the rats in the experimental group did eat. Thus, haloperidol did not simply block the response normally elicited by the reinforcing stimulus; it blocked the *reinforcing consequences* of this response. Because the animals were tested in a drug-free condition, the effects do not seem to have been caused by changes in motor performance. Other investigators (for example, Ettenberg and Duvauchelle, 1988) have shown that haloperidol also prevents the establishment of a conditioned place preference by reinforcing brain stimulation.

Drugs that block dopamine receptors interfere with activational effects of appetitive stimuli, as well as their reinforcing effects. For example, Falk (1972) discovered that when a very hungry rat receives small pieces of food at infrequent intervals—say, every 2 minutes—the animal becomes very active, engaging in a variety of species-typical behaviors. If water is present, the animal will drink copiously, sometimes consuming an amount equal to 30 percent of its body weight during a 3-hour session. The behaviors are not limited to ingestive ones: If a block of wood is present, the rat will gnaw on it; if another male is present, the rat will attack it; and so on. Behaviors elicited by these means are called *adjunctive behaviors*, because they occur as an adjunct to intermittent reinforcement. Salamone (1988) found that an injection of haloperidol blocked these excitatory effects of reinforcing stimuli; the drug abolished adjunctive activity when rats were given small pieces of food every 30 to 360 seconds. The drug did *not* interfere with eating; the animals simply stayed next to the food dish and ate the food when it was delivered. These excitatory effects, then, appear to be caused by the activity of dopaminergic neurons.

Systemic Administration of Dopamine Agonists

If dopamine antagonists interfere with the effects of reinforcing stimuli, then we might expect that dopamine agonists would enhance them. Indeed, they do—and when these drugs are given by themselves, they produce their own reinforcing effect. For example, Gallistel and Karras (1984) found that injections of amphetamine, a dopaminergic agonist, increases the rate at which a rat will press a lever to obtain reinforcing brain stimulation. Spyraki, Fibiger, and Phillips (1982b) found that rats would learn a conditioned place preference if they were given an injection of amphetamine just before being put in a particular chamber.

Probably the most dramatic effect of dopamine agonists is seen in experiments in which animals administer the drugs themselves. In such *self-administration* studies animals are able to press a lever that turns on a pump that injects the drug directly into their veins by means of a flexible plastic tube. Members of a variety of species, including rats, monkeys, and humans, will eagerly and vigorously inject themselves with dopamine agonists such as amphetamine and cocaine (Koob and Bloom, 1988). (I am sure you are aware that the evidence concerning humans did not require laboratory experiments.)

Self-administration of amphetamine and cocaine occurs because of the effects of these drugs on dopaminergic synapses. If the concentration of the solution available to the animal is lowered, the animal compensates for the decreased reinforcing value by increasing its rate of responding. Of course, if the concentration becomes low enough, the animal ceases responding, because the reinforcing effect is simply not worth the effort of pressing the lever. The same effect happens when an animal self-administering amphetamine or cocaine is given a drug that blocks dopamine receptors: At low doses it responds faster, to make up for the diminished reinforcing effect, but it stops responding when high doses are given (Wise and Rompré, 1989).

Local Administration of Drugs

A large body of experimental evidence indicates that the tegmentostriatal pathway, which begins in the ventral tegmental area and terminates in the nucleus accumbens, is the pathway responsible for the reinforcing effects of electrical stimulation of the medial forebrain bundle, for the reinforcing effects of injections of amphetamine and cocaine, and for the reinforcing effects of many natural appetitive stimuli. Any treatment that stimulates dopamine receptors in the nucleus accumbens will reinforce behaviors; thus, animals will press a lever that delivers electrical stimulation of the ventral tegmental area, medial forebrain bundle, or nucleus accumbens itself (Routtenberg and Malsbury, 1969; Crow, 1972; Olds and Fobes, 1981). They will also press a lever that delivers direct injections of very small amounts of dopamine or amphetamine into the nucleus accumbens (Hoebel et al., 1983; Guerin, Goeders, Dworkin, and Smith, 1984). They will *not* press a lever that causes cocaine to be delivered to the nucleus accumbens (Goeders and Smith, 1983). A possible explanation for this puzzling fact is that this drug acts as a local anesthetic as well as a dopaminergic agonist; thus, it may simply block the conduction of action potentials in axons leading out of the nucleus.

If the activation of dopamine receptors in the nucleus accumbens is responsible for reinforcement, then we would expect that the injection of drugs that block these receptors would interfere with reinforcement. And it does. Stellar, Kelley, and Corbett (1983) trained rats to travel through a runway in order to receive electrical stimulation of the medial forebrain bundle. They found that when they injected a dopamine receptor blocker into the nucleus accumbens, they had to turn up the stimulator in order to get the animals to run. That is, the drug reduced the reinforcing value of the electrical brain stimulation. (See *Figure 16.7.*)

Dopaminergic neurons can be selectively killed by the drug 6-HD (6-hydroxydopamine). When injected into the brain, the drug is taken up by the cell bodies, axons, or terminals of these cells, collects inside them, and kills them. (The drug will also kill noradrenergic neurons; but if it is administered along with imipramine, a drug that blocks the reuptake mechanism in these cells, they will be spared.) You will probably not be surprised to learn that 6-HD lesions of the ventral tegmental area, medial forebrain bundle, or nucleus accumbens disrupt the reinforcing effects of electrical stimulation of the brain. For example, Fibiger, Le Piane, Jakubovic, and Phillips (1987) implanted electrodes in the ventral tegmental area of rats and trained them to press a lever that delivered electrical brain stimulation. Next, they injected 6-HD into one side of the medial forebrain bundle, either on the same side of the brain as the stimulating electrode or contralateral to it. The drug destroyed the dopaminergic axons of the tegmentostriatal path; an analysis performed on the brains after the experiment was completed indicated that the level of dopamine in the nucleus accumbens on the lesioned side of the brain had decreased by over 97 percent. As Figure 16.8 shows, the animals with the lesions ipsilateral to the stimulating electrode stopped responding,

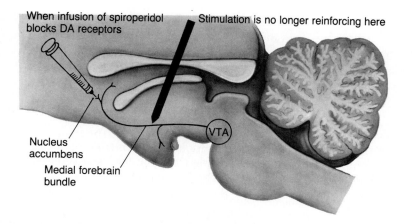

When infusion of spiroperidol blocks DA receptors

Stimulation is no longer reinforcing here

Nucleus accumbens

Medial forebrain bundle

VTA

FIGURE 16.7

An explanation of the experiment by Stellar, Kelley, and Corbett (1983).

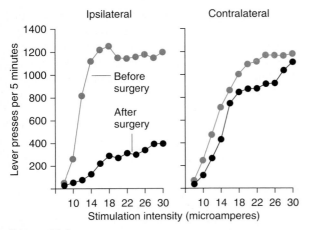

FIGURE 16.8

Lever pressing for reinforcing stimulation of the ventral tegmental area before and after 6-HD lesions of the medial forebrain bundle, ipsilateral or contralateral to the stimulating electrode. (Adapted from Fibiger, H.C., Jakubovic, A., Le Piane, F.G., and Phillips, A.G. *Journal of Neuroscience*, 1987, 7, 3888–3896.)

whereas those with the contralateral lesions responded normally. (See *Figure 16.8.*)

Several types of studies indicate that both cocaine and amphetamine exert their reinforcing effects in the nucleus accumbens, which contains the terminal buttons of the neurons of the tegmentostriatal pathway. First, if drugs that block dopamine receptors are injected into the nucleus accumbens, animals will no longer self-administer cocaine or amphetamine (Roberts and Zito, 1987). Thus, we can conclude that dopamine receptors located in other parts of the brain, which are still intact, are not responsible for the reinforcing effect of these drugs. Second, if 6-HD is infused into the nucleus accumbens, destroying the dopaminergic axons and terminal buttons located there, rats will no longer self-administer cocaine. However, they *will* self-administer apomorphine, a drug that directly stimulates dopamine receptors (Roberts, 1989). Let us see why.

Cocaine acts as a dopamine agonist because it blocks the reuptake of dopamine by the terminal buttons. Thus, if no dopaminergic terminal buttons are present, cocaine can have no effect, because there is no dopamine to be released. However, drugs such as apomorphine, which directly stimulate dopamine receptors, are still ef-

fective, because the 6-HD does not damage the postsynaptic cells, where these receptors are located. In fact, these receptors become supersensitive. *Supersensitivity* occurs when postsynaptic receptors are deprived of their normal input, either through the death of the terminal button or through long-term administration of drugs that block these receptors or prevent the release of the transmitter substance. The postsynaptic neuron manufactures more receptors, apparently to compensate for the lack of normal postsynaptic activity. Roberts (1989) predicted that the development of supersensitivity in the nucleus accumbens should make animals become more sensitive to the effects of drugs such as apomorphine, which directly stimulate dopamine receptors. His predictions were confirmed; he found that after they had received 6-HD lesions of the nucleus accumbens, rats became willing to work harder and harder for injections of apomorphine as supersensitivity developed. (See *Figure 16.9.*)

A third piece of evidence indicating that cocaine and amphetamine produce their reinforcing effect in the nucleus accumbens comes from studies using the *drug discrimination procedure.* This procedure uses the physiological effects of drugs as discriminative stimuli in order to learn something about the nature of these effects (Schuster

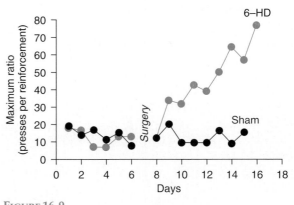

FIGURE 16.9

Behavioral effects of supersensitivity. The graph shows the maximum amount of effort that rats with 6-HD lesions or sham lesions of the nucleus accumbens were willing to expend for the infusion of apomorphine into the nucleus accumbens as a function of time after the lesion. (Adapted from Roberts, D.C.S. *Pharmacology, Biochemistry, and Behavior*, 1989, 32, 43–47.)

and Balster, 1977). An animal is given a drug and then is trained to press one of two levers to receive food. The next day, it receives an injection of saline and is trained to press the other lever. Each day thereafter, it receives either the drug or the saline, and it receives food only if it presses the appropriate lever. Obviously, the presence or absence of feedback from the effects of the drug tells the animal which lever to press. Then on test days the animal is given another drug. If the animal presses the "drug" lever, we can conclude that the feedback feels similar to the first drug; if it presses the "saline" lever, we can conclude that it does not.

Wood and Emmett-Oglesby (1989) trained rats to discriminate between the effects of injections of cocaine and saline and then administered cocaine directly into the brain on test days. They injected the drug into three locations in which dopaminergic terminal buttons are found: the nucleus accumbens, the caudate nucleus, and the prefrontal cortex. They found that the rats pressed the "cocaine" lever only when they had received the drug in the nucleus accumbens; when they received the drug in the caudate nucleus or prefrontal cortex, they pressed the "saline" lever. Thus, to the rats, the effects of an injection of cocaine in the nucleus accumbens felt like the effects of a systemic injection.

Microdialysis Studies

Chapter 5 described a research technique called *microdialysis* that is being adopted by an increasing number of laboratories. As we saw in Chapter 13, microdialysis has been used to measure the relation between hunger and satiety and the release of norepinephrine and serotonin in the hypothalamus. Researchers have also used this technique (and a related method, *voltammetry*) to measure the effects of artificial and natural stimulation on the release of dopamine in the brain.

The results of these studies confirm the results obtained by the use of other methods and provide direct evidence that natural reinforcing stimuli cause the release of dopamine in the nucleus accumbens, a fact that was certainly suspected but had not been proved. Using voltammetry, Phillips, Blaha, and Fibiger (1989) found that when a rat pressed a lever for electrical stimulation of the ventral tegmental area, the stimulation caused the

release of dopamine in the nucleus accumbens. This release was proportional to the effectiveness of the stimulation as a reinforcer. Injections of cocaine increased the rate of lever pressing for the stimulation and also increased the release of dopamine. (See *Figure 16.10*.)

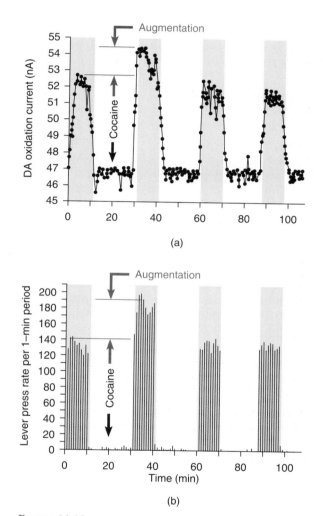

(a)

(b)

FIGURE 16.10

Effects of cocaine on lever pressing for electrical stimulation of the ventral tegmental area and release of cocaine in the nucleus accumbens. Lever presses were reinforced during the periods indicated by the color shading. (a) Release of dopamine, as measured by voltammetry. Note that the release of dopamine is increased temporarily by the injection of cocaine. (b) Number of lever presses. Note that the behavioral results resemble the neurochemical results. (Adapted from Phillips, A.G., Blaha, C.D., and Fibiger, H.C. *Neuroscience and Biobehavioral Reviews*, 1989, *13*, 99–104.)

Other studies have shown that reinforcing electrical stimulation of the medial forebrain or the administration of cocaine or amphetamine cause the release of dopamine in the nucleus accumbens (Moghaddam and Bunney, 1989; Nakahara, Ozaki, Miura, Miura, and Nagatsu, 1989). Even more importantly, natural reinforcers stimulate this release: drinking, induced by dehydration or by an injection of angiotensin; salt intake, induced by sodium depletion; or eating, induced by food deprivation (Blander, Mark, Hernandez, and Hoebel, 1988; Chang, Mark, Hernandez, and Hoebel, 1988; Hernandez and Hoebel, 1988). Figure 16.11 shows the effects of a natural reinforcer (food) on the level of dopamine in the nucleus accumbens. The animal had been trained to press a lever to obtain food; the shaded area indicates the time during which the signal light indicated that lever pressing would be reinforced. (See *Figure 16.11.*)

As I mentioned earlier in this chapter, whether a particular stimulus is reinforcing depends on the physiological condition of the animal. For example, food will reinforce the behavior of a hungry animal but not a satiated one. Another way to change the reinforcing value of a stimulus is to pair it with another one. As we saw in Chapter 13, a conditioned flavor aversion can be established by pairing a particular flavor with treatments that produce illness, such as an injection of lithium chloride. Mark, Blander, Hernandez, and Hoebel (1989) found that although the taste of saccharin normally caused an increase in dopamine release in the nucleus accumbens of naive animals, it caused a *decrease* in dopamine release if the flavor of saccharin had previously been paired with an injection of lithium chloride. Thus, the same stimulus had very different effects on the activity of neurons involved with reinforcement, depending on the animal's prior experience with this stimulus.

As we also saw in Chapter 13, Scott and his colleagues have shown that a conditioned aversion to saccharin changes the response pattern of neurons in the nucleus of the solitary tract (a region that receives taste information from the tongue) to the taste of saccharin; the pattern resembles the response made to quinine, a substance that rats avoid. On the other hand, inducing a salt appetite

by depleting the animals of sodium changed the pattern produced by a salty taste so that it resembled the one produced by the taste of sucrose. Thus, there were two patterns, "good" and "bad." We can hypothesize that the presence of the "good" pattern stimulates the activity of neurons involved in reinforcement, whereas the presence of the "bad" pattern does not—or may even *decrease* this activity.

Dopamine and Neural Plasticity

The fact that the release of dopamine reinforces behavior does not prove that dopamine itself is responsible for synaptic changes affecting learning; possibly, these changes are controlled farther "downstream," by neurons that receive

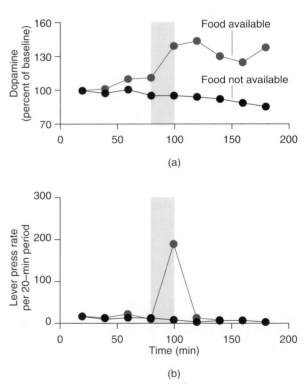

FIGURE 16.11
Effects of lever pressing for food on release of dopamine in the nucleus accumbens. Lever presses were reinforced by food during the period indicated by the color shading. (a) Release of dopamine, as measured by microdialysis. (b) Lever pressing. (Adapted from Hernandez, L., and Hoebel, B.G. *Life Sciences,* 1988, *42,* 1705–1712.)

dopaminergic input or even by neurons that *these* neurons communicate with. In any case, some interesting studies summarized by Stein and Belluzzi (1988) indicate that dopamine does appear to be capable of changing the response characteristics of single neurons.

Stein and Belluzzi prepared hippocampal slices according to the method described in Chapter 15. They recorded from single CA1 pyramidal neurons, which are known to contain dopamine receptors. They attempted to reinforce bursts of neural activity by infusing dopamine or dopamine agonists onto the neuron through a micropipette. Whenever the neuron spontaneously produced a burst of action potentials lasting at least 0.5 second, they applied the dopamine. Figure 16.12 shows the results of administering dop-

amine, cocaine, or saline. *Baseline* refers to periods during which they simply recorded the number of bursts of action potentials. During *reinforcement* periods they followed each burst with the infusion. During *noncontingent* periods they administered infusions that were not paired with the bursts. As you can see, both dopamine and cocaine increased the rate of the bursts, but only when they were applied contingently. (See *Figure 16.12*.)

These findings indicate that if dopamine is administered at the time that cells are already firing, their firing rate will increase. We do not know the mechanism responsible for this phenomenon. If it involves the strengthening of synaptic connections with other neurons in the slice, then it could imply that dopamine itself can reinforce weak

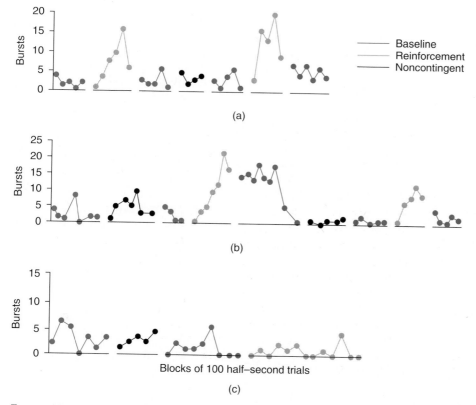

FIGURE 16.12

Instrumental conditioning of single neurons in the CA1 field of the hippocampal formation. (a) Dopamine infusion. (b) Cocaine infusion. (c) Saline infusion. (Adapted from Stein, L., and Belluzzi, J.D., in *Quantitative Analyses of Behavior. Vol. VII: Biological Determinants of Reinforcement and Memory,* edited by M. Commons, R. Church, J. Stellar, and A. Wagner. Hillsdale, N.J.: Lawrence Erlbaum Associates, 1988.)

connections between neurons. Obviously, more research needs to be done.

Tracing the Circuitry of Reinforcing Brain Stimulation: Neurophysiological Studies

For several years investigators believed that electrical stimulation of the medial forebrain bundle was reinforcing because it directly activated ascending dopaminergic axons, thus causing dopamine to be released in the nucleus accumbens. However, subsequent evidence indicates that the electrical stimulation activates dopaminergic neurons indirectly, by means of axons that travel from the forebrain to the ventral tegmental area.

Electrophysiological techniques indicate that electrical stimulation of the medial forebrain bundle activates long, myelinated axons with diameters of 0.5 to 2.0 μm that descend to the ventromedial tegmentum. The cell bodies of these axons probably lie in the basal forebrain region, including the preoptic area and the lateral hypothalamus. Indeed, Phillipson (1979) injected horseradish peroxidase in the ventral tegmental area and found retrograde labeling of cell bodies in these areas. Although dopaminergic and noradrenergic axons do travel through the MFB, they are thin and unmyelinated and are therefore difficult to stimulate electrically.

The evidence for these conclusions about the nature of the stimulated axons comes from several different types of electrophysiological studies, two of which I will describe. The first method used pairs of pulses of electrical current delivered to the MFB to determine the refractory period of the stimulated axons. Yeomans (1975) measured the effectiveness of trains of twenty pulses (ten pairs) as reinforcers of lever pressing. When the pulses were evenly spaced, they produced their maximum effect. However, when the pairs were closely spaced, they were no more effective than ten single pulses. The reason for this result is that once an axon is stimulated, it becomes refractory to further stimulation and cannot respond again until it has recovered. Yeomans found that when the pulse pairs were separated by at least 1.2 msec, the reinforcing effect was as strong as that produced by twenty individual pulses; hence the refractory period for the MFB axons was under 1.2 msec.

From these results and the results of another (more complicated) electrophysiological experiment, Bielajew and Shizgal (1982) calculated that the velocity of action potentials in axons that mediate the reinforcing effect of MFB stimulation is between 2 and 8 meters per second, which implies that they are myelinated and have diameters between 0.5 and 2.0 μm. Thus, they are not monoaminergic neurons, which are thinner and nonmyelinated.

Bielajew and Shizgal (1986) obtained evidence that the axons responsible for the reinforcing effects of electrical stimulation of the MFB are descending, having their origin in the forebrain and terminating in the midbrain. (In contrast, catecholaminergic axons in the MFB are ascending.) The investigators placed electrodes in the rostral

Figure 16.13

Effects of hyperpolarizing and depolarizing electrical stimulation on the effectiveness of reinforcing electrical brain stimulation, observed by Bielajew and Shizgal (1986).

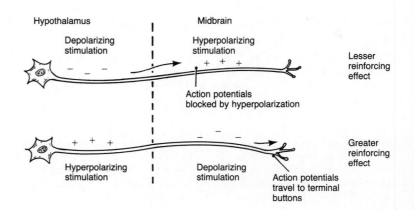

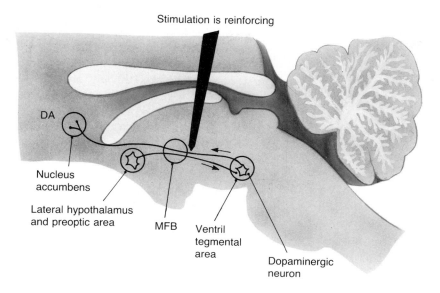

Stimulation is reinforcing

DA

Nucleus
accumbens

Lateral hypothalamus
and preoptic area

MFB   Ventril
tegmental
area

Dopaminergic
neuron

FIGURE 16.14

Effects of MFB stimulation.
When the medial forebrain
bundle is electrically stimulated,
axons of dopaminergic neurons
are indirectly stimulated by way
of the ventral tegmental area.
MFB = medial forebrain bundle.

and caudal ends of the MFB and passed negative (depolarizing) pulses of current through one electrode and positive (hyperpolarizing) pulses through the other. When the depolarizing stimulation was passed through the electrode in the caudal (midbrain) end, the rats pressed the lever rapidly. When the current was reversed, they pressed more slowly. Thus, the stimulation was most effective when the caudal stimulation was depolarizing. These results indicate that the cell bodies of the axons that mediate reinforcement are located rostrally, and the terminal buttons are located caudally. (See *Figure 16.13*.)

In summary, the axons that produce the reinforcing effects of MFB stimulation are not ascending dopaminergic fibers. However, these axons terminate in the ventral tegmental area, where they activate dopaminergic neurons that ascend to the nucleus accumbens. (See *Figure 16.14*.)

Relation of Self-Stimulation to Natural Reinforcement

The experiments with self-stimulation tell us that behaviors can be reinforced by the activation of neurons located in the basal forebrain that send axons to the ventral tegmental area, where they activate dopaminergic neurons whose axons travel to the nucleus accumbens. We also know that the reinforcing effects of natural appetitive

stimuli are abolished by dopamine antagonists and that natural reinforcers increase the release of dopamine in the nucleus accumbens. So this circuit probably is not simply a curiosity for neuroscientists; it plays an important role in reinforcement in the world outside the laboratory. The obvious questions are, then, "When natural reinforcers occur, what stimulates these neurons in the basal forebrain?" and "How does the release of dopamine in the nucleus accumbens reinforce behaviors?"

A tentative answer to the first question comes from studies described in Chapter 13. As we saw, evidence gathered by Rolls and his colleagues indicates that neurons in the lateral hypothalamus of the monkey become active when an animal sees food, but only when it is hungry. These neurons even show sensory-specific satiety. That is, once a monkey has had all it wants of a particular food, the neurons stop responding to the sight of that food but continue to respond to the sight of foods that the animal is still willing to eat. Thus, the activity of these neurons is clearly related to motivation.

As we saw earlier in this chapter, many psychologists believe that the signal for reinforcement is produced by feedback from certain categories of appetitive species-typical responses. Thus, the lateral hypothalamic neurons whose activity was observed by Rolls and his colleagues may produce two effects: stimulation of motivated behavior by means of connections with brain stem motor systems, and stimulation of reinforcement by means of connections with the ventral tegmental area. Of course, it remains to be established that these lateral hypothalamic neurons have these connections.

Rompré and his colleagues (Rompré and Miliaressis, 1985; Rompré and Boye, 1989) have discovered another site in the brain stem in which electrical stimulation has a reinforcing effect: the midline of the rostral pons. Rompré and Wise (1989) found that injections of pimozide reduced the effectiveness of electrical stimulation of the midline pons, which suggests that these neurons appear to be connected somehow to the dopaminergic neurons of the ventral tegmental area. The pons contains many circuits of neurons involved in motor control; thus it is possible that these connections with the ventral tegmental area (if they do exist) provide another pathway through which feedback from appetitive behaviors initiates the process of reinforcement.

Not much progress has yet been made on providing an answer to the second question, "How does the release of dopamine in the nucleus accumbens reinforce behaviors?" Obviously, since activity of the dopaminergic neurons of the tegmentostriatal system reinforces behaviors, there must be some outputs from the nucleus accumbens that are responsible for this effect. Besides receiving dopaminergic input from the ventral tegmental area, the nucleus accumbens receives inputs from the hippocampus and the amygdala (Kelley and Domesick, 1982; Kelley, Domesick, and Nauta, 1982). Its outputs reach motor circuits in the midbrain, especially those that control locomotion (Swanson, Mogenson, Gerfen, and Robinson, 1984). Yang and Mogenson (1987) found that dopamine agonists injected into the nucleus accumbens modulated the effects of hippocampal stimulation on motor activity. Thus, the behavioral effects of at least one part of the limbic system on behavior are modulated by activity of the dopaminergic neurons of the tegmentostriatal system. It remains to be seen if these interactions are responsible for the reinforcing effects described in this chapter.

INTERIM SUMMARY

Olds and Milner discovered that rats would perform a response that caused electrical current to be delivered through an electrode placed in their brain. Subsequent studies found that stimulation of many locations had reinforcing effects but that the medial forebrain bundle produced the strongest and most reliable ones.

Reinforcing brain stimulation appears also to elicit behaviors, or at least to increase the ability of environmental stimuli to elicit behaviors. These effects suggest that the stimulation mimics the feedback from having made an appetitive response, which is the normal condition for reinforcement. This artificial feedback strengthens the connection between neurons that detect stimuli and neurons whose activity produces behaviors. For example, if an animal receives MFB stimulation when it presses a lever, the sight of the lever becomes an eliciting stimulus that produces pressing.

For several years investigators have believed that the catecholamines— norepinephrine and dopamine—play a role in reinforcement. This belief was suggested by the observation that amphetamine and cocaine, potent catecholamine agonists, have strong reinforcing effects. It appears that the most important neurons are dopaminergic cells located in the ventral tegmental area that send their axons to the nucleus accumbens. Systemic injections of dopamine agonists are reinforcing, and systemic injections of dopamine antagonists will block the reinforcing effects of natural stimuli or electrical stimulation of the medial forebrain bundle. Infusions of dopamine antagonists directly into the nucleus accumbens have the same effects as systemic injections. Microdialysis studies have also shown that natural and artificial reinforcers stimulate the release of dopamine in the nucleus accumbens. An increase in the spontaneous response rate of neurons in hippocampal slices can even be increased by contingent infusions of dopamine; thus, single neurons can be instrumentally conditioned.

Electrophysiological studies have shown that the axons directly activated by electrical stimulation of the medial forebrain bundle are myelinated, have a diameter between 0.5 and 2.0 μm, and travel caudally, terminating in the ventral midbrain. There, they activate dopaminergic neurons, which send their axons rostrally, especially to the nucleus accumbens. The axons that are stimulated by the electrical current probably belong to neurons located in the lateral hypothalamus and preoptic area, which fire in response to food-related stimuli capable of reinforcing an animal's behavior. On their way to motor circuits in the brain stem, the axons of these neurons may activate dopaminergic neurons in the ventral tegmental area, producing reinforcement. A similar system of neurons located in the midline of the rostral pons may perform similar functions.

ADDICTION

Drug addiction is one of the most serious problems that our species presently faces. Consider the disastrous effects caused by the abuse of humankind's oldest drug, alcohol: automobile accidents, fetal alcohol syndrome, cirrhosis of the liver, Korsakoff's syndrome, increased rate of heart disease, and increased rate of intracerebral hemorrhage. Smoking (nicotine addiction) greatly increases the chances of dying of lung cancer, heart attack, and stroke; and women who smoke give birth to smaller, less healthy babies. Cocaine addiction often causes psychosis, brain damage, and death from overdose; it produces babies born with severe brain damage and consequent psychological problems; and competition for lucrative markets terrorizes neighborhoods, subverts political and judicial systems, and causes many deaths. The use of "designer drugs" exposes users to unknown dangers of untested and often contaminated products, as several young people discovered when they acquired

Parkinson's disease. Addicts who take their drug intravenously run a serious risk of contracting AIDS. Why do people use these drugs and subject themselves to these dangers?

The answer, as you may have predicted from what you have read in this chapter so far, is that all of these substances stimulate the release of dopamine in the nucleus accumbens; thus, they reinforce the behaviors responsible for their delivery to the body: swallowing, smoking, sniffing, or injecting. The immediate consequences of these drugs are more powerful than the realization that in the long term bad things will happen.

Characteristics of Addictive Substances

Most substances to which people can become addicted produce an excitatory effect, although some, like opiates and alcohol, produce both excitation and inhibition. Most investigators believe that the excitatory effects are the most important in producing addiction.

Opiates

Opium, derived from a sticky resin produced by the opium poppy, has been eaten and smoked for centuries. Morphine, one of the naturally occurring ingredients of opium, is sometimes used as a painkiller but has largely been supplanted by synthetic opiates. Heroin, a compound produced from morphine, is the most commonly abused opiate.

Opiate addiction has several high personal and social costs. First, because heroin is an illegal drug, an addict becomes, by definition, a criminal. Second, the behavioral response to opiates declines with continued use, which means that a person must take increasing amounts of the drug to achieve a "high." The habit thus becomes more and more expensive, and the person often turns to crime to obtain enough money to support his or her habit. (If the addict is a pregnant woman, her infant will also become dependent on the drug, which easily crosses the placental barrier. The infant must be given opiates right after being born and then be given gradually decreasing doses.) Third, an opiate addict often uses unsanitary needles; at present, a substantial percentage of people who inject illicit drugs have been exposed in this way to the AIDS virus. Fourth, the uncertainty about the strength of a given batch of heroin makes it possible for a user to receive an unusually large dose of the drug, with possibly fatal consequences. In addition, dealers typically dilute pure heroin with various adulterants such as milk sugar, quinine, or talcum powder; and dealers are not known for taking scrupulous care with the quality and sterility of the substances they use. Some heroin-induced deaths have actually been reactions to the adulterants mixed with the drugs.

Tolerance and Withdrawal Symptoms. Many people—including many health care professionals—think of heroin as the prototype for addiction. People who habitually take heroin (or other opiates) become physically dependent on the drug. Eddy, Halbach, Isbell, and Seevers (1965) define *physical dependence* as "an adaptive state that manifests itself by intense physical disturbances when the administration of a drug is suspended" (p. 723). In contrast, they define *psychic dependence* as "a condition in which a drug produces a feeling of satisfaction and a psychic drive that requires periodic or continuous administration of the drug to produce pleasure or to avoid discomfort" (p. 723). In fact, as we shall see, the distinction between "physical" and "psychic" dependence reflects a misunderstanding of the process of addiction.

Tolerance is the decreased sensitivity to a drug that comes from its continued use; the drug user must take larger and larger amounts of the drug in order for it to be effective. Once a person has taken an opiate regularly enough to develop tolerance, that person will suffer *withdrawal symptoms* if he or she stops taking the drug. Withdrawal symptoms are primarily the opposite of the effects of the drug itself. That is, heroin produces euphoria; withdrawal from it produces *dysphoria*—a feeling of anxious misery. (*Euphoria* and *dysphoria* mean "easy to bear" and "hard to bear," respectively.) Heroin produces constipation; withdrawal from it produces nausea and cramping. Heroin produces relaxation; withdrawal from it produces agitation.

Most investigators believe that the withdrawal symptoms are produced by the body's attempt to compensate for the unusual condition of heroin intoxication. That is, most systems of the body, including those controlled by the brain, are regulated so that they stay at an optimal value. When a drug artificially changes these systems for a prolonged time, homeostatic mechanisms begin to produce the opposite reaction, thus partially compensating for the disturbance from the optimal value. These compensatory mechanisms account for the fact that more and more heroin must be taken in order to achieve the effects that were produced when the person first started taking the drug (tolerance). They also account for the symptoms of withdrawal: When the person stops taking the drug, the compensatory mechanisms make themselves felt, unopposed by the action of the drug.

Research suggests that there are basically two types of compensatory mechanisms. The first mechanism involves a decrease in the effectiveness of opiates as a neuromodulator. Either opiate receptors become less sensitive or the mechanisms that couple them to ion channels in the membrane become less effective; or both effects occur. A second effect, described by Siegel (1978), involves classical conditioning. When a person takes heroin, the drug produces its primary effects, which in turn activate the homeostatic compensatory mechanisms. The activation of these compensatory mechanisms can become classically conditioned to environmental stimuli present at the time. The stimuli associated with taking the drug—including the paraphernalia involved in preparing the solution of the drug, the syringe, the needle, the feel of the needle in a vein, and even the room in which the drug is taken—serve as conditional stimuli. The homeostatic compensatory responses provoked by the effects of the drug serve as the unconditional response, which becomes conditioned to the environmental stimuli. Thus, once classical conditioning has taken place, the compensatory mechanisms are activated not only by the primary effects of the drug but also *by the stimuli associated with taking the drug*. (See *Figure 16.15.*)

Heroin addiction has provided such a striking example of drug dependence that some authorities have concluded that "real" addiction does not occur unless a drug causes tolerance and with-

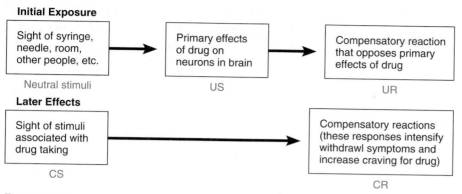

Initial Exposure

| Sight of syringe, needle, room, other people, etc. | → | Primary effects of drug on neurons in brain | → | Compensatory reaction that opposes primary effects of drug |

Neutral stimuli   US   UR

Later Effects

| Sight of stimuli associated with drug taking | ⟶ | Compensatory reactions (these responses intensify withdrawl symptoms and increase craving for drug) |

CS   CR

FIGURE 16.15

The classical conditioning model of drug tolerance proposed by Siegel (1978).

drawal. Without doubt, withdrawal symptoms make it difficult for a person to stop taking heroin—they keep the person hooked, so to speak. However, withdrawal symptoms do not explain why a person *becomes* a heroin addict, nor do they explain why people continue taking the drug. Certainly, people do not start taking heroin so that they will become physically dependent on it and feel miserable when they go without it. In fact, when the cost of a habit gets too high, some addicts stop taking heroin "cold turkey." Doing so is not as painful as most people believe; withdrawal symptoms have been described as similar to a bad case of the flu. After a week or two, when their nervous system adapts to the absence of the drug, they recommence their habit. If their only reason for taking the drug was to avoid unpleasant withdrawal symptoms, they would never be capable of following this strategy. The reason that people take—and continue to take—drugs such as heroin is that the drugs give them a pleasurable "rush"; in other words, the drugs have a reinforcing effect on their behavior.

There are two kinds of evidence that contradict the belief that drug addition is caused by physical dependence. First, some very potent drugs—including cocaine—do not produce physical dependence. That is, people who take the drug do not show tolerance, and if they stop, they do not show any withdrawal symptoms. And yet the people show just as strong an addiction as heroin addicts. Second, some drugs produce physical

dependence (tolerance and withdrawal symptoms) but are not abused (Jaffe, 1985). The reason they are not abused is that they do not have reinforcing effects on behavior.

Effects on Dopaminergic Neurons. Laboratory animals, like humans, will self-administer opiates. As you learned in Chapter 7, opiates act by stimulating specialized receptors on the membranes of neurons located in various parts of the nervous system. When an opiate is administered systemically, it stimulates all of these receptors and produces a variety of effects, including analgesia, hypothermia (lowering of body temperature), sedation, and reinforcement. Opiate receptors in the periaqueductal gray matter are responsible for the analgesia, those in the preoptic area are responsible for the hypothermia, those in the mesencephalic reticular formation are responsible for the sedation, and those in the ventral tegmental area and the nucleus accumbens are responsible for the reinforcement. In addition, opiate receptors in the periaqueductal gray matter appear to be responsible for the withdrawal effects seen in animals with heroin dependency (Wise, 1989).

Animals will self-administer opiates into two regions of the brain known to be involved in the effects of dopamine on reinforcement: the ventral tegmental area and the nucleus accumbens (Bozarth and Wise, 1984; Goeders, Lane, and Smith, 1984). In addition, if a drug that blocks opi-

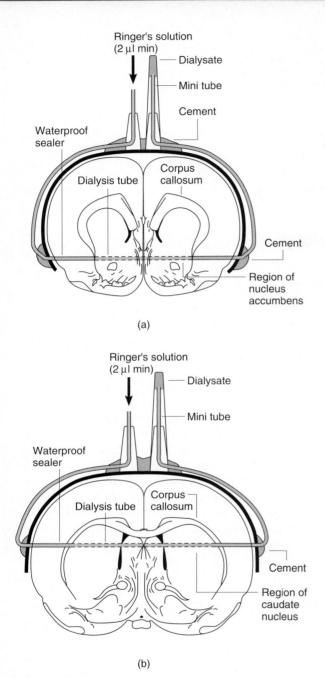

Ringer's solution
(2 μl min)

— Dialysate

— Mini tube

Cement

Waterproof
sealer

Corpus
callosum

Dialysis tube

Cement

Region of
nucleus
accumbens

(a)

Ringer's solution
(2 μl min)

— Dialysate

— Mini tube

Waterproof
sealer

Corpus
callosum

Dialysis tube

Cement

Region of
caudate
nucleus

(b)

Figure 16.16
The microdialysis procedure used by Di Chiara and
Imperato (1987) to measure the release of dopamine.
(a) Nucleus accumbens. (b) Caudate nucleus.
(Adapted from Carboni, E., Imperato, A., Perezzani,
L., and Di Chiara, G. *Neuroscience*, 1989, *28*, 653–661.)

ate receptors is injected into either the ventral
tegmental area or the nucleus accumbens, the reinforcing effect of intravenous heroin is decreased
(Britt and Wise, 1983; Vaccarino, Bloom, and
Koob, 1985). Bozarth and Wise (1984) found that
repeated injection of morphine into the ventral
tegmental area does not seem to produce signs of
withdrawal when the injections stop; however,
repeated injection into the periaqueductal gray
matter *does* lead to withdrawal symptoms, even
though the injections are not reinforcing. Thus,
receptors in different parts of the brain are
responsible for the reinforcing effects of opiates
and the aversive effects produced by opiate
withdrawal.

Several different kinds of experimental evidence indicate that opiates exert their reinforcing
effects in the ventral tegmental area by activating
dopaminergic neurons. First, injection of morphine into the ventral tegmental area increases
the activity of dopaminergic neurons located
there (Matthews and German, 1984). Second, 6-
HD lesions of the tegmentostriatal dopaminergic
neurons disrupts intravenous self-administration of heroin (Bozarth and Wise, 1986). Third,
neurotoxic lesions of the nucleus accumbens
block the reinforcing effects of intravenous heroin
(Zito, Vickers, and Roberts, 1985).

As we saw earlier in this chapter, microdialysis
studies have shown that reinforcing brain stimulation and many natural stimuli that reinforce behaviors cause dopamine to be released in the nucleus accumbens. Di Chiara and Imperato (1987)
constructed special microdialysis tubes that they
inserted into the brain so that they passed through
the nucleus accumbens or the caudate nucleus.
(See *Figure 16.16*.) They found that injections of
opiates caused the release of dopamine, particularly in the nucleus accumbens.

Cocaine and Amphetamine
Cocaine and amphetamine have similar behavioral effects, because both act as dopamine agonists by blocking its reuptake after it is released
by the terminal buttons. In addition, amphetamine directly stimulates the release of dopamine. "Crack," a particularly potent form of cocaine, is smoked and thus enters the blood supply
of the lungs and reaches the brain very quickly.

Because its effects are so potent and so rapid, it is probably the most effective reinforcer of all available drugs.

When people take cocaine, they become euphoric, active, and talkative. They say that they feel powerful and alert. Some of them become addicted to the drug, and obtaining it becomes an obsession to which they devote more and more time and money. Laboratory animals, who will quickly learn to self-administer cocaine intravenously, also act excited and show intense exploratory activity. After receiving the drug for a day or two, rats start showing stereotyped movements, such as grooming, head bobbing, and persistent locomotion (Geary, 1987). If rats or monkeys are given continuous access to a lever that permits them to self-administer cocaine, they often self-inject so much cocaine that they die. In fact, Bozarth and Wise (1985) found that rats that self-administered cocaine were almost three times more likely to die than rats that self-administered heroin. (See *Figure 16.17*.)

One of the alarming effects of cocaine and amphetamine seen in people who abuse these drugs regularly is psychotic behavior: hallucinations, delusions of persecution, mood disturbances, and repetitive behaviors. These symptoms so

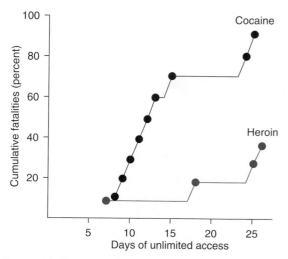

FIGURE 16.17
Cumulative fatalities in groups of rats self-administering cocaine or heroin. (From Bozarth, M.A., and Wise, R.A. *Journal of the American Medical Association*, 1985, 254, 81–83.)

closely resemble those of paranoid schizophrenia that even a trained mental health professional cannot distinguish them unless he or she knows about the person's history of drug abuse. The fact that these symptoms are provoked by dopamine agonists and reduced by drugs that block dopamine receptors suggests that overactivity of dopaminergic synapses is one of the causes of schizophrenia. I will say more about this subject in Chapter 18, which is devoted to the biology of mental disorders.

Usually, a psychotic reaction caused by use of cocaine or amphetamine will subside once the person stops taking the drug. However, the exposure to the drug appears to produce long-term changes in the brain that make the person more likely to display psychotic symptoms if he or she takes the drug later—even months or years later (Sato, Chen, Akiyama, and Otsuki, 1983; Sato, 1986). A study with rats suggests that this effect is produced by long-term changes in the nucleus accumbens. Robinson, Jurson, Bennett, and Bentgen (1988) administered escalating daily doses of amphetamine to rats over a period of five weeks, in a pattern designed to mimic that of people who abuse the drug and become psychotic. Two to three weeks later, the investigators administered a single dose of amphetamine and observed the animals' behavior and measured the release of dopamine in the nucleus accumbens by means of microdialysis. As Figure 16.18 shows, the rates of head and limb movements, sniffing, and dopamine release were much higher in animals that had previously received the amphetamine. (See *Figure 16.18*.)

Nicotine and Caffeine

Stimulant drugs such as nicotine and caffeine may seem rather tame after a discussion of opiates, cocaine, and amphetamine. Nevertheless, these drugs, too, have addictive potential. Fortunately, caffeine is relatively innocuous; most people do not take enough to impair their health or produce serious behavioral effects. Nicotine is a different story. The combination of nicotine and other substances in tobacco smoke is carcinogenic and leads to cancer of the lungs, mouth, throat, and esophagus. Although nicotine is less potent than the "hard" drugs, many more people who

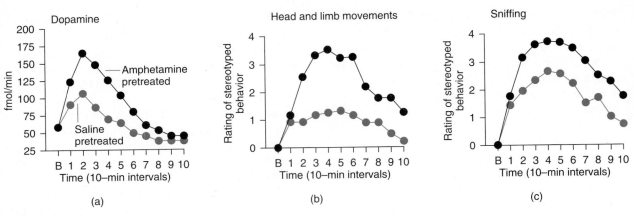

FIGURE 16.18

Sensitization to the effects of amphetamine in rats that had been pretreated for five weeks with amphetamine or saline. (a) Effects of amphetamine on the release of dopamine in the nucleus accumbens. (b) Effects of amphetamine on stereotyped behaviors. (Adapted from Robinson, T.E., Jurson, P.A., Bennett, J.A., and Bentgen, K.M. *Brain Research*, 1988, *462*, 211–222.)

try it go on to become addicts. The addictive potential of nicotine should not be underestimated; many people continue to smoke even when doing so causes serious health problems. For example, Sigmund Freud, whose theory of psychoanalysis stressed the importance of insight in changing one's behavior, was unable to stop smoking even after most of his jaw had been removed because of the cancer that this habit had caused (Brecher, 1972).

As we saw in Chapter 3, caffeine is a phosphodiesterase inhibitor; that is, it suppresses the activity of an enzyme that destroys cyclic nucleotides, the second messengers that transmit information from a postsynaptic receptor to the ion channels in the membrane that they control. Cyclic nucleotides have many other functions as well, so the effects of caffeine are not at all specific. Nevertheless, there is some evidence that caffeine activates dopaminergic neurons (Wise, 1988).

Ours is not the only species willing to self-administer nicotine; so will laboratory animals (Henningfield and Goldberg, 1983). Nicotine stimulates acetylcholine receptors, of course. It also increases the activity level of dopaminergic neurons, which contain these receptors (Svensson, Grenhoff, and Aston-Jones, 1986), and causes dopamine to be released in the nucleus accumbens (Damsma, Day, and Fibiger, 1989).

Figure 16.19 shows the effects of two injections of nicotine or saline on the extracellular dopamine level of the nucleus accumbens, measured by microdialysis probes. (See *Figure 16.19.*)

Wise (1988) notes that because nicotine stimulates the tegmentostriatal dopaminergic system, smoking could potentially make it more difficult for a cocaine or heroin addict to stop taking the drug. As several studies with laboratory animals have shown, if self-administration of cocaine or heroin is extinguished through nonrein-

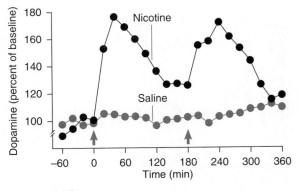

FIGURE 16.19

Release of dopamine in the nucleus accumbens caused by injections of nicotine or saline. The arrows indicate the time of the injections. (From Damsma, G., Day, J., and Fibiger, H.C. *European Journal of Pharmacology,* 1989, *168*, 363–368.)

forcement, an injection of drugs that stimulate dopaminergic neurons can reinstate the responding. A similar "cross-priming" effect from cigarette smoking could potentially contribute to a relapse in people who are trying to abstain. (As we shall see, alcohol also stimulates dopaminergic neurons, so drinking could present the same problem.)

Alcohol and Barbiturates

Alcohol costs society more than any other drug. A large percentage of deaths and injuries caused by motor vehicle accidents are related to alcohol use, and alcohol contributes to violence and aggression. Chronic alcoholics often lose their jobs, their homes, and their families; and many die of cirrhosis of the liver, exposure, or diseases caused by poor living conditions and abuse of their body. Women who drink during pregnancy run the risk of giving birth to babies with the fetal alcohol syndrome, which includes malformation of the head and the brain. (See *Figure 16.20.*) In fact, the leading cause of mental retardation in the Western world today is alcohol consumption by pregnant women (Abel and Sokol, 1986). Thus, understanding the physiological and behavioral effects of this drug is an important issue.

At low doses alcohol produces mild euphoria and has an *anxiolytic* effect—that is, it reduces the discomfort of anxiety. At higher doses it produces incoordination and sedation. In studies with laboratory animals the anxiolytic effects manifest themselves as a release from the punishing effects of aversive stimuli. For example, if an animal is given electric shocks whenever it makes a particular response (say, one that obtains food or water), it will stop doing so. However, if it is then given some alcohol, it will begin making the response again (Koob et al., 1984).

Alcohol probably produces both positive and negative reinforcement. *Positive* reinforcement is reinforcement caused by the presence of an appetitive stimulus, which, as we have seen, is related to the release of dopamine by neurons of the tegmentostriatal system. *Negative* reinforcement is reinforcement caused by the termination of an aversive stimulus. For example, an animal can be trained to press a lever if doing so turns off a loud noise. Similarly, if we find a medication that makes a painful headache go away, we will quickly turn to that medication the next time we have a headache. Negative reinforcement is provided by the anxiolytic effect of alcohol. If a person feels anxious and uncomfortable, then a drug that relieves this discomfort provides at least a temporary escape from an unpleasant situation.

Narrow forehead

Short palpebral fissures

Small nose

Long upper lip with deficient philtrum

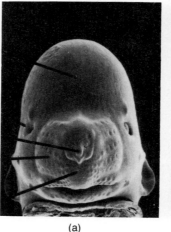
(a)

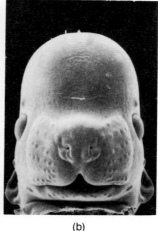
(b)

FIGURE 16.20

A child with fetal alcohol syndrome, along with magnified views of rat fetuses. (a) Fetus whose mother received alcohol during pregnancy. (b) Normal rat fetus. (Photograph courtesy of Katherine K. Sulik.)

The negative reinforcement provided by the anxiolytic effect of alcohol is probably not enough to explain the drug's addictive potential. Other drugs, such as the benzodiazepines ("tranquilizers" such as Valium), are even more potent anxiolytics than alcohol, and yet such drugs are rarely abused. It is probably the unique combination of stimulating and anxiolytic effects—of positive and negative reinforcement—that makes alcohol so difficult for some people to resist.

In low doses alcohol appears to act on the nervous system by stimulating the GABA-benzodiazepine receptor complex (described in Chapter 3). Suzdak et al. (1986) found that alcohol makes GABA receptors become more sensitive. In fact, they discovered a drug (Ro15–4513) that reverses alcohol intoxication, presumably by blocking one of the receptor sites on the GABA-benzodiazepine receptor complex. Figure 16.21 shows two rats who received injections of enough alcohol to make them pass out. The one facing us also received an injection of the alcohol antagonist and appears completely sober. (See *Figure 16.21.*)

This wonder drug is not likely to reach the market soon, if ever. Although the behavioral effects of alcohol may be mediated by benzodiazepine receptors, alcohol has other, potentially fatal effects on all cells of the body. Alcohol destabilizes the membrane of cells, interfering with their functions. Thus, a person who takes some of the alcohol antagonist could then go on to drink himself or herself to death, without becoming drunk in the process. Drug companies naturally fear possible liability suits stemming from such occurrences.

The site (or sites) of action of alcohol in the brain is not yet known. However, the positive reinforcement produced by the drug apparently involves the release of dopamine. Alcohol increases the firing of dopaminergic neurons in the ventral tegmental area (Gessa, Muntoni, Collu, Vargiu, and Mereu, 1985). It also causes the release of dopamine in the nucleus accumbens, as measured by microdialysis (Imperato and Di Chiara, 1986). It remains to be seen just how alcohol activates dopaminergic neurons and causes this dopamine release.

Barbiturates have effects very similar to those of alcohol. In fact, both drugs may act on the GABA-benzodiazepine receptor complex (Maksay and Ticku, 1985). However, if they do so, they act at different sites in the complex; Ro15–4513, the alcohol antagonist, does not reverse the intoxicating effects of barbiturates (Suzdak, Glowa, Crawley, Schwartz, Skolnick, and Paul,

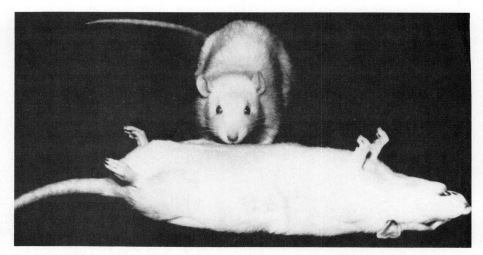

FIGURE 16.21
Effects of Ro15–4513, an alcohol antagonist. Both rats received an injection of alcohol, but the one facing us also received an injection of the alcohol antagonist. (Photograph courtesy of Steven M. Paul, National Institute of Mental Health, Bethesda, Md.)

1986). The effects of alcohol and barbiturates are additive; if a person takes a moderate dose of alcohol and a moderate dose of a barbiturate, the effect can be fatal. Barbiturates do *not* appear to affect dopaminergic neurons (Wood, 1982).

Although the effects of heroin withdrawal have been exaggerated, those produced by barbiturate or alcohol withdrawal are serious and can even be fatal (Julien, 1981). Convulsions caused by alcohol withdrawal are considered to be a medical emergency and are usually treated with benzodiazepines or barbiturates.

Genetics of Addiction

Not everyone is equally likely to become addicted to a drug. Many people manage to drink alcohol moderately, and even many users of potent drugs such as cocaine and heroin use them "recreationally," without becoming dependent on them. There are only two possible sources of individual differences in any characteristic: heredity and environment. Because this book considers the *physiology* of behavior, I will not discuss the role that environment plays in a person's susceptibility to the addicting effects of drugs. Obviously, environmental effects are important; people raised in a squalid environment without any real hope for a better life are more likely to turn to drugs for some temporary euphoria and removal from the unpleasant world that surrounds them. But even in a given environment, poor or privileged, some people become addicts and some do not—and some of these behavioral differences are a result of genetic differences.

Most of the research on the effects of heredity on addiction have been devoted to alcoholism. One of the most important reasons for this focus—aside from the importance of the problems caused by alcohol—is that almost everyone is exposed to alcohol. Most people drink alcohol sometime in their lives and thus receive firsthand experience with its reinforcing effects. The same is not true for cocaine, heroin, and other drugs that have even more potent effects. In most countries alcohol is freely and legally available in local shops, whereas cocaine and heroin must often be purchased in dangerous neighborhoods from unsavory dealers. From what we now know about

the effects of addictive drugs on the nervous system, it seems likely that the results of studies on the heredity of alcoholism will apply to other types of drug addiction as well.

Alcohol consumption is not distributed equally across the population; in the United States 10 percent of the people drink 50 percent of the alcohol (Heckler, 1983). The best evidence for an effect of heredity on susceptibility to alcoholism comes from two main sources: twin studies and cross-fostering studies. As you know, there are two types of twins. Monozygotic twins come from a single fertilized ovum, which splits apart early in development, becoming two independent individuals with identical heredity. Dizygotic twins come from two different ova, fertilized by two different sperms. Thus, they share (on the average) 50 percent of their chromosomes, just like any two siblings. If a trait is influenced by heredity, then we would expect that, with respect to this trait, monozygotic twins would resemble each other more than dizygotic twins. Monozygotic twins (identical twins) have the same body shape, facial characteristics, and hair and eye color, because these traits certainly are influenced by heredity. Many of their personality characteristics are also similar, which tells us that these traits, too, are influenced by heredity. Alcoholism is one of those traits; monozygotic twins are more likely to resemble each other with respect to alcohol abuse than dizygotic twins (Goodwin, 1979).

The second type of heritability study uses children who were adopted by nonrelatives when they were young. A study like this permits the investigator to estimate the effects of family environment as well as genetics. That is, one can examine the effects of being raised by an alcoholic parent, or having a biological parent who is an alcoholic, or both, on the probability of becoming alcoholic. Such a study was carried out in Sweden by Cloninger, Bohmann, Sigvardsson, and von Knorring (1985). Briefly, the study found that heredity was much more important than family environment. But the story is not quite that simple.

In a review of the literature on alcohol abuse Cloninger (1987) notes that many investigators have concluded that there are two principal types of alcoholics: those who cannot abstain but drink consistently, and those who are able to go without drinking for long periods of time but are unable to control themselves once they start. (For convenience, I will refer to these two groups as "steady drinkers" and "bingers.") Steady drinking is associated with antisocial personality disorder, which includes a lifelong history of impulsiveness, fighting, lying, and lack of remorse for antisocial acts. Binge drinking is associated with emotional dependence, behavioral rigidity, perfectionism, introversion, and guilt feelings about one's drinking behavior. Steady drinkers usually begin their alcohol consumption early in life, whereas binge drinkers begin much later. (See *Table 16.1*.)

Steady drinking is strongly influenced by heredity. The Swedish adoption study found that men with fathers who were steady drinkers were almost seven times more likely to become steady drinkers themselves than men whose fathers did not abuse alcohol. Family environment had no measurable effect; the boys began drinking whether or not the members of their adoptive family themselves drank heavily. Very few women become steady drinkers; the daughters of

steady-drinking fathers instead tend to develop *somatization disorder.* People with this disorder chronically complain of symptoms for which no physiological cause can be found, leading them to seek medical care almost continuously. Thus, the genes that predispose a man to become a steady-drinking alcoholic (antisocial type) predispose a woman to develop somatization disorder. The reason for this interaction with gender is not known.

Binge drinking is influenced both by heredity and by environment. The Swedish adoption study found that having a biological parent who was a binge drinker had little effect on the development of binge drinking unless the child was exposed to a family environment in which there was heavy drinking. The effect was seen in both males and females.

The existence of an effect of heredity implies a biological difference. That is, genes affect behavior only by affecting the body. A susceptibility to alcoholism could conceivably be caused by differences in the ability to digest or metabolize alcohol or by differences in the structure of biochemistry of the brain. Most investigators believe that differences in brain physiology are more likely to play a role. Cloninger (1987) notes that many studies have shown that people with antisocial tendencies, which includes the group of steady drinkers, show a strong tendency to seek novelty and excitement. These people are disorderly and distractible (many have a history of hyperactivity as children) and show little restraint in their behavior. They tend not to fear dangerous situations or social disapproval. They are easily bored. They tend to have low levels of 5-HT and dopamine metabolites in their cerebrospinal fluid, which suggests that serotonergic and dopaminergic neurons may be less active than those of other people (Linnoila, 1983; Cloninger, 1986). On the other hand, binge drinkers tend to be anxious, emotionally dependent, sentimental, sensitive to social cues, cautious and apprehensive, fearful of novelty or change, rigid, and attentive to details. Their EEG shows little slow alpha activity, which is characteristic of a relaxed state (Propping, Kruger, and Mark, 1981). When they take alcohol, they report a pleasant relief of tension (Propping, Kruger, and Janah, 1980). Perhaps, as Cloninger

TABLE 16.1
Characteristic features of two types of alcoholism

Feature	Type of Alcoholism	
	Steady	Binge
Usual age of onset (years)	Before 25	After 25
Spontaneous alcohol seeking (inability to abstain)	Frequent	Infrequent
Fighting and arrests when drinking	Frequent	Infrequent
Psychological dependence (loss of control)	Infrequent	Frequent
Guilt and fear about alcohol dependence	Infrequent	Frequent
Novelty seeking	High	Low
Harm avoidance	Low	High
Reward dependence	Low	High

From Cloninger, C.R., *Science*, 1987, *236*, 410–416.

suggests, these personality differences are a result of differences in the sensitivity of neural mechanisms involved in reinforcement, exploration, and punishment.

For example, steady drinkers may have an undersensitive punishment mechanism, which makes them unresponsive to danger and to social disapproval. They may also have an undersensitive reinforcement system, which leads them to seek more intense thrills (including those provided by alcohol) in order to experience pleasurable sensations. Thus, they seek the excitatory (dopamine-stimulating) effect of alcohol. Binge drinkers may have oversensitive punishment systems. Normally, they avoid drinking because of the guilt they experience afterward; but once they begin, and once the sedative effect begins, the alcohol-induced suppression of the punishment system makes it impossible for them to stop.

These hypotheses are merely speculative; we should view them as suggestions for further research rather than explanations of the biological nature of alcoholism. But even if they are wrong, they do give us hope that laboratory research may some day help us understand the causes of addictive behaviors.

INTERIM SUMMARY

Research on the physiology of reinforcement has led to considerable progress in understanding the physiology of drug addiction, which is one of the most serious problems our society faces today. Apparently, all substances that produce addiction have an excitatory effect, although several addictive drugs, such as alcohol and the opiates, produce an inhibitory effect as well. The excitatory effect, correlated with reinforcement, appears to involve the release of dopamine in the nucleus accumbens, as microdialysis studies and studies with dopamine antagonists have shown.

Opiates produce tolerance and withdrawal symptoms, which makes the habit become expensive and makes quitting more difficult; but the primary reason for addiction is the reinforcing effect, not the unpleasant symptoms produced when an addict tries to quit. Tolerance appears to be produced by homeostatic mechanisms, one involving mechanisms coupled to opiate receptors, and another involving classical conditioning of compensatory responses to the environmental stimuli associated with taking the drug. Both the ventral tegmental area and the nucleus accumbens contain opiate receptors that are involved in the reinforcing effects of opiates. Withdrawal symptoms appear to involve opiate receptors on neurons in the periaqueductal gray matter.

Cocaine and amphetamine are potent dopamine agonists and thus serve as potent reinforcers—and substances with a high addictive potential. Nicotine and caffeine also increase the release of dopamine in the nucleus accumbens.

Alcohol has both excitatory and anti-anxiety effects and thus is able to produce both positive and negative reinforcement. Its sedative effects are initiated by stimulation of a receptor associated with the GABA-benzodiazepine complex. Its reinforcing effects involve the release of dopamine in the nucleus accumbens, but how this is accomplished is not known.

Most people who are exposed to addictive drugs—even those with a high abuse potential—do not become addicts. Evidence suggests that the likelihood of addiction, especially to alcohol, is strongly affected by heredity. There may be two types of alcoholism, one related to an antisocial, pleasure-seeking personality (steady drinkers), and another related to a repressed, anxiety-ridden personality (binge drinkers). Some investigators believe that a better understanding of the physiological basis of reinforcement and punishment will help us understand the effects of heredity on susceptibility to addiction.

CONCLUDING REMARKS

Reinforcement mechanisms are responsible for our ability to profit from experience—to learn to make particular responses in particular situations. Unfortunately, because a wide variety of chemicals available naturally or from the chemical laboratory are capable of stimulating these mechanisms, these mechanisms can also be responsible for addictive behaviors. In this chapter I have not addressed legal and moral issues of addiction, but we can hope that understanding the physiological basis of addiction will help us find ways to cope with one of the important problems that faces our society.

In the next chapter I will discuss human communication, verbal and nonverbal. In the section on verbal communication the issue of learning and memory will appear again. Verbal communication involves several different kinds of memories—of the sounds and sight of words, of the movements we make to talk and write, and of the relation between words and the things they signify.

NEW TERMS

adjunctive behavior p. 518
conditioned place
   preference p. 517
drug discrimination
   procedure p. 520

medial forebrain bundle p. 513
nucleus accumbens p. 515
self-administration p. 518
self-stimulation p. 512

supersensitivity p. 520
tegmentostriatal system p. 515
tolerance p. 528
withdrawal symptoms p. 528

SUGGESTED READINGS

Bozarth, M.A. *Methods of Assessing the Reinforcing Properties of Abused Drugs.* New York: Springer-Verlag, 1987.

Commons, M., Church, R., Stellar, J., and Wagner, A. *Quantitative Analyses of Behavior, Volume VII: Biological Determinants of Reinforcement and Memory.* Hillsdale, N.J.: Lawrence Erlbaum Associates, 1988.

Harris, L.S. *Problems of Drug Dependence, 1985.* Washington, D.C.: U.S. Government Printing Office, 1986.

Marlatt, G.A., Baer, J.S., Donovan, D.M., and Kivlahan, D.R. Addictive behaviors: Etiology and treatment. *Annual Review of Psychology,* 1988, *39,* 223–252.

Spitz, H.I., and Rosecan, J.S. *Cocaine Abuse: New Directions in Treatment and Research.* New York: Brunner/Mazel, 1987.

Wise, R.A., and Rompré, P.-P. Brain dopamine and reward. *Annual Review of Psychology,* 1989, *40,* 191–225.

17

Human Communication

539

*V*erbal behaviors constitute one of the most important classes of human social behavior. Our cultural evolution has been possible because we can talk and listen, write and read. Language enables our discoveries to be cumulative; knowledge gained by one generation can be passed on to the next.

The basic function of verbal communication is seen in its effects on other people. When we talk to someone, we almost always expect our speech to induce the person to engage in some sort of behavior. Sometimes, the behavior is of obvious advantage to us, as when we ask for an object or for help performing a task. At other times, we are simply asking for a social exchange: some attention and perhaps some conversation. Even "idle" conversation is not idle, because it causes another person to look at us and say something in return.

But not all human communication is verbal. We also exchange information by means of facial expression and gestures and through our tone of voice. Thus, this chapter describes the physiology of verbal and nonverbal communication: words and emotions.

SPEECH PRODUCTION AND COMPREHENSION: BRAIN MECHANISMS

Studying Speech Disorders

Our knowledge of the physiology of language has been obtained primarily by observing the effects of brain lesions on people's verbal behavior. Although investigators have studied people who have undergone brain surgery or who have sustained head injuries, brain tumors, or infections, most of the observations have been made on people who have suffered strokes, or *cerebrovascular accidents.* The most common type of cerebrovascular accident is caused by obstruction of a blood vessel (almost always an artery, but sometimes a vein). The interruption in blood flow deprives a region of the brain of its blood supply, which causes cells in that region to die.

Most strokes that affect verbal behavior occur in the region of the brain served by the middle ce-

rebral artery. This vessel branches off the internal carotid artery, follows the lateral fissure, and feeds most of the lateral surface of the brain. In addition, branches of the middle cerebral artery penetrate and feed subcortical regions such as the thalamus, basal ganglia, and white matter. The posterior cerebral artery supplies the posterior medial portion of the cerebrum, principally the occipital cortex and underlying white matter. Strokes in its territory sometimes produce reading deficits. Strokes of the anterior cerebral artery, which supplies most of the anterior and dorsal medial region of the cerebral hemispheres, seldom produce language disturbances. (See *Figure 17.1.*)

Study of human brain functions presents difficulties that are not encountered by investigators who use laboratory animals. The brain lesion occurs naturally and is not placed in a specific location by the investigator. In the past scientists possessed only crude techniques to infer the location of a living patient's lesion. To be certain where the lesion was, they had to wait until the patient died so that they could examine the brain. This situation meant that unless the patient died soon after being studied, the brain was usually not available to the investigator. Even if the patient did die soon, the family might not give permission for the brain to be removed and examined. Thus, the development of the CT scanner and, later, the MRI scanner revolutionized the study of the anatomy of verbal behavior. CT scans and MRI scans provide remarkably good views of obstructive strokes, permitting the investigator to see which regions of the brain are damaged. In the past few years these scans have resolved many controversies about the location of damage that produces specific deficits. (See *Figure 17.2.*)

The most important category of speech disorders is *aphasia,* a primary disturbance in the comprehension or production of speech, caused by brain damage. Not all speech disturbances are aphasias. To be classified as aphasic, a patient must have difficulty comprehending, repeating, or producing meaningful speech, and this difficulty must not be caused by simple sensory or motor deficits or by lack of motivation. For example,

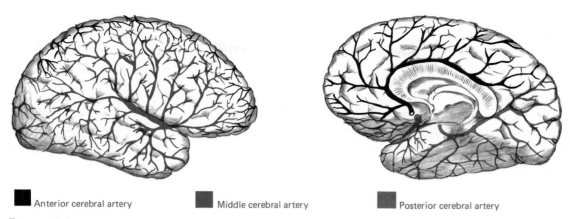

■ Anterior cerebral artery   ■ Middle cerebral artery   ■ Posterior cerebral artery

FIGURE 17.1

Regions of the human cerebral cortex served by the anterior *(black)*, middle *(color)*, and posterior *(gray)* cerebral arteries. (Adapted from Netter, F.H. *The Ciba Collection of Medical Illustrations. Vol. 1: Nervous System.* Summit, N.J.: Ciba Pharmaceutical Products Co., 1953.)

inability to speak caused by deafness or paralysis of the speech muscles is not considered to be aphasia. In addition, the deficit must be relatively isolated; that is, the patient must appear to be aware of what is happening in his or her environment and to comprehend that others are attempting to communicate.

Lateralization

Verbal behavior is a *lateralized* function; most language disturbances occur after damage to the left side of the brain. The best way to determine which side of the brain is dominant for speech is to perform a *Wada test* (named after its inventor). A patient who is about to undergo surgery that might

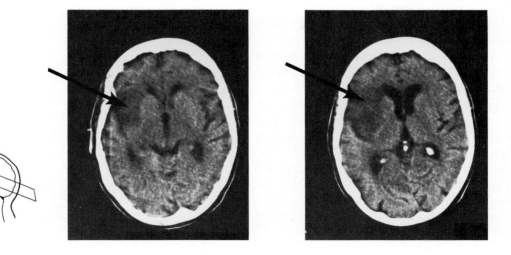

FIGURE 17.2

Two CT scans from a patient with Broca's aphasia. The lesion, located in the left frontal lobe, is indicated by the arrows. (Scans courtesy of Brian Chiango and Jean Dempster, Brigham and Women's Hospital, Boston, Massachusetts.)

encroach on a speech area receives a short-acting anesthetic in one carotid artery and then, when the effects have worn off, in the other. Thus, in a few minutes the involvement of both hemispheres in speech functions can be assessed. In over 95 percent of right-handed people the left hemisphere is dominant for speech. That is, when the left hemisphere is anesthetized, the person loses the ability to speak. However, when the right hemisphere is anesthetized, the person can still talk and carry on a conversation. The figure is somewhat lower in left-handed people: approximately 70 percent (Rasmussen and Milner, 1977). Therefore, unless I say otherwise, you can assume that the brain damage described in the first part of this chapter is located in the left (speech-dominant) hemisphere.

Why is one hemisphere specialized for speech? The perceptual functions of the left hemisphere are more specialized for the analysis of sequences of stimuli, occurring one after the other. The perceptual functions of the right hemisphere are more specialized for the analysis of space and geometrical shapes and forms, the elements of which are all present at the same time. Speech is sequential; it consists of sequences of words, which are composed of sequences of sounds. Thus, it makes sense for the left hemisphere to have become specialized at perceiving speech. In addition, as we saw in Chapter 8, the left hemisphere (in particular, the left parietal lobe) is involved in the execution of sequences of voluntary movements. Perhaps this fact accounts for the localization of neural circuits involved in speech production, as well as speech perception, in the left hemisphere.

Although the circuits *primarily* involved in speech comprehension and production are located in the left hemisphere, it would be a mistake to conclude that the right hemisphere plays no role in speech. As you will see in a subsequent section of this chapter, our ability to understand the meaning of words and the perceptions and memories that we talk about involve neural circuits besides those directly involved in speech. Thus, these circuits, too, play a role in verbal behavior. For example, damage to the right hemisphere produces deficits in people's ability to read maps, perceive spatial relations, and recognize complex geometrical forms. Thus, people with such damage will not be able to talk about things like maps and complex geometrical forms or to understand what other people have to say about them. And as you will see, the right hemisphere is involved in control of rhythm and emphasis of speech and in the expression of feelings of emotion in the tone of voice. Therefore, in some sense, both hemispheres of the brain are involved in speech.

Speech Comprehension: Wernicke's Area

Comprehension of speech obviously begins in the auditory system, which is needed to detect and analyze sounds. But as we shall see, the region of the brain that is most important for speech comprehension (Wernicke's area) is also involved in its production—for transforming perceptions and thoughts into meaningful words.

Wernicke's Aphasia

The primary characteristics of *Wernicke's aphasia* are poor speech comprehension and production of meaningless speech. These characteristics may be related: If one cannot understand what words mean, how can one possibly use them correctly in one's own speech? Wernicke's aphasia is fluent and unlabored; the person does not strain to articulate words and does not appear to be searching for them. The patient maintains a melodic line, with the voice rising and falling normally. When you listen to the speech of a person with Wernicke's aphasia, it appears to be grammatical. That is, the person uses grammatical connecting words like *and* and *but* and employs complex verb tenses and subordinate clauses. However, the words they string together just do not make sense. They often make *paraphasic errors*—substitutions of incorrect words or sounds. For example, *table* might be pronounced as "trable" or "fable." In the extreme, speech deteriorates into a meaningless jumble, illustrated by the following quotation:

Examiner: What kind of work did you do before you came into the hospital?

Patient: Never, now mista oyge I wanna tell you this happened when happened when he rent. His—his kell come down here and is—he got ren something. It happened. In thesse ropiers were with him for hi—is friend—like was. And it just happened so I don't know, he did not bring around anything. And he did not pay it. And he roden all o these arranjen from the pedis on from iss pescid. In these floors now and so. He hadn't had em round here. (Kertesz, 1981, p. 73)

Because of their speech deficit, the ability of people with Wernicke's aphasia to comprehend speech must be assessed by asking them to make nonverbal responses to verbal requests. That is, we cannot assume they do not understand what other people say to them just because they do not give the proper answer. A commonly used test of comprehension assesses their ability to respond to questions by pointing to objects on a table in front of them. For example, they are asked to "Point to the one with ink." If they point to an object other than the pen, they have not comprehended the request. When tested this way, people with severe Wernicke's aphasia show poor comprehension.

A remarkable fact about people with Wernicke's aphasia is that they often seem unaware of their deficit. That is, they do not appear to recognize that their speech is faulty, nor do they recognize that they cannot understand the speech of others. They do not look puzzled when someone tells them something, even though they obviously cannot understand what they hear. Perhaps their comprehension deficit prevents them from realizing that what they say and hear makes no sense. They still follow social conventions, taking turns in conversation with the examiner, even though they do not understand what the examiner says. They remain sensitive to the other person's facial expression and tone of voice and begin talking when he or she asks a question and pauses for an answer. One patient with Wernicke's aphasia made the following responses when asked to name ten common objects:

toothbrush→ "stoktery"
cigarette→ "cigarette"

pen→ "tankt"
knife→ "nike"
fork→ "fahk"
quarter→ "minkt"
pen→ "spentee"
matches→ "senktr"
key→ "seek"
comb→ "sahk"

He acted sure of himself and gave no indication that he recognized that most of his responses were meaningless. The responses he made were not simply new words that he had invented; he was asked several times to name the objects and gave different responses each time (except for cigarette, which he always named correctly).

Even when patients recognize that something is wrong, they appear unsure of what the problem is. The following quotation illustrates this puzzlement.

Examiner: Can you tell me a little bit about why you're here?
Patient: I don't know whata wasa down here for me, I just don't know why I wasn't with up here, at all you, it was neva, had it been walked me today ta died.
Examiner: Uh huh. Okay.
Patient: Sine just don't know why, what is really wrong, I don't know, cause I can eaten treffren eatly an everythin like that I'm all right at home. (Kertesz, 1980)

The patient appears to recognize that she has a problem of some kind, but she is also saying (I think) that at home she can prepare her own meals and otherwise take care of herself.

Karl Wernicke (1874) reported that the aphasia that soon thereafter received his name is produced by damage to the posterior portion of the superior temporal gyrus, now called **Wernicke's area.** Subsequent studies, including recent ones using CT scans, have proved him correct (Kertesz, 1979; Damasio, 1981). However, almost always, the lesion includes more than Wernicke's area, and most investigators believe that a lesion that damages only Wernicke's area will not produce a severe aphasia.

Because the superior temporal gyrus is a region of auditory association cortex, and because a

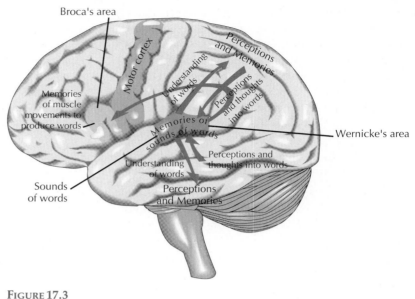

FIGURE 17.3
The location of Wernicke's area in the posterior part of the left superior temporal gyrus and its role in speech. (Broca's area will be described later.)

comprehension deficit is so prominent in Wernicke's aphasia, this disorder has been characterized as a *receptive* aphasia. Some investigators have suggested Wernicke's area is the location of *memories of the sequences of sounds that constitute words*. Thus, the cortex of the superior temporal gyrus recognizes the sounds of words, just as the cortex of the inferior temporal gyrus recognizes the sight of objects. (See *Figure 17.3*.)

Of course, Wernicke's area must do more than perform auditory analyses. After all, people with Wernicke's aphasia have a speech production deficit as well as a speech comprehension deficit. Wernicke believed (and many modern investigators continue to believe) that the superior temporal gyrus is necessary for the formation of a particular class of memories: auditory "images" of words. For example, if a person is asked to say the name of an object, perception of the object evokes neural activity in Wernicke's area that corresponds to the sequence of sounds that constitutes the appropriate word. This neural pattern is transmitted to motor systems in the frontal lobe, which eventually cause movements of the muscles that produce speech. If Wernicke's area is damaged, people will be unable to comprehend words spo-

ken to them; and when they try to produce their own, the lack of adequate auditory patterns will prevent them from producing meaningful speech. (See *Figure 17.3*.)

Wernicke's area must do even more than this. As we saw in Chapter 6, damage to the inferior temporal lobe produces visual agnosia: People are not able to recognize common objects by sight, even though they can perceive fine visual details. But they are aware of their deficit; people with visual agnosia recognize that their visual perception is faulty. The fact that damage to the visual and auditory association areas of the cortex produce such different effects suggests that Wernicke's area plays a special role in thinking as well as in listening and talking.

Auditory Disconnection of Wernicke's Area: Pure Word Deafness

The special role of Wernicke's area in the production of speech is demonstrated by another syndrome: *pure word deafness.* The term for this disorder is apt; people with pure word deafness have a pure disorder, uncontaminated by other problems. Although they are not deaf, they cannot understand speech. As one patient put it, "I can hear you talking, I just can't understand what you're saying." They can detect sounds, and they respond appropriately to nonspeech sounds such as the barking of a dog, the sound of a doorbell, the chirping of a bird, and so on. More significantly, their own speech is excellent.

Pure word deafness is produced by *bilateral* destruction of the primary auditory cortex or by lesions deep in the left temporal lobe that destroy axons that connect Wernicke's area with both the left and the right primary auditory cortex (Coslett, Brashear, and Heilman, 1984). (See *Figure 17.4*.) Wernicke's area is not damaged, which accounts for the patients' ability to produce normal speech. In addition, they can read and write normally, and they often ask people to communicate with them by writing.

Although some authorities do not classify pure word deafness as one of the aphasias, this disorder illustrates the importance of Wernicke's area in the acoustical analysis of words. It also provides an excellent example of a *disconnection syndrome.* Verbal behavior consists of many related skills: perceiving a word, understanding its meaning, thinking of a particular word to express a concept, pronouncing a word, and so on. Although no area of the brain stands in isolation, different regions perform different functions, receiving information from some areas, analyzing this information, and passing on the results of the analysis to other areas. If a particular input to a given area is destroyed, the area is said to be *disconnected* from the source of that input, and it obviously can no longer analyze the information normally received by this pathway. Brain damage that produces pure word deafness deprives Wernicke's area of auditory information and thus abolishes the patient's ability to understand spoken words.

The best way to appreciate the role that Wernicke's area plays in the production of speech is to compare the verbal abilities of people with Wernicke's aphasia with those who have pure word deafness. In both cases the patient is unable to comprehend speech. However, a person with pure word deafness has no problem expressing his or her own thoughts in words and can understand written language. If the only function of Wernicke's area were the recognition of spoken words, then the symptoms of Wernicke's aphasia would be the same as those of pure word deafness. They are not, which suggests that besides being involved in the recognition of sounds, Wernicke's area is involved in the translation of meaning into sounds.

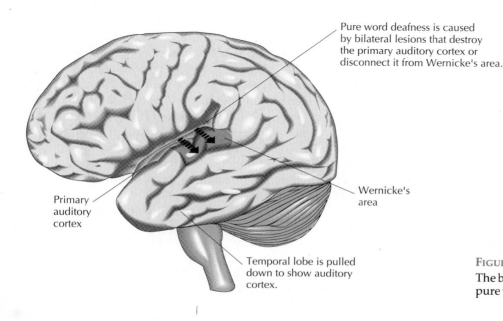

Pure word deafness is caused by bilateral lesions that destroy the primary auditory cortex or disconnect it from Wernicke's area.

Wernicke's area

Primary auditory cortex

Temporal lobe is pulled down to show auditory cortex.

FIGURE 17.4

The brain damage that causes pure word deafness.

Speech Production:
Broca's Aphasia

Another form of aphasia tells us something about the brain mechanisms involved in the production of speech. Unlike Wernicke's aphasia, which is characterized by fluent but meaningless speech, **Broca's aphasia** is characterized by slow, laborious, and nonfluent speech. When trying to converse with patients who have Broca's aphasia, most people find it hard not to try to help them by supplying the words they are obviously groping for. But although they often mispronounce words, the ones they manage to come out with are meaningful. As we saw, the speech of people with Wernicke's aphasia is full of the little words with grammatical meaning, such as *a, the, some, in,* or *about.* These words—called **function words,** because they have important grammatical functions—are almost completely absent in the speech of people with Broca's aphasia. Conversely, **content words**—words that convey meaning, including nouns, adjectives, and adverbs—are sparse in the speech of people with Wernicke's aphasia but rich in the speech of Broca's aphasics. Here is a sample of speech from a man with Broca's aphasia, who is telling the examiner why he has come to the hospital. The dots indicate long pauses.

> Ah . . . Monday . . . ah Dad and Paul [patient's name] . . . and Dad . . . hospital. Two . . . ah doctors . . . , and ah . . . thirty minutes . . . and yes . . . ah . . . hospital. And, er Wednesday . . . nine o'clock. And er Thursday, ten o' clock . . . doctors. Two doctors . . . and ah . . . teeth. Yeah, . . . , fine. (Goodglass, 1976, p. 278)

People with Broca's aphasia can comprehend speech much better than they can produce it. In fact, some observers have said that their comprehension is unimpaired, but as we will see, this is not quite true. Broca (1861) suggested that this form of aphasia is produced by a lesion of the frontal association cortex, just anterior to the face region of the primary motor cortex. Subsequent research proved him to be essentially correct, and we now call the region **Broca's area.** (Refer to **Figure 17.3.**)

Lesions that produce Broca's aphasia are certainly centered in the vicinity of Broca's area. However, although Broca's aphasia has been studied for many years, the anatomical basis of this disorder is still unsettled. For example, damage to the precentral gyrus, as well as Broca's area itself, may contribute to this disorder; Mori, Yamadori, and Furumoto (1989) found that a patient with a lesion restricted to the base of the motor cortex displayed a mild case of Broca's aphasia. Naeser et al. (1989) suggest that damage to axons lying between the lateral surface of the brain and the anterior horn of the lateral ventricle may be critical; they report some cases of patients with extensive cortical damage *without* Broca's aphasia and patients with lesions restricted to the subcortical white matter *with* aphasia. The subcortical lesions disrupt communication between the frontal neocortex and the basal ganglia and cingulate gyrus. Finally, there is evidence that lesions of the basal ganglia—especially the head of the caudate nucleus—can also produce a Broca-like aphasia (Damasio, Eslinger, and Adams, 1984).

Wernicke (1874) suggested (and many modern investigators concur) that Broca's area contains *memories of the sequences of muscular movements that are needed to articulate words.* For example, consider your ability to say the word *ball.* You take a breath, press your lips together, begin expelling air through your vocal cords, and simultaneously open your lips, letting out a small puff of air, forming the sound of the *b.* Your tongue begins in a relaxed position in the middle of your mouth and remains there as you make the vowel sound. Then the end of your tongue moves up and touches the roof of your mouth behind your teeth, remains for a while, and then falls back, forming the sound of the *l.* The word completed, you relax your vocal cords and stop exhaling. (Try saying the word as you read this description again.) Obviously, circuits of neurons somewhere in your brain represent this pattern and, when properly activated, will cause the sequence of movements to be executed. Because damage to the inferior caudal left frontal lobe (including Broca's area) disrupts the ability to articulate words, this region is the most likely candidate for the location of these "programs."

But the speech functions of the left frontal lobe

include more than programming the movements used to speak. In general, three major speech deficits are produced by lesions in and around Broca's area: *agrammatism, anomia,* and *articulation difficulties.* Although most patients with Broca's aphasia will have all of these deficits to some degree, their severity can vary considerably from person to person.

Agrammatism refers to a patient's difficulty in using grammatical constructions. This disorder can appear all by itself, without any difficulty in pronouncing words (Nadeau, 1988). As we saw, people with Broca's aphasia rarely use function words. In addition, they rarely use grammatical markers such as *-ed* or auxiliaries such as *have* (as in *I have gone*). For some reason, they *do* often use *-ing,* perhaps because this ending converts a verb into a noun. A study by Saffran, Schwartz, and Marin (1980) illustrates this difficulty. The following quotations are from agrammatic patients attempting to describe pictures:

Picture of a boy being hit in the head by a baseball

> The boy is catch . . . the boy is hitch . . . the boy is hit the ball. (Saffran, Schwartz, and Marin, 1980, p. 229)

Picture of a girl giving flowers to her teacher

> Girl . . . wants to . . . flowers . . . flowers and wants to . . . . The woman . . . wants to . . . . The girl wants to . . . the flowers and the woman. (Saffran, Schwartz, and Marin, 1980, p. 234)

The second major speech deficit seen in Broca's aphasia is *anomia* ("without name"). Anomia refers to a word-finding difficulty; and because all aphasics omit words or use inappropriate ones, anomia is actually a primary symptom of *all* forms of aphasia. However, because their speech lacks fluency, the anomia of Broca's aphasics is especially apparent; their facial expression and frequent use of sounds like "uh" make it obvious that they are groping for the correct words. In contrast, people with Wernicke's aphasia seldom pause in their speech and appear satisfied with their utterances; thus, their anomia is less apparent.

The third major characteristic of Broca's aphasia is *difficulty with articulation.* Patients mispronounce words, often altering the sequence of sounds. For example, *lipstick* might be pronounced "likstip." Unlike Wernicke's aphasics, people with Broca's aphasia recognize that their pronunciation is erroneous, and they usually try to correct it.

As I said, these three deficits are seen in various combinations in different patients, depending on the exact location of the lesion, and, to a certain extent, on their stage of recovery. Although the anatomical correlates are not yet worked out, we can characterize these deficits hierarchically. On the lowest, most elementary level is control of the sequence of movements of the muscles of speech. The next higher level is selection of the particular "programs" for individual words. Finally, the highest level is selection of grammatical structure, including word order, use of function words, and word endings. Presumably, the control of articulation involves the face area of the primary motor cortex and portions of the basal ganglia; the selection of words, word order, and grammatical markers involves Broca's area and other regions of the frontal association cortex.

So far, I have described Broca's aphasia as a disorder in speech production. In an ordinary conversation Broca's aphasics seem to understand everything that is said to them. They appear to be irritated and annoyed by their inability to express their thoughts well, and they often make gestures to supplement their scanty speech. The marked disparity between their speech and their comprehension often leads people to assume that their comprehension is normal. But it is not. Schwartz, Saffran, and Marin (1980) showed Broca's aphasics pairs of pictures in which agents and objects of the action were reversed: for example, a horse kicking a cow and a cow kicking a horse, a truck pulling a car and a car pulling a truck, and a dancer applauding a clown and a clown applauding a dancer. As they showed each pair of pictures, they read the subject a sentence, for example, *The horse kicks the cow.* The subject's task was to point to the appropriate picture, indicating whether they understood the grammatical construction of the sentence. (See *Figure 17.5.*)

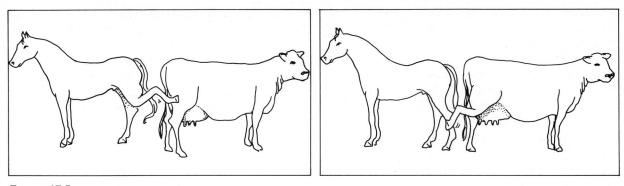

FIGURE 17.5
An example of the stimuli used in the experiment by Schwartz, Saffran, and Marin (1980).

On the average, they scored 62 percent correct, which is not much above chance.

The correct picture in the study by Schwartz and her colleagues was specified by a particular aspect of grammar: word order. The agrammatism that accompanies Broca's aphasia appears to disrupt patients' ability to use grammatical information, including word order, to decode the meaning of a sentence. Thus, their deficit in comprehension parallels their deficit in production. If they heard a sentence such as *The man swats the mosquito,* they would understand that it concerns a man and a mosquito and the action of swatting. Obviously, they would have no trouble figuring out who is doing what to whom. But a sentence such as *The horse kicks the cow* does not provide any extra cues; if the grammar is not understood, neither is the meaning of the sentence.

Other experiments have shown that people with Broca's aphasia have difficulty carrying out a sequence of commands such as ''Pick up the red circle and touch the green square with it'' (Boller and Dennis, 1979). This finding, along with the other symptoms I have described in this section, suggests that an important function of the left frontal lobe is sequencing— of movements of the muscles of speech (producing words) and of words (comprehending and producing grammatical speech).

Verbal Short-Term Memory: Conduction Aphasia

Wernicke (1874) predicted that if a lesion in the inferior parietal lobe were to interrupt the flow of information from the auditory association cortex of the superior temporal gyrus to the speech production area in the inferior frontal lobe (that is, disconnect Wernicke's area from Broca's area), then the person should not be able to repeat speech. However, if the temporal lobe was intact, he or she should be able to comprehend speech; and if the frontal lobe was intact, he or she should be able to produce fluent spontaneous speech. Subsequent observations proved Wernicke to be correct; *conduction aphasia* is produced by damage to the inferior parietal lobe that disrupts subcortical white matter, including axons that connect Wernicke's area with Broca's area (Damasio and Damasio, 1980).

Conduction aphasia is characterized by meaningful (but often paraphasic) fluent speech, relatively good comprehension, but very poor repetition. For example, the spontaneous speech of patient L.B. (observed by Margolin and Walker, 1981) was excellent; he made very few errors and had no difficulty naming objects. In addition, his reading and writing abilities were reasonably good. If their conversation had been overheard by people not familiar with the speech of aphasics, they would be unlikely to notice anything amiss in either his comprehension or his production. At the most, they might suspect the man was slightly hard of hearing, because occasionally he asked the examiner to repeat a question.

But let us see how patient L.B. performed when he was asked to repeat words.

Examiner: bicycle
Patient: bicycle

Examiner:	hippopotamus
Patient:	hippopotamus
Examiner:	blaynge
Patient:	I didn't get it.
Examiner:	Okay, some of these won't be real words, they'll just be sounds. Blaynge.
Patient:	I'm not . . .
Examiner:	blanch
Patient:	blanch
Examiner:	north
Patient:	north
Examiner:	rilld
Patient:	Nope, I can't say.

You will notice that the patient can repeat individual words (all nouns, in this case) but utterly fails to repeat nonwords. Now let us see how he does when he is given three-word sequences.

Examiner:	Up and down.
Patient:	Up and down.
Examiner:	look, car, house
Patient:	I didn't get it.
Examiner:	Save your money.
Patient:	Save your money.
Examiner:	yellow, big, south
Patient:	yellen . . . Can't get it.
Examiner:	They ran away.
Patient:	They ran away.
Examiner:	look, catch, sell
Patient:	like . . . [shakes head, laughs] . . . That's the trouble!

So the patient could repeat single words but not nonwords and could repeat meaningful three-word phrases but not three unrelated words. The important distinction seems to be *meaning*. People with conduction aphasia can repeat speech sounds they hear only if these sounds have meaning. In fact, McCarthy and Warrington (1987) found that patients with conduction aphasia could remember sentences containing six words more easily than lists of three unrelated words.

The symptoms seen in conduction aphasia suggest that there are two routes between the speech mechanisms of the temporal lobe and the frontal lobe (Geschwind, 1965). One simply conveys *speech sounds* to the frontal lobes. We use this pathway to repeat unfamiliar words—for example, when we are learning a foreign language or

trying to repeat a nonword such as *blaynge*. This pathway is damaged in conduction aphasia. The second pathway is based on the *meaning* of words, not the sounds they make. This pathway permitted patient L.B. to repeat single meaningful words or groups of three words that made a meaningful sentence. (See *Figure 17.6.*)

Aphasia in Deaf People

As we saw, damage to Wernicke's area, a region of auditory association cortex, impairs people's ability to comprehend speech. However, their speech is fluent, even though it is meaningless. Is Wernicke's area specialized for verbal comprehension in general, or does it owe its role to the fact that speech is primarily acoustical?

The effects of brain damage in deaf people suggest that, to a certain extent, the location of the brain regions that are essential for speech comprehension depends on the sensory modality used for communication. A well-documented case report by Chiarello, Knight, and Mandel (1982) describes a deaf woman who suffered a stroke that destroyed part of the left parietal lobe, including a region that is essential for normal reading and writing (the *angular gyrus*, discussed in a later section of this chapter.) As you learned in Chapter 7, the primary function of the parietal lobe is somotosensation. In particular, the left parietal lobe is involved in perception of one's own body, including the movement and location of its parts, and the right parietal lobe is involved in perception of the location and shape of objects in the environment. As you learned in Chapter 8, the left parietal lobe, along with the left frontal lobe, is also involved in controlling sequences of voluntary hand movements.

Many deaf people in North America communicate by means of *Ameslan*, a language that is expressed by hand movements. Ameslan is a full-fledged language, having signs for nouns, verbs, adjectives, adverbs, and all the other parts of speech contained in acoustically based languages. People can converse rapidly and efficiently by means of sign language, can tell jokes, and can even make puns based on the similarity between signs. After her stroke, patient L.K., a 66-year-old woman, deaf since she was six months old, could no longer read, write, express herself

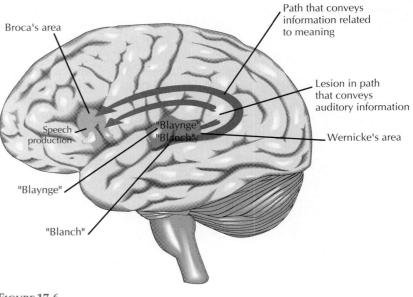

FIGURE 17.6

A hypothetical explanation of conduction aphasia. A lesion that produces conduction aphasia disrupts transmission of auditory information, but not information related to meaning, to the frontal lobe. A patient with conduction aphasia could repeat *blanch* but not *blaynge*.

in sign language, or comprehend other people's signing. Her verbal abilities resembled those of a hearing person with Wernicke's aphasia: She signed fluently but made many errors, she had a severe anomia, and her comprehension of other people's signing was very poor.

When people who can hear receive damage to their left parietal lobe, similar to that of patient L.K., they typically lose the ability to read, write, and perform arithmetical calculations. They also tend to have difficulty with perceptions and memories related to their own bodies; they have trouble recognizing objects placed in their right hand or naming parts of their body. Finally, they have trouble performing sequences of voluntary movements. Patient L.K., too, had these deficits. But people who can hear typically do *not* become aphasic after their left parietal lobe is damaged. If the lesion disrupts axons that connect Wernicke's area with Broca's area, they may show symptoms of conduction aphasia; but as we saw, these symptoms are very different from those shown by patient L.K. Thus, it appears that the left parietal lobe plays a special role in the verbal abilities of

people who communicate by means of hand movements. Damage to a region involved in perception of body parts and their movements impairs a person's ability to produce and comprehend information expressed by hand movements. Thus, speech seems not to be an entirely abstract phenomenon; instead, it seems to be linked to the sensory modalities used to express it.

There are some similarities between the brain mechanisms involved in speech and signing as well as differences. Bellugi, Poizner, and Klima (1989) reported the cases of two patients with damage to the left frontal lobe who showed difficulties with grammar. Thus, although the grammars of spoken languages and signed languages are very different, both are disrupted by lesions of the frontal association cortex.

Memory of Words: Anomic Aphasia

As I already noted, anomia, in one form or other, is a hallmark of aphasia. However, one category of aphasia consists of almost pure anomia, the other symptoms being inconsequential. Speech of patients with anomic aphasia is fluent and grammatical, and their comprehension is excellent, but they have difficulty finding the appropriate words. They often employ *circumlocutions* (literally, "to speak in a roundabout way") to get around missing words. For example, the following quotation is from a patient that some colleagues and I studied (Margolin, Marcel, and Carlson, 1985). We asked her to describe the picture shown in *Figure 17.7.* Her pauses, which are marked with three dots, indicate word-finding difficulties. In some cases, when she could not find a word, she supplied a definition instead or went off on a new track. I have added the words in brackets that I think she intended to use.

Examiner: Tell us about that picture.
Patient: It's a woman who has two children, a son and a daughter, and her son is to get into the . . . cupboard in the kitchen to get out [take] some . . . cookies out of the [cookie jar] . . . that she possibly had made, and consequently he's slipping [falling] . . . the wrong direction [backward] . . . on the . . . what he's standing on [stool], heading to the . . . the cupboard [floor] and if he falls backwards he could have some problems [get hurt], because that [the stool] is off balance.

The patient's anomia was most obvious when we asked her to name pictures of common objects. When a person talks spontaneously, he or she has more flexibility in choosing words. If the person has difficulty finding a word to express a particular thought, he or she can either find a circumlocution or change the subject. But when confronted with a picture, the person must find a particular word, and failure to do so is obvious. On one occasion she correctly named only fourteen of a list of fifty of them. Here is her attempt to name a picture of a carpenter's saw. Note that she tried to remember the word by starting sentences that would use it. She almost, but not quite, got the word. Clearly, she knows what the object is, so her deficit is not one of perception or comprehension.

Patient: I know what it is. I can't tell you— maybe I can. If I was to carry the wood and cut it in half with that . . . you know, if I had to cut the wood down and bring it in . . .
Examiner: You'd use one of these?
Patient: It's called a . . . I have 'em in the garage. They are your . . . You cut the wood with them . . . it . . . sah! . . . ah . . . Ss . . . sahbing . . . sah . . . I can't say it. I know what it is and

FIGURE 17.7

The drawing of the kitchen story, part of the Boston Diagnostic Aphasia Test. (From Goodglass, H., and Kaplan, E. *The Assessment of Aphasia and Related Disorders.* Philadelphia: Lea & Febiger, 1972.)

I can cut the wood with it and it's in my garage . . . .

Anomia has been characterized as a partial amnesia for words. It can be produced by both anterior and posterior lesions (that is, lesions that include Broca's area or Wernicke's area), but only posterior lesions produce a *fluent* anomia. Little is known about the location of lesions that produce anomia without the other symptoms of aphasia, such as comprehension deficits, agrammatism, or difficulties in articulation, except that they generally occur in the left temporal or parietal lobe, usually sparing Wernicke's area. Obviously, when we learn more about the anatomy of pure anomia, we will know more about the anatomy of verbal memories.

Memory of Meanings of Words: Transcortical Sensory Aphasia

As we have seen, Wernicke's area, Broca's area, and their interconnections play a special role in language comprehension and production. They are necessary for recognition of spoken words, comprehension and production of grammatical structure, and articulation of words. But these regions cannot function in isolation. *Recognition* of words is one thing; *comprehension* is another. Similarly, *articulation of words* is one thing; *having something to say* is another. The functions of the verbal areas of the brain that I have described so far have dealt with perception and complex motor sequences, not with meaning.

Words refer to objects, actions, or relations in the world. Thus, the meaning of a word is defined by particular memories associated with it. For example, knowing the meaning of the word *tree* means being able to imagine the physical characteristics of trees: what they look like, what the wind sounds like blowing through their leaves, what the bark feels like, and so on. It also means knowing facts about trees: about their roots, buds, flowers, nuts, wood, and the chlorophyll in their leaves. These memories are not stored in the primary speech areas but in other parts of the brain, especially regions of the association cortex. We can think of Wernicke's area as containing the entries of a dictionary, with the definitions contained in other locations.

Obviously, the ability of the sound of the word *tree* to evoke the memories that define it depends on connections between circuits in Wernicke's area and circuits in other parts of the brain. We hear a word, and its recognition activates the memories associated with it. Similarly, our ability to express a thought in words also depends on these connections, but in reverse: The sight (or thought) of a tree activates the appropriate pattern of activity in the speech areas, resulting in articulation of the proper word.

A syndrome called ***transcortical sensory aphasia*** occurs when the speech areas are disconnected from the posterior association cortex (Kertesz, 1979). Although people with this disorder can recognize words and can talk, they cannot understand what people are saying to them and they have no spontaneous speech of their own. However, they can repeat what they hear; thus, their disorder is the opposite of conduction aphasia.

A classic case of this disorder was reported by Geschwind, Quadfasel, and Segarra (1968). A woman sustained brain damage after inhaling carbon monoxide from a faulty water heater. The lesion bordered the primary speech areas and their interconnections, isolating them from the surrounding cortex. (See *Figure 17.8.*) The woman spent several years in the hospital before she died, without ever saying anything meaningful

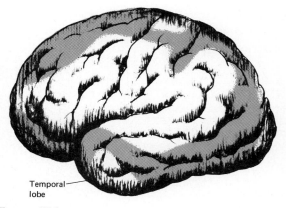

Temporal lobe

FIGURE 17.8

Brain damage (shaded area) produced by inhalation of carbon monoxide, in the patient reported by Geschwind, Quadfasel, and Segarra (1968).

on her own. She did not follow verbal commands or otherwise give signs of understanding them. However, she often repeated what was said to her. The repetition was not parrotlike; she did not imitate accents different from her own, and she sometimes corrected ungrammatical constructions. Often she did not simply repeat words but continued a sequence they started. For example, when an examiner said "Roses are red, violets are blue," she continued with "Sugar is sweet and so are you." She could sing and would do so when someone started singing a song she knew. She even learned new songs from the radio while in the hospital. Remember, though, that she gave no signs of understanding anything she heard or said. Her case supports the hypothesis that the brain mechanisms needed to perceive and recognize words, to learn and remember sequences of words, and to articulate them are different from the brain mechanisms needed to understand the *meaning* of words.

Damage to particular regions of the sensory association cortex can damage particular kinds of information and thus abolish particular kinds of meanings. For example, I met a patient who had recently had a stroke that damaged a part of her right parietal lobe that played a role in spatial perception. She was alert and intelligent and showed no signs of aphasia. However, she was confused about directions and other spatial relations. When asked to, she could point to the ceiling and the floor, but she could not say which was *over* the other. Her perception of other people appeared to be entirely normal, but she could not say whether a person's head was at the *top* or *bottom* of the body.

I wrote a set of multiple-choice questions to test her ability to use words denoting spatial relations. The results of the test indicated that she did not know the meaning of words such as *up, down,* or *under* when they referred to spatial relations, but she could use these words normally when they referred to nonspatial relations. For example, here are some of her incorrect responses when the words referred to spatial relations:

A tree's branches are *under* its roots.
The sky is *down.*
The ceiling is *under* the floor.

She made only ten correct responses on the sixteen-item test. In contrast, she got all eight items correct when the words referred to nonspatial relations like the following:

After exchanging pleasantries, they got
   down to business.
He got sick and threw *up.*

Damage to other parts of the association cortex of the left parietal lobe can produce an inability to name body parts. People who otherwise converse normally cannot reliably point to their elbow, knee, or cheek when asked to do so and cannot name body parts when the examiner points to them. However, they have no difficulty understanding the meaning of other words. Because the parietal lobes deal with somatosensation, it makes sense that the meaning of the names of body parts entails connections between parts of the parietal cortex and the speech areas.

Other investigators have reported deficits that appear to be caused by disconnection between auditory recognition of words and particular categories of information. For example, McCarthy and Warrington (1988) reported the case of a man with left temporal lobe damage (patient T.B.) who was unable to explain the meaning of words that denoted living things. For example, when he was asked to define the word *rhinoceros*, he said "Animal, can't give you any functions." However, when he was shown a picture of a rhinoceros, he said "Enormous, weighs over one ton, lives in Africa." Similarly, when asked what a *dolphin* was, he said "A fish or a bird"; but he responded to a picture of a dolphin by saying "Dolphin lives in water . . . they are trained to jump up and come out . . . In America during the war years they started to get this particular animal to go through to look into ships." When patient T.B. was asked to define the meanings of words that denoted inanimate objects such as lighthouses or wheelbarrows, he had no trouble at all.

The case of patient T.B. raises some interesting issues. His brain damage appears not to have destroyed his knowledge of living things, because once the circuits concerning the information are activated by showing him a picture, he can describe that information very well. But the damage does appear to have disconnected the neural circuits that analyze the sounds of words from the neural circuits that contain that information. Are the connections *from* speech areas *to* the circuits containing the information different from connections going in the opposite direction? And is information about living and nonliving things contained in different parts of the brain?

Some investigators suggest that information about the world is not categorized by the brain in a way that corresponds to categories that we have invented. Damasio (1989) notes that when patients are tested carefully, categories such as "living" or "inanimate" usually break down; for example, a patient who has no difficulty defining inanimate objects may not be able to define musical instruments (which are certainly inanimate). Marshall (1988) suggests that "conceptual" categories may simply reflect the ways in which particular kinds of information are learned (and thus stored in different parts of the brain). For example, he makes the point that some of our information about a particular object is learned through direct visual experience or through looking at pictures featuring the object; other facts may be learned verbally, by listening to what other people tell us. Thus, some information would be stored in the visual association cortex and others in the auditory association cortex. In fact, I once studied a patient with damage to the visual association cortex of the left temporal lobe who could not name pictures of objects, but he could easily name the *actions* depicted in pictures, such as climbing, walking, throwing, hitting, and waving. Perhaps the memories associated with the meanings of actions, because they involve movement of the body, are at least partly represented in the frontal and parietal lobes—and thus were spared by the lesion.

The picture I have drawn so far suggests that comprehension of speech includes a flow of information from Wernicke's area to the surrounding regions of association cortex, and that production of spontaneous speech includes the same connections, operating in reverse. This model is certainly an oversimplification, but it is a useful starting point in conceptualizing basic mental processes. For example, thinking in words probably involves two-way communication between the speech areas and surrounding association cortex (and

subcortical regions such as the hippocampus and amygdala, of course).

Figure 17.9 summarizes some of the information I have discussed so far. Three diagrams illustrate the role of Broca's area, Wernicke's area, and the sensory and motor association cortex in three verbal tasks: repeating a word, speaking "spontaneously" (which actually means talking about one's perceptions or memories, or ideas based on them), and answering a question. (See *Figure 17.9.*)

Motivation to Speak: Transcortical Motor Aphasia

The final aphasic disorder, ***transcortical motor aphasia,*** is characterized by good comprehension and good repetition but very little speech output. The patients just do not say much. Damasio and Van Hoesen (1983) described a case of a 35-year-old woman with transcortical motor aphasia, caused by a stroke. She lay in bed quietly; and although she appeared to understand what was said to her, she made no attempt to speak or to communicate with gestures. Later, when she had largely recovered her ability to speak, she said that she had not talked because she had "nothing to say"; her mind was "empty" and "nothing mattered." She had understood the conversations of the people attending her but had no interest in replying to their questions.

Even several months later, although she had recovered almost normal speech and could communicate well, she reported that she needed some time to prepare her speech and found that she talked slower than she previously did. For a ten-month period after her stroke she had not once tried to write; she assumed that she had lost the ability. However, when the examiners asked her to try, she was able to do so. She readily wrote down what the examiners dictated to her but had difficulty thinking of something to write on her own.

Transcortical motor aphasia is caused by frontal lesions that do not involve Broca's speech area but damage the ***supplementary motor area*** in the superior frontal lobe or the connections between this region and Broca's area (Damasio, 1981; Freedman, Alexander, and Naeser, 1984). (See

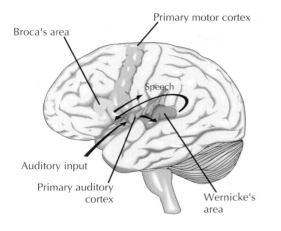

(a) **Repeating a word**

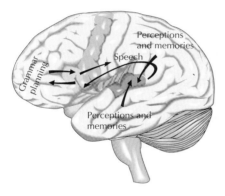

(b) **Spontaneous speech**

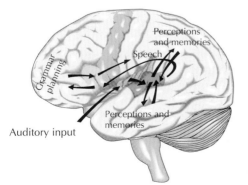

(c) **Answering a question**

Figure 17.10.) The easiest way to keep from confusing transcortical *sensory* aphasia with transcortical *motor* aphasia is to remember that one involves a lesion in the posterior (sensory) cortex and the other involves a lesion in the frontal (motor) cortex.

Little is known about the functions of the supplementary motor area, except that it is involved somehow in the planning of movements and, as the description above suggests, in motivation to talk. Exactly what *that* means is uncertain; we know less about the functions of the frontal lobes than we do about any other part of the brain.

Prosody: Rhythm, Tone, and Emphasis in Speech

When we speak, we do not merely utter words. Our speech has a regular rhythm and cadence, we give some words stress (that is, pronounce them louder), and we vary the pitch of our voice to indicate phrasing and to distinguish between assertions and questions. In addition, we can impart information about our emotional state through the rhythm, emphasis, and tone of our speech. These rhythmic, emphatic, and melodic aspects of speech are referred to as ***prosody.*** The importance of these aspects of speech is illustrated by our use of punctuation symbols to indicate some elements of prosody when we write. For example, a comma indicates a short pause; a period indicates a longer one with an accompanying fall in the pitch of the voice; a question mark indicates a pause and a rise in the pitch of the voice; an exclamation mark indicates that the words are articulated with special emphasis; and so on.

The prosody of people with fluent aphasias, caused by posterior lesions, sounds normal. Their speech is rhythmical, pausing after phrases and sentences, and has a melodic line. Even when the speech of a person with severe Wernicke's aphasia makes no sense, the prosody sounds normal. As Goodglass and Kaplan (1972) note, a person

◀ FIGURE 17.9

Hypothetical explanations of the role of the speech areas and association cortex. (a) In repeating a word. (b) In speaking "spontaneously." (c) In answering a question.

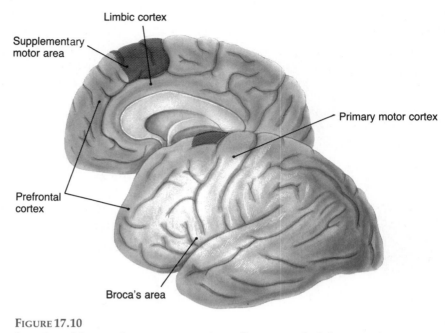

Supplementary motor area

Limbic cortex

Primary motor cortex

Prefrontal cortex

Broca's area

FIGURE 17.10
Location of the supplementary motor area. Damage to the left supplementary motor area in the superior frontal lobe causes transcortical motor aphasia.

with Wernicke's aphasia may "sound like a normal speaker at a distance, because of his fluency and normal melodic contour of his speech." (Up close, of course, we hear the speech clearly enough to realize that it is meaningless.) In contrast, just as the lesions that produce Broca's aphasia destroy grammar, they also severely disrupt prosody. In patients with Broca's aphasia articulation is so labored and words are uttered so slowly that there is little opportunity for the patient to demonstrate any rhythmic elements; and because of the relative lack of function words, there is little variation in stress or pitch of voice.

Evidence from studies of normal people and patients with brain lesions suggests that prosody is a special function of the right hemisphere. This function is undoubtedly related to the more general role of this hemisphere in musical skills and the expression and recognition of emotions; production of prosody is rather like singing, and prosody often serves as a vehicle for conveying emotion.

Weintraub, Mesulam, and Kramer (1981) tested the ability of patients with right-hemi-

sphere damage to recognize and express prosodic elements of speech. In one experiment they showed their subjects two pictures, named one of them, and asked them to point to the appropriate one. For example, they showed them a picture of a greenhouse and a house that was painted green. In speech we distinguish between *greenhouse* and *green house* by stress: *GREEN house* means the former and *GREEN HOUSE* (syllables equally stressed) means the latter. In a second experiment Weintraub and her colleagues tested the subjects' ability simply to detect differences in prosody. They presented pairs of sentences and asked the subjects whether they were the same or different. The pairs of sentences either were identical or differed in terms of intonation (for example, *Margo plays the piano?* and *Margo plays the piano*) or location of stress (for example, *STEVE drives the car* and *Steve drives the CAR*). The patients with right-hemisphere lesions (but not control subjects) performed poorly on both of these tasks. Thus, they showed a deficit in prosodic comprehension.

To test production, the investigators presented two written sentences and asked a question about them. For example, they presented the following pair:

> The man walked to the grocery store.
> The woman rode to the shoe store.

The subjects were instructed to answer questions by reading one of the sentences. Try this one yourself. Read the question below and then read aloud the sentence (above) that answers it.

> Who walked to the grocery store, the man or the woman?

The question asserts that someone walked to the grocery store but asks who that person was. When answering a question like this, people normally stress the requested item of information—in this case they say, "The *man* walked to the grocery store." However, Weintraub and her colleagues found that although patients with right-hemisphere brain damage chose the correct sentence, they either failed to stress a word or stressed the wrong one. Thus, the right hemisphere plays a role in production as well as perception of prosody.

*I*NTERIM SUMMARY

Two regions of the brain are especially important in understanding and producing speech. Wernicke's area, in the posterior superior temporal lobe, is involved with speech perception and is necessary for the production of meaningful speech. Broca's area, in the frontal lobe just rostral to the region of the primary motor cortex that controls the muscles of speech, is involved with speech production. Presumably, Wernicke's area contains memories of the sounds of words, each of which is connected with memories about the properties of the things the words denote. Broca's area contains memories of the sequences of muscular movements that produce words, each of which is connected with its auditory counterparts in the posterior part of the brain. Disconnection syndromes, such as pure word deafness and conduction aphasia, can occur when connections between various components of the mechanisms devoted to language are damaged.

The meanings of words are our memories of objects, actions, and other concepts associated with them. These meanings are memories and are stored in the association cortex, not in the speech areas themselves. Transcortical sensory aphasia consists of damage to these regions or their disconnection from the speech areas. Damage to specific regions of the association cortex effectively "erases" some categories of the meanings of words.

The syndrome of transcortical motor aphasia consists of lack of motivation to speak, even though speech is possible and comprehension is intact. The syndrome tells us that the supplementary motor area plays an important role in motivation to speak, but we know little about the precise meaning of that process.

Prosody includes changes in intonation, rhythm, and stress that add meaning, especially emotional meaning, to the sentences that we speak. The neural mechanisms that control the prosodic elements of speech appear to be in the right hemisphere.

Because so many terms and symptoms were described in this section, I have provided a table that summarizes them. (See *Table 17.1.*)

READING AND WRITING DISORDERS

Relation to Aphasia

With few exceptions, the reading and writing skills of people with aphasia are similar to their speaking and comprehending abilities. For example, patients with Wernicke's aphasia have as much difficulty reading and writing as they do speaking and understanding speech. Patients with Broca's aphasia comprehend what they read about as well as they can understand speech, but their reading aloud is poor, of course. If their speech is agrammatical, so is their writing; and to the extent that they fail to comprehend grammar when listening to speech, they fail to do so when reading. Patients with conduction aphasia gener-

TABLE 17.1
Aphasia syndromes produced by strokes.

	Area of Lesion	Spontaneous Speech	Comprehension	Repetition	Naming	Reading Comprehension	Writing
Wernicke's aphasia	Posterior portion of superior temporal gyrus (Wernicke's area)	Fluent	Poor	Poor	Poor	Poor	Poor
Pure word deafness	Both primary auditory cortices, or connection between them and Wernicke's area	Fluent	Poor	Poor	Good	Good	Good
Broca's aphasia	Frontal cortex rostral to base of primary motor cortex (Broca's area)	Nonfluent	Good	Poor[a]	Poor	Good	Poor
Conduction aphasia	Area of parietal lobe superior to lateral fissure	Fluent	Good	Poor	Good	Good to poor	Good
Anomic aphasia	Various parts of parietal or temporal lobes	Fluent	Good	Good	Poor	Good to poor	Good to poor
Transcortical sensory aphasia	Connections between speech areas and posterior association cortex	Nonfluent or even absent	Poor	Good	Poor	Poor[b]	Poor
Transcortical motor aphasia	Supplementary motor area	Scanty or absent	Good	Good	Good	Good	Good

[a]May be better than spontaneous speech.
[b]Patient may be able to read words without comprehending them.

ally have some difficulty reading; and when they read aloud, they often make semantic paraphasias (saying synonyms for some of the words they read), just as they do when attempting to repeat what they hear. Depending on the location of the lesion, some patients with transcortical sensory aphasia may read aloud accurately but fail to comprehend what they read.

Alexia with Agraphia

Some reading and writing difficulties are not accompanied by aphasia. For example, *alexia with agraphia* includes the inability to read (alexia) or write (agraphia). Most cases of alexia with agraphia are caused by damage to the left *angular gyrus,* a region of the parietal lobe behind the caudal end of the lateral fissure (Dejerine, 1891; Benson and Geschwind, 1969). If the damage is extensive enough, a fluent anomia is often associated with this syndrome. Some investigators believe that the angular gyrus—which receives visual, auditory, and somatosensory input—plays a special role in the integration of polysensory information, including that which is necessary to read and write. (See *Figure 17.11.*)

Pure Alexia

Dejerine (1892) described a remarkable syndrome, which we now call *pure alexia,* or sometimes *pure word blindness* or *alexia without agraphia.* His patient had a lesion in the left occipital lobe and the posterior end of the corpus callosum. The patient lost the ability to read, but he could still write. In fact, if he was shown some of his own writing, he could not read it.

Some colleagues and I studied a man with pure alexia who discovered his ability to write in an in-

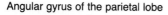

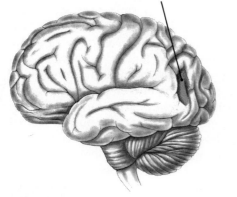

FIGURE 17.11
Location of the angular gyrus. Damage to the left angular gyrus causes alexia with agraphia.

teresting way. A few months after sustaining a head injury that caused his brain damage, he and his wife were watching a service person repair their washing machine. The patient wanted to say something privately to his wife, so he picked up a pad of paper and jotted a note. As he was handing it to her, they suddenly realized with amazement that although he could not read, he was able to write. His wife brought the note to their neurologist, who asked the patient to read it. Although he remembered the gist of the message, he could not read the words.

Although patients with pure alexia cannot read, they can recognize words that are spelled aloud to them; thus, they have not lost their memories of the spellings of words. Pure alexia is obviously a perceptual disorder; it is a disconnection syndrome similar to pure word deafness, except that the problem is with visual input, not auditory input. The disorder is caused by lesions that disconnect the angular gyrus from all visual input (Damasio and Damasio, 1983). Figure 17.12 shows a diagram of the brain damage of Dejerine's original patient. Notice how the two lesions disrupt the path of visual information from both the right and the left visual cortex. The occipital lobe lesion produces blindness in the right visual field, and the callosal lesion prevents visual information from reaching the posterior left hemisphere. (See *Figure 17.12.*)

You will recall from Chapter 6 that visual agnosia is a perceptual deficit in which people with bilateral damage to the visual association cortex cannot recognize objects by sight. Patients with pure alexia do *not* have visual agnosia; they can recognize objects and supply their names. In contrast, people with visual agnosia can still read. Thus, the perceptual analysis of objects and words requires different mechanisms. I find this fact both interesting and puzzling. Certainly, the ability to read cannot have had an effect on the evolution of the human brain, because the invention of writing is only a few thousand years old, and until very recently, the vast majority of the world's population was illiterate. Thus, reading and object recognition use brain mechanisms that undoubtedly existed even before the invention of writing. What is the nature of these mechanisms? What features of the world around

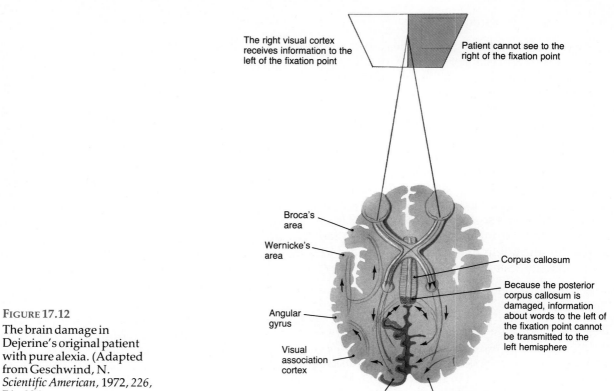

The right visual cortex receives information to the left of the fixation point

Patient cannot see to the right of the fixation point

Broca's area

Wernicke's area

Corpus callosum

Because the posterior corpus callosum is damaged, information about words to the left of the fixation point cannot be transmitted to the left hemisphere

Angular gyrus

Visual association cortex

Left visual cortex   Right visual cortex

FIGURE 17.12
The brain damage in Dejerine's original patient with pure alexia. (Adapted from Geschwind, N. *Scientific American*, 1972, 226, 76–83.)

us require analysis similar to the analysis we use to recognize objects versus words?

The fact that patients with pure alexia can name objects that they see suggests that visual information concerning words and visual information concerning objects are transmitted across different parts of the corpus callosum. Let us see why. In all cases of pure alexia, patients have some sort of visual defect in their right visual field, caused by the left occipital lesion. In some cases the defect is a complete right *homonymous hemianopia*—half-blindness in the same (right) visual field of both eyes. These people cannot see anything presented to the portions of their retinas that send information to the left hemisphere; thus, when they name an object that they see, they are using the visual information that comes from their right hemisphere. Because naming is a function of the *left* hemisphere, the visual information must cross the corpus callosum somewhere.

Figure 17.13 shows a possible explanation. As we saw in Chapter 6, visual information received by the primary visual cortex is sent to the first level of the visual association—the *prestriate cortex.* This region actually consists of a set of subregions that perform the first analysis of visual stimuli. The results of this analysis are then sent on to the *inferior temporal cortex,* where the final stages of the perception of objects takes place. For a person to say the name of the object, the information must be transmitted from the inferior temporal cortex to Wernicke's area and then to Broca's area. The flow of information necessary for this process is shown by black lines with arrowheads indicating the direction of the flow. The broken lines indicate the flow of information disrupted by the lesion; as you can see, the person is able to name objects seen in the left visual field because of the connections between the left and right inferior temporal cortex through the corpus callosum. (See *Figure 17.13.*)

Now let us see why the person cannot read. Normally, information from the prestriate cortex is sent to the angular gyrus, where words are recognized. From there, information is sent on to Wernicke's area and then to Broca's area. The left

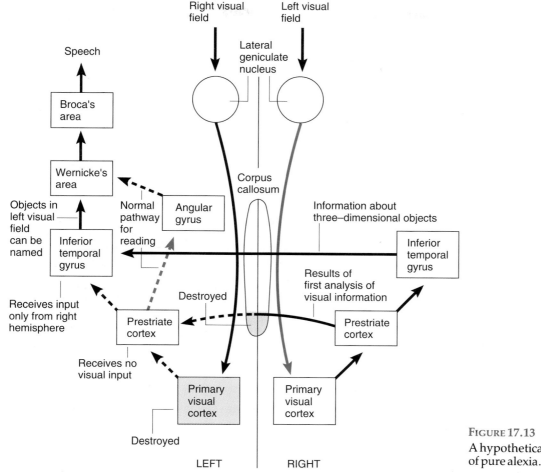

Visual input from retinas

<figure>
FIGURE 17.13

A hypothetical explanation of pure alexia.
</figure>

prestriate cortex receives no input from the left primary visual cortex, because it is destroyed, and receives no input from the right prestriate cortex, because the posterior part of the corpus callosum is destroyed. Thus, the angular gyrus receives no useful input. (See the broken color lines in *Figure 17.13.*)

Toward an Understanding of Writing

Because *pure agraphia*—that is, agraphia unaccompanied by alexia or aphasia—is rare, much less is known about the anatomical basis of writing than about the anatomical basis of reading. Writing depends on knowledge of the words that are to be used, along with the proper grammatical structure of the sentences they are to form. Thus, if a patient is unable to express himself or herself by speech, we should not be surprised to see a writing disturbance as well. Some forms of agraphia are caused by motor disturbances that prevent the person from forming letters well—or drawing pictures or performing other kinds of manual construction skills. As we saw in Chapter 8, lesions of the left parietal lobe cause apraxia, that is, difficulty in making movements—especially a series of movements—on command. You will not be surprised to learn that these lesions also impair writing skills. I think it would be inaccurate to characterize such a disorder as language-related.

Most people first learn the sounds of words,

then learn to say them, then learn to read, and then learn to write. Undoubtedly, reading and writing depend heavily on the skills that are learned earlier. For example, in order to write most words, we must be able to "sound them out in our heads," that is, to hear them and to articulate them subvocally. But if our ability to write most words depends upon a transfer of information between memories of sounds (presumably, in the left superior temporal gyrus) and motor movements that represent those sounds, then damage to the auditory association cortex should not impair written symbols that represent *visually* acquired memories.

This situation does indeed seem to be true. The Japanese language makes use of two kinds of written symbols. *Kanji* symbols are pictographs, adopted from the Chinese language (although they are pronounced as Japanese words). Thus, they represent concepts by means of visual symbols but do not provide a guide to their pronunciation. *Kana* symbols are phonetic representations of syllables; thus, they encode acoustical information. Sasanuma (1975) found that lesions of the left temporal lobe in Japanese patients interfered with the writing of kana symbols (acoustical), but not kanji symbols (visual). In contrast, damage to other regions of the brain usually impairs a patient's ability to write kanji symbols but not kana symbols. Thus, when a Japanese person writes, the behavior utilizes different brain functions, depending on the kinds of symbols being written.

Recall that the case of the deaf woman with aphasia led to a similar conclusion: Her ability to communicate verbally by means of hand movements was impaired by a lesion that damaged somatosensory mechanisms.

Kawamura, Hirayama, and Yamamoto (1989) reported an interesting case of a man with damage to the middle part of the corpus callosum who could write kana symbols with both hands and could write kanji symbols with the right hand but not the left. He could *copy* kanji symbols with his left hand; he just could not write them down when the investigators dictated them to him. (See *Figure 17.14*.) These results indicate that writing these two types of symbols not only involves different mechanisms in the left hemisphere but also crosses the corpus callosum at different locations.

Even English-speaking people write by more than one means. We probably write most long words by spelling out the sequence of sounds. (Try to write a long word such as *antidisestablishmentarianism* from memory and see whether you can do it without saying the word to yourself. If you recite a poem or sing a song to yourself under your breath, you will see that the writing comes to a halt.) This form of writing is similar to the writing of kana symbols. We probably also learn sequences of letters that spell some words the way we learn poems or the lyrics to a song. For example, many Americans learned to spell *Mississippi* with a singsong chant that goes like this: *M*-i-s-s-*I*-s-s-*I*-p-p-*I*, emphasizing the

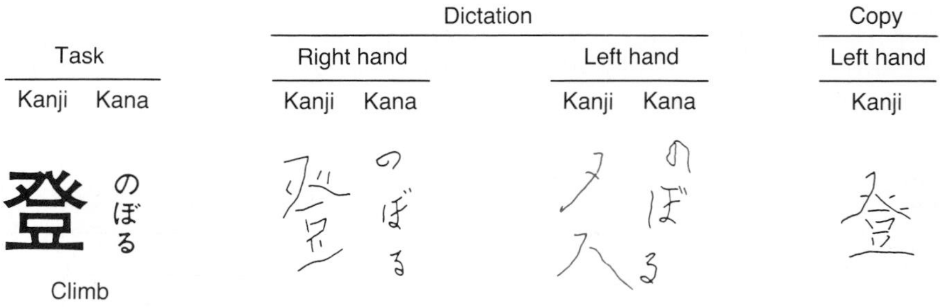

Task		Dictation				Copy
		Right hand		Left hand		Left hand
Kanji	Kana	Kanji	Kana	Kanji	Kana	Kanji

Climb

FIGURE 17.14

The writing of a Japanese patient with damage to the middle part of the corpus callosum. He could write both kanji and kana characters with his right hand, but could not write kanji characters with his left hand (color). He could, however, *copy* kanji characters with his left hand if he was given a model to look at. (From Kawamura, M., Hirayama, K., and Yamamoto, H. *Brain*, 1989, *112*, 1011–1018.)

callosum to speech mechanisms in the left hemisphere, where the letters are pronounced and the words are recognized. (See *Figure 17.16.*)

Phonological Dyslexia

Patients with *phonological dyslexia* can read most words rather well but have great difficulty reading nonwords such as the ones I recently asked you to try to pronounce (Beauvois and Dérouesné, 1979; Dérouesné and Beauvois, 1979). Phonological dyslexia provides further evidence for the existence of word-form reading and phonological reading. Phonetic reading, which is required for reading nonwords or words we have not yet learned, entails some sort of letter-to-sound decoding. Obviously, phonological reading of English requires more than decoding of the sounds produced by single letters, because, for example, some sounds are transcribed as two-letter sequences (such as *th* or *sh*) and the addition of the letter *e* to the end of a word lengthens an internal vowel (*can* becomes *cane*). People with phonological dyslexia have lost the ability to read phonetically. (See *Figure 17.17.*)

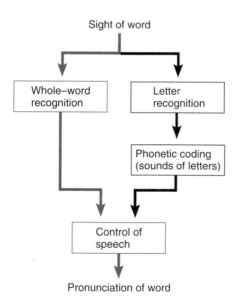

Sight of word

Whole–word recognition

Letter recognition

Phonetic coding (sounds of letters)

Control of speech

Pronunciation of word

FIGURE 17.17
A hypothetical explanation of phonological dyslexia. The damaged processes are shown in gray; the pathway used by the patient is shown in color. Only whole-word reading remains.

Because only a few cases of phonological dyslexia have been reported so far, little is known about the anatomical basis of this disorder.

Direct Dyslexia

Recall that patients with transcortical sensory aphasia can repeat what is said to them but show no signs of understanding what they hear or say. *Direct dyslexia* resembles transcortical sensory aphasia, except that the words in question are written, not spoken (Schwartz, Marin, and Saffran, 1979; Lytton and Brust, 1989). Patients with direct dyslexia are able to read even though they cannot understand the words they are saying. After sustaining a stroke that damaged his left frontal and temporal lobes, Lytton and Brust's patient lost the ability to communicate verbally; his speech was meaningless and he was unable to comprehend what other people said to him. However, he could read words with which he was already familiar. He could *not* read pronounceable nonwords; thus, he had lost the ability to read phonetically. His comprehension deficit seemed complete; when the investigators presented him with a word and several pictures, one of which corresponded to the word, he read the word correctly but had no idea what picture went with it.

The diagram of the reading of a patient with direct dyslexia is identical to that of a person with phonological dyslexia (shown in Figure 17.17). The only difference is that the circuits involved in visual word recognition are not able to connect to circuits involved in word *comprehension*.

Deep Dyslexia

Deep dyslexia is caused by massive damage to the left hemisphere (Coltheart, Patterson, and Marshall, 1987). Most patients have Broca's aphasia as well as a reading deficit. This disorder is particularly interesting because its symptoms combine most of those we have encountered in the reading disorders.

People with deep dyslexia are very poor readers. Those words they successfully read almost always represent concrete objects or actions; the patients almost never successfully read abstract words. In addition, when they attempt to read a concrete word, they often make semantically related substitutions. For example, *dream* might become *sleep; Eskimo* might become *iceman* (Coltheart, Patterson, and Marshall, 1980). The patients cannot read phonetically. If they attempt to read pronounceable nonwords, they usually make no response; or if they do respond, they tend to say a visually related word. For example, one patient said "city" for *cit* and "flute" for *frute* (Patterson and Marcel, 1977). Sometimes, their responses to nonwords obviously have a semantic origin; for example, *rud* was read as *naughty* and *glem* as *jewel,* presumably because they resemble the words *rude* and *gem.*

Figure 17.18 suggests a possible explanation of deep dyslexia. Although the ability to recognize whole words remains, the connections between whole-word recognition and speech programs are gone. Letter recognition and phonetic reading are also gone. The only pathway left involves a connection between whole-word recognition and visual recognition of the tangible objects that correspond to the words. (See *Figure 17.18.*)

In case you were wondering, the reason for the name *deep* dyslexia is that the reading errors the patients make tend to be related to the meaning of the word they are looking at. Metaphorically speaking, meaning is "deeper" than superficial features of words, such as their pronunciation.

Developmental Dyslexias

Some children have great difficulty learning to read and never become fluent readers, even though they are otherwise intelligent. Specific language learning disorders, called ***developmental dyslexias,*** tend to occur in families, which suggests a genetic (and hence biological) component. In addition, most people with developmental dyslexias are male, which suggests a possible link with the Y chromosome or with the presence of androgens during development (Rutter and Yule, 1975).

Several studies (Galaburda and Kemper, 1979; Galaburda et al., 1988) have found evidence that brain abnormalities may be responsible for at least some cases of developmental dyslexia. The investigators obtained the brains of deceased people with histories of developmental dyslexia. In all cases they found abnormalities in the ***planum temporale,*** a part of Wernicke's area. The left planum temporale is normally much larger than the right one (Galaburda, Le May, Kemper, and Geschwind, 1978), but in every dyslexic studied so far, it has been the same size on both sides of the brain. Even more significantly, the microscopic appearance of this region was abnormal. Figure

FIGURE 17.18
A hypothetical explanation of deep dyslexia. The damaged processes are shown in gray; the pathway used by the patient is shown in color. Presumably, the sight of the word produces an internal image of the object it represents, which is then named.

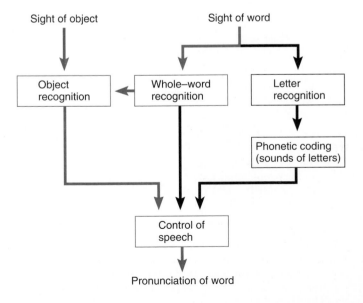

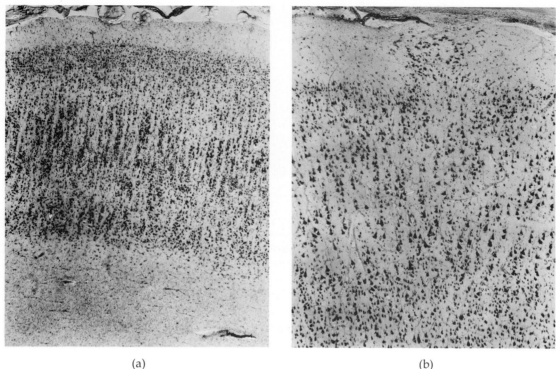

(a)   (b)

FIGURE 17.19

Photomicrographs of the left planum temporale (a portion of Wernicke's area) (a) of a normal person. (b) Of a person with developmental dyslexia. Nissl stain. (Photographs courtesy of A. Galaburda.)

17.19 shows a section through the left planum temporale of a normal person (a) and of a dyslexic accident victim (b). Notice the regular columnar arrangement of cells in the normal brain but not in the brain of the dyslexic accident victim. (See *Figure 17.19.*) Galaburda and Kemper (1979) observed that certain cells apparently failed to migrate during development and were left in the location they occupied during an earlier fetal stage. Cortical neurons develop in the central core of the brain before the twentieth week of gestation and then migrate to the position they are to occupy in the mature brain (Rakic, 1972). It appears that in this case something prevented normal migration of these cells.

Geschwind and Behan (1984) noted that investigators have long recognized that a disproportionate number of people with developmental dyslexias are also left-handed. Furthermore, clinical observations suggested a relation between left-handedness and various immune disorders. Therefore, Geschwind and Behan studied a group of left-handed and right-handed people to see whether the relations were statistically significant. They found that they were: The left-handed subjects were ten times more likely to have specific learning disorders (10 percent versus 1 percent) and two and one-half times more likely to have immune disorders (8 percent versus 3 percent). The immune disorders included various thyroid and bowel diseases, diabetes, and rheumatoid arthritis. Of course, although the relation was statistically significant, it was not perfect. After all, there are many healthy left-handed people.

Geschwind and Behan suggested that left-handedness, developmental dyslexia, and immune disorders are causally related. They noted that although the superior temporal gyrus develops one to two weeks earlier on the right, the left superior temporal gyrus ultimately becomes larger (Chi, Dooling, and Gilles, 1977). In fact, retardation in the rate of development may be the mechanism that causes the left language area to become larger than the corresponding region of the right hemisphere; by growing more slowly, it ultimately achieves a larger size. Perhaps dyslexia occurs when the development of the left hemisphere is suppressed so much that it fails to develop normally. This suppression would cause left-handedness as well. Several studies reviewed by Galaburda and Geschwind (1982) suggested that testosterone slows brain development and suppresses development of the thymus, an important part of the immune system. This effect might account for the fact that males with a family history of specific learning disorders are much more likely than females to exhibit developmental dyslexias. The hypothesis is interesting, but much research has yet to be done to test it experimentally.

INTERIM SUMMARY

Brain damage can produce reading and writing disorders. All cases of aphasia are accompanied by writing deficits that parallel the speech production deficits and by reading deficits that parallel the speech comprehension deficits. The reading and writing abilities of a person with pure word deafness, which is not an aphasic disorder, are generally good. The first reading and writing disorders to be identified that were not accompanied by aphasia were pure alexia and alexia with agraphia. Pure alexia is caused by lesions that produce blindness in the right visual field and that destroy fibers of the posterior corpus callosum. Alexia with agraphia is usually caused by lesions of the left angular gyrus. At least two different types of dysgraphia—phonological and orthographic—have been observed, which indicates that several different brain mechanisms are involved in the process of writing.

Research in the past few decades has discovered that acquired reading disorders (dyslexias) can fall into one of several catego-

ries, and the study of these disorders has provided neuropsychologists and cognitive psychologists with thought-provoking information that has helped them understand how normal people read. Developmental dyslexia appears to involve abnormal development of parts of the brain that play a role in language. A better understanding of the components of reading and writing may help us develop effective teaching methods that will permit people with dyslexia to take advantage of the abilities that they do have.

COMMUNICATION OF EMOTIONS

Not all human communication is conveyed by means of spoken or written words. We also communicate our feelings through tone of voice, facial expression, gestures, and body postures. Research by Ekman and his colleagues (Ekman and Friesen, 1971; Ekman, 1980) tends to confirm Darwin's hypothesis that facial expression of emotion uses an innate, species-typical repertoire of movements of facial muscles (Darwin, 1872/1965). For example, Ekman and Friesen (1971) studied the ability of members of an isolated tribe of people in New Guinea to recognize facial expressions of emotion produced by westerners. They had no trouble doing so and themselves produced facial expressions that westerners readily recognized. Figure 17.20 shows four photographs taken from videotapes of a man from this tribe reacting to stories designed to evoke facial expressions of sadness, disgust, happiness, and anger. I am sure that you will have no trouble recognizing which is which. (See *Figure 17.20*.)

Because the same facial expressions were used by people who had not previously been exposed to each other, Ekman and Friesen concluded that the expressions were unlearned behavior patterns. In contrast, different cultures use different words to express particular concepts; production of these words does not involve innate responses but must be learned.

Investigators have not yet determined whether other means of communicating emotions, such as tone of voice or hand movements, are learned or are at least partly innate. However, as we will see, some progress has been made in

FIGURE 17.20

A member of an isolated New Guinea tribe, studied by Ekman and Friesen, making faces when told stories. (a) "Your friend has come and you are happy." (b) "Your child had died." (c) "You are angry and about to fight." (d) "You see a dead pig that has been lying there a long time." (From Ekman, P. *The Face of Man: Expressions of Universal Emotions in a New Guinea Village.* New York: Garland STPM Press, 1980.)

studying the anatomical basis of expressing and recognizing emotions.

Emotional behaviors are species-typical reactions—physiological and behavioral—to situations that are important to us. As James (1884) and Lange (1887) pointed out over one hundred years ago, feelings of emotions appear to be provided by feedback from these reactions. (See *Figure 17.21.*) As we saw in Chapter 14, the amygdala plays an important role in emotions, because it provides a link between the detection of emotion-producing stimuli and autonomic, hormonal, and behavioral reactions to them.

The issue in this chapter is not the brain mechanisms that produce emotional reactions but the brain mechanisms involved in recognizing that a particular situation has emotional significance for the person involved, in recognizing the emotional

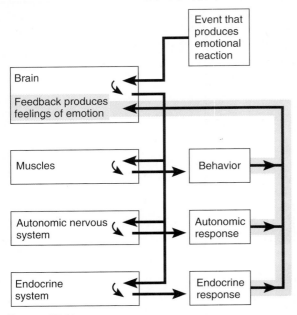

FIGURE 17.21

A diagrammatic representation of the James-Lange theory of emotion. An event in the environment triggers behavioral, autonomic, and endocrine responses. Feedback from these responses produces feelings of emotions.

state of another person expressed in their facial gestures and tone of voice, and in expressing their emotional state to other people.

Studies with Normal Subjects

Recognition of Other People's Emotions

We recognize other people's feelings by means of vision and audition—seeing their facial expressions and hearing their tone of voice and choice of words. Several studies by Bryden, Ley, and colleagues have found that the right hemisphere plays a more important role than the left hemisphere in comprehension of emotion. The rationale for these studies is that each hemisphere directly receives information from the contralateral part of the environment. For example, when a person looks directly ahead, visual stimuli to the left of the fixation point (seen with *both* eyes) are transmitted to the right hemisphere, and stimuli to the right are transmitted to the left hemisphere. Of course, the hemispheres exchange informa-

tion by means of the corpus callosum, but it appears that this transcommissural information is not as precise and detailed as information that is directly received. Similarly, although each hemisphere receives auditory information from both ears, the contralateral projections are richer than the ipsilateral ones. Thus, when stimuli are presented to the left visual field or left ear, the right hemisphere receives more specific information than the left hemisphere does.

In studies of hemispherical differences in visual recognition, stimuli are usually presented with a *tachistoscope* (literally, "seen most swiftly"), which flashes an image in a specific part of the visual field so fast that the subject does not have time to move his or her eyes. Many studies (reviewed by Bryden and Ley, 1983) have shown that the left hemisphere is better than the right at recognizing words or letter strings. Knowing what you do about the verbal functions of the left hemisphere, this finding will come as no surprise to you. However, when a person is required to discriminate among different faces or detect differences in the tilt of lines presented to one side of the visual field, the right hemisphere performs better than the left.

Ley and Bryden (1979) prepared cartoon drawings of five different people, each displaying one of five facial expressions, ranging from negative to neutral to positive. (See *Figure 17.22.*) They showed these drawings briefly in the right or left visual field, one at a time. After each presentation they showed the same face or a different one in the center of the visual field (to both hemispheres) and asked the subjects to say whether the same emotion was presented. When the experimenters showed the subjects neutral or mild expressions, the hemispheres performed approximately the same. However, when the experimenters showed the subjects strong expressions, the right hemisphere judged them more accurately. (See *Figure 17.23.*)

When auditory stimuli are presented to one ear, most subjects recognize words better when the right ear (left hemisphere) hears them, but they recognize music or nonverbal environmental sounds better when the left ear (right hemisphere) hears them (Bryden and Ley, 1983). Bryden, Ley, and Sugarman (1982) presented

FIGURE 17.22

The faces and expressions used as stimuli in the study by Ley and Bryden. (From Ley, R.G., and Bryden, M.P. *Brain and Language,* 1979, *7,* 127–138.)

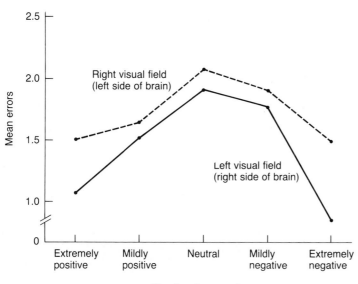

FIGURE 17.23

Mean errors in ratings of facial expressions of emotion in drawings presented to the right or left side of the brain. (Data from Ley, R.G., and Bryden, M.P. *Brain and Language,* 1979, *7,* 127–138.)

subjects with little melodies played in the major or minor mode. Most westerners perceive major tunes as happy and minor ones as sad. The investigators simultaneously presented a different melody to each ear and asked the subjects to pay attention to only one of them and say whether it was happy or sad. When the modes of the melodies were different, subjects judged the one presented to the left ear (right hemisphere) more accurately than the one presented to the right ear. Again, the study suggests the superiority of the right hemisphere in judging emotional connotation.

Ley and Bryden (1982) also investigated perception of tone of voice by similar means. They simultaneously presented different verbal messages with a different (happy, neutral, or sad) tone of voice to each ear and asked the subjects to attend to the message presented to one ear and report on its verbal content and emotion. Most of the subjects more accurately detected the verbal content of the message when it was presented to the left hemisphere and more accurately detected the emotional tone of the voice when it was presented to the right hemisphere. The results suggested that when a message is heard, the right hemisphere assesses the emotional expression of the voice, while the left hemisphere assesses the meaning of the words.

Expression of Emotion

When people show emotions with their facial muscles, the left side of the face usually makes a more intense expression. For example, Sackheim and Gur (1978) cut photographs of people who were posing emotions into right and left halves,

prepared mirror images of each of them, and pasted them together. They found that the left halves were more expressive than the right ones. (See *Figure 17.24*.) Because motor control is contralateral, the results suggest that the right hemisphere is more expressive than the left.

Moscovitch and Olds (1982) made more natural observations of people in restaurants and parks and found that the left side of their faces appeared to make stronger expressions of emotions. They confirmed these results in the laboratory by analyzing videotapes of people telling sad or humorous stories.

Studies with Neurological Patients

Long ago, Babinski (1914) noted that people with right-hemisphere damage often acted indifferent or euphoric, which suggested that this hemisphere was involved in either the recognition or expression of emotions. Later, Goldstein (1948) observed that people with left-hemisphere damage were more likely to exhibit what he called a *catastrophic reaction,* a strong display of sadness and despair caused by their neurological deficit. In contrast, damage to the right hemisphere, even when it resulted in paralysis of the left side of the body, was more likely to be met with indifference. These results suggest that when the left side of a person's brain is damaged, the intact right hemisphere recognizes the loss and consequently expresses grief. However, when the right side is damaged, the person may be able to acknowledge the deficit verbally but fails to react emotionally.

I once met a man who had sustained a right-

FIGURE 17.24

An example of a stimulus used by Sackheim and Gur (1978). (a) Original photo. (b) Composite of the right side of the man's face. (c) Composite of the left side of the man's face. (Reprinted with permission from *Neuropsychologia, 16,* H.A. Sackheim and R.C. Gur. Lateral asymmetry in intensity of emotional expression. Copyright 1978, Pergamon Journals, Ltd.)

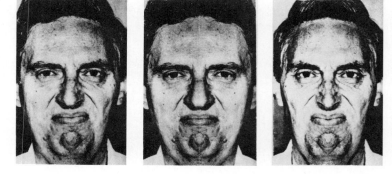

(a)   (b)   (c)

hemisphere stroke. Even though his left arm and leg were paralyzed, he was cheerful and indifferent to his disability. He even attempted several times to walk down the stairs, although he did acknowledge, when asked why he was in a wheelchair, that he could not move the left side of his body. He was alert and intelligent and received superior scores on the verbal components of an intelligence test, so his failure to react emotionally to his deficit cannot be explained by a simple comprehension deficit. His ability to talk about his condition was in sharp contrast to his ability to appreciate its meaning to his own existence.

Recognition of Other People's Emotions

Damage to the right hemisphere (especially the area posterior to the central sulcus) appears to impair the recognition of emotions being expressed by other people. For example, Heilman, Scholes, and Watson (1975) presented patients who had right or left lesions of the temporal-parietal region with sentences with neutral content (such as *The boy went to the store*), said in a happy, sad, angry, or indifferent tone of voice. Patients with right-hemisphere damage judged the emotion being expressed less accurately. Tucker, Watson, and Heilman (1977) performed a similar experiment, this time requiring the subjects simply to say whether the tone of voice of two sentences was the same or different. Again, right-hemisphere damage impaired the subjects' ability to discriminate the tone of voice more than left-hemisphere damage did.

Heilman, Watson, and Bowers (1983) presented an interesting case of a man with pure word deafness who could not comprehend the meaning of speech but who had no difficulty identifying the emotion being expressed by its intonation. This case demonstrates that comprehension of words and recognition of tone of voice are independent functions.

Visual recognition of emotions, as well as auditory recognition, also appears to be a right-hemisphere function more than a left-hemisphere function. DeKosky, Heilman, Bowers, and Valenstein (1980) found that right-hemisphere damage, more than left-hemisphere damage, disrupted patients' ability to discriminate among different facial expressions of emotion. In addition, Bowers and Heilman (1981) reported the case of a patient with a large tumor of the posterior right hemisphere who could accurately distinguish among faces of different people but not among different emotional expressions. In contrast, he had no trouble recognizing the emotional content of voices. Thus, although recognition of different faces and recognition of different expressions are both primarily right-hemisphere tasks, their anatomical basis differs.

Hemispheric differences in the recognition of emotions is seen in children as well as adults. Voeller, Hanson, and Wendt (1988) showed pictures of the faces of children expressing happiness, sadness, anger, or fright to children (mean age = 8 years, 3 months) with damage to the right or left hemisphere. The children with the right-hemisphere damage had much more difficulty identifying the expressions. The authors pointed out that misidentifying the emotions of other children could potentially cause serious problems with their socialization.

Expression of Emotion

Left-hemisphere lesions do not usually impair vocal expressions of emotion. For example, a person with Wernicke's aphasia usually modulates his or her voice according to mood. Even people with Broca's aphasia, who exhibit deficits in prosodic expression, can laugh and express emotions by tone of voice when uttering expletives. (When a Broca's aphasic says "Damn!" he sounds as if he means it.) However, right-hemisphere lesions do impair expression of emotion, both facially and by tone of voice.

Buck and Duffy (1980) showed slides that were designed to elicit expressions of emotions to patients with damage to the right or left hemisphere. For example, they showed a picture of a starving child and a crying woman. The investigators found that people with right-hemisphere damage showed fewer facial expressions of emotion. Heilman, Watson, and Bowers (1983) asked patients with unilateral brain lesions to *pose* expressions of emotions and found no differences between right and left lesions. However, they suggest a plausible explanation for this failure. As you know, people with Broca's aphasia often exhibit an oral and facial apraxia, having difficulty making particular movements on command. Thus, they have difficulty responding to the suggestion to smile but nevertheless smile spontaneously when they are told a joke. (You have probably noticed how difficult it is to smile when someone asks you to do so while taking your picture. In contrast, a smile occurs automatically when we are amused. Sometimes, we even have to fight to suppress a smile when we do not want to offend someone who has said or done something foolish.) So far, no one has compared the effects of left and right brain lesions on people's ability to *pose* expressions of emotions.

Morrow, Urtunski, Kim, and Boller (1981) obtained evidence that the decreased tendency of patients with right-hemisphere lesions to respond emotionally is not restricted to facial expression. To assess the motor effects of emotional stimuli, they recorded changes in skin conductivity, which presumably correlate with alterations in sweat production and blood flow—and hence with autonomic arousal. When they presented emotionally loaded stimuli, they found that patients with right-hemisphere damage exhibited less intense changes than those with left-hemisphere damage.

Ross (1981; Gorelick and Ross, 1987) suggested that the comprehension and expression of emotions are performed by neural circuits in the right hemisphere similar to those in the left hemisphere that are necessary for the comprehension and expression of speech. For example, he found three patients with frontal lesions who could recognize emotions portrayed by facial expressions or tone of voice but who could not express their own emotions, and he found a patient with a posterior lesion who could express but not comprehend emotions. Obviously, these cases correspond to Broca's and Wernicke's aphasia. In addition, he found cases of what he called *transcortical sensory aprosodia* and *global aprosodia*. (See *Figure 17.25.*) Although more cases will have to be observed before we can evaluate the accu-

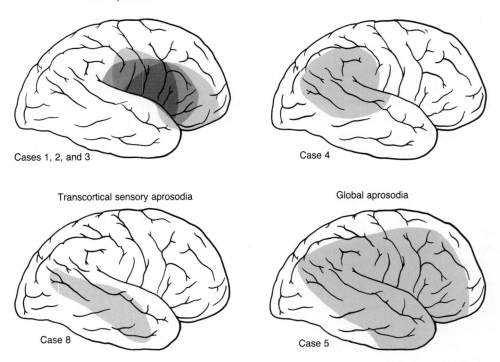

FIGURE 17.25

Brain damage that caused different forms of aprosodia. (From Ross, E.D. *Archives of Neurology*, 1981, *38*, 561–569. Copyright 1981, American Medical Association.)

racy of Ross's conclusions, his results suggest interesting similarities in the functions of the hemispheres with respect to different types of information.

*I*NTERIM SUMMARY

An important form of nonverbal communication is the use of facial expressions to show our feelings. Expression and comprehension of emotions involve the right hemisphere more than the left. Studies with normal people have shown that people can judge facial expressions, tone of voice, or mode of music better when the information is presented to the right hemisphere than when it is presented to the left hemisphere. In addition, the left halves of people's faces tend to be more expressive than the right halves, and emotional hand gestures are produced more often by the left hand. (As you know, control of movement is contralateral.)

Damage to the right hemisphere is more likely to produce deficits in expression and comprehension of emotions conveyed by tone of voice or by facial expression than damage to the left hemisphere. In fact, people with right-hemisphere lesions sometimes do not even react emotionally to their own neurological deficits. Perhaps the right hemisphere contains mechanisms of emotional comprehension and expression that

are parallel to the mechanisms of speech comprehension and expression in the left hemisphere, but further research will be needed to confirm this possibility.

*C*ONCLUDING REMARKS

Many people have pointed out that our ability to communicate with each other by means of speech and writing is the most important distinguishing feature of the human species. Because such communication is so important, most people are fascinated by the specific language disorders caused by brain damage. Verbal communication involves memories of the sounds of words and their visual appearance when written, of the movements of the muscles neccessary to pronounce or write them, of the relation between the words and our knowledge of objects and events in the world (that is, the word's meanings), and of the grammatical relations among words that define sentence structure. Neuropsychological research is helping us understand how the brain accomplishes such verbal tasks.

Because the expression of emotions is less specific and is not as rule-governed as verbal communication, not as much is presently known about this topic. We will examine an aspect of pathological emotional conditions—affective disorders—in the next (and final) chapter.

NEW TERMS

agrammatism p. 547
alexia with agraphia p. 559
angular gyrus p. 559
anomia p. 547
aphasia p. 540
Broca's aphasia p. 546
Broca's area p. 546
catastrophic reaction p. 572
cerebrovascular
    accident p. 540
circumlocution p. 551
conduction aphasia p. 548
content word p. 546

deep dyslexia p. 565
developmental dyslexia p. 566
direct dyslexia p. 565
disconnection syndrome p. 545
function word p. 546
homonymous hemianopia p. 560
orthographic dysgraphia p. 563
paraphasic error p. 542
phonetic reading p. 563
phonological dysgraphia p. 563
phonological dyslexia p. 565
planum temporale p. 566
prosody p. 555

pure agraphia p. 561
pure alexia p. 559
pure word deafness p. 544
supplementary motor
    area p. 554
tachistoscope p. 570
transcortical motor
    aphasia p. 554
transcortical sensory
    aphasia p. 552
Wernicke's aphasia p. 542
Wernicke's area p. 543
word-form dyslexia p. 564

SUGGESTED READINGS

Caplan, D. *Neurolinguistics and Linguistic Aphasiology*. Cambridge, England: Cambridge University Press, 1987.

Coltheart, M., Patterson, K., and Marshall, J.C. *Deep Dyslexia*, 2nd ed. London: Routledge and Kegan Paul, 1987.

Heilman, K.M., and Satz, P. *Neuropsychology of Human Emotion*. New York: The Guilford Press, 1983.

Kertesz, A. *Localization in Neuropsychology*. New York: Academic Press, 1983.

Kolb, B., and Whishaw, I.Q. *Fundamentals of Human Neuropsychology*, 3rd ed. New York: W.H. Freeman, 1989.

Plum, F. *Language, Communication, and the Brain*. New York: Raven Press, 1988.

Mental Disorders

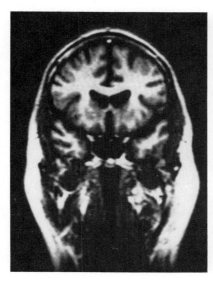
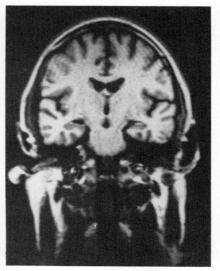

*M*ost of the discussion in this book has concentrated on the physiology of normal, adaptive behavior. This chapter summarizes research on the nature and physiology of mental disorders—of syndromes characterized by maladaptive behavior. The symptoms of mental disorders include deficient or inappropriate social behaviors; illogical, incoherent, or obsessional thoughts; inappropriate emotional responses, including depression, mania, or anxiety; and delusions and hallucinations. Research in recent years indicates that many of these symptoms are caused by abnormalities in the brain: structural and biochemical.

The most serious mental disorders are called *psychoses.* The two most important psychoses, schizophrenia and the major affective disorders, can disrupt people's behavior so severely that they cannot survive without the care of others. Their thoughts seem so different from those of other people that past generations concluded that these disorders were caused by possession by inhuman devils. *Neuroses* are generally less severe. People with neuroses are often unhappy, but most of them can reason logically and do not have hallucinations or delusions. They often have good insight into their problems and can articulate them well. In some cases, however, even neurotic disorders can seriously interfere with people's lives. This chapter discusses two of the most serious neuroses, panic disorder and obsessive compulsive disorder.

SCHIZOPHRENIA

Description

Schizophrenia is the most common psychosis, afflicting approximately 1 percent of the world's population. Descriptions of symptoms in ancient writings indicate that the disorder has been around for thousands of years (Jeste, Del Carmen, Lohr, and Wyatt, 1985). *Schizophrenia* is probably the most misused psychological term in existence. The word literally means "split mind," but it does *not* imply a split or multiple personality. People of-

ten say that they "feel schizophrenic" about an issue when they really mean that they have mixed feelings about it. A person who sometimes wants to build a cabin in Alaska and live off the land and at other times wants to take over the family insurance business may be undecided, but he or she is not schizophrenic. The man who invented the term, Eugen Bleuler, intended it to refer to a break with reality, caused by disorganization of the various functions of the mind, so that thoughts and feelings no longer worked together normally.

Schizophrenia is characterized by two categories of symptoms, positive and negative. *Positive symptoms* are those that make themselves known by their presence. These include thought disorders, hallucinations, and delusions. A *thought disorder*—disorganized, irrational thinking—is probably the most important symptom of schizophrenia. Schizophrenics have great difficulty arranging their thoughts logically and sorting out plausible conclusions from absurd ones. In conversation they jump from one topic to another, as new associations come up. Sometimes, they utter meaningless words or choose words for their rhyme rather than for their meaning. *Delusions* are beliefs that are obviously contrary to fact. Delusions of *persecution* are false beliefs that others are plotting and conspiring against oneself. Delusions of *grandeur* are false beliefs in one's power and importance, such as a conviction that one has godlike powers or has special knowledge that no one else possesses. Delusions of *control* are related to delusions of persecution; the person believes, for example, that he or she is controlled by others through such means as radar or tiny radio receivers implanted in his or her brain.

The third positive symptom of schizophrenia is *hallucinations,* which are perceptions of stimuli that are not actually present. The most common schizophrenic hallucinations are auditory, but they can also involve any of the other senses. The typical schizophrenic hallucination consists of voices talking to the person. Sometimes, they order the person to do something; sometimes, they scold the person for his or her unworthiness; sometimes, they just utter meaningless phrases.

Olfactory hallucinations are also fairly common; often they contribute to the delusion that others are trying to kill the person with poison gas.

In contrast to the positive symptoms, the *negative symptoms* of schizophrenia are known by the absence of normal behaviors: flattened emotional response, poverty of speech, lack of initiative and persistence, inability to experience pleasure, and social withdrawal (Crow, 1980; Andreasen and Olsen, 1982). Negative symptoms are not specific to schizophrenia; they are seen in many neurological disorders that involve brain damage, especially to the frontal lobes. As we will see later in this chapter, evidence suggests that these two sets of symptoms result from different physiological disorders: Positive symptoms appear to involve excessive activity in some neural circuits that include dopamine as a neurotransmitter, and negative symptoms appear to be caused by brain damage. Many researchers believe that these two sets of symptoms involve a common set of underlying causes.

Heritability

One of the strongest pieces of evidence that schizophrenia is a biological disorder is that it appears to be heritable. Two approaches have established a linkage between schizophrenia and genes: adoption studies and twin studies.

Kety, Rosenthal, Wender, and Schulsinger (1968) performed one of the earliest and best-known adoption studies. Kety and his colleagues identified a group of schizophrenic people who had been adopted when they were children. They found that the incidence of schizophrenia in the adopted families of the patients was exactly what would be expected in the general population. Thus, it did not appear that the patients became schizophrenic because they were raised in a family of schizophrenics. However, the investigators did find an unusually high incidence of schizophrenia in the patients' *biological* relatives (parents and siblings), even though they were not raised by and with them—and probably, in most cases, did not even know them. The results clearly favor the conclusion that a tendency to develop schizophrenia is heritable.

Twin studies have produced similar results. These studies take advantage of the fact that monozygotic twins have identical genotypes, whereas the genetic similarity between dizygotic twins is, on the average, 50 percent. Investigators study records to identify pairs of twins in which at least one member has received a diagnosis of schizophrenia or perhaps of a related but milder condition, such as schizotypal personality disorder. If both twins have been diagnosed as having schizophrenia, then they are said to be *concordant*. If only one has received this diagnosis, the twins are said to be *discordant*. Thus, if a disorder has a genetic basis, the percentage of monozygotic twins concordant for the diagnosis will be higher than that for dizygotic twins. As many studies have shown, this is exactly what occurs (Gottesman and Shields, 1976). One of the more recent studies found that the concordance rate for monozygotic twins was over five times higher than the concordance rate for dizygotic twins (Farmer, McGuffin, and Gottesman, 1987).

If schizophrenia were a simple trait produced by a single gene, we would expect to see this disorder in at least 50 percent of the children of two schizophrenic parents if the gene were dominant. If it were recessive, all children of two schizophrenic parents should become schizophrenic. However, the actual incidence is less than 50 percent, which means either that several genes are involved, or that having a "schizophrenia gene" imparts a *susceptibility* to develop schizophrenia, the disease itself being triggered by other factors. Perhaps, in certain kinds of environments, the susceptible individual develops schizophrenia or at least a schizotypal personality disorder. As we will see, evidence suggests that one of the inherited traits may include susceptibility to a virally triggered autoimmune disorder that disrupts the functioning of the brain and eventually causes brain damage.

If the susceptibility hypothesis is true, then we would expect that some people carry a "schizophrenia gene" but do not express it; that is, their environment is such that schizophrenia is never triggered. One such person would be the nonschizophrenic member of a pair of monozygotic twins discordant for schizophrenia. The logical

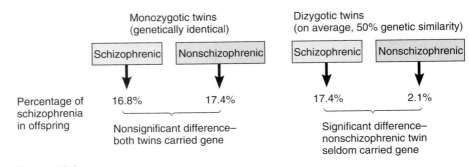

FIGURE 18.1

An explanation for evidence that people can have an unexpressed "schizophrenia gene."

way to test this hypothesis is to examine the children of both members of discordant pairs. Gottesman and Bertelsen (1989) found that the percentage of schizophrenic children was identical for both members of such pairs: 16.8% for the schizophrenic parents and 17.4% for the nonschizophrenic parents. For the dizygotic twins the percentages were 17.4% and 2.1%, respectively. These results provide strong evidence for heritability of schizophrenia and also support the conclusion that carrying a "schizophrenia gene" does not mean that a person will necessarily become schizophrenic. (See *Figure 18.1.*)

Studies have suggested two possible locations for a "schizophrenia gene": chromosome 5 and a special region of the X chromosome. Bassett, McGillivray, Jones, and Pantzar (1988) found a schizophrenic man with a schizophrenic uncle, both of whom had an abnormality of the long arm of chromosome 5; they had three copies of this arm rather than two. The abnormality suggested that this region might be a worthwhile place to look for a defective gene. Sherrington et al. (1988) used DNA markers to study five families in Iceland and two in England that had some schizophrenic members, and they found evidence that implicated this location. However, other studies (Kennedy et al., 1988; St. Clair et al., 1989) failed to confirm the results. Thus, unless the correlation in the first study was accidental, we must conclude that there is more than one gene that can produce a susceptibility to schizophrenia.

A second candidate is found on the X chromosome. Normally, if a dominant gene is found on the X chromosome, the trait associated with it will occur with equal frequency in both males and females. However, there is a special location on the short arm of the X chromosome that normally exchanges genetic material with the short arm of the Y chromosome during sperm production in males, through a process that geneticists call *crossing-over*. This region is called the *pseudoautosomal segment* because genes there act as if they were on an autosome (that is, nonsex chromosome). (See *Figure 18.2.*)

The exact location of the point at which the chromosomes cross over is variable; thus, depending on the exact location of a particular gene found here, it will sometimes cross over to the Y chromosome and sometimes remain on the X chromosome; thus, it will sometimes be found on the X chromosome in a man's sperms and sometimes on the Y chromosome. If the "schizophrenia gene" ends up on the Y chromosome, a father will give it to his sons; if it ends up on the X chromosome, he will give it to his daughters.

Crow, DeLisi, and Johnstone (1989) found that when a family contains more than one schizophrenic child, the children are more likely to be of the same sex when the history of schizophrenia is on the father's side, but not when it is on the mother's. This difference suggests that the "schizophrenia gene" is found near the end of the X chromosome. The ratio of same-sex to mixed-

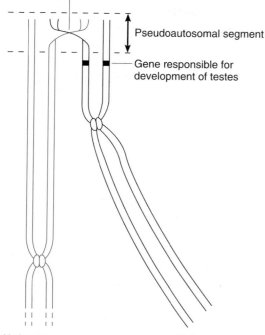

Exact point of
crossing–over varies

Pseudoautosomal segment

Gene responsible for
development of testes

X chromosome
(most of long arm not shown)

Y chromosome

FIGURE 18.2

Crossing-over between an X chromosome and a Y
chromosome in the pseudoautosomal segment during
sperm production. (Adapted from Crow, T.J., DeLisi,
L.E., and Johnstone, E.C. *British Journal of Psychiatry*,
1989, *155*, 92–97.)

sex pairs of schizophrenic siblings was 3:1 in families with a paternal history of schizophrenia,
which, according to the authors, gives clues about
the precise location of the hypothetical gene.

Evidence suggests that schizophrenia can
sometimes be caused by nongenetic factors.
Schwarzkopf, Nasrallah, Olson, Coffman, and
McLaughlin (1989) found that if a schizophrenic
person does not have relatives with a schizophrenic disorder, the person is more likely to have had
a history of complications at or around the time
of childbirth. Thus, brain damage not related to
heredity may also be a cause of schizophrenia.

Some investigators have attempted to find
other traits that correlate with schizophrenia,
traits that may make it possible to detect the presence of even an unexpressed "schizophrenia
gene" (that is, a "schizophrenia gene" in a person

without the disorder). For example, many studies
have found that difficulty in tracking a smoothly
moving object with the eyes is highly correlated
with schizophrenia. Up to 85 percent of all schizophrenics show abnormal tracking, as compared
with under 10 percent in nonschizophrenics.
Approximately half of the first-degree relatives
(children, parents, and siblings) of schizophrenic
people show this abnormality, even if they
themselves are not schizophrenic (Holzman et al.,
1974; Rea, Sweeney, Solomon, Walsh, and
Frances, 1989). Allen and Sarich (1988) conclude
that the data suggest that a single gene is responsible for both schizophrenia and abnormal eye
tracking. Presumably, a brain abnormality is responsible for the two conditions.

Pharmacology of Schizophrenia:
The Dopamine Hypothesis

Pharmacological evidence suggests that the positive symptoms of schizophrenia are caused by a
biochemical disorder. The explanation that has
accrued the most evidence is the *dopamine hypothesis,* which suggests that schizophrenia is caused
by overactivity of the mesolimbic and mesocortical dopaminergic neurons, projecting from the
ventral tegmental area to the basal forebrain,
limbic cortex, and neocortex. (These circuits were
described in Chapter 16.)

Effects of Dopamine Agonists
and Antagonists

The treatments for most physiological disorders are developed after we understand their
causes. For example, once it was discovered that
diabetes was caused by the lack of a hormone produced by the pancreas, researchers were able to
extract a substance from pancreatic tissue (insulin) that would alleviate the symptoms of this disease. However, in some cases treatments are discovered before the causes of the disease. For
example, natives of tropical regions discovered
that tea made from the bark of the cinchona tree
would prevent death from malaria many years before scientists discovered that this disease is
caused by microscopic parasites that are transmitted in the saliva of a certain species of mos-

quito. (The bark of the cinchona tree contains quinine, now used to treat malaria.)

In the case of schizophrenia a treatment was discovered before its causes were understood. (In fact, its causes are *still* not completely understood.) The discovery was accidental (Snyder, 1974). Antihistamine drugs were discovered in the early 1940s and were found to be useful in the treatment of allergic reactions. Because one of the effects of histamine release is a lowering of blood pressure, a French surgeon named Henri Laborit began to study the effects of antihistamine drugs on the sometimes-fatal low blood pressure that can be produced by surgical shock. He found that one of the drugs, promethazine, had an interesting effect: It reduced anxiety in his presurgical patients without causing mental confusion.

Laborit's findings spurred drug companies to examine other antihistamine drugs for sedative effects. Paul Charpentier, a chemist with a French drug company, developed *chlorpromazine,* which appeared to be promising from tests with animals. Laborit tried the drug in humans and found that it had profound calming effects but did not seem to decrease the patient's alertness. This drug produced "not any loss in consciousness, nor any change in the patients' mentality but a slight tendency to sleep and above all 'disinterest' for all that goes on around him" (Laborit, 1950, quoted by Snyder, 1974). Chlorpromazine was tried on patients with a variety of mental disorders: mania, depression, anxiety, neuroses, and schizophrenia (Delay and Deniker, 1952a, 1952b). The drug was not very effective in treating neuroses or affective psychoses, but it had dramatic effects on schizophrenia.

The discovery of the antipsychotic effects of chlorpromazine profoundly altered the way in which physicians treated schizophrenic patients and made prolonged hospital stays unnecessary for many of them (the patients, that is). The efficacy of antipsychotic drugs has been established in many double-blind studies (Baldessarini, 1977). They actually eliminate, or at least diminish, the patients' symptoms; they do not simply mask them by tranquilizing the patients. Although some antipsychotic drugs do have tranquilizing effects, these effects are not related to the amount of relief the patients receive from their

psychotic symptoms. Moreover, antipsychotic drugs can have either activating or calming effects, depending upon the patient's symptoms. An immobile patient becomes more active, whereas a furiously active patient who is suffering from frightening hallucinations becomes more calm and placid. The results are not just a change in the patient's attitudes; the hallucinations and delusions go away, or at least become less severe.

Since the discovery of chlorpromazine, many other drugs have been discovered that relieve the positive symptoms of schizophrenia. All have one property in common: They block dopamine receptors. In fact, the better a drug blocks D_2 dopamine receptors, the more effectively it reduces the symptoms of schizophrenia (Creese, Burt, and Snyder, 1976). Other drugs that interfere with dopaminergic transmission, such as reserpine (which prevents the storage of monoamines in synaptic vesicles), α-methyl *p*-tyrosine (which blocks the synthesis of dopamine), and apomorphine (which stimulates dopamine autoreceptors and hence inhibits the release of dopamine), either facilitate the antipsychotic action of drugs such as chlorpromazine or themselves exert antipsychotic effects (Tamminga, Burrows, Chase, Alphs, and Thaker, 1988).

Another category of drugs has the opposite effect, namely, the production of the positive symptoms of schizophrenia. The drugs that can produce these symptoms have one known pharmacological effect in common: They act as dopamine agonists. These drugs include amphetamine, cocaine, and methylphenidate (which block the reuptake of dopamine) and L-DOPA (which stimulates the synthesis of dopamine). The symptoms that these drugs produce can be alleviated with antipsychotic drugs, which further strengthens the argument that these drugs exert their therapeutic effects by blocking dopamine receptors.

An example of the psychosis-inducing effect of amphetamine was demonstrated by Griffith, Cavanaugh, Held, and Oates (1972). The investigators recruited a group of people who had a history of amphetamine use and gave them large doses (10 mg) of dextroamphetamine every hour for up to five days. (Experimentally, it would have been better to study nonusers. Ethically, it was better not to introduce this drug to people who did not normally use it.) None of the subjects had prior histories of psychotic behavior. All seven volunteers became psychotic within two to five days. They became suspicious and began to believe that the experimenters were trying to poison them. One developed a delusion that an electric dynamo was controlling his thoughts. Most had auditory hallucinations. Similar symptoms—the classic positive symptoms of schizophrenia—are seen today in many people who abuse cocaine.

The fact that dopamine antagonists relieve the positive symptoms of schizophrenia and dopamine agonists produce them suggests that schizophrenia may be caused by an abnormality of some sort in dopaminergic pathways.

The Search for Abnormalities in Dopamine Transmission in the Brains of Schizophrenic Patients

The dopamine hypothesis suggests that schizophrenia is caused by the overactivity of dopaminergic synapses. There is little evidence to suggest that the production and release of dopamine in the brains of schizophrenic patients is abnormal (Wyatt, Kirch, and DeLisi, 1988). In fact, several studies have found *decreased* levels of the principal breakdown product of dopamine (homovanillic acid) in the cerebrospinal fluid. However, as we shall see later in this chapter, the ventricles of patients with schizophrenia tend to be larger than those of nonschizophrenics; thus, the substance could simply be diluted in a larger pool of CSF (Reynolds, 1989). In any event, most investigators have studied the possibility that too many dopamine receptors are present on the postsynaptic membrane at dopaminergic synapses. This overabundance of dopamine receptors would increase the size of the postsynaptic potentials at dopaminergic synapses. Two types of analyses have been made: postmortem measurements in the brains of deceased schizophrenic patients and PET scans after treatment with radioactive ligands for dopamine receptors.

Postmortem measurements of dopamine receptors are performed by removing the regions of the brain that contain dopaminergic terminals, homogenizing the tissue, extracting the cell membranes, and incubating them with a radioactive ligand of dopamine receptors. The degree of radioactivity of the tissue reveals the relative number of dopamine receptors. (This method was discussed in more detail in Chapter 5.) Jaskiw and Kleinman (1988) reviewed twelve such studies published between 1978 and 1987 and found that ten of them observed an increase in the number of D_2 dopamine receptors present in the neostriatum (caudate nucleus and putamen).

Measurements of levels of D_2 receptors in the brains of living schizophrenic patients have yielded mixed results. Wong et al. (1986) administered a radioactive ligand for D_2 receptors and used a PET scanner to measure the radioactivity in the caudate nucleus. Their results suggested that the number of D_2 receptors was 30 to 100 percent higher in the brains of schizophrenic patients. However, Farde et al. (1990) and Martinot et al. (1990), using even more specific ligands for D_2 receptors, found no differences between the level of these receptors in schizophrenic and normal brains.

What conclusion can we make? Farde and his colleagues studied young patients who had just been diagnosed as being schizophrenic. The patients had not yet been given an antipsychotic medication, so the results of the study were not contaminated by possible effects of the medication. Many—perhaps most—of the schizophrenic patients used in previous studies (including the postmortem studies) had received antipsychotic drugs. This issue is important; several studies have shown that the administration of an antipsychotic medication for several days increases the number of D_2 receptors in the neostriatum of laboratory animals (Burt, Creese, and Snyder, 1977). Indeed, Farde and his colleagues found that the level of D_2 receptors in a patient who had been receiving an antipsychotic medication was elevated. Thus, it would seem premature to conclude that schizophrenia is caused by increased numbers of D_2 dopamine receptors.

The failure to obtain solid, unambiguous evidence that dopaminergic synapses are hyperactive in schizophrenic patients does not mean that the dopamine hypothesis should be abandoned. For one thing, investigators may have been looking in the wrong part of the brain. The neostriatum contains many dopamine receptors, which makes this region the easiest one in which to study their concentration. If schizophrenia were caused by a genetic defect that created an overproduction of dopamine receptors, then we would expect to find more of the receptors in the neostriatum. But what we know about the functions of the dopaminergic pathways in the brain would not make us suspect that the neostriatum would be involved in schizophrenia. The neostriatum is involved in motor control. A deficiency in the release of dopamine in the neostriatum causes Parkinson's disease; thus, we would expect that excessive dopaminergic activity there would cause excessive movement, not schizophrenia.

The nucleus accumbens and the prefrontal cortex, which also receive input from dopaminergic neurons, seem to be much better candidates than the neostriatum. As we saw in Chapter 16, the activity of dopaminergic terminal buttons in the nucleus accumbens appears to be a vital link in the process of reinforcement. In addition, the prefrontal cortex plays an important role in making plans and shifting strategies in order to adapt one's behavior to changes in environmental contingencies. Overactivity of either or both of these systems could conceivably produce the positive symptoms of schizophrenia.

Let us consider the dopaminergic neurons involved in reinforcement. As we saw, drugs that strongly reinforce behaviors (such as cocaine and amphetamine) also produce the positive symptoms of schizophrenia. Perhaps the two effects of the drugs are related. If reinforcement mechanisms were activated at inappropriate times, then inappropriate behaviors—including delusional thoughts—might be reinforced. At one time or other, all of us have had some irrational thoughts, which we normally brush aside and forget. But if neural mechanisms of reinforcement became active while these thoughts were occurring, we would tend to take them more seriously. In time, full-fledged delusions might develop.

Even if dopaminergic neurons are directly involved in the production of the symptoms of schizophrenia, it is possible that nothing is wrong with dopaminergic neurons or dopamine receptors; the abnormality could lie elsewhere. For example, some investigators suggest that schizo-

phrenia is actually caused by damage to GABA-secreting neurons that normally inhibit dopaminergic neurons (Reynolds, 1989). Decreased inhibitory control of dopaminergic neurons would result in their overactivity. If this hypothesis is correct, then treatment with dopamine receptor blockers does not correct an abnormality in dopaminergic neurons or D_2 receptors but simply compensates for the excessive activity of dopaminergic neurons caused by decreased inhibitory control.

Another possibility is that schizophrenia is caused by the *overactivity* of neurons that *excite* dopaminergic neurons. Freed (1989) has proposed that antipsychotic drugs produce their therapeutic effects by decreasing the sensitivity of glutamate receptors on neurons in the mesolimbic and mesocortical dopaminergic pathways. Because glutamate is an excitatory transmitter substance, the decrease in sensitivity would reduce the activation of the dopaminergic neurons. In support of this hypothesis Freed, Cannon-Spoor, and Rodgers (1989) found that after mice had received an antipsychotic drug (haloperidol) for twenty-eight days, they showed a reduced behavioral response to quisqualic acid, a glutamate agonist.

Remaining Problems

Because of two primary pieces of evidence—that dopamine agonists produce the positive symptoms of schizophrenia and dopamine antagonists relieve them—the dopamine hypothesis is likely to be with us until it is proved to be correct or until it is replaced with a better one. As we saw in the previous section, we still do not have good evidence that schizophrenia is caused by an abnormality in dopaminergic neurons or dopamine receptors. There are other problems with the hypothesis, too.

The first problem is simple: The symptoms of up to one-third of all schizophrenic patients are not substantially reduced by antipsychotic drugs. One possible explanation is that individual differences could exist in the permeability of the blood-brain barrier to these drugs or in metabolic processes relating to dopaminergic activity. However, a PET scan study by Wolkin et al. (1989) found that an antipsychotic drug produced equal levels of dopamine receptor blockade in the brains of schizophrenics, regardless of whether the patients responded to the drug. Thus, the possibility remains that schizophrenia can be caused by more than one kind of biochemical abnormality.

The second problem is slightly more complex. It involves a motor problem that most investigators believe is a side effect of antipsychotic drugs: *tardive dyskinesia.* A common side effect of antipsychotic drugs is symptoms of Parkinson's disease, including loss of facial expression, muscular rigidity, and tremors. These symptoms are acute; they occur immediately and can be reduced by decreasing the dose of the drug. In most cases they disappear spontaneously. A much more serious symptom is **tardive dyskinesia,** which occurs in approximately 10 percent of the patients who receive these drugs. *Tardus* means ''slow'' and *dyskinesia* means ''faulty movement''; thus, tardive dyskinesia is a late-developing movement disorder. This syndrome includes peculiar facial tics and gestures, including tongue protrusion, cheek puffing, and pursing of the lips. In some cases speech is affected. Sometimes, writhing movements of the hands and trunk are also seen.

Tardive dyskinesia appears to be the opposite of Parkinson's disease. Indeed, dyskinesia commonly occurs when patients with Parkinson's disease receive too much L-DOPA. In schizophrenic patients tardive dyskinesia is made *worse* by discontinuing the antipsychotic drug and is improved by increasing the dose. The symptoms are also intensified by dopamine agonists such as L-DOPA or amphetamine (Baldessarini and Tarsy, 1980). Therefore, the disorder appears to be produced by an overstimulation of dopamine receptors. If it is, why should it be originally caused by antipsychotic drugs, which are dopamine antagonists?

The answer seems to be provided by a phenomenon called **denervation supersensitivity** in which, within a few days after the nerve to a muscle is cut, the muscle develops an increased sensitivity to acetylcholine. That is, a given amount of acetylcholine produces a larger effect than it previously did. This phenomenon is caused by an increase in the number of postsynaptic acetylcholinergic receptors on the muscle (Miledi, 1959). Presumably, the decreased input to the muscle in-

duces a regulatory mechanism to increase the muscle's sensitivity to acetylcholine.

Investigators have found that neurons, as well as muscles, can develop denervation supersensitivity (Baldessarini and Tarsy, 1980). If a particular input ceases to be active, regulatory mechanisms increase the neuron's sensitivity to that input. Thus, in the case of tardive dyskinesia, blocking dopamine receptors in the caudate nucleus causes a compensatory supersensitivity to this transmitter substance. This supersensitivity results in dyskinesia when the drug is withdrawn. In cases in which the antipsychotic medication continues for a long time, the supersensitivity becomes so great that it overcompensates for the effects of the drug, causing the tardive dyskinesia to occur even while the drug is still being administered.

So far, so good. But consider this question: Why do schizophrenic patients not develop ''tardive schizophrenia''? If positive symptoms of schizophrenia are alleviated by drugs that block dopamine receptors, we should expect denervation supersensitivity to cause *schizophrenic* symptoms, as well as motor symptoms, to recur. They do not; a rebound effect is *not* seen in the symptoms of schizophrenia even when the drug treatment is prolonged. (See *Figure 18.3.*) There are two possible explanations to this puzzle. First, the reduction of the symptoms of schizophrenia may not be related to the blockade of dopamine receptors; that is, the dopamine hypothesis may be wrong. Second, there may be a fundamental difference in the physiology of neurons that receive dopaminergic input. Those in the neostriatum may respond to dopamine antagonists with supersensitivity, whereas those located elsewhere (say, in the nucleus accumbens or the prefrontal cortex) may not develop supersensitivity.

Just to complicate an already complicated story, I should tell you that not all investigators believe that the primary cause of tardive dyskinesia is antipsychotic medication. If it is not, then the absence of ''tardive schizophrenia'' does not contradict the dopamine hypothesis. Crow, Cross, Johnstone, Owen, Owens, and Waddington (1982) note that dyskinesias had been reported in schizophrenic patients long

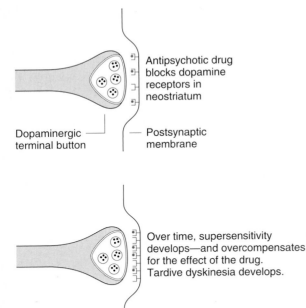

Antipsychotic drug blocks dopamine receptors in neostriatum

Dopaminergic terminal button

Postsynaptic membrane

Over time, supersensitivity develops—and overcompensates for the effect of the drug. Tardive dyskinesia develops.

FIGURE 18.3

Supersensitivity caused by drugs that block dopamine receptors. Tardive dyskinesia occurs, but not "tardive schizophrenia."

before antipsychotic drugs were discovered. They cite the following quotation from Kraepelin (1919):

> The spasmodic phenomena in the musculature of the face and speech, which often appear, are extremely peculiar disorders . . . . Some of them resemble movements of expression, wrinkling of the forehead, distortion of the corners of the mouth, irregular movements of the tongue and lips . . . . Connected with these are further smacking and clicking of the tongue . . . [and] tremors of the muscles of the mouth . . . . Several patients continually carried out peculiar sprawling, irregular [jerky] outspreading movements . . . . (p. 83)

Thus, tardive dyskinesia is not a new phenomenon, introduced with the advent of antipsychotic medication. Crow and his colleagues also reported that dyskinesias were at least as prevalent in a group of schizophrenic patients who had never received drug treatment as in those who

had. In addition, they found no differences in either D_1 or D_2 receptors in the brains of deceased patients with or without a history of movement disorders. (See *Figure 18.4.*) There is no doubt that dyskinesias are made worse by dopaminergic agonists and are alleviated by dopaminergic antagonists, but the study by Crow and his colleagues suggests that supersensitivity may not be the cause. Clearly, this issue merits further research on both theoretical and practical grounds.

Schizophrenia as a Neurological Disorder

So far, I have been discussing the physiology of the positive symptoms of schizophrenia—principally, hallucinations, delusions, and thought disorders. These symptoms are plausibly related to one of the known functions of dopaminergic neurons: reinforcement. But the negative symptoms of schizophrenia—social withdrawal, flattened emotional reaction, and poverty of thought and speech—are very different. Whereas the positive symptoms are unique to schizophrenia (and to amphetamine or cocaine psychosis), the negative symptoms are similar to those produced by brain damage caused by several different means. Many pieces of evidence suggest that the negative symptoms of schizophrenia are a result of brain damage.

Evidence for Brain Damage in Schizophrenia

Although schizophrenia has been traditionally labeled as a psychiatric disorder, most patients with schizophrenia exhibit neurological symptoms that suggest the presence of brain damage. These symptoms include catatonia; facial dyskinesias; unusually high or low rates of blinking; staring and avoidance of eye contact; absent blink reflex in response to a tap on the forehead; episodes of deviation of the eyes (especially to the right), accompanied by speech arrest; paroxysmal bursts of jerky eye movements; very poor visual pursuit of a smoothly moving object; inability to move the eyes without moving the head; poor pupillary light reactions; and continuous elevation of the brows, causing characteristic horizontal creasing of the forehead (Stevens, 1982a). Although these symptoms can be caused

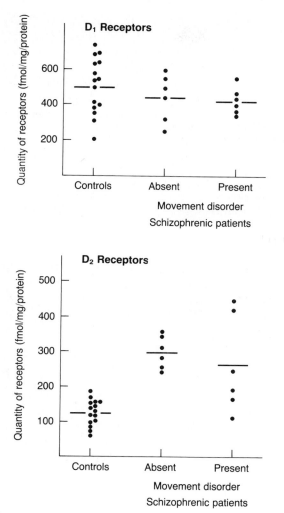

FIGURE 18.4

Quantity of D_1 and D_2 receptors in the brains of controls and schizophrenic patients with and without movement disorders. (From Crow, T.J., Cross, A.J., Johnstone, E.C., Owen, F., Owens, D.G.C., and Waddington, J.L. *Journal of Clinical Psychopharmacology,* 1982, *2,* 336–340. © The Williams & Wilkins Co., Baltimore.)

by a variety of neuropathological conditions and are hence not unique to schizophrenia, their presence suggests that schizophrenia may be associated with brain damage of some kind.

Several studies have found evidence of brain damage from CT and MRI scans of schizophrenic patients. For example, Weinberger and Wyatt (1982) obtained CT scans of eighty chronic schizo-

phrenics and sixty-six normal controls of the same mean age (twenty-nine years). Without knowledge of the patients' diagnoses, they measured the area of the lateral ventricles in the scan that cut through them at their largest extent, and they expressed this area relative to the area of brain tissue in the same scan. The relative ventricle size of the schizophrenic patients was more than twice as great as that of normal control subjects. (See *Figure 18.5.*) The most likely cause of the enlarged ventricles is therefore loss of brain tissue; thus, the CT scans provide evidence that chronic schizophrenia is associated with brain damage.

Figure 18.6 shows MRI scans from the brains of a schizophrenic patient and a normal volunteer that illustrate the difference that is often seen between them. (Of course, not all schizophrenic brains are as abnormal as this one.) You can easily see the enlargement of the posterior horns of the lateral ventricles. In addition, the corpus callosum is almost completely absent; presumably, it failed to develop normally. (See *Figure 18.6.*)

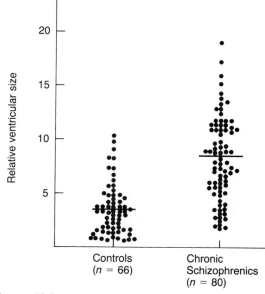

FIGURE 18.5

Relative ventricular size in chronic schizophrenics and controls. (From Weinberger, D.R., and Wyatt, R.J., in *Schizophrenia as a Brain Disease,* edited by F.A. Henn and H.A. Nasrallah. New York: Oxford University Press, 1982.)

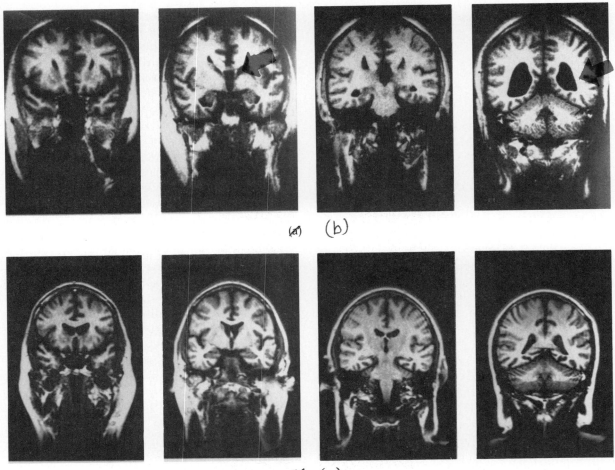

FIGURE 18.6
MRI scans. (a) A normal subject. (b) A person with schizophrenia. Arrows mark the almost complete absence of the corpus callosum and enlarged posterior horns of the lateral ventricles. (From Andreasen, N.C. *Science*, 1988, *239*, 1381–1388.)

Bogerts (1989) compared CT scans of fifty-four schizophrenic patients and age-matched controls, making careful measurements of all the ventricles and major fissures and sulci. He found evidence for a loss of tissue in the frontal lobes, anterior temporal lobes, and hypothalamus. There was no relation between any of his measurements and the duration of the illness, which suggests that the changes in the brain occur early in life. Andreasen (1988) notes that the brains of many schizophrenic patients show abnormalities in the shape of the corpus callosum and hippo-campus, which are embryologically related. This fact suggests that the abnormalities may occur during brain development.

Causes of the Brain Damage

As we saw earlier, schizophrenia is a heritable disease, but its heritability is less than perfect. Why do fewer than half the children of parents with chronic schizophrenia become schizophrenic? A possible answer is that what is inherited is a susceptibility to the damaging effects of a viral disease. If a child with schizophrenic parents contracts the disease, he or she is likely to develop brain damage. If a person without a family history of schizophrenia contracts the same disease, brain damage is unlikely.

No direct evidence for virally induced schizophrenia exists, but evidence reveals similarities between schizophrenia and known viral disorders. There is no doubt that viruses can cause brain damage. One example is the herpes simplex virus, which normally hides in the trigeminal nerve ganglion. From time to time, the virus emerges from its hiding place, following branches of the trigeminal nerve to the region around the mouth, where it produces harmless cold sores. In rare instances the virus goes the other way and enters the brain, where it damages neurons in the limbic cortex that borders the frontal and temporal lobes. In addition, the virus that caused the 1918 influenza epidemic caused brain damage in many patients and produced illnesses that resembled schizophrenia (Menninger, 1926).

Stevens (1988) notes some interesting similarities between schizophrenia and a known neuropathological condition, multiple sclerosis. As we saw in Chapter 2, multiple sclerosis appears to be an autoimmune disease—triggered by a virus—in which the patient's own immune system attacks myelin. The natural histories of multiple sclerosis and schizophrenia are similar in several ways. Both diseases are more prevalent and more malignant in people who spent their childhood in latitudes far from the equator. Both diseases are more common in people with low socioeconomic status, who live in crowded, deprived conditions. Both diseases are characterized by one of three general courses: (1) attacks followed by remissions, many of which produce no residual deficits; (2) recurrent attacks with only partial remissions, causing an increasingly major deficit; or (3) an insidious onset with a steady and relentless progression, leading to permanent and severe deficits. These similarities suggest that schizophrenia, like multiple sclerosis, could be a virally induced autoimmune disease.

There is evidence that suggests that at least some cases of schizophrenia may involve an autoimmune process. Olivia and Torrey (1985) found high levels of interferon in 24 percent of patients with schizophrenia but only 3 percent of control subjects. The presence of this compound suggests that immune system is particularly active. In addition, Sugiura et al. (1989) found auto-antibodies against various components of the brain in the blood of 28 percent of the schizophrenic patients that they studied. (Unfortunately, the investigators did not make comparisons with normal controls.)

Schizophrenia could also be caused by brain damage produced by obstetrical problems. I mentioned earlier in this chapter that some monozygotic twins are discordant for schizophrenia; that is, one of them develops schizophrenic and the other does not. In these cases the schizophrenic twin is more likely to have undergone complications during delivery (Gottesman and Bertelsen, 1989).

A third possible cause of schizophrenia is interference with normal prenatal brain development. Several studies show that people born during the winter months are more likely to develop schizophrenia later in life. Torrey, Torrey, and Peterson (1977) suggest that the causal factor could be seasonal variations in nutritional factors or—more likely—variations in toxins or infectious agents in air, water, or food. The fact that known viruses such as rubeola (measles), rubella (German measles), and varicella (chicken pox) show similar seasonality suggests that the causal factor might be a virus. The "seasonality effect" is seen more strongly in poor, urban locations, where people are at greater risk for viral infections (Machon, Mednick, and Schulsinger, 1983).

A seasonally related virus could affect either a pregnant woman or her newborn infant. Two pieces of evidence suggest that the damage is done prenatally. First, brain development is more susceptible to disruption prenatally than postnatally. Second, a study of the offspring of women who were pregnant during an epidemic of type A2 influenza in Finland during 1957 showed an elevated incidence of schizophrenia (Mednick, Machon, and Huttunen, 1990). The increased incidence was seen only in the children of women who were in the second trimester of their pregnancy when the epidemic occurred. (See *Figure 18.7.*) Presumably, the viral infection produced toxins that interfered with the brain development

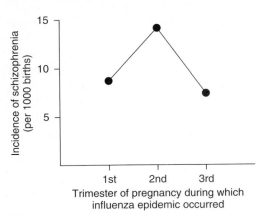

Figure 18.7
Incidence of schizophrenia in the offspring of women who were pregnant during the 1957 influenza epidemic in Finland. (Prepared from data of Mednick, S.A., Machon, R.A., and Huttunen, M.O. *Archives of General Psychiatry*, 1990, 47, 292.)

of some of the fetuses, resulting in the development of schizophrenia later in life.

Relation Between Brain Damage and Positive and Negative Symptoms

The evidence reviewed in the previous two subsections indicates that schizophrenia is associated with brain damage, which may occur prenatally, during childbirth, or postnatally. Presumably, developmental problems or brain damage that occurs during childbirth is not related to hereditary factors, but postnatal brain damage may be caused by an autoimmune disease triggered in a genetically susceptible individual by a virus. Even if the brain damage associated with schizophrenia can really be caused by three different means, we would at least expect some similarity in the location of the damage.

As we have seen, CT and MRI scans have found that schizophrenia is associated with damage to the frontal lobes, anterior temporal lobes, and hypothalamus. Miller (1988) suggests that schizophrenia should be viewed as a progressive disorder—that an abnormality in the brain causes excessive activation of some neurons. (He leaves open the question of just what neurons are involved. Presumably, damage to a set of inhibitory neurons—caused by any of the three means

outlined above—could produce this activation.) The activity of these neurons causes overactivity of the neurons they excite, which produces the positive symptoms of schizophrenia. Eventually, the continuous activation leads to neural degeneration, in a manner similar to that produced by injections of excitatory amino acids.

Miller's hypothesis suggests that positive and negative symptoms are part of the same process; the positive symptoms are produced by the overactivity, and the negative symptoms are produced by the ensuing brain damage. He suggests that some research effort should be devoted to investigating the possibility that the damage could be prevented by reducing the overactivity, perhaps through the administration of NMDA antagonists. (As we saw in Chapter 15, NMDA receptors are involved in excitotoxic neural damage.)

A different hypothesis is proposed by Weinberger (1988), who believes that the brain damage associated with schizophrenia occurs early in life and that the negative symptoms are produced by hypoactivity of the frontal lobes. As I mentioned earlier, the negative symptoms of schizophrenia are not peculiar to this disorder but are seen in many people who have sustained brain damage, particularly to the frontal lobes.

One of the most reliable tests of the functions of the dorsolateral prefrontal cortex is the Wisconsin Card Sort Test (WCST). In this test subjects are presented with a deck of cards that contain patterns that differ in number, shape, and color. The cards contain between one and four objects having one of four shapes and one of four different colors. The subjects are instructed to pick up the cards, one at a time, and place each of them in one of four piles, according to the number, shape, or color. The experimenter does not tell the subjects what the criterion is; he or she simply says "right" or "wrong" after each response. Once the subjects learn to respond appropriately (which usually does not take very long), the experimenter changes the criterion without warning. For example, if the first criterion was number, the second one might be color. People with damage to the dorsolateral prefrontal cortex learn the first task as rapidly as normal subjects do, but they have great difficulty switching their strategy when the criterion changes; they persist with the outmoded strategy. Thus, one of the functions of the dorso-lateral prefrontal cortex is related to behavioral flexibility.

Weinberger, Berman, and Zec (1986) tested schizophrenic patients and normal control subjects on a computerized version of the WCST, in which patterns were presented on a color video screen and subjects had to respond by pressing one of four switches. While the subjects were performing the task, they breathed air containing radioactive xenon. An array of detectors arranged around the subjects' heads measured the radioactive decay of the xenon, permitting a computer to calculate the regional blood flow. (See *Figure 18.8.*)

Weinberger and his colleagues found that the schizophrenic patients performed poorly on the task, just as subjects with lesions of the dorsolateral prefrontal cortex do. In addition, whereas the lateral prefrontal cortex of the normal subjects showed an increased blood flow during the card-sorting task, the cortex of the schizophrenic subjects did not. The results are shown in Color Plate 5.4, which was presented earlier to illustrate the measurement of regional cerebral blood flow. The two scans on the left were made while the subjects were performing a simple number-matching task that is not impaired by lesions of the dorsolateral prefrontal cortex; as you can see, the blood flow is similar for both groups. The two scans on the right were made during the sorting task; in this case only the normal subjects showed signs of increased activation of the lateral prefrontal cortex. (See *Color Plate 5.4.*)

What might cause the "hypofrontality" that Weinberger and his colleagues have observed? They believe that the primary cause may be subcortical lesions or abnormalities that reduce the dopaminergic input to the prefrontal cortex. In fact, Weinberger, Berman, and Illowsky (1988) found that the concentration of a dopamine breakdown product in the cerebrospinal fluid of schizophrenic patients (homovanillic acid, or HVA) was correlated with the activity of the prefrontal cortex, as measured by regional cerebral blood flow. That is, subjects with evidence for higher levels of activity of dopaminergic neurons had frontal lobes that were more active. In addition, studies with monkeys indicate that destruction of

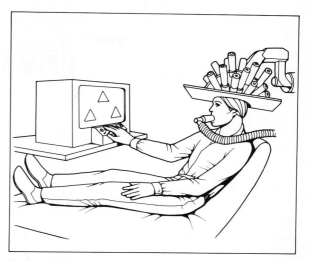

FIGURE 18.8

The automated card-sorting task and the apparatus for determining regional cerebral blood flow. (Adapted from Weinberger, D.R., Berman, K.F., and Zec, R.F. *Archives of General Psychiatry*, 1986, *43*, 114–124.)

the dopaminergic input to the prefrontal cortex lowers its metabolic rate and leads to cognitive dysfunctions (Brozowski, Brown, Rosvold, and Goldman, 1979; Schwartzman, Alexander, Grothusen, and Stahl, 1987).

Of course, this hypothesis must be reconciled with the dopamine hypothesis, which states that the positive symptoms of schizophrenia are produced by *hyperactivity* of dopaminergic synapses. Weinberger, Berman, and Zec (1986) suggest that the inhibition of the prefrontal cortex causes an excitation of the mesolimbic system. In fact, Pycock, Kerwin, and Carter (1980) found that 6-HD lesions of the prefrontal cortex of rats (that is, destruction of the dopaminergic input) increased the activity of dopaminergic terminals in the nucleus accumbens and the neostriatum. Perhaps, then, the negative symptoms of schizophrenia are caused by *hypoactivity* of dopaminergic neurons in the frontal lobes and the positive symptoms are caused by *hyperactivity* in the nucleus accumbens. (See *Figure 18.9.*)

In the interest of clarity and brevity, I have been selective in my review of research on schizophrenia. This puzzling and serious disorder has stimulated many ingenious hypotheses and

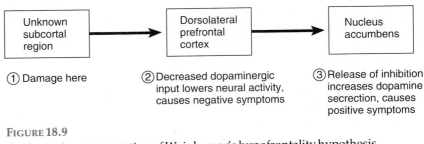

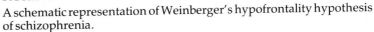

FIGURE 18.9

A schematic representation of Weinberger's hypofrontality hypothesis of schizophrenia.

much research. Some hypotheses have been proved wrong; others have not yet been adequately tested. Possibly, future research will find that all of these hypotheses (including the ones I have discussed) are incorrect, or that one that I have not mentioned is correct. However, I am impressed with recent research, and I believe that we have real hope of finding the causes of schizophrenia in the near future. With the discovery of the causes we can hope for the discovery of methods of prevention.

INTERIM SUMMARY

Researchers have made considerable progress in the past few years in their study of the physiology of mental disorders, but many puzzles still remain. Schizophrenia consists of positive and negative symptoms, the former involving the presence of an unusual behavior and the latter involving the absence of a normal behavior. Because schizophrenia is at least somewhat heritable, it appears to have a biological basis. But evidence indicates that not all cases are caused by heredity, and some people who appear to carry a "schizophrenia gene" do not become schizophrenic. The location of this gene (if, indeed, a single gene exists) may be the long arm of chromosome 5 or the end of the X chromosome, in the pseudoautosomal segment.

The dopamine hypothesis—inspired by the findings that dopamine antagonists alleviate the positive symptoms of schizophrenia and that dopamine agonists increase or

even produce them—is still dominant. This hypothesis states that the positive symptoms of schizophrenia are caused by hyperactivity of dopaminergic synapses. There is no evidence that an abnormally large amount of dopamine is released, but some studies indicate that the brains of schizophrenic patients contain increased numbers of D_2 dopamine receptors in the neostriatum. However, some investigators have suggested that the increase is caused by the administration of antipsychotic drugs. It is still possible that an abnormality exists in the dopaminergic systems that project to the nucleus accumbens or prefrontal cortex. The involvement of dopamine in reinforcement could plausibly explain the positive effects of schizophrenia.

The fact that some patients are not helped by antipsychotic drugs poses an unsolved problem for the dopamine hypothesis. In addition, the existence of tardive dyskinesia, presumably a result of supersensitivity of dopamine receptors provoked by the administration of antipsychotic drugs, raises the question of why a tardive schizophrenia is not also observed. On the other hand, some studies suggest that the disorder can occur even in patients who have not received antipsychotic medication.

CT and MRI scans indicate that brain damage is associated with the negative symptoms of schizophrenia. Studies of the epidemiology of schizophrenia suggest that, as in multiple sclerosis, one of the causes may be an autoimmune process produced by an infection in people who are genetically vulnerable. In addition, the disorder may be caused by obstetrical problems or by toxins (such as those produced by viral infections) that are present during pregnancy.

Miller suggests that positive symptoms are created by the removal of inhibitory control on dopaminergic neurons, which causes both positive symptoms and, through overstimulation, brain damage. His hypothesis suggests that the brain damage occurs over a period of time. Weinberger suggests that the brain damage occurs early and that it decreases the dopaminergic input to the dorsolateral prefrontal cortex, causing hypoactivity and accounting for the negative symptoms. The positive symptoms occur because the low activity of the prefrontal cortex causes an increase in the dopaminergic system that projects to the nucleus accumbens.

MAJOR AFFECTIVE DISORDERS

Affect, as a noun, refers to feelings or emotions. Just as the primary symptom of schizophrenia is disordered thoughts, the *major affective disorders* (also called *mood disorders*) are characterized by disordered feelings.

Description

Feelings and emotions are essential parts of human existence; they represent our evaluation of the events in our lives. In a very real sense, feelings and emotions are what human life is all about. The emotional state of most of us reflects what is happening to us: Our feelings are tied to events in the real world, and they are usually the result of reasonable assessments of the importance these events have for our lives. But for some people, affect becomes divorced from reality. These people have feelings of extreme elation (*mania*) or despair (*depression*) that are not justified by events in their lives. For example, depression that accompanies the loss of a loved one is normal, but depression that becomes a way of life, and will not respond to the sympathetic effort of friends

and relatives or even to psychotherapy, is pathological.

Almost everyone experiences some depression from time to time, mostly caused by events that sadden us. This form of depression is called *reactive depression* because it occurs as a reaction to events in the world. The form of depression seen in the major affective disorders is quite different. It seems to be an intrinsic characteristic of the person rather than a reaction to the environment; thus, it is referred to as *endogenous depression.*

There are two principal types of major affective disorders. The first type is characterized by alternating periods of mania and depression—a condition called *bipolar disorder.* This disorder afflicts men and women in approximately equal numbers. Episodes of mania can last a few days or several months, but they usually take a few weeks to run their course. The episodes of depression that follow generally last three times as long as the mania. The second type is *unipolar depression,* or depression without mania. This depression may be continuous and unremitting or, more typically, may come in episodes. Unipolar depression strikes women two to three times more often than men. Mania without periods of depression sometimes occurs, but it is rare.

Severely depressed people usually feel extremely unworthy and have strong feelings of guilt. The affective disorders are dangerous; a person who suffers from endogenous depression runs a considerable risk of death by suicide. Depressed people have very little energy, and they move and talk slowly, sometimes becoming almost torpid. At other times they may pace around restlessly and aimlessly. They may cry a lot. They are unable to experience pleasure; they lose their appetite for food and sex. Their sleep is disturbed; they usually fall asleep readily but awaken early and find it difficult to get to sleep again. (In contrast, people with reactive depression usually have trouble falling asleep and do not awaken early.) Even their body functions become depressed; they often become constipated, and secretion of saliva decreases.

Episodes of mania are characterized by a sense of euphoria that does not seem to be justified by circumstances. The diagnosis of mania is partly a matter of degree—one would not call exuberance and a zest for life pathological. People with mania usually exhibit nonstop speech and motor activity. They flit from topic to topic and often have delusions, but they lack the severe disorganization that is seen in schizophrenia. They are usually full of their own importance and often become angry or defensive if they are contradicted. Frequently, they go for long periods without sleep, working furiously on projects that are often unrealistic. (Sometimes, their work is fruitful; George Frederic Handel wrote *The Messiah*, one of the masterpieces of choral music, during one of his periods of mania.)

Heritability

The tendency to develop an affective disorder appears to be heritable. For example, Rosenthal (1971) found that close relatives of people who suffer from affective psychoses are ten times more likely to develop these disorders than people without afflicted relatives. Of course, this study does not prove that genetic mechanisms are operating; relatives have similar environments as well as similar genes. However, Gershon, Bunney, Leckman, Van Eerdewegh, and DeBauche (1976) found that if one member of a set of monozygotic twins was afflicted with an affective disorder, the likelihood that the other twin was similarly afflicted was 69 percent. In contrast, the concordance rate for dizygotic twins was only 13 percent. Furthermore, the concordance rate for monozygotic twins appears to be the same whether the twins were raised together or apart (Price, 1968). The heritability of the affective disorders implies they have a physiological basis.

For a while, it looked as if the locus of a gene responsible for bipolar disorder had been found. Egeland et al. (1987) studied a large Amish family that contained several members with bipolar disorder. They correlated the presence or absence of the disorder with the presence or absence of various proteins in the blood that are controlled by genes with known locations. They concluded that the gene appeared to be located at the tip of the short arm of chromosome 11. However, several studies failed to confirm their results in other families (Byerley et al., 1989), and finally, after having found more family members and reanalyzing the data, Kelsoe et al. (1989) concluded that the earlier study was mistaken.

Physiological Treatments

There are four effective biological treatments for endogenous depression: monoamine oxidase (MAO) inhibitors, the tricyclic antidepressant drugs, electroconvulsive therapy (ECT), and sleep deprivation. Bipolar disorder is effectively treated by lithium salts. The response of these disorders to medical treatment provides additional evidence that they have a physiological basis. Furthermore, the fact that lithium is very effective in treating bipolar affective disorders but not unipolar depression suggests that there is a fundamental difference between these two illnesses.

Prior to the 1950s there was no effective drug treatment for depression. In the late 1940s clinicians noticed that some drugs used for treating tuberculosis seemed to elevate the patient's mood. Researchers subsequently found that a derivative of these drugs, iproniazid, reduced symptoms of psychotic depression (Crane, 1957). Iproniazid inhibits the activity of MAO, which destroys excess monoamine transmitter substances within terminal buttons. Thus, the drug increases the release of dopamine, norepinephrine, and serotonin. Other MAO inhibitors were soon discovered. Unfortunately, MAO inhibitors can have harmful side effects. The most common problem is the *cheese effect*. Many foods (for example, cheese, yogurt, wine, yeast breads, chocolate, and various fruits and nuts) contain *pressor amines*—substances similar to catecholamines. Normally, these amines are deactivated by MAO, which is present in the blood and in other tissues of the body. But a person who is being treated with an MAO inhibitor may suffer a serious sympathetic reaction after eating food containing pressor amines. The pressor amines simulate the effects of increased activity of the sympathetic nervous system, increasing blood pressure and heart rate. The reaction can raise blood pressure enough to produce intracranial bleeding or cardiovascular collapse.

Fortunately, another class of antidepressant drugs was soon discovered that did not produce a cheese effect: the *tricyclic antidepressants*. These drugs were found to inhibit the reuptake of 5-HT and norepinephrine by terminal buttons. By retarding reuptake, the drugs keep the neurotransmitter in contact with the postsynaptic receptors, thus prolonging the postsynaptic potentials. Thus, both the MAO inhibitors and the tricyclic antidepressant drugs are monoaminergic agonists.

A depressed patient does not respond immediately to treatment with MAO inhibitors or to one of the tricyclic antidepressant drugs; improvement in symptoms is not usually seen before two to three weeks of drug treatment. In contrast, the effects of ECT are more rapid. (ECT was described in Chapter 15.) A few seizures induced by ECT can often snap a person out of a deep depression within a few days. Although prolonged and excessive use of ECT causes brain damage, resulting in long-lasting impairments in memory (Squire, 1974), the judicious use of ECT during the interim period before antidepressant drugs become effective has undoubtedly saved the lives of some suicidal patients (Baldessarini, 1977). In addition, some severely depressed people are not helped by drug therapy; for them, occasional ECT is the only effective treatment.

The therapeutic effect of *lithium,* the drug used to treat bipolar affective disorders, is very rapid. This drug, which is administered in the form of lithium carbonate, is most effective in treating the manic phase of a bipolar affective disorder; once the mania is eliminated, depression usually does not follow (Gerbino, Oleshansky, and Gershon, 1978). Many clinicians and investigators have referred to lithium as psychiatry's wonder drug: It does not suppress normal feelings of emotions, but it leaves patients able to feel and express joy and sadness to events in their lives. Similarly, it does not impair intellectual processes; many patients have received the drug continuously for years without any apparent ill effects (Fieve, 1979). Reifman and Wyatt (1980) calculated that during a ten-year period in the United States lithium treatment saved at least $4 billion in treatment costs and lost productivity.

Investigators have not yet discovered the pharmacological effects of lithium that are responsible for its ability to eliminate mania. Some suggest that the drug stabilizes the population of certain classes of neurotransmitter receptors in the brain, thus preventing wide shifts in neural sensitivity. A later section will describe research with other drugs that suggests the relevance of receptor sensitivity to the treatment of the affective disorders.

Role of Monoamines

The fact that depression can be treated effectively with tricyclic antidepressants and MAO inhibitors, both of which are monoamine agonists, suggested the *monoamine hypothesis:* Depression is caused by insufficient activity of monoaminergic neurons. Because the symptoms of depression do not respond to potent dopamine agonists such as amphetamine or cocaine, most investigators have focused their research efforts on the other two monoamines: norepinephrine and serotonin.

The Monoamine Hypothesis

As we saw, the dopamine hypothesis of schizophrenia receives support from the fact that dopamine agonists can produce the symptoms of schizophrenia. Similarly, the monoamine hypothesis of depression receives support from the fact that depression can be caused by monoamine antagonists. Many hundreds of years ago, an alkaloid extract from *Rauwolfia serpentina,* a shrub of Southeast Asia, was found to be useful for treating snakebite, circulatory disorders, and insanity. Modern research has confirmed that the alkaloid, now called reserpine, has both an antipsychotic effect and a hypotensive effect (that is, it lowers blood pressure). The effect on blood pressure precludes its use in treating schizophrenia, but the drug is still occasionally used to treat patients with high blood pressure.

Reserpine has a serious side effect: It can cause depression. In fact, in the early years of its use as a hypotensive agent, up to 15 percent of the people who received it became depressed (Sachar and Baron, 1979). Reserpine acts on the membrane of synaptic vesicles in the terminal buttons of monoaminergic neurons, making the membranes "leaky," so that the neurotransmitters are lost from the vesicles and are destroyed by MAO. Thus, the drug serves as a potent norepinephrine, dopamine, and serotonin antagonist. The pharmacological and behavioral effects of reserpine complement the pharmacological and behavioral effects of the drugs used to treat depression—MAO inhibitors and most of the tricyclic antidepressants. That is, a monoamine antagonist produces depression, whereas monoamine agonists alleviate it.

Several studies have found that suicidal depression is related to decreased CSF levels of *5-HIAA* (5-hydroxyindoleacetic acid), a metabolite of serotonin that is produced when serotonin is destroyed by MAO. A decreased level of 5-HIAA implies that less 5-HT (serotonin) is being produced and released in the brain. Träskmann, Åsberg, Bertilsson, and Sjöstrand (1981) found that CSF levels of 5-HIAA in people who had attempted suicide were significantly lower than those of controls. In a follow-up study of depressed and potentially suicidal patients, 20 percent of those with levels of 5-HIAA below the median subsequently killed themselves, whereas none of those with levels above the median committed suicide. More recent studies have confirmed these results (Roy, De Jong, and Linnoila, 1989).

Sedvall et al., (1980) analyzed the CSF of healthy, nondepressed volunteers. The families of subjects with unusually low levels of 5-HIAA were more likely to include people with depression. The results suggest that serotonin metabolism or release is genetically controlled and that it is linked to depression. Thus, these findings clearly support the monoamine hypothesis.

Long-Term Changes in Receptor Sensitivity

Although researchers have known for a long time that depression does not respond immediately to antidepressant medication, they investigated the effects of these drugs by studying their acute, immediate pharmacological effects in animals. In recent years the approach to the study of the pharmacological effects of antidepressant drugs has changed. Perhaps the acute effects of the drugs, such as the blocking of monoamine reuptake and the inhibition of MAO, are not the pharmacological effects that relieve the symptoms of depression. Instead, the relevant effects may take two to three weeks to develop, because the delay in symptom reduction takes this long.

Sulser and Sanders-Bush (1989) reviewed research that suggests that the long-term effect of most, if not all, biological treatments for depression causes a *subsensitivity* of postsynaptic noradrenergic β receptors. The subsensitivity, which is just the opposite of denervation supersensitivity, appears to be caused by a decreased number of β receptors. Table 18.1 illustrates some of the drugs and other biological treatments that are effective in reducing the symptoms of depression and that also reduce the sensitivity of β receptors. To be effective, these treatments must be applied chronically, over many days; subsensitivity is not produced by short-term treatment. (See *Table 18.1*.)

As you can see, a wide variety of antidepressant treatments—drugs that block the reuptake of 5-HT or norepinephrine, MAO inhibitors, GABA agonists, a phosphodiesterase inhibitor, ECT, and sleep deprivation—all affect the sensitivity of noradrenergic β receptors. (I will discuss the significance of sleep deprivation later.) The change in sensitivity of the noradrenergic β receptors takes about as much time as the therapeutic response does. Electroconvulsive therapy, the treatment that produces the quickest therapeutic effects, also produces the fastest change in sensitivity of β receptors. (The mechanism by which ECT affects these receptors is not known.) In addition, reserpine, which can produce symptoms of depression, makes β receptors *super*sensitive (Leonard, 1982).

Studies have suggested that at least one of the ways that antidepressant treatments produce subsensitivity of β receptors is by first stimulating them. This finding implies that the subsensitivity is a regulatory response, just as supersensitivity is a response to drugs that block receptors or prevent the release of the neurotransmitter. For example, Janowsky, Steranka, and Sulser (1981) made unilateral lesions in the locus coeruleus, which contains noradrenergic neurons. They then administered long-term desipramine treatments and observed subsensitivity only on the nonlesioned side. Desipramine is a noradrenergic agonist by virtue of its ability to block the reuptake of norepinephrine. Thus, it could have no effect

TABLE 18.1

Antidepressant treatments that produce subsensitivity of noradrenergic β receptors.

Antidepressant drugs that block reuptake of 5-HT and norepinephrine (NE)

Chlorimipramine
Imipramine
Amitriptyline

Antidepressant drugs that predominantly block reuptake of NE

Desipramine
Nisoxetine

Antidepressant drugs that predominantly block reuptake of 5-HT

Fluvoxamine
Sertraline
Fluoxetine

Antidepressant drugs that block MAO

Pargyline
Nialamide
Tranylcypromine
Moclobemide

Antidepressant drugs that act as GABA agonists

Fengabine
Bupropion

Antidepressant drugs that act as phosphodiesterase inhibitors

Rolipram

Electroconvulsive therapy

REM sleep deprivation

SOURCE: Adapted from Sulser, F., in *Typical and Atypical Antidepressants: Molecular Mechanisms,* edited by E. Costa and G. Racagni. New York: Raven Press, 1982; and Sulser, F., and Sanders-Bush, E., in *Tribute to B.B. Brodie,* edited by E. Costa. New York: Raven Press, 1989.

thesis with injections of PCPA prevents antidepressant drugs from making noradrenergic β_2 receptors become less sensitive. Thus, therapeutic effects of antidepressant treatment appear to require the participation of serotonergic neurons.

Little can be said about the physiological relevance of the subsensitivity of β receptors. For example, desipramine acts acutely as a noradrenergic agonist, but its chronic effect would appear to classify it as a noradrenergic antagonist. What, then, is the net effect of this drug on the noradrenergic synapses? Are antidepressant treatments correcting overactivity or underactivity of noradrenergic synapses? We still do not have enough information to answer these questions.

As you learned in Chapter 16, reinforcement involves the release of dopamine in the nucleus accumbens. Because inability to experience pleasure is one of the most important symptoms of depression, we might expect to find some involvement of dopaminergic neurons in this disorder. However, Reynecke, Allin, Russell, and Taljaard (1989) found that chronic desipramine treatment had no effect on the sensitivity of D_1 or D_2 dopamine receptors in the nucleus accumbens; nor did it affect the release of dopamine by electrical stimulation. Therefore, of the three monoamines, only serotonin and norepinephrine have been shown to play a role in depression.

Role of Circadian Rhythms

One of the most prominent symptoms of depression is disordered sleep. The sleep of people with endogenous depression tends to be shallow; slow-wave delta sleep (stages 3 and 4) is reduced and stage 1 is increased. Sleep is fragmented; people tend to waken frequently, especially toward the morning. In addition, REM sleep occurs earlier, the first half of the night contains a higher proportion of REM periods, and REM sleep contains an increased number of rapid eye movements (Kupfer, 1976; Vogel, Vogel, McAbee, and Thurmond, 1980). (See *Figure 18.10.*)

REM Sleep Deprivation

One of the most effective antidepressant treatments is sleep deprivation, either total or selec-

on the lesioned side, because the noradrenergic axons there had degenerated.

As we saw earlier, suicidally depressed people have low levels of 5-HIAA in their cerebrospinal fluid, which implies that the serotonergic neurons in their brains are hypoactive. There appears to be an important link between serotonergic and noradrenergic neurons; Sulser and Sanders-Bush (1989) note that studies have shown that destruction of 5-HT neurons or the blocking of 5-HT syn-

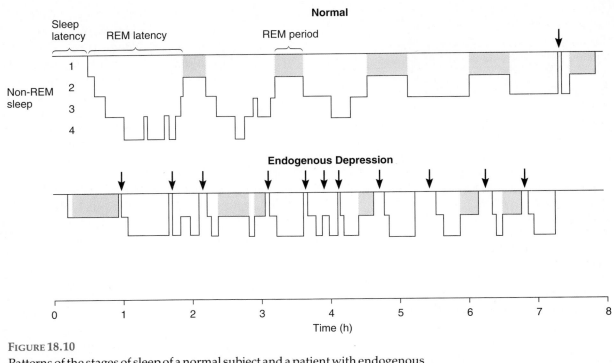

FIGURE 18.10

Patterns of the stages of sleep of a normal subject and a patient with endogenous depression. Note the reduced sleep latency, reduced REM latency, reduction in slow-wave sleep (stages 3 and 4), and general fragmentation of sleep (arrows) in the depressed patient. (From Gillin, J.C., and Borbély, A.A. *Trends in Neurosciences*, 1985, *8*, 537–542.)

tive. Selective deprivation of REM sleep, accomplished by monitoring people's EEG and awakening them whenever they show signs of REM sleep, alleviates depression (Vogel et al., 1975; Vogel, Buffenstein, Minter, and Hennessey, 1990). The therapeutic effect, like that of the antidepressant medications, occurs slowly, over the course of several weeks. Some patients show long-term improvement even after the deprivation is discontinued; thus, it is a practical as well as an effective treatment. In addition, regardless of their specific pharmacological effects, other treatments for depression suppress REM sleep, delaying its onset and decreasing its duration. These facts suggest that REM sleep and mood might somehow be causally related.

Scherschlicht, Polc, Schneeberger, Steiner, and Haefely (1982) examined the effects of twenty antidepressant drugs on the sleep cycles of cats and found that all of them profoundly reduced REM sleep and most of them increased slow-wave

sleep. In an extensive review of the literature Vogel, Buffenstein, Minter, and Hennessey (1990) found that all drugs that suppressed REM sleep (and produced a rebound effect when their administration was discontinued) acted as antidepressants. These results suggest that the primary effect of antidepressant medication may be to suppress REM sleep, and the changes in mood may be a result of this suppression. However, some drugs that relieve the symptoms of depression (such as iprindole and trimipramine) do not suppress REM sleep. Thus, suppression of REM sleep cannot be the *only* way that antidepressant drugs work.

Studies of families with a history of endogenous depression also suggest a link between this disorder and abnormalities in REM sleep. For example, Giles, Roffwarg, and Rush (1987) found that first-degree relatives of people with depression are likely to show a short REM sleep latency, even if they have not yet had an episode of depression. Giles, Biggs, Rush, and Roffwarg (1988) found that the members of these families who had the lowest REM latency had the highest risk of subsequently becoming depressed. Abnormalities in REM sleep are seen early in life; Coble, Scher, Reynolds, Day, and Kupfer (1988) found that newborn infants of mothers with a history of endogenous depression showed patterns of REM sleep that were different from those of the infants of mothers without such a history.

Vogel, Neill, Hagler, and Kors (1990) have developed what they believe to be an animal model of depression, which may be useful in studying the physiological basis of this disorder. They gave young rats injections of clomipramine (an antidepressant drug that blocks the reuptake of 5-HT) twice a day from age eight days to twenty-one days. This early treatment appears to have affected the development of the brain; perhaps, the authors suggest, it permanently decreased the sensitivity of postsynaptic serotonin receptors. Later, when the rats reached maturity, they showed many of the symptoms of endogenous depression: decreased sexual behavior, increased irritability, and decreased pleasure-seeking behavior (specifically, decreased willingness to work for reinforcing brain stimulation or for a taste of sucrose). The animals' sleep was also altered; the latency to the first bout of REM sleep was shorter, and the proportion of REM sleep was higher. The animals even responded to antidepressant treatment; imipramine and REM sleep deprivation both increased sexual behavior.

Total Sleep Deprivation

Total sleep deprivation also has an antidepressant effect. Unlike specific deprivation of REM sleep, which takes several weeks to reduce depression, total sleep deprivation produces immediate effects (Wu and Bunney, 1990). Figure 18.11 shows the mood rating of a patient who stayed awake one night; as you can see, the depression was lifted by the sleep deprivation but returned the next day, after a normal night's sleep. (See *Figure 18.11.*)

Wu and Bunney suggest that during sleep, a substance is produced that has a *depressogenic* effect. That is, the substance produces depression in a susceptible person. Presumably, this sub-

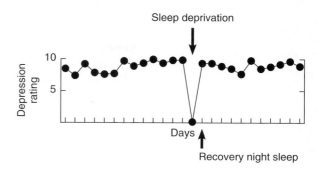

FIGURE 18.11

Changes in the depression rating of a depressed patient produced by a single night's total sleep deprivation. (From Wu, J.C., and Bunney, W.E. *American Journal of Psychiatry*, 1990, *147*, 14–21.)

stance is produced in the brain and acts as a neuromodulator. During waking, this substance is gradually metabolized and hence inactivated. Some of the evidence for this hypothesis is presented in Figure 18.12. The data are taken from eight different studies (cited by Wu and Bunney, 1990) and show self-ratings of depression of people who did and did not respond to sleep deprivation. (Total sleep deprivation improves the mood of patients with endogenous depression approximately two-thirds of the time.) People who responded to the sleep depression started the day depressed, but their mood gradually improved. This improvement continued through the sleepless night and during the following day. The next night they were permitted to sleep normally, and their depression was back the next morning. The data are consistent with the hypothesis that sleep produces a substance with a depressogenic effect. (See *Figure 18.12.*)

An alternative interpretation of the results we just saw is that waking might produce a substance with *antidepressant* effects, which is destroyed during sleep. However, Wu and Bunney point out that several studies have found that for some subjects a short nap reinstates the depression that had been reduced by sleep deprivation. In some cases a nap as short as 90 seconds (timed by EEG monitoring) can eliminate the beneficial effects of sleep depression. They conclude that the simplest hypotheses is that a nap produces a sudden secretion of a substance that causes depression. It

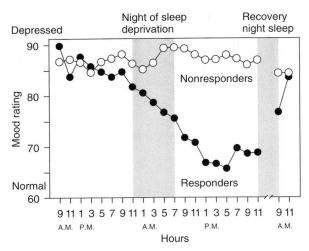

FIGURE 18.12

Mean mood rating of responding and nonresponding patients deprived of one night's sleep as a function of the time of day. (From Wu, J.C., and Bunney, W.E. *American Journal of Psychiatry,* 1990, *147,* 14–21.)

seems less likely that a nap could be responsible for the sudden *destruction* of a substance with an antidepressant effect.

The relation between the antidepressant effects of REM sleep deprivation and that of total sleep deprivation are unclear. They may very well be produced by different means, because one is slow and long-lasting, whereas the other is fast and short-lived. At the present time, total sleep deprivation does not provide a practical way of reducing people's depression, but biochemical comparisons made in people before and after sleep depression may provide some useful information about the physiological causes of depression.

Role of Zeitgebers

Yet another phenomenon relates depression to sleep and waking—or, more specifically, to the phenomena responsible for circadian rhythms. Some people become depressed during the winter season, when days are short and nights are long. The symptoms of this form of depression, called **seasonal affective disorder,** are somewhat different from those of major depression; both forms include lethargy and sleep disturbances, but seasonal depression includes a craving for car-

bohydrate and an accompanying weight gain. (As you will recall, people with major depression tend to lose their appetite.)

Seasonal affective disorder can be treated by exposing people to bright light for several hours a day (Rosenthal et al., 1985). As you will recall, circadian rhythms of sleep and wakefulness are controlled by the activity of the suprachiasmatic nucleus of the hypothalamus. Light serves as a *zeitgeber;* that is, it synchronizes the activity of the biological clock to the day-night cycle. It is possible that people with seasonal affective disorder require a stronger-than-normal zeitgeber to reset their biological clock.

Many people are sensitive to seasonal changes in the hours of sunlight and darkness. Ninety-two percent of the respondents to a survey by Kasper et al. (1989a) said that they noticed seasonal changes in their mood, 27 percent reported that these changes caused problems, and 4 percent reported problems severe enough to qualify as a seasonal affective disorder. Kasper et al. (1989b) recruited people with "winter blahs" through newspaper advertisements. They excluded people with evidence of a true seasonal affective disorder and exposed the others to bright light each day. They found that the exposure to bright light improved the mood of the subjects with the "blahs," whereas the mood of normal subjects was not changed. Of course, a placebo effect may have affected the results, but it is difficult to imagine how one could design a double-blind study in which subjects would spend a few hours each day under a bright light without noticing it. In any case, the study suggests that we should consider increasing the level of illumination in the home or workplace. The only negative aspect of the change would seem to be a higher electric bill.

It is possible that all the phenomena discussed in this section are related in a fundamental way. Goodwin, Wirz-Justice, and Wehr (1982) have suggested that all affective disorders are caused by a disturbance in circadian rhythms. As we saw in Chapter 9, several hormonal and biochemical systems (such as the secretion of growth hormone) are linked to various stages of sleep. In a depressed person some of these systems may become uncoupled from the normal control mechanisms, so that specific components of interrelated systems occur at the wrong times. One of the consequences of this uncoupling could be the production of a depressogenic substance during sleep.

Ehlers, Frank, and Kupfer (1988) have proposed an intriguing hypothesis that integrates behavioral and biological evidence. They suggest that some cases of depression may be triggered by the loss of social zeitgebers. They note that in humans social interactions, as well as light, may serve as zeitgebers. For example, people tend to synchronize their daily rhythms to those of their spouses. After loss of a spouse, people's daily schedules are usually disrupted, and, of course, many of them become depressed.

Ehlers and her colleagues (1988) suggest that some people may be especially susceptible to the disruptive effects of changes in social contacts and regular daily routines. This susceptibility could represent one of the genetic contributions toward developing mood disorders. Almost everyone becomes depressed, at least for a period of time, after the loss of a loved one. Other events that change a person's daily routine, such as the birth of an infant or the loss of a job, can also precipitate a period of depression. Perhaps people who "spontaneously" become depressed are reacting to minor changes in their daily routine that disrupt their biological rhythms. Clearly, this interesting hypothesis deserves further research.

INTERIM SUMMARY

The major affective disorders include bipolar affective disorder, with its cyclical episodes of mania and depression, and unipolar depression. Heritability studies suggest that genetic anomalies are at least partly responsible for these disorders. Endogenous depression can be successfully treated by MAO inhibitors, tricyclic antidepressant drugs (which block the reuptake of norepinephrine and serotonin), electroconvulsive therapy, and sleep deprivation. Bipolar disorder can be successfully treated by lithium salts.

Several lines of evidence suggest that depression is caused by abnormalities in monoamine metabolism, release, or transmission. Indeed, low levels of 5-HIAA (a serotonin metabolite) in the cerebrospinal fluid correlate with attempts at suicide. Early studies focused on the acute effects of tricyclic antidepressant drugs and MAO inhibitors, which are NE and 5-HT agonists. However, because the effects of antidepressant treatment are delayed, more recent investigations have studied the chronic effects, which are quite different. Research indicates that all effective treatments for depression reduce the number or sensitivity of postsynaptic noradrenergic β receptors. This effect occurs only if the system of serotonergic neurons is intact.

Sleep disturbances are characteristic of affective disorders. In fact, total sleep deprivation rapidly (but temporarily) reduces depression in many people, and selective deprivation of REM sleep does so slowly (but more lastingly). In addition, almost all effective antidepressant treatments suppress REM sleep. Finally, a specific form of depression, seasonal affective disorder, can be treated by exposure to bright light, the zeitgeber that resets the biological clock. Clearly, the mood disorders are somehow linked to biological rhythms, perhaps through their regulatory effects on receptors or neuromodulators.

ANXIETY DISORDERS

As we have just seen, the affective disorders are characterized by unrealistic extremes of emotion: depression or elation (mania). The *anxiety disorders* are characterized by unrealistic, unfounded fear and anxiety. This section will describe two of the anxiety disorders that appear to have biological causes: panic disorder and obsessive compulsive disorder.

Panic Disorder

Description

People with *panic disorder* suffer from episodic attacks of acute anxiety—periods of acute and unremitting terror that grip them for variable lengths of time, from a few seconds to a few hours. The estimated incidence of panic disorder is between 1 and 2 percent of the population (Robbins et al., 1984). Women are approximately twice as likely as men to suffer from panic disorder. The disorder usually has its onset in young adulthood; it rarely begins after age thirty-five (Woodruff, Guze, and Clayton, 1972).

Panic attacks include many physical symptoms, such as shortness of breath, clammy sweat, irregularities in heartbeat, dizziness, faintness, and feelings of unreality. The victim of a panic attack often feels that he or she is going to die. Anxiety is a normal reaction to many stresses of life, and none of us is completely free from it. In fact, anxiety is undoubtedly useful in causing us to be more alert and to take important things seriously. However, the anxiety we all feel from time to time is obviously different from the intense fear and terror experienced by a person gripped by a panic attack.

Between panic attacks, many people with panic disorder suffer from *anticipatory anxiety*—the fear that another panic attack will strike them. This anticipatory anxiety often leads to the development of a serious phobic disorder: *agoraphobia* (*agora* means "open space"). According to the American Psychiatric Association's official *Diagnostic and Statistical Manual III-R*, agoraphobia associated with panic attacks is a fear of "being in places or situations from which escape might be difficult (or embarrassing) or in which help might not be available in the event of a panic attack . . . . As a result of this fear, the person either restricts travel or needs a companion when away from home." Agoraphobia can be severely disabling; some people with this disorder have stayed inside their houses or apartments for years, afraid to venture outside.

Possible Causes

Because the physical symptoms of panic attacks are so overwhelming, many patients reject the suggestion that they have a mental disorder, insisting that their problem is medical. In fact, they may be correct: A considerable amount of evidence suggests that panic disorder may have biological origins. First, the disorder appears to be hereditary; there is a higher concordance rate for

the disorder between monozygotic twins than between dizygotic twins (Slater and Shields, 1969), and almost 30 percent of the first-degree relatives of a person with panic disorder also have panic disorder (Crowe, Noyes, Pauls, and Slymen, 1983). The pattern of panic disorder within a family tree suggests that the disorder is caused by a single, dominant gene (Crowe, Noyes, Wilson, Elston, and Ward, 1987).

Panic attacks can be triggered in people with a history of panic disorder by giving them injections of lactic acid (a by-product of muscular activity) or by having them breathe air containing an elevated amount of carbon dioxide (Gaffney, Fenton, Lane, and Lake, 1988; Woods, Charney, Goodman, and Heninger, 1988). Cowley and Arana (1990) report that between 40 and 60 percent of people with such a history will react to an injection on a particular occasion.

Susceptibility to lactate-induced panic attacks appears to be at least partly heritable. Balon, Jordan, Pohl, and Yeragani (1989) infused forty-five normal subjects with sodium lactate and found that ten of them had panic attacks. The investigators obtained the family history of their subjects, using an interviewer who did not know which subjects had had panic attacks. They found that over 24 percent of the relatives of the subjects with the panic attacks themselves had a history of anxiety disorders, compared with less than 8 percent in the nonresponders.

Several studies have measured cerebral blood flow by means of PET scans during panic attacks triggered by an injection of lactate. Reiman et al. (1986) found that the activity of the parahippocampal gyrus rose just before the panic attack occurred, and that the activity of the anterior ends of the temporal lobes was elevated during the attack itself. Reiman, Fusselman, Fox, and Raichle (1989) produced anticipatory anxiety in normal subjects by leading them to believe that they were about to receive an intensely painful electric shock. (The subjects received a mild shock at the beginning of the experiment to make them believe what the experimenters said, but they did not actually receive a strong shock.) The PET scan showed that in normal subjects, too, anxiety produces increased activity of the temporal poles. (See *Color Plate 18.1*.)

Reiman and his colleagues note that studies with laboratory animals also suggest that the temporal poles are involved in anxiety reactions. For example, stimulation of this region in monkeys produces autonomic responses and facial expressions indicating fear, and humans with epilepsy caused by a focus in the anterior temporal lobes often report feelings of anxiety and fear just before their seizures occur. Of course, even if the anterior temporal cortex is involved in an anxiety reaction, we have no reason to suspect that panic disorder is caused by an abnormality in this region; the reaction could be provoked by an abnormality elsewhere in the brain.

Anxiety disorders are usually treated by a combination of behavior therapy and a benzodiazepine. As we saw in Chapter 3, benzodiazepines have strong *anxiolytic* ("anxiety dissolving") effects. The brain possesses benzodiazepine receptors, which are part of the GABA receptor complex. When a benzodiazepine agonist binds with its receptor, it increases the sensitivity of the GABA binding site and produces an anxiolytic effect. On the other hand, when a benzodiazepine *inverse agonist* occupies the receptor site, it reduces the sensitivity of the GABA binding site and *increases* anxiety. Anxiety disorders, then, might be caused by a diminished number of benzodiazepine receptors or by the secretion of a neuromodulator that acts as an inverse agonist at benzodiazepine receptors.

As we saw earlier in this chapter, rats who receive an antidepressant medication (clomipramine) early in life later develop the symptoms of depression, which can be reduced by an antidepressant drug or by REM sleep deprivation. Similarly, fearfulness can be produced in cats by prenatal administration of a benzodiazepine tranquilizer. Marczynski and Urbancic (1988) gave pregnant cats injections of diazepam (Valium) and assessed the fearfulness of the offspring of these cats when they were one year old. They found that the animals showed restlessness and anxiety in novel situations. This fearfulness could be reduced with an injection of diazepam. Afterward, they measured the level of benzodiazepine receptors in the animals' brains and found a decrease in the hypothalamus, frontal cortex, anterior parietal cortex, and midline thalamus.

Thus, fearfulness appears to be associated with a decreased number of benzodiazepine receptors and, presumably, lower sensitivity to the endogenous benzodiazepine agonist, whatever that may be.

Obsessive Compulsive Disorder

Description

As the name implies, people with an *obsessive compulsive disorder* suffer from *obsessions*—thoughts that will not leave them—and *compulsions*—behaviors that they cannot keep from performing. Obsessions are seen in a variety of mental disorders, including schizophrenia. However, unlike schizophrenics, people with obsessive compulsive disorder recognize that their thoughts and behaviors are senseless and desperately wish that they would go away. Compulsions often become more and more demanding, until they interfere with people's careers and daily lives.

The incidence of obsessive compulsive disorder is approximately 2 percent. Females are slightly more likely than males to have this diagnosis. Like panic disorder, obsessive compulsive disorder most commonly begins in young adulthood (Robbins et al., 1984). People with this disorder are unlikely to marry, perhaps because of the common obsessional fear of dirt and contamination or because of the shame associated with the rituals they are compelled to perform, which causes them to avoid social contacts (Turner, Beidel, and Nathan, 1985).

Most compulsions fall into one of four categories: *counting, checking, cleaning,* and *avoidance.* For example, people might repeatedly check burners on the stove to see that they are off and windows and locks to be sure that they are locked. Davison and Neale (1974) reported the case of a woman who washed her hands more than five hundred times a day because she feared being contaminated by germs. The hand washing persisted even when her hands became covered with painful sores. Other people meticulously clean their apartment or endlessly wash, dry, and fold their clothes. Some become afraid to leave home because they fear contamination and refuse to touch other members of their family. If they do accidentally become "contaminated," they usually have lengthy purification rituals. (See *Table 18.2*.)

Some investigators believe that the compulsive behaviors seen in obsessive compulsive disorder are forms of species-typical behaviors—for example, grooming, cleaning, and attention toward sources of potential danger—that are released from normal control mechanisms by a brain dysfunction (Wise and Rapoport, 1988).

Possible Causes

Evidence is beginning to accumulate suggesting that obsessive compulsive disorder may have a genetic origin. Family studies have found that this disorder is associated with a neurological disorder that appears during childhood (Pauls and Leckman, 1986; Pauls, Towbin, Leckman, Zahner, and Cohen, 1986). This disorder, *Tourette's syndrome,* is characterized by muscular and vocal tics: facial grimaces, squatting, pacing, twirling, barking, sniffing, coughing, grunting, or repeating specific words (especially vulgarities). Pauls and his colleagues believe that the two disorders are produced by the same single, dominant gene. It is not clear why some people with the faulty gene develop Tourette's syndrome early in childhood and others develop obsessive compulsive disorder later in life.

Not all cases of obsessive compulsive disorder have a genetic origin; the disorder sometimes occurs after brain damage caused by various means, such as birth trauma, encephalitis, and head trauma (Hollander et al., 1990). As we saw in the first part of this chapter, schizophrenia, too, appears to have both hereditary and nonhereditary causes.

Several studies using PET scans have found evidence of increased glucose metabolism in the frontal lobes, caudate nucleus, and cingulate gyrus (Baxter et al., 1987, 1989; Swedo et al., 1989). These three structures are closely interconnected, and investigators have long considered them to be involved in emotional reactions. In fact, some patients with severe obsessive compulsive disorder have been successfully treated with surgical destruction of the cingulum bundle, a group of axons that connects the prefrontal and cingulate cortex with the limbic cortex of the temporal lobe (Ballantine, Bouckoms, Thomas, and Giriunas,

TABLE 18.2

Reported obsessions and compulsions of child and adolescent patients.

Major Presenting Symptom	Percent Reporting Symptom at Initial Interview
Obession	
Concern or disgust with bodily wastes or secretions (urine, stool, saliva), dirt, germs, environmental toxins, etc.	43
Fear something terrible might happen (fire, death/illness of loved one, self, or others)	24
Concern or need for symmetry, order, or exactness	17
Scrupulosity (excessive praying or religious concerns out of keeping with patient's background)	13
Lucky/unlucky numbers	18
Forbidden or perverse sexual thoughts, images, or impulses	14
Intrusive nonsense sounds, words, or music	11
Compulsion	
Excessive or ritualized hand washing, showering, bathing, toothbrushing, or grooming	85
Repeating rituals (going in/out of door, up/down from chair, etc.)	51
Checking doors, locks, stove, appliances, car brakes, etc.	46
Cleaning and other rituals to remove contact with contaminants	23
Touching	20
Ordering/arranging	17
Measures to prevent harm to self or others (e.g., hanging clothes a certain way)	16
Counting	18
Hoarding/collecting	11
Miscellaneous rituals (e.g., licking, spitting, special dress pattern)	26

SOURCE: From Rapoport, J.L. *Journal of the American Medical Association,* 1988, *260,* 2888–2890.

1987). Obviously, because a brain lesion cannot be undone, these operations are performed only in severe cases, after behavior therapy and drug therapy have been found to be ineffective.

By far, the most effective treatment of obsessive compulsive disorder is drug therapy. So far, three effective drugs have been found: clomipramine, fluoxetine, and fluvoxamine. Although these drugs are also effective antidepressants, their antidepressant action does not seem to be related to their ability to relieve the symptoms of obsessive compulsive disorder. For example, Leonard et al. (1989) compared the effects of clomipramine and desipramine (an antidepressant drug) on the symptoms of children and adolescents with severe obsessive compulsive disorder. For three weeks all patients received a placebo. Then for five weeks half of them received

clomipramine (CMI) and the other half received desipramine (DMI), on a double-blind basis. At the end of that time, the drugs were switched. As Figure 18.13 shows, CMI was a much more effective drug; in fact, when the patients were switched from CMI to DMI, their symptoms got worse. (See *Figure 18.13*.)

All of the effective antiobsessional drugs are specific blockers of 5-HT reuptake; thus, they are specific serotonergic agonists. In general, serotonin has an inhibitory effect on species-typical behaviors, which has tempted several investigators to speculate that these drugs alleviate the symptoms of obsessive compulsive disorder by reducing the strength of the washing, cleaning, and danger avoidance behaviors that may underlie this disorder.

*I*NTERIM SUMMARY

The anxiety disorders severely disrupt some people's lives. People with panic disorder periodically have panic attacks, during which they experience intense symptoms of autonomic activity and often feel as if they were going to die. Frequently, panic attacks lead to the development of agoraphobia, an avoidance of being away from a safe place, such as home. Panic disorder is at least partly heritable, which suggests that it has biological causes.

Panic attacks can be triggered in many susceptible people by inhalation of air containing an elevated amount of carbon dioxide or by giving them an injection of lactic acid or a lactate salt. During a panic attack people show increased activity of the anterior ends of the temporal lobes.

Panic attacks can be alleviated by the administration of a benzodiazepine, which suggests that the disorder may involve decreased numbers of benzodiazepine receptors or an inadequate secretion of an endogenous benzodiazepine agonist. Cats given a benzodiazepine prenatally will become especially fearful when they reach adulthood, and the treatment decreases the number of benzodiazepine receptors in parts of their brain.

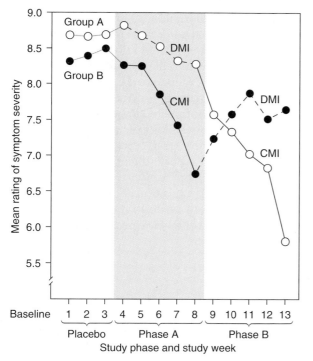

FIGURE 18.13

Mean rating of symptom severity of patients with obsessive compulsive disorder treated with desipramine (DMI) or clomipramine (CMI). (From Leonard, H.L., Swedo, S.E., Rapoport, J.L., Koby, E.V., Lenane, M.C., Cheslow, D.L., and Hamburger, S.D. *Archives of General Psychiatry,* 1989, *46,* 1088–1092.)

Obsessive compulsive disorder is characterized by obsessions—unwanted thoughts—and compulsions—uncontrollable behaviors, especially those involving cleanliness and attention to danger. Some investigators believe that these behaviors represent overactivity of species-typical behavioral tendencies.

Obsessive compulsive disorder has a heritable basis and is related to a neurological disorder characterized by tics and strange verbalizations, Tourette's syndrome. It can also be caused by brain damage at birth, encephalitis, and head injuries. PET scans indicate that people with obsessive compulsive disorder tend to show increased glucose metabolism in the frontal lobes, caudate nucleus, and cingulate gyrus, structures that are probably involved in emotional reactions. The destruction of the cingulum bundle, which links them with the anterior temporal lobe, reduces the symptoms, as do drugs such as clomipramine, which specifically block the reuptake of serotonin. Some investigators believe that clomipramine and related drugs alleviate the symptoms of obsessive compulsive disorder by increasing the activity of serotonergic pathways that play an inhibitory role on species-typical behaviors.

C ONCLUDING REMARKS

Schizophrenia, the major affective disorders, and the anxiety disorders are serious problems. Early in this century most psychiatrists believed that the psychoses, at least, were caused by brain abnormalities; but with the ascendancy of psychotherapy, this belief fell into disrepute. For several years most therapists believed that mental disorders were caused by people's social relations (particularly during infancy), and very few biologists were involved in research on mental disorders. More recently, the discovery of the hereditary basis of these disorders and the efficacy of drug treatment has convinced both clinicians and scientists that the serious mental disorders reflect abnormalities in brain structure or biochemistry. We have seen some of the important hypotheses being investigated by researchers today and some of the progress that has been made in understanding and treating the disorders. The future offers hope to people who suffer from the major mental disorders and to their families and friends.

A personal note: You are now at the end of the book (as you well know), and you have spent a considerable amount of time reading my words. While working on this book, I have tried to imagine myself talking to someone who is interested in learning something about the physiology of behavior. As I mentioned in the preface, writing is often a lonely activity, and the imaginary audience helped keep me company. If you would like to turn this communication into a two-way conversation, write to me—my address is given at the end of the preface.

NEW TERMS

agoraphobia p. 602
anticipatory anxiety p. 602
anxiety disorder p. 601
bipolar disorder p. 593
chlorpromazine p. 582
compulsion p. 603
delusion p. 578
denervation supersensitivity p. 585

endogenous depression p. 593
hallucination p. 578
5-HIAA p. 596
lithium p. 595
major affective disorder p. 593
monoamine hypothesis p. 595
negative symptom (of schizophrenia) p. 579

neurosis p. 578
obsession p. 603
obsessive compulsive disorder p. 603
panic disorder p. 601
positive symptom (of schizophrenia) p. 578
psychosis p. 578

SUGGESTED READINGS

Depue, R.A., and Iacono, W.G. Neurobehavioral aspects of affective disorders. *Annual Review of Psychology,* 1989, *40,* 457–492.

Goodwin, D.W., and Guze, S.B. *Psychiatric Diagnosis,* 3rd ed. New York: Oxford University Press, 1984.

Kaplan, H.I., and Sadock, B.J. *Comprehensive Textbook of Psychiatry, 5th ed.* Baltimore, Md.: Williams and Wilkins, 1988.

Miller, R. Schizophrenia as a progressive disorder: Relations to EEG, CT, neuropathological and other evidence. *Progress in Neurobiology,* 1989, *33,* 17–44.

Nasrallah, H.A., and Weinberger, D.R. *Handbook of Schizophrenia, Vol. 1: The Neurology of Schizophrenia.* Amsterdam: Elsevier Science Publishers, 1986.

Schulz, S.C., and Tamminga, C.A. *Schizophrenia: A Scientific Focus.* New York: Oxford University Press, 1988.

GLOSSARY

Absorptive phase.   The phase of metabolism during which nutrients are absorbed from the digestive system. Glucose and amino acids constitute the principal source of energy for cells during this phase. Stores of glycogen are increased, and excess nutrients are stored in adipose tissue in the form of triglycerides.

Acetylcholine (ACh).   A neurotransmitter found in the brain, spinal cord, ganglia of the autonomic nervous system, and postganglionic terminal buttons of the parasympathetic division of the autonomic nervous system.

Acetylcholinesterase (AChE).   The enzyme that destroys acetylcholine soon after it is liberated by the terminal buttons, thus terminating the postsynaptic potential.

Achromatopsia.   Inability to discriminate among different hues; caused by damage to the visual association cortex.

Acquired dyslexia.   Reading deficit in someone who could previously read; caused by brain damage.

ACTH.   See *adrenocorticotropic hormone (ACTH).*

Actin.   Actin and myosin are the proteins that provide the physical basis for muscular contraction. See Figures 8.1 and 8.2.

Action potential.   The brief electrical impulse that provides the basis for conduction of information along an axon. The action potential results from brief changes in membrane permeability to sodium and potassium ions. See Figures 2.17 and 2.24.

Activational effects.   See under *hormone.*

Adaptation.   Decreasing sensitivity to a stimulus that is applied continuously.

Adenohypophysis.   See under *pituitary gland.*

Adenosine triphosphate (ATP).   A molecule of prime importance to cellular energy metabolism: The conversion of ATP to adenosine diphosphate (ADP) liberates energy. ATP can also be converted to cyclic AMP, which serves as an intermediate messenger in the production of postsynaptic po-

tentials by some neurotransmitters and in the mediation of the effects of peptide hormones. See also *adenylate cyclase* and Figure 3.9.

Adenylate cyclase.   An enzyme that converts ATP to cyclic AMP when the postsynaptic receptor to which it is bound is stimulated by the appropriate substance. It is important in mediating the intracellular effects of many neurotransmitters and peptide hormones. See also *adenosine triphosphate (ATP)* and Figure 3.9.

ADH.   See *vasopressin.*

Adipose tissue.   Fat tissue, composed of cells that can absorb nutrients from the blood and store them in the form of lipids during the absorptive phase or release them in the form of fatty acids and ketones during the fasting phase.

Adipsia.   Complete lack of drinking; can be produced by lesions of the lateral hypothalamus or the region around the anteroventral tip of the third ventricle.

Ad libitum.   Literally, "to the desire." More generally, "as much as is wanted.'

Adrenal gland.   An endocrine gland located atop the kidney. The *adrenal cortex* produces steroid hormones such as corticosterone, androstenedione, and aldosterone. The *adrenal medulla,* controlled by sympathetic nerve fibers, secretes epinephrine and norepinephrine.

Adrenalin.   See *epinephrine.*

Adrenocorticotropic hormone (ACTH).   A hormone produced and liberated by the anterior pituitary gland in response to corticotropin-releasing hormone, produced by the hypothalamus. ACTH stimulates the adrenal cortex to produce various steroid hormones.

Adrenogenital syndrome.   A condition characterized by hypersecretion of androgens by the adrenal cortex. The result, in females, is masculinization of the external genitalia.

Affect.   An emotional state of strong feelings, either positive or negative.

Affective attack. A highly emotional attack of one animal upon another; can be elicited by electrical stimulation of certain regions of the brain.

Afferent. Toward a structure; all neurons afferent to the central nervous system convey sensory information.

Afterdischarge. Abnormally slow and synchronous electrical discharges recorded by the EEG; produced by electrical stimulation of the brain and characteristic of seizures.

Agonist. Literally, a contestant, or one who takes part in the contest. An agonistic drug facilitates the effects of a particular neurotransmitter on the postsynaptic cell. An agonistic muscle produces or facilitates a particular movement. Antonym: antagonist.

Agoraphobia. Fear of being away from home or other protected places. See *panic attack.*

Agrammatism. One of the usual symptoms of Broca's aphasia; difficulty in comprehending or properly employing grammatical devices, such as verb endings and word order.

Agraphia. Inability to write, caused by brain damage.

Aldosterone. A hormone of the adrenal cortex that causes the retention of sodium by the kidneys.

Alexia. Inability to read, caused by brain damage.

All-or-none law. States that once an action potential is triggered in an axon, it is propagated, without decrement, to the end of the fiber.

Alpha activity. Smooth electrical activity of 8 to 12 Hz recorded from the brain. Alpha activity is generally associated with a state of relaxation.

Alpha motor neuron. A neuron whose cell body is located in the ventral horn of the spinal cord or in one of the motor nuclei of the cranial nerves. Stimulation of an alpha motor neuron results in contraction of the extrafusal muscle fibers upon which its terminal buttons synapse.

Alzheimer's disease. A degenerative brain disorder of unknown origin; causes progressive memory loss, motor deficits, and eventual death. Acetylcholine-secreting neurons are the first to be affected.

Amacrine cell. Neuron in the retina that interconnects adjacent ganglion cells and the inner arborizations of the bipolar cells.

Amino acid. A molecule that contains both an amino group and a carboxyl group. Amino acids are linked together by peptide bonds and serve as the constituents of proteins.

Amino acid autoradiography. A neuroanatomical technique that permits the tracing of efferent pathways from a region of the brain. A radioactive amino acid such as proline is injected into a region, where it is taken up by neurons and incorporated into proteins. These radioactive proteins are carried by axoplasmic transport to the terminal buttons. The location of the terminal buttons is determined by means of autoradiography.

Amino group. NH_2; two atoms of hydrogen attached to an atom of nitrogen.

Amitriptyline. A monoamine agonist: retards re-uptake by the terminal buttons.

Ammon's horn. The hippocampus proper; part of the hippocampal formation; consists of fields CA1–CA4 (for *cornu Ammonis*).

Amphetamine. A catecholamine agonist: facilitates neurotransmitter release, stimulates postsynaptic receptors (slightly), and retards re-uptake by the terminal buttons.

AMPT. See *α-methyl-p-tyrosine (AMPT).*

Amygdala. The term commonly used for the *amygdaloid complex*, a set of nuclei located in the base of the temporal lobe. The amygdala is a part of the limbic system.

Analgesia. Lack of sensitivity to pain.

Androgen. A male sex steroid hormone. Testosterone is the principal mammalian androgen.

Androgen insensitivity syndrome. A condition, also called *testicular feminization*, caused by a congenital lack of functioning androgen receptors. Because androgens cannot exert their effects, a person with XY sex chromosomes develops as a female, with female external genitalia. Because the fetal testes produce Müllerian-inhibiting substance, neither the Wolffian nor the Müllerian systems develop into internal sex organs.

Androgenization. The process initiated by exposure of the cells of a developing animal to androgens. Exposure to androgens causes embryonic sex organs to develop as male and produces certain changes in the brain. See also *hormone.*

Androstenedione. An androgen secreted by the adrenal cortex of both males and females.

Angiotensin. See under *renin.*

Angiotensinogen. See under *renin.*

Angular gyrus. A gyrus in the parietal lobe; the left angular gyrus is important for verbal functions, especially reading.

Anion. See under *ion.*

Anomia. Difficulty in finding (remembering) the appropriate word to describe an object, action, or attribute; one of the symptoms of aphasia.

Anorexia nervosa. A disorder that most frequently afflicts young women; exaggerated concern with overweight that leads to excessive dieting and often compulsive exercising; can lead to starvation.

ANS. See *autonomic nervous system (ANS).*

Antagonist. An antagonistic muscle produces a

movement contrary or opposite to the one being described. An antagonistic drug opposes or inhibits the effects of a particular neurotransmitter on the postsynaptic cell. Antonym: agonist.

Anterior. See Figure 4.1.

Anterior nuclei (of thalamus). A group of three nuclei of the thalamus (anterodorsal, anteromedial, and anteroventral); part of the limbic system; receive input from the hippocampus (via the fornix columns) and mammillary bodies of the hypothalamus; send axons to the cingulate gyrus.

Anterior pituitary gland. See under *pituitary gland*.

Anterograde amnesia. Amnesia for events that occur after some disturbance to the brain, such as head injury, electroconvulsive shock, or certain degenerative brain diseases.

Anterograde degeneration. Rapid degeneration of an axon distal to its point of damage.

Antipsychotic drug. A drug that reduces or eliminates the symptoms of psychosis. Antischizophrenic drugs appear to exert their effect by antagonizing dopaminergic synapses.

Aphagia. Complete lack of eating; can be produced by lesions of the lateral hypothalamus.

Aphasia. Difficulty in producing or comprehending speech not produced by deafness or a simple motor deficit; caused by brain damage.

Apperceptive visual agnosia. See under *visual agnosia*.

Apraxia. Difficulty in carrying out purposeful movements, in the absence of paralysis or muscular weakness.

Aprosodia. Difficulty in producing or comprehending those aspects of speech that are conveyed by changes in intonation or emphasis; apparently related to difficulties in the communication or perception of emotions.

Arachnoid membrane. The middle layer of the meninges, between the outer dura mater and inner pia mater. The subarachnoid space beneath the arachnoid membrane is filled with cerebrospinal fluid, which cushions the brain.

Arcuate nucleus. The hypothalamic nucleus that contains the cell bodies of the neurosecretory cells that produce the hypothalamic hormones.

Area postrema. A region of the medulla where the blood-brain barrier is weak. Systemic poisons can be detected there and can initiate vomiting.

Association cortex. Those regions of cortex that receive information from the sensory areas (sensory association cortex) or that project to the primary motor cortex (motor association cortex); plays an important role in perception, learning, and planning.

Associative visual agnosia. See under *visual agnosia*.

Astrocyte (astroglia). A glial cell that provides support for neurons of the central nervous system. Astrocytes also participate in the formation of scar tissue after injury to the brain or spinal cord.

ATP. See *adenosine triphosphate (ATP)*.

Atrial natriuretic peptide (ANP). A peptide secreted by the atria of the heart when blood volume is higher than normal. It increases water and sodium excretion; inhibits renin, vasopressin, and aldosterone secretion; and inhibits sodium appetite.

Auditory nerve. The auditory nerve has two principal branches. The *cochlear nerve* transmits auditory information, and the *vestibular nerve* transmits information related to balance.

Autonomic ganglion. See under *ganglion*.

Autonomic nervous system (ANS). The portion of the peripheral nervous system that controls the body's vegetative function. The *sympathetic division* mediates functions that accompany arousal; the *parasympathetic division* mediates functions that occur during a relaxed state.

Autoradiography. A procedure that locates radioactive substances in body tissue, usually in the brain or spinal cord. The tissue is sliced, mounted on a microscope slide, and covered with a photographic emulsion or piece of film. The radiation exposes the emulsion, which is subsequently developed.

Autoreceptor. A receptor molecule located on a neuron that responds to the neurotransmitter or neuromodulator that the neuron itself secretes. Some autoreceptors are located on the presynaptic membrane; they participate in the regulation of the amount of neurotransmitter that is synthesized and released.

Axoaxonic synapse. The synapse of a terminal button upon the axon of another neuron, near its terminal buttons. These synapses mediate presynaptic inhibition.

Axodendritic synapse. The synapse of a terminal button of the axon of one neuron upon the dendrite of another neuron.

Axon. A thin, elongated process of a neuron that can transmit action potentials toward its terminal buttons, which synapse upon other neurons, gland cells, or muscle cells.

Axon hillock. The initial part of the axon, at the junction of the axon and soma. It is capable of producing an action potential and generally has a slightly lower threshold of excitation than the rest of the axon.

Axoplasmic transport. An active mechanism involving proteins similar to actin and myosin that propel substances down the axons from the soma to the terminal buttons. A slower form of axoplasmic transport carries substances in the opposite direction.

Axosomatic synapse. The synapse of a terminal button of the axon of one neuron upon the membrane of the soma of another neuron.

Balint's syndrome. A syndrome caused by bilateral damage to the parieto-occipital region; includes *optic ataxia* (difficulty in reaching for objects under visual guidance), *ocular apraxia* (difficulty in visual scanning), and *simultanagnosia* (difficulty in perceiving more than one object at a time).

Baroreceptor. A special receptor that transduces changes in barometric pressure (chiefly within the heart or blood vessels) into neural activity.

Basal ganglia. Caudate nucleus, globus pallidus, putamen, and amygdala. The first three are important parts of the motor system.

Basic rest-activity cycle (BRAC). A 90-minute cycle (in humans) of waxing and waning alertness, controlled by a biological clock in the caudal brain stem; during sleep, it controls cycles of REM sleep and slow-wave sleep.

Basilar artery. An artery found at the base of the brain, connecting the blood supplies of the vertebral and carotid arteries.

Basilar membrane. A membrane in the cochlea of the inner ear; contains the organ of Corti, the receptor organ for hearing.

Basolateral group. The phylogenetically newer portion of the amygdaloid complex.

Benzodiazepine. A class of drug with anxiolytic ("tranquilizing") effects; works by activating benzodiazepine receptors coupled to GABA receptors on neurons, making the latter more sensitive to the neurotransmitter.

Beta activity. Irregular electrical activity of 1 to 30 Hz recorded from the brain. Beta activity is generally associated with a state of arousal.

Bilateral. On both sides of the midline of the body.

Bipolar affective disorder. A psychosis characterized by cyclical periods of mania and depression; effectively treated with lithium carbonate.

Bipolar neuron. A neuron with only two processes— a dendritic process at one end and an axonal process at the other end. (See Figure 2.8.) *Bipolar cells* constitute the middle layer of the retina, conveying information from the receptor cells to the ganglion cells, whose axons give rise to the optic nerves.

Blindsight. The ability of a person to reach for objects located in his or her "blind" field; occurs after damage restricted to the primary visual cortex.

Blob. The central region of a module of the primary visual cortex, revealed by a stain for cytochrome oxidase; contains wavelength-sensitive neurons; part of the parvocellular system.

Blood-brain barrier. A barrier produced by the astrocytes and cells in the walls of the capillaries in the brain; this barrier permits passage of only certain substances.

Botulinum toxin. An acetylcholine antagonist: prevents release by terminal buttons.

BRAC. See *basic rest-activity cycle (BRAC)*.

Brain stem. The "stem" of the brain, from the medulla to the midbrain, excluding the cerebellum.

Bregma. The junction of the sagittal and coronal sutures of the skull. It is often used as a reference point for stereotaxic brain surgery.

Broca's area. A region of frontal cortex, located just rostral to the base of the left primary motor cortex, that is necessary for normal speech production. Damage to this region results in *Broca's aphasia*, characterized by agrammatism and extreme difficulty in speech articulation.

Brown adipose tissue. Fat cells densely packed with mitochondria, which can generate heat; important in hibernating animals and thought to play an important role in converting excessive calories of nutrients into heat rather than increased size of fat deposits.

Bruce effect. Termination of pregnancy caused by the odor of a pheromone in the urine of a male other than the one that impregnated the female; first identified in mice.

Bulimia. Bouts of excessive hunger and eating; often seen in people with anorexia nervosa.

Cable properties. Passive conduction of electrical current, in a decremental fashion, down the length of an axon, similar to the way in which electrical current traverses a submarine cable.

Caffeine. An alkaloid drug found in coffee, chocolate, and other commonly ingested substances; blocks the activity of phosphodiesterase, an enzyme that destroys cyclic nucleotides, the second messengers in the response of many cells to neurotransmitters, neuromodulators, or peptide hormones.

Calcarine fissure. A horizontal fissure on the inner surface of the posterior cerebral cortex; the location of the primary visual cortex.

Calpain. A proteolytic (protein-cleaving) enzyme; thought to cause some of the cellular changes responsible for long-term potentiation by cleaving spectrin, a protein found immediately inside the neural membrane.

Cannula. A small tube that may be inserted into the body to permit introduction of chemicals or removal of fluid for analysis.

Carboxyl group. COOH; two atoms of oxygen and one atom of hydrogen bound to a single atom of carbon.

Carotid artery. An artery, the branches of which serve the rostral portions of the brain.

Cataplexy. A symptom of narcolepsy; complete paralysis that occurs during waking. Cataplexy is thought to be related to REM sleep mechanisms.

Catecholamine. A class of biologically active amines that includes the neurotransmitters dopamine, norepinephrine, and epinephrine.

Cation. See under *ion.*

Caudal. See Figure 4.1.

Caudate nucleus. A telencephalic nucleus, one of the basal ganglia. The caudate nucleus is principally involved with inhibitory control of movement.

CCK. See *cholecystokinin (CCK).*

Central canal. The narrow tube, filled with cerebrospinal fluid, that runs through the length of the spinal cord.

Central nervous system (CNS). The brain and spinal cord.

Central sulcus. The sulcus that separates the frontal lobe from the parietal lobe.

Central tegmental tract. An alternative name for the ventral noradrenergic bundle, which carries fibers of noradrenergic neurons from regions of the medulla and from the locus coeruleus and the subcoerulear area of the pons to the hypothalamus.

Cerebral aqueduct. A narrow tube interconnecting the third and fourth ventricles of the brain.

Cerebral cortex. The outermost layer of gray matter of the cerebral hemispheres.

Cerebrospinal fluid (CSF). A clear fluid, similar to blood plasma, that fills the ventricular system of the brain and the subarachnoid space surrounding the brain and spinal cord.

Chemoreceptor. A receptor that responds, by means of receptor potentials or neural impulses, to the presence of a particular chemical.

Chlorpromazine. A dopamine antagonist: blocks postsynaptic receptors. It is the most commonly prescribed antischizophrenic drug.

Cholecystokinin (CCK). A hormone secreted by the duodenum that regulates gastric motility and causes the gallbladder (cholecyst) to contract, expelling bile into the digestive system; also found in neurons in the brain, where it may serve as a neurotransmitter or neuromodulator.

Choline acetyltransferase. The enzyme that transfers the acetate ion from acetyl coenzyme A to choline, producing the neurotransmitter acetylcholine.

Chorda tympani. A branch of the facial nerve (seventh cranial nerve) that passes beneath the eardrum; conveys taste information from the anterior part of the tongue and controls the secretion of some salivary glands.

Chorea. A movement disorder characterized by uncontrollable jerky movements.

Choroid plexus. Highly vascular tissue that protrudes into the ventricles and produces cerebrospinal fluid.

Chromosome. Strand of DNA, with associated proteins, found in the nucleus; carries genetic information.

Ciliary muscles. Muscles arranged around the lens of the eye; control the shape of the eye to focus images of near or distant objects on the retina.

Cingulate gyrus. A strip of limbic cortex lying along the lateral walls of the groove separating the cerebral hemispheres, just above the corpus callosum.

Circadian rhythm. A daily rhythmical change in behavior or physiological process.

Citric acid cycle. See *Krebs cycle.*

Classical conditioning. A learning procedure. When a stimulus that initially produces no more than an orienting response is followed several times by an *unconditional stimulus* that produces a defensive or appetitive response (the *unconditional response*), the first stimulus (now called a *conditional stimulus*) itself evokes the response (now called a *conditional response*).

CNS. Central nervous system; the brain and spinal cord.

Cocaine. A drug that retards the re-uptake of the catecholamines, especially dopamine; a potent dopamine agonist.

Cochlea. The snail-shaped structure of the inner ear that contains the auditory transducing mechanisms.

Cochlear microphonics. Electrical activity recorded from the cochlear nerve that corresponds to the sound vibrations received at the oval window.

Cochlear nerve. See under *auditory nerve.*

Commissure. A fiber bundle that interconnects corresponding regions on each side of the brain.

Conditional response (CR). See under *classical conditioning.*

Conditional stimulus (CS). See under *classical conditioning.*

Conditioned emotional response. A classically conditioned response that occurs when a neutral stimulus is followed by an aversive stimulus; usually includes autonomic, behavioral, and endocrine components such as changes in heart rate, freezing, and secretion of stress-related hormones.

Conditioned food aversion.   The avoidance of a relatively unfamiliar food that previously caused (or was followed by) illness.

Conduction aphasia.   Damage to the connections between Wernicke's area and Broca's area; results in the inability to repeat words that are heard, although they can usually be understood and responded to appropriately.

Cone.   See under *photoreceptor*.

Consolidation.   The process by which short-term memories are converted into long-term memories.

Constructional apraxia.   Difficulty in drawing pictures or diagrams or in making geometrical constructions of elements such as building blocks or sticks; caused by brain damage, especially to the right parietal lobe.

Contralateral.   Residing in the side of the body opposite to the reference point.

Coolidge effect.   The restorative effect of introducing a new female sex partner to a male that has apparently become ''exhausted'' by sexual activity.

Cornea.   The transparent outer surface of the eye, in front of the iris and pupil.

Corpus callosum.   The largest commissure of the brain, interconnecting the areas of neocortex on each side of the brain.

Corpus luteum.   After ovulation, the ovarian follicle develops into a corpus luteum and secretes estradiol and progesterone.

Correctional mechanism.   In a regulatory process, the mechanism that is capable of changing the value of the system variable.

Corticobulbar pathway.   A bundle of axons from the neocortex (principally the primary motor cortex) to the nuclei of the fifth, seventh, and twelfth cranial nerves in the medulla, which control movements of the face and tongue.

Corticomedial group.   The phylogenetically older portion of the amygdaloid complex.

Corticospinal pathway.   The system of axons that originates in the cortex (especially the primary motor cortex) and terminates in the ventral gray matter of the spinal cord. Axons of the *lateral corticospinal tract* cross the midline in the medulla and synapse on spinal motor neurons and interneurons that control the arms and hands. Axons of the *ventral corticospinal tract* cross the midline near their site of termination in the spinal cord and primarily control movements of the trunk muscles.

CR.   Conditional response. See under *classical conditioning*.

Cranial nerve.   One of a set of twelve pairs of nerves that exit from the base of the brain.

Cranial nerve ganglion.   See under *ganglion*.

Cross section.   See Figure 4.2.

CS.   Conditional stimulus. See under *classical conditioning*.

CSF.   See *cerebrospinal fluid (CSF)*.

CT scanner.   A device that uses a computer to analyze data obtained by a scanning beam of X-rays to produce a two-dimensional picture of a ''slice'' through the body.

Cyclic adenosine monophosphate (cyclic AMP).   Intermediate messenger in the production of postsynaptic potentials by some neurotransmitters and in the mediation of the effects of peptide hormones. See also *adenylate cyclase*.

Cyclic guanosine monophosphate (cyclic GMP).   Similar in form and function to cyclic adenosine monophosphate, except that guanosine substitutes for adenosine. See also *cyclic adenosine monophosphate* and *adenylate cyclase*.

Cyclic nucleotide.   A compound such as cyclic AMP or cyclic GMP, important in mediating the intracellular effects of many neurotransmitters and peptide hormones. See also *adenylate cyclase*.

Cytoplasm.   The viscous, semiliquid substance contained in the interior of a cell.

DA.   See *dopamine (DA)*.

Decerebrate.   Describes an animal whose brain stem has been transected.

Declarative memory.   Memory that can be verbally expressed, such as memory for events in a person's past. The ability to form new declarative memories is disrupted by lesions of the hippocampal formation or related structures.

Decremental conduction.   Conduction of a subthreshold stimulus along an axon, according to its cable properties.

Decussation.   Crossing of a fiber to the other side of the brain.

Deep dyslexia.   A language disorder caused by massive damage to the left hemisphere; characterized by Broca's aphasia (usually) and difficulty reading words other than concrete nouns.

Defeminizing effect.   Effect of a hormone present early in development; reduces or prevents the later development of anatomical or behavioral characteristics typical of females. See also *masculinizing effect*.

Delayed conditioning.   A classical conditioning procedure in which the unconditional stimulus is presented just before the conditional stimulus is turned off (both stimuli are turned off at the same time).

Delta activity. Regular, synchronous electrical activity of approximately 1 to 4 Hz recorded from the brain. Delta activity is generally associated with slow-wave sleep.

Dementia. Loss of cognitive abilities such as memory, perception, verbal ability, and judgment. Common causes are multiple strokes or Alzheimer's disease.

Dendrite. Treelike process attached to the soma of a neuron, which receives messages from the terminal buttons of other neurons.

Dendritic spine. Small buds on the surface of a dendrite, upon which terminal buttons from other neurons synapse.

Dendrodendritic synapse. Synaptic connections between dendrites of adjacent neurons.

Denervation supersensitivity. Increased sensitivity of the neural postsynaptic membrane or motor endplate to the neurotransmitter; caused by damage to the afferent axons or long-term blockage of neurotransmitter release.

Dentate gyrus. Part of the hippocampal formation; receives inputs from the entorhinal cortex via the perforant path and projects to the CA3 field of the hippocampus proper (Ammon's horn).

2-Deoxyglucose (2-DG). A sugar that interferes with the metabolism of glucose.

Deoxyribonucleic acid (DNA). A long, complex macromolecule consisting of two interconnected helical strands. Strands of DNA, along with their associated proteins, constitute the chromosomes, which contain the genetic information of the animal.

Depolarization. Reduction (toward zero) of the membrane potential of a cell from its normal resting potential of approximately -70 mV.

Desynchrony. Irregular electrical activity recorded from the brain, generally associated with periods of arousal. See also *beta activity.*

Detector. In a regulatory process, a mechanism that signals when the system variable deviates from its set point.

Deuteranopia. An inherited form of defective color vision in which red and green hues are confused. "Green" cones appear to be filled with "red" cone opsin.

Developmental dyslexia. Reading difficulty in a person of normal intelligence and perceptual ability; of genetic origin or caused by prenatal or perinatal factors.

2-DG. See *2-deoxyglucose (2-DG).*

Diabetes mellitus. A disease that results from insufficient production of insulin, thus causing, in an untreated state, a high level of blood glucose.

Diencephalon. See Table 4.1.

Diffusion. Movement of molecules from regions of high concentration to regions of low concentration.

L-Dihydroxyphenylalanine. See *L-DOPA.*

Discriminative stimulus. A stimulus that signifies that a particular response will be followed by a particular event; in an instrumental conditioning task, a discriminative stimulus indicates that a response will be reinforced.

DNA. See *deoxyribonucleic acid (DNA).*

L-DOPA. The levorotatory isomeric form of dihydroxyphenylalanine; the precursor of the catecholamines dopamine, norepinephrine, and epinephrine. It is often used to treat Parkinson's disease because of its effect as a dopamine agonist.

DOPA decarboxylase. The enzyme that converts the L-DOPA to the neurotransmitter dopamine.

Dopamine (DA). A neurotransmitter; one of the catecholamines.

Dopamine β-hydroxylase. The enzyme that converts dopamine to the neurotransmitter norepinephrine; the conversion occurs within synaptic vesicles.

Dorsal. See Figure 4.1.

Dorsal columns. Vertically oriented bundles of axons in the dorsal spinal cord; convey somatosensory information to the brain.

Dorsal lateral geniculate nucleus. See under *lateral geniculate nucleus.*

Dorsal motor nuclei of the vagus. Nuclei of the tenth cranial nerve; control parasympathetic functions of the vagus nerve, such as the secretion of insulin.

Dorsal root. See under *spinal root.*

Dorsal root ganglion. See under *ganglion.*

Dorsal tegmental bundle. An alternative name for the dorsal noradrenergic bundle, which carries fibers of noradrenergic neurons from the locus coeruleus to various forebrain structures.

Dorsolateral column. A fiber bundle in the spinal cord that contains serotonergic axons that mediate opiate-induced analgesia.

Dorsolateral pathway. The system of axons that travel from the brain stem to the spinal cord, primarily those of the *rubrospinal tract,* which controls muscles that move the forelimbs.

Drive reduction hypothesis. The hypothesis that reinforcement occurs when a drive (presumed to be aversive) is reduced; for example, when hunger is reduced by eating.

Duodenum. The portion of the small intestine immediately adjacent to the stomach.

Dura mater. The outermost layer of the three meninges.

Dynorphin.   See under *endogenous opiate*.

Dyslexia.   A term that refers to a variety of reading disorders.

EEG.   See *electroencephalogram (EEG)*.

Efferent.   Away from a structure; efferent axons of the central nervous system control the muscles and glands.

Electroconvulsive shock (ECS).   A brief electrical shock, applied to the head, that results in electrical seizure and convulsions. It is used therapeutically to alleviate severe depression and experimentally (in animals) to study the consolidation process.

Electrode.   A conductive medium (generally made of metal) that can be used to apply electrical stimulation or to record electrical potentials.

Electroencephalogram (EEG).   Electrical brain potentials recorded by placing electrodes on or in the scalp or on the surface of the brain.

Electrolyte.   An aqueous solution of a material that ionizes—namely, a soluble acid, base, or salt.

Electromyogram (EMG).   Electrical potential recorded from an electrode placed on or in a muscle.

Electro-oculogram (EOG).   Electrical potentials from the eyes, recorded by means of electrodes placed on the skin around them; detects eye movements.

Electrostatic pressure.   The attractive force between atomic particles charged with opposite signs, or the repulsive force between atomic particles charged with the same sign.

Embolus.   A piece of matter (such as a blood clot, fat, or bacterial debris) that dislodges from its site of origin and occludes an artery. In the brain, an embolus can lead to a stroke.

Endocrine gland.   A gland that liberates its secretions into the extracellular fluid around capillaries and hence into the bloodstream.

Endogenous opiate.   A class of peptides secreted by the brain or pituitary gland that act as opiates; includes the *endorphins, dynorphins,* and *enkephalins.*

β-Endorphin.   See under *endogenous opiate*.

Endplate potential.   The postsynaptic potential that occurs on the membranes of muscle fibers in response to release of acetylcholine by terminal buttons.

Enkephalin.   See under *endogenous opiate*.

Entorhinal cortex.   A region of the limbic cortex that provides the major source of input to the hippocampal formation.

Enzyme.   A protein that facilitates a biochemical reaction without itself becoming part of the end product.

EOG.   See *electro-oculogram (EOG)*.

Ependyma.   The layer of tissue around blood vessels and on the interior walls of the ventricular system of the brain.

Epinephrine.   A hormone, secreted by the adrenal medulla, that produces physiological effects characteristic of the sympathetic division of the autonomic nervous system.

EPSP.   See under *postsynaptic potential*.

Equilibrium.   A balance of forces, during which the system is not changing.

Estradiol.   The principal estrogen of many mammals, including humans.

Estrogen.   A class of sex hormones that cause maturation of the female genitalia, growth of breast tissue, and development of other physical features characteristic of females. Estrogens are also necessary for normal sexual behavior of most mammals other than primates.

Estrous cycle.   A cyclic change in the hormonal level and sexual receptivity of subprimate mammals.

Estrus.   That portion of the estrous cycle during which a female is sexually receptive.

Evoked potential.   A regular series of alterations in the slow electrical activity recorded from the central nervous system, produced by a sensory stimulus or an electrical shock to some part of the nervous system.

Excitatory postsynaptic potential (EPSP).   See under *postsynaptic potential*.

Exocrine gland.   A gland that liberates its secretions into a duct.

Extension.   Movements of limbs that tend to straighten their joints; the opposite of flexion. The muscles that support the weight of a four-legged animal are those that produce extension.

Extracellular fluid.   All body fluids outside cells: interstitial fluid, blood plasma, and cerebrospinal fluid.

Extrafusal muscle fiber.   One of the muscle fibers that are responsible for the force exerted by a muscular contraction.

Fasting phase.   The phase of metabolism during which nutrients are not available from the digestive system. Glucose, amino acids, fatty acids, and ketones are derived from glycogen, protein, and adipose tissue during this phase.

Fatty acid.   A substance of importance to metabolism during the fasting phase. Fats can be broken down to fatty acids and glycerol. Fatty acids can be metabolized by most cells of the body. Their basic structure is an alkyl group (CH) attached to a carboxyl group (COOH).

Feature detector. A neuron whose synaptic connections with afferent neurons cause it to respond when particular classes of stimuli, with characteristic features, are detected.

Fimbria. A fiber bundle that runs along the lateral surface of the hippocampal complex, connecting this structure with other regions of the forebrain. The fibers of the fimbria become the *fornix* as they course rostrally from the hippocampal formation. The *precommissural fornix* conveys axons from the medial septum to the hippocampus, and from the hippocampus to the lateral septum. The *fornix columns* convey axons from the subiculum to the anterior thalamic nuclei and to the mammillary bodies of the hypothalamus.

Fissure. A major groove in the surface of the brain. A smaller groove is called a sulcus.

Fixation. The chemical preparation and preservation of body tissue, usually with formalin.

Flexion. Movements of the limbs that tend to bend their joints; opposite of extension.

Focal epilepsy. A condition in which recurrent seizures are produced by hyperirritability of a localized region of the brain, especially the medial temporal lobe or orbital frontal lobe.

Follicle. A small secretory cavity. The *ovarian follicle* consists of epithelial cells surrounding an oocyte, which develops into an ovum.

Follicle-stimulating hormone (FSH). The hormone of the anterior pituitary gland that causes development of an ovarian follicle and the maturation of its oocyte into an ovum.

Foramen. A normal passage that allows communication between two cavities of the body. The *intervertebral foramen* permits passage of the spinal nerves through the vertebral column. The *foramens of Magendie and Luschka* permit the passage of cerebrospinal fluid out of the fourth ventricle and into the subarachnoid space. The *foramen of Monro* interconnects the lateral and third ventricles.

Forebrain. See Table 4.1.

Formalin. The aqueous solution of formaldehyde gas; the most commonly used tissue fixative.

Fornix. See under *fimbria.*

Fornix columns. See under *fimbria.*

Fourth ventricle. See under *ventricle.*

Fovea. The region of the retina that mediates the most acute vision of birds and higher mammals. Color-sensitive cones constitute the only type of photoreceptor found in the fovea.

Frontal section. See Figure 4.2.

FSH. See *follicle-stimulating hormone (FSH).*

GAD. See *glutamic acid decarboxylase (GAD).*

Gamete. A mature reproductive cell; a sperm or ovum.

Gamma-aminobutyric acid (GABA). An important inhibitory transmitter substance.

Gamma motor neuron. A lower motor neuron whose terminal buttons synapse upon intrafusal muscle fibers.

Ganglion. A collection of neural cell bodies, covered with connective tissue, located outside the central nervous system. *Autonomic ganglia* contain the cell bodies of postganglionic neurons of the sympathetic and parasympathetic branches of the autonomic nervous system. *Dorsal root ganglia (spinal nerve ganglia)* contain cell bodies of afferent spinal nerve neurons. *Cranial nerve ganglia* contain cell bodies of afferent cranial nerve neurons. The *basal ganglia* include the amygdala, caudate nucleus, globus pallidus, and putamen; in this case the term *ganglion* is a misnomer, since the basal ganglia are actually brain nuclei.

Ganglion cells. Neurons located in the retina; receive visual information from bipolar cells; their axons give rise to the optic nerve.

Gene. The functional unit of the chromosome, which directs synthesis of one or more proteins.

Gestagen. A group of hormones that promote and support pregnancy. Progesterone is the principal mammalian gestagen.

GH. See *growth hormone (GH).*

Glia (glial cells). The supportive cells of the central nervous system—the astroglia, oligodendroglia, and microglia.

Globus pallidus. One of the basal ganglia; an excitatory structure of the extrapyramidal motor system.

Glucagon. A pancreatic hormone that promotes the conversion of liver glycogen into glucose.

Glucocorticoid. One of a group of hormones of the adrenal cortex that are important in protein and carbohydrate metabolism, secreted especially in times of stress.

Glucose. A simple sugar, of great importance in metabolism. Glucose and ketones constitute the major sources of energy for the brain.

Glucostatic hypothesis. A hypothesis that states that the level or availability of glucose in the interstitial fluid determines whether an organism is hungry or satiated.

Glutamic acid (glutamate). An amino acid; an important excitatory transmitter substance.

Glutamic acid decarboxylase (GAD). The enzyme that converts glutamic acid into GABA, an important inhibitory transmitter substance.

Glycerol (glycerin). A trihydric alcohol; the breakdown of triglycerides (fats stored in adipose tissue) yields fatty acids and glycerol; can be converted by the liver into glucose.

Glycine. An amino acid; an important inhibitory transmitter substance.

Glycogen. A polysaccharide often referred to as *animal starch.* The hormone glucagon causes conversion of liver glycogen into glucose.

Golgi apparatus. A complex of parallel membranes in the cytoplasm that wraps the products of a secretory cell.

Golgi tendon organ. The receptor organ at the junction of the tendon and muscle that is sensitive to stretch.

Gonadotropic hormone. A hormone of the anterior pituitary gland that has a stimulating effect on cells of the gonads. See *follicle-stimulating hormone (FSH)* and *luteinizing hormone (LH).*

Granule cell. Small, granular cells. The granule cells of the dentate gyrus are part of the trisynaptic circuit; they send axons to the CA3 field of Ammon's horn.

Growth hormone (GH). A hormone that is necessary for the normal growth of the body before adulthood; also called *somatotropic hormone (STH).*

Gyrus. A convolution of the cortex of the cerebral hemispheres, separated by sulci or fissures.

Hair cell. The receptive cell of the auditory or vestibular apparatus.

6-HD. See *6-hydroxydopamine (6-HD).*

Hepatic portal system. The system of blood vessels that drain the capillaries of the digestive system, travel to the liver, and divide again into capillaries.

Hertz (Hz). Cycles per second; a measure of frequency of vibration.

Heterosynaptic facilitation. The ability of the activity of one synapse on a cell to increase the effectiveness of another synapse, belonging to another neuron, on the same cell; thought to be an essential feature of learning.

5-HIAA. See *5-hydroxyindoleacetic acid (5-HIAA).*

Hindbrain. See Table 4.1.

Hippocampal formation. A forebrain structure of the temporal lobe, constituting an important part of the limbic system; includes the hippocampus proper (Ammon's horn), dentate gyrus, and subiculum.

Histology. The microscopic study of tissues of the body.

Homeostasis. The process by which the body's substances and characteristics (such as temperature and glucose level) are maintained at their optimal level.

Homoiothermous. A "warm-blooded" animal, which regulates its body temperature by altering its metabolic activity.

Horizontal cell. Neuron in the retina that interconnects adjacent photoreceptors and the outer arborizations of the bipolar cells.

Horizontal section. See Figure 4.2.

Hormone. A chemical substance liberated by an endocrine gland that has effects on target cells in other organs. *Organizational effects* of a hormone affect tissue differentiation and development; for example, androgens cause prenatal development of male genitalia. *Activational effects* of a hormone are those that occur in the fully developed organism; many of them depend upon the organism's prior exposure to the organizational effects of hormones.

Horseradish peroxidase (HRP). An enzyme extracted from the horseradish root; can be made visible by special histological techniques. Since it is taken up by terminal buttons or by severed axons and is carried by axoplasmic transport, it is useful in anatomical studies.

5-HTP decarboxylase. The enzyme that converts 5-hydroxytryptophan (5-HTP) to the neurotransmitter 5-hydroxytryptamine (5-HT, or serotonin).

H-Y antigen. A protein produced by a gene on the Y chromosome that appears to play an essential role in converting the primordial gonads of the embryo into testes.

Hydrocephalus. A condition in which all or some of the brain's ventricles are enlarged. *Obstructive hydrocephalus* occurs when the normal flow of cerebrospinal fluid is impeded, increasing the intraventricular pressure. *Hydrocephalus ex vacuo* occurs when brain tissue degenerates and the ventricles expand to take up the space the tissue formerly occupied.

6-Hydroxydopamine (6-HD). A chemical that is selectively taken up by axons and terminal buttons of noradrenergic or dopaminergic neurons and that acts as a poison, damaging or killing them.

5-Hydroxyindoleacetic acid (5-HIAA). A breakdown product of the neurotransmitter serotonin.

5-Hydroxytryptamine (5-HT). An indolamine transmitter substance; also called *serotonin.*

5-Hydroxytryptophan (5-HTP). Derived from the amino acid tryptophan; converted to the neurotransmitter 5-hydroxytryptamine (5-HT) by the enzyme 5-HTP decarboxylase.

Hyperpolarization. An increase in the membrane potential of a cell, relative to the normal resting potential. Inhibitory postsynaptic potentials (IPSPs) are hyperpolarizations.

Hypnagogic hallucinations. A symptom of narcolepsy; vivid dreams that occur just before a person falls asleep; accompanied by sleep paralysis.

Hypoglycemia. A low level of blood glucose.

Hypothalamic hormone. A hormone produced by cells of the hypothalamus that affects the secretion and production of hormones of the anterior pituitary gland. The effects are excitatory in the case of releasing hormones and inhibitory in the case of inhibitory hormones.

Hypothalamic-hypophyseal portal system. A system of blood vessels that connect capillaries of the hypothalamus with capillaries of the anterior pituitary gland. Hypothalamic hormones travel to the anterior pituitary gland by means of this system.

Hypovolemia. See under *volumetric thirst.*

Hz. See *hertz (Hz).*

Imipramine. A noradrenergic agonist; retards reuptake of norepinephrine by terminal buttons; one of the most commonly used tricyclic antidepressants.

Immune system. The system by which the body protects itself from foreign proteins. In response to an infection, the white blood cells produce antibodies that attack and destroy the foreign antigen.

Incus. One of the bones of the middle ear, shaped somewhat like an anvil. See Figures 7.2 and 7.3.

Inferior. See Figure 4.1.

Inferior colliculi. Protrusions on top of the midbrain that relay auditory information to the medial geniculate nucleus.

Inferior temporal cortex. In monkeys, the highest level of visual association cortex, located on the inferior surface of the temporal lobe.

Inhibitory postsynaptic potential (IPSP). See under *postsynaptic potential.*

Instrumental conditioning. A learning procedure whereby the effects of a particular behavior in a particular situation increase (reinforce) or decrease (punish) the probability of the behavior; also called *operant conditioning.*

Insulin. A pancreatic hormone that facilitates entry of glucose and amino acids into the cell, facilitates conversion of glucose into glycogen, and facilitates transport of fats into adipose tissue.

Interstitial fluid. The fluid that bathes the cells of the body, filling the space between the cells of the body (the "interstices").

Intervertebral foramen. See under *foramen.*

Intracellular fluid. The fluid contained within cells.

Intrafusal muscle fiber. A muscle fiber that functions as a stretch receptor, arranged parallel to the extrafusal muscle fibers, thus detecting muscle length; also called *muscle spindle.*

Intraperitoneal (IP). Pertaining to the peritoneal cavity, the space surrounding the abdominal organs.

Intromission. Insertion of one part into another, especially of a penis into a vagina.

Ion. A charged molecule; *cations* are positively charged, and *anions* are negatively charged.

Ion channel. A specialized protein molecule that permits specific ions to enter or leave cells. *Voltage-dependent ion channels* open or close according to the value of the membrane potential. *Neurotransmitter-dependent ion channels* open when they detect molecules of the appropriate neurotransmitter or molecules of a cyclic nucleotide that serves as a second messenger.

IP. See *intraperitoneal (IP).*

Iproniazid. A monoamine agonist; deactivates monoamine oxidase and thus prevents destruction of extravesicular monoamines in the terminal buttons.

Ipsilateral. Located on the same side of the body as the point of reference.

IPSP. See under *postsynaptic potential.*

Isotonic. Equal in osmotic pressure to the contents of a cell. A cell placed in an isotonic solution neither gains nor loses water.

Kainic acid. A molecule similar to glutamic acid that destroys neurons with which it comes in contact, apparently by causing continuous excitation; used to produce brain lesions that spare axons that pass through the area containing the cells targeted for destruction.

Ketone. An organic acid consisting of two hydrocarbon radicals attached to a carbonyl group (CO). Ketones are produced from the breakdown of fats and can be utilized by the brain; they are often called *ketone bodies.*

Kindling. The establishment of a seizure focus by daily administration of a small amount of localized electrical brain stimulation; used to produce animal models of focal epilepsy.

Kinesthesia. Perception of the body's own movements.

Korsakoff's syndrome. Permanent anterograde amnesia (inability to learn new information) caused by brain damage resulting from chronic alcoholism or malnutrition.

Krebs cycle (citric acid cycle, tricarboxylic acid cycle). A series of chemical reactions that involve oxidation of pyruvate. The Krebs cycle takes place on the cristae of the mitochondria and supplies the principal source of energy to the cell.

Lateral. See Figure 4.1.

Lateral corticospinal tract. See under *corticospinal pathway.*

Lateral fissure. The fissure that separates the temporal lobe from the overlying frontal and parietal lobes.

Lateral geniculate nucleus. A group of cell bodies within the lateral geniculate body of the thalamus. The *dorsal lateral geniculate nucleus* receives fibers from the retina and projects fibers to the primary visual cortex.

Lateral hypothalamus. A region of the hypothalamus that contains cell bodies and diffuse fiber systems. Destruction of the lateral hypothalamus produces a relative lack of spontaneous movement, adipsia, aphagia, and weight loss, from which the animal at least partially recovers.

Lateral lemniscus. A band of fibers running rostrally through the medulla and pons; carries fibers of the auditory system.

Lateral preoptic area. See under *preoptic area.*

Lateral ventricle. See under *ventricle.*

Lee-Boot effect. The increased incidence of false pregnancies seen in female animals that are housed together; caused by a pheromone in the animals' urine; first observed in mice.

Lemniscal system. The somatosensory fibers of the lateral or trigeminal lemniscus, as contrasted with the extralemniscal system, a polysynaptic pathway that ascends through the reticular formation.

Leupeptin. A drug that inactivates calpain, an enzyme that cleaves spectrin, a protein present just inside the neural membrane.

LH. See *luteinizing hormone (LH).*

Limbic cortex. Phylogenetically old cortex, located at the edge ("limbus") of the cerebral hemispheres; part of the limbic system.

Limbic system. A group of brain regions including the anterior thalamic nuclei, amygdala, hippocampus, limbic cortex, and parts of the hypothalamus, as well as their interconnecting fiber bundles.

Locus coeruleus. A dark-colored group of noradrenergic cell bodies located in the pons near the rostral end of the floor of the fourth ventricle.

Long-term memory. Relatively stable memory, as opposed to short-term memory.

Long-term potentiation. An increase in the excitability of neurons in the trisynaptic circuit of the entorhinal cortex and hippocampal formation, caused by repeated electrical stimulation; thought to be related to learning and to the phenomenon of kindling.

Lordosis. A spinal sexual reflex seen in many four-legged female mammals; arching of the back in response to approach of a male or to touching the flanks, which elevates the hindquarters.

Lower motor neuron. A neuron located in the intermediate horn or ventral horn of the gray matter of the spinal cord or in one of the motor nuclei of the cranial nerves, the axon of which synapses on muscle fibers.

Luteinizing hormone (LH). A hormone of the anterior pituitary gland that causes ovulation and development of the ovarian follicle into a corpus luteum.

Macroelectrode. A relatively large electrode (larger than a microelectrode) that is used to record evoked potentials or spontaneous EEG activity.

Magnocellular system. The phylogenetically older portion of the visual system, named after the magnocellular layers of the lateral geniculate nucleus. Responsible for perception of form, movement, depth, and small differences in brightness.

Malleus. One of the bones of the middle ear, shaped somewhat like a hammer. See Figures 7.2 and 7.3.

Mammillary body. A protrusion of the bottom of the brain at the posterior end of the hypothalamus, containing the medial and lateral mammillary nuclei.

MAO. See *monoamine oxidase (MAO).*

Masculinizing effect. Effect of a hormone present early in development; promotes the later development of anatomical or behavioral characteristics typical of males. See also *defeminizing effect.*

Massa intermedia. A bridge of tissue across the third ventricle that connects the right and left portions of the thalamus.

Medial. See Figure 4.1.

Medial forebrain bundle (MFB). A fiber bundle that runs in a rostral-caudal direction through the basal forebrain and lateral hypothalamus.

Medial geniculate nucleus. A group of cell bodies within the medial geniculate body of the thalamus; part of the auditory system.

Medial lemniscus. A fiber bundle that ascends rostrally through the medulla and pons, carrying fibers of the somatosensory system.

Medial preoptic area. See *preoptic area.*

Medulla oblongata (usually medulla). The most caudal portion of the brain, immediately rostral to the spinal cord.

Meiosis. The process by which a cell divides to form gametes (sperms or ova).

Membrane. A structure consisting principally of lipid molecules that defines the outer boundaries of a cell and also constitutes many of the cell organelles, such as the Golgi apparatus.

Membrane potential. The electrical charge across a cell membrane; the difference in electrical potential inside and outside the cell; expressed as inside voltage relative to outside voltage (e.g., -70 mV signifies that the inside is 70 mV negative to the outside).

Meninges (singular: meninx). The three layers of tissue that encase the central nervous system: the dura mater, arachnoid membrane, and pia mater.

Mesencephalon. See Table 4.1.

Messenger ribonucleic acid (mRNA). See under *ribonucleic acid.*

Metabolism. The sum of all physical and chemical changes that take place in an organism, including all reactions that liberate energy. See also *absorptive phase* and *fasting phase.*

Metencephalon. See Table 4.1.

α-Methyl-p-tyrosine (AMPT). A substance that interferes with the activity of tyrosine hydroxylase and thus prevents the synthesis of dopamine and norepinephrine.

MFB. See *medial forebrain bundle (MFB).*

Microelectrode. A very fine electrode, generally used to record activity of individual neurons.

Microglia. Small glial cells that serve as phagocytes.

Micrometer (μm). Unit of measurement; one-millionth of a meter, or one-thousandth of a millimeter.

Midbrain. See Table 4.1.

Midsagittal plane. The plane that divides the body in two symmetrical halves through the midline.

Mitochondrion. A cell organelle in which the chemical reactions of the Krebs cycle take place.

Mitosis. Duplication and division of a somatic cell into a pair of daughter cells.

Monoamine. A class of amines that includes indolamines (e.g., serotonin) and catecholamines (e.g., dopamine and norepinephrine).

Monoamine oxidase (MAO). A class of enzymes that destroy the monoamines: dopamine, norepinephrine, and serotonin.

Monosynaptic stretch reflex. A reflex consisting of the afferent axon of the intrafusal muscle fiber synapsing upon an alpha motor neuron, and the efferent axon of the alpha motor neuron synapsing on the extrafusal muscle fibers in the same muscle. When a muscle is quickly stretched, the monosynaptic stretch reflex causes it to contract.

Morphology. Physical shape and structure.

Motor end plate. Region of the membrane of a muscle fiber upon which the terminal buttons of the efferent axon synapse.

Motor neuron (motoneuron). A neuron whose stimulation results in contractions of muscle fibers.

Motor unit. A motor neuron and its associated muscle fibers.

mRNA. See under *ribonucleic acid (RNA).*

Müllerian-inhibiting substance. A peptide secreted by the fetal testes that inhibits the development of the Müllerian system, which would otherwise become the female internal sex organs.

Müllerian system. The embryonic precursors of the female internal sex organs.

Multipolar neuron. A neuron with a single axon and numerous dendritic processes originating from the somatic membrane.

Muscle spindle. See *intrafusal muscle fiber.*

Myelencephalon. See Table 4.1.

Myelin. A complex fatlike substance produced by the oligodendroglia in the central nervous system and by the Schwann cells in the peripheral nervous system, which surrounds and insulates myelinated axons.

Myosin. Actin and myosin are the proteins that provide the physical basis for muscular contraction. See Figures 8.1 and 8.2.

Naloxone. A drug that blocks opiate receptors and thus blocks the effects of endogenous and exogenous opiates; used in treating opiate overdoses and in experimental investigations.

Narcolepsy. A sleep disorder characterized by periods of irresistible sleep, attacks of cataplexy, sleep paralysis, and hypnagogic hallucinations.

NE. See *norepinephrine (NE).*

Negative feedback. A process whereby the effect produced by an action serves to diminish or terminate that action. Regulatory systems are characterized by negative feedback loops.

Neocortex. The phylogenetically newest cortex, including the primary sensory cortex, primary motor cortex, and association cortex.

Neostriatum. The caudate nucleus and putamen.

Neural integration. The process by which inhibitory and excitatory postsynaptic potentials summate and control the rate of firing of a neuron.

Neuraxis. An imaginary line drawn through the center of the length of the central nervous system, from the bottom of the spinal cord to the front of the forebrain.

Neuroglia. The formal name for *glia.*

Neurohypophysis. See under *pituitary gland.*

Neuromodulator.   A naturally secreted substance that acts like a neurotransmitter except that it is not restricted to the synaptic cleft but diffuses through the interstitial fluid. Presumably, it activates receptors on neurons that are not located at synapses.

Neuromuscular junction.   The synapse between the terminal buttons of an axon and a muscle fiber.

Neurosecretory cell.   A neuron that secretes a hormone or hormonelike substance into the interstitial fluid.

Neurotransmitter.   See under *transmitter substance.*

Neurotransmitter-dependent ion channel.   See under *ion channel.*

Nigrostriatal bundle.   A bundle of axons originating in the substantia nigra and terminating in the neostriatum (caudate nucleus and putamen).

Nissl substance.   Cytoplasmic material dyed by cell-body stains (Nissl stains).

NMDA receptor.   A specialized glutamate receptor that controls a calcium channel that is normally blocked by Mg^{2+} ions; involved in long-term potentiation, seizures, brain damage produced by anoxia, and learning.

Node of Ranvier.   A naked portion of a myelinated axon, between adjacent oligodendroglia or Schwann cells.

Noradrenalin.   See *norepinephrine.*

Norepinephrine (NE).   A neurotransmitter found in the brain and in the terminal buttons of postganglionic fibers of the sympathetic division of the autonomic nervous system.

Nucleolus.   An organelle within the nucleus of a cell that produces the ribosomes.

Nucleus.   1. The central portion of an atom. 2. A spherical structure, enclosed by a membrane, located in the cytoplasm of most cells and containing the chromosomes. 3. A histologically identifiable group of neural cell bodies in the central nervous system.

Nucleus accumbens.   A nucleus of the basal forebrain near the septum; receives dopamine-secreting terminal buttons from neurons of the ventral tegmental area; thought to be involved in reinforcement and attention.

Nucleus basalis of Meynert.   A nucleus of the basal forebrain that contains most of the acetylcholine-secreting neurons that send axons to the neocortex; degenerates in patients with Alzheimer's disease.

Nucleus of the solitary tract.   A nucleus of the medulla that receives information from visceral organs and from the gustatory system; appears to play a role in sleep.

Nucleus raphe magnus.   One of the nuclei of the raphe; contains serotonin-secreting neurons that project to the dorsal gray matter of the spinal cord via the dorsolateral columns; involved in analgesia produced by opiates.

Olfactory bulb.   The protrusion at the end of the olfactory nerve; receives input from the olfactory receptors.

Oligodendroglia.   A type of glial cell in the central nervous system that forms myelin sheaths.

Operant conditioning.   See *instrumental conditioning.*

Opsin.   A class of protein that, together with retinal, constitutes the photopigments that are responsible for the transduction of visual information in the eye.

Optic chiasm.   A cross-shaped connection between the optic nerves, located below the base of the brain, just anterior to the pituitary gland.

Optic disk.   See under *optic nerve.*

Optic nerve.   The second cranial nerve, carrying visual information from the retina to the brain. The *optic disk* is formed at the exit point from the retina of the fibers of the ganglion cells that form the optic nerve.

Optic radiation.   The band of axons that project from the dorsal lateral geniculate nuclei of the thalamus to the primary visual cortex.

Organizational effects.   See under *hormone.*

Organ of Corti.   The receptor organ situated on the basilar membrane of the inner ear.

Oscilloscope.   A laboratory instrument capable of displaying a graph of voltage as a function of time on the face of a cathode ray tube.

Osmometric thirst.   Thirst produced by an increase in the osmotic pressure of the interstitial fluid relative to the intracellular fluid, thus producing cellular dehydration.

Osmosis.   Movement of ions through a semipermeable membrane, down their concentration gradient.

Outer plexiform layer.   The layer of the retina that contains synapses between the arborizations of bipolar cells, horizontal cells, and photoreceptors.

Oval window.   An opening in the bone surrounding the cochlea. The baseplate of the stapes presses against a membrane exposed by the oval window and transmits sound vibrations into the fluid within the cochlea.

Ovarian follicle.   See *follicle.*

Paleostriatum.   The globus pallidus.

Panic attack.   Episodic periods of symptoms such as shortness of breath, irregularities in heartbeat, and other autonomic symptoms, accompanied by intense fear. Fear of having a panic attack is called *anticipatory anxiety;* often leads to agoraphobia.

Parabrachial nucleus. A nucleus of the pons; relays gustatory information from the nucleus of the solitary tract of the medulla to the thalamic taste area.

Parachlorophenylalanine (PCPA). A substance that blocks the action of the enzyme tryptophan hydroxylase and hence prevents synthesis of serotonin (5-HT).

Paradoxical sleep. See *REM sleep.*

Paraphasic error. A speech error characterized by unintended or transposed syllables, words, or phrases.

Parasympathetic division. See under *autonomic nervous system (ANS).*

Paraventricular nucleus. A hypothalamic nucleus that contains cell bodies of neurons that produce antidiuretic hormone and oxytocin, and transport it through their axons to the posterior pituitary gland.

Parkinson's disease. A neurological disease that is characterized by fine tremor, rigidity, and difficulty in movement. Caused by degeneration of the nigrostriatal bundle.

Parvocellular system. The phylogenetically newer portion of the visual system, named after the parvocellular layers of the lateral geniculate nucleus; responsible for perception of color and fine details.

PCPA. See *parachlorophenylalanine (PCPA).*

A chain of amino acids joined together by peptide bonds. Many peptides produced by cells of the brain serve as neurotransmitters, neuromodulators, or hormones. Proteins are long peptides.

Perforant path. The system of axons that travel from cells in the entorhinal cortex to the dentate gyrus of the hippocampal formation.

Periaqueductal gray matter. The region of the midbrain that surrounds the cerebral aqueduct; contains neural circuits that control aggressive behavior and female sexual behavior and opiate-sensitive cells that mediate analgesia.

Peripheral nervous system (PNS). The cranial nerves, spinal nerves, and peripheral ganglia.

Permeability. The degree to which a membrane permits passage of a particular substance.

PGO waves. Bursts of phasic electrical activity originating in the pons, followed by activity in the lateral geniculate nucleus and visual cortex; a characteristic of REM sleep.

Phagocytosis. The process by which cells engulf and digest other cells or debris caused by cellular de-

generation; the cells that perform this function are *phagocytes.*

Pheromone. A chemical released by one animal that affects the behavior or physiology of another animal; usually smelled or tasted.

Phosphodiesterase. A class of enzymes that deactivate cyclic nucleotides.

Phosphorylation. The addition of phosphate to a protein, thus altering its physical characteristics.

Photoreceptor. The receptor cell of the retina, which transduces photic energy into electrical potentials. *Cones* are maximally sensitive to one of three different wavelengths of light and hence encode color vision, whereas all *rods* are maximally sensitive to light of the same wavelength and hence do not encode color vision.

Physostigmine. An acetylcholine agonist; inactivates acetylcholinesterase.

Pia mater. The layer of the meninges adjacent to the surface of the brain.

Pinocytosis. Pinching off of a bud of cell membrane, which travels to the interior of the cell; used to incorporate substances present in the interstitial fluid and to recycle pieces of the membrane used for producing synaptic vesicles.

Pituitary gland. The "master endocrine gland" of the body, attached to the base of the brain. The *anterior pituitary gland* (adenohypophysis) secretes hormones in response to the hypothalamic hormones. The *posterior pituitary gland* (neurohypophysis) secretes oxytocin or antidiuretic hormone in response to stimulation from its neural input.

Placebo. An inert substance given to an organism in lieu of a physiologically active drug; used experimentally to control for the effects of mere administration of a drug.

Platelet. A cell fragment that is necessary for the formation of blood clots.

Plexus. A network formed by the junction of several adjacent nerves.

PNS. The peripheral nervous system: the cranial nerves, spinal nerves, and peripheral ganglia.

Poikilothermous. Not capable of regulating body temperature by producing heat endogenously. Most poikilothermous animals regulate their body temperature but must approach or avoid sources of heat to do so.

Pons. The region of the brain rostral to the medulla and caudal to the midbrain.

Population EPSP. An evoked potential recorded from portions of the trisynaptic circuit of the hippocampal formation that represents the EPSPs of a population of neurons; long-term potentiation is detected by recording the population EPSP.

Posterior.   See Figure 4.1.

Posterior pituitary gland.   See under *pituitary gland.*

Postganglionic neurons.   Neurons of the autonomic nervous system that synapse directly upon their target organ.

Postsynaptic membrane.   The cell membrane opposite the terminal button in a synapse; the membrane of the cell that receives the message.

Postsynaptic potential.   Alterations in the membrane potential of a postsynaptic neuron, produced by liberation of transmitter substance at the synapse. *Excitatory postsynaptic potentials (EPSPs)* are depolarizations and increase the probability of firing of the postsynaptic neuron. *Inhibitory postsynaptic potentials (IPSPs)* are hyperpolarizations and decrease the probability of neural firing.

Postsynaptic receptor.   A receptor molecule in the postsynaptic membrane of a synapse that detects the presence of a neurotransmitter and controls neurotransmitter-dependent ion channels, thus producing excitatory or inhibitory postsynaptic potentials.

Precommissural fornix.   See under *fimbria.*

Predatory aggression.   Attack of one animal directed at an individual of another species, on which the attacking animal normally preys.

Preganglionic neuron.   The efferent neuron of the autonomic nervous system whose cell body is located in a cranial nerve nucleus or in the intermediate horn of the spinal gray matter and whose terminal buttons synapse upon postganglionic neurons in the autonomic ganglia.

Preoptic area.   An area of cell bodies (usually divided into the *lateral preoptic area* and *medial preoptic area*) just rostral to the hypothalamus. Some investigators refer to the preoptic area as a part of the hypothalamus, although embryologically they are derived from different tissue.

Prestriate cortex.   A region of visual association cortex; receives fibers from the striate cortex and from the superior colliculi and projects (in primates) to the inferior temporal cortex.

Presynaptic.   Referring to a neuron that synapses upon another one. See also *postsynaptic.*

Presynaptic membrane.   The membrane of a terminal button that lies parallel to the postsynaptic membrane.

Primary motor cortex.   The precentral gyrus, which contains neurons that control movements of skeletal muscles.

Primary sensory cortex.   Regions of cortex whose primary input is from one of the sensory systems.

Primordial.   In embryology, refers to the undeveloped early form of an organ.

Progesterone.   A steroid hormone produced by the ovary; maintains the endometrial lining of the uterus during the later part of the menstrual cycle and during pregnancy; along with estradiol, promotes receptivity in female mammals with estrous cycles.

Projection.   The efferent connection between neurons in one specific region of the brain and those in another region.

Prolactin.   A hormone of the anterior pituitary gland, necessary for production of milk and (in some subprimate mammals) development of a corpus luteum. Occasionally called luteotropic hormone.

Propranolol.   A noradrenergic antagonist; blocks postsynaptic β-noradrenergic receptors.

Prosody.   The use of changes in intonation and emphasis to convey meaning in speech besides that specified by the particular words; an important means of communication of emotion.

Prosopagnosia.   The inability to recognize people by the sight of their faces.

Prosthesis.   A device used to substitute for a missing or damaged part of the body.

Protanopia.   An inherited form of defective color vision in which red and green hues are confused. "Red" cones appear to be filled with "green" cone opsin.

Protein.   A long peptide that can serve in a structural capacity or as an enzyme.

Protein kinase.   An enzyme that attaches a phosphate (PO_4) to a protein and thereby causes it to change its shape. Protein kinases are activated by cyclic nucleotides and open ion channels by phosphorylating membrane proteins.

Psychosurgery.   Destruction of brain tissue to treat behavioral disorders in the absence of verified brain damage.

Pure word deafness.   The ability to hear, to speak, and (usually) to write, without being able to comprehend the meaning of speech; caused by bilateral temporal lobe damage.

Putamen.   One of the nuclei that constitute the basal ganglia. The putamen and caudate nucleus compose the neostriatum.

Pylorus.   The ring of smooth muscle at the junction of the stomach and duodenum that controls the release of the stomach contents.

Pyramidal cell.   A category of large neurons with a pyramid shape; found in the cerebral cortex and Ammon's horn of the hippocampal formation.

Pyramidal tract. A fiber bundle that contains axons of the lateral and ventral corticospinal tracts.

Raphe. A group of nuclei located in the reticular formation of the medulla, pons, and midbrain, situated along the midline.

Receptive field. That portion of the visual field in which the presentation of visual stimuli will produce an alteration in the firing rate of a particular neuron.

Receptor blocker. A drug that attaches to postsynaptic receptors without stimulating them, thus preventing the neurotransmitter from acting on them.

Receptor cell. A specialized type of cell that transduces physical stimuli into slow, graded receptor potentials.

Receptor molecule. A protein molecule situated in the membrane of a cell that is sensitive to a particular chemical, such as a neurotransmitter or hormone. When the appropriate chemical stimulates a receptor site, changes take place in the membrane or within the cell.

Receptor potential. A slow, graded electrical potential produced by a receptor cell in response to a physical stimulus. Receptor potentials alter the firing rate of neurons upon which the receptor cells synapse.

Red nucleus. A large nucleus of the midbrain that receives inputs from the cerebellum and motor cortex and sends axons to the spinal cord via the rubrospinal tract and to various subcortical motor nuclei.

Reflex. A stereotyped glandular secretion or movement produced as the direct result of a stimulus.

REM sleep. A period of desynchronized EEG activity during sleep, at which time dreaming, rapid eye movements, and muscular paralysis occur; also called *paradoxical sleep.*

Renin. A hormone that causes the conversion of *angiotensinogen* in the blood into *angiotensin;* sympathetic stimulation of the kidney, or reduction of its blood flow, results in the liberation of renin. Angiotensin produces thirst, constricts blood vessels (thus raising blood pressure), and stimulates the adrenal cortex to produce aldosterone, a hormone that stimulates the kidney to retain sodium.

Reserpine. A monoamine antagonist; makes synaptic vesicles leaky, so that the neurotransmitter (dopamine, norepinephrine, or serotonin) cannot be kept inside.

Resting potential. The membrane potential of a neuron when it is not being altered by excitatory or inhibitory postsynaptic potentials; approximately -70 mV.

Reticular formation. A large network of neural tissue located in the central region of the brain stem, from the medulla to the diencephalon.

Reticulospinal tract. A bundle of axons that travel from the reticular formation to the gray matter of the spinal cord; controls the muscles responsible for postural movements.

Retina. The neural tissue and photoreceptive cells located on the inner surface of the posterior portion of the eye.

Retrograde amnesia. Amnesia for events that preceded some disturbance to the brain, such as a head injury or electroconvulsive shock.

Re-uptake. The re-entry of a transmitter substance just liberated by a terminal button back through its membrane, thus terminating the postsynaptic potential that is induced in the postsynaptic neuron.

Rhodopsin. A particular opsin found in rods.

Ribonucleic acid (RNA). A complex macromolecule composed of a sequence of nucleotide bases attached to a sugar-phosphate backbone. *Messenger RNA (mRNA)* delivers genetic information from a portion of a chromosome to a ribosome, where the appropriate amino acids are assembled to produce the polypeptide coded for by the active portion of the chromosome.

Ribosome. A cytoplasmic structure, made of protein, that serves as the site of production of proteins translated from mRNA.

RNA. See *ribonucleic acid (RNA).*

Rod. See under *photoreceptor.*

Rostral. See Figure 4.1.

Round window. An opening in the bone surrounding the cochlea of the inner ear that permits vibrations to be transmitted, via the oval window, through the fluids and receptive tissue contained within the cochlea.

Rubrospinal tract. See under *dorsolateral pathway.*

Sagittal section. See Figure 4.2.

Saltatory conduction. Conduction of action potentials by myelinated axons; the action potential "jumps" from one node of Ranvier to the next.

Satellite cell. A cell that serves to support neurons of the peripheral nervous system, such as the Schwann cells that provide the myelin sheath.

Satiety. Cessation of hunger, produced by adequate and available supplies of nutrients.

Schwann cell. A cell in the peripheral nervous system that is wrapped around a myelinated axon, providing one segment of its myelin sheath.

SCN. See *suprachiasmatic nucleus (SCN).*

Scotoma. A region of blindness within an otherwise-normal visual field, produced by localized damage somewhere in the visual system.

Semicircular canal. One of the three ringlike structures of the vestibular apparatus that transduce changes in head rotation into neural activity.

Sensory coding. Representation of sensory events in the form of neural activity.

Sensory modality. A particular form of sensory input, such as vision, audition, or olfaction.

Sensory transduction. The process by which sensory stimuli are transduced into slow, graded receptor potentials.

Septum. A portion of the limbic system, lying between the walls of the anterior portions of the lateral ventricles.

Serotonin. An alternative name for the neurotransmitter 5-hydroxytryptamine (5-HT); named because of its constricting effect on blood vessels.

Set point. The optimal value of the system variable in a regulatory mechanism. The set point for human body temperature, recorded orally, is approximately 37°C.

Sexually dimorphic nucleus. A nucleus in the preoptic area that is much larger in males than in females; first observed in rats.

SFO. See *subfornical organ (SFO)*.

Short-term memory. Immediate memory for sensory events that may or may not be consolidated into long-term memory.

Single unit. An individual neuron.

Sleep apnea. Failure to breathe while asleep. Periods of sleep apnea occur in normal people, but when they are especially frequent, they substantially disturb sleep and pose a risk to life in infants and old or debilitated people.

Slow-wave sleep. Non-REM sleep, characterized by synchronized EEG activity during its deeper stages.

Smooth muscle. Nonstriated muscle innervated by the autonomic nervous system, found in the walls of blood vessels, in sphincters, within the eye, in the digestive system, and around hair follicles.

Sodium-potassium pump. A metabolically active process in the cellular membrane that extrudes sodium from and transports potassium into the cell.

Solitary nucleus. See *nucleus of the solitary tract*.

Soma. A cell body or, more generally, the body.

Somatosenses. Bodily sensation; sensitivity to such stimuli as touch, pain, and temperature.

Somatosensory cortex. The gyrus caudal to the central sulcus, which receives many projection fibers from the somatosensory system.

Somatotropic hormone (STH). See *growth hormone (GH)*.

Species-typical behavior. A behavior that is typical of all or most members of a species of animal, especially a behavior that does not appear to have to be learned.

Spectrin. A protein that lies just inside the neural membrane; thought to be involved in the structural changes that accompany long-term potentiation. See also *calpain*.

Spinal nucleus of the bulbocavernosus. A nucleus located in the lower spinal cord; in laboratory rodents the nucleus has been found to be sexually dimorphic, being present only in males.

Spinal root. A bundle of axons surrounded by connective tissue that occurs in pairs, which fuse and form a spinal nerve. The *dorsal root* contains afferent fibers, whereas the *ventral root* contains efferent fibers.

Stapes. One of the bones of the inner ear, shaped somewhat like a stirrup. See Figures 7.2 and 7.3.

Stereotaxic apparatus. A device that permits the experimenter to place an object such as an electrode or cannula into a specific part of the brain.

Steroid hormone. A hormone of low molecular weight, derived from cholesterol. Steroid hormones affect their target cells by attaching to receptors found within the cell.

STH. See *growth hormone (GH)*.

Striate cortex. Primary visual cortex.

Stria terminalis. A long fiber bundle that connects portions of the amygdala with the hypothalamus.

Subarachnoid space. The fluid-filled space between the arachnoid membrane and the pia mater.

Subcortical. Located within the brain, as opposed to being located on its cortical surface.

Subfornical organ (SFO). A small organ located in the confluence of the lateral ventricles, attached to the underside of the fornix; contains neurons that detect the presence of angiotensin in the blood and excite neural circuits that initiate drinking.

Subiculum. Part of the hippocampal formation. See under *fimbria*.

Substantia nigra. A darkly stained region of the tegmentum, which communicates with the neostriatum via the nigrostriatal bundle.

Sulcus. A groove in the surface of the cerebral hemisphere, smaller than a fissure.

Superior. See Figure 4.1.

Superior cerebellar peduncle. One of the three pairs of bands of white matter connecting the cerebellum and brain stem.

Superior colliculi. Protrusions on top of the midbrain; part of the visual system.

Suprachiasmatic nucleus (SCN). A nucleus situated atop the optic chiasm; contains a biological clock responsible for organizing many of the body's circadian rhythms.

Supraoptic nucleus. A hypothalamic nucleus that contains cell bodies of neurons that produce antidiuretic hormone and transport it through their axons to the posterior pituitary gland.

Sympathetic division. See under *autonomic nervous system (ANS)*.

Synapse. A junction between the terminal button of an axon and the membrane of another neuron.

Synaptic cleft. The space between the presynaptic membrane and the postsynaptic membrane.

Synaptic vesicle. A small, hollow, beadlike structure found in terminal buttons. Synaptic vesicles contain transmitter substance.

Synchrony. High-voltage, low-frequency electroencephalographic activity, characteristic of slow-wave sleep or coma. During synchrony, neurons are presumably firing together in a regular fashion.

System variable. That which is controlled by a regulatory mechanism; for example, temperature in a heating system.

Tardive dyskinesia. A movement disorder that occasionally occurs after prolonged treatment with antischizophrenic medication, characterized by involuntary movements of the face and neck, sometimes interfering with speech.

Target cell. The type of cell that is directly affected by a hormone or nerve fiber.

Tectospinal tract. A bundle of axons that travel from the tectum to the spinal cord; coordinates head and trunk movements with eye movements.

Tectum. The roof of the midbrain, comprising the inferior and the superior colliculi.

Tegmentum. The portion of the midbrain beneath the tectum, containing the red nucleus and nuclei of various cranial nerves.

Telencephalon. See Table 4.1.

Terminal button. The rounded swelling at the end of an axonal process that synapses upon another neuron, muscle fiber, or gland cell.

Testicular feminization. See *androgen insensitivity syndrome*.

Testosterone. The principle androgen found in males.

Theta activity. EEG activity of 5–8 Hz. Theta activity of the hippocampus is an important indication of its physiological state.

Third ventricle. See under *ventricle*.

Threshold of excitation. The value of the membrane potential that must be reached in order to produce an action potential.

Trace conditioning. A classical conditioning procedure; the unconditional stimulus follows the conditional stimulus by a short interval of time.

Transmitter substance. A chemical that is liberated by the terminal buttons of an axon and produces an EPSP or an IPSP in the membrane of the postsynaptic cell; also called *neurotransmitter*.

Transverse section. See Figure 4.2.

Tricarboxylic acid cycle. See *Krebs cycle*.

Tricyclic antidepressant. A class of drugs, named for their molecular structure, that are used to treat depression.

Trigeminal lemniscus. A bundle of fibers running parallel to the medial lemniscus; conveys afferent fibers from the trigeminal nerve to the thalamus.

Triglyceride. The form of fat storage in adipose cells; consists of a molecule of glycerol joined with the three fatty acids: stearic acid, oleic acid, and palmitic acid.

Trisynaptic circuit. The recurrent circuit formed by connections between the entorhinal cortex, dentate gyrus, and CA1 and CA3 fields of Ammon's horn. Repeated stimulation of this circuit leads to long-term potentiation of the extracellular population spike.

Tritanopia. An inherited form of defective color vision in which hues with short wavelengths are confused. "Blue" cones are either lacking or faulty.

Tryptophan. An amino acid; the precursor for 5-HT (serotonin).

Tryptophan hydroxylase. The enzyme that converts tryptophan to 5-hydroxytryptophan (5-HTP).

Tyrosine. An amino acid; the precursor of the catecholamines: dopamine, norepinephrine, and epinephrine.

Tyrosine hydroxylase. The enzyme that converts tyrosine to L-DOPA, the immediate precursor of dopamine.

Unconditional response (UR). See under *classical conditioning*.

Unconditional stimulus (US). See under *classical conditioning*.

Unipolar depression. A psychosis; unremitting depression, or periods of depression that do not alternate with periods of mania.

Unipolar neuron. A neuron with a long, continuous fiber that has dendritic processes on one end and axonal processes and terminal buttons on the other. The fiber connects with the soma of the neuron by means of a single, short process.

Vagus nerve. The largest of the cranial nerves, conveying efferent fibers of the parasympathetic division of the autonomic nervous system to organs of the thoracic and abdominal cavities. The vagus nerve also carries nonpainful sensory fibers from these organs to the brain.

Vasopressin. A hormone secreted by the posterior pituitary gland that causes the kidneys to excrete a more concentrated urine, thus retaining water in the body; also called *antidiuretic hormone (ADH)*.

Ventral. See Figure 4.1.

Ventral amygdalofugal pathway. The diffuse system of fibers connecting portions of the amygdala with various forebrain structures.

Ventral corticospinal tract. See under *corticospinal pathway*.

Ventral horn (of gray matter of spinal cord). Location of the cell bodies of alpha and gamma motor neurons of the spinal cord.

Ventral posterior nucleus (of thalamus). The thalamic nucleus that projects to the primary somatosensory cortex.

Ventral root. See under *spinal root*.

Ventral tegmental area. A nucleus in the ventral tegmentum that contains dopamine-secreting neurons whose axons project to the forebrain, especially to the cortex and nucleus accumbens; thought to be important in arousal and reinforcement.

Ventricle. One of the hollow spaces within the brain, filled with cerebrospinal fluid, including the *lateral*, *third*, and *fourth ventricles*.

Ventrolateral nucleus (of thalamus). A nucleus that receives inputs from the cerebellum and sends axons to the primary motor cortex.

Ventromedial nucleus of the hypothalamus (VMH). A large nucleus of the hypothalamus located near the walls of the third ventricle; important in controlling female sexual behavior.

Ventromedial pathways. The vestibulospinal, tectospinal, and reticulospinal tracts.

Vertebral artery. An artery, the branches of which serve the posterior region of the brain.

Vestibular nerve. See under *auditory nerve*.

Vestibulospinal tract. A bundle of axons from the vestibular nuclei of the brain stem to the gray matter of the spinal cord; controls postural movements in response to information from the vestibular system.

Visual agnosia. Deficits in visual perception in the absence of blindness; caused by brain damage. *Apperceptive visual agnosia* is a failure to perceive objects, even though detection of individual components is relatively normal. *Associative visual agnosia* is the inability to name objects that are perceived visually, even though the form of the perceived object can be matched with similar objects.

VMH. See *ventromedial nucleus of the hypothalamus (VMH)*.

Voltage-dependent ion channel. See under *ion channel*.

Volumetric thirst. Thirst produced by *hypovolemia*, or reduction in the amount of extracellular fluid. Volumetric thirst is produced by baroreceptors in the right atrium of the heart and by reduced blood flow from the kidneys.

Vomeronasal organ. A sensory organ in some species that detects the presence of certain chemicals, especially when a liquid is actively sniffed; mediates the effects of some pheromones.

Wernicke's area. A region of auditory association cortex on the left temporal lobe of humans, which is important in the comprehension of words and the production of meaningful speech. *Wernicke's aphasia*, which occurs as a result of damage to this area, results in fluent but meaningless speech.

Whitten effect. The synchronization of the menstrual or estrous cycles of a group of females, which occurs only when a male (or his pheromone) is present.

Wolffian system. The embryonic precursors of the male internal sex organs.

Word-form dyslexia. A disorder in which a person can read a word only after spelling out the individual letters; caused by brain damage.

REFERENCES

Abel, E.L., and Sokol, R.J. Fetal alcohol syndrome is now a leading cause of mental retardation. *Lancet*, 1986, *2*, 1222.

Adams, D.B. Defense and territorial behaviour dissociated by hypothalamic lesions in the rat. *Nature*, 1971, *232*, 573–574.

Adams, D.B. Brain mechanisms for offense, defense, and submission. *Behavioral and Brain Sciences*, 1979, *2*, 201–241.

Adams, D.B. Hormone-brain interactions and their influence on agonistic behavior. In *Hormones and Aggressive Behavior*, edited by B.B. Svare. New York: Plenum Press, 1983.

Adams, D.B. Ventromedial tegmental lesions abolish offense without disturbing predation or defense. *Physiology and Behavior*, 1986, *38*, 165–168.

Adams, D.B., Gold, A.R., and Burt, A.D. Rise in female-initiated sexual activity at ovulation and its suppression by oral contraceptives. *New England Journal of Medicine*, 1978, *299*, 1145–1150.

Adams, R.D. The anatomy of memory mechanisms in the human brain. In *The Pathology of Memory*, edited by G.A. Talland and N.C. Waugh. New York: Academic Press, 1969.

Adey, W.R., Bors, E., and Porter, R.W. EEG sleep patterns after high cervical lesions in man. *Archives of Neurology*, 1968, *19*, 377–383.

Adieh, H.B., Mayer, A.D., and Rosenblatt, J.S. Effects of brain antiestrogen implants on maternal behavior and on postpartum estrus in pregnant rats. *Neuroendocrinology*, 1987, *46*, 522–531.

Adolph, E.F. Measurements of water drinking in dogs. *American Journal of Physiology*, 1939, *125*, 75–86.

Aggleton, J.P., Hunt, P.R., and Rawlins, J.N.P. The effects of hippocampal lesions upon spatial and nonspatial tests of working memory. *Behavioural Brain Research*, 1986, *19*, 133–146.

Akil, H., Mayer, D., and Liebeskind, J.C. Antagonism of stimulation-produced analgesia by Naloxone, a narcotic antagonist. *Science*, 1976, *191*, 961–962.

Akil, H., Watson, S.J., Young, E., Lewis, M.E., Khachaturian, H., and Walker, J.M. Endogenous opioids: Biology and function. *Annual Review of Neuroscience*, 1984, *7*, 223–255.

Albert, D.J., Dyson, E.M., Walsh, M.L., and Petrovic, D.M. Cohabitation with a female activates testosterone-dependent social aggression in male rats independently of changes in serum testosterone concentration. *Physiology and Behavior*, 1988, *44*, 735–740.

Albert, D.J., Dyson, M., Petrovic, D.M., and Walsh, M.L. Activation of aggression in female rats by normal males and by castrated males with testosterone implants. *Physiology and Behavior*, 1988, *44*, 9–13.

Albert, D.J., Petrovic, D.M., and Walsh, M.L. Competitive experience activates testosterone-dependent social aggression toward unfamiliar males. *Physiology and Behavior*, 1989a, *45*, 723–727.

Albert, D.J., Petrovic, D.M., and Walsh, M.L. Ovariectomy attenuates aggression by female rats cohabiting with sexually active sterile males. *Physiology and Behavior*, 1989b, *45*, 225–228.

Albrecht, D.G. *Analysis of visual form.* Doctoral dissertation, University of California, Berkeley, 1978.

Albright, T.D., Desimone, R., and Gross, C.G. Columnar organization of directionally selective cells in visual area MT of the macaque. *Journal of Neurophysiology*, 1984, *51*, 16–31.

Alexander, M.P., and Albert, M.L. The anatomical basis of visual agnosia. In *Localization in Neuropsychology*, edited by A. Kertesz. New York: Academic Press, 1983.

Allen, J.S., and Sarich, V.M. Schizophrenia in an evolutionary perspective. *Perspectives in Biology and Medicine*, 1988, *32*, 132–153.

Allen, L.S., Hines, M., Shryne, J.E., and Gorski, R.A. Two sexually dimorphic cell groups in the human brain. *Journal of Neuroscience*, 1989, *9*, 497–506.

Allison, T., and Chichetti, D. Sleep in mammals: Ecological and constitutional correlates. *Science,* 1976, *194,* 732–734.

Al-Maskati, H.A., and Zbrozyna, A.W. Cardiovascular and motor components of the defence reaction elicited in rats by electrical and chemical stimulation in amygdala. *Journal of the Autonomic Nervous System,* 1989, *28,* 127–132.

Amenomori, Y., Chen, C.L., and Meites, J. Serum prolactin levels in rats during different reproductive states. *Endocrinology,* 1970, *86,* 506–510.

Amir, S. Stimulation of the paraventricular nucleus with glutamate activates interscapular brown adipose tissue thermogenesis in rats. *Brain Research,* 1990, *508,* 152–155.

Anand, B.K., and Brobeck, J.R. Hypothalamic control of food intake in rats and cats. *Yale Journal of Biology and Medicine,* 1951, *24,* 123–140.

Anderson, R.H., Fleming, D.E., Rhees, R.W., and Kinghorn, E. Relationships between sexual activity, plasma testosterone, and the volume of the sexually dimorphic nucleus of the preoptic area in prenatally stressed and non-stressed rats. *Brain Research,* 1986, *370,* 1–10.

Andersson, B. The effect of injections of hypertonic NaCl solutions in different parts of the hypothalamus of goats. *Acta Physiologica Scandinavica,* 1953, *28,* 188–201.

Andreasen, N.C. Brain imaging: Applications in psychiatry. *Science,* 1988, *239,* 1381–1388.

Andreasen, N.C., and Olsen, S.A. Negative vs positive schizophrenia: Definition and validation. *Archives of General Psychiatry,* 1982, *39,* 789–794.

Anonymous. Effects of sexual activity on beard growth in man. *Nature,* 1970, *226,* 867–870.

Applegate, C.D., Frysinger, R.C., Kapp, B.S., and Gallagher, M. Multiple unit activity recorded from the amygdala central nucleus during Pavlovian heart rate conditioning in the rabbit. *Brain Research,* 1982, *238,* 457–462.

Arendash, G.W., and Gorski, R.A. Effects of discrete lesions of the sexually dimorphic nucleus of the preoptic area or other medial preoptic regions on the sexual behavior of male rats. *Brain Research Bulletin,* 1983, *10,* 147–154.

Arnauld, E., Dufy, B., and Vincent, J.D. Hypothalamic supraoptic neurons: Rates and patterns of action potential firing during water deprivation in the unanesthetized monkey. *Brain Research,* 1975, *100,* 315–325.

Arnold, A.P., and Jordan, C.L. Hormonal organization of neural circuits. In *Frontiers in Neuroendocrinology, Vol. 10,* edited by L. Martini and W.F. Ganong. New York: Raven Press, 1988.

Artmann, H., Grau, H., Adelman, M., and Schleiffer, R. Reversible and non-reversible enlargement of cerebrospinal fluid spaces in anorexia nervosa. *Neuroradiology,* 1985, *27,* 103–112.

Asanuma, H., and Rosén, I. Topographical organization of cortical efferent zones projecting to distal forelimb muscles in monkey. *Experimental Brain Research,* 1972, *13,* 243–256.

Aschoff, J. Circadian rhythms: General features and endocrinological aspects. In *Endocrine Rhythms,* edited by D.T. Krieger. New York: Raven Press, 1979.

Aserinsky, N.E., and Kleitman, N. Regularly occurring periods of eye motility and concomitant phenomena during sleep. *Science,* 1955, *118,* 273–274.

Aston-Jones, G. Behavioral functions of locus coeruleus derived from cellular attributes. *Physiological Psychology,* 1985, *13,* 118–126.

Aston-Jones, G., and Bloom, F.E. Activity of norepinephrine-containing locus coeruleus neurons in behaving rats anticipates fluctuations in the sleep-waking cycle. *The Journal of Neuroscience,* 1981a, *1,* 876–886.

Aston-Jones, G., and Bloom, F.E. Norepinephrine-containing locus coeruleus neurons in behaving rats exhibit pronounced responses to non-noxious environmental stimuli. *Journal of Neuroscience,* 1981b, *1,* 887–900.

Aston-Jones, G., Ennis, M., Pieribone, V.A., Nickell, W.T., and Shipley, M.T. The brain nucleus locus coeruleus: Restricted afferent control of a broad efferent network. *Science,* 1986, *234,* 734–737.

Avenet, P., Hoffman, F., and Lindemann, B. Transduction in taste receptor cells requires cAMP-dependent protein kinase. *Nature,* 1988, *331,* 351–354.

Avenet, P., and Lindemann, B. Perspectives of taste reception. *Journal of Membrane Biology,* 1989, *112,* 1–8.

Babinski, J. Contribution à l'étude des troubles mentaux dans l'hémiplégie organique cérébrale (anosognosia). *Revue Neurologique,* 1914, *27,* 845–848.

Baddeley, A. Implications of neuropsychological evidence for theories of normal memory. *Philosophical Transactions of the Royal Society of London,* 1982, *298,* 59–72.

Bailey, C.H., and Chen, M. Structural plasticity at identified synapses during long-term memory in *Aplysia. Journal of Neurobiology,* 1989, *20,* 356–372.

Baldessarini, R.J. *Chemotherapy in Psychiatry.* Cambridge, Mass.: Harvard University Press, 1977.

Baldessarini, R.J., and Tarsy, D. Dopamine and the

pathophysiology of dyskinesias induced by anti-psychotic drugs. *Annual Review of Neuroscience*, 1980, *3*, 23–42.

Balint, R. Seelenlahmung des "Schauens", optische Ataxie, raumliche Storung der Aufmerksamkeit. *Monatsschr. Psychiat. Neurol.*, 1909, *25*, 51–81.

Ballantine, H.T., Bouckoms, A.J., Thomas, E.K., and Giriunas, I.E. Treatment of psychiatric illness by stereotactic cingulotomy. *Biological Psychiatry*, 1987, *22*, 807–819.

Balon, R., Jordan, M., Pohl, R., and Yeragani, V.K. Family history of anxiety disorders in control subjects with lactate-induced panic attacks. *American Journal of Psychiatry*, 1989, *146*, 1304–1306.

Bambridge, B., and Gijsbers, K. The role of tonic neural activity in motivational processes. *Experimental Neurology*, 1977, *56*, 370–385.

Bandler, R.J., Chi, C.C., and Flynn, J.P. Biting attack elicited by stimulation of the ventral midbrain tegmentum of cats. *Science*, 1972, *177*, 364–366.

Bandler, R.J., and Flynn, J.P. Control of somatosensory fields for striking during hypothalamically elicited attack. *Brain Research*, 1972, *38*, 197–201.

Barkley, M.S., Geschwind, I.I., and Bradford, G.E. The gestational pattern of estradiol, testosterone, and progesterone secretion in selected strains of mice. *Biology of Reproduction*, 1979, *20*, 33–38.

Bartus, R.T., Dean, R.L., Beer, B., and Lippa, A.S. The cholinergic hypothesis of geriatric memory dysfunction. *Science*, 1982, *217*, 408–417.

Basbaum, A.I., and Fields, H.L. Endogenous pain control mechanisms: Review and hypothesis. *Annals of Neurology*, 1978, *4*, 451–462.

Basbaum, A.I., and Fields, H.L. Endogenous pain control systems: Brainstem spinal pathways and endorphin circuitry. *Annual Review of Neuroscience*, 1984, *7*, 309–338.

Bassett, A.S. Chromosome 5 and schizophrenia: Implications for genetic linkage studies. *Schizophrenia Bulletin*, 1989, *15*, 393–402.

Bassett, A.S., McGillivray, B.C., Jones, B., and Pantzar, J.T. Partial trisomy chromosome 5 cosegregating with schizophrenia. *Lancet*, 1988, *1*, 799–801.

Baxter, L.R., Phelps, M.E., Mazziotta, J.C., Guze, B.H., Schwartz, J.M., and Selin, C.E. Local cerebral glucose metabolic rates in obsessive-compulsive disorder. *Archives of General Psychiatry*, 1987, *44*, 211–218.

Baxter, L.R., Schwartz, J.M., Mazziotta, J.C., Phelphs, M.E., Pahl, J.J., and Guze, B.H. Cerebral glucose metabolic rates in non-depressed obsessive com-pulsives. *American Journal of Psychiatry*, 1989, *145*, 1560–1563.

Baylis, G.C., Rolls, E.T., and Leonard, C.M. Selectivity between faces in the responses of a population of neurons in the cortex in the superior temporal sulcus of the monkey. *Brain Research*, 1985, *342*, 91–102.

Baylis, P.H., and Thompson, C.J. Osmoregulation of vasopressin secretion and thirst in health and disease. *Clinical Endocrinology*, 1988, *29*, 549–576.

Bazett, H.C., McGlone, B., Williams, R.G., and Lufkin, H.M. Sensation. I. Depth, distribution, and probable identification in the prepuce of sensory end-organs concerned in sensations of temperature and touch: Thermometric conductivity. *Archives of Neurology and Psychiatry (Chicago)*, 1932, *27*, 489–517.

Beach, F.A. Cerebral and hormonal control of reflexive mechanisms involved in copulatory behavior. *Physiological Review*, 1967, *47*, 289–316.

Beal, M.F., Kowall, N.W., Ellison, D.W., Mazurek, M.F., Swartz, K.J., and Martin, J.B. Replication of the neurochemical characteristics of Huntington's disease by quinolinic acid. *Nature*, 1986, *321*, 168–171.

Bean, N.J. Modulation of agonistic behavior by the dual olfactory system in male mice. *Physiology and Behavior*, 1982, *29*, 433–437.

Bean, N.J., and Conner, R. Central hormonal replacement and home-cage dominance in castrated rats. *Hormones and Behavior*, 1978, *11*, 100–109.

Bean, N.J., and Wysocki, C.J. Vomeronasal organ removal and female mouse aggression: The role of experience. *Physiology and Behavior*, 1989, *45*, 875–882.

Beauvois, M.F., and Dérouesné, J. Phonological alexia: Three dissociations. *Journal of Neurology, Neurosurgery and Psychiatry*, 1979, *42*, 1115–1124.

Beauvois, M.F., and Dérouesné, J. Lexical or orthographic dysgraphia. *Brain*, 1981, *104*, 21–45.

Beckstead, R.M., Morse, J.R., and Norgren, R. The nucleus of the solitary tract in the monkey: Projections to the thalamus and brainstem nuclei. *Journal of Comparative Neurology*, 1980, *190*, 259–282.

Beecher, H.K. *Measurement of Subjective Responses: Quantitative Effects of Drugs*. New York: Oxford University Press, 1959.

Beeman, E.A. The effect of male hormone on aggressive behavior in mice. *Physiological Zoology*, 1947, *20*, 373–405.

Beidler, L.M. Physiological properties of mammalian taste receptors. In *Taste and Smell in Vertebrates*, edited by G.E.W. Wolstenholme. London: J.&A. Churchill, 1970.

Beitz, A.J. The organization of afferent projections to the midbrain periaqueductal gray of the rat. *Neuroscience*, 1982a, *7*, 133–159.

Beitz, A.J. The sites of origin of brain stem neurotensin and serotonin projections to the rodent nucleus raphe magnus. *Journal of Neuroscience*, 1982b, *7*, 829–842.

Bell, A.P., Weinberg, M.S., and Hammersmith, S.K. *Sexual Preference: Its Development in Men and Women.* Bloomington: Indiana University Press, 1981.

Bellisle, F., Lucas, F., Amrani, R., and Le Magnen, J. Deprivation, palatability and the micro-structure of meals in human subjects. *Appetite*, 1984, *5*, 85–94.

Bellringer, J.F., Pratt, H.P.M., and Keverne, E.B. Involvement of the vomeronasal organ and prolactin in pheromonal induction of delayed implantation in mice. *Journal of Reproduction and Fertility*, 1980, *59*, 223–228.

Bellugi, U., Poizner, H., and Klima, E.S. Language, modality and the brain. *Trends in Neurosciences*, 1989, *12*, 380–388.

Benedek, G., Obal, F., Lelkes, Z., and Obal, F. Thermal and chemical stimulation of the hypothalamus heat detectors: The effects on the EEG. *Acta Physiologica Hungaria*, 1982, *60*, 27–35.

Benson, D.F., and Geschwind, N. The alexias. In *Handbook of Clinical Neurology, Vol. 4*, edited by P. Vinken and G. Bruyn. Amsterdam: North-Holland, 1969.

Benson, D.F., and Greenberg, J. Visual form agnosia. *Archives of Neurology*, 1969, *20*, 82–89.

Benzing, W.C., and Squire, L.R. Preserved learning and memory in amnesia: Intact adaptation-level effects and learning of stereoscopic depth. *Behavioral Neuroscience*, 1989, *103*, 538–547.

Berger, T.W., Berry, S.D., and Thompson, R.F. Role of the hippocampus in classical conditioning of aversive and appetitive behaviors. In *The Hippocampus, Vol. 4*, edited by R.L. Isaacson and K.H. Pribram. New York: Plenum Press, 1986.

Berger, T.W., and Orr, W.B. Hippocampectomy selectively disrupts discrimination reversal conditioning of the rabbit nictitating membrane response. *Behavioural Brain Research*, 1983, *8*, 49–68.

Berkun, M.A., Kessen, M.L., and Miller, N.E. Hunger-reducing effects of food by stomach fistula versus food by mouth measured by a consummatory response. *Journal of Comparative and Physiological Psychology*, 1952, *45*, 550–554.

Berlucchi, G., Maffei, L., Moruzzi, G., and Strata, P. EEG and behavioral effects elicited by cooling of

medulla and pons. *Archives Italiennes de Biologie*, 1964, *102*, 372–392.

Bermant, G., and Davidson, J.M. *Biological Bases of Sexual Behavior*. New York: Harper & Row, 1974.

Bernard, C. *Leçons de Physiologie Expérimentale Appliquée à la Médicine Faites au Collège de France, Vol. 2.* Paris: Bailliere, 1856.

Bernstein, I.L. Learned taste aversion in children receiving chemotherapy. *Science*, 1978, *200*, 1302–1303.

Bernstein, I.L. Meal patterns in "free running humans." *Physiology and Behavior*, 1981, *27*, 621–624.

Bernstein, I.L., Zimmerman, J.C., Czeisler, C.A., and Weitzman, E.D. Meal patterns in "free running humans." *Physiology and Behavior*, 1982, *27*, 621–623.

Berthier, N.E., and Moore, J.W. The nictitating membrane response: An electrophysiological study of the abducens nerve and nucleus and the accessory abducens nucleus in rabbit. *Brain Research*, 1983, *258*, 201–210.

Besson, J.M., Guilbaud, G., Abdelmoumene, M., and Chaouch, A. Physiologie de la nociception. *Journal of Physiology (Paris)*, 1982, *78*, 7–107.

Bielajew, C., and Shizgal, P. Behaviorally derived measures of conduction velocity in the substrate for rewarding medial forebrain bundle stimulation. *Brain Research*, 1982, *237*, 107–119.

Bielajew, C., and Shizgal, P. Evidence implicating descending fibers in self-stimulation of the medial forebrain bundle. *Journal of Neuroscience*, 1986, *6*, 919–929.

Birch, L.L., McPhee, L., Shoba, B.C., Steinberg, L., and Krehbiel, R. "Clean up your plate": Effects of child feeding practices on the conditioning of meal size. *Learning and Motivation*, 1987, *18*, 301–317.

Birch, L.L., McPhee, L., Sullivan, S., and Johnson, S. Conditioned meal initiation in young children. *Appetite*, 1989, *13*, 105–113.

Blake, L., Jarvis, C.D., and Mishkin, M. Pattern discrimination thresholds after partial inferior temporal or lateral striate lesions in the monkey. *Brain Research*, 1977, *120*, 209–220.

Blander, D.S., Mark, G.P., Hernandez, L., and Hoebel, B.G. Angiotensin and drinking induce dopamine release in the nucleus accumbens. *Neuroscience Abstracts*, 1988, *14*, 527.

Blank, D.L., and Wayner, M.J. Lateral preoptic single unit activity: Effects of various solutions. *Physiology and Behavior*, 1975, *15*, 723–730.

Blass, E.M., and Epstein, A.N. A lateral preoptic osmosensitive zone for thirst. *Journal of Comparative and Physiological Psychology*, 1971, *76*, 378–394.

Blass, E.M., and Kraly, F.S. Medial forebrain bundle lesions: Specific loss of feeding to decreased glucose utilization in rats. *Journal of Comparative and Physiological Psychology,* 1974, *86,* 679–692.

Blaustein, J.D., and Feder, H.H. Cytoplasmic progestin receptors in guinea pig brain: Characteristics and relationship to the induction of sexual behavior. *Brain Research,* 1979, *169,* 481–497.

Blaustein, J.D., and Feder, H.H. Nuclear progestin receptors in guinea pig brain measured by an in vitro exchange assay after hormonal treatments that affect lordosis. *Endocrinology,* 1980, *106,* 1061–1069.

Blaustein, J.D., and Olster, D.H. Gonadal steroid hormone receptors and social behaviors. In *Advances in Comparative and Environmental Physiology, Vol. 3.,* edited by J. Balthazart. Berlin: Springer-Verlag, 1989.

Blaza, S. Brown adipose tissue in man: A review. *Journal of the Royal Society of Medicine,* 1983, *76,* 213–216.

Blest, A.D. The function of eyespot patterns in insects. *Behaviour,* 1957, *11,* 209–256.

Bliss, T.V.P., and Lømo, T. Long-lasting potentiation of synaptic transmission in the dentate area of the anaesthetized rabbit following stimulation of the perforant path. *Journal of Physiology (London),* 1973, *232,* 331–356.

Bloch, G.J., and Gorski, R.A. Cytoarchitectonic analysis of the SDN-POA of the intact and gonadectomized rat. *Journal of Comparative Neurology,* 1988, *275,* 604–612.

Bloch, V., Hennevin, E., and Leconte, P. Interaction between post-trial reticular stimulation and subsequent paradoxical sleep in memory consolidation processes. In *Neurobiology of Sleep and Memory,* edited by R.R. Drucker-Colín, and J.L. McGaugh. New York: Academic Press, 1977.

Block, M., and Zucker, I. Circadian rhythms of rat locomotor activity after lesions of the midbrain raphe nuclei. *Journal of Comparative and Physiological Psychology,* 1976, *109,* 235–247.

Blumer, D. Temporal lobe epilepsy and its psychiatric significance. In *Psychiatric Aspects of Neurologic Disease,* edited by D.F. Benson and D. Blumer. New York: Grune & Stratton, 1975.

Blumer, D., and Walker, A.E. The neural basis of sexual behavior. In *Psychiatric Aspects of Neurologic Disease,* edited by D.F. Benson and D. Blumer. New York: Grune & Stratton, 1975.

Bogerts, B. The role of limbic and paralimbic pathology in the etiology of schizophrenia. *Psychiatry Research,* 1989, *29,* 255–256.

Bolhuis, J.J., Fitzgerald, R.E., Dijk, D.J., and Koolhaas, J.M. The corticomedial amygdala and learning in an agonistic situation in the rat. *Physiology and Behavior,* 1984, *32,* 575–579.

Boller, F., and Dennis, M. (eds.). *Auditory Comprehension: Clinical and Experimental Studies with the Token Test.* New York: Academic Press, 1979.

Bonvallet, M., and Sigg, B. Etude électrophysiologique des afférences vagales au niveau de leur pénétration dans le bulbe. *Journal of Physiology (Paris),* 1958, *50,* 63–74.

Booth, D.A. The physiology of appetite. *British Medical Bulletin,* 1981, *37,* 135–140.

Borbély, A.A., and Tobler, I. Endogenous sleep-promoting substances and sleep regulation. *Physiological Reviews,* 1989, *69,* 605–670.

Bornstein, B., Stroka, H., and Munitz, H. Prosopagnosia with animal face agnosia. *Cortex,* 1969, *5,* 164–169.

Bouchard, C. Genetic factors in obesity. *Medical Clinics of North America,* 1989, *73,* 67–81.

Boulos, Z., Rosenwasser, A.M., and Terman, M. Feeding schedules and the circadian organization of behavior in the rat. *Behavioural Brain Research,* 1980, *1,* 39–65.

Bowers, D., and Heilman, K.M. A dissociation between the processing of affective and nonaffective faces. Paper presented at the meeting of the International Neuropsychological Society, Atlanta, 1981.

Bowersox, S.S., Kaitin, K.I., and Dement, W.C. EEG spindle activity as a function of age: Relationship to sleep continuity. *Brain Research,* 1985, *63,* 526–539.

Boynton, R.M. *Human Color Vision.* New York: Holt, Rinehart and Winston, 1979.

Bozarth, M.A., and Wise, R.A. Anatomically distinct opiate receptor fields mediate reward and physical dependence. *Science,* 1984, *224,* 516–517.

Bozarth, M.A., and Wise, R.A. Toxicity associated with long-term intravenous heroin and cocaine self-administration in the rat. *Journal of the American Medical Association,* 1985, *254,* 81–83.

Bozarth, M.A., and Wise, R.A. Involvement of the ventral tegmental dopamine system in opioid and psychomotor stimulant reinforcement. In *Problems of Drug Dependence, 1985,* edited by L.S. Harris. Washington, D.C.: U.S. Government Printing Office, 1986.

Brackett, N.L., and Edwards, D.A. Medial preoptic connections with the midbrain tegmentum are essential for male sexual behavior. *Physiology and Behavior,* 1984, *32,* 79–84.

Bradbury, M.W.B. *The Concept of a Blood-Brain Barrier.* New York: John Wiley & Sons, 1979.

Bradford, J.M.W. Research on sex offenders. *Psychiatric Clinics of North America,* 1983, *6,* 715–731.

Brady, J.V., and Nauta, W.J.H. Subcortical mechanisms in emotional behavior: Affective changes following septal forebrain lesions in the albino rat. *Journal of Comparative and Physiological Psychology*, 1953, *46*, 339–346.

Brala, P.M., and Hagen, R.L. Effects of sweetness perception and caloric value of a preload on short term intake. *Physiology and Behavior*, 1983, *30*, 1–9.

Bray, G.A. Effect of caloric restriction on energy expenditure in obese patients. *Lancet*, 1969, *2*, 397–398.

Brecher, E.M. *Licit and Illicit Drugs*. Boston: Little, Brown & Co., 1972.

Breedlove, S.M., and Arnold, A. Hormone accumulation in a sexually dimorphic motor nucleus of the rat spinal cord. *Science*, 1980, *210*, 564–566.

Breedlove, S.M., and Arnold, A. Sex differences in the pattern of steroid accumulation by motoneurons of the rat lumbar spinal cord. *Journal of Comparative Neurology*, 1983, *215*, 211–216.

Breedlove, S.M., Jacobson, C.D., Gorski, R., and Arnold, A.P. Masculinization of the female rat spinal cord following a single neonatal injection of testosterone propionate but not estradiol benzoate. *Brain Research*, 1982, *237*, 173–181.

Breger, L., Hunter, I., and Lane, R.W. The effects of stress on dreams. *Physiological Issues Monograph Number 27*. New York: International University Press, 1971.

Breisch, S.T., Zemlan, F.P., and Hoebel, B.G. Hyperphagia and obesity following serotonin depletion by intraventricular *p*-chlorphenylalane. *Science*, 1976, *192*, 382–384.

Bridges, R.S. A quantitative analysis of the roles of dosage, sequence and duration of estradiol and progesterone exposure in the regulation of maternal behavior in the rat. *Endocrinology*, 1984, *114*, 930–940.

Bridges, R.S., DiBiase, R., Loundes, D.D., and Doherty, P.C. Prolactin stimulation of maternal behavior in female rats. *Science*, 1985, *227*, 782–784.

Bridges, R.S., and Ronsheim, P.M. Prolactin (PRL) regulation of maternal behavior in rats: Bromocriptine treatment delays and PRL promotes the rapid onset of behavior. *Endocrinology*, 1990, *126*, 837–848.

Britt, M.D., and Wise, R.A. Ventral tegmental site of opiate reward: Antagonism by a hydrophilic opiate receptor blocker. *Brain Research*, 1983, *258*, 105–108.

Broberg, D.J., and Bernstein, I.L. Cephalic insulin release in anorexic women. *Physiology and Behavior*, 1989, *45*, 871–874.

Broca, P. Remarques sur le siège de la faculté du langage articulé, suivies d'une observation d'aphemie (perte de la parole). *Bulletin de la Société Anatomique (Paris)*, 1861, *36*, 330–357.

Browman, L.G. Light in its relation to activity and estrous rhythms in the albino rat. *Journal of Experimental Zoology*, 1937, *75*, 375–388.

Brown, T.H., Ganong, A.H., Kairiss, E.W., Keenan, C.L., and Kelso, S.R. Long-term potentiation in two synaptic systems of the hippocampal brain slice. In *Neural Models of Plasticity: Experimental and Theoretical Approaches*, edited by J.H. Byrne and W.O. Berry. San Diego: Academic Press, 1989.

Brownell, K.D., Greenwood, M.R.C., Stellar, E., and Shrager, E.E. The effects of repeated cycles of weight loss and regain in rats. *Physiology and Behavior*, 1986, *38*, 459–464.

Brozowski, T.J., Brown, R.M., Rosvold, H.E., and Goldman, P.S. Cognitive deficit caused by regional depletion of dopamine in prefrontal cortex of rhesus monkey. *Science*, 1979, *205*, 929–932.

Bruce, H.M. A block to pregnancy in the mouse caused by proximity of strange males. *Journal of Reproduction and Fertility*, 1960a, *1*, 96–103.

Bruce, H.M. Further observations of pregnancy block in mice caused by proximity of strange males. *Journal of Reproduction and Fertility*, 1960b, *2*, 311–312.

Bryden, M.P., and Ley, R.G. Right-hemispheric involvement in the perception and expression of emotion in normal humans. In *Neuropsychology of Human Emotion*, edited by K.M. Heilman and P. Satz. New York: Guilford Press, 1983.

Bryden, M.P., Ley, R.G., and Sugarman, J.H. A left ear advantage for identifying the emotional quality of tonal sequences. *Neuropsychologia*, 1982, *20*, 83–87.

Buchsbaum, M.S., Mendelson, W.B., Duncan, W.C., Coppola, R., Kelsoe, J., and Gillin, J.C. Topographical cortical mapping of EEG sleep stages during daytime naps in normal subjects. *Sleep*, 1982, *5*, 248–255.

Buck, R., and Duffy, R.J. Nonverbal communication of affect in brain damaged patients. *Cortex*, 1980, *16*, 351–362.

Buddington, R.W., King, F.A., and Roberts, L. Emotionality and conditioned avoidance responding in the squirrel monkey following septal injury. *Psychonomic Science*, 1967, *8*, 195–196.

Buggy, J., and Johnson, A.K. Preoptic-hypothalamic periventricular lesions: Thirst deficits and hypernatremia. *American Journal of Physiology*, 1977, *233*, R44–R52.

Buijs, R.M., and Van Heerikhuize, J.J. Vasopressin and oxytocin release in the brain—a synaptic event. *Brain Research*, 1982, *252*, 71–76.

Bukowiecki, L., Folléa, N., Vallières, J., and Leblanc, J. β-adrenergic receptors in brown-adipose tissue:

Characterization and alterations during acclimation of rats to cold. *European Journal of Biochemistry*, 1978, *92*, 189–196.

Burt, D.R., Creese, I., and Snyder, S.H. Antischizophrenic drugs: Chronic treatment elevated dopamine receptor binding in brain. *Science*, 1977, *196*, 326–328.

Burton, M.J., Rolls, E.T., and Mora, F. Effects of hunger on the responses of neurons in the lateral hypothalamus to the sight and taste of food. *Experimental Neurology*, 1976, *51*, 668–677.

Buzsáki, G. Two-stage model of memory trace formation: A role for "noisy" brain states. *Neuroscience*, 1989, *31*, 551–570.

Buzsáki, G., and Gage, F.H. Mechanisms of action of neural grafts in the limbic system. *Canadian Journal of Neurological Sciences*, 1988, *15*, 99–105.

Buzsáki, G., Gage, F.H., Czopf, J., and Björklund, A. Restoration of rhythmic slow activity (theta) in the subcortically denervated hippocampus by fetal CNS transplants. *Brain Research*, 1987, *400*, 334–347.

Byerley, W., Mellon, C., O'Connell, P., Lalouel, J.-M., Nakamura, Y., Leppert, M., and White, R. Mapping genes for manic-depression and schizophrenia with DNA markers. *Trends in Neurosciences*, 1989, *12*, 46–48.

Byrne, J.H., and Gingrich, K.J. Mathematical model of cellular and molecular processes contributing to associative and nonassociative learning in *Aplysia*. In *Neural Models of Plasticity: Experimental and Theoretical Approaches*, edited by J.H. Byrne and W.O. Berry. San Diego: Academic Press, 1989.

Cahill, G.M., and Menaker, M. Effects of excitatory amino acid receptor antagonists and agonists on suprachiasmatic nucleus responses to retinohypothalamic tract volleys. *Brain Research*, 1989, *479*, 76–82.

Cain, W.S. Olfaction. In *Stevens' Handbook of Experimental Psychology. Vol. 1. Perception and Motivation*, edited by R.C. Atkinson, R.J. Herrnstein, G. Lindzey, and R.D. Luce. New York: John Wiley & Sons, 1988.

Calhoun, J. Population density and social pathology. *Scientific American*, 1962, *206*, 139–148.

Callaway, C.W., Lydic, R., Baghdoyan, H.A., and Hobson, J.A. Pontogeniculoocipital waves: Spontaneous visual system activity during rapid eye movement sleep. *Cellular and Molecular Neurobiology*, 1987, *2*, 105–149.

Campfield, L.A., Brandon, P., and Smith, F.J. On-line continuous measurement of blood glucose and meal pattern in free-feeding rats: The role of glucose in meal initiation. *Brain Research Bulletin*, 1985, *14*, 605–617.

Card, J.P., and Moore, R.Y. Ventral lateral geniculate nucleus efferents to the rat suprachiasmatic nucleus exhibit avian pancreatic polypeptide-like immunoreactivity. *Journal of Comparative Neurology*, 1982, *206*, 390–396.

Card, J.P., and Moore, R.Y. The suprachiasmatic nucleus of the golden hamster: Immunohistochemical analysis of cell and fiber distribution. *Neuroscience*, 1984, *13*, 415–431.

Card, J.P., Riley, J.N., and Moore, R.Y. The suprachiasmatic hypothalamic nucleus: Ultrastructure of relations to optic chiasm. *Neuroscience Abstracts*, 1980, *6*, 758.

Carew, T.J., Hawkins, R.D., and Kandel, E.R. Differential classical conditioning of a defensive withdrawal reflex in *Aplysia californica*. *Science*, 1983, *219*, 397–400.

Carlson, H.E., Gillin, J.C., Gorden, P., and Snyder, F. Absence of sleep-related growth hormone peaks in aged normal subjects and in acromegaly. *Journal of Clinical Endocrinology and Metabolism*, 1972, *34*, 1102–1105.

Carlson, N.R., and Thomas, G.J. Maternal behavior of mice with limbic lesions. *Journal of Comparative and Physiological Psychology*, 1968, *66*, 731–737.

Carpenter, C.R. Sexual behavior of free ranging rhesus monkeys (*Macaca mulatta*). I. Specimens, procedures and behavioral characteristics of estrus. *Journal of Comparative Psychology*, 1942, *33*, 113–142.

Carr, C.E., and Konishi, M. Axonal delay lines for time measurement in the owl's brainstem. *Proceedings of the National Academy of Sciences, USA*, 1989, *85*, 8311–8315.

Carrive, P., Bandler, R., and Dampney, A.L. Somatic and autonomic integration in the midbrain of the unanesthetized decerebrate cat: A distinctive pattern evoked by excitation of neurones in the subtentorial portion of the midbrain periaqueductal grey. *Brain Research*, 1989, *483*, 251–258.

Carrive, P., Dampney, R.A.L., and Bandler, R. Excitation of neurones in a restricted portion of the midbrain periaqueductal grey elicits both behavioural and cardiovascular components of the defense reaction in the unanesthetised decerebrate cat. *Neuroscience Letters*, 1987, *81*, 273–278.

Cassell, M.D., and Gray, T.S. The amygdala directly innervates adrenergic (C1) neurons in the ventrolateral medulla in the rat. *Neuroscience Letters*, 1989, *97*, 163–168.

Chang, F.-C.T., and Scott, T.R. Conditioned taste aversions modify neural responses in the rat nucleus tractus solitarius. *Journal of Neuroscience*, 1984, *4*, 1850–1862.

Chang, F.-L.F., and Greenough, W.T. Lateralized effects of monocular training on dendritic branching in adult split-brain rats. *Brain Research*, 1982, *232*, 283–292.

Chang, V.C., Mark, G.P., Hernandez, L., and Hoebel, B.G. Extracellular dopamine increases in the nucleus accumbens following rehydration or sodium repletion. *Society for Neuroscience Abstracts*, 1988, *14*, 527.

Chattarji, S., Stanton, P.K., and Sejnowski, T.J. Commissural synapses, but not mossy fiber synapses, in hippocampal field CA3 exhibit associative long-term potentiation and depression. *Brain Research*, 1989, *495*, 145–150.

Chi, J.G., Dooling, E.C., and Gilles, F.H. Gyral development of the human brain. *Annals of Neurology*, 1977, *1*, 86–93.

Chiarello, C., Knight, R., and Mandel, M. Aphasia in a prelingually deaf woman. *Brain*, 1982, *105*, 29–51.

Chiba, T., and Murata, Y. Afferent and efferent connections of the medial preoptic area in the rat: A WGA-HRP study. *Brain Research Bulletin*, 1985, *14*, 261–272.

Chorover, S.L., and Schiller, P.H. Short-term retrograde amnesia in rats. *Journal of Comparative and Physiological Psychology*, 1965, *59*, 73–78.

Chung, S.K., McVary, K.T., and McKenna, K.E. Sexual reflexes in male and female rats. *Neuroscience Letters*, 1988, *94*, 343–348.

Chwalbinska-Moneta, J. Role of hepatic portal osmoreception in the control of ADH release. *American Journal of Physiology*, 1979, *236*, E603–E609.

Clancy, A.N., Macrides, F., Singer, A.G., and Agosta, W.C. Male hamster copulatory responses to a high molecular weight fraction of vaginal discharge: Effects of vomeronasal organ removal. *Physiology and Behavior*, 1984, *33*, 653–660.

Clark, A.W., Hurlbut, W.P., and Mauro, A. Changes in the fine structure of the neuromuscular junction of the frog caused by black widow spider venom. *Journal of Cell Biology*, 1972, *52*, 1–14.

Clarke, P.G.H., and Whitteridge, D. A comparison of stereoscopic mechanisms in cortical visual areas V1 and V2 of the cat. *Journal of Physiology (London)*, 1978, *275*, 92–93.

Clemens, L.G. Influence of prenatal litter composition on mounting behavior of female rats. *American Zoologist*, 1971, *11*, 617–618.

Clemente, C.D., and Chase, M.H. Neurological sub-

strates of aggressive behavior. *Annual Review of Physiology*, 1973, *35*, 329–356.

Cloninger, C.R. A unified biosocial theory of personality and its role in the development of anxiety states. *Psychiatric Development*, 1986, *3*, 167–226.

Cloninger, C.R. Neurogenetic adaptive mechanisms in alcoholism. *Science*, 1987, *236*, 410–416.

Cloninger, C.R., Bohmann, M., Sigvardsson, S., and von Knorring, A.-L. Psychopathology in adopted-out children of alcoholics. The Stockholm Adoption Study. *Recent Developments in Alcoholism*, 1985, *3*, 37–51.

Clugston, G.A., and Garlick, P.J. The response of protein and energy metabolism to food intake in lean and obese man. *Human Nutrition: Clinical Nutrition*, 1982, *36C*, 57–70.

Coble, P.A., Scher, M.S., Reynolds, C.F., Day, N.L., and Kupfer, D.J. Preliminary findings on the neonatal sleep of offspring of women with and without a prior history of affective disorder. *Sleep Research*, 1988, *16*, 120.

Coburn, P.C., and Stricker, E.M. Osmoregulatory thirst in rats after lateral preoptic lesions. *Journal of Comparative and Physiological Psychology*, 1978, *92*, 350–361.

Coil, J.D., Hankins, W.B., Jenden, D.J., and Garcia, J. The attenuation of a specific cut-to-consequences association by antiemetic agents. *Psychopharmacology*, 1978, *56*, 21–25.

Coirini, H., Magarinos, A.M., DeNicola, A.F., Rainbow, T.C., and McEwen, B.S. Further studies of brain aldosterone binding sites employing new mineralocorticoid and glucocorticoid receptor markers in vitro. *Brain Research*, 1985, *12*, 212–216.

Collier, T.J., Quirk, G.J., and Routtenberg, A. Separable roles of hippocampal granule cells in forgetting and pyramidal cells in remembering spatial information. *Brain Research*, 1987, *409*, 316–328.

Coltheart, M., Patterson, K., and Marshall, J.C. *Deep Dyslexia*. London: Routledge & Kegan Paul, 1980.

Coltheart, M., Patterson, K., and Marshall, J.C. *Deep Dyslexia*, 2nd edition. London: Routledge & Kegan Paul, 1987.

Comarr, A.E. Sexual function among patients with spinal cord injury. *Urologia Internationalis*, 1970, *25*, 134–168.

Commins, D., and Yahr, P. Lesions of the sexually dimorphic area disrupt mating and marking in male gerbils. *Brain Research Bulletin*, 1984, *13*, 185–193.

Conner, R.L., and Levine, S. Hormonal influences on aggressive behaviour. In *Aggressive Behaviour*, edited by S. Garattini and E.B. Sigg. New York: John Wiley & Sons, 1969.

Cook, K.S., Min, H.Y., Johnson, D., Chaplinsky, R.J., Flier, J.S., Hunt, C.R., and Spiegelman, B.M. Adipsin: A circulating serine protease homolog secreted by adipose tissue and sciatic nerve. *Science*, 1987, *237*, 402–405.

Cooper, J.R., Bloom, F.E., and Roth, R.H. *The Biochemical Basis of Neuropharmacology*, 5th ed. New York: Oxford University Press, 1987.

Corkin, S., Sullivan, E.V., Twitchell, T.E., and Grove, E. The amnesic patient H.M.: Clinical observations and test performance 28 years after operation. *Society for Neuroscience Abstracts*, 1981, *7*, 235.

Coslett, H.B., Brashear, H.R., and Heilman, K.M. Pure word deafness after bilateral primary auditory cortex infarcts. *Neurology*, 1984, *34*, 347–352.

Cotman, C.W., Monaghan, D.T., and Ganong, A.H. Excitatory amino acid neurotransmission: NMDA receptors and Hebb-type synaptic plasticity. *Annual Review of Neuroscience*, 1988, *11*, 61–80.

Cowley, D.S., and Arana, G.W. The diagnostic utility of lactate sensitivity in panic disorder. *Archives of General Psychiatry*, 1990, *47*, 277–284.

Crane, G.E. Iproniazid (Marsilid) phosphate, a therapeutic agent for mental disorders and debilitating diseases. *Psychiatry Research Reports*, 1957, *8*, 142–152.

Crawford, M.P. The relation between social dominance and the menstrual cycle in female chimpanzees. *Journal of Comparative Psychology*, 1940, *30*, 483–513.

Creese, I., Burt, D.R., and Snyder, S.H. Dopamine receptor binding predicts clinical and pharmacological potencies of antischizophrenic drugs. *Science*, 1976, *192*, 481–483.

Crick, F., and Mitchison, G. The function of dream sleep. *Nature*, 1983, *304*, 111–114.

Criswell, H.E., and Rogers, F.B. Narcotic analgesia: Changes in neural activity recorded from periaqueductal gray matter of rat brain. *Society for Neuroscience Abstracts*, 1978, *4*, 458.

Crone, C. Facilitated transfer of glucose from blood to brain. *Journal of Physiology (London)*, 1965, *181*, 103–113.

Crow, T.J. A map of the rat mesencephalon for electrical self-stimulation. *Brain Research*, 1972, *36*, 265–273.

Crow, T.J. Molecular pathology of schizophrenia: More than one disease process? *British Medical Journal of Clinical Research*, 1980, *280*, 66–68.

Crow, T.J., Cross, A.J., Johnstone, E.C., Owen, F., Owens, D.G.C., and Waddington, J.L. Abnormal involuntary movements in schizophrenia: Are they related to the disease process or its treatment? Are they associated with changes in dopamine receptors? *Journal of Clinical Psychopharmacology*, 1982, *2*, 336–340.

Crow, T.J., DeLisi, L.E., and Johnstone, E.C. Concordance by sex in sibling pairs with schizophrenia is paternally inherited. *British Journal of Psychiatry*, 1989, *155*, 92–97.

Crowe, R.R., Noyes, R., Pauls, D.L., and Slymen, D. A family study of panic disorder. *Archives of General Psychiatry*, 1983, *40*, 1065–1069.

Crowe, R.R., Noyes, R., Wilson, A.F., Elston, R.C., and Ward, L.J. A linkage study of panic disorder. *Archives of General Psychiatry*, 1987, *44*, 933–937.

Culebras, A., and Moore, J.T. Magnetic resonance findings in REM sleep behavior disorder. *Neurology*, 1989, *39*, 1519–1523.

Czeisler, C.A., Kronauer, R.E., Allan, J.S., Duffy, J.F., Jewett, M.E., Brown, E.N., and Ronda, J.M. Bright light induction of strong (type 0) resetting of the human circadian pacemaker. *Science*, 1989, *244*, 1328–1332.

Damasio, A.R. Disorders of complex visual processing: Agnosias, achromatopsia, Balint's syndrome, and related difficulties of orientation and construction. In *Principles of Behavioral Neurology*, edited by M.-M. Mesulam. Philadelphia: F.A. Davis, 1985.

Damasio, A.R. Category-related recognition defects and the organization of meaning systems. *Trends in Neurosciences*, 1990, *13*, 95–98.

Damasio, A.R., and Damasio, H. The anatomic basis of pure alexia. *Neurology*, 1983, *33*, 1573–1583.

Damasio, A.R., Damasio, H., and Van Hoesen, G.W. Prosopagnosia: Anatomic basis and behavioral mechanisms. *Neurology*, 1982, *32*, 331–341.

Damasio, A.R., and Van Hoesen, G.W. Emotional disturbances associated with focal lesions of the limbic frontal lobe. In *Neuropsychology of Human Emotion*, edited by K.M. Heilman and P. Satz. New York: Guilford Press, 1983.

Damasio, A.R., Yamada, T., Damasio, H., Corbett, J., and McKee, J. Central achromatopsia: Behavioral, anatomic, and physiologic aspects. *Neurology*, 1980, *30*, 1064–1071.

Damasio, H. Cerebral localization of the aphasias. In *Acquired Aphasia*, edited by M.T. Sarno. New York: Academic Press, 1981.

Damasio, H., and Damasio, A. The anatomical basis of conduction aphasia. *Brain*, 1980, *103*, 337–350.

Damasio, H., Eslinger, P., and Adams, H.P. Aphasia following basal ganglia lesions: New evidence. *Seminars in Neurology*, 1984, *4*, 151–161.

Damsma, G., Day, J., and Fibiger, H.C. Lack of tolerance to nicotine-induced dopamine release in the nucleus accumbens. *European Journal of Pharmacology*, 1989, *168*, 363–368.

D'Andrade, R. Sex differences and cultural institutions. In *The Development of Sex Differences*, edited by E. Maccoby. Stanford, Calif.: Stanford University Press, 1966.

Danguir, J. Intracerebroventricular infusion of somatostatin selectively increases paradoxical sleep in rats. *Brain Research*, 1986, *367*, 26–30.

Danguir, J. Internal milieu and sleep homeostasis. In *Sleep Peptides: Basic and Clinical Approaches*, edited by S. Inoué and D. Schneider-Helmert. Berlin: Springer-Verlag, 1988.

Danguir, J., and Nicolaïdis, S. Intravenous infusion of nutrients and sleep in the rat: An ischymetric sleep regulation hypothesis. *American Journal of Physiology*, 1980, *238*, E307–E312.

Danielsen, E.H., Magnuson, D.J., and Gray, T.S. The central amygdaloid nucleus innervation of the dorsal vagal complex in rat: A *Phaseolus vulgaris* leucoagglutinin lectin anterograde tracing study. *Brain Research Bulletin*, 1989, *22*, 705–715.

Darwin, C. *The Expression of the Emotions in Man and Animals*. Chicago: University of Chicago Press, 1872/1965.

Davidson, J.M. Characteristics of sex behavior in male rats following castration. *Animal Behaviour*, 1966, *14*, 266–272.

Davidson, J.M. Hormones and sexual behavior in the male. In *Neuroendocrinology*, edited by D.T. Krieger and J.C. Hughes. Sunderland, Mass.: Sinauer Associates, 1980.

Davidson, J.M., Camargo, C.A., and Smith, E.R. Effects of androgen on sexual behavior in hypogonadal men. *Journal of Clinical Endocrinology and Metabolism*, 1979, *48*, 955–958.

Davis, J.D., and Campbell, C.S., Peripheral control of meal size in the rat: Effect of sham feeding on meal size and drinking rate. *Journal of Comparative and Physiological Psychology*, 1973, *83*, 379–387.

Davison, G.C., and Neale, J.M. *Abnormal Psychology: An Experimental Clinical Approach*. New York: John Wiley & Sons, 1974.

Daw, N.W. Colour-coded ganglion cells in the goldfish retina: Extension of their receptive fields by means of new stimuli. *Journal of Physiology (London)*, 1968, *197*, 567–592.

Daw, N.W., Brunken, W.J., and Parkinson, D. The function of synaptic transmitters in the retina. *Annual Review of Neuroscience*, 1989, *12*, 205–226.

De Andres, I., Gutierrez-Rivas, E., Nava, E., and Reinoso-Suarez, F. Independence of sleep-wakefulness cycle in an implanted head "encéphale isolé." *Neuroscience Letters*, 1976, *2*, 13–18.

De Bold, A.J. Atrial natriuretic factor: A hormone produced by the heart. *Science*, 1985, *230*, 767–770.

De Bold, A.J., Borenstein, H.B., Veres, A.T., and Sonnenberg, H. A rapid and potent natriuretic response to intravenous injection of atrial myocardial extracts in rats. *Life Science*, 1981, *28*, 89–94.

de Castro, J.M. A microregulatory analysis of spontaneous fluid intake by humans: Evidence that the amount of liquid ingested and its timing is mainly governed by feeding. *Physiology and Behavior*, 1988, *43*, 705–714.

de Castro, J.M., and de Castro, E.S. Spontaneous meal patterns of humans: Influence of the presence of other people. *American Journal of Clinical Nutrition*, 1989, *50*, 237–247.

de Castro, J.M., McCormick, J., Pedersen, M., and Kreitzman, S.N. Spontaneous human meal patterns are related to preprandial factors regardless of natural environmental constraints. *Physiology and Behavior*, 1986, *38*, 25–29.

Dejerine, J. Sur un cas de cécité verbale avec agraphia, suivi d'autopsie. *Comptes Rendus des Séances de la Société de Biologie et de Ses Filiales*, 1891, *3*, 197–201.

Dejerine, J. Contribution à l'étude anatomo-pathologique et clinique des différentes variétés de cécité verbale. *Comptes Rendus des Séances de la Société de Biologie et de Ses Filiales*, 1892, *4*, 61–90.

De Jonge, F.H., Louwerse, A.L., Ooms, M.P., Evers, P., Endert, E., and van de Poll, N.E. Lesions of the SDN-POA inhibit sexual behavior of male Wistar rats. *Brain Research Bulletin*, 1989, *23*, 483–492.

DeKosky, S., Heilman, K.M., Bowers, D., and Valenstein, E. Recognition and discrimination of emotional faces and pictures. *Brain and Language*, 1980, *9*, 206–214.

Delay, J., and Deniker, P. Le traitement des psychoses par une methode neurolytique derivée d'hibernothéraphie; le 4560 RP utilisée seul une cure prolongée et continuée. *Comptes Rendus Congrès des Médecins Aliénistes et Neurologistes de France et des Pays de Langue Française*, 1952a, *50*, 497–502.

Delay, J., and Deniker, P. 38 cas des psychoses traitées par la cure prolongée et continuée de 4560 RP. *Comptes Rendus Congrès des Médecins Aliénistes et Neurologistes de France et des Pays de Langue Française*, 1952b, *50*, 503–513.

DeLong, M. Motor functions of the basal ganglia: Single-unit activity during movement. In *The Neurosciences: Third Study Program*, edited by F.O. Schmitt and F.G. Worden. Cambridge, Mass.: MIT Press, 1974.

Dement, W.C. The effect of dream deprivation. *Science,* 1960, *131,* 1705–1707.

Denlinger, S.L., Patarca, R., and Hobson, J.A. Differential enhancement of rapid eye movement sleep signs in the cat: A comparison of microinjection of the cholinergic agonist carbachol and the β-adrenergic antagonist propranolol on pontogeniculooccipital wave clusters. *Brain Research,* 1988, *473,* 116–126.

Deol, M.S., and Glucksohn-Waelsch, S. The role of inner hair cells in hearing. *Nature,* 1979, *278,* 250–252.

Depaulis, A., Bandler, R., and Vergnes, M. Characterization of pretentorial periaqueductal gray matter neurons mediating intraspecific defensive behaviors in the rat by microinjections of kainic acid. *Brain Research,* 1989, *486,* 121–132.

Dérouesné, J., and Beauvois, M.F. Phonological processing in reading: Data from alexia. *Journal of Neurology, Neurosurgery and Psychiatry,* 1979, *42,* 1125–1132.

Desimone, R., Albright, T.D., Gross, C.G., and Bruce, D. Stimulus-selective properties of inferior temporal neurons in the macaque. *Journal of Neuroscience,* 1984, *8,* 2051–2062.

Desmond, N.L., and Levy, W.B. Anatomy of associative long-term synaptic modification. In *Long-Term Potentiation: From Biophysics to Behavior,* edited by P.W. Landfield and S. Deadwyler. New York: A.R. Liss, 1988.

Deutsch, J.A. The cholinergic synapse and the site of memory. In *The Physiological Basis of Memory,* edited by J.A. Deutsch. New York: Academic Press, 1983.

Deutsch, J.A., and Gonzalez, M.F. Gastric nutrient content signals satiety. *Behavioral and Neural Biology,* 1980, *30,* 113–116.

Deutsch, J.A., and Hardy, W.T. Cholecystokinin produces bait shyness in rats. *Nature,* 1977, *266,* 196.

DeValois, R.L., Abramov, I., and Jacobs, G.H. Analysis of response patterns of LGN cells. *Journal of the Optical Society of America,* 1966, *56,* 966–977.

DeValois, R.L., Albrecht, D.G., and Thorell, L. Cortical cells: Bar detectors or spatial frequency filters? In *Frontiers in Visual Science,* edited by S.J. Cool and E.L. Smith. Berlin: Springer-Verlag, 1978.

De Valois, R.L., and De Valois, K.K. *Spatial Vision.* New York: Oxford University Press, 1988.

De Valois, R.L., Thorell, L.G., and Albrecht, D.G. Periodicity of striate-cortex-cell receptive fields.

Journal of the Optical Society of America, 1985, *2,* 1115–1123.

Diamond, D.M., Dunwiddie, T.V., and Rose, G.M. Characteristics of hippocampal primed burst potentiation *in vitro* and in the awake rat. *Journal of Neuroscience,* 1988, *8,* 4079–4088.

Diamond, D.M., and Weinberger, N.M. Role of context in the expression of learning-induced plasticity of single neurons in auditory cortex. *Behavioral Neuroscience,* 1989, *103,* 471–494.

Di Chiara, G., and Imperato, A. Preferential simulation of dopamine release in the nucleus accumbens by opiates, alcohol, and barbiturates: Studies with transcerebral dialysis in freely moving rats. *Annals of the New York Academy of Sciences,* 1987, *473,* 367–381.

Dickinson, C., and Keverne, E.B. Importance of noradrenergic mechanisms in the olfactory bulbs for the maternal behaviour of mice. *Physiology and Behavior,* 1988, *43,* 313–316.

Dixon, A.K. *The effect of olfactory stimuli upon the social behaviour of laboratory mice (Mus musculus L).* Doctoral dissertation, Birmingham University, Birmingham, England, 1973.

Dixon, A.K., and Mackintosh, J.H. Effects of female urine upon the social behaviour of adult male mice. *Animal Behaviour,* 1971, *19,* 138–140.

Dobelle, W.H., Mladejovsky, M.G., and Girvin, J.P. Artificial vision for the blind: Electrical stimulation of visual cortex offers hope for a functional prosthesis. *Science,* 1974, *183,* 440–444.

Doetsch, G.S., and Erickson, R.P. Synaptic processing of taste quality information in the nucleus tractus solitarius of the rat. *Journal of Neurophysiology,* 1970, *33,* 490–507.

Donahoe, J.W., Crowley, M.A., Millard, W.J., and Stickney, K.A. A unified principle of reinforcement: Some implications for matching. In *Quantitative Analyses of Behavior. Vol. 2. Matching and Maximizing Accounts,* edited by M.L. Commons, R.J. Herrnstein, and H. Rachlin. New York: Ballinger, 1982.

Dornan, W., and Malsbury, C.W. Neuropeptides and male sexual behavior. *Neuroscience and Biobehavioral Reviews,* 1989, *13,* 1–15.

Doty, R.L., Ford, M., Preti, G., and Huggins, G.R. Changes in the intensity and pleasantness of human vaginal odors during the menstrual cycle. *Science,* 1975, *190,* 1316.

Dowling, J.E. A new retinal neuron—the interplexiform cell. *Trends in Neurosciences,* 1979, *2,* 189–191.

Dowling, J.E. *The Retina: An Approachable Part of the*

Brain. Cambridge, Mass.: Harvard University Press, 1987.

Drachman, D.A., and Leavitt, J. Human memory and the cholinergic receptor. *Archives of Neurology,* 1974, *30,* 113–121.

Dray, A. The physiology and pharmacology of mammalian basal ganglia. *Progress in Neurobiology,* 1980, *14,* 221–335.

Dunnett, S.B., Lane, D.M., and Winn, P. Ibotenic acid lesions of the lateral hypothalamus: Comparison with 6-hydroxydopamine-induced sensorimotor deficits. *Neuroscience,* 1985, *14,* 509–518.

Durie, D.J. Sleep in animals. In *Psychopharmacology of Sleep,* edited by D. Wheatley. New York: Raven Press, 1981.

Dykes, R.W. Parallel processing of somatosensory information: A theory. *Brain Research Reviews,* 1983, *6,* 47–115.

Dykes, R.W., Rasmusson, D.D., and Hoeltzell, P.B. Organization of primary somatosensory cortex in the cat. *Journal of Neurophysiology,* 1980, *43,* 1527–1545.

Eddy, N.B., Halbach, H., Isbell, H., and Seevers, M.H. Drug dependence: Its significance and characteristics. *Bulletin of the World Health Organization,* 1965, *32,* 721–733.

Edwards, D.A. Mice: Fighting by neonatally androgenized females. *Science,* 1968, *161,* 1027–1028.

Edwards, M.A., and Adams, D.B. Role of midbrain central gray in pain-induced defensive boxing of rats. *Physiology and Behavior,* 1974, *23,* 113–121.

Egeland, J.A., Gerhard, D.S., Pauls, D.L., Sussex, J.N., Kidd, K.K., Allen, C.R., Hostetter, A.M., and Housman, D.E. Bipolar affective disorders linked to DNA markers on chromosome 11. *Nature,* 1987, *325,* 783–787.

Eguchi, K., and Satoh, T. Characterization of the neurons in the region of solitary tract nucleus during sleep. *Physiology and Behavior,* 1980, *24,* 99–102.

Ehlers, C.L., Frank, E., and Kupfer, D.J. Social zeitgebers and biological rhythms. *Archives of General Psychiatry,* 1988, *45,* 948–952.

Ehrenkranz, J., Bliss, E., and Sheard, M. Plasma testosterone: Correlation with aggressive behavior and social dominance in man. *Psychosomatic Medicine,* 1974, *36,* 469–475.

Ehrhardt, A.A., and Meyer-Bahlburg, H.F.L. Effects of prenatal sex hormones on gender-related behavior. *Science,* 1981, *211,* 1312–1318.

Ekman, P. *The Face of Man: Expressions of Universal Emotions in a New Guinea Village.* New York: Garland STPM Press, 1980.

Ekman, P., and Friesen, W.V. Constants across cultures in the face and emotion. *Journal of Personality and Social Psychology,* 1971, *17,* 124–129.

Elias, M. Serum cortisol, testosterone and testosterone binding globulin responses to competitive fighting in human males. *Aggressive Behavior,* 1981, *7,* 215–224.

Ellison, G.D., and Flynn, J.P. Organized aggressive behavior in cats after surgical isolation of the hypothalamus. *Archives Italiennes de Biologie,* 1968, *106,* 1–20.

Engen, T. Method and theory in the study of odor preferences. In *Human Responses to Environmental Odors,* edited by A. Turk, J.W. Johnston, and D.G. Moulton. New York: Academic Press, 1974.

Engen, T. *The Perception of Odors.* New York: Academic Press, 1982.

Ennis, M., and Aston-Jones, G. Potent excitatory input to the nucleus locus coeruleus from the ventrolateral medulla. *Neuroscience Letters,* 1986, *71,* 299–305.

Ennis, M., and Aston-Jones, G. Excitatory synaptic transmission from paragigantocellularis to locus coeruleus: A new amino acid pathway in brain. *Journal of Neuroscience,* 1988, *8,* 3644–3657.

Enroth-Cugell, C., and Robson, J.G. The contrast sensitivity of retinal ganglion cells of the cat. *Journal of Physiology (London),* 1966, *187,* 517–552.

Epstein, A.N., and Sakai, R.R. Angiotensin-aldosterone synergy and salt intake. In *Brain Peptides and Catecholamines in Cardiovascular Regulation,* edited by J.P. Buckley and C.M. Ferrario. New York: Raven Press, 1987.

Errington, M.L., Lynch, G.. and Bliss, T.V.P. Long-term potentiation in the dentate gyrus: Induction and increased glutamate release are blocked by D(-)aminophosphonovalerate. *Neuroscience,* 1987, *20,* 279–284.

Eslinger, P.J., and Damasio, A.R. Severe disturbance of higher cognition after bilateral frontal lobe ablation: Patient EVR. *Neurology,* 1985, *35,* 1731–1741.

Ettenberg, A., and Duvauchelle, C. Haloperidol blocks the conditioned place preferences induced by rewarding brain stimulation in rats. *Behavioral Neuroscience,* 1988, *102,* 687–691.

Evans, C.M., Mackintosh, J.H., Kennedy, J.F., and Robertson, S.M. Attempts to characterise and isolate aggression reducing olfactory signals from the urine of female mice. *Mus musculus L. Physiology and Behavior,* 1978, *20,* 129–134.

Evarts, E.V. Sensorimotor cortex activity associated with movements triggered by visual as compared to somesthetic inputs. In *The Neurosciences: Third*

Study Program, edited by F.O. Schmitt and F.G. Worden. Cambridge, Mass.: MIT Press, 1974.

Everitt, B.J., Herbert, J., and Hamer, J.D. Sexual receptivity of bilaterally adrenalectomised female rhesus monkeys. *Physiology and Behavior,* 1972, *8,* 409–415.

Falck, B., Hillarp, N.-Å. Thieme, G., and Torp, A. Fluorescence of catechol amines and related compounds condensed with formaldehyde. *Journal of Histochemistry and Cytochemistry,* 1962, *10,* 348–364.

Falk, J.L. The nature and determinants of adjunctive behavior. In *Schedule Effects: Drugs, Drinking, and Aggression,* edited by R.M. Gilbert and J.D. Keehn. Toronto: University of Toronto Press, 1972.

Fallon, J.H. Topographic organization of ascending dopaminergic projections. *Annals of the New York Academy of Sciences,* 1988, *537,* 1–9.

Fang, F.G., Moreau, J.O., and Fields, H.L. Dose-dependent antinociceptive action of neurotensin microinjected into the rostroventromedial medulla of the rat. *Brain Research,* 1987, *426,* 171–174.

Fanselow, M.S. Naloxone attenuates rat's preference for signaled shock. *Physiological Psychology,* 1979, *7,* 70–74.

Farde, L., Wiesel, F.-A., Stone-Elander, S., Halldin, C., Nördstrom, A.-L., Hall, H., and Sedvall, G. D_2 dopamine receptors in neuroleptic-naive schizophrenic patients: A positron emission tomography study with [^{11}C]raclopride. *Archives of General Psychiatry,* 1990, *47,* 213–219.

Farmer, A., McGuffin, P., and Gottesman, I. Twin concordance in DSM-III schizophrenia. *Archives of General Psychiatry,* 1987, *44,* 634–641.

Fava, M., Copeland, P.M., Schweiger, U., and Herzog, M.D. Neurochemical abnormalities of anorexia nervosa and bulimia nervosa. *American Journal of Psychiatry,* 1989, *146,* 963–971.

Fazeli, M.S., Errington, M.L., Dolphin, A.C., and Bliss, T.V.P. Long-term potentiation in the dentate gyrus of the anaesthetized rat is accompanied by an increase in protein efflux into push-pull cannula perfusates. *Brain Research,* 1988, *473,* 51–59.

Ferguson, N.B.L., and Keesey, R.E. Effect of a quinine-adulterated diet upon body weight maintenance in male rats with ventromedial hypothalamic lesions. *Journal of Comparative and Physiological Psychology,* 1975, *89,* 478–488.

Fibiger, H.C., Le Piane, F.G., Jakubovic, A., and Phillips, A.G. The role of dopamine in intracranial self-stimulation of the ventral tegmental area. *Journal of Neuroscience,* 1987, *7,* 3888–3896.

Fibiger, H.C., Murray, C.L., and Phillips, A.G. Lesions

of the nucleus basalis magnocellularis impair long-term memory in rats. *Society for Neuroscience Abstracts,* 1983, *9,* 332.

Fieve, R.R. The clinical effects of lithium treatment. *Trends in Neurosciences,* 1979, *2,* 66–68.

Finkelstein, J.W., Roffwarg, H.P., Boyar, R.M., Kream, J., and Hellman, L. Age-related change in the twenty-four-hour spontaneous secretion of growth hormone. *Journal of Clinical Endocrinology and Metabolism,* 1972, *35,* 665–670.

Fisher, C., Byrne, J., Edwards, A., and Kahn, E. A psychophysiological study of nightmares. *Journal of the American Psychoanalytic Association,* 1970, *18,* 747–782.

Fisher, C., Gross, J., and Zuch, J. Cycle of penile erection synchronous with dreaming (REM) sleep: Preliminary report. *Archives of General Psychiatry,* 1965, *12,* 29–45.

Fitzpatrick, D., Itoh, K., and Diamond, I.T. The laminar organization of the lateral geniculate body and the striate cortex in the squirrel monkey *(Saimiri sciureus). Journal of Neuroscience,* 1983, *3,* 673–702.

Fitzsimons, J.T. Drinking by rats depleted of body fluid without increase in osmotic pressure. *Journal of Physiology (London),* 1961, *159,* 297–309.

Fitzsimons, J.T. Thirst. *Physiological Reviews,* 1972, *52,* 468–561.

Fitzsimons, J.T., and Le Magnen, J. Eating as a regulatory control of drinking in the rat. *Journal of Comparative and Physiological Psychology,* 1969, *3,* 273–283.

Fitzsimons, J.T., and Moore-Gillon, M.J. Drinking and antidiuresis in response to reductions in venous return in the dog: Neural and endocrine mechanisms. *Journal of Physiology (London),* 1980, *308,* 403–416.

Fleming, A., and Rosenblatt, J.S. Olfactory regulation of maternal behavior in rats. II. Effects of peripherally induced anosmia and lesions of the lateral olfactory tract in pup-induced virgins. *Journal of Comparative and Physiological Psychology,* 1974, *86,* 233–246.

Fleming, A., Vaccarino, F., and Luebke, C. Amygdaloid inhibition of maternal behavior in the nulliparous female rat. *Physiology and Behavior,* 1980, *25,* 731–745.

Fleming, A., Vaccarino, F., Tambosso, L., and Chee, P. Vomeronasal and olfactory system modulation of maternal behavior in the rat. *Science,* 1979, *203,* 372–374.

Fleming, A.S., Cheung, U., Myhal, N., and Kessler, Z. Effects of maternal hormones on "timidity" and attraction to pup-related odors in female rats. *Physiology and Behavior,* 1989, *46,* 449–453.

Flock, A. Transducing mechanisms in the lateral line canal organ receptors. *Cold Spring Harbor Symposia on Quantitative Biology*, 1965, *30*, 133–146.

Flock, A. Physiological properties of sensory hairs in the ear. In *Psychophysics and Physiology of Hearing*, edited by E.F. Evans and J.P. Wilson. London: Academic Press, 1977.

Floody, O.R. Hormones and aggression in female mammals. In *Hormones and Aggressive Behavior*, edited by B.B. Svare. New York: Plenum Press, 1983.

Floody, O.R., and Pfaff, D.W. Aggressive behavior in female hamsters: The hormonal basis for fluctuations in female aggressiveness correlated with estrous state. *Journal of Comparative and Physiological Psychology*, 1977, *91*, 443–464.

Flynn, J., Vanegas, H., Foote, W., and Edwards, S. Neural mechanisms involved in a cat's attack on a rat. In *The Neural Control of Behavior*, edited by R.F. Whalen, M. Thompson, M. Verzeano, and N. Weinberger. New York: Academic Press, 1970.

Foote, S.L., Bloom, F.R., and Aston-Jones, G. The nucleus locus coeruleus: New evidence of anatomical and physiological specificity. *Physiological Reviews*, 1983, *63*, 844–914.

Fouriezos, G., and Wise, R.A. Pimozide-induced extinction of intracranial self-stimulation: Response patterns rule out motor or performance deficits. *Brain Research*, 1976, *103*, 377–380.

Foutz, A.S., Mitler, M.M., Cavalli-Sforza, L.L., and Dement, W.C. Genetic factors in canine narcolepsy. *Sleep*, 1979, *1*, 413–421.

Freed, W.J. An hypothesis regarding the antipsychotic effect of neuroleptic drugs. *Pharmacology, Biochemistry and Behavior*, 1989, *32*, 337–345.

Freed, W.J., Cannon-Spoor, H.E., and Rodgers, C.R. Attenuation of the behavioral response to quisqualic acid and glutamic acid diethyl ester by chronic haloperidol administration. *Life Sciences*, 1989, *44*, 1303–1308.

Freedman, M., Alexander, M.P., and Naeser, M.A. Anatomic basis of transcortical motor aphasia. *Neurology*, 1984, *34*, 409–417.

Freeman, P.H., and Wellman, P.J. Brown adipose tissue thermogenesis induced by low level electrical stimulation of hypothalamus in rats. *Brain Research Bulletin*, 1987, *18*, 7–11.

Friedman, M.I., and Bruno, J.P. Exchange of water during lactation. *Science*, 1976, *191*, 409–410.

Friedman, M.I., Tordoff, M.G., and Ramirez, I. Integrated metabolic control of food intake. *Brain Research Bulletin*, 1986, *17*, 855–859.

Fruhstorfer, B., Mignot, E., Bowersox, S., Nishino, S.,
Dement, W.C., and Guilleminault, C. Canine narcolepsy is associated with an elevated number of α_2-receptors in the locus coeruleus. *Brain Research*, 1989, *500*, 209–214.

Fuller, C.A., Lydic, R., Sulzman, F.M., Albers, H.E., Tepper, B., and Moore-Ede, M.C. Circadian rhythm of body temperature persists after suprachiasmatic lesions in the squirrel monkey. *American Journal of Physiology*, 1981, *241*, R385–R391.

Fulton, J.F., and Bailey, P. Tumors in the region of the third ventricle: Their diagnosis and relation to pathological sleep. *Journal of Nervous and Mental Disorders*, 1929, *69*, 1–25, 145–164, 261–277.

Funakoshi, M., and Ninomiya, Y. Neural code for taste quality in the thalamus of the dog. In *Food Intake and Chemical Senses*, edited by Y. Katsuki, M. Sateo, S.F. Takagi, and Y. Oomura. Tokyo: University of Tokyo Press, 1977.

Fuster, J.M. Inferotemporal units in selective visual attention and short-term memory. *Journal of Neurophysiology*, 1990, in press.

Fuster, J.M., and Jervey, J.P. Inferotemporal neurons distinguish and retain behaviorally relevant features of visual stimuli. *Science*, 1981, *212*, 952–955.

Gabrieli, J.D.E., Cohen, N.J., and Corkin, S. The impaired learning of semantic knowledge following bilateral medial temporal-lobe resection. *Brain and Cognition*, 1988, *7*, 157–177.

Gaffney, F.A., Fenton, B.J., Lane, L.D., and Lake, C.R. Hemodynamic, ventilatory, and biochemical responses of panic patients and normal controls with sodium lactate infusion and spontaneous panic attacks. *Archives of General Psychiatry*, 1988, *45*, 53–60.

Gagne, P. Treatment of sex offenders with medroxyprogesterone acetate. *American Journal of Psychiatry*, 1981, *138*, 644–646.

Galaburda, A., and Geschwind, N. Dyslexia update. *Neurology and Neurosurgery Update Series*, 1982, *3*, 1–7.

Galaburda, A., and Kemper, T.L. Observations cited by Geschwind, N. Specializations of the human brain. *Scientific American*, 1979, *241*, 180–199.

Galaburda, A.M. The pathogenesis of childhood dyslexia. In *Language, Communication, and the Brain*, edited by F. Plum. New York: Raven Press, 1988.

Galaburda, A.M., LeMay, M., Kemper, T.L., and Geschwind, N. Right-left asymmetries in the brain. *Science*, 1978, *199*, 852–856.

Galaburda, A.M., Sherman, G.F., Rosen, G.D., Aboitiz, F., and Geschwind, N. Developmental dyslexia: Four consecutive patients with cortical anomalies. *Annals of Neurology*, 1985, *18*, 222–233.

Gall, C., Brecha, N., Karten, H.J., and Chang, K.-J. Localization of enkephalin-like immunoreactivity to identified axonal and neuronal populations of the rat hippocampus. *Journal of Comparative Neurology*, 1981, *198*, 335–350.

Gallagher, M., Kapp, B.S., McNall, C.L., and Pascoe, J.P. Opiate effects in the amygdala central nucleus on heart rate conditioning in rabbits. *Pharmacology, Biochemistry and Behavior*, 1981, *14*, 497–505.

Gallagher, M., Rapp, P.R., and Fanelli, R.J. Opiate antagonist facilitation of time-dependent memory processes: Dependence upon intact norepinephrine function. *Brain Research*, 1985, *347*, 284–290.

Gallistel, C.R., and Karras, D. Pimozide and amphetamine have opposing effects on the reward summation function. *Pharmacology, Biochemistry, and Behavior*, 1984, *20*, 73–77.

Gandelman, R., and Simon, N.G. Spontaneous pup-killing by mice in response to large litters. *Developmental Psychobiology*, 1978, *11*, 235–241.

Gandelman, R., and Simon, N.G. Postpartum fighting in the rat: Nipple development and the presence of young. *Behavioral and Neural Biology*, 1980, *28*, 350–360.

Gandelman, R., and vom Saal, F.S. Pup-killing in mice: The effects of gonadectomy and testosterone administration. *Physiology and Behavior*, 1975, *15*, 647–651.

Garcia, J., and Koelling, R.A. Relation of cue to consequence in avoidance learning. *Psychonomic Science*, 1966, *4*, 123–124.

Gaw, A.C., Chang, L.W., and Shaw, L.-C. Efficacy of acupuncture on osteoarthritic pain. *New England Journal of Medicine*, 1975, *293*, 375–378.

Gazzaniga, M.S. *The Bisected Brain*. New York: Appleton-Century-Crofts, 1970.

Gazzaniga, M.S., and LeDoux, J.E. *The Integrated Mind*. New York: Plenum Press, 1978.

Geary, N. Cocaine: Animal research studies. In *Cocaine Abuse: New Directions in Treatment and Research*, edited by H.I. Spitz and J.S. Rosecan. New York: Brunner/Mazel, 1987.

Gebhardt, G.F. Opiate and opioid peptide effects on brain stem neurons: Relevance to nociception and antinociceptive mechanisms. *Pain*, 1982, *12*, 93–140.

Geelen, G.L., Keil, L.C., Kravik, S.E., Wade, C.E., Thrasher, T.N., Barnes, P.R., Pyka, G., Nesvig, C., and Greenleaf, J.E. Inhibition of plasma vasopressin after drinking in dehydrated humans.

American Journal of Physiology, 1984, *247*, R968–R971.

Gentil, C.G., Mogenson, G., and Stevenson, J.A.F. Electrical stimulation of septum, hypothalamus and amygdala and saline preference. *American Journal of Physiology*, 1971, *220*, 1172–1177.

Gerbino, L., Oleshansky, M., and Gershon, S. Clinical use and mode of action of lithium. In *Psychopharmacology: A Generation of Progress*, edited by M.A. Lipton, A. DiMascio, and K.F. Killam. New York: Raven Press, 1978.

Gershon, E.S., Bunney, W.E., Jr., Leckman, J., Van Eerdewegh, M., and DeBauche, B. The inheritance of affective disorders: A review of data and hypotheses. *Behavior Genetics*, 1976, *6*, 227–261.

Geschwind, N. Disconnexion syndromes in animals and man. *Brain*, 1965, *88*, 237–294, 585–644.

Geschwind, N., Quadfasel, F.A., and Segarra, J.M. Isolation of the speech area. *Neuropsychologia*, 1968, *6*, 327–340.

Geschwind, N.A., and Behan, P.O. Laterality, hormones, and immunity. In *Cerebral Dominance: The Biological Foundations*, edited by N. Geschwind and A.M. Galaburda. Cambridge, Mass.: Harvard University Press, 1984.

Gessa, G.L., Muntoni, F., Collu, M., Vargiu, L., and Mereu, G. Low doses of ethanol activate dopaminergic neurons in the ventral tegmental area. *Brain Research*, 1985, *348*, 201–204.

Gesteland, R.C. The neural code: Integrative neural mechanisms. In *Handbook of Perception: Vol. VIA. Tasting and Smelling*, edited by E.C. Carterette and M.P. Friedman. New York: Academic Press, 1978.

Ghiraldi, L., and Svare, B. Unpublished observations cited in Svare, B. Recent advances in the study of female aggressive behavior in mice. In *House Mouse Aggression: A Model for Understanding the Evolution of Social Behavior*, edited by S. Parmigiani, D. Mainardi, and P. Brain. London: Gordon and Breach, 1989.

Giantonio, G.W., Lund, N.L., and Gerall, A.A. Effect of diencephalic and rhinencephalic lesions on the male rat's sexual behavior. *Journal of Comparative and Physiological Psychology*, 1970, *73*, 38–46.

Gibbs, J., Young, R.C., and Smith, G.P. Cholecystokinin decreases food intake in rats. *Journal of Comparative and Physiological Psychology*, 1973, *84*, 488–495.

Giles, D.E., Biggs, M.M., Rush, A.J., and Roffwarg, H.P. Risk factors in families of unipolar depression. I. Psychiatric illness and reduced REM latency. *Journal of Affective Disorders*, 1988, *14*, 51–59.

Giles, D.E., Roffwarg, H.P., and Rush, A.J. REM latency concordance in depressed family members. *Biological Psychiatry*, 1987, *22*, 910–924.

Giordano, A.L., Ahdieh, H.B., Mayer, A.D., Siegel, H.I., and Rosenblatt, J.S. Cytosol and nuclear estrogen receptor binding in the preoptic area and hypothalamus of female rats during pregnancy and ovariectomized, nulliparous rats after steroid priming: Correlation with maternal behavior. *Hormones and Behavior*, 1990, *24*, 232–255.

Gladue, B.A., Green, R., and Hellman, R.E. Neuroendocrine response to estrogen and sexual orientation. *Science*, 1984, *225*, 1496–1499.

Glendenning, K.K. Effects of septal and amygdaloid lesions on social behavior of the cat. *Journal of Comparative and Physiological Psychology*, 1972, *80*, 199–207.

Glick, Z., Teague, R.J., and Bray, G.A. Brown adipose tissue: Thermic response increased by a single low protein, high carbohydrate meal. *Science*, 1981, *213*, 1125–1127.

Goeders, N.E., Lane, J.D., and Smith, J.E. Self-administration of methionine enkephalin into the nucleus accumbens. *Pharmacology, Biochemistry, and Behavior*, 1984, *20*, 451–455.

Goeders, N.E., and Smith, J.E. Cortical dopaminergic involvement in cocaine reinforcement. *Science*, 1983, *221*, 773–775.

Gold, R.M., Jones, A.P., Sawchenko, P.E., and Kapatos, G. Paraventricular area: Critical focus of a longitudinal neurocircuitry mediating food intake. *Physiology and Behavior*, 1977, *18*, 1111–1119.

Goldberg, J.M., and Fernandez, C. Vestibular mechanisms. *Annual Review of Physiology*, 1975, *37*, 129–162.

Goldfoot, D.A. Olfaction, sexual behavior, and the pheromone hypothesis in rhesus monkeys: A critique. *American Zoologist*, 1981, *21*, 153–164.

Goldfoot, D.A., Krevetz, M.A., Goy, R.W., and Freeman, S.K. Lack of effect of vaginal lavages and aliphatic acids on ejaculatory responses in rhesus monkeys: Behavioral and chemical analyses. *Hormones and Behavior*, 1976, *7*, 1–28.

Goldstein, A., Pryor, G.T., Otis, L.S., and Larsen, F. On the role of endogenous opioid peptides: Failure of naloxone to influence shock escape threshold in the rat. *Life Sciences*, 1976, *18*, 599–604.

Goldstein, K. *Language and Language Disturbances*. New York: Grune & Stratton, 1948.

Golgi, C. *Opera Omnia, Vols. I and II*. Milan: Hoepli, 1903.

Golterman, N.R., Rehfeld, J.F., and Røigaard-Petersen, H. *In vivo* biosynthesis of cholecystokinin in rat cerebral cortex. *Journal of Biological Chemistry*, 1980, *255*, 6181–6185.

Gonzalez, M.F., and Deutsch, J.A. Vagotomy abolishes cues of satiety produced by gastric distension. *Science*, 1981, *212*, 1283–1284.

Goodglass, H. Agrammatism. In *Studies of Neurolinguistics*, edited by H. Whitaker and H.A. Whitaker. New York: Academic Press, 1976.

Goodglass, H., and Kaplan, E. *Assessment of Aphasia and Related Disorders*. Philadelphia: Lea & Febiger, 1972.

Goodwin, D.W. Alcoholism and heredity: A review and hypothesis. *Archives of General Psychiatry*, 1979, *36*, 57–61.

Goodwin, F.K., Wirz-Justice, A., and Wehr, T.A. Evidence that the pathophysiology of depression and the mechanisms of action of antidepressant drugs both involve alterations in circadian rhythms. In *Typical and Atypical Antidepressants: Clinical Practice*, edited by E. Costa and G. Racagni. New York: Raven Press, 1982.

Gorelick, P.B., and Ross, E.D. The aprosodias: Further functional-anatomical evidence for the organisation of affective language in the right hemisphere. *Journal of Neurology, Neurosurgery, and Psychiatry*, 1987, *50*, 553–560.

Gormezano, I. Classical conditioning: Investigations of defense and reward conditioning in the rabbit. In *Classical Conditioning II*, edited by A.H. Black and W.R. Prokasy. New York: Appleton-Century-Crofts, 1972.

Gorski, R.A., Gordon, J.H., Shryne, J.E., and Southam, A.M. Evidence for a morphological sex difference within the medial preoptic area of the rat brain. *Brain Research*, 1978, *148*, 333–346.

Gotsick, J.E., and Marshall, R.C. Time course of the septal rage syndrome. *Physiology and Behavior*, 1972, *9*, 685–687.

Gottesman, I.I., and Bertelsen, A. Confirming unexpressed genotypes for schizophrenia. *Archives of General Psychiatry*, 1989, *46*, 867–872.

Gottesman, I.I., and Shields, J. A critical review of recent adoption, twin, and family studies of schizophrenia: Behavioral genetics perspectives. *Schizophrenia Bulletin*, 1976, *2*, 360–401.

Gould, K.B., Lee, A.F.S., and Morelock, S. The relationship between sleep and sudden infant death. *Annals of the New York Academy of Sciences*, 1988, *533*, 62–77.

Gouras, P. Identification of cone mechanisms in monkey ganglion cells. *Journal of Physiology (London)*, 1968, *199*, 533–538.

Goy, R.W., Bercovitch, F.B., and McBrair, M.C. Behavioral masculinization is independent of genital masculinization in prenatally androgenized female rhesus macaques. *Hormones and Behavior,* 1988, *22,* 552–571.

Gray, C., Freeman, W.J., and Skinner, J.E. Chemical dependencies of learning in the rabbit olfactory bulb: Acquisition of the transient and spatial pattern change depends on norepinephrine. *Behavioral Neuroscience,* 1986, *100,* 585–596.

Gray, J.A., Whitsett, J.M., and Ziesenis, J.S. Hormonal regulation of aggression toward juveniles in female house mice. *Hormones and Behavior,* 1978, *11,* 310–322.

Gray, T.S., Carney, M.E., and Magnuson, D.J. Direct projections from the central amygdaloid nucleus to the hypothalamic paraventricular nucleus: Possible role in stress-induced adrenocorticotropin release. *Neuroendocrinology,* 1989, *50,* 433–446.

Green, D.M., and Swets, J.A. *Signal Detection Theory and Psychophysics.* New York: John Wiley & Sons, 1966.

Green, J.D., and Arduini, A.A. Hippocampal electrical activity in arousal. *Journal of Neuophysiology,* 1954, *17,* 533–557.

Green, J.D., Clemente, C., and DeGroot, J. Rhinencephalic lesions and behavior in cats. *Journal of Comparative Neurology,* 1957, *108,* 505–545.

Greenberg, R., and Pearlman, C.A. Cutting the REM nerve: An approach to the adaptive role of REM sleep. *Perspectives in Biology and Medicine,* 1974, *17,* 513–521.

Greenberg, R., Pillard, R., and Pearlman, C. The effect of dream (stage REM) deprivation on adaptation to stress. *Psychosomatic Medicine,* 1972, *34,* 257–262.

Greenough, W.T., Juraska, J.M., and Volkmar, F.R. Maze training effects on dendritic branching in occipital cortex of adult rats. *Behavioral and Neural Biology,* 1979, *26,* 287–297.

Greenough, W.T., and Volkmar, F.R. Pattern of dendritic branching in occipital cortex of rats reared in complex environments. *Experimental Neurology,* 1973, *40,* 491–504.

Gregory, E., Engle, K., and Pfaff, D. Male hamster preference for odors of female hamster vaginal discharges: Studies of experiential and hormonal determinants. *Journal of Comparative and Physiological Psychology,* 1975, *89,* 442–446.

Griesbacher, T., Leighton, G.E., Hill, R.G., and Hughes, J. Reduction of food intake by central administration of cholecystokinin octapeptide in the rat is dependent upon inhibition of brain peptidases. *British Journal of Pharmacology,* 1989, *96,* 236–242.

Griffith, J.D., Cavanaugh, J., Held, N.N., and Oates, J.A. Dextroamphetamine: Evaluation of psychotomimetic properties in man. *Archives of General Psychiatry,* 1972, *26,* 97–100.

Grossmann, K., Thane, K., and Grossmann, K.E. Maternal tactual contact of the newborn after various conditions of mother-infant contact. *Developmental Psychology,* 1981, *17,* 158–169.

Grossman, S.P., and Grossman, L. Parametric study of the regulatory capabilities of rats with rostromedial zona incerta lesions: Responsiveness to hypertonic saline and polyethylene glycol. *Physiology and Behavior,* 1978, *21,* 431–440.

Guerin, G.F., Goeders, N.E., Dworkin, S.I., and Smith, J.E. Intracranial self-administration of dopamine into the nucleus accumbens. *Society for Neuroscience Abstracts,* 1984, *10,* 1072.

Gulevich, G., Dement, W.C., and Johnson, L. Psychiatric and EEG observations on a case of prolonged (264 hours) wakefulness. *Archives of General Psychiatry,* 1966, *15,* 29–35.

Haas, R.H. Thiamin and the brain. *Annual Review of Nutrition,* 1988, *8,* 483–515.

Haeberich, F.J. Osmoreception in the portal system. *Federation Proceedings,* 1968, *27,* 1137–1141.

Halasz, P., Pal, I., and Rajna, P. K-complex formation of the EEG in sleep: A survey and new examinations. *Acta Physiologica Hungaria,* 1985, *65,* 3–35.

Hall, W.G. A remote stomach clamp to evaluate oral and gastric controls of drinking in the rat. *Physiology and Behavior,* 1973, *11,* 897–901.

Hall, W.G., and Blass, E.M. Orogastric determinants of drinking in rats: Interaction between absorptive and peripheral controls. *Journal of Comparative and Physiological Psychology,* 1977, *91,* 365–373.

Halmi, K.A. Anorexia nervosa: Recent investigations. *Annual Review of Medicine,* 1978, *29,* 137–148.

Halpern, M. The organization and function of the vomeronasal system. *Annual Review of Neuroscience,* 1987, *10,* 325–362.

Hansen, S., Köhler, C., and Ross, S.B. On the role of the dorsal mesencephalic tegmentum in the control of masculine sexual behavior in the rat: Effects of electrolytic lesions, ibotenic acid and DSP4. *Brain Research,* 1982, *240,* 311–320.

Harbaugh, R.E., Reeder, T.M., Senter, H.J., Knopman, D.S., Baskin, D.S., Pirozzolo, F., Chui, H.C., Shetter, A.G., Bakay, R.A.E., Leblanc, R., Watson, R.T., DeKosky, S.T., Schmitt, F.A., Read, S.L., and Johnston, J.T. Intracerebroventricular bethanechol chloride infusion in Alzheimer's disease. *Journal of Neurosurgery,* 1989, *71,* 481–486.

Harlan, R.E., Shivers, B.D., Kow, L.-M., and Pfaff,

D.W. Intrahypothalamic colchicine infusions disrupt lordotic responsiveness in estrogen-treated female rats. *Brain Research*, 1982, *238*, 153–167.

Harmon, L.D., and Julesz, B. Masking in visual recognition: Effects of two-dimensional filtered noise. *Science*, 1973, *180*, 1194–1197.

Harris, E.W., and Cotman, C.W. Long-term potentiation of guinea pig mossy fiber responses is not blocked by N-methyl-D-aspartate antagonists. *Neuroscience Letters*, 1986, *323*, 132–137.

Harris, G.W., and Jacobsohn, D. Functional grafts of the anterior pituitary gland. *Proceedings of the Royal Society of London, B.*, 1951–1952, *139*, 263–267.

Harris, R.B.S., Bruch, R.C., and Martin, R.J. In vitro evidence for an inhibitor of lipogenesis in serum from overfed obese rats. *American Journal of Physiology*, 1989, *257*, R326–R336.

Hart, B. Sexual reflexes and mating behavior in the male dog. *Journal of Comparative and Physiological Psychology*, 1967, *66*, 388–399.

Hart, B. Gonadal hormones and sexual reflexes in the female rat. *Hormones and Behavior*, 1969, *1*, 65–71.

Hart, B.L. Hormones, spinal reflexes, and sexual behaviour. In *Determinants of Sexual Behaviour*, edited by J.B. Hutchinson. Chichester, England: John Wiley & Sons, 1978.

Hartmann, E. *The Biology of Dreaming*. Springfield, Ill.: Charles C Thomas, 1967.

Haseltine, F.P., and Ohno, S. Mechanisms of gonadal differentiation. *Science*, 1981, *211*, 1272–1277.

Hawke, C. Castration and sex crimes. *American Journal of Mental Deficiency*, 1951, *55*, 220–226.

Hawkins, R.D., Abrams, T.W., Carew, T.J., and Kandel, E.R. A cellular mechanism of classical conditioning in *Aplysia*: Activity-dependent amplification of presynaptic facilitation. *Science*, 1983, *219*, 400–405.

Hebb, D.O. *The Organization of Behaviour*. New York: Wiley-Interscience, 1949.

Heckler, M.M. *Fifth Special Report to the U.S. Congress on Alcohol and Health*. Washington, D.C.: U.S. Government Printing Office, 1983.

Heilman, K.M., Rothi, L., and Kertesz, A. Localization of apraxia-producing lesions. In *Localization in Neuropsychology*, edited by A. Kertesz. New York: Academic Press, 1983.

Heilman, K.M., Scholes, R., and Watson, R.T. Auditory affective agnosia: Disturbed comprehension of affective speech. *Journal of Neurology, Neurosurgery, and Psychiatry*, 1975, *38*, 69–72.

Heilman, K.M., Watson, R.T., and Bowers, D. Affective disorders associated with hemispheric disease. In *Neuropsychology of Human Emotion*, edited

by K.M. Heilman and P. Satz. New York: Guilford Press, 1983.

Heimer, L., and Larsson, K. Impairment of mating behavior in male rats following lesions in the preoptic-anterior hypothalamic continuum. *Brain Research*, 1966/1967, *3*, 248–263.

Hellhammer, D.H., Hubert, W., and Schurmeyer, T. Changes in saliva testosterone after psychological stimulation in men. *Psychoneuroendocrinology*, 1985, *10*, 77–81.

Hendrickson, A.E., Wagoner, N., and Cowan, W.M. Autoradiographic and electron microscopic study of retino-hypothalamic connections. *Zeitschrift für Zellforschung und Mikroskopische Anatomie*, 1972, *125*, 1–26.

Henke, P.G. The telencephalic limbic system and experimental gastric pathology: A review. *Neuroscience and Biobehavioral Reviews*, 1982, *6*, 381–390.

Hennevin, E., Hars, B., and Block, V. Improvement of learning by mesencephalic reticular stimulation during postlearning paradoxical sleep. *Behavioral and Neural Biology*, 1989, *51*, 291–306.

Henningfield, J.E., and Goldberg, S.R. Nicotine as a reinforcer in human subjects and laboratory animals. *Pharmacology, Biochemistry, and Behavior*, 1983, *19*, 989–992.

Hering, E. *Outlines of a Theory of the Light Sense*. 1905. Translated by L.M. Hurvich and D. Jameson. Cambridge, Mass.: Harvard University Press, 1965.

Hernandez, L., and Hoebel, B.G. Food reward and cocaine increase extracellular dopamine in the nucleus accumbens as measured by microdialysis. *Life Sciences*, 1988, *42*, 1705–1712.

Herz, A., Albus, K., Metys, J., Schubert, P., and Teschemacher, H. On the central sites for the antinociceptive action of morphine and fentanyl. *Neuropharmacology*, 1970, *9*, 539–551.

Hess, R.H., Baker, C.L., and Zihl, J. The "motion-blind" patient: Low-level spatial and temporal filters. *Journal of Neuroscience*, 1989, *9*, 1628–1640.

Hetherington, A.W., and Ranson, S.W. Hypothalamic lesions and adiposity in the rat. *Anatomical Record*, 1942, *78*, 149–172.

Heuser, J.E. Synaptic vesicle exocytosis revealed in quick-frozen frog neuromuscular junctions treated with 4-aminopyridine and given a single electrical shock. In *Society for Neuroscience Symposia, Vol. II*, edited by W.M. Cowan and J.A. Ferrendelli. Bethesda, Md.: Society for Neuroscience, 1977.

Heuser, J.E., and Reese, T.S. Evidence for recycling of synaptic vesicle membrane during transmitter release at the frog neuromuscular function. *Journal of Cell Biology*, 1973, *57*, 315–344.

Heuser, J.E., Reese, T.S., Dennis, M.J., Jan, Y., Jan, L., and Evans, L. Synaptic vesicle exocytosis captured by quick freezing and correlated with quantal transmitter release. *Journal of Cell Biology*, 1979, *81*, 275–300.

Hill, A.J., and Best, P.J. Effects of deafness and blindness on the spatial correlates of hippocampal unit60activity in the rat. *Experimental Neurology* 1981, *74*, 204–217.

Hilton, S.M., and Zbrozyna, A.W. Amygdaloid region for defense reactions and its afferent pathway to the brain stem. *Journal of Physiology (London)*, 1963, *165*, 160–173.

Himmi, T., Boyer, A., and Orsini, J.C. Changes in lateral hypothalamic neuronal activity accompanying hyper- and hypoglycemias. *Physiology and Behavior*, 1988, *44*, 347–354.

Himms-Hagen, J. Current status of nonshivering thermogenesis. In *Assessment of Energy Metabolism in Health and Disease*, edited by J.W. Kinney. Columbus, Ohio: Ross Laboratories, 1980.

Hitchcock, J., and Davis, M. Lesions of the amygdala, but not of the cerebellum or red nucleus, block conditioned fear as measured with the potentiated startle paradigm. *Behavioral Neuroscience*, 1986, *100*, 11–22.

Hoebel, B.G., Monaco, A.P., Hernandez, L., Aulisi, E.F., Stanley, B.G., and Lenard, L. Self-injection of amphetamine directly into the brain. *Psychopharmacology*, 1983, *81*, 158–163.

Hoebel, B.G., and Teitelbaum, P. Weight regulation in normal and hypothalamic hyperphagic rats. *Journal of Comparative and Physiological Psychology*, 1966, *61*, 189–193.

Hogan, S., Himms-Hagen, J., and Coscina, D.V. Lack of diet-induced thermogenesis in brown adipose tissue of obese medial hypothalamic-lesioned rats. *Physiology and Behavior*, 1985, *35*, 287–294.

Hollander, E., Schiffman, E., Cohen, B., Rivera-Stein, M.A., Rosen, W., Gorman, J.M., Fyer, A.J., Papp, L., and Liebowitz, M.R. Signs of central nervous system dysfunction in obsessive-compulsive disorder. *Archives of General Psychiatry*, 1990, *47*, 27–32.

Holmes, G. The cerebellum of man. *Brain*, 1939, *62*, 21–30.

Holzman, P.S., Proctor, L.R., Levy, D.L., Yasillo, N.J., Meltzer, H.Y., and Hurt, S.W. Eye tracking dysfunction in schizophrenic patients and their relatives. *Archives of General Psychiatry*, 1974, *31*, 143–151.

Hood, L. Antibody genes: Arrangements and rearrangements. In *Molecular Genetic Neuroscience*, edited by F.O. Schmitt, S.J. Bird, and F.E. Bloom. New York: Raven Press, 1982.

Horne, J.A. A review of the biological effects of total sleep deprivation in man. *Biological Psychology*, 1978, *7*, 55–102.

Horne, J.A. The effects of exercise on sleep. *Biological Psychology*, 1981, *12*, 241–291.

Horne, J.A. *Why We Sleep: The Functions of Sleep in Humans and Other Mammals*. Oxford, England: Oxford University Press, 1988.

Horne, J.A., and Harley, L.J. Human SWS following selective head heating during wakefulness. In *Sleep '88*, edited by J. Horne. New York: Gustav Fischer Verlag, 1989.

Horne, J.A., and Minard, A. Sleep and sleepiness following a behaviourally "active" day. *Ergonomics*, 1985, *28*, 567–575.

Horne, J.A., and Moore, V.J. Sleep effects of exercise with and without additional body cooling. *Electroencephalography and Clinical Neurophysiology*, 1985, *60*, 347–353.

Horne, J.A., and Pettitt, A.N. High incentive effects on vigilance performance during 72 hours of total sleep deprivation. *Acta Physiologica*, 1985, *58*, 123–139.

Horne, J.A., and Staff, L.H.E. Exercise and sleep: Body heating effects. *Sleep*, 1983, *6*, 33–38.

Horowitz, R.M., and Gentili, B. Dihydrochalcone sweeteners. In *Symposium: Sweeteners*, edited by G.E. Inglett. Westport, Conn.: Avi Publishing, 1974.

Horton, J.C., and Hubel, D.H. Cytochrome oxidase stain preferentially labels intersection of ocular dominance and vertical orientation columns in macaque striate cortex. *Society for Neuroscience Abstracts*, 1980, *6*, 315.

Hrdy, S.B. Infanticide as a primate reproductive strategy. *American Scientist*, 1977, *65*, 38–47.

Huang, Y.H., and Mogenson, G.J. Neural pathways mediating drinking and feeding in rats. *Experimental Neurology*, 1972, *37*, 269–286.

Hubel, D.H., and Livingstone, M.S. Segregation of form, color, and stereopsis in primate area 18. *Journal of Neuroscience*, 1987, *7*, 3378–3415.

Hubel, D.H., and Wiesel, T.N. Laminar and columnar distribution of geniculo-cortical fibers in the macaque monkey. *Journal of Comparative Neurology*, 1972, *146*, 421–450.

Hubel, D.H., and Wiesel, T.N. Functional architecture of macaque monkey visual cortex. *Proceedings of the Royal Society of London*, 1977, *198*, 1–59.

Hubel, D.H., and Wiesel, T.N. Brain mechanisms of vision. *Scientific American*, 1979, *241*, 150–162.

Hubel, D.H., Wiesel, T.N., and Stryker, M.P. Anatomical demonstration of orientation columns in macaque monkeys. *Journal of Comparative Neurology*, 1978, *177*, 361–380.

Hudspeth, A.J. Extracellular current flow and the site of transduction by hair cells. *Journal of Neuroscience*, 1982, *2*, 1–10.

Hudspeth, A.J. The cellular basis of hearing: The biophysics of hair cells. *Science*, 1985, *230*, 745–752.

Hudspeth, A.J., and Jacobs, R. Stereocilia mediate transduction in vertebrate hair cells. *Proceedings of the National Academy of Sciences, USA*, 1979, *76*, 1506–1509.

Hughes, J., Smith, T.W., Kosterlitz, H.W., Fothergill, L.A., Morgan, B.A., and Moris, H.R. Identification of two related pentapeptides from the brain with potent opiate agonist activity. *Nature*, 1975, *258*, 577–579.

Humphrey, A.L., and Hendrickson, A.E. Radial zones of high metabolic activity in squirrel monkey striate cortex. *Society for Neuroscience Abstracts*, 1980, *6*, 315.

Hyman, B.T., Van Hoesen, B.G., and Damasio, A.R. Alzheimer's disease: Glutamate depletion in the hippocampal perforant pathway zone. *Annals of Neurology*, 1987, *22*, 37–40.

Hyman, B.T., Van Hoesen, G.W., Damasio, A.R., and Barnes, C.L. Alzheimer's disease: Cell-specific pathology isolates the hippocampal formation. *Science*, 1984, *225*, 1168–1170.

Ibuka, N., and Kawamura, H. Loss of circadian rhythm in sleep-wakefulness cycle in the rat by suprachiasmatic nucleus lesions. *Brain Research*, 1975, *96*, 76–81.

Iggo, A., and Andres, K.H. Morphology of cutaneous receptors. *Annual Review of Neuroscience*, 1982, *5*, 1–32.

Imperato, A., and Di Chiara, G. Preferential stimulation of dopamine-release in the accumbens of freely moving rats by ethanol. *Journal of Pharmacology and Experimental Therapeutics*, 1986, *239*, 219–228.

Ingelfinger, F.J. The late effects of total and subtotal gastrectomy. *New England Journal of Medicine*, 1944, *231*, 321–327.

Inouye, S.-I., Takahashi, J.S., Wollnik, F., and Turek, F.W. Inhibitor of protein synthesis phase shifts a circadian pacemaker in mammalian SCN. *American Journal of Physiology*, 1988, *255*, R1055–R1058.

Inouye, S.T., and Kawamura, H. Persistence of circadian rhythmicity in mammalian hypothalamic "island" containing the suprachiasmatic nucleus. *Proceedings of the National Academy of Sciences, USA*, 1979, *76*, 5961–5966.

Insel, T.R., and Harbaugh, C.R. Lesions of the hypothalamic paraventricular nucleus disrupt the initiation of maternal behavior. *Physiology and Behavior*, 1989, *45*, 1033–1041.

Institute of Medicine. *Sleeping Pills, Insomnia, and Medical Practice*. Washington, D.C.: National Academy of Sciences, 1979.

Ito, M. Neuronal events in the cerebellar flocculus associated with an adaptive modification of the vestibulo-ocular reflex of the rabbit. In *Control of Gaze by Brain Stem Neurons, Developments in Neuroscience*, edited by R. Baker and A. Berthoz. Amsterdam: Elsevier, 1977.

Iwai, E., and Mishkin, M. Further evidence of the locus of the visual area in the temporal lobe of the monkey. *Experimental Neurology*, 1969, *25*, 585–594.

Iwai, E., Osawa, Y., and Umitsu, Y. Elevated visual pattern discrimination limen in monkeys with total removal of inferotemporal cortex. *Japanese Journal of Physiology*, 1979, *29*, 749–765.

Iwata, J., Chida, K., and LeDoux, J.E. Cardiovascular responses elicited by stimulation of neurons in the central amygdaloid nucleus in awake but not anesthetized rats resemble conditioned emotional responses. *Brain Research*, 1987, *418*, 183–188.

Iwata, J., LeDoux, J.E., Meeley, M.P., Arneric, S., and Reis, D.J. Intrinsic neurons in the amygdaloid field projected to by the medial geniculate body mediate emotional responses conditioned to acoustic stimuli. *Brain Research*, 1986, *383*, 195–214.

Jacklet, J.W. The cellular mechanisms of circadian clocks. *Trends in Neurosciences*, 1978, *1*, 117–119.

Jacobs, B.L., Asher, R., and Dement, W.C. Electrophysiological and behavioral effects of electrical stimulation of the raphe nuclei in cats. *Physiology and Behavior*, 1973, *11*, 489–496.

Jacobs, B.L., and McGinty, D.J. Effects of food deprivation on sleep and wakefulness in the rat. *Experimental Neurology*, 1971, *30*, 212–222.

Jacobs, K.M., Mark, G.P., and Scott, T.R. Taste responses in the nucleus tractus solitarius of sodium-deprived rats. *Journal of Physiology (London)*, 1988, *406*, 393–410.

Jacobson, C.D., Csernus, V.J., Shryne, J.E., and Gorski, R.A. The influence of gonadectomy, androgen exposure, or a gonadal graft in the neonatal rat on the volume of the sexually dimorphic nucleus of the preoptic area. *Journal of Neuroscience*, 1981, *1*, 1142–1147.

Jacquet, Y.F. Conditioned aversion during morphine maintenance in mice and rats. *Physiology and Behavior*, 1973, *11*, 527–541.

Jaffe, J.H. Drug addiction and drug abuse. In *The Pharmacological Basis of Therapeutics, Vol. 7,* edited by L.S. Goodman and A. Gilman. New York: Macmillan, 1985.

James, W. What is an emotion? *Mind*, 1884, *9*, 188–205.

James, W. *Principles of Psychology.* New York: Henry Holt, 1890.

James, W.P.T., and Trayhurn, P. Thermogenesis and obesity. *British Medical Bulletin*, 1981, *27*, 43–48.

Janowitz, H.D., and Grossman, M.I. Some factors affecting the food intake of normal dogs and dogs with esophagostomy and gastric fistula. *American Journal of Physiology*, 1949, *159*, 143–148.

Janowitz, H.D., and Hollander, F. The time factor in the adjustment of food intake to varied caloric equipment in the dog: A study of the precision of appetite regulation. *Annals of the New York Academy of Sciences*, 1955, *63*, 56–67.

Janowsky, A., Steranka, L.R., and Sulser, F. Role of neuronal signal input in the down-regulation of central noradrenergic receptor function by antidepressant drugs. Paper presented at the Annual Meeting of the Society for Neuroscience, 1981.

Jaskiw, G., and Kleinman, J. Postmortem neurochemistry studies in schizophrenia. In *Schizophrenia: A Scientific Focus,* edited by S.C. Schulz and C.A. Tamminga. New York: Oxford University Press, 1988.

Jasper, J.H., and Tessier, J. Acetylcholine liberation from cerebral cortex during paradoxical (REM) sleep. *Science*, 1969, *172*, 601–602.

Jeffress, L.A. A place theory of sound localization. *Journal of Comparative and Physiological Psychology*, 1948, *41*, 35–39.

Jeste, D.V., Del Carmen, R., Lohr, J.B., and Wyatt, R.J. Did schizophrenia exist before the eighteenth century? *Comprehensive Psychiatry*, 1985, *26*, 493–503.

Jiang, C.L., and Hunt, J.N. The relation between freely chosen meals and body habitus. *American Journal of Clinical Nutrition*, 1983, *38*, 32–40.

Johns, M.A., Feder, H.H., Komisaruk, B.R., and Mayer, A.D. Urine-induced reflex ovulation in anovulatory rats may be a vomeronasal effect. *Nature*, 1978, *272*, 446–448.

Johnson, A., Josephson, R., and Hawke, M. Clinical and histological evidence for the presence of the vomeronasal (Jacobson's) organ in adult humans. *Journal of Otolaryngology*, 1985, *14*, 71–79.

Johnson, A.K., and Cunningham, J.T. Brain mechanisms and drinking: The role of lamina terminalis-associated systems in extracellular thirst. *Kidney International*, 1987, *32*, S35–S42.

Johnson, M.K., Kim, J.K., and Risse, G. Do alcoholic Korsakoff's syndrome patients acquire affective reactions? *Journal of Experimental Psychology: Learning, Memory, and Cognition*, 1985, *11*, 22–36.

Johnston, D., Hopkins, W.F., and Gray, R. The role of norepinephrine in long-term potentiation at mossy-fiber synapses in the hippocampus. In *Neural Models of Plasticity: Experimental and Theoretical Approaches,* edited by J.H. Byrne and W.O. Berry. San Diego: Academic Press, 1989.

Jones, B.E., and Beaudet, A. Distribution of acetylcholine and catecholamine neurons in the cat brain stem studied by choline acetyltransferase and tyrosine hydroxylase immunohistochemistry. *Journal of Comparative Neurology*, 1987, *261*, 15–32.

Jones, B.E., Bobillier, P., and Jouvet, M. Effets de la destruction des neurones contenant des catécholamines du mésencéphale sur le cycle veille-sommeils du chat. *Comptes Rendus de la Societe de Biologie (Paris)*, 1969, *163*, 176–180.

Jones, D.T., and Reed, R.R. G_{olf}: An olfactory neuron specific-G protein involved in odorant signal transduction. *Science*, 1989, *244*, 790–795.

Jones, R. Anomalies of disparity in the human visual system. *Journal of Physiology*, 1977, *264*, 621–640.

Jouvet, M. Recherches sur les structures nerveuses et les mécanismes responsables des différentes phases du sommeil physiologique. *Archives Italiennes de Biologie*, 1962, *100*, 125–206.

Jouvet, M. The role of monoamines and acetylcholine-containing neurons in the regulation of the sleep-waking cycle. *Ergebnisse der Physiologie*, 1972, *64*, 166–307.

Jouvet, M. Paradoxical sleep and the nature-nurture controversy. *Progress in Brain Research*, 1980, *53*, 331–346.

Juji, T.M., Satake, Y., Honda, Y., and Doi, Y. HLA antigens in Japanese patients with narcolepsy: All the patients were CR2 positive. *Tissue Antigens*, 1984, *24*, 316–319.

Julien, R.M. *A Primer of Drug Action.* San Francisco: W.H. Freeman, 1981.

Kadekaro, M., Cohen, S., Terrell, M.L., Lekan, H., Gary, H., and Eisenberg, H.M. Independent activation of subfornical organ and hypothalamo-neurohypophysial system during administration of angiotensin II. *Peptides*, 1989, *10*, 423–429.

Kahn, A., Blum, D., Rebuffat, E., Sottiaux, M., Levitt, J., Bochner, A., Alexander, M., Grosswasser, J., and Muller, M.F. Polysomnographic studies of infants who subsequently died of sudden infant death syndrome. *Pediatrics*, 1988, *82*, 721–727.

Kales, A., Scharf, M.B., Kales, J.D., and Soldatos, C.R. Rebound insomnia: A potential hazard following withdrawal of certain benzodiazepines. *Journal of the American Medical Association*, 1979, *241*, 1692–1695.

Kales, A., Tan, T.-L., Kollar, E.J., Naitoh, P., Preston, T.A., and Malmstrom, E.J. Sleep patterns following 205 hours of sleep deprivation. *Psychosomatic Medicine*, 1970, *32*, 189–200.

Kalra, P.S., Simpkins, J.W., Luttge, G., and Kalra, S.P. Effects on male sexual behavior and preoptic dopamine neurons of hyperprolactineaemia induced by MtTW15 pituitary tumors. *Endocrinology*, 1983, *113*, 2065–2071.

Kanamori, N., Sakai, K., and Jouvet, M. Neuronal activity specific to paradoxical sleep in the ventromedial medullary reticular formation of unrestrained cats. *Brain Research*, 1980, *189*, 251–255.

Kandel, E.R., and Schwartz, J.H. Molecular biology of learning: Modulation of transmitter release. *Science*, 1982, *218*, 433–443.

Kaneko, N., Debski, E.A., Wilson, M.C., and Whitten, W.K. Puberty acceleration in mice. II. Evidence that the vomeronasal organ is a receptor for the primer pheromone in male mouse urine. *Biology of Reproduction*, 1980, *22*, 873–878.

Karacan, I., Salis, P.J., and Williams, R.L. The role of the sleep laboratory in diagnosis and treatment of impotence. In *Sleep Disorders: Diagnosis and Treatment*, edited by R.J. Williams and I. Karacan. New York: John Wiley & Sons, 1978.

Karacan, I., Williams, R.L., Finley, W.W., and Hursch, C.J. The effects of naps on nocturnal sleep: Influence on the need for stage-1 REM and stage 4 sleep. *Biological Psychiatry*, 1970, *2*, 391–399.

Karlson, P., and Luscher, M. "Pheromones": A new term for a class of biologically active substances. *Nature*, 1959, *183*, 55–56.

Kasper, S., Rogers, S.L.B., Yancey, A., Schulz, P.M., Skwerer, R.G., and Rosenthal, N.E. Phototherapy in individuals with and without subsyndromal seasonal affective disorder. *Archives of General Psychiatry*, 1989a, *46*, 837–844.

Kasper, S., Wehr, T.A., Bartko, J.J., Gaist, P.A., and Rosenthal, N.E. Epidemiological findings of seasonal changes in mood and behavior: A telephone survey of Montgomery County, Maryland. *Archives of General Psychiatry*, 1989b, *46*, 823–833.

Katayama, Y., DeWitt, D.S., Becker, D.P., and Hayes, R.L. Behavioral evidence for cholinoceptive pontine inhibitory area: Descending control of spi-

nal motor output and sensory input. *Brain Research*, 1986, *296*, 241–262.

Katsuki, Y. In *Sensory Communication*, edited by W.A. Rosenblith. Cambridge, Mass.: MIT Press, 1961.

Kawamura, M., Hirayama, K., and Yamamoto, H. Different interhemispheric transfer of kanji and kana writing evidenced by a case with left unilateral agraphia without apraxia. *Brain*, 1989, *112*, 1011–1018.

Keithley, E.M., and Schreiber, R.C. Frequency map of the spiral ganglion in the cat. *Journal of the Acoustical Society of America*, 1987, *81*, 1036–1042.

Kelley, A.E., and Domesick, V.B. The distribution of the projection from the hippocampal formation to the nucleus accumbens in the rat: An anterograde and retrograde horseradish peroxidase study. *Neuroscience*, 1982, *7*, 2321–2335.

Kelley, A.E., Domesick, V.B., and Nauta, W.J.H. The amygdalostriatal projection in the rat—an anatomical study by anterograde and retrograde tracing methods. *Neuroscience*, 1982, *7*, 615–630.

Kelly, D.H., Walker, A.M., Cahen, L.A., and Shannon, D.C. Periodic breathing in siblings of SIDS victims. *Pediatric Research*, 1980, *14*, 645–650.

Kelso, S.R., and Brown, T.H. Differential conditioning of associative synaptic enhancement in hippocampal brain slices. *Science*, 1986, *232*, 85–87.

Kelso, S.R., Ganong, A.H., and Brown, T.H. Hebbian synapses in hippocampus. *Proceedings of the National Academy of Sciences, USA*, 1986, *83*, 5326–5330.

Kelsoe, J.R., Ginns, E.I., Egeland, J.A., Gerhard, D.S., Goldstein, A.M., Bale, S.J., Pauls, D.L., Long, R.T., Kidd, K.K., Conte, G., Housman, D.E., and Paul, S.M. Re-evaluation of the linkage relationship between chromosome 11p loci and the gene for bipolar affective disorder in the Old Order Amish. *Nature*, 1989, *342*, 238–243.

Kemble, E.D., and Nagel, J.A. Failure to form a learned taste aversion in rats with amygdaloid lesions. *Bulletin of the Psychonomic Society*, 1973, *2*, 155–156.

Kemp, D.T. Stimulated acoustic emissions from within the human auditory system. *Journal of the Acoustical Society of America*, 1978, *64*, 1386–1391.

Kennedy, J.L., Giuffra, L.A., Moises, H.W., Cavalli-Sforza, L.L., Pakstis, A.J., Kidd, J.R., Castiglione, C.M., Sjögren, B., Wetterberg, L., and Kidd, K.K. Evidence against linkage of schizophrenia to markers on chromosome 5 in a northern Swedish pedigree. *Nature*, 1988, *336*, 167–170.

Kent, E., and Grossman, S.P. Evidence for a conflict interpretation of anomalous effects of rewarding brain stimulation. *Journal of Comparative and Physiological Psychology*, 1969, *69*, 381–390.

Kertesz, A. *Aphasia and Associated Disorders: Taxonomy, Localization, and Recovery.* New York: Grune & Stratton, 1979.

Kertesz, A. Personal communication, 1980.

Kertesz, A. Anatomy of jargon. In *Jargonaphasia,* edited by J. Brown. New York: Academic Press, 1981.

Kessler, S., Guilleminault, C., and Dement, W.C. A family study of 50 REM narcoleptics. *Acta Neurologica Scandinavica,* 1974, *50,* 503–512.

Kety, S.S., Rosenthal, D., Wender, P.H., and Schulsinger, K.F. The types and prevalence of mental illness in the biological and adoptive families of adopted schizophrenics. In *The Transmission of Schizophrenia,* edited by D. Rosenthal and S.S. Kety. New York: Pergamon Press, 1968.

Keverne, E.B., and de la Riva, C. Pheromones in mice: Reciprocal interactions between the nose and brain. *Nature,* 1982, *296,* 148–150.

Keverne, E.B., and Michael, R.P. Sex-attractant properties of ether extracts of vaginal secretions from rhesus monkeys. *Journal of Endocrinology,* 1971, *51,* 313–322.

Kiang, N.Y.-S. Discharge patterns of single fibers in the cat's auditory nerve. Cambridge, Mass.: MIT Press, 1965.

King, B.M., and Frohman, L.A. Hypothalamic obesity: Comparison of ratio-frequency and electrolytic lesions in male and female rats. *Brain Research Bulletin,* 1986, *17,* 409–413.

Kinnamon, J.C., and Roper, S.D. Evidence for a role of voltage-sensitive apical K$^+$ channels in sour and salt taste transduction. *Chemical Senses,* 1988, *13,* 115–121.

Kinnamon, S.C., Dionne, V.E., and Beam, K.G. Apical localization of K$^+$ channels in taste cells provides the basis for sour taste transduction. *Proceedings of the National Academy of Sciences, USA,* 1988, *85,* 7023–7027.

Kinsey, A.C., Pomeroy, W.B., Martin, C.E., and Gebhard, P.H. *Sexual Behavior in the Human Female.* Philadelphia: Saunders, 1943.

Kinsley, C., and Svare, B. Prenatal stress reduces intermale aggression in mice. *Physiology and Behavior,* 1986, *36,* 783–785.

Kinsley, C.H., Konen, C.M., Miele, L., Ghiraldi, L., and Svare, B. Intrauterine position modulates maternal behaviors in female mice. *Physiology and Behavior,* 1986, *36,* 793–799.

Kirchgessner, A.L., and Sclafani, A. PVN-hindbrain pathway involved in the hypothalamic hyperphagia-obesity syndrome. *Physiology and Behavior,* 1988, *42,* 517–528.

Klaus, M.H., Jerauld, R., Krieger, N.C., McAlpine, W., Steffa, M., and Kennell, J.H. Maternal attachment: Importance of the first postpartum days. *New England Journal of Medicine,* 1972, *286,* 460–463.

Kleitman, N. The nature of dreaming. In *The Nature of Sleep,* edited by G.E.W. Wolstenholme and M. O'Connor. London: J.&A. Churchill, 1961.

Kleitman, N. Basic rest-activity cycle—22 years later. *Sleep,* 1982, *4,* 311–317.

Klopfer, P.H., Adams, D.J., and Klopfer, M.S. Maternal "imprinting" in goats. *Proceedings of the National Academy of Sciences, USA,* 1964, *52,* 911–914.

Klüver, H., and Bucy, P.C. Preliminary analysis of functions of the temporal lobes in monkeys. *Archives of Neurology and Psychiatry (Chicago),* 1939, *42,* 979–1000.

Knobil, E. A hypothalamic pulse generator governs mammalian reproduction. *News in Physiological Sciences,* 1987, *2,* 42–43.

Knoll, J. Satietin: A centrally acting potent anorectic substance with a long-lasting effect in human and mammalian blood. *Polish Journal of Pharmacology and Pharmacy,* 1982, *34,* 3–16.

Koch, K.W., and Fuster, J.M. Unit activity in monkey parietal cortex related to haptic perception and temporary memory. *Experimental Brain Research,* 1989, *76,* 292–306.

Koenig, J.H., and Ikeda, K. Disappearance and reformation of synaptic vesicle membrane upon transmitter release observed under reversible blockage of membrane retrieval. *The Journal of Neuroscience,* 1989, *9,* 3844–3860.

Kolarsky, A., Freund, K., Machek, J., and Polak, O. Male sexual deviation. Association with early temporal lobe damage. *Archives of General Psychiatry,* 1967, *17,* 735–743.

Komisaruk, B.R., and Larsson, K. Suppression of a spinal and a cranial nerve reflex by vaginal or rectal probing in rats. *Brain Research,* 1971, *35,* 231–235.

Komisaruk, B.R., and Steinman, J.L. Genital stimulation as a trigger for neuroendocrine and behavioral control of reproduction. *Annals of the New York Academy of Sciences,* 1987, *474,* 64–75.

Koob, G.F., and Bloom, F.E. Cellular and molecular mechanisms of drug dependence. *Science,* 1988, *242,* 715–723.

Koob, G.F., Thatcher-Britton, K., Britton, D., Roberts, D.C.S., and Bloom, F.E. Destruction of the locus coeruleus or the dorsal NE bundle does not alter the release of punished responding by ethanol and chlordiazepoxide. *Physiology and Behavior,* 1984, *33,* 479–485.

Koopmans, H.S. The role of the gastrointestinal tract in the satiation of hunger. In *The Body Weight Regulatory System: Normal and Disturbed Mechanisms,* edited by L.A. Cioffi, W.P.T. James, and T.B. Van Italie. New York: Raven Press, 1981.

Korn, J.H., and Moyer, K.E. Behavioral effects of isolation in the rat: The role of sex and time of isolation. *The Journal of Genetic Psychology*, 1968, *113*, 263–273.

Kornhuber, H.H. Cerebral cortex, cerebellum, and basal ganglia: An introduction to their motor functions. In *The Neurosciences: Third Study Program*, edited by F.O. Schmitt and F.G. Worden. Cambridge, Mass.: MIT Press, 1974.

Kozlowski, S., and Drzewiecki, K. The role of osmoreception in portal circulation in control of water intake in dogs. *Acta Physiologica Polonica*, 1973, *24*, 325–330.

Kraepelin, E. *Dementia Praecox*. 1919. Translated by R.M. Barclay. Facsimile edition. New York: Krieger, 1971.

Kral, J.G. Surgical treatment of obesity. *Medical Clinics of North America*, 1989, *73*, 251–264.

Kraly, F.S. Drinking elicited by eating. In *Progress in Psychobiology and Physiological Psychology, Vol. 14*, edited by A.N. Epstein and A. Morrison. New York: Academic Press, 1990.

Kraly, F.S., and Corneilson, R. Angiotensin II mediates drinking elicited by eating in the rat. *American Journal of Physiology*, 1990, *258*, R436–R442.

Kraly, F.S., and Specht, S.M. Histamine plays a major role for drinking elicited by spontaneous eating in rats. *Physiology and Behavior*, 1984, *33*, 611–614.

Kramer, F.M., Jeffery, R.W., Forster, J.L., and Snell, M.K. Long-term follow-up of behavioral treatment for obesity: Patterns of weight regain among men and women. *International Journal of Obesity*, 1989, *13*, 123–136.

Kreuz, L., and Rose, R. Assessment of aggressive behavior and plasma testosterone in a young criminal population. *Psychosomatic Medicine*, 1972, *34*, 321–332.

Krieger, M.S., Conrad, L.C.A., and Pfaff, D.W. An autoradiographic study of the efferent connections of the ventromedial nucleus of the hypothalamus. *Journal of Comparative Neurology*, 1979, *183*, 785–816.

Krieger, M.S., and Pfaff, D.W. Projections from mesencephalic central grey in the rat. Unpublished paper, 1980. Cited by Pfaff, 1980.

Krueger, J.M., Davenne, D., Walter, J., Shoham, S., Kubillus, S.L., Rosenthal, R.S., Martin, S.A., and Biemann, K. Bacterial peptidoglycans as modulators of sleep. II. Effects of muramyl peptides on the structure of rabbit sleep. *Brain Research*, 1987, *402*, 258–266.

Krueger, J.M., Pappenheimer, J.R., and Karnovsky, M.L. Sleep-promoting effects of muramyl peptides. *Proceedings of the National Academy of Sciences, USA*, 1982a, *79*, 6102–6106.

Krueger, J.M., Pappenheimer, J.R., and Karnovski, M.L. The composition of sleep-promoting factor isolated from human urine. *Journal of Biological Chemistry*, 1982b, *257*, 1664–1669.

Krug, M., Lössner, B., and Ott, T. Anisomycin blocks the late phase of long-term potentiation in the dentate gyrus of freely moving rats. *Brain Research Bulletin*, 1984, *13*, 39–42.

Kuffler, S.W. Neurons in the retina: Organization, inhibition and excitation problems. *Cold Spring Harbor Symposium on Quantitative Biology*, 1952, *17*, 281–292.

Kuffler, S.W. Discharge patterns and functional organization of mammalian retina. *Journal of Neurophysiology*, 1953, *16*, 37–68.

Kukorelli, T., and Juhasz, G. Sleep induced by intestinal stimulation in cats. *Physiology and Behavior*, 1977, *19*, 355–358.

Kupfer, D.J. REM latency: A psychobiologic marker for primary depressive disease. *Biological Psychiatry*, 1976, *11*, 159–174.

Laborit, H. La thérapeutique neuro-végétate du choc et de la maladie post-traumatique. *Presse Medicale*, 1950, *58*, 138–140. Cited by Snyder, 1974.

Labruyere, J., Fuller, T.A., Olney, J.W., Price, M.T., Zorumski, C., and Clifford, D. Phencyclidine and ketamine protect against kainic acid-induced seizures and seizure-related brain damage. *Society for Neuroscience Abstracts*, 1986, *12*, 344.

Lahmeyer, H.W. Sleep in craniopagus twins. *Sleep*, 1988, *11*, 301–306.

Lancet, D. Vertebrate olfactory reception. *Annual Review of Neuroscience*, 1986, *9*, 329–355.

Land, E.H. The retinex theory of colour vision. *Proceedings of the Royal Institute of Great Britain*, 1974, *47*, 23–57.

Land, E.H. The retinex theory of color vision. *Scientific American*, 1977, *237*, 108–128.

Lange, C.G. *Über Gemüthsbewegungen*. Leipzig: T. Thomas, 1987.

Langston, J.W., Ballard, P., Tetrud, J., and Irwin, I. Chronic parkinsonism in humans due to a product of meperidine-analog synthesis. *Science*, 1983, *219*, 979–980.

Langston, J.W., Irwin, I., Langston, E.B., and Forno, L.S. Pargyline prevents MPTP-induced parkinsonism in primates. *Science*, 1984, *225*, 1480–1482.

Lankenau, H., Swigar, M.E., Bhimani, S., Luchins, S.,

and Quinlon, D.M. Cranial CT scans in eating disorder patients and controls. *Comprehensive Psychiatry*, 1985, *26*, 136–147.

Larue-Achagiotis, C., and Le Magnen, J. Effect of long-term intravenous insulin infusion on body weight on food intake in intravenous versus intraperitoneal routes. *Appetite*, 1985a, *6*, 319–329.

Larue-Achagiotis, C., and Le Magnen, J. Feeding rate and responses to food deprivation as a function of fast-induced hypoglycemia. *Behavioral Neuroscience*, 1985b, *99*, 1176–1180.

Laschet, U. Antiandrogen in the treatment of sex offenders: Mode of action and therapeutic outcome. In *Contemporary Sexual Behavior: Critical Issues in the 1970's*, edited by J. Zubin and J. Money. Baltimore: Johns Hopkins University Press, 1973.

Lasek, R.J., Gainer, H., and Przybylski, R.J. Transfer of newly synthesized proteins from Schwann cells to the squid gaint axon. *Proceedings of the National Academy of Sciences (U.S.A.)*, 1974, *71*, 1188–1192.

Lavie, P., Pratt, H., Scharf, B., Peled, R., and Brown, J. Localized pontine lesion: Nearly total absence of REM sleep. *Neurology*, 1984, *34*, 1118–1120.

Lawrence, D.G., and Kuypers, G.J.M. The functional organization of the motor system in the monkey. I. The effects of bilateral pyramidal lesions. *Brain*, 1968a, *91*, 1–14.

Lawrence, D.G., and Kuypers, G.J.M. The functional organization of the motor system in the monkey. II. The effects of lesions of the descending brainstem pathways. *Brain*, 1968b, *91*, 15–36.

LeBlanc, J., and Cabanac, M. Cephalic postprandial thermogenesis in human subjects. *Physiology and Behavior*, 1989, *46*, 479–482.

LeDoux, J.E., Iwata, J., Cicchetti, P., and Reis, D.J. Different projections of the central amygdaloid nucleus mediate autonomic and behavioral correlates of conditioned fear. *Journal of Neuroscience*, 1988, *8*, 2517–2529.

LeDoux, J.E., Iwata, J., Pearl, D., and Reis, D.J. Disruption of auditory but not visual learning by destruction of intrinsic neurons in the rat medial geniculate body. *Brain Research*, 1986, *371*, 395–399.

LeDoux, J.E., Ruggiero, D.A., Forest, R., Stornetta, R., and Reis, D.J. Topographic organization of convergent projections to the thalamus from the inferior colliculus and spinal cord in the rat. *Journal of Comparative Neurology*, 1987, *254*, 123–146.

LeDoux, J.E., Ruggiero, D.A., and Reis, D.J. Projections to the subcortical forebrain from anatomically defined regions of the medial geniculate body in the rat. *Journal of Comparative Neurology*, 1985, *242*, 182–213.

LeDoux, J.E., Sakaguchi, A., and Reis, D.J. Subcortical efferent projections of the medial geniculate nucleus mediate emotional responses conditioned to acoustic stimuli. *Journal of Neuroscience*, 1984, *4*, 683–698.

Lehman, M.N., Silver, R., Gladstone, W.R., Kahn, R.M., Gibson, M., and Bittman, E.L. Circadian rhythmicity restored by neural transplant: Immunocytochemical characterization with the host brain. *Journal of Neuroscience*, 1987, *7*, 1626–1638.

Lehman, M.N., and Winans, S.S. Vomeronasal and olfactory pathways to the amygdala controlling male hamster sexual behavior: Autoradiographic and behavioral analyses. *Brain Research*, 1982, *240*, 27–41.

Leibowitz, S.F., Weiss, G.F., and Shor-Posner, G. Hypothalamic serotonin: Pharmacological, biochemical and behavioral analyses of its feeding-suppressive action. *Clinical Neuropharmacology*, 1988, *11*, 551–571.

Leibowitz, S.F., Weiss, G.F., Walsh, U.A., and Viswanath, D. Medial hypothalamic serotonin: Role in circadian patterns of feeding and macronutrient selection. *Brain Research*, 1989, *503*, 132–140.

Leibowitz, S.F., Weiss, G.F., Yee, F., and Tretter, J.B. Noradrenergic innervation of the paraventricular nucleus: Specific role in control of carbohydrate ingestions. *Brain Research Bulletin*, 1985, *14*, 561–567.

Le Magnen, J. Hyperphagie provoquée chez le rat blanc par l'altération du méchanisme de satiéte périphérique. *Comptes Rendus de la Société de Biologie*, 1956, *147*, 1753–1757.

Le Magnen, J., and Tallon, S. Enregistrement et analyse préliminaire de la "périodicité alimentaire spontanée" chez le rat blanc. *Journal of Physiology (Paris)*, 1963, *55*, 286–297.

Le Magnen, J., and Tallon, S. La périodicité spontanée de la prise d'aliments *ad libitum* du rat blanc. *Journal of Physiology (Paris)*, 1966, *58*, 323–349.

Lenard, H.G., and Schulte, F.J. Polygraph sleep study in cranipagus twins (where is the sleep transmitter?). *Journal of Neurology, Neurosurgery and Psychiatry*, 1972, *35*, 756–762.

Leon, M. Plasticity of olfactory output circuits related to early olfactory learning. *Trends in Neurosciences*, 1987, *10*, 434–438.

Leonard, B.E. On the mode of action of mianserin. In *Typical and Atypical Antidepressants: Molecular Mechanisms*, edited by E. Costa and G. Racagni. New York: Raven Press, 1982.

Leonard, H.L., Swedo, S.E., Rapoport, J.L., Koby, E.V., Lenane, M.C., Cheslow, D.L., and Hamburger, S.D. Treatment of obsessive-compulsive disorder with clomipramine and desipramine in children and adolescents: A double-blind cross-over comparison. *Archives of General Psychiatry*, 1989, *46*, 1088–1092.

Lepkovsky, S., Lyman, R., Fleming, D., Nagumo, M., and Dimick, M. Gastrointestinal regulation of water and its effect on food intake and rate of digestion. *American Journal of Physiology*, 1957, *188*, 327–331.

Leventhal, A.G., Rodieck, R.W., and Dreher, B. Retinal ganglion cell classes in cat and Old World monkey: Morphology and central projections. *Science*, 1981, *213*, 1139–1142.

Levine, A.S., and Morley, J.E. Neuropeptide Y: A potent inducer of consummatory behavior in rats. *Peptides*, 1984, *5*, 1025–1029.

Levine, J.D., Gordon, N.C., and Fields, H.L. The role of endorphins in placebo analgesia. In *Advances in Pain Research and Therapy, Vol. 3*, edited by J.J. Bonica, J.C. Liebeskind, and D. Albe-Fessard. New York: Raven Press, 1979.

Levine, J.D., Rosenwasser, A.M., Yanovski, J.A., and Adler, N.T. Circadian activity rhythms in rats with midbrain raphe lesions. *Brain Research*, 1986, *384*, 240–249.

Levy, W.B., and Steward, O. Temporal contiguity requirements for long-term associative potentiation/depression in the hippocampus. *Neuroscience*, 1983, *8*, 791–797.

Ley, R.G., and Bryden, M.P. Hemispheric differences in recognizing faces and emotions. *Brain and Language*, 1979, *7*, 127–138.

Ley, R.G., and Bryden, M.P. A dissociation of right and left hemispheric effects for recognizing emotional tone and verbal content. *Brain and Cognition*, 1982, *1*, 3–9.

Li, C.-S., Kaba, H., Saito, J., and Seto, K. Excitatory influence of the accessory olfactory bulb on tuberoinfundibular arcuate neurons of female mice and its modulation by oestrogen. *Neuroscience*, 1989, *29*, 201–208.

Liebelt, R.A., Bordelon, C.B., and Liebelt, A.G. The adipose tissue system and food intake. In *Progress in Physiological Psychology*, edited by E. Stellar and J.M. Sprague. New York: Academic Press, 1973.

Lind, R.W., and Johnson, A.K. Central and peripheral mechanisms mediating angiotensin-induced thirst. In *The Renin Angiotensin System in the Brain*, edited by D. Ganten, M. Printz, M.I. Phillips, and B.A. Schölkens. Berlin: Springer-Verlag, 1982.

Lind, R.W., Thunhorst, R.L., and Johnson, A.K. The subfornical organ and the integration of multiple factors in thirst. *Physiology and Behavior*, 1984, *32*, 69–74.

Lindsley, D.B., Schreiner, L.H., Knowles, W.B., and Magoun, H.W. Behavioral and EEG changes following chronic brain stem lesions in the cat. *Electroencephalography and Clinical Neurophysiology*, 1950, *2*, 483–498.

Lindvall, O. Dopamine pathways in the rat brain. In *The Neurobiology of Dopamine*, edited by A.S. Horn, J. Korb, and B.H.C. Westerink. New York: Academic Press, 1979.

Linnoila, M., Virkkunen, M., Scheinin, M., Nirutila, A., Rimon, R., and Goodwin, F.K. Low cerebrospinal fluid 5-hydroxyindoleacetic and concentration differentiates impulsive from nonimpulsive violent behavior. *Life Sciences*, 1983, *33*, 2609–2614.

Lisk, R.D. The regulation of sexual "heat." In *Biological Determinants of Sexual Behaviour*, edited by J.B. Hutchison. New York: John Wiley & Sons, 1978.

Lisk, R.D., Pretlow, R.A., and Friedman, S. Hormonal stimulation necessary for elicitation of maternal nest-building in the mouse (*Mus musculus*). *Animal Behaviour*, 1969, *17*, 730–737.

Liuzzi, F.J., and Lasek, R.J. Astrocytes block axonal regeneration in mammals by activating the physiological stop pathway. *Science*, 1987, *237*, 642–645.

Livingstone, M.S., and Hubel, D.H. Effect of sleep and arousal on the processing of visual information in the cat. *Nature*, 1981, *291*, 554–561.

Livingstone, M.S., and Hubel, D.H. Thalamic inputs to cytochrome oxidase-rich regions in monkey visual cortex. *Proceedings of the National Academy of Sciences, USA*, 1982, *79*, 6098–6101.

Livingstone, M.S., and Hubel, D.H. Psychophysical evidence for separate channels for the perception of form, color, movement, and depth. *Journal of Neuroscience*, 1987, *7*, 3416–3468.

Livingstone, M.S., and Hubel, D. Segregation of form, color, movement, and depth: Anatomy, physiology, and perception. *Science*, 1988, *240*, 740–749.

Loewenstein, W.R., and Mendelson, M. Components of receptor adaptation in a Pacinian corpuscle. *Journal of Physiology (London)*, 1965, *177*, 377–397.

Loewenstein, W.R., and Rathkamp, R. The sites for mechano-electric conversion in a Pacinian corpuscle. *Journal of General Physiology*, 1958, *41*, 1245–1265.

Lomas, D.E., and Keverne, E.B. Role of the vomeronasal organ and prolactin in the acceleration of puberty in female mice. *Journal of Reproduction and Fertility*, 1982, *66*, 101–107.

Lømo, T. Frequency potentiation of excitatory synaptic activity in the dentate area of the hippocampal formation. *Acta Physiologica Scandinavica*, 1966, *68* (Suppl. 227), 128.

LoTurco, J.J., Coulter, D.A., and Alkon, D.L. Enhancement of synaptic potentials in rabbit CA1 pyramidal neurons following classical conditioning. *Proceedings of the National Academy of Sciences, USA*, 1988, *85*, 1672–1676.

Louis-Sylvestre, J., and Le Magnen, J. A fall in blood glucose level precedes meal onset in free-feeding rats. *Neuroscience and Biobehavioral Reviews*, 1980, *4*, 13–16.

Luiten, P., Koolhaas, J., de Boer, S., and Koopmans, S. The corticomedial amygdala in the central nervous system organization of agonistic behavior. *Brain Research*, 1985, *332*, 283–297.

Lund, J.S., and Boothe, R.G. Interlaminar connections and pyramidal neuron organization in the visual cortex, area 17, of the macaque monkey. *Journal of Comparative Neurology*, 1975, *159*, 305–334.

Lydic, R., McCarley, R.W., and Hobson, J.A. The time-course of dorsal raphe discharge, PGO waves and muscle tone averaged across multiple sleep cycles. *Brain Research*, 1983, *274*, 365–370.

Lydic, R., Schoene, W.C., Czeisler, C.A., and Moore-Ede, M.C. Suprachiasmatic region of the human hypothalamus: Homolog to the primate circadian pacemaker? *Sleep*, 1980, *2*, 355–361.

Lynch, G., Larson, J., Kelso, S., Barrionuevo, G., and Schottler, F. Intracellular injections of EGTA block induction of long-term potentiation. *Nature*, 1984, *305*, 719–721.

Lynch, G., Muller, D., Seubert, P., and Larson, J. Long-term potentiation: Persisting problems and recent results. *Brain Research Bulletin*, 1988, *21*, 363–372.

Lynds, P.G. Olfactory control of aggression in lactating female housemice. *Physiology and Behavior*, 1976, *17*, 157–159.

Lytton, W.W., and Brust, J.C.M. Direct dyslexia: Preserved oral reading of real words in Wernicke's aphasia. *Brain*, 1989, *112*, 583–594.

MacDonnell, M.F., and Flynn, J.P. Control of sensory fields by stimulation of hypothalamus. *Science*, 1966, *152*, 1406–1408.

MacFadyen, U.M., Oswald, I., and Lewis, S.A. Starvation and human slow-wave sleep. *Journal of Applied Physiology*, 1973, *35*, 391–394.

Machne, S., Calma, I., and Magoun, H.W. Unit activity of central cephalic brain stem in EEG arousal. *Journal of Neurophysiology*, 1955, *18*, 547–558.

Machon, R.A., Mednick, S.A., and Schulsinger, F. The interaction of seasonality, place of birth, genetic risk and subsequent schizophrenia in a high risk sample. *British Journal of Psychiatry*, 1983, *143*. 383–388.

Magnes, J., Moruzzi, G., and Pompeiano, O. Synchronization of the EEG produced by low-frequency electrical stimulation of the region of the solitary tract. *Archives Italiennes de Biologie*, 1961, *99*, 33–67.

Maier, S.F., Drugan, R.C., and Grau, J.W. Controllability, coping behavior, and stress-induced analgesia in the rat. *Pain*, 1982, *12*, 47–56.

Maksay, G., and Ticku, M.K. Dissociation of [^{35}S]t-butylbicyclophosphorothionate binding differentiates convulsant and depressant drugs that modulate GABAergic transmission. *Journal of Neurochemistry*, 1985, *44*, 480–486.

Malinow, R., and Miller, J.P. Postsynaptic hyperpolarization during conditioning reversibly blocks induction of long-term potentiation. *Nature*, 1986, *321*, 175–177.

Mallow, G.K. The relationship between aggression and cycle stage in adult female rhesus monkeys (*Macaca mulatta*). *Dissertation Abstracts*, 1979, *39*, 3194.

Malsbury, C.W. Facilitation of male rat copulatory behavior by electrical stimulation of the medial preoptic area. *Physiology and Behavior*, 1971, *7*, 797–805.

Mann, F., Bowsher, D., Mumford, J., Lipton, S., and Miles, J. Treatment of intractable pain by acupuncture. *Lancet*, 1973, *2*, 57–60.

Mann, M.A., Konen, C., and Svare, B. The role of progesterone in pregnancy-induced aggression in mice. *Hormones and Behavior*, 1984, *18*, 140–160.

Mantyh, P.W. Connections of midbrain periaqueductal gray in the monkey. II. Descending efferent projections. *Journal of Neurophysiology*, 1983, *49*, 582–594.

Marczynski, T.J., and Urbancic, M. Animal models of chronic anxiety and "fearlessness." *Brain Research Bulletin*, 1988, *21*, 483–490.

Margolin, D.I., Marcel, A.J., and Carlson, N.R. Common mechanisms in dysnomia and post-semantic surface dyslexia: Processing deficits and selective attention. In *Surface Dyslexia: Neuropsychological and Cognitive Studies of Phonological Reading*, edited by M. Coltheart. London: Lawrence Erlbaum Associates, 1985.

Margolin, D.I., and Walker, J.A. Personal communication, 1981.

Mariani, A.P. Biplexiform cells: Ganglion cells of the primate retina that contact photoreceptors. *Science*, 1982, *216*, 1134–1136.

Mark, G.P., Blander, D.S., Hernandez, L., and Hoebel, B.G. Effects of salt intake, rehydration and conditioned taste aversion (CTA) development on dopamine output in the rat nucleus accumbens. *Appetite*, 1989, *12*, 224.

Mark, G.P., and Scott, T.R. Conditioned taste aversions affect gustatory activity in the NTS of chronic decerebrate rats. *Neuroscience Abstracts*, 1988, *14*, 1185.

Mark, V.H., Ervin, F.R., and Yakovlev, P.I. The treatment of pain by stereotaxic methods. *Confina Neurologica*, 1962, *22*, 238–245.

Markowitsch, H.J. Diencephalic amnesia: A reorientation towards tracts. *Brain Research Reviews*, 1988, *13*, 351–370.

Marshall, J.C. Sensation and semantics. *Nature*, 1988, *334*, 378.

Martinot, J.-L., Peron-Magnan, P., Huret, J.-D., Mazoyer, B., Baron, J.-C., Boulenger, J.P., Loc'h, C., Maziere, B., Caillard, V., Loo, H., and Syrota, A. Striatal D_2 dopaminergic receptors assessed with positron emission tomography and [^{76}Br]bromospiperone in untreated schizophrenic patients. *American Journal of Psychiatry*, 1990, *147*, 44–50.

Maruniak, J., Desjardins, C., and Bronson, F. Dominant-subordinate relationships in castrated male mice bearing testosterone implants. *American Journal of Physiology*, 1977, *233*, 495–499.

Masters, W.H., Johnson, V.E., and Kolodny, R.C. *Human Sexuality*. Boston: Little, Brown & Co., 1982.

Mather, P., Nicolaïdis, S., and Booth, D.A. Compensatory and conditioned feeding responses to scheduled glucose infusions in the rat. *Nature*, 1978, *273*, 461–463.

Mathews, D.F. Response patterns of single neurons in the tortoise olfactory epithelium and olfactory bulb. *Journal of General Physiology*, 1972, *60*, 166–180.

Matsumoto, A., Micevych, P.E., and Arnold, A.P. Androgen regulates synaptic input to motoneurons of the adult rat spinal cord. *Journal of Neuroscience*, 1988, *8*, 4168–4176.

Matthews, R.T., and German, D.C. Electrophysiological evidence for excitation of rat ventral tegmental area dopaminergic neurons by morphine. *Neuroscience*, 1984, *11*, 617–626.

Mauk, M.D., Steinmetz, J.E., and Thompson, R.F. Classical conditioning using stimulation of the inferior olive as the unconditioned stimulus. *Proceedings of the National Academy of Sciences, USA*, 1986, *83*, 5349–5353.

Maunsell, J.H.R., and Van Essen, D.C. The connections of the middle temporal visual area (MT) and their relationship to a cortical hierarchy in the macaque monkey. *Journal of Neuroscience*, 1983, *3*, 2563–2586.

Mawson, A.R. Anorexia nervosa and the regulation of intake: A review. *Psychological Medicine*, 1974, *4*, 289–308.

Mayer, A.D., and Rosenblatt, J.S. Prepartum changes in maternal responsiveness and next defense in *Rattus norvegicus*. *Journal of Comparative Psychology*, 1984, *98*, 177–188.

Mayer, D.J., and Liebeskind, J.C. Pain reduction by focal electrical stimulation of the brain: An anatomical and behavioral analysis. *Brain Research*, 1974, *68*, 73–93.

Mayer, D.J., Price, D.D., Rafii, A., and Barber, J. Acupuncture hypalgesia: Evidence for activation of a central control system as a mechanism of action. In *Advances in Pain Research and Therapy, Vol. 1*, edited by J.J. Bonica, and D. Albe-Fessard. New York: Raven Press, 1976.

Mayer, J. Regulation of energy intake and the body weight: The glucostatic theory and the lipostatic hypothesis. *Annals of the New York Academy of Science*, 1955, *63*, 15–43.

Mazur, A. Hormones, aggression, and dominance in humans. In *Hormones and Aggressive Behavior*, edited by B.B. Svare. New York: Plenum Press, 1983.

Mazur, A., and Lamb, T. Testosterone, status, and mood in human males. *Hormones and Behavior*, 1980, *14*, 236–246.

McCann, M.J., Verbalis, J.G., and Stricker, E.M. LiCl and CCK inhibit gastric emptying and feeding and stimulate OT secretion in rats. *American Journal of Physiology*, 1989, *256*, R463–R468.

McCarley, R.W. The biology of dreaming sleep. In *Principles and Practices of Sleep Disorders in Medicine*, edited by M.H. Kryger, T. Roth, and W.C. Dement. New York: Saunders, 1989.

McCarley, R.W., and Hobson, J.A. The form of dreams and the biology of sleep. In *Handbook of Dreams: Research, Theory, and Applications*, edited by B. Wolman. New York: Van Nostrand Reinhold, 1979.

McCarthy, R.A., and Warrington, E.K. The double dissociation of short-term memory for lists and sentences. *Brain*, 1987, *110*, 1545–1563.

McCarthy, R.A., and Warrington, E.K. Evidence for modality-specific meaning systems in the brain. *Nature*, 1988, *334*, 428–435.

McClintock, M.K. Menstrual synchrony and suppression. *Nature*, 1971, *229*, 244–245.

McClintock, M.K., and Adler, N.T. The role of the female during copulation in wild and domestic

Norway rats (*Rattus norvegicus*). *Behaviour*, 1978, *67*, 67–96.

McCormick, D.A., Steinmetz, J.E., and Thompson, R.F. Lesions of the inferior olivary complex cause extinction of the classically conditioned eyeblink response. *Brain Research*, 1985, *359*, 120–130.

McCormick, D.A., and Thompson, R.F. Cerebellum: Essential involvement in the classically conditioned eyelid response. *Science*, 1984, *223*, 296–299.

McEwen, B.S. Gonadal steroid influences on brain development and sexual differentiation. In *Reproductive Physiology IV*, edited by R.O. Greep. Baltimore: University Park Press, 1983.

McGaugh, J.L. Involvement of hormonal and neuromodulatory systems in the regulation of memory storage. *Annual Review of Neuroscience*, 1989, *12*, 255–288.

McGaugh, J.L., and Herz, M.J. *Memory Consolidation*. San Francisco: Albion, 1972.

McGaugh, J.L., Introini-Collison, I.B., and Nagahara, A.H. Memory-enhancing effects of posttraining naloxone: Involvement of β-noradrenergic influences in the amygdaloid complex. *Brain Research*, 1988, *446*, 37–49.

McGinty, D.J., and Sterman, M.B. Sleep suppression after basal forebrain lesions in the cat. *Science*, 1968, *160*, 1253–1255.

McGrath, M.J., and Cohen, D.B. REM sleep facilitation of adaptive waking behavior: A review of the literature. *Psychological Bulletin*, 1978, *85*, 24–57.

McKenna, T.M., Weinberger, N.M., and Diamond, D.M. Responses of single auditory cortical neurons to tone sequences. *Brain Research*, 1989, *481*, 142–153.

McNaughton, B.L., Barnes, C.A., Rao, G., Baldwin, J., and Rasmussen, M. Long-term enhancement of hippocampal synaptic transmission and the acquisition of spatial information. *Journal of Neuroscience*, 1986, *6*, 565–571.

McNaughton, B.L., Leonard, B., and Chen, L. Cortical-hippocampal interactions and cognitive mapping: A hypothesis based on reintegration of the parietal and inferotemporal pathways for visual processing. *Psychobiology*, 1989, *17*, 230–235.

Meddis, R. The evolution of sleep. In *Sleep Mechanisms and Functions*, edited by A. Mayes. London: Van Nostrand Reinhold, 1983.

Meddis, R., Pearson, A., and Langford, G. An extreme case of healthy insomnia. *Electroencephalography and Clinical Neurophysiology*, 1973, *35*, 213–214.

Mednick, S.A., Machon, R.A., and Huttunen, M.O. An update on the Helsinki influenza project. *Archives of General Psychiatry*, 1990, *47*, 292.

Meijer, J.H., and Rietveld, W.J. Neurophysiology of the suprachiasmatic circadian pacemaker in rodents. *Physiological Reviews*, 1989, *69*, 671–707.

Meijer, J.H., van der Zee, E.A., and Dietz, M. Glutamate phase shifts circadian activity rhythms in hamsters. *Neuroscience Letters*, 1988, *86*, 177–183.

Meisel, R., and Pfaff, D.W. RNA and protein synthesis inhibitors: Effects on sexual behavior in female rats. *Brain Research Bulletin*, 1986, *12*, 187–193.

Mendelsohn, F.A.O., Quirion, R., Saavedra, J.M., Aguilera, G., and Catt, K.J. Autoradiographic localization of angiotensin II receptors in rat brain. *Proceedings of the National Academy of Sciences, USA*, 1984, *81*, 1575–1579.

Menninger, K.A. Influenza and schizophrenia. An analysis of post-influenzal "dementia praecox" as of 1918 and five years later. *American Journal of Psychiatry*, 1926, *5*, 469–529.

Meredith, M., and O'Connell, R.J. Efferent control of stimulus access to the hamster vomeronasal organ. *Journal of Physiology*, 1979, *286*, 301–316.

Merigan, W.H. Chromatic and achromatic vision of macaques: Role of the P pathway. *Journal of Neuroscience*, 1989, *9*, 776–783.

Merigan, W.H., and Eskin, T.A. Spatio-temporal vision of macaques with severe loss of Pb retinal ganglion cells. *Vision Research*, 1986, *26*, 1751–1761.

Mesulam, M.-M., Mufson, E.J., Wainer, B.H., and Levey, A.I. Central cholinergic pathways in the rat: An overview based on an alternative nomenclature. *Neuroscience*, 1983, *10*, 1185–1201.

Metherate, R., and Weinberger, N.M. Acetylcholine produces stimulus-specific receptive field alterations in cat auditory cortex. *Brain Research*, 1989, *480*, 372–377.

Miledi, R. Acetylcholine sensitivity of partially denervated frog muscles. *Journal of Physiology (London)*, 1959, *147*, 45–46P.

Miller, G.A. The magical number seven plus or minus two: Some limits on our capacity for processing information. *Psychological Review*, 1956, *63*, 81–97.

Miller, G.A., and Taylor, W.G. The perception of repeated bursts of noise. *Journal of the Acoustical Society of America*, 1948, *20*, 171–182.

Miller, J.D., Faull, K.F., Bowersox, F.S., and Dement, W.C. CNS monoamines and their metabolites in canine narcolepsy: A replication study. *Brain Research*, 1990, *509*, 169–171.

Miller, N.E., Sampliner, R.I., and Woodrow, P. Thirst reducing effects of water by stomach fistula versus water by mouth, measured by both a consummatory and an instrumental response. *Journal of Comparative and Physiological Psychology*, 1957, *50*, 1–5.

Miller, R. Schizophrenia as a progressive disorder: Relations to EEG, CT, neuropathological and other evidence. *Progress in Neurobiology*, 1988, *33*, 17–44.

Miller, V.M., and Best, P.J. Spatial correlates of hippocampal unit activity are altered by lesions of the fornix and entorhinal cortex. *Brain Research*, 1980, *194*, 311–323.

Milner, B. Memory disturbance after bilateral hippocampal lesions. In *Cognitive Processes and the Brain*, edited by P. Milner and S. Glickman. Princeton, N.J.: Van Nostrand, 1965.

Milner, B. Memory and the temporal regions of the brain. In *Biology of Memory*, edited by K.H. Pribram and D.E. Broadbent. New York: Academic Press, 1970.

Milner, B., Corkin, S., and Teuber, H.-L. Further analysis of the hippocampal amnesic syndrome: 14-year follow-up study of H.M. *Neuropsychologia*, 1968, *6*, 317–338.

Miselis, R.R., Shapiro, R.E., and Hand, P.J. Subfornical organ efferents to neural systems for control of body water. *Science*, 1979, *205*, 1022–1025.

Miselis, R.R., Weiss, M.L., and Shapiro, R.E. Modulation of the visceral neuraxis. In *Circumventricular Organs and Body Fluids*, edited by P.M. Gross. Boca Raton, Fla.: CRC Press, 1987.

Mishkin, M. Visual mechanisms beyond the striate cortex. In *Frontiers in Physiological Psychology*, edited by R.W. Russell. New York: Academic Press, 1966.

Mishkin, M. Memory in monkeys severely impaired by combined but not by separate removal of amygdala and hippocampus. *Nature*, 1978, *273*, 297–298.

Mishkin, M. A memory system in the monkey. *Philosophical Transactions of the Royal Society of London*, 1982, *298*, 85–95.

Mishkin, M., Malamut, B., and Bachevalier, J. Memories and habits: Two neural systems. In *Neurobiology of Learning and Memory*, edited by G. Lynch, J.L. McGaugh, and N.M. Weinberger. New York: Guilford Press, 1984.

Mobbs, C.V., Harlan, R.E., Burrous, M.R., and Pfaff, D.W. An estradiol-induced protein synthesized in the ventral medial hypothalamus and transported to the midbrain central gray. *Journal of Neuroscience*, 1988, *8*, 113–118.

Moghaddam, B., and Bunney, B.S. Differential effect of cocaine on extracellular dopamine levels in rat medial prefrontal cortex and nucleus accumbens: Comparison to amphetamine. *Synapse*, 1989, *4*, 156–161.

Mok, D., and Mogenson, G.J. Contribution of zona incerta to osmotically induced drinking in rats. *American Journal of Physiology*, 1986, *251*, R823–R832.

Moltz, H., Lubin, M., Leon, M., and Numan, M. Hormonal induction of maternal behavior in the ovariectomized nulliparous rat. *Physiology and Behavior*, 1970, *5*, 1373–1377.

Monaghan, D.T., and Cotman, C.W. Distribution of NMDA-sensitive L-³H-glutamate binding sites in rat brain as determined by quantitative autoradiography. *Journal of Neuroscience*, 1985, *5*, 2909–2919.

Money, J. Components of eroticism in man: Cognitional rehearsals. In *Recent Advances in Biological Psychiatry*, edited by J. Wortis. New York: Grune & Stratton, 1960.

Money, J., and Ehrhardt, A. *Man & Woman, Boy & Girl*. Baltimore: Johns Hopkins University Press, 1972.

Money, J., Schwartz, M., and Lewis, V.G. Adult erotosexual status and fetal hormonal masculinization and demasculinization: 46,XX congenital virilizing adrenal hyperplasia and 46,XY androgen-insensitivity syndrome compared. *Psychoneuroendocrinology*, 1984, *9*, 405–414.

Montarolo, P.G., Goelet, P., Castellucci, V.F., Morgan, J., Kandel, E.R., and Schacher, S. A critical time period for macromolecular synthesis in long-term heterosynaptic facilitation in *Aplysia*. *Science*, 1986, *234*, 1249–1254.

Mook, D. Some determinants of preference and aversion in the rat. *Annals of the New York Academy of Sciences*, 1969, *157*, 1158–1170.

Moore, B.O., and Deutsch, J.A. An antiemetic is antidotal to the satiety effects of cholecystokinin. *Nature*, 1985, *315*, 321–322.

Moore, R.Y. Effects of some rhinencephalic lesions on retention of conditioned avoidance behavior in cats. *Journal of Comparative and Physiological Psychology*, 1964, *53*, 540–548.

Moore, R.Y., and Bernstein, M.E. Synaptogenesis in the rat suprachiasmatic nucleus demonstrated by electron microscopy and synapsin I immunoreactivity. *Journal of Neuroscience*, 1989, *9*, 2161–2162.

Moore, R.Y., Card, J.P., and Riley, J.N. The suprachiasmatic hypothalamic nucleus: Neuronal ultrastructure. *Neuroscience Abstracts*, 1980, *6*, 758.

Moore, R.Y., and Eichler, V.B. Loss of a circadian adrenal corticosterone rhythm following suprachiasmatic lesions in the rat. *Brain Research*, 1972, *42*, 201–206.

Moore-Gillon, M.J., and Fitzsimons, J.T. Pulmonary vein–atrial junction stretch receptors and the inhibition of drinking. *American Journal of Physiology*, 1982, *242*, R452–R457.

Morales, F.R., Boxer, P.A., and Chase, M.H. Behavioral state-specific inhibitory postsynaptic potentials impinge on cat lumbar motoneurons during active sleep. *Experimental Neurology*, 1987, *98*, 418–435.

Moran, T.H., Shnayder, L., Hostetler, A.M., and McHugh, P.R. Pylorectomy reduces the satiety action of cholecystokinin. *American Journal of Physiology*, 1989, *255*, R1059–R1063.

Mori, E., Yamadori, A., and Furumoto, M. Left precentral gyrus and Broca's aphasia: A clinicopathologic study. *Neurology*, 1989, *39*, 51–54.

Morris, G.O., Williams, H.L., and Lubin, A. Misperception and disorientation during sleep deprivation. *Archives of General Psychiatry*, 1960, *2*, 247–254.

Morris, N.M., Udry, J.R., Khan-Dawood, F., and Dawood, M.Y. Marital sex frequency and midcycle female testosterone. *Archives of Sexual Behavior*, 1987, *16*, 27–37.

Morris, R.G.M., Anderson, E., Lynch, G., and Baudry, M. Selective impairment of learning and blockade of long-term potentiation by an *N*-methyl-D-aspartate receptor antagonist, AP5. *Nature*, 1986, *319*, 774–776.

Morris, R.G.M., Garrud, P., Rawlins, J.N.P., and O'Keefe, J. Place navigation impaired in rats with hippocampal lesions. *Nature*, 1982, *297*, 681–683.

Morrow, L., Urtunski, P.B., Kim, Y., and Boller, F. Arousal responses to emotional stimuli and laterality of lesion. *Neuropsychologia*, 1981, *19*, 65–72.

Moruzzi, G., and Magoun, H.W. Brain stem reticular formation and activation of the EEG. *Electroencephalography and Clinical Neurophysiology*, 1949, *1*, 455–473.

Mos, J., Lammers, J.H., van der Poel, A.M., Bermon, B., Meelis, W., and Kruk, M.R. Effects of midbrain central gray lesions on spontaneously and electrically induced aggression in the rat. *Aggressive Behavior*, 1983, *9*, 133–155.

Moscovitch, M., and Olds, J. Asymmetries in emotional facial expressions and their possible relation to hemispheric specialization. *Neuropsychologia*, 1982, *20*, 71–81.

Mountcastle, V.B. Modality and topographic properties of single neurons of cat's somatic sensory cortex. *Journal of Neurophysiology*, 1957, *20*, 408–434.

Mountcastle, V.B., Lynch, J.C., Georgopoulos, A., Sakata, H., and Acuna, C. Posterior parietal association cortex: Command functions for operations

within extra-personal space. *Journal of Neurophysiology*, 1975, *38*, 871–908.

Moushegian, G., and Rupert, A.L. Relations between the psychophysics and the neurophysiology of sound localization. *Federation Proceedings*, 1974, *33*, 1924–1927.

Mukhametov, L.M. Sleep in marine mammals. In *Sleep Mechanisms*, edited by A.A. Borbély and J.L. Valatx. Munich: Springer-Verlag, 1984.

Muller, R.U., and Kubie, J.L. The effects of changes in the environment on the spatial firing of hippocampal complex-spike cells. *Journal of Neuroscience*, 1987, *7*, 1935–1950.

Murray, E.A., Davidson, M., Gaffan, D., Olton, D.S., and Suomi, S. Effects of fornix transection and cingulate cortical ablation on spatial memory in rhesus monkeys. *Experimental Brain Research*, 1989, *74*, 173–186.

Nachman, M., and Ashe, J.H. Effects of basolateral amygdala lesions on neophobia, learned taste aversions, and sodium appetite in rats. *Journal of Comparative and Physiological Psychology*, 1974, *87*, 622–643.

Nadeau, S.E. Impaired grammar with normal fluency and phonology. *Brain*, 1988, *111*, 1111–1137.

Naeser, M.A., Palumbo, C.L., Helm-Estabrooks, N., Stiassny-Eder, D., and Albert, M.L. Severe nonfluency in aphasia: Role of the medial subcallosal fasciculus and other white matter pathways in recovery of spontaneous speech. *Brain*, 1989, *112*, 1–38.

Nafe, J.P., and Wagoner, K.S. The nature of pressure adaptation. *Journal of General Psychology*, 1941, *25*, 323–351.

Naitoh, P., Kales, A., Kollar, E.J., Smith, J.C., and Jacobson, A. Electroencephalographic activity after prolonged sleep loss. *Electroencephalography and Clinical Neurophysiology*, 1969, *27*, 2–11.

Nakahara, D., Ozaki, N., Miura, Y., Miura, H., and Nagatsu, T. Increased dopamine and serotonin metabolism in rat nucleus accumbens produced by intracranial self-stimulation of medial forebrain bundle as measured by in vivo microdialysis. *Brain Research*, 1989, *495*, 178–181.

Nakamura, S., Kimura, F., and Sakaguchi, T. Postnatal development of electrical activity in the locus coeruleus. *Journal of Neurophysiology*, 1987, *58*, 510–524.

Nakano, I., and Hirano, A. Loss of large neurons of the medial septal nucleus in an autopsy case of Alzheimer's disease. *Journal of Neuropathology and Experimental Neurology*. 1982, *41*, 341.

Nakashima, T., Kimmelman, C.P., and Snow, J.B.

Vomeronasal organs and nerves of Jacobson in the human fetus. *Acta Otolaryngologia*, 1985, *99*, 226–271.

Nathans, J., Piantanida, T.P., Eddy, R.L., Shows, T.B., and Hogness, D.S. Molecular genetics of inherited variation in human color vision. *Science*, 1986, *232*, 203–210.

Nauta, W.J.H. Hypothalamic regulation of sleep in rats: Experimental study. *Journal of Neurophysiology*, 1946, *9*, 285–316.

Nauta, W.J.H. Some efferent connections of the prefrontal cortex in the monkey. In *The Frontal Granular Cortex and Behavior*, edited by J.M. Warren and K. Akert. New York: McGraw-Hill, 1964.

Neff, W.D. The brain and hearing: Auditory discriminations affected by brain lesions. *Annals of Otology, Rhinology and Laryngology*, 1977, *86*, 500–506.

Nelson, D.O., and Johnson, A.K. Subfornical organ projections to nucleus medianus: Electrophysiological evidence for angiotensin II synapses. *Federation Proceedings*, 1985, *44*, 1010.

Newman, E.A., and Evans, C.R. Human dream processes as analogous to computer programme clearance. *Nature*, 1965, *206*, 54.

Nichols, D.G. Brown adipose tissue mitochondria. *Biochimica et Biophysica Acta*, 1979, *549*, 1–29.

Nichols, D.S., Thorn, B.E., and Berntson, G.G. Opiate and serotonergic mechanisms of stimulation-produced analgesia within the periaqueductal gray. *Brain Research Bulletin*, 1989, *22*, 717–724.

Nicolaïdis, S. Early systemic responses to orogastric stimulation in the regulation of food and water balance: Functional and electrophysiological data. *Annals of the New York Academy of Sciences, USA*, 1969, *151*, 1176–1203.

Nicolaïdis, S. Short-term and long-term regulation of energy balance. *Proceedings of the International Congress of Physiological Sciences*, 1974, *10*, 122–123.

Nicolaïdis, S. What determines food intake? The ischymetric theory. *NIPS*, 1987, *2*, 104–107.

Nicolaïdis, S., Danguir, J., and Mather, P. A new approach of sleep and feeding behaviors in the laboratory rat. *Physiology and Behavior*, 1979, *23*, 717–722.

Nicoll, R.A., Alger, B.E., and Nicoll, R.A. Enkephalin blocks inhibitory pathways in the vertebrate CNS. *Nature*, 1980, *287*, 22–25.

Niijima, A. Afferent discharges from osmoreceptors in the liver of the guinea pig. *Science*, 1969a, *166*, 1519–1521.

Niijima, A. Afferent impulse discharge from glucoreceptors in the liver of the guinea pig. *Annals of the New York Academy of Sciences*, 1969b, *157*, 690–700.

Niijima, A. Glucose-sensitive afferent nerve fibers in the hepatic branch of the vagus nerve in the guinea pig. *Journal of Physiology*, 1982, *332*, 315–323.

Nilsson, O.G., Shapiro, M.L., Gage, F.H., Olton, D.S., and Björklund, A. Spatial learning and memory following fimbria-fornix transection and grafting of fetal septal neurons to the hippocampus. *Experimental Brain Research*, 1987, *67*, 195–215.

Noirot, E. Selective priming of maternal responses by auditory and olfactory cues from mouse pups. *Developmental Psychobiology*, 1972, *5*, 371–387.

Noirot, E., Goyens, J., and Buhot, M.C. Aggressive behavior of pregnant mice towards males. *Hormones and Behavior*, 1975, *6*, 9–17.

Norgren, R., and Grill, H. Brain-stem control of ingestive behavior. In *The Physiological Mechanisms of Motivation*, edited by D.W. Pfaff. New York: Springer-Verlag, 1982.

Norman, R.L., and Spies, H.G. Cyclic ovarian function in a male macaque: Additional evidence for a lack of sexual differentiation in the physiological mechanisms that regulate the cyclic release of gonadotropins in primates. *Endocrinology*, 1986, *118*, 2608–2609.

Nose, H., Morita, M., Yawata, T., and Morimoto, T. Continuous determination of blood volume on conscious rats during water and food intake. *Japanese Journal of Physiology*, 1986, *36*, 215–218.

Novin, D., Robinson, B.A., Culbreth, L.A., and Tordoff, M.G. Is there a role for the liver in the control of food intake? *American Journal of Clinical Nutrition*, 1983, *9*, 233–246.

Novin, D., VanderWeele, D.A., and Rezek, M. Hepatic-portal 2-deoxy-D-glucose infusion causes eating: Evidence for peripheral glucoreceptors. *Science*, 1973, *181*, 858–860.

Nowlis, G.H., and Frank, M. Qualities in hamster taste: Behavioral and neural evidence. In *Olfaction and Taste, Vol. 6*, edited by J. LeMagnen and P. MacLeod. Washington, D.C.: Information Retrieval, 1977.

Numan, M. Medial preoptic area and maternal behavior in the female rat. *Journal of Comparative and Physiological Psychology*, 1974, *87*, 746–759.

Numan, M. Maternal behavior. In *The Physiology of Reproduction*, edited by E. Knobil and J. Neill. New York: Raven Press, 1988.

Numan, M., Rosenblatt, J.S., and Komisaruk, B.R. Medial preoptic area and onset of maternal behavior in the rat. *Journal of Comparative and Physiological Psychology*, 1977, *91*, 146–164.

Numan, M., and Smith, H.G. Maternal behavior in rats: Evidence for the involvement of preoptic projections to the ventral tegmental area. *Behavioral Neuroscience*, 1984, *98*, 712–727.

Nuñez, A.A., and Casati, M.J. The role of efferent connections of the suprachiasmatic nucleus in the control of circadian rhythms. *Behavioral and Neural Biology*, 1979, *25*, 263–267.

Oaknin, S., Rodriguez del Castillo, A., Guerra, M., Battaner, E., and Mas, M. Change in forebrain Na,K-ATPase activity and serum hormone levels during sexual behavior in male rats. *Physiology and Behavior*, 1989, *45*, 407–410.

O'Connell, R.J., and Meredith, M. Effects of volatile and nonvolatile chemical signals on male sex behaviors mediated by the main and accessory olfactory system. *Behavioral Neuroscience*, 1984, *98*, 1083–1093.

O'Keefe, J., and Conway, D.H. On the trail of the hippocampal engram. *Physiological Psychology*, 1980, *8*, 229–238.

O'Keefe, J., and Dostrovsky, T. The hippocampus as a spatial map: Preliminary evidence from unit activity in the freely moving rat. *Brain Research*, 1971, *34*, 171–175.

Olds, J. Commentary. In *Brain Stimulation and Motivation*, edited by E.S. Valenstein. Glenview, Ill.: Scott, Foresman, 1973.

Olds, M.E., and Fobes, J.L. The central basis of motivation: Intracranial self-stimulation studies. *Annual Review of Psychology*, 1981, *32*, 523–574.

Olivia, T.P., and Torrey, E.F. Serum interferon in patients with psychosis. *American Journal of Psychiatry*, 1985, *142*, 1184.

Olton, D.S. Memory functions and the hippocampus. In *Neurobiology of the Hippocampus*, edited by W. Siefert. New York: Academic Press, 1983.

Olton, D.S., Collison, C., and Werz, M.A. Spatial memory and radial arm maze performance in rats. *Learning and Motivation*, 1977, *8*, 289–314.

Olton, D.S., and Papas, B.C. Spatial memory and hippocampal function. *Neuropsychologia*, 1979, *17*, 669–682.

Olton, D.S., and Samuelson, R.J. Remembrance of places past: Spatial memory in rats. *Journal of Experimental Psychology: Animal Behavior Processes*, 1976, *2*, 97–116.

Oomura, Y. Significance of glucose, insulin and free fatty acid on the hypothalamic feeding and satiety neurons. In *Hunger: Basic Mechanisms and Clinical Implications*, edited by D. Novin, W. Wyrwicka, and G. Bray. New York: Raven Press, 1976.

Panksepp, J. Aggression elicited by electrical stimulation of the hypothalamus in albino rats. *Physiology and Behavior*, 1971, *6*, 321–329.

Panksepp, J., Pollack, A., Krost, K.P., Mieker, R., and Ritter, M. Feeding in response to repeated protamine zinc insulin injections. *Physiology and Behavior*, 1975, *14*, 487–493.

Park, C.R., Johnson, L.H., Wright, J.H., and Bastel, H. Effect of insulin on transport of several hexoses and pentoses into cells of muscle and brain. *American Journal of Physiology*, 1957, *191*, 13–18.

Parsons, B., Rainbow, T.C., and McEwen, B.S. Organizational effects of testosterone via aromatization on feminine reproductive behavior and neural progestin receptors in rat brain. *Endocrinology*, 1984, *115*, 1412–1417.

Patterson, K., and Kay, J.A. How word-form dyslexics form words. Paper presented at the meeting of the British Psychological Society Conference on Reading, Exeter, England, 1980.

Patterson, K.E., and Marcel, A.J. Aphasia, dyslexia, and the phonological coding of written words. *Quarterly Journal of Experimental Psychology*, 1977, *29*, 307–318.

Patterson, P.H., and Chun, L.L.Y. The influence of non-neural cells on catecholamine and acetylcholine synthesis and accumulation in cultures of dissociated sympathetic neurons. *Proceedings of the National Academy of Sciences (U.S.A.)*, 1974, *71*, 3607–3610.

Patton, G. The course of anorexia nervosa. *British Medical Journal*, 1989, *299*, 139–140.

Pauls, D.L., and Leckman, J.F. The inheritance of Gilles de la Tourette's syndrome and associated behaviors. *New England Journal of Medicine*, 1986, *315*, 993–997.

Pauls, D.L., Towbin, K.E., Leckman, J.F., Zahner, G.E.P., and Cohen, D.J. Gilles de la Tourette's syndrome and obsessive-compulsive disorder. *Archives of General Psychiatry*, 1986, *43*, 1180–1182.

Pavlides, C., Greenstein, Y.J., Grudman, M., and Winson, J. Long-term potentiation in the dentate gyrus is induced preferentially on the positive phase of theta rhythms. *Brain Research*, 1988, *439*, 383–387.

Pavlov, I.P. "Innere Hemmung" der bedingten Reflexe und der Schlaf—ein und derselbe Prozesz. *Skandinavisches Archiv für Physiologie*, 1923, *44*, 42–58.

Peck, J., and Novin, D. Evidence that osmoreceptors mediating drinking in rabbits are in the lateral preoptic area. *Journal of Comparative and Physiological Psychology*, 1971, *74*, 134–147.

Peck, J.W., and Blass, E.M. Localization of thirst and antidiuretic osmoreceptors by intracranial injections in rats. *American Journal of Physiology*, 1975, *5*, 1501–1509.

Pedersen, C.A., Ascher, J.A., Monroe, Y.L., and Prange, A.F. Oxytocin induces maternal behavior in virgin female rats. *Science*, 1982, *216*, 648–649.

Pedersen, C.A., Caldwell, J.D., Johnson, M.F., Fort, S.A., and Prange, A.J. Oxytocin antiserum delays onset of ovarian steroid-induced maternal behavior. *Neuropeptides*, 1985, *6*, 175–182.

Penfield, W., and Jasper, H. *Epilepsy and the Functional Anatomy of the Human Brain*. Boston: Little, Brown & Co., 1954.

Penfield, W., and Rasmussen, T. *The Cerebral Cortex of Man: A Clinical Study of Localization*. Boston: Little, Brown & Co., 1950.

Perkins, A.T., and Teyler, T.J. A critical period for long-term potentiation in the developing rat visual cortex. *Brain Research*, 1988, *439*, 25–47.

Perlmutter, L.S., Siman, R., Gall, C., Seubert, P., Baudry, M., and Lynch, G. The ultrastructural localization of calcium-activated protease "calpain" in rat brain. *Synapse*, 1988, *2*, 79–88.

Perrigo, G., Bryant, W.C., and vom Saal, F.S. Fetal, hormonal and experiential factors influencing the mating-induced regulation of infanticide in male house mice. *Physiology and Behavior*, 1989, *46*, 121–128.

Perrigo, G., Bryant, W.C., and vom Saal, F.S. A unique neural timing system prevents male mice from harming their own offspring. *Animal Behaviour*, 1990, *39*, 535–539.

Perry, V.H., Oehler, R., and Cowey, A. Retinal ganglion cells that project to the dorsal lateral geniculate nucleus in the macaque monkey. *Neuroscience*, 1984, *12*, 1101–1123.

Perryman, R.L., and Thorner, M.O. The effects of hyperprolactinaemia on sexual and reproductive function in men. *Journal of Andrology*, 1981, *5*, 233–242.

Persky, H. Reproductive hormones, moods, and the menstrual cycle. In *Sex Differences in Behavior*, edited by R.C. Friedman, R.M. Richart, and R.L. Vande Wiele. New York: John Wiley & Sons, 1974.

Persky, H., Lief, H.I., Strauss, D., Miller, W.R., and O'Brien, C.P. Plasma testosterone level and sexual behavior of couples. *Archives of Sexual Behavior*, 1978, *7*, 157–173.

Pert, C.B, Snowman, A.M., and Snyder, S.H. Localization of opiate receptor binding in presynaptic membranes of rat brain. *Brain Research*, 1974, *70*, 184–188.

Petsche, H., Stumpf, C., and Gogolák, G. The significance of the rabbit's septum as a relay station be-

tween the midbrain and the hippocampus: The control of hippocampal arousal activity by septum cells. *Electroencephalography and Clinical Neurophysiology*, 1962, *13*, 202–211.

Pfaff, D.W., and Keiner, M. Atlas of estradiol-concentrating cells in the central nervous system of the female rat. *Journal of Comparative Neurology*, 1973, *151*, 121–158.

Pfaff, D.W., and Sakuma, Y. Deficit in the lordosis reflex of female rats caused by lesions in the ventromedial nucleus of the hypothalamus. *Journal of Physiology*, 1979, *288*, 203–210.

Pfaff, D.W., and Schwartz-Giblin, S. Cellular mechanisms of female reproductive behaviors. In *The Physiology of Reproduction*, edited by E. Knobil and J. Neill. New York: Raven Press, 1988.

Phillips, A.G., Blaha, C.D., and Fibiger, H.C. Neurochemical correlates of brain-stimulation reward measured by ex vivo and in vivo analyses. *Neuroscience and Biobehavioral Reviews*, 1989, *13*, 99–104.

Phillips, M.I., and Felix, D. Specific angiotensin II receptive neurons in the cat subfornical organ. *Brain Research*, 1976, *109*, 531–540.

Phillipson, O.T. Afferent projections to the ventral tegmental area of Tsai and interfascicular nucleus: A horseradish peroxidase study in the rat. *Journal of Comparative Neurology*, 1979, *187*, 117–143.

Piéron, H. *Le Problème Physiologique du Sommeil*. Paris: Masson, 1913.

Pilleri, G. The blind Indus dolphin, *Platanista indi*. *Endeavours*, 1979, *3*, 48–56.

Plant, T.M. Gonadal regulation of hypothalamic gonadotropin-releasing hormone release in primates. *Endocrinology Reviews*, 1986, *7*, 75–88.

Pleim, E.T., and Barfield, R.J. Progesterone versus estrogen facilitation of female sexual behavior by intracranial administration to female rats. *Hormones and Behavior*, 1988, *22*, 150–159.

Poggio, G.F., and Fischer, B. Binocular interaction and depth sensitivity in striate and prestriate cortex of behaving rhesus monkey. *Journal of Neurophysiology*, 1977, *40*, 1392–1405.

Poggio, G.F., and Poggio, T. The analysis of stereopsis. *Annual Review of Neuroscience*, 1984, *7*, 379–412.

Pohl, C.R., and Knobil, E. The role of the central nervous system in the control of ovarian function in higher primates. *Annual Review of Physiology*, 1982, *44*, 583–593.

Pompeiano, O., and Swett, J.E. EEG and behavioral manifestations of sleep induced by cutaneous nerve stimulation in normal cats. *Archives Italiennes de Biologie*, 1962, *100*, 311–342.

Rogers, B.C., Barnes, M.I., Mitchell, C.L., and Tilson, H.A. Functional deficits after sustained stimulation of the perforant path. *Brain Research*, 1989, *493*, 41–50.

Rogers, R.C., and Novin, D. The neurological aspects of hepatic osmoregulation. In *The Kidney in Liver Disease*, second edition, edited by M. Epstein. Amsterdam: Elsevier, 1983.

Roland, P.E. Metabolic measurements of the working frontal cortex in man. *Trends in Neurosciences*, 1984, *7*, 430–435.

Roldan, E., Alvarez-Pelaez, R., and Fernandez de-Molina, A. Electrographic study of the amygdaloid defense response. *Physiology and Behavior*, 1974, *13*, 779–787.

Rolls, B.J., Rowe, E.A., Rolls, E.T., Kingston, B., Megson, A., and Gunary, R. Variety in a meal enhances food intake in man. *Physiology and Behavior*, 1981, *26*, 215–221.

Rolls, E.T. Neuronal activity related to the control of feeding. In *Neural and Humoral Controls of Food Intake*, edited by R. Ritter and S. Ritter. New York: Academic Press, 1986.

Rolls, E.T. Functions of the primate hippocampus in spatial processing and memory. In *Neurobiology of Comparative Cognition*, edited by D.S. Olton and R.P. Kesner. Hillsdale, N.J.: Lawrence Erlbaum Associates, 1989a.

Rolls, E.T. Visual information processing in the primate temporal lobe. In *Models of Visual Perception: From Natural to Artificial*, edited by M. Imbert. Oxford, England: Oxford University Press, 1989b.

Rolls, E.T., and Baylis, G.C. Size and contrast have only small effects on the responses to faces of neurons in the cortex of the superior temporal sulcus of the monkey. *Experimental Brain Research*, 1986, *65*, 38–48.

Rolls, E.T., Baylis, G.C., Hasselmo, M.E., and Nalwa, V. The effect of learning on the face selective responses of neurons in the cortex in the superior temporal sulcus of the monkey. *Experimental Brain Research*, 1989, *76*, 153–164.

Rolls, E.T., Murzi, E., Yaxley, S., Thorpe, S.J., and Simpson, S.J. Sensory-specific satiety: Food-specific reduction in responsiveness of ventral forebrain neurons after feeding in the monkey. *Brain Research*, 1986, *368*, 79–86.

Rolls, E.T., Rolls, B.J., Kelly, P.H., Shaw, S.G., Wood, R.J., and Dale, R. The relative attenuation of self-stimulation, eating and drinking produced by dopamine-receptor blockade. *Psychopharmacologia*, 1974, *38*, 219–230.

Rompré, P.-P., and Boye, S. Localization of reward-rel-evant neurons in the pontine tegmentum: A moveable electrode mapping study. *Brain Research*, 1989, *496*, 295–302.

Rompré, P.-P., and Miliaressis, E. Pontine and mesencephalic substrates of self-stimulation. *Brain Research*, 1985, *359*, 246–259.

Rompré, P.-P., and Wise, R.A. Opioid-neuroleptic interaction in brainstem self-stimulation. *Brain Research*, 1989, *477*, 144–151.

Roper, S.D. The cell biology of vertebrate taste receptors. *Annual Review of Neuroscience*, 1989, *12*, 329–353.

Rose, G. Physiological and behavioral characteristics of dentate granule cells. In *Neurobiology of the Hippocampus*, edited by W. Seifert. London: Academic Press, 1983.

Rose, G.A., and Williams, R.T. Metabolic studies of large and small eaters. *British Journal of Nutrition*, 1961, *15*, 1–9.

Rose, J.E., Brugge, J.F., Anderson, D.J., and Hind, J.E. Phase-locked response to low-frequency tones in single auditory nerve fibers of the squirrel monkey. *Journal of Neurophysiology*, 1967, *30*, 769–793.

Roselli, C.E., Handa, R.J., and Resko, J.A. Quantitative distribution of nuclear androgen receptors in microdissected areas of the rat brain. *Neuroendocrinology*, 1989, *49*, 449–453.

Rosén, I., and Asanuma, H. Peripheral inputs to the forelimb area of the monkey motor cortex: Input-output relations. *Experimental Brain Research*, 1972, *14*, 257–273.

Rosenblatt, J.S., and Aronson, L.R. The decline of sexual behavior in male cats after castration with special reference to the role of prior sexual experience. *Behaviour*, 1958a, *12*, 285–338.

Rosenblatt, J.S., and Aronson, L.R. The influence of experience on the behavioural effects of androgen in prepuberally castrated male cats. *Animal Behaviour*, 1958b, *6*, 171–182.

Rosenfield, M.E., and Moore, J.W. Red nucleus lesions disrupt the classically conditioned membrane response in rabbits. *Behavioural Brain Research*, 1983, *10*, 393–398.

Rosenthal, D. A program of research on heredity in schizophrenia. *Behavioral Science*, 1971, *16*, 191–201.

Rosenthal, N.E., Sack, D.A., James, S.P., Parry, B.L., Mendelson, W.B., Tamarkin, L., and Wehr, T.A. Seasonal affective disorder and phototherapy. *Annals of the New York Academy of Sciences*, 1985, *453*, 260–269.

Rosenzweig, M.R. Experience, memory, and the brain. *American Psychologist*, 1984, *39*, 365–376.

Ross, E.D. The aprosodias: Functional-anatomic organization of the affective components of language in the right hemisphere. *Archives of Neurology,* 1981, *38,* 561–569.

Rosser, A.E., and Keverne, E.B. The importance of central noradrenergic neurons in the formation of an olfactory memory in the prevention of pregnancy block. *Neuroscience,* 1985, *16,* 1141–1147.

Rothman, S.M., and Olney, J.W. Excitotoxicity and the NMDA receptor. *Trends in Neurosciences,* 1987, *10,* 299–302.

Rothwell, N.J., and Stock, M.J. A role for brown adipose tissue in diet-induced thermogenesis. *Nature,* 1979, *281,* 31–35.

Routtenberg, A., and Malsbury, C. Brainstem pathways of reward. *Journal of Comparative and Physiological Psychology,* 1969, *68,* 22–30.

Rowland, N.E. Peripheral and central satiety factors in neuropeptide Y-induced feeding in rats. *Peptides,* 1988, *9,* 989–992.

Roy, A., De Jong, J., and Linnoila, M. Cerebrospinal fluid monoamine metabolites and suicidal behavior in depressed patients. *Archives of General Psychiatry,* 1989, *46,* 609–612.

Rozin, P., and Kalat, J.W. Specific hungers and poison avoidance as adaptive specializations of learning. *Psychological Review,* 1971, *78,* 459–486.

Rubin, B.S., and Barfield, R.J. Priming of estrous responsiveness by implants of 17B-estradiol in the ventromedial hypothalamic nucleus of female rats. *Endocrinology,* 1980, *106,* 504–509.

Rudy, J.W., and Sutherland, R.J. The hippocampal formation is necessary for rats to learn and remember configural discriminations. *Behavioural Brain Research,* 1989, *34,* 97–109.

Rumelhart, D.E., McClelland, J.L., and the PDP Research Group. *Parallel Distributed Processing: Explorations in the Microstructure of Cognition.* Cambridge, Mass.: MIT Press, 1986.

Rusak, B., and Boulos, Z. Pathways for photic entrainment of mammalian circadian rhythms. *Photochemistry and Photobiology,* 1981, *34,* 267–273.

Rusak, B., and Groos, G. Suprachiasmatic stimulation phase shifts rodent circadian rhythms. *Science,* 1982, *215,* 1407–1409.

Rusak, B., Meijer, J.H., and Harrington, M.E. Hamster circadian rhythms and phase-shifted by electrical stimulation of the geniculohypothalamic system. *Brain Research,* 1989, *493,* 283–291.

Rusak, B., and Morin, L.P. Testicular responses to photoperiod are blocked by lesions of the suprachiasmatic nuclei in golden hamsters. *Biology of Reproduction,* 1976, *15,* 366–374.

Russchen, F.T., Amaral, D.G., and Price, J.L. The afferent connections of the substantia innominata in the monkey, *Macaca fascicularis. Journal of Comparative Neurology,* 1986, *242,* 1–27.

Russek, M. Hepatic receptors and the neurophysiological mechanisms controlling feeding behavior. In *Neurosciences Research, Vol. 4,* edited by S. Ehrenpreis. New York: Academic Press, 1971.

Russell, M.J. Human olfactory communication. *Nature,* 1976, *260,* 520–522.

Russell, M.J., Switz, G.M., and Thompson, K. Olfactory influences on the human menstrual cycle. Paper presented at the meeting of the American Association for the Advancement of Science, San Francisco, June 1977.

Rutter, M., and Yule, W. The concept of specific reading retardation. *Journal of the American Academy of Child Psychiatry,* 1975, *16,* 181–197.

Ryback, R.S., and Lewis, O.F. Effects of prolonged bed rest on EEG sleep patterns in young, healthy volunteers. *Electroencephalography and Clinical Neurophysiology,* 1971, *31,* 395–399.

Ryle, G. *The Concept of Mind.* San Francisco: Hutchinson, 1949.

Saayman, G.S. Aggressive behaviour in free-ranging chacma baboons (*Papio ursinus*). *Journal of Behavioral Science,* 1971, *1,* 77–83.

Sachar, E.J., and Baron, M. The biology of affective disorders. *Annual Review of Neuroscience,* 1979, *2,* 505–518.

Sachs, B.D., and Meisel, R.L. The physiology of male sexual behavior. In *The Physiology of Reproduction,* edited by E. Knobil and J. Neill. New York: Raven Press, 1988.

Sackheim, H.A., and Gur, R.C. Lateral asymmetry in intensity of emotional expression. *Neuropsychologia,* 1978, *16,* 473–482.

Saffran, E.M., Schwartz, M.F., and Marin, O.S.M. Evidence from aphasia: Isolating the components of a production model. In *Language Production,* edited by B. Butterworth. London: Academic Press, 1980.

Sahu, A., Kalra, P.S., and Kalra, S.P. Food deprivation and ingestion induce reciprocal changes in neuropeptide Y concentrations in the paraventricular nucleus. *Peptides,* 1988, *9,* 83–86.

St. Clair, D.M., Blackwood, D., Muir, W., Baillie, D., Hubbard, A., Wright, A., and Evans, H.J. No linkage of chromosome 5q11-q13 markers to schizophrenia in Scottish families. *Nature,* 1989, *339,* 305–309.

Saitoh, K., Maruyama, N., and Kudoh, M. Sustained response of auditory cortex units in the cat. In *Brain Mechanisms of Sensation,* edited by Y. Katsuki, R.

Norgren, and M. Sato. New York: John Wiley & Sons, 1981.

Sakai, F., Meyer, J.S., Karacan, I., Derman, S., and Yamamoto, M. Normal human sleep: Regional cerebral haemodynamics. *Annals of Neurology*, 1979, *7*, 471–478.

Sakai, K. Some anatomical and physiological properties of pontomesencephalic tegmental neurons with special reference to the PGO waves and postural atonia during paradoxical sleep in the cat. In *The Reticular Formation Revisited*, edited by J.A. Hobson and M.A. Brazier. New York: Raven Press, 1980.

Sakai, K. Anatomical and physiological basis of paradoxical sleep. In *Brain Mechanisms of Sleep*, edited by D. McGinty, A. Morrison, R.R. Drucker-Colín, and P.L., Parmeggiani. New York: Spectrum, 1985.

Sakai, K., and Jouvet, M. Brain stem PGO—on cells projecting directly to the cat dorsal lateral geniculate nucleus. *Brain Research*, 1980, *194*, 500–505.

Sakai, R.R., Nicolaïdis, S., and Epstein, A.N. Salt appetite is suppressed by interference with angiotensin II and aldosterone. *American Journal of Physiology*, 1986, *251*, R762–R768.

Sakuma, Y., and Akaishi, T. Cell size, projection path, and localization of estrogen-sensitive neurons in the rat ventromedial hypothalamus. *Journal of Neurophysiology*, 1987, *57*, 1148–1159.

Sakuma, Y., and Pfaff, D.W. Facilitation of female reproductive behavior from mesencephalic central grey in the rat. *American Journal of Physiology*, 1979a, *237*, R278–R284.

Sakuma, Y., and Pfaff, D.W. Mesencephalic mechanisms for integration of female reproductive behavior in the rat. *American Journal of Physiology*, 1979b, *237*, R285–R290.

Sakuma, Y., and Pfaff, D.W. Convergent effects of lordosis-relevant somatosensory and hypothalamic influences on central gray cells in the rat mesencephalon. *Experimental Neurology*, 1980a, *70*, 269–281.

Sakuma, Y., and Pfaff, D.W. Excitability of female rat central gray cells with medullary projections: Changes produced by hypothalamic stimulation and estrogen treatment. *Journal of Neurophysiology*, 1980b, *44*, 1012–1023.

Salamone, J.D. Dopaminergic involvement in activational aspects of motivation: Effects of haloperidol on schedule-induced activity, feeding, and foraging in rats. *Psychobiology*, 1988, *16*, 196–206.

Saller, C.F., and Stricker, E.M. Hyperphagia and increased growth in rats after intraventricular injection of 5,7-dihydroxytryptamine. *Science*, 1976, *192*, 385–387.

Salm, A.K., Modney, B.K., and Hatton, G.I. Alterations in supraoptic nucleus ultrastructure of maternally behaving virgin rats. *Brain Research Bulletin*, 1988, *21*, 685–691.

Sananes, C.B., and Campbell, B.A. Role of the central nucleus of the amygdala in olfactory heart rate conditioning. *Behavioral Neuroscience*, 1989, *103*, 519–525.

Sasanuma, S. Kana and kanji processing in Japanese aphasics. *Brain and Language*, 1975, *2*, 369–383.

Sassenrath, E.N., Powell, T.E., and Hendrickx, A.G. Perimenstrual aggression in groups of female rhesus monkeys. *Journal of Reproduction and Fertility*, 1973, *34*, 509–511.

Satinoff, E., and Prosser, R.A. Suprachiasmatic nuclear lesions eliminate circadian rhythms of drinking and activity, but not of body temperature, in male rats. *Journal of Biological Rhythms*, 1988, *1*, 1–22.

Sato, M. Acute exacerbation of methamphetamine psychosis and lasting dopaminergic supersensitivity—a clinical survey. *Psychopharmacology Bulletin*, 1986, *22*, 751–756.

Sato, M., Chen, C.-C., Akiyama, K., and Otsuki, S. Acute exacerbation of paranoid psychotic state after long-term abstinence in patients with previous methamphetamine psychosis. *Biological Psychiatry*, 1983, *18*, 429–440.

Sawchenko, P.E., Gold, R.M., and Leibowitz, S.F. Evidence for vagal involvement in the eating elicited by adrenergic stimulation of the paraventricular nucleus. *Brain Research*, 1981, *225*, 249–269.

Scammell, T.E., Schwartz, W.J., and Smith, C.B. No evidence for a circadian rhythm of protein synthesis in the rat suprachiasmatic nuclei. *Brain Research*, 1989, *494*, 155–158.

Schenck, C.H., Bundlie, S.R., Ettinger, M.G., and Mahowald, M.W. Chronic behavioral disorders of human REM sleep: A new category of parasomnia. *Sleep*, 1986, *9*, 293–308.

Schenkel, E., and Siegel, J.M. REM sleep without atonia after lesions of the medial medulla. *Neuroscience Letters*, 1989, *98*, 159–165.

Scherschlicht, R., Polc, P., Schneeberger, J., Steiner, M., and Haefely, W. Selective suppression of rapid eye movement sleep (REMS) in cats by typical and atypical antidepressants. In *Typical and Atypical Antidepressants: Molecular Mechanisms*, edited by E. Costa and G. Racagni. New York: Raven Press, 1982.

Schiffman, P.L., Westlake, R.E., Santiago, T.V., and Edelman, N.H. Ventilatory control in parents of victims of the sudden infant death syndrome. *New England Journal of Medicine*, 1980, *302*, 486–491.

Schreiner, L., and Kling, A. Rhinencephalon and behavior. *American Journal of Physiology*, 1956, *184*, 486–490.

Schulkin, J., Marini, J., and Epstein, A.N. A role for the medial region of the amygdala in mineralocorticoid-induced salt hunger. *Behavioral Neuroscience*, 1989, *103*, 178–185.

Schuster, C.R., and Balster, R.L. The discriminative stimulus properties of drugs. *Advances in Behavioral Pharmacology*, 1977, *1*, 85–138.

Schwartz, D.H., McClane, S., Hernandez, L., and Hoebel, B.G. Feeding increases extracellular serotonin in the lateral hypothalamus of the rat as measured by microdialysis. *Brain Research*, 1989, *479*, 349–354.

Schwartz, M.F., Marin, O.S.M., and Saffran, E.M. Dissociations of language function in dementia: A case study. *Brain and Language*, 1979, *7*, 277–306.

Schwartz, M.F., Saffran, E.M., and Marin, O.S.M. The word order problem in agrammatism. I. Comprehension. *Brain and Language*, 1980, *10*, 249–262.

Schwartz, W.J., and Gainer, H. Suprachiasmatic nucleus: Use of ^{14}C-labelled deoxyglucose uptake as a functional marker. *Science*, 1977, *197*, 1089–1091.

Schwartz, W.J., Gross, R.A., and Morton, M.T. The suprachiasmatic nuclei contain a tetrodotoxin-resistant circadian pacemaker. *Proceedings of the National Academy of Sciences, USA*, 1987, *84*, 1694–1698.

Schwartz, W.J., Reppert, S.M., Eagan, S.M., and Moore-Ede, M.C. In vivo metabolic activity of the suprachiasmatic nuclei: A comparative study. *Brain Research*, 1983, *274*, 184–187.

Schwarzkopf, S.B., Nasrallah, H.A., Olson, S.C., Coffman, J.A., and McLaughlin, J.A. Perinatal complications and genetic loading in schizophrenia: Preliminary findings. *Psychiatry Research*, 1989, *27*, 233–239.

Schwartzman, R.J., Alexander, G.M., Grothusen, J.R., and Stahl, S. CNS glucose metabolic changes in the stages of the MPTP primate model of Parkinson's disease. *Neurology*, 1987, *37*, 338.

Sclafani, A. Neural pathways involved in the ventromedial hypothalamic lesion syndrome in the rat. *Journal of Comparative and Physiological Psychology*, 1971, *77*, 70–96.

Sclafani, A., and Aravich, P.F. Macronutrient self-selection in three forms of hypothalamic obesity. *American Journal of Physiology*, 1983, *244*, R686–R694.

Sclafani, A., and Nissenbaum, J.W. Robust conditioned flavor preference produced by intragastric starch infusions in rats. *American Journal of Physiology*, 1988, *255*, R672–R675.

Scouten, C.W., Burrell, L., Palmer, T., and Caganske, C.F. Lateral projections of the medial preoptic area are necessary for androgenic influence on urine marking and copulation in rats. *Physiology and Behavior*, 1980, *25*, 237–243.

Scoville, W.B., and Milner, B. Loss of recent memory after bilateral hippocampal lesions. *Journal of Neurology, Neurosurgery and Psychiatry*, 1957, *20*, 11–21.

Seagraves, M.A., Goldberg, M.E., Deny, S., Bruce, C.J., Ungerleider, L.G., and Mishkin, M. The role of striate cortex in the guidance of eye movements in the monkey. *The Journal of Neuroscience*, 1987, *7*, 3040–3058.

Seal, J., Gross, C., Doudet, D., and Bioulac, B. Instruction-related changes of neuronal activity in area 5 during a simple forearm movement in the monkey. *Neuroscience Letters*, 1983, *36*, 145–150.

Sedvall, G., Fyrö, B., Gullberg, B., Nybäck, H., Wiesel, F.-A., and Wode-Helgodt, B. Relationship in healthy volunteers between concentrations of monoamine metabolites in cerebrospinal fluid and family history of psychiatric morbidity. *British Journal of Psychiatry*, 1980, *136*, 366–374.

Segal, K.R., and Pi-Sunyer, F.X. Exercise and obesity. *Medical Clinics of North America*, 1989, *73*, 217–236.

Seubert, P., Baudry, M., Dudek, S., and Lynch, G. Calmodulin stimulates the degradation of brain spectrin by calpain. *Synapse*, 1987, *1*, 20–24.

Shaikh, M.B., Shaikh, A.B., and Siegel, A. Opioid peptides within the midbrain periaqueductal gray suppress affective defense behavior in the cat. *Peptides*, 1988, *9*, 999–1004.

Shaikh, M.B., and Siegel, A. Naloxone-induced modulation of feline aggression elicited from midbrain periaqueductal gray. *Pharmacology, Biochemistry, and Behavior*, 1989, *31*, 791–796.

Shallice, T. Phonological agraphia and the lexical route in writing. *Brain*, 1981, *104*, 413–429.

Shammah-Lagnado, S.J., Negrao, N., and Ricardo, J.A. Afferent connections of the zona incerta: A horseradish peroxidase study in the rat. *Neuroscience*, 1985, *15*, 109–134.

Shapiro, C.M., Bortz, R., Mitchell, D., Bartel, P., and Jooste, P. Slow-wave sleep: A recovery period after exercise. *Science*, 1981, *214*, 1253–1254.

Shapiro, M.L., Simon, D.K., Olton, D.S., Gage, F.H., Nilsson, O., and Björklund, A. Intrahippocampal grafts of fetal basal forebrain tissue alter place fields in the hippocampus of rats with fimbria-fornix lesions. *Neuroscience*, 1989, *32*, 1–18.

Sharp, P.E., McNaughton, B.L., and Barnes, C.A. Spontaneous synaptic enhancement in hippocampi of rats exposed to a spatially complex environment. *Society for Neuroscience Abstracts*, 1983, *9*, 647.

Sherrington, R., Brynjolfsson, J., Petursson, H., Potter, M., Dudleston, K., Barraclough, B., Wasmuth, J., Dobbs, M., and Gurling, H. Localization of a susceptibility locus for schizophrenia on chromosome 5. *Nature*, 1988, *336*, 164–167.

Shik, M.L., and Orlovsky, G.N. Neurophysiology of locomotor automatism. *Physiological Review*, 1976, *56*, 465–501.

Shimizu, N., Oomura, Y., Novin, D., Grijalva, C., and Cooper, P.H. Functional correlations between lateral hypothalamic glucose-sensitive neurons and hepatic portal glucose-sensitive units in rat. *Brain Research*, 1983, *265*, 49–54.

Shoham, S., and Krueger, J.M. Muramyl dipeptide-induced sleep and fever: Effects of ambient temperature and time of injections. *American Journal of Physiology*, 1988, *255*, R157–R165.

Sidman, M., Stoddard, L.T., and Mohr, J.P. Some additional quantitative observations of immediate memory in a patient with bilateral hippocampal lesions. *Neuropsychologia*, 1968, *6*, 245–254.

Siegal, A., and Skog, D. Effect of electrical stimulation of the septum upon attack behavior elicited from the hypothalamus in the cat. *Brain Research*, 1970, *23*, 371–380.

Siegel, J.M. Behavioral functions of the reticular formation. *Brain Research Reviews*, 1979, *1*, 69–105.

Siegel, J.M. A behavioral approach to the analysis of reticular formation unit activity. In *Behavioral Approaches to Brain Research*, edited by T.E. Robinson. New York: Oxford University Press, 1983.

Siegel, J.M. Pontomedullary interactions in the generation of REM sleep. In *Brain Mechanisms of Sleep*, edited by D.J. McGinty, R. Drucker-Colín, A. Morrison, and P.L. Parmeggiani. New York: Raven Press, 1985.

Siegel, J.M., and McGinty, D.J. Pontine reticular formation neurons: Relationship of discharge to motor activity. *Science*, 1977, *196*, 678–680.

Siegel, R.M., and Andersen, R.A. Motion perceptual deficits following ibotenic acid lesions of the middle temporal area (MT) in the behaving monkey. *Society for Neuroscience Abstracts*, 1986, *12*, 1183.

Siegel, S. A Pavlovian conditioning analysis of morphine tolerance. In *Behavioral Tolerance: Research and Treatment Implications*, edited by N.A. Krasnegor. Washington, D.C.: NIDA Research Monographs, 1978.

Silva, N.L., and Boulant, J.A. Effects of osmotic pressure, glucose, and temperature on neurons in preoptic tissue slices. *American Journal of Physiology*, 1984, *247*, R335–R345.

Silverman, M.S., Grosof, D.G., De Valois, R.L., and Elfar, S.D. Spatial-frequency organization in primate striate cortex. *Proceedings of the National Academy of Sciences, USA*, 1989, *86*, 711–715.

Silverstein, L.D., and Levy, C.M. The stability of the sigma sleep spindle. *Electroencephalography and Clinical Neurophysiology*, 1976, *40*, 666–670.

Simpson, J.B., Epstein, A.N., and Camardo, J.S., Jr. The localization of dipsogenic receptors for angiotensin II in the subfornical organ. *Journal of Comparative and Physiological Psychology*, 1978, *92*, 581–608.

Sims, E.A.H., and Horton, E.S. Endocrine metabolic adaptation to obesity and starvation. *American Journal of Clinical Nutrition*, 1968, *21*, 1455–1470.

Sinclair, D. *Cutaneous Sensation*. London: Oxford University Press, 1967.

Sinclair, D. *Mechanisms of Cutaneous Sensatión*. Oxford, England: Oxford University Press, 1981.

Singer, A.G., Agosta, W.C., O'Connell, R.J., Pfaffman, C., Bowen, D.V., and Field, F.H. Dimethyl disulfide: An attractant pheromone in hamster vaginal secretion. *Science*, 1976, *191*, 948–949.

Singer, A.G., Clancy, A.N., Macrides, F., and Agosta, W.C. Chemical studies of hamster vaginal discharge: Effects of endocrine ablation and protein digestion on behaviorally active macromolecular fractions. *Physiology and Behavior*, 1984, *33*, 639–643.

Singer, J. Hypothalamic control of male and female sexual behavior in female rats. *Journal of Comparative and Physiological Psychology*, 1968, *66*, 738–742.

Sirevaag, A.M., Black, J.E., Shafron, D., and Greenough, W.T. Direct evidence that complex experience increases capillary branching and surface area in visual cortex of young rats. *Developmental Brain Research*, 1988, *43*, 299–304.

Sitaram, N., Moore, A.M., and Gillin, J.C. Experimental acceleration and slowing of REM ultradian rhythm by cholinergic agonist and antagonist. *Nature*, 1978, *274*, 490–492.

Sitaram, N., Weingartner, H., and Gillin, J.C. Human serial learning: Enhancement with arecholine and choline and impairment with scopolamine. *Science*, 1978, *201*, 271–276.

Sitaram, N., Wyatt, R.J., Dawson, S., and Gillin, J.C. REM sleep induction of physostigmine infusion during sleep. *Science*, 1976, *191*, 1281–1283.

Slater, B., and Shields, J. Genetical aspects of anxiety. *British Journal of Psychiatry Special Publication No. 3, Studies of Anxiety.* Ashford, Kent: Headley Bros., 1969.

Slotnick, B.M. Disturbances of maternal behavior in the rat following lesions of the cingulate cortex. *Behaviour,* 1967, *29,* 203–236.

Slotnick, B.M., McMullen, M.F., and Fleischer, S. Changes in emotionality following destruction of the septal area in albino mice. *Brain, Behavior and Evolution,* 1974, *8,* 241–252.

Smith, C. Sleep states and learning: A review of the animal literature. *Neuroscience and Biobehavioral Reviews,* 1985, *9,* 157–168.

Smith, D.J., Perotti, J.M., Crisp, T., Cabral, M.E.Y., Long, J.T., and Scalzitti, J.M. The μ opiate receptor is responsible for descending pain inhibition originating in the periaqueductal gray region of the rat brain. *European Journal of Pharmacology,* 1988, *156,* 47–54.

Smith, G.P., and Gibbs, J. The satiating effect of cholecystokinin. In *Control of Appetite,* edited by M. Winick. New York: John Wiley & Sons, 1988.

Smith, G.P., Gibbs, J., and Kulkosky, P.J. Relationships between brain-gut peptides and neurons in the control of food intake. In *The Neural Basis of Feeding and Reward,* edited by B.G. Hoebel and D. Novin. Brunswick, Maine: Haer Institute, 1982.

Smith, G.P., and Jerome, C. Effects of total and selective abdominal vagotomies on water intake in rats. *Journal of the Autonomic Nervous System,* 1983, *9,* 259–271.

Snyder, F. Towards an evolutionary theory of dreaming. *American Journal of Psychiatry,* 1966, *123,* 121–136.

Sofroniew, M.V., and Weindl, A. Projections from the parvocellular vasopressin and neurophysin containing neurons of the SCN. *American Journal of Anatomy,* 1978, *153,* 391–430.

Solomon, P.R., and Moore, J.W. Latent inhibition and stimulus generalization of the classically conditioned nictitating membrane response in rabbits (*Oryctolagus cuniculus*) following dorsal hippocampal ablation. *Journal of Comparative and Physiological Psychology,* 1975, *89,* 1192–1203.

Sørensen, T.I.A., Price, R.A., Stunkard, A.J., and Schulsinger, F. Genetics of obesity in adult adoptees and their biological siblings. *British Medical Journal,* 1989, *298,* 97–90.

Speedie, L.J., Rothi, L.J., and Heilman, K.M. Spelling dyslexia: A form of cross-cuing. *Brain and Language,* 1982, *15,* 340–352.

Sperry, R.W. Brain bisection and consciousness. In *Brain and Conscious Experience,* edited by J. Eccles. New York: Springer-Verlag, 1966.

Spinelli, D.H., and Jensen, F.E. Plasticity: The mirror of experience. *Science,* 1979, *203,* 75–78.

Spinelli, D.H., Jensen, F.E., and DiPrisco, G.V. Early experience effect on dendritic branching in normally reared kittens. *Experimental Neurology,* 1980, *62,* 1–11.

Spoendlin, H. The innervation of the cochlear receptor. In *Basic Mechanisms in Hearing,* edited by A.R. Møeller. New York: Academic Press, 1973.

Sprague, J.M., Berlucchi, G., and Rizzolatti, G. The role of the superior colliculus and pretectum in vision and visually guided behavior. In *Handbook of Sensory Physiology. Vol. VII/3. Central Processing of Visual Information, Part B: Visual Centers in the Brain,* edited by R. Jung. Berlin: Springer-Verlag, 1973.

Spyraki, C., Fibiger, H.C., and Phillips, A.G. Attenuation by haloperidol of place preference conditioning using food reinforcement. *Psychopharmacology,* 1982a, *77,* 379–382.

Spyraki, C., Fibiger, H.C., and Phillips, A.G. Dopaminergic substrates of amphetamine-induced place preference conditioning. *Brain Research,* 1982b, *253,* 185–193.

Squire, L.R. Stable impairment in remote memory following electroconvulsive therapy. *Neuropsychologia,* 1974, *13,* 51–58.

Squire, L.R. The neuropsychology of human memory. *Annual Review of Neuroscience,* 1982, *5,* 241–273.

Squire, L.R., Amaral, D.G., Zola-Morgan, S., Kritchevsky, M., and Press, G. Description of brain injury in the amnesia patient N.A. based on magnetic resonance imaging. *Experimental Neurology,* 1989, *105,* 23–35.

Squire, L.R., Haist, F., and Shimamura, A.P. The neurology of memory: Quantitative assessment of retrograde amnesia in two groups of amnesia patients. *Journal of Neuroscience,* 1989, *9,* 828–839.

Squire, L.R., and Moore, R.Y. Dorsal thalamic lesions in a noted case of chronic memory dysfunction. *Annals of Neurology,* 1979, *6,* 503–506.

Squire, L.R., Shimamura, A.P., and Amaral, D.G. Memory and the hippocampus. In *Neural Models of Plasticity: Experimental and Theoretical Approaches,* edited by J.H. Byrne and W.O. Berry. San Diego: Academic Press, 1989.

Squire, L.R., Zola-Morgan, S., and Chen, K.S. Human amnesia and animal models of amnesia: Performance of amnesia patients on tests designed for the monkey. *Behavioral Neuroscience,* 1988, *102,* 210–221.

Stallone, D., and Nicolaïdis, S. Increased food intake

and carbohydrate preference in the rat following treatment with the serotonin antagonist metergoline. *Neuroscience Letters,* 1989, *102,* 319–324.

Stanley, B.G., Magdalin, W., and Leibowitz, S.F. A critical site for neuropeptide Y-induced eating lies in the caudolateral paraventricular/perifornical region of the hypothalamus. *Society for Neuroscience Abstracts,* 1989, *15,* 894.

Stanley, B.G., Schwartz, D.H., Hernandez, L., Hoebel, B.G., and Leibowitz, S.F. Patterns of extracellular norepinephrine in the paraventricular hypothalamus: Relationship to circadian rhythm and deprivation-induced eating behavior. *Life Sciences,* 1989, *45,* 275–282.

Stanley, B.G., Schwartz, D.H., Hernandez, L., Leibowitz, S.F., and Hoebel, B.G. Pattern of extracellular 5-hydroxyindoleacetic acid (5-HIAA) in the paraventricular hypothalamus (PVN): Relation to circadian rhythm and deprivation-induced eating behavior. *Pharmacology, Biochemistry, and Behavior,* 1989, *33,* 257–260.

Stanton, P.K., and Sarvey, J.M. Blockade of long-term potentiation in rat hippocampal CA1 region by inhibitors of protein synthesis. *Journal of Neuroscience,* 1984, *4,* 3080–3088.

Staubli, U., Larson, J., Thibault, O., Baudry, M., and Lynch, G. Chronic administration of a thiol-proteinase inhibitor blocks long-term potentiation of synaptic responses. *Brain Research,* 1988, *444,* 153–158.

Staubli, U., and Lynch, G. Stable hippocampal long-term potentiation elicited by "theta" pattern stimulation. *Brain Research,* 1987, *435,* 227–234.

Stebbins, W.C., Miller, J.M., Johnsson, L.-G., and Hawkins, J.E. Ototoxic hearing loss and cochlear pathology in the monkey. *Annals of Otology, Rhinology and Laryngology,* 1969, *78,* 1007–1026.

Steen, S.N., Oppliger, R.A., and Brownell, K.D. Metabolic effects of repeated weight loss and regain in adolescent wrestlers. *Journal of the American Medical Association,* 1988, *260,* 47–50.

Stefanick, M.L., and Davidson, J.M. Genital responses in noncopulators and rats with lesions in the medial preoptic area or midthoracic spinal cord. *Physiology and Behavior,* 1987, *41,* 439–444.

Steffens, A.B. Influence of reversible obesity on eating behavior, blood glucose, and insulin in the rat. *American Journal of Physiology,* 1975, *228,* 1738–1744.

Stein, L. Self-stimulation of the brain and the central stimulant action of amphetamine. *Federation Proceedings,* 1964, *23,* 836–850.

Stein, L., and Belluzzi, J.D. Operant conditioning of individual neurons. In *Quantitative Analyses of Behavior. Vol. VII. Biological Determinants of Reinforcement and Memory,* edited by M. Commons, R. Church, J. Stellar, and A. Wagner. Hillsdale, N.J.: Lawrence Erlbaum Associates, 1988.

Steinhausen, W. Über den experimentellen Nachweis der Ablenkung der Cupula terminalis in der intakten Bogengangsampulle des Labyrinths bei der thermischen und adäquäten rotatorischen Reizung. *Zeitschrift fur Hals-, Nasen- und Ohrenheilkunde,* 1931, *29,* 211–216.

Steinmetz, J.E., Lavond, D.G., and Thompson, R.F. Classical conditioning in rabbits using pontine nucleus stimulation as a conditioned stimulus and inferior olive stimulation as an unconditioned stimulus. *Synapse,* 1989, *3,* 225–233.

Steinmetz, J.E., Logan, C.G., Rosen, D.J., Thompson, J.K., Lavond, D.G., and Thompson, R.F. Initial localization of the acoustic conditioned stimulus projection system to the cerebellum essential for classical eyelid conditioning. *Proceedings of the National Academy of Sciences, USA,* 1987, *84,* 3531–3535.

Steinmetz, J.E., Rosen, D.L., Chapman, P.F., Lavond, D.G., and Thompson, R.F. Classical conditioning of the rabbit eyelid response with a mossy fiber stimulation CS. I. Pontine nuclei and middle cerebellar peduncle stimulation. *Behavioral Neuroscience,* 1986, *100,* 871–880.

Stellar, J.R., Kelley, A.E., and Corbett, D. Effects of peripheral and central dopamine blockade on lateral hypothalamic self-stimulation: Evidence for both reward and motor deficits. *Pharmacology, Biochemistry, and Behavior,* 1983, *18,* 433–442.

Stephan, F.K., and Nuñez, A.A. Elimination of circadian rhythms in drinking activity, sleep, and temperature by isolation of the suprachiasmatic nuclei. *Behavioral Biology,* 1977, *20,* 1–16.

Stephan, F.K., and Zucker, I. Circadian rhythms in drinking behavior and locomotor activity of rats are eliminated by hypothalamic lesion. *Proceedings of the National Academy of Sciences, USA,* 1972, *69,* 1583–1586.

Steriade, M., Paré, D., Bouhassira, D., Deschênes, M., and Oakson, G. Phasic activation of lateral geniculate and perigeniculate thalamic neurons during sleep with ponto-geniculo-occipital waves. *Journal of Neuroscience,* 1989, *9,* 2215–2229.

Sterman, M.B., and Clemente, C.D. Forebrain inhibitory mechanisms: Cortical synchronization induced by basal forebrain stimulation. *Experimental Neurology,* 1962a, *6,* 91–102.

Sterman, M.B., and Clemente, C.D. Forebrain inhibitory mechanisms: Sleep patterns induced by basal forebrain stimulation in the behaving cat. *Experimental Neurology,* 1962b, *6,* 103–117.

Stern, J.M. A revised view of the multisensory control of maternal behaviour in rats: Critical role of tactile inputs. *Ethoexperimental Approaches to the Study of Behavior,* edited by R.J. Blanchard, D.C. Blanchard, S. Parmigiani, and P.F. Brain. The Hague: Nijhoff Publishing Co., 1989a.

Stern, J.M. Maternal behavior: Sensory, hormonal, and neural determinants. In *Psychoendocrinology,* edited by S. Levine and F.R. Brush. New York: Academic Press, 1989b.

Stern, J.M., and McDonald, C. Ovarian hormone-induced short-latency maternal behavior in ovariectomized virgin Long-Evans rats. *Hormones and Behavior,* 1989, *23,* 157–172.

Sternbach, R.A. *Pain: A Psychophysiological Analysis.* New York: Academic Press, 1968.

Stevens, J.R. Neurology and neuropathology of schizophrenia. In *Schizophrenia as a Brain Disease,* edited by F.A. Henn and H.A. Nasrallah. New York: Oxford University Press, 1982.

Stevens, J.R. Schizophrenia and multiple sclerosis. *Schizophrenia Bulletin,* 1988, *14,* 231–241.

Stevens, S.S., and Newman, E.B. Localization of actual sources of sound. *American Journal of Psychology,* 1936, *48,* 297–306.

Stewart, W.B., Kauer, J.S., and Shepherd, G.M. Functional organization of the rat olfactory bulb analysed by the 2-deoxyglucose method. *Journal of Comparative Neurology,* 1979, *185,* 715–734.

Stoyva, J., and Metcalf, D. Sleep patterns following chronic exposure to cholinesterase-inhibiting organophosphate compounds. *Psychophysiology,* 1968, *5,* 206.

Stricker, E.M., and Zigmond, M.J. Recovery of function after damage to central catecholamine-containing neurons: A neurochemical model for the lateral hypothalamic syndrome. *Progress in Psychobiology and Physiological Psychology,* 1976, *6,* 121–188.

Striem, B.J., Pace, U., Zehavi, U., Naim, M., and Lancet, D. Sweet tastants stimulate adenylate cyclase coupled to GTP-binding protein in rat tongue membranes. *Biochemical Journal,* 1989, *260,* 121–126.

Stunkard, A.J., Sørensen, T.I.A., Harris, C., Teasdale, T.W., Chakraborty, R., Schull, W.J., and Schulsinger, F. An adoption study of human obesity. *New England Journal of Medicine,* 1986, *314,* 193–198.

Sturup, G.K. Correctional treatment and the criminal sexual offender. *Canadian Journal of Correction,* 1961, *3,* 250–265.

Sugiura, M., Yokoi, Y., Maruyama S., Ishido, T., Tokunaga, Y., and Sasaki, K. Detection of anti-cerebral autoantibodies in schizophrenia and Alzheimer's disease. *Journal of Clinical and Laboratory Immunology,* 1989, *28,* 1–3.

Sullivan, R.M., and Leon, M. One-trial olfactory learning enhances olfactory bulb responses to an appetitive conditioned odor in 7-day-old rats. *Developmental Brain Research,* 1987, *35,* 301–311.

Sullivan, R.M., Wilson, D.A., and Leon, M. Norepinephrine and learning-induced plasticity in infant rat olfactory system. *Journal of Neuroscience,* 1989, *9,* 3998–4006.

Sulser, F., and Sanders-Bush, E. From neurochemical to molecular pharmacology of antidepressants. In *Tribute to B.B. Brodie,* edited by E. Costa. New York: Raven Press, 1989.

Supple, W.F., and Kapp, B.S. Response characteristics of neurons in the medial component of the medial geniculate nucleus during pavlovian differential fear conditioning in rabbits. *Behavioral Neuroscience,* 1989, *103,* 1276–1286.

Sutherland, R.J., and Rudy, J.W. Configural association theory: The role of the hippocampal formation in learning, memory, and amnesia. *Psychobiology,* 1989, *17,* 129–144.

Suzdak, P.D., Glowa, J.R., Crawley, J.N., Schwartz, R.D., Skolnick, P., and Paul, S.M. A selective imidazobenzodiazepine antagonist of ethanol in the rat. *Science,* 1986, *234,* 1243–1247.

Svare, B. Psychobiological determinants of maternal aggressive behavior. In *Aggressive Behavior: Genetic and Neural Approaches,* edited by E.C. Simmel, M.E. Hahn, and J.K. Walters. Hillsdale, N.J.: Lawrence Erlbaum Associates, 1983.

Svare, B. Recent advances in the study of female aggressive behavior in mice. In *House Mouse Aggression: A Model for Understanding the Evolution of Social Behavior,* edited by S. Parmigiani, D. Mainardi, and P. Brain. London: Gordon and Breach, 1989.

Svare, B., Betteridge, C., Katz, D., and Samuels, O. Some situational and experiential determinants of maternal aggression in mice. *Physiology and Behavior,* 1981, *26,* 253–258.

Svare, B., and Gandelman, R. Postpartum aggression in mice: Experiential and environmental factors. *Hormones and Behavior,* 1973, *4,* 323–334.

Svare, B., and Gandelman, R. Postpartum aggression in mice: The influence of suckling stimulation. *Hormones and Behavior,* 1976, *7,* 407–416.

Svare, B., Mann, M.A., Broida, J., and Michael, S. Maternal aggression exhibited by hypophysectomized parturient mice. *Hormones and Behavior,* 1982, *16,* 455–461.

Svejda, M.J., Campos, J.J., and Emde, R.N. Mother-infant "bonding": failure to generalize. *Child Development,* 1980, *51,* 775–779.

Svensson, T.H., Grenhoff, J., and Aston-Jones, G. Midbrain dopamine neurons: Nicotinic control of firing patterns. *Society for Neuroscience Abstracts,* 1986, *12,* 1154.

Swaab, D.F., and Fliers, E. A sexually dimorphic nucleus in the human brain. *Science,* 1985, *228,* 1112–1115.

Swaab, D.F., and Hofman, M.A. Sexual differentiation of the human hypothalamus: Ontogeny of the sexually dimorphic nucleus of the preoptic area. *Developmental Brain Research,* 1988, *44,* 314–318.

Swanborg, R.H. Experimental allergic encephalomyelitis. *Methods in Enzymology,* 1988, *162,* 413–421.

Swanson, L.W., and Cowan, W.M. The efferent connections of the suprachiasmatic nucleus of the hypothalamus. *Journal of Comparative Neurology,* 1975, *160,* 1–12.

Swanson, L.W., Köhler, C., and Björklund, A. The limbic region. I. The septohippocampal system. In *Handbook of Chemical Neuroanatomy. Vol. 5. Integrated Systems of the CNS, Part I,* edited by A. Björklund, T. Hökfelt, and L.W. Swanson. Amsterdam: Elsevier Science Publishers, 1987.

Swanson, L.W., Mogenson, G.J., Gerfen, C.R., and Robinson, P. Evidence for a projection from the lateral preoptic area and substantia innominata to the "mesencephalic locomotor region" in the rat. *Brain Research,* 1984, *295,* 161–178.

Swedo, S.E., Schapiro, M.B., Grady, C.L., Cheslow, D.L., Leonard, H.L., Kumarn, A., Friedland, R., Rapoport, S.I., and Rapoport, J.L. Cerebral glucose metabolism in childhood-onset obsessive-compulsive disorder. *Archives of General Psychiatry,* 1989, *46,* 518–523.

Szymusiak, R., and McGinty, D. Sleep-related neuronal discharge in the basal forebrain of cats. *Brain Research,* 1986a, *370,* 82–92.

Szymusiak, R., and McGinty, D. Sleep suppression following kainic acid–induced lesions of the basal forebrain. *Experimental Neurology,* 1986b, *94,* 598–614.

Szymusiak, R., and McGinty, D. Sleep-waking discharge of basal forebrain projection neurons in cats. *Brain Research Bulletin,* 1989, 22, 423–430.

Szymusiak, R., and Satinoff, E. Ambient temperature–

dependence of sleep disturbances produced by basal forebrain damage in rats. *Brain Research Bulletin,* 1984, *12,* 295–305.

Takahashi, Y. Growth hormone secretion related to the sleep waking rhythm. In *The Functions of Sleep,* edited by R. Drucker-Colín, M. Shkurovich, and M.B. Sterman. New York: Academic Press, 1979.

Takeuchi, L., Davis, G.M., Plyley, M., Goode, R., and Shephard, R.J. Sleep deprivation, chronic exercise and muscular performance. *Ergonomics,* 1985, *28,* 591–601.

Tamminga, C.A., Burrows, G.H., Chase, T.N., Alphs, L.D., and Thaker, G.K. Dopamine neuronal tracts in schizophrenia: Their pharmacology and *in vivo* glucose metabolism. *Annals of the New York Academy of Sciences,* 1988, *537,* 443–450.

Tanabe, T., Iino, M., Ooshima, Y., and Takagi, S.F. An olfactory area in the prefrontal lobe. *Brain Research,* 1974, *80,* 127–130.

Tanabe, T., Iino, M., and Takagi, S.G. Discrimination of odors in olfactory bulb, pyriform-amygdaloid areas, and orbitofrontal cortex of the monkey. *Journal of Neurophysiology,* 1975, *38,* 1284–1296.

Tarjan, E., Denton, D.A., and Weisinger, R.S. Atrial natriuretic peptide inhibits water and sodium intake in rabbits. *Regulatory Peptides,* 1988, *23,* 63–75.

Teitelbaum, P., and Stellar, E. Recovery from the failure to eat produced by hypothalamic lesions. *Science,* 1954, *120,* 894–895.

Terenius, L., and Wahlström, A. Morphine-like ligand for opiate receptors in human CSF. *Life Sciences,* 1975, *16,* 1759–1764.

Thach, W.T. Correlation of neural discharge with pattern and force of muscular activity, joint position, and direction of intended movement in motor cortex and cerebellum. *Journal of Neurophysiology,* 1978, *41,* 654–676.

Thomas, G.J. Memory: Time binding in organisms. In *Neuropsychology of Memory,* edited by L.R. Squire and N. Butters. New York: Guilford Press, 1984.

Thompson, R.F. Neural circuit for classical conditioning of the eyelid closure response. In *Neural Models of Plasticity: Experimental and Theoretical Approaches,* edited by J.H. Byrne and W.O. Berry. San Diego: Academic Press, 1989.

Thorell, L.G., De Valois, R.L., and Albrecht, D.G. Spatial mapping of monkey V1 cells with pure color and luminance stimuli. *Vision Research,* 1984, *24,* 751–769.

Thornton, S.N., de Beaurepaire, R., and Nicolaïdis, S. Electrophysiological investigation of cells in the region of the anterior hypothalamus firing in relation to blood pressure and volaemic changes. *Brain Research*, 1984, *299*, 1–7.

Tootell, R.B.H., Silverman, M.S., and De Valois, R.L. Spatial frequency columns in primary visual cortex. *Science*, 1981, *214*, 813–815.

Tootell, R.B.H., Silverman, M.S., De Valois, R.L., and Jacobs, G.H. Functional organization of the second cortical visual area in primates. *Science*, 1983, *220*, 737–739.

Tootell, R.B.H., Silverman, M.S., Switkes, E., De Valois, R.L. The organization of cortical modules in primate striate cortex. *Society for Neuroscience Abstracts*, 1982, *218*, 707.

Tordoff, M.G. How do non-nutritive sweeteners increase food intake? *Appetite*, 1988, *11*, 5–11.

Tordoff, M.G., and Friedman, M.I. Hepatic portal glucose infusions decrease food intake and increase food preference. *American Journal of Physiology*, 1986, *251*, R192–R196.

Tordoff, M.G., and Friedman, M.I. Hepatic control of feeding: Effect of glucose, fructose, and mannitol. *American Journal of Physiology*, 1988, *254*, R969–R976.

Tordoff, M.G., Hopfenbeck, J., and Novin, D. Hepatic vagotomy (partial hepatic denervation) does not alter ingestive responses to metabolic challenges. *Physiology and Behavior*, 1982, *28*, 417–424.

Tordoff, M.G., Schulkin, J., and Friedman, M.I. Further evidence for hepatic control of salt intake in rats. *American Journal of Physiology*, 1987, *253*, R444–R449.

Torrey, E.F., Torrey, B.B., and Peterson, M.R. Seasonality of schizophrenic births in the United States. *Archives of General Psychiatry*, 1977, *34*, 1065–1070.

Tourney, G. Hormones and homosexuality. In *Homosexual Behavior*, edited by J. Marmor. New York: Basic Books, 1980.

Träskmann, L., Åsberg, M., Bertilsson, L., and Sjöstrand, L. Monoamine metabolites in CSF and suicidal behavior. *Archives of General Psychiatry*, 1981, *38*, 631–636.

Triandafillou, J., and Himms-Hagen, J. Brown adipose tissue in genetically obese (*fa/fa*) rats: Response to cold and diet. *American Journal of Physiology*, 1983, *244*, E145–E150.

Trulson, M.E., and Jacobs, B.L. Raphe unit activity in freely moving cats: Correlation with level of behavioral arousal. *Brain Research*, 1979, *163*, 135–150.

Tsou, K., and Jang, C.S. Studies on the site of analgesia action of morphine by intracerebral microinjection. *Scientia Sinica*, 1964, *13*, 1099–1109.

Tucker, D.M., Watson, R.T., and Heilman, K.M. Affective discrimination and evocation in patients with right parietal disease. *Neurology*, 1977, *27*, 947–950.

Tunturi, A.R. A difference in the representation of auditory signals for the left and right ears in the isofrequency contours of right middle ectosylvian auditory cortex in the dog. *American Journal of Physiology*, 1952, *168*, 712–727.

Turkenburg, J.L., Swaab, D.F., Endert, E., Louwerse, A.L., and van de Poll, N.E. Effects of lesions of the sexually dimorphic nucleus on sexual behavior of testosterone-treated female Wistar rats. *Brain Research Bulletin*, 1988, *21*, 215–224.

Turner, A.M., and Greenough, W.T. Differential rearing effects on rat visual cortex synapses. I. Synaptic and neuronal density and synapses per neuron. *Brain Research*, 1985, *329*, 195–203.

Turner, S.M., Beidel, D.C., and Nathan, R.S. Biological factors in obsessive-compulsive disorders. *Psychological Bulletin*, 1985, *97*, 430–450.

Ungerleider, L.G., and Mishkin, M. Two cortical visual systems. In *Analysis of Visual Behavior*, edited by D.J. Ingle, M.A. Goodale, and R.J.W. Mansfield. Cambridge, Mass.: MIT Press, 1982.

Urca, G., and Nahin, R.L. Morphine-induced multiple unit changes in analgesic and rewarding brain sites. *Pain Abstracts*, 1978, *1*, 261.

Uttal, W.R. *The Psychobiology of Sensory Coding*. New York: Harper & Row, 1973.

Vacas, M.I., Lowenstein, P.R., and Cardinali, D.P. Testosterone decreases β-adrenoceptor sites in rat pineal gland and brain. *Journal of Neural Transmission*, 1982, *53*, 49–57.

Vaccarino, F.J., Bloom, R.E., and Koob, G.F. Blockade of nucleus accumbens opiate receptors attenuates intravenous heroin reward in the rat. *Psychopharmacology*, 1985, *86*, 37–42.

Vallbo, Å.B. Muscle spindle response at the onset of isometric voluntary contractions in man: Time differences between fusimotor and skeletomotor effects. *Journal of Physiology (London)*, 1971, *218*, 405–431.

Vandenbergh, J.G., Witsett, J.M., and Lombardi, J.R. Partial isolation of a pheromone accelerating puberty in female mice. *Journal of Reproductive Fertility*, 1975, *43*, 515–523.

Van den Berghe, G. Metabolic effects of fructose in the liver. In *Current Topics in Cellular Regulation*, edited by B.L. Horecker and E.R. Stadtman. New York: Academic Press, 1978.

van de Poll, N.E., Taminiau, M.S., Endert, E., and

Louwerse, A.L. Gonadal steroid influence upon sexual and aggressive behavior of female rats. *International Journal of Neuroscience*, 1988, *41*, 271–286.

van der Lee, S., and Boot, L.M. Spontaneous pseudopregnancy in mice. *Acta Physiologica et Pharmacologica Néerlandica*, 1955, *4*, 442–444.

Vanderwolf, C.H. Hippocampal electrical activity and voluntary movement in the rat. *Electroencephalography and Clinical Neurophysiology*, 1969, *26*, 407–418.

Vanderwolf, C.H., Kramis, R., Gillespie, L.A., and Bland, B.G. Hippocampal rhythmical slow activity and neocortical low voltage fast activity: Relations to behavior. In *The Hippocampus. Vol. 2. Neurophysiology and Behavior*, edited by R.L. Isaacson and K.H. Pribram. New York: Plenum Press, 1975.

Van Eekelen, J.A.M., and Phillips, M.I. Plasma angiotensin II levels at moment of drinking during angiotensin II intravenous infusion. *American Journal of Physiology*, 1988, *255*, R500–R506.

Van Hoesen, G.W., and Damasio, A.R. Neural correlates of cognitive impairment in Alzheimer's disease. In *Handbook of Physiology: Section I. The Nervous System, Vol. V, Higher Functions of the Brain*, edited by F. Plum. Bethesda, Md.: American Physiological Society, 1987.

Vergnes, M. Déclenchement de réactions d'aggression interspécifique après lésion amygdalienne chez le rat. *Physiology and Behavior*, 1975, *14*, 271–276.

Vergnes, M. Contrôle amygdalien de comportements d'aggression chez le rat. *Physiology and Behavior*, 1976, *17*, 439–444.

Verney, E.B. The antidiuretic hormone and the factors which determine its release. *Proceedings of the Royal Society of London, B.*, 1947, *135*, 25–106.

Victor, M., Adams, R.D., and Collins, G.H. *The Wernicke-Korsakoff Syndrome*. Philadelphia: F.A. Davis, 1971.

Voci, V.E., and Carlson, N.R. Enhancement of maternal behavior and nest behavior following systemic and diencephalic administration of prolactin and progesterone in the mouse. *Journal of Comparative and Physiological Psychology*, 1973, *83*, 388–393.

Voeller, K.K.S., Hanson, J.A., and Wendt, R.N. Facial affect recognition in children: A comparison of the performance of children with right and left hemisphere lesions. *Neurology*, 1988, *38*, 1744–1748.

Vogel, G.W., Buffenstein, A., Minter, K., and Hennessey, A. Drug effects on REM sleep and on endogenous depression. *Neuroscience and Biobehavioral Reviews*, 1990, *14*, 49–63.

Vogel, G.W., Neill, D., Hagler, M., and Kors, D. A new animal model of endogenous depression: A summary of present findings. *Neuroscience and Biobehavioral Reviews*, 1990, *14*, 85–91.

Vogel, G.W., Thurmond, A., Gibbons, P., Sloan, K., Boyd, M., and Walker, M. REM sleep reduction effects on depression syndromes. *Archives of General Psychiatry*, 1975, *32*, 765–777.

Vogel, G.W., Vogel, F., McAbee, R.S., and Thurmond, A.J. Improvement of depression by REM sleep deprivation: New findings and a theory. *Archives of General Psychiatry*, 1980, *37*, 247–253.

Volicer, L., and Loew, C. Penetration of angiotensin II into the brain. *Neuropharmacologia*, 1975, *10*, 631–636.

vom Saal, F.S. Models of early hormonal effects on intrasex aggression in mice. In *Hormones and Aggressive Behavior*, edited by B.B. Svare. New York: Plenum Press, 1983.

vom Saal, F.S. Time-contingent change in infanticide and parental behavior induced by ejaculation in male mice. *Physiology and Behavior*, 1985, *34*, 7–15.

vom Saal, F.S., and Bronson, F.H. *In utero* proximity of female mouse fetuses to males: Effect on reproductive performance during later life. *Biology of Reproduction*, 1980a, *22*, 777–780.

vom Saal, F.S., and Bronson, F.H. Sexual characteristics of adult female mice are correlated with their blood testosterone levels during prenatal development. *Science*, 1980b, *208*, 597–599.

von Békésy, G. *Experiments in Hearing*. New York: McGraw-Hill, 1960.

von Frey, M. The distribution of afferent nerves in the skin. *Journal of the American Medical Association*, 1906, *47*, 645.

Waldbillig, R.J. Offense, defense, submission, and attack: Problems of logic and lexicon. *The Behavioral and Brain Sciences*, 1979, *2*, 227–228.

Walsh, L.L., and Grossman, S.P. Dissociation of responses to extracellular thirst stimuli following zona incerta lesions. *Pharmacology, Biochemistry, and Behavior*, 1978, *8*, 409–415.

Ward, I. Prenatal stress feminizes and demasculinizes the behavior of males. *Science*, 1972, *175*, 82–84.

Ward, I., and Weisz, J. Maternal stress alters plasma testosterone in fetal mice. *Science*, 1980, *207*, 328–329.

Warrington, E.K., and James, M. Visual apperceptive agnosia: A clinico-anatomical study of three cases. *Cortex*, 1988, *24*, 1–32.

Warrington, E.K., and Shallice, T. Word-form dyslexia. *Brain*, 1980, *103*, 99–112.

Warrington, E.K., and Weiskrantz, L. Amnesia: A disconnection syndrome? *Neuropsychologia,* 1982, *20,* 233–248.

Waterhouse, B.D., Sessler, F.M., Cheng, J.-G., Woodward, D.J., Azizi, S.A., and Moises, H.C. New evidence for a gating action of norepinephrine in central neuronal circuits of mammalian brain. *Brain Research Bulletin,* 1988, *21,* 425–432.

Webb, W.B. *Sleep: The Gentle Tyrant.* Englewood Cliffs, N.J.: Prentice-Hall, 1975.

Webb, W.B. Some theories about sleep and their clinical implications. *Psychiatric Annals,* 1982, *11,* 415–422.

Webster, H.H., and Jones, B.E. Neurotoxic lesions of the dorsolateral pontomesencephalic tegmentum-cholinergic cell area in the cat. II. Effects upon sleep-waking states. *Brain Research,* 1988, *458,* 285–302.

Weinberger, D.R. Schizophrenia and the frontal lobe. *Trends in Neurosciences,* 1988, *11,* 367–370.

Weinberger, D.R., Berman, K.F., and Illowsky, B.P. Physiological dysfunction of dorsolateral prefrontal cortex in schizophrenia. III. A new cohort and evidence for a monoaminergic mechanism. *Archives of General Psychiatry,* 1988, *45,* 609–615.

Weinberger, D.R., Berman, K.F., and Zec, R.F. Physiologic dysfunction of dorsolateral prefrontal cortex in schizophrenia. I. Regional cerebral blood flow evidence. *Archives of General Psychiatry,* 1986, *43,* 114–124.

Weinberger, D.R., and Wyatt, R.J. Brain morphology in schizophrenia: *In vivo* studies. In *Schizophrenia as a Brain Disease,* edited by F.A. Henn and H.A. Nasrallah. New York: Oxford University Press, 1982.

Weingarten, H.P. Conditioned cues elicit feeding in sated rats: A role for learning in meal initiation. *Science,* 1983, *220,* 431–432.

Weingarten, J.P., Chang, P.K., and McDonald, T.J. Comparison of the metabolic and behavioral disturbances following paraventricular- and ventromedial-hypothalamic lesions. *Brain Research Bulletin,* 1985, *14,* 551–559.

Weintraub, S., Mesulam, M.-M., and Kramer, L. Disturbances in prosody: A right-hemisphere contribution to language. *Archives of Neurology,* 1981, *38,* 742–744.

Weiskrantz, L. Residual vision in a scotoma: A follow-up study of ''form'' discrimination. *Brain,* 1987, *110,* 77–92.

Weiskrantz, L., and Warrington, E.K. Conditioning in amnesia patients. *Neuropsychologia,* 1979, *17,* 187–194.

Weiskrantz, L., Warrington, E.K., Sanders, M.D., and Marshall, J. Visual capacity in the hemianopic field following a restricted occipital ablation. *Brain,* 1974, *97,* 709–728.

Weisz, D.J., Clark, G.A., Yank, B., Thompson, R.F., and Solomon, P.R. Activity of dentate gyrus during NM conditioning in rabbit. In *Conditioning: Representation of Involved Neural Functions,* edited by C.D. Woody. New York: Plenum Press, 1982.

Weisz, D.W., Solomon, P.R., and Thompson, R.F. The hippocampus appears necessary for trace conditioning. *Bulletin of the Psychonomic Society,* 1980, *16* (Abstract).

Weitzman, E.D. Sleep and its disorders. *Annual Review of Neuroscience,* 1981, *4,* 381–418.

Welle, S.L., Nair, K.S., and Campbell, R.G. Failure of chronic β-adrenergic blockade to inhibit overfeeding-induced thermogenesis in humans. *American Journal of Physiology,* 1989, *256,* R653–R658.

Welner, S.A., Dunnett, S.B., Salamone, J.D., MacLean, B., and Iversen, S.D. Transplantation of embryonic ventral forebrain grafts to the neocortex of rats with bilateral lesions of nucleus basalis magnocellularis ameliorates a lesion-induced deficit in spatial memory. *Brain Research,* 1988, *463,* 192–197.

Wernicke, C. *Der Aphasische Symptomenkomplex.* Breslau, Poland: Cohn & Weigert, 1874.

Whipple, B., and Komisaruk B.R. Analgesia produced in women by genital self-stimulation. *Journal of Sex Research,* 1988, *24,* 130–140.

Whitehead, R.G., Rowland, M.G.M., Hutton, M., Prentice, A.M., Müller, E., and Paul, A. Factors influencing lactation performance in rural Gambian mothers. *Lancet,* 1978, *2,* 178–181.

Whitehouse, P.J., Price, D.L., Struble, R.G., Clark, A.W., Coyle, J.T., and DeLong, M.R. Alzheimer's disease and senile dementia: Loss of neurons in the basal forebrain. *Science,* 1982, *215,* 1237–1239.

Whitfield, I.C., and Evans, E.F. Responses of auditory cortical neurons to stimuli of changing frequency. *Journal of Neurophysiology,* 1965, *28,* 655–672.

Whitten, W.K. Occurrence of anestrus in mice caged in groups. *Journal of Endocrinology,* 1959, *18,* 102–107.

Wiener, S.I., Paul, C.A., and Eichenbaum, H. Spatial and behavioral correlates of hippocampal neuronal activity. *Journal of Neuroscience,* 1989, *9,* 2737–2763.

Wiesner, B.P., and Sheard, N. *Maternal Behaviour in the Rat.* London: Oliver and Brody, 1933.

Wilska, A. Eine Methode zur Bestimmung der Horschwellenamplituden der Tromenfells bei verscheideden Frequenzen. *Skandinavisches Archiv für Physiologie*, 1935, *72*, 161–165.

Wilson, D.A., and Leon, M. Spatial patterns of olfactory bulb single-unit responses to learned olfactory cues in young rats. *Journal of Neurophysiology*, 1988, *59*, 1770–1782.

Winans, S.S., and Powers, J.B. Olfactory and vomeronasal deafferentation of male hamsters: Histological and behavioral analyses. *Brain Research*, 1977, *126*, 325–344.

Winn, P., Tarbuck, A., and Dunnett, S.B. Ibotenic acid lesions of the lateral hypothalamus: Comparison with electrolytic lesion syndrome. *Neuroscience*, 1984, *12*, 225–240.

Winograd, T. Frame representations and the declarative-procedural controversy. In *Representation and Understanding: Studies in Cognitive Science*, edited by D. Bobrow and A. Collins. New York: Academic Press, 1975.

Winslow, J.T., Ellingoe, J., and Miczek, K.A. Effects of alcohol on aggressive behavior in squirrel monkeys: Influence of testosterone and social context. *Psychopharmacology*, 1988, *95*, 356–363.

Winslow, J.T., and Miczek, J.A. Social status as determinants of alcohol effects on aggressive behavior in squirrel monkeys (*Saimiri sciureus*). *Psychopharmacology*, 1985, *85*, 167–172.

Winslow, J.T., and Miczek, J.A. Androgen dependency of alcohol effects on aggressive behavior: A seasonal rhythm in high-ranking squirrel monkeys. *Psychopharmacologia*, 1988, *95*, 92–98.

Wise, R.A. Psychomotor stimulant properties of addictive drugs. *Annals of the New York Academy of Sciences*, 1988, *537*, 228–234.

Wise, R.A. Opiate reward: Sites and substrates. *Neuroscience and Biobehavioral Reviews*, 1989, *13*, 129–133.

Wise, R.A., and Rompré, P.-P. Brain dopamine and reward. *Annual Review of Psychology*, 1989, *40*, 191–225.

Wise, S.P., and Rapoport, J.L. Obsessive compulsive disorder: Is it a basal ganglia dysfunction? *Psychopharmacology Bulletin*, 1988, *24*, 380–384.

Wolf, G., Schulkin, J., and Simson, P.E. Multiple factors in the satiation of salt appetite. *Behavioral Neuroscience*, 1984, *98*, 661–673.

Wolkin, A., Barouche, F., Wolf, A.P., Rotrosen, J., Fowler, J.S., Shiue, C.-Y., Cooper, T.B., and Brodie, J.D. Dopamine blockade and clinical response: Evidence for two biological subgroups of schizophrenia. *American Journal of Psychiatry*, 1989, *146*, 905–908.

Wong, D.F., Wagner, H.N., Tune, L.E., Dannals, R.F., Pearlson, G.D., Links, J.M., Tamminga, C.A., Broussolle, E.P., Ravert, H.T., Wilson, A.A., Toung, J.K.T., Malat, J., Williams, J.A., O'Tuama, L.A., Snyder, S.H., Kuhar, M.J., and Gjedde, A. Positron emission tomography reveals elevated D_2 dopamine receptors in drug-naive schizophrenics. *Science*, 1986, *234*, 1558–1563.

Wong-Riley, M. Personal communication, 1978. Cited by Livingstone and Hubel, 1982.

Woo, C.C., Coopersmith, R., and Leon, M. Localized changes in olfactory bulb morphology associated with early olfactory learning. *Journal of Comparative Neurology*, 1987, *236*, 113–125.

Wood, D.M., and Emmett-Oglesby, M.W. Mediation in the nucleus accumbens of the discriminative stimulus produced by cocaine. *Pharmacology, Biochemistry, and Behavior*, 1989, *33*, 453–457.

Wood, P.L. Actions of GABAergic agents on dopamine metabolism in the nigrostriatal pathway of the rat. *Pharmacology and Experimental Therapeutics*, 1982, *222*, 674–679.

Woodruff, M.L., and Bownds, M.D. Amplitude, kinetics, and reversibility of a light-induced decrease in guanosine 3',5'-cyclic monophosphate in isolated frog receptor membranes. *Journal of General Physiology*, 1979, *73*, 629–653.

Woodruff, R.A., Guze, S.B., and Clayton, P.J. Anxiety neurosis among psychiatric outpatients. *Comprehensive Psychiatry*, 1972, *13*, 165–170.

Woods, S.W., Charney, D.S., Goodman, W.K., and Heninger, G.R. Carbon dioxide–induced anxiety. *Archives of General Psychiatry*, 1988, *45*, 43–52.

Wu, J.C., and Bunney, W.E. The biological basis of an antidepressant response to sleep deprivation and relapse: Review and hypothesis. *American Journal of Psychiatry*, 1990, *147*, 14–21.

Wyatt, R.J., Kirch, D.G., and DeLisi, L.E. Biochemical, endocrine, and immunologic studies of schizophrenia. In *Comprehensive Textbook of Psychiatry*, 5th ed., edited by H.I. Kaplan and B.J. Sadock. Baltimore: Williams and Wilkins, 1988.

Wysocki, C.J. Neurobehavioral evidence for the involvement of the vomeronasal system in mammalian reproduction. *Neuroscience and Biobehavioral Reviews*, 1979, *3*, 301–341.

Wysocki, C.J., and Beauchamp. G.K. Ability to smell androsterone is genetically determined. *Proceedings of the National Academy of Sciences, USA*, 1984, *81*, 4899–4902.

Yamamoto, T., Yuyama, N., and Kawamura, Y. Central processing of taste perception. In *Brain Mechanisms of Sensation*, edited by Y. Katsuki, R. Norgren, and M. Sato. New York: John Wiley & Sons, 1981.

Yang, C.R., and Mogenson, G.J. Hippocampal signal transmission to the pedunculopontine nucleus and its regulation by dopamine D_2 receptors in the nucleus accumbens: An electrophysiological and behavioural study. *Neuroscience*, 1987, *23*, 1041–1055.

Yau, K.W., and Baylor, D.A. Cyclic GMP-activated conductance of retinal photoreceptor cells. *Annual Review of Neuroscience*, 1989, *12*, 289–327.

Yee, F., MacLow, C., Chan, I.N., and Leibowitz, S.F. Effects of chronic paraventricular nucleus infusion of clonidine and α-methyl-*para*-tyrosine on macronutrient intake. *Appetite*, 1987, *9*, 127–138.

Yeo, C.H., Hardiman, M.J., Glickstein, M., and Steele-Russell, I. Lesions of cerebellar nuclei abolish the classically conditioned nictitating membrane response. *Society for Neuroscience Abstracts*, 1982, *8*, 22.

Yeomans, J.S. Quantitative measurement of neural post-stimulation excitability with behavioral methods. *Physiology and Behavior*, 1975, *15*, 593–602.

Yeung, J.C., and Rudy, T. Sites of antinociceptive action of systemically injected morphine: Involvement of supraspinal loci as revealed by intracerebroventricular injection of naloxone. *Journal of Pharmacology and Experimental Therapeutics*, 1980, *215*, 626–632.

Young, W.G., and Deutsch, J.A. Intragastric pressure and receptive relaxation in the rat. *Physiology and Behavior*, 1980, *25*, 973–975.

Zarbin, M.A., Innis, R.B., Wamsley, J.K., Snyder, S.H., and Kuhar, M.J. Autoradiographic localization of cholecystokinin receptors in rodent brain. *Journal of Neuroscience*, 1983, *3*, 877–906.

Zeki, S. The construction of colours by the cerebral cortex. *Proceedings of the Royal Institute of Great Britain*, 1984, *56*, 231–257.

Zeki, S., and Shipp, S. The functional logic of cortical connections. *Nature*, 1988, *335*, 311–317.

Zeki, S.M. The cortical projections of foveal striate cortex in the rhesus monkey. *Journal of Physiology*, 1978a, *277*, 227–244.

Zeki, S.M. The third visual complex of rhesus monkey prestriate cortex. *Journal of Physiology*, 1978b, *277*, 245–272.

Zeki, S.M. The representation of colours in the cerebral cortex. *Nature*, 1980, *284*, 412–418.

Zito, K.A., Vickers, G., and Roberts, D.C.S. Disruption of cocaine and heroin self-administration following kainic acid lesions of the nucleus accumbens. *Pharmacology, Biochemistry, and Behavior*, 1985, *23*, 1029–1036.

Zola-Morgan, S., and Squire, L.R. Amnesia in monkeys following lesions of the mediodorsal nucleus of the thalamus. *Annals of Neurology*, 1985a, *17*, 558–564.

Zola-Morgan, S., and Squire, L.R. Medial temporal lesions in monkeys impair memory in a variety of tasks sensitive to human amnesia. *Behavioral Neuroscience*, 1985b, *99*, 22–34.

Zola-Morgan, S., Squire, L.R., and Amaral, D.G. Human amnesia and the medial temporal region: Enduring memory impairment following a bilateral lesion limited to field CA1 of the hippocampus. *Journal of Neuroscience*, 1986, *6*, 2950–2967.

Zola-Morgan, S., Squire, L.R., and Amaral, D.G. Lesions of the amygdala that spare adjacent cortical regions do not impair memory or exacerbate the impairment following lesions of the hippocampal formation. *Journal of Neuroscience*, 1989a, *9*, 1922–1936.

Zola-Morgan, S., Squire, L.R., and Amaral, D.G. Lesions of the hippocampal formation but not lesions of the fornix or the mammillary nuclei produce long-lasting memory impairment in monkeys. *Journal of Neuroscience*, 1989b, *9*, 898–913.

Zola-Morgan, S., Squire, L.R., Amaral, D.G., and Suzuki, W.A. Lesions of perirhinal and parahippocampal cortex that spare the amygdala and hippocampal formation produce severe memory impairment. *Journal of Neuroscience*, 1989, *9*, 4355–4370.

NAME INDEX

SUBJECT INDEX

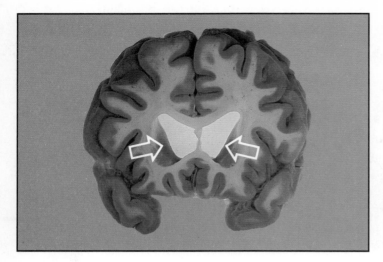

COLOR PLATE 8.1
A slice through the brain of a person who had Huntington's chorea. The arrowheads indicate the location of the caudate nuclei, which are severely degenerated. As a consequence of the degeneration, the lateral ventricles (open spaces in the middle of the slice) have enlarged. Compare the caudate nuclei and lateral ventricles of this plate with those shown in Color Plate 8.2. (Courtesy of Anthony D'Agostino, Good Samaritan Hospital, Portland, Oregon.)

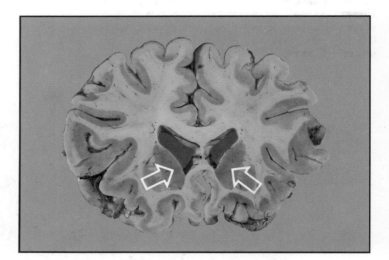

COLOR PLATE 8.2
A slice through a normal human brain, showing the normal appearance of the caudate nuclei (arrowheads) and lateral ventricles. (Courtesy of Harvard Medical School/Betty G. Martindale.)

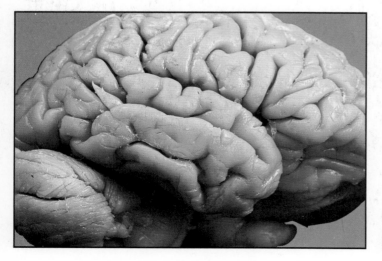

COLOR PLATE 15.1
A lateral view of the right side of a normal brain. (© Dan McCoy/Rainbow)

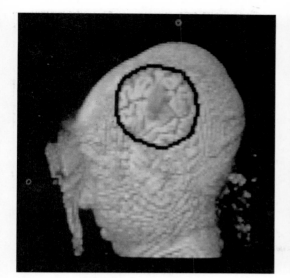

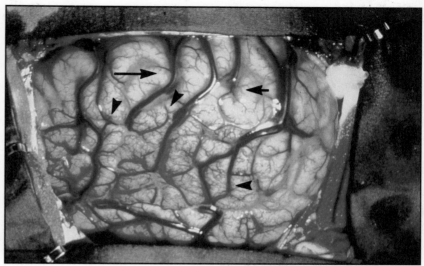

COLOR PLATE 5.5

Seizure focus. (a) A computer display of a composite scan of the head of a seven-year-old girl, made from a series of PET and MRI scans. The purple spot shows the seizure focus, whose metabolic activity is higher than the rest of the brain.

(b) A photograph of the surface of the skull made during surgery. Long arrows point to the primary motor cortex; short arrows point to the primary somatosensory cortex; arrowheads point to the seizure focus. You can see that the large blood vessels are smaller in this region but that the small blood vessels contained within the pia mater are dilated. (From Levin, D. N., Hu, X., Tan, K. K., Galhotra, S., Pelizzari, C. A., Chen, G. T. Y., Beck, R. N., Chen, C.-T., Cooper, M. D., Mullan, J. F., Hekmatpanah, J., and Spire, J.-P. *Radiology*, 1989, *172*, 783–789. Reprinted by permission.)

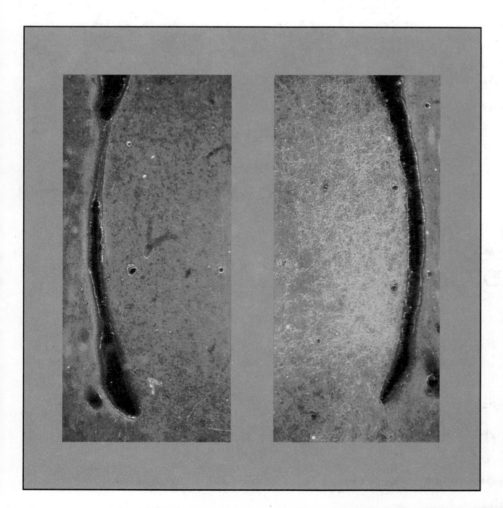

COLOR PLATE 5.6

Frontal sections through half of the septum (a region of the forebrain) of two rats, arranged side by side for comparison. Both brains were stained with a special dye linked to an antibody for vasopressin, a peptide hormone and transmitter substance. The dye shows up as a bright yellow. (a) The brain of a male whose testes were removed three months previously. The loss of the male sex hormones produced by the testes has caused the vasopressin-secreting axons to disappear. (b) The brain of a normal male. (Histological material courtesy of Geert DeVries, University of Massachusetts.)

PHYSIOLOGY
OF BEHAVIOR